A Garland Series

CLASSICS OF

ENGLISH LEGAL HISTORY

IN THE MODERN ERA

One Hundred and Forty-Two
Rare and Important Titles
Reproduced in Facsimile
in One Hundred and Eleven Volumes

Selected by

David S. Berkowitz

Samuel E. Thorne

William Hawkins

A TREATISE
OF THE
PLEAS OF THE CROWN

in two volumes
Vol. II

Garland Publishing, Inc.
New York & London • 1978

Bibliographical note:
This facsimile has been made
from a copy in the British Library
(1471.K.21)

The volumes in this series are printed on
acid-free, 250-year-life paper.

Library of Congress Cataloging in Publication Data

Hawkins, William, 1673-1746.
A treatise of the pleas of the crown.

(Classics of English legal history in the modern era)
Reprint of the 1716-21 ed. printed by E. Nutt for
J. Walthoe, London.
Includes index.
1. Pleas of the crown. I. Title. II. Series.
KD7869.H39 1979 345'.41'072 77-86642
ISBN 0-8240-3079-6

Printed in the United States of America

A TREATISE OF THE PLEAS OF THE CROWN:

OR A

SYSTEM of the Principal Matters relating to that SUBJECT, digested under their proper Heads.

BOOK II.

By *WILLIAM HAWKINS*,
of the *Inner-Temple*, Esq;.

In the *SAVOY*,

Printed by Eliz. Nutt and R. Gosling, (Assigns of Edward Sayer, *Esq*;) for J. Walthoe in the *Middle-Temple-Cloysters*; and J. Walthoe, *jun.* against the *Royal-Exchange* in *Cornhill*. 1721.

To the Right Honourable

THOMAS, Lord *PARKER*,

Baron of *MACCLESFIELD*,

AND

Lord High Chancellor of *Great Britain*.

My LORD,

THE Experience I have ſo often had of your Lordſhip's Goodneſs, cannot but encourage me to hope for the Continuance of it: And the Succeſs of my former Endeavours under the Protection of your Lordſhip's Name, is a ſufficient Aſſurance, That if I can be ſo happy as to have your Lordſhip's Approbation and Encouragement, I need not deſire any other.

NOR is my Application to your Lordſhip in Behalf of a Common Law Treatiſe, any way diſcouraged by your Lordſhip's Removal to the Station you at preſent adorn; for tho' the Publick Good, and his Majeſty's Service, have put you under a Neceſſity of leaving the Common Law Courts, yet nothing can ever make you ceaſe from being the moſt aſſured Friend, and Patron, as well as the moſt exquiſite Maſter of the Common Law. And the Greateſt Lovers of it have the leſs Regret for the Loſs of your Lordſhip's Preſence among them, from the Honour the Law it ſelf has received by your Lordſhip's Advancement, whereby the World has been effectually convinc'd, That nothing ſo much conduces to make a

Consummate Chancellor, as the most perfect Skill and Experience in the Common Law.

It is with the utmost Pleasure we observe your Lordship with so much Steadiness adhere to those stated Boundaries of Property, which our Ancestors have always had in such high Veneration, and which your Lordship never departs from, but in such Cases, wherein evident Equity, Common Sense, and Natural Justice, undeniably point out an Exception.

It is to your Lordship we are obliged for the Removal of that Vulgar Prejudice, That the Rules of Law and Equity could not possibly be reconciled: As your Lordship had formerly convinced us, That there is nothing in the Common Law rightly understood, that is any way repugnant to Equity, you have now given us the like Satisfaction, That there is no Rule of Equity skillfully applied, that in the least contradicts the true Reason of the Common Law.

I am,

My Lord,

With the greatest Respect,

Your Lordship's most dutiful,

and most obliged Servant,

William Hawkins.

AN ANALYSIS OF THE Second BOOK OF THE Pleas of the Crown.

ALL Courts of criminal Jurisdiction are Courts of Record, (ch. 1. sect. 14.) and derive their Authority from the Crown, ch. 1. sect. 1, *&c.*

The Principal Courts of this Kind, are,

1. The Court of the Lord High Steward, ch. 2.
2. The Court of King's Bench, ch. 3.
3. The Court of the Constable and Marshall, ch. 4.
4. The Court of the Justices of *Oyer* and *Terminer*, ch. 5.
5. The Court of Justices of Gaol-Delivery, ch. 6.
6. The Court of the Justices of Assise and *Nisi prius*, ch. 7.
7. The Court of Sessions of Justices of Peace, ch. 8.
8. The Court of the Coroner, ch. 9.
9. The Sheriff's Torn, ch. 10.
10. The Court-Leet. ch. 11.

The first Thing to be done in order to the bringing a Criminal to Justice is to arrest him.

Arrests are either without Process from a Court of Record, or by Vertue of such Process.

And first, Arrests without such Process, are either,

1. By Private Persons, or,
2. By Publick Officers.

Arrests of this Kind by Private Persons are either,

1. Such as are commanded and enjoined by Law, (ch. 12. sect. 1 *to* 8.) or,
2. Such as are permitted by Law, ch. 12. sect. 8 *to* 18.) or,
3. Such as are rewarded by Law, ch. 12. sect. 22, *&c.*

Arrests of this King by Publick Officers, are either,

1. By Watchmen, (ch. 13. sect. 1 *to* 7.) or,
2. By Constables, (ch. 13. sect. 7 *to* 12.) or,
3. By Bailiffs of Towns, (ch. 13. sect. 12.) or,
4. By Justices of Peace, which are either,
   1. By Parol, (ch. 13. sect. 14.) or,
   2. By Warrant, ch. 13. sect. 15. *to the End of the Chapter.*

Persons arrested are either to be bailed, ch. 15.

Or committed, ch. 16.

Persons may be criminal in preventing the bringing of Offenders to Publick Justice, several Ways,

1. Before any Arrest made,
2. After an Arrest.

Persons may be so guilty before any Arrest made,
1. By opposing an Arrest, ch. 17. sect. 1.
2. By suffering a Criminal to escape, ch. 17. sect. 2, 4.
3. By flying from an Arrest, ch. 17. sect. 3. ch. 49. sect. 14, 15, 16.

Persons may be so Guilty after an Arrest, either in Respect of an Arrest of themselves, or of others.

Their Offence in Respect of an Arrest of themselves, if without Force, is called an Escape, ch. 17. sect. 5.

If with Force, is called a Breach of Prison, ch. 18.

Their Offence in Respect of the Arrest of others, is either,
1. Without Force, or,
2. With Force.

Such Offences, without Force, come under the Notion of Escapes, and are either,
1. By Officers, (ch. 19) or,
2. By Private Persons, ch. 20.

Such Offences with Force come under the Notion of Rescous, ch. 21.

Secondly, Arrests by Process from a Court of Record may be made by Vertue of two Kinds of Process,
1. Upon such as is awarded by the Discretion of the Court, upon a bare Suggestion, or the Knowledge of the Justices.
2. Upon such as is awarded on an Appeal, Indictment, or Information.

Process of the first Kind is generally called an Attachment, (ch. 22.) and lies either against,
1. The Officers of the Court, as,
   1. Sheriffs, and Bailiffs, ch. 22. sect. 2 *to* 6.
   2. Attorneys, ch. 22. sect. 6 *to* 12.
   3. Other Officers of the Court, ch. 22. sect. 12.
   4. Jurors, ch. 22. sect. 14 *to* 25. or,
2. Against others, as,
   1. Inferior Judges, ch. 22. sect. 25 *to* 30.
   2. Counsellors, ch. 22. sect. 30.
   3. Gaolers, ch. 22. sect. 31.
   4. Any other Persons whatsoever, ch. 22. sect. 33. *to the End of the Chapter.*

Process on an Appeal, Indictment, or Information, supposes such Appeal, Indictment, or Information to be first exhibited.

An Appeal is either,
1. By an Innocent Person, which may either be by Writ, or by Bill, ch. 23.
2. By an Offender confessing himself Guilty, who is commonly called an Approver, ch. 24.

Indictments (ch. 25.) are of two Kinds,
1. Such as are grounded on the Common Law, ch. 25. sect. 53 *to* 101.
2. Such as are grounded on Statute, ch. 25. sect. 101 *to* 120.

Informations are of two Kinds,
1. Such as are merely the Suit of the King, ch. 26. sect. 1 *to* 17.
2. Such as are partly the Suit of the King, and partly the Suit of the Party, ch. 26. sect. 17. *to the End of the Chapter.*

Process on an Appeal, Indictment, or Information, may be either considered,
1. In General, without any Particular Regard to Process of Outlawry, ch. 27. sect. 1 *to* 113.
2. In Particular, with Regard to such Process only, ch. 27. sect. 113 *to the End of the Chapter.*

A Criminal being brought into Court is to be arraigned, or put upon his Trial, the Manner whereof may be considered,
1. As it relates to all Criminals in general, ch. 28.
2. As it relates to Principals and Accessaries in Particular, ch. 29.

The Party being arraigned, either,
1. Stands Mute, (ch. 30.) or,
2. Confesses, (ch. 31.) or,
3. Pleads.

Pleas are either,
1. Dilatory, or,
2. In Chief.

The Dilatory are either,
1. Declinatory, or,
2. In Abatement, ch. 34.

The Declinatory are either,
1. Of the Privilege of Sanctuary, (ch. 32.) or,
2. Of the Benefit of the Clergy, ch. 33.

Pleas in Chief are either,
1. In Bar, or,
2. The General Issue, ch. 38.

The Principal Pleas in Bar are,
1. That of *Autrefoits acquit*, ch. 35.
2. That of *Autrefoits attaint* or *convict*, ch. 36.
3. That of Pardon, ch. 37.

The Plea of Not Guilty is triable either,
1. By the Country, or,
2. By the Peers, (ch. 44.) or,
3. By Battel, ch. 45.

In order for a Trial by the Country a Jury must be returned,
1. From the proper County, ch. 40.
2. By proper Process, ch. 41.
3. Before a proper Court, ch. 42.

The

The Jurors being returned into Court may in many Cases be challenged.

Such challenges may be considered either,

1. Without any particular Regard to Aliens, or,
2. As they particularly relate to Aliens, ch 43. sect. 34 *to the End of the Chapter.*

Those of the first Kind, are either,

1. Such as may be taken on the Part of the King, (ch. 43. sect. 2. 3.) or,
2. Such as may be taken on the Part of the Prisoner,

A Challenge may be taken on the Part of a Prisoner, either,

1. Peremptorily, (ch. 43. sect. 5 *to* 10.) or,
2. For Cause, ch. 43. sect. 10 *to* 34.

The Jury being sworn, are to be gnided by their Evidence, ch. 46.

Whereupon they must give some Verdict, either General or Special, ch. 47.

Judgments in Criminal Cases are of two Kinds,

1. Such as expresly sentence the Party to the Punishment proper for his Crime.
2. Such as give no such express Sentence.

Of Judgments by such express Sentence there are two Kinds,

1. Such as are fix'd and stated, and always the same for the same Species of Crimes, ch. 48. sect. 2 *to* 14.
2. Such as are discretionary and variable according to the different Circumstances of each Case, ch. 48. sect. 14 *to* 21.

Of Judgments which give no such express Sentence, there are also two Kinds,

1. Outlawry, ch. 48. sect. 21, 22, 23.
2. Abjuration, ch. 48. sect. 24.

The most considerable Consequences of an Attainder, *&c.* are,

1. The Forfeiture of Lands and Goods, ch. 49. sect. 1 *to* 42.
2. The Loss of the Wife's Dower, ch. 49. sect. 42 *to* 47.
3. The Corruption of Blood, ch. 49. sect. 47 *to the end of the Chapter.*

Forfeitures of Lands and Goods are either,

1. By the Common Law, (ch. 49. sect. 1. *to* 18) or,
2. By Statute, ch. 49. sect. 18 *to* 30.

Judgments may be avoided either,

1. Without Writ of Error, ch. 50. sect. (10 *to* 17.) or,
2. By Writ of Error.

They may be avoided by Writ of Error, either,

1. For Faults apparent in the Record, ch. 50. sect 1.) or,
2. For Matters *dehors* the Record, ch. 50. sect. 2 *to* 10.

The Party condemned is either to be.

1. Reprieved, (ch. 51. sect. 8, 9.) or,
2. Executed; ch. 51. sect. 1 *to* 8.

A TREA-

BOOKS Printed for *J. Walthoe.*

In Folio.

1. SErjeant *Salkeld*'s Reports, 2 Vols.
2. *Hawkins*'s Treatise of the Pleas of the Crown.
3. *Farresley*'s Reports in the first Year of Queen *Anne*.
4. *Lutwyche*'s Reports and Entries, 2 Vols.
5. Sir *Bartholomew Shower*'s Reports, 2 Vols.
6. Sir *Orlanho Bridgman*'s Conveyances, 4th Edition.
7. Modern Cases in the 2d and 3d of Q. *Anne*.
8. *D'Anvers*'s Abridgment of the Law, 2 Vols.
9. A Collection of Entries by Sir *Creswell Levinz*.
10. Cases adjudged in the Court of Chancery, three Parts, 2d Edition.
11. *Dyer*'s Reports, with new References and Cases.
12. *Benloe*'s Reports, and *Dalison*'s.
13. The Reports of *Robert Keilway*, Esq;
14. The Law of Real Actions, by *George Booth*, Esq;
15. Baron *Puffendorf*, of the Law of Nature and Nations, with *Barbarett*'s Notes, 3d Edit.
16. The Lives of the Primitive Fathers, by *William Cave*, D. D.
17. The Works of the famous *Nicholas Matchiavel*.
18. An Exposition of the 39 Articles, by Dr. *Burnet*.
19. Dr. *Burnet*'s History of the Reformation of the Church of *England*.
20. Compleat History of the most Remarkable Transactions at Sea, by *Josiah Burchet*, Esq;

In Octavo and Twelves.

21. *Cursus Cancellariæ*, or the Practise of the Court of Chancery.
22. Reports in the Court of Chancery.
23. Sir *Matthew Hale*'s History of the Law.
24. The Rules of the Courts at *Westminster*, 2 Vols.
25. The Statute Law concerning Trials in Cases of Treason.
26. Lord Chief Justice *Scroggs*, of Courts-Leet and Baron.
27. The Law against Bankrupts, by Serjeant *Goodinge*, 3d Edition.
28. The Law of Ejectments, 2d Edition.
29. *Watson*'s Clergyman's Law, or the compleat Incumbent, in 2 Vols.
30. The Law of Last Wills and Testaments.
31. The Impartial Lawyer.
32. The compleat Sheriff, to which is now added the Law of Replevins.
33. The New *Retorna Brevium*.
34. The Modern Conveyancer, or Conveyancing improved, 3d Edition.
35. The compleat Attorney and Solicitor in all the Courts at *Westminster*, 4th Edition.
36. Legal Provisions for the Poor, 4th Edit.
37. An Abridgment of *Coke* on *Littleton*.
38. A Compendium of the Laws of *England*, by *H. Curson*, Esq;
39. Tenants Law, or the Law of Landlords and Tenants, 8th Edition.
40. Laws concerning Trade and Tradesmen, 12ves.
41. *Enchiridion Clericale*, or Precedents for Young Clerks.
42. Cases in Law relating to Justices of the Peace, by *S. Blackerby*, Esq;
43. Mr. *Blackerby*'s Justice of Peace's Companion.
44. Trials *Per pais*, or the Law of *England* concerning Juries, with a Treatise of Evidence.
45. The Laws of Replevins, Distresses, &c.
46. Lord *Hale*'s Pleas of the Crown.
47. Baron and Feme, or the Law of Husband and Wife.
38. The Law of Commons and Commoners, shewing the several Kinds thereof.
49. *Brown* of Fines and Recoveries, 5th Edition, with Additions.
50. The Office and Duty of Executors, by *Wentworth*, with Additions.
51. Sir *Edward Lutwyche*'s Reports, in *English*, 2 Vols.
52. The Office and Authority of a Justice of Peace, by *William Nelson*, Esq; the 7th Edition.

A

TREATISE

OF THE

PLEAS

OF THE

CROWN.

BOOK II.

CHAP. I.

Of Courts of criminal Jurisdiction in general.

HAVING in the first Book endeavoured to shew the Nature of criminal Offences, I am now to shew, in what Manner the Offenders are to be brought to Punishment; and in Order hereto I shall consider,

1. The Nature of the Courts which have Jurisdiction over such Offences.
2. In what Manner the Offenders are to be proceeded against by such Courts.

And

And first, for the better Understanding of the Nature of such Courts, I shall premise some Considerations concerning them in general, and then consider the Nature of the principal of them in particular.

As to the Nature of such Courts in general, I shall consider,

1. What is requisite to the Constitution of their Authority.
2. What is incidental to all such Courts in general.

S.P.C. 54, 55.

Sect. 1. As to the first Point I shall take it for granted, That the King being the supream Magistrate of the Kingdom, and intrusted with the whole executive Power of the Law, no Court whatsoever can have any such Jurisdiction, unless it some Way or other derive it from the Crown.

Dalt. ch. 1. S. P. C. 54 b. 4 Inst. 71. 2 R 3. 11 a. Speed 521, 524. 1 Rol. Ab. 535.

Sect. 2. Yet it seems, That the King himself cannot sit in Judgment upon any Indictment, because he is one of the Parties to the Suit; and therefore where it is said in some of our ancient Histories, that our Kings have sometimes sate in Person with the Justices at the Arraignment of great Offenders, probably it ought not to be intended that they came as Judges, but as Spectators only, for the greater Solemnity of the Proceeding.

[a] 4 Inst. 70, 71. 2 Inst. 103. 8 H. 4. 13 b. 14. a. 20. 2 R. 3. 11. [b] Madox *History of the* Exchequer, *from Fol.* 5, *to* 17, *and Fol.* 56. *to* 85. Dalton ch. 1. [c] 28 Ass. pl. 52. [d] 4 Inst. 73.

Sect. 3. And it is said by [a] Sir *Edward Coke*, That the King has committed and distributed all his whole Power of Judicature to several Courts of Justice; and though it may be argued with the highest Probability both from the Nature of the Thing, and the constant Tenor of our [b] ancient Records and Histories since the Conquest, and also from the Form of all Process in the King's Bench, and Chancery, which is always made returnable before the [c] King himself, That in old Time our Kings in Person, often determined Causes between Party and Party, proper for those Courts; yet at this Day, by the long, constant and uninterrupted Usage of many Ages, our [d] Kings seem to have delegated their whole judicial Power to the Judges of their several Courts, which by the same immemorial Usage have gained a known and stated Jurisdiction, regulated by certain and established Rules, which our Kings themselves cannot alter without an Act of Parliament.

6 H. 7. 4. b. 5. a. Bro. Pat 53. 4 Inst. 125, 127. 6 Co. 11. b. 12 a.

Sect. 4. For it seems to be clearly agreed, That the King cannot give any Addition of Jurisdiction to an ancient Court, but that all such Courts must be holden in such Manner, and proceed by such Rules, and in such Cases only, as their known Usage has limited and prescribed; and from hence it follows, That as the Court of King's Bench cannot be authorized to determine a mere real Action between Subject and Subject, so neither can the Court of Common Pleas to inquire of Felony or Treason.

4 Inst 87. 1 Sid. 338.

Sect. 5. Nay it is said by some, That the King is so far restrained by the ancient Forms in all Cases of this Nature, that his Grant of a judicial Office for Life, which has been accustomed to be granted only at Will, is void.

42 Ass. 12, 13. 4 Inst. 164. Bro. Commission, 15, 16 F.N.B 110. b. Bro. Indictment 22, 38. See 12 Co. 31.

Sect. 6 And the Law is so jealous of any Kind of Innovation, in a Matter so highly concerning the Safety of the Subject, as not to endure any the least Deviation from the old known stated Forms, however immaterial it may seem, as will be more fully shewn, *Ch.* 5. *Sect.* 1.

Sect. 7. And from the like Reason it follows, that Commissions to [a] seize the Goods and imprison the Bodies of all Persons, who shall be notoriously suspected of Felonies or Trespasses, without any Indictment or other legal Process against them, are illegal and void.

Sect. 8. And it is said, That the King cannot grant any new Commission whatsoever, that is not warranted by ancient Precedents, however necessary it may seem, and conducive to the publick Good; and therefore [b] Commissions to assay Weights and Measures, being of a new Invention, were condemned by Parliament; and it is said by [c] Sir *Edward Coke*, That the King could not authorize Persons to take Care of Rivers and the Fishery therein, according to the Method prescribed by the Statute of *Westm.* 2. *Ch.* 47. before the making of that Statute.

Sect. 9. As all Judges must derive their Authority from the Crown, by some Commission warranted by Law, they must also exercise it in a legal Manner, and hold their Courts in their proper Persons; for they cannot act by [d] Deputy, nor any Way transfer their Power to another, as the Judges of Ecclesiastical Courts may.

Sect. 10. [f] But it seems, That regularly where there are divers Judges of a Court of Record, the Act of any one of them is effectual, especially if their [g] Commission do not expresly require more.

Sect. 11. It hath been [h] resolved, That by the Common Law, all Patents of the Justices of either Bench, Barons of the Exchequer, Sheriffs, Escheators, Commissioners of *Oyer* and *Terminer*, Gaol-Delivery, and of the Peace, are determined by the Death of the King who made them. Also it seems [i] certain, That at the Common Law (before 1 *Ed.* 6. 7. set forth more at large, *Ch.* 6.) if one had been convicted of any Offence before any such Commissioners, and the King had died before Judgment, no Judgment at all could have been given, because the King was dead for whom the Judgment was to have been given, and because the Authority of the Judges was determined. Also it is said, that at [k] Common Law a Person attainted in the Time of a former King, could not have been executed without a new Warrant. Yet it hath been adjudged, That the Authority of a [l] Coroner or Verderor ceases not by the Demise of the King in whose Reign they were chosen; and that the Office of a [m] Sheriff, in such Places where he is chosen by a Corporation, having by its Charter the Inheritance of the Office, does not determine by the Demise of the King; from whence it seems also to follow, That no other Corporation Officer, who by the Charter is invested with any judicial Authority, loses it by such Demise.

Sect. 12. And to prevent the Disorders and other Inconveniences, which may happen upon the Death of a King, from the want of Persons armed with competent Authority to execute the Laws, before the Successor can have Time to appoint others, it was enacted by 7 & 8 *Gul.* 3. 27. *That no Commission either Civil or Military, shall cease, determine, or be void, by Reason of the Death and Demise of his said late Majesty, or of any of his Heirs or Successors, Kings or Queens of this Realm; but that every such Commission shall be, continue, and remain in full Force and Vertue, for the Space of six Months next after any such Death or Demise, unless in the mean Time superseded, determined, or made void by the next and immediate Successor, to whom the Imperial Crown of this Realm, according to the Act of Settlement in the said Statute before mentioned, is limited and appointed to go, remain, or descend.*

Sect. 13. And it is farther enacted by 1 *Anne*, 8. Par. 2. *That no Patent or Grant of any Office or Imployment, either Civil or Military, hereafter to be made, shall cease, determine, or be void, by Reason of the Death or Demise of*

any

[a] 42 Aff. 5. Bro. Commission, 3, 15, 16. 2 Inst. 54.

[b] 4 Inst. 163, 245. 18 E. 3 ch. 1, 4.

[c] 2 Inst. 478.

[d] 1 Rol. Abr. 382. b. 6 Mod. 87. 9 E 4. 30. b. 31. a. Bro. Judges, 11.

[e] Latch 7.

[f] Bro. Coron. 201. 14 H 4. 34. b. 35. a.

[g] 23 Aff. pl. 7, 39 H. 6 41. b. 42. a.

S P. C. 53. *Letters* B. C. Con. Dalis. 24, 25. Hob. 70. 2 Rol. A. 673. Crompt. 121.

[h] 27 Aff 23. 2 Rol Ab. 677. G.

[i] Dalis. 15. Benloe 79. Dy. 165. pl. 2. 1 And. 44. 4 E. 4. 44. Bro. Judges, 32.

1 E. 5. 1. Crom. Jur. 126. a.

[i] 7 Co. 31.

[k] 1 Aff. pl 8. Bro Coron. 66.

[l] Dalis. 15. Dy. 165. pl. 2. 2 Inst. 175. 1 Levin. 120. Bro. Coron. 201. Commission, 19. Crom Jur. 126. a. *But this is made a Query,* 4 E 4. 44 b. *and* Bro Officer, 25. *and denied in* S. P. C. fol. 49 *Letters* B. C

[m] 7 Co. 30. b.

any King or Queen of this Realm, but that every such Patent or Grant shall be, continue, and remain in full Force for six Months, next after any such Death or Demise, unless in the mean Time superseded, determined, or made void by the next immediate Successor, to whom the Crown is limited and appointed to go, remain or descend.

And it is farther enacted, Par. 5. *That no Commission of Assize,* Oyer *and* Terminer, *general Gaol-Delivery, or of Association, Writ of Admittance, Writ of* Si non omnes, *Writ of Assistance, or Commission of the Peace, shall be determined by the Death of any King or Queen of this Realm; but every such Commission and Writ shall be and continue in full Force for six Months next ensuing, notwithstanding such Demise, unless superseded and determined by the next Successor: And also no original Writ, Writ of* Nisi prius, *Commission, Process or Proceedings whatsoever in, or issuing out of, any Court of Equity, nor any Process or Proceeding upon any Office or Inquisition, nor any Writ of* Certiorari, *or* Habeas Corpus, *in any Matter or Cause, either Criminal or Civil, nor any Writ of Attachments, or Process for Contempt,* &c. *shall be determined, abated, or discontinued, by the Demise of any King or Queen of this Realm; but every such Writ,* &c. *shall remain in full Force, to be proceeded upon as if such King or Queen had lived.*

As to the second Point, *viz.* What is incidental to all such Courts in general, I shall only take Notice of the following Particulars;

Sect. 14. First, That all Courts of this Kind must be Courts of [a] Record; for a Court which is not of Record, can neither impose any Fine on an Offender, nor award a *Capias* against him, nor even hold Plea of a common Trespass *Vi & armis*; And from hence it clearly follows, That no Proceedings of any Court of criminal Jurisdiction, can be removed into a Superior, but by Writ of Error or *Certiorari*; and that no Averment can be taken against the Truth of any Thing recorded in any such Court; [b] And that all Courts of Common Law, that have Power given them to fine and imprison, are thereby made Courts of Record.

Sect. 15. Secondly, That [c] all such Courts may injoin the People to keep Silence under a Pain, and impose reasonable Fines, not only on such as shall be convicted before them of any Crime on a formal Prosecution, but also on all such as shall be guilty of any Contempt in the Face of the Court, as by giving opprobrious Language to the Judge, or obstinately refusing to do their Duty as Officers of the Court; and it is said, That all such Courts, except the Court-Leet, may also imprison all such Offenders; Also it seems, [d] That even a Court-Leet is so far intrusted with the keeping of the Peace within its own Precinct, that the Steward of it may by Recognizance bind any Person to the Peace, who shall make an Affray in his Presence, sitting the Court, or may commit him to Ward, either for want of Sureties, or by Way of Punishment, without demanding any Sureties of him, in which Case he may afterwards impose a Fine according to his Discretion; from whence it follows *à fortiori*, that other superior Courts of Record have the like Power.

Sect. 16. Thirdly, That no [e] Judge of any such Court is compellable to deliver his Opinion before-hand, in Relation to any Question which may after come judicially before him.

Sect. 17. That no such Judge is any way punishable for a mere [f] Error of Judgment, as hath been more fully shewn in the first *Book, Chapter* 72. *Sect.* 6.

[a] 2 Inst. 311, 312. Reg. 111. b. F. N. B. 85. f. 16. a. 239. d. 1 Rol. Ab. 543. E. F. pl. 3. Co. Lit. 117. b. 260. a. 2 Lev. 93. 1 Mod. 215. 3 Lev. 205. 8 Co. 38. b.

[b] Salk. 200.

[c] 11 H 6 12. b. 1 Rol. Ab. 219. Y. 8 Co. 38. b. 11 Co. 43. b. Cro. E. 581. 1 Sid. 145. Brook Leet, 12, 36.

[d] F. N. B 82. Dalton ch. 1. Lamb. ch. 3. 10 H. 6. 10. b. Cromp. 7. 11 Co 43. b. *seems contrary.*

[e] 1 H 7 26. a. 3 Inst. 29.

[f] 27 Ass. pl. 23. 2 Rol. A. 77. G. Bro. Indictment, 17. Cromp. 121, 122. Salk. 201.

 Sect.

Sect. 18. It is questioned, Whether all Courts of Record may not discharge any Person arrested, during his Journeying to or from such Courts, or necessary Attendance there by Process from any other Court: However it seems to be agreed, That any such Court may discharge a Person who shall be so arrested in the Face of it. Lamb. 403. *Query* 1 Keb. 845. 1 Lev. 159. 1 Brown. 15. Raym. 100. Bro. Privilege 35. Crompt. 180.

CHAP. II.

Of the Court of the High Steward of England.

AND now I am to consider the Nature of the principal Courts of criminal Jurisdiction in particular, and

1. Of the Court of the High Steward of *England.*
2. The Court of King's Bench.
3. The Court of the Constable and Marshal.
4. The Court of the Justices of *Oyer* and *Terminer.*
5. The Court of the Justices of Gaol-Delivery.
6. The Court of the Justices of Assize and *Nisi prius.*
7. The Court of the Sessions of the Justices of the Peace.
8. The Court of the Coroners.
9. The Sheriff's Torn.
10. The Court-Leet.

The Office of High Steward of *England,* which anciently was Hereditary, not having been granted to any one since the Reign of King *Henry* the Fourth, but only *pro hac vice,* either for the Trial of a Peer on an Indictment for a capital Offence, or for the Determination of the Pretensions of those who claim to hold by Grand Serjeanty, to do certain honourable Services to the King at his Coronation: It seems needless to make a particular Inquiry, concerning the Authority of the Court of this High Officer, of which very little Mention is made in our ancient Records, or Law-Books; and therefore I shall content my self with remarking in this Place in general, That anciently the Duty of this Office consisted in supervising and regulating next under the King the Administration of Justice, and all other Affairs of the Realm, whether Civil or Military, and that no one under the Degree of Nobility is capable of so honourable a Post; and for the particular Manner of executing this Office in the Trial of a Peer, I shall refer the Reader to the Chapter concerning the Trial of Peers. 3 Inst. 58, 59. Madox *History of the* Exchequer, 33, *&c.* Crompton *of Courts,* 84. Fleta, lib. 2. Ca. 2. 3. 13 H. 8. 11. b. 3 Inst. 59. S. P. C. 152. infra ch. 8. s. 1.

CHAP. III.

Of the Court of King's Bench.

Vide supra, Ch. 1. S. 3. *and* Madox, ch. 19.

Sect. 1. THE whole Jurisdiction which is now distributed among the several Courts of *Westminster-hall*, seems in the first Reigns after the Conquest, to have been lodged in one Court, commonly called the King's Court, wherein Justice is said to have been administred sometimes by the King himself in Person, and sometimes by the High Justicier, who was an [a] Officer of very great Authority, and used in the King's Absence beyond-sea to govern the Realm as Vice-Roy.

[a] Madox, fol. 21 *and* 135. 1 Rol. Ab. 94. *Letter* A. *and* 95. *Letter* B. 2 Inst. 24, 25, 26.

Sect. 2. Out of this Court the Courts of [b] Common Pleas and Exchequer seem to have been derived, some Time before the making of the Statute of *Magna Charta*; the former of which Courts properly determines Pleas merely Civil, and the latter those relating to the Revenue of the Crown. And after the [c] Erection of these Courts, the supreme Court seems by Degrees to have obtained the Name of the Court of King's Bench, and hath always retained a supreme Jurisdiction in all criminal Matters, and also in certain personal Causes, and is still [d] supposed to have always the King himself in Person sitting in it.

[b] *See* Madox, Chap. 19. *Query* 2 Inst. 21, 22, 23. 1 Inst. 71.

[c] Madox, 543.

[d] Dyer, 187. pl. 6. Madox 543, 544. Crompton *of Courts*, 78. B.

For the better understanding the Nature of this Court, I shall consider the following Particulars:

1. In what Manner it corrects all Kinds of Misdemeanours of all Persons in general.
2. How far it reforms inferiour Courts.
3. How far its Presence suspends the Power of all other Courts.
4. What Rules are to be observed in the Form of its Proceedings.

See 16 Ca. 1. ca. 10. sec. 2. 11 Co. 98. 4 Inst. 71.

Sect. 3. As to the first Point, it is certain, That this Court is intrusted with the highest Jurisdiction, not only over all capital Offences, but also all other Misdemeanours whatsoever of a publick Nature, tending either to a Breach of the Peace, or to the Oppression of the Subject, or to the raising of Faction, Controversy, or Debate, or to any Manner of Misgovernment; so that whatsoever Crime is manifestly against the Publick Good, it comes within the Conusance of this Court, though it do not directly injure any particular Person; neither can any private Subject, who has not forfeited his Right to the Protection of the Law, suffer any kind of unlawful Violence or gross Injustice against his Person, Liberty, or Possessions, from any Person whatsoever, without a proper Remedy from this Court, not only for Satisfaction of the private Damage, but also for the exemplary Punishment of the Offender.

Sect. 4. Neither is it necessary in a Prosecution of any such Offence in this Court, to shew a Precedent of the like Crime formerly punished here, agreeing with the present in all its Circumstances; for this Court being the *Custos Morum* of all the Subjects of the Realm, where-ever it meets with an Offence contrary to the first Principles of common Justice, and

1 Sid. 168. *See the Preamble of* 16 Ca. 1.

and of dangerous Consequence to the Publick, if not restrained, will adapt such a Punishment to it as is suitable to the Heinousness of it.

Sect. 5. And so high a Trust doth the Law repose in the Justice and Integrity of this Court, as generally to leave it to the Discretion of its Judges to inflict such Fine and Imprisonment, and even infamous Punishment on Offenders, as the Nature of the Crime, considered in all its Circumstances, shall require; neither doth it confine them to make use of their own Prison, but leaves them at Liberty to commit Offenders to any Prison in the Kingdom, which they shall think most proper, and doth not suffer any other Court to remove or bail any Persons condemned to Imprisonment by them.

Mo. 666. pl. 913. 1 Sid. 145.

Sect. 6. Also this Court hath such a sovereign Jurisdiction in criminal Matters, that it may proceed as [a] well on Indictments found before other Courts, and removed into this by *Certiorari*, as on Indictments or Informations originally commenced in it, whether the Courts before whom such Indictments were found be determined or suspended, or still *in esse*, and whether the Proceedings be grounded on the Common Law, or on some Statute making a new Law concerning an old Offence, and appointing certain Justices to execute it, as the Statutes of [b] forcible Entries, and the [c] Statute of *Philip* and *Mary*, against Persons taking away Females under the Age of sixteen Years from their [d] Guardians, *&c.* Neither doth a Statute which appoints, That all Crimes of a certain Denomination shall be tried before certain Judges, exclude the Jurisdiction of this Court without express negative Words; upon which Ground it hath been resolved, That [e] 33 *H.* 8. 12. which enacts, That all Treasons, *&c.* within the King's House, shall be determined before the Lord Steward of the King's House, *&c.* doth not restrain this Court from proceeding against such Offences: But where a Statute creates a [f] new Offence, which was not taken Notice of by the Common Law, and erects a new Jurisdiction for the Punishment of it, and prescribes a certain Method of Proceeding, it seems questionable, how far this Court has an implied Jurisdiction in such a Case.

[a] Dalis. 25.
44 E. 3. 31 b. Cromp. Jurisd. 131.
[b] 9 Co. 118. *See* B. 1. Ch. 64. S. 51.
[c] Cro. Ca. 465. 2 Lev. 179. 2 Mod. 128, 129, 130.
[d] 3 Keb. 75, 94, 106, 273.
[e] 2 Inst. 549. 2 Jones 53.
[f] *See* 1 Sid. 296. *the Books above cited and the Chapter concerning* Indictments.

Sect. 7. But it is certain, That the Law has so high a Regard to this Court, that it will not suffer a [g] Record regularly removed into it from an inferiour one, to be remanded [h] after the Term in which it came in, (except in some few [i] special Cases;) [k] yet if the Justices perceive, that there is any Practice in endeavouring to remove any such Record, or that the sole Intention of such Removal is the Delay of Justice, they may on their Discretion refuse to receive such Record, and may before it is filed remand it back again, for the greater Expedition of Justice; and upon this [k] Ground, as I suppose, where one who had pleaded Not guilty to an Appeal below, and at his Trial had challenged so many of his Jury, that the Inquest could not be taken for want of Jurors, whereupon a new *Distringas* was awarded, removed himself into the Court of King's Bench, he was ordered to be remanded: Also by the Construction of the Statutes, which impower the Common Law Courts of *Westminster*, to grant a [l] *Nisi prius* for the Trial of Issues joined in those Courts, the Justices of the King's Bench may grant such Trial, as well in Cases of Treason and Felony as in other common Cases; because, for such Trial, not the Record it self is sent down, but only the Transcript of it.

[g] 22 Ed. 3. 6. b. 29 Ass. 43. 40 Ass. 29. 1 Rol. Ab. 534. G. 2. 492. K. 1. 4 Inst. 73. S. P. C. 158.
[h] 1 Rol. Re. 85.
[i] Cro. Car. 297. 1 Saunders, 97, 99. 1 Lev. 223. 1 Sid. 329.
[k] 4 Inst. 74, 75. 16 E. 4. 5. a. Bro. Coron. 162.

Sect. 8. And it is recited by 6 *H.* 8. 6. *That divers Felons and Murderers, upon feigned and untrue Surmises, had oftentimes removed, as well their Bodies as their Indictments, by Writ, and otherwise, before the King in his Bench, and could not by the Order of the Law be remitted and sent down to the Justices* of

[l] 4 Inst. 74. Ray. 364.

of Gaol Delivery, or of the Peace, nor other Justices, nor Commissioners, to proceed upon them after the Course of the Common Law. And thereupon it is enacted, *That the Justices of the King's Bench have full Authority by their Discretions, to remand and send down, as well the Bodies of all Felons and Murtherers, brought or removed before the King in his Bench, as their Indictments, into the Counties where the same Murders or Felonies have been committed and done; and to command all Justices of Gaol Delivery, Justices of Peace, and all other Justices and Commissioners, and every of them, to proceed and determine, upon all the aforesaid Bodies and Indictments so removed, after the Course of the Common Law, in such Manner as the same Justices of Gaol Delivery, Justices of Peace, and other Commissioner's, or any of them, might or should have done, if the said Prisoners or Indictments had never been brought into the said King's Bench.*

Cromp. Jur. 213.

Sect. 9. In the Construction of this Statute it seems to have been holden, That it shall not be extended by Equity to High Treason.

Ray. 367.

Sect. 10. As to the second Point, *viz.* How far the Court of King's Bench reforms inferior Courts, there is no Doubt, but that this Court, being the highest Court of Common Law, hath not only Power to reverse erroneous Judgments given by inferior Courts, but also to punish all inferior Magistrates, and all Officers of Justice, for all wilful and corrupt Abuses of their Authority, against the known, obvious, and common Principles of natural Justice, but not for mere Mistakes, which an honest well-meaning Man may innocently fall into.

Sect. 11. As to the third Point, *viz.* How far the Presence of this Court suspends the Power of all other Courts, it is certain, That this being the [a] supreme Court of *Oyer* and *Terminer*, Gaol Delivery, and *Eyre*, doth so far suspend the Power of all other Justices of this Kind, in the County wherein it sits during the Time of its sitting in it, (if such Justices have [b] Notice of its sitting there, and even without such [c] Notice, as some say,) that all Proceedings commenced before any such Justices during such Time are void; yet it [d] seems, That such Justices may proceed upon Indictments taken in a foreign County and removed before them, because the Court of King's Bench hath nothing to do with such Indictments, unless they be removed into it. Also there seems to be the same Reason, That such Justices may proceed on Indictments taken before them, of Offences in the same County before the Term; for it is said in [e] *Keilway*, That if an Appeal be commenced before Justices in *Eyre*, and afterwards another Appeal be brought in the King's Bench, it will be a good Plea that another Appeal is depending; which shews that the King's Bench ought not without a *Certiarari, &c.* to intermeddle in an Appeal, whereof another Court is legally possessed before; and the Reason seems to be the same as to Indictments: And it is said in the same [f] Book, That if the King's Bench and Justices in *Eyre* are in one County, yet this shall not change the Power of the Justices in *Eyre*, but that if the King will make Process for any Thing not commenced before the Justices of *Eyre*, as to such Thing their Power is ceased; by which it seems to be implied, that as to what was commenced before them their Power continues: However, it is certainly the [g] safest way for any of the Justices above mentioned, proceeding on any such Indictment, to have a Special Commission for that Purpose, and it is most adviseable, that such Commission bear *Teste* in the Term.

[a] H. P. C. 156. 9 Co. 118. b. 27 Aff. pl. 1. 3 Inst. 27. 4 Inst. 73.
[b] 21 H. 7. 29. b. Bro. Commission, 10. Vide infra Ch. 5. f. 2.
[c] 4 Inst. 73.
[d] 4 Inst. 73. Dy. 286. pl. 45.
[e] Keilw. 152. b.
[f] Keilw. 153.
[g] 3 Inst. 24. 4 Inst. 73. H. P. C. 156, 157.

Sect. 12. As to the fourth Point, What Rules are to be observed in the Form of the Proceedings of this Court, it seemeth, That all Process upon [h] Writs of Appeal, and also all Process upon [i] Indictments removed hither by *Certiorari* from a foreign County, ought to be made returnable

[h] Co. Entries, 57. b. 58. b. 60. a.
[i] Co. Entries, 354. b. 355. b. 356. b. 358. a.

coram nobis ubicunque fuerimus, but that all Process upon [a] Bills of Appeal against one *in custodia Mareschalli*, and perhaps also upon [b] Indictments commenced in the King's Bench, ought to be returnable *coram nobis apud Westmonasterium*: Also it has been [c] resolved, That where the Court proceeds on an Offence committed in the same County wherein it sits, the Process may be made returnable immediately; but that where it proceeds on an Offence removed by *Certiorari* from another, there must be fifteen Days between the *Teste* and Return of every Process.

[a] Co. Entries, 52. a. b 58. b. 60 a.
[b] Co. Entries, 352 a. 353 b. 361. a. Con. Co. Entries, 300. a. 363. a.
[c] 9 Co. 118. b. Co Lit. 134. b. 1 Lev. 61. 1 Sid. 72. 2 Rol. Ab. 626. pl. 4, 5. 2 Inst. 550, 568.

CHAP. IV.

Of the Court of the Constable and Marshal.

FOR the better understanding the Nature of this Court, it may not be improper to premise some general Considerations concerning the ancient Jurisdiction of those high Officers before whom it is holden.

Sect. 1. As to the Office of High Constable of *England*, which anciently was hereditary, the same being esteemed of too high Authority to be safely intrusted with any Subject, but only *pro hac vice*, since the Reign of King *Henry* the eighth, and there being very little to be found in our ancient Records and Histories, concerning the particular Power or Authority of this high Officer, our most learned Antiquaries seem to be able to give us little more than their own Conjectures concerning this Matter. However there is no Doubt, but that he was an Officer of very great Power both in War and Peace; and indeed his very Name imports no less, for the Word Constable signifying in general a Commander or Officer, he who was called Constable of *England*, or the King's Constable, or sometimes, by way of Eminency, the Constable, without any other Addition, cannot but be thought to have been a Person of the highest Command and Authority; and the Statute of 13 *R.* 2. (which is at large set forth in the following Part of this Chapter,) restraining his Jurisdiction to Things touching War, not determinable by the Common Law, in relation to which it requires him to proceed according to ancient Usage, clearly supposes him to have an ancient established Authority concerning these Matters: And it seems to have been somewhat doubtful, before the making of the said Statute, Whether the Constable and Marshal had not a general Jurisdiction over all Contracts whatsoever made beyond-sea.

Dy. 285. b. 4 Inst. 127.

Madox *History of the Exchequer*, *fol.* 27, 28, 29.

Madox, 27.

Madox, 28.

48 E. 3. 3. 13 H. 4 4, 5.

Sect. 2. Neither do there seem to be any greater Footsteps in Antiquity, of the original Institution of the Office of the Lord Marshal, or of his Power, or Authority; for anciently there were several Officers of the King's Houshold, who were called Marshals, as the Marshals of his [a] Horses, of his [a] Birds, and of his [a] Measures, who had certain Salaries allotted them, for the Management or well ordering of the Things committed to their Charge. And in the ancient Records relating to those Officers, there seems no more to be meant by having the Marshalsy of a Thing, than to have the Oversight, or Charge, or Ordering of it: Also in our old Records, there are some Officers taken Notice of by the Name of Marshals, who are mentioned only in general to have been Servants of the King's Houshold, without any farther Account of the Nature

[a] Madox, 30.

Madox, 30, 31.

Madox, 29, 30.

1 Rol. Ab. 527. K. ture of their Office, or Duty in particular. However, we find that in the 22d Year of King *Edw.* 3. the Parliament granted Fifteenths on divers Conditions, one of which was, That there should be no Mareschalsy in *England*, except the Mareschalsy of the King, and of the Guardian of *England*, when the King shall be out of *England*. And it seems clear, That there was one Marshal superior to the rest, who was sometimes called the Master-Marshal, at other Times the King's Marshal, the Marshal of *England*, or the Earl Marshal, being an Officer of very great Authority both in War and Peace, whose principal Office in [a] Time of War, was to regulate the Incampments of the Army, and to assign to the Troops their respective Posts in the Day of Battel; and in [b] Time of Peace, to provide for the Security of the King's Person in his Palace, to distribute the Lodgings there, and to preserve Peace and Order in the King's Houshold, and to be assistant to the Constable in determining Causes, and also to [c] execute the Orders both of the Court of the Constable, wherein he himself sat as Judge, and of the [d] Court of the High Steward, to which he seems to have been only an Officer.

Madox, 31, 32, 33.
[a] Fleta.Lib.2. Ca. 4. Co. Lit. 74.
[b] Madox, 33.
[c] 4 Inst. 123. *Cases in Parliament*, 60.
[d] Fleta, Lib.2. Ca. 3.

Sect. 3. But whatever might be the original Institution of these Officers, or the Nature of their Authority, it is certain their Jurisdiction is at present declared, limited and restrained by certain Acts of Parliament, before the making whereof, we have scarce any Thing memorable on Record concerning this Matter.

Madox, 29.

Sect. 4 And first it is enacted by 8 *R.* 2. 5. as followeth, *Because divers Pleas concerning the Common Law, and which by the Common Law ought to be examined and discussed, are of late drawn before the Constable and Marshal of* England, *to the great Damage and Disquietness of the People: It is agreed and ordained, That all Pleas and Suits touching the Common Law, and which ought to be examined and discussed at the Common Law, shall not hereafter be drawn or holden by any Means before the foresaid Constable and Marshal, but that the Court of the same Constable and Marshal shall have that which belongeth to the same Court, and that the Common Law shall be executed and used, and have that which to it belongeth, and the same shall be executed and used, as it was accustomed to be used in the Time of King* Edward.

Sect. 5. And it is farther declared by 13 *R.* 2. 2. in the following Words, *Because that the Commons do make a grievous Complaint, that the Court of the Constable and Marshal hath incroached to him and daily doth incroach Contracts, Covenants, Trespasses, Debts and Detinues, and many other Actions pleadable at the Common Law, in great Prejudice of the King, and of his Courts, and to the great Grievance and Oppression of the People: Our Lord the King, willing to ordain a Remedy against the Prejudices and Grievances aforesaid, hath declared in this Parliament, by the Advice and Assent of the Lords Spiritual and Temporal, the Power and Jurisdiction of the said Constable, in the Form that followeth: To the Constable it pertaineth to have Cognizance of Contracts touching Deeds of Arms and of War out of the Realm, and also of Things that touch War within the Realm, which cannot be determined nor discussed by the Common Law, with other Usages and Customs to the same Matters pertaining, which other Constables heretofore have duly and reasonably used in their Time. Joining to the same, That every Plaintiff shall declare plainly his Matter in his Petition, before that any Man be sent for to answer thereunto. And if any will complain, That any Plea be commenced before the Constable and Marshal, that might be tried by the Common Law of the Land, the same Plaintiff shall have a Privy-Seal of the King without Difficulty, directed to the said Constable and Marshal, to surcease in that Plea, until it be discussed by the Kings Council, if that Matter ought of Right to pertain to that Court, or otherwise to be tried by the Common Law of the Realm of* England, *and also that they surcease in the mean Time.*

Sect. 6. And it is farther enacted by 1 *H* 4. 14. as followeth, *For many great Inconveniences and Mischiefs, that often have happened, by many Appeals made within the Realm of* England *before this Time, it is ordained and stablished from henceforth, That all the Appeals to be made of Things done within the Realm, shall be tried and determined by the good Laws of the Realm, made and used in the Time of the King's noble Progenitors; and that all the Appeals to be made of Things done out of the Realm, shall be tried and determined before the Constable and Marshal of* England *for the Time being: And moreover, it is accorded and assented, That no Appeal be from henceforth made, or in any wise pursued in Parliament in Time to come.*

For the better understanding of the Construction of these Statutes, and the Nature of this Court, I shall examine the following Particulars:

1. How far the said Court hath Conusance of Points of Honour in general.
2. Whether it can punish private Persons for marshalling Funerals.
3. Whether it can be holden by a Lord Marshal alone without a Constable.
4. Whether its Power as to Appeals of Treason be superseded by 26 or 35 *H.* 8. or 5 and 6 *Ed.* 6. 11. or 1 and 2 *Ph.* and *Mar.* 10.
5. By what Law, and in what Manner it proceeds.
6. Whethet it may be prohibited if it exceeds its Jurisdiction.
7. Whether it can be holden by Commission.

Sect. 7. As to the first Point, it is observable, That the above mentioned Statute of 13 *R.* 2. declares the Jurisdiction of this Court, in Relation to Things done within the Realm in these Words, *To the Constable pertaineth Conusance, &c. of Things that touch War within the Realm, which cannot be determined nor discussed by the Common Law:* From whence it seems to follow, That this Court has nothing to do with a mere Civil Matter, no way relating to War, and therefore the Proceedings of the Court of the Lord Marshal, in the Time of King *Charles* the first, for bare scandalous Words, reflecting on the [a] Honour or Gentility of Families, seem no way to be maintained; yet it seems to be taken for granted in some [b] Books, That Disputes concerning Precedency, and Points of Honour, and Satisfaction therein, are proper for this Court: Neither do I find, That the Proceedings therein against Persons for falsly assuming the Name and Arms of honourable Families, were censured or disallowed by the [c] learned Members of the Committee of the House of Commons in the Year 1639. who were appointed to inquire into the Abuses of this Court. And it seems to be [d] admitted in the Argument of *Oldis*'s Case, That all Matters of this Nature are proper for this Court; yet it seems to be a large Interpretation to make these Things relate to War, so as to come within the Declaration above mentioned; and the Rule laid down in [e] *Rolle's Reports*, that the Marshal has Power given him where the Common Law gives no Remedy, seems no way maintainable from the said Statute; for it doth not say in general, That to the Constable pertaineth Conusance of Things, which cannot be determined by the Common Law, but of Things of War, *&c.* which cannot be thereby determined; [f] neither is it a conclusive Argument, that a Matter which is remediless by the Common Law, must have a Remedy from some other Law; yet inasmuch as by the Preamble of the said Statute,

[a] Rushworth's Coll. Part 2. Vol. 2. 1055, 1056.

[b] Hob. 128. 1 Rol.Re. 87. 2 Lev. 134. Show. 353. 1 Sid, 353. 1 Lev. 230.

[c] Rushorth's Coll. Part 2. Vol 2. 1055, 1056.

[d] *Parliament Cases*, 64, 65.

[e] 1 Rol. Re. 87.

[f] 13 H. 4. 4. b. 5. a.

tute, its chief Intention appears to be to prevent Incroachments on the Common Law; and ſuch Proceedings in Matters whereof the Common Law hath no Conuſance, cannot be ſaid any way to incroach upon it: And inaſmuch as the ſaid Statute is wholly declarative, and hath no negative Words; and the conſtant Practice, which is the beſt Interpreter of Laws, and the general Opinion of Lawyers ſeem to countenance ſuch Proceedings, I ſhall not take upon me to determine how far they may be warrantable.

Sect. 7. As to the ſecond Point, *viz.* Whether this Court can puniſh private Perſons for Marſhalling Funerals; though it ſhould be granted, That the Marſhalling publick Funerals belongs to the Heralds, who are Attendants on this Court, and that no other Perſons without their Licence can lawfully intermeddle herein; yet it does by no Means follow, That the Marſhal has Power to puniſh thoſe who ſhall be guilty of any ſuch Incroachment; but the proper Remedy ſeems to be by Action on the Caſe at Common Law, and not by a Suit in this Court, which by the above mentioned Statutes of 8 and 13 *R.* 2. has Cognizance only of ſuch Matters, which cannot be determined nor diſcuſſed by the Common Law: And this ſeems to be the principal Reaſon of Dr. *Oldis*'s Caſe, wherein a Suit in the Marſhal's Court againſt one *Donmille*, for taking upon him without Licence to paint Arms and Eſcutcheons, and cauſing them to be fixed to Herſes, and providing and lending Palls for Funerals, and painting Arms for one who had no Right to their Uſe at the Funeral, and marſhalling ſeveral Funerals, *&c.* was prohibited by the Court of Exchequer, upon great Deliberation, with the Advice of the reſt of the Judges, and the Judgment was afterwards confirmed by the Houſe of Lords.

1 Lev. 230. 1 Sid. 353. Show. Rep. 353.

Caſes in Parliament, 58, *&c.*

Sect. 8. As to the Third Point, *viz.* Whether this Court can be holden by the Lord Marſhal alone without the Conſtable, it was ſtrongly inſiſted in the [a] Arguments made uſe of in Dr. *Oldis*'s Caſe, That the Lord Marſhal cannot hold this Court without the Conſtable; and this was alſo the Opinion of the [b] above mentioned learned Committee of the Houſe of Commons in the Year 1639. And it is certain, That all our ancient [c] Law-Books and [d] Reports, which ſpeak of this Court, ſpeak of it either as the Court of the Conſtable and Marſhal, or of the Conſtable [e] only; and it is obſervable, that the above mentioned Statute of 13 *R.* 2. which in the Preamble ſpeaks of this Court, as the Court of the Conſtable and Marſhal, in the Body of the Act mentions the Conſtable only. And it is farther remarkable, That where-ever the Conſtable is mentioned together with the Marſhal, as Judge of this Court, he is always put before him; which ſeems to intimate, that he is look'd upon as the principal Judge of it: And it is agreed by [f] all, That the Marſhal cannot determine an Appeal of Death, or Treaſon, without a Conſtable; but on the other Side it may be argued, That the Reaſon why an Appeal of a capital Matter neceſſarily requires a Conſtable as well as Marſhal, is, becauſe 1 *H.* 4. which orders how ſuch an Appeal ſhall be brought, is expreſs, That it ſhall be tried and determined before the Conſtable and Marſhal of *England* for the Time being; whereas the other Statutes only provide againſt the Incroachments of this Court, and do not mention in what Manner or before whom it ſhall be holden; but they ſeem to refer ſuch Queſtions to ancient Uſage; ſo that if [g] before theſe Statutes the Court was uſually holden before the Conſtable and Marſhal jointly and ſeverally, [h] according to the common Uſage of other Courts, which generally may be holden before one Judge in the Abſence of

[a] *Caſes in Parliament*, 65, 66.

[b] Ruſhworth's Coll. Pt. 2. Vol. 2. 1056.

[c] S.P.C. 65. Cromp Juriſdiction, 82. 2 Inſt. 51. 3 Inſt. 123. Co.Lit.261.a. 391.b.

[d] 13 H.4.46. 37 H.3.5.a. 48 E.3.3.b. 37 H.6.20.b. 21.a.

[e] 3c H.6.6.G. 13 H.4.5.a.

[f] 1 Inſt.74.b. Ruſhworth's Coll. Pt. 2. Vol. 1. 107, 112, *&c.* *Caſes in Parliament*, 61. 1 Lev. 230. Hutton, 3.

[g] *Caſes in Parliament*, 60, 61.

[h] *See* Ch. 1. S. 10.

of the rest, it seems a reasonable Construction of the said Statutes to allow this Court still to be so holden; neither is it probable, That the Lord Marshal upon the Extinguishment of the hereditary Office of the Constable, should from Time to Time in the [a] Reigns of King *Henry* the eighth, Queen *Elizabeth*, and King *James* the first, hold this Court by himself without any Constable, and also often be assisted therein by the Judges of the Common Law, unless it were then well known, that such his Proceeding was warranted by the ancient and established Usage of his Court; and it is very extraordinary, That our Judges and Lawyers should [b] generally take it as a Thing granted, that the Marshal is at this Day the proper Judge of Points of Honour, *&c.* if it were imagined that he has no Power to act without the Concurrence of a Constable.

[a] *Cases in Parliament*, 60, 61. 4 Inst. 126.

[b] Hob. 121. 1 Rol. Re 87. 2 Lev. 134. Show. 353. 1 Sid. 353. 1 Lev. 236.

Sect. 9. As to the fourth Point, *viz.* Whether the Power of this Court as to Appeals of Treason, be superseded by the Statutes of 26 *H.* 8. 13. or 35 *H.* 8. 2. or 5 and 6 *Ed.* 6. 11. or 1 and 2 *Ph.* and *Mar.* 10. it is observable that it is enacted by the said Statutes of *H* 8. and *Ed.* 6. *That all manner of Treasons,* &c. *done out of this Realm shall from thenceforth be inquired, heard and determined before the Justices of the King's Bench, or before Commissioners,* &c. *in like Manner, to all Intents and Purposes, as if they had been done in the same Shire wherein they shall be inquired of,* &c. And it is enacted by the said Statute of 1 and 2 *Phil.* and *Mar.* 10. *That from thenceforth all Trials for any Treason, shall be had and used only according to the due Order and Course of the Common Law*: Yet it hath been adjudged, That none of these Statutes take away the Jurisdiction of this Court in Relation to such Treason: For the said Statutes of *H.* 8. and *Ed.* 6. being wholly in the Affirmative, and it being their chief Intention to supply a Defect in the Common Law, which had provided no Method for the Trial of such Offences by Jury, they shall not without express Words be construed to take away the Authority of an ancient Court, confirmed by Parliament; and therefore the above mentioned Expression, That all such Treasons shall be tried by the King's Bench, *&c.* shall be taken to purport no more than that the King's Bench, *&c.* shall have Authority to try them; and as to the 1 and 2 *Ph.* and *Ma.* the plain Import thereof, seems to be to restore the ancient Manner of Trial by the Course of the Common Law to all Treasons within its Jurisdiction, which had been much altered by some Statutes in the former Reigns, and this is fully satisfied by abolishing all Innovations, in the Proceedings at Common Law, and has no Relation to Cases no way within its Conusance.

Cases in Parliament 62. Rushworth's Coll. Part 2. Vol 1. 107. 4 Inst. 124.

Rushworth's Coll. Part 2. Vol 1. 107. Dyer 131. pl. 75. 3 Inst. 24. 4 Inst. 124.

Sect. 10. As to the fifth Point, *viz.* By what Law and in what Manner this Court proceeds, there is no Doubt but that it ought to follow its own Customs and Usages so far as they go, and in Cases omitted the Rules of the [a]Civil Law: And because this is not a Court of Common Law, a [b]Condemnation in it for a capital Offence causes neither Forfeiture of Lands nor Corruption of Blood; neither can an Error in its Proceedings be remedied by Writ of Error, but only by Appeal to the King: And yet the Judges of the Common Law take Notice of the Jurisdiction of this Court, and give Credit to a Certificate of its Judges, for the Trial of an [d] Issue concerning its Proceedings; [d] for the Civil Law is as much the Law of the Land, in such Cases wherein it has been always used, as the Common Law is in others.

[a] 3 Inst. 125. 2 Inst. 51. 1 Inst 261. 37 H 6. 3. b. 20 b.

[b] 3 Inst. 125 Rushworth's Coll. Part 2. Vol. 1. 107, 113, *&c.* *Cases in Parliament*, 62. 2 Inst. 51.

[c] 3 Inst. 125, 341. *Cases in Parliament* 62.

[d] 30 H 6 6 b. 37 H. 6 3. b. 20 b. 21. a.

Sect. 11. It is questioned, Whether the [e] King have any Remedy in this Court against an Offender, by way of Indictment or Information by the Attorney-General.

[e] Hutt 3.

Sect. 12. As to the sixth Point, *viz.* Whether this Court may be prohibited if it exceeds its Jurisdiction, it is expresly resolved in *Oldis's* Case, That the said Court being holden before the Lord Marshal only, may be prohibited by the Courts of the Common Law if it exceed its Jurisdiction, and it is strongly insisted on in the Argument of that Case, That the Court of the Constable and Marshal, may also be prohibited; but there having been no Court holden before a Constable and Marshal for these many Years, and there seeming to be small Likelihood of its being revived, I shall refer the Reader for the farther Examination of this Matter to the learned Sir *Bartholomew Shower's* Report of the said Case.

Cases in Parliament 61, 65.

Sect. 13. As to the seventh Point, *viz.* Whether the said Court can be holden by Commission; it seems to be the better Opinion of the Court in *Parker's* Case, That during the Lunacy of an Earl Marshal, it may well be holden before Commissioners deputed to exercise his Office; and it seems hard to say, That such Commissions, founded on the plain Necessity of the Case, and intended to prevent a Failure of Justice, as to Cases of which no other Court hath Conusance, are against the Purview of the Petition of Right, made in the third Year of the Reign of King *Charles* the first; which, complaining that Commissions had been granted for the Trial of certain capital Offences and other Outrages, by the Martial Law, under Pretence whereof divers of the King's Subjects had been put to Death, prays that from thenceforth no Commissions of like Nature might issue forth to be executed as aforesaid.

1 Lev. 230. 1 Sid. 353.

CHAP. V.

Of the Court of the Justices of Oyer *and* Terminer.

FOR better understanding of the Nature of the Courts of the Justices of *Oyer* and *Terminer* and Gaol Delivery, I shall premise some Considerations concerning them in general, and then consider the Nature of each of them in particular.

Sect. 1. But in the first Place, it may not be improper to remark, That the Prerogative authorizing these or any other Justices, is inseparably united to the Crown, not only by the Common Law, but also by Statute, to which Purpose it is enacted by 27 *H.* 8. 24. *That no Person or Persons, of what Estate, Degree, or Condition soever they be, shall have any Power or Authority to make any Justices of Eyre, Justices of Assize, Justices of Peace, or Justices of Gaol Delivery: But that all such Officers and Ministers shall be made by Letters Patent under the King's Great Seal, in the Name and by the Authority of the King's Highness, in all Shires, Counties Palatine,* Wales, &c. *or any other his Dominions,* &c. *any Grants, Usages, Allowance, or Act of Parliament to the contrary notwithstanding.*

Lamb. B. 1. ch. 5. Co. Lit. 114. 1 Lev. 219.

As to what belongs to Justices of *Oyer* and *Terminer*, and Gaol Delivery in general I shall examine:

1. By what Kind of Instruments they must be constituted.
2. How their Authority may be suspended, revived or determined.

3. How far the precise Letter of their Commissions must be observed by such Justices.
4. What Form is to be observ'd in the Adjournment of such Commissions.
5. How far the Power given by them, may be extended by other Commissions to other Justices, or committed to fewer than were appointed by the former.
6. Whether such Justices can sit in one County to try Offences in another.
7. Where their Records are to be kept after they are determined.
8. Whether the same Justices at the same Time may execute both Commissions.

Sect. 1. As to the first Point, *viz.* By what Kind of Instrument such Justices must be constituted; it seems to be laid down as a general Rule in some of the old Books, That though a Justice may be discharged by Writ under the Great Seal, yet that he cannot be made a Justice by such Writ, but only by [a] Commission: And it seems to be holden, both by [b] Sir *Edward Coke* and Sir [c] *Matthew Hale*, If any such Justices have their Authority by Writ, though made in the same Form and Words, that a legal Commission ought to have, yet their Proceedings are void; and yet it seems, That nothing more is meant by these Expressions, if strictly examined, than that all such Justices must derive their Authority from such Instruments as are of a known, stated, and allowed Form, warranted by ancient Precedents; and 'tis only a Dispute of Words, whether such Instruments are to be called Writs or Commissions; for if you take the Import of the Word *Writ* from [d] *Finch*'s Definition of it, who says, That it is a *Latin* Letter of the King's, from his higher Courts of Record, in Parchment, sealed with his Seal, and *tested* by him, it seemeth that the most approved Forms of Commissions of *Oyer* and *Terminer*, *&c.* may well enough come under the general Notion of Writs, which by the last mentioned [e] Author are divided into Writs Original and Commissional: And accordingly we find, That Commissions of *Oyer* and *Terminer*, Association, and *si non omnes*, granted upon special Occasions, are called Writs both by the [f] Register, and also by [g] *Fitzherbert*, who yet seems not to approve of this general Notion of the Word *Writ*, and says, that these Commissions should not properly be called Writs. Also it is said, by Sir *Edward Coke* in his Comment on the Statute of *Westminster*, the second, *Ch.* 32. which mentions the Writ of *Oyer* and *Terminer*, that Commissions were anciently granted by Writ, by which he seems to imply, That they are otherwise granted at this Day; but he doth not tell us the Distinction between a Writ and Commission; neither can I find that the modern Precedents differ from the old ones; but on the contrary, that it hath always been agreed, That it is the safest Way to follow the old ones: But I must confess, That I cannot find a certain Instance from any [h] Book of Authority, wherein general Commissions of *Oyer* and *Terminer* are called Writs. However, as to the Resolutions of the Judges in 42 *Ass. pl.* 12, 13. which are but briefly and obscurely reported, and yet seem to be the chief Foundation of what is said in the later Books relating to this Matter, the Authority thereof seems to amount to no more than these two following Points: First, That Justices appointed by Commission to hear and determine certain Offences, cannot receive an additional Power by Writ directing them to inquire of other Offences; and this seems to be the Sense of [i] *Staundford* and [k] *Fitzherbert*

[a] Long. Quinto. Ed.4.13.27.b. 42 Ass. pl. 12, 13. Bro. Ass. 384. Commission, 16, 18. Indictment, 22, 38. 29 Finch 247.

[b] 4 Inst 164.

[c] H.P.C. 161.

[d] Finch 237. *See* Theloal's *Digest of Originals*, 1. b. 2. b.

[e] Finch, 312, 318. *See* Theloal, 2 b.

[f] Register. 123.b. 124 b.

[g] F.N.B. 110, 111. Cromp. Jurisdiction, 131.

[h] Vide infra, Sect. 3.

[i] S P.C. 94.A.

[k] Fitz. Enditement, 7. *See* Br. Commission 16, 18. Indictment, 22, 38, 39.

[c] 12 Co. 31.

a 12 Co. 31. *herbert* in relation to this Matter. [a] Secondly, That Writs impowering Persons to inquire of Offences, without authorizing them also to determine them, are illegal, except in such Cases wherein they are allowed by ancient Usage, as were [b] Writs of this Kind to Sheriffs before the Statute of 28 *E.* 3. 9. And therefore where it is generally said in some [c] Books, That Commissions have been directed to certain Persons to inquire of certain Offences, in order to have them afterwards tried before other Justices, it seems that it ought to be understood, that such Commissions were in the common Form of Commissions of *Oyer* and *Terminer*, though they be spoken of only as Commissions of Inquiry As to the Resolution in the *Long* [d] *Quinto* of *Edward* the fourth, which is the other principal Authority concerning this Matter, the Import thereof seems to be no more than this, That a Person cannot legally be associated to Justices of Assize, by a Writ directed to such Justices, reciting a Commission of Association to such Person, and commanding the Justices to receive him, unless there be also produced a Commission of Association directed to such Person; for that the King cannot make a Justice by such Writ directed to others; by which it seems to be implied, That by a proper Writ he may do it. And it is certain, That the Commission of Association directed to the Party himself, is called a Writ both by the [e] Register, [f] *Fitzherbert*, and [g] *Finch*, and also by [h] Sir *Edward Coke*, as well as the Writ of Admittance directed to the other Justices. However it seems clearly to be agreed by all these Books, That the best Rule of judging of the Validity of any such Commissions, is their Conformity to known and ancient Precedents, and this seems to be the best Reason of the Resolution in 1 *And.* 196. wherein it is adjudged, That a Commission to a Corporation, appointing some of its principal Members to be Justices of Gaol Delivery, together with those whom the King should appoint from Time to Time, was void: For such an Authority depending on the precarious Appointment of of other Justices, is not agreeable to the known Forms of such Commissions; but the other Reason given in that Book, for such newly appointed Justices not joining with the former, because their Authority commences at several Times seems not conclusive; for the Authority of Justices, appointed by Writ of Association, is of a subsequent Commencement from that of the Justices in the first Commission; and yet it is certain, That such may act jointly together, as will more fully appear in the following Chapter.

b Register, 121. S. P. C. 84.

c 1 And. 106. See Pl. Com. 390.

d Fol 111. 112. 29 b. 137, 138.

e Register, 124. b.

f F. N. B. 111.

g Finch, 318.

h 4 Inst. 107.

Sect. 2. As to the second Point, *viz.* How the Authority of such Justices may be suspended, revived or determined, there is no Doubt, but that their Power is wholly suspended by the Court of King's Bench sitting in the same County for which they are commissioned, during the Time of such sitting, especially if they have Notice thereof, as hath been more fully shewn *Chap.* 3. *Sect.* 10. and it seems, That their Jurisdiction is revived of Course, when the said Court no longer sits there, without any Writ of *Procedendo, &c.* Also it is certain, that their [h] Authority may be suspended by a Writ of *Supersedeas*, which is grantable on Proof that their Commission was unduly granted, in which Case their Power may be restored by a Writ of *Procedendo*, without any new Commission. But a Commission once determined, cannot be revived by any Writ of *Procedendo*, nor the Justices authorized anew without another Commission.

h Register, 124, 125. 12 Ass 21. 4 Inst. 163. H. P. C. 162.

Sect. 3. Such Commissions may be determined expresly or impliedly; expresly, by an absolute Repeal or Countermand from the King; impliedly, several Ways. 4 Inst. 163.

Sect. 4 First, by the Demise of the King by whom they were granted; but this Mischief is in a great Measure obviated by late Statutes, as hath been more fully shewn, *Ch.* 1. *sect.* 11, 12, 13.

Sect. 5. Secondly, According to some Opinions, by the Justice's Acceptance of any new Name of Dignity, as of that of Duke, Knight, or Serjeant, *&c.* But this is remedied by 1 *Ed.* 6. 7. by which it is enacted, *That if any Person being in any of the King's Commissions whatsoever, shall fortune to be made or created Duke, Archbishop, Marquess, Earl, Viscount, Baron, Bishop, Knight, Justice of the one Bench or of the other, or Serjeant at Law, or Sheriff, yet that notwithstanding he shall remain Commissioner*, &c. But it hath been questioned, Whether the Dignity of a Baronet which has been created since that Statute, be within the Equity of it? Bro. Commission.4,22. Cro. Ca. 104. Lit. Rep. 81.

Sect. 6. Thirdly, By holding a Session without adjourning it, if the Commission have no Time limited for its Continuance; as where it is appointed *pro hac vice* only; but if it be granted for a certain Time, or *quamdiu nobis placuerit*, it does not necessarily require any Adjournment; and therefore, if the Court holden by Vertue of such Commission, break up without any Adjournment, or upon a void one, as being made without the Consent of the Majority of the Commissioners, yet it may be holden again on a new Summons. Crom. Jur. 125. b. H. P. C. 161. 4 Inst. 165. Bro. Commission. 12. Dalis 24, 25. Vide Dyer 205. pl. 5. 4 Inst. 165. 1 Leon 270. 10 Ed. 4. 7.

Sect. 7. Fourthly, By granting a new Commission to other Persons of the same Nature with the former, though but for Part of the District for which the former was granted, as some say: And whether [a] such new Commission be for a certain Time, or *pro hac vice* only; yet the former Commissions shall remain [b] in Force, so far as they are consistent with the later; and therefore it seems certain, that a Commission of the Peace is not determined, as to its Authority relating to the Peace, by a new Commission to hear and determine Felonies. But it hath been [c] holden, That it is determined as to its Authority relating to Felonies; but this seems justly questionable, not only as being contrary to common Practice, but also because Justices of the Peace, as such, seem to have Authority by 34 *E.* 3. to hear and determine Felonies, without any special Clause in their Commission, for that Purpose, as will more fully be shewn *Ch.* 8. But it seems certain, That a Commission of [d] Gaol-Delivery shall not be determined by a new Commission of *Oyer* and *Terminer*, because they are of different Natures. [e] Also it seems to be clear not only from 2 *&* 3 *Ph.& Mar.* 18. set forth more at large, *Sect.* 12. but also in Cases not within the Statute, that a Commission of the Peace for a certain Town determines not the Authority of the Corporation, having a Grant from the King, That the Mayor and his Successors shall be Justices of the Peace within its Limits, because such a Grant is irrevocable. [f] Also it seems certain, That no new Commission doth determine an old one, unless the former Commissioners have Notice of it.

[a] Bro. Commission 7.
[b] Bro. Commission. 8, 24.
[c] Bro. Commission. 8.
[d] Bro. Commission. 24.
[e] Bro. Commission. 5.
[f] H.P.C. 162. 4 Inst. 165. 34 Ass. 8. Bro. Commission.6, 14.
[g] H P.C. 162. 4 Inst. 165. Keilw. 116. Crom. Jur. 125. b.
[h] 34 Ass. 8. Bro. Commission. 14. Moor. 186. pl. 333. H P. C. 162. 4 Inst. 165. Dyer 355. pl. 36.

Sect. 8. Such Notice may be given expresly or impliedly; expresly, by [g] shewing the new Commission to the former Commissioners, which certainly determines the Power of all those to whom it is shewn; impliedly, two manner of Ways.

Sect. 9. I. By [h] holding a Session by Force of the new Commission, which seemeth to be agreed to be a Matter so notorious, that the first Justices shall be presumed to have Notice of it.

H. P. C. 162. 4 Inst. 165. Bro. Commission, 6. Keilw. 116.

Sect. 10. II. According to the general Opinion, by proclaiming the new Commission in the County.

Sect. 11. As the Authority of the Justices appointed by any former Commission, is determined by the Grant of a new one in the Manner abovementioned, so likewise were all Proceedings before such Justices discontinued at the Common Law; to remedy which Inconvenience it was enacted by 1 *Ed.* 6. 7. Par. 6. *That no manner of Process, or Suit made, sued, or had before any Justices of Assize, Gaol-Delivery, Oyer and Terminer, Justices of Peace, or other of the King's Commissioners, shall not in any wise be discontinued by the making and publishing of any new Commission or Association, or by altering the Names of the Justices of Assize, Gaol-Delivery, Oyer and Terminer, Justices of Peace, or other the King's Commissioners, but that the new Justices of Assize, Gaol-Delivery, and of the Peace, and other Commissioners, may proceed in every Behalf, as if the old Commissions, Justices and Commissioners, had still remained and continued not altered.*

1 Sid 348. 2 Keb. 292. Bro. Coro. 178.

Sect. 12. And it farther enacted by 2 & 3 *Ph. & Mar.* 18. *That all and singular Commissions granted to any City or Town-Corporate, not being a County in it self, for the keeping of their Peace, and Delivery of the Prisoners remaining in the Gaols of any such City or Town-Corporate, shall stand, remain, and be good, and available and effectual in the Law, to all Intents, Constructions and Purposes, the granting of any like Commission of Peace or Gaol-Delivery, to any Commissioner or Commissioners for the Conservation of the Peace, or Delivery of the Prisoners remaining in the Gaol of any Shire, Lathe, Rape, Riding, or Wapentake within the Realm of* England, *bearing Date after the said Commission or Commissions granted as is aforesaid, to any such City or Town-Corporate, not being, as aforesaid, a County in it self, to the contrary notwithstanding.*

Dalis. 25.

Sect. 13. As to the third Point, *viz.* How far the precise Letter of such Commissions must be observed by the Justices, it is said to be agreed, That if a Commission of *Oyer* and *Terminer, &c.* be awarded to certain Persons to inquire at such a Place, they can neither open their Commission at another, nor adjourn it thither, nor give Judgment there; and that if they do, all their Proceedings shall be esteemed as *coram non judice:* Yet it is agreed, That Justices appointed by Commission *pro hac vice*, may adjourn their Commission from one Day to another, though there be no Words in their Commission to such Purpose; for nothing can be more reasonable, than to intend that a general Commission authorizing Persons to do a Thing, does implicitly allow them convenient Time for the doing of it.

12 Ass pl. 21. Crom. Jur. 136. Long. quinto E. 4. 133. a. Dalis. 25. 3 Inst. 31. H. P. C. 160. Bro. Commission, 18. Kelynge 57.

Sect. 14. As to the fourth Point, *viz.* What Form is to be observed in the Adjournment of such Commissions, having already in the foregoing Part of this Chapter, in the 6th and 13th Sections, incidentally treated of the principal Questions relating to this Matter, I shall only take Notice in this Place, That it seems most proper to [a] enter all such Adjournments in the Present Tense; yet it is said, That the Entry of of them in the Preter-Tense, is made good by the Multitude of Precedents: [b] However it is said, That the Court will never intend that there was an Adjournment, if no Entry at all were made of it.

[a] Raym. 115.

[b] 1 Sid. 348. 2 Keb. 284, 294.

Sect. 15. As to the fifth Point, *viz.* How far the Power given by such Commissions, may be extended by new ones to other Justices, or committed to fewer than were appointed by the former; it is certain, That new Commissioners of this Kind may be added to the former, by a Writ or Commission of Association, which setting forth the Purport of the former Commission, declares the King's Pleasure to associate to the Persons, appointed by the first, those to whom such new Writ or Commisſion is directed, provided that ſuch new Juſtices attend at the Times and Places appointed by the former; and it is uſual to direct another Writ to the former Juſtices, commanding them to admit ſuch new Juſtices as their Aſſociates with the Proviſo abovementioned; and the Writ to the Perſons ſo aſſociated is always Patent, and that to the other Juſtices to admit them is Cloſe. But it hath been [a] reſolved, That the firſt Juſtices are not bound by ſuch Writ to admit the Perſons named in it as their Aſſociates, unleſs they produce ſuch Patent of Aſſociation as is abovementioned directed to themſelves, as hath been more fully ſhewn in the firſt Section of this Chapter. And it hath been [b] queſtioned, Whether a ſpecial Commiſſion of Aſſociation, relating only to a particular Cauſe, can aſſociate the Perſons named in it to Juſtices appointed by a general Commiſſion? Alſo it hath been holden, That the King can grant but one Patent of Aſſociation to one Commiſſion.

Regiſter 124. F. N. B. 111. B. Finch 318, 319. H. P. C. 159, 162. 4 Inſt. 165. [a] Long. quinto E. 4. 137. [b] Long. quinto E. 4. 111, 112, 130, 131. Fitz. Aſſize 17. 32 H. 6. 10.

Sect. 16. If after Juſtices have ſate by Vertue of a Commiſſion, and taken divers Indictments, and awarded Proceſs thereon, they ſhall all, or ſome of them die, the King may grant a new Commiſſion to thoſe who are living only, or to others, commanding them to continue the Proceedings begun, and to proceed upon ſuch Proceſs, and to hear and determine all the Offences in the former Commiſſion: And thereupon the King ſhall ſend a Writ unto the Executors of the Juſtices who are dead, to ſend the Rolls, Records, and Proceſſes touching the Premiſſes, before the new Commiſſioners, *&c.*

Regiſter 128. F. N. B. 111. D. 113, 114.

Sect. 17. After a VVrit of Aſſociation, it is uſual to make out a Writ of *ſi non omnes*, directed both to the firſt Juſtices, and alſo to thoſe who are ſo aſſociated to them, which reciting the Purport of the two former Commiſſions, commands the Juſtices, That if all of them cannot conveniently be preſent, ſuch a Number of them may proceed, *&c.*

Regiſter 124. F. N. B. 111.

Sect. 18. As to the ſixth Point, *viz.* Whether ſuch Juſtices may ſit in one County to try Offences in another? it ſeems agreed, That regularly all Offences are to be inquired of, heard, and determined in the County wherein they were committed, and that the King cannot authorize the taking of them in another; yet it was adjudged in the Caſe of the City of *Glouceſter*, That if the King grant to a City the Privilege of being a County of it ſelf, diſtinct from the County within which it lies, with a *Salvo* or Reſervation, That the Juſtices of *Oyer* and *Terminer*, *&c.* for the County at large, may ſtill ſit in ſuch City, ſuch Reſervation makes the City ſtill remain Part of the County for ſuch Purpoſe, and conſequently, that an Indictment found within ſuch City, of an Offence in the County at large, is good. Alſo it is certain, That by a ſpecial Cuſtom, Indictments of Offences within a County, may be taken in a Place out of it, as they are in Fact taken both for *Middleſex* and *London* at the Seſſions-Hall at *Newgate*, which ſtands in *London*; for it ſhall be intended, That at the original Diviſion of *London* from *Middleſex*, there was a ſpecial Proviſion made for this Purpoſe. Alſo it is certain, That the King may grant a ſpecial Commiſſion of *Oyer* and *Terminer*, to ſit in one County for hearing and determining Offences, whereof Indictments have been found in another: But it is agreed, That the Trial muſt be by the Jurors of the proper County.

3 Inſt. 27. H. P. C. 162, 163. Dy. 286. pl. 45. Poph. 16, 17. 1 And. 291, 292. 3 Inſt. 27. H. P. C. 162, 163. Dy. 286. pl. 45. Raym. 193. Popham 17. 3 Inſt. 27. H. P. C. 162, 163. Dy. 286. pl. 45. Pl. Com. 396.

Sect. 19. As to the ſeventh Point, *viz.* Where the Records of ſuch Juſtices are to be kept after they are determined, it is enacted by 9 *Ed.* 3. 5. *That Juſtices of Aſſize, Gaol-Delivery, and of Oyer and Terminer, ſhall ſend all their Records and Proceſſes determined and put in Execution, to the Exchequer at* Michaelmas, *every Year once, to be delivered there; and the Trea-*

14 H. 7. 25 b.

surer and Chamberlains, which for the Time shall be, having the Sight of the Commissions of such Justices, shall receive the same Records and Processes of the said Justices under their Seals, and keep them in the Treasury, as the Manner is; so that the Justices always do first take out the Estreats of the said Records and Processes against them, to send to the Exchequer as they were wont before.

9 H 7. 9 a. b. Bro. Commission, 17, 24. Crom Jur. 126. b. H. P. C. 160. Fitz. Coro. 47. 9 H 7. 9.

Sect. 20. As to the eighth Point, *viz.* Whether the same Justices at the same Time may execute both the Commission of *Oyer* and *Terminer*, and also that of Gaol-Delivery? It seems certain at this Day, That the same Persons being authorized by both these Commissions, may proceed by Vertue of the one in those Cases, wherein they have no Jurisdiction by the other, and execute both at the same Time, and make up their Records accordingly; but this doth not seem to have been clearly agreed in former Times.

And now I am to consider the Nature of each of the abovementioned Commissions in particular; and first of that of *Oyer* and *Terminer*, concerning which I shall endeavour to shew;

1. Its several Kinds.
2. To what Cases the Jurisdiction given by it doth extend.
3. To whom, and on what Occasions it is grantable.

As to the first Point, these Commissions are of two Kinds:

1. General.
2. Special.

4 Inst. 161, 163. Crom. Jur. 131 Pl. Com. 384. b. 2 Inst. 419. Register 123.

Sect. 21. At this Day the common Form of such a General Commission, is to authorize the Persons to whom it is directed, or three or four of them, of which Number either such or such particular Persons among them are specially appointed to be, to inquire by the Oaths of lawful Men, and by other Means, of all Treasons, Felonies, and Misdemeanors, being specially mentioned, and of all others, in such and such Counties, and to hear determine the same at certain Days and Places to be appointed by them, &c. For which Purpose the King acquaints them, That he hath sent a Writ to the Sheriffs of such Counties, commanding them to return a Jury before them, at such Days and Places as shall be notified by them, in order to make Inquiries of such Offences, &c.

34 Ass. pl. 8. 42 Ass. pl. 5. 2 Inst. 419.

Sect. 22. It is observable, That the abovementioned Commission makes no mention of the Suit of the Party; but it seems to have been anciently the most common Form of such Commissions to direct the Justices to hear and determine Offences, as well at the Suit of the Party as of the King.

Of Special Commissions of *Oyer* and *Terminer*, there are many Precedents in our ancient Law Books; as first,

[a] Regist. 123. F. N. B. 110. [b] Register 125, 127. F. N. B. 112, 113. [c] Register 126. F. N. B. 112. Letter C.

Sect. 23. 1. [a] For the inquiring and determining of some particular enormous Violence done to the Party, at whose Complaint the Commission is sued.

Sect. 24. 2. [b] Or for inquiring and determining of Trespasses done to the Possessions of a Bishoprick, while the Temporalities were in the King's Hands.

Sect. 25. 3. [c] Or for inquiring and determining of Injuries offered to Merchants, &c. under Pretence that their Ships were wrecked.

Sect. 26. 4. Or for inquiring and determining of Oppressions of Under-Sheriffs and Bailiffs, and other Officers; after which the King may send a Writ to the High Sheriff, commanding him as far as in him lies, to remove such Persons from their Offices till such Inquiries be made.

Register 126. F. N. B 112. *Letters* D. E.

Sect. 27. 5. Or for inquiring into the Want of Reparations of Sea-Walls, Ditches, Gutters, Sewers, Bridges, *&c.*

Register 127, 128.

Sect. 28. 6. For hearing and determining the Right and Title of certain Persons claiming an Office, *&c.* Yet we find in *Dyer*, That the Defendant, sued before such Commissioners, demurred to the Jurisdiction of the Court; and it seems not to be clearly settled there whether such Commission be good.

F. N. B. 113. Crom. Jur. 132. Dyer 175. pl. 25, 26.

Sect. 29. It is observable, That some of these special Commissions are mentioned to be granted at the Complaint of the [a] particular Persons supposed to be aggrieved; others at the Complaint of [b] divers Persons in general without naming them, and [c] others without any Complaint at all.

2 Inst. 419. [a] Register 123. a. 125. a. b. 126. a. 127. a. [b] Register 125. b. [c] Register 127. a.

Sect. 30. Also there are Precedents of other Commissions of like Nature, granted on particular Occasions: But such special Commissions having been of late much disused, I shall refer the Reader for a more exact Knowledge of them to the *Register*, and *Fitzherbert*'s *Natura Brevium*.

Sect. 31. As to the second Point, *viz.* To what Cases the Jurisdiction given by the Commission of *Oyer* and *Terminer* doth extend; it is generally said, That the Justices have no Power from it to proceed against any Persons, but those who are indicted before themselves, because the Words of it are, That they shall inquire hear, and determine; by which it seems to be implied, That they must inquire of an Offence before they proceed to hear and determine it: But this Reasoning depending wholly on the Wording of general Commissions, which are made in such Form, doth by no Means prove that a special Commission of *Oyer* and *Terminer*, reciting an Indictment of a particular Person, and authorizing the Justices to send for and proceed upon it to try the Offender, is not good; and accordingly we find, That the Attainder of *Dudley*, afterwards Earl of *Leicester*, by Vertue of such a Commission, was not objected against on this Account, in the Arguments concerning it, reported at large in *Plowden*'s *Commentaries*.

Bro Commission. 24. 4 Inst. 164. H. P. C. 161. 12 Co. 32. Crom. Jur. 131, 132. Plow. Com. 385, 386, *&c.*

Sect. 32. It seems to be [a] agreed, That where a Statute prohibits a Thing, and does not appoint in what Court it shall be punished, the Offender may be indicted before Justices of *Oyer* and *Terminer*, because the King hath a Prerogative of suing in what Court he will. But it hath been [b] adjudged, That if such Statute appoint that the Offence shall be determined in any of the King's Courts of Record, it can be proceeded against only in one of the Courts of *Westminster-Hall*; because those being the highest Courts of Record, shall be intended to be only spoken of *secundum excellentiam*; and if the Act should be taken literally to intend any Court of Record whatsoever, the Sheriff's Turn, Court-Leet, and Pie-powders, and all other inferior Courts of Record, would be within the Purview of it: And it is farther reasonable to construe the Statute to extend to the said Courts of *Westminster* only, because the King's Attorney always attends there, whose Office it is, if the Defendant plead a special Plea to make a Replication; yet both Sir *Edward Coke* and Sir *Matthew Hale* seem to be of Opinion, That on a Statute so worded, the Prosecution may be in any Court of *Oyer* and *Terminer*. And indeed seeing the abovementioned Limitation of such Suits to Courts of Record, is no more than the Law would have implied, if it had not been expres-

[a] Dy. 236. pl. 24. Crom. Jur. 132. 4 Inst. 164. [b] Dy. 236 pl. 24. 6 Co. 19. b. 20. a. Cro Jac. 538. Cro. Eliz. 737. Cro. Ca. 146. Salk. 178. 4 Inst. 164, 165. H. P C. 161.

sed: And it is agreed, That if it had not been expressed, the Suit might be in any Court of *Oyer* and *Terminer*, it may be reasonably argued, that it may be brought in any such Court notwithstanding such Limitation, according to the common Maxim, *quod expressio eorum quæ tacitè insunt, nihil operatur*; especially considering that the Court holden before Justices of *Oyer, &c.* is a Court of Record of a very high Nature, and much regarded by the Law. And as to the Objection, That the Construction contended for, would extend such Suits to all inferior Courts of Record, it may be answered, that it would only extend them to such Courts of a general Jurisdiction, wherein Suits of like Nature may properly be brought, and not to Courts of a limited Authority, instituted for special Purposes, and confined either to Offences at the Common Law, as the Court-Leet and Sheriff's Turn are, or to Contracts of a special Nature, as the Court of Pie-powders is: As to the Objection, That it is most reasonable to construe the Statute, to intend only such Courts wherein the King's Attorney attends, the same may be said in Relation to Prosecutions on Statutes, which mention no Court at all wherein they shall be brought; and yet it seems to be certain, That such Prosecutions may be brought in any Court of *Oyer* and *Terminer*: Neither do I find any Reason assigned, why the King's Prerogative, of choosing in what Court he will commence a Suit, should be restrained without express Words in this Case, where Courts are mentioned in general, more than in the others where they are not mentioned at all. Besides it ought to be considered, That if such Prosecutions are to be confined to the Courts of *Westminster*, no Offence against any such Statute in any County, but that wherein the King's Bench sits, could be indicted at all; for it is certain, That no Offence can be inquired of out of the County wherein it was committed: Also since 21 *Jac.* 1. 4. set forth more at large in the Chapter concerning *Informations*, which restrains all Prosecutions whatsoever on Penal Statutes to their proper Counties, (as the Construction of the said Statute is now settled,) if Suits on such Statutes could be brought only in *Westminster-Hall*, no Offences out of *Middlesex* could be prosecuted at all.

Fitz. Essoign. 173.

Dy. 236. pl. 24.

Sect. 33. As to the third Point, *viz.* To what Persons, and on what Occasions, Commissions of *Oyer* and *Terminer* are grantable, it is enacted by the Statute of *Westminster* 2. Chap. 29. *That a Writ of Trespass*, (ad audiendum & terminandum,) *from henceforth shall not be granted before any Justices, except Justices of either Bench, and Justices in Eyre, unless it be for an heinous Trespass, where it is necessary to provide speedy Remedy, and our Lord the King of his special Grace hath thought it good to be granted.*

Sect. 34. And it is farther enacted by 2 *E.* 3. Ch. 2. *That Oyers and Terminers shall not be granted but before Justices of the one Bench or the other, or the Justices Errants, and that for great Hurt or horrible Trespasses, and of the King's Special Grace, after the Form of the Statute abovementioned.*

Sect. 35. Also it is enacted by 34 *Ed.* 3. 1. *That Writs of Oyer and Terminer be granted according to the Statutes thereof made, and that the Justices which shall be thereto assigned, be named by the Court, and not by the Party.*

Sect. 36. It may perhaps be argued from the general Words of these Statutes, That no Commission of *Oyer* and *Terminer* ought to be granted to any, but such Justices as are therein mentioned, and on such special Occasions. And Sir *Edward Coke* in his Comment on the said Statute of *Westminster* 2. does not shew whether all such Commissions in general are meant to be restrained by it, or such only as are of a particular Nature; yet if the Intention of the said Statutes be fully examined, it seems reasonable to confine the Purview of them to special Commissions of *Oyer*

2 Inst. 418.

and *Terminer*, granted at the Complaint of particular Perſons, upon ſome great Injury ſuggeſted to have been done to them; not only for that ſuch ſpecial Commiſſions, for redreſſing of a particular Grievance at the Suit of the Party, ſeem to come more properly and generally under the Notion of Writs, than general Commiſſions iſſued by the King as the common Diſpenſer of Juſtice to his People, without any particular Application from, or Regard to any particular Perſon; but alſo becauſe there may be a Miſchief to the Subject from ſuch ſpecial Commiſſions, which cannot be feared from the general ones; for the Party who ſues out ſuch a ſpecial Commiſſion, may thereupon take out a Writ to the Sheriff, commanding him to arreſt the Goods ſuppoſed to be wrongfully taken away, and to keep them in ſafe Cuſtody till ſome Order be made concerning them, by the Juſtices aſſigned to determine the Matter, which may be very inconvenient to the Perſon complained of: Neither can it be imagined, That the Statute intended to reſtrain general Commiſſions to enormous Treſpaſſes, which could not but hinder the due Execution of Juſtice, which requires the Puniſhment of all Kinds of Miſdemeanors, of which ſuch Commiſſioners are the uſual and proper Judges. But it is reaſonable indeed, That ſuch ſpecial Commiſſions ſhould not be granted but upon urgent Occaſions; and accordingly we find Precedents for the ſuperſeding of them, where the King has been informed, that he was impoſed upon in granting them on a Suggeſtion, that the Injury complained of was of a heinous Nature, where in Truth it was but a ſlight inconſiderable Treſpaſs.

Theolal's Digeſt of Writs 1, 2. & ſupra Sect. 1. 2 Inſt. 419.

Regiſter 126, 127. 2 Inſt. 419. F.N.B. 112. f.

Regiſter 124, 125. 12 Aſſ. pl. 21.

For other Particulars concerning the Proceedings of Juſtices of *Oyer* and *Terminer*, ſee the Chapter concerning *Approver*, and the Chapter concerning *Proceſs againſt the Jury*.

CHAP. VI.

Of the Court of the Juſtices of Gaol-Delivery.

FOR the better underſtanding of the Nature of the Commiſſion of Gaol Delivery, I ſhall conſider,

1. What ought to be the Form of it.
2. What Juriſdiction the Juſtices authorized by it have by the Common Law.
3. What by Statute.
4. In what Place they ought to hold their Seſſions.

Sect. 1. As to the firſt Point, having already ſhewn that all judicial Commiſſions muſt be agreeable to ancient Precedents, I ſhall only ſhew in this Place, the Purport of the moſt uſual Commiſſion of Gaol-Delivery, which is a Patent in Nature of a Letter from the King to certain Perſons, appointing them his Juſtices, or two or three of them, of which Number either ſuch or ſuch a particular Perſon among them is eſpecially required to be, and authorizing them to deliver his Gaol, at ſuch a Place, of the Priſoners in it; for which Purpoſe it commands them to meet at ſuch Place, at the Time which they themſelves ſhall appoint, and

Chap. 1. *from* Sect. 4 *to* Sect. 9. *and* Chap. 5. Sect. 1.

4 Inſt. 168. Cromp. Ju. 125.

and informs them, That for the ſame Purpoſe the King hath commanded his Sheriff of the ſame County, to bring all the Priſoners of the ſame Gaol, and their Attachments before them, at ſuch Day to be appointed by them.

H. P. C. 158. 4 Inſt. 168, 169. Bro. Coron. 179. 12 Co. 32.

Sect. 2. As to the ſecond Point, *viz.* What Juriſdiction Juſtices of Gaol-Delivery have by the Common Law; it ſeems to be clear, That they may by Common Law proceed upon any Indictment of Felony or Treſpaſs, found before other Juſtices, againſt any Perſon in the Priſon mentioned in their Commiſſion, and not determined; and therefore thoſe Words in the Statute of 4 *E.* 3. Ch. 2. *That the Juſtices aſſigned to deliver the Gaols ſhall have Power to deliver the ſame Gaols of thoſe that ſhall be indicted before the Juſtices of Peace,* ſeem only to be in Affirmance of the Common Law; and herein the Authority of theſe Juſtices differs from that of Juſtices of *Oyer* and *Terminer,* who regularly can proceed only againſt Perſons indicted before themſelves, as hath been more fully ſhewn in the precedent Chapter, *Sect.* 31.

[a] Cro. Eliz. 90, 179. Bro. Commiſſion 24. 1 And. 111. Fitz. Coron. 47. [b] 1 And. 111. 112. H. P. C. 158. 4 Inſt. 168.

Sect. 3. But it is ſaid in ſome [a] Books, That Juſtices of Gaol-Delivery, as ſuch, have no Power to take any Indictment; but the common Opinion, that they have ſuch Power, ſeems much more agreeable to Reaſon; for [b] ſurely it cannot but be implied in their Commiſſion to deliver Priſons of their Priſoners, That they muſt have Authority to make ſuch Deliverance by due Courſe of Law, which cannot be without a Proclamation, if there be no Proſecution, or a proper Trial if there be one, in Order to which there muſt be an Accuſation of Record, without which the Priſoner cannot be arraigned or tried.

[c] S. P. C. 183. *Letter* A. 2 Rol. Rep. 12. Crom. Jur. 28. Fitz. Coron. 47. 1 And. 111.

Sect. 4. Alſo it hath been [c] holden, That Juſtices of Gaol-Delivery, as ſuch, have no Power to deliver the Gaol of Perſons committed for High Treaſon, perhaps for this Reaſon, becauſe this being a Crime of ſo high a Nature, and againſt the King himſelf, ſhall not be included in the general Words of a Commiſſion, nor tried without the King's ſpecial Direction; and this Opinion ſeems to be much favoured by the Preamble of the Statute of 3 *H.* 5. Ch. 7. wherein it is recited, *That the Puniſhment of counterfeiting Money,* (which is a Species of Treaſon,) *pertaineth not to any Judges of the Realm, but to the King's Juſtices before himſelf, or to ſpecial Commiſſioners thereto aſſigned*; and thereupon it is enacted, *That Juſtices of Aſſiſe ſhall have Power by the King's Commiſſion to hear and determine the Offence abovementioned*: Yet the contrary Opinion is not only warranted by very great [d] Authorities, but alſo ſeems to be more agreeable to Reaſon; for ſince the Words of the Commiſſion are general, and include all Priſoners alike without any Exception, why ſhould thoſe who are accuſed of Treaſon, be conſtrued to be out of the Meaning of them more than others? eſpecially conſidering, That the greater the Crime is for which a Man is impriſoned, the greater Hardſhip it is for him to lie under the Terror of a Proſecution for it, without being admitted to an Opportunity of clearing his Innocence; And the Statute of 1 *Ed.* 6. 7. which authorizes ſubſequent Commiſſioners of Gaol-Delivery, to give Judgment of Death againſt ſuch as were found guilty before other Commiſſioners of Gaol-Delivery, of Treaſon, *&c.* and reprieved before Judgment, clearly ſuppoſes ſuch Juſtices to have Power in Treaſon as well as in other Caſes.

[d] 4 Inſt. 169. H. P. C. 159. 1 And. 112. *and the next* Ch. Sect. 4.

Fitz. Coron. 7.

Sect. 5. It ſeems clear from the Words of the Commiſſion, That theſe Juſtices have nothing to do with any Perſons not in Cuſtody of the Priſon mentioned in it, except in ſome ſpecial Caſes; for if Part only of thoſe who were Accomplices to the ſame Felony be in ſuch Priſon, and other Part of them out of it; ſuch Juſtices for the Neceſſity of the Caſe, may [a] receive an Appeal against those who are out of the Prison, as well as those who are in it; which Appeal after the Trial of such Prisoners, shall be removed into the King's Bench, and Process shall issue from thence against the rest: But if those out of Prison should be omitted in such Appeal, they could never be put into any other, because there can be but one Appeal for one Felony. Also it is said both by [b] *Staundford*, and [c] *Hale*, That such Justices may receive an Appeal by Bill against one let to Bail. But I cannot find any Authority in the [d] Books, cited by them for that Purpose, to warrant this Opinion; for though it be true, That the Court of King's Bench may receive an Appeal by Bill, against one for whom Bail is filed, as being *in Custodia Mareschalli*; yet this seems to depend on the particular Usage of that Court. And I do not find it said in any Book, That those who are bailed by any other Court, are looked upon as Prisoners in the Prison belonging to such Court, but only in the Custody of their Sureties, who may detain them where-ever they please: However, it seems to be agreed by all the Books abovementioned, That such Justices have no more to do with one let to Mainprize, than if he were at large, because such Person can in no Sense be said to be a Prisoner, since it is not in the Power of his Sureties to detain him in their Custody, as will be more fully shewn in the Chapter concerning *Bail*.

[a] 9 H. 4. 1. b. 4 Co. 47. b. S. P. C. 64. D.

[b] S. P. C. 64. C. D. 65 A. 159, 160.

[c] H. P. C. 132, 179. *Quære* 4 Inst. 169.

[d] 32 H. 6. 4. a. 39 H. 6. 27. b. 9 H. 4. 2. a. 13 H. 4. 10. b. 21 H. 7. 33. a. Fitz. Mainprize 12, 13. Dy. 99. pl. 62. Bro. Appeal 11, 19, 51, 123.

Sect. 5. It seems clear, That such Justices have not only Power to discharge such Prisoners, as upon their Trial shall be acquitted; but also all such against whom, upon Proclamation made, no Evidence shall appear to indict them; which neither Justices of Peace, nor Justices of *Oyer* and *Terminer* can do.

4 Inst. 167. Fitz. Coron. 47. H. P. C. 158.

Sect. 6. Also there seems to be no Doubt, but that the Justices of Gaol-Delivery may award Execution, against such Prisoners as have been outlawed for Felony before Justices of Peace.

15 H. 7. 5. b. 4 Inst. 169. H. P. C. 158.

Sect. 7. Also notwithstanding the Commission of Justices of Gaol-Delivery be in Strictness determined after the End of their Session, yet it seems to be settled at this Day, That they have Power either to order the Execution or Reprieve, of the Persons who have been condemned before them.

Dyer 205. pl. 5. H. P. C. 160. cont. Cromp. Jur. 126. *Quære* S. P. C. 132. *Letter* B.

Sect. 8. Also it is said by some, That the Justices of Gaol-Delivery may by the Common Law punish those who unduly bail Prisoners, as being guilty of a negligent Escape; but it seems needless strictly to examine this Matter, since they have certainly such Power by Statute, as will be more fully shewn in the following Part of this Chapter.

S. P. C. 77. a. 25 E. 3. 39. a.

As to the third Point, *viz.* What Jurisdiction Justices of Gaol-Delivery have by Statute, I shall consider the same,

1. In Relation to Appellees.
2. To irregular Bailment of Prisoners.
3. To Sheriffs, *&c.* refusing to receive Prisoners.
4. To Persons convicted before former Justices.
5. To Offences created by Statute.

Sect. 9. As to the first Particular, it is enacted by 28 *E.* 1. *That they may award Process into a foreign County against those who shall be appealed before them by an Approver*, as shall be more fully shewed in the Chapter concerning *Approvers*.

Sect. 10. As to the second Particular, *viz.* The Power of such Justices in Relation to the Bailment of Prisoners, it is enacted by 27 *Ed.* 1. *cap.* 3. commonly called the Statute *De finibus, That Justices of Assise shall deliver the Gaols of Counties where they take Assises,* &c. *and inquire if Sheriffs or any other, have let out by Replevin Prisoners not repleviable, or have offended in any Thing contrary to the Form of the Statute of* Westminster, 1 Cap. 15. *and whom they shall find guilty, they shall chasten and punish in all Things according to the Form of the Statute aforesaid.*

F. N. B. 251. H. H. P. C. 158. 3 Inst. 169. *Sect.* 11. But this Statute mentioning only Justices of Assise, it may perhaps be questioned, whether it is to be extended by Equity, to Justices of Gaol-Delivery by special Commission, not being Justices of Assise.

Sect. 12. However, it is enacted by 4 *Ed.* 3. *cap.* 2. *That Justices assigned to deliver Gaols, shall have Power to enquire of Sheriffs, Gaolers, and other in whose Ward Persons indicted before Wardens of the Peace shall be, if they make Deliverance, or let to Mainprize any so indicted, which be not mainpernable, and to punish the said Sheriffs, Gaolers and others, if they do any Thing against this Act.*

Sect. 13. It is observable, that this Statute saith only in general, That such Justices shall have Power to punish the Offenders therein mentioned, without saying, That they shall punish them according to the
S. P. C. 77. a. Form of the Statute of *Westminster* 1. as the abovementioned Statute *de finibus* does; yet it is said, That they may punish them according to the Form of the said Statute of *Westminster,* as much as if it had been expressed.

Sect. 14. Also it is enacted by 1 & 2 *Ph. & Mar.* 13. *That if any Justice of the Peace of the* Quorum, *or Coroner, shall offend against the Purview of the said Statute, either as to bailing Prisoners, or taking their Examinations, or the Information of those that bring them before them, or not putting the same in Writing, or not certifying them to the next Gaol-Delivery, or not putting in Writing the Evidence given to a Jury on a Coroner's Inquest of Murder or Manslaughter, or not binding over material Witnesses against Persons accused of Felony, to give Evidence at the next general Gaol-Delivery, or not certifying such Evidence, and also such Recognizances,* &c. *the Justices of Gaol-Delivery of the Place where such Offence shall be committed upon due Proof thereof by Examination before them, shall for every such Offence set such Fine as they shall think meet,* &c.

Sect. 15. As to the third Particular, *viz.* The Power of such Justices in Relation to Sheriffs, *&c.* refusing to receive Prisoners, it is enacted by 4 *E.* 3. *cap.* 10. *That Justices of Gaol-Delivery shall punish Sheriffs and Gaolers, refusing to take Felons into their Custody from Constables and Townships, without being paid for such Receipt.*

Sect, 16. As to the fourth Particular, *viz.* The Power of such Justices, in Relation to Persons convicted before former Justices, it is enacted by 1 *Ed.* 6. *cap.* 7. *That where any Person or Persons shall be found guilty of any Treason or Felony, for the which Judgment of Death should or may ensue, and shall be reprieved to Prison without Judgment at that Time given against him, her, or them so found guilty, those Persons that at any Time hereafter, shall by the King's Letters Patent be assigned Justices to deliver the Gaol, where any such Person or Persons found guilty shall remain, shall have full Power and Authority to give Judgment of Death against such Person so found guilty, and reprieved, as the same Justices, (before whom such Person or Persons was or were found guilty,) might have done, if their Commission of Gaol-Delivery had remained and continued in full Force and Strength.*

Sect. 17. It hath been holden, That this Statute extends not to Convictions before Justices of *Oyer* and *Terminer*, not only because Convictions before Justices of Gaol-Delivery only are mentioned, but because the Proceedings before Justices of *Oyer* and *Terminer*, after the *Oyer* determined, ought to remain in the King's Bench, and the Records before the Justices of Gaol-Delivery with the *Custos Rotulorum*. 11 Co. 33. Bro. Oyer & Terminer.

Sect. 18. Also it seemeth, That since the Statute speaks only of Persons reprieved before Judgment, it gives subsequent Commissioners no Manner of Power over Persons condemned by former Justices; and therefore it hath been holden, That if a Person condemned by former Justices, plead a Pardon before their Successors, they have no Power to allow it, but that the Record ought to be removed by *Certiorari* into the King's Bench, and the Prisoner also by *Habeas Corpus*, and that there the Pardon shall be allowed or disallowed. And from the same Reason it seems to follow, That subsequent Justices have no Power from this Statute to award the Execution of Persons condemned by former Justices, and reprieved by them: But if Judgment had not been given by the former Justices, there is no Doubt but that the subsequent ones might by force of this Statute, have allowed the Pardon, or given Judgment, and awarded Execution, *&c.* as the first might have done. Also it hath been adjudged, That not only such subsequent Justices as are authorized by the same King by whom the former were commissioned, but also that the Justices of the next King have the like Power by Virtue of this Statute. Dalison 10. Quare Dy. 165. pl. 4. 7 Co. 31. b. Dalison 10.

Sect. 19. As to the fifth Particular, *viz.* The Jurisdiction of Justices of Gaol-Delivery in Relation to Offences created by Statute; By 33 *H.* 8. 9. Par. 20. They may punish those who keep unlawful Gaming-Houses, or use unlawful Games. By 5 *Eliz.* 9. Par. 9. They have Jurisdiction over Perjury and Subornation of Perjury against the Form of that Statute. By 8 *Eliz.* 3. They may punish those who transport Sheep alive. By 23 *Eliz.* 1. Par. 9. They may enquire of, hear and determine Offences against that Statute in not coming to Church; and generally they have the like Power in other Statutes, creating new Offences, which it would be too tedious particularly to set down in this Place.

As to the fourth general Point of this Chapter, *viz.* In what Place Justices of Gaol-Delivery ought to hold their Sessions, it is enacted by 6 *Ric.* 2. 5. *That Justices assigned to take Assizes and deliver Gaols, shall hold their Sessions in the principal and chief Towns of every of the Counties where the Shire-Courts of the same Counties were then holden, or hereafter should be holden.* For other Matters relating to these Justices, see Chapter 7. concerning *Justices of Assise and* Nisi Prius, and the Chapter concerning *Process.*

CHAP.

CHAP. VII.

Of the Court of the Justices of Affise *and* Nisi Prius.

Sect. 1. THE Power of Justices of Assise, whether as such, or as Justices of *Nisi Prius*, in Relation to criminal Matters, depending wholly on Statute, I shall only take Notice of the principal Branches of their Jurisdiction of this Kind, given them by several Acts of Parliament; and for more particular Inquiries concerning their Authority in other Cases, and the Nature, Extent, and End of their Commission shall refer the Reader to Sir *Edward Coke*'s *4th Institute*, *fol.* 158, *&c.* and to his *12th Report*, *fol.* 32. and to Mr. *Crampton*'s *Treatise concerning the Jurisdiction of Courts*, *fol.* 204. *&c.*

The most considerable Parts of their Jurisdiction in criminal Matters, proper to be considered in this Place, are such as relate,

1. To the Delivery of Gaols.
2. To Counterfeiters of Money.
3. To Appellees.
4. To Conspirators, Maintainers, and other Offenders of the like Nature.
5. To Offences of Sheriffs, Gaolers, and other Officers.
6. To capital Offences tried by Writ of *Nisi Prius*.
7. To the Counties for which such Justices of Assise may be commissioned.

Sect. 2. As to the first of these Particulars, it is enacted by 27 *Ed.* 1. commonly called the Statute *de finibus*, *cap.* 3. *That Justices assigned to take Assises, in every County where they do take Assises, as they be appointed incontinent after the Assises taken in the Shires, shall remain both together if they be lay; And if one of them be a Clerk, then one of the most discreet Knights of the Shire being associate to him that is a Layman by the King's Writ, shall deliver the Gaols of the Shires, as well within Liberties as without, of all Manner of Prisoners, after the Form of the Gaol-Deliveries of those Shires, before times used. And the same Justices shall inquire then, if Sheriffs or any other have let out by Replevin Persons not repleviable*, &c.

Sect. 3. Also it is recited by 2 *Ed.* 3, 2. *That Offenders had been greatly encouraged, because the Justices of Gaol-Delivery and of* Oyer *and* Terminer, *had been procured by great Men against the Form of the said Statute of 27 Ed.* 1. and thereupon it is enacted, *That such Justices shall not be made against the Form of the said Statute.*

S. P. C. 57.b. Raym. 375. H. P. C. 164. 12 Co. 32. *Sect.* 4. It seems to have been the most general Opinion in the Construction of the abovementioned Statute of 27 *Ed.* 1. That the Purview of it extends only to Cases of Felony; and this is farther confirmed by the Recital of the Statute of 3 *H.* 5. set forth more at large in the following Part of this Chapter, by which it is declared, That no Judges but those of the King's Bench, or special Commissioners, have Power to
S.P.C. 57, 58. punish Counterfeiters of Money. Also it is argued, That the Purview of

 the

the faid Statute of 3 *H.* 5. impowering Juftices of Affife, having the King's Commiffion for fuch Purpofe, to hear and determine the Offences of fuch Perfons, would be vain and to no Purpofe, if fuch Juftices, as fuch, had Power over fuch Offences before, by Virtue of the faid former Statute: And yet perhaps the contrary Opinion is the more plaufible; for fince the faid Statute is intended for the greater Expedition of Juftice, and the Words of it expreffly extend to all Manner of Prifoners, why fhould they be reftrained by a violent Interpretation, inconfiftent with the natural and obvious Senfe of them? And fince Juftices of Gaol-Delivery, armed only with a general Commiffion to deliver Gaols of the Prifoners in them, are, according to the better Opinion at this Day, authorized to deliver fuch Gaols of Perfons accufed of Treafon, as well as of others committed for Crimes of an inferior Nature, why fhould not the faid Statute, the Intent whereof is to give Juftices of Affife like Power with Juftices of Gaol-Delivery, be conftrued to give them as large a Power? And as to the Arguments drawn from the Opinion of the Makers of the abovementioned Statute of 3 *H.* 5. it may be anfwered, That perhaps the Purport of the faid Recital may amount to no more than this, that no other Judges but thofe therein mentioned, would venture to take upon them a Power to try fuch Offences, becaufe it was not clearly fettled that they had Authority to do it. Vide infra fect. 9. Vide fupra cap. 6. fect. 4

Sect. 5. It feems to be the general Opinion, That Juftices of Affife, as fuch, by force of the faid Statute of 27 *E.* 1. may deliver Gaols without any fpecial Commiffion for that Purpofe; and this feems to be moft agreeable to the Purview of the faid Statute, if fuch Juftices be Laymen; for feeing the Act provides only, That if one of them be a Clerk, then one of the Knights of the County being affociate by Writ to him that is a Layman fhall deliver the Gaols; and makes no mention of any fuch Writ where both are Laymen; but only fays in general, That in fuch Cafe they fhall remain both together, it feems to imply that Laymen being Juftices of Affife fhall have fuch Power of Courfe. H. P. C. 164. S. P. C. 57. b. Crom Jur. 126. Dyer 99. pl. 62.

Sect. 6. As to the fecond particular, *viz.* The Power of thefe Juftices in Relation to Counterfeiters of Money, it is recited by the Statute of 3 *H.* 5. *cap.* 7. *That Counterfeiting, Clipping, Wafhing, and other Falfity of Money, had then of late abounded, for that the Punifhment of the fame pertaineth not to any Judges of the Realm, but to the King's Juftices before himfelf, or fpecial Commiffioners thereto affigned,* &c. and thereupon it is enacted, *That the King's Juftices affigned to take Affifes in all the Counties of* England, *fhall have Power by the King's Commiffions, to hear and determine in their Seffions, as well of the Counterfeiting and of the bringing fuch falfe Money into the Realm, as of Clipping, Wafhing, and every other Falfity of the faid Money.* *See the precedent Chap. Sect. 4. and the 15th Sect. of this Chapter.*

Sect. 7. It feems clear from the manifeft Purport of this Statute, That Juftices of Affife can claim no Power from it over any of the Offences therein mentioned, without a fpecial Commiffion for fuch Purpofe; but this Statute being wholly in the Affirmative, and no way intended to abridge but inlarge the Jurifdiction of fuch Juftices; It feems clear, That if they had Authority as Juftices of Gaol-Delivery, by Vertue of the abovementioned Statute *De finibus*, without any fpecial Commiffion, to deliver Perfons in Prifon for fuch Crimes, (which Queftion is more fully handled in the precedent Part of this Chapter) they may ftill lawfully proceed upon the faid Statute in the fame Manner as before. S. P. C. 58. H. P. C. 164 Supra fect. 4. Cro. Jur. 126.

Sect. 8. As to the third Particular, *viz.* The Power of Juftices of Affife in relation to Appellees, it is enacted by 28 *Ed.* 1. commonly called the Statute *De Appellatis, That fuch Juftices may award Procefs into any foreign County againft Perfons appealed by Approvers, and proceed againft them,* &c.

Dyer 99. pl. 62. 12 Co. 32. *Sect.* 9. It is made a Doubt in *Dyer's Reports*, by what Warrant Justices of Assise hold Plea of an Appeal of Robbery; and it is there holden, That they do it by Vertue of the Commission of Gaol-Delivery: But it seems, that it ought not to be intended to be the Meaning of this Report, That Justices of Assise have no Jurisdiction as to an Appeal of Robbery, without an express Commission of Gaol-Delivery; for since Justices of Assise, as such, have Power by the abovementioned Statute *De finibus* to deliver Gaols of all manner of Prisoners, after the Form of the Gaol-Deliveries of the Shires wherein they sit, why should they not by Force of those general Words, deliver such Gaols of Persons proceeded against by way of Appeal commenced before them, as well as of those proceeded against by way of Indictment, as it seems to be taken for granted in other Books that they may? (22 Ed. 4. 19. a. Bro. Appeal. 113. 4 Inst. 159.) And therefore it seems to be reasonable to take the abovementioned Report of *Dyer* in this Sense, That Justices of Assise may hold Plea of Appeals of Robbery by the Commission of Gaol-Delivery, given them implicitly by the said Statute *De finibus*, in respect whereof they seem to have all the Power of Justices of Gaol-Delivery, whether given them by the Common Law or by Statute, as fully appears from what immediately follows the abovementioned Passage in the said Report, wherein it is said, That the Statute of 2 or 3 *H.* 7. gives Justices of Assise the Power by express Words as to Appeals of Death (Dyer 99. pl. 62. 3 H. 7. ch. 1.); but it is certain, that the said Statute of *H.* 7. does not expresly mention Justices of Assise, but saith only, That the Wife, *&c.* may commence an Appeal before the Sheriff and Coroners, or before the King in his Bench, or Justices of Gaol-Delivery; and yet it is holden in the said Report, That this Statute expresly extends to Justices of Assise; from which it seems manifestly to follow, That such Justices are taken to be included under the general Notion of Justices of Gaol-Delivery. (13 Co. 32. 4 Inst. 159.)

Sect. 10. As to the fourth Particular, *viz.* The Power of Justices of Assise in relation to Conspirators, Maintainers, and other Offenders of the like Nature, it is enacted by 28 *Ed.* 1. commonly called *Articuli super chartas*, ch. 10. *That Justices assigned to take Assises, when they come into the Country to do their Office, shall upon every Plaint made unto them of Conspirators, false Informers, and evil Procurers of Dozens, Assises, Inquests, and Juries, award Inquests thereupon without Writ, and shall do Right to the Plaintiffs without Delay.* And it is farther enacted by 4 *Ed.* 3. 11. *That the Justices of Assise, whensoever they come to hold their Sessions, or to take Inquests upon* Nisi Prius, *shall inquire, hear, and determine, as well at the Suit of the King as at the Suit of the Party, of Maintainors, Bearors, Conspirators,* &c. And the like is ordained by 20 *Ed.* 3. 6. by which it is enacted, *That such Justices shall have Commissions to inquire of Maintainers and common Embraceors,* &c.

Register 188. *Sect.* 11. Also it is enacted by 5 *Ed.* 3. 10. *That the Justices before whom any Assise, Inquest or Jury shall pass, may inquire and determine the Offence of any Juror in taking Money of either Party,* &c.

Sect. 12. But it is ordained by 38 *Ed.* 3. 12. *That no Justice,* &c. *inquire of Office of the said Offence, but only at the Suit of the Party, or of other,* &c.

Sect. 13. And it is farther enacted by 32 *H.* 8. ch. 9. *That the Justices of Assise of every Circuit within this Realm, and elsewhere within the King's Dominions, shall in every County within their Circuits, twice in the Year cause open Proclamation to be made, as well of the said Statute as of all others made against unlawful Maintenance, Champerty, Embracery,* &c.

Sect. 14. As to the fifth Particular, *viz.* The Power of Justices of Assise

Assise in Relation to the Offences of Sheriffs, Gaolers, and other Officers, it is enacted by 20 *Ed.* 3. 6. *That Justices of Assise shall have Commissions sufficient to inquire of Sheriffs, Eschcators, Bailiffs of Franchises and their Ministers, and of the Gifts which they take to execute their Office,* &c.

Sect. 15. Also it is enacted by 23 *H.* 6. 10. *That Justices of Assises in their Sessions, shall have Power to inquire, hear and determine of Office without special Commission, of and upon all Sheriffs, Under-Sheriffs, Clerks, Bailiffs, Gaolers, Coroners, Stewards, Bailiffs of Franchises, or any other Officer or Minister doing contrary to the said Statute, as by extorting Money for the omitting of an Arrest, or shewing Ease or Favour to those who shall be arrested, or by admitting Persons to Bail, or denying them the Benefit of it, contrary to the Form of the said Statute.*

Sect. 16. Also it is enacted by 1 *H.* 8. 7. *That Justices of Assise and of the Peace, shall have Authority to inquire of and determine, as well by Examination as by Presentment, the Defaults of Coroners in not taking an Inquest without Fee or Reward, on the View of the Body of any Person slain by Misadventure.*

Sect. 17. As to the Sixth Particular, *viz.* The Power of Justices of Assise, in Relation to capital Offences tried by Writ of *Nisi Prius*, it is enacted by 14 *H.* 6. 1. *That the Justices before whom Inquisitions, Inquests and Juries, shall be taken by the King's Writ of* Nisi Prius, *shall have Power in all the Cases of Felony and Treason, to give their Judgments, as well where a Man is acquit of Felony or of Treason, as where he is thereof attainted, the Day and Place where the said Inquisitions, Inquests, and Juries be so taken, and then from thenceforth to award Execution to be made by Force of the same Judgments.* Raym. 367.

Sect. 18. In the Construction of this Statute it hath been holden, That if the Plaintiff in Appeal be nonsuited before Justices of *Nisi Prius*, they have no Power to arraign the Defendant at the Suit of the King on the Declaration in the Appeal, as Justices before whom an Appeal is originally commenced may do: And the Reason of this Construction seems to be this, because the Statute only mentioning that Justices of *Nisi Prius* shall give Judgment where the Defendant is acquitted or attainted, leaves their Jurisdiction upon a Nonsuit as it was before. But it seems certain, That on the Acquittal of an Appellee such Justices have Power to inquire of the Abettors, and also of the sufficiency of the Plaintiff to answer the Damages; for since the Statute of *Westminster* 2. Ch. 12. gives such Power to the Justices before whom an Appeal shall be heard and determined; and now by Force of 14 *H.* 6. it may be heard and determined before Justices of *Nisi Prius*, it seems necessarily to follow, that Justices of *Nisi Prius* shall have such Power since the said Statute of 14 *H.* 6. And from the same Reasoning it seems also to follow, That such Justices may give Judgment for the Damages; but constant Experience hath over-ruled it to the contrary.

22 Ed.4.19.a. Dy. 120. pl. 12. Crom. Jur. 212. 4 Inst. 160. 22 Ed.4.19.a. 10Ed.4 14 b. 2 Inst. 386. Bro. Nisi Prius 27.

Sect. 19. As to the seventh Particular, *viz.* For what Counties Justices of Assise may be commissioned, it is enacted by 8 *Ric.* 2. 2. *That no Man of Law shall be from thenceforth Justice of Assises, or of the common Deliverance of Gaols, in his own Country.*

Sect. 20. Also it is enacted by 33 *H.* 8. Ch. 24. *That no Justice, nor other Man learned in the Laws of this Realm, shall use, nor exercise the Office of Justice of Assise within any County where the said Justice was born, or doth inhabit, on Pain of* 100 *l.* &c. *Provided that the said Act shall not extend to any Person who shall be Clerk of Assises, and Associate to any Justice of Assise, nor to any Mayor, Sheriff, Recorder, Steward, Bailiff, Sewter, or other Officer being born or dwelling within any City, Borough, or Town within this Realm of* England, &c. *Nor to Justices of either Bench for taking, hearing, or determining Assises in the one Bench or the other, nor to the Justices, Justice Clerks, or Clerk of Assises, in the Dutchy and County Palatine of* Lancaster.

CHAP.

CHAP. VIII.

Of the Court of Sessions of Justices of Peace.

BEFORE I come to consider the Nature of the Court of Sessions of Justices of Peace, I shall premise,

1. In what Manner Conservators of the Peace were provided by the Common Law.
2. In what Manner Justices of Peace have been ordained by the several Statutes concerning them.
3. How they are to be commissioned in Pursuance of those Statutes.
4. What is most observable from the said Statutes and Commissions.

As to the first Point it seems, that Conservators of the Peace by the Common Law, were of two Sorts;

1. Those who in respect of their Offices had Power to keep the Peace, but were not simply called by the Name of Conservators of the Peace, but by the Name of such Offices.
2. Those who were constituted for this Purpose only, and were simply called by the Name of Conservators or Wardens of the Peace.

[a] Lamb B. 1. Ch. 3. Dalt. Ch. 1. [b] Bro. Recognizance 14, 19. Dalt. Ch. 1. [c] Lamb B. 1. Ch. 3.

Sect. 1. And first of those of the first Sort, of which the King's [a] Majesty is certainly the Principal, from whom all Authority of this Kind was originally derived, and who still continues to have the same in his own Person; yet it is said, [b] That he cannot take a Recognizance for the keeping the Peace, because it is a Rule in Law, that no one can take any Recognizance, who is not either a Justice of Record, or by Commission; also it seems certain, That [c] no Duke, Earl, or Baron, as such, have any greater Authority to keep the Peace than mere private Persons.

[d] Dalt. Ch. 1. Lamb B. 1 Ch. 3. Crompt. 6. b.

Sect. 2. The [d] Lord Chancellor or Lord Keeper of the Great Seal, the Lord High Steward of *England*, the Lord Marshal, and Lord High Constable of *England*, and every Justice of the King's Bench, and, as some say, the Lord Treasurer, have, as incident to their Offices, a general Authority to keep the Peace throughout all the Realm, and to award Process for the Surety of the Peace, and to take Recognizances for it. And the Master of the Rolls hath also the like Power, either as incident to his Office, or at least by Prescription.

[e] 10 H. 6. 7. b. Lamb B. 1. Ch. 3.

Sect. 3. Also every [e] Court of Record, as such, hath Power to keep the Peace within its own Precincts, as hath been more fully shewn, *Ch.* 1. *Sect.* 15. And the Justices of Gaol-Delivery may take Surety of the Peace from a Prisoner before them, who was committed for not finding such Surety.

Sect. 4. Alſo every Sheriff is a principal [a] Conſervator of the Peace within his County, and may without Doubt, *ex Officio*, award Proceſs of the Peace, and take Surety for it; and it ſeems the better [b] Opinion, That the Security ſo taken by him is by the Common Law looked on as a Recognizance or Matter of Record, and not as a common Obligaligation, or Matter *in Pais* only; for that it is taken by him by Vertue of the King's Commiſſion, by which he is intruſted with the Cuſtody of the County, and conſequently has by it an implied Power of keeping the Peace within ſuch County; and it is a general [c] Rule, That whatſoever is done by Vertue of the King's Commiſſion ought to be taken as a Matter of Record.

[a] Lamb. B. 1. Ch. 3. 12 H. 7. 17. b. Bro. Peace 13 Cro. Car. 26.
[b] Bro. Recognizance 5. F.N.B. 81. d. 82. Dalt. Ch. 11. Lamb. B. 1. Ch. 13. *Quære* Bro. Recognizance 5, 14, 16, 18
[c] *See the Books above cited.*

Sect. 5. Alſo every [d] Coroner is another principal Conſervator of the Peace within the County of which he is a Coroner, and may certainly bind any Perſon to the Peace who makes an Affray in his Preſence; But it ſeems the better Opinion, That he has no Authority to grant Proceſs for the Peace; and it ſeems clear, That the Security taken by him for the keeping of the Peace, (except only where it is taken by him as Judge of his own Court for an Affray done in ſuch Court,) is not to be looked on as a Recognizance, but as an Obligation; becauſe it is not taken by one who acts as a Judge of Record, or by the King's Commiſſion, as all [e] Recognizances ought to be.

9 E. 4. 30. b. 31. a.
[d] Cromp. 6. Lamb B. 1. Ch. 3.
[e] *See the Books cited* S. 1. *Letter* b *and* S. 4 *Letter* b.

Sect. 6. Alſo every High and Petit Conſtable are by the Common Law Conſervators of the Peace within their ſeveral Limits, and may take ſuch Order for the keeping of the ſame, as hath been more fully ſhewn, *B.* 1. *Ch.* 63. *S.* 13, 14, *&c.*

Crompt. 6. b.

Secondly, Conſervators of the Peace by the Common Law, who were conſtituted for that Purpoſe only, and were ſimply called by the Name of Conſervators or Keepers of the Peace, were of two Kinds:

1. Ordinary.
2. Extraordinary.

Thoſe of the firſt Kind were either,

1. By Tenure, or
2. By Election, or
3. By Preſcription.

Sect. 7. Conſervators of the Peace by Tenure were thoſe who held Lands of the King by this Service, among others, of being Conſervators of the Peace, within ſuch a Diſtrict.

Lamb B. 1. Ch. 3.

Sect. 8. Conſervators of the Peace by Election, were thoſe who were choſen to ſuch Office in Purſuance of the King's Writ to ſuch Purpoſe, (as all Sheriffs anciently were and as Coroners ſtill are,) by the Freeholders of a County in the County-Court; after which Election it was uſual for the King to ſend another Writ to the Perſons ſo choſen, commanding them diligently to attend their ſaid Office till they ſhould receive a Command from the King to the contrary.

Lamb B. 1. Ch. 3.

Sect. 9. Conſervators of the Peace by Preſcription, were thoſe who claimed ſuch Power from an immemorial Uſage in themſelves, and their Predeceſſors or Anceſtors, or thoſe whoſe Eſtate they had in certain Lands, to exerciſe the like Power, which wholly depended upon ſuch Uſage both as to its Extent, and the Manner in which it was to be exerciſed.

Bro. Peace 18. Preſcription 79. 22 Ed. 4. 35. b. Lamb B. 1. Ch. 3.

[a] 21 Ed. 4. 67. a.

Sect. 10. It is [a] questioned indeed by some, Whether any such Power can be claimed by Usage? Yet if the Power of holding Pleas and even Courts of Record, which of are so high a Nature, and imply a Power of keeping the Peace within their own Precincts, may be claimed by Usage, as it seems to be [b] certain, that they may; it seems strange that the bare Authority of keeping the Peace in a certain District may not as well be claimed by such Usage.

[b] Co. Lit. 114 b. Doctor and Student B. 1. Ch. 7.

Sect. 11. It [c] seems, That the Power of such Conservators of the Peace, whether by Tenure, Election, or Prescription was no greater than that of Constables at this Day, unless it were enlarged by some special Grant or Prescription.

[c] Dalt. B. 1. fol 3. Crompt 6. b.

Sect. 12. The extraordinary Conservators of the Peace were Persons specially commissioned, in Times of imminent Danger either from Rebels or foreign Invaders, to take care of and defend such a particular District committed to their Charge, and to preserve the Peace within the Limits of it; and these had Power to command the Sheriff with his whole *Posse* to aid and assist them.

Lamb. B. 1. Ch. 3.

Sect. 13. And now I am in the second Place to shew, in what Manner Justices of Peace have been ordained by the several Statutes concerning them, the first whereof is 1 *Ed.* 3. *Ch.* 16. which is in the following Words, *For the better keeping and Maintenance of the Peace, the King willeth that in every County, good Men and lawful, which be no Maintainers of Evil, or Barretors in the Country, shall be assigned to keep the Peace.*

Sect. 14 And it is farther enacted by 4 *Ed.* 3, 2. *That there shall be assigned good and lawful Men in every County to keep the Peace; and at the Time of the Assignments mention shall be made, that such as shall be indicted or taken by the said Keepers of the Peace, shall not be let to Mainprise by the Sheriffs, nor by none other Ministers, if they be not mainpernable by the Law; nor that such as shall be indicted, shall not be delivered but at the Common Law. And the Justices assigned to deliver the Gaols, shall have Power to deliver the same Gaols of those that shall be indicted before the Keepers of the Peace; and that the said Keepers shall send their Indictments before the Justices,* &c.

Sect. 15. And it is farther enacted by 18. *Ed.* 3. 2.*That two or three of the best Reputation in the Counties, shall be assigned Keepers of the Peace by the King's Commission. And at what Time need shall be, the same with other wise and learned in the Law shall be assigned by the King's Commission, to hear and determine Felonies, and Trespasses done against the Peace in the same Counties, and to inflict Punishment reasonably according to the Law and Reason, and the Manner of the Deed.*

Sect. 16. And it is farther enacted by 34 *Ed.* 3. 1. *That in every County of* England, *shall be assigned for the keeping of the Peace, one Lord, and with him three or four of the most worthy in the County, with some Learned in the Law, and they shall have Power to restrain the Offenders, Rioters, and all other Barretors, and to pursue, arrest, take and chastise them according to their Trespass or Offence; and to cause them to be imprisoned and duly punished according to the Law and Customs of the Realm, and according to that which to them shall seem best to do by their Discretion and good Advisement; and also to inform them, and to inquire of all those that have been Pillors and Robbers in the Parts beyond the Sea, and be now come again, and go wandering, and will not labour as they were wont in Times past; and to take and arrest all those that they may find by Indictment, or by Suspicion, and to put them in Prison, and to take of all them that be not of good Fame, where they shall be found, sufficient Surety and Mainprise of their Good Behaviour towards the King and his People, and the other duly to punish, to the Intent that the People be not by such Rioters or Rebels troubled nor endamaged, nor the Peace blemished, nor Merchants nor other passing by the Highways of the Realm disturbed, nor put in the Peril which may happen of such Offenders; and also to hear and determine at the King's Suit, all Manner of Felonies and Trespasses done in the same County according to the Laws and Customs aforesaid.*

Sect. 17. And it is enacted by 17 *R.* 2. 10. *That in every Commission of the Peace through the Realm, where need shall be, two Men of Law of the same County where such Commission shall be made, shall be assigned to go and proceed to the Deliverance of Thieves and Felons, as often as they shall think it expedient.*

Sect. 18. And it is farther enacted by 2 *H.* 5. Stat. 1. Ch. 4. *That the Justices of Peace in every Shire named of the* Quorum, *(except Lords, and the Justices of either Bench, and the Chief Baron, and Serjeants at Law, and the King's Attorney for the Time that they shall be occupied in the King's Service,) shall be resiant in the same Shire, and shall make their Sessions four Times by the Year,* viz. *in the first Week after* Michaelmas, Epiphany, Easter, *and the Translation of St.* Thomas *the Martyr, and oftner if Need be, and that the same Justices hold their Sessions throughout* England *in the same Weeks every Year.* 36 Ed. 3. 12. Lambert B 4. Ch. 19. Crompt. 123.

Sect. 19. Also it is enacted by 2 *H.* 5. Stat. 2. Ch. 1. *That Justices of Peace shall be made in the Counties of* England, *of most sufficient Persons dwelling in the same Counties, by the Advice of the Chancellor and of the King's Counsel, without taking other Persons dwelling in foreign Counties to execute such Office, except the Lords and the Justices of Assises to be named by the King and his Counsel; and except all the King's Chief Stewards of the Lands and Seigniories of the Dutchy of* Lancaster, *in the North Parts, and in the South, for the Time being.*

Sect. 20. Also it is enacted by 1 *Mar.* Sess. 2. Ch. 8. *That no Person having or using the Office of a Sheriff of any County, shall use or exercise the Office of a Justice of Peace, by Force of any Commission or otherwise, in any County where he shall be Sheriff, during the Time only that he shall exercise the said Office, or Sheriffwick: And that all Acts done by such Sheriff by Authority of any Commission of the Peace, during the Time abovesaid, shall be void.* Crompt. 121.

Sect. 21. Also there are many other Statutes concerning the Power of Justices of Peace, all of which it would be endless to enumerate; therefore I have only taken Notice of those which concern their Authority in general; and for those which concern the particular Branches of it, I shall refer the Reader to the Books which treat principally of this Subject.

Sect. 22. As to the third Point, *viz.* In what Manner Justices of the Peace are to be commissioned in Pursuance of the several Statutes concerning them; it is observable, That the Commission of the Peace hath often been altered in several Reigns, and that the present Form of it was settled by the Judges about the thirty-third Year of Queen *Elizabeth*, and is in Substance as followeth: 4 Inst. 171. Lamb. B. 1. Ch. 9.

Sect. 23. Beginning with a Salutation from the King to the several Persons named in it, it afterwards assigns them and every one of them, jointly and severally the King's Justices, to keep the Peace in such a County; and to cause to be kept all Statutes made for the Good of the Peace and quiet Government of the People, as well within Liberties as without; and to punish all those who shall offend against any of the said Statutes; and to cause all those to come before them, or some of them, who shall threaten any of the People as to their Persons, or the burning of their Houses, in order to compel them to find Surety for the Peace or Good Behaviour; and if they shall refuse to find such Surety, to cause them to be safely kept in Prison till they shall find it.

Sect. 24. Then it goes on and assigns them, and every two or more of them, (of which Number either such or such a particular Person among them is specially required to be,) Justices to inquire by the Oath of good and lawful

ful Men of the same County, of all Felonies, Witchcrafts, Inchantments, Sorceries, Magick Art, Trespasses, Forestallers, Regraters, Ingrossers, and Extortions whatsoever, and of all other Offences of which Justices of the Peace may lawfully inquire; also of all those who shall go or ride armed, *&c.* or in Companies, to the Disturbance of the Peace; and also of all Innholders and others who shall offend in the Abuse of Weights or Measures, or selling of Victuals, *&c.* and also of all Sheriffs, Bailiffs, Stewards, Constables, Gaolers, and other Officers, who shall be faulty in the Execution of their Offices; and to inspect all Indictments taken before them, or any of them, or other former Justices of the Peace for the same County; and to make and continue Process against all the Persons so indicted till they shall be taken, or render themselves, or be outlawed; and to hear and determine all the Felonies, and other Offences aforesaid: Provided that if a Case of Difficulty shall arise, they shall not proceed to give Judgment, except in the Presence of some Justice of one of the Benches or of Assise.

Sect. 25. And then it commands them to make Inquiries of the Premisses, and to hear and determine the same at certain Days and Places, which they or any such two or more of them shall appoint.

Sect. 26. And then it goes on and commands the Sheriff of the County to return before them at certain Days and Places to be made known to him by them, such and so many lawful Men of his Bailiwick, by whom the Truth of the Premisses may be best known and inquired.

Sect. 27. And then concludes, by assigning some one of them Keeper of the Rolls of the Peace in the same County; and commanding him to cause to be brought before himself and his Fellows, at the said Days and Places, the Writs, Precepts, Processes, and Indictments aforesaid.

And now I am in the fourth Place to shew, What is most observable from the said Statutes and Commissions; in order to which I shall endeavour to shew,

1. What Statutes concerning the Peace may be executed by such Justices.
2. How far the Justices of Peace for a County may act out of it, or within a Liberty.
3. What Commissions of this Kind require a special Suit to the King for the granting of them.
4. How far such Justices have Power to proceed on Indictments not taken before themselves.
5. By what Name they are to be described.
6. What Authority they have in Relation to Felonies.
7. What in relation to Treason, *Præmunire*, and Misprision of Treason.
8. What in relation to inferior Offences.

Lamb. B. 1. Ch. 9. Dalt. Ch. 5. Crompt. 7, 8.

Sect. 28. As to the first Point, *viz.* What Statutes concerning the Peace may be executed by such Justices, it seems certain, That by Vertue of the said Commission they may execute all Statutes whatsoever, made for the better keeping of the Peace, and consequently those of *Winchester* and *Westminster*, and all others concerning the Peace made before the Reign of *Edward* the third, in whose Time Justices of Peace were first instituted; for all these Statutes were expresly mentioned in the ancient Commissions of the Peace, and have always been undoubtedly taken to be included in the general Words of the present Commission; and yet none of the Statutes which ordain the Office of Justices of Peace, say any Thing concerning

 ing

ing the Execution of the said former Statutes, so that the Power of Justices of Peace in relation to those Statutes, seems intirely to depend on the King's Commission, and yet hath always been unquestionably allowed; from whence it appears, That regularly the King by his Commission, may authorize whom he pleases to execute an Act of Parliament.

As to the second Point, *viz.* How far the Justices of Peace for a County may act out of it or within a Liberty? It is said, That they have no coercive Power when out of the County; and therefore that an Order of Bastardy, or for Payment of Labourers Wages made by them out of the County, is not binding; yet it is said, That Recognizances and Informations voluntarily taken before them in any Place, are good: And it is to be observed, Cro.Car.211, 212.

Sect. 29. That the Justices of Peace for a County have by their Commission, an express Authority as well within Liberties as without; from whence it seems clearly to follow, That they may execute their Office within a Town, which has a special Commission of the Peace for its own Limits, unless such Commission have a Clause, that no other Justices, except those named in it, shall any way concern themselves in the keeping of the Peace within the Liberties of such Town; and it may be questioned, whether such a special Clause in such a Commission, do absolutely make void the Act of any County-Justice within such Town? since the Commission for the County seems as fully to give those named in it a Jurisdiction over all such Towns within the Precinct of it, as such Commission for a Town doth exclude them: And the Justices for the County seem to be under no Necessity of informing themselves of the Contents of a Commission, which they have nothing to do with; yet if they have express Notice given them of such a restraining Clause, and proceed to act within such Town in Defiance of it, they may perhaps be punishable for their Contempt of the King's Prohibition; and yet perhaps it may be questioned whether their Acts be void, for the Reasons abovementioned. Lamb. B. 1. Ch. 9. Lamb. B. 1. Ch. 9 Cont.Cromp. 8. 20 H.7.6,7,8.

Sect. 30. As to the third Point, *viz.* What Commissions of this Kind require a special Suit to the King for granting of them; it seems agreed, That notwithstanding all such Commissions must be in the King's Name, as hath been more fully shewn, *Ch.* 5. *Sect.* 1. yet there is not any need of a special Suit or Application to, or Warrant from the King, for the granting of them; for this is only requisite for such as are of a particular Nature, as constituting the Mayor of such a Town and his Successors, perpetual Justices of the Peace within their Liberties, *&c.* which Commissions are neither revocable by the King, nor determinable by his Death, as the common Commission for the Peace is, which is made of Course by the Lord Chancellor, according to his Discretion. Lamb. B. 1. Ch. 5. Brook Commission 5. Dalt. Ch. 3. 1 Lev. 219.

Sect. 31. As to the fourth Point, *viz.* How far Justices of Peace have Power to proceed on Indictments not taken before themselves, it is certain, That subsequent Justices of Peace may proceed upon Indictments taken before their Predecessors, but this seems chiefly to depend upon 11 *H.* 6. 6. which, *reciting the Inconvenience that Pleas and Processes upon Indictments before Justices of Peace had often been discontinued by making of new Commissions of the Peace, to the great Loss of the King,* &c. *ordains that such Pleas, Suits, and Processes before Justices of the Peace, shall not be discontinued by new Commissions of the Peace, but stand in Force: And that the new Justices, after that they have the Records of the same Pleas and Processes before them, may continue, and finally hear and determine the same,* &c. And this is farther confirmed by 1 *Ed.* 6. 7. Par. 6. But it is certain That they cannot proceed Cromp 2. 9. Cromp. 9. H. P. C. 166, 167.

proceed on an Indictment taken before a Coroner, or Justices of *Oyer* and *Terminer*, or Gaol-Delivery, nor deliver Persons suspected by Proclamation: But by 1 *Ed.* 4. 2. they are enabled to proceed on Indictments taken before the Sheriff at his Torn.

Sect. 32. As to the fifth Point, By what Name such Justices are to be described, it is observable, That they are expresly commissioned by the Name of Justices of Peace; and in no Part of their Commission are called by the Name of Keepers of the Peace, yet, inasmuch as by 18 *E.* 3. 2. which is one of the first Statutes made concerning their Institution, they are expresly called Keepers of the Peace, and the principal End of their Office is for the keeping of the Peace, and their usual Description in *Certiorari's* is by the Name of Keepers of the Peace; it hath been adjudged, That the Caption of an Indictment, (whereof Justices of Peace have Conusance,) *coram* A. B. *&* C. D. *Custodibus Pacis & Justiciariis Domini Regis* in such a Place, is good, without expresly naming them Justices of Peace. Also it hath been resolved, That the Description of Justices of Peace by the Name of *Justiciarii Domini Regis ad pacem conservandam*, &c. is good without saying, *ad pacem Domini Regis*, for that it is necessarily implied.

2 Rol. Ab 95.

The King and Howkins, Mich. 3 Geor.

Sect. 33. As to the sixth Point, *viz.* What Authority Justices of Peace have in Relation to Felonies, it is observable, That such of the said Justices as are of the *Quorum* only, are expresly authorized to inquire of, and hear and determine Felonies and Trespasses, and that the abovementioned Statute of 18 *E.* 3. after it hath ordained, *That some Persons shall be assigned Keepers of the Peace by the King's Commission*, saith in another distinct Clause, *That at what Time need shall be, the same shall be assigned by the King's Commissions to hear and determine Felonies and Trespasses*, &c. From whence it is inferred, That Justices of Peace have no Power to hear and [a] determine Felonies, unless they be authorized so to do by the express Words of their Commission: And this Opinion is farther confirmed by the Authority of the Year-Books of [b] 2 *R.* 3. 9. *a. b.* and 12 *H.* 7. 25. *a.* wherein it is adjudged, That a *Certiorari* to remove certain Indictments taken before Justices of Peace was not good, because it named them only Justices of Peace, without adding that they were also assigned to hear and determine Felonies, *&c.* Yet it seems, That it may probably be argued for the contrary Opinion, that the Statute of 34 *E.* 3. 1. is express, that the Persons assigned for the keeping of the Peace, shall have Power among other Things to hear and determine Felonies and Trespasses, *&c.* And this seems to be the Principal Ground of the Resolution in the Case of *Barnes* and *Constantine*, wherein it is adjudged, That the setting forth of an Indictment in a Declaration as taken before Justices of Peace, being also assigned to hear and determine Felonies, *&c.* was well justified upon *Oyer* of the Record, wherein it was entred as taken before Justices of Peace, without adding, That they were assigned to hear and determine Felonies, *&c.*. And as to the Authority of *Staundford* and *Hale*, it may be answered, That their Opinion is expresly grounded on the wording of the Statute of 18 *E.* 3. And it does not appear that they considered the Purport of 34 *E.* 3. As to the Authority of 2 *R.* 3. 9. it may be answered, That the *Certiorari* therein mentioned, was for the Removal of an Indictment for counterfeiting Coin, and that the Power of Justices of Peace to take such an Indictment, depends wholly upon the Statute of 3 *H.* 5. 7. whereby it is enacted, *That the Justices of Peace throughout the Realm, shall have Power by the King's Commissions to inquire of the said Offence.* And as to what is said in 12 *H.* 7. 25. it may be answered, that the *Certiorari* therein mentioned was to remove certain Indictments, but it doth not appear from the Book what those Indictments were; so that it is pos-

[a] Crompt. 120. b. S. P. C. 53. a. 58. *and* 96. *Letter* E. H. P. C. 165, 207.

[b] Brook Indictment 32, 50.

Cro Jac. 32. Yelv. 46. 2 Roll. Rep., 151. Dy. 69. pl. 29.

sible they might be of a special Nature, not within the general Purview of 34 *E.* 3. *sed Quare.* However it is certain, That such a Clause in the Commission of Justices to hear and determine Felonies, *&c.* gives them no Jurisdiction over an Offence, which by Statute, is specially appointed to be determined by Justices of *Oyer* and *Terminer*, because such Justices shall be intended to mean such Justices of *Oyer* and *Terminer* only, which properly and usually are so called, and not those who are distinctly known by another Name. And from hence it follows, That Justices of Peace have no Power to take an Indictment upon the Statute of 5 *Eliz.* 14. concerning Forgery, nor on the 2 *&* 3 *Ed.* 6. 24. against Accessaries in one County to Felonies in another, nor on any other Statute which specially limits the Jurisdiction of determining any other Felony to other Justices of a particular Denomination. Yet inasmuch as all Felonies include in them a Breach of the Peace, and 2 *&* 3 *Ph. & Mar.* 10. which directs Justices of Peace to take the Examinations of all such Persons as shall be committed by them for Felony, seems to suppose them to have a general Power of committing all Persons accused of any Kind of Felony, and the general Practice has always been agreeable hereto; it is said, That Justices of Peace may take the Examination of Persons brought before them for any Kind of Felony, and commit them to Prison, and also take the Information of the Prosecutors upon Oath, and bind them over to prosecute, and to commit those who shall refuse to be so bound, if it appear that they can give material Evidence. Also inasmuch as the said Statute of 2 *&* 3 *Ph. & Mar.* 10. and also 1 *&* 2 *Ph. & Mar.* 13. direct Justices of Peace, in Case of Homicide and other Felonies, to take the Examination of the Offenders, and the Information of others, and to certify the same to the Justices of Gaol-Delivery; it hath been generally thought adviseable for Justices of Peace to proceed no farther in Relation to any Felonies, though within their Commission, except only Petit Larcenies.

H. P. C. 165. 9 Co. 118. b. Cro. El. 87, 601, 697. 2 Roll. Abr. 96. pl. 2.

Dalton Ch. 20. H. P. C. 167, 168.

H. P. C. 169.

Sect. 34. As to the seventh Point, *viz.* What Authority Justices of Peace have in relation to Treason, *Præmunire*, and Misprision of Treason; it seems to be agreed, That notwithstanding none of these Offences are within the Letter of their Commission, yet inasmuch as they are against the Peace of the King, and of the Realm, any Justice of Peace may, either upon his own Knowledge, or the Complaint of others, cause any Person to be apprehended for any such Offence. And it is the Opinion both of *Dalton* and Sir *Matthew Hale*, That such Justice may take the Examination of the Person so apprehended, and the Information of all those who can give material Evidence against him, and put the same in Writing, and also bind over such who are able to give any such Evidence to the King's Bench, or Gaol-Delivery, and certify his Proceedings to the same Court, to which he shall bind over such Informers. And this Opinion seems to be agreeable to constant Practice, especially since the Statutes of 1 *&* 2 *Ph. & Mar.* 13. and 2 *&* 3 *Ph. & Mar.* 10. which directing Justices of Peace to proceed in this Manner against Persons brought before them for Felony, seem to give them a discretionary Power of proceeding in like Manner against Persons accused of the abovementioned Offences.

Lamb. 226.

Dalt. Ch. 90. H. P. C. 168.

Sect. 35. Also by 3 *H.* 5. Ch. 7. *Justices of Peace shall have Power by the King's Commissions to inquire of Counterfeiting, Clipping, Washing, and other Falsity of Money of the Land, and thereupon to make Process by* Capias *only, against those who before them shall be thereof indicted.*

Sect. 36. And by 5 *El.* 1. Sect. 3. *Justices of Peace may inquire of the Offence of maintaining the Pope's Power, and shall certify every Presentment made*

made before them of any such Offence, into the King's Bench, within forty Days after it shall be made, &c.

1 Leon. 239. *Sect.* 37. And by 23 *E.* 1. Sect. 8. *They may inquire of all Offences against that Act, or against the Acts of the first, fifth, or thirteenth Years of the said Queen's Reign, touching acknowledging of the King's supream Government in Causes Ecclesiastical, or other Matters touching the Service of God, or coming to Church, or Establishment of true Religion in this Realm, within one Year and a Day after every such Offence committed.*

Sect. 38. As to the eighth Point, *viz.* What Authority Justices of Peace have in Relation to inferior Offences, it would be endless to enumerate all the Offences within their Jurisdiction, concerning which there have been such great Numbers of Statutes; and therefore I shall content my self in this Place with observing, that by the abovementioned Statute of 34 *Ed.* 3. 1. and also by the express Words of their Commission, they are impowered to hear and determine all Trespasses, which is a Word of a very general Extent, and in a large Sense not only comprehends all inferior Offences, which are properly and directly against the Peace, as Assaults and Batteries, and such like, but also all others which are so only
[a] 6Mod. 128. by Construction; as all Breaches of the Law in general are [a] said to be: Yet it hath been of late settled, that Justices of Peace have no Jurisdi-
[b] Salk. 406. Crompt. 120. [b] Lamb. B. 1. Ch. 12. ction over [b] Forgery or Perjury at the Common Law, the principal Reason of which Resolution as I apprehended, was, that inasmuch as the chief End of the Institution of the Office of these Justices, was for the Preservation of the Peace against personal Wrongs, and open Violence; and the Word Trespass in its most proper and natural Sense, is taken for such kind of Injuries, it shall be understood in that Sense only in the said Statute and Commission, or at the most to extend to such other Offences only as have a direct and immediate Tendency to cause such
[c] 1 Lev. 139. 1 Sid. 271. 1 Keb. 559, 772, 788, 931. 2 Keb. 138. Contra Cro. Jac. 421. Tr. 13 Annæ. [d] Latch. 173. Poph. 208. Breaches of the Peace, [c] as Libels, and such like, which on this Account have been adjudged indictable before Justices of Peace: And for this Reason, principally as I apprehended, the Court of the King's Bench in the Case of one *Pitt*, since the abovementioned Resolution concerning Perjury and Forgery, refused to quash an Indictment found at a Session of the Peace for a Libel, but ordered the Defendant to demur to it, if he thought fit. [d] And upon the like Reason perhaps the former Opinion, That one may be indicted before Justices of Peace for being a common Night-Walker and Haunter of Bawdy-Houses, may not be thought to contradict the abovementioned Resolution.

Cro. Jac. 32. Yelv. 46. Con. 2. Roll. Rep. 151. *Sect.* 39. And Justices of Peace by Vertue of the abovementioned Statute of 34 *Ed.* 3. 1. seem to have a Jurisdiction over Barretors, and such like Offenders whether they be mentioned in their Commission or not. And it seems clear, That Justices of Peace have Jurisdiction of all inferior Crimes within their Commission, whether such Crimes be
King and Loggain. mentioned in any Statute concerning them or not; for that all such Crimes are either directly, or at least by Consequence, and Judgment of Law, against the Peace, and upon this Ground principally, as I apprehended, it was lately resolved, That they may take an Indictment of Extortion.

Sect. 40. And now I am to consider the Nature of the Court of these Justices Sessions, by which we understand an Assembly of two or more of them, whereof one is of the *Quorum*, at a certain Day and Place before appointed, in order to inquire, hear and determine, in Pursuance of their Commission, of any Causes or Matters therein contained. And for the better understanding hereof, I shall consider the following Particulars:

1. By whom, and in what Manner such Court is to be summoned and appointed.
2. What Persons are bound to give their Attendance at it.
3. Whether it have any Power over its own Members.
4. The Difference between general, and special, and Quarter-Sessions.

Sect. 41. As to the first Point, It seems clear from the express Words of the Commission, That any two such Justices, whereof one is of the *Quorum*, may hold such Court at such Days and Places as shall be appointed by them, and that the Sheriff is bound to return proper Juries, and that the *Custos Rotulorum* ought to bring the Rolls of the Peace before them, *&c.* Lamb. B. 4. Ch. 2. & 20.

Sect. 42. And from hence it seems to follow, That any two such Justices may direct their Precept under their *Teste* to the Sheriff, for the Summons of a Session of the Peace, thereby commanding him to return a Grand Jury before them, or their Fellow Justices at a certain Day and Place, and to give Notice to all Stewards, Constables, and Bailiffs of Liberties to be present and do their Duties at such Day and Place, and to proclaim in proper Places throughout his Bailiwick, that such Sessions will be holden at such Day and Place, and to attend there himself to do his Duty, *&c.* Lamb. B. 4. Ch. 2.

Sect. 43. And it is said, That such a Precept by any two such Justices, cannot be superseded by any of their Fellows, but only by Writ out of Chancery. Lamb. B. 4. Ch. 2. Crompt. 122. b.

Sect. 44. It is said, That such Justices may hold such a Session without any such Summons, which seems to be a well grounded Opinion, as to their proceeding on Indictments before taken before themselves or others, or on other particular Occasions, for which there is no need either for the Attendance of Grand-Jurors, or Officers, *&c.* Lamb. B. 4. Ch. 2.

Sect. 45. As to the second Point, *viz.* What Persons are bound to give their Attendance at the Court of Sessions, there is no Doubt but that the Sheriff, (who is bound both to return his Precept, and also to take the Charge of all the Prisoners who shall be committed to him) and also all Constables of Hundreds, who are to make their Presentments required by several Statutes, (as that of Huy and Cry, and those relating to Highways and Ale-houses, *&c.* and also all Bailiffs of Franchises, and all Persons returned on a Jury, and the *Keeper of the House of Correction, *&c.* are bound to attend on every such Summons as is abovementioned, on Pain of being amerced for their Default at the Discretion of the Court, *&c.* Lamb. B. 4. Ch. 3. *See the Statute of* Winchester, *and* B. 1. Ch. 78. S. 22. *and* Ch. 76. S. 45. * Vide 7 Jac. c. 4.

Sect. 46. As to the third Point, *viz.* Whether the Court of Sessions have any Power over its own Members; it seems certain, That it hath no Authority to amerce any Justice of Peace for his Non-Attendance at any such Court, as the Justices of Assise may for the Absence of any such Justice at the Gaol-Delivery; for it is a general Rule, That *inter pares non est potestas*, it being reasonable rather to refer the Punishment of Persons in a judicial Office, in relation to their Behaviour in such Office, to other Judges of a superior Station, than to those of the same Rank with themselves; and therefore it seems to have been holden, That if a Justice of Peace at the Sessions who is not of the *Quorum*, shall use such Expressions towards another who is of the *Quorum*, for which if he were a private Person, he might be committed or bound to his Good Behaviour; yet the Sessions hath no Authority to commit him, or to bind him to his Good Behaviour: And yet it seems to be agreed, That if a Justice of Peace give just Cause Lamb. B. 4. Ch. 3. Crompt. 122. a. Fitz. Justices de Peace 3. Lamb. B. 4. Ch. 3. Crompt. 122. a.

to any Person to demand the Surety of the Peace against him, he may be compelled by any other Justice to find such Security, as hath been shewn in the first Book; for the Publick Peace requires an immediate Remedy in all such Cases.

Ch. 50. Sect. 5.

Sect. 47. As to the fourth Point, *viz.* The Difference between General and Special and Quarter-Sessions, Mr. *Lambard* seems to make no Distinction between General and Quarter-Sessions, but to take them as synonymous Terms? But it seems the better Opinion, That Quarter-Sessions are a Species only of General Sessions, and that such Sessions only are properly called General Quarter-Sessions, which are holden in the four Quarters of the Year in Pursuance of the abovementioned Statute of 2 *H.* 5. 4. set forth more at large in the fifteenth Section of this Chapter; and that any other Sessions holden at any other Time for the general Execution of the Authority of Justices of Peace, which by the abovementioned Statute, Justices of the Peace are authorized to hold oftener than at the Times therein specified, if Need be, may be properly called General Sessions; and that those holden on a special Occasion for the Execution of some particular Branch of their Authority, may properly be called Special Sessions.

Lamb. B. 4. Ch. 19.
Lamb. B. 4. Ch. 20.
Salk. 474. pl. 11. 476. pl. 14. 480. pl. 29. 482. pl. 34.

CHAP. IX.

Of the Court of the Coroner.

Sect. 1. CORONERS are [a] ancient Officers by the Common Law; so [b] called, because they deal principally with the Pleas of the Crown, and [c] were of old Time the principal Conservators of the Peace within their County; and there still ought to be a certain Number of them in every County; in [d] some more, in others less, according as the Usage hath been.

[a] 2 Inst. 31. S. P. C. 48, 49.
[b] 4 Inst. 271. 2 Inst. 31.
[c] Ch. 8. Sect. 3.
[d] F. N. B. 397. 4 Inst. 271. 2 Inst. 175.

Before I come to the particular Consideration of their Duty and Authority, it may not be improper to premise the following Particulars:

1. What Persons are qualified to be Coroners.
2. In what Manners they are to be placed in their Office.
3. How they may be discharged.

Sect. 2. As to the first Point, it is enacted by the Statute of *Westminster* 1. Ch. 10. in the following Words, *Forasmuch as mean Persons and indiscreet, now of late are commonly chosen to the Office of Coroners, where it is requisite, that Persons honest, loyal, and wise, should occupy such Offices: It is provided, That through all Shires sufficient Men shall be chosen to be Coroners of the most loyal and most wise Knights, which know, will, and may best attend upon such Offices, and which lawfully shall attach and present Pleas of the Crown.*

Sect. 3. It is observable, That this Statute seems expresly to require that none under the Degree of Knighthood shall be chosen a Coroner, and that the Statute of *Merton*, Chapter the Third, which was made near forty Years before, seems to suppose, That all Coroners were Knights: And it is farther remarkable, That in the Writ *De Coronatore exonerando*, it is mentioned as a sufficient Cause for the Discharge of a Coroner, that he is not

23 Ass. pl. 7. 4 Inst. 271.
Register 177. b. F. N. B. 164.

not a Knight; yet inasmuch as the principal Intent of putting those Words into the Statute, was to prevent the choosing of Persons of mean Ability, which is sufficiently answered, by choosing Men of good Substance and Credit: And it has been generally found impracticable to find Knights enough in any County willing to undertake this Office, and the constant Usage of many late Ages, which is the best Interpreter of Laws, hath suffered Persons of good Ability, under the Degree of Knights, to be chosen and continue Coroners, without any Objection against them on this Account; it seems certain, That at this Day it is no good Cause to remove a Coroner, that he is not a Knight. For why should not such Usage be as well allowed to make such an Explanation of the Law concerning Coroners, as it unquestionably hath done of that relating to the Representatives of a County in Parliament, who by the Writ for their Election are expresly required to be *duo Milites gladio cincti*, and yet may certainly be well chosen in Pursuance of that Writ, though they be under the Degree of Knights? S. P. C. 48. e. 2 Leon. 160, 161. F. N B. 164. 2 Inst. 176. Co. Lit. 109. b.

Sect. 4. It is farther enacted by 14 *E.* 3. 8. *That no Coroner be chosen, unless he have Land in Fee sufficient in the same County, whereof he may answer to all manner of People.*

Sect. 5. As to the second Point, *viz.* In what Manner Coroners are to be placed in their Office, it is observable, That they do not receive their Authority from the King's Commission, but from the Election of the County, in Pursuance of the King's Writ, issuing out of, and afterwards returned into the Chancery: And this is the Reason why their Authority does not determine by the Demise of the King, as that of all Judges, acting by the King's Commission only, regularly does, as hath been more fully shewn, *Chap.* 1. *Sect.* 11.

Sect. 6. The abovementioned Writ for the Election of a Coroner is in this Form: First it recites the Death or Discharge of one or more former Coroners, and then commands the Sheriff to cause one other or more, as the Case is, to be chosen, in a full County-Court, by the Assent of the County, according to the Form of the Statute in that Case made and provided; who having taken his Oath in the usual Manner, may do all Things which belong to the Office of a Coroner, *&c.* and then it concludes with commanding the Sheriff to certify to the Court the Name of the Person chosen, *&c.* *See the Form of such Certificate in Rastal's Entries* 133.

Sect. 7. A Coroner, being chosen by Vertue of such Writ, shall be sworn by the Sheriff, that he will lawfully do what belongs to the Office of a Coroner, *&c.* S. P C. 49 d. F. N. B. 163. M. 4 Inst. 271.

Sect. 8. And inasmuch as he is chosen by the County, if he be insufficient, and not able to answer such Fines and other Duties in respect of his Office, as he ought, the County, as his Superior, shall answer for him. 2 Inst. 174, 175.

Sect. 9. And it is enacted by 28 *E.* 3. 6. *That all Coroners of the Counties, shall be chosen in the full Counties by the Commons of the same Counties, of the most meet and lawful People, that shall be found in the same Counties, to execute the said Office: Saved always to the King and other Lords, who ought to make such Coroners, their Seigniories and Franchises.*

From this Statute the two following Points are observable.

Sect. 10. First, that all such Elections are appointed by it to be made by the Commons of the Counties, without mentioning Freeholders; and yet inasmuch as the said Statute was made in Affirmance of the Common Law, and [a] none but Freeholders are Suitors to the County-Court, F. N. B. 164. S. P. C. 49 B. [a] 2 Inst. 99. 2 Rol. Abr. 121. F.

Court, and the Uſage hath always been, both before and ſince the ſaid Statute, for ſuch only to vote, it is certain that none but Freeholders have a Voice at any ſuch Election.

Sect. 11. Secondly, That it is clearly ſuppoſed by the ſaid Statute, that not only the King, but alſo other Lords have the Franchiſe of making Coroners: From whence it ſeems reaſonable to infer, That the King may lawfully claim ſuch Franchiſe by Preſcription, and that other Lords may claim it by Grant from the Crown; but it is a Privilege of ſo high a Nature, that no Subject can well intitle himſelf to it by Preſcription only.

Co. Lit. 114. a.

Sect. 12. As to the third Point, *viz.* In what Manner Coroners may be diſcharged from their Office; it is certain, That if any of them be ſo far engaged in any other publick Buſineſs in the County, that he cannot have Leiſure enough to attend the Office of a Coroner; or if he be choſen Verderor of a Foreſt, or if he have not ſufficient Lands in the ſame County, whereon to live according to his State and Degree, or if he be diſabled either by old Age, or any inveterate Diſeaſe, as the Palſy, or the like, to execute his Office, as he ought, and as ſome ſay, if he follow any common Trade, he may be diſcharged by the Writ *De Coronatore exonerando*, which being directed to the Sheriff, after a Recital of the particular Cauſe of the Diſcharge of ſuch Coroner, commands him to cauſe another to be choſen in his Room.

Regiſter 177. a. b. F. N. B. 163, 164. S. P. C. 48. *Letter* E. 8 Co. 41. b. 2 Inſt. 32.

Sect. 13. But if any Writ of this Kind be grounded on an untrue Suggeſtion, the Coroner may procure a Commiſſion from the Chancery to inquire of the Truth of it, and to return the Inquiry before the King into the Chancery; and if upon ſuch Commiſſion the Suggeſtion be diſproved, the King may make a *Superſedeas* to the Sheriff, that he do not remove ſuch Coroner; or if he have removed him, That he ſuffer him to execute the Office as he did before.

Regiſter 177. b 178. a. F.N.B. 164. d. S. P. C. 49.

And now I am particularly to conſider the Duty and Authority of a Coroner; for the better underſtanding whereof I ſhall examine the following Points:

1. In what Places he hath a Juriſdiction.
2. How far he is impowered, and in what Manner he ought to take an Inquiſition.
3. How far to receive and proceed on a Bill of Appeal.
4. How far to receive and proceed on the Appeal of an Approver.
5. How far to take the Abjuration of a Felon.
6. How far the Act of any one of them ſhall be as effectual as if it had been done by all.
7. In what Caſes he may lawfully take a Fee for the Execution of his Office.
8. In what Caſes a Matter recorded by, or found before him, admits of no Traverſe.

As to the firſt Point, *viz.* In what Places a Coroner hath Juriſdiction, I ſhall conſider:

1. How far he hath a Juriſdiction of Offences committed on the Sea.
2. How far a Coroner of the County may intermeddle with Offences done within the Verge of the Court, and *vice verſa*.

Sect. 14. As to the firſt Particular, it is laid down as a general Rule by [a] ſome, That he may inquire of a Felony committed on the Arms of the Sea, where a Man may ſee from the one Side to the other; but by others,

[a] Owen 122. Moor 892. pl. 1255. H. P. C. 171. S. P. C. 51. *Letter* K.

thers, who seem to be more accurate, his [a] Power is confined to such Parts of the Sea, where a Man standing on the one Side, may see what is done on the other: But it seems to be [b] agreed, That he hath no Jurisdiction of Offences committed in the open Sea, between the high and low Water-Mark when the Tide is in; but that he hath an Authority over Offences committed in such Places when the Tide is out.

[a] Fitz. Coron. 399. 4 Inst. 140. 2 Rol. Abr. 169 pl. 7.
[b] 3 Inst. 113. 5 Co. 107.
[c] 2 Leon. 160. 4 Co. 46 b.
[d] 2 Leon. 160. 4 Co. 46. b.

Sect. 15. As to the second Particular, *viz.* How far a Coroner of the County may intermeddle with Offences done within the Verge of the Court, *& vice versa*; it is said, That at the Common Law, as the Coroner of the King's House had nothing to do with an Offence committed in the County out of the Verge, so neither had the Coroner of the County any Thing to do with an Offence committed within the Verge. And therefore it seems, That before the Statute of *Articuli super Chartas*, if a Person had been killed any where within the Verge of the Court, and the King had removed his Court before the Coroner of the King's House had taken an Indictment, no Coroner at all had any Jurisdiction of the Fact; not the Coroner of the County, because he had nothing to do with what happened within the Verge of the Court; nor the Coroner of the King's-House, because his Authority ceased when the Place where the Matter happened, ceased to be within the Verge of the Court; and this seems to be confirmed by the Statute of *Articuli super Chartas*, Ch. 3. whereby it is recited, that before the making of that Act, *Many Felonies committed within the Verge had been unpunished, because the Coroners of the County had not been authorized to inquire of Felonies done within the Verge, but the Coroner of the King's House, which never continued in one Place, by Reason whereof there can be no Trial made in due Manner, nor the Felons put in Exigent, nor outlawed, nor any Thing presented in the Circuit, the which had been to the great Damage of the King, and nothing to the Preservation of the Peace:* And thereupon it is ordained, *That from thenceforth in Cases of the Death of Men, whereof the Coroners Office is to make View and Inquest, it shall be commanded to the Coroner of the County, that he with the Coroner of the King's House, shall do as belongeth to his Office, and enrol it, &c.* It is said indeed by Sir *Edward Coke*, That if a Murder had been committed within the Verge, and the King had removed before any Indictment taken by the Coroner of the Verge, the Coroner of the County might have inquired of the same at the Common Law, *ne maleficia remanerent impunita:* But since no Authority is cited by him for the Maintenance of this Opinion, and the Argument brought to prove it is founded on a mistaken Supposition, inasmuch as it doth by no Means follow, That such Offences would be dispunishable if they could not be inquired of by the Coroner of the County, since they might certainly be indicted before Justices of *Oyer* and *Terminer*, or of the Peace, who have a general Jurisdiction throughout the whole County; the contrary Opinion seems rather the more plausible, as being more agreeable to the Purport of the said Statute, and the general Tenor of our Law Books.

2 Inst. 550.
2 Inst. 549. 4 Co. 46 b. 47. a. 4 Co. 47.

Sect. 16. But it is certain, That an Indictment taken before the Coroner of the County, and the Coroner of the King's House, of an Offence not appearing by the Indictment it self, to have happened within the Verge of the Court, is insufficient; for that every material Part of an Indictment ought to be found by the Oaths of the Indictors, and cannot be supplied with any Averment; and it doth not appear by the Indictment, that the Coroner of the King's House had any Authority to take it, and it shall not be said to be void, and *coram non judice* as to the Coroner of the King's House, and good as to the Coroner of the County, inasmuch as the Record is entire, and the Indictment was taken entirely

4 Co. 47. 2 Inst. 550.

before both; and peradventure the Jury was directed principally by the Coroner of the House, and the Witnesses examined and sworn by him.

4 Co. 46. a. 3 Inst. 134. 2 Leon. 160. *the same Case, but no Resolution.*

Sect. 17. It hath been resolved, That if the same Person be Coroner of the County, and also of the King's House, an Indictment of Death taken before him as Coroner both of the King's House, and of the County, is good, because the Mischief expressed in the Statute, is remedied as well when both Offices are in the same Persons as when they are in divers.

Sect. 18. Also it is enacted by 33 *H.* 8. 12. Par. 1. & 3. *That all Inquisitions upon the View of Persons slain within any of the King's Palaces or Houses, or any other House or Houses, at such Time as his Majesty shall happen to be there demurrant or abiding in his Royal Person, shall be taken by the Coroner for the Time being of the King's Houshold, without any adjoining or assisting of another Coroner of any Shire within this Realm, by the Oath of twelve or more of the Yeomen, Officers of the King's Houshold, returned by the two Clerks Controllers, the Clerks of the Check, and the Clerks Marshals, or one of them, for the Time being, of the said Houshold, to whom the said Coroner of the same Houshold shall direct his Precept, which Coroner shall be from Time to Time appointed by the Lord Great Master, or Lord Steward for the Time being; and that the said Coroner shall certify under his Seal, and the Seals of such Persons as shall be sworn before him, all such Inquisitions before the said Lord Master or Lord Steward,* &c.

As to the second general Point, *viz.* How far a Coroner is impowered, and in what Manner he ought to take an Inquisition, I shall consider his Authority of this Kind,

1. In Relation to Death.
2. In Relation to other Matters.

As to his Authority to take an Inquisition of Death, I shall examine,

1. In what Cases and in what Manner he ought to take such Inquisition.
2. What farther Care must be taken by him for the Prosecution of the Offender, after taking the Inquisition.
3. What high Credit the Law gives to it.

Bract. 121. Fleta B. 1. Ch. 25.

Sect. 19. As to the first of these Particulars, it is enacted by 4 *E.* 1. commonly called the Statute *de officio Coronatoris, That the Coroner upon Information, shall go to the Places where any be slain, or suddenly dead or wounded, and shall forthwith command four of the next Towns, or five or six, to appear before him in such a Place; and when they are come thither, the Coroner upon the Oath of them shall inquire in this Manner; that is to wit, if they know where the Person was slain, whether it were in any House, Field, Bed, Tavern, or Company, and who were there. Likewise it is to be inquired who were culpable, either of the Act, or of the Force, and who were present, either Men or Women, and of what Age soever they be, (if they can speak or have any Discretion.) And how many soever be found culpable by Inquisition in any of the Manners aforesaid, they shall be taken and delivered to the Sheriff, and shall be committed to the Gaol: And such as be founden, and be not culpable, shall be attached until the coming of the Justices, and their Names shall be written in the Coroners Rolls. If it fortune any such Man be slain, which is found in the Fields, or in the Woods, first it is to be inquired whether he were slain in the same Place or not. And if he were brought and laid there, they shall do as much as they can, to follow*

 low

low their Steps that brought the Body thither, whether he were brought upon a Horse, or in a Cart. It shall be inquired also, if the dead Person were known, or else a Stranger, and where he lay the Night before, and if any be found culpable of the Murder, the Coroner shall immediately go unto his House, and shall inquire what Goods he hath, and what Corn he hath in his Grange; and if he be a Freeman, they shall inquire how much Land he hath, and what it is worth yearly, and further, what Corn he hath upon the Ground. And when they have thus inquired upon every Thing, they shall cause all the Land, Corn, and Goods to be valued, in like Manner as if they should be sold incontinently, and thereupon they shall be delivered to the whole Township, which shall be answerable before the Justices for all. And likewise of his Freehold, how much it is worth yearly over and above the Service due to the Lords of the Fee, and the Land shall remain in the King's Hands, until the Lords of the Fee have made Fine for it. And immediately upon these Things being inquired, the Bodies of such Persons being dead or slain shall be buried. In like Manner it is to be inquired of them that be drowned, or suddenly dead, and after such Bodies are to be seen, whether they were so drowned or slain, or strangled by the Sign of a Cord tied strait about their Necks, or about any of their Members, or upon any other Hurt found upon their Bodies, whereupon they shall proceed in the Form abovesaid; and if they were not slain, then ought the Coroner to attach the Finders, and all other in Company.

Sect. 20. *Also all Wounds ought to be viewed, the Length, Breadth, and Deepness, and with what Weapons, and in what Part of the Body the Wound or Hurt is, and how many be culpable, and how many Wounds there be, and who gave the Wound; all which Things must be inrolled in the Roll of the Coroners. Also Horses, Boats, Carts, &c. whereby any are slain, that properly are called Deodands, shall be valued and delivered unto the Towns as before is said.*

Sect. 21. It is observable, That this Statute being wholly Directory and in Affirmance of the Common Law, doth neither restrain the Coroner from any Branch of his Power, nor excuse him from the Execution of any Part of his Duty not mentioned in it, which was incident to his Office before; and from hence it follows, That though the Statute mention only his taking Inquiries of the Death of Persons slain or drowned or suddenly dead, yet he may and ought to inquire of the Death of all Persons whatsoever who die in Prison, to the end that the Publick may be satisfied, whether such Persons came to their End by the common Course of Nature, or by some unlawful Violence, or unreasonable Hardships put on them by those under whose Power they were confined.

Fitz. Coron. 421. 3 Inst. 52, 91. Bro. Coron. 168. S. P. C. 51.

Sect. 22. And the like Reason also seems to be the best Ground of the Resolution which we find in some [a] Books, That there is no Necessity that it appear in a Coroner's Inquest, that it was taken by the Oaths of Persons of the next adjacent Towns, but that it is sufficient to say, That it was taken by the Oaths of lawful Person of the County, inasmuch as such Inquisitions being good before the said Statute, which is wholly Declaratory, must needs be so still; but it [b] seems, That it ought to appear in every such Inquisition at what Place, and by what Jurors by Name it was taken, and that such Jurors were sworn, and that the Reason given in some Books that such Inquests shall be intended to have been taken by the Men of the next Towns seems very harsh, if it be supposed necessary to be taken by such Persons; for that such Intendment would be contrary to the general Rule of the Law which will not suffer any material Part of an Indictment to be taken by Intendment.

[a] 1 Sid. 204. 1 Keb. 723, 744, 745. Con. Latch. 166. Poph. 210. Co. Ent. 354.

[b] Cro. El. 31.

1 Sid. 204. 1 Keb. 745.

Sect. 23.

[a] Fitz.Coron. 107. S.P.C. 51.G. 2 Levin. 141. Latch. 166. Noy 87. 2 R 3. 2. pl. 5. 21 Ed 4. 70. b. H. P. C. 170. Poph. 209. [b] Fitz.Coron. 329, 339, 421. H. P. C. 170. S. P. C. 51. 1 Keb. 278. pl. 74. [c] 21 Ed 4. 70. b. 2 R. 3. 2 pl. 5. S. P. C. 51. H. P. C. 170. Bro. Coron. 167, 173. [d] S. P. C. 51. H. P. C. 170. 2 Lev 141. Latch. 166. 1 Vent. 352. Poph. 209. Salk. 190, 377. Noy 87. 2 Rol. Abr. 96. pl. 3. 1 Rol. Rep. 217. [e] *The King and* Cawſey. Hillary 3 Georg.

Sect. 23. Alſo it is farther remarkable, that the Statute doth not expreſly ſay, That the Coroner ſhall take his Inqueſt on the View of the dead Body, and that an Inqueſt otherwiſe taken by him, ſhall be void: And yet it is clearly agreed by all the [a] Books, That a Coroner has no Manner of Power to take an Inquiſition of Death without a View of the Body, and that any ſuch Inqueſt taken by him without ſuch View, is meerly void. And for this Reaſon it hath been [b] adjudged, That if a dead Body in a Priſon, or other Place, whereon an Inqueſt ought to be taken, be interred, or ſuffered to lie ſo long, that it putrify before the Coroner hath viewed it, the Gaoler or Townſhip ſhall be amerced. Alſo it hath been [c] reſolved, That a Coroner may lawfully within convenient Time, as the Space of fourteen Days after the Death, take up a dead Body out of the Grave in order to view it, not only for the taking of an Inqueſt where none hath been taken before; but alſo for the taking of a good one, where an inſufficient one hath been taken before. But if the Body cannot be [d] found, or have lain ſo long before the Coroner hath viewed it, that he can be no Way aſſiſted from the View in the taking of his Inqueſt; or if there be Danger of infecting People in digging of it up, the Inqueſt ought not to be taken by the Coroner, (unleſs he have a ſpecial Writ or Commiſſion for that Purpoſe) but by Juſtices of Peace, or other Juſtices authorized to inquire of, hear and determine Felonies, *&c.* who ſhall take the Inqueſt on the Teſtimony of Witneſſes; but none can take an Inqueſt on View in any Caſe, but the Coroner.

Sect. 24. If a [e] Coroner take an Inqueſt after a Body hath been ſo long buried, that it may reaſonably be preſumed, that the View of it could be of no Manner of Uſe for the Information of the Jurors, the Court into which the Inquiſition is returned will in Diſcretion refuſe to receive or file it, upon Affidavit of the whole Circumſtances of the Proceeding.

[f] Latch. 166. *See* Poph. 209.

Sect. 25. [f] Yet it is not neceſſary, That the Inquiſition be taken in the very ſame Place where the Body was viewed; for it hath been reſolved, That an Inquiſition taken at *D.* on the View of a Body lying dead at *L.* may be good.

[g] 4 H. 7. 18 b. Fitz Forfeiture 10. S. P. C. 183. *Letter* D. Keilw. 67. Daliſ. 32. Moore 29. pl. 95.

Sect. 26. As the Coroner hath no Power from the ſaid Statute, nor from 3 *H.* 7. 1. to inquire of any Acceſſories to a Felony after the Fact; ſo neither hath he any ſuch Power by the [g] Common Law; for he has nothing to do with any but thoſe who ſome Way or other cauſed the Party's Death: And therefore it hath been reſolved, That an Indictment of *J. S.* before a Coroner for having received and comforted one who had been guilty of a Murder, is void.

[h] S.P.C. 183. *Letters* C D. 2 Lev. 141, 152. Keilw. 68. b. H. P. C. 170. Bro. Coron. 151. 8 Ed. 4. 4. a. vide infra Section.

Sect. 27. But it is certain, That a Coroner may inquire of the Acceſſories before the Fact, as well as of the Principals; and that he [h] alſo may inquire, whether any in ſuch Manner found to have been guilty, did fly for the Offence; for which Flight they forfeit all their Goods and Chattels.

[i] Keilw. 67. [k] Aleyn 51.

Sect. 28. Alſo it is [i] certain, That a Coroner may and ought to inquire of all the Circumſtances of the Party's Death, and alſo of all Things which occaſioned it; and [k] therefore it is ſaid, That if it be found by his Inqueſt, that the Perſon deceaſed was killed by a Fall from a Bridge into a River, and that the Bridge was out of Repair by the Default of the Inhabitants of ſuch a Town, and that theſe Inhabitants are bound to repair it, the Townſhip ſhall be amerced.

Sect. 29.

I

Sect. 29. Also it is agreed, That if a Coroner be remiss in coming to do his Office when he is sent for, *&c.* he shall be amerced, by Virtue of the abovementioned Statute *De coronatoribus.* Also it is farther enacted by 3 *H.* 7. 1. *That if any Person be slain or murdered in the Day, and the Murderer escape untaken, the Township where the said Deed is so done, shall be amerced for the said Escape, and that the Coroner have Authority to inquire thereof upon the View of the Body dead: And that if any Coroner be remiss and make not Inquisitions upon the View of the Body dead, he shall forfeit for every Default an hundred Shillings.* S P.C. 51. H. Salk. 377. Fitz. Coron. 292. H. P. C. 170.

Sect. 30. As to the second Particular, *viz.* What farther Care must be taken by a Coroner for the Prosecution of the Offender, after taking an Inquisition of Death against him, it is farther enacted by the said Statute of 3 *H.* 7. 1. *That after the Felony found, the Coroners deliver their Inquisitions afore the Justices of the next general Gaol-Delivery, in the Shire where the Inquisition is taken, the same Justices to proceed against such Murderers if they be in the Gaol, or else the same Justices to put the same Inquisitions afore the King in his Bench. And if any Coroner do not in such Manner certify his Inquisition, he shall forfeit an hundred Shillings.*

Sect. 31. Also it is enacted by 1 & 2 *Ph. & Mar.* 13. *That every Coroner, upon any Inquisition before him found, whereby any Person or Persons shall be indicted for Murder or Manslaughter, or as Accessary or Accessaries to the same, before the Murder or Manslaughter committed, shall put in Writing the Effect of the Evidence given to the Jury before him, being material: And shall bind all such by Recognizance or Obligation, as do declare any Thing material to prove the same, to appear at the next general Gaol-Delivery to be holden within the County, City, or Town-Corporate where the Trial thereof shall be, then and there to give Evidence against the Party so indicted at the Time of the Trial, and shall certify as well the same Evidence, as such Bond or Bonds in Writing, as he shall take, together with the Inquisition or Indictment before him taken and found, at or before the Time of his said Trial thereof to be had or made: And in Case any Coroner shall offend in any Thing contrary to the true Intent and Meaning of this Act, the Justices of Gaol-Delivery of the Shire, City, Town, or Place where such Offence shall happen to be committed, upon due Proof thereof, by Examination before them, shall for every such Offence set such Fine on every such Coroner, as they shall think meet, and estreat the same, as other Fines and Amerciaments assessed before Justices of Gaol-Delivery ought to be.*

Sect. 32. And it is enacted by 1 *H* 8. 7. *That if any Coroner shall not endeavour himself to do his Office upon any Person dead by Misadventure, he shall forfeit forty Shillings.*

Sect. 33. As to the third Particular, *viz.* What high Credit the Law gives to an Inquisition of Death found before a Coroner, it seems [a] certain, That anciently the Judges would not receive a Verdict, acquitting a Person of the Death of a Man found against him by a Coroner's Inquest, unless the Jury so acquitting the Defendant, had found at the same Time what other Person did the Fact, or by what other Means the Party came to his Death; because it appeared by the Coroner's View upon Record, that a Person was killed: But it is [b] agreed, That the Judges cannot compel a Jury to make such farther Inquiry on an Acquittal of a Defendant from any other Indictment, because it doth not in such Manner appear of Record by any such Inquisition, that a Person is dead: And it seems hard to reconcile the said Practice of compelling a Jury to find such farther Matter with Reason in any Case, unless it appear in the Course of the Evidence by what other Means not mentioned in the Indictment, the Party lost his Life; for it seems strange, That a Jury should

[a] 13 E. 4. 3. pl. 7. 37 Aff. pl. 13. 11 H. 4. 93. pl. 51. 14 H. 7. 2. pl. 7. Fitz. Coron. 213. Keilway 686. S. P. C. 181. *Letters* B. C. Finch of Law 415. Brock Appeal, 42, 122. Bro. Indictment 10, 35. Bro. Coron. 32, 39, 52, 117.

[b] *See the Books above cited.*

be in any Case compelled to find a Matter upon their Oaths, which they have no Evidence to support; and therefore if it no Way appear to them, by what other Means the Death in question was occasioned, it seems difficult to maintain that it shall not be sufficient for them to declare so to the Court.

Sect. 34. How high a Credit is given by the Law to a Coroner's Inquisition of Self-Murder, or of the Flight of a Person indicted for the Death of another, will be more fully shewn in the three last Sections of this Chapter.

Sect. 35. As to the second general Point, *viz.* What Authority a Coroner hath to take an Indictment of other Matters, it is expressly said in some [a] Books, That a Coroner hath no Power *Ex officio* to inquire of any Felony, but only of the Death of a Man upon View. And both [b] *Staundford* and [c] *Hale* seem to speak doubtfully of this Matter, upon the Authority of those Books; and [d] Sir *Edward Coke* seems expressly to declare his Opinion, That a Coroner hath no Power to take an Indictment in any other Case: Yet since it is expressly declared by the abovementioned [e] Statute *De officio Coronatoris,* That a Coroner ought to inquire of the Breakers of Houses; and it is said by [f] *Britton,* That he may inquire of Rape, and of the Breach of a Prison, and such Power hath never been expressly taken from him, it seems hard to say, That he may not still make such Inquiries if he please; for as to the Authority of 27 *Ass* 55. & 35 *H.* 6. 27. *b.* which are cited for the Maintenance of the contrary Opinion, it may be answered, That this Point is not resolved in either of those Books, but only spoken of incidentally; for the very Point resolved in 27 of *Assises,* seems to be no more than this, That a Coroner hath no Power to take an Indictment of an Accessary after the Fact; and that which is said in 35 *H.* 6. concerning this Matter, is only brought in by Way of Argument concerning a Point of a quite different Nature.

[a] 35 H. 6. 27. b. 27 Ass. pl. 55. a. Fitz. Coron. 206. Bro. Appeal 111.
[b] S. P. C. 51. I K.
[c] H. P. C. 171.
[d] 4 Inst. 271. 2 Inst. 147.
[e] *See the Statute at large.*
[f] Britton 3.

Sect. 36. However there seems to be no Doubt but that the Coroner may and ought to inquire of Treasure-trove, concerning which it is enacted by the said Statute of 4 *E.* 1. *De officio Coronatoris, That a Coroner being certified by the King's Bailiffs, or other honest Men of the Country, shall go to the Places where Treasure is said to be found.* And it is farther enacted in the following Part of the same Statute in these Words, *A Coroner ought also to inquire of Treasure that is found, who were the Finders, and likewise who is suspected thereof: And that may be well perceived where one liveth riotously, haunting Taverns, and hath done so of long Time; hereupon he may be attached for this Suspicion by four or six, or more Pledges, if he may be found.*

Bracton, B. 3. Ch. 6.

Sect. 37. It is also said, That a Coroner may inquire of Royal Fishes, as Sturgeons, Whales, &c.

S. P. C. 51. K. Bracton 120. b.

Sect. 38. As to the third general Point, *viz.* How far a Coroner is impowered to receive and proceed on a Bill of Appeal, I shall endeavour to shew,

1. How far he is authorized to receive such Appeal.
2. How far to proceed upon it.
3. In what Manner it may be removed by *Certiorari.*

Sect. 39. As to the first of these Particulars, it appears clearly from the abovementioned [a] Statute of 4 *E.* 1. *De officio Coronatoris,* and also from our ancient [b] Law Books, That a Coroner in the County-Court may receive an Appeal of any Felony or Maihem, upon the Plaintiff's

[a] *See the Statute at large.*
[b] Bract. 122. a. b. 147. Fleta, lib. 1. cap. 25. Britton, fol. 5. S. P. C. 64. 22 Ass 97, 98. Finch 321.

finding sufficient Pledges to the Sheriff for the Prosecution of the Suit. And it is observable, That the said Books generally mention the Coroner as the Person before whom such Appeal is to be commenced, without joining any other with him; from whence it seems clearly to be intimated, That the Coroner is the [b] only Person who hath a Jurisdiction in this Matter; and that at Common Law he might [c] receive such Appeal without the Concurrence of any other, as he certainly may the Appeal of an Approver, *&c.* But it being provided by the Statute of *Westminster* 1. *cap.* 10. That the Sheriff shall have Counter-Rolls with the Coroners, it seems, That no Appeal since that Statute is well commenced before the Coroner, [d] unless the Sheriff be also present, in order to take a Counter-Roll of the Proceeding: But it seems, That the Sheriff by Vertue of this Statute, is no more a Judge of the Matter than he was before; and therefore where it is said by the Statute of 3 *H.* 7. 1. That an Appeal of Felony may be commenced before the Sheriff and Coroners of the County where it was done, it seems reasonable to intend the Meaning of the Statute to be, that it may be commenced before them in the same Manner as before, and not without express [e] Words to make any Alteration of the Jurisdiction given them by the Common Law.

Sect. 40. But it is [f] certain, That a Coroner hath no Power to receive a Bill of Appeal of any Offence done out of the County whereof he is Coroner, because the Offender cannot be tried by the County: But it is [f] agreed, That he may receive the Appeal of an Approver, or take the Abjuration of one, who acknowledges a Felony done by him in any County, because that after such Confessions there is no Need of any Trial.

Sect. 41. As to the second Particular, *viz.* How far a Coroner may proceed upon such Appeal, it seems [g] probable, That before the Statute of *Magna Charta, cap.* 17. Coroners might try Offenders as well as receive Accusations against them; but it is [h] agreed, That they cannot proceed so far since that Statute, by which it is enacted, *That no Sheriff, Constable, Coroner, or other Bailiff of the King, shall hold Pleas of the Crown.* Also it is agreed, [i] That Process may be awarded in the County-Court on such Appeals till the Exigent; but [k] it seems questionable, whether such Process may properly be said to be awarded by the Sheriff and Coroner jointly, since the Coroner being the only Judge, as I have endeavoured to prove, *Sect.* 38. it seems to be most proper that the Process be awarded by him only: Neither doth it seem clear, That the abovementioned Statute of *Magna Charta*, doth restrain the Coroner from awarding an Exigent, and thereon outlawing an Appellee; for since, as it is agreed by all, an Offender might become attainted by an Abjuration of a Felony made before a Coroner, why not as well by an Outlawry pronounced by him? And accordingly we find it taken for granted in some of the [l] old Books of the best Authority since this Statute, that Appellees may be outlawed for not appearing on Process before the Coroner.

Sect. 42. As to the third Particular, *viz.* In what Manner an Appeal before the Coroner may be removed by *Certiorari*, there [m] is no Doubt but that it may be removed either into the King's Bench or Chancery, by *Certiorari* directed to the Coroners and Sheriff. But it hath been [n] resolved, That it cannot be removed by such Writ directed to the Sheriff only, because the Coroner is the Judge, and the Sheriff hath only a Counter-Roll by Vertue of the above-mentioned Statute of *Westm.* 1. *cap.* 10.

[a] Con. 17 Ass. pl. 5. Bro. Appeal. 56 H.P.C. 171. S P.C. 52 D. 64 *Letter* B.
[b] 2 Inst. 176. 4 H. 6 16. a. Bro. Appeal. 44
[c] H P.C. 172.
[d] 39 H. 6. 41. a. 4 H. 6 16. a. Contra Bro. Appeal 44.
[e] *Quære* S P. C. 64. b.
[f] H P.C 171, 172. S. P. C 52. D. 53. Fitz. Coron. 437.
[g] *See* Dalton's Sheriff, cap. 106.
[h] 22 Ass. 97, 98. Bract. 147. a. Fleta, lib. 1. cap 25. 2 Inst. 30, 31, 32. Bro. Appeal. 56, 62 Coron. 82.
[i] S, P. C 64. H. P. C. 171.
[k] Contra S. P. C. 64. H. P. C. 171.
[l] 27 Ass. 47. 22 Ass 97. Fitz. Coron. 184. Con. Bro. Appeal 82. *Quære* Bro. Appeal. 109. S. P. C. 64 H. P C 171.
[m] S. P. C. 64. *Letter* B. 70. *Letter* C. H. P. C. 171, 172. 2 Inst. 176.
[n] 14 H. 4 15 b. 16. a. Bro. Appeal. 44. 2 Inst. 176. S P C. 64 *Letter* B. 70. *Letter* C

Sect. 43. As to the fourth general Point, *viz.* How far a Coroner is authorized to receive and proceed on the Appeal of an Approver, there is no Doubt but that the Coroner alone may receive such Appeal, [a] whether the Offence were committed in the same or in any other County, and may also award Process to the Sheriff against the Appellee, being in the same County, till it come to the Exigent; and it [b] seems, That it may be probably argued, that he may award Process even to an Outlawry, as hath been more fully shewn in the forty-first Section of this Chapter: But it is certain, That he cannot award any Process against an Appellee in a foreign County, but must leave it to the [c] Justices of Gaol-Delivery, or others, before whom the Appeal is afterwards recorded, who shall award Process against such Appellees in such Manner, as shall be more fully set forth in the Chapter concerning *Approvers*.

Sect. 44. As to the fifth general Point, *viz.* How far a Coroner is authorized to take the Confession and Abjuration of a Felon, there seems to be no Doubt but that he may record the Confession of the Breach of Prison by any Felon, *&c.* and also the [d] Confession of any Felony by an Approver; but the Law relating to these Matters being in great Measure obsolete, it seems needless over nicely to inquire into it; also it is certain that he might take an Abjuration, but this not having been in Use since 21 *Jac.* 1.28. *Sect.* 6. 7. by which it is enacted, *That no Sanctuary or Privilege of Sanctuary, shall be admitted or allowed in any Case,* I shall only touch upon it, and take Notice, That at the Common Law, if a Person accused of any Felony (except [e] Sacrilege,) [f] whether in the same or any other County, for which he was liable to Judgment of [g] Death, and not charged with [h] High Treason, nor (as [i] some say) with Petit Treason, had fled to any [k] Church or Church-yard, and within [l] forty Days confessed himself guilty before the Coroner, and declared all the particular [m] Circumstances of the Offence, and thereupon taken the Oath in that Case provided, (the [n] Substance whereof was that he abjured the Realm, and would depart as soon as possible, at the Port which should be assigned him, and never return without Leave from the King, *&c.*) he saved his Life, if he observed the Terms of the Oath, by going with all [o] convenient Speed the nearest Way to the Port assigned, *&c.* but he was [p] attainted of the Felony by such Abjuration without more, and consequenrly forfeited his Lands and Goods, *&c.*

Sect. 45. As to the sixth general Point, *viz.* How far the Act of any one Coroner is as effectual as if it were done by all, it seems clear, That [q] where-ever Coroners are authorized to act as Judges, as in the taking of an [r] Inquisition of Death, or receiving an Appeal of Felony, *&c.* the Act of any one of them, who first proceeds in the Matter, is of the same Force as if all had joined in it; but it is said, That after [s] such Proceeding by one of them, the Act of any other will be void: Also it seems certain, That where Coroners are impowered only to act [t] ministerially, as in the Execution of Process directed to them upon the Default or Incapacity of the Sheriff, all their Acts will be void wherein they do not all join.

Sect. 46. As to the seventh general Point, *viz.* In what Cases a Coroner may lawfully take a Fee for the Execution of his Office, it is enacted by the Statute of *Westm.* 1. *cap.* 10. which was made in Affirmance of the Common Law, 2 *Inst.* 176. [u] *That no Coroner demand or take any Thing of any Man to do his Office, upon Pain of great Forfeiture to the King.*

[a] H.P.C. 172. S.P.C. 53. a. *See Section* 40.
[b] S.P.C. 73. H.P.C. 172.
[c] S.P.C 53.73. H.P.C. 172. Fitz. Co. 462. 29 Ed. 3. 42.
[d] Vid. Sect. 36 & 49.
[e] Fitz. Coron. 420. S.P.C. 117. *Letter* B. 3 Inst. 115.
[f] Sup. Sect. 40.
[g] Bro. Coron. 183. S.P.C. 123. *Letter* A. Finch of Law 388, 389.
[h] Bro. Coron. 181. S.P.C. 116. G. Finch of Law 388.
[i] S.P.C. 116. *Letter* G. 117. *Letter* A. Bro. Coron. 181. Finch 388.
[k] S.P.C. 116. *Letter* F. 3 Inst. 115. Finch of Law 388.
[l] S.P.C. 117, 118. 3 Inst. 117.
[m] S.P.C. 117. *Letter* E. Fitz. Co. 54. 3 H. 7. 12. pl. 6.
[n] S.P.C. 119, 120. Finch of Law 389.
[o] 7 H. 7. 7. pl. 11. Bro. Coron. 145. S.P.C. 121,
[p] Fitz. Coron. 425. S.P.C. 122. c, Finch of Law 389. 3 Inst. 217.
[q] S.P.C. 53. a. 14 H. 4. 34. b.
[r] Vid. supra Ch. 1. S. 10.
[s] Fitz. Co. 107 S.P.C. 52. A. H.P.C. 172.
[t] S.P.C. 53. 14 H. 4. 34, 35. a. 39 H. 6. 40. b. 41, 42.
[u] *See* Book 1. Ch. 68.

Sect. 47. But it is enacted by 3 *H.* 7. 1. *That a Coroner have for his Fee upon every Inquisition taken upon the view of a Body slain* 13 s. 4 d. *of the Goods and Chattels of the Slayer and Murderer, if he have any Goods; and if he have no Goods, of such Amerciaments as shall fortune any Township to be amerced for the Escape of the Murderer,* &c.

Sect. 48. But the Coroners endeavouring to extend this Statute to Persons slain by Misadventure, it was enacted by 1 *H.* 8. 7. *That upon a Request made to a Coroner to come and inquire upon the View of any Person slain, drowned, or otherwise dead by Misadventure, the said Coroner shall diligently do his Office, without taking any Thing therefore, upon Pain to every Coroner that will not endeavour himself to do his Office, (as afore is said) or that taketh any Thing for doing of his Office upon every Person dead by Misadventure, for every Time forty Shillings.*

As to the eighth general Point, *viz.* In what Cases a Matter recorded by, or found before a Coroner, admits of no Traverse, I shall consider the same in Relation,

1. To Abjurations or Confessions made before him.
2. To Escapes.
3. To Flights.
4. To Self-Murders.

Sect. 49. As to the first Particular, it is said, That his Record of an [a] Abjuration, or of the Confession of [b] breaking a Prison, or of the Confession of a Felony by an [c] Approver, is of so great Authority, as not only to estop the Party from taking any Traverse to his having made such Confession, but also from alledging that what was said by him was extorted by Duress, or other unfair Means. Also it seems that if the Party plead, That he is not the same Person who abjured, *&c.* and the [d] Coroner record that he is the same Person, such Record is conclusive, *&c.* But in these [e] Cases it seems, That the Judge for the better Information of his Conscience, may in his Discretion if he think fit, take an Inquiry from the People living next to the Place, of the whole Circumstances of the Matter, *&c.*

Sect. 50. As to the second Particular, *viz.* That relating to Escapes found before a Coroner, it is [f] said, That if it be found by a Coroner's Inquest, that a Murder was committed in such a Town, and that the Murderer escaped untaken, the Township cannot traverse such Escape, because it makes them only liable to an Amercement, *& de minimis non curat Lex.*

Sect. 51. As to the third Particular, *viz.* That relating to a Flight found before a Coroner, it seems, That if a Person indicted of a Murder by a Coroner's Inquest, be also found to have fled for it, and afterwards upon his Trial be [g] acquitted of the Murder, and also found not to have fled for it; yet he shall forfeit his Goods, because such a finding that he did not fly by a Jury, who as some say, had nothing to do with it, and ought not to have been charged with such Inquiry, shall not controll the Coroner's Inquest, which is of such Authority, that immediately upon the Flight, the Party's Goods shall be delivered to the Township, which shall be answerable for them. Also it seems [h] generally to be taken for granted, That the Party has no Remedy whatsoever to traverse such Flight found against him by a Coroner's Inquest; for that such Inquest is of very great Authority, [i] inasmuch as all Persons of the neighbouring

[a] H. P. C. 171. Fitz Co. 134. S. P. C. 51. *Letter* B.
[b] S. P. C. 31. *Letter* H 52. *Letter* B. 25 E 3. 43. pl. 35. Fitz. Coron. 134, 243, 435.
[c] Fitz. Coron. 118, 169. 12 Assises, pl. 29.
[d] Fitz. Coron. 124. S. P. C. 52. Letter B.
[e] Fitz. Coron. 118, 134, 169. 12 Ass. 29. Bro. Coron. 75.
[f] S. P. C. 34. *Letters* A. B. 35. *Letter* F. 183. *Letter* D. *See* Fitz. 352.
[g] 13 H. 4. 13. pl. 6. Fitz. Forfeiture 29, 32, 35. 5 Co. 109 b. Dyer 238. pl. 36. H. P. C. 271.
[h] Bro. Coron 151. 8 E. 4. 4 a. 2 Lev. 141. Bro. Traverse per sans ceo, 229 3 Keb. 564, 566.
[i] 2 Inst. 147, 148. 3 Keb. 366.

Towns, above the Age of twelve Years, are bound to attend at the taking of it; and yet I cannot find any direct Resolution settling this Point; but on the contrary it is certain, That Sir *William Staundford* makes a Query of it, and the Reason abovementioned, which is brought to support the great Credit of such Inquests, holds as strongly against the traversing them as to the Point of the Offence, in which respect it is at this Day generally holden that they may be traversed, as will be more fully shewn in the next Section. And surely the other Reason which is given for this Opinion, That the Party only forfeits his Chattels by such finding, and therefore shall not traverse it, because the Law reckons Chattels among those *minima de quibus non curat Lex*, is very harsh and unaccountable; and it is very hard to say, That a Man shall be liable to forfeit all his Goods, which may perhaps be all that he is worth, by an [a] Inquest taken in his Absence, without either hearing him, or giving him an Opportunity of defending himself.

Sect. 52. As to the fourth Particular, *viz.* That relating to Self-Murder found before a Coroner, it is strongly holden in some [b] Books, that no Inquest of this Kind admits of any Traverse; but the contrary Opinion being also holden by [b] Books of as great Authority, and seeming also to be more agreeable to the general Tenor of the Law in other Cases; it seems to be the better Opinion, That such Inquest being moved into the King's Bench by *Certiorari*, may be there traversed by the Executor or Administrator of the Person deceased, and perhaps also [c] by the King or the Lord of the Manor, *&c.*

Sect. 53. Also if it [d] appear, That a Coroner hath been guilty of any corrupt Practice in the taking of an Inquisition, it seems that a *Melius inquirendum* shall be awarded for the taking a new one by special Commissioners, who shall not proceed on the View of the Body, but on the Testimony of Witnesses; and the Coroner shall have nothing to do in the taking such new Inquest, because it appears from his former Misbehaviour, that he is not fit to be trusted; but [e] where his Inquisition is quashed for a Defect in Point of Form only, he may and ought to take a new one, in like Manner as if he had not taken any before.

[a] 3 Inst. 55. 2 Lev 141. H. P. C. 29. 1 Vent. 181, 182.

[b] 8 Ed. 4. 4. a. Bro. Coron. 151. 2 Lev. 141, 152. 2 Keb. 859. 2 Jon. 198. 1 Vent. 278. 3 Keb. 564, 566, 604, 800.

[c] *See the Books above cited.*

[d] Cro. El. 371. 3 Keb. 800. 856. 1 Mod. 82. Salkeld 190. 2 Keb. 859. 1 Vent. 181, 182, 352. 3 Mod. 80, 100, 238. Con. 2 Jones 198.

[e] 2 Rol. Abr. 32. pl. 5. 21 Ed. 4. 70. b. Salkeld 190.

CHAP.

CHAP. X.

Of the Sheriff's Torn.

Sect. 1. THE Sheriff's Torn is the King's Court of Record, holden before the Sheriff for redressing of common Grievances within the County; for the better understanding of the Nature whereof I shall examine the following Points.

Finch 241.) F. N. B. 82.

1. The original Institution of this Court.
2. At what Time and in what Place it must be holden.
3. What Persons owe Suit to it.
4. What Authority the Sheriff (or his Steward) hath as Judge of it.
5. What Kind of Offences are inquirable in it.
6. Within what Place such Offences must arise.
7. By what Jurors and in what Manner Indictments in it ought to be found.
8. In what Manner they are to be proceeded upon.
9. In what Manner they are to be traversed and determined.

Sect. 2. As to the first Point it is observable, That by the [a] Common Law, every Sheriff ought to make his Torn or Circuit throughout every Hundred in his County twice in the Year, in order to hold a Court in every such Hundred for the Reformation of common Grievances, and the Preservation of the Peace and good Government of the Kingdom. For which Purpose all the [b] Inhabitants of such Hundreds, being above the Age of twelve Years, and not specially privileged, (in such Manner as shall be more fully set forth under the third Point,) are bound to attend at such Courts in order to make Inquiries of all such Offences; and also to give Security to the Publick for their good Behaviour, by taking an Oath to be faithful to the King, and to observe his Laws, and also by incorporating themselves into some Free-Pledge or Tithing, which formerly signified a certain Number of Families living together in the same Precinct, the Masters whereof were every one of them mutually bound for each other, and punishable for the Default of any Member of any such Family, in not appearing to answer for himself on any Accusation made against him.

[a] Co. 9. Preface. Dalton's Sheriff 385. Magna Charta 35. 2 Inst. 70, 71, 73, 122. Bro. Leet 42. Britton 71. [b] *See the Books above cited.* Fleta B. 1. Ch. 27. Bract. 124. b. 2 Inst. 121. Lambard of Constables 8. Keilw. 141. a.

Sect. 3. And the better inforcing of this Order seems anciently to have been the principal End of holding this Court, the Style whereof even to this Day must be *Curia visus franci plegii Domini Regis tenta apud* C. *coram viceecomite in turno suo tali die, &c.* But it hath been resolved, That the Law doth not take Notice of any such Court, under the Style of *Turn' Vicecom' tent. tali die*; for the Word *Torn* properly taken, doth not signify the Sheriff's Court, but his Perambulation.

2 Inst. 71, 72. Dalt. Sheriff 385, 391. Fitz. Leet 11.

Sect. 4. As to the second Point, *viz.* At what Time, and in what Place, this Court is to be holden, it is said, That at the Common Law, it might be holden at any Place within the Hundred, and as often as the Sheriff thought fit: But this having been found to give the Sheriff too great a Power of oppressing the People, by holding his Court at such

6 H. 7. 2 b. Dalt. Sheriff 390. Contra Co. Lit. 115. Kitchin 44 b. Dalt. Sheriff 390.

Times and Places at which they could not conveniently attend, in order thereby for his own Advantage, to increase the Number of his Amercements, it was enacted by the Statute of *Magna Charta* 35. *That no Sheriff or his Bailiff, shall make his Torn through a Hundred but twice in a Year, and at the Place accustomed,* viz. *once after* Easter, *and again after the Feast of St.* Michael; *and that the View of Frank pledge shall be at the Term of St.* Michael.

Sect. 5. And it is farther enacted by 31 *E.* 3. Ch. 15. *That every Sheriff shall make his Torn yearly, one Time within the Month after* Easter, *and another Time within the Month after St.* Michael; *and if they hold them in other Manner, that then they shall lose their Torn for the Time.*

Sect. 6. And it seems [a] certain, That since these Statutes the Sheriff is indictable for holding this Court at another Time, than what is therein limited, or at an unusual Place.

Sect 7. Also it hath been [b] resolved, That an Indictment found at a Sheriff's Torn, appearing to have been holden at another Time, is void.

Sect. 8. But it is observable, That neither of these Statutes do expressly mention a Court-Leet, and therefore it is said in some [c] Books, That they do not extend to it; neither do I find any Resolution, that an ancient Court-Leet holden at any other Time, or at an unusual Place, is void: But on the contrary it is [d] said, That a Court-Leet may be holden at any Place within the Precinct which the Lord thinks fitting. And it seems to be [e] agreed, That a Prescription to hold such Court oftner than twice in the Year is good; which seems hardly reconcileable with the general Rule of Law, That no Prescription can stand good against a Statute which has negative Words, if a Court-Leet be construed to be within the Purview of the abovementioned Statutes. It is true indeed, That both Sir *Edward Coke* and *Kitchin* endeavour to solve this Difficulty, by offering a Distinction that the said Rule extends not to Statutes made in Affirmance of the Common Law; but it is questionable how far this will amount to a good Answer, since it seems to be holden by [f] others of good Authority, that the said Statutes were not made in Affirmance of the old Law, but are introductory of a new one; yet it is certainly safest to hold a Court-Leet at the Times accustomed, for it is [g] said, That if it be holden at an unusual Time it is void. And it [h] seems, That no Court-Leet granted since the Statute, can be holden at any other Time than what is limited by it, because every such Court is derived out of the Torn, to which the Statute certainly did extend.

Sect. 9. It hath been [i] holden, That in every Caption of an Indictment taken in a Sheriff's Torn, or Court-Leet, the Day whereon it was taken ought to be set forth, that it may appear not to have been on a Sunday.

Sect. 10. As to the third Point, *viz.* What [k] Persons owe Suit to the Sheriff's Torn, it is certain, That regularly all Persons above the Age of twelve Years, are by the Common Law bound to appear at this Court in their proper Persons, and that no Persons so bound to appear, are within the Benefit of the Statute of [l] *Merton*, Ch. 10. which allows Suit-Service to be performed by Attorney. And that not only Masters of Families, but also all their Servants are bound to pay such Suit, and that every [m] Master may be amerced for suffering a Servant to continue with him a Year and a Day, without being put into the Decennary, *&c.*

[a] Dy. 151. pl. 4. Keilw. 192. Dalt. Sheriff, 390, 391.
[b] 38 H. 6. 7. a. 6 H 7. 2 b 3. a. S. P. C. 84. *See* 2 Danv. Ab. 256. pl. 14. 2 Inst. 71. 2 Saund. 290.
[c] Bro. Leet 23. 2 Leon. 74. 1 Rol. Rep. 201.
[d] 8 H. 7. 4. b. Kitchin 44. b. Owen 35. Dalis 61.
[e] Co. Lit. 115. a. Kitchin 8. 44. Cro. El. 125, 245. 1 Rol. Rep. 201.
[f] Dalt. Sheriff 390. 6 H. 7. 2. b.
[g] 38. H. 6. 7. a. Fitz. Leet 2. Bro Leet 32. 2 Saund. 291.
[h] Cro. El. 245. Con. 2 Inst. 72. 2 Saund. 291.
[i] 2 Keb. 731. 1 Vent. 107. 2 Saund. 290.
[k] *See* Sect. 2.
[l] 2 Inst, 99.
[m] 41 E 3. 26. b. 45 E 3. 26. b.

Sect. 11. But [a] Tenants in Ancient Demesne are privileged by the Common Law from coming to this Court, unless they and their Ancestors have Time out of Mind used to come to it: Also [b] Parsons of Churches have the like Privilege by the Common Law; and all [c] Peers of the Realm, and Women have the same Privilege by the Statute of *Marlebridge, cap.* 10. (and perhaps by the Common Law,) unless their Presence be specially required for some particular Cause.

Sect. 12. Also it seems [d] clear, That by the Common Law, as well as the said Statute of *Marlebridge, cap.* 10. no Man can be obliged to do Suit to any such Court, within the Precincts whereof he doth not reside, in respect of any Lands which he may have within the Jurisdiction of it; for that no Suit of this Kind is due in Respect of the Tenure of any Lands, but only in Respect of the personal Residence of the Party. And [e] if a Man have a House which stands upon the Precincts of two Leets, it is said, That he shall do his Suit to the Court within the Jurisdiction of which his Bed-chamber lies: And if [f] one have a House and Family in two Leets, it seems that he ought to do his Suit to that, wherein for the most part he personally resides, but no Man can be of two Leets; and therefore one who lives within a [g] private Leet, cannot be obliged to do Suit to the Sheriff's Torn, or to any other grand Leet, unless such private Leet, for some Default of the Lord, be seized into the King's Hands, or [h] unless the Lord of the Leet neglect to hold his Court.

[a] F.N.B. 161. Letter C. Dalt. Sheriff 387.
2 Inst. 121. Quære Bro. Leet 38.
[b] F.N.B. 160. c.
2 Inst. 121. Regist. 175.
[c] 2 Inst. 120, 121. Register 175. F.N.B. 160, 161. Dalt. Sheriff 186. Bract. 124. b.
[d] Regist. 175. F.N.B. 160, Dalt. Sheriff 387.
[e] 2 Inst. 122. Dalt. Sheriff 387.
[f] 2 Inst. 122. Dalt. Sheriff 387.
[g] 2 Inst. 122. See 19 H. 6. 1. 33 H. 6. 9.
[h] Cro. Jac. 584. Finch 246. Dalt. Sheriff 388.

As to the fourth Point, *viz.* What Authority the Sheriff (or his [i] Steward,) hath as Judge of this Court, I shall consider the same in Relation,

1. To Indictments.
2. To Fines and Amercements in general.
3. To the Appointment of Constables.

See the next Chapter, Sect. 3.
[i] Dalt. Sher. 388.

Sect. 13. As to the first of these Points, it seems, That by the Common Law he might proceed to [k] hear and determine any Offence within his Jurisdiction, being indicted before him and requiring a Trial. But it is clear, that he is restrained from this Power by the Statute of *Magna Charta, cap.* 17. By which it is enacted, *That no Sheriff, Constable, or other Bailiff of the King, shall hold Pleas of the Crown*: And it seems, That this Statute also extends to the [l] Stewards of Courts Leet, who cannot deliver any Persons indicted before them of Felony, but must refer them to the Justices of Gaol-Delivery; neither can they try any Person indicted before them of any other Offence, and therefore there is no Remedy to avoid such Presentments before them as are traversable, but [m] by removing them into the King's Bench, *&c.* as will be more fully shewn under the ninth Point,

[k] Dalt. Sheriff 400.
[l] 2 Inst. 32. Dalt. Sheriff 400.
[m] 8 H. 4. 17. a. Bro. Leet 11. 27. H. 8. 2. Kitch 22, 23. H. P. C. 175. 1 Ed. 3. Ch. 17.

Sect. 14. But it is certain, That the abovementioned Statute of *Magna Charta* 17. doth neither restrain the Sheriff's Torn, nor the Court-Leet, from taking [n] Indictments or Presentments, or awarding Process thereon in the same Manner as before; but this Power of awarding such Process, having been abused by the Sheriffs in their Torns, was taken from all of them, (except those of *London*,) but not from any Court-Leet, by 1 *E.* 4. 2. which is more fully set forth under the eighth general Point of this Chapter.

[n] Kitchin 42. b. Finch 386. 1 Ed. 3. Ch. 17.
[o] Dalt. Sher. 400, 401.

As to the ſecond Point, *viz.* The Sheriff's Authority in his Torn in relation to Fines, and Amercements, I ſhall conſider,

1. In what Caſes he may, and in what Manner he ought to impoſe a Fine.
2. In what Caſes he ought to award an Amercement.
3. In what Manner ſuch Amercement is to be awarded and affeered.
4. In what Manner ſuch Fine or Amercement is to be recovered.
5. What farther Penalty may be added to ſuch Fine or Amercement.

Sect. 15. As to the firſt Particular, it ſeems clear, That the Sheriff's Power in this Court is ſtill the ſame as anciently it was, in all Caſes not within either of the abovementioned Statutes of *Magna Charta* or 1 *E.* 4. from whence it follows, That he ſtill continues a Judge of Record, and may impoſe a Fine on all ſuch as ſhall be guilty of [a] any Contempt in the Face of the Court; alſo there ſeems to be no Doubt, but that he may impoſe what reaſonable Fine he ſhall think fitting, upon a [b] Suitor refuſing to be ſworn, or upon a [c] Bailiff refuſing to make a Panel, *&c.* or upon a [d] Tithingman neglecting to make his Preſentment, or upon one of the Jury [e] refuſing to preſent the Articles wherewith they are charged, or upon a Perſon duly choſen [f] Conſtable, refuſing to be ſworn.

Sect. 16. But it hath been [g] reſolved, That all ſuch Fines ought to be ſeverally impoſed on each particular Offender, and not jointly upon all of them, except where a whole Vill is to be fined; in which Caſe, for the Neceſſity of the Thing, a joint Fine upon all is good.

Sect. 17. As to the ſecond Particular, *viz.* In what Caſes the Sheriff in his Torn ought to award an Amercement, it ſeems that he hath a diſcretionary Power [h] either to award a Fine or Amercement for Contempts to the Court, as for a Suitor's refuſing to be ſworn, *&c.* Alſo there ſeems to be no Doubt, but that at the Common Law he might, as the Steward of a Court-Leet ſtill may, award an [i] Amercement of any Perſon indicted for an Offence not Capital within his Juriſdiction, without any farther Proceeding or Trial: And it ſeems to be taken for granted in [k] ſome Books, That he might in ſuch Caſes impoſe a Fine on the Offender if he thought fit; and the Statute of 1 *Ed.* 4. 2. which reſtrains him from levying any Fines or Amercements on Indictments found before him, clearly ſuppoſes him to have had a Power of impoſing ſuch Fines; from all which it ſeems probable, that in ſuch Caſes he had, and that the Steward of a Court-Leet ſtill hath a Power, either to amerce or fine the Offender, eſpecially if the [l] Crime were any Way enormous, as an Affray accompanied with wounding, *&c.*

Sect. 18. As to the third Particular, *viz.* In what Manner ſuch Amercement is to be awarded and affeered, it ſeems, That if by an Amercement be meant the Judgment, that the Party ſhall be *in miſericordia Domini Regis*, this being a [m] judicial Act, ought to be the Act of the Court only, and requires not the Concurrence or Aſſent of the Jury or any other, as appears from the conſtant Form of all Entries: Neither do I ſee any Reaſon why ſuch an Award of a *Miſericordia* by a Judge of a Court-Leet, ſhould expreſs any certain Sum for which the Party ſhould be *in Miſericordia*, except in ſuch Caſes only where no other Perſon is afterwards to affeer it; for in other Caſes the Award of a *Miſericordia* is only in order to authorize others to fix the Sum, which the

[a] *See* Book 1. Ch. 21. Sect. 11. *and the firſt* Chapter *of this Book*, Sect. 15.
[b] Fitz. Leet 11. Dalt. Sheriff 400. 2 Inſt. 142, 143. 44 E. 3. 19 b.
[c] 7 H. 6. 12.
[d] 10 H. 6. 7 b. 8 Co. 38. b.
[e] *See* 8 Co. 38. b 39. a. Dalt. Sheriff 401. Dy. 211. b.
[f] 8 Co. 38. Dalt. Sheriff 400.
[g] 1 Rol. Rep. 33, 73. 11 Co. 42. b. 43. b. Dyer 211. b.
[h] Dalt. Sheriffs 400. Fitz. Leet 11. *See* 8 Co. 39, 40. Kitchin 43. b.
[i] Bro. Leet Keilw. 66. Finch 468. Kitchin 51, 52
[k] Fitz. Torn 4. 8 E. 4. 5. pl. 15 Dalt. Sheriff 401.
[l] 8 Ed. 4. 5. pl. 15.
[m] 1 Jones 301. Cro. Car. 275. 8 Co. 38. b. 40. b.

Party is to pay to the King for his Default; and in such [a] Cases the Courts of *Westminster-hall*, never do more than award that the Party be *in Misericordia*, without mentioning any Sum in certain; and there seems no Reason, why the Judge of a Court-Leet should not follow the same Rule; and accordingly I find the Opinion of the Lord Chief Justice [b] *Hobart*, which is the chief Ground of a Resolution in [c] *Levinz*'s third Report, That every such Award of an Amercement must express a certain Sum, * over-ruled of late by the Court of King's Bench.

Sect. 19. But if by an Amercement be meant, the taxing or reducing to a Certainty, the Sum to be paid by the Party to the King, upon the Award of his being *in Misericordia*; it [d] seems, That if it be for an Offence indicted, it ought to be done by certain Officers called Affeerors, being specially chosen and sworn for this Purpose. It is true [e] indeed, That the common Entry of an Amercement upon a Presentment in a Court-Leet is, that the Party is amerced, or *in Misericordia* to such a Sum, without distinguishing between the Award of the *Misericordia*, and the Assessment of the Amercement, or shewing by whom they are made; yet in Judgment of Law the Award of the *Misericordia* is the Act of the Court only, and the Assessment of the Sum to be paid the Act of the Affeerers, and so it ought to be pleaded. But if the [f] Amercement be for a Contempt to the Court, it may be settled by the Judge himself, and needs no other Affeerment; for [g] the Judge of every Court of Record is the most proper Judge of all Contempts offered to such Court; and an Amercement of this Kind is in [h] Nature of a Fine, and called so in some [i] Books; and it seems to be a general [k] Rule, That no Fine for a Contempt is within the Statutes which require that Amercements be affeered.

Sect. 20. As to the fourth Particular, *viz.* In what Manner such [l] Fines and Amercements are to be recovered; it seems, That the King or Lord have an Election of common Right, either to distrain for them or to bring an Action of Debt; for the better understanding of the Nature of which Remedies, I shall first lay down some Rules concerning both of them in common, and then descend to each of them in particular.

As to what concerns the said Remedies in common, I shall lay down the following Rules:

Sect. 21. First, That it is safest in every Avowry, or Declaration of this Kind, expresly to [m] shew that the Offence was committed within the Jurisdiction of the Court; for if it were not, all the Proceedings were *coram non Judice*; and a Court shall not be presumed to have a Jurisdiction, where it doth not appear to have one. But perhaps it is not necessary to alledge in the Presentment it self, That [n] the Offence arose within the Jurisdiction of the Court; yet it is certainly adviseable to have such an Allegation, and that [o] perhaps may supply the want of the Averment of Juridiction in the Pleadings.

Sect. 22. Secondly, That it is [p] adviseable expresly to alledge, that the Offence was committed as well as that it was presented, &c. yet I cannot find any express Opinion to this Purpose; but on the contrary it is observable, That the [r] Precedents of Pleadings of this Kind in the best Authors, do not expresly aver that the Offence was committed, but only that it was presented, and that it arose in such a Place within the Jurisdiction of the Court, &c. It is true indeed, that it hath been generally [f] holden, That in an Avowry or Declaration for an Amercement

in

[a] 8 Co. 40. b. See Rastal's Entries 553. a b. 606. F. N. B. 76. Letter A.
[b] Hobart 129. 1 Rol. Abr. 542. pl. 5.
[c] 3 Lev. 206. 3 Mod 138.
* Salk. 56.
[d] 8 Co. 40. b. 3 Lev. 206. See Rastal's Entries 606. a b. Kitchin 46. See Keilw. 66. a. 3 Keb. 362.
[e] Kitchin 51, 52, 53.
[f] Rastal's Entries 151 b. 7 H. 6. 12 b. 10 H. 6. 7.
[g] 8 Co. 40, 41. 2 Leon. 242. 3 Mod 138.
[h] Brook Amercement 50.
[i] Savil 93. Co. Entries 572. 8 Co. 38. b. Rast. Ent. 553. 8 Co. 38, &c. 2 Inst. 196.
[k] Magna Charta 14. W. 1. 18.
[l] Rastal's Ent. 151. 553, 606. 2 H. 4. 24. b. 10 H. 6. 7. Cro. E. 581. Raym. 68. Savil 93, 94.
[m] Hob. 129. See Rastal's Ent 553. a b. Co Ent. 572, 573.
[n] Hob. 129.
[o] See Rastal's Ent. 606.
[p] 2 Rol. Rep. 40. Raym. 337. Salk. 107, 108.
[r] Rastal's Entries 151, 553. 606. Co. Ent 573.
[f] Moor 75. Cro. Jac. 582. Cro. El. 748. 885. 886. 3 Leon. 7, 8. 1 Leon 242.

in a Court-Baron, it is as necessary to alledge that the Offence was committed, as that it was presented: But to this it may be answered, That a Court-Baron is not a Court of Record, and consequently not of so high Authority as the Sheriff's Torn or a Court-Leet; neither are Presentments in a Court-Baron, nor even in any other Court whatsoever, so highly credited by the Law as those made in a Torn or Leet, which admit of no Traverse to the Truth of them, except in some special Cases, as will be more fully shewn under the ninth general Point of this Chapter.

Sect. 23. Thirdly, That it is safest in [a] setting forth a Presentment, or an Affeerment of an Amercement, to shew the Names of the Presentors and Affeerors; yet I cannot find this done in any of [b] *Rastal*'s Precedents; and some have said, That it is necessary to set forth the Names of the Presentors in an Action of Debt, but not in Replevin.

Sect. 24. Fourthly, That it is adviseable to shew, that proper [c] Notice was given of the holding of this Court, yet this I find omitted in some [d] Precedents; and perhaps the contrary Opinion may be the better, for that every Court of Record shall be presumed to observe all necessary previous Incidents for the holding of it, and all Persons within its Jurisdiction shall be intended to have Notice of it. And for the like Reason perhaps, it is not necessary in an Avowry for a [e] Distress for such Fine or Amercement, to shew that the Party had previous Notice what it was.

As to the Recovery of such Fines and Amercements by Way of Distress, I shall observe,

Sect. 25. First, That it seems to be [f] settled at this Day, That a Distress is incident of common Right to every Fine and Amercement in a Sheriff's Torn or Court-Leet, whether the same belong to the King or to a Subject, if the Offence for which they were imposed be of common Right incident to the Jurisdiction of such Courts; but [g] if such Offence were only the Neglect of a Duty created by Custom, it is questionable whether it do not require the like Custom for a Distress, though the Duty be of a publick Nature; but if it be for the [h] private Benefit of a Subject, it seems clear that no Distress is incident to it without a special Custom.

Sect. 26. Secondly, That the Sheriff, or Lord of a Leet, may for such Fines or Amercements distrain the Goods of the Offender in [i] any Lands within the County or Precinct of the Leet, of whomsoever they shall be holden, except [k] only in such Lands which shall be in the King's Hands; for that all such Lands, while they continue in the King's Possession, are wholly out of the Jurisdiction of such Courts.

Sect. 27. Thirdly, That such a Distress may lawfully be taken in the [l] Highway; for that the Statute of *Marlebridge*, *cap.* 15. which prohibits the taking of a Distress there, is to be intended only of Distresses taken for Services due by Way of Tenure of Lands.

Sect. 28. Fourthly, That such Fines and Amercements being for a personal Offence, no [m] Stranger's Beasts can lawfully be distrained for them, though they have been levant and couchant on the Lands of the Offender.

Sect. 29. Fifthly, That it seems to be [n] agreed, That where any such Court is in the King's Hands, the Goods distrained for such Fines and Amercements may lawfully be sold, after they have been kept a reasonable Time, as the Space of sixteen [o] Days; and it seems the better

2 [o] Opinion,

[a] Keilw. 66. a. 3 Keb. 362. Co. Ent. 572. 773.
[b] Rastal 553, 606.
9 E. 4. 40. b.
[c] 10 H. 7. 15. pl. 12. 1 Vent. 105. Raym. 204. Coke's Ent. 572, 573. Rast. Entries 553, 606. 1 Rol. Abr. 365. pl. a. 468. pl. b. 2 Rol. Abr. 136. 1 Rol. Rep. 201.
[d] Co. Ent. 572, 573. Rastal's Ent. 553, 606.
[e] 45 E. 3. 9. a. b. Rast. Ent. 553. 606.
[f] 1 Rol. Abr. 665. f. 666. pl. 2, 3. 1 Ro. Re. 201. 11 Co. 45. a. 8 Co. 41. Cro. Jac. 382. 10 H. 7. 15. pl. 12. 10 H. 6. 7. Con. 11 H. 7. 14. a. 21 H. 7. 40. b.
[g] 1 Vent. 105. Raym. 204. 2 Keb. 701. 739. 745.
[h] 1 Ro. R. 76. 11 Co. 44. b.
[i] 2 H. 4. 24. b. 47 E. 3. 13. a. Bro. Leet 28, 41. Fitz. Avowry 194. 1 Rol. Abr. 670. L. 1, 2, 3, 4. 2 Inst. 104.
[k] 47 Ed. 3. 12, 13. Fitz. Dist. 15. 1 Rol. Abr. 670. pl. 5.
[l] 2 Inst. 131. 47 E. 3. 13. a. 1 And. 72.
[m] 47 E. 3. 13. a. 41 E. 3. 26. b. Bro. Distr. 3. F. N. B. 100. H. Owen 146. Noy 20. Con. 1 Rol. A. 669. pl. 20.
[n] Hetley 62. Finch 476.
[o] Hetley 62.

[a] Opinion, That where any such Court is in the Hands of a common Person, if the Goods were distrained for an Offence of a publick Nature, they may be sold of common Right, without any special Custom for that Purpose.

Sect. 30. Sixthly, That no Bailiff can lawfully distrain for any such Fine or Amercement, without a special [b] Warrant for so doing, which must be set forth by him in an Avowry or Justification of such a Distress.

Sect. 31. As to the Recovery of such Fines and Amercements by Action of Debt, being scarce able to find any Thing remarkable concerning this Matter, except what hath been already taken Notice of, I shall content my self with this one Observation, That the Defendant shall [c] not be suffered to wage his Law in any such Action, because it is grounded on the Act of a Court of Record.

Sect. 32. As to the fifth Particular, *viz.* What farther Penalty may be added to such Fines and Amercements, there seems to be no Doubt, but that upon a Presentment of a common Nusance in a Torn or Leet, the Sheriff or Steward may either amerce the Person presented, and [d] also order him to remove the Nusance by such a Day, under Pain of forfeiting a certain Sum, or may order him to remove it under such a Pain [e] without amercing him at all. But it seems doubtful, Whether such Person be bound at his Peril, to take Notice of and obey such Order, being made in his [f] Absence, unless express Notice be given him of it; but if he have such Notice it seems clear, That he shall forfeit the Pain upon a Presentment at another Court, that he hath not removed such Nusance, [g] without any farther Proceeding: Also it seems, That no such Pain can be affeered to any [h] lesser Sum than what is at first set; and it is said, That every such Pain when forfeited, may be recovered [i] either by Distress or Action of Debt, in the same Manner as a Fine or Amercement may be: And this Point seeming to be agreed by most of the Books cited in the Margent, it seems probable, That the Reason of the Judgment is mistaken in *Fletcher* and *Ingram*'s Case, as reported by Mr. Serjeant [k] *Salkeld*, wherein the contrary Opinion is said to have been holden.

Before I come to the Third Point, *viz.* The Authority of the Sheriff as Judge of the Torn, in Relation to the Appointment of Constables, I shall in brief premise some Considerations concerning the Antiquity and Nature of the Office of a Constable.

Sect. 33. And first, as to the Antiquity of the Office of a Constable, it [l] seems to be the better Opinion, That both Constables of Hundreds, which are commonly called High Constables, and also Constables of Tithings, which are at this Day commonly called Petit Constables or Tithingmen, and were anciently called Chief Pledges, were by the Common Law, and not first ordained by the Statute of *Winchester*, *cap.* 6. as it is holden by [m] some that they were; for that Statute doth not say, That there shall be such Officers constituted, but clearly seems to suppose that there were such before the making of it.

Sect. 34. As to the Nature of this Office, there seems to be no Doubt but that the [n] original Institution of it was for the better Preservation of the Peace; for which Purpose a Constable is said to be authorized by the Common Law to [o] arrest Felons, and also all suspicious Persons that go abroad in the Night, and sleep by Day, or resort to Bawdy-

[a] 3 H. 7. 4. 6. b. 8 Co. 41. b. 1 Rol. Rep. 76. Noy 17. *Quary* Het 62. 1 Bulst. 53. 11 H. 7. 14. a. 21 H. 7. 40. b.
[b] 3 Mod. 138. Cro. El. 698, 748. Moor 574. pl. 789, 607. pl. 839. 2 Keb. 745. Salk. 108.
[c] 10 H. 6. 7. Co. Lit. 295. Fit Ley, 5. 43. 2 Rol. Abr. 106. pl. 1, 2, 8.
[d] *See* Kitchin 51, 52. 53.
[e] *See* Kitchin 51, 52, 53. Co. Entr. 573. 1 Rol. Abr. 468 pl. 6. Cro. Jac 382.
[f] 1 Rol. Abr. 468. pl. 6. 2 Rol. Abr. 136. 1 Rol. Re. 201, Aleyn 78. 5 Mod. 130, 131.
[g] Co. Ent. 573.
[h] 3 Leon. 7, 8. Moor 75. pl. 205. Co. Ent. 573. Bro. Leet 37.
[i] 8 Co. 41. b. Keilw. 66. b. Cro. Jac, 382. 1 Rol. Rep. 201. 1 Rol. Abr. 468. pl. 6. Contra Bro. Leet 37.
[k] Salk. 131. *See* 5 Mod. 96, 130, 131.
[l] Salk. 175, 381. 12 H. 7. 18. a. Owen 105. Finch 336. Kitch. 47, 48. 4 Inst. 265. Poph. 13. Contra Cro. El. 375, 376. Lamb. Constables 5, 9, 10. 6 Co. 77. b.
[m] Lamb. Constable, 5. 4 Inst. 267.
[n] *See the Books cited*, Sect. 33.
[o] *See* Ch. 12.
[p] Kitchin 48. 13 H. 7. 10. b.

Houses, or keep suspicious Company, and to surpress *Affrays: And to the same End also it [a] seems, That he ought by the ancient Common Law, to present at the Torn or Leet all those within his Precinct, who have not been admitted into some Tithing and sworn to the King's Allegiance; and it seems that he still ought by the Law in [b] use at this Day, to present all Offences inquirable in the Torn or Leet; yet in the Oath set down by *Kitchin*, he only swears to present all Bloodsheds, Outcries, Affrays, and Rescouses done within his Office.

* B. 1 Ch 63. [a] Lamb Constable, 5, 6, &c. 45 E. 3. 27. [b] *See* Rast. Entries 151. Crompt. 212. Dalt. Sheriff 388. Kitchin 47.

Sect. 35. Also it is [c] said, That a Constable was at the Common Law a subordinate Officer to the Conservators of the Peace: and consequently since the Office of such Conservators hath been disused, and Justices of Peace constituted in their Stead, it hath been always holden, That the Constable is the proper Officer to a Justice of Peace, and bound to execute his Warrants; and therefore it hath been [d] resolved, That where a Statute authorizes a Justice of Peace to convict a Man of a Crime, and to levy the Penalty by Warrant of Distress, without saying to whom such Warrant shall be directed, or by whom it shall be executed, the Constable is the proper [e] Officer to serve such Warrant, and indictable for disobeying it.

[c] Salk 380, 381. [d] 5 Mod. 130. Salk. 175. [e] Salk. 381. 2 Rol. Rep. 78.

Sect. 36. Yet in as much as the Office of a Constable is wholly ministerial and no way Judicial, it seems, That he may appoint a Deputy to execute a [f] Warrant directed to him, when by Reason of Sickness, Absence, or otherwise, he cannot do it himself. For the Publick Good requires, That there should be always some Officer ready at Hand to execute such Warrants, and the too rigorous Restraint of the Service of them to the proper Officer, could not but sometimes Cause a Failure of Justice; yet I do not find it settled, That a Constable can make a Deputy without some such special Cause.

[f] 1 Rol. Abr. 591. A. Moor 845. Crompt. 222. 3 Bulst 77. Dalt. cap. 1. 1 Rol. Rep. 274. 1 Sid. 355. 1 Lev. 233. March 30. *Quære* 2 Keb. 309. 1 Sid. 355.

For the better understanding of the Authority of the Sheriff, as Judge of the Torn, in Relation to the Appointment of Constables, I shall consider the following Particulars:

1. Whether the Sheriff in his Torn hath Power to make or remove a Constable.
2. What Persons are privileged from being Constables.
3. In what Manner Persons duly chosen Constables, may be punished for refusing to be sworn.
4. What Remedy Persons having a Right to this Office, or to be discharged, may have to be admitted into, or restored to it, or discharged of it.
5. What Power Justices of Peace have in Relation to these Matters.

Sect. 37. As to the first Particular, *viz.* Whether the Sheriff in his Torn, hath Power to make or remove a Constable, it being said in some [g] Books, That both High and Petit Constables are to be chosen and appointed by the Sheriff in his Torn; and by [h] others, that they are to be chosen by the Decennary, it seems difficult to determine to whom this Power doth of common Right belong; yet it seems clear, That whether a Constable be to be chosen by the Sheriff or Decennary, yet he is to be sworn and placed in his Office by the Sheriff, as being judge of the Court. Also it seems certain, That a Custom for choosing a Constable either Way, is good; and it seems to have been the Opinion of the Makers of 13 & 14 *Car.* 2. 12. That the Lords of the Courts-Leet have this Power of

[g] Dalt. Sheriff 400. 1 Rol. Rep. 34. [h] 2 Jones 212. Lamb. Constable 8. Salk 175.

Common Right; for the said Statute, on the Neglect of such Lords to appoint a Constable, gives to Justices of Peace the sole Power of making one; from whence it seems probable, That the Makers of that Statute thought that the like Power did originally belong of common Right to such Lords, and consequently to the Sheriff in his Torn, where there is no Court-Leet: But [a] it hath been said, That a Custom in a Town that the Inhabitants shall serve the Office of Constable by Turns, according to the Situation of their several Houses, is not good; for that by such a Course it may come to a Woman's Turn to be Constable, as Inhabitant of one of those Houses; yet we find such Customs allowed to be good in later Books; and it seems, That the Consequence of the Reasoning abovementioned may well be denied, since such Woman in such Case may procure another to serve for her.

Sect. 38. However it seems clear, That the Sheriff or Steward having Power to place a [b] Constable in his Office, have by Consequence a Power of removing him.

Sect. 39. As to the second Particular, *viz.* What Persons are privileged from being Constables, it [c] seems certain, That if a sworn Attorney or other Officer of any of the Courts of *Westminster-hall* be chosen into this Office, he may have a Writ of Privilege for his Discharge; for that all such Officers, being bound to give their personal Attendance to such Courts, shall be privileged from all such inferior Offices, which it is apparent that for the most Part they cannot personally execute: And it hath been resolved, That such Officers shall have this Privilege, not only where there is no special Custom concerning the Election of Constables, but [d] also where they are chosen by a particular Custom, in respect of their Estates or otherwise; for that no such Custom shall be intended to be more ancient than the Usages of those Courts, and therefore shall give way to them; And upon the like Reasons I find it [e] taken for granted, That practising Barresters at Law, and the Servants of Members of Parliament, have the same Privilege, but I know not of any Resolution to this Purpose.

Sect. 40. Also it hath been resolved, That an [f] Alderman of *London* is not compellable to be a Constable, for that as an Alderman he is bound to be present in the City for the good Government of it.

Sect. 41. But [g] it hath been holden, That a Captain of the King's Guards, being presented to serve as Constable, in Pursuance of a Custom in respect of his Lands in a Town, cannot claim this Privilege; for that notwithstanding he be bound by his Office to personal Attendance on the King's Person, yet such Office being of late Institution, shall not prevail against an ancient Custom: Also it [h] seems, That a practising Physician being chosen Constable in Pursuance of such Custom, has no Remedy for his Discharge; for that there are no Precedents of this Kind, and his Calling is private; yet if such an Officer, or a [i] Gentleman of Quality who hath no such Office, or a practising Physician, be chosen Constable of a Town, which has sufficient Persons besides to execute this Office, and no special Custom concerning it, perhaps he may be relieved by the King's Bench: But it [k] seems, That even a Custom cannot exempt fitting Persons from serving the Office of Constable, where there are not sufficient besides them to execute it. Yet these Points seem not to be settled, as appears by the various Opinions in the Books concerning this Matter, which are very differently reported.

[a] Cro. Car. 389. 2 Keb 309, 578. 1 Lev. 266. 1 Sid. 355.

[b] Bulst. 174.

[c] Noy 112, 113. March 30. Cro. Ca. 389. 2 Keb. 477.

[d] 2 Keb. 508. pl. 84. Cro. Ca. 389. 1 Lev. 265, 266.

[e] 1 Mod 22. 2 Keb. 578. 1 Mod. 13.

[f] 1 Jon. 462. Cro. Ca. 585.

[g] See 2 Keb. 309. 1 Sid. 272, 355. 1 Lev. 233. 1 Keb 933.

[h] 2 Keb. 578. 1 Mod. 22.

[i] 1 Keb 439. Con. 2 Keb. 578.

[k] Sid. 272. See 1 Keb. 933.

Sect. 42. It is alledged in the Petition of the *London* Surgeons, whereon the Statute of 5 *H.* 8. *cap.* 6. is made, *That the Wardens and Fellowship of the Craft and Mystery of Surgeons infranchised in the City of* London, *not passing in Number twelve Persons, for the continual Service and Attendance that they at all Hours and Times give to the King's People, have been exempted and discharged from all Offices and Business, wherein they should use or bear any Manner of Armour or Weapon,* &c. And thereupon it is enacted and established, *That from thenceforth the said Wardens and Fellowship be discharged, and not chargeable of Constableship, Watch, and all Manner of Office bearing any Armour,* &c. *and also that the said Act extend to all Barber-Surgeons admitted and approved to exercise the said Mystery of Surgeons, according to the Form of the Statute made in that Behalf, so that they exceed not, nor be at any Time above the Number of twelve Persons.*

2 Keb 578. *Sect.* 43. And it seems, That by the Equity of this Statute, and the ancient Custom of the Realm, all Surgeons have been allowed the like Privilege.

Sect. 44. Also it is enacted by 32 *H.* 8. 40. *That the President of the Commonalty and Fellowship of the Science and Faculty of Physick in* London, *and the Commons and Fellows of the same, shall not be chosen Constables in the City of* London *or Suburbs of the same,* &c. Yet it seems to have been holden, That the Equity of this Act doth not extend to other Physicians not mentioned in it; perhaps for this Reason, because Physicians have no such special Custom for their Discharge as Surgeons are said to have.

Vide supra Sect. 41.

Sect. 45. Also it is enacted 6 *W.* 3. 4 which hath been continued by subsequent Statutes, *That all Persons using the Art of an Apothecary, who have been brought up and served as Apprentices in the said Art for seven Years, according to the Statute of* 5 Eliz. *shall be freed and exempted from the Office of Constable, in the Counties and Places where they live, for so long as they use and exercise the said Art.*

Sect. 46. As to the third Particular, *viz.* In what Manner Persons duly chosen Constables may be punished for refusing to be sworn, it seems, That no Person can lawfully be committed for such Refusal without more; but it is said, That if the Party be present in the Court he may be fined, and that if he be absent, and have a certain Time and Place appointed him for the taking of the Oath before a Justice of Peace, and have also express Notice of such Appointment, and be presented at the next Court, for having refused to take it accordingly, he may be amerced: Also it seems, That in either Case he may be indicted either at the Sessions of the Peace, or before Justices of *Oyer* and *Terminer*: And it is adviseable in all Pleadings in any Action concerning such a Fine or Amercement, and in all Indictments for such Refusal, specially and expresly to set forth the Manner of every such Election, Appointment, Notice, and Refusal, and [a] before whom the Court was holden: And it hath been adjudged, That it is insufficient to say in general, that the Party was [b] *Debito modo electus*, or *Legitime electus*, or that he had [c] Notice thereof, without setting forth the special Circumstances of such Notice, *&c.* Also it is [d] said to have been adjudged, That an Indictment for not finding a sufficient Person to serve the Office of Constable, without shewing that the Party refused to serve it himself, is insufficient; and it is said not to be sufficient to shew, That a Man was presented and returned to be a Chief Pledge, without shewing that there were other inferior Pledges.

Cro. Car. 567. Co. Ent. 572. 5 Mod. 130. Salk. 175. 8 Co. 38.

[a] 1 Mod. 24. [b] 5 Mod. 96, 129.

[c] Aleyn 78. 5 Mod. 96, 129, 130, 131. 1 Keb. 418. Vide supra fol. 66. [d] 1 Keb. 416. 6 Co. 77. b.

Sect. 47. As to the fourth Particular, *viz.* What Remedy Persons having a Right to be Constables or to be discharged, may have to be admitted into or restored to their Office, or discharged of it; it seems clear at this Day, That the Court of King's Bench having the supream Controll of all inferior Jurisdictions, may upon the Complaint of any Person apprehending himself to be unjustly aggrieved in any such Respect, award a Writ to the Judge of the Court, thereby commanding him to swear, restore, or discharge the Party as the Case shall be; whereupon if such Judge do not obey such Writ, nor an *Alias* and *Pluries* to the same Purpose, nor return a sufficient Cause to the Court to justify his not obeying it, the Court will at last award a peremptory *Mandamus*. 1 Rol. Abr. 535, *Letter* I. 541. pl. 5, 6. 2 Rol Rep. 82. Con. 1 Bulst. 174.

Sect. 48. Also it hath been holden, That a Person duly chosen Constable at a Court Leet, and refused to be sworn by the Steward, may be relieved by the Sessions of the Peace; but this Point shall be more fully considered in the next Section. 2 Jon. 212.

Sect. 49. As to the fifth Particular, *viz.* What Power Justices of Peace have in Relation to these Matters, it is observable, That the Constable being a principal Peace-Officer, and it being necessary for the Preservation of the Peace, that every Vill should be furnished with one; the Justices of Peace have ever since the Institution of their Office, taken upon them as Conservators of the Peace, not only to swear Constables which have been chosen at a Torn or Leet, but also to nominate and swear those who have not been chosen at any such Court, on the Neglect of the Sheriffs or Lords to hold their Courts, or to take Care that such Officers are appointed in them; also it seems, That such Justices have always used for good Cause to displace such Officers which have been so chosen and sworn by them; and this Power of Justices of Peace having been confirmed by the uninterrupted Usage of many Ages shall not now be disputed, but shall be presumed to have been grounded on sufficient Authority. And some have carried this Point so far, as to allow the Justices at their Sessions to swear one who was chosen at the Leet, and unduly rejected by the Steward, who had sworn another in his Place. Salk. 175. pl. 1, 2. 176. 1 Mod. 13. 2 Jon. 212. 1 Bulst. 174. Aleyn 78. Dalt. Ch. 121. fol. 366, 367. 1 Bulst. 174. Salk. 176. Con. 1 Bulst. 174.

Sect. 50. However it is certain, That Justices of Peace had Power to nominate and swear Constables on the Default of the Torn or Leet, before the Statute of 13 & 14 *Car.* 2. 12. Par. 15. and therefore, that they have such Authority in some Cases not mentioned in that Statute, which reciting, *That the Laws and Statutes for apprehending Rogues and Vagabonds had not been duly executed, sometimes for want of Officers, by Reason Lords of Manors do not keep Court-Leets every Year for the making of them*; doth *enact*, *That in Case any Constable, Headborough, or Tythingman shall die or go out of the Parish, any two Justices of Peace may make and swear a new Constable, Headborough, or Tythingman, until the said Lord shall hold a Court, or until next Quarter-Sessions, who shall approve of the said Officers so made and sworn as aforesaid, or appoint others, as they shall think fit; and if any Officer shall continue above a Year in his or their Office, that then in such Case the Justices of Peace in their Quarter-Sessions may discharge such Officers, and may put another fit Person in his or their Place until the Lord of the said Manor shall hold a Court as aforesaid.* *See the Books cited in the precedent Section.*

As to the fifth general Point of this Chapter, *viz.* What Kind of Offences are inquirable in the Sheriff's Torn, I shall premise the following Observations,

4 Inst. 261. Crompt. 213.

1. That it is no certain Rule, That such Offences as are omitted in 18 *E.* 2. concerning the View of Frank-Pledge are not within the Jurisdiction of the Torn or Leet.

Fitz. Torn, 5. infr. Sect 52.

2. That Offences made Treason or Felony or in any other Manner, having a Restraint by Statute superadded to that of the Common Law, are not inquirable here in Respect of any such Statute, but only as Offences at the Common Law; for that the Jurisdiction of these Courts is wholly confined to Offences at Common Law.

Keilw. 66. b.

3. That no Offence whatsoever is cognisable in any such Court, unless it arose since the holding of the last Court.

Offences inquirable in this Court are either,

1. Capital, or
2. Not Capital.

The Capital are either,

1. Treasons, or
2. Felonies.

[a] Cromp. 212. b. Dalt. Sheriff 292. 7 H. 6. 12. b. 10 H. 6. 7. a. *Quære* Bro. Leet 26. [b] 9 H. 6. 44 b. [c] Inf. Sect. 58. [d] Kitchin 8, 9, 22. H. P. C. 173. 6 H. 7. 4. b. 5. a. *See the next Section.* [e] 10 H. 6 7. a. Kitchin 9, 10. Cromp. 212. Dalt. Sheriff 392. [f] 9 H. 44. b. 22 E. 4 22. b. 7 H. 6. 12. Fitz. Torn 5. 5. 40 Ass. 30. Bro. Leet, 18, 26. Finch 241. Kitchin 22. [g] Kitchin 22. 18 E. 2. View of Frank-pledge. 2 Inst. 181. 22 E 4. 22. 6 H. 7. 4. b. 5. a. Fitz. Torn. 5. Leet 3.

Sect. 51. And first as to Treasons, it is said in [a] some Books, That the Sheriff in his Torn may inquire of them all in general, and in [b] others, that he may inquire of all which are not against the King's Person; but I can find no Reason given for this Distinction: And since it is a general Rule, That Offences are inquirable in this Court, in Respect of their being of a publick Nature, on which Account the lowest Offences against the King, as [c] Mortmains and Purprestures, and such like, are inquirable in it,; it seems strange, That the highest should be exempted. However it is [d] clear, That the Sheriff has no Power to inquire of any Offence made Treason by Statute, as of a Treason, but only as it was an Offence at Common Law.

Sect. 52. Secondly, As to Felonies, it is also generally said in [e] some Books, That the Sheriff in his Torn may inquire of all Kinds of Felonies, and in [f] others, That he may inquire of all except of the Death of a Man, or Rape, of the first of which it is said, That he cannot inquire, because it is not a common Nusance, but only a Wrong to a single Person: But if this Reasoning be the only Foundation of this Opinion, it seems difficult to maintain it; for if an Assault aud Battery of a single Person being accompanied with bloodshed or Robbery, be inquirable in this Court, in respect of the Enormity of the Offence, and the Danger to the Publick from suffering such Offenders to go unrestrained, it seems strange if such an Assault proceed to Murder, that it should not be inquirable in it also: But it is [g] said, That the Sheriff cannot inquire of Rape as of a Felony, because it is made a Felony by the Statute of *Westminster* 2. 34. by which it is enacted, That he who ravishes a Woman, shall have Judgment of Life and Member: But if this Statute had only repealed the 13th of *Westminster* 1. (by which this Offence, which was a Felony at Common Law, was made a Trespass only,) it seems that it would have restored the Jurisdiction of the Sheriff's Torn over it as a Felony, because then it would have been a Felony by the Common Law again; but now it being a Felony only by the Statute, it is inquirable as a Trespass only in this Court.

Offences not Capital inquirable in the Sheriff's Torn, are either,

1. Such as amount to an actual Trespass, or
2. Such as do not amount to such a Trespass.

Sect. 53. And first, As to such Offences amounting to an actual Trespass it is agreed, [a] That an Assault and Battery is inquirable here, if there be any Bloodshed in it, but otherwise not; because in such Case it is not looked on as a common Grievance, but as an Injury to a particular Person.

Sect. 54. Secondly, That all [b] Affrays are also inquirable here, for that they are *in terrorem Populi.*

Sect. 55. Thirdly, That the common [c] breaking of Hedges, Walls, or Dykes, may also be inquired of in this Court, but not the breaking of any particular Hedge, for that it is no common Grievance.

Sect. 56. Fourthly, Also it is commonly said, That all [d] Pound Breaches may be inquired of in this Court, as being common Grievances, in direct Contempt of the Authority of the Law, by which Pounds are provided for the legal Detainment of Distresses till they shall be delivered by due Course of Law.

Sect. 57. Offences under the Degree of Capital, not amounting to an actual Trespass, and inquirable in this Court, either immediately concerning the King's Interest, or do not.

Sect. 58. As to those which immediately concern the King's Interest, it seems to be agreed, That all [e] Purprestures or Incroachments upon the King, and [f] Alienations in Mortmain, and [g] Seisures of Treasure-trove, or of [h] Waifs or [h] Estrays, or Goods [h] wrecked, belonging to the King, may be inquired of in this Court: But it seems [i] questionable, Whether a Prescription in a Court-Leet to inquire of the Seisure of such Things belonging to the Lord of it, being a Subject, be good or not, since it is against the general [k] Rule of the Law for the Court-Leet to take Conusance of Trespasses done to the private Damage of the Lord, because that would make him his own Judge?

Sect. 59. As to Offences of this Kind, which do not immediately concern the King's Interest, it seems to be a general [l] Rule, That all common Nusances are indictable in this Court; as all Annoyances to common Bridges or Highways, [m] Bawdy-houses, &c. and also all other such like Offences, as [n] selling corrupt Victuals or exposing them to Sale, [o] breaking the Assise of Beer and Ale, neglecting to hold a [p] Fair or Market in Pursuance of a Grant or Prescription: Also it seems, That the keeping of [q] false Weights or Measures is indictable in this Court, whether it appear that they were actually made Use of or not: Also it is said, That all common Disturbers of the Peace may be here indicted, as [r] Barretors, [r] common Scolds, [r] Eves-droppers, and also all common Oppressors, as [s] Usurers, &c. and also all [t] dangerous and suspicious Persons as Vagabonds; or those who go abroad in the Night, and sleep in the Day, or those who inordinately haunt Taverns, having no visible Means to live by, &c. And also all [u] Suitors to the Court who shall make Default, &c. And [x] also all those who shall levy a Hue and Cry without Cause, or shall neglect to levy one where they ought, or to pursue one rightly levied.

Sect.

18 E. 4. 5. b. Dy. 233, pl. 14. 1 R. 3. 1. a. 4 H. 6. 18. 18 E. 2 View of Frank-pledge. Kitch. 37, 38. [b] 4 H. 6. 10. a. 1 R. 3. 1. a. Bro. Leet 15. Kitchin 11. [c] Kitch. 11. Bro. Leet 26. 22 E. 4, 23. Finch 241. [d] Dalt. Sheriff 394. Kitch. 11, 37. Contra 4. Leon. 12. [e] Dalt. Sheriff 393. [f] Kitch. 23, 38, 39. [g] Kitch. 40. 18 E. 2 View of Frank-pledge. [h] Kitch. 12, 13, 23, 40. Dalt. Sheriff 393. Crompt. 213. [i] 44 E. 3. 19. pl. 14. [k] 1 Saunders 135. Raym. 160. 12 H. 4. 8. b. [l] 1 R. 3. 1. 4 H. 6. 10. 22 E. 4 22, 23. 1 Rol. Abr. 541, 542, 543. [m] Kitch. 11. [n] 1 R. 3. 1. Bro. Leet 1. 4 Inst. 261. Kitch. 11. 23. [o] 2 Inst. 72. 4 E. 4 24. 4 Inst. 262. Rol. Ab. 543. [p] Cromp. 212. [q] 18 E. 2 View of Frank-pledge. Con. Kitch. 11. b. Dalt Sh. 395. [r] Kitch. 11. Hob 246. [s] Cromp. 212. Dalt. Sh. 394. [t] 18 E. 2 View of Frank-pledge. Kitch. 11. [u] Kich. 10. b. [x] Dalt. Sheriff 394. 18 E. 2. View of Frank-pledge.

Sect. 60. Alſo [a] it is ſaid, That every Vill within the Precinct of a Torn, is indictable in it for not having a Pair of Stocks, and ſhall forfeit five Pounds.

Sect. 61. Alſo by [b] Statute, many other Offences are inquirable in this Court, which it would be too long to enumerate in this Place.

Sect. 62. But it hath been [c] reſolved, That a Man cannot be amerced in a Court-Leet for ſurcharging a Common, becauſe this only concerns the private Intereſt of the Inhabitants.

Sect. 63. Yet it hath been [d] holden, That if there be a By-Law made in a Court-Leet, in Purſuance of a Cuſtom to make By-Laws, That no one ſhall receive a poor Man to be his Tenant, who ſhall be chargeable to the Town, under a certain Penalty; and afterwards an Inhabitant offend againſt ſuch By-Law, he may be preſented at the Court-Leet and compelled to pay ſuch Penalty: But if ſuch By-Laws be valid, it ſeems clear, That they depend entirely on the Cuſtom, and are not binding of common Right; for that the Court-Leet, as ſuch, hath nothing to do with ſuch Matters of a private Nature: And how far any ſuch Court may receive, from a ſpecial Cuſtom, a new collateral Power of a different Nature from what naturally belongs to it, may deſerve to be conſidered; but it [e] ſeems, That of common Right any Court with the Aſſent of the Tenants, may make By-Laws under certain Penalties, in Relation to Matters properly within the Conuſance of ſuch Court, as the Reparation of the Highways, *&c.* Alſo there [f] ſeems to be no Doubt, but that by Cuſtom a Court-Baron may make By-Laws, for the well regulating of Commons and ſuch like private Matters; and therefore where a Court-Leet and Baron are holden together at the ſame Place, as they uſually are, it ſeems, That what is tranſacted therein in Relation to publick Matters, ſhall be applied to the [g] Juriſdiction of the Court-Leet, and what is done in Relation to private Matters, ſhall be intended to be done by the Court-Baron.

Sect. 64. As to the ſixth general Point of this Chapter, *viz.* Within what Place Offences indictable in the Sheriff's Torn muſt ariſe, it ſeemeth that it is not material, Whether ſuch [h] Offences did ariſe within the Hundred in which the Torn is holden or not; for though the Sheriff ought to hold his Torn in every particular Hundred, yet it ſeems, That in each of them he holds it for the whole County; and it is certain, That he hath a general Juriſdiction throughout the whole; yet it ſeems, That the Jurors ſhall not be charged on their [i] Oaths to preſent any Offences, but thoſe ariſing within their particular Hundreds: Alſo it is provided by the Statute of *Marlbridge*, *cap.* 10. That thoſe who have Tenements in different [k] Hundreds, ſhall not be compelled to come to any Torn, but only in the Bailiwick wherein they ſhall be converſant: Alſo it [l] ſeems clear, That no Offence ariſing within the Precincts of a Leet is inquirable in the Torn, unleſs there have been a Neglect to preſent it in the Leet: But after ſuch a Neglect it ſeems the better [m] Opinion, That it is inquirable in the Torn, leaſt otherwiſe there ſhould be a Failure of Juſtice: Yet it ſeems certain, That in pleading you [n] cannot juſtify the Proceedings of the Sheriff's Torn againſt any Offence ariſing within a Leet, without expreſsly alledging that the Leet had neglected to inquire of it; for that ſuch a Neglect is not to be preſumed, where it doth not appear.

Sect. 65. As to the ſeventh general Point of this Chapter, *viz.* By what Jurors, and in what Manner, Indictments in the Sheriff's Torn ought to be found, it is enacted by the Statute of *Weſtminſter*, 2. 13. *That the Sheriff ſhall take no Inqueſt either* ex Officio, *or by Virtue of the King's Writ,*

[a] Kirch. 13. *See the next Chapter.*
[b] *See* Kitch. 12. 2 Danv. Ab. 291.
[c] 1 Rol. Abr. 541. 2 Rol Abr. 83. pl. 7.
[d] 1 Rol Ab. 542. pl. 11, 12. Lane 55, 56.
[e] 11. H. 7. 14. 21 H 7. 40 b. 5 Co. 63. Hob 212. Kitch. 45.
[f] 1 Danv. 735. pl. 10. 737 pl. 1, 2, 3. Kitch. 78.
[g] *See* Ch. 11. Sect 6.
[h] Dalton's Sheriff 385. Finch 241, 242. Cro. Jac. 551. *ſeems contrary.*
[i] Cromp. 212. Dalt. Sheriff 388.
[k] 2 Inſt 120, 122.
[l] 1 Rol Ab. 543. *Letter* D. Crompt. 212. a. Co Lit. 168 b. Bro. Preſentment 1. Dalt Sheriff 395, 396. 3 Keb 230.
[m] *See the Books above cited, and* 10 H. 4. 4 a. 12 H. 7. 18. Mo. 607. Finch 246. Cro. Jac. 584, 551. Cont. 4 Inſt. 261.
[n] Cro. Jac. 551.

2 Inſt, 387,

Writ, but by twelve lawful Men at the least, who shall put their Seals to such Inquisitions; and the same is also provided as to Bailiffs of Franchises.

Sect. 66. In the Construction of this Statute it hath been holden, That if there be more than twelve Jurors, and all agree to the Inquisition, all must set their Seals to it; but that it is sufficient, if twelve of them only agree, for those twelve to set their Seals. Dalt. Sheriff 389.

Sect. 67. And it is farther enacted by 1 *R.* 3. *cap.* 4. *That no Officer return or impanel any Person to be taken or put in any Inquiry in any Sheriff's Torn, but such as be of good Name and Fame, and having Freehold to the yearly Value of* 20 s. *or Copyhold to the yearly Value of* 26 s. 8 *d. on Pain of* 40 s. &c. *And that every such Indictment before any Sheriff in his Torn otherwise taken, shall be void.*

Sect. 68. And *Note*, That Courts-Leet seem to be within the Letter of the said Statute of *Westminster* 2. and are said by some to be within the Equity of the said Statute of 1 *R.* 3. but this seems questionable; for it is said, by some Books, That any Person happening to be present at a Court-Leet, or to be riding by the Place where it is holden, may for the want of Jurors be compelled by the Steward to be sworn, whether he be Resident within the Precincts of the Leet or not; by which it seems to be implied, That any Person whatsoever is capable of being put upon the Jury in a Court-Leet. 2 Inst. 388. S. P. C. 85. b. 7 H. 6 13. a. 12 H. 7. 18 b. Bro. Leet 14. 3 H 7. 4. b.

Sect. 69. And to prevent the altering or imbezilling of any such Indictment, it is enacted by 1 *E.* 3. Stat. 2. Ch. 17. *That the Sheriffs and Bailiffs of Franchises, and all other that do take Indictments in their Torns, or elsewhere, where Indictments ought to be made, shall take such Indictment by Roll indented, whereof the one Part shall remain with the Indictors, and the other Part with him that taketh the Inquest; so that the Indictments shall not be imbezilled as they have been in Times past; and so that one of the Inquests may shew the one Part of the Indenture to the Justices, when they come to make Deliverance.* 2 Inst. 388. S. P. C. 85. a

Sect. 70. And there is no Doubt, But that this Statute extends as well to Courts-Leet, as to the Sheriff's Torn. Keilw. 141. a. 148. a.

Sect. 71. Also there are many particular Customs and Usages in Relation to the taking of Indictments in these Courts; but it seems to have been anciently the most general Course, to impanel not only a Grand Jury, but also a Jury of twelve Men, which was commonly called the Petit Jury; and that all Offences were first presented by the Headboroughs, and the Presentments affirmed by the Petit Jury, before they were brought to the Grand Jury: However it seems, That no Exception can be taken to any such Indictment, in Respect of the Non-observance of any such Custom or Usage; for that no Averment lies against the Acts of a Court of Record, and every Judge of such Court shall be presumed to act according to the Rules of it. Dalt. Sheriff 388, 389. Crompt. 212, 213. Keilw. 66. b. 9 H. 6. 44 b.

Sect. 72. What is above said concerning Indictments taken before the Sheriff in his Torn, is to be intended of such only as are taken before him *ex Officio*; for that he is restrained to take any such Indictment, by Virtue of any Writ or Commission by 28 *E.* 3. 9. *Which reciting that the People had suffered many Mischiefs, for that Sheriffs of divers Counties, by Virtue of Commissions and general Writs granted to them at their own Suit, for their singular Profit to gain of the People, had made and taken divers Inquests, to cause to indict the People at their Will, and had taken Fine and Ransom of them to their own Use, and had delivered them; whereas such Persons indicted were not brought before the King's Justices to have Deliverance, doth thereupon enact, for to eschew all such Mischief, that all such Commissions and Writs before made be utterly repealed, and that from thenceforth no such Commissions nor Writs shall be granted.*

F. N. B. 92. e. 144. i. 250. A. Cro. E. 371. Salk. 190. 2 Inst. 388. H. P. C. 103, 104. 173. S. P. C. 77. F. G. 84. A. Dalt. Sheriff 388, 389. 3 Mod. 238. Book 1. Ch. 29. Sect. 20, 24.

Sect. 73. Yet it seemeth not to be clearly settled, Whether by Virtue of this Statute, all such Writs and Commissions, and the Proceedings thereon, be made wholly void or not?

Sect. 74. As to the eighth general Point of this Chapter, *viz.* In what Manner Indictments in the Sheriff's Torn are to be proceeded upon, it is recited by 1 *E.* 4. 2. *That many of the King's People by inordinate and infinite Indictments and Presentments of Felonies and other Offences, taken before Sheriffs at their Torns or Law-Days, (which were oftentimes affirmed by Jurors having no Conscience, nor any Freehold, and often by the Sheriff's menial Servants) had been arrested and imprisoned, and constrained to make grievous Fines and Ransoms, after which they had been enlarged out of Prison, and the said Indictments and Presentments imbezilled and withdrawn.* And thereupon it is enacted, *That all indictments and Presentments before any of the King's Sheriffs in his Counties, except in* London, *their Under-Sheriffs, Clerks, Bailiffs or Ministers at their Torns or Law-Days, they nor any of them shall have Power to attach, arrest, or put in Prison, or to levy or take any Fine or Amercement of any Person so indicted or presented, by Reason of any such Indictment or Presentment, but that the said Sheriffs and Under-Sheriffs, Clerks or Bailiffs, and their Ministers, shall deliver all such Indictments and Presentments to the Justices of Peace, at their next County-Sessions on Pain of* 40 l. *And that the said Justices of Peace shall have Power to award Process upon all such Indictments and Presentments as the Law doth require, and in like Form as if the said Indictments and Presentments were taken before the said Justices of Peace; and also to arraign and deliver all such Persons so indicted and presented before the said Sheriffs,* &c. *And such Persons which shall be indicted or presented of Trespass, shall make such a Fine as shall seem lawful by their Discretions. And the Estreats of the said Fines and Amercements shall be inrolled, and by Indenture be delivered to the said Sheriffs, Under-Sheriffs, their Clerks, Baillffs, or Ministers, or some of them, to the Use and Profit of him that was Sheriff at the Time of such Indictments or Presentments taken. And if any of the said Sheriffs, their Under-Sheriffs, Clerks, Bailiffs, or their Ministers, do arrest, attach, or put in Prison, or cause any Fine or Ransom to be taken, or levy any Amercement, of any Person or Persons so indicted or presented, by Reason or Colour of any such Indictment or Presentment taken before them at their Torns or Law-Days above rehearsed, before that they have Process from the said Justices of Peace, or Estreats delivered out, of the said Indictments or Presentments so brought, delivered, and presented to them, that then the Sheriffs which so do, shall forfeit an Hundred Pounds.*

Sect. 75. It is observable, That by the Words of this Statute, Justices of Peace may award Process on any such Indictments, in like Manner as if they had been taken before themselves; and yet it is clear, That if the Sheriff's Torn had no Authority to take the Indictment removed before such Justices, they have no Power to proceed upon it, as they might have done if it had been taken before themselves; for the Statute in giving them such Power to proceed upon Indictments in the Sheriff's Torn, must be intended to mean such only as were there lawfully taken, not those which were void *ab initio*, as being taken *coram non Judice*; nor is there the least Intimation in the Statute of an Intent to inlarge the Sheriff's Power in taking Indictments, but the whole Purport of it is to restrain him from proceeding on them. And to this Purpose it hath been so largely construed, That not only the Judge of the Court is punishable for awarding such Process, but also the Officer for obeying it.

S. P. C. 87. D. 4 E. 4. 31. a. Fitz. Torn 3.

1 Jon. 301. Cro. Ca. 275.

Sect. 76. As to the ninth general Point of this Chapter, *viz.* In what Manner Indictments in the Sheriff's Torn are to be traversed and determined; it seems to be [a] agreed, That a Presentment by [b] twelve or more in a Torn or Leet, of any Offence within the Jurisdiction of the Court, being neither Capital nor concerning any Freehold, subjects the Party to a Fine or Amercement without any farther Proceeding, and binds him for ever after the Day on which it is found, and admits of no Traverse to the Truth of it; but [c] some say, That the Party may have a Writ of false Presentment against the Jurors, the same Day on which the Indictment is found, yet it seems agreed, That no Instance can be shewn of any such Writ being actually brought: But if the Presentment concern the Party's Life or [d] Freehold, as if it charge him with not repairing such a Highway, which he is charged to be bound to repair by the Tenure of his Land; it seems clear, That he may remove it into the King's Bench and traverse it; but not if it barely charge his Person, as for digging a Ditch in the Highway, or not cutting the Branches of his Trees hanging over it, &c. Also it [e] seems, That a Man may in like Manner traverse an Indictment of an Offence wholly out of the Jurisdiction of a Court-Leet; as of an Affray or Nusance done out of the Precinct of it, or of the Non-Appearance of a Person at a Leet, who lives out of the Precinct of it. But if the Affray or Nusance were within the Precinct of the Leet, it seems, That no one can traverse it in Respect of his own not living in it; and that a Person who lives within the Precinct of a Leet, shall have no Traverse to a Presentment for not appearing at it.

[a] Finch 386. Keilw. 52. a. 66. b. 3 Mod 138. Dyer 13. pl. 45.

[b] Keilw. 141. a. 45 E. 3. 26. b. 27. a.

[c] Fitz. Bar. 271. Keilw. 66. b. 41 Ed. 3. 28.

[d] 5 H. 7. 4. a. Br. Trav. 183. Keilw. 52, 66, 67. Dy. 13. pl 64.

[e] Keilw. 66, 67. 41 E. 3. 27.

Sect. 77. But it seems certain, That at this Day, neither the Torn nor Leet, have any Power to try any Traverse whatsoever, as hath been more fully shewn, *Sect.* 13. But it is certain, That the Justices of Peace may by Force of the abovementioned Statute of 1 *E.* 4. try a Man indicted of Felony before the Sheriff in his Torn: Also it seems, That they may try a Person upon any other Indictment in the Torn, which is traversable at Common Law, but that they have no Power to take any Traverse of any other Indictment in the Torn; for that the Words of the Statute are only, *That they may award Process on any such Indictments, as if they had been taken before themselves, and also arraign and deliver the Persons indicted,* which must be intended of those indicted of Felony, who only are said to be arraigned, *And that Persons indicted of Trespass, shall make Fines,* &c. *by their Discretion,* without saying, That they shall be tried; by which it seems to be implied, That Persons so indicted shall be fined, as they usually were before in the Torn, and still are in the Leet, and that in some Cases without any farther Trial, as is more fully shewn in the precedent Section.

CHAP.

CHAP. XI.

Of the Court-Leet.

Finch 246.
[a] Sect. 45, &c.
[b] Sect. 10, &c.
[c] Sect. 13, &c.
[d] Sect. 17, &c.
[e] Sect. 33, &c.
[f] Sect. 51, &c.
[g] Sect. 64, &c.
[h] Sect. 65, &c.
[i] Sect. 74, &c.
2 Inst. 71, 72.
22 Ed. 4. 22.

Sect. 1. A Court-Leet is a Court of Record having the ſame Juriſdiction within ſome particular Precinct, which the Sheriff's Torn hath in the County: And therefore ſince it hath been ſhewn in the precedent Chapter, at what [a] Time and in what Place the Sheriff's Torn is to be holden, and what Perſons owe Suit to it, and [b] what Authority the Judge of it hath in Relation to his Proceeding on [c] Indictments, and alſo in Relation to [d] Fines and Amercements, and the [e] Appointment of Conſtables; and having alſo ſhewn what [f] Kind of Offences are inquirable in this Court, and within what [g] Place ſuch Offences muſt ariſe, and by what [h] Jurors, and in what Manner, Indictments in it are to be found, and in what Manner they are to be [i] proceeded upon, traverſed and determined; and ſince the Court-Leet hath regularly the very ſame Juriſdiction with the Sheriff's Torn as to all theſe Points, except in ſome ſpecial Caſes, which have been already taken Notice of in the Chapter concerning the Sheriff's Torn; I ſhall refer the Reader to the ſaid Chapter for all theſe Particulars, and ſhall only conſider in this Place,

1. The End of inſtituting the Court-Leet.
2. How far it exempts thoſe who live within its Precincts from the Torn.
3. How far it is ſubject to the Overſight of the Torn.
4. For what Cauſes it may be forfeited.
5. What ought to be the Form of a Caption of an Indictment in it.

11 H. 7. 18.
2 Inſt. 71, 72.
1 Jon. 283.
6 Co. 77. b.
Dyer 30. pl. 209.
13 H. 4. 9.
11 Co. 42.
1 Rol. Rep. 32. 73.
1 Rol. Abr. 211. A. C.

Sect. 2. As to the firſt Point it ſeems, That anciently all People who now owe Suit to any Court-Leet, were bound to come to the Sheriff's Torn, in order there to take the Oath of Allegiance to the King, and to be incorporated into ſome Tithing, and for ſuch other Purpoſes as are ſet forth more at large in the precedent Chapter, *Sect.* 2. But it being more for the Eaſe of the People, to have Courts of this Kind holden in their own Townſhips or Manors; by Degrees, Grants of ſuch Courts were obtained from the King for moſt Manors and Towns, not only by the Lords of Manors, but alſo by other Perſons, who had no Lands in the Places for which they obtained ſuch Grants: And for a Recompence to ſuch Grantees, for the Charge and Trouble they were ſuppoſed to have been at in procuring ſuch Grants, it was uſual for the Inhabitants who had the Benefit of them, to agree to pay a certain Sum of Money, called Capitage, or *certum Letæ, &c.* at every ſuch Court-Leet; and for the Non-payment of this Duty or Refuſal to preſent it, ſuch Grantees may preſcribe to amerce the Defaulters, and to diſtrain for the Amercement; but no ſuch Preſcription ſhall be allowed for any other Matter whatſoever of a private Nature.

Sect. 3. As to the ſecond Point, *viz.* How far a Court-Leet exempts thoſe who live within the Precincts of it from the Torn, it ſeems to be a general [a] Rule, That no Man can be within two Leets at the ſame Time, and in the ſame Reſpect; from whence it follows, That he who reſides within the Precincts of a Leet, the Lord whereof doth duly hold his Court, cannot be compelled to come to the Torn, or any other ſuperior Leet, for the taking the Oath of Allegiance, or any other ſuch like Purpoſe, which may be as well anſwered by his Attendance at his own Leet: Yet if ſuch private Leet have not the general Juriſdiction of the Torn, but be [b] ſpecially granted for two or three Articles of it only; it ſeems, That the Inhabitants within its Precinct muſt attend the Sheriff's Torn for all ſuch Matters of which ſuch private Leet hath no Juriſdiction: Alſo it [c] ſeems to be a good Preſcription for a Grand Leet, (to which other inferior Leets may be ſubordinate in the ſame Manner as that is to the Torn,) to oblige the Chief Pledges, and a certain Number of the Inhabitants of every Town within its Precinct, to appear at every ſuch Grand Leet, to inquire of ſuch Offences as have not been inquired of in the inferior Leets.

[a] Dalt. Sheriff 402, 403. 1 Jon. 283. 6 Co 77. b. 18 H. 6. 13. Fitz Leet 1. Cro. Jac 584. *See* Ch. 10. Sect. 12. Con. Kitch. 34. 1 Rol. Abr. 542. b.
[b] Keilw. 141. a. 142. a. 2 Rol. Abr. 203. pl 7.
[c] Cro Jac 583. Raym. 204. Cro. Car. 75, 76. *See* Ch. 10. Sect. 12, 64.

Sect. 4. As to the third Point, *viz.* How far the Court-Leet is ſubject to the Overſight of the Torn; it is ſaid, That the Sheriff's Torn as an [d] Overſeer of this Court, is to inquire whether the Tithings be whole or no, and to preſent Defaults that are not redreſſed in the Leet; and it ſeems alſo, That it may of common Right inquire of the Concealment of Offences inquirable in Leets, and of the Defaults of the Lords of ſuch Courts: However it [e] ſeems clear, That a Preſcription to this Purpoſe is good. And there is no Doubt, but that if a Leet be [f] ſeized into the King's Hands, all thoſe who owed Suit to it ought to come to the Torn.

[d] Finch 246. *See* Ch. 10. Sect. 64. Dalt. Sheriff 387, 391.
[e] Cro Jac. 584.
[f] 2 Rol. Abr. 203. pl. 7. Finch 246.

Sect. 5. As to the fourth Point, *viz.* For what Cauſes a Court-Leet may be forfeited, it ſeems, That this being a Franchiſe not intended to be granted for the private Benefit of the Grantee, but for the Good of the Publick, from the more eaſy and convenient Adminiſtration of Juſtice, ſhall not only be forfeited by Acts of groſs and palpable Oppreſſion and Injuſtice, [g] but alſo by bare Omiſſions, in not making it anſwer the End of its Inſtitution; as in the not [h] puniſhing Offenders in the ſame Manner as the Law requires, or in [i] neglecting to hold a Court when it ought to be holden, (at leaſt if ſuch Neglects be often repeated, and without a reaſonable Excuſe,) or in not [k] providing an able Steward to diſcharge the Office, or in not taking Care to have ſuch other Officers, or other Things as are neceſſary for the Execution of Juſtice, as Conſtables, and Ale-taſters, *&c.* and [l] Pillory and Tumbrel; but it is [m] ſaid, That a Vill may be bound by Preſcription to provide a Pillory and Tumbrel, and [n] that every Vill is bound of common Right to provide a Pair of Stocks. *Quære.*

[g] Co. Lit. 233. a. Kitch. 33. Cro. Jac. 155. 9 Co. 50. 2 Rol. Abr. 155. O. 11 Ed. 4. 1. 2 H. 7. 11. b.
[h] 1 Jon. 383. Keilw. 148. b. 152. a.
[i] Kitch. 33.
[k] 1 Jon. 283.
[l] Fitz Leet 12. Cro Eliz. 125. 698. Mo. 573, 574, 607. 1 Jon. 283.
[m] Cro. Eliz. 698. Mo. 607.
[n] Kitch 13. a. Carter 29. Con. Moor 374, 573. 1 Jon. 283.

Sect. 6. As to the fifth Point, *viz.* What ought to be the Form of the Caption of an Indictment in a Court-Leet, it hath been [o] reſolved, 1. That the Caption of an Indictment, *ad Cur. Viſ. Franc. Pleg. cum Cur. Baron. &c.* is good; for that the Words *cum Cur. Baron.* ſhall be rejected; and it cannot but be intended that the Indictment was taken by that Court, which alone hath the Colour of Authority to take it.

[o] Vide ſupra Ch 10 Sect. 9. Salk. 195.

Sect. 7. 2. That the not ſetting forth in the Caption, whether ſuch Court be holden by Grant or Preſcription, is helped by the Multitude of Precedents.

Salk. 200.

CHAP. XII.

Of Arrests by private Persons.

HAving thus endeavoured to shew the Nature of the Courts which have Jurisdiction over criminal Offences, I am now to shew in what Manner Offenders are to be proceeded against by such Courts; and in Order hereto shall consider,

1. How they are to be apprehended.
2. In what Manner and in what Cases they are to be bailed.
3. In what Cases and in what Manner they are to be committed to Prison.
4. How far they and their Assistants are punishable for an Hindrance in bringing them to publick Justice.

As to the first of these Points I shall consider,

1. In what Manner such Offenders are to be apprehended by private Persons.
2. In what Manner by publick Officers.
3. In what Cases it is lawful to break open Doors in order to apprehend them.

As to Arrests of such Offenders by private Persons, I shall examine,

1. Where Arrests of this Kind are commanded and injoined by Law.
2. Where they are permitted by Law.
3. Where they are rewarded.

Sect. 1. As to the first Point it seems clear, That [a] all Persons whatsoever who are present when a Felony is committed, or a dangerous Wound given, are bound to apprehend the Offender, on Pain of being fined and imprisoned for their Neglect, [b] unless they were under Age at the Time.

Sect. 2. And for this [c] Cause, by the Common Law if any Homicide be committed, or dangerous Wound given, whether with or without Malice, or even by [d] Misadventure or Self-defence, in any Town or in the [e] Lanes or Fields thereof, in the Day-time, and the Offender escape, the Town shall be amerced, and if out of a Town, the [f] Hundred shall be amerced.

Sect. 3. And since the Statute of *Winchester cap.* 5. which ordains that [g] walled Towns shall be kept shut from Sun-setting to Sun-rising, if the Fact happen in any such Town by Night or by Day, and the Offender escape, the Town shall be amerced.

[a] 3 Inst. 53, 139, 152. H. P. C. 89, 90. 3 H. 7 cap. 1. 2 Inst. 52. Fitz. Coron. 293.
[b] Fitz. Coron. 395.
[c] H. P. C. 89, 90. 3 H. 7. cap. 1. 3 Inst. 53. 4 Inst. 183. Cro. Car. 252. 3 Leon. 207. Fitz. Coron. 238, 293, 299, 352, 425. Cont. 1 Leon. 107.
[d] 2 Inst. 315. Fitz. Coron. 302.
[e] Dy. 210. pl. 25.
[f] S. P. C. 34. E. P.
[g] S. P. C. 34. a. 3 Inst. 53. 7 Co 6. b. 7 a.

Sect. 4. And as all [a] private Persons are bound to apprehend all those, who shall be guilty of any of the Crimes abovementioned in their View; so also are they with the utmost Diligence to pursue, and endeavour to take all those who shall be guilty thereof out of their View, upon a Hue and Cry levied against them.

[a] H. P. C. 90. 3 Inst. 117. 2 Inst. 172.

Sect. 5. [b] Hue and Cry is the Pursuit of an Offender from Town to Town till he be taken, which all who are present when a Felony is committed, or a dangerous Wound given, are by the Common Law as well as by Statute, bound to raise against the Offenders who escape, on Pain of Fine and Imprisonment: Also it [c] seems certain, That a Man may lawfully raise it against one who sets upon him in the Highway to rob him: Also it is enacted by the Statute of [d] *Winchester, cap.* 4. That Hue and Cry shall be levied upon any Stranger who shall not obey the Arrest of the Watch in the Night-time; and [e] 21 *E.* 1. which was made against Trespassers in Forests, Chases, Parks, and Warrens, seems to allow the levying thereof upon any such Offenders. But if a Man take upon him to [f] levy a Hue and Cry without sufficient Cause, he shall be punished as a Disturber of the Peace.

[b] 3 Inst. 116, 117. Dalt. Justice, Ch. 28. 109. 2 Inst. 172. Fitz. Coron. 395. Cro. El. 654. Crompt. 178, 179.
[c] 9 E 4. 26. b.
[d] 13 Ed. 1.
[e] Keble's Statutes, fol. 59.
[f] 29 E 3. 39. Fitz. Tresp. 252. Crompt. 179. 21 H. 7. 28. a.

Sect. 6. In order rightly to raise a Hue and Cry, you ought to go to the Constable of the next Town, and declare the Fact, and [g] describe the Offender, and the Way he is gone; whereupon the Constable ought immediately, whether it be Night or Day, to raise his own Town, and make a Search for the Offender; and upon the not finding him, to send the like Notice with the utmost Expedition, by Horsemen as well as Footmen, to the Constables of all the neighbouring Towns, who ought in like Manner to search for the Offender, and also to give Notice to their neighbouring Constables, and they to the next, till the Offender be found.

[g] 3 Inst 116. Dalt. Justice cap. 28, 109. H. P. C. 91. Cromp. 178, 179.

Sect. 7. Also every [h] private Person is bound to assist an Officer demanding his Help for the taking of a Felon, or the suppressing an Affray, or apprehending the Affrayers, *&c.*

[h] Ch. 13 Sect. 5.

Arrests of Offenders by private Persons permitted by Law, are either,

1. By their own Authority, or
2. By a Warrant from a Justice of Peace.

Arrests of this Kind by their own Authority, are either,

1. In Respect of Treason or Felony, or
2. In Respect of inferior Offences.

Arrests of this Kind in Respect of Treason or Felony are either,

1. For the Suspicion of such Crimes already done, or supposed to have been done, or,
2. To prevent their being done.

As to such Arrests for such Suspicion, I shall endeavour to shew,

1. What are sufficient Causes of Suspicion.
2. By whom the Person arrested must be suspected.
3. Whether any such Cause will justify an Arrest, where no Treason or Felony at all hath been committed, *&c.*
4. In what Manner an Arrest for such Suspicion is to be justified in Pleading.

Sect.

Sect. 8. As to the first Particular, *viz.* What are sufficient Causes of Suspicion, I shall take Notice of some of the Principal of them, which are generally agreed to justify the Arrest of an innocent Person for Felony, as

Sect. 9. 1. The common [a] Fame of the Country: but it [b] seems, That it ought to appear upon Evidence, in an Action brought for such an Arrest, that such Fame had some probable Ground.

Sect. 10. 2. The [c] living a vagrant, idle, and disorderly Life, without having any visible Means to support it.

Sect. 11. 3. The being in [d] Company with one known to be an Offender, at the Time of the Offence; or [e] generally at other Times keeping Company with Persons of scandalous Reputations.

Sect. 12. 4. The being found in such Circumstances as induce a strong Presumption of Guilt; as [f] coming out of a House wherein Murder has been committed, with a bloody Knife in one's Hand; or being found in [g] Possession of any Part of Goods stolen, without being able to give a probable Account of coming honestly by them.

Sect. 13. 5. The behaving one's self in such Manner as betrays a Consciousness of Guilt; as [h] where a Man being charged with a Treason or Felony, says nothing to it, but seems tacitly by his Silence to own himself Guilty; or where a Man accused of any such Crime, upon hearing that a Warrant is taken out against him, doth abscond.

Sect. 14. 6. The being [i] pursued by an Hue and Cry.

Sect. 15. As to the second Particular, *viz.* By whom the Person must be suspected, upon such an Arrest for Suspicion; it seems to be [k] agreed, That the Law hath so tender a Regard to the Liberty and Reputation of every Person, that no Causes of Suspicion whatsoever, let the Number and Probability of them be never so great, will justify the Arrest of an innocent Man, by one who is not himself induced by them to suspect him to be guilty, whether he make such Arrest of his own Head, or in Obedience to the Commands of a private Person, or even of a [l] Constable.

Sect. 16. As to the third Particular, *viz.* Whether any such Cause of Suspicion will justify an Arrest where no Treason or Felony at all hath been committed, or dangerous Wound given: It is holden in some [m] Books, That none of the abovementioned Causes will in any Case justify the arresting a Man for the Suspicion of a Crime, where in Truth no such Crime hath been committed either by him or any other Person whatsoever. But howsoever this Rule may in general be true, it seems very hardly maintainable in the Case of the Arrest of an innocent Person upon a Hue and Cry levied against him, in such a Place where his Character is unknown, and with such other Circumstances, that the People of the Country have no Reason to presume it groundless; for in such Cases, it would be a great Inconvenience to discourage Persons from following a Hue and Cry, with that Vigour and Diligence, which the Law expects, and the Publick Good requires, by making them liable to an Action if it should in the Event prove to have been levied without sufficient Cause, which they cannot take Time to examine without delaying their Pursuit: And since the Person injured by such an ill-grounded Hue and Cry, has a good Action against him that raised it, there seems to be no Necessity, that he should also have a Remedy against another. And this Opinion seems to be the more plausible, for that among the [n] Books [o] cited to maintain the contrary, [p] that which alone doth directly affirm it, seems to go upon an Argument manifestly inconclusive; for it says, That an Hue and Cry is not a sufficient Authority to arrest a Man unless a Felony be done, because the Words of

[a] 2 H. 7. 15. b. 16. 5 H. 7. 4. b. 5. a. 11 E. 4. 4. b. Dy. 236. p. 26. Bridg. 62. 7 E. 4. 20. a. H. P. C. 91. Keilw. 81. Pult. 13. a.
[b] 2 Inst. 52. Crom. 98, 99. S. P. C. 97. Bracton 143.
[c] 7 E. 4. 20. a. 17 E. 4. 5. b. H. P. C. 91. Poult. 13. b.
[d] 7 E. 4. 20. a. Keilw. 71. Poult. 13. a. H. P. C. 91.
[e] 2 Inst. 52. Crompt. 98.
[f] 11 E. 4. 4. b. 12 Co. 92.
[g] 7 E. 4. 20. a. Cro. E. 901. Cro. Jac. 190, 191. Pult. 136. H. P. C. 91. 12 Co. 92. Moor 600. pl. 828.
[h] Crom. 98, 99. Fitz. Cor. 24.
[i] 29 El. 871. 29 E. 3. 39. Fitz. Tresp. 252. 5 H. 7. 5. a. 21 H. 7. 28. a. H. P. C. 91.
[k] 10 H. 7. 17. b. 2 H. 7. 15. b. 16. a. 5 H. 7. 4. b. 5. a. 7 Ed. 4. 20. a. 20 E. 4. 6. b. 11 E. 4. 4. b. Cro. El. 871. H. P. C. 93. 12 Co. 92.
[l] 10 H. 7. 17. b. 2 H. 7. 15. b. 16. a. 17 E. 4. 5. a. b.
[m] 2 Inst. 173. Cro. Jac. 194. H. P. C. 91. 2 H. 7. 3. a. 27 H. 8. 23. a. 8 E. 4. 3. b. 3 Inst. 118. b. Fitz. Tresp. 252. 29 E. 3. 39. 2 Rol. Abr. 559. D.
[n] 29 E. 3. 39. 11 E. 4. 4. b. 2 H. 7. 15.
[o] 2 Inst. 173.
[p] 5 H. 7. 5. a.

the Statute of *Westminster* 1. *cap.* 9. are, That all Men shall be ready upon Hue and Cry to arrest Felons; but where no Felony is done, there can be no Felon, *&c.* to which it may be replied, That this Argument, if it prove any Thing, proves that none but Felons can be arrested on a Hue and Cry, which seems to be manifestly false; for it is agreed by all the Books, That if a Felony be actually committed, an innocent Person on whom a Hue and Cry for it is levied, may lawfully be arrested: Also there seems to be no Doubt, but that he who barely attempts to rob a Man, or who dangerously wounds him, may safely be pursued and taken by a Hue and Cry, and yet there is no Pretence to call such a Person a Felon. Vide supra Sect. 4, 5.

Sect. 17. And if it be granted lawful to arrest a Man on a Hue and Cry where no Felony hath been committed; from the like Grounds it seems also to follow, That it is lawful to arrest a Man on the Warrant of a Justice of Peace, where no Felony hath been committed; but this Point shall be more fully considered in the next Chapter.

Sect. 18. As to the fourth Particular, *viz.* In what Manner an Arrest for such Suspicion is to be justified in Pleading; it seems to be certain, That whoever would justify the Arrest of an innocent Person, by Reason of any such Suspicion, must not only shew that he suspected the Party [a] himself, but must also set forth the [b] Cause which induced him to have such a Suspicion, that it may appear to the Court to have been a sufficient Ground for his Proceeding: Also it seems [c] certain, That regularly he ought expresly to shew, that the very same Crime for which he made the Arrest, was actually committed. But [d] if a Man have several Causes of such Suspicion, he is not bound to insist upon some one of them only, but may alledge them all; for that the Replication *De son tort demesne*, answers the whole. And [e] where a Man arrests another, who is actually guilty of the Crime for which he is arrested, it seems, That he needs not in justifying it, set forth any special Cause of his Suspicion, but may say in general, that the Party feloniously did such a Fact, for which he arrested him, *&c.*

[a] Vide supra Sect. 15.
[b] 2 Inst. 52. Finch 340. 17 E. 4. 5. a. b. 1 E. 4. 20. a. Bridgm. 62. 7 H. 4. 35.
[c] 8 E. 4. 3. b. 27 H. 8. 23 a. Cro. Jac. 194. Finch 340.
[d] 7 E. 4. 20. a. 17 E 4. 5. a. b. Bridgm. 62. Finch 394. 4 H. 7. 1. b. 2. a.
[e] 10 E. 4. 17. b. Fitz. Faux Imprisonm. 5.

Sect. 19. As to the arresting of Offenders by private Persons of their own Authority, permitted by Law for the Prevention of Treason or Felony only intended to be done; it [f] seems, that any one may lawfully lay hold on another, whom he shall see upon the Point of committing a Treason or Felony, or doing any Act which would manifestly endanger the Life of another, and may detain him so long till it may reasonably be presumed, that he hath changed his Purpose; and upon this Ground it [g] seemeth to be the better Opinion, That not only a Constable, but any private Person, who shall see another expose an Infant in the Street, and refuse to take it away, may lawfully apprehend and detain him, till he shall consent to take Care of it.

[f] 9 E. 26. b. *See* B. 1 Ch. 60. Sect. 23.
[g] Popham 12. 13. Owen 98. Moor 284.

Sect. 20. As to the Arrest of Offenders by private Persons of their own Authority, permitted by Law, for inferior Offences; it [h] seems clear, That regularly no private Person can of his own Authority arrest another for a bare Breach of the Peace after it is over; for if an Officer cannot justify such an Arrest, without a Warrant from a Magistrate, surely *à fortiori*, a private Person cannot: Yet it is holden by [i] some, That any private Person may lawfully arrest a suspicious Night-walker, and detain him till he make it appear, that he is a Person of good Reputation. Also it hath been [k] adjudged, That any one may lawfully apprehend a common notorious Cheat, going about the Country with false Dice, and being actually caught playing with them, in order to have him before a Justice of Peace; for the publick Good requires the utmost Discouragement

[h] *See* B. 1. Ch. Ch. 63. Sect. 13, 14, 17.
[i] Latch. 173. 4 H. 7. 18 b. Poph. 208. *Quære* 4 H. 7. 1. b. 2. a. 5 H. 7. 5. a. 2 Inst. 52.
[k] 1 Jon. 249. Cro. Ca. 234. 2 Rol. Abr. 546. C. 2.

of all such Persons, and the restraining of private Persons from arresting them without a Warrant from a Magistrate, would often give them an Opportunity of escaping: And from the Reason of this Case it seems to follow, That the Arrest of any other Offenders by private Persons, for Offences in like Manner scandalous and prejudicial to the Publick, may be justified.

Cromp 147. 14 H 8. 16.2. *Sect.* 21. As to Arrests of such Offenders by private Persons, having a Warrant from a Justice of Peace permitted by Law, there is no Doubt but that where the Law authorizes Justices of Peace to direct their Warrants to such Persons, it doth implicitly authorize the Execution of them by them.

As to the third general Point of this Chapter, *viz.* In what Cases the Arrests of Offenders by private Persons are rewarded by Law, I shall give a short Account of the Statutes concerning this Matter, in Relation,

1. To Robbers in Highways.
2. To Counterfeiters and Clippers of the Coin.
3. To Shoplifters, and other Offenders of like Nature.
4. To Burglars and felonious Breakers of Houses.

Sect. 22. And first as to Robbers in Highways it is enacted by 4 & 5 *W. & M.* 8. *That whoever shall apprehend and take one or more Thief or Robber in any Highway or Road in* England *or* Wales, *and prosecute him or them till he or they be convicted of any Robbery, committed in or upon any Highway, Passage, Field, or open Place, shall receive from the Sheriff of the County where such Robbery and Conviction shall be, without paying any Fee for the same, for every such Offender so convicted* 40 l. *within one Month after such Conviction and Demand thereof made, by tendring a Certificate to the said Sheriff under the Hand or Hands of the Judge or Justices before whom such Felon or Felons shall be convicted; and in Case any Dispute shall arise, between the Persons so apprehending any the said Thieves and Robbers touching their Right to the said Reward, That then the said Judge or Justices so respectively certifying, shall by their said Certificate direct and appoint the said Reward to be paid in such Shares and Proportions as to them shall seem just and reasonable. And if any such Sheriff shall die or be removed before the Expiration of one Month after such Conviction and Demand made, That then the next Sheriff shall pay the same within one Month after Demand and Certificate brought as aforesaid: And the Sheriff making Default in paying the said Sum, shall forfeit double as much.*

Sect. 23. And it is farther enacted, *That if any Person shall be killed by any such Robber in endeavouring to apprehend, or making Pursuit after him, the Executors or Administrators,* &c. *of such Person, shall receive* 40 l. *from the Sheriff,* &c. *upon Certificate delivered under the Hands and Seals of the Judge or Justices of Assize for the County where the Fact was done, or the two next Justices of the Peace, of such Person being so killed, which Certificate the said Judge or Justices, upon sufficient Proof before them made, are immediately required to give without Fee or Reward.*

Sect. 24. And it is farther enacted, *That every Person who shall so take, apprehend, prosecute, or convict such Robber as aforesaid, shall have as a farther Reward, the Horse, Furniture and Arms, Money and other Goods of such Robber, that shall be taken with him; any their Majesties Right or Title, Bodies Politick or Corporate, or the Right or Title thereunto of the Lord of any Manor or Franchise, or of him or them lending or letting the same to Hire to any such Robber notwithstanding: Provided, That this shall not be extended to take away the Right of any Person to such Horses, Furniture, and Arms, Money or other Goods, from whom the same were before feloniously taken.*

Sect. 25. Secondly, As to Counterfeiters and Clippers of the Coin, it is enacted by 6 & 7 *Gul.* 3. 17. *That whoever shall apprehend any Person who shall counterfeit any of the current Coin of this Realm, or for Lucre clip, wash, file, or otherwise diminish the same, or shall cause to be brought into the Kingdom any clipt, false, or counterfeit Coin, and prosecute such Person to Conviction, shall have from the Sheriff of the County where such Conviction shall be, forty Pounds upon the Judge's Certificate,* &c.

Sect. 26. Thirdly, As to Shoplifters, *&c.* it is enacted by 10 & 11 *W.* 3. 23. *That whosoever shall take and prosecute to Conviction, any Person who by Night or Day, shall in any Shop, Warehouse, Coach-house or Stable, privately and feloniously steal any Goods, Wares, or Merchandizes, of the Value of* 5 s. (*though such Shop,* &c. *were not broken, and though no Person were in such Shop,* &c.) *or shall assist, hire, or command any Person to commit such Offence, shall have a Certificate thereof* Gratis *from the Judge or Justices, expressing the Parish or Place where such Felony was committed; and if any Dispute shall happen about the Right to such Certificate, the Judge or Justices shall direct and appoint the said Certificate into so many Shares, to be divided among the Persons therein concerned, as to the said Judge,* &c. *shall seem reasonable, which Certificate (before any Benefit has been made of it) may be once assigned over, and no more, and the original Proprietor or Assignee shall by Virtue thereof, be discharged from all Parish and Ward Offices, within the Parish or Ward wherein the Felony was committed; and the said Certificate shall be enrolled by the Clerk of the Peace of the County, for the Fee of one Shilling: And in Case any Person happen to be slain by any such Felons by endeavouring to apprehend them, his Executors,* &c. *shall have the like Reward,* &c.

Sect. 27. Fourthly, As to Burglars and felonious Breakers of Houses, it is enacted by 5 *Annæ* 31. *That every Person who shall take any one guilty of Burglary, or the felonious breaking and entring any House in the Day-time, and prosecute them to Conviction, shall receive above the Reward given by the abovementioned Statute of* 10 & 11 W. 3. *the Sum of* 40 l. *within one Month after such Conviction*; concerning which the same Rules in Effect are prescribed, as are provided by the abovementioned Statute of 4 & 5 *W.* 3. 8. concerning the Reward of 40 *l.* to be paid to those who shall apprehend a Highway-man.

CHAP. XIII.

Of Arrests by publick Officers.

ARRESTS of Offenders by publick Officers, are either by Vertue of Process from some Court of Record, or without such Process.

Arrests of this Kind by Vertue of such Process, shall be considered hereafter in their proper Place.

Arrests by publick Officers without such Process, are either

1. By Watchmen.
2. By Constables.
3. By Bailiffs of Towns, or
4. By Justices of Peace.

Sect. 1.

Sect. 1. But before I consider the Nature of each of these in particular, I shall take it for granted, That where-ever any such Arrest may be justified by a private Person, in every such Case, *a fortiori* it may be justified by any such Officer. As to Arrests by Watchmen, I shall first premise in what Manner Watch is to be kept in every Town, and then shall shew the Power of the Watchmen.

Sect. 2. And first as to the keeping Watch in every Town, it is enacted by the Statute of *Winchester*, Ch. 4. *That from thenceforth all Towns be kept as it had been used in Times passed, That is to wit, from the Day of* Ascension *unto the Day of* St. Michael, *in every City six Men shall keep at every Gate, in every Borough twelve Men, in every Town six or four, according to the Number of Inhabitants of the Town, and shall watch the Town continually all Night, from the Sun-setting to the Sun-rising.*

Sect. 3. And it farther enacted by 5 *H.* 4. 3. *That the Watch to be made upon the Sea-Coasts through the Realm, shall be made by the Number of the People in the Places, and in Manner and Form as they were wont to be made in Times past, and that in the same Case the Statute of* Winchester *be observed and kept; and that in the Commissions of the Peace this Article be put in, That the Justices of Peace have Power thereof to make Inquiry in their Sessions from Time to Time, and to punish them which be found in Default after the Tenor of the said Statute.*

Sect. 4. It hath been resolved, That a Stranger who is not an Inhabitant of a Town, [a] cannot be compelled by Vertue of the said Statute of *Winchester* to keep Watch in it; but it seems to be agreed, That every Inhabitant is bound to keep it in his Turn, or to [b] find another sufficient Person to keep it for him; from whence it follows, That he is indictable for a Refusal: But it is [c] not agreed, That he may be committed by the Constable till he consent to do his Duty.

[a] Cro. El. 204.

[b] Vide Co. Lit. 70. a.

[c] Cro. El. 204.

Sect. 5. As to the Power of Watchmen, it is farther enacted by the said Statute of *Winchester*, Ch. 4. *That if any Stranger do pass by the Watch, he shall be arrested until Morning. And if no Suspicion be found, he shall go quit; and if they find Cause of Suspicion, they shall forthwith deliver him to the Sheriff, and the Sheriff may receive him without Damage, and shall keep him safely until he be acquitted in due Manner. And if they will not obey the Arrest, they shall levy Hue and Cry upon them, and such as keep the Town shall follow with Hue and Cry with all the Town and the Towns near, and so Hue and Cry shall be made from Town to Town, until that they be taken, and delivered to the Sheriff as before is said: And for the Arrestments of such Strangers none shall be punished.*

Poph 208. Latch. 173. *Sect.* 6. It is holden, That this Statute was made in Affirmance of the Common Law, and that every private Person may by the Common Law arrest any suspicious Night-walker, and detain him till he give a good Account of himself, as hath been more fully shewn in the precedent Chapter, Section 20.

Secondly, As to such Arrests by Constables, I shall endeavour to shew,

1. How far they may be justified by their own Authority.
2. How far by Vertue of a Warrant from a Justice of Peace.

Sect. And first, As to the justifying of such Arrests by the Constable's own Authority; it seems difficult to find any Case, wherein a Constable is impowered to arrest a Man for a Felony committed or attempted, in which a private Person might not as well be justified in doing it: But the chief Difference between the Power and Duty of a Constable and a private Person in Respect of such Arrests seems to be this, That the [a] former has the greater Authority to demand the Assistance of others, and is liable to the severer Fine for any Neglect of this Kind, and has no sure Way to discharge himself of the Arrest of any Person apprehended by him for Felony, [b] without bringing him before a Justice of Peace in order to be examined, as shall be more fully shewn in the 16th Chapter, whereas a private Person having made such an Arrest, needs only to deliver his Prisoner into the Hands of the Constable.

[a] 3 Inst. 158. Lamb. Constable 12. 17 E. 4. 5. a. b. 3 H. 7. 1. a. 2 H. 7 15. b.
[b] H. P. C. 91, 112. 10 E. 4. 17. b.

Sect. 8. But it is said, That a Constable hath Authority not only to arrest those whom he shall see actually engaged in an Affray, but also to detain them till they find Sureties of the Peace, as hath been more fully shewn in the [c] first Book; whereas a private Person seems to have no other Power in a bare Affray, not attended with the Danger of Life, but only to stay the [d] Affrayers till the Heat be over, and then deliver them to the Constable, and also to stop those whom he shall see coming to join either Party: But it is difficult to find any Instance wherein a Constable hath any greater Power than a private Person over a Breach of the Peace out of his View; and it seems clear, That he cannot justify an Arrest for any such Offence, without a Warrant from a Justice of Peace, *&c.*

[c] Ch. 63. Sect. 14, 17.
[d] B. 1. Ch 63. Sect. 11, 12.

Sect. 9. As to the justifying such Arrests by Constables, by Vertue of a Warrant from a Justice of Peace, it seems [e] clear, That such an Arrest unlawfully made by a Constable without a Warrant, cannot be made good by a Warrant taken out afterwards; also it hath been [f] holden, That if a Constable after he hath arrested the Party by Force of any such Warrant suffer him to go at large, upon his Promise to come again at such a Time and find Sureties, he cannot afterwards arrest him by Force of the same Warrant: However, if the Party return and put himself again under the Custody of the Constable, it seems, that it may be probably argued, That the Constable may lawfully detain him and bring him before the Justice in Pursuance of the Warrant; for if a Person taken by Vertue of a civil Process and voluntarily suffered by the Sheriff to escape, may afterwards upon his Return to the Prison be kept by the Sheriff by Vertue of the same Process, unless the Plaintiff rather chuse to take Advantage of the Escape against the Sheriff; surely *a fortiori* upon an Arrest for a Crime, in which Case it is to be presumed, that the Publick Good requires that the Party be brought to Justice, it shall likewise be lawful to detain a Person returning to the Officer after such an Escape: However as the Law seems [g] not to be settled in Relation to such an Escape after an Arrest by Vertue of civil Process; so neither doth it seem to be clear in Relation to an Escape after an Arrest by Force of such a Warrant from a Justice of Peace.

[e] Dy. 244. pl. 61. Fitz Bar. 248. Crompt. 149. a. 2 Keb. 705. Dalt. cap. 117. fol. 338.
[f] Cromp. 148. 2 Keb. 206. Dalt cap. 117. 13 E. 4 9. a.
[g] See 1 Danv. Abr. 633. pl. 4. 635. pl. 1 r. Hob. 202. 1 Lev. 21. Cro. Ca. 75. 2 Keb. 206.

Sect. 10. But it seems clear, That a Constable cannot justify any Arrest by [h] Force of a Warrant from a Justice of Peace, which expresly appears in the Face of it, to be for an Offence whereof a Justice of Peace hath no Jurisdiction, or to bring the [i] Party before him at a Place out of the County for which he is a Justice. But it seems, That he both may and ought to execute a general Warrant to bring a Person before a Justice of Peace, to answer such Matters as shall be objected against him on the Part of the King; for that the Officer ought to presume, That the Justice hath a Jurisdiction of the Matter, which he takes [k] Conusance of, unless the contrary appear; and it may often endanger the Escape of the Party to

[h] 14 H. 8 16. Crompt. 147, 148.
[i] Crompt. 149. b.
[k] Dalt. cap. 117.

make known the Crime he is accuſed of. But it ſeems to be very queſtionable, Whether a Conſtable can juſtify the Execution of a general Warrant to ſearch for Felons or ſtoln Goods, becauſe ſuch Warrant ſeems to be illegal in the very Face of it; for that it would be extreamly hard to leave it to the Diſcretion of a common Officer to arreſt what Perſons, and ſearch what Houſes he thinks fit: And if a Juſtice cannot legally grant a blank Warrant for the Arreſt of a ſingle Perſon, leaving it to the Party to fill it up, ſurely he cannot grant ſuch a general Warrant, which might have the Effect of a hundred blank Warrants.

Dalt. cap. 117. Crompt. 147, 148. Cro. Jac. 81. H. P. C. 93. 3 Inſt. 177. *Yet ſee a Precedent of this kind,* Dalt. 114. Dalt. cap. 117.

Sect. 11. Yet perhaps it is the better Opinion at this Day, That any Conſtable, or even private Perſon, to whom a Warrant ſhall be directed from a Juſtice of Peace to arreſt a particular Perſon for Felony, or any other Miſdemeanour within his Juriſdiction, may lawfully execute it, whether the Perſon mentioned in it be in Truth guilty or innocent, and whether he were before indicted of the ſame Offence or not, and whether any Felony were in Truth committed or not; for however the Juſtice himſelf may be puniſhable for granting ſuch a Warrant without ſufficient Grounds, it is reaſonable that he alone be anſwerable for it, and not the Officer, who is not to examine or diſpute the Reaſonableneſs of his Proceeding; and therefore it ſeems that the old Books, (cited in the foregoing Chapter, Sect. 15, 16.) which ſay generally, That no one can juſtify an Arreſt upon a Suſpicion of Felony, unleſs he himſelf ſuſpect the Party, and unleſs the Felony were in Truth committed, ought to be intended only of Arreſts made by a Perſon of his own Head, or in Obedience to the Command of a Conſtable, or other ſuch like miniſterial Officer, and not of ſuch as are made in Purſuance of the Warrant of a Juſtice of Peace; for inaſmuch as it ſeems to have been the conſtant and allowed Practice of late, to make out Warrants on the Suſpicion of Felony, before any Indictment hath been found againſt the Perſon ſuſpected; and the ſame ſeems to be countenanced by 1 & 2 *Ph. & Mar.* 13. and 2 & 3 *Ph. & Mar.* 10. which direct in what Manner Perſons brought before Juſtices of Peace upon Suſpicion, ſhall be examined in order to their being committed or bailed; and ſince the ancient [a] Opinion, That a Juſtice of Peace cannot make out a Warrant againſt a Man for Felony, who has not been indicted before, hath been [b] contradicted by conſtant Experience; and ſince in the very ſame [c] Report in which this Rule is laid down, That a Juſtice of Peace cannot make a Warrant againſt a Perſon who has not been indicted; it ſeems nevertheleſs to be agreed, That ſuch a Warrant is a good Juſtification for the Officer; and ſince none of the [d] Books cited by Sir *Edward Coke* to maintain the contrary Opinion mention the Caſe of an Arreſt by force of a Warrant from a Juſtice of Peace, but generally relate only to Arreſts by private Perſons of their own Authority, or by the Command of a Conſtable; and ſince too the [e] Caſe, which is fulleſt to the Purpoſe, wherein it is reſolved, That an Arreſt of a Perſon by the Command of a Biſhop for ſaying, That he was not bound to pay Tithes, could not be juſtified by Force of the [f] Statute, which authorized Biſhops to arreſt Perſons for Hereſy, for which this Reaſon is given among others, That the Biſhop himſelf could not juſtify ſuch an Arreſt, and conſequently could not authorize another to make it; it may be anſwered, That the Reſolution in that Caſe doth not wholly depend upon this Reaſon, but rather perhaps upon theſe, that the Biſhop's Command was by Parol only, and not by Writing, and that the Statute gave him no Juriſdiction over Points not Heretical; and that the Power of impriſoning Perſons

Crompt. 147, 148. Dalt. Juſtice, cap. 118. 14 H 8. 16. *See* Ch. 12. Sect 15. Cont 4 Inſt. 177. H. P. C. 93, 94.

Dalt cap. 118, 121. 6 Mod. 179. Cro. E. 130. 1 Leon. 187.

[a] 4 Inſt. 177. 14 H. 8. 16. [b] 6 Mod. 179. [c] 14 H. 8. 16. Bro. Faux Impriſonment 33. [d] 2 H. 7. 3 pl. 9 15. pl. 1. 4 H. 7. 2. a. 5 H. 7. 4. 5. 10 H. 7. 17. 20 H. 7. 12. 7 E 4 20. 8 E. 4. 3. b. 9 E. 4. 26. b. 10 E. 4. 17 b. 11 E. 4. 4. b. 13 E. 4. 9. a. 17 E. 4. 5. 7 E. 4. 35. Dyer 236. [e] 10 H. 7. 17. [f] 2 H. 4. ch. 15.

Persons for meer Matters of Opinion ought to be strictly construed: And farther, since the Party injured by an Arrest on a Justice's Warrant, hath a good Action against the Justice who granted it, if he did it maliciously of his own Head, in order to oppress or defame the Party, without any probable Ground of Suspicion; and therefore there is no Necessity of giving a farther Remedy against the Officer who obeys the Warrant: And farther, since it is in general a great Discouragement to Officers, to subject them to Actions for endeavouring to serve the Publick, by paying Obedience to the Precepts of those whose Officers they are; it would certainly be very difficult at this Day, to maintain an Action against them for any Arrest of this Kind, unless the Warrant appear to be for a Matter whereof the Justice has no Jurisdiction. It seems indeed to be holden in *Broucher*'s Case in *Croke*'s second Report, That where an Officer arrests a Man by Force of a Warrant from a Magistrate, *pro certis Causis*, without shewing any Cause in particular, he cannot justify himself in an Action brought against him for such Arrest, without setting forth the particular Cause in his Plea; and yet in this very Report it seems to be allowed, That such a general Warrant is good; and if so, it seems strange, That the Officer should not be justified by setting forth the Truth of his Case; since if there were no good Cause to justify the granting of the Warrant, the Magistrate ought to answer for it, not the Officer.

Cro. El. 130. 1 Leon. 187.

Cro. Jac. 81.

Sect. 12. Thirdly, As to such Arrests by Bailiffs of Towns, it is enacted by the abovementioned Statute of *Winchester*, Ch. 4. *That in great Towns being walled, the Gates shall be closed from the Sun-setting until the Sun-rising, and that no Man do lodge in the Suburbs, nor in any Place out of the Town, from nine of the Clock until Day, without his Host will answer for him: And the Bailiffs of Towns every Week, or at the least every fifteenth Day, shall make Inquiry of all Persons being lodged in the Suburbs, or in foreign Places of the Towns; and if they do find any that have lodged or received any Strangers or suspicious Persons against the Peace, the Bailiffs shall do Right therein.* And surely it cannot be doubted, but that by Force hereof such Bailiffs may lawfully arrest and detain any such Stranger, being found under probable Circumstances of Suspicion, till he shall give a good Account of himself.

Sect. 13. Fourthly, As to such Arrests by Justices of Peace, I shall first take it for granted, That where-ever an Arrest of this Kind by a private Person, or inferior Officer acting of their own Authority, is either permitted or enjoined by the Law, in every such Case, *a fortiori*, such an Arrest by a Justice of Peace in Person, is also permitted or enjoined.

H. P. C. 93.

Arrests by the Command of Justices of Peace, as such, are either,

1. By Parol
2. By Warrant.

Sect. 14. And first, As to such Arrests by Parol, it seems, That any such Justice may lawfully by Word of Mouth, authorize any one to arrest another, who shall be guilty of any actual Breach of the Peace in his Presence, or shall be engaged in a Riot in his Absence, as hath been more fully shewn in the first Book, Ch. 65. S. 16.

Dalt. cap. 117.

As to such Arrests by the Warrant of a Justice of Peace, I shall endeavour to shew,

1. In what Cases a Warrant for such an Arrest may lawfully be made by such a Justice.
2. In what Form it ought to be made.
3. How it is to be executed.

As to the first Point, I shall consider,

1. For what Offences such a Warrant may be granted.
2. Upon what Evidence.

Sect. 15. And first as to the Offences for which such a Warrant may be granted, there seems to be no Doubt, but that it may be lawfully granted by any Justice of Peace for Treason, Felony or *Præmunire*, or any other Offence against the Peace, as hath been more fully shewn in the Chapter concerning *Justices of Peace*: Also it seems clear, That wherever a Statute gives to any one Justice of Peace a Jurisdiction over any Offence, or a Power to require any Person to do a certain Thing ordained by such Statute, it impliedly gives a Power to every such Justice to make out a Warrant to bring before him any Person accused of such Offence, or compellable to do the Thing ordained by such Statute; for it cannot but be intended, that a Statute giving a Person Jurisdiction over an Offence, doth mean also to give him the Power incident to all Courts, of compelling the Party to come before him. And it would be to little Purpose to authorize a Man to require another to do a Thing, if it were to be understood that the Person authorized had no Power to compel the Party to come before him.

Supra Ch. 8. Sect 33, 34. Dalt. cap. 117. 12 Co 130, 131.

Sect. 16. But it seems, That anciently no one Justice of Peace could legally make out a Warrant for an Offence against a Penal Statute, or other Misdemeanour, cognizable only by a Sessions of two or more Justices; for that one single Justice of Peace hath no Jurisdiction of such Offence, and regularly those only who have a Jurisdiction over a Cause can award Process concerning it. Yet the long, constant, universal, and uncontrolled Practice of Justices of Peace seems to have altered the Law in this particular, and to have given them an Authority in Relation to such Arrests, not now to be disputed.

Dalt. cap. 117. Bro. Peace 6. 6 Mod. 179.

Sect. 17. But I do not find any good Authority, That a Justice can justify sending a general Warrant to search all suspected Houses in general for stolen Goods, as hath been more fully shewn, *Sect.* 10.

H. P. C. 93. 4 Inst. 177. b.

Sect. 18. Secondly, As to the Evidence on which such a Warrant is to be granted, it seems probable, That the Practice of Justices of Peace in Relation to this Matter also, is now become a Law, and that any Justice of Peace may justify the granting of a Warrant for the Arrest of any Person upon strong Grounds of Suspicion for a Felony or other Misdemeanour, before any Indictment hath been found against him. Yet inasmuch as Justices of Peace claim this Power rather by Connivance, than any express Warrant of Law, and since the undue Execution of it may prove so highly prejudicial to the Reputation as well as the Liberty of the Party, a Justice of Peace cannot well be too tender in his Proceedings of this Kind, and seems to be punishable not only at the Suit of the King, but also of the Party grieved; if he grant any such Warrant groundlesly

6 Mod. 179. *Quære* Dalt. 117. Con. 14 H. 8. 16.

groundlesly and maliciously, without such a probable Cause, as might induce a candid and impartial Man to suspect the Party to be guilty. Cro. El. 130. 1 Leon. 187.

Sect. 19. And since both *Coke* and *Hale* seem to disapprove of such Warrants granted upon Suspicion, and the old Books seem generally to disallow all Arrests for the Suspicion of Felony made by any other Person whatsoever except the very Person who hath the Suspicion; it is certainly a safe Way of Proceeding for him, who hath the Suspicion to make the Arrest in his proper Person, and to get a Warrant from a Justice of Peace to the Constable to keep the Peace. 4 Inst. 177. H P C. 93. Supr. Sect. 10. Ch. 12. Sect. 15.

Sect. 20. And perhaps there may be this Difference between the Warrant of a Justice of Peace, for such Causes which he has not Authority to hear and determine as Judge without the Concurrence of others, and such Warrant for an Offence which he may so determine, without the Concurrence of any other: That in the former Case, inasmuch as he rather proceeds ministerially than judicially, if he act corruptly, he is liable to an Action at the Suit of the Party, as well as to an Information at the Suit of the King: But in the latter Case he is punishable only at the Suit of the King, for that regularly no Man is liable to an Action for what he doth as Judge. Cro. E. 130. 1 Leon. 187. 1 Danv. Abr. 179. pl. 1, 2, 6.

As to the second Point, *viz.* In what Form such a Warrant is to be made; I shall lay down the following Rules:

Sect. 21. 1. That [a] it ought to be under the Hand and Seal of the Justice who makes it out. [a] Dalt. cap. 117.

Sect. 22. 2. That it [b] ought to set forth the Year and Day wherein it is made, That in an Action brought upon an Arrest made by Vertue of it, it may appear to have been prior to such Arrest. 3 Inst. 76. 14 H. 8. 16. [b] Dalt. cap. 117.

Sect. 23. 3. That it is [c] safe, but perhaps not necessary, in the Body of the Warrant to shew the Place where it was made; yet it seems necessary to set forth the County in the Margin, at least if it be not set forth in the Body. *See the Precedents in* Dalt. cap. 121. [c] Dalt. cap. 117, 121. Lamb. 85 86.

Sect. 24. 4. That it may be made either in the Name of the King, or of the Justice himself, as appears from the Precedents above referred to. Crompt. 147. 232, &c.

Sect. 25. 5. [d] That if it be for the Peace or Good Behaviour, it is adviseable to set forth the special Cause upon which it is granted; but if it be for Treason or Felony, or other Offence of an enormous Nature, it is said, That it is not necessary to set it forth; and it seems to be rather discretionary, than necessary to set it forth in any Case. [d] Dalt. c. 117. Supra Sec. 10.

Sect. 26. 6. [a] That such a Warrant may be either general, to bring the Party before any Justice of Peace of the County, or special, to bring him before the Justice only who granted it. [a] Dalt. cap. 117. 1 Rol. Rep. 375. 5 Co. 59 b.

Sect. 27. 7. [b] That it may be directed to the Sheriff, Bailiff, Constable, or to any indifferent Person by Name, who is no Officer; for that the Justice may authorize any one to be his Officer, whom he pleases to make such, yet it is most advisable to direct it to the Constable of the Precinct wherein it is to be executed; [c] for that no other Constable, and *a fortiori* no private Person, is compellable to serve it. Bro. Peace 9. [b] Dalt. cap. 117. Cromp. 147. 14 H. 8. 16 Bro. Peace 6. Salk. 176. [c] Salk. 176.

As to the third Point, *viz.* In what Manner such Warrant is to be executed, I shall lay down the following Rules,

Sect. 28. 1. That a Bailiff or a Constable, if they be sworn and commonly known to be Officers, and act within their own Precincts,

8 E. 4. 14 a. 14 H. 7. 9. b. 6 Co. 54. 9 Co. 69.

need not ſhew their Warrant to the Party, notwithſtanding he demand the Sight of it, but that theſe and all other Perſons whatſoever making an Arreſt, ought to acquaint the Party with the Subſtance of their Warrants, and that all private Perſons to whom ſuch Warrants ſhall be directed, and even Officers if they be not ſworn and commonly known; and even theſe, if they act out of their own Precincts muſt ſhew their Warrants, if demanded.

Dalt. cap. 117. 8 E. 4. 14. a.

Sect. 29. 2. That the Sheriff having ſuch Warrant directed to him, may authorize others to execute it; but that every other Perſon to whom it is directed, muſt perſonally execute it; yet it ſeems, That any one may lawfully aſſiſt him.

Salk. 176.

Sect. 30. 3. That if a Warrant be generally directed to all Conſtables, no one can execute it out of his own Precinct; but if it be directed to a particular Conſtable by Name, he may execute it any where within the Juriſdiction of the Juſtice.

CHAP. XIV.

Where Doors may be broken open in Order to make an Arreſt.

Sect. 1. AND now I am to conſider in what Caſes it is lawful to break open Doors in order to apprehend Offenders; and to this Purpoſe I ſhall premiſe, That the Law doth never allow of ſuch *Extremities but in Caſes of Neceſſity; and therefore, That no one can juſtify the breaking open another's Doors to make an Arreſt, unleſs he firſt ſignify to thoſe in the Houſe the Cauſe of his coming, and requeſt them to give him Admittance.

* 27 Aſſ. 35. 4 Inſt. 177. 5 Co. 91, 92. Dalt. cap. 78. H. P. C. 90. Fitz. Execution 252.

Sect. 2. But where a Perſon authorized to arreſt another who is ſheltered in a Houſe, is denied quietly to enter into it, in order to take him; it ſeems generally to be agreed, That he may juſtify breaking open the Doors in the following Inſtances.

[a] 27 Aſſ. 35. 12 Co. 131. 4 Inſt. 131. [b] Moor 606, 668. [c] Dalt. cap. 78. Cromp. 170. b [d] Moor 606, 668. Cro. El. 908. Yelv. 28. Dalt. cap. 78. [e] 2 Jones 233, 234.

Sect. 3. 1. Upon a [a] *Capias* grounded on an Indictment for any Crime whatſoever, or upon a [b] *Capias* from the [c] King's Bench or Chancery, to compell a Man to find Sureties for the Peace or Good Behaviour, or even upon a Warrant from a Juſtice of Peace for ſuch Purpoſe.

Sect. 4. 2. Upon a [d] *Capias utlagatum*, or *Capias pro fine*, in any Action whatſoever.

Sect. 5. 3. Upon the [e] Warrant of a Juſtice of Peace, for the levying of a Forfeiture in Execution of a Judgment or Conviction for it grounded on any Statute which gives the whole, or but Part of ſuch Forfeiture to the King, and authorizes the Juſtice of the Peace to give ſuch Judgment or Conviction for it.

[f] Dalt. cap. 22 & 78. [g] H. P. C. 90, 93. Dalt. cap 78. 13 E. 4. 9. a. [h] 13 E. 3. 7. b.

Sect. 6. 4. Where a [f] Forcible Entry or Detainer is either found by Inquiſition before Juſtices of Peace, or appears upon their View.

Sect. 7. 5. [g] Where one known to have committed a Treaſon or Felony, or [h] to have given another a dangerous Wound, is purſued either with or without a Warrant, by a Conſtable or private Perſon: But where one lies under a probable Suſpicion only, and is not indicted, it ſeems the

3 better

better [a] Opinion at this Day, That no one can justify the breaking open Doors in Order to apprehend him.

Sect. 8. 6. Where an [b] Affray is made in an House in the View or Hearing of a Constable; or where those who have made an Affray in his Presence fly to a House, and are immediately pursued by him, and he is not suffered to enter; in order to suppress the Affray in the first Case, or to apprehend the Affrayers in either Case.

Sect. 9. 7. Where-ever a [c] Person is lawfully arrested for any Cause and afterwards escapes, and shelters himself in a House.

Sect. 10. Also it is enacted by 3 & 4 *Jac.* 1. Par. 35. *That upon any lawful Writ, Warrant, or Process, awarded to any Sheriff or other Officer, for the taking of any Popish Recusant, standing excommunicated for such Recusancy, it shall be lawful, if need be, to break open any House.*

Sect. 11. But it hath been resolved, That where Justices of Peace are by Vertue of a Statute, authorized to require Persons to come before them, to take certain Oaths prescribed by such Statute, the Officer cannot lawfully break open the Doors of the Persons who shall be named in any Warrant made in Pursuance of such Statute, in order to be brought before the Justices to take such Oath, because such Warrant is not grounded on a precedent Offence; neither doth it appear, That the Party either is or will be guilty of any: But it seems clear, That if an Officer enter into any House to serve any such Warrant, and the Doors of the House be locked upon him, being in such House, he or his Friends may justify breaking them open, in order to regain his Liberty; for that even in the Execution of Civil Process, the Law allows of the breaking open Doors in the like Circumstances.

[a] H P. C. 91. 4 Inst. 117. Con. 13 E. 9 a. B.o. Coron. 159. Dalt. cap. 78. Fitz Bar. 110.

[b] H. P. C. 134, 135. Cromp. 170. b. Dalt. cap. 78. Bro. Faux Imprisoment 6.

[c] 6 Mod. 173, 174.

Palm. 52, 53. Cro. Jac. 555.

CHAP. XV.

Of Bail.

Sect. 1. AND now I am to consider in what Manner, and in what Cases Offenders are to be bailed; as to which it is to be observed, That where-ever a Person is brought before a Justice of Peace upon an Accusation of Treason or Felony, he must be either bailed or committed, unless it manifestly appear that no such Crime was committed, or that the Cause for which alone the Party was suspected, was totally groundless; in which Cases only it is lawful to discharge him without Bail.

H. P. C. 98. Crompt. 154.

For the better understanding of the Nature of Bail, I shall consider the following Points:

1. The Nature of Bail and Mainprize in general.
2. What shall be said to be sufficient Bail.
3. The Offence of taking insufficient Bail.
4. The Offence of granting it where it ought to be denied.

5. The

5. The Offence of denying, delaying or obstructing it where it ought to be granted.
6. In what Cases it is grantable.
7. In what Form it is to be taken.
8. What shall forfeit the Recognizance.

And first, As to the Nature of Bail and Mainprise in general, I shall endeavour to shew,

1. In what Respects they agree.
2. In what they differ.

Sect. 2. As to the first Particular it seems, That the Words Bail and Mainprise, are often used promiscuously in our [a] Law-Books and [b] Acts of Parliament, as signifying one and the same Thing; and it is [c] certain, That Bail and Mainprise agree in this Notions that they save a Man from Imprisonment in the common Gaol, by his Friends undertaking for him before certain Persons for that Purpose authorized, that he shall appear at a certain Day, and answer the Crime with which he is charged, and be justified by the Law.

Sect. 3. As to the second Particular, The chief, if not the [d] only, Difference between Bail and Mainprise seems to be this, That a Man's Mainpernors are [e] barely his Sureties, and cannot justify the detaining or imprisoning of him themselves, in order to secure his Appearance: But that a Man's Bail are looked upon as his [f] Gaolers of his own choosing; and that the [g] Person bailed is in the Eye of the Law for many Purposes, esteemed to be as much in the Prison of the Court by which he is bailed, as if he were in the actual Custody of the proper Gaoler. But I do not find this Point clearly settled in Relation to any other Court besides the King's Bench, as hath been more fully shewn *Ch.* 6. *Sect.* 4. However it seems certain in every Bailment, That if the Party bailed be [h] suspected by his Bail as likely to deceive them, he may be detained by them, and enforced to appear according to the Condition of the Recognizance, or may be [i] brought by them before a Justice of Peace, by whom he shall be committed, unless he find new Sureties.

Sect. 4. As to the second Point, *viz.* What shall be said to be sufficient Bail, it seems to be [k] agreed, That no Person ought in any Case to be bailed for Felony by less than two; and it is [l] said to be the Practice of the King's Bench, not to admit any Person to bail upon a *Habeas Corpus* on a Commitment for Treason or Felony without four Sureties: Also [m] it seems to have been anciently an established Rule, That none under the Degree of Subsidy-men, should be admitted to bail any Person for a capital Crime: But the Manner of granting Taxes by Way of Subsidy having been of late for many Years disused, this Rule at present seems to be of little Use: But the only sure Way of proceeding in this Case, is to take Care that every one of the Bail be of Ability sufficient to answer the Sum in which they are bound, which [n] ought never to be less than forty Pounds for a capital Crime, but may be as much higher as the Justices in Discretion shall think fit to require, upon Consideration of the Ability and Quality of the Prisoner, and the Nature of the Offence: And if it shall seem doubtful, whether the Persons who offer themselves to be Sureties, be able to answer such Sum; it is [o] said, That the Person who is to take the Bail, may examine them on their Oaths concerning their Sufficiency: And if a Person who has Power to take Bail be so far imposed

[a] Dalt. cap. 114. Lamb. 340. 4 Inst. 180.
[b] 1 Rich. 3 3. 3 H. 7. 3. 1 & 2 Ph. & Ma. 13.
[c] H. P. C. 96. Dalt. cap 114.
[d] 4 Inst. 179, 180.
[e] Fitz Mainprise 12, 13. Bro Mainprise 89. Coke Bail & Mainprize, Ch. 3. *and the Books cited under Letter* f. g. h.
Cont. 4 H. 6. 8. pl. 21. 32 H. 6. 4. pl. 3.
[f] H. P. C. 98. Fitz. Mainprise 12, 13.
[g] S P C. 64 D. 21 H 7. 33 pl. 26. 22 H. 6 59. pl. 13. 39 H. 6. 27. pl. 39. 32 H. 6. 4. pl. 3. Supra Ch. 6. Sect. 4.
[h] Fitz. Mainprise 12, 13 Dalt. cap. 114. Brook Mainprise 99
[i] H. P. C 96. Dalt. cap. 114.
[k] H. P. C. 97. Dalt cap 114. *See* 10 Co 101.
[l] Style's Practical Register 110.
[m] Dalt cap. 70. & 114. H P. C. 97.
[n] Dalt. cap. 114. H. P C. 97.
[o] Dalt. cap. 114. Cromp. 194.

posed upon as to suffer a Prisoner to be bailed by insufficient Persons, it is said, That either he, or any other Person who hath Power to bail him, may require the Party to find better Sureties, and to enter into a new Recognizance with them, and may commit him on his Refusal, for that insufficient Sureties are as no Sureties. H. P. C. 96. Dalt. cap. 70. & 114.

Sect. 5. But Justices must take Care, That under pretence of demanding sufficient Surety, they do not make so excessive a Demand, as in effect amounts to a Denial of Bail; for this is looked on as a great Grievance, and is complained of as such by 1 *W & M. Sess.* 2. by which it is declared, *That Excessive Bail ought not to be required.*

Sect. 6. As to the third Point, *viz.* the Offence of taking insufficient Bail, it seems clear; That wherever a Sheriff, in pursuance of the Statute of *Westminster, cap.* 15. Or Justices of Peace in pursuance of the subsequent Statutes, grounded on the said Statute of *Westminster* 1. and set forth more at large in the following part of this Chapter, shall admit any Person to bail for Felony, with insufficient Sureties, who shall not afterwards appear according to the Condition of the Recognisance, the Justices of Assise may, by force of 27 *Ed.* 1. *chap.* 3. commonly called the Statute *de finibus levatis*, impose such Fine on such Sheriff or Justices of Peace, as to such Justices of Assise in their Discretion shall seem proper. But if a Prisoner, who is bailed by insufficient Sureties, do appear according to the Condition of the Recognisance, it seems that those who admitted him to bail are safe, inasmuch as the End of the Law is answered, and the Appearance of the Prisoner as effectually procured by such Sureties, as if they had been never so sufficient. Vide Supra. cap. 6. Sect. 10, 11, &c. Dalt. cap. 114. H. P. C. 97. Dalt. cap. 114. H. P. C. 97.

Sect. 7. As to the fourth point, *viz.* The Offence of granting Bail where it ought to be denied: There is no doubt but that the bailing of a Person who is not baileable by Law, is punishable either at Common Law, as a negligent Escape, as shall be more fully shewn in the Chapter concerning Escapes, or as an Offence against the several Statutes concerning Bail. S. P. C. 53. F. 77. A. 25 E. 3. 39. Pl. 22. Fitz. Eschape 4 Coron. 246. H. P. C. 97. 113.

Sect. 8. And first it is enacted by the Statute of *Westminster* 1. 15. *That if the Sheriff, or any other, let any go at large by Surety, that is not replevisable, if he be Sheriff, or Constable, or any other Bailiff of Fee, which hath keeping of Prisons, and be thereof attainted, he shall lose his Fee and Office for ever. And if the Under-Sheriff, Constable, or Bailiff of such as have Fee for keeping of Prisons, do it contrary to the Will of his Lord, or any other Bailiff being not of Fee, they shall have three Years Imprisonment, and make Fine at the King's Pleasure.*

Sect. 9. Also it is enacted by 27 *Ed.* 1. commonly called the Statute *de finibus levatis, cap.* 3. *That the Justices assigned to take Assises,* &c. *when they deliver the Gaols,* &c. *shall inquire if Sheriffs, or any other, have let out by Replevin Prisoners not replevisable, or have offended in any Thing contrary to the Form of the said Statute of* Westminster 1. *and whom they shall find Guilty they shall chasten and punish in all things, according to the Form of the said Statute.* Vide Supra. Chap. 6. Sect. 10, 11, &c.

Sect. 10. And it is farther enacted by 4 *Ed.* 3. 2. *That at the time of the Assignment of Keepers of the Peace, mention shall be made, that such as shall be indicted, or taken by them, shall not be let to Mainprise by the Sheriffs, nor by none other Ministers, if they be not mainpernable by Law; nor that none who are indicted shall be delivered but by the Common Law. And that the Justices assigned to deliver the Gaols, shall have Power to inquire of Sheriffs, Gaolers, and others, in whose Ward such Persons indicted shall be, if they make Deli-* Vide Supra. Cap. 6. Sect. 12, 13.

verance, or let to Mainprise, any so indicted, which be not mainpernable; and to punish the said Sheriffs, Gaolers, and others, if they do any thing against the said Act.

Sect. 11. And it is enacted by 1 & 2 *Ph. & Mar.* 13. *That no Justice or Justices of Peace, shall let to Bail or Mainprise any Person or Persons, which, for any Offence or Offences, by them, or any of them committed, be declared not to be replevised or bailed, or be forbidden to be replevised or bailed, by the abovementioned Statute of* Westminster *the* first, cap 15. *And that the Justices of Gaol-Delivery of the Place where such Justices of the Peace shall be guilty of such Offence, upon due Proof thereof, by Examination before them, shall for every such Offence set such Fine on every such Justice, as the same Justices of Gaol-Delivery shall think meet*, &c.

Sect. 12. It hath been resolved, That it is no Excuse for Justices of Peace admitting a Person to bail, who was in Truth committed for a Cause not bailable by Law, that they did not know that he was committed for such Cause; and that no other Cause of his Commitment was mentioned in his *Mittimus* but the Suspicion of Felony; for that they ought, at their Peril, to have informed themselves of the Cause for which the Party was committed, that they might be satisfied that he was bailable by Law.

Poph. 96. Dalt.cap.114.

Sect. 13. As to the fifth Point, *viz.* The Offence of denying, delaying, or obstructing Bail where it ought to be granted; this seems to be a Misdemeanour, not only by the Statute, but also by the Common Law, and punishable thereby as an Offence against the Liberty of the Subject, not only by Action at the Suit of the Party wrongfully imprisoned, but also by indictment at the Suit of the King.

Vide 14 H. 7. 7. Pl. 19. H. P. C. 97. Dalt.cap. 114

Sect. 14. But it seems clear, That he who has Power to bail another is not bound to demand of him to find his Sureties, and to forbear committing him 'till he shall refuse to find them; but may well justify his Commitment, unless the Party himself shall offer his Sureties.

H. P. C. 97. Dalt.cap. 114 14 H. 7. 10.a. Bro. Peace, 7. Mainprise, 39.

Sect. 15. The principal Statutes relating to this Offence, are the abovementioned Statute of *Westminster* 1. 15. and the Statute *de finibus, cap.* 3. and 31 *Car.* 2. *cap.* 2. commonly called the *Habeas Corpus* Act: By the first whereof it is enacted, *That if any withhold Prisoners replevisable, after that they have offered sufficient Surety, he shall pay a grievous Amerciament to the King. And if he take any Reward for the Deliverance of such, he shall pay double to the Prisoner, and also shall be in the great Mercy of the King.* And by the later of the said Statutes it is enacted, *That Justices of Assise shall inquire if Sheriffs, or any other, have offended in any thing contrary to the said Statute of* Westminster, *and whom they shall find Guilty they shall punish in all things according to the Form of the said Statute.*

Sect. 16. Also it is recited by the above mentioned Statute of 31 *Car.* 2. *That great Delays had been used by Sheriffs, Gaolers, and other Officers, to whose Custody the King's Subjects had been committed for criminal, or supposed criminal Matters; in making Return of Writs of* Habeas Corpus, *by standing out an* Alias *and* Pluries, *and sometimes more, and by other Shifts to avoid their yielding Obedience to such Writs, contrary to their Duty, and the known Laws of the Land, whereby many Subjects had been long detained in Prison, in such Cases where by Law they were bailable*, &c. And thereupon it is enacted, *That whensoever any Person shall bring any* Habeas Corpus *directed unto any Person whatsoever, for any Person in his Custody, and the said Writ shall be served upon the said Officer, or left at the Gaol or Prison with any of the Under-Officers, Under-Keepers, or Deputy of the said Officers or Keepers, that the said Officer or Officers, his or their Under-Officers, Under-Keepers, or Deputies, shall, within three Days after*

after such Service thereof (unless the Commitment were for Treason or Felony plainly and specially expressed in the Warrant of Commitment) upon Payment or Tender of the Charges of bringing the said Prisoner, to be ascertained by the Judge or Court that awarded the same, and endorsed on the said Writ, not exceeding 12 d. *per Mile, and on Security given by his own Bond, to pay the Charges of carrying back the Prisoner if he should be remanded, and that he will not make any Escape by the Way, make Return of such Writ, and bring, or cause to be brought, the Body of the Party so committed, or restrained, unto or before the Lord Chancellor, or Lord Keeper, or the Judges or Barons of the Court from which the said Writ shall issue, or such other Persons before whom the said Writ is made returnable, according to the Command thereof; and shall then likewise certify the true Causes of his Detainer or Imprisonment, unless the Commitment be in a Place beyond twenty Miles distance,* &c. *and if beyond the distance of twenty, and not above one hundred Miles, then within the Space of ten Days, and if beyond the Distance of one hundred Miles, then within the Space of twenty Days.*

Sect. 17. And it is further enacted, Par. 3. *That all such Writs shall be marked in this Manner,* Per Statutum tricesimo primo Caroli Secundi Regis; *and shall be signed by the Person that awards the same. And if any Person shall be, or stand committed or detained as aforesaid, for any Crime, unless for Treason or Felony, plainly expressed in the Warrant of Commitment, in the Vacation-time, it shall be lawful for such Person so committed or detained (other than Persons Convict, or in Execution by legal Process) or any one on his Behalf, to complain to the Lord Chancellor, or Lord Keeper, or any Justice of either Bench, or Baron of the Exchequer of the Degree of the Coif; and the said Lord Chancellor,* &c. *Justice or Baron, on view of the Copy of the Warrant of the Commitment, or otherwise on Oath that it was denied, are authorized and required, on Request in writing by such Person, or any in his Behalf, attested and subscribed by two Witnesses, who were present at the Delivery of the same, to grant an* Habeas Corpus *under the Seal of the Court whereof he shall be one of the Judges, to be directed to the Officer in whose Custody the Party shall be, returnable* immediate *before the said Lord Chancellor,* &c. *Justice or Baron; and on Service thereof as aforesaid, the Officer,* &c. *in whose Custody the Party is, shall within the times respectively before limited, bring him before the said Lord Chancellor, Justice or Baron before whom the said Writ is returnable; and in Case of his absence, before any other of them, with the Return of such Writ, and the true Causes of the Commitment and Detainer. And thereupon, within two Days after the Party shall be brought before them, the said Lord Chancellor, Justice or Baron, before whom the Prisoner shall be brought as aforesaid, shall discharge the said Prisoner from his Imprisonment; taking his Recognizance, with one or more Sureties, in any Sum according to their Discretions, having Regard to the Quality of the Prisoner and Nature of the Offence, for his Appearance in the King's Bench the Term following, or in such other Court wherein the Offence is properly cognisable, as the Case shall require; and then shall certify the said Writ with the Return thereof, and the Recognisance, into such Court; unless it be made appear to the said Lord Chancellor,* &c. *that the Party so committed is detained upon a Legal Process, Order or Warrant, out of some Court that hath Jurisdiction of criminal Matters; or by some Warrant signed and sealed with the Hand and Seal of any of the said Justices or Barons, or some Justice or Justices of the Peace, for such Matters or Offences, for the which by Law the Prisoner is not bailable.*

Sect. 18. But it is provided, Par. 4. *That if any Person shall have willfully neglected by the space of two whole Terms after his Imprisonment, to pray a* Habeas Corpus *for his Enlargment, he shall not have a* Habeas Corpus *to be granted in Vacation-time, in Pursuance of this Act.*

Sect. 19. And it is farther enacted, Par. 5. *That if any Officer,* &c *shall neglect or refuse to make the Returns aforesaid, or to bring the Body of the Prisoner according to the Command of the said Writ, within the respective Times aforesaid, or shall not within six Hours after Demand deliver a true Copy of the Commitment,* &c. *he shall forfeit for the first Offence* 100 l. *for the second* 200 l. *and be made uncapable to hold his Office,* &c.

Sect. 20. And it is farther enacted, Par. 6. *That no Person who shall be set at large upon any* Habeas Corpus, *shall be again imprisoned for the same Offence by any Person whatsoever, other than by the legal Order and Process of such Court wherein he shall be bound by Recognisance to appear, or other Court having Jurisdiction of the Cause, on pain of* 500 l.

Sect. 21. And it is farther enacted, Par. 7. *That if any Person who shall be committed for Treason or Felony, plainly and specially expressed in the Warrant of Commitment; upon his Prayer or Petition in open Court the first Week of the Term, or the first Day of the Sessions of Oyer and Terminer, or general Gaol-Delivery, to be brought to his Trial, shall not be indicted some time in the next Term, Sessions of Oyer and Terminer, or general Gaol-Delivery after such Commitment, the Justices of the said Courts shall, upon Motion in open Court, the last Day of the Term, or Sessions, set at Liberty the Prisoner upon Bail; unless it appear upon Oath, that the Witnesses for the King could not be produced the same Term,* &c. *And if such Prisoner, upon his Prayer,* &c. *shall not be indicted and tried the second Term, or Sessions, he shall be discharged from his Imprisonment.*

Sect. 22. And it is farther enacted, Par 10. *That it shall be lawful for any Prisoner, as aforesaid, to move and obtain his* Habeas Corpus *as well out of the Chancery or Exchequer, as the King's Bench or Common Pleas: And if the said Lord Chancellor or Lord Keeper, or any Judge or Judges, Baron or Barons for the time being, of the degree of the Coif, of any of the Courts aforesaid, in the Vacation-time, upon View of the Copy of a Warrant of Commitment or Detainer, or on Oath made that such Copy was denied, shall deny any Writ of* Habeas Corpus, *by this Act required to be granted, being moved for as aforesaid, they shall severally forfeit to the Party grieved, the Sum of* 500 l.

Sect. 23. But it is provided, Par. 18. *That after the Assises proclaimed for that County where the Prisoner is detained, no Person shall be removed from the common Gaol upon any* Habeas Corpus *granted in pursuance of this Act; but upon such* Habeas Corpus *shall be brought before the Judge of Assise in open Court, who thereupon shall do what to Justice shall appertain.* But it is provided nevertheless, Par. 19. *That after the Assises are ended, any Person detained may have his* Habeas Corpus *according to the Direction of this Act.*

Sect. 24. It is observable, that this Statute makes the Judges liable to an Action at the Suit of the Party grieved in one Case only, which is the refusing to award a *Habeas Corpus* in Vacation-time; and seems to leave it to their Discretion in all other Cases, to pursue its Directions in the same manner as they ought to execute all other Laws, without making them subject to the Action of the Party, or to any other express Penalty or Forfeiture: And this is most agreeable to the general Reason of the Law, which regularly will not suffer a Judge to be liable to an Action for what he does as Judge.

B. 1. ch. 72. S. 6. & B. 2. ch. 1. S. 17.

As to the fifth Point, *viz.* In what Cases Bail is grantable, I shall endeavour to shew,

1. Where it is grantable by a Sheriff.
2. Where by a Justice of Peace.
3. Where by Justices of Gaol-Delivery.
4. Where by the Courts of *Westminster* Hall.

As

As to the first Point, I shall first consider, where Bail is grantable by a Sheriff *ex officio*; and secondly, where by Virtue of a Writ.

Sect. 25. As to the first Particular, it is holden [a] by some, That by the Common Law the Sheriff might, by Vertue of his Office, as principal Conservator of the Peace, bail any Person arrested on Suspicion of Felony or for any other Offence which is bailable.

Sect. 26. Also it hath been holden, [b] that a Constable had the like Power by the Common Law: And it may [c] probably be inferred from the Recitals of the Writs of Mainprize in the Register, That by the Common Law the Sheriff had Power to bail Persons indicted of Larceny [d] in a Court Leet, and also Persons indicted as [d] Accessories to a Felony, and Persons appealed by [e] Approvers, after the Death of the Approvers, *&c.* But it seems that the Sheriff [f] had no Power *ex officio*, to bail any Person indicted of any Crime before Justices of Peace. And it is certain, [g] That neither the Sheriff, nor Constable, could, in any of the Cases abovementioned, take Bail by Recognisance, but only by Obligation. And some [h] have holden, That the Statutes which impower Justices of Peace to admit Persons to bail, on an Accusation of Felony, and particularly prescribe in what Manner they shall do it, have taken away all Power of this kind from the Sheriff and Constable; yet others seem to be of another Opinion, because the said Statutes are wholly in the Affirmative.

Sect. 27. But it seems certain, [i] That by the Common Law, the Sheriff might bail any Person who was indicted before him at his Torn, for Felony, or any other Crime that is bailable; because he might both award Process, and also give Judgment against the Person so indicted: And it is a general [k] Rule, That whosoever is Judge of the Offence, may bail the Offender. But it is holden, [l] that at this Day the Sheriff has lost this Power, by reason of 1 *Ed.* 4. *cap.* 2. set forth more at large *cap.* 10. *sect.* 74. by which it is enacted, That the Sheriff shall not proceed on any such Indictment, but shall remove it to the next Sessions of the Peace.

As to the second Particular, it seems, That Bail is grantable by a Sheriff by Vertue of the following Writs.

1. That of *Odio* & *Atia*.
2. That of Mainprize.
3. That of *Homine replegiando*.

Sect. 28. But having already, in *Book* 1. *Cap.* 29. *Sect.* 20 and 24. incidentally shewn the Nature of the first of these Writs, which seems to be in great Measure obsolete at this Day, I shall refer the Reader to what is there said concerning it.

Sect. 29. Secondly, Of the Writ of Mainprize little Notice is taken in the late Books; yet the Law relating to it seems to be still in Force in many Cases; and consequently in such Cases, those who are bailable, and have been refused the Benefit of Bail, may still by Vertue thereof be delivered out of Prison (upon their finding Sureties [m] to the Sheriff that they will appear and answer to the Crimes alledged against them, before the Justices in the Writ mentioned, *&c.*) as those [n] who are imprisoned for a slight Suspicion of Felony, or indicted of Larceny [o] before the Steward of a Leet, or of Trespass [p] before Justices of Peace, and many other [q] Persons, all which it will be needless to enumerate.

[a] Dalison 11. See the Preamble of 13 Ed. 1. Cap. 15. Register. 83. b. 269. S. P. C. 74. letter D. Fitz. coron. 297. contra 2 Inst. 190.
[b] Dalison. 11. Contra 2 Inst. 190.
[c] Register. 269 a.
[d] Register. 270.
[e] Register. 269. b.
[f] Register. 133. b. 270. b. 271. a. b.
[g] Supra. cap. 8. Sect. 4, 5. Dalison. 11.
[h] Dalison. 11.
[i] H. P. C. 106. 2 Inst. 190. Register. 269.
[k] Lamb. 342, 348. S. P. C. 74. Letter E. 2 Inst. 190.
[l] H. P. C. 106.
[m] Register. 269. 270.
[n] F. N. B. 250. b. Register. 269. a.
[o] F. N. B. 250. C. Register. 269. a. 2 Inst. 290.
[p] F. N. B. 250. G. 251. C. Register. 133. b. 270. b. 271. b.
[q] F. N. B. 250. 251. Register. 269, &c.

[a] H. P. C. 104. [b] 2 Inst. 190. *Sect.* 30. But as to that which is said in general, both by Sir *Matthew Hale* [a] and Sir *Edward Coke*, [b] in relation to this Matter, from which it may seem to have been the Opinion of those Authors, That no Writ of Mainprize is grantable at this Day; it may be answered, That this is to be understood [c] only of the Writ of Mainprize, for Persons indicted before the Sheriff in his Torn, in relation to whom he has no judicial Power at this Day, and consequently no Power to bail them *ex officio*; from whence it follows, That the Writ of Mainprize for such Persons, being grounded on a Suggestion that the Sheriff had unjustly refused before to admit them to bail, cannot now be proper, because he cannot be said to have unjustly refused to do a thing which he had no Power to do. But this can be no manner of Reason why the Writ of Mainprize should not be still grantable in other Cases.

[c] F. N. B. 250. A. 4 Inst. 182. Coke, Bail and Mainprise, cap. 10. Vide Supra. Cap. 10. S. 72, 74

F. N. B. 66, 67, 68. Register, 78, 79. *Sect.* 31. Thirdly, As to the Writ of *Homine replegiando*, there seems to be no doubt but that at the Common Law the Sheriff might deliver any Persons out of Prison by Vertue of this Writ, except in those special Cases mentioned in the Statute of *Westminster* 1. *cap.* 15. which is set forth more at large in the next Section: And if he had returned, that the Plaintiff had been eloigned out of the County by the Defendant, he might afterward, by Vertue of a *Capias in Withernam* against such Defendant, whether he were a Peer or Commoner, have taken and imprisoned him till the Plaintiff should be replevied. But the Writ of *Homine replegiando* has been much disused of late, in such Cases wherein Justices of Peace have been authorised to admit Persons to bail; yet whether the Statutes which gave such Authority to Justices of Peace, being wholly in the Affirmative, do take away the Sheriff's Power in the Cases mentioned in those Statutes, may deserve to be considered. However there can be no doubt but that in other Cases the Writ of *Homine replegiando*, and *Capias in Withernam*, are very proper and effectual Remedies.

Register, 79 a. F. N. B. 68 C.

Vide Supra. Section. 26

1 Syd. 210.

Sect. 32. But for the better understanding the Sheriff's Power in this Particular, I shall set down, and endeavour to explain so much of the said Statute of *Westminster* 1. *cap.* 15. as relates to it, which is enacted as followeth, *Forasmuch as Sheriffs, and others who have taken and kept in Prison Persons detected of Felony, and incontinent have let out by Replevin such as were not replevisable, and have kept in Prison such as were replevisable, because they would gain of the one Party, and grieve the other: And forasmuch as before this time it was not determined which Persons were replevisable, and which not; but only those that were taken for the Death of a Man, or by Commandment of the King, or of the Justices, or for the Forest: It is provided, and by the King Commanded, that such Prisoners as before were outlawed, and they which have abjured the Realm, Provors, and such as be taken with the Manner, and those which have broken the King's Prison, Thieves openly defamed and known, and such as be appealed by Provors, so long as the Provors be living (if they be not of good Name) and such as be taken for House burning feloniously done, or for false Money, or for Counterfeiting the King's Seal, or Persons excommunicate, taken at the Request of the Bishop, or for manifest Offences, or for Treason touching the King himself, shall be in no wise replevisable by the common Writ, nor without Writ: But such as be indicted of Larceny by Enquests taken before Sheriffs, or Bailiffs by their Office, or of light Suspicion, or for Petit Larceny, that amounteth not above the value of*
2 Inst. 190. *Twelve Pence, if they were not accused of some other Larceny aforetime, or accused of Receipt of Thieves or Felons, or of Commandment, or Force, or of Aid in*
2 Inst. 190. *Felony done, or accused of some other Trespass, for which one ought not to lose Life or Member, and a Man approved by a Provor, after the Death of the Provor (if*

he be no common Thief, nor defamed) ſhall be henceforth let out by ſufficient Surety, whereof the Sheriff will be anſwerable, and that without giving ought of their Goods.

For the better Expoſition hereof, I ſhall diſtinctly conſider,

1. That part of the Preamble which declares, what Perſons had always been agreed not to be repleviſable.
2. That part of the Purview which ſhews what other Perſons ſhall not be repleviſable.
3. That which ſhews what Perſons ſhall be repleviſable.

Of thoſe who by the Preamble are declared to have always been agreed to be irrepleviſable, there are four kinds.

1. *Thoſe who are taken for the Death of a Man.*
2. *Thoſe who are taken by the Commandment of the King.*
3. *Thoſe who are taken by the Commandment of the Juſtices.*
4. *Thoſe who are taken for the Foreſt.*

Sect. 33. As to the firſt of theſe Particulars, it is obſervable that the Statute declares generally, That thoſe impriſoned for the Death of a Man have always been taken to be irrepleviſable, without making any diſtinction between ſuch Homicide as is malicious, and that which happens by Miſadventure, or in Self-Defence. And it is further to be obſerved, that the Statute of *Glouceſter, cap.* 9. provides, *That where a Man kills another by Misfortune, or in his Defence, or in other Manner without Felony, he ſhall be put in Priſon 'till the next coming of the Juſtices in Eyre, or Juſtices aſſigned to the Gaol-Delivery,* &c. And agreeably hereto we find, That all Perſons in general, who are taken for the Death of a Man, are excepted out of the Writ [a] *de Homine replegiando:* And that even the Superior [b] Courts, which are not reſtrained by theſe Statutes, have yet been always cautious of bailing Perſons impriſoned for any Homicide, except in ſuch ſpecial Caſes as ſhall be ſet forth more at large in the following part of this Chapter. (2 Inſt. 186. 2 Inſt. 315. [a] Regiſter, 77. b. F.N.B. 66.E. [b] 25 Ed 3. 42. pl. 27.)

Sect. 34. Alſo it ſeems agreed, That Juſtices of Peace, who have Power at this Day to bail a Man arreſted for a light Suſpicion of Homicide, cannot Bail any ſuch Perſon for Manſlaughter, or even excuſable Homicide, if it manifeſtly appear that he was guilty of the Fact, let it be never ſo plain that it cannot amount to Murder, as ſhall be ſhewn more at large in the following Part of this Chapter. (41 Aſſ. pl. 14. 37 Aſſ. pl. 12. 29 Aſſ. 44. 1 Ro. Re. 268. 44 Ed 3. 38. pl. 34. 21 Ed. 4. 71. a.)

Sect. 35. And it is enacted by 3 *H.* 7. 1. *That if it happen, that any Perſon named as Principal, or Acceſſary, be acquitted of any Murder at the King's Suit, within the Year and Day, that then the ſame Juſtices before whom he is acquitted, ſhall not ſuffer him to go at large, but either remit him to Priſon, or bail him, after their Diſcretion, 'till the Year and Day be paſſed.*

Sect. 36. As to the ſecond Particular, *viz.* That concerning thoſe who are taken by the Commandment of the King, it ſeems, That the Words of the Statute concerning them are to be underſtood of ſuch only as are impriſoned either by the King's Perſonal Command, or by the Command of his Privy Council, which is looked upon to be as it were incorporated with him, and to ſpeak with his Mouth; and accordingly we find the exception in the Writ of *Homine replegiando,* relating to Perſons impriſoned by the King, thus expreſſed in the Regiſter, *Niſi capti ſunt per ſpeciale preceptum noſtrum*; by which it ſeems to be implied, That this Exception is (2 Inſt. 186, 187. S. P. C. 72. E. 1 Rol. Rep. 134. Dalt. cap. 114. Regiſter, 77. b.)

not

not to be applied generally to every Command whatſoever of the King: To which it may be added, That if it were to be underſtood in ſo large a Senſe, it would extend even to thoſe who are taken by a *Capias* in a Perſonal Action, for that every ſuch *Capias* is the Commandment of the King; but it ſeems certain, That a Defendant taken by ſuch a *Capias* is replevilable by the Common Law. But Perſons impriſoned by the ſpecial Command of the King, or of his Privy Council, are ſo far from being replevilable by the Sheriff, that they have formerly [a] been adjudged not to be bailable even by the Court of King's Bench: However, at this Day the Law is otherwiſe declared and ſettled by Parliament, as ſhall be ſhewn more at large in the following part of this Chapter.

S. P. C. 72. E.

[a] 1. And 298. 1 Rol. Rep. 134, 192, pl. 31, 32. 219. 1 Leon. 70. Bro Mainpriſe, 37. Contra Moor 839. 1. And 158.

Sect. 37. As to the third Particular, *viz.* That concerning Perſons impriſoned by the Command of the Juſtices, it is obſervable, that the Exception in the Writ of *Homine replegiando*, in the Regiſter,[b] concerning Perſons ſo impriſoned, is reſtrained to thoſe who are taken by the ſpecial Command of the King's Chief Juſtice. But by *Fitzherbert*[c] and *Staundford*,[d] *Coke*[e] and *Dalton*,[f] the Words of the Statute relating to Perſons ſo impriſoned, ſeem to be underſtood in a large Senſe, of any of the King's Juſtices in general, as of thoſe of Aſſiſe, as well as of thoſe of the Courts of *Weſtminſter* Hall. But it ſeems that they are not to be underſtood generally of Perſons impriſoned by any Command whatſoever of ſuch Juſtices, for that thoſe who are impriſoned by their ordinary Command, not by way of Puniſhment, but in order only to be ſafely kept, are ſaid to be replevilable by the Sheriff, in Caſes not prohibited by the Statute; and therefore it ſeems, That they muſt be taken in a more reſtrained Senſe, of thoſe only who are impriſoned by the abſolute Command of ſuch Juſtices by way of Puniſhment, as for a Miſdemenour done in their Preſence, or for other Contempts, or ſuch like Matters, which lie rather in their Diſcretion than in their ordinary Power; and it ſeems that a Commitment by the Chief Juſtice, without ſhewing any Cauſe whatſoever, ſhall be intended to be for ſome ſuch Matter; and there can be no doubt but that a Perſon under ſuch a Commitment is irreplevilable by the Sheriff. Alſo it hath been holden, That a Perſon ſo committed is not bailable upon a *Habeas Corpus*: But how far Perſons committed by the abſolute Command of one Court, are bailable by another, ſhall be more fully conſidered in the following Part of this Chapter.

[b] Regiſter, 77. b.
[c] F. N. B. 66 E.
[d] S. P. C. 73.
[e] 2 Inſt. 187.
[f] Dalt. cap. 114.

S. P. C. 73. Dalt. cap. 114. F. N. B. 251. B.

S. P. C. 73. Dalt. cap. 114. 24 Ed. 3. 33. pl. 25.

1 Rol. Rep. 131.

Sect. 38. As to the fourth Particular, *viz.* That concerning thoſe who are impriſoned for the Foreſt, who alſo are excepted out of the Writ [a] of *Homine replegiando*; it ſeemeth that the ſaid Exception is to be underſtood as well of Foreſts in the Hands of Subjects, [b] as of thoſe in the Hands of the King; but it ſeems, that it is to be underſtood ſtrictly of proper Foreſts only, and not to be extended [c] by Equity to Chaſes or Parks. And as to Impriſonments for Offences in Foreſts, the Law has been much mitigated by later Statutes; for it is recited by 1 *Ed.* 3. *cap.* 8. *That divers Perſons had been undone by the chief Keepers of Foreſts*, &c. *againſt the Form of the Great Charter* [d] *of the Foreſt, and againſt the Declaration* [e] *made by King* Edward 1. *by which he granted, That Treſpaſſes done, in his Foreſt, of Vert and Veniſon, ſhould be preſented at the next Swainmote, before the Foreſters*, &c. *and that ſuch Preſentments made before ſuch Foreſters*, &c. *ſhould by the Oaths of Knights, and other diſcreet and lawful Men*, &c. *by the common Aſſent of all the ſaid Miniſters, be ſolemnly written, and with their Seals enſealed: And that if any Indictment ſhould be in any other Manner made, that the ſame ſhould be void.* And thereupon it is ordained, *That from thenceforth no Man ſhall be taken nor impriſoned for Vert or Veniſon, unleſs he be taken with the Manner*,

[a] Regiſter, 77. b. 4 Inſt. 314.
[b] Vide 1 Inſt. 2. a. 233. a.
[c] Regiſter, 80. b. F. N. B. 67. d Vide Plowd. Com. 124. a.
[d] 9 H. 3. 10. & 16.
[e] 34 Ed. 1. commonly called, *Ordinatio Foreſtæ*.

 or

or else indicted after the Form before specified: And then the chief Warden shall let him to mainprise 'till the Eyre of the Forest, without any thing taken for his Deliverance, And if the said Warden will not so do, he shall have a [c] *Writ out of the Chancery,* &c. *to be at Mainprise 'till the Eyre. And if the Warden shall not obey such Writ, the Plaintiff shall have a* [f] *Writ to the Sheriff to attach the said Warden before the King, at a certain Day,* &c. *And the Sheriff (the Verders being called to him) shall deliver him that is so taken, by good Mainprise, in the Presence of the Verders, and shall deliver the Names of the Mainpernors to the same Verders, to answer in the Eyre before the Justices,* &c. And it is farther enacted, by 7 *R.* 2. 4. That *No Man shall be imprisoned by any Officer of the Forest without due Indictment, or being taken with the Manner, or trespassing in the Forest,* &c.

[c] F. N. B. 67. A. Register, 80. b.
[f] F. N. B. 67. B. Register, 80. b.

Sect. 39. And *Note*, That Persons so indicted, or taken with the Mannor, being imprison'd by such Officers, have their Election either to be mainprized by twelve Mainpernors, by Vertue of the Writ of *Homine replegiando*, given by the said Statute of 1 *Ed.* 3. 9. or to be bailed upon a *Habeas Corpus*, by the Judges of *Westminster* Hall, *&c.* And if a Person be imprisoned for any Offence relating to the Forest, without having been first indicted for it, or taken with the Manner, there seems to be no doubt but that he may have an Action of False Imprisonment, and may also be mainprised or bailed in the Manner abovementioned.

4 Inst. 290. Register, 80. b. F. N. B. 67. A. B. C.
45 Ed. 37 pl. 8. 4 Inst. 290. Register, 80. a. b.

And now I am to consider that part of the Purview of the above recited Statute of *Westminster*, 1. 15. which shews what other Persons are not replevisable, of which there are two Sorts.

1. Such as are excluded from the Benefit of a Replevin, in respect of the Notoriety of their Offence.
2. Such as are excluded from it in respect of the Hainousness of the Crime alledged against them.

Persons excluded from the Benefit of a Replevin, in respect of the Notoriety of their Offence, are of two kinds.

1. Those who by an express or implied Judgment, Sentence or Conviction, or their own Confession, appear to be Guilty.
2. Those who are under violent Presumptions of Guilt.

Sect. 40. And first, Of those who by Judgment, Sentence, Conviction or Confession, appear to be Guilty, some are excluded from the Benefit of a Replevin by the express Words of the Statute, as *Those who are outlawed, or have abjured the Realm*; *Persons excommunicate, taken at the request of the Bishop, and Provors.* And all other [a] Persons who are condemned, or convicted of Felony, or any other [b] heinous Crime whatsoever, whether by their own Confession, or by Verdict General or Special; [c] and also all those [d] who on their Examination own themselves guilty of a Felony alledged against them, and are charged in their *Mittimus* with the Felony so confessed, seem to be excluded from it by Parity of Reason, and the manifest Intent of the Statute; for [e] Bail is only proper where it stands indifferent whether the Party be Guilty or Innocent of the Accusation against him, as it often does before his Trial; but where that Indifferency is removed, it would, generally speaking, be absurd to bail him: And agreeably hereto the Statute of 2 *H.* 5. *cap.* 2. provides, even as to civil Causes, *That if upon a Writ of* Certiorari, *or* Corpus cum causa, *out of Chancery, it shall be returned that the Prisoner is condemned*

[a] S. P. L. 74. H. P. C. 101. Dalt. cap 114. 1 Rol. Rep. 268. 15 H. 7. 9. Pl. 8. Kelynge 90. 3 Bulst. 113, 114.
[b] Vide infra. S. 44.
[c] Dy. 179. pl. 42. 1 Bulst. 87, 88. 15 H. 7. 9. a.
[d] 3 Bulst. 114. 1 Rol. Rep. 268. 4 Inst. 178.
[e] 2 Inst. 188. Dyer 179. pl. 42. H. P. C. 100, 101.

condemned by judgment given against him, he shall be remanded, &c. Also 23 *H. 6. cap.* 10 which ordains, That Sheriffs, *&c.* shall let out of Prison Persons in their Custody by force of any Writ, *&c.* in Personal Actions, or on Indictments of Trespass, by sufficient Sureties, *&c.* expresly excepts *All such as shall be in their Ward by Condemnation, Execution,* &c. And therefore it cannot but be reasonable to intend, That the said Statute of *Westminster* 1. put the Cases of Persons outlawed and excommunicate as Examples only; meaning thereby to intimate, That all other Persons under the like Circumstances, should be in like manner irreplevisable: Yet it is certain, that the Court of King's Bench may, in their Discretion, in some special Cases, bail a Person upon an Outlawry of Felony; as [a] where he pleads that he is not of the same Name, and therefore not the same Person with him that was outlawed; or alledges [b] any other Error in the Proceedings. Also it seems, That the Court of King's Bench, or Justices of Gaol-Delivery, may bail [c] a Person convicted of Manslaughter, or, as some say, of any other Felony, for which he afterwards gets the King's Pardon. And [d] there seems to be no doubt at this Day, but that they may also bail any Person who is found guilty before them of Homicide in Self-defence, or by Misadventure. Also it is certain, That if a Person appear to be imprisoned for an Excommunication, in a Cause of which the Spiritual Court hath no Conusance, he may be delivered either upon a *Habeas Corpus,* or by quashing or superseding the Writ of *Excommunicato capiendo.*

See the Books above cited.
H. P. C. 101. S. P. C. 74. Letter A. 2 Inst. 188.
[a] 5 H. 7. 16. pl. 7.
[b] 19 H. 6. 2. a.
[c] Brook Mainprise. 94. H. P. C. 101. 105.
[d] H. P. C. 101. 105. F. N. B. 246. c. *Contra* Fitz. Coron. 297. 354. *Quære* S. P. L. 74. D.

Secondly, Of those who are under violent Presumptions of Guilt, and in that respect are excluded by the Statute from the Benefit of a Replevin, there are several kinds.

2 Inst. 188.

Sect. 41. I. *Those who are taken with the Manner* (or rather *Mainer,* that is, with the thing stolen, as it were, in their Hands) and by Parity of Reason, those who are taken freshly upon a Hue and Cry.

H. P. C. 101.
H. P. C. 101.

Sect. 42. II. *Those who have broken the King's Prison,* and by the same reason those who have broken any other Prison, which the Law presumes that no Innocent Person will do.

Vide cap. 18. S. 1 & 4. 2 Inst. 188.

Sect. 43. III. *Those who are appealed by Provors,* who regularly are not bailable, because the Approver, by confessing his own Guilt, induces a strong Presumption against those whom he accuses of the same Crime of which he owns himself guilty; yet by the express Words of the Statute, *If the Person appealed by an Approver be of good Reputation, he may be bailed, even in the Life of the Approver; and, unless he be a notorious Felon, he may be bailed after his Death.* And by Parity of Reason, he may also be bailed if the Approver waive [a] his Appeal, or be vanquished, [b] unless there be some other Cause to detain him in Prison, as the Appeal of some other Approver, *&c.* And if a Person disabled by Law to become an Approver, as one attainted, [c] *&c.* appeal another of High Treason, it seems that the Person so appealed ought to be bound [d] to his Good Behaviour towards the King: But [e] if such Person had appealed him of Felony only, it seems that he ought to have been wholly discharged, if there had been no other Accusation against him.

H. P. C. 102. 2 Inst. 188.
Register, 269. b.
[a] 25 Ed. 3. 42. pl. 27. H. P. C. 102. Fitz. Mainprise, 1. 2 Inst 288.
[b] 25 Ed. 3. 42. pl. 31. Fitz. Mainprise, 2.
[c] H. P. C. 192.
[d] Fitz. coron. 387.
[e] Bro. coron. 81. 211. 17 Ass. pl. 4. 11 Ass. pl. 27.

Sect. 44. IV. *Thieves openly known and notorious,* who, as it seems, ought not to be bailed for any fresh Felony, whereof there is probable Evidence against them. But how far Persons accused of any Crime, shall be so far esteemed likely to have committed it, from their former scandalous Behaviour, as to be presumed guilty upon slight Evidence, seems in great measure to be left to the Discretion [f] of the Person who hath Power to bail them; who, upon consideration of the Circumstances of the whole Matter,

[f] H. P. C. 102.

ter, and the Probabilities of both Sides, if he find it reasonable strongly to presume them to be guilty, ought not to bail but commit them.

Sect. 45. V. *Persons taken for open and manifest Offences*, which seems to be understood of inferior Crimes of an enormous Nature, under the degree of Felony, as dangerous Riots, [a] favouring of High Treason, [b] scandalous Extortions, Conspiracies, [c] by Justices, *&c.* violent and exorbitant Rescouses [d] of Persons arrested by vertue of the King's Writs, Misprision [e] of Treason, *Præmunire*, [f] Maim, and such like heinous Offences, whereof no one who is notoriously Guilty, seems to be bailable by the Intent of this Statute; for notwithstanding in the latter Part of it, it be said generally, That those who are accused of a Trespass, for which a Man shall not lose Life or Member, are replevisable; yet upon the Construction of the whole it seems reasonable to qualify the Generality of that Expression with this Limitation, that such Accusation ought to be either on a light Suspicion, or if it be on plain and unquestionable Evidence that the Offence ought to be inconsiderable, for if all Persons whatsoever shall be replevisable for Offences not touching Life or Member, let their Guilt be never so notorious, the abovementioned general unlimited Clause, that those who are taken for open Offences shall be irreplevisable, must be restrained to Felonies and Offences touching Member, which seems contrary to the most obvious reasonable Purport of it, and also to common Practice, and that allowed general Rule, That Bail is only then proper where it stands indifferent whether the Party were Guilty or Innocent; *sed quære.* Yet it seems to be in great measure left to the Discretion of the Person who has Power to admit others to bail, to judge in what Cases their Crime is so flagrant and enormous, that they ought not to have the Benefit of it.

[a] Dalt. cap. 114.
[b] Bro Mainprise 62. 42 Ass. pl. 5.
[c] Coke Bail & Mainprize, Ch. 5. 27 Ass. pl. 12.
[d] Keilw. 165. b. Fitz. Execution 147. 13 H. 7. 21. b. Rastal 380. pl. 6.
[e] H. P. C. 168.
[f] 6 H. 7. 1. b.
Supr. Sect 44.

Of those who are excluded by the Purview of the said Statute, from the benefit of a Replevin, in respect of the heinousness of the Crime alledged against them, there are four kinds.

1. *Those who are taken for Arson.*
2. *Those who are taken for false Money.*
3. *Those who are taken for falsifying the King's Seal.*
4. *Those who are taken for Treason, which touches the King himself.*

Sect. 46. And all such Persons being expresly declared to be irreplevisable, it seems clear, That they can in no Case be delivered out of Prison by the Sheriff, either by Vertue of the said Writ of *Homine replegiando*, or without it: Yet if a Person at large be accused before a Sheriff, on a light Suspicion of any of these, or of any other of the abovementioned Crimes, which always have been agreed to be irreplevisable, as of Homicide, *&c.* it seems by no means to follow either from the Words or Intention of the Statute, That the Sheriff is bound to keep him in Prison 'till he be delivered by due Course of Law; but in such a Case it seems to be more reasonable, that he take Surety of him to appear in a proper Court to answer such Accusation; for it seems extreamly harsh, and contrary to the first Principles of the Law, which favours nothing more than the Liberty of the Subject, to put an Officer under a Necessity of depriving a Man of his Liberty upon every Accusation of such a Crime, be it never so weakly grounded. And the Words of the Statute, declaring Persons to be irreplevisable for such Crimes, seem clearly applicable to such only as are under an actual Imprisonment, and not to those who are barely accused; for that none can be properly said

to

to be replevied, but those who being actually imprisoned, are, upon finding Pledges, delivered out of Custody; from which it follows, That Persons not imprisoned are not within the Statute: Nay, the Law is so far from obliging a Sheriff to imprison a Man on every Accusation whatsoever of such Crimes, that it subjects him, as well as any other Person, to an Action of False Imprisonment, if he does it without a reasonable Ground; as hath been more fully shewn in the Chapters concerning Arrests. But if a Person be actually under an Arrest, either of a Magistrate or private Person, for any of the abovementioned Crimes, it seems clear from the express Words of the Statute, that the Sheriff cannot replevy him; and it seems, that at the Common Law he ought to have safely detained the Party so arrested 'till he could have obtained his legal Deliverance, and that the Person so arrested had no Remedy but by Indictment or Action of False Imprisonment against those who arrested and delivered him to the Sheriff, on a groundless Suspicion. But how far the Law may at this Day be altered in this Point, by the universal and allowed Practice of Sheriffs receiving no Person into their Custody, for any Crime, without the Warrant of some Magistrate, shall be more fully considered in the next Chapter.

2 Inst. 185. 40 Ass. 33.

Sect. 47. It is certain, That the Court of King's Bench still may, and always might, bail Persons in Custody for any of these Crimes, notwithstanding this Statute; yet in Discretion it seldom uses this Power but in very special Cases, as shall be shewn in the following Part of this Chapter.

And now I am to consider that Part of the Purview of the said Statute, which shews what Persons are replevisable; for the better understanding whereof, I shall endeavour to explain.

1. The Branch relating to Persons accused as Principals.
2. That which concerns those who are charged as Accessories.

2 Inst. 190. S. P. C. 74. Letter C H. P. C. 106. Dalt cap 114. 29 Ass. pl. 44. 16 Ed. 4. 5. pl. 4. Coke Bail & Mainprise, cap. 5. Register 270. b. 271.

Sect. 48. As to the first Branch, First, *Those who are indicted of Larceny by Inquests taken before Sheriffs, or Bailiffs, by their Office,* that is, before Sheriffs in their Torns, and Lords in their Leets, are expresly declared to be replevisable; and according to some Opinions, those who are indicted, or appealed in any other Court, of any other Felony, not expresly declared by the Statute to be irreplevisable, as Robbery or Burglary, *&c.* are replevisable by the Sheriff, *ex officio,* without Writ, within the Equity of this Clause: Yet the Authorities which are brought to warrant this Opinion, relate only to the Bailment of Persons by superior Courts, upon Indictments or Appeals of such Crimes before such Courts, and do by no means prove that such Persons are replevisable by the Sheriff *ex officio,* without Writ: And it is observable, that the Writs of Mainprize in the Register, for Persons indicted only of Trespass, before Justices of Peace, expresly declare, That such Persons cannot be delivered out of Prison without the King's special Command; from whence it seems to follow, That such Persons are not within the common Benefit of a Replevin by the Sheriff, without some such special Command. And if Persons indicted of Trespass only, before Justices of Peace, are not within the ordinary Remedy of a Replevin by the Sheriff without a Writ, surely it cannot be thought, that Persons indicted of higher Crimes, and before Superior Courts, can be any way intituled to it: However, inasmuch as the said Statute of *Westminster* 1. expresly allows Persons indicted of

Larceny before the Sheriff the ordinary Remedy of a Replevin, and expressly excludes some other particular Felonies, and says nothing of others, it seems a reasonable Construction of the Statute, That the Sheriff might by Vertue of it, either with or without Writ, replevy those who were indicted before himself, or at a Court-Leet, of those other Felonies not expressly excepted, as well as those indicted of Larceny only. And the Statute leaving such a Latitude to the Sheriff in relation to the Persons so indicted before himself, or at a Court Leet, it hath been usual for superior Courts, (who though they be not within the Statute, have yet always had a great Regard to the Rules prescribed by it) to use the same Liberty in relation to such Crimes, and sometimes greater, for such special Reasons, and in such special Cases, as shall be set forth more at large in the following part of this Chapter. Yet notwithstanding the Statute seems generally to allow the Benefit of a Replevin to all those who are indicted of Larceny, *&c.* without any Limitation; yet it hath been always construed to intend only that such Persons indicted of a Grand Larceny, Register, 269. as are of a good Reputation, shall be replevisable; and therefore if there 2 Inst. 190. be strong Presumptions of their Guilt, it seems that they ought not to be H. P. C. 100. bailed; but this is in great Measure to be left to Discretion. 16 Ed. 4. 5. S. P. L. 74 c

Sect. 49. Secondly, *Those who are imprisoned for a light Suspicion*, are likewise declared by the Statute to be replevisable; yet notwithstanding the Words are general, it hath always been taken to be the Intent of Register, 83 b 269. them, That the Persons so imprisoned ought to be of a good Reputation: F. N. B. 250. c. Also it seems clear, That the Statute means only such Persons as are imprisoned for Crimes not expressly excepted by it from the Benefit of a Replevin; 2 Inst. 190. and therefore that this Branch cannot extend to Persons imprisoned for the Treasons mentioned in the Statute, Arson, or Homicide, but only to those taken for Larceny, Robbery, Burglary, and such like Felonies, *&c.*

Sect. 50. Thirdly, Those who are imprisoned *for Petit Larceny, which does not amount above the value of* 12 d. are also declared by the Statute to be replevisable, *if they have not been accused of some other Larceny before:* And it seems to be agreed, That there is no Necessity that such Persons 2 Inst 190. be of good Reputation; yet upon the Construction of the whole Statute, Register, 269. b if such Persons be taken with the Manner, or confess the Fact, *&c.* or F. N. B. 250. c. their Crime be otherwise open and manifest, it seems that they ought not to be bailed; but if there be any Colour of Probability for their Innocence, Vide Supra Sect. 45. it seems most agreeable to the Intention of the Statute to bail them.

Sect. 51. Fourthly, *Persons accused of other Trespass, for which a Man ought not to lose Life or Member*, are declared by the Statute to be replevisable; yet perhaps the generallity of this Clause is restrained by that other Clause which declares, That Persons taken for open and manifest Offences shall not be replevied, as hath been more fully shewn *Sect.* 45.

Sect. 52. Fifthly, The Appellee of an Approver is also expressly declared to be bailable after the Death of the Approver, unless he be a notorious Felon. But having already incidentally shewn *Sect.* 43. in what Cases such an Appellee is replevisable, I shall refer the Reader, for this Matter, to what is there said concerning it.

Sect. 53. Secondly, As to the Branch concerning those who are charged as Accessories, which is in the following Words, *Those who are accused of the receipt of Thieves or Felons, or of Commandment, or of Force,* or *or of Aid of Felony done, shall be replevisable*, &c. it is observable, That notwithstanding the Statute mentions only those who are Accessory by receiving Felons, or by Commandment, Force or Aid, yet all those who are accessory to a Felony any[a] other way, as by Persuasion or any other Procurement, or Abetment, have always been taken to be within the Equity of it; and most [b] of the Books relating to this Matter seem generally to hold, That all Accessories, whether to Homicide or any other Felony, are bailable 'till the Principal be convicted, or attainted; and that they are bailable even after such Conviction or Attainder, upon their [c]pleading to the Indictment, and do not express any Limitation or Restriction, that they be of good Fame, or but slightly suspected, *&c.* And in the Case [e] of 25 *Ed.* 3. 44. *pl* 14. wherein a Person appealed of Murder, as having holden the deceased in his Arms while the other killed him, was not let to Mainprise, the Reason given for it by the Reporter is, because the Defendant was in a manner a Principal; for that otherwise being an Accessory only, he ought to have been let to Mainprise by the Intent of the Statute. Yet I find it made a Query in the Year Book of 21 [f] *Ed.* 4. Whether Accessories are to be let to bail of Course? And perhaps it may be more reasonable to intend, in the above-cited Case of 25 *Ed.* 3. That such Person was denied the Benefit of Mainprise by reason of the Notoriety of his Guilt; for it seems clear, both from the [g]*Register*, [h]*Fitzherbert*, and [i]*Dalton*, That Accessories to Felonies are not to be bailed unless they be of good Reputation; and if the want of a good Reputation, which is at most but a very slight Inducement to presume them guilty of a particular Crime, be a good Cause to exclude them from the Benefit of Mainprise, which is given them by the general Words of the Statute, it seems strange, that strong and unquestionable Evidence of their Guilt should not much more exclude them from it; especially considering that it is an allowed Rule, [k] That Bail is only proper where it stands indifferent whether the Person accused were guilty or innocent. And since later Statutes have, in many Cases, excluded Accessories before the Fact from the Benefit of the Clergy, it seems absurd to say, That Persons notoriously guilty of being Accessory to Crimes which exclude them from the Benefit of the Clergy, shall be admitted to Bail; whereas if they had been committed to Prison on the like Evidence of Guilt, as Principals, for Felonies within the Benefit of the Clergy, or even for inferior Offences of an enormous Nature, they could not have had the like Priviledge: And therefore, since the general Words of the Statute concerning the replevysing of Accessories, are agreed to receive the above-mentioned Limitations, That they ought to be of a good Reputation, and also to plead first to the Indictment, if the Principal be attainted; why should it not be reasonable to admit this farther Restriction, That their Guilt be not notorious? which seems admitted to be implied in most of the other Clauses of the Statute, which yet are penned in as general Words as that relating to Accessories. But this Matter seems at this Day to be put beyond all Question, by 31 *Car.* 2. *cap.* 2. Par. 21. By which it is recited, *That many times Persons charged with Petit Treason, or Felony, or as Accessories thereunto, are committed on Suspicion only, whereupon they are bailable or not, according as the Circumstances making out that Suspicion, are more or less weighty*, &c. And thereupon it is enacted, *That no Person so charged, shall be removed or bailed by Vertue of that Act, in other manner than he might before.* From which it seems clearly to follow, That where there are strong Presumptions of Guilt, against a Person so charged, he neither was bailable before that Statute, nor is now bailable by Vertue of it.

[a] Register. 270. S. P. C. 71. F. N. B. 250. E. H. P. C. 100.
[b] S. P. C. 71. Bro Mainprise, 6, 11. 22, 54. 58. H. P. C. 100. Coke Bail & Mainprise. Cap. 5. Dy. 120. pl. 10. 25 Ed. 3. 42. pl. 14 40 Ed. 42. pl. 21. 50 Ed. 3. 15. a. 29 Ass. 44. 40 Ass 8.
[c] S. P. C. 71. H. P. C. 100. Bro Mainprise 58, 64 40 Ed. 3. 42. pl. 22. 43 Ed. 3. 17. 40 Ass. 8. Cont. 27 Ed. 3. 94. pl 3
[e] Fitz. coron. 135.
[f] 21 Ed. 4. 71 Bro Mainprise, 78.
[g] Register. 270.
[h] F. N. B. 250. e.
[i] Dalt. cap. 114.
[k] Supra Sect. 40.

As to the second Point, *viz.* In what Cases Bail is grantable by a Justice of Peace, I shall endeavour to shew,

1. How far it is grantable by Construction of the Statutes and Commission which give Justices of Peace a Jurisdiction over certain Crimes, without saying any thing concerning the Power of granting Bail.

2. How far it is grantable by the Statutes specially relating to the Power of granting Bail.

Sect. 54. As to the first Point it seems, That where-ever Justices of Peace have Jurisdiction of a Crime, they may bail the Person indicted before them of such Crime, upon such Circumstances for which other Courts might bail the Person so indicted before them; for that it seems to be a good general Rule, That so far as any Persons are Judges of any Crime, so far they have Power of bailing a Person indicted before them of such Crime: And upon this Ground it seems clear, That any two Justices of Peace, whereof one is of the *Quorum*, may, of common Right, bail Persons indicted before the Sessions of Justices of Peace, for that any two such Justices may hear and determine the Indictment. * Also it hath been holden, That any one Justice of Peace hath the like Power in relation to Persons so indicted, because every such Justice being a Judge of the Court which is to determine the Offence, seems consequently to have a discretionary Power of judging whether it be bailable, and of admitting the Party to bail. And this seems to be implied by the Statute of 1 *Ric.* 3. *cap.* 3. which giving one Justice of Peace Power of bailing Persons arrested for Felony, *in like Form as if such Persons had been indicted at Sessions,* clearly supposes, that if such Persons had been indicted at Sessions, they might have been bailed by any one Justice: And if any one Justice of Peace had such Power of bailing the Persons so indicted at Sessions, before the Statutes specially relating to the Power of Justices of Peace in granting Bail, it seems, That he has still the same Power in relation to Persons so indicted of any bailable Crime under the degree of Felony, because the said Statutes seem not to restrain him in any such Case, under the degree of Felony, from any Power which he lawfully might claim before. Also it seems to be agreed, That any one Justice of Peace might always in his Discretion either bail or imprison one who has given another a dangerous Wound, according as it shall appear from the whole Circumstances, that the Party is most likely to live or dye, for that every such Justice being a principal Conservator of the Peace, the Offence at present being only an enormous Breach thereof, and no Felony, seems properly to come under his Conusance.

H. P. C. 105. 106. Coke Bail & Mainprise, Chap. 6. Lamb. 347. 348. *See the Books above cited. Cromp. 197. 234. 235. H. P. C. 105. B. 1. Chap. 63. Sect. 19.

Sect. 55. As to the second Point, *viz.* How far Bail is grantable by Justices of Peace, by Vertute of the Statutes specially relating to their Power of granting Bail, it is recited by 1 *R.* 3. *cap.* 3. *That divers Persons had been daily arrested and imprisoned for Suspicion of Felony, sometime of Malice, and sometime of a light Suspicion, and so kept in Prison, without Bail or Mainprize, to their great Vexation and Trouble: And thereupon it is enacted, That every Justice of Peace in every Shire, City or Town, may, by his or their Discretion, let such Prisoners and Persons so arrested to Bail or Mainprise, in like Form as though the same Prisoners, or Persons, were indicted thereof of Record, before the same Justices at their Sessions.*

Sect. 56. But it is recited, by 3 *H.* 7. *cap.* 3. *That by Colour of the said Statute of* 1 R. 3. *divers Persons which were not mainpernable, were oftentimes let to Bail and Mainprise by Justices of Peace, against the due Form of Law,*

whereby

whereby many Felons had escaped, to the great Displeasure of the King, and Annoiance of his Liege People; and thereupon it is enacted, *That the Justices of Peace in every Shire, City, and Town, or two of them at the least, whereof one to be of the* Quorum, *have Authority and Power to let any such Prisoners, or Persons mainpernable by Law, that have been imprisoned within their several Counties, City or Town, to Bail or Mainprise, unto their next general Sessions, or unto the next general Gaol Delivery of the same Goals, in every Shire, City, or Town, as well within Franchises as without, where any Gaols be, or hereafter shall be: And that the said Justices of Peace, or one of them, so taking any such Bail or Mainprise, do certify the same at the next general Sessions of the Peace, or the next general Gaol Delivery of any such Gaol, in every such County, City or Town, next following after any such Bail or Mainprise so taken, on pain to forfeit to the King for every Default thereupon recorded,* 10 l. *And that the aforesaid Act, giving Authority and Power in the Premises, to any Justice of the Peace by himself, be in that behalf utterly void, and of none effect.*

Sect. 57. And it is recited, by 1 & 2 *Ph. & M.* 13. *That since the said Statute of* 3 H. 7. *one Justice of Peace, in the Name of himself, and one other of the Justices his Companion, not making the said Justice Party nor Privy unto the Case wherefore the Prisoner should be bailed, had oftentimes by sinister Labor and Means, set at large the greatest and notablest Offenders, such as be not replevisable by the Laws of this Realm; and yet the rather to hide their Affections in that behalf, had signified the Cause of their Apprehension to be only for Suspicion of Felony, whereby the said Offenders had and did daily escape Punishment,* &c. And thereupon it is enacted, *That from the first Day of* April *then next coming, no Justice or Justices of Peace, shall let to Bail or Mainprise any such Person or Persons, which for any Offence or Offences, by them or any of them committed, be declared not to be replevised, or be forbidden to be replevised or bailed by the above-mentioned Statute of* Westminster 1.

Sect. 58. And it is farther enacted, *Par.* 3. *That any Person or Persons arrested for Manslaughter or Felony, or Suspicion of Manslaughter or Felony, being bailable by the Law, shall not be let to Bail or Mainprise by any Justices of the Peace if it be not in open Sessions, except it be by two Justices of Peace at the least, whereof one to be of the* Quorum, *and the same Justices to be present together at the time of the said Bailment or Mainprise; which Bailment or Mainprise they shall certify in Writing subscribed or signed with their own Hands, at the next general Gaol-Delivery to be holden within the County where the said Person or Persons shall be arrested or suspected.*

Sect. 59. And it is farther enacted, Par. 4. *That the said Justices, or one of them, being of the* Quorum, *when any such Prisoner is brought before them for any Manslaughter or Felony, before any Bailment or Mainprize, shall take the Examination of the said Prisoner, and Information of them that bring him, of the Fact and Circumstances thereof, and the same, or as much thereof as shall be material to prove the Felony, shall put in Writing before they make the same Bailment; which said Examination, together with the said Bailment, the said Justices shall certify at the next general Gaol-Delivery, to be holden within the Limits of their Commission.*

Sect. 60. And it is farther enacted, Par. 5. *That the said Justices shall have Authority to bind all such by Recognisance or Obligation, as do declare any thing material, to prove the said Offences or Felonies, to appear at the next general Gaol-Delivery to be holden within the County, City, or Town Corporate where the Trial thereof shall be, and then and there to give Evidence against the Party at the time of his Trial; and shall certify as well the same Evidence, as such Bond or Bonds in writing, as he shall take, at or before the time of his said Trial thereof to be had or made. And in case any Justice of Peace of* Quorum, *shall*

shall offend in any thing, contrary to the true intent and meaning of this Act; the Justices of Gaol-Delivery, where such Offence shall happen to be committed, upon due Proof thereof, by Examination before them, shall for every such Offence, set such Fine on every of the same Justices, as the same Justices of Gaol Delivery shall think meet, &c.

Sect. 61. But it is provided, Par. 6. *That Justices of Peace, and Coroners, within the City of* London, *and the County of* Middlesex, *and in other Cities, Boroughs, and Towns Corporate, shall within their several Jurisdictions, have Authority to let to bail Felons and Prisoners, in such Manner and Form as they had been before accustomed; and also shall take Examinations and Bonds, as is aforesaid, upon every Bailment by them made, and certify every such Bailment, Bond and Examination, at the next general Gaol-Delivery,* &c.

From these Statutes the following Particulars appear most observable.

Sect. 62. First, That it seems clearly to be imply'd by the above-mentioned Statute of 1 *R.* 3. 3. which authorised any one Justice of Peace to bail a Person on a slight Suspicion of Felony, in like manner as if such Person had been indicted at Sessions, That before that Statute, Justices of Peace could bail those only for Felony, who had been indicted of it before them. And by Parity of Reason it seems also to follow, That they had no Power to bail Persons for any other Crime before such Indictment, unless it were an Offence directly tending to the Breach of the Peace, the bailing of Persons for which seems properly to come under their Conusance as Conservators of the Peace: And therefore it seems difficult to maintain the Power of one Justice of the Peace to bail a Person for any other Crime, unless it be by some Statute limited to the Connusance of one Justice, or the Party have been indicted for it at Sessions, because the Commission in giving a Justice a general Jurisdiction over any Crime, shall be construed so far only to give him a Power to bail a Person accused of it, as it makes him a Judge of it, which he cannot be till it come regularly before him by Indictment; and the Statutes above-mentioned specially relating to the Power of Justices of Peace, in granting Bail, expresly require the Connusance of two Justices. Coke, Bail and Mainprise, cap. 6. Supra. Sect. 54.

Sect. 63. Secondly, That Justices of Peace have no Power to bail any Person not replevisable by the above-mentioned Statute of *Westminster* 1. 15. from whence it seems to follow, That a Person under the actual Commitment or Arrest of any other Magistrate, or even of a private Person, for any Crime declared to be irreplevisable by that Statute, as Treason against the King's Person, Arson, *&c.* cannot be delivered from his Imprisonment by the Bailment of any Justice of Peace. Yet if a Person at large be only accused of any such Crime, on a slight Suspicion, before a Justice of Peace, it seems that the Justice ought not to commit him, but to take Surety of him to appear before a proper Court, as hath been more fully shewn in relation to the Sheriff, *Sect.* 46. And inasmuch as the above-mentioned Statute of 1 & 2 *Ph. & M.* 13. expresly mentions the bailing of Persons for Manslaughter, as well as for other Felonies, there can be no Doubt, but that Justices of Peace may, by Force thereof, safely bail any Person imprisoned on a slight Suspicion of a Fact, clearly appearing to be no higher an Offence than Manslaughter, and much more if it appear to amount to no more than Homicide by Misadventure, or in Self-defence. Yet it seems to be agreed, That such Justices must, at their Peril, take care that the Offence in Truth amounted not to Murder; and that they ought in no case to bail any Person who manifestly appears to Vide Supra. Section. 33, 34. 1 Rol. Rep. 268. Dalt cap 114. H. P. C. 99.

 have

Lamb. 346, 347. have been guilty of any of the Homicides above-mentioned, either by his own Confession, or the Notoriety of the Fact, not only because the above-mentioned Statute of *Westminster* 1. 15. which is the Pattern prescribed by 1 & 2 *Ph. & M.* for the direction of Justices of Peace in relation to Bail, expresly excludes all Persons from the Benefit of it which are guilty of open and manifest Offences; but also because the Statute of *Glocester*, *cap.* 9. is express, That all Persons who are guilty of Homicide, by Misadventure or in Self-defence, shall be kept in Prison 'till the next coming of the Justices Itinerant, or of Gaol-Delivery.

Supra Sect. 44, 45. 2 Inst. 314, 315.

Sect. 64. Thirdly, That the chief Import of these Statutes is to shew in what Manner Persons are to be bailed by Justices of Peace, and not to declare what Persons are bailable by them; in relation to which Matter, the old Rules of the Statute of *Westminster* 1. are generally still to be followed, which extending only to criminal Offences punishable in the ordinary way by Indictment before the Sheriff, *&c.* give no Power to bail Persons taken on Process in Civil Actions, or for Contempts to Superior Courts, as by Process of Rebellion out of Chancery. And therefore by a reasonable Construction of all these Statutes, Justices of Peace have no Power in any such Cases to admit any Person to bail.

Dalt. cap 114. Cromp 152. H. P. C. 105.

Sect. 65. As to the third Point, *viz.* Where Bail is grantable by the Justices of Gaol-Delivery, it seems to be clearly settled [a] at this Day, That such Justices may bail any Person convicted before them of Homicide by Misadventure, or in Self-defence, the better to enable him to purchase his Pardon: And if a Person convicted of Manslaughter before such Justices, purchase his Pardon, it seems, that they may [b] bail him, even after their Sessions is determined, 'till the next Sessions of Gaol-Delivery, that he may come in then and plead his Pardon, for that the Power of such Justices seems [c] to continue for such Purposes after their Sessions. Also [d] if a Man be convicted of Manslaughter before such Justices, against plain Evidence, it is said that they may bail him till the next Sessions of Gaol-Delivery, in order to purchase his Pardon in the mean time. But it seems, [e] That Justices of Peace have no Power to bail a Man in any of these Cases, because they are tied up for the most Part to the Rules prescribed by the above-mentioned Statute of *Westminster* 1. But this Statute not [f] extending to Justices of Gaol-Delivery, seems to leave them a discretionary Power in those Cases, wherein it restrains the Sheriff from admitting Persons to bail. And therefore if a Defendant in an Appeal of Death, plead an Excommunication in Disability of the Plaintiff, it seems to be holden by *Staundford*, [g] That such Justices may bail the Defendant from Day to Day, till the Plaintiff shall be absolved, for that otherwise the Defendant might lee in Prison for ever, without any Opportunity of coming to his Trial. But it is observable, That the Books [h] which are cited for the Maintenance of this Opinion, speak only of an Appeal of Robbery: Yet if Justices of Gaol-Delivery have such Power of bailing Persons in the Case of Death, on the Circumstances above-mentioned, as it seems agreed in the Cases above-cited that they have, I do not find any Reason why they may not as well upon other such like Circumstances, bail Persons indicted or appealed before them of any other Crime, in such manner as the Court of King's Bench may do, as shall be more fully shewn under the next Point.

[a] Cromp. 154. a. H. P. C. 101, 104, 105. Fitz. Coron. 361. Dalt cap 114. F.N.B. 246. c. S. P. C. 15. C. 16. D. Con. 25 Ed. 3 42. pl. 27. S P. C. 74. D. Fitz. Coron. 354. Mainprise, 1.
[b] Crompt. 153. b. Bro. Mainprise, 94. H. P. C. 101.
[c] Vide Supra. cap 6. Sect. 7.
[d] Cromp. 154. a.
[e] H. P. C. 104, 105. Vide Supra. Sect. 63. Cont. Dalt cap 114.
[f] 2 Inst. 185. 186.
[g] S.P.C. 72. f.
[h] Fitz. Mainprise, 6. 3 Ass. pl. 12. Salk. 61. *seems contrary.*

As to the Fourth Point, *viz.* Where Bail is grantable by the Courts of *Westminster-Hall*, I shall endeavour to shew.

1

1. Where

1. Where it is grantable by the Court of King's Bench.
2. Where by the other Courts of *Westminster-Hall.*

As to the first of these Points I shall consider,

1. Where Bail is grantable by the Court of King's Bench, to a Person imprisoned by the King's special Command, or by the Order of his Privy Council.
2. Where to a Person committed by either House of Parliament.
3. Where to one committed by the Court of Chancery.
4. Where to one committed by an Inferior Court of Record.
5. Where to one expresly excluded by the abovementioned Statute of *Westminster* 1. Chap. 15. from the common Benefit of a Replevin by the Sheriff.

Sect. 66. As to the first of these Particulars, *viz.* Where Bail is grantable by the Court of King's Bench to a Person imprisoned by the King's special Command, or by the Order of the Privy Council; I do not find but that where-ever [a] a Commitment by the Privy Council hath specially expressed the Crime for which the Party hath been committed, this Court has always admitted him to bail, on the like Circumstances on which, in Discretion, it will grant Bail on other Commitments: [b] And where-ever it has appeared, that Persons have been imprisoned by colour of an usurped Authority, pretended to be derived from any Patent whatsoever, contrary to Law, it seems that the said Court hath always discharged the Persons so imprisoned, without Bail. But there have been formerly many Opinions, [c] That Persons committed by the Special Command of the King, or of his Privy Council, without expressing any other Cause of the Commitment, were not bailable by any Court whatsoever, without some Intimation of the King's Consent to such Bailment, by Letter from the Privy Council, or otherwise. And a Distinction [d] was taken by some between a Commitment by one of the Privy Council, and a Commitment by the whole Body; and that the former ought indeed to set forth some other Cause of the Commitment besides the Command of the Person who made it; but that the latter needed not any.

Sect. 67. But this Matter came afterwards to be very solemnly debated in the famous Case [e] of Sir *John Corbet*, and others, who being imprisoned by a Warrant from the Privy Council, about the third Year of the Reign of King *Charles* the First, moved the Court of King's Bench to admit them to Bail upon their *Habeas Corpus*; whereon it was returned, That they were detained in the Prison of the *Fleet* by the special Command of the King, signified to the Warden by a Warrant of some of the Members of the Privy Council, in which Warrant no other Cause of the Imprisonment was contained but such Special Command: And it was strongly urged on the Behalf of the Prisoners, That such Imprisonment is against the Statute of *Magna Charta, chap.* 29. which provides, *That no Freeman shall be taken or imprisoned, and that the King will not pass upon him, nor condemn him, but by the Judgment of his Peers, or the Law of the Land*; and also against many other Statutes [f] made in Affirmance of *Magna Charta*, by which it is ordained, *That no Man shall be taken by Petition, or Suggestion, made to the King or to his Council, unless it be by Indictment or Presentment, or by Process by Original Writ; and that no Man shall be imprisoned,* &c. *without being brought to answer by due Process of Law; nor be put to answer without Presentment before Justices, or matter of Record, or by due Process, and Writ Original.*

[a] 5 Mod 78. 1 Syd. 143. 1. And 297. 298. 1 Leon. 70. Palm. 559.

[b] 1 Leon. 70. 1. And 297.

[c] 33 H.6.28. b. 1. And 298. 1 Rol. Rep. 134, 192. pl. 31, 32, 219. pl. 22. Con. Mo. 839. 1 And 158. See the Arguments on the *Habeas Corpus* concerning Loans, 81, 82, &c.

[d] 1 Leon. 70. 71.

[e] See the Arguments on the *Habeas Corpus* concerning Loans, & Rushworth's Collections, 1 Part. Fol. 458, &c.

[f] 25 Ed. 3. 4. 28 Ed. 3. 3. 42 Ed. 3. 3.

Original. And it was argued, That the Liberty of the Subject would be precarious, and lie at the King's Mercy, if Persons who happen to incur his Displeasure, for what perhaps the Law esteems no Crime, should by means of such a Commitment be liable to be for ever imprisoned, without any Possibility of Redress; and that it seems inconsistent with natural Justice to expose a Man to so severe a Punishment for a supposed Crime alledged against him, without giving him an Opportunity of clearing himself by a lawful Trial. And it was farther urged, That, according to the Opinion of Sir *John Markham*, in the time of King *Edward* the Fourth, the King could not so much as arrest a Man upon Suspicion of Treason or Felony, as any of his Subjects may; for that if the King should do Wrong, the Party could have no Action against him. Also it was insisted, That the Preamble of the Statute of *Westminster* 1. 15. which declares, That Persons imprisoned by the King's Command have always been taken to be irreplevisable, must be intended only of a Replevin by the common Writ *de Homine replegiando*, or by the Sheriff, *ex officio*, without Writ, for that it speaks only of a Replevin by Sheriffs and others; and therefore shall not be taken to extend to superior Courts: And it was never thought, that the Court of King's Bench was restrained by it from bailing Persons imprisoned for Homicide; and yet all such are equally declared by the Statute to be irreplevisable: Also many Precedents were alledged, whereby it appeared, That Persons committed by the King's special Command had been discharged upon Writs of *Habeas Corpus*.

1 H. 7. 4. b.

Sect. 67. But on the other Side it was argued, That such Commitments could not reasonably be intended to be against the Purview of the Statutes above-cited, inasmuch as the said Statute of *Westminster* 1. 15. which was made in the very next Reign after that in which the Statute of *Magna Charta* was made, it was declared to be a settled and undoubted Point, That Persons committed by the Command of the King (which, as it seems to be agreed, is to be understood of the King's special, absolute, and extrajudicial Command) are not replevisable; and it cannot be imagined that so high a Regard should be paid to such a Commitment, if it were thought to be illegal, and contrary to *Magna Charta*. And it was insisted, That Commitments of this kind have often been allowed by the Courts [a] of Justice, and are mentioned by Authors [b] of the best Credit since the above-cited Statutes, without any the least Objection to their Legality, and as depriving the Party imprisoned by them from the common Benefit of the Writ of Replevin. And it was also strongly urged, That there are often secret Causes not fit to be divulged, which may make it necessary for the Safety of the State, in some particular Circumstances, to restrain some Persons from their Liberty for a certain time, and that the King, who is entirely entrusted with the Management of State-Affairs, shall be presumed always to act for the Publick Good; and that it is immodest for any of his Courts to question the Justice of his Proceedings of this kind, which the Law seems wholly to have left to his Wisdom, or to suffer a Suggestion that he abuses his Prerogative to cover Oppression; and that the Subject is in no danger of perpetual Imprisonment on this Account, for that the Court of King's Bench hath always used a discretionary Power over such Commitments, as well as all others, and therefore upon special Circumstances of Hardship, may admit Persons under such Commitments to Bail; but that where there was nothing extraordinary in the Case, it had been the general Course of the Court not to do it without a special Order from the Council for it, as appeared

Vide Supra Sect.

[a] Vide Supra Sect. 66.
[b] S. P. C. 72, 73. F. N. B. 66. E.

Rushworth's Collections, part 1. fol. 510.

appeared from the Examination of most of the Precedents relating to this Matter. And therefore in the Case abovementioned the Court of King's Bench was unanimous in Opinion, That Sir *John Corbet*, and the other Gentlemen so committed by the King's Special Command, as is abovementioned, had no Right, *prima facie*, to demand the Benefit of Bail, without the Consent of the Council, and therefore remanded them.

1 Ro. Re. 219. See the Arguments abovementioned, pag 81.

Sect. 68. But this Matter being afterwards considered in Parliament, and it being the general Opinion, That the chief Reason why those Gentlemen incurred the King's Displeasure was their Refusal to pay the Loans, which, as they insisted, were demanded of them without sufficient Authority; and it being evident, That if there were no certain legal Remedy for the Liberty of the Subject against such a Strain of the Prerogative, no Man could be safe in maintaining his Property, either in Parliament, or out of it, against a disputed Demand from the Crown, but would be liable to a discretionary Imprisonment, and that under colour of Law, without any certain Redress from the Law; it was thought necessary on this Occasion to draw up the famous Petition of Right, which was afterwards assented to by the King, wherein, among other things, the Lords and Commons complain to the King, *That against the Tenour of of the above* * *cited Statutes, divers Subjects had then of late been imprisoned, without any Cause shewed; and when for their Deliverance they had been brought before Justices by Writs of* Habeas Corpus, *there to undergo and receive as the Court should order; and their Keepers commanded to certify the Causes of their Detainer, no Cause had been certified, but that they were detained by his Majesty's special Command, signified by the Lords of his Privy Council, and yet were returned back to several Prisons, without being charged with any thing to which they might make Answer according to the Law: And thereupon the said Lords and Commons, among other things, humbly pray, That no Freeman, in any such manner as is before mentioned, be imprisoned, or detained,* &c.

Rushworths Collections 1. part, 428, 473, 499, &c.

Rushworth's Collections, Part 1. Fol. 613.

* Supra Section. 66.

Sect. 69. And it seems to have been generally agreed, since the time of this Petition, That where-ever any Commitment by the Privy Council hath not expressed, with some convenient Certainty, the Crime alledged against the Party, he ought to be bailed upon his *Habeas Corpus*.

Vide Cro. Car. 507, 579, 593.

Sect. 70. And for the greater Security of the Liberty of the Subject, against Commitments by the Command of the King, or of his Privy Council, it is farther *provided and enacted*, by 16 *Car.* 1. *cap.* 10. *Par.* 8. *That if any Person shall be committed, restrained of his Liberty, or suffer Imprisonment by the Command or Warrant of the King's Majesty, in his own Person, or by the Command or Warrant of the Council-Board, or, of any of the Lords or others of his Majesty's Privy Council; That in every such Case, every such Person upon Demand or Motion to the Judges of the King's Bench or Common Pleas, in open Court, shall without Delay, upon any Pretence whatsoever, for the ordinary Fees usually paid for the same, have forthwith granted unto him a Writ of* Habeas Corpus, *to be directed generally unto all and every Sheriffs, Gaoler, Minister, Officer, or other Person in whose Custody the Party committed or restrained shall be, and such Sheriff,* &c. *shall, at the return of the said Writ, and according to the Command thereof, on due and convenient Notice thereof given unto him, at the Charge of the Party who requireth or procureth such Writ, and on Security by his own Bond given, to pay the Charges of carrying back the Prisoner, if he shall be remanded by the Court,* &c. *which Charges shall be ordered by the Court, bring or cause to be brought the Body of the Party before the Judges of the Court, from whence the same Writ shall issue, in open Court, and shall then likewise certify the true Cause of such his Detainer or Imprisonment, and thereupon* the

[a] See 1 Sid. 78
1 Keb 305. pl. 15, 17.

the Court, within three Court-Days after such Return made and delivered [a] *in open Court, shall proceed to examine and determine whether the Cause of such Commitment, appearing upon the said Return, be just and legal or not, and shall thereupon do what to Justice shall appertain, either by delivering, bailing, or remanding the Prisoner: And if any thing shall be otherwise wilfully done, or omitted to be done by any Judge, Justice, Officer, or other Person aforementioned, contrary to the true meaning hereof, That then such Person so offending shall forfeit to the Party grieved, his treble Damages,* &c.

Sect. 71. But it is provided Par. 9. *That the above-recited Clause shall extend only to the Warrants and Directions of the Council-Board, and to the Commitments, Restraints and Imprisonments of any Person or Persons, made, commanded or awarded, by the King's Majesty, his Heirs or Successors, in their own Person, or by the Lords and others of the Privy Council, and every one of them.*

Sect. 72. As to the second Particular, *viz.* Where Bail is grantable by the Court of King's Bench, to a Person imprisoned by either House of Parliament, There can be no Doubt but that the highest Regard is to be paid to all the Proceedings of either of those Houses, and that where-ever the Contrary does not plainly and expressly appear, it shall be presumed that they act within their Jurisdiction, and agreeably to the Usages of Parliament, and the Rules of Law and Justice: And therefore, where-ever it stands indifferent upon the Return of a *Habeas Corpus,* whether a Commitment by either of those Houses were strictly legal or not, and the Parliament be still sitting, I can find no Precedent that the Prisoner hath been bailed by the Court of King's Bench. And it cannot but be expected, that those Houses would be apt to resent an Attempt of this kind, which might seem to carry with it an implicit Reflection on their Honour, as unjustly depriving a Subject of his Liberty, and putting him under a Necessity of demanding Justice from another Court, by unreasonably refusing to restore him to it; which surely shall never be intended, where their Proceedings are capable of a more favourable Construction. And therefore in the Lord *Shaftsbury*'s Case, who, upon his *Habeas Corpus* in the King's Bench, was returned to have been committed by the House of Lords for his high Contempt committed against that House, the Court would not take notice of any Exceptions against the Form of the Commitment, as that it was too general, and did not express the Nature of the Contempt, or in what Place it was committed, *&c.* for that it shall be presumed, That it was such for which the Lords might lawfully make such an Order, and no other Court shall prescribe to them in what Form they ought to make it. But if it be demanded, in case a Subject should be committed by either of those Houses, for a Matter manifestly out of their Jurisdiction, what remedy can he have? I answer, That it cannot well be imagined that the Law, which favours nothing more than the Liberty of the Subject, should give us a Remedy against Commitments by the King himself, appearing to be illegal, and yet give us no manner of Redress against a Commitment by our fellow Subjects, equally appearing to be unwarranted. But as this is a Case, which, I am perswaded, will never happen, it seems needless over nicely to examine it.

1 Mod. 144, 145.

Sect. 73. However it seems agreed, That a Person committed for a Contempt, by the Order of either House of Parliament, may be discharged by the Court of King's Bench after a Dissolution, or Prorogation of the Parliament, whether he were committed during the Sessions, or afterwards; for that all the Orders of Parliament are determined by a

Dissolution, or Prorogation; and all Matters, before either House, must be commenced anew at the next Parliament, except only in the Case of a Writ of Error: And if the Subject should be deprived of his Liberty till the next Parliament, which perhaps may not meet again in many Years, no one could say when his Imprisonment would end. 1 Keb. 371, 887, 388. 1 Syd. 245. 1 Lev. 165. 1 Mod. 155, 157.

Sect. 74. But it is holden in *Shower's Reports*, That a Lord committed by the House of Lords, on an Impeachment of Treason, and afterwards pardoned, cannot be discharged by the Court of King's Bench, because the Impeachment being in a Superior Court, the Pardon must be pleaded there; and the Commitment being by the Lords, the King's Bench cannot take Conusance of it. Yet it seems to have been taken for granted in the Lord *Stafford*'s Case, That the Court of King's Bench may, in their Discretion, bail a Lord upon an Impeachment of High Treason, which in that Case they refused to do, not as a Matter out of their Power, but as a thing which they were not bound to do, and improper on Consideration of the whole Circumstances. And though the Reasons above cited from *Shower*'s *Reports*, seem proper to prove, That the Court of King's Bench cannot discharge a Prisoner from any Impeachment in Parliament whatsoever; yet they seem by no means to prove, that they cannot bail him. But it is observable, That it doth not clearly appear, from either of the above mentioned Reports, whether any Parliament were sitting at the Time of the Motions for such Discharge and Bailment, or not; but it is certainly most likely to prevail in such a Motion, when no Parliament is sitting, nor likely soon to sit, and after the Party hath been long in Prison; because, in such a Case, if he should not be bailed, he might be perpetually imprisoned for a Crime, without any Opportunity of making his Defence. Shower's, 100. Raymond, 381.

Sect. 75. As to the third Particular, *viz.* Where Bail is grantable by the King's Bench, to a Person committed by the Court of Chancery; little is said in the Books, except in the Reign of King *James* the first, at the time when Sir *Edward Coke* was Chief Justice, when this Matter was very much litigated, and occasion'd great Heats between the two Courts, and several Persons committed to the *Fleet* by the Chancellor, were bailed by the Court of King's Bench, upon Exceptions to the Generality of the Form of the Commitments, as [a] not shewing the time of the Commitment, or setting [b] forth only the Command of the Lord Chancellor as the Ground of the Imprisonment, without mentioning any Crime at all, or mentioning the Crime in [c] general Terms, as for a Contempt to the Court of Chancery, without shewing what the Contempt was, or at what time committed: And one [d] *Glanvil*, who was generally committed by the command of the Lord Chancellor, without setting forth any Cause of such Command, seems to have been bailed upon Examination of the Merits of the Decree, for disobeying whereof he was in truth committed; whereby it appeared that the Decree related to a Matter before adjudged at the Common Law, which was thought contrary to the Purport of the [f] Statutes of 27 *Ed.* 3. 1. & 4 *H.* 4. 23. But this Proceeding being resented by the Lord Chancellor, the said *Glanvil* was afterwards recommitted by him for the same Matter, and yet was afterwards, on another *Habeas Corpus*, bailed the second time by the Court of King's Bench: But I have not met with any Precedent of this kind of late Years; and how far the long Disuse of such like Proceedings may have lessened the Authority of the Cases above mentioned, may deserve to be considered. However, it cannot but be expected, That,

[a] 1 Rol. Rep. 192, pl. 31. 218, pl. 19.
[b] Moor. 839. 1 Rol. Rep. 219, pl. 21.
[c] 1 Rol. Rep. 192, pl. 31, 32. 218, pl. 19, 20. 219, pl. 23.
[d] 1 Rol. Rep. 111, 219. Moor, 838. 2 Bulst. 301. Cro. Jac. 343. like Case 3 Bulst. 115. 1 Rol. Rep. 277.
[f] Vide 1 Rol. Rep. 277. 3 Bulst. 115. Dalison. 81. 3 Leon. 18.

That the Superior Courts will pay the highest Regard to one anothers Proceedings, and be ready to presume, That they are agreeable to Law, unless the Contrary appear, or the Case be very particular and extraordinary, which may perhaps reasonably induce them, in some Circumstances, to make Exceptions from those general Rules, which in common Cases usually govern their Discretion. But what Case in particular may be said to be of so extraordinary a Nature, it would be needless and presumptuous for me to endeavour to examine. But as to the Case above mentioned, which was formerly so much litigated, concerning the Chancery's giving Relief against a Judgment of Law, since it seems to be settled at this Day, That the Chancery may, in some Cases, give Relief against the unequitable Use of such a Judgment, especially as to a Point not relievable by Law; whenever it stands indifferent, whether the Matter examined by Chancery, after a Judgment at Law, be of such a Nature as is proper for Relief in Chancery, or not; it is not probable, That any other Court of *Westminster-Hall* will easily presume that it is not, when the Chancellor, who is the proper Judge, hath determined that it is: And agreeably hereto it hath been adjudged, That a Commitment from Chancery, for Disobedience to a Decree, is good, without shewing what the Decree was.

Vaughan, 130, 140 Seems contrary.

Vide Book 1. Ch. 19. Sect. 17.

1 Mod. 155. Moor, 840. pl. 1135.

Sect. 76. As to the fourth Particular, *viz.* Where Bail is grantable by the Court of King's Bench to one committed by an Inferior Court of Record; it seems, That this Court, having the supreme Controul of all inferior Courts, may, in Discretion, on Consideration of the whole Circumstances of any Case whatsoever, bail any Person who shall appear to have been unjustly or hardly deprived of his Liberty by any Inferior Court. And therefore, where-ever it shall clearly and expresly appear, that a Person hath been committed by any such Court, for a Matter which either is in Truth no Crime at all, or, if it be a Crime, is not within the Jurisdiction of such Court, there can be no Doubt but that it is a proper Motion to the King's Bench to bail him. But in what other Cases in particular one may hope for the like Success in a Motion of this kind it seems difficult to determine; for that every such Case depends upon its particular Circumstances, which have great Weight with the Court in its Determinations of this kind, in which it is in great measure left to its Discretion. And therefore, tho' perhaps it may bail a Man on a Commitment by a Mayor of a Town, or a Justice of Peace, or other inferior Magistrate, for a Contempt, without shewing the particular Nature of it; yet it cannot be expected, that it will with like readiness bail a Man on such a general Commitment by a Court of a higher [a] Dignity, as a Court of Oyer and Terminer, or any other Court of *Westminster-Hall*; to the Honour of whose Proceedings the greatest Regard is always to be given; and on this ground chiefly, as I suppose, where a Person on a *Habeas Corpus*, was returned to have been committed by an Order of the Exchequer, for not paying a Fine of 50 *l.* by the Ecclesiastical Commissioners imposed upon him, the Court of King's Bench [b] refused to bail him, though it was not shewn wherefore the said Fine was imposed. And as a great Regard is always paid to the Dignity of the Court by which the Party is committed; so is it likewise to the Notoriety of the Offence; and therefore, where a Person convicted of buying and selling old Money, before Justices of Oyer and Terminer, was committed in Execution for the Fine, by an Order of the Court, not strictly formal, yet the Court of King's Bench refused [c] to bail him, for this Reason chiefly, because he was in execution, and his Commitment

Vaughan, 157. Vide 6 Mod 73, &c.

See Bushels Case in Vaughan's Reports.

2 Bulst. 139, 140.

[a] See the precedent Section, and Cro. Jac 219. & Vaughan 139, 140.

[b] Cro. Car. 579.

[c] 1 Sid. 144, 186, 320.

4 ment

ment was defective only in point of Form. Also where Persons taken in Execution for their Fines to the King, set on them by a Sessions of Justices of Peace, have not only brought their *Habeas Corpus*, but also their Writ of Error in the King's Bench, and assigned Errors, yet the Court has refused to bail them. But I take it for granted, in those Cases which are but briefly reported, That it appeared upon the whole Record, That such Fines were legally imposed. Also it seems, That the said Court has sometimes been induced to deny Persons committed by other Courts, by Warrants not strictly formal, the Benefit of Bail, for the Enormity, dangerous Tendency, or Obstinacy [a] of their Offence, which if it had been attended with less aggravating Circumstances might not have excluded them from it. Also the said Court, in determining whether it be proper to bail a Man committed by another Court, usually considers all the other Circumstances of the Case, as the Length [b] and Hardship [c] of the Imprisonment, and such like, in order to give such a Determination upon the whole, as may be most agreeable to the Honour and Prerogative of the Crown, and the Liberty and Safety of the Subject.

Salk. 348. 5 Mod. 19, 20, &c. Vide March, 52, 53. 1 Sid. 288. 289. 1 Sid. 320. pl. 10. 144.

[a] 1 Bulst. from 48. to 54. 1 Rol Rep. 220, pl. 14. 337, pl. 52. 411, pl. 54.
[b] 1 Rol. Rep. 218. pl. 19. 337. pl. 51. 2 Bulst 140.
[c] Latch. 12.

Sect. 77. But it seems to be agreed, That no one can in any Case controvert the Truth of the Return to a *Habeas Corpus*, or plead or suggest any Matter repugnant to it: Yet it hath been holden, That a Man may confess and avoid such a Return, by admitting the Truth of the Matters contained in it, and suggesting others not repugnant, which take off the effect of them. And upon this Ground, where one *Swallow*, a Citizen of *London*, was committed for refusing to accept the Office of an Alderman of the said City to which he had been elected, and the Custom of the City justifying a Commitment for such a Refusal, and the Election and Refusal were set forth in the Return to the *Habeas Corpus*; he filed a suggestion in the Crown-Office, That he was an Officer of the King's Mint, and that all such Officers were exempted from all City Offices, both by Prescription and by the King's Charter; and thereupon the Patent of the Grant of his Office, and also the Patent of the Exemption being inrolled in the Court, he was discharged.

1 Sid. 287, 288.

Sect. 78. Also the Court will sometimes examine by Affidavit, the Circumstances of a Fact on which a Prisoner brought before them by an *Habeas Corpus* hath been indicted, in order to inform themselves, on Examination of the whole Matter, whether it be reasonable to bail him or not. And agreeably hereto, where one *Jackson*, who had been indicted of Piracy before the Sessions of Admiralty, on a malicious Prosecution, brought his *Habeas Corpus* in the said Court in order to be bailed, the Court examined the whole Circumstances of the Fact by Affidavits, upon which it appeared, That the Prosecutor himself, if any one, was Guilty, and carry'd on the present Prosecution to skreen himself; and thereupon the Court, in Consideration of the Unreasonableness of the Prosecution, and the Uncertainty of the Time when another Sessions of Admiralty might be holden, admitted the said *Jackson* to bail, and committed the Prosecutor till he should find Bail to answer the Facts contained in the Affidavits.

5 Mod 323. 454. 455. 2 Jo. 222.

Trin. 4 Georg.

Sect. 79. As to the fifth Particular, *viz.* Where Bail is grantable by the Court of King's Bench, to one excluded by the above-mentioned Statute of *Westminster* 1. *chap.* 15. from the common Benefit of a Replevin by the Sheriff; It cannot be doubted, but that notwithstanding neither [d] the Judges of this, nor of any other Superior Court of Justice, are strictly within

[d] 2 Inst. 185, 186, 189. H P. C. 104. Salk. 61.

[a] 3 Bulst. 113. 1 Rol. Rep. 168. Supra. Sect. 33. Latch. 12. S. P. C. 74, 75. 5 Mod. 454, 455. [b] Kelyng. 90. [c] Dyer. 179. pl. 42. 1 Bulst. 87, 88. [d] 1 Rol. Rep. 268. 3 Bulst. 113, 114. Vide Supra Sect 33. [e] 5 H. 7. 16. pl 7. 2 Inst. 188. H. P. C. 101. S. P. C. 74. Letter A. [f] 19 H. 6. 2. a. S. P. C. 74. Letter A. 2. Inst. 188. 1 Syd. 316. [g] Crompton's Justice, 154. pl 22. [h] 5 Mod. 454 455. 1 Sid. 78. 1 Bulst. 85. Palm. 558, 559. 1 Keb. 305. 306. 48 Ed. 3. 22 a. [i] 3 Ass. pl. 12. 13 Ed. 4, 8. pl. 3. Bro Mainprise, 48. 73. S. P. C. 72. Letter B. [k] Latch 12. Cro. Jac. 356. Co. Lit. 289. a. [l] 2 Inst. 53, 55, 615. 4 Inst. 290. Vaughan, 154, 155, 156, 157. 2. And 297. Dalison, 81. 3 Leon. 18. 2 Jo. 13, 14, 17. 2 Mod. 198. 306.

within the Purview of that Statute; yet [a] they will always, in their Discretion, pay a due Regard to the Rules prescribed by it, and not admit a Person to Bail who is expresly declared by it to be irreplevisable, without some particular Circumstance in his favour: And therefore it seems difficult to find an Instance where Persons attainted [b] of Felony, or but convicted thereof by Verdict general or [c] special, or notoriously [d] guilty of Treason or Manslaughter, &c. by their own Confession or otherwise, have been admitted to the Benefit of Bail, without some special Motive to induce the Court to grant it: As where [e] a Person taken by a *Capias utlagatum*, on an Appeal of Felony by the Name of *J. S.* Gentleman, pleads that his Name is *J. S.* Yeoman, and not Gentleman, and so he is not the same Person who was outlawed, in which Case the Court in Discretion may bail him; for untill the Plea be determined, it appears not whether he were the Person intended or not. Or where [f] a Person outlawed alledges an Error in the Record, in which Case also the Court, *ex gratia*, may bail him, especially if the Error be apparent. Or where a Man is convicted [g] of Felony, upon Evidence by which it plainly appears to the Court that he is not guilty of it; in which Case even the Justices of Gaol-Delivery may bail him. Or where [h] it appears to the Court that the Prosecutor of an Indictment, or the Plaintiff in an Appeal, hath unreasonably delayed his Prosecution; as where two *Nihils* are returned upon two Writs of *Scire facias*, awarded against a Plaintiff in an Appeal, removed by *Certiorari* into the King's Bench, and the Prisoner hath lain a long time under Confinement. Or where [i] the Defendant in an Appeal hath pleaded an Excommunication in Disability of the Plaintiff; in which case it is apparent, That the Plaintiff cannot proceed at present; and if the Defendant should be kept in Prison till the Plaintiff be absolved, he might be a Prisoner for Life. Or where [k] it appears to the Court, That the Defendant may be in danger of losing his Life, either by Famine, or a dangerous Distemper, &c. if he continue longer in Prison.

As to the second Point, *viz.* In what Cases Bail is grantable by the other Courts of *Westminster-Hall*: I shall consider,

1. How far it is grantable by such Courts, to Persons committed for Causes under the Degree of Treason or Felony.
2. How far to Persons committed for Treason or Felony.

Sect. 80. As to the first Point, *viz.* How far Bail is grantable by the said Courts, to Persons committed for Causes under the Degree of Treason or Felony, it seems, [l] That the Courts of Common Pleas and Exchequer, at any time during Term, and the Court of Chancery, either in Term or Vacation, may award a *Habeas Corpus* by the Common Law, for any Person committed for any such Cause, and thereupon discharge him, if it shall clearly appear by the Return, That the Commitment was against Law (as being made by one who had no Jurisdiction of the Cause, or for a Matter for which by Law no Man ought to be punished) or bail him, if it shall be doubtful whether the Commitment were legal or not, &c. However it is certain at this Day, That by force of the *Habeas Corpus* Act, Par. 3. & 10. set forth more at large *Sect.* 17. & 22. any of the said Courts, in Term-time, and any Judge of either Bench, or Baron of the Exchequer, being of the Degree of the Coif, in the Vaca-

2 tion,

tion, may award a *Habeas Corpus* for any Prisoner whatsoever, who is bailable by the Intent of that Act, and thereupon bail him.

Sect. 81. As to the second Point, *viz.* How far Bail is grantable by the said Courts to Persons committed for Treason or Felony, it is observable, That the above-mentioned Clauses of the said *Habeas Corpus* Act extend not to Persons committed for Treason or Felony, plainly and specially expressed in the Warrant of Commitment; neither do I find any printed Case, wherein Persons committed for such Crimes have been bailed either by the Courts of Common Pleas or Exchequer. However it is certain, That in some Cases Persons committed for Felony are bailable by the Court of Chancery. But our Law-Books being generally silent in relation to these Matters, I shall refer the Reader for the more accurate Knowledge of them, to Observation and Experience.

See Vaughan 156, 157. 2 Jo. 14.

Register, 271. a. b

Sect 82. As to the seventh general Point of this Chapter, *viz.* In what Form Bail is to be taken; it seems to be the Practice of the Court of King's Bench in admitting a Person to Bail, who is actually present [a] in Court, upon an Indictment or Appeal [b] of Felony, or other Crime, punishable with loss [c] of Member, to take [d] a several Recognisance to the King in a certain Sum from each of the Bail, that the Prisoner shall appear at a certain Day, &c. and also, That the Bail shall be liable for the Default of such Appearance, &c. Body for Body. And [e] it seems to be left to the Discretion of Justices of Peace, in admitting any Person to Bail for Felony, to take the Recognisance either in a certain Sum, or else Body for Body. But [f] where a Person is bailed by the Court of King's Bench, before the Return of a *Capias* awarded against him for Felony, or (as it seems to be implied in the Book cited in the Margin that he may be,) or by any Court for a Crime of an Inferior Nature, it seems, That the Recognisance ought to be only in a certain Sum of Money, and not Body for Body. However it is certain [g] at this Day, That Persons bound Body for Body, are not liable on the forfeiture of the Recognisance, to such Punishment to which the Principal is to be adjudged, if found Guilty, but only to be fined, &c.

[a] 1 Bulst. 45.
[b] 2 Jon. 210.
[c] 1 Lev. 106. Contra 1 Sid. 211.
[d] 4 Inst. 178. 1 Bulst. 45. 21 H. 7. 20. pl. 3. Con. 1 Syd. 210. Vide 2 Jo. 222.
[e] H. P. C. 97. Crompt. Justice 235. a. 4 Inst. 178. Dalt. cap 127. *seems contrary.*
[f] 1 Bulst. 45.
[g] 4 Inst. 178. S. P. C. 65. Fitz. Mainprise, 13. 21 H. 7. 20. Pl 3. H. P. C. 97. Contra Fitz. Mainprise. 12.

Sect. 83. As to the eighth general Point of this Chapter, *viz.* What shall forfeit the Recognisance: If on a bailment for Felony, the usual [h] Form, *ad Standum recto de felonia prædicta, et ad respondendum Domino Regi,* be made use of, and at the Trial the Party stand obstinately mute, it may reasonably be argued, that in Strictness the Recognisance is forfeited, for [i] that the Expressions above-mentioned seem to import at least thus much, That the Prisoner shall make some Answer; and at the Common Law, before the Statute [k] of *Marlebridge chap.* 28. if a Person under Bail had insisted on his Privilege as a Clerk, and refused to answer to the Crime alledged against him, his Sureties were to be amerced; and though the said Statute have in that Case excused the Bail, yet an obstinate Refusal to answer in other Cases may perhaps remain as it was at the Common Law. Mr. *Dalton* [l] indeed seems to be of another Opinion, because the Words above-mentioned are always used of Course: But it seems strange, That Words should be looked on as idle and insignificant because they are most usual and proper. However, if late Practice and Experience have been agreeable to the above-mentioned Opinion of Mr. *Dalton,* as I apprehend that they have, they will certainly be of great Force to maintain it: And indeed it must be confessed, That if a Man's Bail, who are his Gaolers of his own choosing, do as effectually secure his Appearance, and put him as much under the Power of the Court as if he had been in the Custody of the proper Officer, they seem

[h] Dalt. cap. 127. S. P. L. 77. Letter C. 4 Inst. 178.
[i] S. P. C. 77. c.
[k] 2 Inst. 150. 4 Inst. 178.
[l] Dalt. cap. 127.

to have answered the end of the Law, and to have done all that can be reasonably required of them: But howsoever the Law may stand in relation to this Case, it is certain, That if Persons be bound by Recognisance, that *J. S.* shall appear in the King's Bench the first Day of such a Term, to answer to such an Information against him, and not depart till he shall be discharged by the Court, and afterwards the Attorney General enter a *Nolle prosequi* as to that Information, and exhibit another, on which the Defendant is convicted, and refuses to appear in Court after personal Notice, the Recognisance is forfeited; for being express that the Party shall not depart till he be discharged by the Court, it cannot be satisfy'd unless he be forth-coming, and ready to answer to any other Information exhibited against him whilst he continues not discharged, as much as to that which he was particularly bound to answer to. But in such Case it seems, That the Recognisance shall not be forfeited by the Party's not appearing in Court the first Day of every Term, after he hath pleaded to the Information, as it may be before he hath pleaded.

Queen and Redpath, 11 Ann.

CHAP. XVI.

Of Commitments.

AND now I am to consider in what Cases, and in what Menner, Offenders are to be committed, for the better Understanding whereof, I shall examine,

1. What kinds of Offenders are to be committed.
2. By whom.
3. To what Prison.
4. What is to be done previous to their Commitment.
5. What ought to be the Form of it.
6. At whose Charges they are to be sent to Prison.
7. To what Court the Commitment is to be certified.
8. By what means the Party may be discharged from such Commitment.

Sect. 1. As to the first Point, There is no Doubt but that Persons apprehended for Offences which are not bailable; and also all Persons who neglect to offer Bail for Offences which are bailable, must be committed.

Sect. 2. And it is said, That wheresoever a Justice of Peace is impowered by any Statute to bind a Person over, or to cause him to do a certain thing, and such Person being in his Presence shall refuse to be bound, or to do such thing, the Justice may commit him to the Gaol, to remain there till he shall comply.

Sect. 3. As to the second Point, *viz.* by whom such Persons are to be committed, it seems to be agreed by all the Old [a] Books, That wheresoever a Constable, or private Person, may justify the arresting another for a Felony or Treason, he may also justify the sending or

[a] 10 H. 4. 7. a. 7 Ed. 4. 20 a. 3 Ed. 4. 26. b. 27. a. 20 Ed. 4. 6. b. 10 Ed. 4. 17. b. 18. a. 5 H. 7. 4. b. 5 a. 2 H. 7. 3. b. 11 Ed. 4. 4. b.

2 bringing

bringing him to the common Gaol, and that every Private Person has as much Authority in cases of this kind as the Sheriff, or any other Officer, and may justify such Imprisonment by his [a] own Authority, but not by the Command of another. But [b] inasmuch as it is certain, That a Person lawfully making such an Arrest may justify bringing the Party to the Constable, in order to be carried by him before a Justice of Peace; and inasmuch as the Statutes of 1 & 2 *Ph. & M.* 13. and 2 & 3 *Ph. & M.* 10. which direct in what manner Persons brought before a Justice of Peace for Felony shall be examined by him in order to their being committed or bailed, seem clearly to suppose, That all such Persons are to be brought before such Justice for such purpose; and inasmuch as the Statute of 31 *Car.* 2. commonly called the *Habeas Corpus* Act, seems to suppose, That all Persons who are committed to Prison, are there detained by Vertue of some Warrant in Writing, which seems to be intended of a Commitment by some Magistrate; and the constant Tenour of the late Books, Practice and Opinions, are agreeable hereto: It is certainly most advisable at this Day, for any Private Person who arrests another for Felony, to cause him to be brought as soon as conveniently he may, before some Justice of Peace, that he may be committed or bailed by him.

[a] 5 H. 7. 4. b. 5. a. Fitz. False Imprisf. 8.
[b] 9 Ed. 4. 26. b. 27. a. 10 Ed. 4. 17. b. H. P. C. 91, 112.

H. P. C. 91, 112. Dalt. cap. 118.

Sect. 4. But it is certain, [c] That the Privy Council, or any one or two of them, or a Secretary of State, may lawfully commit Persons for Treason, and for other Offences against the State, as in all Ages they have done.

[c] 1 And 298. Palm. 558. 1 Sid. 78. 1 Leon. 70, 71. Sir William Wyndham's Case, Trin. 2 Georg. Sal. 347.

As to the third Point, *viz.* To what Prison such Offenders are to be committed, I shall observe,

1. That the Prison ought to be in the Realm of *England.*
2. That regularly it ought to be a Common Prison.

Sect. 5. As to the first of these Particulars, it is enacted by 31 *Car.* 2. 12. *That no Subject of this Realm, being an Inhabitant, or Resiant of this Kingdom of* England, *Dominion of* Wales, *or Town of* Berwick upon Tweed, *shall or may be sent Prisoner into* Scotland, Ireland, Jersey, Guernsey, Tangier, *or into Parts, Garrisons, Islands, or Places beyond the Seas, which then were, or at any time hereafter should be, within or without the Dominions of his Majesty, his Heirs or Successors; and that every such Imprisonment is by the said Statute enacted and adjudged to be illegal, and that every Subject so imprisoned, shall have an Action of False Imprisonment,* &c. *and recover treble Costs, and no less Damages than five Hundred Pounds against the Person making such Warrant, who shall also incur a* Præmunire.

Sect. 6. As to the second of the above-mentioned Particulars, It is enacted by 14 *Ed.* 3. 10. as followeth, *In the right of the Gaols which were wont to be in ward of the Sheriffs, and annexed to their Bailiwicks; it is assented and accorded, That they shall be rejoined to the Sheriffs, and the Sheriffs shall have the Custody of the same Gaols, as before this time they were wont to have; and they shall put in such Under-keepers for whom they will answer.* And this is confirmed by 19 *H.* 7. *chap.* 10. Also it is recited by 5 *H.* 4. 10. *That divers Constables of Castles, within the Realm, being assigned Justices of Peace by the King's Commission, had by colour of such Commission, used to take People to whom they bore evil Will, and imprison them within the said Castles, till they had made Fine and Ransom with the said Constables for their Deliverance.* And thereupon it is enacted, *That none be imprisoned by any Justice of the*

the Peace, but only in the Common Gaol; saving to Lords and others which have Gaols their Franchise in this Case.

Sect. 7. And it [a] seems, That the King's Grant since this Statute to private Persons to have the Custody of Prisoners committed by Justices of Peace, is void. And it is said, That none can claim a Prison as a Franchise, unless he have also a Gaol-delivery.

Sect. 8. It seems to be [b] agreed, That if a Person be arrested in one County, for a Crime done in it, and fly into another, and be re-taken there, he may be brought before a Justice of the County where the Offence was done, and be committed by him to the Gaol of such County. But it seems to be the stronger [c] Opinion, That if one who hath committed an Offence in one County, fly into another before he be taken, and be pursued and arrested in such County, he ought to be brought before a Justice of the County where he is taken, and be committed by him to the common Gaol of the same County, [d] whether it lie in such County or another; [e] unless there be some special Reason to the Contrary, as an apparent Danger that the Party may be rescued from such Prison by Rebels, *&c.* And it seems to be laid down as a Rule, by some Books, [f] That any Offender may be committed to the Gaol next to the Place where he was taken, whether it lie in the same County or not.

Sect. 9. It is [g] said, That if a Constable bring a Felon to Gaol, and the Gaoler refuse to receive him, the Town where he is Constable ought to keep him till the next Gaol-Delivery. But [h] in other Cases it seems, That regularly no one can justify the detaining a Prisoner in Custody out of the common Gaol, unless there be some particular Reason for so doing; as if the Party be so dangerously [i] sick that it would apparently hazard his Life to send him to the Gaol, [k] or there be evident Danger of a Rescous from Rebels, *&c.* Yet constant Practice seems to authorise a Commitment to a Messenger; and it is [l] said, That it shall be intended to have been made in order for the carrying of the Party to Gaol.

Sect. 10. As Prisoners ought to be committed at first to the proper Prison, so ought they not to be removed from thence, except in some special Cases. And to this Purpose it is enacted by 31 *Car.* 2. *chap.* 2. Par. 9. *That if any Subject of this Realm, shall be committed to any Prison, or in Custody of any Officer or Officers whatsoever, for any criminal, or supposed criminal Matter; that the said Person shall not be removed from the said Prison and Custody, into the Custody of any other Officer or Officers, unless it be by* Habeas Corpus, *or some other legal Writ; or where the Prisoner is delivered to the Constable, or other inferiour Officer, to carry such Prisoner to some common Gaol; or where any Person is sent by Order of any Judge of Assise, or Justice of the Peace, to any common Workhouse, or House of Correction; or where the Prisoner is removed from one Prison or Place to another, within the same County, in order to a Trial, or Discharge by due Course of Law; or in case of sudden Fire, or Infection, or other Necessity; upon Pain that he who makes out signs or countersigns, or obeys or executes such Warrant, shall forfeit to the Party grieved one Hundred Pounds for the first Offence, two Hundred Pounds for the second,* &c.

Sect. 11. As to the fourth Point, *viz.* What ought to be done previous to the Commitment of such Offenders, it is enacted by 2 *&* 3 *Ph. & M.* 10. *That every Justice or Justices, before whom any Person shall be brought for Manslaughter, or Felony, or for Suspicion thereof, before he or they shall commit or send such Prisoner to Ward, shall take the Examination of such Prisoner, and Information of those that bring him, of the Fact and Circumstances thereof; and the same, or as much thereof as shall be material to prove the Felony,*

[a] See 1 And. 345. Cro. El. 829, 830. 9 Co. 119. b. Sal. 343.
[b] H. P. C. 93. Dalt. cap. 118. Cromp. 172, b. 173, a.
[c] Dalt. cap. 118. Crompt. 72, b. H. P. C. 92. 93. 11 Ed. 4. 4, b. 5, a. 13 Ed. 4. 8, b. 9, a. Pl. Com. 37, a. Keilw. 45, b. Contra 2 Bulst. 264. 11 Ed. 4. 7. a. b.
[d] Keilw. 45, b. 11 Ed. 4. 5, a
[e] 11 Ed. 4. 4, b. 5, a. 7, a. b.
[f] Keilw. 45, b. 22 Ed. 4. 34, b.
[g] H. P. C. 114. 10 H. 4. 7. pl. 2. Fitz. Escape, 8. Dalt. cap. 118. Bro. faux. Imprisonment. 25.
[h] 20 Ed. 4. 6, b. Bro. faux. Imprisonment. 21, 27. 11 Ed. 4. 7. a. b.
[i] 2 Ed. 4. 8. b
[k] 11 Ed. 4. 4, b. 5, a.
[l] Sal. 347.

shall put in writing within two Days after the said Examination, and the same shall certify in such Manner and Form, and at such Time, as they should and ought to do, if such Prisoner, so committed or sent to Ward, had been bailed, or let to Mainprize, upon such Pain as in 1 *&* 2 Ph. & M. 13. *is limited and appointed, for not taking or not certifying such Examinations,* &c. *And it is farther enacted, That the said Justices shall have Authority to bind all such by Recognisance or Obligation, as do declare any thing material to prove the said Manslaughter, or Felony, to appear at the next General Gaol-Delivery to be holden within the County, City, or Town Corporate, where the Trial of the said Manslaughter, or Felony, shall be, then and there to give Evidence against the Party; and that the said Justices shall certify the said Bonds taken before them, in like manner as they ought to certify the Bonds mentioned in the said former Act,* &c. See Chap. 15. Sect. 60.

Sect. 12. It seems that a Justice of Peace ought not to detain a Prisoner by Vertue of this Statute, in order to examine him, any longer than is necessary for such Purpose, for which it is said, That the space of three Days is a reasonable time. Cro. E. 829, 830.

As to the fifth Point, *viz.* What ought to be the Form of a Commitment, the following Rules are to be observed.

Sect. 13. 1. It must be in Writing, under the Hand and Seal of the Person by whom it is made, and expressing his Office, or Authority, and the Time and Place at which it is made, and must be directed to the Gaoler, or the Keeper of the Prison. 2 Inst. 52, 591. Dalt. cap 125. H. P. C. 94.

Sect. 14. 2. It may be made either in the Name of the King, and only tested by the Person who makes it, or it may be made by such Person in his own Name. Dalt. cap. 125.

Sect. 15. 3. It may command the [a] Gaoler to keep the Party in safe and close Custody; for if every Gaoler be bound [b] by the Law to keep his Prisoner in such Custody, surely it can be no fault in a *Mittimus* to command him so to do.

Sect. 16. 4. It ought to set forth the Crime alledged against the Party with convenient [c] Certainty, whether the Commitment be by the Privy [d] Council, or any other Authority; otherwise the Officer [e] is not punishable, by reason of such *Mittimus*, for suffering the Party to escape: And the Court, before whom he is removed by *Habeas Corpus*, ought to discharge or bail him: And this doth not only hold where [f] no Cause at all is expressed in the Commitment, but also where it it so loosely set forth, that the Court cannot adjudge whether it were a reasonable Ground of Imprisonment; as [g] where one was committed for manifold Contumacy to the High Commission-Court, or for [h] refusing to answer before them to certain Articles, or [i] for insolent Behaviour and Words spoken at the Council-Table, *&c.* And it is holden by Sir [k] *Edward Coke*, in his second Institute, That a Commitment for High Treason, or Felony in general, without shewing the Species of the Offence, is not good; yet in [l] another part of the same Book, such general Commitments seem to be allowed by him to be good: And there are Precedents of Commitments for Felony in general, in good [m] Authors. And [n] it hath been resolved, That Commitments for High Treason in general are good.

[a] Sir William Wyndham's Case, Trin. 2. Georg.
[b] 8 Co. 100. 9 Co 87, b. Dalt. cap. 118.
[c] H. P. C. 94. Dalt. cap 125. 2 Inst. 52, 591.
[d] 16 Car. 1. cap. 10. Cro. Car. 133, 507, 579, 593. 2 And 298. Contra 1 Ro. Re. 134. 1 Leon. 71. Ch. 15. Sect. 66, to 72.
[e] 2 Inst. 591. H. P. C. 109. Infra. cap. 17. Palm. 558.
[f] Cro. Car. 579, 793, 507. Barkham's & Lawson's Case. Palmer, 558.
[g] 1 Rol Rep. 245.
[h] 1 Rol. Rep. 220, 245.
[i] Cro. Car. 133, 579. 2 Bulst. 139, 140.
[k] 2 Inst. 591. 5 Mod. 85.
[l] 2 Inst. 52.
[m] Crompt. 233, b. Dalt. cap. 125.
[n] 1 Sid. 78. 2 And 298. 1 Keb. 305. Palmer, 558. Sir William Wyndham's Case, Trin. 2 Georg.

Sect. 15.

Sect. 17. 5. It is ſafe to ſet forth, That the Party is charged upon Oath; but this is not neceſſary, for it hath been [a] reſolved, That a Commitment for Treaſon, or for Suſpicion of it, without ſetting forth any particular Accuſation, or Ground of the Suſpicion, is good.

Sect. 18. 6. Every ſuch *Mittimus* ought to have a lawful Concluſion, [b] *viz.* That the Party be ſafely kept till he be delivered by Law, or by order of Law, or by due Courſe of Law; or that he be kept till farther [c] Order, (which ſhall be intended of the Order of Law) or to the like Effect. And if the Party be committed only for want of Bail, it ſeems [d] to be a good Concluſion of the Commitment, That he be kept till he find Bail. But a Commitment, [e] till the Perſon who makes it ſhall take further Order, ſeems not to be good. And it ſeems, That the Party committed by ſuch, or any other irregular *Mittimus*, may be bailed.

Sect. 19. As to the ſixth Point, *viz.* At whoſe Charge Offenders are to be ſent to Priſon, it is enacted by 3 *Jac.* 1. 10. *That every Perſon and Perſons, that ſhall be committed to the common or uſual Gaol within any County or Liberty within this Realm, by any Juſtice or Juſtices of the Peace, for any Offence or Miſdemeanour, having Means or Ability thereunto, ſhall bear their own reaſonable Charges, for ſo conveying or ſending them to the ſaid Gaol, and the Charges alſo of ſuch as ſhall be appointed to guard them to ſuch Gaol, and ſhall ſo guard them thither. And if any ſuch Perſon or Perſons ſo to be committed, ſhall refuſe at the time of their Commitment and ſending to the ſaid Gaol, to defray the ſaid Charges, or ſhall not then pay or bear the ſame, that then ſuch Juſtice or Juſtices of the Peace, ſhall and may by Writing under his or their Hand and Seal, or Hands and Seals, give Warrant to the Conſtable or Conſtables of the Hundred, or Conſtable or Tythingman of the Tything, or Townſhip where ſuch Perſon or Perſons ſhall be dwelling and inhabit, or from whence he or they ſhall be committed, or where he or they ſhall have any Goods within the County or Liberty, to ſell ſuch, and ſo much of the Goods and Chattels of the ſaid Perſons, as by the Diſcretion of the ſaid Juſtice, or Juſtices of the Peace, ſhall ſatisfy and pay the Charges of ſuch his or their conveying or ſending to the ſaid Gaol; the Appraiſement to be made by four of the honeſt Inhabitants of the Pariſh or Tything where ſuch Goods or Chattels ſhall remain and be, and the Overplus of the Money which ſhall be made thereof, to be delivered to the Party to whom the ſaid Goods ſhall belong.*

Sect. 20. And it is farther enacted, *That if the ſaid Perſons ſhall not have, or be known to have, any Goods or Chattels, which may be ſold for the Purpoſe aforeſaid, within the County or Liberty, an indifferent Aſſeſſment ſhall be made by the Conſtables and Church-Wardens, and two or three other the honeſt Inhabitants of the Pariſh, or Tything, where ſuch Offenders ſhall be taken or apprehended, the ſaid Taxation being allowed under the Hand of one or more Juſtice or Juſtices of the Peace, if there be ſuch Conſtables or Church-Wardens there inhabiting; and in default of them, by four of the principal Inhabitants of the ſaid Pariſh, Townſhip or Tything, where ſuch Offenders ſhall be taken or apprehended: And if any ſo aſſeſſed ſhall refuſe to pay their ſaid Taxation, then the Juſtice or Juſtices of Peace by whom the ſaid Offenders ſhall be committed to Priſon, or any Juſtice of Peace near adjoining, ſhall and may give Warrant as aforeſaid, to the Conſtable, Tythingman, or other Officer there, to diſtrain the Goods of any ſo aſſeſſed, which ſhall refuſe to pay the ſame, and to ſell the ſame; and that ſuch Perſon or Perſons ſo authoriſed, ſhall have full Power ſo to diſtrain, and by Appraiſment of four ſubſtantial Inhabitants of the ſaid Place, to ſell a ſufficient Quantity of the Goods and Chattels of the ſaid Perſon ſo refuſing, for the levying of the ſaid Taxation; and if any Overplus of the Money come by the Sale thereof, the ſame to be delivered to the Owner.*

[a] Sir William Wyndham's Caſe, Trin. 2 Geor. Dalt. cap. 125. Cromp. 233. b. 2 Inſt. 52. Palm. 558, 559.
[b] 2 Inſt. 52, 591. H. P. C. 94. Crompt. 233. b. Dalt. cap. 124.
[c] 1 Lev. 230 contra Cro. Car. 558.
[d] 6 Mod. 73, 74.
[e] 2 Inſt. 52, 591. 1 Rol. Rep. 220. 1 Lev. 230. Cro. Car. 579. con. 3 Bulſt. 48, 49. 1 Rol. Rep. 410.

Sect. 21. As to the seventh Point, *viz.* To what Court such Commitments are to be certified, it is enacted by 3 *H.* 7. 3. *That every Sheriff, Bailiff of Franchise, and every other Person, having Authority or Power of keeping of Gaol, or of Prisoners for Felony, do certify the Names of every such Prisoner in their keeping, and of every Prisoner to them committed for any such Cause, at the next general Gaol-Delivery, in every County or Franchise where any such Gaol shall be, there to be Calender'd before the Justices of the Deliverance of the same Gaol, whereby they may, as well, for the King as for the Party, proceed to make Deliverance of such Prisoners according to Law, on pain to forfeit to the King for every Default there recorded, one hundred Shillings.*

Sect. 22. As to the eighth Point, *viz.* By what means a Person under such a Commitment may be discharged, It seems, That a Person legally committed for a Crime, certainly appearing to have been done by some one or other, cannot be lawfully discharged by any one but by the King, till he be acquitted on his Trial, or have an *Ignoramus* found by the Grand Jury, or none to prosecute him, on a Proclamation for that purpose by the Justices of Gaol-Delivery. But if a Person be committed on a bare Suspicion, without any Appeal or Indictment, for a supposed Crime, where afterwards it appears that there was none, as for the Murder of a Person thought to be dead, who afterwards is found to be alive; it hath been holden, That he may be safely dismissed without any farther Proceeding, for that he who suffers him to escape is properly punishable only as an Accessary to his supposed Offence; and it is impossible that there should be an Accessary where there can be no Principal; and it would be hard to punish one for a Contempt, in disregarding a Commitment founded on a Suspicion, appearing in so uncontested a Manner to be groundless.

Keilw. 34. 3 Inst. 209, 210. H. P. C. 54. 95.

Keilw. 34. H. P. C. 109, 110, 114.

CHAP. XVII.

Of Hindrances in bringing Offenders to publick Justice, &c.

HAVING shewn in what Manner Criminals are to be arrested, bailed or committed, I am now to consider in what Manner they and their Assistants are punishable for an Hindrance in bringing them to publick Justice. And in order hereto I shall examine,

1. How far they are punishable for an Offence of this kind, before an Arrest made.
2. How far after an Arrest.

Sect. 1. As to the first Point, It is [a] certainly an Offence of a very high Nature, to oppose one who lawfully endeavours to arrest another for Treason, or Felony. And some [b] have said, That the Person who so opposes an Arrest for Treason, whereof he knows the Party to have been guilty, is thereby guilty of the Treason; and that he who so opposes an Arrest for Felony, is an Accessory to the Felony. And if it be

[a] H. P. C. 116. [b] S. P. C. 31. Letter B. Crompt. 38. b. 26 Ass. 47. Fitz Justice of Peace. 114, 231. Contra H. P. C. 116. Fitz. Coron. 333. 2 Inst. 590.

a H. P. C. 218, 219. 2 Inst. 183. Moore, 8. pl. 29. S. P. C. 41. Letter E.

a general [a] Rule, That whoever knowing a Person to have committed any such Crime receives and comforts him, and endeavours to favour and aid him in the making his Escape, thereby becomes a Principal in the Case of Treason, and an Accessory in the Case of Felony, though he use no Force in giving such Assistance to the Offender; it seems strange that he who so far takes part with him as to fight in his Defence from Justice, should not be at least equally guilty. And therefore it seems reasonable to understand the Books above cited, which seem to contradict this Opinion, to intend no more than that it is not Felony in the Party himself, who is attacked in order to be arrested, to save himself from the Arrest by such Resistance.

b S. P. L. 32. Letter I. 9 H. 4. 1. Pl. 3. 26 Ass. 47.

Sect. 2. [b] But if a Person, knowing another to have been guilty of such a Crime, barely receive him, and permit him to escape, without giving him any manner of Advice, Assistance or Encouragement in it, as by directing him how to do it in the safest manner, or furnishing him with Money, Provisions, or other Necessaries, it seems he is guilty of a high Misdemeanour only, but no capital Offence.

H. P. C. 111, 271.

Sect. 3. Also it is certain, That the Party himself who flies from such an Arrest, is not thereby guilty of a capital Offence, but only liable to forfeit his Goods, when such Flight is found against him, in such manner as hath been already shewn, *Chap.* 9. *Sect.* 51. and shall be also more fully considered hereafter.

Sect. 4. How far a Vill, which suffers one who has been guilty of Homicide to escape, is liable to be amerced, hath been already shewn, *Chap.* 12. *Sect.* 2, 3.

Offences of this kind, after an Arrest made, may be considered in relation either,

1. To the Party under such an Arrest. Or,
2. To others.

Such Offences by the Party himself are either without or with Force.

H. P. C. 108. 2 Inst. 589, 590.

Sect. 5. And first, As to such Offences by the Party himself, without Force, which seem properly to come under the Notion of Escapes, there is little remarkable in the Books; and therefore I shall content my self with taking notice, That as all Persons are bound to submit themselves to the Judgment of the Law, and to be ready to be justified by it; whoever, in any Case, refuses to undergo that Imprisonment which the Law thinks fit to put upon him, and frees himself from it by any Artifice, before such time as he is delivered by due Course of Law, is guilty of a high Contempt, punishable with Fine and Imprisonment. And if it be so great a Crime for one not arrested to fly, in order to save himself from Imprisonment for a capital Offence, surely it must be at least as great a Crime, for one who is actually under the Custody of the Law for any such Crime, by any indirect means to free himself from it. And some [c] have holden, That such an Escape amounts to Felony: But this Opinion seems to be over severe, and not to be maintained by the [d] Book cited to prove it.

Cro Car. 210. 1 Ass. pl. 6. c S. P. C. 31. Letter A. d 2 Ed. 3. 2. pl. 4. Fitz. Coron. 149.

CHAP.

CHAP. XVIII.

Of breaking Prison.

SUCH Offences by the Party himself, accompanied with Force, come under the Notion of Prison-breaches; which I shall consider,

1. As they stand by the Common Law.
2. On the Statute *de frangentibus Prisonam*, which was made in the first Year of King *Edward* 2.

Sect. 1. And first as to Prison-breaches, as they stood by the Common Law; it seems the better Opinion, [a] That all such Offences were Felonies, if the Party were lawfully in Prison for any Cause whatsoever, whether Criminal or Civil, and whether he were actually in the Walls of a Prison, or only in the Stocks, or in the Custody of any Person who had lawfully arrested him; and it seems not to have been any way material whether the Prison did belong to the King, or to the Lord of a Franchise; not only for that every Person who is under a lawful Imprisonment, may properly enough be called the King's Prisoner; but also because it is allowed, [b] That whoever breaks from any such Imprisonment, since the Statute *de frangentibus Prisonam*, is guilty of Felony: From whence it seems clearly to follow, That he must have been in like manner guilty before that Statute, the Purport whereof is not to make any Offences Felonies which were not so before, but only to restrain some of those which were. And it [c] seems also to be clear, That the Confession of such Offence before the Coroner is not traversable by the Common Law; which is not altered as to this Point by the Statute.

[a] Bracton, Lib. 3. ch. 9. Briton, fol. 17. S. P. C. 30. 2 Inst. 589. H. P. C. 87. Contra S. P. C. 31. Letter D. 33. Letter H. 1 H. 7. 6. pl. 2. Bro. Coron. 130. Cro. Car. 210. 2 Inst. 589.

[b] Vide infra. Sect 4.

[c] Vide Supra Ch. 9. Sect. 49.

Sect. 2. And now I am to consider these Offences, as they stand by the said Statute, for the better understanding whereof I shall first set down the Words of the Statute, and then endeavour to shew in what Manner they are to be understood.

Sect. 3. And first, the Words of the Statute are as follows, *De prisonariis prisonam frangentibus, Dominus Rex vult & præcipit, quod nullus de cætero, qui prisonam fregerit, subeat judicium vitæ vel membrorum pro fractione prisonæ tantum, nisi causa, pro qua captus & imprisonatus fuerit, tale judicium requirat, si de illa secundum legem & consuetudinem terræ fuisset convictus, licet temporibus præteritis aliter fieri consuevit.* For the better understanding of the Construction whereof, I shall consider the following Points,

2 Inst. 589

1. What shall be said to be a Prison, within the meaning of this Statute.
2. How far the Imprisonment ought to be well grounded.
3. What shall be said to be a breaking of Prison.
4. For what Crime the Party ought to be imprisoned, to make the Offence of breaking the Prison Felony, within the Intent of the Statute.

5. Whether

5. Whether the Offence of breaking Prison can ever amount to High Treason.

6. At what Time, and in what Manner, the Offender is to be proceeded against.

7. In what Manner he is to be indicted.

8. In what Manner those are to be punished for a Breach of Prison, who are within the Benefit of the Statute.

Sect. 4. As to the first Point, *viz.* What shall be said to be a Prison [a] within the meaning of the Statute; it seems clear, That any Place whatsoever, wherein a Person under a lawful Arrest for a supposed Crime, is restrained of his Liberty, whether in the Stocks or Street, or in the common Gaol, or the House of a Constable or private Person, or the Prison of the Ordinary, is properly a Prison within the Statute; for Imprisonment [b] is nothing else but a Restraint of Liberty.

Sect. 5. As to the second Point, *viz.* How far the Imprisonment ought to be well grounded, it is clear, [c] That if a Person be taken upon a *Capias*, awarded on an Indictment or Appeal against him, for a supposed Treason, or Felony, he is within the Statute if he break the Prison, whether any such Crime were in Truth committed by him or any other Person, or not; for that there is an Accusation against him on Record, which makes his Commitment lawful be he never so innocent, and the Prosecution never so groundless.

Sect. 6. Also if an Innocent Person be committed by a lawful *Mittimus* on such a Suspicion of a Felony, actually done by some other, as will justify his Imprisonment, though he be neither indicted nor appealed, he is certainly [d] within the Statute if he break the Prison, for that he was legally in Custody, and ought to have submitted to it till he had been discharged by due course of Law.

Sect. 7. But if no [e] Felony at all were done, and the Party be neither indicted nor appealed, it seems clear, That no *Mittimus* for such a supposed Crime will make him guilty within the Statute by breaking the Prison, for that his Imprisonment was unjustifiable.

Sect. Also if a Felony were done, yet if there were no just Cause of Suspicion, either to arrest or commit the Party, it seems clear, That if his *Mittimus* be not in such Form [f] as the Law requires, his breaking of the Prison cannot be Felony, because the Lawfulness of his Imprisonment in such Case depends wholly on the *Mittimus*; which if it be not according to Law, the Imprisonment will have nothing to support it. But if the Party were taken up for such strong [g] Causes of Suspicion as will be a good Justification both of his Arrest and Commitment, but happen to be committed by an informal Warrant, it seems, that it may be probably argued, That it will be Felony [h] in him to break the Prison; for if by the ancient Common Law, any private Person might, of his own Authority, justify both an Arrest and Commitment, for Treason or Felony, on a reasonable Cause of Suspicion, as it seems probable [i] from the Tenor of all the old Books that he might; and if the Necessity of a *Mittimus* [k] from a Magistrate, depend rather on the constant settled Practice of Justices of Peace than any direct Law, it seems difficult to maintain that a Slip in want of Form of such a *Mittimus*, should make it lawful for the Prisoner to break the Prison, whereas by the old Law it would have been Felony in such a Case to have broken it, without any such *Mittimus* at all. And on the other side, if the Party be taken up

[a] Fitz. Coron. 158, 290, 312, 48, 164, 250, 419. 22 Aff pl. 85. Cro. Car. 210. 2 Inst. 589, 590. H. P. C. 107. Dyer 99. pl. 60. Cromp. 38, 39.

[b] S. P. C. 30. D.

[c] 2 Inst. 590. H. P. C. 109. Bro. Escape. 29. See Book 1. Chap. 28. Sect. 11, 12.

[d] H. P. C. 109. 2 Inst. 590. Dyer 99. pl. 60. Cromp. 38. a.

[e] H. P. C. 109. 2 Inst. 590. 591. Contra 2 Leon. 166.

[f] Vide Chap. 16. Sect. 12, 13, 14, 15, 16.

[g] Vide Supra Ch. 12. Sect. 8, 9, &c.

[h] Bro. Escape. 29. 42 Aff. 5.

[i] Vide Supra. Ch. 12 & Ch. 15 Sect. 3.

[k] Vide 5 Mod. 80.

up for such slight causes of Suspicion of a Felony actually done, as will not in Strictness justify the Arrest, yet if the Justice before whom he is brought think them of such Weight as to require a Commitment, and do accordingly send the Party to Gaol by a regular *Mittimus*, it seems very dangerous for him to break the Prison; for the Practice of Justices of Peace in making such Commitments, being now grown into settled Law, it seems reasonable, that their *Mittimus* be a good Justification of the Imprisonment which it commands, for a Crime within their Jurisdiction regularly brought before them; from whence it follows, That to break from such Imprisonment must be unlawful. And therefore, since it doth not appear, that there hath been any direct Resolution of these Points, perhaps it may be reasonable to understand what is more generally said by Sir [a] *Edward Coke*, and Sir [b] *Matthew Hale*, in relation to this Matter, according to the above-mentioned Distinctions.

Vide infra, Sect. 14.

[a] 2 Inst. 591.
[b] H. P. C. 109.

As to the third Point, *viz.* What shall be said to be a breaking of Prison, within the Meaning of this Statute, the following Rules are to be observed.

Sect. 8. 1. There must be an actual [c] Breaking; for every Indictment for this Offence, as a Felony, must have the Words *felonicè fregit prisonam*, which seem necessarily to import the use of some real Force or Violence, and not such only as may be implied by the Construction of Law, in any Act done in Contempt of it; and therefore, if without any Obstruction a Prisoner go out of the Prison Doors, being opened by the Consent or Negligence of the Gaoler, or otherwise escape without using any kind of Force or Violence, he is guilty of a Misdemeanour only, but not of a Felony, and the Gaoler is punishable in such manner as shall be set forth more at large in the next Chapter.

[c] 2 Inst. 590. H. P. C. 108. S. P. C. 31. Letter A.
[d] Supra Sect. 5.

Sect. 9. 2. Such Breaking must be either by the Prisoner himself, or by others through his Procurement, or at least with his Privity; for if the Prison be broken by others, without his Procurement or Consent, and he escape through the Breach so made, it seems the better [e] Opinion that he cannot be indicted for the Breaking, but only for the Escape.

[e] 2 Inst. 589. H. P. C. 108. S. P. C. 30. Letter E. 31 Letter B. Fitz. Coron. 48. 1 H. 7. 6. a.

Sect. 10. 3. Such Breaking must not be necessitated by an inevitable Accident, happening without any fault of the Prisoner; as where [f] the Prison is fired by Lightning, or otherwise, without his Privity, and he breaks it open to save his Life.

[f] 15 H. 7. 1. 2 Pl. Com. 136. 2 Inst. 590. H. P. C. 108.

Sect. 11. 4. It seems, That no Breach of Prison will amount to Felony, unless the Prisoner escape; for if the Breaking of a Prison by a Stranger, in order to free the Prisoners who are in it, be not Felony, unless the Prisoners go out of it, as it is said [g] that it is not, it seems *a fortiori*, That such a Breach by the Prisoner himself, who lies under so much stronger a Temptation to it, cannot be Felony, unless he do escape.

[g] Keilw. 87. a.

As to the fourth Point, *viz.* For what Crime the Party must be imprisoned, to make his breaking the Prison Felony within the Meaning of the Statute, the following Rules are to be observed.

Sect. 12. 1. It is not material, whether the Offence for which he was imprisoned were capital at the time of this Statute, or were made so by subsequent Statutes; for since all Breaches of Prison were Felonies by the Common Law, which is restrained by the Statute in respect only

H. P. C. 108.

of Imprisonment for Offences not capital; when an Offence becomes capital, it is as much out of the benefit of the Statute, as if it had always been so.

Sect. 13. 2. The Offence for which the Party was imprisoned must be a Capital one at the time of the Offence, and not become such by Matter subsequent; as where [a] *A.* is committed to Prison for a dangerous Wound given to *B.* and breaks the Prison, and then *B.* dies: For though to some Intents such Offence be esteemed capital from the time of the first Act, yet inasmuch as it was in Truth but a Trespass at the time of the breaking of the Prison, and it was then uncertain whether it would ever become capital; and it becomes such afterwards *ab initio*, by Fiction only, for some special Purposes, and Fictions of Law are never carried farther than the Necessity of those particular Cases, which were the Cause of the inventing them doth require; they shall never be construed to exempt a Person from the Advantage of a beneficial Law made in Favour of Life, who is clearly within the Letter, and doth not plainly appear to be out of the Meaning of it. However, it seems certain, That such an Offender breaking Prison, while it is uncertain whether his Offence will become capital, is highly punishable for his Contempt, by Fine and Imprisonment, *&c.*

[a] H. P. C. 108, 219. 2 Inst. 591. Pl. Com. 258, b. 401, a. 11 H. 4. 12. b. S. P. C. 33. A.

11 H. 4. 12. b. S. P. C. 35. Letter H.

Sect. 14. 3. If the Party be only arrested for, and in his *Mittimus* charged with a Crime which does not require judgment of Life or Member, as Petit Larceny, or Homicide *se defendendo*, or by Misadventure, and the Offence, in Truth, be no greater than the *Mittimus* doth suppose it to be, it is clear, from the express Words of the Statute, That a Breaking of the Prison cannot amount to Felony. And if the Offence for which the Party is committed, be supposed in the *Mittimus* to be of such a Nature as requires a capital Judgment, yet if in the Event it be found to be of an inferior Nature, and not to require such a Judgment, it seems difficult to maintain, That the Breaking of the Prison on a Commitment for it can be Felony; for the Words of the Statute are, *Nisi causa pro qua captus & imprisonatus fuerit, tale judicium requirit*; and here it appears, That the Offence, which is the Cause of his Imprisonment, doth not require such a Judgment; and it is hard to say, That a Mistake of the Nature of the Crime, by the Person who makes the Arrest or *Mittimus*, should so far prejudice the Party, as to make his Escape amount to Felony by reason of such Mistake, which otherwise would have been but a Trespass. Also it seems to be agreed, That if a Person be committed for a supposed Felony, where no Felony hath been done, he is not guilty of Felony for breaking the Prison; from whence it clearly appears, That in that Case the Law doth not so far regard the Charge contained in the *Mittimus*, where there is no good Ground to support it, as in respect thereof to exclude the Party from the Benefit of the Statute; and yet in that Case the Party is as much accused of a capital Offence as in the Case in question; so that it is clear, That the Law doth not so much respect the Hainousness of the Charge against the Party, as of the very Crime which is the subject of the Charge: And this will farther appear if it be considered, That the Accusation cannot be said to be the Cause which requires Judgment of Life or Member, but the Offence which supports the Accusation; and if there be no such Offence, there is, in Truth, no Cause which requires such a Judgment. On the other side, If the Offence, which was the Cause of the Commitment, be in Truth of such a Nature as requires a capital Judgment, but in the *Mittimus* be supposed to be of an inferior Degree; it may probably be argued, That the Party's breaking

H. P. C. 110. 2 Inst. 590.

ing of the Prison is Felony within the meaning of the Statute; for the Cause of his Arrest and Commitment is the Fact for which he was arrested and committed, and that does in Truth require Judgment of Life, though the Nature of it be mistaken in the *Mittimus*, which does no way alter the Judgment of Law in relation to the Guilt of it. But there appearing no express Resolution of these Points, and the [a] Authors who have expounded this Statute seeming rather to incline to a different Opinion, I shall leave these Matters to the Judgment of the Reader. [a] 2 Inst. 590, 591. H P. C. 109, 110.

Sect. 15. 4. It is not material, Whether the Party who breaks his Prison, were under an Accusation only, or actually attainted of the Crime charged against him; and yet the Words of the Statute are *si causa tale judicium requirit*: And it cannot be properly said, That the Offence of one attainted doth require such a Judgment, (for that there ought not to be a second Judgment against one already condemned) but only that it did require it; and it is a settled Rule, that all Statutes are to be construed strictly in Favour of Life, and that no parallel Case, which comes within the same Mischief, shall be construed to be within the Purview of it, unless it can be brought within the Meaning of the Words: Yet considering that the manifest Purport and Meaning of the Words of the Statute taken all together, is no more than this, That the Breaking of Prison shall not be a capital Offence, unless the Crime for which the Party was in Prison be also a capital Offence; and it is frequent, in the Construction of Penal Laws, to bring Persons within the Purview of them by being within the meaning of the Words, though not in strict Grammar properly within the very Letter; and it would be extreamly harsh to imagine, that the Makers of the Statute could intend a greater Favour to Persons appearing to be guilty, and actually under the Condemnation of the Law, than to Persons under an Accusation only: There can be no Doubt, but that Persons attainted, breaking Prison, are as much guilty within the Meaning of the above-mentioned Exception as any others. S. P. C. 32. Letters A, B, C, D. See Book 1. Ch. 32. Sect. 2, 3, 4.

Sect. 16. As to the fifth Point, *viz.* Whether the Offence of breaking Prison can ever amount to High Treason; it seems clear, That a Person committed for High Treason becomes guilty of Felony only, and not of High Treason, by breaking the Prison and escaping singly, without letting out any other Prisoner; for that no Offence is to be construed High Treason, which is not either within the Purview of 25 *Ed.* 3. or of some subsequent Statute relating to Treason; but if other Persons committed also for High Treason escape together with him, and his intention in breaking the Prison were to favour their Escape as well as his own, he seems to be guilty of High Treason in respect of their Escape, for that there are no Accessories in High Treason; and such Assistance given to Persons committed for Felony, will make him who gives it an Accessory to the Felony, and by the same reason a Principal in the Case of High Treason. But this Offence coming more properly under the Notion of Rescous than of the breaking of Prison, shall be more fully considered in the Chapter concerning Rescous. Book 1. Ch. 17. Sect. 2. 2 Inst. 590. S. P. C. 32. Letter F. 1 H. 6. 5. b.

Sect. 17. As to the sixth Point, *viz.* At what Time and in what Manner the Offender is to be proceeded against, it is said, That he may be arraigned for this Offence before he be convicted of the Crime for which he was imprisoned; for that it is not material whether he were guilty of such Crime or not, neither is he punishable as an Accessory in respect thereof, but as a principal Offender in respect of the Breach of H. P. C. 110, 116. 2 Inst. 592.

Prison it self; on which account this Case differs from that of a Rescous or voluntary Escape, as shall be shewn more at large in the following Chapters.

Fitz. Enditement. 30. 1 H. 7. 6. pl. 2.

Sect. 18. It seems clear, That the Sheriff's Return of a Breach of Prison, is not a sufficient Ground to arraign the Prisoner for it, unless he be also indicted.

H. P. C. 109. 2 Inst. 591. Fitz. Enditements, 18.

Sect. 19. As to the seventh Point, *viz.* In what Manner an Offender is to be indicted for a Breach of Prison, it is certain, That every Indictment of this kind, to bring the Offender within the Intention of the Statute, must specially set forth his Case in such a manner that it may appear that he was lawfully in Prison, and for such a Crime as requires Judgment of Life or Member; and that it is not sufficient to say in general, *Quod felonice fregit prisonam.* And it seems, That the same Rules which are required for an Indictment of an Escape, set forth at large in the next Chapter, are generally to be observed in Indictments of breaking Prison.

Book 1. Ch. 20. Sect. 1. Ch. 59 Sect. 1. H. P. C. 116. S. P. C. 35. H. 11 H. 4. 12. b.

Sect. 20. As to the eighth Point, *viz.* In what manner those are to be punished who are within the Benefit of the Statute, by being freed from that severe Judgment for the Breach of Prison, to which by the Common Law they would have been liable: There seems to be no Doubt, but that whoever breaks from any lawful Imprisonment is still punishable as for a High Misprision by Fine and Imprisonment; for that every capital Offence doth include in it a Misprision, and may be proceeded against as such only, if the King please; and it cannot be thought the Meaning of the Statute in ordaining, That such Offences shall not be punished as capital ones, to intend, That they shall not be punished at all.

CHAP. XIX.

Of Escapes suffered by Officers.

HAVING shewn in the precedent Chapters, how far the Party himself, under a lawful Arrest for a Crime charged against him, is punishable for unlawfully freeing himself from such Arrest, without waiting for his Deliverance by due Course of Law, I shall now in the second Place, consider Offences of this Kind in Relation to others. And

1. Such as are without Force.
2. Such as are accompanied with Force.

Such Offences, without Force, come under the Notion of Escapes, which are either,

1. By Officers. Or,
2. By Private Persons.

As

As to Escapes suffered by Officers, I shall endeavour to shew the following Particulars.

1. What shall be judged an Escape.
2. Where such Escape is to be esteemed voluntary, and where negligent.
3. Where the Prisoner may be re-taken after an Escape.
4. Whether the Escape is excused by such a Re-taking; or by killing the Prisoner if he cannot be re-taken.
5. In what Manner the Officer suffering an Escape is to be indicted.
6. How an Escape is to be tried and adjudged.
7. How a voluntary Escape is to be punished.
8. How a negligent one.

As to the first Point, *viz.* What shall be adjudged an Escape, the following Rules are to be observed.

Sect. 1. I. There must be an actual Arrest, and therefore, If [a] an Officer, having a Warrant to arrest a Man, see him shut up in a House, and challenge him as his Prisoner, but never actually have him in his Custody, and the Party get free, the Officer cannot be charged with an Escape.

Sect. 2. II. As there must be an actual Arrest, such Arrest must [b] also be justifiable, for if it be either for a supposed Crime, where no such Crime was committed, and the Party neither indicted nor appealed, or for such a slight Suspicion of an actual Crime, aud by such an irregular *Mittimus* as will neither justify the Arrest nor Imprisonment, the Officer is not guilty of an Escape by suffering the Prisoner to go at large: And it seems to be a good general Rule, That where-ever an Imprisonment is so far irregular, that it will be no Offence in the Prisoner to break from it by Force, it can be no Offence in the Officer to suffer him to escape.

Sect. 3. III. As the Imprisonment must be justifiable, so must it be also for a Criminal Matter; and some [c] are said to have holden, That no Escape is criminal, but where the Commitment is for Felony. However it is certain, That the Escape of one committed for Petit Larceny [d] only, is criminal; and it seems most agreeable to the general Reason of the Law, That the Escape of a Person committed for any other Crime whatsoever, should also be criminal. For surely, where-ever the publick Justice requires, That a Person be committed for a Crime; it likewise requires, That he be safely kept under such Commitment, and consequently may reasonably demand publick Satisfaction from the Officer to whose Custody he is committed, if he neglect to keep him as he ought.

Sect. 4. IV. As the Imprisonment must be justifiable, and for some Crime, so must its Continuance, at the time of the Escape, be grounded on that Satisfaction which the publick Justice demands from such Crime; for if a Prisoner be acquitted, [e] and detained only for his Fees, it will not be criminal to suffer him to escape, though the Judgment were, That he be discharged paying his Fees; so that till they be paid, the first Imprisonment continued lawful, as before; for inasmuch as he is detained, not as a Criminal, but only as a Debtor, his Escape cannot be more criminal than that of any other Debtor; yet if a Person convicted of a Crime, be condemned to Imprisonment for a certain Time,

[a] Coron 76. 9 H. 4. 1. pl. 3. 27 Assis. pl. 1. Fitz. Coron. 249. Bro. Escape, 22.

[b] Fitz. Coron. 224. 42 Ass. pl. 5. Bro. Escape, 27, 29. 5 Mod. 414, 415, 416. Contra 2 Leon. 166. See Ch. 18. Sect. 5, 6, 7, 8.

[c] Fitz. Coro. 248. S. P. C. 33. Letter H.

[d] Fitz. Coro. 430, 431. S. P. C. 33. Letter H.

[e] Bro. Escape 16. 21 H. 7. 7. S. P. C. 34. Letter F.

and also till he pay his Fees, and he escape after such time is elapsed, without paying them, perhaps such Escape may be criminal, for that it was part of the Punishment, that the Imprisonment be continued till the Fees should be paid; but it seems, that this is to be intended where the Fees are due to others as well as to the Gaoler, for otherwise the Gaoler will be the only Sufferer by the Escape, and it will be hard to punish him for suffering an Injury to himself only, in the Non-payment of a Debt in his Power to release.

Sect. 5. V. It is an Escape, in some Cases, to suffer a Prisoner to have greater Liberty than by the Law he ought to have; as to admit a Person to bail, [a] who by Law ought not to be bailed, but to be kept in close Custody; or to permit [b] a Prisoner to go out of the Limits of the Prison: Yet some [c] seem to have holden, That in this last Case it shall not be adjudged an Escape, unless the Prisoner be found to have had an Intention to escape; but it will be difficult to maintain, That the Offence of the Gaoler can depend on the Intention of the Prisoner.

Sect. 6. VI. If [d] the Gaoler so closely pursue the Prisoner, who flies from him, that he re-take him without losing sight of him, the Law looks on the Prisoner so far in his Power all the time, as not to adjudge such a Flight to amount at all to an Escape: But if the Gaoler once lose sight of the Prisoner, and afterwards re-take him, he seems in strictness to be guilty of an Escape; and *à fortiori* therefore, [e] if he kill him in the Pursuit, he is in like manner Guilty, though he never lost sight of him, and could not otherwise take him, not only because the King loses the Benefit he might have had from the Attainder of the Prisoner, by the Forfeiture of his Goods, *&c.* but also because the Publick Justice is not so well satisfied by the killing him in such an extrajudicial Manner.

Sect. 7. VII. While the Privileges of Sanctuaries were allowed, if a Sheriff, conducting a Prisoner to Gaol, had brought him in the way, through the Limits of such a Franchise, and the Prisoner had claimed the Privilege of it, and by that means got free, it seems, [f] that the Sheriff was guilty of an Escape, for that it was his fault, by bringing his Prisoner that way to Gaol, to give him an Opportunity of claiming the Franchise.

Sect. 8. VIII. Also while the Law allowed those who had the Benefit of the Clergy, to free themselves from Prison in certain Cases, by making their Purgation before the Ordinary, it was an Escape [g] in the Ordinary, to suffer such Persons to deliver themselves by it, in such Cases in which they ought not to have been admitted to it.

Sect. 9. IX. If [h] a Prisoner be rescued by Enemies, the Gaoler is not guilty of an Escape, as he would have been by the better Opinion, if he had been rescued by Subjects, because there is a legal Remedy against them.

Sect. 10. As to the second Point, *viz.* Where such Escape is to be esteemed voluntary, and where negligent, There [i] can be no Doubt, but that where-ever an Officer, who hath the Custody of a Prisoner, charged with and Guilty of a Capital Offence, doth knowingly give him his Liberty, with an Intent to save him, either from his Trial or Execution, he is guilty of a voluntary Escape, and thereby involv'd in the Guilt of the same Crime of which the Prisoner was guilty, and stood charged with. And it seems to be the Opinion of Sir *Matthew Hale*, [k] That in some Cases an Officer may be adjudged guilty of such Escape, who hath not such Intent, but only means to give his Prisoner that Liberty which

See Fitz. Coron. 430. S. P. C. 34. Letter E.

[a] 25 Ed. 3. 39. pl. 22. H. P. C. 113. Fitz. Escape, 4. Fitz. Coron. 246.

[b] Fitz. Coron. 242.

[c] Fitz. Coro. 431. S. P. C. 133. Letter E.

[d] Fitz. Coro. 236, 400. S. P. C. 33. Letters B. C. Bro. Escape, 14, 32, 49, 52. 10 H. 7. 25. b. 26. a. 6 H. 7. 11. b. 12. a.

[e] Fitz. Coro. 328, 346. S. P. C. 33. Letters B. C. See Book 1. Ch. 28. Sect. 11, 12.

[f] Bro. Escap. 38, 50. 2 H. 4. 15. pl. 14. Fitz. Coron. 222, 316. but 27 Ass. 54. and Bro. Escape, 24. seem contrary.

[g] Fitz. Coro. 16. 27 H. 6. 7. b. S. P. C. 33. Letters G. H. Vide 23 H. 8. 11.

[h] Bro. Escap. 10, 32, 52. 6 H. 7. 11. b. 12. a. 10 H. 7. 25. b. 26. a. 29 Ass. 34. Bro. Escape. 16. seems contrary.

[i] See Cro. Car 492. S. P. C. 32. Letter I.

[k] H. P. C. 113.

which by the Law he hath no Colour of Right to give him; as where a Gaoler bails a Prisoner who is not bailable. But it seems agreed, That a Person who hath Power to bail, is guilty only of a negligent Escape, by bailing one who is not bailable; neither can I meet with any Authority in other Books, to support the above-mentioned Opinion, That the bailing of one who is not bailable, by one who hath no Power to bail, must necessarily be esteemed a voluntary Escape; but the contrary Opinion seems more agreeable to the Purview of 5 *Ed.* 3. 8. set forth more at large in the subsequent part of this Chapter: Also there are some Cases wherein an Officer seems to have been found [a] to have knowingly given his Prisoner more Liberty than he ought to have had, as to go out of the Prison on his Promise of returning, or to go among his Friends, to find some who would warrant Goods to be his own, which he is suspected to have stoln, and yet seems to have been only adjudged guilty of a negligent Escape. But it must be confessed, That in these Cases, the Prisoner was only accused of Larceny; and it doth not appear, whether he were bailable or not, and generally the old Cases concerning this Subject, are so very briefly reported, that it is very difficult to make an exact state of the Matter from them; however thus much seems clear, That if in the Cases above-mentioned, the Officer were only guilty of a negligent Escape, in suffering the Prisoner to go out of the Limits of the Prison, without any Security for his Return, he could not have been guilty in a higher Degree, if he had taken Bail for his Return; from which it seems reasonable to infer, That it cannot be in all Cases a general Rule, that an Officer is guilty of a voluntary Escape by bailing his Prisoner, whom he hath no Power to bail; but that the Judgment to be made of all Offences of this kind, must depend on the Circumstances of the Case, as the Heinousness of the Crime with which the Prisoner is charged, the Notoriety of his Guilt, the Improbability of his returning to render himself to Justice, the Intention of the Officer, the Motives on which he acted, *&c.*

Supra. Sect. 5.

[a] Fitz. Coro. 242, 316, 431. S. P. C. 33.

Sect. 11. Neither is it a certain Rule, That an Officer, who unlawfully, knowingly, and willingly suffers a Capital Offender to escape, is in all Cases to be adjudged guilty of a voluntary Escape; for where an Ordinary suffered a Clerk, attainted, being committed to his Custody, to free himself from Imprisonment, by making his Purgation, he might be truly said, to have suffered such Prisoner to escape unlawfully, knowingly, and willingly, and yet it seems, [b] that he was guilty only of a negligent Escape, for that he did not save the Prisoner from Execution, which was excused by the Privilege of the Clergy, but only from the Imprisonment.

[b] Fitz. Coro. 18, 370. Escape, 1. S. P. C. 34. G. 141. B. 15 H. 7. 9. pl. 8.

Sect. 12. As to the third Point, *viz.* In what Cases a Prisoner may be re-taken after an Escape; it seems to be clearly agreed, by all the Books, [c] That an Officer making a fresh Pursuit after a Prisoner, who hath escaped through his Negligence, may re-take him at any time after, whether he find him in the same, or in a different [d] County. And it is said generally in some Books, [e] That an Officer who hath negligently suffered a Prisoner to escape, may re-take him where-ever he finds him, without mentioning any fresh Pursuit; and indeed, since the Liberty gained by the Prisoner is wholly owing to his own Wrong, there

[c] Fitz. Trespass, 94. Escape, 2. Coron. 236. Bro. Escape, 49, 32, 52. 13 Ed. 4. 9. 2 Ed. 4. 6. b.

[d] 33 H. 6. 52. b 53. a. 3 Co. 44, b. 52. Bro. Escape, 4. Fresh Suit, 3, 5. Contra Keilw. 3. a.

[e] Fitz. Coron. 236, 400, 313, 335. S. P. C. 117. Letter C. Bro. Execution, 58, 151. 27 H. 8. 1. a. 13 H. 7. 1. b. F. N. B. 130.

seems

ſeems to be no reaſon he ſhould take any manner of Advantage from it. But where a Gaoler hath voluntarily ſuffered a Priſoner to eſcape, it is ſaid by ſome, [a] That he can no more juſtify the re-taking him, than if he had never had him in Cuſtody before, becauſe by his own free Conſent he hath admitted, that he hath nothing to do with him. And it ſeems to be holden by Sir *William Staundforde*, [b] That after a Gaoler hath been fined for ſuffering a Priſoner negligently to eſcape, he cannot afterwards re-take him; but the Book [c] on which alone he ſeems to ground his Opinion, doth not fully come up to it; for the Purport of it ſeems to be no more than this, That a Gaoler's re-taking of a Priſoner, after he hath been fined for an Eſcape, ſhall be to no purpoſe, for that it is contrary to the Record, by which it appears, that the Priſoner hath been at large; by which it ſeems only to be intended, That a Gaoler, who hath been fined for an Eſcape, ſhall not avoid the Judgment of his Fine by re-taking the Priſoner: But I do not ſee how it can be collected from hence, that he cannot juſtify the re-taking him.

[a] 2 Jon 21, 22, 45. 3 Co 52. b. Cro. Jac. 659. Query 1 Danv. Abr. 633 pl 4. 535 pl. 11.
[b] S. P. C 33. Letter E
[c] 13 Eed. 4. 9. Fitz. Eſcape, 2. Bro. Eſcape 35.

Sect. 13. As to the fourth Point, *viz.* How far an Eſcape is excuſed by re-taking the Priſoner, or by killing him if he cannot be re-taken; perhaps it is the better Opinion, [d] That where-ever a Priſoner, by the Negligence of his Keeper, gets ſo far out of his Power that the Keeper loſes ſight of him, the Keeper is finable at the diſcretion of the Court, notwithſtanding he re-took him immediately after; for it ſeems agreed, That this is to be adjuded a negligent Eſcape, which implies an Offence, and conſequently that it muſt be puniſhable. It is true indeed, That in an Action againſt a Gaoler, for ſuffering one arreſted in a Civil Action to eſcape, it is a good Excuſe for the Gaoler, that before the Action brought, he re took the Priſoner upon freſh Suit, which is well maintained by ſhewing that he purſued him immediately after Notice of the Eſcape, though it were ſome Hours after it, and re-took him; but it does not from hence follow, that the like Excuſe will ſerve for the negligent Eſcape of a Criminal, becauſe this is an Offence againſt the Publick, but the other is only a private Damage to the Party: Neither will it be the like Hardſhip to the Officer, to be expoſed to ſuch Puniſhment as the Court, in diſcretion, ſhall think fit to impoſe upon him for the negligent Eſcape of a Criminal, as it would be to be liable to an Action of Eſcape, for ſuffering a Perſon in his Cuſtody, in a Civil Action, to eſcape; for that in the former Caſe the Court would moderate his Fine according to the Circumſtances of the whole Matter, and would certainly mitigate, if not wholly excuſe it, if he ſhould appear to have taken all reaſonable Care: But in the other Caſe, if he ſhould be liable to an Action, his Judgment would not lie in the diſcretion of the Court, but he would be bound to pay the whole Debt, for which the Party was in his Cuſtody, if the Eſcape ſhould be adjudged againſt him. However it is certain, that it will be no advantage to a Gaoler to re-take his Priſoner, after he has been fined for the Eſcape, as hath been ſhewn in the Precedent Section; alſo it is clear, that he cannot excuſe himſelf by killing a Priſoner in the Purſuit, though he could not poſſibly re-take him; but muſt, in ſuch Caſe, be content to ſubmit to ſuch Fine as his Negligence ſhall appear to deſerve.

[d] S. P. C. 33. H. P. C 114. ſeems contray.

See the Books cited Sect. 6. 1 Rol. Abr. 808. 1 Dan. Abr. 633 pl. 4. Vide 8 Gul. 26. S. 8.

Vide Supra. Sect. 6.

[d] 27 Aſſ pl. pl. 9. Bro. Eſcape, 22. Fitz. Aſſiſe, 247.

Sect. 14. As to the fifth Point, *viz.* In what Manner the Officer, ſuffering an Eſcape, is to be indicted, it ſeems clear, That every Indictment for an Eſcape, whether negligent or voluntary, muſt expreſsly ſhew, that the Party was actually [d] in the Defendant's Cuſtody for a Crime, Action, or Commitment for it; and that [e] it is not ſuffi-

[e] Salk. 272. 5 Mod. 414, 415.

cient to say, that he was in the Defendant's Custody, and charged with such a Crime; for that a Person in Custody may be so charged, and yet not be in Custody by reason of such Charge: And it seems also, that every such Indictment must expressly shew that the Prisoner went at large, which is most properly [a] expressed by the Words *exivit ad largum.* Also it seems necessary, to shew the Time when the Offence was committed, for which the Party was in Custody, not only [b] that it may appear, that it was prior to the Escape, but also [c] that it was subsequent to the last general Pardon. Also it seems clear, That every Indictment for a voluntary Escape, must alledge that the Defendant *felonicè & voluntariè* A. B. *ad largum ire permisit*; and must [d] also shew the Species of the Crime for which the Party was imprisoned; for it is not sufficient to say in general, That he was in Custody for Felony, *&c.* for that no one can be punished in this Degree, but as involved in the Guilt of the Crime for which the Party was in his Custody; and therefore the particular Crime must be set forth, that it may appear, that the Principal is attainted for the very same Crime, if it were Felony, or that it was in Truth committed, if High Treason. But it seems questionable, [e] whether such Certainty, as to the Nature of the Crime, be necessary in an Indictment for a negligent Escape, for that it is not material in this Case, whether the Person who escaped were guilty or not.

[a] Bro. Escape. 52. 10 H. 7. 26. a.
[b] Contra 2 Leon 166. Bro. Escape. 17. Cro. El. 752.
[c] Henly 13.
[d] Cro. El. 752. Hetley, 73. S. P. C. 95. A. H. P. C. 110, 111, 206. 8 Ed. 4. 3. pl. 6.
[e] See Keilw. 192, 194.

Sect. 15. As to the sixth Point, *viz.* In what manner an Escape is to be tried and adjudged, it is to be observed, That where Persons being present in a Court of Record, are committed to Prison by such Court, the Keeper of the Gaol is bound to have them always ready, whenever the Court shall demand them of him; and if he shall fail to produce them at such Demand, the Court will adjudge him guilty of an Escape, without any farther Inquiry, unless he have some reasonable Matter to alledge in his Excuse, as that the Prison was set on Fire, or broken open by Enemies, *&c.* for he shall be concluded,[e] by the Record of the Commitment, to deny that the Prisoners were in his Custody: And some [f] have holden, That if the Gaoler say nothing in Excuse of such an Escape, it shall be adjudged voluntary; but I cannot find any Resolution to this purpose; and where it stands indifferent, whether an Escape be negligent or voluntary, it seems difficult to maintain that it ought to be adjudged a Crime of so high a Nature, without a previous Trial.

S. P. C. 34, 35. Fitz. Coron. 466.
[e] 11 H. 6. 49. b. 12 H. 6. 2, b. 3. S. P. C. 35.
[f] S. P. C. 34. G. 39 H. 6. 33, 34.

Sect. 16. As to other Prisoners who are not so committed, but are in the Custody of a Gaoler, Sheriff, Constable, or other Person, by any other means whatsoever, it seems agreed, [g] That the Person who has them in Custody is in no Case punishable for their Escape, except in some special Cases, untill it be presented; for the better understanding whereof I shall endeavour to shew,

[g] S. P. C. 35.

1. Before whom such Presentments are to be made.
2. In what Cases they are traversable.

Sect. 17. As to the first Point, It is enacted by the Statute of *Westminster* 1. *Chap.* 3. *That nothing be demanded nor taken, nor levied by the Sheriff, nor by any other, for the Escape of a Thief, or Felon, until it be judged for an Escape by the Justices in Eyre; and that he who does otherwise, shall restore to him or them that have paid it, as much as he or they have taken or received, and as much also unto the King.*

[a] 27 Ass. pl. 1, 9. 21 Ass. pl. 12. S. P. C. 35. 2 Inst. 166.

Sect. 18. It hath been adjudged,[a] That this Statute restrains not the Court of King's Bench from receiving such Presentments, for that its Jurisdiction includes in it that of Justices in Eyre, and this Court is it self, the Highest Court of Eyre.

Sect. 19. It is farther enacted, by 31 *Ed.* 3. 14. *That the Escape of Thieves and Felons, and the Chattels of Felons, and of Fugitives, and also Escapes of Clerks Convict, out of their Ordinary's Prison, from thenceforth to be judged before any of the King's Justices, shall be levied from time to time, as they shall fall, as well of the Time past as time to come.* By which it seems to be implied, That other Justices, as well as those in Eyre, may take Cognisance of Escapes; and it is certain, That Justices of Gaol-Delivery may punish Justices of Peace for a negligent Escape, in admitting Persons to Bail, who are not bailable.

Vide Supra Ch. 6. S. 10, 11, 12, 13, 14. S. P. C. 35.

Sect. 20. And it is farther enacted, by 1 *Rich.* 3. *Chap.* 3. *That Justices of Peace shall have Authority to enquire, in their Sessions, of all manner of Escapes of every Person arrested and imprisoned for Felony.*

S P. C. 35. Letter F.

Sect. 21. As to the second Particular, in what Cases such Presentments are traversable; It is laid down as a Rule, by Sir *William Staundford*, That where-ever an Escape is finable, the Presentment of it is traversable; but that where the Offence is amerciable only, there the Presentment is of it self conclusive; such Amercements being reckoned among those *minima de quibus non curat lex*; and this Distinction seems to be well warranted by the Old[b] Books; and in what Cases Escapes are finable, and where amerciable only, shall be considered in the following part of this Chapter, *Sect.* 31, 33, 35.

[b] 21 Ass. pl. 12. 27 Ass. pl. 9, 27. Fitz. Coron. 291, 328, 345, 346, 352.

Sect. 22. As to the seventh Point, *viz.* In what manner a voluntary Escape is to be punished, it seems to be generally[c] agreed, That such Escape amounts to the same kind of Crime, and is punishable in the same degree, as the Offence of which the Party was guilty, and for which he was in Custody, whether it be Treason, Felony or Trespass; and whether the Person escaping were actually committed to some Gaol, or under an Arrest only and not committed; and whether he were attainted, or only accused[d] of such Crime, and neither indicted nor appealed: And it is said to be no Excuse of such Escape, that the Prisoner had been acquitted on an Indictment of Death, and only committed till the Year and Day be passed, to give the Widow, or Heir of the Deceased, an opportunity of bringing their Appeal.

[c] S. P. C. 32. I. H. P. C. 113. Bro. Coron. 112. 27 Ass. 62. 11 H. 4. 12. b. [d] H. P. C. 114, 115. Dyer 99. pl. 60. Fitz Escape, 3. 27 Ass. pl. 62.

Sect. 23. Also such an Escape, suffered by one who wrongfully takes upon him the keeping of a Gaol, seems to be[e] punishable in the same manner as if he were never so rightfully intituled to such Custody, for that the Crime is in both Cases of the very same ill Consequence to the Publick; and there seems to be no reason that a wrongful Officer should have greater Favour than a rightful, and that for no other reason but because he is a wrongful one.

[e] Bro. Escape, 18, 23. 2 Ro. Re. 246. Fitz. Assise, 252. 39 H. 6. 33, 34. Quere 27 Ass. pl. 27. H P. C. 114.

Sect. 24. Also if the Warrant of Commitment do plainly and expressly charge the Party with Treason or Felony, but in some other respect be not strictly formal, yet it seems, that it may[f] be probably argued, that the Gaoler suffering an Escape, is as much punishable as if the Warrant were perfectly right; for it would be highly inconvenient to suffer Gaolers to take advantage of a slip of this kind in Commitments, which, being generally made by Persons of no great knowledge in the Law, cannot be expected to be always agreeable to its Forms; and therefore, if they be good in Substance, the publick Good seems to require, that

[f] Salk. 272, 348. Contra H. P. C. 114. 2 Inst. 590, 591, 592. Salk 347. See Ch. 16. & Ch. 18. Sect. 5, 6, 7

that the Gaoler be as much bound to observe them, as if they were never so exactly made.

Sect. 25. But it seems to be agreed, That no Escape can amount to a capital Offence, unless the Cause for which the Party was committed, [a] were actually such at the time of the Escape; and therefore, if a Gaoler suffer one to escape who is committed for having given a dangerous Wound to another, who afterwards dies of such Wound, yet is he not guilty of Felony, for that the Offence of the Prisoner was but a Trespass at the time of the Escape; and though by a Fiction of Law it be afterwards, for some Purposes, esteemed a Felony from the time of the giving of the Wound, yet since it is, in truth, no Felony till the Death of the Party, it shall be afterwards construed such in respect of those only who were privy to the giving of the Wound.

[a] H. P. C. 114. 219. See Ch. 16. Sect. 19. 11 H. 4. 12. b.

Sect. 26. Also it seems clear, That he who suffers another to escape, who was in his Custody for Felony, cannot be arraigned for such Escape as for a Felony, untill the Principal be attainted; for that he who suffers such Escape, is, by the better Opinion, not punishable in this Degree, but as an Accessory to the Felony; and it is a Rule, That no Accessory ought to be tried till the Principal be attainted, as shall be more fully shewn hereafter: Yet it seems certain, [b] that one accused of such an Escape, may be indicted and tried for a Misprision, before the Attainder of the principal Offender, for that whether such Offender were guilty or innocent it was a high Contempt to suffer him to escape: And if the Commitment were for High Treason, and the Person committed actually guilty of it, it seems, that the Escape is immediately punishable as High Treason also, whether the Party escaping be ever convicted of such Crime or not; for that there are no Accessories in High Treason, but all who are guilty of assisting the Party guilty of such Crime, in such a manner as would make them Accessories to a Felony, are accounted Principals in the Treason, as shall be more fully shewn in the Chapter concerning Principal and Accessory.

H. P. C. 110, 215. 216. Fitz. Coron. 158. Query 27 Ass. 62. Contra Crompton, 58.

[b] H. P. C. 116. Fitz. Coron. 158. See Ch. 18. Sect. 20. H. P. C. 110, seems contrary.

H. P. C. 116.

Sect. 27. Also it seems to be clear, That no one is punishable in this degree for a voluntary Escape, but the Person only who is actually guilty of it; and therefore, that the principal Gaoler is only finable for a voluntary Escape suffered by his Deputy, for that no one shall suffer capitally for the Crime of another.

Salkield, 272. H. P. C. 113. 114.

As to the eighth Point, *viz.* in what manner a negligent Escape is to be punished, I shall endeavour to shew,

1. How such Escape is punishable by the Common Law.
2. How by Statute.

Sect. 28. As to the first Particular, I shall take it for granted at this Day, that whoever *de facto* occupies the Office of Gaoler is liable to answer for such an Escape; and that it is no way material whether his Title to the Office be legal or not.

H. P. C. 114. 2 Rol. Rep. 146. Bro. Escape, 18, 23.

Sect. 29. Also I take it to be the better Opinion, That [c] a Sheriff is as much liable to answer for an Escape suffer'd by his Bailiff, as if he had actually suffer'd it himself, and that [d] the Court may charge either the Sheriff or Bailiff for such an Escape; and that if a Deputy Gaoler be not sufficient [c] to answer a negligent Escape, his Principal must answer for him: But

Query 27 Ass. 27. Vide Supra. Sect. 23.

[c] Fitz. Coron. 317.

[d] Salk. 272. H. P. C. 113. 2 Levin. 71.

But if the Gaoler who suffers an Escape, have an Estate [a] for Life, or Years, in the Office, I do not find it agreed how far he in Reversion is liable to be punished.

Sect. 30. It seems the better Opinion, That one negligent Escape will not amount to a Forfeiture of the Gaoler's Office, as one voluntary [b] one will; Yet if a Gaoler suffer many negligent Escapes, it is said that he puts it in the Power of the Court to oust him of his Office by its Discretion.

Sect. 31. It seems to be certain, That where-ever a Person is found guilty upon an Indictment, or Presentment, of a negligent Escape of a Criminal actually in his Custody, he ought to be condemned in a certain Sum to be paid to the King, which seems most properly to be called a Fine; but this doth not clearly appear from the Old Books, for in some [c] of them it seems to be taken as a Fine, in others [d] as an Amercement, and in others it is spoken of generally, as an Imposition of a certain Sum, and without any [e] mention either of Fine or Amercement. But where the Books speak of the Punishment of a Vill, or Hundred, for suffering a Felon to escape without being arrested, they seem always to take it as an Amercement, and not as a Fine: And where a Sheriff, having returned a *Cepi Corpus* into the King's Bench, on a *Capias* against a Man on an Indictment of Felony, does not bring him in at the Day, it seems, [f] That he is, by the Course of the said Court, to be amerced, not fined.

Sect. 32. It hath been holden, [g] That a negligent Escape may be pardoned by the King before it happens, but that a voluntary one cannot be so pardoned; but this shall be more fully considered in the Chapter concerning Pardon.

Sect. 33. And it seems, [h] That by the Common Law, the Penalty for suffering the negligent Escape of a Person attainted, was of Course 100 *l.* and for suffering such Escape of a Person indicted and not attainted, was 5 *l.* [i] but if the Person escaping were neither attainted nor indicted, it seems that it was left to the Discretion of the Court to assess such a reasonable Forfeiture as should seem proper; and [k] if the Party had twice escaped, it seems, that the Penalties above-mentioned were of course to be doubled; yet it seems, that the Forfeiture was to be no greater for suffering [l] a Prisoner, committed on two several Accusations to escape, than if he had been committed but on one.

Sect. 34. As to the second Particular, *viz.* In what manner Offences of this kind are punishable by Statute, it is recited by 5 *Ed.* 3. *Ch.* 8. *That Persons indicted of Felonies in times past, had removed the Indictments before the King, and there yielded themselves, and by the Marshals of the King's Bench had been incontinently let to Bail, and after had done many evil Deeds,* &c. And thereupon it is enacted, *That such Enditees and Appellees shall be safely and surely kept in Prison, as belongeth to them, according to the Charge which the said Marshals shall have of the Justices; and if any Marshal shall do otherwise, at the Complaint of every Man that will complain, the Justices shall do him Right during the Terms; and in the end of the Terms, upon their rising, the said Marshals shall choose before the said Justices, before they depart their Places, in what Town they will keep such Prisoners, at their Peril: And in the same Town they shall allow to them Houses to keep such Prisoners at their own Costs and Charges; and there they shall keep them in Prison, and shall not suffer them to go wandring abroad, neither by Bail nor without Bail. And if any such Prisoner be found wandring out of Prison, by Bail or without Bail, and*

[a] 39 H. 6. 33, 34. 2 Rol. A. 155. Letters M. N. 3 Levin. 288. 2 Levin. 81.
[b] Bro forfeiture of Offices. 27. 2 R A. 155. Letter N.
[c] 8 H. 5. 2. Fitz. Coron. 84, 292.
[c] S. P. C. 35. H. Bro Escape, 16. Rastal's Ent. 583. b.
[d] Fitz. Coro. 335.
[e] 25 Ed. 3. 39. pl. 22. 27 Ass. pl. 9. S. P. C. 65. 26 Ass. pl. 51. H. P. C. 113 Fitz. Coron. 196, 291, 370. Graunt. 39. Escape, 4. See the Book Supra Ch 12. Sect. 2.
[f] Fitz. Esch. 7. 40 Ass pl. 42.
[g] 3 H. 7. 15. pl. 30. 8 H. 5. 2. pl. 6. Fitz. Graunt. 37.
[h] S. P. C. 35. K. H. P. C. 113. Fitz Coron. 370.
[i] S. P. C. 35. K. H. P. C. 113. 27 Ass. pl. 9. 40 Ass. pl. 42. 25 Ed. 3. 39. pl. 22. H. P. C. 113. Fitz. Coron. 454.
[k] S. P, C 33. K. Fitz. Coron. 422.
[l] Fitz. Coro. 196. 26 Ass. pl. 51.

that be found at the King's Suit, or at the Suit of the Party, the Marshals which shall be found thereof guilty, shall have half a Year's Imprisonment, and be ransomed at the King's Will; and the Justices shall thereof make Enquiry when they see time; and as to the Marshals, it shall be done within the Verge that which Reason will. And in case that the Marshals suffer by their Assent such Prisoners to escape, they shall be at the Law, as before the time of the Statute they had been. And the King intendeth not by this Statute to lose the Escape, where he ought to have the same.

Sect. 35. Also it is enacted by 19 *H.* 7. 10. *That every Sheriff have the Custody of the King's Common Gaols, during the time of his Office, except all Gaols whereof any Person or Persons have the keeping of Estate of Inheritance: And that all Letters Patents made for term of Life, or Years, of the keeping of the said Gaols,* &c. *shall be annulled and void.* And then it is recited by the said Statute, *That divers Persons before that time, for Treason and Felonies had been taken, some for Suspection of the same Deeds, and some upon Indictments, and thereupon brought to the same Gaols, and sometime remained in the keeping of the Persons that so arrested them for the said Causes, and that such Persons, by colour of Negligence, subtilly and craftily, and oftentimes for favour, Mede, Affection or Corruption, suffered the said Offenders to escape, as if it had been by Negligence, to the overt and express Impediment of Justice: And when such Escapes had been found before Justices having Authority to enquire thereof, and thereupon the Parties convicted, or yielded themselves to make Fine for the same, small Fines had been set in those Causes, to the little Dread and Fear, and great Imboldning of the Offenders, by means whereof, great and arrant Felons, and heinous Murderers had escaped,* &c. And thereupon it is enacted, *That for every negligent Escape from any Sheriff, having the keeping of any Gaol, or from any Constable of Castle, or other, being Keeper of any Gaols where such Prisoners accustomably have been, or shall be kept, of Persons indicted of High Treason being in their keeping, that no less Fine be set or made for every such Escape, than* 100 *Marks, and more, by the Discretion of the Justices that shall assess such Fines: And for every Escape of Persons escaping being in their keeping for Suspection of High Treason, no less Fine to be set ne made than* 40 l. *and for every Escape of Persons indicted of Murder, or Petit Treason,* 20 l. *at least, and more, by the Discretion of the Justices that shall assess such Fines: And for every Escape of Persons suspected of Murder or Petit Treason,* 10 l. *or more, by the Discretion of the Justices that shall assess such Fines: And for every Person escaping, being in their keeping, indicted of Felony, other than Murder or Treason,* 10 l. *And for every Person suspected of Felony, other than Murder or Treason,* 100 *Shillings, or more, by the Discretion of the Justices, after the Manner and Quantity of their Demerits, saving to every Person such Right and Title to any such Escapes and Fines for the same, or to be quit of such Escapes, or of any other Escapes, as they had, or ought to have had at the time of the making of the said Act.*

CHAP. XX.

Of Escapes suffered by private Persons.

HAVING in the precedent Chapter endeavoured to shew the nature of Escapes suffered by Officers, I am now in the second Place to consider, the nature of such Escapes suffered by private Persons: But the Law being generally the same in relation to such Escapes, as in relation to those suffered by Officers, I shall refer the Reader, for the general Learning of this kind, to what is said in the former Chapter concerning Escapes suffered by Officers, and shall content my self in this Place with considering the two following Particulars.

H. P. C. 112.

1. Where a private Person is to be adjudged guilty of such an Escape.
2. In what Manner he is to be punished.

Sect. 1. As to the first Point, It seems to be a good general Rule, That where-ever any Person hath another lawfully in his Custody, whether upon an Arrest made by himself or another, he is guilty [a] of an Escape, if he suffer him to go at large, before he hath discharged himself of him by delivering him over to some other who by Law ought to have the Custody of him.

[a] See Ch. 12. H. P. C. 112.

Sect. 2. And therefore, If a private Person arrest another for Suspicion of Felony, and deliver him into the Custody of another private Person, who receives him, and suffers him to go at large, it is said, [b] That both of them are guilty of an Escape, the first, because he should not have parted with him, till he had delivered him into the Hands of a publick Officer; the later, because having charged himself with the Custody of a Prisoner, he ought, at his Peril, to have taken care of him.

[b] H. P. C. 112. 44 Aff. pl. 12. Bro. Escape, 31. 43 Ed. 3. 36. pl. 55. Fitz. Coron. 454. Escape, 3.

Sect. 3. But if a private Person, having made such an Arrest, have delivered over his Prisoner to the proper Officer (as the Sheriff, [c] or his Bailiff, [d] or a Constable, [e]) from whose Custody the Prisoner escapes, the Party who made the Arrest is not chargeable with it.

[c] Fitz. Coro. 345.
[d] Fitz. Coro. 328, 337. S. P. C. 34. D.
[e] H. P. C. 112.

Sect. 4. But if no Officer will receive such Prisoner into his Custody, it seems [f] to be the safest way to deliver him into the Custody of the Township where the Person who arrested him lives, or perhaps of that where the Arrest was made, which shall be bound to keep him till the next Gaol-Delivery; but if such Township refuse also to receive him, I do not see how the Person who made that Arrest can discharge himself of him before the next Gaol-Delivery, unless he can, in the mean time procure him to be bailed.

[f] 10 H. 7. pl. 2. Fitz. Escape, 8. H. P. C. 114.

Sect. 5. Neither can such private Person excuse himself of the Escape of such a Prisoner, by alledging, That he delivered him over to a Sheriff, or other Officer, without shewing to whom, in particular, by

Fitz. Coron. 345.

Name, he so delivered him, that the Court may certainly know who is answerable for him.

Sect. 6. As to the second Point, *viz.* In what manner a private Person is punishable for such an Escape, I shall take it for granted that if it were voluntary, he is punishable in the same manner as an Officer, for which I shall refer the Reader to the former Chapter; and if it were negligent, he is punishable by Fine and Imprisonment, at the Discretion of the Court, as the Law is settled by 19 *H.* 7. 10. The Words whereof, so far as they relate to this Purpose, are as follows, *And if any Person hereafter have any Prisoner in his keeping, arrested for Suspection of Felony, Treason, or Murder, and that Person that is so arrested, escape by negligent keeping before that he be brought to the Gaol, that Person from whom he so escaped, shall forfeit for every Person that doth so escape, such Fines as shall be set by the Discretion of the Justices that shall have Authority to assess such Fines, as the Cause shall require, and the same Forfeiture to go to them that be intituled to have such Forfeitures at the time of making the said Act.* H. P. C. 112. Bro. Coron. 112. 27 Ass. 62.

CHAP. XXI.

Of Rescous.

THE Offence of a Stranger, in forcibly freeing another from an Arrest, comes under the notion of Rescous, which in most Instances is of the same nature with the Offence of breaking Prison, which hath been already considered in the eighteenth Chapter; and therefore it seems sufficient for the Declaration of the Nature of this Crime, to shew,

1. In what Cases it agrees with the Offence of breaking Prison. And
2. In what it differs.

And first, This Offence agrees with that of breaking Prison in the following Particulars.

Sect. 1. I. Whatever is such a Prison, that the Party himself was, by the Common Law, guilty of Felony by breaking from it, in every such Case a Stranger was guilty of as high a Crime at least, in rescuing him from it. 2 Inst. 589. S. P. C. 30, 31. and the Cases cited Ch. 18. Sect. 1. & 4.

Sect. 2. II. Where-ever [a] the Imprisonment is so far groundless, or irregular, or for such a Cause, or the breaking of it is occasioned by such a Necessity, *&c.* that the Party himself breaking the Prison, is, either by the Common Law, or by the Statute *de frangentibus Prisonam*, saved from the Penalty of a capital Offender, a Stranger who rescues him from such an Imprisonment, is in like manner also excused; *& sic è converso.* [a] See Ch. 18. S. P. C. 30, 31. H. P. C. 116.

Sect. 3. III. As the Party himself seems not to be guilty of Felony by breaking the Prison unless he go out of it; so neither is a Stranger unless the Prisoner actually go out of the Prison. Keilw. 87. a. Bro. Escape. 52.

Sect.

Fitz. Enditement, 30. 1 H. 7. 6. pl. 2.

Sect. 4. IV. As the Sheriff's Return, that a Prisoner hath broken the Prison, is not a sufficient Ground to arraign him for such Offence, unless he be indicted also for it; so neither is his Return of a Rescous a good Ground for the Arraignment of the Rescuer, unless he be indicted.

Vide Supra. Ch. 18. S. 19. & Ch. 19. S. 14. Dyer. 164. pl. 60.

Sect. 5. V. As an Indictment of breaking Prison, and also an Indictment of Escape, must specially set forth the Nature and Cause of the Imprisonment, and the special Circumstances of the Fact in question, so also must an Indictment of Rescous.

Vide Supra. Ch. 18. Sect. 20.

Sect. 6. VI. As those who break Prison are still punishable, as for a high Misprision, by Fine and Imprisonment, in those Cases wherein they are saved from Judgment of Death, by the Statute *de frangentibus prisonam*, so also are those who rescue such Prisoners in the like Cases, in the same manner punishable.

2. The Offence of Rescous differs from that of breaking Prison in the following Particulars.

Vide Supra. Ch. 18. S. 16.

Sect. 7. I. Whereas a Person committed for High Treason, who breaks the Prison and escapes, is guilty of Felony only, unless he lets others also escape whom he knows to be committed for High Treason, in which Case he is guilty of High Treason, not in respect of his own breaking of the Prison, but of the Rescous of the others. A Stranger [a] who rescues a Person committed for and guilty of High Treason, knowing him to be so committed, is in all Cases guilty of High Treason; and by some [b] he is in like manner guilty, whether he knew that the Prisoners were committed for High Treason or not; but this Opinion is not proved by the Authority of the Case [c] on which it seems to be grounded.

Sect. 8. II. Whereas a Prisoner who breaks the Prison, may be arraigned [d] for such Offence before he be arraigned of the Crime for which he was imprisoned; he who rescues one imprisoned for Felony cannot, according to the better [e] Opinion, be arraigned for such Offence as for a Felony, till the principal Offender be first attainted; but if the Person rescued were imprisoned for High Treason, the Rescuer may immediately be arraigned, for that in High Treason all are Principals; also it seems, that he may be immediately proceeded against for a Misprision only, if the King please.

[a] S. P. C. 11. C. 32. F. H. P. C. 109. Dalt. fol. 228. 1 Jo. 455. 1 H. 6. 5. b. Fitz. Coron. 2. Bro. Treas. 11.

[b] Cro. Car. 583.

[c] 1 H. 6. 5. b.

[d] Supra Ch. 18. Sect. 17.

[e] Vide Supra. Ch. 19. H. P. C. 116. S. P. C. 43. Letter B. seems contray.

CHAP. XXII.

Of Attachment.

HAVING shewn in what manner Offenders may be apprehended without Process from a Court of Record, I am now to shew in what Manner they may be brought into Court by such Process, of which there are two sorts.

1. Such as may be awarded by the Discretion of the Justices upon a bare Suggestion, or their own Knowledge, without any Appeal, Indictment, or Information.

2. Such as can be awarded only upon such Accusations.

Sect. 1. And first, I shall consider the nature of the first of these, which is generally called an Attachment, and is properly grantable in Cases of Contempts, against which, for the most part, all Courts of Record generally, but more especially those of *Westminster-Hall*, and above all the Court of King's Bench, may proceed, in a summary Manner according to their Discretion; and if they happen to be done by a Person present in the Court, and appear either from the Confession of the Party on his Examination upon Oath, or by the View or immediate Observation of the Judges themselves, the Court may immediately record the Crime, and commit the Offender, and also inflict such farther Punishment as shall seem proper: And if such Offences be done by a Person not present in Court, and be complained of by Affidavit, the Court will either make a Rule on the Party to attend at a certain Day, in order to answer the matter of the Complaint against him; or else will make a Rule upon him, to shew Cause why an Attachment should not be granted against him; or else, if the Offence were of a very exorbitant Nature, as for Words of Contempt of the Court it self, will grant an Attachment on the first Complaint, without any such Rule to shew Cause; and the Party who is ordered to attend the Court in pursuance of such Rule, ought regularly to appear in proper Person, and not by Attorney, as also must every one against whom an Attachment is granted; and if the Offence be of an heinous Nature, and the Person attending the Court upon such a Rule to answer it, or appearing upon an Attachment, be apparently guilty, the Court will generally commit him immediately, in order to answer Interrogatories, to be exhibited against him in relation to such Contempt. But if there be any favourable Circumstances to extenuate or excuse the Offence, or if it appear doubtful whether the Party were guilty of it or not, the Court will generally, in their Discretion, suffer the Party, having first given Notice of his intention to the Prosecutor, to enter into a Recognisance to answer such Interrogatories; and if no such Interrogatories be exhibited within four Days after such Recognisance, will discharge the Recognisance upon Motion; yet if the Party do not make such Motion, and the Interrogatories be exhibited after the four Days, the Court will compell him to answer them: But in all the Cases above-mentioned, if the Party fully purge himself upon Oath, in his Answer to such Interrogatories, of the whole matter charged upon him, the Court will discharge him of the Contempt, and leave the Prosecutor to proceed against him for the Perjury if he thinks fit: But if the Party confess part of the Contempts in his Answer to such Interrogatories, and deny others, the Court will not discharge him from the Contempts so denied, but will proceed farther to examine the Truth of them, and will inflict such Punishment as from the whole shall appear to be reasonable; neither will the Court discharge the Party upon a shifting or evasive Answer to any material Part of the Charge against him, but will punish him in the same manner as if he had confessed it.

Fitz Corody 4. Rastal 268. pl. 4, 5. Raym. 376. Cro. Car. 146. 1 Rol. Rep. 315. Salk. 84. 3 H. 7. 6. pl. 4. 22 Ed. 4. 33 b. 34. 6 Mod. 73. 6 Mod. 73. The Queen and Barber, Mich. 11. Annæ. 6 Mod. 73. 2 Jon. 178. 2 Jo. 178.

But for the better understanding in what Cases the Court may proceed in the manner above-mentioned against such Offenders, I shall endeavour to shew,

1. Where it may so proceed against the Ministers of the Court.
2. Where against others.

As to the first of these Points I shall consider,

1. Where it may so proceed against Sheriffs, Bailiffs of Franchises, and Sherifs Bailiffs.
2. Where against Attorneys, and others acting as such.
3. Where against other Officers.
4. Where against Jurors.

As to the first of these Points I shall endeavour to shew,

1. Where the Court may so proceed against Sheriffs, Bailiffs of Franchises, and Sheriffs Bailiffs, for not executing a Writ.
2. Where for doing it oppressively.
3. Where for not doing it effectually.
4. Where for making a false Return.

Sect. 2. As to the first Particular, *viz.* In what Cases the Court may proceed in the manner above-mentioned against Sheriffs, *&c.* for not executing a Writ; It seems clear from the general reason of the Law, which gives all Courts of Record a kind of discretionary Power over all Abuses, by their own Officers, in the Administration or Execution of Justice, which bring a Disgrace on the Courts themselves, as not taking sufficient Care to prevent them; that where ever it shall appear, that any such Officers have been guilty of any corrupt Practice in not serving any Writ, as where they refuse to do it unless paid an unreasonable Gratuity from the Plaintiff, or receive a Bribe from the Defendant, or give him notice to remove his Person or Effects, in order to prevent the service of any Writ, the Court which awarded it may punish such Offences in such manner as shall seem proper, by Attachment, *&c.* as well as the Court of King's Bench, which has a general Superintendency over all Crimes whatsoever (as the Star Chamber [a] had also formerly) but commonly leaves Offences of this kind, in relation to Causes in other Courts, to be punished by such Courts to which they more immediately belong. But if there neither appear to have been any palpable Corruption in the Case, nor particular Obstinacy, as by disobeying a special Rule of the Court, in relation to the Service of such Writ, nor other extraordinary Circumstances of wilfull Negligence, the Judgment whereof is to be left to the Discretion of the Court, it seems not to be usual to grant an Attachment in such Cases, but to leave the Party to his ordinary remedy against the Officer, which he may have either by serving him with Rules to return the Writ, *&c.* or by suing him for the Damage sustained by his Negligence, in an Action of Escape, or on the Case, or by taking out an *Alias* [b] and *Pluries*, which if the Sheriff do not execute, an Attachment, directed to the Coroners, goes against him of course, unless he give a good Excuse for his not having done it.

Dy. 218. pl. 4.

[a] Hob. 62, 263, 264. Noy. 101.

Hob. 264. *Lasely versus* Weston. See Fitz. process, 13, 104.

[b] F. N. B. 38. C. 47. C. 265. F. Finch 237.

Sect. 3. As to the second Particular, *viz.* Where the Court may proceed in the Manner above-mentioned, against a Sheriff, or Bailiff, *&c.* for an oppressive Practice in the Execution of a Writ; it is every Day's Practice to grant Attachments for Misdemeanours of this kind, as for using needless Force, Violence and Terror, in making an Arrest, or by breaking open Doors where by Law it is not justifiable, and there is no plausible

5 Mod. 314, 315. Hob. 62, 263, 264.

plausible Excuse for doing it, or treating the Persons arrested basely and inhumanly, or keeping them in Custody till they consent to pay Money for their Deliverance, or making an Arrest without due Authority, as by force of a blank [a] Warrant, filled up with the Name of a special Bailiff by the Party himself, or Bailiff, without the Privity or subsequent Agreement of the Sheriff; yet I have sometimes known Attachments of this kind denied, in respect of the common use of the Practice, which by Experience hath been found to be almost necessary in some Cases to prevent the Defendants having notice of the intended Arrest, and therefore, if it shall appear to the Court, that there was any such reasonable Cause for such a Proceeding, it will be a great Inducement to excuse, if not wholly to dispence with it.

11 H 6. 41. b. 43 a.

[a] Noy. 101. Moor, 770. pl. 1064. 2 Rol. Abr. 278. H.

Sect. 4. As to the third Particular, *viz.* Where the Court may proceed in the Manner above-mentioned, against a Sheriff, or Bailiff, *&c.* for not executing a Writ effectually; it seems clear, That where any such Officer is guilty of a corrupt Practice in depriving the Party who sues out a Writ of that Benefit and Advantage which he ought to have from the Execution of it, he is liable to be punished in the Manner above-mentioned, as if he levy a Debt by vertue of an Execution, and keep the Money in his own Hands, and imbezil it: But unless there appear some gross and palpable Corruption in a Sheriff neglecting to return a Writ which hath been executed by him, or to bring in the Body or Money, *&c.* according to his Return, the Court will hardly grant an Attachment against him immediately, but will rather proceed against him by Rules to return the Writ, *&c.* and if he do not obey them, will increase the Amercements upon him till he do, or perhaps grant an Attachment for the Contempt: And [b] if the Sheriff return, That he sent the Process to the Bailiff of a Liberty, who hath given him no answer, a *non omittas* shall be awarded to the Sheriff: And if he return, That he sent the Process to such Bailiff, who hath returned a *cepi Corpus*, or such like matter, and the Bailiff bring not in the Body or Money, *&c.* at the Day, by the better [c] Opinion the Bailiff shall be amerced, and a Writ [d] shall issue to the Sheriff, to distrain the Bailiff to bring in the Body, *&c.*

[b] Fitz. Process, 13, 32.

[c] Rastal 109. Capias pl. 20. 189. pl. 20, 21, 22. 670. pl. 2. 36 H. 6. 1. Contra Bro. Process, 25. Fitz. Return de Vicont. 35. 3 H. 7. 11. 47 Ass. pl. 6.

[d] Fitz. Process, 12, 14, 104, 122, 132, 135, 225. Execution, 101. Retornde vicount, 35. 27 Ed. 3. 83. pl. 8. 27 Ed. 3. 77. pl. 9.

Sect. 5. As to the fourth Particular, *viz.* Where the Court may proceed in the Manner above-mentioned, against a Sheriff, *&c.* for making a false return to a Writ; There seems [e] to be no doubt, but that wherever any such Officer endeavours to impose upon a Court, by making a Return to a Writ of a Matter known by him to be false, he is, in strictness, liable to be punished in this manner for his Contempt: Yet it seems, That the Court will not easily be prevailed on to proceed in this manner for a bare false Return, but will rather leave the Party injured by it to his remedy, by an Action on the Case, unless there be some extraordinary circumstances of Hardship or Oppression. as where [f] an Officer who had arrested one on a *Capias*, returned, That he had taken him, but that the Party was so sick, that he could not bring in his Body at the Day for fear of endangering his Life, where in Truth the Party had been all the while in good Health, and was only detained under such pretence, in order to extort Money from him, *&c.*

Rastal. 109. Capias, pl. 20. Bro. Process, 25, 48, 113, 115. Bro Return, 96, 99. 5 Ed. 4. 43. pl. 13. 38 Ed. 3. 1. b. 39 Ed. 3. 3. 8 H. 5. 2. pl. 8. [e] Fitz. Process, 5. Bro. Surmise, pl. 14. 11 H. 19. Retorn de Brief, 100. Rastal Habeas Corpus, 7. [f] 11 H 6. 42. b.

As to the second Point, *viz.* In what Cases the Court may proceed in the Manner above-mentioned, against Attorneys, and others acting as such, I shall endeavour to shew,

1. Where it may so proceed against them, for appearing for a Person without sufficient Authority.
2. Where for injustice to their Clients.
3. Where for other Contempts to the Court, or dishonest Practice.

Sect. 6. As to the first of these Particulars, *viz.* Where the Court may proceed, in the Manner above mentioned, against Attorneys, and others acting as such, for appearing for any Person without sufficient Authority; There is no doubt [a] but that it may so proceed against them, for taking upon them to prosecute or defend a Suit for another, without any manner of Directions from him; also if they have in Truth a Warrant from the Party, but do not cause it to be recorded before Judgment, it seems [b] that they are in strictness liable to an Attachment, for that the Court takes no judicial Notice of any such Warrant not of Record; yet [c] if in such Case it appear, upon Examination, that the Warrant of Attorney happened not to be recorded, through the Negligence of the Officer, or some such like Accident, attended with no corrupt Practice in the Attorney, it seems, that the Court would never easily be prevailed on to proceed in this Manner against the Attorney; and much less at this Day, since he is liable by Statute to a certain pecuniary Forfeiture for every Offence of this kind.

[a] 38 Ed. 3. 8. b. 41 Ed. 3. 1. pl. 3. Rastal. 582. pl. 28. 16 Ed. 4. 5. b.

[b] Rastal. 96. pl. 3.

[c] Fitz. Judgment, 96. 41 Ed. 3. 1. pl. 3. 38 Ed. 3. 8. b. 4 Ed. 4. 13. pl. 31. 16 Ed. 4. 5. b. Rastal 582. pl. 28.

Sect. 7. For it is enacted by 32 *H.* 8. 30. made perpetual by 2 *Ed.* 6. 32. and by 18 *El.* 14. and 4 & 5 *Anna* 16. *That the Plaintiff's Attorney shall file his Warrant the same Term he declares, and the Defendant's Attorney the same Term he appears, on pain of forfeiting ten Pounds, and also suffering such Imprisonment, as by the Discretion of the Justices of the Court, where any such Default shall fortune to be, shall be thought convenient.*

Cokes Entries, 167.

Sect. 8. And it seems, That since these Statutes, it hath not been usual to grant Attachments in these Cases, without some apparent Circumstances of Fraud, or other Corruption.

Vide Dyer, 180. pl. 48. Rastal 289. pl. 2.

Sect. 9. But howsoever a regular Attorney may be excused from an Attachment, for not having recorded his Warrant, those have no reason to expect the like favour from the Court, who take upon them to appear for others as Attorneys, without having been admitted and sworn as such, for these are liable to an Attachment for every Appearance, whether their Warrant were recorded or not.

Rastal. 93. pl. 3.

Sect. 10. As to the second Particular, *viz.* Where the Court may proceed in the Manner above-mentioned against Attorneys, and others acting as as such, for Injustice to their Clients; It is every Day's Practice to move for it against them, for base and unfair Dealing towards their Clients in the way of Business, as for protracting Suits by little Shifts and Devices, and putting the Parties to unnecessary Expences in order to raise their Bills, or demanding Fees for Business which never was done, or for refusing to deliver up to their Clients, Writings with which they had been intrusted, in the way of Business, or Money which has been recovered and received by them to their Clients Use, and for other such like gross and palpable Abuses: But the Court will seldom grant an Attachment for the detainer of such Writings or Money, without first making a Rule on the Attorney to deliver them to the

See 4 H. 4. Ch. 18. 3 Ja. 1. 7.

the Party; also it will justify an Attorney's detaining such Writings or Money for his Security till he be paid all his just Fees; nor will it ever interpose in this Manner as to any Writings or Money received by an Attorney on any other Account, except only in his way of Business as an Attorney, but will leave the Party to his ordinary remedy by Action. Salk. 87. pl. 7.

Sect. 11. As to the third Particular, *viz.* Where the Court may proceed in the Manner above-mentioned, against Attorneys, and others acting as such, for other Contempts to the Court, or dishonest Practice, it seems, That it may not only proceed in such Manner against them for Disobedience of its Rules, after Notice given them of such Rules, either expressly or impliedly; but also, for any such ill Practice as is against the known and obvious Rules of Justice and common Honesty; as for Forging [a] a Writ, or any other matter of Record, [b] or but attempting to do it; or for taking out a *Capias*, [c] which has no Original to warrant it; or for receiving [d] Money of the Client for suing out an Original, and also for the Fine due thereon to the King, where, in Truth, no Original has been sued out, nor any Fine paid to the King; or for endeavouring to impose upon the Court, as [e] by causing an Action to be brought against one in it by Collusion, without any just ground, in order thereby to intitle the Party to the Privilege of the Court, and afterwards, upon the examination of the Matter in Court, giving a false Account of it; or [f] for giving directions to a Sheriff concerning what Persons he should return on a Panel; and for other Misdemeanours of the like Nature.

[a] Cro. Car. 74. Dyer. 241. pl. 50. 244. pl. 58. [b] Fitz. Attachment, 7. [c] 20 H. 6. 37. a. Fitz. Attachment, 3. [d] Cro. Car. 74. [e] 16 Ed. 4. 5. Bro. Privilege, 43. [f] Moore, 882. pl. 1237.

Sect. 12. As to the third Point, *viz.* Where the Court may proceed in the Manner above-mentioned, against other Officers of the Court; There being scarce any thing of this kind to be met with in the Books, I shall only observe, That it seems clear, from the general Reason of the Law, which gives all Courts of Record a kind of discretionary Power in the Government of their own Officers, that any such Court may proceed in such manner against any such Officer, not only for refusing to execute its Commands, or for executing them irregularly, remissly, [g] or oppressively, but also for all kinds of Oppression or Injustice done by them in the Execution of their Offices, or by Colour of them.

Vide Supra. Sect. 1. Fitz. Offic del. Court, 12. Rastal. 329. pl. 8. 268. pl. 5. Dy. 218. pl. 4. [g] Fitz. Trespass, 73. 33 H. 6. 55. b. 56. a.

Sect. 13. As to the fourth Point, *viz.* In what Cases the Court may proceed in the Manner above-mentioned, against Jurors, It is observable, that Jurors may be considered either in a Ministerial Capacity, *viz.* as Persons bound to attend the Court, in order to perform the Duty for which they are returned, untill they shall be discharged; or in a Judicial Capacity, *viz.* as Judges of the Fact which is to be tried or inquired by them; and therefore, for the better understanding of this Matter, I shall consider,

1. How far Jurors are punishable in the manner above-mentioned, in their Ministerial Capacity.
2. How far in their Judicial.

As to the first Particular, it seems clear, That Jurors are punishable in the Manner above-mentioned in their Ministerial Capacity, in the following Instances.

Sect. 14. I. For making Default; as where more than one of the Persons returned on a Jury, do appear; but not a sufficient Number to take an Enquest, 48 Ed. 3. 30.

Enqueſt, and ſome [a] of the others come within View of the Court, or into the ſame Town [b] in which the Court is holden, but refuſe to come into the Court to be ſworn; in which Caſes, upon Proof of ſuch Matter, the Court [c] may, at the Prayer of the Party, order the Jurors who appeared, to inquire what is the Yearly Value of ſuch Defaulters Lands, and after ſuch Inquiry made, either ſummon them to appear, on pain of forfeiting ſuch Sum as their Lands have been found to be worth by the Year, or ſome leſſer [d] Sum, or impoſe [e] a Fine of the like Sum upon them, without any farther Proceeding. But it ſeems, [f] That ſuch Juror ſhall be liable to loſe his Iſſues only for ſuch Default, and not the yearly Value of his Lands, unleſs the Party pray it: But a Juror [g] who hath actually appeared, and after makes Default, is ſaid to be ſubject to ſuch Forfeiture of the yearly Value of his Lands, whether the Party pray it or not, becauſe his Contempt appears to the Court by its own Record; yet [h] even in this Caſe the Court, in Diſcretion, will ſometimes only impoſe a ſmall Fine. Alſo it is ſaid, That no Juror ſhall be ſubject to ſuch Penalty, where [i] the Inqueſt could not be taken if he had appeared, as where but five of the Jurors ſummoned on an Aſſiſe, have had a View of the Land. Alſo it ſeems, [k] That a Juror who makes Default without ever coming into the Town wherein the Court is holden, is liable only to loſe his Iſſues, or to be amerced, but not to be fined: And it is ſaid, That he ſhall neither [l] be fined nor amerced if the Defendant be eſſoined on the Day on which the Jury was to appear, for that his Appearance in ſuch Caſe would be to no purpoſe; and it ſeems [m] queſtionable whether a Juror be amerciable for not appearing at the Return of a *Sicut alias Venire facias*, where the firſt *Venire* was not ſerved; neither doth a Juror ſeem to be amerciable at all, at the Day of the Return of the firſt *Venire* [n] *facias*, except before Juſtices errant, or of Oyer and Terminer, *&c.*

Sect. 15. II. For refuſing to to be ſworn when they do appear; for which, as it ſeems, [o] every Court of Record may of common Right impoſe ſuch a reaſonable Fine on any one returned on a Grand or Petit Jury, as ſhall ſeem convenient.

Sect. 16. III. For refuſing [p] to give any Verdict at all.

Sect. 17. IV. For endeavouring to impoſe upon the Court; as where [q] a Petit Jury offer a Verdict to the Court, as agreed to by their whole Number, where, in Truth, ſome of them have not agreed to it; or where [r] they agree upon two Verdicts, and firſt to offer one of them to the Court, and to ſtand to it, if the Court ſhall expreſs no Diſatisfaction to it; but if the Court ſhall diſlike it, then to give the other.

Sect. 18. V. For misbehaving themſelves after their Departure from the Bar; as where they [s] do not all keep together till they have given their Verdict; or where any [t] of them carry any thing eatable with them in their Pockets; or eat [u] or drink, or otherwiſe refreſh themſelves without Leave from the Court, before they have given their Verdict, though they were agreed [x] on it, and were alſo all the time in the Cuſtody of the Bailiff appointed to take Care of them.

[a] Raſtal. 267. b. pl. 2. 268. a. pl. 3. [b] Raſtal. 267. b. pl. 1. 30 Aſſ. pl. 3, 42. 48 Ed. 3. 30. Bro. Jurors, 25, 26. 20 Aſſ. pl. 11. [c] Raſtal. 267. b. pl. 12, 268. a. pl. 3. 4 Ed. 4. 37. a. 9 H. 4. 5. a. 20 Aſſ. pl. 11. 8 Co. 41. a. [d] Raſtal. 267. b. pl. 2. [e] Raſtal. 267. pl. 2. 268. pl. 3. [f] Fitz. Peine, 1, 2. 30 Aſſ. 42. 4 H. 6. 7. a. 4 Ed. 36. b. 37. a. 36 H. 6. 27. a. Bro. Jurors, 15, 18. 26. Enqueſt, 42. [g] Fitz. Challenge, 47. 36 H. 6. 27. a. [h] Fitz. Office de Court, 12. [i] Fitz. Peine, 3. 9 H. 4. 5. a. [k] 10 E. 4. 19. [l] 10 Ed. 4. 19. 30 Aſſ. pl. 17. Quere 48 Ed. 3. 12. a. 12 Aſſ. pl. 14. Fitz. Aſſiſe, 65. [m] 1 H. 7. 8. a. [n] Fitz. Aſſ. 136, 466. 11 Aſſ. pl. 7. Bro. Amercement, 68. See the Chapter of Proceſs againſt Jurors. [o] 2 Inſt. 242, 143. 44 Ed. 3. 19. b. 8 Co. 38. b. 7 H. 6. 12. b. [p] Vaughan 152. Noy. 49. 3 Bulſt. 173. 9 H. 6. 44. b. [q] 29 Aſſ. pl. 27. Bro. Jurors, 28. 40 Aſſ. pl. 10. 1 Rol. Abr. 219. pl. 4. [r] Cro. El. 779. [s] 14. H. 7. 29 b. 30. Vaughan, 151. [t] Dyer 78. pl. 41. [u] Dyer 218. pl. 4. Vaughan, 152. Cro. Jac. 21. Fitz. Examination, 17. Bro. Jurors, 13. [x] Raſtal. 268 pl. 4, 5.

Sect. 19. VI. For sending [a] for, or receiving Instructions from either of the Parties concerning the Matter in question, and therefore [b] much more for receiving a Bribe.

Sect. 20. As to the second Particular, *viz.* How far Jurors are punishable in the Manner above-mentioned, in their judicial Capacity, It seems to be the current Opinion of the Old Books, that Jurors are not subject to any Prosecution for a false Verdict, except by way of Attaint: And there seem to be very few ancient Precedents, for the Punishment either of a Grand or Petit Jury, meerly for giving a Verdict against Evidence, or the Direction of the Court, either in a Criminal or Civil Matter. It is said [c] indeed in *Fitzherbert*'s Abridgment of a Case in the time of King *Richard* II. That the Judge told the Jury, upon their acquitting a common Thief of an Indictment, That they should be bound to their Behaviour for their Lives: But this was only the sudden Opinion of a Judge; and it doth not appear, that the Jurors were afterwards actually so bound, in pursuance of the said Opinion; and *Fitzherbert* makes a Query in his Abridgment of the Case, by what Law they could be so bound: And as to those three [d] other Cases in the time of King *Edward* III. wherein it is said, That a Juror was committed for refusing to agree with the other eleven, it may be answered, That it is said [e] in the first of those Cases, *That such Juror staid his Companions a Day and a Night, without agreeing with them, and this without Reason*; from whence it is reasonable to intend, That there might be some Circumstances of Misbehaviour, as an obstinate perverse Resolution, right or wrong, to find a Verdict one way, and not to consult with the other Jurors, nor hear their Reasons, *&c.* And in the last of the [f] said Cases it is said, That the Juror committed by the Justices of Assise, for refusing two Days and a Night to agree with his Companions, and saying, That he would rather dye in Prison than agree with them, was afterwards discharged by the Justices of the Common Bench, upon the adjournment of the Assise thither. And it was part [g] of the Charge against *Empson*, who was indicted in the beginning of the Reign of King *Henry* VIII. for a great Complication of Offences, That he had committed a Jury to ward, and bound them to appear before the King and his Council, and afterwards, on their Appearance, fined them (though with the Concurrence of the rest of the Council) in the Sum of 8 *l.* a-piece, for refusing to find a Person guilty of an Indictment of Larceny, upon sufficient Evidence; yet it is said in *Dalison*'s [h] Reports of Cases, in the third and fourth years of *Philip* and *Mary*, That it was agreed, that Justices of Assise, Oyer and Terminer, Gaol-Delivery, or Peace, have no Power indeed to assess Fines on Jurors who make a false Oath before them, but that they may give them a Day before themselves, or the King's Council; by which it seems to be implied, That such Jurors were then thought to be some way or other Punishable by such Judges, or at least by the King's Council; for otherwise it would be to little purpose to bind them to appear before them. Also it seems to be holden by Sir *Edward Coke*, [i] That though a Jury be no way punishable for Convicting a Man upon an Indictment against Evidence, yet they might be charged in the Star-Chamber for their Partiality in finding a manifest Offender not guilty: And about [k] the later end of the Reign of Queen *Elizabeth*, a Jury was committed and fined, and bound to the Good Behaviour, for finding one *Wharton* guilty of Manslaughter only, against clear Evidence, and the Direction of the Court, upon an Indictment of Murder: And it is said in *Palmer*'s [l] Reports, That Jurors, who go against

[a] Rastal 329. b. pl. 8. Hob. 114. Fitz. Exami. 17.
[b] 40 Ass. 43.
See Book 1. Ch. 72. S. 4.
[c] Fitz. Coro. 108. Vaughan, 152.
[d] Fitz Imprisonment, 4. Judgment 89. Verdict 40.
[e] 8 Ass. pl. 35. Vaughan, 151. 2 Jon. 16, 17.
[f] 41 Ass. pl. 11. 41 Ed 3. 31. Vaugh. 151.
[g] Raymond, 88, 89.
[h] Dalison, 18.
[i] 12 Co. 23, 24.
[k] Yelv. 23. Noy. 48, 49.
[l] Palmer, 363.

against the Directions of the Court are to be fined: And there are several instances in the beginning of the Reign of King *Charles* II. wherein it was resolved, That both Grand [a] and Petit [b] Juries were finable by the Justices of Gaol Delivery, for going against plain Evidence, and the Directions of the Court; but these Proceedings were always thought Grievous, and were complained [c] of in the House of Commons; and this Question was at last fully considered and debated in *Bushel*'s Case, who having been committed by the Justices of Oyer and Terminer at the *Old Baily*, brought his *Habeas Corpus* in the Court of Common Pleas, to which it was returned, That he was committed for the Fine of forty Marks, imposed on him for having, with other Jurors, acquitted certain Defendants of an Indictment for an unlawful Assembly, against full and manifest Evidence, and against the Direction of the Court in matter of Law; and upon this Return he was discharged, and the Return was adjudged insufficient, for not setting forth particularly [d] so much of the Evidence that it might appear that it was full and manifest; and likewise [e] for not setting forth, That the Defendant did know, and believe it to have been full and manifest; and also, [f] for not shewing what the Direction of the Court was, and in what manner the Defendant found against it. And it was also resolved, [g] That Petit Jurors are in no Case finable for giving a Verdict against the Evidence delivered in Court, whether they be liable to an Attaint for such Verdict or not, not only for that the Jury are by Law the proper Judges of matter of Fact, as the Judges are of matter of Law, and therefore ought to be free in their Judgment of it, without being over-ruled by the Judges, who, strictly speaking, have no more to do with the Judgment of the Fact, than the Jurors have with the Judgment of the matter of Law; neither is it possible that a Judge can certainly know that a Juror acts corruptly in giving his Verdict contrary to the strength of the Evidence delivered in Court; for he may be influenced by his own personal Knowledge of the Truth of the Fact, of the Credit of the Witnesses, the Reputation of the Parties, and many other Circumstances unknown to the Judge, and well known to the Jury, for which Cause the Law provided, That all Issues should be tried by the Neighbourhood of the Place in which they are supposed to arise, because Neighbours are presumed to have better Knowledge than others of what concerns their Neighbours. And for these Causes, and other such like, the Court of King's Bench granted an Information against a Town-Clerk, for publishing an Order of the Court against Jurors, who had found a Person guilty of Manslaughter only, upon an Indictment of Murder, by which Order the said Jurors were declared to be justly suspected of Bribery, and declared uncapable of holding an Office, *&c.*

[a] 1 Syd. 229, 230. 2 Keb. 180.
[b] 1 Syd. 272, 273. Raym. 88, 89, 138. 1 Keb. 769, 938. 2 Keb. 404.
[c] 1 Syd. 338. 2 Keb. 180, 181.
[d] Vaughan, 142. 2 Jon. 16, 17.
[e] Vaughan, 142. 2 Jon. 16, 17.
[f] Vaughan, 143.
[g] Vaughan, 144, 145. 3 Keb. 352. 2 Jon 16. Vide Hob. 114. Contra 3 Keb. 352.

Hilary, 10 Ann. Queen & Wakefield.

Sect. 21. Yet if it shall plainly appear in any Case, that Jurors are perfectly satisfied of the Truth of a Fact, whereupon they declare to the Court, that they find it in such a particular Manner, and the Court directly tell them, That upon the Fact so found, as they have agreed it to be, the Judgment of the Law is such or such, and therefore, that they ought to give a Verdict accordingly, yet they obstinately insist upon a Verdict contrary to such a Direction; it seems agreeable to the general Reason of the Law, that the Jurors are finable by the Court in such a Case, unless an Attaint lies against them, for otherwise they would be dispunishable for so palpable a Partiality, in taking upon them to judge of matters of Law, with they have nothing to do with, and are presumed to

2 Jon. 15, 16. Vaughan, 144, 145. Palm. 363.

to be ignorant of, contrary to the express Direction of one who by the Law is appointed to direct them in such Matters, and is to be presumed of Ability to do it.

Sect. 22. Also if a Judge, for the better Direction and Information of a Jury, shall ask them their Opinions concerning such a particular Fact, and they shall refuse to answer him, and obstinately insist to deliver in their Verdict as they think fit, contrary to his Direction, it seems questionable, whether they may not be fined in such a Case also, unless an Attaint lie against them; for that it is the Duty of Jurors to take the Advice and Information of the Court, in order to be governed by it as far as shall be consistent with their Consciences. Bracton 288. b. 289. 2 Jon 15, 16. Vaughan, 144.

Sect. 23. Also if a Jury shall refuse to find an Office for the King, upon full Evidence, it hath been holden, That they may be fined, for that in such Case they are not liable to an Attaint, and their finding does not determine any Man's Right, and the King, in many Cases, hath no other Remedy; yet it seems questionable, how far at this Day these Reasons may be thought conclusive; and it seems, that they hold as strongly for the Punishment of Grand Jurors refusing to find an Indictment of High Treason; and yet it will be hard to maintain, That such Jurors are any way punishable for such a Refusal. Moor, 730. 3 Leon. 148. Vaughan, 153. 9 H. 6. 44. b

Sect. 24. But if a Petit Jury in a Leet, conceal a Matter presentable by them, it is a good Custom that they may be amerced for such Concealment, being found by the Grand Jury; and by 3 *H.* 7. 1. set forth more at large Book 1. Ch. 59. S. 1. *If an Inquest conceal any matter inquirable before Justices of Peace, another Inquest may be impanelled to inquire of such Concealments, and the Concealers may be amerced by the Discretion of such Justices.* 9 H. 6. 44. b

Having shewn in what Cases the Ministers of the Court are punishable in the manner above-mentioned, I am now to shew, in what Cases others may be so punished; and for this purpose I shall endeavour to shew,

1. Where inferior Judges are punishable in such manner.
2. Where Counsellors.
3. Where Gaolers.
4. Where any Person whatsoever.

As to the first Point, I shall endeavour to shew, where inferior Judges are in such manner punishable,

1. For proceeding without Jurisdiction.
2. For proceeding unjustly, oppressively, or irregularly.
3. For refusing to do Justice.
4. For Contempts of superior Courts.

Sect. 25. As to the first of these Particulars, *viz.* In what Cases inferior Judges are punishable in the Manner above-mentioned, for proceeding without Jurisdiction; it seems, [a] That the Court of King's Bench having a general Superintendency over all inferior Courts, may in strictness award an Attachment against any such Court usurping a Jurisdiction no way belonging to it, and putting the Subject to unnecessary Vexation by colour of a judicial Proceeding wholly unwarranted by [a] 41 Ass. pl. 30. Salk. 201. 1 Keb. 484. Palm. 564.

by Law, and therefore [a] prohibited by it; yet in these Cases it seems to be rather the more usual [b] way, first to award a Writ of Prohibition to such Court, and afterwards an Attachment upon its proceeding after such Prohibition, and not to grant a Rule to shew Cause why an Attachment should not go in the first Instance, unless there be some extraordinary Circumstances in the Case; as where [c] the Steward of a Leet is guilty of a double Usurpation, as of holding Plea of a Matter which arose out of his Precinct, and which, if it had arisen within his Precinct, would not have been within the Jurisdiction of his Court; or where [d] the Judge of an inferior Court refuses to receive a Plea that the Cause of Action arose out of his Jurisdiction; or where [e] any Judge takes Cognisance of a Cause to which he himself is a Party; or where the Judge of a Court-Baron is privy to a Practice of splitting [f] a Cause of Action for more than forty Shillings into lesser Sums, in order to bring it within the Jurisdiction of the Court; but in this last Case, there seem to be more instances [g] of Prohibitions than Attachments; and in the Cases above-mentioned, and all others of the like Nature, it seems to lie wholly in the Discretion of the Court to grant either.

Sect. 26. As to the second Particular, *viz.* In what Cases inferior Judges are punishable in the Manner above-mentioned, for acting unjustly, oppressively, or irregularly; it is not easy to meet with Cases of this kind in the Books, there being seldom any thing in them so remarkable as to be thought worth reporting; but it seems to be common Practice, to grant Attachments against the Judges of such Courts for any Practice contrary to the plain Rules of natural Justice, though it have been never so long used in such Courts; as for denying a Defendant a Copy of the Declaration against him, and going on to Trial, or giving Judgment against him without giving him any manner of Notice, or Time to make his Defence; or for taking of unreasonable [h] Distresses, either on mesne Process, or Execution; or for compelling [i] a Defendant to give exorbitant Bail; or for proceeding contrary to the Prohibition [k] of a Statute, as [l] by amercing a Clergyman according to his spiritual Benefice; or by assessing [m] an Amercement without any affeerment by the Tenants of the Manor; or by [n] taking Money of a Plaintiff or Defendant for vicious Pleading.

Sect. 27. As to the third Particular, *viz.* In what Cases inferior Judges are punishable in the Manner above-mentioned, for refusing to do Justice; It seems clear, from the general Reason of the Law, and the common Practice of the Court of King's Bench in Cases of this Nature, That the said Court may, in its Discretion, award an Attachment against any such Judge, obstinately and perversely, and without any colour of a reasonable Excuse, refusing to proceed at all, or to give Judgment, or award Execution, in a Matter brought regularly before him; for all such Delays of Justice are not only grievous to the Suitor, but bring a Disgrace upon the Law it self: Yet if there be no extraordinary Circumstances in any such Delay, to bring the Judge under a reasonable Suspicion of Corruption, it seems the more usual Method to take out a Writ to such Judge, commanding him to do the thing, of the Delay whereof you complain; and if such Writ be not obeyed, to take out an *Alias & Pluries*, or to take [o] out the *Alias & Pluries* together with the first Writ; and thereupon, if the Judge refuse to comply, to take out an Attachment against him at the Suit of the King and of the Party, which may either be returnable into the Court of King's Bench, or at

[a] Vide 19 H. 6. 54. b. 9 H. 6. 61. F. N. B. 270. c.
[b] Register, 145. 146. F. N. B. 239. H. 240. B. 1 Syd. 464. 6 Mod. 90. 2 Inst. 312. 2 Rol. Abr. 317. Letter I.
[c] 41 Ass. 30. Fitz. Leete. 9. Bro. Leete, 18, 31.
[d] Vaughan and Hodges Paschæ, 11. Annæ.
[e] Salk. 201. pl. 3.
[f] Palmer 564. 1 Keb. 484.
[g] 19 H. 6. 54. 2 Rol. Abr. 317. I. pl. 1. 6 Mod. 90. 2 Keb. 617. 1 Ventries, 65, 73. 1 Keb. 484. 1 Syd. 464.
[h] Salk. 201. 3 Keb. 92.
[i] 2 Jon. 178.
[k] F. N. B. 76. D. 160. B. 165. C. 166 D. 270. C. 9 H. 6. 61. 19 H. 6. 54.
[l] F. N. B. 76. B. C. D.
[m] F. N. B. 76. D.
[n] F. N. B. 270. A. B. C. 2 Inst. 122. Fitz. Attachment, 8.
[o] F. N. B. 68. E. Infra. Sect. 34.

at the Party's election into the Court of Common Pleas, except in some special [a] Cases; and this seems [b] to be the proper Remedy to compel the Lord of a Mannor to hold a Court for the determining of a Writ of Right Patent, or a Writ [c] of Right Close; or to compel the Judge of any inferior Court, whether of Record [d] or not, to proceed [e] in a Plea, or to give Judgment, [f] or to award Execution. [g]

Sect. 28. As to the fourth Particular, *viz.* In what Cases inferior Judges are punishable in the Manner above-mentioned, for Contempts of superior Courts: There is no doubt but that Justices [h] of Peace, or Commissioners [i] of Sewers, may be so punished for proceeding in any Matter before them, after a *Certiorari* delivered to them, or the Judge of a Spiritual [k] or Civil [l] Law Court, for proceeding in a Cause, after Notice of a Rule to shew Cause why a Prohibition should not go, or a Judge of any inferior Common Law Court, for proceeding in a Cause after a *Habeas Corpus*, or Writ of Error allowed; or a Sheriff, [m] for proceeding in Replevin, or other Cause, in the County-Court, after a *Supersedeas, Pone,* or *Recordare*. Also a Rule [n] has been granted to shew Cause why an Attachment should not go against the Steward of a Wapentake for proceeding after a Tolt, though this be only a Contempt to the County-Court.

Sect. 29. Also Justices of Peace may be punished in the Manner above-mentioned, for acting in a Contemptuous manner against the Determination of the Court of King's Bench; as where an Order of Settlement, specially setting forth the Circumstances of the Case, is removed into the said Court, and quashed there, by the Judgment of the Court, upon the Merits; and yet the Justices of Peace afterwards make another Order to remove the same Person to the same Place, for the very same Cause, without regarding the Judgment of the Court, though it were well known to them, and insisted on by the Parties.

Sect. 30. As to the second Point, *viz.* In what Cases Counsellors are punishable in the Manner above-mentioned, it seems clear, That notwithstanding they are neither Officers of any Court, nor invested with any judicial Office, but barely practise as Counsellors, yet [o] inasmuch as they have a special Privilege to practise the Law, and their Misbehaviour tends to bring a Disgrace upon the Law it self, they are punishable for any foul Practice as other Ministers of Justice are.

Sect. 31. As to the third Point, *viz.* In what Cases Gaolers are punishable in the Manner above-mentioned, it seems clear, That they are not only punishable in this Manner, as all other Officers are, by the Courts to which they more immediately belong, for any gross Misbehaviour in their Offices, or Contempts of the Rules of such Courts, but they are also punishable by any other Courts for disobeying Writs of *Habeas Corpus* awarded by such Courts, and not bringing up the Prisoner at the Day prefixed by such Writs. Also it seems clear, [p] That it is no excuse for not obeying a Writ of *Habeas Corpus ad subjiciendum*, that the Prisoner did not tender the Fees due to the Gaoler: Also [q] it seems to be the better Opinion, That the want of such a Tender is no Excuse for not obeying a Writ of *Habeas Corpus ad faciendum & recipiendum*; however [r] it is certain, That if the Gaoler bring up the Prisoner by vertue of such *Habeas Corpus*, the Court will not turn him over till the Gaoler be paid all his Fees, [s] nor, as some [t] say, till he be paid all that is due to him for the Prisoner's Diet, for that a Gaoler is compellable [u] to find his Prisoner Sustenance; but this is denied by others. [x]

[a] F. N. B. 62. o. 230. e. 63. b. 67. b. 13. h. 14. a.
[b] F. N. B. 3. e. 13. a.
[c] F. N. B. 12. e.
[d] Rastals Entries, 83. b. pl. 4.
F. N. B. 20. b. 153. d. 243. d.
[e] F. N. B. 12. e. 13. a. Rastal's Entries, 83. b. pl. 4.
[f] F. N. B. 153. b. c. 243. d.
[g] F. N. B. 20. a. b.
[h] Moor, 677. pl. 921. Yelv. 32. 1 Keb. 93.
[i] 1 Mod. 44.
[k] 2 Jon. 47.
[l] 1 Rol. Rep. 315.
[m] F. N. B. 13. b. 14. a. Fitz. Replevin, 31. 43 Ed 3. 26. Fitz. Process, 168. Action sur le Case, 39.
[n] Burgh & Blunt, Hil. 3 Geor.
[o] 6 Mod, 137. See Book 1. Ch. 83. S. 26.
[p] 1 Keb. 272. pl. 57.
[q] March 89. 1 Keb. 280. pl. 79. 2 Jon. 178. Contra 1 Keb. 566. pl 11.
[r] 2 Jon. 178.
[s] 2 Rol. Abr. 32. B.
[t] 1 Rol. Rep. 338, 339. Contra 2 Rol. Abr. 32. B.
[u] Co. Lit. 295. a. 9 Co. 87. b.
[x] Pl. Com. 68. a. 2 Rol. Abr. 32. B.

Sect. 32. Also it seems, That the Court of King's Bench, which has a general [a] Superintendency over all Persons who are in any respect Ministers of Justice, may award an Attachment against any Gaoler using a Prisoner barbarously and inhumanly; yet it is said, [b] That a Gaoler is no way punishable for keeping a Debtor in Irons. And it seems agreed at this Day, That a Gaoler shall not be punished in the Manner above mentioned, for the bare Escape of a Person in his Custody by Civil Process; but that the Party grieved by such Escape ought to take his Remedy by Action.

Sect. 33. As to the fourth Point, *viz.* In what Cases any Person whatsoever is punishable in the Manner above-mentioned; it seems, That even Peers of the Realm, whether Spiritual or Temporal, are liable to such Punishment for some Contempts, as for rescuing [c] a Person arrested by due Course of Law, or for proceeding in a Cause against [d] the King's Writ of Prohibition, or for disobeying other [e] Writs, wherein the King's Prerogative, or the Liberty [f] of the Subject are nearly concerned; but it doth not [g] seem clear that it is a certain general Rule, that a Peer is punishable in this manner for Disobedience of all Writs whatsoever; and it seems [h] certain, That no Peer is liable to an Attachment for not appearing on a Jury; therefore it seems, That what is said [i] in some Books in general, That an Attachment lies against Peers, for Contempts ought to be understood of such only as are of an enormous [k] Nature, as those above-mentioned, and others [l] of the same kind, about which it is difficult to lay down any certain particular Rules; however it is certain, that all other Persons are liable to an Attachment for Contempts, all the particular instances whereof it would be endless to enumerate, and therefore I shall only take notice of the most remarkable, which seem reducible to the following Heads.

1. Contempts of the King's Writs.
2. Contempts in the Face of a Court.
3. Contemptuous Words, or Writings, concerning the Court.
4. Contempts of the Rules or Awards of the Court.
5. Abuses of the Process of the Court.
6. Forgeries of Writs, and other Deceits of the like kind, tending to impose on the Court.

Sect. 34. As to the first Particular, *viz.* Where Persons are punishable in the Manner above-mentioned for Contempts of the King's Writs; it seems that it may reasonably be argued, That all such Writs, being in the King's Name, and importing some lawful Command or Prohibition from him, which every Subject is in Duty bound to obey, every Disobedience [m] of any of them being a Contempt of the King's Authority, is, in strictness, punishable in the manner above-mentioned, if the Court, in Discretion, shall think fit so to proceed: Yet it doth not seem to have been usual for the Court to proceed in this manner for a bare Nonfesance, in not performing the Command of the first Writ in any Case whatsoever. But [n] it seems clear, That an Attachment lies of Course for the Non performance of the Demand of a *Pluries*, which may in some Cases, if not in all, be taken out together with the *alias*, at the same time with the first Writ: Also it seems, That the Court may in any special Case, in which it shall seem proper, make a Rule to compell the Party to whom the first Writ is directed, to execute it; and, if

[a] 6 Mod. 137.
[b] 2 Inst. 381. 2 Rol. Abr. 806. c. 1. 807. pl. 2. 3 Co 44.
[c] Fitz P.ocess. 114, 161 Retorn de vicount, 74. 1 H. 5. 14. a. Dyer 212. pl. 36. 27 H. 8. 22. b. Crompton Jur. 14. a.
[d] 21 Ed. 3. 3. pl. 7.
[e] 2 R. A. 228. Letter A. 234. pl. 3. 8 Ed 4. 17. a Vide 25 Ed. 3 Ch. 6. F. N. B. 47. c Fitz quare non admisit 7 Bro. Contempt, 5. 8 Co. 60.
[f] 11 H. 4 15 b Fitz. Withernam. 4.
[g] 21 Ed. 3. 3. pl. 7. F. N. B. 33. e
[h] Dyer, 319. pl. 98.
[i] Fitz. Process, 198. Cro. El. 170. 2 Rol. Abr. 234. pl. 3. Bro. Contempt, 3, 19. 6 Co. 54 a. Finch, 355.
[k] Dyer, 315. pl. 98. Hob. 61. 21 Ed. 3. 59. b. Rastal 313. pl. 19, 20. 29 Ass pl. 33.
[l] Cro. El 503, 170. 1 Rol. Abr. 220. pl. 12. 221 pl. 13. 3 Inst. 142.
[m] 1 Mod. 44. 5 Mod 314, 315. Fitz. quare non admisit 7
[n] Fitz. Suggestion, 25. 43 Ass. 39 Rastal. 457. pl. 7. Finch. 237. 11 H. 4. 86. Fitz Counter 34. Suggestion. 25. F. N. B. 68. e.

Supra Sect 27.

if ſuch Rule ſhall be diſobeyed, there can be no doubt but that the Court may proceed againſt ſuch Diſobedience in the ſame manner as they uſually do againſt the Diſobedience of any other Rule: Alſo it ſeems [a] to be common Practice to grant Attachments upon Affidavits of Contempts to the King's Writs, by acting contrary to the Purport of them. Alſo there can be no doubt, but that if a Sheriff ſhall in any Caſe return to the Court, That a Perſon arreſted, [b] or Goods ſeiſed, [c] or Poſſeſſion of Lands delivered [d] by him, by Vertue of the King's Writ, were reſcued or violently taken from him, &c. the Court may award an Attachment againſt the Reſcuers. Alſo it is certain, That the Court hath, in ſome Caſes, awarded an Attachment upon Affidavits of a Reſcous, where the Officer hath not returned one; yet this was anciently [e] looked on as irregular, and of late the Court has refuſed to grant an Attachment in any Caſe for a Reſcous, unleſs the Officer will return it; for that it hath been found by Experience, that Officers will often take upon them to ſwear a Reſcous, where they will not venture to return one.

[a] F. N. B. 165 B. 166. B, C, D. 170. C. 173. E. 174. A, B. 175. B. Fitz. Suggeſtion, 9. 8 Co. 60. Supra. Sect. 33.
[b] Fitz. Attachment, 1. Proceſs, 56. Fitz. Retorn de vicount, 74. 37 H. 6. 27. b. Dy. 212. pl. 36.
[c] Jon. 39.
[e] Fitz. Attachment, 5. 38 Ed. 3. 9. b.
[d] Salk. 321, 7
[e] Fitz. Suggeſion, 25

Sect. 35. As to the ſecond Particular, *viz.* Where Perſons are puniſhable in the Manner above-mentioned, for Contempts in the Face of the Court; it ſeems clear, That all Perſons are puniſhable in this manner, not only for making an actual Breach of the Peace, but alſo for any heinous Miſdemeanour in the Face of the Court; as [f] for giving falſe, trifling, and contradictory Anſwers upon an Examination in Court concerning one's Ability to be Bail for another, in an Action depending in the Court, or concerning any other ſuch like Matter in queſtion before the Court, and to be determined by the Examination of the Parties; or [g] for any contemptuous Behaviour towards any Judge in the Face of the Court, as by charging him with Injuſtice, and praying for an Information againſt him, &c.

[f] Cro. Car. 146 7 H 6. 25. pl. 10.
[g] Raym. 376.

Sect. 36. As to the third Particular, *viz,* Where Perſons are puniſhable in the Manner above-mentioned, for contemptuous Words, or Writings, concerning the Court; it ſeems needleſs to put any Inſtances of this kind, which are generally ſo obvious to common Underſtanding, and therefore I ſhall only obſerve, That ſometimes Attachments have been granted for contemptuous Words concerning the Rules of the Court, without making any Rule to ſhew Cauſe why ſuch Attachments ſhould not be granted, becauſe it would be vain to ſerve him with a ſecond Rule who has deſpiſed the firſt.

Salk. 84.

Sect. 37. As to the fourth Particular, *viz.* Where Perſons are puniſhable in the Manner above-mentioned, for Contempts of the Rules or Awards of the Court; There is nothing more frequent than to proceed in this Manner for Contempts of this kind; as where [f] a Defendant in an Action of Account being adjudged to account before Auditors, refuſes to do it, unleſs they will allow ſuch an Acquittance, which was diſallowed by the Court before; or [g] where one who has ſubmitted to an Arbitration by Rule of Court, being afterward perſonally ſerved with a Copy of the Award, and required to perform it, refuſes to do it; or where one, refuſing to pay the Coſts taxed by the Maſter, for that ſuch a Taxation is, in Judgment of Law, a Taxation by the Court: But it ſeems, That generally an Attachment is not grantable for Diſobedience of any Rule, unleſs the Party have been perſonally ſerved with it; nor for Diſobedience of a Rule at *Niſi Prius,* unleſs it be

43 Aſſ. pl, 39
[f] Fitz. Impriſonment, 18. and Vide Fitz Accompt, 23. 84. 109. 112. 29 Ed. 3 35. b.
[g] 1 Mod. 21. Salk. 71 pl. 4. 83 pl. 1. Vide 9 & 10 Guil. 3. 15.

Salk. 84.

be made a Rule of Court, nor for Disobedience of a Rule made by a Judge at his Chamber, unless it be entred.

Sect. 38. As to the fifth Particular, *viz.* Where Persons are punishable in the Manner above-mentioned, for Abuses of the Process of the Court, There are so many instances of this kind that it would be in vain to go about to enumerate them all, and therefore I shall only take notice of some of the Principal of them, as,

Hob. 264.

[a] 8 H. 4. 17. Fitz. Coron. 73.

Sect. 39. First, The taking out such Process without any Colour of Right to it; as where one sues out Execution without any Judgment to warrant it, *&c*, or where a Woman brings an Appeal [a] of the Death of her Husband, whom she knows to be alive.

Style Rep. 239, 343.

Sect. 40. Secondly, The making use of such Process as a Stale to help the Jurisdiction of an inferior Court; as where one arrests another by a *Latitat*, in order by that means to bring him within the Limits of an inferior Court, and when he has got him there drops the *Latitat* and proceeds in the inferior Court.

[b] Fitz. Corpus cum Causa, 3. 14 H. 7. 6. b. 7. a. 6 Co. 60. a. Savil. 14.

[c] 7. H. 6. 45. a.

Sect. 41. Thirdly, Making use of such Process in a vexatious manner; as where a Person who has brought an Action in one Court, does afterwards sue the same Defendant, for the very same Cause, in another Court, while the first Action is still depending, in which Case the Defendant seems to have an Election either to move for an Attachment, [b] or to bring an Action [c] on the Case for such a vexatious Proceeding against him.

[d] Hob. 264. Dyer, 249. pl. 84. Vide 8 El. 2.

Sect. 42. Fourthly, Making use of such Process any other way to serve the purposes of Oppression or Injustice; as where [d] one arrests another at my Suit, without my Privity, in order to make some undue Advantage from him, *&c.*

[e] Dyer, 241, pl. 50. 244. pl. 58.

[f] 6 Mod. 310

[g] Dyer, 245. pl. 61. Bro. Privilege, 43.

[h] 6 Mod. 16. Savil. 31.

Sect. 43. As to the sixth Particular, *viz.* Where Persons are punishable in the Manner above-mentioned for forging of Writs, and other Deceits of the like kind, tending to impose on the Court; nothing can be more frequent than to proceed in such manner for Offences of this kind, as for altering [e] the *Teste* of Writs, or for filling [f] them up after they are sealed, or [g] for bringing groundless Actions, in order to intitle the Parties to the Privilege of the Court, or for getting [h] Judgment in Ejectment, by Affidavit of the Service of a Declaration on one who was procured to personate the Tenant, or for any such like Practices.

CHAP.

CHAP. XXIII.

Of Appeal.

BEFORE we examine the Nature of ſuch Proceſs, as is grounded on an Appeal, Indictment, or Information, it may not be improper, firſt to conſider the Nature of each of theſe in Particular. And firſt of Appeals, of which there are two ſorts,

1. By an Innocent Perſon.
2. By an Offender confeſſing himſelf Guilty, who is commonly called an Approver.

Sect. 1. And Firſt, Of an Appeal by an Innocent Perſon, which is the Party's private Action; proſecuting alſo for the Crown, in reſpect of the Offence againſt the Publick, which he may do two ways, (Finch of Law, 310, 311. Plow. Com. 476.)

1. By Writ.
2. By Bill.

Sect. 2. As to the Writ of Appeal, I ſhall only take Notice in this Place, That it is an Original iſſuing out of Chancery, and returnable in the King's Bench only; and for the Form of it I ſhall refer the Reader to the latter part of this Chapter, wherein I ſhall endeavour to ſhew for what Defects it may be abated.

Sect. 3. Alſo I ſhall refer the Reader to the ſame Place, for the Form of a Bill of Appeal, and ſhall not here take any farther Notice of it, than by obſerving that it muſt contain greater Certainty than a Writ of Appeal, and is in the Lieu both of the Writ and Declaration, and ſhewing before what Courts, and againſt whom it may be proſecuted.

Sect. 4. And firſt, There is no doubt [a] but that any Appeal may be ſued by Bill in the King's Bench againſt any Perſon *in cuſtodia Mareſchalli*, either by an actual Commitment, or by having Bail filed for him in that Court; but [b] not againſt one who is mainpriſed *de die in diem*, for that ſuch a one cannot be ſaid to be *in cuſtodia Mareſchalli*. And it hath been reſolved, [c] That if the Appellee be arraigned and tried the ſame Term, there is no neceſſity to file the Bill againſt him. Alſo [d] it ſeems clear, That if a Defendant appear in the ſaid Court on a void Writ of Appeal, he may be committed to the Marſhalſey, and then declared againſt *in cuſtodia Mareſchalli*; but where a Defendant appears on a Writ not void, but voidable only, as for the want of an Addition, *&c.* it was once [e] holden, That he could not be committed, nor declared againſt *in cuſtodia Mareſchalli*; but ought to be diſcharged. But the contrary hereto ſeems to be now ſettled in the Caſe of *Reeves* [f] againſt *Trundal*, who, appearing in the Court on a Writ of Appeal of Death, demanded Oyer of

[a] Cro. El. 605, 695. S. P. C. 64. Letters C. D. H. P. C. 179. 17 Aſſ. pl. 5. 17 Ed. 3. 13. pl. 40.
[b] 4 Inſt. 180. 1 Bulſt. 74.
[c] 1 Jo. 425. Cro. Car. 532. 1 Rol. Ab. 536. K.
[d] Cro. El. 694, 695.
[e] Cro. El. 605, 695.
[f] Paſche, 3. Georg.

Like Case between Smith and Bowen, Mich. 7 Annæ.

of the Writ, and pleaded in Abatement the want of an Addition; and thereupon the Court abated the Writ, and suffered him to be arraigned by Bill *in custodia Marescballi*: And surely this cannot but seem more reasonable than to suffer a Prisoner under so heavy an Accusation, to which he is still liable, to go at large without a Trial; neither do I find any reason given why a Prisoner appearing on a voidable Writ, should have a greater Advantage than on a void one.

Keilw. 152, b. pl. 4.

Sect. 5. Secondly, It is also holden, That an Appeal may be commenced before Justices in Eyre, which, as I suppose, must be intended of an Appeal by Bill, for that all Writs of Appeal must be returnable in the King's Bench.

2 Inst. 418, 420.

Sect. 6. Thirdly, Also it seems clearly to follow, from the Purport of the Statute of *Westminster*, 2. Ch. 29. That Bills of Appeal may be commenced and determined before Justices, specially assigned, in special Cases, and for certain Causes, to hear and determine them.

[a] Bro. Appeal, 11, 19, 51, 123. Dyer, 201. pl. 67. S. P. C. 64. Letter C. H. P. C. 148.

Sect. 7. Fourthly, It is certain, [a] That Commissioners of Gaol-delivery may receive a Bill of Appeal against any Prisoner of the Gaol which they are authorised to deliver. Also it is generally holden, That they may receive such a Bill against a Person who has been let to Bail by them, but not against one who has been let to Mainprise. And it hath been resolved, That if part of the Accomplices to the same Felony be in the Prison which such Justices are to deliver, and the others be not in it, the Justices shall receive an Appeal against them all, which, after the Trial of those that are in the Prison, shall be removed into the King's Bench, where the others shall be proceeded against. But these three last Points, having been already more largely considered, Chap. 6. Sect. 5. I shall refer the Reader to what is there said concerning them.

Vide Supra. fol. 28, 29, 30. Dy. 99. pl. 62.

Sect. 8. Fifthly, It seems to follow, from the Purport of the Statutes which have been generally construed to authorize Justices of Assise to deliver Gaols without any special Commission of Gaol-delivery, that they may receive Bills of Appeal in the same manner as Commissioners of Gaol-delivery may.

[b] Coro. 95. [c] Vide S. P. C. 65. Letter A. 2 Inst. 420. H. P. C. 179. 2 H. 4. 19. pl. 12. Bro. Appeal, 18. [d] 44 Ed. 3. 44. pl. 57. See Bro. Appeal, 11.

Sect. 9. Sixthly, It seems to be holden in *Fitzherbert*'s Abridgment, [b] That Justices of Peace have Power to receive Appeals by Vertue of 34 *Ed.* 3. 1. which enacts, That they shall hear and determine all manner of Felonies and Trespasses in the same County, *&c.* But there is much greater Authority [c] for the contrary Opinion; and the Case in the [d] *Year-Book*, in the Abridgment whereof the said Opinion of *Fitzherbert* is insinuated, is plainly mistaken, for that it makes no manner of mention of Justices of Peace, but only of Justices of Gaol-delivery; to which may be added, That the above-mentioned Statute of 34 *Ed.* 3. 1. which empowers Justices of Peace to hear and determine Felonies, *&c.* is express, That they shall have Power so to do at the King's Suit, which must be either taken to exclude the Suit of the Party, or to signify little or nothing.

[e] See Ch. 9. Sect. 39, 40, 41. [f] See Ch. 9. Sect. 42. [g] H. P. C. 180. S. P. C. 65. a. 1 Inst. 74. a. b. Vide infra, Sect. 28.

Sect. 10. Seventhly, It is certain, That an Appeal may be commenced [e] by Bill, before the Sheriff and Coroner, and removed [f] from them into the King's Bench, by *Certiorari*, as hath been more fully shewn, Chap. 9.

Sect. 11. Eighthly, It seems to be agreed, [g] That an Appeal by the Course of the Civil Law, in Nature of a Bill of Appeal by the Common Law, may be sued before the Constable and Marshal for some Felonies

Felonies done out of the Realm, in relation whereunto it is enacted by 1 *H.* 4. 14. as followeth, *For many great Inconveniencies and Mischiefs that often have happened by many Appeals made within the Realm before this time, it is ordained from henceforth, That all Appeals to be made of things done within the Realm, shall be tried and determined by the good Laws of the Realm: And that all Appeals to be made of things done out of the Realm, shall be tried and determined before the Constable and Marshal of* England *for the time being.*

Sect. 12. In the Construction of this Statute, it seems to have been agreed, [a] That if any of the King's Subjects kill any other of his Subjects in any foreign Realm, the Wife, or Heir of the Deceased may have an Appeal of his Death, before the Constable and Marshal, who shall proceed according to the Civil [b] Law, and give Sentence by the Testimony of Witnesses, or Combat: From whence it follows, [c] That no such Sentence can corrupt the Blood of the Appellee, for that such Corruption can only be caused by a Judgment by course of the Common Law. Also [d] it seems to be clear, That no such Appeal can be prosecuted before the Marshal alone without a Constable.

Sect. 13. It hath been holden, [e] That if a Man die in *England*, of a Wound given him in a foreign Realm, he may be appealed by the intent of this Statute, before the Constable and Marshal, for that it is certain That he cannot be tried by the Common Law; and it cannot be thought the meaning of the Statute in restraining the Civil Law, in Cases within the Conusance of the Common, to restrain it also in Cases which the Common Law had nothing to do with, and which were properly cognisable by the Civil Law, and by that only; for the only end of such a Construction would be to cause a Failure of Justice.

Sect. 14. It is farther enacted by the said Statute of 1 *H.* 4. 14. *That no Appeals be from thenceforth made, or in any wise pursued in Parliament, in any time to come.*

[a] S. P. C. 65. Letter B. 1 Inst. 74. a. 13 H. 4. 5. a.
[b] 4 Inst. 155. 1 Inst. 74, 391. b. Supra Ch. 4. Sect. 10. Bro. Jurisdict. 103.
[c] See B. 1. Ch. 37. Sect. 8. and Ch. 4. of this Book Sect. 10. and 1 Inst. 391. a.
[d] See Ch. 4. Sect. 8. Letter f. Hutt. 3. 1 Inst. 74, b.
[e] S. P. C. 65. Letter B. 1 Inst 74. b. B. 1. Ch. 31. Sect. 11.

Appeals considered, as to the Matter of them, are of two kinds.

1. Not Capital.
2. Capital.

Sect. 15. And first, of those not Capital, whereof there were anciently several kinds; as Appeals *de pace*, *de plagis*, and *de Imprisonamento*, as well as Appeals of *Mayhem*; but the former of these having been out of use, and turned to Actions of Trespass, for these many hundred Years, I shall only consider the Nature of an Appeal of *Mayhem*; for the better Understanding whereof, I shall endeavour to shew,

Fleta Lib. 1. cap. 41. Bract. Lib. 3. cap. 25. 4 Inst. 182. 1 Inst. 126. b.

1. Of what *Mayhems* it lies.
2. What ought to be the form of the Writ, Bill, and Declaration.
3. What Defence may be made by the Appellee.
4. How the *Mayhem* shall be tried, and where the Trial shall be peremptory.

Sect. 16. As to the first Point, *viz.* Of what *Mayhems* an Appeal lies; I shall take it for granted, That notwithstanding every [f] Hurt whatsoever done to a Man's Body, whereby he is less able in Fighting, may perhaps, properly enough, in a large Sense, be called a *Mayhem*, and [g] will certainly subject the Person who occasion'd it to the Payment

[f] See B. 1. Ch. 44.
[g] 2 Jo. 205. Hob. 134.

of Damages, in an Action of Trespass by the Party grieved, whether it were malicious, or happened through Accident or Misadventure; yet [a] an Appeal of *Mayhem* cannot be maintained for any such Hurt, unless it were accompanied with some evil Intention in the Person who caused it; for surely the Law, in requiring that the Word Felony be made use of in every such Appeal, (as will be more fully shewn under the next Point) cannot imply less than that the Fact must be attended with some odious Circumstances. Yet it seems clear, That if a Man striking at another with such an evil Intent, as would subject him to an Appeal of *Mayhem*, if the Person struck at should be maimed, shall happen to miss him, and strike a third Person, and maim him, he is liable [b] to an Appeal of *Mayhem* at his Suit, whether he had any kind of Ill-will against him or not.

[a] 13 H. 7. 14. pl. 5.

[b] Bro. Appeal, 157. 13 H. 7. 14. pl. 5. See B. 1. Ch. 31. Sect. 41.

As to the second Point, *viz.* What ought to be the Form of the Writ, Bill, and Declaration, I shall only take Notice in this Place,

Sect. 17. First, That the Word *Mayhemiavit* [c] is so necessary in every such Writ, Bill, or Declaration, that it can be supplied by no other Word of the like Sense, nor by any Circumlocution whatsoever.

Sect. 18. Secondly, That in every such Writ, Bill, or Declaration, the *Mayhem* must [d] be laid to have been done *Felonicè*, and yet the Defendant is not at this Day subject to the loss of Member from such an Appeal, as anciently [e] he was, in which respect the Law seems to have required the use of the Word *Felonicè*.

Sect. 19. Thirdly, [f] That it is in the Election of the Plaintiff to declare against him who actually gave the Wound, as the Principal Offender, and against those who abetted him, as Accessories; or else to declare against them all as Principals.

Sect. 20. Fourthly, That if a Man bring a Writ of Appeal of *Mayhem*, and count of Battery, he abates the Writ, because the Writ supposes no Battery, and therefore is not pursued by such a Declaration as it ought to be. But for other Particulars relating to the Form of Appeals, I shall refer the Reader to the Books [g] of Entries.

Sect. 21. As to the third Point, *viz.* What Defence may be made by the Appellee; being able to find little or nothing Particular concerning Pleas in Abatement by such an Appellee, I shall refer the Reader for that Matter, to what is said concerning Pleas in Abatement of Appeals in general, in the latter part of this Chapter, and only take notice in this Place of the following Particulars.

[c] 1 Inst. 126. b.

[d] 1 Inst. 127. a. Bro. Appeal, 72, 86, 143.

[e] See B. 1. Ch, 44. Sect. 3. 1 Inst, 127. a Pulton 17. a.

[f] 41 Ass. 16. 40 Ass. 9. Fitz. Trespass, 199. Coron. 11, 228. S. P. C. 44. Letter F. Contra Bro. Appeal, 154. Bro. Appeal, 60. Fitz. Coron. 110.

[g] Coke Entries, 50, 51. Rastel's Entries, 45, 46.

1. Where a Recovery in another Action may be pleaded in Bar of an Appeal of *Mayhem*.
2. Where and in what Manner *son Assault demesne*, and other Matters of the like Nature may be so pleaded.
3. Whether an Arbitrament, or an Accord with Satisfaction, may be so pleaded.
4. What kind of Release may be so pleaded.
5. Where a Nonsuit in a former Action.
6. That [h] the Appellee cannot wage his Law.

[h] 1 Inst. 295. a. Vide 48 Ed. 3, 6. Fitz. Ley, 36.

Sect. 22. As to the first of these Particulars, *viz.* Where a Recovery in another Action may be pleaded in Bar of an Appeal of *Mayhem*;

It seems clear, That notwithstanding a Recovery [a] in an Appeal of *Mayhem* cannot be pleaded in Bar of an Action of Trespass for the Battery with which the *Mayhem* was accompanied, because [b] in such an Appeal the *Mayhem* only is considered distinct from the Battery; yet [c] a Recovery in an Action of Trespass, for an Assault, Battery, and Wounding, may be pleaded in Bar of an Appeal of *Mayhem*, appearing by proper Averments to be brought for the same Trespass; for it shall be intended that the Jury in giving Damages for the Wounding, included the Maim, and no Man shall be liable to double Vexation for one and the same thing; yet [d] in such a Case if the Appellee shall make it appear, by a special Replication, that the Maim hath been occasioned since the Verdict in the Action of Trespass, by some subsequent Mortification, Dryness, or shrinking of the Part, by reason of the Wound, perhaps he may avoid such Plea by such special Matter; but the Court will not intend it unless it be specially shewn.

Sect. 23. As to the second Particular, *viz.* Where, and in what manner *son Assault demesne*, and other Matters of the like Nature, may be pleaded in Bar of an Appeal of *Mayhem*; It seems clear, that it is a good Plea in Bar of such an Appeal, That [e] the Plaintiff first assaulted the Defendant, and would have beaten and killed him, unless he had defended himself against him, *&c.* Or that [f] the Plaintiff first assaulted the Defendant, who fled from Place to Place, till he was reduced to a necessity of Fighting, *&c.* And in some Books [g] it seems to be holden in general, That *son Assault demesne* may be pleaded in Bar of any such Appeal without any such special Circumstances in favour of the Defendant: Yet how far a trifling Assault may justify a grievous *Mayhem*, as the cutting off of a Leg, or Hand, *&c.* unless it happened accidentally in the Scuffle, without any barbarous Intention, may well deserve to be considered. However [h] it seems clear, That if the Maim in the Declaration be laid in *A.* and the Defendant justify the same Maim, by reason of an Assault made upon him by the Plaintiff in *B.* he needs not traverse the maiming of the Plaintiff in *A.* or in any other Place, for it is apparent, that the same Maim could not be given but in one and the same Place, and therefore being justified in any one Place it is well answered. Also it seems [i] clear, That a Man cannot justify the maiming another in the Defence of his Possessions, but only in the Defence of his Person. Also it is certain, [k] That a Defendant cannot give in Evidence on the general Issue, that the Plaintiff first assaulted him, but must specially plead it.

Sect. 24. As to the third Particular, *viz.* Where an Arbitrement, or Accord with Satisfaction, may be pleaded in Bar of an Appeal of *Mayhem*, it clearly seems to be admitted in the Pleadings, [l] in some Books, and is said [m] to have been adjudged in a Roll, not printed, That notwithstanding every such Appeal must suppose the Fact to have been done feloniously, yet inasmuch as at this Day it subjects not the Appellee to the Loss of Member, but only to Damages, *&c.* as an Action of Trespass doth it may be well barred either by an Arbitrament, or an Accord with Satisfaction executed.

Sect. 25. As to the fourth Particular, *viz.* What kind of Release may be pleaded in Bar of an Appeal of *Mayhem*; There can be no doubt, but that in a Release of all manner of Appeals, [n] or a Release of all manner of Actions, or a Release of all manner of Demands, [o] might always be pleaded in Bar of such an Appeal; and that a Release of all manner

[a] 22 Aff. pl. 82. Fitz. Coro. 110, 181. 4 Co. 43. 43 Aff. 39.
[b] Bro. Appeal, 60.
[c] 4 Co. 43. a. 1 Leon. 318, 319. 43 Aff. pl. 3.
[d] 1 Leon. 318, 319.
[e] 2 Rol. Ab. 547. letter F. Rastals Entries. 45.
[f] 2 Rol. Ab. 112. letter B. 25 Ed. 3. 42. pl. 21. See B. 1. Ch. 60. Sect. 23.
[g] 27 Ed. 3. 94. pl. 1. 41 Aff pl. 21. Fitz. Coro. 142. 1 Keb. 921. 1 Syd. 246.
[h] 41 Aff. pl. 21. Bro. Visne, 74. Bro. Traverse, 173.
[i] 2 Rol. Ab. 548. pl. 5. 2 Inst. 316.
[k] 2 Inst. 282, 283. 2 Inst. 316.
[l] 35 H. 6. 39. b. 30. a. 6 H. 7. 1. pl. 1. Fitz. Coro. 63. 6 Co. 44. a.
[m] 9 Co. 78. b.
[n] Littleton, Sect. 501.
[o] Littleton, Sect. 508.

[a] 1 Inst. 288

1 Inst. 288.

manner of Actions [a] personal may also be pleaded in Bar of it at this Day, because the Appellant shall recover in it nothing but Damages; but while it subjected the Appellee to the loss of Member, it seems questionable, whether it could be barred by a Release of Actions personal, because it seems to have been then esteemed an Action of a higher Nature, and not properly to have come under the Notion of a personal Action.

Sect. 26. As to the fifth Particular, *viz.* Where a Nonsuit in a former Action may be pleaded in Bar of an Appeal of *Mayhem*; It seems clear, [b] That a Nonsuit in any such Appeal, after the Plaintiff hath appeared to it, may be pleaded in Bar of any other. Also [c] it seems to have been adjudged, That it may also be pleaded in Bar of an Action of Trespass brought for the same Maim, and also for the Battery with which it was accompanied; yet howsoever the Law may stand in relation to this matter; if such Action be brought for the Battery only, without mentioning the *Mayhem*, I see not how it can be barred by such a Nonsuit, because it is generally holden, That in an Appeal of *Mayhem* no Consideration [d] can be had of the Battery, but only of the *Mayhem*; and if so, it seems strange, that a Nonsuit in such an Appeal should bar an Action of a different Nature, brought for a Matter which the Appeal had nothing to do with. However [e] it seems clear, That a Nonsuit in an Action of Trespass is no Bar of an Appeal of *Mayhem*. Also I take it for granted, That a Nonsuit in an Appeal of *Mayhem*, before the Plaintiff hath appeared to it, is not [f] a Bar of any other Appeal, or Action, because the Writ, for what appears to the contrary, might be purchased by a Stranger, in the Name of the Plaintiff.

[b] 43 Aff. pl. 39.
40 Aff. pl. 1.
1 Inst. 139 a
Fitz. Coron. 214.
[c] 43 Aff. pl. 39.
Bro. Appeal, 138.

[d] Bro. Appeal, 60.
Fitz. Coron. 110, 182.
Vide Supra. Sect. 22.
[e] Bro. Appeal, 138,
Fitz. Ley. 36
[f] 1 Inst. 139. a.

Sect. 27. As to the fourth Point, *viz.* How the *Mayhem* shall be tried, and where the Trial shall be peremptory; There [g] is no doubt but that if the Defendant put it in issue whether the Plaintiff were maimed or not, and pray that the Part which was hurt be viewed by the Court, in order to have it adjudged on such View, whether there be any *Mayhem* or not, the Court may take a View of the Part, and on such View determine the Matter; or if there remain a doubt upon the View, may [h] award a Writ to the Sheriff to return some able Physicians and Surgeons, for the better Information of the Court. But it seems, That the Court cannot proceed to such a Trial by their View, unless the Defendant pray it: And in such Case it seems, [i] That they are not bound to try it in such Manner, but may order a Trial by a Jury, at which it is said, [k] That they may, if they think fit, order that the Jury shall have a view of the Wound: And because the Court hath such a discretionary Power in relation to such View, it has been resolved, [l] That the Plaintiff in the Appeal must appear in proper Person, and not by Attorney, because that would put the View out of the Power of the Court. And it seems to be agreed, [m] That an Adjudication made upon such View, is peremptory and conclusive to each Party.

[g] 28 Aff. pl. 5.
8 H. 4. 21. pl. 1.
2 Rol. Abr. 578. letter F.

[h] 28 Aff. pl. 5.
Rastal's Entries, 46. pl. 5, 6.
28 Ed. 3. 94. pl. 1.
[i] 6 H. 7. 1. pl. 1.
21 H. 7. 33. pl 30.
21 H. 7. 40. pl. 58.
41 Aff. pl. 27.
[k] 22 Aff. pl. 82. Vide 21 H. 7. 33. pl 30.
[l] 2 Inst. 313.
[m] 6 H. 7. 1. pl. 1.
28 Aff. pl. 5.
21 H. 7. 33. pl. 30.
37 Aff. pl. 9.
26 Aff. pl. 32.

Sect. 28. It seems to be holden, That the Defendant, in an Appeal of Maim, may in some Cases wage Battel; but I find no Instance in which Battel hath been actually waged in such an Appeal.

Secondly, Of Capital Appeals there are two kinds,

1. Of Treason.
2. Of Felony.

Sect. 29. And first of Appeals of Treason, which, as it is said, [a] might be sued anciently not only before the Parliament, but also before other Courts of Common Law, as well as before the Constable and Marshal, and were determinable by Battel, Verdict, or otherwise, according to the Course of the several Courts before which they were commenced. But it is certain, That such Appeals before the Parliament are taken away by 1 *H.* 4. 14. set forth more at large in the fourteenth Section of this Chapter. But I do not see any reason why Appeals of Treason, done in the Realm, before other Courts of Common Law, which had before Jurisdiction thereof, should be construed to be taken away by that Statute, which by ordaining, *That Appeals of Things done within the Realm, shall be tried and determined by the good Laws of the Realm,* cannot be intended to restrain any Appeal determinable wholly by those Laws, as all the Appeals before the Courts of Common Law seem always to have been. However, since there has been no Instance of any such Appeal, before any Court of Common Law, either since the making of the said Statute, nor for many Years before, the Law relating to such Appeals seems wholly obsolete at this Day. But as for Appeals before the Constable and Marshal, of Treasons done out of the Realm, it seems clear, That the Law in relation to them is still in Force, as it always hath been; for the said Statute of 1 *H.* 4. 14. by ordaining, *That Appeals of Things done out of the Realm, shall be tried and determined before the Constable and Marshal,* seems clearly rather to affirm than weaken their Jurisdiction in relation to such Treasons. Also it hath been adjudged, that the Statutes which ordain, That Treasons done out of the Realm shall be tried in the King's Bench, *&c.* do not take away the Jurisdiction of the Constable and Marshal, in relation to Appeals of such Treasons, as hath been more fully shewn Chap. 4. Sect. 9. And agreeably hereto, an Appeal of Treason, supposed to have been committed beyond Sea, was actually commenced in the seventh Year of the Reign of King *Charles* the First, by *Donald* Lord *Rea*, against *David Ramsey*, Esq; before the Constable and Marshal, who, for want of sufficient Proof to clear the Truth of the Accusation, actually awarded, That a Duel should be fought between the said Appellant and Appellee, for the final Determination of the Matter.

[a] 3 Inst. 132 Bract. 118, 119. Fleta Lib. 1. Ch. 21. S. P.C. 78. Letter C. Contra Bro. Appeal 46.

4 Inst. 124. H. P. C. 180. *seems contrary.*

Rushworth's Collect. Part 2. Vol. 1. from fol. 112. to 128.

Of Appeals of Felony there are four principal kinds,

1. Of Death.
2. Of Larceny.
3. Of Rape.
4. Of Arson.

But before I examine the Nature of each of these in Particular, I shall premise some Things in general concerning what Persons are capable of bringing them, as

Sect. 30. First, That [b] the Infancy, Old Age, or other Imbecillity of the Plaintiff, is no good Objection against his bringing an Appeal, tho' it take from the Defendant the benefit of waging Battel, and in that respect put him in a worse Condition than he would be in if the Appeal were brought by a Person capable of fighting; for inasmuch as the Defendant has proper means for his Acquittal, by putting himself upon a Trial

[b] Moor 461. pl. 646. H. P. C. 183, 184. Keilw. 120. a S. P. C. 60. Letter D. See the Books under cited. Con. 45 Ed. 3. 25. pl. 36. 41 Ass. pl. 14

Trial by his Country, and the Imbecillity of the Plaintiff is wholly owing to the Act of God, and no ways lessens the Injury complained of by him, it is not reasonable he should suffer any Disadvantage from it. And agreeably hereto it seems to have been settled [a] of late times, contrary to the numerous Authorities [b] in the old Books, That the Parol shall not demur in an Appeal for the Nonage of the Plaintiff. Yet it is certain, [c] That an Infant must prosecute such Suit by a Guardian; and it is said, [d] That he shall be nonsuited for the Non-appearance of such Guardian, upon Demand, at any Day whereon he is demandable, notwithstanding an Allegation that he was not able to come by reason of Sickness, or other such like Excuse. And there [e] is a Case wherein the Court refused to inlarge the Day of such Guardian's Appearance upon a Surmise of his Sickness. But notwithstanding the Guardian be so necessary in the Prosecution of such a Suit, yet if the Infant come into Court, and say he will relinquish it, and yet the Guardian will prosecute it; the Court may, [f] in Discretion, discharge such Guardian, and assign another, for it is not reasonable that an Infant be bound to continue a Suit against his Will, which demands nothing but Revenge, and will be chargeable to him.

Sect. 31. Secondly, [g] That a Woman may sue any other Appeal except that of the Death of an Ancestor; for that the Statute of *Magna Charta*, 34. which ordains, *That no Man shall be imprisoned on the Appeal of a Woman, for the Death of any one but her own Husband*, restrains not any other Appeal whatsoever.

Sect. 32. Thirdly, That an Ideot, [h] or Person born Deaf and Dumb, or one attainted [i] of Treason or Felony, or but outlawed [k] in a Personal Action (so long as such Attainder or Outlawry continue in force) cannot bring any Appeal whatsoever.

And now I am more particularly to consider the Nature of an Appeal of Death in particular, for the better understanding whereof, I shall examine the following Points.

1. Within what time it must be brought.
2. In what County.
3. By whom.

Sect. 33. As to the first Point, *viz.* Within what time an Appeal of Death must be brought, it is enacted by the Statute of *Glocester*, Ch. 9. *That an Appeal* (which from the Purport of the whole Statute hath been construed [l] to be meant only of an Appeal of Death) *shall stand in effect, and shall not be abated for default of fresh Suit, if the Party shall sue within the Year* [m] *and the Day after the Deed done.* And it hath been holden, [n] That the computation of such Year and Day is to be made from the Time of the Wound which occasioned the Death, and not from the Time of the Death; and this Opinion seems somewhat to be favour'd by the Letter of the Statute, which is, That the Party shall sue within the Year and Day after the Deed done, but no Deed is done at the time of the Death, but at the time of the Wound; yet the contrary Opinion is settled [o] to be Law, and is certainly most agreeable to the Intent of the Statute, the plain Import whereof seems to be, That the Appellant shall not be adjudged to have made default of fresh Suit, unless he have been negligent a Year and a Day; but negligent he could

[a] 27 H. 8. 11 pl. 25. Keilw. 120. pl. 66. S P. C. 60. D H. P. C. 183. Smith and Bowen, Mich. 7 Annæ.
[b] 2 Inst. 320. 32 Aff. pl. 8. Dyer 137. pl. 24. 11 H. 4. 94. pl. 56. 13 Aff. pl. 10. 17 Ed. 4. 2. pl. 4. Bro. Appeal, 116. Fitz. Age. 57, 83. 21 Aff. pl. 4. 27 Ed. 3. 83. pl. 2. 21 Ed. 3. 23. pl. 16.
[c] 27 H. 8. 11, pl. 25.
[d] Noy 88. Latch 173.
[e] Noy 88. Latch 173.
[f] 1 Rol. Abr. 288. D. Styles 456. Vide Salk. 176, 177.
[g] Co. Lit. 25 b. 2 Inst. 68. Fitz. Coron. 357. S P. C. 60. F. H. P. C. 184.
[h] H. P. C. 183. S P. C. 60. D. 98, C.
[i] 11 Aff. pl. 27.
[k] 17 Aff. pl. 26. Bro. Appeal, 118, 146. Fitz Utlagary, 47.
[l] S. P. C. 62. Letter B. Infra. Sect. 48.
[m] Bro. Appeal, 37. 22 Ed. 4. 39. b.
[n] S. P. C. 63. Letter A.
[o] 4 Co. 42. b. 2 Inst. 320. 3 Inst. 53.

not be as to the bringing an Appeal before the Party was actually dead, because till then no Appeal lay. And agreeably hereto it seems also to be settled, [a] That if a Person become Accessory after the Death, by receiving the Offender, an Appeal lies against him, at any time within the Year and Day after such Receipt, because till then the Appellant could not possibly be guilty of any Negligence as to the bringing of an Appeal against the Receiver. Also if an Appeal had been abated by the Demise of the King, before 1 *Ed.* 6. Ch. 7. (by which this Mischief is provided against) it seems [b] clear, That the Appellant might have sued a Re-attachment against the Appellee, within the Year and Day after such Demise, for that he was in no default, and otherwise would have been without remedy.

Sect. 34. It seems, That the Year and Day in any of the Cases abovementioned, are to be computed from the beginning of the Day, on which the Death, or Receipt, *&c.* happened, and not from the precise Minute, or Hour, because regularly the Law makes no Fraction of a Day; and therefore [c] if the Party dye at any time the first Day of *January*, the Year shall end the first Day of *January* following.

Sect. 35. As to the second Point, *viz.* In what County an Appeal of Death must be brought; I shall take it for granted, That it is a local [d] Action, and consequently cannot be brought in a foreign County. But if a Person happen to dye in one County of a Wound received in another, it is said, [e] That the Appellant had, by the Common Law, his Election to bring his Appeal in either County, and that in every such Case the Trial ought [f] to be at the Bar, and by a Jury returned [g] from the Body of each of those Counties. But since the making of 2 & 3 *Ed.* 6. 24. by which it is enacted, *That in such Cases, the Party to whom Appeal of Murder shall be given by the Law, may commence, take, and sue Appeal of Murder in the same County where the Person feloniously stricken, or poisoned, shall die,* &c. I take it for granted, That such an Appeal, in the County wherein the Party died, may be tried by a Jury of such County without the joinder of any other.

I shall not in this Place examine in what County Accessories to Murder are to be appealed or tried, but shall refer the Consideration thereof to the Chapter concerning the Arraignment of the Principal and Accessory.

As to the third Point, *viz.* By whom an Appeal of Death is to be brought, I shall endeavour to shew,

1. Where it may be brought by a Wife.
2. Where by an Heir.

1. As to an Appeal by a Wife, the following Particulars seem most observable.

Sect. 36. First, She must be able to prove, not only that she was wholly innocent herself of the Death complained of, but also that she was the Lawful Wife of the Deceased, at the time of his Death; for it seems to be clearly settled, [h] That *N'unques accouple in loial matrimonie* is a good Plea in such an Appeal, and triable by the Bishop's Certificate, who, if the Marriage were unlawful, by reason of a Precontract, or Consan-

[a] 26 Aff. pl. 52. 3 Inst. 53. S. P. C. 63. Letter B. 2 Inst. 320.

[b] 2 H. 7. 10. pl. 5. Bro. Appeal, 81, 10 Ed. 4. 13. pl. 7. Fitz. Re-attachment, 8. 7 Co. 30.

[c] Vide 5 Co. 1 Co. Lit. 130. b. 255. A. Contra 3 Inst. 53.

[d] 18 Ed. 3. 32. pl. 6. S. P. C. 63. D. Fitz. Forfeiture, 14. Dyer, 38. pl. 50, &c.

[e] 3 H. 7. 12. pl. 4. 4 H. 7. 18. pl. 10. Fitz. Coron. 59, 60. *But the Preamble of 2 & 3 Ed. 6. 24. seems contrary.*

[f] Dy. 46. pl. 8.

[g] 3 H. 7. 12. pl. 4. Finch, 410. 411. Dy. 46. pl. 8.

Vide Infra, Sect. 59. & 60.

[h] 2 Inst. 68. 28 Ed. 3. 91 pl. 4. 50 Ed. 3 15. 27 Aff. pl. 3. 11 H. 4. 14. a. b. S. P. C. 59. A B. H. P. C. 181. 1 Inst. 33. b.

Consanguinity, or otherwise, ought to certify against the Appellant. Also it is laid down as a Rule in the Old Books, [a] That a Wife may have an Appeal of the Death of her Husband *inter brachia sua interfecti & non aliter*. By which Words, *inter brachia sua*, according to Sir *Edward Coke*, [b] it is to be understood, That the deceased had the Wife lawfully in possession at his Death; and if this be the meaning of them, thus much at least seems to follow, That if the Husband were divorced from the Wife at his Death, though by a voidable Sentence, she cannot maintain an Appeal. Yet it is generally holden, That a Wife who hath eloped from her Husband may have an Appeal of his Death, as shall be more fully shewn in the next Section. And *Staundforde* [c] seems to understand the import of the expression above-mentioned to be this, That the Wife ought to have had the Deceased in her View, and to have been present at his Death, which is most certainly not necessary at this Day. But finding little more said concerning this Matter in any other Modern Book, I shall leave the farther Consideration thereof to others.

Sect. 37. Secondly, In some Cases a Woman may have an Appeal of the Death of her Husband, where she cannot claim Dower of his Lands, as where the Husband was attainted [d] of High Treason at the time of his Death; for after the Attainder he was still her Husband as much as before, and [e] it is the Loss of her Husband which is the Cause of the Appeal. Also where a Woman elopes from her Husband, it is said, That she may have an Appeal [f] of his Death, though not a Writ of Dower; for by the Common Law she might have had both; and the Statute of *Westminster* 2. Ch. 34. which takes from her the later, leaves the other as before.

Sect. 38. Thirdly. If such Appellant take another Husband either before, or pending the Appeal, she puts [g] an end to it for ever; for, being given her only from a regard to her Widowhood, it cannot but cease when that determines, and being once barred, it is barred for ever. And on this ground it seems also to be certain, [h] That if she marry after Judgment in Appeal, she cannot pray Execution. However it seems clear, That in such a Case the Appellee shall not [i] be discharged without the King's Pardon: But I do not find it settled [k] what ought to be done with the Appellee in such a Case. But thus much seems to be certain, That the King cannot proceed against him by way of Indictment, because he is attainted already; and therefore it may probably be argued, That the Court may award Execution against him, either *ex Officio*, or at least at the demand of the King, for otherwise he would save his Life by reason of the Attainder by which he is adjudged to lose it.

Secondly, as to the Appeal of Death by an Heir, the following particulars seem most remarkable.

Sect. 39. First, If the deceased had a Wife at the time of his Death, and such Wife were wholly innocent of it, she [l] only, and not the Heir, hath a Right to the Appeal, and whether she bring one or wholly neglect it, and though she dye or marry within the Year and Day, the Heir cannot bring an Appeal; and the reason hereof, according to *Keilwey*, [m] is this, That the Appeal being once out of the Blood, shall

[a] Bract. Lib. 3. cap. 29. Fleta Lib 1. cap. 35. S. P. C. 58. C.
[b] 2 Inst. 68. 317.
[c] S. P. C. 59.
[d] 27 Ass. pl. 41. 35 H. 6. 57. b. 58. Bro. Appeal, 131. Fitz Coro. 21. Co. Litt. 33. b. 7 Co. Calvin's Case, 13. b. S. P. C. 59.
[e] Bro. Appeal, 148.
[f] Bro. Appeal, 17. 1 Inst. 33. b. S. P. C. 59. C. Contra 2 Inst. 317.
[g] H. P. C. 181. S. P. C. 59. letter B. 2 Inst. 69. 20 H. 6. 43. b. Bro. Appeal, 148.
[h] 11 H. 4. 48. b. Bro. Appeal, 109, 112, 148. con. 21 E. 4. 73. b. *See also the Books above cited.*
[i] Bro. Appeal, 27. 3 Inst. 209. 210. 2 H. 7. 10. pl. 5. 8 H. 4. 22. pl. 7. Fitz. Scire facias, 41. 38 H. 6. 13. pl. 26. 9 H. 7. 5. b. S. P. C. 166. letter A.
[k] 3 Leon. 83. Vide 21 Ed. 4. 72. b. 73.
[l] Keilw. 120. pl. 65. H. P. C. 181, 182. S. P. C. 59. E. 20 H. 6. 43.
[m] Keilw. 120. pl. 65.

not return to it again: Yet [a] if the Wife herself had a share in the Guilt, the Heir may have an Appeal against her. But if the Petit Treason be pardoned by the Parliament, it seems, [b] That the Heir can bring no Appeal; for he cannot bring it for the Murder only, because the Petit Treason includes in it Murder and more, and being the greater Offence drowns the less, and therefore the Pardon of it seems to pardon the Murder also.

Sect. 40. Secondly, Every such Appellant must be Heir [c] general to the deceased, by the Course of the Common Law, unless [d] the Heir general had himself a share in the Guilt, in which Case the next Heir shall have an Appeal against him. But a Father cannot [e] have an Appeal of the Death of his Son, because he cannot be his Heir. Neither [f] can any one bring an Appeal of the Death of a Person attainted of Treason or Felony, except his Wife, because he can have no Heir. Neither shall a special [g] Heir, by the Custom of Borough-English, or otherwise, have an Appeal of the Death of his Ancestor, because he is not his next general Heir; and yet he is inheritable to such of his Lands to which the Custom extends, *&c.* And for the like reason, if the deceased, at the time of his Death, had two Sons, the Elder whereof is attainted of Treason, or Felony, neither [h] of them can have an Appeal; not the Elder, because of the Attainder; not the Younger, because he cannot be Heir to his Father while he has an Elder Brother; who, though he be looked upon as dead in Law to some Purposes, is yet in Truth alive, and capable of forfeiting all the Privileges belonging to the Heir, though not of taking benefit from any of them. But notwithstanding a younger Son cannot bring an Appeal of the Death of the Father, while there is an Elder Son of the same Father living; yet if the eldest Son be by one Venter, and the middle and younger Son by another, and the middle Son be killed, the youngest only shall have an Appeal of his Death, because he only is his Heir, as being of the whole Blood with him: And therefore, [i] it is no good Plea to an Appeal for the Death of a Brother, That the Appellant has *J. S.* an Elder Brother living, without shewing, that *J. S.* was of the whole Blood to the deceased.

Sect. 41. Thirdly, If an Appeal be once commenced by an Heir, who dies hanging the Suit, it seems to be agreed, [k] by almost all the Books, That no other Heir can afterwards proceed in such Appeal, or commence a new one; for that this is a Personal Action, given to the Heir in respect to his immediate Relation to the Person killed, at the time of his Death, and like other Personal Actions, shall die with the Person. But some [l] have holden, That if the first Heir die within the Year and Day, without commencing an Appeal, the next Heir may bring one. But this is made a doubt by others, [m] and the generality [n] of the Books seem to favour the contrary Opinion, as being more agreeable to the Reason of the Case above-mentioned, and the general Tenor of the Law in relation to Appeals, which in no Case, that I know of, will suffer the Right of bringing one to be transferred from one to another; and therefore, as in Case [o] where the deceased hath a Wife at the time of his Death, who dies within the Year and Day, the Heir hath no Right to an Appeal; so if he have an Heir at his Death, in whom the Right of the Appeal is vested, and such Heir die within the Year

[a] Cro. Car. 531, 532. 1 Jon. 425. 18 Ed. 4. 1. pl. 3. Fitz. Coro. 459. H. P. C. 181, 182. S. P. C. 59. D.

[b] Dy. 50. pl. 4. 1 Leon. 326.

[c] 27 Ed. 3. 83. pl. 2. Fitz. Coron. 322. H. P. C. 182. S. P. C 59. F. 27 Ass. pl. 25.

[d] H. P. C. 182. Fitz. Coro. 459. S. P. C. 60. Letter B.

[e] Fitz. Coro. 41. Bro. Appeal, 116, 131. 2 Ass. pl. 3.

[f] S. P. C. 59. F. H. P. C. 182.

[h] S. P. C. 60. Letter A. 1 Inst. 8. a. 13. a.

20 H. 6. 43. b. Fitz. Coro. 235. But Fitz. Coron. 322. *seems contrary.*

[i] 7 Ed. 4 15. pl. 13. Fitz. Coro. 28. Bro. Appeal, 94. S. P. C. 60. E.

[k] 11 H. 4. 11. b. 12. a. 9 H. 7. 5. b. 16 H. 7. 15. pl. 14. S. P. C. 59. G. H. P. C. 182. Bro. Appeal, 39, 88, 104, 141, 144.

[l] 16 H. 7. 15. pl. 14. Bro. Appeal, 156. 11 H. 4. 11. b.

[m] S. P. C. 59. G. Dy. 69. pl. 31.

[n] 20 H. 6. 43. b. 11 H. 4. 12. a. H. P. C. 182. Bro. Appeal, 39, 88, 104, 141, 144.

[o] Supra Sect. 39.

and Day, it seems, That no other Heir shall have an Appeal. Yet it is holden, [a] by Sir *Matthew Hale*, and some others, That if the first Heir get Judgment in an Appeal of Death, and die, his Heir may sue Execution. But this is doubted of by Sir *William Staundford*, [b] and seems contrary to many [c] of the old Books, and not easily reconcileable with the Reason of the Cases above-mentioned. But whether in this Case the Court may [d] not award Execution, either *ex officio*, or at the Demand of the King, may deserve to be considered, for the Reasons given *Section* 38. Also if a Person who is killed have no Wife at the time of his Death, and no issue but Daughters, and all those Daughters die within the Year and Day, it may reasonably be argued, That the Heir Male may have an Appeal, because the Right of bringing one never vested in any other before. But finding this Case in none of the Books, I shall leave it to be more fully considered by others.

[a] H. P. C. 182. 13 H. 4. 6. pl. 14. 11 H. 4. 11. b
[b] S. P. C. 59. I
[c] 33 H. 6. 13. pl. 26. 9 H. 7. 5. b. 6. a. 16 H. 7. 15. pl. 14. 11 H. 4. 11. b 12. a. Bro. Appeal, 141, 144, 156.
[d] 2 Leon. 83 *seems contrary.*

Sect. 42. Fourthly, Every such Appellant must not only be Heir general to the deceased, but also Heir male; and this depends upon *Magna Charta*, Ch. 35. by which it is enacted, *That no one shall be taken or imprisoned on the Appeal of a Woman for the Death of any one but her own Husband.* And the Judges are so far bound to take notice of this Statute, That if a Woman bring an Appeal of the Death of her Father, or any other but her Husband, they ought, [d] *ex officio*, to abate the Writ, though the Defendant take no Exception to it. But it is said, [e] That by the Common Law an Heir female might have brought an Appeal of the Death of her Ancestor, as well as an Heir male. And it seems [f] to be the better Opinion at this Day, That the Heir male of the deceased, who derives his Blood through a Female, may have an Appeal, as the Uncle being Heir on the part of the Mother, or the Grandson by a Daughter, *&c.* and yet the Mother in the first Case, and the Daughter in the second, could have had no Appeal; for inasmuch as by the Common Law, such Mother and Daughter had not only a Right to bring such Appeal, but also to have such Right derived through them to others, it seems hard to construe the Statute by depriving them of the former to take from them the other also; especially considering, That an Heir Male, who derives his Blood through Females, seems no way less worthy to bring an Appeal, than if he had derived it through Males; and all Statutes whatsoever, which are made in Abridgment of any Right of the Subject ought to be strictly construed.

[d] Fitz. Office de Court, 7. 10 Ed. 4. 7. pl. 18.
[e] 2 Inst. 68. 1 Inst. 25.
[f] H. P. C. 182, 183. 2 Inst. 68. Fitz. Coro. 385. *the contrary adjudged by all the Judges, in the Exchequer Chamber, but one.* 20 H. 6. 43. Quere 17 Ed. 4. 1. pl. 1. 1 Inst. 25. S. P. C. 58. B. C. Bro. Appeal, 104.

Sect. 43. Fifthly, In every such Appeal, by one, as Heir to the deceased, it must specially [g] appear by the Writ, or at least by the Count, in what manner he is so.

[g] 21 Ed. 3. 23 pl. 16. 45 Ed. 3. 25. pl. 36. 27 Ass. pl. 25. S. P. C. 81. Letter A. 1 Bulst. 71, 75. H. P. C. 187.

And now I am come to an Appeal of Larceny, for the better understanding whereof, I shall consider,

1. **By whom it may be brought.**
2. **Against whom.**
3. **In what County.**
4. **Within what time.**
5. **Where there shall be a Restitution of the Goods stoln.**

As to the first Point, *viz.* By whom an Appeal of Larceny may be brought, the following Particulars seem most remarkable.

Sect. 44. First, There is no necessity that the Appellant have the absolute Property of the Goods stoln; for it seems agreed that a Carrier, or even a Servant, [a] to whom Goods are delivered to be carried to a certain Place, or Churchwardens [b] having Possession of the Goods of a Church, or in general, any Person whatsoever, [c] who is so far intrusted with the Goods of another as in Judgment of Law to have the Possession, and not the bare Charge of them, may have an Appeal of Larceny against any one who shall steal them, for that they have a special kind of Property in them against all Strangers: And it seems that they may either bring a general [d] Appeal as for their own Goods, or a Special [e] one for the Goods of *J. S.* in their Custody. Also it is said, That a Person who hath been robbed of his Goods, still continues to have so far the Possession as well as the Property of them, that he may bring an Appeal of Larceny against any one who shall steal them from the Robber, as shall be more fully shewn in the next Section. But it seems [f] clear, That no one can maintain such an Appeal who has the bare Charge of Goods without a Possession, as a Butler or Cook, who in my own House have the Charge of my Goods, for that in such a Case the whole Possession, as well as the absolute Property, in the Judgment of Law always continues in me. Also it is certain, That a Villain cannot [g] have an Appeal of Larceny against his Lord, for any of his Goods taken by the Lord, because [h] the Lord by seizing them makes them his own. But it is agreed, [i] That a Villain may have an Appeal of Death or of Rape against his Lord. Also it seems clear at this [k] Day, That any Tenant, who is not a Villain, may have an Appeal of Larceny against his Lord.

Sect. 45. Secondly, There is no necessity that the Wrong for which such an Appeal is brought, were immediately done to the Person of the Appellant; for if a Servant be robbed of the Master's Goods in his Custody, the Master [l] may bring the Appeal as well as the Servant, and in such Case he who first commences it shall prevent [m] the other. Also if one be robbed of Goods wherein another is jointly interested with him, and die, the Survivor [n] may bring an Appeal. Also if I be robbed by *A.* who afterwards is robbed of the same Goods by *B.* it is said, [o] That I may have an Appeal of Larceny against *B.* because *A.* claiming no Property, but taking the Goods meerly as a Felon, had, in Judgment of Law, neither any Property nor Possession in them, but the same wholly continued in me. But if the Goods had been taken from me by a Trespasser, under the pretence of some Title, and such Trespasser had been robbed of them, it seems that I could have had no Appeal for them. Neither can an Executor [p] bring an Appeal for a Larceny from the Testator, because such Larceny, at the time when it was committed, was no injury to the Executor, but to the Testator only; and therefore the Appeal for it being a meer personal Action, and wholly vested in the Testator, there is no doubt but that it dies with him, as all other Actions for mere Torts do.

[a] Fitz Coro 100. Latch 127. S P. C. 60. F.
[b] 11 H. 4. 12. pl. 25. 12 H. 7. 27. b. 28, 29. 37 H. 6. 30, 31.
[c] 2 Ed. 4. 15. b. 2 Ri. 3. 22. pl. 53. 3 H. 7. 12. pl. 9. 5 H. 7. 18. pl. 11. 21 H. 7. 14. pl. 23. Bract. Lib. 3. cap. 26. See B. 1. Ch. 33. S. 3. S. P. C. 60. F.
[d] Keilw. 70. pl. 7.
[e] Bract. lib. 3. cap. 26. Fitz. Coron. 100. 11 H. 4. 18. Bro. gard d'Eglise, 6. Bro. Coron. 142. Bro. Appeal, 91.
[f] 3 Inst. 108. See B. 1. Ch. 33. S. 6.
[g] H. P. C. 184. S. P. C. 60. F. Fitz. Coron. 17. Bro. Coron. 216. Bro. Appeal, 34.
[h] Lit. Sect. 177.
[i] Lit. Sect. 189, 190. H. P. C. 184.
[k] S. P. C. 62. Letter A.
[l] H P. C. 184

[m] Latch 127. [n] H. P. C. 184. S. P. C. 61. Fitz. Coron. 392. [o] H. P. C. 184. S. P. C. 61. Fitz. Coro. 39, 79. 13 Ed. 4. 3. pl. 7. Keilw. 160. b. Bro. Appeal, 100. 4 H. 7. 5. b. See B. 1. Ch. 33. S. 9. [p] H. P. C. 184. S. P. C. 60. F.

Sect.

Sect. 46. As to the second Point, *viz.* Against whom an Appeal of Larceny may be brought; having incidentally shewn what is most considerable relating to this Point under the former, I shall only take notice in this place, That this, or any other Appeal lies against an Infant, [a] as well as against a Person of full Age, and against a Feme covert, [b] in the same manner as if she were sole, without taking notice of the Husband.

Sect. 47. As to the third Point, *viz.* In what County such Appeal is to be brought: There is no doubt, but that, like all other [c] Appeals, it is a Local Action, and must be brought in the County where the Felony complained of was done. Yet if one rob me in the County of *A.* and afterwards carry my Goods into the County of *B.* I have my Election [d] either to bring an Appeal of Robbery in the County of *A.* or an Appeal of Larceny in the County of *B.* because the Possession as well as the Property of the Goods continued in me, in Judgment of Law, after the Robbery; and therefore, in what Place soever the Robber keeps them from me, he feloniously injures me in the Possession as well as Property of them, and consequently may properly enough be said to steal them from me: Yet he shall be appealed for the Robbery in the first County only, [e] for there only he was guilty of a taking from the Person, without which there can be no Robbery. Also [f] if one take me from the County of *A.* into the County of *B.* and there rob me, he shall be appealed for the Robbery in the County of *B.* only, for he was guilty only of a Trespass in the County of *A.* But [g] if one bring my Goods into the County of *B.* by reason of a Menace in the County of *A.* it may be questioned which is the proper County for the bringing of the Appeal.

Sect. 48. As to the fourth Point, *viz.* Within what time an Appeal of Larceny is to be brought; It seems to be agreed [h] at this Day, that it may be sued at any time, as well after as within the Year and Day, if the Plaintiff have made fresh Suit; for that the Statute of *Glocester*, Chap. 9. which requires, That an Appeal be brought within the Year and Day, hath been construed [i] to intend no other Appeal but that of Death; and the Common Law seems to have limited no certain time for the bringing of an Appeal, but to have suffered it to be brought at any time by one who had made fresh Suit; the Nature whereof shall be more fully considered in the Fiftieth Section. But it seems, That one who has been guilty of a gross neglect in pursuing the Offender, may be barred of such an Appeal as well within the Year and Day as after; for that the Common Law seems [k] in all Appeals to have required, that the Appellant should have made fresh Suit; and the said Statute of *Glocester*, which takes away the necessity of it in Appeals of Death brought within the Year and Day, extends not to other Appeals.

Sect. 49. As to the fifth Point, *viz.* In what Cases there shall be a Restitution of the Goods stoln, I shall premise, That until [l] such Goods are seiz'd to the use of the King, or of some other Person claiming them under the Crown, as being Waifs, or the Goods of a Felon, *&c.* the rightful Owner, without any fresh Suit or Appeal, may seize them wherever he finds them; but they shall not be restored to them after such Seizure by others, without bringing his Appeal, *&c.* And for the better understanding in what Cases a Restitution of the Goods so seiz'd shall be awarded on such an Appeal, I shall examine the following Particulars.

[a] S. P. C. 62. a. H. P. C. 185.
[b] Bro. Coro. 50. 15 Ed. 4. 1. pl. 2. S. P. C. 62. A H. P. C. 185. Vide Fitz. Coron. 17.
[c] Supra Sect. 35.
11 H. 4. 93. pl. 53. Fitz. Coro. 437. Bro. Appeal, 35. Dyer, 38, 39, 40.
[d] 7 H. 4. 43. pl. 9. Dy. 39. pl. 56. 40. pl. 66 4 H. 7. 5. b 6. a S. P. C. 63. G. 26 Ass. pl. 32 7 Co. 2. a Fitz. Coro. 62, 79. Fitz. Assise, 446. Bro. Aqpeal, 35. B. 1. Ch. 33. S. 9
[e] H. P. C. 184. 7 Co. 2. a Contra Keilw. 160 b
[f] S. P. C. 63. Letter F. Infra. Sect. 71
[g] S. P. C. 63. letter F.
[h] H. P. C. 185. S. P. C. 62. Letter B. 165. D. Bro. Appeal, 37, 62. 7 H. 4. 44. pl. 9. Contra 22 Ass. pl. 97.
[i] Supra Sect. 33.
[k] 2 Inst. 319.
[l] 21 Ed. 4. 16, pl. 7. Fitz. Estray, 2. Avowry, 151. S. P. C. 186. 5 Co. 109.

1. Whether it necessarily require a fresh Suit.

2. What shall be esteemed a fresh Suit.

3. By whom, and in what manner, such fresh Suit shall be inquired and adjudged.

4. How far the Appeal must be prosecuted.

5. Whether the Appellant's Title to such Restitution shall be preferred to any subsequent Title claimed in the Goods.

6. Whether there shall be such a Restitution on any other Prosecution besides that of Appeal.

7. Whether there shall be a Restitution to any Goods not mentioned in the Appeal.

Sect. 50. As to the first Particular, *viz.* Whether such Restitution necessarily require a fresh Suit; It so fully appears to do so by almost all the Books [a] relating to this Matter, that it seems needless to cite Authorities to prove it.

Sect. 51. As to the second Particular, *viz.* What shall be esteemed a fresh Suit; It seems to have been anciently holden, [b] That to make a fresh Suit, the Party ought to have raised a Hue and Cry with all convenient Speed, and also to have taken the Offender: But at this Day it seems to be settled, [c] That if the Party have been guilty of no gross Neglect, but have used all reasonable Care, and Diligence in inquiring after, pursuing, and apprehending the Felon, he ought to be allowed to have made sufficient fresh Suit, whether any Hue and Cry were levied or not, and whether such Offender were taken by means of such Pursuit, or without any Assistance from it.

Sect. 52. As to the third Particular, *viz.* By whom, and in what manner, such fresh Suit shall be inquired and adjudged; It seems, [d] That it is usual and proper to make such Inquiry by the same Jury that tries the principal Matter; and it is certain, That upon the finding of the fresh Suit by such Jury, the Court may award a Restitution: And in such Cases wherein the Appellee is condemned without any Trial, as where he is convicted by his own Confession, or outlawed, or stands mute, *&c.* it seems, That the Court may make such Inquiry by any [e] Inquest of Office, returned for such Purpose, and on their finding the fresh Suit award a Restitution: But in either Case such Inquest is but an Inquest [f] of Office, and perhaps is not absolutely necessary, but required chiefly for the Satisfaction of the Conscience of the Judges, in a matter which, if they think fit, they may, by the Purport of some Authorities, [g] examine themselves, as they generally may (according to some [h] Opinions) any matters whatsoever inquirable by an Inquest of Office, especially [i] if the Parties interested in the thing in question be willing that they should do so: And agreeably hereto it is holden, in the best Authors, [k] That the judging of fresh Suit lies in the Discretion of the Court; and there is a Case [l] wherein a Writ of Restitution of the Goods stoln was actually awarded, without making any Inquiry of the fresh Suit; but in the Book wherein this Case is reported, it is made a Query, whether such Inquiry ought not to be made at the Return of such Writ.

Sect. 53. As to the fourth Particular, *viz.* How far the Appeal must be prosecuted in order to intitle the Appellant to a Restitution,

[a] See the Authorities cited to the three next Sections.

[b] Fitz. Coro. 379, 319, 392. S. P. C. 62. 165. 2 Rich. 3. 13. a.

[c] Bro. Fresh Suit, 1, 6. 7 H. 4. 44. pl. 9. S. P. C. 62. letter B. 165. D. Query Hetley, 64, 65.

[d] 4 Ed. 4. 11. b. S. P. C. 166. Letter B.

[e] 8 H. 4. 1. pl. 2. 7 H. 4. 31. pl. 16. 2 Rich. 3. 13 pl. 31. 10 H. 4. 5. pl. 18. Contra S. P. C. 166. Letter B.

[f] S. P. C. 166 Letter B. *and see the Books cited to the other points of this Section.* and Rastal's Entries, 52, 53.

[g] Vide Fitz. Coro. 379, 392.

[h] 14 H. 4. 9. b. 3 H. 6. 29. b 8 H. 6. 5. a Yel. 152. 1 Brownl. 214. 1 Sid. 442. pl. 15. Contra Latch 213. 3 Leon. 150, 213.

[i] Cro. Jac. 415. pl. 3. 2 Saund. 106, 107.

[k] H. P. C. 185. S. P. C. 62. Letter B.

[l] 21 Ed. 4. 16. pl. 7. Fitz Coron. 42. Bro. Fresh Suit, 4. Vide S. P. C. 166. Letter A. 2 Leon. 108.

it seems, That anciently the Appellant could in no Case be intitled to a Restitution, unless [a] the Appellee were attainted at his Suit; and therefore, if several Appeals were commenced against the same Person, by several Plaintiffs, and the Appellee were attainted at the Suit of one of them, no [b] other could have a Restitution, because the Appellee [c] being once attainted, could not be afterwards attainted again: But [d] it seems to be settled at this Day, That there is no such necessity that the Appellee be attainted at the Suit of the Appellant; and therefore in the Case above mentioned, after such Attainder at the Suit of one Appellant, it shall be inquired by an Inquest of Office, Whether the Appellee were guilty of the Facts complained of in the other Appeals, and made fresh Suit, *&c.* and upon such matter found by such Inquest, a Restitution shall be awarded, *&c.* Also [e] if an Appellee die in Prison, it seems, That the like Inquiry shall be made by Inquest of Office, and thereupon a Restitution awarded, *&c.* And [f] if an Appellee be outlawed, or have the Benefit of his Clergy before Conviction, or stand mute, or challenge peremptorily above twenty Jurors, or break from Prison, perhaps a Restitution shall be awarded upon such an Inquest's finding the fresh Suit, without any farther Inquiry whether the Appellee were guilty or not; because, by refusing to take his Trial, he tacitly seems to admit himself Guilty. Also if one bring an Appeal against two, whereof one is attainted, and the other acquitted; yet [g] it seems, he shall have a Restitution. But [h] if both the Appellees had been acquitted, it seems, That the Appellant should never have his Goods again, though it were expressly found that they were his Goods, but he shall forfeit them to the King for his false Appeal. But *Quære* if this ought not to be understood of such Goods only [i] as were before seised to the King's Use, as having been waived, *&c.*

Sect. 54. As to the fifth Particular, *viz.* Whether the Appellant's Title to such Restitution, shall be preferred to any subsequent Title gained in the Goods; It seems clear, That the Appellant's Title to such Restitution shall not [k] be barred by any Seisure of such Goods, as being Waifs, or Estrays, or the Goods of Felons, *&c.* nor [l] even by a Sale of them, *bonâ fide*, made in Market overt, *&c.* And by the like reason it is certain, That the Prosecutor of an Indictment, since 21 *H.* 8. 11. set forth more at large in the next Section, shall not be barred of his Restitution by any such Seisure, or Sale, *&c.*

Sect. 55. As to the sixth Particular, *viz.* Whether there shall be a Restitution of the Goods stoln, upon any other Prosecution besides that of Appeal; It seems to be clearly agreed, [m] That by the Common Law it could not be had upon any other Prosecution whatsoever: But to remedy this Inconvenience, it is enacted by 21 *H.* 8. 11. *That if any Felon or Felons, do rob, or take away any Money, Goods or Cattels, from any of the King's Subjects, from their Persons or otherwise, within this Realm, and thereof the said Felon or Felons be indicted, and after arraigned of the said Felony, and found guilty thereof, or otherwise attainted by reason of Evidence given by the Party so robbed, or Owner of the said Money, Goods or Cattels, or by any other by their Procurement; that then the Party so robbed, or Owner, shall be restored to his said Money, Goods and Cattels; and that as well the Justices of Gaol-delivery, as other Justices, afore whom any such Felon or Fe-*

[a] 44 Ed. 3. 44. pl, 57. Fitz. Coron. 95, 162, 318, 319. Avowry, 151. S. P. C. 165, Letter D. 166
[b] Fitz. Coro. 95.
[c] Vide infra, in the Chapter concerning Judgment. Contra 4 Ed. 4. 11. b
[d] S. P. C. 166 7 H 4 31. pl. 16. Fitz. Coron. 81, 194, 379, 380.
[e] Fitz. Coro. 379. Forfeiture, 15. S. P. C. 166
[f] 21 Ed 4. 16. pl. 7. 10 H. 4. 5 pl. 18. 40 Ass. 39. 2 R. 3. 13. pl. 31. 8 H. 4. 1. pl. 2. 26 Ass. 32. Fitz. Coron. 42, 71, 194, 217. 379, 466 S P. C. 166 2 Leon. 108
[g] S. P. C. 166
[h] Fitz Coron. 367 368 5 Co. 110. a
[i] Vide Supra Sect. 48. 5 Co. 110. a S. P. C. 186. Contra 3 Inst. 227.
[k] S. P. C. 186 5 Co. 109. 21 Ed. 4. 16. pl. 7. Keling, 35, 47. See the Books cited Sect. 49 Query Hetley, 64, 65. Fitz. Avowry, 151. Coron. 71, 318, 319. Bro. Appeal, 24.
[l] Keling, 34, 47. Query Moor, 360. Popham, 84. 1 And 344.
[m] 4 H. 7. 5. pl. 1. Fitz. Coron. 62, 460. S. P. C. 66. Letter E. 165, 167, Letter A. H. P. C. 212. Latch. 144.

lons

lons shall be found Guilty, or otherwise attainted, by reason of Evidence given by the Party so robbed, or Owner, or by any other by their Procurement, have Power by the said Act to award from time to time, Writs of Restitution for the said Money, Goods and Chattels, in like manner as though any such Felon or Felons were attainted at the Suit of the Party in Appeal.

Sect. 56. Sir *William Staundford,* [a] in his Construction of this Statute, seems to incline to an Opinion, That the Party may have a Restitution by vertue of it without making any fresh Suit; and this seems to be agreeable to Practice, and the Purport of the first part of the Statute, which seems to require no more in order to intitle the Party to a Restitution, than that the Indicter be found Guilty, or otherwise attainted by his Evidence, *&c.* Yet if it shall plainly appear to the Court, That the Party hath been guilty of a gross Neglect in prosecuting the Offender, it may reasonably be argued, That he is not intitled to a Restitution; for the latter part of the Statute, by ordaining, That Writs of Restitution shall be awarded as though the Felon had been attainted in an Appeal, seems to imply, That it is a sufficient Favour, within the Intention of the Makers of the Statute, to the Prosecutor of an Indictment, to give him a like Remedy for a Restitution of his Goods as the Common Law gave to the Plaintiff in an Appeal; but it is certain, [b] That the Plaintiff in an Appeal, who appears to have been guilty of such a Neglect, cannot demand a Restitution by the Common Law. And the Construction I would contend for will appear the more reasonable, if it be considered, that it hardly can be imagined to be the Intention of the Makers of the Statute, to give the Party a greater Benefit from a Conviction grounded on his own Evidence, as a Conviction on an Indictment may be, than from a Conviction on the Evidence of others, as a Conviction in Appeal must be. However if it shall appear to the Court, upon the Evidence at the Trial, or otherwise, That the Party has been reasonably diligent in prosecuting the Offence, I readily grant, That the Justices may, if they think fit, in their Discretion award a Restitution, without making any Inquiry concerning the fresh Suit; but this seems to be no more than they may also do in Appeal, if they think fit, as I have already more fully endeavoured to shew in Section 52.

[a] S. P. C. 167

[b] Supra Sect. 50, 51, and 52.

Sect. 57. As to the seventh Particular, *viz,* Whether there shall be a Restitution to any Goods not mentioned in the Appeal; There is no [c] doubt, but that if a Man be robbed of several Goods by the same Person, either at the same or different times, and such Goods be seised as Waifs, *&c.* and afterwards the Party, in his Appeal for the Robbery, mention some of those Goods only, and omit the rest, and the Appellee be convicted, *&c.* the Appellant shall be restored to such of the Goods only as were mentioned in the Appeal, and the rest shall be confiscated, not only in respect of that Favour which the Law presumes that the Appellant beareth to the Felon, in making the Charge against him easier than it ought to have been, which might possibly have given him an Opportunity to have escaped, but also because, as it seemeth, the Restitution ought regularly to be grounded on the Record of the Appeal, and by that no other Goods can appear to have been stoln than what are mentioned in it: But whether an Appellant, who had, before his Appeal brought, lawfully regained the Possession of his Goods stoln, shall forfeit to the King such of them as he leaves out of his Appeal, doth neither clearly appear from the principal [d] Case concern-

[c] Fitz. Coro. 100. H. P. C. 184. 3 Inst. 227. 5 Co. 110. a. S. P. C. 186.

Vide Supra Sect. 49, & 54.

[d] Fitz. Coo. 100.

concerning this matter, nor from any of the Books above-cited, which ſeem chiefly to rely on the Authority of it. But there is a ſpecial [a] Caſe wherein the Appellant ſhall recover things which were neither ſtoln from him, nor mentioned in his Appeal; as where the Appellee ſells [b] the things ſtoln, or exchanges [c] them for ſome other thing, before the Appeal brought, and the Money taken on the Sale, or thing given in Exchange, are ſeiſed to the King's Uſe, *&c.* in which Caſe they ſhall be delivered to the Appellant, on the Conviction of the Appellee, though they were never in his Poſſeſſion before; for he appears to be in no manner of fault, and there is no reaſon that he ſhould be prejudiced by the Act of the Felon. And I take it for granted, That in all theſe Caſes the Law is the ſame at this Day in relation to a Reſtitution, by force of the above-cited Statute of 21 *H.* 8. to the Proſecutor of an Indictment.

[a] Vide Fitz. Coron. 323. Bro. Reſtitution, 22. Property, 34. 2 Bulſt. 310.
[b] Noy. 128.
[c] Cro. El. 661.

And now I am come to an Appeal of Rape, for the better underſtanding of the Nature whereof, I ſhall conſider,

1. By whom, and in what manner it may be brought.
2. In what County.
3. Within what time.

Sect. 58. As to the firſt Point, *viz,* By whom, and in what manner an Appeal of Rape may be brought; It ſeems, [d] That by the Common Law, it might be brought by any Woman who had been raviſhed, againſt the Raviſher, whether ſuch Perſon raviſhed were the Nief [e] of the Raviſher, or a Free Woman, and whether ſhe were a Virgin, Wife, or Widow; neither [f] do I find that ſhe could be barred of her Appeal at the Common Law, for conſenting after the Rape, to the Raviſher, as ſhe may [g] be at this Day, by force of the Statutes of *Weſtminſter* 2. 34. & 6 *Ric.* 2. 6. But it ſeems, That a Woman lawfully married, can neither [h] by the Common Law, nor by force of any Statute, bring ſuch an Appeal without her Husband, as one married *de facto* only, and not *de jure,* perhaps may.

Sect. 59. But howſoever the Common Law might ſtand in relation to Appeals of Rape, it ſeems, That they were wholly taken away by the Statute of *Weſtminſter* 1. 13. by which the Offence of Rape was reduced to a Treſpaſs only, and conſequently puniſhable only by an Action, or Indictment of Treſpaſs: But afterwards, Appeals of Rape were given again by the Statute of *Weſtminſter* 2. 34. by which it is enacted, *That if a Man from thenceforth do raviſh a Woman married, Maid, or other, where ſhe did not conſent, neither before nor after, he ſhall have Judgment of Life and Member. And likewiſe where a Man raviſheth a Woman married, Lady, Damoſel, or other, with Force, although ſhe conſent after, he ſhall have ſuch Judgment as before is ſaid, if he be attainted at the King's Suit, and there the King ſhall have the Suit.*

Sect. 60. It ſeems to be ſo clear, [i] That this Statute impliedly gives an Appeal to the Woman who does not conſent to the Raviſher, that it ſeems needleſs to endeavour to prove it; but it is obſervable, [k] That the Statute does not reſtore the old Common Law in relation to ſuch Appeals, as it would have done if it had only repealed the above-mentioned of *Weſtminſter* 1. 13. but makes a new Law in relation to them; from

[d] Bracton, 147, 148. Fleta Lib. 1. cap. 25. Sect. 14. 2 Inſt. 180. See Book 1. Ch. 41. Sect. 7. Contra 2 Inſt. 433. 1 Inſt. 123. b
[e] Littleton, Sect. 190. Contra Fitz. Coron. 17. S.P.C. 98. b
[f] Vide Bract. 147. S.P.C. 61, 148. Letter A.
[g] Vide 2 Inſt. 433, 43 . Infra Sect. 59 60, 61.
[h] 8 H 4 21. pl. 2. 11 H. 4. 14. S.P.C. 98. b
[i] 47 Aſſ. 6. Littleton, Sect. 190. 2 Inſt. 433. S.P.C. 6, 81 Contra Fitz. Utlagary, 49. Bro. Coron. 169.
[k] Vide Supra Ch. 10. Sect. 52.

from whence it follows, That all Appeals of Rape at this Day, must [a] conclude *contra formam Statuti.*

Sect. 61. It is farther enacted, by 6 *Rich.* 2. 6. in the following Words, *Against the Offenders and Ravishers of Ladies, and the Daughters of Noblemen, and other Women in every part of the Realm, in these Days offending more violently, and much more than they were wont: It is ordained and stablished, That wheresoever, and whensoever such Ladies, Daughters, and other Women aforesaid be ravished, and after such Rape do consent to such Ravishers, That as well the Ravishers as they that be ravished, and every of them, be from thenceforth disabled, and by the same Deed be unable to have or challenge all Inheritance, Dower, or joint Feoffment after the Death of their Husbands and Ancestors. And that incontinently in this Case, the next of the Blood of those Ravishers, or of them that be ravished, to whom such Inheritance, Dower, or joint Feoffment ought to revert, remain, or fall after the Death of the Ravisher, or of her that is so ravished, shall have Title; that is to say, after the Rape to enter upon the Ravisher, or her that is ravished, and their Assigns, and Land-Tenants, in the same Inheritance, Dower, or joint Feoffment, and the same to hold in State of Inheritance: And that the Husbands of such Women, if they have Husbands, or if they have no Husbands in Life, that then the Fathers, or other next of their Blood, have from thenceforth the Suit to pursue, and may sue against the same Offenders and Ravishers in this Behalf, and to have them thereof convict of Life, and of Member, although the same Women after such Rape, do consent to the said Ravishers. And the Defendant in this Case shall not be received to wage Battel, but the Truth of the Matter shall be tried by Inquisition of the Countrey. Saving always to our Lord the King, and to other Lords of the Realm, all their Escheats of the said Ravishers, if peradventure they be thereof convict.*

[a] 9 Ed. 4 26. a. Fitz. Enditement, 18. Dyer, 202. pl. 68. Vide infra, Sect. 70.

In the Construction of this Statute the following Points have been holden.

Sect. 62. First, That [b] in an Appeal brought upon it by a Husband for the Rape of his Wife, it is a good Plea, That the Appellant and Woman ravished were never lawfully married, which shall be tried by the Bishop's Certificate, who, if the Marriage were unlawful by reason of a Precontract, *&c.* ought to certifie against the Appellant.

Sect. 63. Secondly, That there is no [c] necessity to alledge, That the Woman did consent to the Ravisher, in a Count which rehearses the Statute, and concludes that the Rape was against the Form of it; which implies, that the Woman consented, *&c.*

Sect. 64. Thirdly, That [d] if a Woman who hath neither Husband nor Father, be ravished by her next of Kin, and consent to him, the next of Kin to the Ravisher shall have the Appeal.

Sect. 65. Fourthly, That [e] whosoever happens at the time to be next Heir to the Person so ravished, and consenting, *&c.* shall have the Appeal, and also enter [f] into the Lands of the Person ravished, and retain them against any other who shall afterwards happen by matter *ex post facto* to become Heir; and therefore where a Woman having Issue only a Daughter, consents to a Ravisher, and the Daughter enters, and then a Son is born to such Woman, the Daughter shall retain the Lands, because she took them by Vertue of a Title given by the Statute which first vested in her as a Purchaser, and never was in any Ancestor.

[b] 11 H. 4. 13, 14. Fitz. Coron. 86, 228. Bro. Parliament, 89.

[c] 11 H 4. 14. Fitz. Coron. 86, 228. S. P. C. 81. Letter C. Dy. 312. pl. 86, 202. pl. 68.

[d] 2 Inst. 434 Vide Supra. Sect. 39, 40,

[e] S. P. C. 61. b.

[f] Fitz. Assize 27. 5 Ed. 4 6. a 9 H 7. 25. a Long quinto 5 Ed. 4. 60, 61. 1 Co. 95. a 98, 137, b. 3 Co. 61. a. 62. a. Pl. Com. 56. b

Sect. 66. Fifthly, That [a] the next in Remainder or Reversion, to whom the Lands of the Woman who consents to a Ravisher would come if she were dead, shall enter and retain her Lands by Vertue of the Statute, provided he be of Kin to her, albeit another Person be nearer; yet it seems, That the Person so intitled to the Lands cannot have an Appeal of Rape where there is another nearer of Kin; for though the Clause relating to the Entry into the Lands seems to intitle such of the next of Kin, to whom the Inheritance would fall after the Death of the Party, whether they be absolutely nearest or not; yet the Clause relating to the Appeal seems to extend to none but the Husband, or Father, or very next of Kin.

[a] Long quinto, Ed. 4. 58, 59, 60. Bro. Entry Congeable, 94 5 Ed. 4. 5. pl. 24 Fitz. Assize, 27.

Sect. 67. Sixthly, That it is not [b] sufficient in setting forth the Title of the Person claiming the Lands by Vertue of the Statute, to say in general, That he is next of Blood to whom the Inheritance would fall, *&c.* without shewing specially in what manner he is so, *&c.*

[b] Long quinto, Ed. 4. 58. Pl. Com. 42. 43.

Sect. 68. Seventhly, That it is not [c] conclusive Evidence to prove the Woman's Consent to the Ravisher to shew, That she lived with him some Years as his Wife, and had a Child by him, if all the time she was under his Power, and never at her Liberty.

[c] Long quinto, Ed. 4. 59. 60, 61. Bro. Entry Congeable, 94 5 Ed. 4. 5. pl. 24.

Sect. 69. Eighthly, That [d] if the Party ravished and consenting to the Ravisher, be under the Age of twelve Years, she shall not lose her Lands by the Intent of the Statute, for that the Consent of a Woman under that Age is looked upon as given by one uncapable of Discretion, and therefore is not regarded by the Law.

[d] Pl. Com. 364. See 1 Danv. Abr. 698. pl. 12. 699. 700. Letter B. 1 Inst. 79.

Sect. 70. Ninthly, That [e] in Appeals brought on this Statute, the Count ought to rehearse it: But I do not find any Resolution cited to maintain this Opinion. It is true indeed, That in the Year Book of 11 *H.* 4. 13. 14. the Statute is recited in an Appeal grounded on it: But it is not there said to be necessary to be so recited; neither do I find any Reason given why an Appeal may not as well be grounded on this Statute without reciting it, as on the Statute of *Westminster* 2, 34. as [f] it is agreed that it may be: If it be said, [g] That the Common Law gave the same Appeal as is given by the Statute of *Westminster* 2. and therefore there is no need to recite it; but that there never was such an Appeal at the Common Law as is given by the Statute of *Rich.* 2. and therefore the Appeal grounded on it ought to recite it; it may be answered, That the said Statute of *Westminster* [h] does not revive the old Common Law in relation to such Appeals, but makes a new Law in relation to them; so that Appeals brought upon it, do altogether as much depend upon it, as those brought on the Statute of *Rich.* 2. do on that. Neither [i] does there appear to be any such Rule, That in Indictments, or Actions grounded on Statutes which give a remedy in Cases which were no way provided for by Law, there is a necessity to recite such Statutes; and indeed at best it seems but Surplus to recite what the Court is bound *ex officio* to take Notice of.

[e] S P. C. 61. Letter C See 1 H. 6. 1 pl. 1. Bro. Rape, 4

[f] S. P. C. 81. Letter C. See 1 H. 6. 1. pl. 1. Bro. Rape, 4

[g] Vide 5 H. 7. 17. pl. 10

[h] Supra Sect. 59, 60.

[i] 5 H. 7. 17. pl. 10. Cro. Car. 564. 6 Mod. 140.

Sect. 71. As to the second Point, *viz.* In what County an Appeal of Rape may be brought; There is no doubt, but that this, like all other [k] Appeals, is a local Action, and consequently ought to be brought in the County wherein the Felony was done. And therefore if a Man take a Woman by Force in one County, and carry her into another, and there ravish her, the Appeal [l] shall be brought only in the County wherein the Rape was committed; for the Taking in the other was no more

[k] Supra Sect. 35, 47.

[l] 3 H. 7. 12. pl. 4 Fitz. Visne, 28. Bro. Appeal, 83. S. P. C. 63. Letters E, F. H. P. C. 186.

more than a Treſpaſs, and needs not be taken Notice of at all in the Appeal of the Rape; and if it be, is only looked upon as Surplus.

Sect. 72. As to the third Point, *viz.* In what Time an Appeal of Rape may be brought; It ſeems, That at this Day it may be brought in any reaſonable [a] Time, the Judgment [b] whereof lies in the Diſcretion of the Court, for that at the Common Law there was no certain Time limited for the bringing of it; and the Statute of *Weſtminſter* 1. 13. by which the Offence of Rape was turned into a Treſpaſs, and forty Days limited for the Suit of the Perſon raviſhed, is repealed; and the Statute of *Gloucester* 9. which requires that Appeals be brought within the Year and Day, extends only to Appeals of Death; and the Statute of *Weſtminſter* 2. 34. which makes Rape a Felony again, limits no Time for the bringing of it, but leaves it to the Conſtruction of Law, which ſhall be agreeable to the ancient Rules of Law in ſuch Points, wherein the Statute is ſilent.

Sect. 73. And now I am come to an Appeal of Arſon; [c] but the Learning relating to it, ſeeming to be altogether obſolete at this Day, I ſhall refer the Reader to the Old [d] Books for it.

Having thus endeavoured to ſhew in what Courts Appeals may be brought, and the ſeveral Kinds of them, and examined the Particulars which ſeemed moſt properly to come under the Conſideration of each Kind, I ſhall now proceed to examine ſome other matters concerning them, wherein I ſhall conſider them all together. As

1. In what Caſes the Appellant and Appellee are to appear in proper Perſon, and where by Attorney, or Guardian.
2. How the Appellant ought to declare.
3. How he may be nonſuited.
4. For what Faults the Writ may be abated.
5. What may be pleaded in Bar of an Appeal.
6. Where the Appellant and his Abettors ſhall render Damages to the Appellee for a falſe Appeal.
7. Where the Appellant is to be fined.

Sect. 74. As to the firſt Point, *viz.* In what Caſes the Appellant and Appellee are to appear in proper Perſon, and where by Attorney, or Guardian: It ſeems, That by the Common Law neither [e] Plaintiff nor Defendant in any Appeal whatſoever, whether of Felony, or Mayhem, [f] could make an Attorney, but muſt appear either by Guardian, [g] or in proper Perſon, on every [h] Day of Continnance, except in ſome ſpecial Caſes; as where the Defendant being convicted in an Appeal of Felony pray'd the Benefit of his Clergy, and the Plaintiff reply'd, that he had been twice married, in which Caſe he might [i] be admitted to go on with the Suit by Attorney, becauſe he had nothing more to do but to get a Certificate of the Bigamy from the Biſhop, which, as it was [k] ſaid, any Stranger might procure as well as the Plaintiff. *Sed Quære*; for it is ſaid, [l] That none can demand Execution but the Plaintiff, and that the Plaintiff cannot do it but in proper Perſon; from whence it ſeems reaſonable to argue, That he ought, in all other Caſes, as well to carry on his Suit in proper Perſon. But it ſeems [m] clear, That after a Defendant is acquitted, he may appear by Attorney for the Recovery of his Damages againſt the Abettors, *&c.* And it is enacted [n] by 3 *H.* 7. 1. *That*

[a] S. P. C. 63. Letter C. H. P. C. 186.
[b] Vide Supra Sect. 51, 52 Littleton, 69 1 Inſt. 56. Supra Sect. 33, 48.
[c] 1 Inſt. 288. a
[d] Fleta. lib. 1. cap. 37. Bract. Lib. 3. cap. 27.
[e] 2 Inſt. 313. Salk. 59, 62, 64. Bro. Attorney, 64, 78. 2 Ri. 3. 13. pl. 38. Bro. Appeal, 112. Raſtal's Entries, 47.
[f] 2 Inſt. 313. F. N. B. 27. F Contra Fitz. Attorney, 104. 21 H. 7. 39. pl. 54.
[g] Supra Sect. 30.
[h] 1 H. 7. 27. pl. 3. Fitz. Utlagary, 34.
[i] 40 Aſſ. 17. Fitz. Attorney, 39, 90. 40 Ed. 3. 42. pl. 23. S. P. C. 135. Vide Fitz. Coron. 13.
[k] 11 H. 4. 11. b. S. P. C. 135. Fitz. Coron. 13.
[l] 21 Ed. 4. 72. 73.
[m] 8 Ed. 4. 3. pl. 5. Fitz. Attorney, 24.
[n] F. N. B. 26.

That the Appellant in any Appeals of Murder or Death of a Man, where Battel by the course of Common Law lies not, may make Attorney and appear in the same, in the said Appeals after they be commenced, to the End of the Suit and Execution of the same. But [a] if a Defendant or Plaintiff appear and plead by Attorney where they ought not, and the Court receive the Plea and adjourn the Cause, it seems. That the Appeal is discontinued, because such Appearance was meerly void in Law.

[a] Salk. 59,62

As to the second Point, *viz.* In what Manner the Appellant ought to declare; I shall refer the Reader for Precedents of Counts in Appeal, to *Staundford's* [b] *Pleas of the Crown*, and the Books [c] of *Entries*, and shall in this Place consider only the following Particulars.

[b] S P. C. 78, 79.
[c] Rastal's & Coke's Entries, Titles Appeal & Mort.

1. In what Manner such Count must pursue the Writ.
2. How it ought to set forth the Substance and Manner of Fact.
3. How the Circumstances of Time and Place.
4. Whether one and the same Count ought to be against those who do not appear as well as against those who do appear, and against the Accessories as well as the Principals.

Sect. 75. As to the first Point, *viz.* In what manner the Count in Appeal must pursue the Writ; I shall take it for granted, That this, like all other Counts in other Actions, must in Substance [d] agree with the Writ, which shall be abated if the Count vary from it in any material Point. And therefore in a Common Appeal of Death, if the Appellant declare, That the Appellee traiterously killed the Person deceased, as he was going to succour the King in his Wars, the Writ shall be abated [e] because that contains no Charge of Treason. So also if the Plaintiff, in an Appeal of Mayhem, declares, That the Appellee beat as well as maimed him, the Writ shall be abated [f] because that mentions not any Battery.

[d] Finch of Law, 357.
[e] Bro. Appeal, 12. 45 Ed. 3. 25. pl. 36. 21 Ed. 3. 23. pl. 16. S. P. C. 78. Letter C.
[f] Fitz Coro. 110. Supra Sect. 20.

As to the second Point, *viz.* In what manner the Count in Appeal ought to set forth the Substance and Manner of the Fact, I shall observe the following Particulars.

Sect. 76. 1. That where several are present at the Fact, and one only actually does it, and the others abet and encourage him, it is in the Election of the Plaintiff, either to suppose [g] in his Declaration, That every one of them did the Fact, because in such a Case the Act of one is, in the Judgment of the Law, the Act of all; or to shew the special [h] manner of the Case as in Truth it was, and set forth the Fact to have been done only by the Person who did it, and the others to have been his Abettors, *&c.*

Sect. 77. II. That no *Periphrasis*, [i] or Circumlocution whatsoever, will supply the want of those Words of Art, which the Law hath appropriated for the Description of the Offence; from whence it follows, That an Appeal of Death cannot [k] amount to a Charge of Murder without the Word *Murdravit*, let it be never so exact and particular in setting forth the Malice and all other Circumstances of the killing; neither [l]

[g] 11 H. 4. 13. b. 4 H. 7. 18. pl. 10. S P. C. 44. Letter B. 80 Letters C.D. Supra Sect. 19. H. P. C. 187. Bro Rape, 2, 3 See the Chapter of the Arraignment of Principal & Accessory.
[h] 4 Co. 41. Fitz. Coro. 97, 216, 40 Ass. 25. 44 Ed. 3. 38. pl. 31. Rastal's Entries, 43. b. 45. pl. 1. 46. pl. 2. 47. pl. 3. Coke's Entries, 57, *&c.*
[i] 5 Co. 121. b. [k] Dy. 261. pl. 26. Cro. Jac. 20. Salk. 377. 9 Ed. 4. 26. b.

[a] can an Appeal of Rape be sufficient without the Word *Rapuit*; nor [b] an Appeal of Larceny without the word *Cepit*; nor [c] an Appeal of Mayhem without the Word *Mayhemiavit*; nor any [d] of the Appeals abovementioned without the Word *Felonicè*.

Sect. 78. III. That in every Appeal of Larceny [e] it must expresly appear whose the Goods were that were stoln, and in every Appeal of Death [f] who the Person was that was killed; because otherwise it cannot appear that the Plaintiff is intitled to the Appeal; yet an Indictment *de morte* [g] *cujusdam ignoti*, or for feloniously stealing [h] the Goods *cujusdam ignoti*, is good; for it is sufficient, That the Person injured was under the Protection of the Law.

Sect. 79. IV. That in an Appeal of Rape the Fact seems to be sufficiently [i] declared, by shewing, That the Defendant *felonicè rapuit* the Woman, without adding the Words *carnaliter cognovit*, or any others tantamount, or first shewing the particular Manner of the Terror or Violence, and then concluding, That the Defendant *sic felonicè rapuit*. Also it seems, [k] That the like general Manner of setting forth the Fact, is sufficient in an Appeal of Larceny; but it seems to be usual, in Appeals of Larceny, to set forth the Price of the Things stoln; but whether this be necessary for any other Purpose than to shew, That the Crime amounts to Grand Larceny, and to ascertain the Goods, in Order thereby the better to intitle the Appellant to a Restitution, I leave to be considered. But [l] in an Appeal of Mayhem it seems necessary, first, To set forth particularly in what Manner the Hurt was done, and the Consequences following it, and then to conclude, That the Defendant *sic felonicè mayhemiavit* the Appellor. Also it seems clear, [m] That in an Appeal of Death it is necessary, not only from the Statute of *Glocester* [n] Ch. 9. which requires, That an Appeal of Death shall declare the Deed; but also from the Common Law, first, To set forth in the Count all the special Circumstances of the Fact, and [o] then to conclude, That the Appellee *sic felonicè murdravit* the Party; and this being the Appeal most in Use at this Day, it may not be improper to set down these following Rules concerning this Matter.

Sect. 80. I. That every such Count ought to set forth in what Part [p] of the Body the Wound was given; in which Respect, the same Certainty seems to be required in Appeals as in Indictments; and therefore, if the Count say only that the Wound was given *circa pectus*, it seems to be vicious, as it hath been resolved, [q] That an Indictment in the like Manner uncertain is, because it doth not ascertain the Part wounded, which, for what appears, might have been the Neck, Arm, or Belly; and for the like Reason such Count seems also to be vicious, if it say, That the Wound was in the Hand, or Leg, or Arm, without [r] shewing whether it were the right or left; neither [s] is such an Uncertainty holpen by laying other Wounds with sufficient Certainty, if there be a general Conclusion that the Party died of the Wounds above mentioned, because the Death being as much imputed to the Wound that is insufficiently laid, as to the others, it appears not but that it might be chiefly owing to that which is insufficiently laid, and therefore the Whole is insufficient. But it hath been resolved, That it is sufficient in an Indictment of Death, and therefore it seems also to be sufficient in an Appeal, to shew, That the Wound

[a] S. P. C. 81. Letter B. 24. Letter D. 96. Letter D. 9 Ed. 4 26. 20 H. 7. 7. a. 1 Inst. 124. a.
[b] Fitz Enditement, 2, 8. S. P. C. 96. Letter B. H. P. C. 207.
[c] Supra Sect. 17.
[d] S. P. C. 94. 96. Letter C. H. P. C. 206, 207. 20 H. 7. 7. a. 1 Bulst. 93. Cro. Jac. 25. Dy. 202. pl. 67. Quære 1 H. 6. 1. pl. 1. Contra Fitz. Enditement, 26. Dy. 69. pl. 28.
[e] Rastal's Entries, 53, b. 54, 55.
[f] Fitz. Enditement 10. S. P. C. 95. Letter G. 181. b. 22 Ass. 94.
[g] H. P. C. 207. 22 Ass. 94. Fitz. Coro. 159. S. P. C. 94. Letter G. 181, b. 1 Ass. pl. 7. Dyer 99 pl. 61.
[h] Fitz. Enditement, 9, 12. H. P. C. 207. S. P. C. 95. Letter G. 181, b. Dy. 99. pl. 61. Keilw. 25. b. Moor, 466. 18 Ass. pl. 15 Contra 9 H. 6 45. b.
[i] Dy. 202. pl. 67. 11 H. 4. 13. Fitz. Coron. 86. S. P. C. 81. Letter C. H. P. C. 187. 51, 52, 53. 318, 319.
[q] 4 Co. 40. b.

[k] See Rastal's Entries, 53, b. 54, 55. [l] See Rastal's Entries, 45, 46. and Coke's Entries, 50, b. [m] See Rastal's Entries, 46, b. 47, &c. Coke's Entries, 53, b. 54, &c. Salkeld, 377. 2 Inst. 2 Lev. 140, 141. 5 Co. 120, 121, 122. 4 Co. 41, 42. [n] 2 Inst. 315. [o] 4 Co. 47, a. [p] 2 Inst. 318. 5 Co. 121, b. [r] 5 Co. 121, b. [s] 4 Co. 40. b.

[a] 4 Co. 41. l. 4. 5 Co. 121. b. Cro. Jac. 95 pl. 23. Con. Cro El. 137 pl 10.
[b] 4 Co. 41. pl. 4. H. P. C. 207.

was given in the left [a] Part of the Belly, or in the left Part of the Side, or in the left Hand, or in the left Arm, or in the Face, or in the Breast, or in the Belly, or even in the Forepart of the Body, in which Case the Word *Body* shall be understood of the Trunk of the Body, between the Neck and Thighs. And it hath been resolved, [b] That where there is such a sufficient Certainty, the Addition of a farther uncertain or unintelligible Description, will do no Hurt; as where a Wound is laid *in finistra parte ventris circa umbelicum*, &c. in which Case the last Words shall be rejected as abundant and Surplus.

[c] S. P. C. 79. Letters C. D. 2 Inst. 318. 4 Co. 40. b. 5 Co. 122. a.
[d] S. P. C. 79. Letters C. D
[e] 5 Co. 121. b. 122. a.

Sect. 81. II. Such Count ought also [c] to shew the Length and Breadth of the Wound, that it may appear to the Court that it was mortal; but it is said, [d] That anciently this was not required: And if a Man be shot, or run through the Body, with a Bullet, or Sword, *&c.* it seems [e] sufficient to say, That the Defendant, with Malice, *&c.* struck the Person killed in such a Part of his Body, and gave him in such Part *Mortale vulnus penetrans in & per corpus*, &c. for this sufficiently shews, That the Wound was mortal. Also in some Cases it is impossible to shew the Length and Breath of the Wound, as where a Limb is cut off, and [f] therefore it is plain, That in such Cases it cannot be required.

[f] 2 Inst. 318. 5 Co 122. a. 4 Co. 41. b. 42. a.
[g] Palmer 282. 3 Mod. 202.
[h] 5 Co. 122. 1 Bulst. 124
[i] Cro Jac, 635. See H P C. 207 and Yel. 28.
[k] 5 Co. 122. vide Dy. 99. pl. 63.

Sect. 82. III. It is not safe, [g] in any such Count, to omit the Word *percussit*, where the Fact will bear it; and by the Authority of some [h] Books this cannot be supplied, in such Cases, by the Words *dedit mortale vulnus*, &c. nor by any other: Yet in *Croke*'s [i] *Reports* this Opinion seems to be questioned, neither do I find any Reason given why the Word *percussit* should be of such absolute necessity, for it is not so much as pretended in *Long*'s [k] Case, which seems to be the chief Foundation of this Opinion, That this is a Word of Art appropriated to this Use; but all that seems there contended for is, That where the Death was occasioned by any external Violence, coming under the Notion of Striking, it must expresly appear, That a Stroke was given. Nor does the Law admit of a less exact Certainty, as to the setting forth the Fact, where the Death was occasioned by any other Means, as by Poison, *&c.* for it hath been resolved, [l] That an Indictment (which in this respect seems not to differ from an Appeal) setting forth, That *J. S.* persuaded the Person deceased to take a certain poisonous Potion under the Notion of a Medicine, and that the deceased, *Nesciens præd' potum cum veneno fore intoxicatum, sed fidem adhibens dictæ persuasioni dicti* J. S. *recepit & bibit* is insufficient, because it doth not expresly say, That the Party received and drank the Poison. And it was also resolved, That the Want of such Certainty is not supply'd by these Words immediately following, *Per quod idem* N. *immediate post receptionem veneni prædicti per tres horas immediatè sequentes languebat & obiit*, &c. and yet there cannot well be a stronger Implication that the Poison was taken and drunk by him; for it being the strict [m] Rule of Law in these Cases to have the Substance of the Fact expressed with precise Certainty, the Judges will suffer no argumentative Certainty whatsoever to induce them to dispense with it. For if they should once be prevailed with to do it in one Case, the like Indulgence would be expected from them in others nearly resembling it, and then in others resembling those, and no one could say where this might end; which could not but endanger the subverting of one of the most fundamental Principles of the Law, by given Room to Judges by Arguments from what the Jury have found to convict a Man of a Fact which they have not found.

[l] 4 Co. 44. b. 3 Mod. 202.
[m] 4 Co. 44 b.

Sect. 83. IV. Such Count ought [a] alſo expreſsly to ſhew that the Party died of the Hurt ſpecially ſet forth; and it hath been reſolved [b] That an Indictment, and from the ſame Reaſon it ſeems that an Appeal, ſetting forth that the Defendant choaked the Deceaſed, *qua ſuffocatione obiit*, inſtead of *de qua ſuffocatione*, &c. is erroneous; yet where the Death was cauſed by divers Poiſons, or Wounds, *&c.* the Count may ſay in general that the Party died of the ſeveral Poiſons or Wounds above mentioned, without [o] ſaying That he died of any one of them in particular; for perhaps the Truth of the Caſe might be, That none of them alone, but all together, cauſed the Death. Or [c] the Count in ſuch Caſe perhaps may ſay, That the Party died of the firſt Poiſon or Wound, and that he would have died of the ſecond if he had not died of the firſt, and alſo that he would have died of the third, if he had not died of the two firſt.

Sect. 84. V. If the Killing were with a Weapon, the Count muſt [d] ſhew with what Weapon in particular, and yet if upon the Evidence it ſhall appear that the killing was not by ſuch Weapon, but by ſome other, the Variance [e] is immaterial, and the Appellee ought to be convicted, as ſhall be ſhewn more at large under the Chapter of *Evidence.* And if the killing were not by a Weapon, but by ſome other Means, as by poiſoning, drowning, ſuffocating, burning, or the like, the Count [f] muſt ſet forth the Circumſtances of the Fact as ſpecially as the Nature of it will admit. But in ſuch Caſes, where no Weapon was uſed, it cannot but be abſurd to require the Mention of one in the Appeal, and therefore the Statute of *Glouceſter* Chap. 9. which directs generally, That in all Appeals of Death the Weapon muſt be ſet forth, is to be intended only [g] of ſuch Killing in which a Weapon was uſed: For the Law is ſo far from requiring it in other Caſes, that it will not ſuffer an Appeal of Killing by a Weapon to be maintained by Evidence of Killing by any other Means in which no Weapon was uſed; neither will it ſuffer an Appeal of Killing by any of thoſe Means without the Help of a Weapon, to be maintained by Evidence of Killing by a Weapon, as ſhall alſo be ſhewn more at large in the Chapter above referred to.

Sect. 85. It hath been adjudged, [h] That the Words *vi & armis* are not neceſſary in ſuch Appeal, becauſe they are ſo fully implied.

Sect. 86. As to the third Point, *viz.* In what Manner the Count in Appeal muſt ſet forth the Circumſtances of Time and Place, it is enacted by the Statute of *Glouceſter*, Chap. 9, *That if an Appeal declare the Deed, the Year, the Day, the Hour, the Time of the King, and the Town where the Deed was done, and with what Weapon, the Appeal ſhall ſtand in Effect*, &c. And tho' this more particularly relate [i] to Appeals of Death, yet it ſeems alſo to be generally a good Rule as to the Circumſtances of Time and Place in other Appeals, and therefore I ſhall conſider them all together, and firſt premiſe [k] That no Omiſſion of any of theſe Circumſtances, where the Law requires them to be expreſsly ſet forth, can be aided by the Conviction of the Defendant; and then for the better underſtanding in what Caſes the Law requires them to be expreſsly ſet forth, I ſhall endeavour to ſhew what Certainty the Count in every Appeal ought to ſhew.

1. The Hour.
2. The Day.
3. The Year and Time of the King.
4. The Place where the Deed was done.

[a] 2 Inſt. 318.
[b] 1 Rol. Rep. 137. pl. 20.
[o] 3 Inſt. 50, 135. Quære 4 Co. 40, b.
[c] 44 Ed. 3. 38. pl. 31. 40 Aſſ. pl. 25. S. P. C. 80. Letter C. 4 Co. 40. b. Raſtal's Entries 46. pl. 2. 47 pl. 3, 4, 49. pl. 6. 51. pl. 11.
[d] 2 Inſt. 318. 3 Mod. 158. See the Stat. of Glouceſt. Chap. 9.
[e] 2 Inſt. 319. H. P. C. 265. 9 Co. 67.
[f] 2 Inſt. 318, 319.
[g] 2 Inſt. 318, 319.
[h] Smith and Bowen. Mich. 7 An.
[i] 2 Inſt. 317.
[k] 1 R. A. 781 Letter N.

Sect. 87. As to the firſt of theſe Particulars, *viz.* With what Certainty the Count in Appeal ought to ſet forth the Hour, it is obſervable that all the [a] Precedents of ſuch Counts (excepting only one,[b]) in Appeals of Larceny in *Raſtal's* Entries, which ſeems to be the only Book of Authority in which any ſuch Counts are to be found; and alſo all the Precedents in *Coke* and *Raſtal* of ſuch Counts in Appeals of [c] *Mayhem*, take Notice of the Hour, as well as thoſe in Appeals of Death; [d] and therefore certainly it is not ſafe wholly to omit it; yet it hath been holden, [e] That ſuch an Omiſſion is not fatal, even in an Appeal of Death, becauſe the Common Law did not require the mention of the Hour, and the Statute above mentioned is in the Affirmative. Yet if the Hour as well as Day be ſet forth in the Allegation of the Offence of the Principal, it is ſaid to be fatal to mention the Day only in the Allegation of the Offence of the Acceſſory. But it ſeems that there is no Neceſſity in any Caſe preciſely to alledge, That the Fact was done at ſuch an Hour, but that it is ſufficient to ſay, That it was done about ſuch Hour, as appears from every [f] one of the Precedents in *Coke* and *Raſtal*, in which the Hour is mentioned, and alſo from other [g] good Authorities; yet we find the contrary Opinion holden by three Judges againſt two in *Bulſtrode's* [h] Reports. But it ſeems [i] certain that a Miſtake of the Hour will not be material upon Evidence.

Sect. 88. As to the ſecond of the above mentioned Particulars, *viz.* With what Certainty the Count in Appeal ought to ſet forth the Day, There can be no Doubt but that every ſuch Count muſt ſet forth the Day on which the Fact was done, as appears from all the Precedents cited in the foregoing Section; and alſo from the common Form of all other Declarations in all Actions whatſoever, as well as of Indictments, for which it is needleſs to cite Authorities. And if the Fact happened in the Night, it ſeems [k] moſt proper to alledge it in *nocte ejuſdem diei.* But it is ſaid not to [l] be ſufficient to alledge the Fact done about ſuch a Day, or between ſuch a Day and ſuch a Day, but that the very Day muſt be preciſely ſet forth. And it ſeems to be inſufficient to alledge [m] it on the Feaſt-Day of ſuch a Saint, without an Addition, if there be another Saint of the ſame Name, as on St. *John's* Day, without ſhewing which Saint is meant, *viz.* the Baptiſt or Evangeliſt. Alſo [n] it ſeems to be erroneous to ſet forth the Fact on an impoſſible Day, as on the thirty-firſt of *June*, or thirtieth of *February*, for this is of no more Effect than to mention no Day at all. Alſo it ſeems clear that an Appeal of Death muſt not only ſet forth the Day when the Hurt was given, but alſo the Day when the Party died of it, as appears from all the Precedents [o] of this Kind both in *Coke* and *Raſtal*; and alſo from the manifeſt Reaſon of the Thing, [p] that it may appear that the Party died within the Year and Day after the Stroke, in which Caſe [q] only the Law intends that the Death was occaſioned by it. And it is [r] ſaid not to be ſufficient to alledge, That the Defendant aſſaulted the Party at a certain Day, and feloniouſly ſtruck him, without expreſsly adding, That he ſtruck him *adtunc & ibidem*; and yet both Sentences being joined with the Copulative, it is the moſt natural Import of the whole, That the Stroke and Aſſault were both at the ſame Time, *&c.* and ſuch Certainty ſeems to be ſufficient in Declarations [s] in civil Actions, and even in Indictments [t] of Treſpaſſes. But in Indictments and Appeals of Death a more expreſs Certainty is ſaid to be required, becauſe the Stroke which cauſed the Death, being a Crime

[a] Raſtal's Entries 53. pl. 1, 2, 3, 54. pl. 4, 5.
[b] Raſtal's Entries, 55. pl. 6.
[c] Coke's Entries, 50. b. 51. pl. 2. 52. pl. 3. Raſtal's Entries, 45. pl. 1, 2, 3, 4.
[d] Coke's Entries, 53. pl. 4. 56. pl. 5. 57. pl. 6. 59 pl. 7. Raſtal's Entries, 43. b. 46 pl. 31. 47. pl. 3. 4 48. b. 49. pl. 6. 50. pl. 10, *&c.*
[e] S. P. C. 80. b. 1 Bul. 82. H. P. C. 187.
[f] Coke's Entries, 50. b. 51. pl. 2. 52. pl. 3. 53. pl. 4. 56. pl. 5. 57. pl. 6. 59. pl. 7. Raſtal's Entries, 43. b. 45. pl. 1, 2, 3, 4. 46. pl. 2 47. pl. 3. 4 48. b. 49. pl. 6. 50. pl. 10 57. pl. 11. &c.
[g] 2 Inſt. 318. Salk. 59. pl. 2.
[h] 1 Bulſt. 77. 80, 81, 82, 83. Vide 3 Mod. 158.
[i] H.P.C. 264. 2 Inſt. 318.
[k] 2 Inſt. 318.
[l] 2 Inſt. 318.
[m] Bro. indict. 47. 3 H. 7. 5. pl. 2.
[n] Moore, 555. pl. 723.
[o] See Citations in the precedent Section
[p] 2 Inſt. 318. Bro. Indictment. 41.
[q] Book 1. Ch. 31. Sect. 9, 10.
[r] Dy. 28. as in the Margin Dy. 8. pl. 28. See B. 1. Ch. 64. Sect. 42. Keilw. 100 Quære.
[s] Cro. Jac. 362. 443.
[t] Cro Ca. 271. 525.
[q] Cro. Jac. 41. See B. 1 Ch. 64. Sect. 42. 1 Rol. Rep. 295.

of a different Nature, and much higher than the Assault, may be well enough intended to have happened at a different Time; and therefore the precise Time of each must be certainly expressed. And even this may be vitiated by a Repugnancy in the Conclusion; for if the Assault and Stroke be alledged in the Premisses on the tenth of *December*, and the Death subsequent on the twentieth of *December* following, and then it be alledged in the Conclusion, that the Defendant in such manner feloniously murdered the Party on the tenth of *December* aforesaid, the whole is naught for the Repugnancy; [a] because the Party could not be said to have been murdered, 'till he was dead: And tho' to some Purposes by a Fiction of Law the Offence of the Defendant after the Death of the Party, is punish'd as a Felony from the time of the Stroke; yet in Truth and Propriety of Speech (which must be observed in legal Proceedings) it is not a Felony but only a Trespass 'till the Death; yet if in such Conclusion it had been alledged that the Defendant in such Manner feloniously murdered the Party on the twentieth of *December* aforesaid, it had been sufficient. But it is said [b] to be the better Way to conclude generally, That the Defendant in such Manner feloniously murdered the Party. And it is certain [c] that a Mistake of the Day will not be material upon Evidence.

Sect. 89. It hath been holden that an Allegation of the Day, *prima facie* somewhat uncertain, may be holpen by the apparent Sense of the whole; as where [d] it is alledged, That the Principal such a Day made the Assault and gave the Stroke, and that the Party died on such a subsequent Day, *&c.* and that *A. B.* was *adtunc & ibidem abettans* the said Principal to do the Felony and Murder aforesaid, in which Case it is said that the Words) *adtunc & ibidem*, from the manifest Import of the whole, shall be referred to the Time of the Stroke; because by that only the Felony which *A. B.* is charged to have abetted was done. Yet if *A. B.* had been said to have been present at the Time of the Felony and Murder aforesaid, *scilicet*, on the Day of the Stroke, *tunc & ibidem* abetting the Felony and Murder aforesaid, *&c.* it seems [e] that the Appeal is insufficient as to the said *A. B.* for the Repugnancy; because he is expresly alledged to have been present, and to have abetted the Principal, at the Time of the Felony and Murder, which must be taken for the Time of the Death, by which the Offence, which was before but a Trespass, became Felony and Murder; but by being present at the Time of the Death, it is impossible he could abet a Stroke given so long before, and therefore it is repugnant and inconsistent in such a Manner to alledge it. Nor is such a Repugnancy any way holpen by the subsequent Allegation of the very Day of the Stroke, coming after the Word *Scilicet*, for it is apparent that the Time of the Felony, could not be on the Day of the Stroke, and therefore it rather adds to than helps the Fault to alledge that it was. But [f] the best Way of alledging such Abatement had been to have set forth, That the said *A. B.* was *præsens, auxilians*, &c. *ad feloniam & murdrum prædictum in forma prædicta faciend'.*

Sect. 90. As to the third Particular, *viz.* With what Certainty the Count in Appeal ought to set forth the Year and Time of the King, there can be no Doubt but that every such Count must expresly set forth in what Year the Fact was done, as appears from the known Form of all other Counts, and also of Indictments. And in an Appeal of Death it is certainly necessary [g] to set forth not only the Year in which the Stroke was given, but also that in which the Death happened, that it may appear that the Death happened within the Year and Day after the Stroke. But it seems clear from all the Precedents, That it is sufficient to shew in what

[a] 4 Co. 42. 47. H. P. C. 207. 2 Inst. 318. Noy 45. Hetley 35. Dy. 50. pl. 9. 10. Quære Cro. El. 739. pl. 12.

[b] 4 Co. 42. 47. 2 Inst. 318.

[c] H. P. C. 264. 2 Inst. 318.

[d] Vide Dyer 164. 60. b. Cro. El. 176. Quære Cro. El. 739 pl. 12.

[e] 4 Co. 42.

[f] 4 Co. 42.

[g] 2 Inst. 318. 319. Bro. Indictment 41. Book 1. Ch. 31. S. 9. 10.

Year of the King's Reign the Fact was done, and the Death happened, without ſhewing the Year of the Lord. Alſo it hath been adjudged, [a] that it is ſufficient to alledge the Fact in ſuch a Year of ſuch a King, without ſaying it was in ſuch a Year of his Reign, becauſe it is clearly implied.

Sect. 91. As to the fourth Particular, *viz.* With what certainty the Count in Appeal ought to ſet forth the Place where the Deed was done, there can be no doubt but that every Count in an Appeal of Death muſt ſhew [b] the Place where the Death happened, as well as that where the Hurt was given, and this with the ſame [c] preciſe Certainty and Freedom from Repugnancy [d] as is required in Relation to the Time of the Death and Hurt, for which I ſhall refer the Reader to the 89th and 90th Sections of this Chapter, wherein what is ſaid in Relation to the Time of the Hurt and Death is equally applicable to the Place. Alſo it ſeems that a Miſtake of the Place is not [e] material upon Evidence upon not Guilty pleaded, any more than a Miſtake of the Time, provided the Fact be proved at ſome other Place in the ſame County.

Sect. 92. But it ſeems to be not only neceſſary in an Appeal of Death to alledge ſome Place both of the Death and Hurt, and in every Count in every other Appeal to alledge ſome Place; where the Fact was committed, but alſo that ſuch Allegation be in a proper Place for the better Underſtanding whereof I ſhall premiſe, That if the Truth will bear it, it is ſafeſt [f] to lay it in a Town, as the Statute of *Glouceſter* above-mentioned directs; but if it were done out of a Town, it ſeems that you may lay it in any other Place from whence a Viſne may come; in Relation to which Matter the Law being in great Meaſure ſuperſeded in civil Actions by the Statute *For the Amendment of the Law*, and chiefly in Uſe in criminal Cauſes, it may not be improper in this Place more fully to conſider it, and for that Purpoſe I ſhall lay it down as a good general Rule, That a Viſne may come from any Place, which is of ſo ſmall a Compaſs, that all who live in or near it may reaſonably be preſumed to have ſome Knowledge of the Perſons living in it, and therefore are eſteemed the moſt proper Judges of the Facts done within its Limits, as being moſt likely to be proved by Witneſſes, and charged upon Perſons with whoſe Integrity and Reputation they are beſt acquainted. And upon this Ground it hath been adjudged, That a Viſne may come not only from a Town, but from [g] a Ward, a [h] Pariſh, Hamlet, [i] Burgh, Manor, [k] Caſtle, [l] or even from a Foreſt, [m] or other Place known [n] out of a Town. Alſo it ſeems [o] clear that whenſoever a Place is generally alledged in Pleading, the Law will intend it to be a Vill unleſs it be mentioned with ſome Addition which ſhews the contrary; or [p] be alledged within a City or Vill, in which Caſe it would be abſurd to take it for a Vill of it ſelf; yet [q] if in Truth there be no ſuch Town, nor Hamlet, nor Place known out of a Town; or [r] if a Fact alledged in a Foreſt, were done in ſome Vill in the Foreſt not mentioned in the Record, the Defendant may plead it in Abatement. Alſo if a Fact done in a Vill within a Pariſh which contains divers Vills, be in the Count in an Appeal alledged generally in the Pariſh, or [r] a Fact done in a City, which contains divers Pariſhes, be in the Count in an Appeal alledged generally in the City, it ſeems [ſ] that the Defendant may plead ſuch Matter in Abatement, for otherwiſe he could take no Advantage of the Inſufficiency of the Allegation, becauſe the Place named as it ſtands

[a] Lev 140. See 1 Sid. 140.
[b] Hetl. 35. Cro. El. 137. pl. 10. 738. pl 11. 739. pl 12.
[c] Dy. 68. pl 28.
[d] Noy 45. Dy. 50 pl 9. 10. Cro. Eliz. 196. pl. 13.
[e] H. P. C. 264, 265. Salk. 288.
[f] Fitz. Coro. 80. 2 Inſt. 319. 3 Mod. 158. Salk. 59. 60.
[g] Yel. 159. 1 Sid. 178. Cro. Jac. 222.
[h] 6 Co. 14. Co. Litt. 125. b. Salk. 60.
[i] Co. Lit. 125. b. Cro. El. 866. 1 Sid. 326.
[k] 2 Rol. A. 612. pl. 6, 7. 613. pl. 1. 614 pl 8. 618 pl. 2. Co. Litt. 125. Cro Jac 405.
[l] 2 Rol. A. 618. pl. 1. 621. pl. 21 Co. Lit. 125. b.
[m] Cro. El. 200. pl. 26. 1 Sid. 326. 2 Rol. A. 621. pl 26. Bro. Appeal 19. Vide Co. Lit. 125 b. Con. Bro. Appeal 127.
[n] 6 H. 7. 3. pl. 1. Co. Litt. 125. a. b. 2 Inſt 319 1 Sid. 326.
[o] Bro Pleadings 61. Co. Litt. 125. b. 2 Rol. A. 54. pl. 30, 31, 32. 1 Sid. 88. con. 1 Sid. 326. [p] Cro. El. 732. 1 Sid. 326. [q] Bro. Pleadings 61. 6 H 7. 3. pl. 1. 2 Rol. A. 621. pl. 26. 7 H 4 27. a. See 2 Rol. A. 616. pl. 2, 3, 4, 5, 6, 7. 1 Sid 88. [r] Cro. El. 200. 7 H. 4. 27 a. 2 Rol. A. 621. pl. 26. [ſ] See the Caſes cited under Letter O. 7 H. 4. 27. a Salk. 59. 60. Co. Litt. 125. b. 4 Co. 14. b. 2 Inſt. 319.

on the Record, must, till the Contrary be shewn, be intended to contain no more than one Town, or Parish, on which Supposition a Visne may well come *de vicineto* [a] *civitatis*, which does not exclude the City, but takes in the City and its Neighbourhood within its Jurisdiction, whether such City be within a County, [b] or be a County of itself; excepting only the City of [c] *London*, from whence it seems that no Visne can come, not only by Reason of the Largeness of its Extent, but also because it hath been the constant Usage of Pleading to shew the Ward and Parish in which a Fact alledged [d] in *London*, was done.

Sect, 92. It hath been adjudged that no [e] Visne can come from the *Wild* of *Sussex*, not only by Reason of the Largeness of its Extent, but also because it shall be taken for a Wood without Inhabitants, and therefore it would seem inconsistent to award the Return of a Jury from it. And yet it hath been holden [f] that a Visne may come from a Park; also it seems to be the general Opinion, That a Visne may come from a Forest, as hath been more fully shewn in the Precedent Section, from whence it may plausibly be argued that it may come as well from such a *Wild*, supposing it to be a Wood. Also it seems [g] to be questionable whether a Visne may not come from a Walk in a Forest, being alledged as a Place in which a Fact was done; but it seems clear that no Visne can come from it, if it be alledged only as a Liberty, for that no Visne can come from a Thing incorporeal, [h] but only from a Place. Also it hath been holden that no Visne [i] can come from the Scite of a Manor, perhaps for this Reason, because it doth not properly signifie a Place, but rather the Limits and Scituation of a Place.

Sect. 93. As to the fourth Point, *viz.* Whether one and the same Count in Appeal ought to be against those who do not appear, as well as against those who do appear, and against the Accessories as well as the Principals. It is said [i] by Sir *Matthew Hale*, That in an Appeal against *A. B.* and *C* if *A.* only appear, yet the Plaintiff ought to count against them all, by the better Opinion. And the like seems also to be holden by Sir *William Staundforde* [k] and *Brook* [l]; yet the Point adjudged in the Principal [m] Case, which seems to be the chief Foundation of these Opinions, seems to be no more than this, That where an Appellant hath had Judgment and Execution in one Appeal, he shall not afterwards have another against Persons not named in the first. And all the Precedents that I can find, either in *Coke* [n] or *Rastal*, [o] of Counts in Appeals, wherein some of the Defendants have not appeared, do indeed mention the Persons absent, as well as those present, and shew in what Manner they were guilty, yet are all of them express that the Appellant *instanter appellat* those that appear only; and that he would in like Manner appeal those that are absent, if they were present; by which it seems clearly to be implied, That when they shall appear there shall be another Declaration against them, and that the present Declaration is esteemed only as a Declaration against those that do appear. Neither do I find any Difference in the Precedents above-mentioned, as to the Form of such Counts in Relation to this Matter, where the Persons not appearing are Accessories, from that wherein they are Principals. But whether the omitting of a Person in one Appeal be always a good Bar to the charging of him in another, shall be considered in the following Part of the Chapter, wherein I shall treat of the Nature of Pleas in Bar to Appeals.

Sect, 94. As to the third Point, *viz.* How the Appellant may be nonsuited, it is generally holden in some Books, [p] That by the Common Law,

Contra Fitz Nonsuit. 15 34. Quære Bro. Nonsuit. 6. 20 H. 6 44. pl. 30. 2 Bulst. 19.

[a] 2 Rol. A. 622. pl. 31, 32, 35, 36, 37, 38. 623. pl. 41, 42. 8 H. 5. 10, pl. 20. Cro. Jac. 307, 308. Con. S. P. C. 155. b.
[b] See the Authorities cited under Letter M.
[c] 1 Sid. 178. pl. 10. Cro. Jac. 307, 308 2 Rol. A. 622. pl. 39. Cro. Jac. 150. pl. 10. Quære Cro. El. 732. Con. S. P. C. 154. Letter C. 2 Rol A. 617. E. 1
[d] Cr El. 732.
[e] 1 Sid. 88. 2 Rol. 617. pl. 2. Hob. 266.
[f] 1 Syd. 327.
[g] 2 Lev. 307. contra 1 Sid. 326. 2 Lev. 307. Contra 1 Sid. 326. 1 Sid. 327.
[h] 1 Sid. 326.
[i] 2 Rol. A. 618. pl. 3. 1 H. P. C. 188.
[k] S. P. C. 65. Letter C.
[l] Brook Appeal 28.
[m] 9 H. 4. 1. pl. 7. See 4 Co. 47. Dyer 120. pl. 10.
[n] Cokes' Entries 50. b.
[o] Rastal's Entries 46. pl. 2. 47. pl. 4. 50. pl. 10. 51. pl. 11. 13. 15. 53. pl. 2, 3, 54. pl. 4. See 47 Ass. pl. 6.
[p] Bro. Nonsuit 44. Co Litt. 139. b 1 Rol. A. 131. E. pl. 3, 4, 5. 132. pl 6, 7, 8, 9, 10. 3 Ed. 4 11. b.

if a Plaintiff in any Action whatsoever be demanded at any Day of Continuance before Judgment, and do not appear, either in [a] proper Person, or by Attorney or Guardian, as the Law requires, he shall be nonsuited, whatsoever [b] Excuse he may have for his Absence. But it is enacted by 2 *H.* 4. 7. *That if the Verdict pass against the Plaintiff, the same Plaintiff shall not be nonsuited.* And since the Statute it hath been adjudged [c] That if a Defendant in an Appeal of Murder be found guilty of Manslaughter only, the Appellant cannot be nonsuited; but it doth not appear whether this Resolution be grounded on the said Statute, or on the Common Law; for it seems difficult to maintain that such a Verdict which finds the Substance of the Fact shall be said to pass against the Appellant, in which Case only the Nonsuit is taken away by the Statute. And therefore perhaps a Nonsuit in this Case may not be suffered by the Common Law, which seems not to have permitted a Nonsuit after a full Verdict, except in such Cases only whereupon some Doubt remained with the Court, as may be reasonably argued from the Authorities above cited under Letter. But it seems that an Appellant may be nonsuited after a special [d] Verdict, or after a Demurrer [e] and Argument thereupon.

Sect. 95. As to the fourth Point, *viz.* For what Faults the Writ may be abated, I shall premise that in Order to take Advantage of a Defect in the Writ it self, the Appellee [f] ought to demand Oyer of it, which he must do in open [g] Court. And for the better understanding for what Faults such Writ shall be abated, I shall consider the following Particulars.

1. Where it may be abated by the Court *ex Officio.*

2. Where upon the Exception, or Plea of the Party, but not without such Exception or Plea.

4. What Defects of this Kind may be amended, which without such Amendment might abate the Writ.

As to the first Particular it seems, That the Writ may be abated by the Court *ex Officio*, [h] for the following Faults, whether the Party take Notice of them or not; as,

Sect. 96. I. [i] Where a Writ or Declaration wants those Words of Art which are appropriated by Law for the Description of the Offence; as where an Appeal of Burglary [k] has the Word *Burgaliter* instead of *burgulariter*, or *burglariter*; or an Appeal of Rape wants the Word *rapuit*, [l] or any Appeal wants the Word *Felonice*. [m]

Sect. 97. II. Where the Declaration varies from the Writ; as [n] by laying the Offence in the Reign of a present King, where the Writ supposed it to have been in the Reign of a former King. Or by giving the Defendant a Name different from that in the Writ; as where the Writ [o] calls him *A. B.* of C. Alderman, and the Declaration *A. B.* of *C.* Esquire. Or where the Declaration is otherwise [p] defective in not pursuing the Writ, or in not setting forth both the Substance [q] and Circumstances [r] of the Fact with that Certainty which the Law requires: Or in [s] laying the Offence in a different Country, from that in which the Writ was brought.

Sect. 98. III. Where [t] the Declaration doth not conclude *contra formam Statuti* in such Cases where by Law it ought.

Sect. 99. IV. Where the Sense is defective for want of a material Word in the Writ; as [u] if the Conclusion be *ibi hoc breve*, &c. without the Word *habeas*; Or where there is a false Concord in the Writ, as *hos* [x] or *hanc breve*; or the singular [y] Number instead of the Plural; or (as some [z] seem to hold generally) any other false *Latin*; or even the Use

[a] Vide supra Sect. 74.
[b] Noy. 88. Lutw. 173. Vide Supra Sect. 30.
[c] Moor. 407. pl. 546. Cro. El. 465.
[d] 2 Jon. 1.
[e] Co. Lit. 139 b. 2 Jones 1. See 20 H. 6. 44. pl. 30. and the Authorities cited under Letter E.
[f] 2 Bulst. 19. 3 Bulst. 243.
[g] Between Widdrinton and Charlton agreed. Mich. 10 Annæ.
[h] Finch of Law. 226. 2 Danv. Abr. 252. Supra Sect. 42.
[i] Vide supra Sect 77.
[k] 4 Co. 39.
[l] Supra Sect. 77.
[m] Supra Sect. 18, 77.
[n] Fitz, Brief 219. 236.
[o] Yel. 120.
[p] Supra Sect. 75.
[q] Supra Sect. 75, &c.
[r] Supra Sect. 86, &c. Cro. El. 196.
[s] Supra Sect. 35, 47. 71. Bro. Appeal 38.
[t] Supra Sect. 60.
[u] Fitz. Coro. 121. S. P. C. 82. Letter A.
[x] 9 H. 7. 16. pl. 8.
[y] 10 Ed. 3. 1. pl. 2. [z] H. P. C. 189. S. P. C. 82. Letter A. 5 Co. 121.

of a Word which is not *Latin*, tho' [a] by the Change or Addition of a Letter it might be made ſo. But it ſeems that ſuch Faults in the Declaration are not fatal if the Writ or Bill on the File be right, as ſhall be ſhewn more at large in the following Part of this Chapter.

Sect. 100. V. Generally where the Writ, or Declaration are any otherwiſe defective in not obſerving the legal Form, as [b] where in a Writ of Appeal ſued by Husband and Wife, the Concluſion is in the Name of the Wife only: Or where the Writ omits [c] either the Name of Baptiſm, or Surname, of the Appellant or Appellee, being under the Degree of Nobility, which alone can give ſo high [d] a Name of Dignity as to ſupply the want of a Surname.

As to the ſecond Particular, *viz.* Where the Writ may be abated upon the Plea or Exception of the Party, but not without ſuch Plea or Exception, I ſhall endeavour to ſhew,

1. Where it may be ſo abated for the want of fifteen Days between the *Teſte* and the Return of the Writ.
2. Where for a *Miſnoſmer* or wrong Addition
3. Where for a Defect in the Addition of the Appellant or Appellee.
4. Where for the Multiplicity of Action.
5. Where for making of *J. S.* a Defendant, when there is no ſuch Perſon.
6. Whether the Defendant may have more than one of ſuch Pleas or Exceptions.

Sect. 101. As to the firſt Point, *viz.* Where a Writ of Appeal may be abated upon the Exception or Plea of the Party for the want of fifteen Days between its *Teſte* and Return. If the Party, before he hath pleaded in chief, do ſpecially ſhew to the Court ſuch a Defect in the Writ, the later Authorities [e] ſeem to incline that it ought to be abated, becauſe the Writ is the Foundation of the whole Proceeding, and the Law ſeems to be in nothing more curious than in ſtrictly keeping up its legal Forms. Yet it hath been reſolved, [f] That ſuch a Defect is ſalved by the Party's coming in and pleading in chief without taking Advantage of it: Alſo it hath been adjudged, That where the Original is right, all Defects in the Meſne Proceſs are ſalved by the Party's Appearance, as ſhall be ſhewn more at large in the Chapter concerning Proceſs.

Sect. 102. As to the ſecond Point, *viz.* Where a Writ of Appeal may be abated, upon the Exception or Plea of the Party, for a *Miſnoſmer* or wrong Addition, it ſeems to be agreed; [g] That if there be a Miſtake in the Writ or Declaration as to the Name of Baptiſm [h] or Surname [i] of the Appellant [k] or Appellee; or [l] as to the Town, Pariſh or County, Eſtate, Degree or Myſtery, whereof they are ſaid to be, as where [m] one who is neither by Birth, Office, Creation or Reputation an Eſquire, or Gentleman, is named with either of thoſe Additions; or where a Gentleman by Birth, who follows a Trade or Husbandry, is named [n], with the Addition of the Trade or Husbandry, and not of Gentleman; or where a Peer, who has more than one Name of Dignity, is not named [o] by the moſt Noble; or where a Gentleman or Gentlewoman [p] is named Spinſter; or a Yeoman [q] is named Gentleman; or [r] if there be no ſuch Town, Pariſh nor Hamlet, nor Place known out of a Town, as that whereof either the Appellant or Appellee are ſaid to be; and the Appellee before [ſ] Imparlance, plead ſuch Matter in Abatement, and thereon Iſſue is joined and found for him,

[a] 2 H. 4 8. pl. 35.

[b] Fitz. Brief 252.

[c] Finch of Law 253. 27 H. 6. 3. pl. 24. 2 Inſt. 665.

[d] Finch 253. 8 Ed. 4. 24. pl. 2. 2 Inſt. 666. 25 Ed. 3. 39. pl. 6.

[e] Salkeld 63. pl. 4. vide 2 Inſt. 667. Cro Jac 424. pl. 8. 1 Ventris 7. 1 Sid. 406. contra 12 Ed. 4. 11. Bro. Error 169.

[f] Salkeld 63 pl. 4.

[g] Finch 363. 364.

[h] 9 H. 5. 1 pl. 3.

[i] H. P. C. 243. Raſtal's Entries 49 51. b. 54 pl. 4. See the Chapter concerning Pleas to Felony.

[k] 9 H. 5. 1. pl. 3.

[l] Bro. Appeal 44. Raſtal's Entries. 108. 11 H 6. 11. pl. 25. pl. 51. 2 Inſt. Entries 108. 35 H. 6. 55. 10 Ed. 4. 12. pl. 10. 2 Inſt. 667. 668.

[m] 2 Inſt. 668. 6. Co. 67.

[n] 14 H. 6. 15. 668, 669.

[o] 2 Inſt. 669.

[p] 2 Inſt. 668.

[q] 5 H. 7. 16. pl. 7. 10 Ed. 4. 16. pl. 19. Raſtal's Thelo... Lib. 11. Chap. 4. Sect 19.

[r] Salkeld 59.

[ſ] Finch 434. 21 Ed. 4. 7. 2. b.

[a] 9 H. 5. 1. 3. pl. Bro. Appeal 38. [b] Bro. Addition 44. [c] Rastal's Entries. 50. pl. 10. 54 pl. 4.

the Writ ought to be abated. And it seems [a] also to have been holden, That if the Appellant after Imparlance confess that he hath brought his Appeal by a wrong Name, the Writ shall be abated: But it is said [b] to be no Fault to give an Esquire the Addition of Gentleman, *& sic è converso*. Also if one [c] who is usually known and called by the Surname of *B.* be so named in the Appeal, and the Appellee plead that his Name is *C.* and not *B.* and the Appellant reply that the Appellee is, and at the time of the Purchase of the Original, was as well known by the Name of *B.* as by the Name of *C.* and this be confessed and found for him, it avoids the Plea of the Misnosmer. And if one who hath his usual Abode at *B.* and hath been sometime seen at *C.* be named of *C.* in an Appeal, it hath been questioned [d] whether this be such a Fault as will abate the Writ; because sometimes Appellees may not have any known Dwelling; but if that happen to be the Case, surely it is safest to reply it, and then there seems to be little doubt but it may make good the naming of the Party of any Place wherein he has at any time been. And if a Place where he dwells, and is a House-Keeper, and also another Place where he keeps his Wife and Family be well known, it seems that the Writ may name him of either of such Places, or perhaps of both of them, but is abateable unless it name him of one of them.

[d] 1 Sid. 325. Vide 10 Ed. 4 12, pl. 10. 4 H. 6. 4. pl. 9

Sect. 103. As to the third Point, *viz.* Where a Writ of Appeal may be abated by the Exception or Plea of the Party, for a Defect in the Addition of the Appellant or Appellee, it seems that the Common Law in no Case [e] requires any other Description of an Appellant or Appellee, but by their Name of Baptism and Surname, unless they be of the Degree of a Knight, [f] or of some higher Dignity; in which Cases, whether the Name of Dignity be ancient, or (as some say [g]) of a new Creation, as that of Baronet, *&c.* it ought to be added to the Name of Baptism and Surname; and if it be of the Degree of Nobility, it ought [h] to supply the Place of the Surname. And it seems that the Law was [i] so curious in this Particular, that if a Plaintiff in any Action gained a new Name of Dignity hanging a Writ, he made it abateable, but this Inconvenience is remedied by 1 *Ed.* 6. 7. Sect. 3. by which it is enacted, *That if any Plaintiff in any Manner of Action shall be made a Duke, Archbishop, Marquess, Earl, Viscount, Baron, Bishop, Knight, Justice of either Bench, or Serjeant at Law depending the same Action, that such Action for such Cause shall not be abateable or abated.* But it hath been holden [k] that the Dignity of a Baronet is not in this Statute, because there was no such Dignity at the time of the making of it.

[e] 2 Inst. 665. 666. 11 H. 4. 40. pl. 3. 11 H. 6. 11. pl. 25. 10 Ed. 4. 16. pl. 19. [f] 11 H. 4 40. pl. 3. 14 H. 6. 14. b. [g] Hob. 129. 2 Rol. A. 469. pl. 10. 2 Inst. 666, 667. contra Latch. 169. [h] Supra Sect. [i] 32 H. 6. 29. b. Contra 24 E. 3. 25. pl. 14. 26. pl. 21. 25. Ed. 3. 39. pl. 6. [k] 1 Sid. 40. Littleton's Rep. 81. Cro. Ca. 104.

Sect. 104. To prevent [l] the Inconvenience of troubling one Person for another, which cannot but often happen if there be no other additional Description of the Defendant, it is enacted, by 1 H. 5. Chap. 5. *That in every original Writ of Actions personal, Appeals, and Indictments, and in which the Exigent shall be awarded, to the Names of the Defendants in such Writs Original, Appeals and Indictments, Additions shall be made of their Estate or Degree, or Mystery, and of the Towns or Hamlets, or Places and Counties, of the which they were or be, or in which they be or were conversant. And if by Process upon the said Original Writs, Appeals or Indictments, in the which the said Additions be omitted, any Outlawries be pronounced, that they be void, frustrate and holden for none. And that before the Outlawries pronounced, the said Writs and Indictments shall be abated by the Exception of the Party, wherein the same the said Additions be omitted.*

[l] 21 E. 4. 72. 2 Inst. 870.

Sect. 105. For the better Explication of this Statute, so far as it relates to the Subject of this Treatise, I shall first premise, That [a] generally such Additions in *English* are as good as in *Latin*; and where there are several Defendants of different Names and the same Addition, it is [b] safest to repeat the Addition after each of their Names, applying it particularly to every one of them; and where a Father hath the same Name and the same Addition with a Defendant being his Son, the Writ is [c] abateable unless it add the Addition of *Puisne* to the other Additions; but where the Father is the Defendant, it is said that there is no need of the Addition of *Eigne*. [d] And if the Son be *in Custodia Mareschalli*, and so declared against, it is said that the Count is good without the Addition of *Puisne*, unless the Father of the same Name and Additions be also in the Custody of the Marshal. And for the better understanding of the Nature of the several Additions required by the Statute abovementioned, I shall endeavour to shew,

[a] 1 Sid. 101. 1 Keb. 12.
[b] Bro. Additions 3.
[c] 37 H. 6. 29. pl. 10. 39 H. 6. 46. 4 Ed. 3. 31. pl. 11.
[d] Salkeld 7.

1. What is a sufficient Addition of the Estate or Degree.
2. What of the Mystery.
3. What of the Town, Hamlet, Place, or County, of the Appellee.
4. How the Defect of an Addition may be salved.

Sect. 106. As to the first Particular, *viz.* What is a sufficient Addition of the Estate or Degree of the Appellee, I shall observe; First, That is necessary to shew the present Estate or Degree of the Appellee [e] at the Time of the Writ, in which Respect this Addition, and also the Addition of the Mystery differs from that of the Place, which is sufficiently set forth by naming the Appellee late of such a Place.

[e] 9 Ed. 4, 2. pl. 8. 22 Ed. 4. 13. pl. 35. 21 H. 6. 3. pl. 4. 2 Inst. 670.

Sect. 107. Secondly, That such Addition must be expressed in such a Manner that it may plainly appear to refer to the Appellee; for it hath been resolved, That to name the Appellee Son of *A.* of *B.* Butcher, is insufficient, because Butcher refers to *A.* rather than to the Appellee.

Sect. 108. Thirdly, That [f] a Bishop of an *Irish* Diocese may be as well described by the Addition of his Bishoprick, as an *English* Bishop may by the Addition of an *English* one; (as it seems to be admitted in the Year-Book of 21 *H.* 6 3. pl. 4.) But it seems [g] clear, That no one can be well described by the Addition of a temporal Dignity in *Ireland*, or any other Nation besides our own, because no such Dignity can give a Man a higher Title here than that of Esquire.

[f] See Theo. Lib. 6. cap. 15. Sect. 8.
[g] 2 Inst. 667.

Sect. 109. Fourthly, That the Degree of a Serjeant [h] at Law is a good Addition, from whence it may reasonably be argued that a Degree in either University is also a good Addition, as it is holden by Sir *Edward* [i] *Coke* without Question; yet this is made a Query by *Theloal*, [k] and it is holden in the Year-Book of 35 *H.* 6, 55, and admitted by Sir *Edward Coke* in the very Place abovecited, That a Doctor in Divinity may have the Addition of Clerk, which seems not easily reconcileable with the Opinion that the Degree of a Doctor is a good Addition; for if it were, why should not the Writ be abateable for having the Addition of Clerk instead of it, contrary to the allowed Rule [l] in other Cases, that the most worthy Addition is to be used?

[h] Theloal. Lib. 6. Ch. 15. Sect. 12.
[i] 2 Inst. 668.
[k] Theloal Book 6. Ch. 15. Sect. 13.
[l] Vide supra Sect. 102.

Sect. 110. Fifthly, That *Generosus* [m] or *Armiger*, [n] are either of them, good Additions for the Estate and Degree of a Man; *Generosa* [o] for that of

[m] 2 Inst. 667, 668.
[n] 2 Inst. 667 Bro. Addition 44. 50.
[o] 2 Inst. 668.

a Woman; and Yeoman [a] and Labourer [b] are alſo good Additions for the Eſtate and Degree of a Man, but not for that of a Woman; and Widow [c] or Single [d] Woman, or as ſome [e] ſay, Wife of *J. S.* are all of them good Additions of the Eſtate and Degree of a Woman, but no ſuch like Addition is good for the Eſtate and Degree of a Man. And Spinſter [f] is a good Addition for the Eſtate and Degree of a Woman, and perhaps alſo for that of a Man.

Sect. 111. Sixthly, That Burgeſs [g] and Citizen, and Servant, [h] are all of them too general, and therefore not good Additions of the State or Degree either of Man or Woman.

Sect. 112. As to the ſecond Particular, *viz.* What is a ſufficient Addition of the Myſtery of an Appellee; having firſt premiſed that the Word *Myſtery* [i] includes all lawful Arts, Trades and Occupations; And [k] that if one under the Degree of a Gentleman have divers of ſuch Arts, Trades or Occupations, he may be named by any of them, I ſhall endeavour to ſhew,

1. What Additions of this Kind are clearly good.
2. What are clearly inſufficient.
3. What are queſtionable.

Sect. 113. And firſt, the following Additions of this Kind clearly ſeem to be good, as Husband-man, [l] Merchant, [m] Broker, [n] Taylor, [o] Point-maker, [p] Smith, [q] Miller, [r] Carpenter, [ſ] Cook, [t] Brewer, [u] Baker, [x] Butcher [y] Pariſh-Clerk, [z] Mercer [aa] Fiſh-Monger, [bb] Dier, [cc] School-Maſter, [dd] Scrivener, and ſuch like.

Sect. 114. Secondly, The following Additions of this Kind clearly ſeem to be inſufficient, as Maintainer, [ee] Extortioner, [ff] Thief, [gg] Vagabond, [hh] Heretick, [ii] common Informer, and ſuch like.

Thirdly, The following Additions of this Kind ſeem to be queſtionable as,

Sect. 115. Firſt, Farmer, which by the better [kk] Opinion ſeems to be an inſufficient Addition, becauſe if any Myſtery be implied in the Notion of it, it is that of Husbandry, of which Husbandman is the proper Addition.

Sect. 116. Secondly, Chamberlain, Butler, and Pantler, which are holden [ll] to be inſufficient Additions, becauſe they denote only a ſpecial Kind of Officer, or Servant, and imply nothing, which in the common Underſtanding of the Words, comes under the Notion of a Myſtery. And from this Ground it ſeems to follow, that neither Groom [mm] nor Page are good Additions, and yet in ſome [nn] of the old Books they ſeem to have been ſo admitted,

Sect. 117. Thirdly, Hoſteler, which hath been holden [pp] to be a good Addition, and ſeems properly enough to come under the Notion of a Myſtery. And tho' it hath been reſolved, [qq] That any one who keeps an Inn may be ſued by the Addition of a Labourer, upon the Cuſtom of the Realm, for want of due Care of the Goods of his Gueſts; becauſe whoever keeps a common Inn, is in that reſpect liable to anſwer for ſuch Defects, by whatſoever Addition he may be ſtyled, yet this does by no

[a] 2 Inſt. 668. Bro. Addition 3, 47, 50.
[b] Bro. Addition 5. 39.
[c] Fitz. Adition 5. Bro. Addition 64, 66. Theloal. Lib. 6. cap. 15. Sect. 4.
[d] Fitz. Addition 5. 14 Ed. 4. 7. pl. 12. Bro. Addition 64, 66. Theloal lib. 6. cap. 15. Sect. 4.
[e] 1 H. 4. 5. b. 4 H. 6. 4. pl. 9. Quære Cro. E. 198. Dy. 47. pl. 2, 3, 4.
[f] Dyer 46. pl. 2, 3. 47. pl. 5. 88. pl. 107. 1 Sid. 247.
[g] 2 Inſt. 668.
[h] 2 Inſt. 668. Bro. Addition 42. 50. 55. 56. con Bro. Addition 5.
[i] 2 Inſt. 668. 669.
[k] Bro. Addition, 44. 2 Inſt. 668.
[l] Bro. Addition 44. 50.
[m] Bro. Addition 40. 50. 66
[n] 9 H. 6. 65. pl. 19. Theloal. lib. 6. ca. 15. Sect. 5.
[o] Bro. Addition. 15. 39.
[p] 7 H. 6. 1. pl. 7.
[q] 21 H. 6. 54. pl. 9. 22 H. 6. 53. a.
[r] Bro. Additions 39. 51.
[ſ] Bro. Additions 15. 22. 39.
[t] 14 H. 6. 15. pl. 51. Theloal. Lib. 6. cap. 15. Sect. 6.
[u] Fitz. utlagary 32. 37. 5 H. 5. 7. pl. 16.
[x] 6 Ed. 4. 3. pl. 10.
[y] Bro. Additions 42.
[z] Bro. Additions 52, 62.
[aa] 2 Inſt. 668.
[bb] 19 H. 6. 51. pl. 9.
[cc] 5 H. 5. 7. pl. 16.
[dd] 2 Leon. 186.
[ee] 9 H. 6. 65. pl. 19. 2 Inſt. 668. 22 Ed. 4. 1. pl. 1. 2 Inſt. 668
[ff] 9 H. 6. 65. pl. 19.
[gg] 22 Ed. 4. 1. pl. 2 Inſt. 668
[hh] 22 Ed. 4. 1. pl. 1.
[ii] 1 Roll. Rep. 190.
[kk] Theloal. Lib. 6. cap. 15. Sect. 9. 2 Inſt. 668. Bro. Addition 10, 28 H. 6. 4. pl. 18.
[ll] Bro. Addition 50, 58. 2 Inſt. 668. Theloal. Lib. 6. cap. 15. Sect. 10.
[mm] 2 Inſt. 668.
[nn] Bro. Addition, 50, 58. Fitz. coro. 43. 21 Ed. 4. 71.
[pp] Bro. Addition, 35. 21 H. 6. 50. pl. 3.
[qq] 22 H. 6. 21. Theloal. lib. 6. cap. 5.

Means prove such Person may not as well be sued by the Addition of Hosteler, but only that he may be sued as well under any other Addition.

As to the Third Particular, *viz.* What is a good Addition of the Town, Hamlet, Place, or County of the Appellee, I shall observe;

Sect. 117. First, That it is a good Addition of this Kind to name the Appellee late [a] of such a Town, in which respect this Addition differs from that of the Estate, Degree or Mystery. And it is said that if a Defendant be named of *A.* and late of *B.* it is sufficient to prove either Addition.

Sect. 118, Secondly, That the constant Course of Precedents hath made it a sufficient Addition of this Kind, to name the Defendant of a City which is a County [b] of it self, as *de Londino* [c] *De Norwico*, &c. without more, by which it shall be intended that he lives in the County as well as City of *London* and *Norwich*, &c. unless he shew the contrary, tho' Part of each of these Cities lie out of their Counties. However it is certain, that it is not sufficient to name a Defendant *Londini* [d] or *Bristolia*, &c. because that imports only that he belongs to such Town, and not that he resides there. Also it seems clear, [e] That it is not sufficient to name a Defendant of any Town which is not a County of it self, without shewing in what County it lies. Also if [f] a Man be named of a Parish which contains more Towns, or Hamlets, or Places known out of any Town, or Hamlet, the Defendant may plead such Matter in Abatement, because such an Addition does not pursue the Statute; but a Parish shall be intended to contain no more than one Town, unless the contrary be shewn.

Sect, 119. Thirdly, That if there be two Towns in a County of the same principal Name, with different Additions to distinguish them from one another, as *Great Dale*, and *Little Dale*, or *Upper Dale*, and *Lower Dale*, and the Defendant be named only of the principal Town without any Addition, as of *Dale* only, the Defendant may plead [g] that there are two *Dales* in the same County called *Great Dale* and *Little Dale*, and none without an Addition, *&c.* Or according to some Opinions [h] either in this Case where there are two different Towns called *Dale*, or even where there is but one Town sometimes called *Southdale*, and sometimes *Northdale*, but never simply *Dale* without an Addition, the Defendant may plead that there is no such Town as *Dale*, in the same County, because Parcel of a Name cannot be said to be the Name. But if there be two Towns of the same Name in a County without any Addition to distinguish them, as it sometimes happens where they lie at a Distance from one another, I do not find any Authority that it is not sufficient in such Case to name the Defendant generally of either of such Towns, without adding any Thing to distinguish it from the other.

Sect. 120, Fourthly, That if an Appellee live in a Hamlet of a Town, it is said [i] to be in the Election of the Appellant to name him either of the Hamlet or of the Town; but it seems that this is to be intended only of such Hamlets which are so far esteemed to be Parts of a Town, that those who live in them are in common Speech indifferently styled sometimes of the Hamlet and sometimes of the Town; for I see not how the Addition of the Town can be proper, where the Party lives in a Place known by a distinct Name, and not Parcel of it.

Sect. 121. Fifthly, That if an [k] Appellee live in a Place known by a a special Name, and lying out of any Town or Hamlet, he may be well

[a] Vide supra Section 106. 21 Ed. 4. 15. pl. 1. 19 H. 6. 66. pl. 6. 1 Ed. 4. 1. pl. 3. 1 Ed. 4. 2. pl. 6. 7. Dyer 213. pl. 44. &c. 9 H. 6. 66. pl. 6. Theloal. lib. 6. cap. 14. Sect. 17.

[b] 2 Inst. 669.

[c] 4 Ed. 4. 16. pl. 30. 21 Ed. 4. 15. pl. 1. 27 H. 6. 4. pl. 26. 35 H. 6. 12. pl. 21.

[d] 35 H 6. 12. pl. 21. 7 H. 6. 1. pl. 7. 4 Ed. 4. 19. pl. 23

[e] Cro. Jac. 167

[f] 2 Inst. 669. vide supra Sect 92. 102. Theloal Lib. 6. cap. 14. Sect. 20. 35. H. 6. 30. pl. 37.

[g] 7 H. 6. 39. a b 19 H. 6. 35. pl. 77. 8 H. 5. 8. pl. 8. 21 Ed. 4. 51. 10 H. 7. 4. pl. 5. 10 H. 6. 5. pl. 16. Rastal's Entries 47. a.

[h] 3 H. 6. 8. pl. 8. 14 H. 6. 23. pl. 68. Theloal. Lib. 6. cap. 14. Sect. 23. contra 7 H. 6. 45. pl. 285.

[i] Theloal. Lib. 6. cap. 14 Sect. 14. 2 Inst. 669. 35 H. 6. 30. pl. 37. 14 H. 6. 23. pl. 68. Inst. 669.

[k] 2 Inst. 669. 21 Ed. 4. 37. pl. 1. Fitz. Brief. 467. 7 H. 4. 27. a.

named of such Place; but if he live in any Place known within a Town or Hamlet, it is said to be safest to name him of the Town or Hamlet.

2 Inst. 669. 3 H. 6. 31. pl. 21. 2 Theloal. Lib. 6. cap. 14. Sect. 6. 7, 9. *Sect.* 122. Sixthly, That the Addition of the Place of Habitation of a Wife is sufficiently shewn by shewing that of the Husband, because it shall be intended that the Wife lives where the Husband does.

[a] 35 H. 6. 12. pl. 21. Bro. Error 69. Cro. Jac. 610. 2 Rol. Rep. 225. 1 Rol. A. 780. pl. 5. 2 Inst. 670. 7 H. 6. 39. a b. seems contrary. [b] 1 Sid. 247. 1 Keb. 885. [c] Pasch. 3. Georgii. *Sect.* 123. As to the fourth Particular, *viz*; How the Defect of an Addition may be salved, it hath been adjudged; [a] That if an Appellee named with an insufficient Addition, or without any, appear and plead to the Appeal, he cannot afterwards take Advantage of the Defect of the Addition, because by his Appearance and Plea he admits himself to be the Person intended. And some have holden, [b] That the Party by his bare Appearance salves the want of an Addition, or a bad one; but this seems contrary to almost all the Authorities above cited in Relation to this Matter, which seem to admit that the Party before other Matter pleaded may take Advantage either of the Want of an Addition or of a bad one. And accordingly it was lately [c] adjudged in an Appeal of Death between *Reeve* and *Trundal*, that the Want of an Addition of the Appellee was a good Plea in Abatement, and the Writ of Appeal was abated by such Plea.

[d] S P. C 82. 82. Letters C. D. H. P. C. 189. Bro. brief 192. Cro. El. 695. Fitz. brief. 548. 774. [e] 10 H. 4. 4. pl. 13. S. P. C 82. Letter D. Fitz. coro. 269. 465. See 4 Ed. 3. 9. pl. 21. [f] Supra, ch. 9. Sect. 39. 40. 41. *Sect.* 124. As to the fourth Point abovementioned, *viz.* Where a Writ of Appeal may be abated upon the Exception or Plea of the Party for the Multiplicity of Action, it seems [d] clear, That after an Appellant hath appeared on a Writ of Appeal, or even on a Bill of Appeal removed into the Court of King's-Bench from before the Sheriff and Coroners by *Certiorari*, if he commence a new Appeal for the same Matter, the Appellee may plead in Abatement that such prior Appeal is still depending, *&c.* But it seems [e] clear, That it is no Plea in Abatement of a Writ of Appeal, that the Appellant hath brought a Bill of Appeal for the same Matter before the Sheriff and Coroners, because such Bill is not of so high a Nature as a Writ of Appeal, but is said to be only in Nature of a Plaint till it be removed into the King's Bench, which seems [f] to depend on the Statute of *Magna Charta* 17, since which Statute the Sheriff and Coroner cannot proceed to Trial upon a Bill of Appeal, as perhaps they might have done by the Common Law. But after such Bill of Appeal before the Sheriff and Coroners is removed into the King's Bench, if the Plaintiff bring a Writ of Appeal for the same Matter, it is holden [g] by *Staundforde*, and seems to be admitted in the Year Book of 4 H. 6. 14, 15, and both by *Fitzherbert* [h] and *Brook* [i] in their Abridgments of the said Year-Book, that the Appellee may plead in Abatement that such Bill of Appeal is depending, because after it is removed into the King's-Bench, it is of as high a Nature as a Writ of Appeal. Yet Sir *Matthew Hale* [k] seems to be of Opinion that such Bill so removed is not pleadable in Abatement 'till the Plaintiff hath appeared thereon; perhaps for this Reason, that before the Plaintiff hath appeared it doth not appear of Record that he hath prosecuted the Suit in the King's Court, because the *Certiorari* might have been taken out by a Stranger. Upon which Ground it seems to have been resolved [l] that it is no good Plea in Abatement of an Appeal, that the Plaintiff hath purchased another Writ of Appeal returnable at such a Day, *&c.* and that such Writ was delivered of Record to the Sheriff, because it might be for what appears upon the Record, That the first Appeal was so far prosecuted by a Stranger, but in the same Case it is admitted that such prior Appeal depending will abate the second, where it appears on Record that the same Plaintiff hath appeared and sued it, as in praying of Process, *&c.*

[g] S. P. C 82. Letter D.
[h] Fitz. coro. 4.
[i] Bro. Appeal 44.
[k] H. P. C. 189.
[l] 7 H. 7. 6. pl. 10. Fitz. Brief 192. Bro. Appeal 87. S. P. C. 82. Letter C.

Sect. 125. As to the fifth Point, *viz.* Where a Writ of Appeal may be abated for the making of *J. S.* the Defendant, where there is no such Person, it seems clear, [a] That if there be divers Defendants in an Appeal, and one of them who does not appear be misnamed either as to the Surname, or Name of Baptism, or be described by a wrong Addition, or were dead before the Writ purchased, any of the Defendants who do appear may plead, That whereas the Appeal is sued out against *A. B.* of *C.* in the County of *D.* Yeoman, there was not at the Time of the Purchase of the Writ, nor hath been since, any such Person as *A. B. in rerum natura* as by the Writ is supposed, whereon if Issue be joined, if the Appellant cannot prove that there now is, or was at the Time when the Writ was purchased, such a Person of such Name and Addition as by the Writ are supposed, it seems that the Verdict ought to go against him, whereupon the Writ shall be abated as to all the Defendants. But it is not [b] adviseable in such a Case to plead that there was not at the Time of the Purchase of the Writ, *&c.* any such Person as *A. B.* of *C.* in the County of *D.* Yeoman, because it implies a Negative pregnant. Also if a Defendant misnamed or described by a wrong Addition do appear, it seems to be agreed [c] that no other Defendant besides himself can plead the *Misnosmer* or wrong Addition, But I do not find it to be agreed [d] That such a Plea by one Defendant shall abate the Writ as to any other besides himself; but if such Matter when pleaded by another on the Non-appearance of the Defendant, will abate the Writ as to all, it seems, difficult to give a Reason why, it should not have the like Effect when pleaded by the Party himself.

Sect. 126. As to the sixth Point, *viz.* Whether the Appellee may have more than one such Plea or Exception, there seems to be no Doubt but that if a Defendant in an Appeal, or even in an Indictment of Felony, think it proper to make use of never so many Pleas or Exceptions of this kind, requiring all of them the same kind of Trial, he may take Advantage of them all, [e] unless [f] they be repugnant to one another. Also it seems to be the better Opinion, [g] That he shall have the like Advantage, where such Pleas or Exceptions do not all of them require the same kind of Trial, but some of them are triable by Matter of Record, and others by the Country. And if such Pleas or Exceptions be all of them triable by the Country, it seems to have [h] been generally agreed, That the Defendant must at the same time plead also with them all his Matters in Bar, if he have any such, and also plead over to the Felony (unless where he hath admitted the Fact by the Matter pleaded in Bar) But if the Plea in Abatement be triable by Matter of Record, it is holden in some Books [i] that the Defendant is not bound to plead over to the Felony, till such Plea in Abatement be found against him. But [k] the greater Number of Precedents, and constant Practice of late seem to be otherwise. However it seems clear, [l] That whatsoever Matters are pleaded in Abatement of an Appeal or Indictment of Felony, and found against the Defendant, yet he may afterwards plead over to the Felony. And in these Respects such an Appeal and Indictment differ from Appeals [m] of *Mayhem* and all civil Actions whatsoever, except only Asizes of Mortdancestor [n], Novel [o] Disseisin, Nusance [p] and *Juris utrum*; [q] for it seems to be a settled Rule, That in Appeals of *Mayhem* and all other civil

[a] Dyer 348. pl. 14. H. P. C. 189. S. P. C. 82. Letter E. Rastal's Entries 49. a 52. a. Fitz. coro. 15. 43. 64. 26 H. 6. 6. pl. 6. 21 H. 7. 34. pl. 35. 7 H. 4. 27. pl. 4.

[b] Bro. Appeal 111. 6 H. 7. 7. pl. 2. 21 Ed. 4. 71. 72.

[c] S. P. C. 82. Letter E. See the Books above cited.

[d] 21 H 7. 31. pl. 13. 5 Ed. 4. 3. pl. 14. 7 H. 4. 27. pl 4. S P. C. 82. Letter E.

[e] Finch of Law, 363, 364. 385. 4 H 6. 15. b. 16. a. Bro Appeal 44.

[f] S. P. C. 82. Letter E.

[g] Finch of Law 364. Quære 4 H. 6. 16. a. Bro. Appeal 44.

[h] Finch of Law, 363. 364. 385. 21 Ed. 4. 71. pl. 56. Reeves and Trundal Pasche 3 Georgii. Dy. 88. pl. 107. Rastal's Entries 49, a. b. 3 Mod. 266,

267. Quære 6 H. 7. 7. pl. 2. Shower's Reports 47. [i] Bro. Appeal 48. 66. 1 H. 6. 1. pl. 1. 27 Afs. pl. 3. [k] Cro. E. 695. 10 H. 4. 4. pl. 14 4 H 6. 15. b 1 H. 6. 1. pl. 1. Rastal's Entries 47. a. [l] Finch of Law 363, 364. 385. 27 Afs. pl. 3. 1 H. 6. 1. pl. 1. [m] Cro. El. 495. pl. 14. Popham 115. Owen 59, 60. Moor 457. pl. 628. Noy 36. [n] Finch of Law 385. 418. 40 Ed. 3. 29. b. 39 Afs. pl. 13. [o] 1 Ed. 3. 11. pl. 33. Dy. 319. pl. 82. 4 H. 6. 16. a. 1 Jon 413. S. P. C. 82. Letters E. Cro. Ca. 520. Finch of Law 363, 364. 385. [p] Finch of Law 363. 385. [q] 40 Ed. 3. 29. b. Finch of Law 363. 385.

Actions,

Actions, those abovementioned only excepted, if a Plea in Abatement, triable by the Country, [a] be found against the Defendant, he shall not [b] be suffered afterwards to plead any new Matter, but final Judgment shall be given against him. Also it seems to be agreed [c] that in all other Actions, except those abovementioned, if a Defendant together with a Plea in Abatement plead also a Plea in Bar, or the general Issue, he waives the Plea in Abatement; and the Plea in Bar or general Issue only shal. be tried.

Sect. 127. And now I am in the third Place to consider, What Faults of this Kind are amendable, which without such Amendment would abate the Writ. It is to be observed, That Appeals are expresly excepted out of 8 *H.* 6. 12. which is the principal Statute of Amendments: also it seems [d] to be generally taken for granted, That no criminal Prosecution whatsoever is within any other Statute of Amendments, or any of the Statutes of *Jeofailes*; from whence it follows that no Defect is amendable in an Appeal, but such only as is amendable by the Common Law. And therefore it seems to be the better Opinion, That no false [e] *Latin* in a Writ or Bill of Appeal, nor Omission of a Word, [f] nor even of a Letter, [g] nor other Defect or Variance [h] from the proper legal Form, can be amended, because no such Fault is amendable by the Common Law without the Consent [i] of the Parties, except only in Actions wherein the King [k] is a Party. It seems indeed to be generally holden in some Books, [l] That such Faults in a Writ are amendable where the *Cursitor* varies from his Instructions, in the Names [m] or Additions of the Parties, or other like Matters which he must take from his Instructions. But what is said in such Books in relation to this Matter seems to be intended of such Writs only as are within the Purview of the Statutes of Amendments, and therefore cannot be applied to Appeals; yet it seems that a Misprision in the Count is amendable by the Common Law, as well in an Appeal as in any other Action, before it is entered on the Record; and so it seems that the Year [n] Book of 7 *H.* 4. 27. is to be intended, in which a Mistake in the Declaration in laying the Fact in an improper Visne, was suffered to be amended. Also it seems that after the Count is entred on the Record, a Variance in it from the Writ, if a meer Misprision, may be amended by it, as it seemed to be agreed in an Appeal of Death between *Smith* and *Bowen*, [o] wherein the Word *Murdum* in the Count on the Record was adjudged to be amendable by the Word *Murdrum* in the Bill on the File.

As to the Fifth general Point, *viz.* What may be pleaded in Bar of an Appeal, having already in the former Part [p] of this Chapter endeavour'd to shew what may be pleaded in Bar of an Appeal of *Mayhem*, and intending in the later Part of the Book to consider the Learning relating to Pleas in Bar of criminal Prosecutions in general, I shall in this Place only examine the Nature of Pleas in Bar of Appeals of Felony in particular, and for that Purpose having premised that by the better Opinion [q] at this Day, no special Plea in Justification of the killing shall be admitted in an Appeal of Death, but that in every such Case the general Issue is to be pleaded, I shall consider.

1. What Pleas will be good Bars of an Appeal of Felony by shewing that the Plaintiff had never any Right to bring it.

2. Whether a *Retraxit* or Nonsuit in a former Appeal of this kind will be good Bars of another.

3. Whether a Discontinuance.

[a] Vide Cro. El. 203. pl. 34. Dyer 228 pl. 45. Yelv. 36.
[b] 1 Sid. 252. pl. 22. 1 Lev. 163. 1 Inst. 33. Yelv. 112. Aleyn 65, 66.
[c] Cro. El. 495. Owen 59. Noy 36. Moor 457. Popham 115. Vide Thelo. Lib. 15. cap. 5.
[d] Vide Salkeld 51. 1 Bulst. 142. 144.
[e] 9 H. 7. 16. pl. 8. 1 Bulst. 142. 144. 4 H. 6. 16. pl. 16. Bro. Amend. 62.
[f] Fitz. Coro. 121. 13 Ass. pl. 10.
[g] Fitz. Amendment 68.
[h] Fitz. Variance 59. 8 Co. 156 b. 4 H. 6. 16. pl. 16.
[i] Fitz. Amendments 63.
[k] 8 Co. 156. b. 4 H. 6. 16. pl. 16. 40 Ass. pl. 26.
[l] Mo. 866. pl. 1196. 1 Rol. 138. pl. 13. Cro. El. 644. pl. 49. Quære Hob. 128.
[m] 2 Ventris 46. 49. 130. 152. 1 Sid. 412. pl. 8. Hob. 118. Hutton 56, 57. Cro Car. 74. Littleton's Rep. 50.
[n] Fitz. Coro. 80.
[o] Mich. 9. Anno.
[p] Sect. 22, 23, 24, 25, 26.
[q] See B. 1 Chap. 28. S. 3.

4. Whether an Abatement of a former Appeal.

5. Where the bringing of an Appeal of this Kind against one Person shall be a Bar of any subsequent Appeal against any other Person not named in the first.

6. Where a Release will be a good Bar of an Appeal of this Kind.

7. Where the Appellant may be barred as to one Appellee, and continue his Suit against the rest.

8. Whether any, and which of these Pleas, are consistent with the general Issue.

Sect. 128. As to the first Particular, *viz.* What Pleas will be good Bars of such an Appeal by shewing that the Plaintiff had never any Right to bring it, it seems to be a good general [a] Rule, That any Plea of this Kind is good which shews that the Plaintiff wants any of those Requisites which the Law makes necessary to entitle him to the Appeal. And therefore in an Appeal of Death by a Woman it is a good Plea, that [b] she was never lawfully married to the Deceased; or [c] that she hath not continued a Widow since his Death, but hath taken another Husband. Also in an Appeal of Death by one as Heir, it is a good Plea, that *A. B.* at the time [d] of the Writ was and still is Heir of the Deceased; or [e] that one of the Defendants was the Wife of the Deceased, and made a Defendant by Covin to exclude her from her Appeal; or that the Plaintiff is a Bastard [f] and not legitimate. And where one brings an Appeal as Brother and Heir, it is a good Plea, That he is not [g] Brother and Heir as by his Writ and Declaration he hath supposed, or [h] that he hath an Elder Brother by the same Father and Mother still alive; or where one brings an Appeal as Cousin and Heir, *viz.* Brother of *A. B.* Father of the deceased, it is a good Plea, That he is not Cousin [i] and Heir, *viz.* Brother of *A. B.* Father of the deceased, *&c*, as by his Writ and Declaration he hath supposed. Also [k] it is a good Plea in any Appeal of Death, That the Plaintiff hath slipt his Time in not bringing the Appeal within the Year and Day after the Death of the Person supposed to have been killed. Also it is a good [l] Plea in an Appeal of Robbery, That the Plaintiff is a Villain to the Defendant. And it is a good [m] Plea in an Appeal of Rape by a Man and a Woman, That the Plaintiffs were never lawfully married. And [n] it is a good Plea in Bar of any Appeal of Felony, That the Plaintiff is an Ideot, or that he was born deaf and dumb. Also it is said by Sir *William Staundforde*, [o] That it is a good Plea in Bar of any such Apeal, That the Plaintiff is attainted of Treason or Felony; however [p] it seems that such Attainder is no perpetual Bar, but only during the Time it continues in Force.

Sect. 129. As to the second Particular, *viz.* Where a *Retraxit* or Nonsuit in a former Appeal of this Kind will be good Bars of another; I take it to be clear, [q] That a *Retraxit* of any such Appeal is a Bar of all subsequent Appeals of the same Kind; for it seems to be a general settled Rule, That a *Retraxit* of any Action whatsoever is a Bar of all others of the like or inferior Nature. Also it seems to be certain, That a Nonsuit on a Bill [r] of Appeal, whether commenced in the Court of King's Bench, or before Justices [s] of Gaol-Delivery, or before the Sheriff [t] and Coroners, or a Nonsuit after [u] Declaration on a Writ of Appeal, is a Bar of all other Appeals of the same Kind; because no such Bill or Declaration shall be received, unless [x] the Appellant have first appeared in proper Person; and it seems to be agreed by all the Books, That a Nonsuit

[a] S. P. C. 98. H. P. C. 190.
[b] Supra Sect. 36. S. P. C. 98.
[c] Supra Sect. 38. S. P. C. 98.
[d] Rastal's Entries 50 pl 8.
[e] Rastal's Entries 50 pl. 9.
[f] Rastal's Entries 49. a.
[g] Rastal's Entries 49. a. b.
[h] Supra Section 40. Letter 1.
[i] Rastal's Entries 49. a.
[k] S. P. C. 98.
[l] Supra Sect. 44. Letter b. S. P. C. 98.
[m] Supra Section 62. S. P. C. 98. Letter b.
[n] Supra Section 32. S. P. C. 98. Letter c.
[o] S P C. 98. Letter c.
[p] Supra Sect. 32.
[q] 1 Inst. 138. b. 139. a. H. P C. 190. 8 Co. 58. 62.
[r] S. P. C. 148. Letters a. b.
[s] 10 H. 4 4. pl. 14.
[t] S. P. C. 148. Letters a. b. 22 Ass. pl. 97.
[u] H. P. C. 190. S. P. C. 148. Letters a. b. Cro. El. 605.
[x] Salkeld 64. Vide f. n. b. 26. Letter p.

ſuit after ſuch an Appearance is peremptory. Alſo it is holden generally in ſome Books, [a] That a Nonſuit after Appearance is a peremptory Bar to the Appellant, without adding that he muſt alſo have declared; from whence, and alſo from the general Reaſon of the Thing, it may be reaſonably argued, That if it any way appear on Record that the Appellant who was nonſuited in a former Appeal, did actually appear and proſecute ſuch Appeal, as by praying [b] of Proceſs on it, *&c.* he ſhall be barred in any other Appeal of the ſame Kind. But it ſeems [c] that the bare taking out of a Writ of Appeal, and cauſing it to be delivered of Record to the Sheriff, and a Nonſuit upon it, is no Bar of a ſecond Appeal, becauſe it doth not appear of Record, but that it might be done by a Stranger; and notwithſtanding ſome Books [d] ſeem to hold generally, that any Nonſuit in Appeal is peremptory, yet it ſeems to be in great Meaſure ſettled [e] at this Day, that ſuch Nonſuit ought to be after an Appearance in proper Perſon of Record.

Sect. 130. As to the third Particular, *viz.* Whether a Diſcontinuance of a former Appeal of this Kind will be a good Bar of another, it is holden [f] by the Reporter of the Year-Book of 16 *Ed.* 4. That a Diſcontinuance of one Appeal is a Bar of any other, becauſe the Life of the Appellee was once put in Jeopardy by the firſt Appeal; but this Reaſon proves as ſtrongly that the Abatement of an Appeal where the Writ was good ſhall be a Bar of another; for by an Appeal ſo abated the Life of the Appellee is as much put in Jeopardy as by an Appeal that is diſcontinued; and yet it ſeems to be agreed at this Day, That ſuch an Abatement of an Appeal cannot regularly be a Bar of another, as ſhall be more fully ſhewn in the next Section. Nor can I find it any where adjudged, That the Diſcontinuance of one Appeal is a Bar of another. It is true indeed, that in *Braaley* [g] and *Banks*'s Caſe, the Appellee was totally diſcharged upon a Diſcontinuance. But the Reaſon hereof ſeems to have been, not that the Diſcontinuance would be of it ſelf a Bar to any other Appeal, but becauſe the Year and Day were paſſed, and conſequently there could be no other Appeal, and the Appellee had alſo been before convicted on an Indictment, and had his Clergy, and conſequently could not be proceeded againſt at the Suit of the King. However, Granting the Opinion aforementioned to be Law, that the Diſcontinuance of one Appeal ſhall be a good Bar of any other; ſurely it is to be intended of ſuch a Diſcontinuance only, as happens after the Appearance of the Appellant, for the Reaſons given in the precedent Section, in relation to a Nonſuit.

Sect. 131. As to the fourth Particular, *viz.* Whether an Abatement of a former Appeal of this Kind will be a good Bar of another, it ſeems clear, That if an Appeal by a Wife abate by her taking another Husband, or an Appeal by an Heir abate by his Death, there can be no [h] other Appeal. But the Reaſon hereof ſeems not ſo much to depend on the Abatement, as on the Marriage in the firſt Caſe, and the Death in the ſecond, which, as it ſeems the better [i] Opinion, would of themſelves have abated a ſubſequent Appeal, whether any had been brought before or not. Yet I find it holden generally in ſome [k] of the Old Books, that an Appeal once determined, cannot revive; and in [l] others, that where an Appeal of Maihem, which in this Reſpect ſeems not to differ from other Appeals, is abated without the Default of the Party, he may have a new one, by which it ſeems to be implied, that if it abated by his Default he cannot have a new one; and this Opinion ſeems alſo to be confirmed by ſome

[a] 22 Aſs. pl. 97. 47 Ed. 3. 16 pl. 27. Bro. Appeal 28. 71. Fitz. coro. 184. 1 Inſt. 139. a. Vide 4 H. 6. 16 a. Supra Sect. 26. 9 H. 4. 2. b. 3. a. 47 Aſs. pl. 7.

[b] Vide 7 H. 7. 6. pl. 10.

[c] S. P. C. 148. Letter a. 7 H. 7. 6. pl. 10. 1 Sid. 32.

[d] 27 Aſs pl. 7. Cro. El. 605. Vide 4 H 6. 16. a. 1 Sid. 32.

[e] See the Books cited to the other Prints of this Section.

[f] 16 Ed. 4. 11. pl. 7. Bro. Appeal 103. Vide S. P. C. 59. G.

[g] 1 Bulſt. 141. Cro. Jac. 283, 284. Yelv. 204.

[h] Vide S. P. C. 147. Letter e. H. P. C. 200.

[i] Vide ſupra Sect. 38, 39, 41.

[k] 6 H. 4. 6. pl. 29. Bro. Appeal 10.

[l] 50 Ed. 3. 1. pl. 2. Bro. Appeal 16.

other

other [a] Old Books, but it is denied [b] by others. However, I take it to be settled [c] at this Day, That where there continues to be a Plaintiff, not disabled to prosecute, he shall not be barred in a second Appeal by an Abatement of the first.

Sect. 132. As to the fifth Particular, *viz.* Where the bringing of an Appeal of this Kind, against one Person will be a Bar of any subsequent Appeal against any other Person not named in the first; it is said, [d] That anciently one might have had two Appeals for the same Fact, one against the Principal, the other against the Accessary. And even at this Day, if one be robbed of the same [e] Goods, at several times, or receive different [f] Maims, whether at the same or at several times; or a Woman be ravish'd more than once, whether by the same or by different Persons, it seems clear that several Appeals lie for each distinct Offence. But it seems to be generally [g] agreed at this Day, That after one hath brought an Appeal of Felony against one Person, who is thereon attainted and hanged; he may be barred by it in any subsequent Appeal, for the very same Crime, against any other Person not named in the first; whether such subsequent Appeal, against the Person so omitted in the first, be brought against him as Principal, or as Accessary [h] before the Fact, or even as Accessary after the Fact, unless where he happens to be so Accessary after the first Appeal was commenced; in which Case it is certain that he is liable to such second [i] Appeal, because it was impossible to charge him in the first. But otherwise, after an Attainder had on the first Appeal, the Law seems to disallow the bringing of a second; for this Reason, That where an Appellant has so far had his Revenge in one Appeal, he shall not be indulged in the bringing of another, which his own Laches only made necessary. Also it seems to be [k] clear, That if one bring an Appeal of Felony against another, who is either acquitted by Verdict, or otherwise finally discharged by any other Matter, which will peremptorily bar any other Appeal against him by the same Appellant, for the same Fact, the Appellant may also be barred in any other Appeal for the same Fact, against any other Person whatsoever; perhaps for this Reason, That he who appears to have brought an ill-grounded Action of so high a Nature, or to have so far made Default in the Prosecution of such an Action as to be for ever barred from bringing another against the same Defendant, shall not be thought worthy to bring another against any other Person whatsoever. But I cannot be satisfied with the Reason which some of the Books seem to give why all the Defendants must be named in one Appeal; which is this, That the Statute of *Magna Charta* 34, by which is provided, *That none shall be imprisoned upon the Appeal of a Woman, for the Death of any other than her own Husband*, speaks only of Appeal in the singular Number, from whence it is said to be collected, that all the Defendants must be named in one Appeal. But by what kind of Argument this Collection is made, I do not find, nor do I see why twenty Appeals brought by the same Woman, if the Law would permit so many, are not as much within the Letter and Meaning of the Statute as one Appeal. And where the Law does permit the bringing of a second Appeal against the same Person, as it is clear that in some Cases it does, it may reasonably be argued, That he may as well bring it against others also; As [g] where the first is abated, and there still continues to be a Plaintiff, not disabled to prosecute, [n] and in some other Cases: For if an Appellant be not barred by the Abatement of his first Appeal, from bringing a second against those who had Vexation by the first, and were legally discharged from it, why should he be barred by it, as to those who were not concerned in it?

[a] 9 H. 5. 1. pl 3. Bro Appeal 38 44. 4 H. 6. 16. a.
[b] Bro. Appeal 53. 118, 146. 13 Ass. pl. 10.
[c] Vide supra Sect. 4.
[d] S. P. C. 65. Letter C.
[e] S. P. C. 65. Letter d.
[f] 9 H. 4. 2. a. 11 H. 4. 14. a. Bro. Appeal 28.
[g] Bro. Appeal 32. 11 H. 4. 13. b. 14. a.
[h] H. P. C. 190. S. P. C. 65. Letters 98. Letter C. Bro. Appeal 14. 28. 4 Co. 47. b. Vide supra Ch. 6 Sect. 5.
[i] Keilw. 83. a. seems contrary as to Appeals of Robbery.
[k] 28 Ed. 3. 90. pl. 138. 26 Ass. pl. 42. Keilw. 83. a. 4 Co. 44. b. 48. a.
[l] 47 Ed. 3. 16. pl. 27. Fitz. 1 Cro. 104. 9 H. 4. 2. a. H. P. C. 188, 190. 190 S. P. C. 98. Letter c. 47 Ass pl. 7.
[m] 28 Ed. 3. 90. pl 138. 4 Co. 48.
[n] See the precedent Section.

Sect.

Sect. 133. As to the sixth Particular, *viz.* Where a Release will be a good Bar of an Appeal of this Kind, it seems clear, That a Release of all manner of Actions, or of all Actions [a] Criminal, or of all Actions [b] Mortal, or of all Actions concerning *Pleas of the Crown*, or of all [c] Appeals, or of all [d] Demands, will be a good Bar of any such Appeal. But it [e] seems that a Release of all Actions Personal will not bar such an Appeal, because that an Appeal in which the Appellee is to have Judgment of Death, is higher than an Action Personal, and not properly called an Action Personal. Also it seems [f] clear, That whatsoever the Nature of the Release may be, it shall not wholly discharge the Appeal, unless it were made before it was commenced; for if it be subsequent to the Appeal, it shall only discharge it as to the Suit of the Plaintiff, and after Judgment given for such Discharge, he shall be arraigned on the Appeal at the King's Suit, as shall be shewn more at large in the Chapter of Indictments. Also it is [g] certain, That no Release shall discharge a Person attainted, without the King's Pardon.

Sect. 134. As to the seventh Particular, *viz.* Where the Appellant may be barred as to one Appellee, and continue his Suit against the rest, it [h] seems, That if he be barred by a Release given, or *Retraxit* entred as to one, or by being vanquished in Battel by one, yet he may continue his Suit against the rest, because he is to have a several Execution against every one of them. Yet in an Appeal against divers, whether they plead the same or several Issues, it hath been adjudged, [i] That a Nonsuit against one, at the Trial of any one of the Issues, is a Nonsuit as to all, of which this seems to be the best Reason, That [k] such a Nonsuit operates in Nature as a Release of the whole. But whether [l] the Discontinuance of an Appeal, as to one Appellee, shall have the like Construction as to all, may deserve to be considered.

Sect. 135. As to the eighth Particular, *viz.* Whether any, and which of the Pleas abovementioned are consistent with the general Issue, it seems agreed at this Day, That if the Defendant in an Appeal of Death, by a [m] Wife, plead *Nunques accouple in loial Matrimony*, [n] or in an Appeal of Death, by one as Heir, plead that the Appellant is a Bastard, [o] or that he hath an elder Brother of the whole Blood alive, or in [p] any Appeal of Death plead that the Person supposed to have been killed, was dead above a Year before the Purchase of the Writ, or that [q] the Appellant hath formerly brought an Appeal for the same Fact against another Person, who was thereon attainted and hanged, or generally [r] any other Plea, not amounting to an implied Confession of the Fact, as a Release, *&c.* Whether it be triable by Matter [s] of Record, or by *Pais*; and whether it [t] deny that the Appellant had ever any Right to the Appeal, or admit that he once had a Right, but shew that he is now barred; he may, together, with such Plea in Bar, plead also Not guilty to the Felony. And if such Plea be triable by the Common Law, unless the Appellant reply both to that, and also to the Plea of Not guilty, he discontinues the Appeal; but [u] if it be not triable by the Common Law, the Defendant needs only to reply to it, and not to the Felony, till after such Plea has been tried. But it is holden in many Books [x] of good Authority, That a Man shall not be admitted to plead a Release, and the general Issue also, because it is repugnant at the same time to insist that the Crime is re-

[a] Littleton Sections 500, 501.
[b] 1 Inst. 287. b. 288. a.
[c] Littleton Section 501.
[d] Littleton Section 508.
[e] Littleton Section 500, 501. Contra Fitz. Release 46. Quære Bro. Appeal 29. 21 Ed. 4. 72. 9 H. 4. 2. pl. 8. Vide supra Section 25.
[f] Fitz. coro. 12. S. P. C. 148. Letter B. H. P. C. 200. Rastal's Entry 43. pl. 8. 48. a.
[g] Supra. Sect. 38, 42.
[h] H. P. C. 190. 21 Ed. 4. 72. a. b. 2 R 3. 9. pl. 18. Bro. Appeal 111, 120.
[i] Cro. El. 460. pl. 6. Dyer 120. pl. 11. 7 H. 6. 27. pl. 19. 27 Ed. 3. 87. pl. 45. 2 Roll's Ab. 133 Letter H. 1 Inst. 139. 1 Sid 378. pl 7 Bro Discontinuance *de process* 20.
[k] Hob. 180.
[l] Vide 7 H. 6. 27. pl. 19 30 Ass pl. 36. 39 Ed. 3. 3. a. 38 Ass. pl. 17. 27 Ed 3. 87. pl. 45.
[m] 3 Leon. 268. Cro. El 223.
[n] 7 Ed. 4. 15. pl. 3. Quære 14 Ed. 4. 7. pl. 10.
[o] Rastal's Entries 49. pl. 5. 7 Ed. 4. 15. pl. 3. Quære 14 Ed. 4. 7. pl. 10. [o] 21 H. 6. 29 a. [p] 22 Ed. 4. 39. b. [q] 9 H. 4. 2. pl. 7. [r] 21 H. 6. 29. a 22 Ed. 4. 39. b. 40. Rastal's Entries 49. pl. 6. 7. 50. pl. 8. 583. b. 584. S. P. C. 98. Letter D. Keil. 188, 189. [s] 21 H. 6. 28, 29. 4 H. 7. 5. pl. 1. 9 H. 4. 2. pl. 7 35 H. 6. 57. pl. 2. 8 Ed. 4. 3. pl. 6. Con. Bro. Apeal 14. 48. 4 H. 7. 5. b. 6. a [t] 7 Ed. 4. 14 pl. 3. 21 H. 6. 29. a. [u] Cro. El. 223. 3 Leon. 268. [x] S. P. C. 68. Letter D. Finch 385, 386. H. P. C. 190, 191. Hob. 170, 171.

leased, and [a] yet that there was no such Crime committed to be released. But I do not find this Point any where adjudged; and as to the Argument abovementioned, from the Repugnancy of the Plea of a Release, to the general Issue, it may be answered, That a Man may reasonably take a Release to free himself from Trouble, from the Suspicion of a Crime, of which he would by no means own himself guilty; and in Appeals of Death after a Plea of [b] *Autrefoits convict* by Verdict, and even after the Plea of [c] *Autrefoits convict* by Confession, and Clergy thereon had, the general Issue has been received; and yet such Pleas as much imply a Confession of the Fact, as the Plea of a Release. And in *Smith*'s Case, who was indicted of High Treason in the beginning of his present Majesty's Reign, for the Murder of Colonel *Parks*, after a Plea of a Pardon, the general Issue was received. However, I do not find it any where holden, That the Plea of a Release may not be pleaded, if the Defendant think fit, without Pleading the general Issue. Also it seems questionable, [d] Whether any other Plea in Bar, whether triable by Matter of Record, or by *Pais*, may not also be received without Pleading the general Issue, as it seems clear, That in some Cases it may, [e] as where it declines the Jurisdiction of the Court, [f] or would be prejudicial to the Defendant by infranchising the Plaintiff, as where a Villain brings an Appeal of Robbery against his Lord, who pleads the Villenage in Bar, in which Case he shall not be compelled to plead Not guilty, because that would amount to an Infranchisement of the Plaintiff; by supposing that the Fact, if committed, needs a Defence, which it cannot do unless the Plaintiff have a Property, which if he be a Villain, he cannot have against his Lord. Also, It seems clear, That [g] if any of the Bars abovementioned, except that of a Release, be suffered to be pleaded without the general Issue, and be found against the Defendant, they do not conclude him from pleading the general Issue afterwards; and as to the Plea of a Release, whether that being pleaded without the general Issue, and found against the Defendant, do conclude him at this Day to plead the general Issue afterwards, may deserve to be considered for the Reasons abovementioned. [h] But it seems, That if a Demurrer to the Court be adjudged against an Appellee, he shall not be admitted to plead either in Bar, or the general Issue, but shall be condemned, as shall be shewn more at large in the Chapter of Demurrers.

Sect. 136. As to the sixth general Point, *viz.* Where the Appellant shall render Damages to the Appellee for a false Appeal, having premised that by the Common Law a Defendant may [i] recover Damages for a false and malicious Appeal, against the Appellant and his Abettors, by a Writ of Conspiracy, or an Action on the Case, in the Nature of such Writ, as hath been more fully shewn in Book 1. [k] I shall here endeavour to shew in what Cases, and in what Manner, he may, if he chuse rather so to proceed, recover such Damages by the Statute of *Westminster* 2. 12. which was made for his speedier Remedy, and is enacted as followeth,

Sect. 137. *Forasmuch as many through Malice intending to grieve others, do procure false Appeals to be made, of Homicides and other Felonies, by Appellors, having nothing to satisfie the King for their false Appeal, nor to the Parties appealed for their Damages: It is ordained, That when any being appealed of Felony, surmised upon him, doth acquit himself in the King's Court in due Manner, either at the Suit of the Appellor, or of our Lord the King, the Justices be-*

[a] Hob. 270, 271.
[b] 1 Bulst. 141. Yelv. 204. Cro Jac. 283. 4 Co. 45.
[c] And. 68.
[d] Finch 385. S. P. C. 151. Letter A. 22 Ed. 4. 39. b. 40. Shower's Reports 47.
[e] Widdrington and Charlton, Trin. 11. Annæ. 50 Ed 3. 15. 28 Ed. 3. 91. pl. 4. 27 Ass. pl. 41. 35 H. 6. 57. pl. 2. 8 Ed. 4. 3. pl. 6.
[f] Keilw. 175. pl. 10. 91. pl. 1. 186. pl. 3. Rastal's Entries 54 a.
[g] 18 Ed. 3. 32 pl. 4. H. P. C. 191. S. P. C. 98. Letter D. Vide Littleton, Section 192, 193, 194. 208.
[h] 14 Ed. 4. 7. pl. 10. 50 Ed. 3. 15, 16. a. 28 Ed. 91. pl. 4. S. P. C. 98. Letter D. Fitz. Coro. 429. 27 Ass. pl. 3. Contra 7 Ed. 4. 15 pl. 3. Keilw. 100. H. P. C. 190, 191. Finch 385, 386.
[k] H. P. C. 243. Sect. 2 and 3.

14 Ed. 4. 7. pl. 10. Keilw. 100. [i] Inst. 283. Keilw. 27. a. S. P. C. 167. b. [k] Book 1.

fore whom the Appeal ſhall be heard and determined, ſhall puniſh the Appellor, by a Year's Impriſonment; and the Appellor ſhall nevertheleſs reſtore to the Parties appealed their Damages, according to the Diſcretion of the Juſtices, having Reſpect to the Impriſonment or Arreſtment, that the Party appealed hath ſuſtained by Reaſon of ſuch Appeals, and to the Infamy that they have incurred by the Impriſonment, or otherwiſe; and ſhall nevertheleſs make a grievous Fine unto the King. And if peradventure ſuch Appellor be not able to recompence the Damages, it ſhall be inquired by whoſe Abetment, by Malice, the Appeal was commenced, if the Party applealed deſire it. And if it be found by the ſame Inqueſt, that any Man is Abettor through Malice, he ſhall be diſtrained by a judicial Writ at the Suit of the Party appealed to come before the Juſtices. And if he be lawfully convict of ſuch malicious Abetment, he ſhall be puniſhed by Impriſonment and Reſtitution of Damages, as before is ſaid of the Appellor.

And for the better underſtanding this Statute, I ſhall endeavour to ſhew how the ſeveral Parts of it have been expounded.

Sect. 138. And firſt, Whereas the Words of the Preamble are, *That many through Malice procure falſe Appeals to be made by Appellors, having nothing,* &c. And in the Purview it is ſaid, *That it ſhall be inquired by whoſe Abetment, by Malice, the Appeal was commenced,* &c. *And if it be found that any Man is an Abettor, through Malice,* &c. In all which Places the Malice is expreſly referred to the Procurers and Abettors only, and in no part of the Statute to the Appellant, it is holden by [a] ſome, That where-ever an Appellee is acquitted of an Appeal of Felony, he ſhall recover Damages by Force of this Statute againſt the Appellant, except only where he hath been indicted of the ſame Felony before. And it muſt be confeſſed, That in the [b] Reports and Entries [c] relating to this Matter, Damages ſeem generally of Courſe to have been awarded againſt the Appellant, on the Acquittal of the Appellee in all other Caſes, without any finding that the Appeal was malicious. Yet it is holden by [d] others, That the Appellant is no more within the Intent of the Statute, than his Abettors, unleſs his Appeal were grounded on Malice. And if it be conſidered, That where the Appellant is to render Damages by Force of the Statute, he is alſo, by the expreſs Words of it, to have a Year's Impriſonment, and to be grievouſly ranſomed to the King; ſurely it cannot be imagined that the Makers of the Statute intended in any Caſe to expoſe him to ſo ſevere a Puniſhment, for a legal Proſecution, which he has reaſonable Evidence to induce him to commence, though it may not be ſufficient to induce a Jury to convict the Defendant. Neither do I ſee any Reaſon why the bringing an Appeal againſt one who hath been before indicted, by a ſufficient Indictment [e] of the very ſame [f] Crime, which is agreed [g] not to be within the Meaning of the Statute, ſhould be the only excepted Caſe; eſpecially conſidering that any other Caſe, wherein the Appellant plainly appears to proceed on a probable Ground of Suſpicion, is within the Reaſon given in many Books [h] for the the Favour ſhewn to the Appellant, where the Appellee has been indicted before; which is this, that the Appellant had Cauſe and Evidence to purſue the Appeal, and it appears to the Court that it was not merely founded on Malice. And this is alſo one of the Reaſons given in the [i] Books, why the Appellant is not to render Damages, by the Intent of the Statute, where the Appellee in an Appeal of Murder is found guilty of Homicide, *ſe defendendo* only. And as to the general Expreſſions of the

[a] 1 Inſt. 139. b. 2 Inſt. 384. Vide Littleton, Section 208. 22 Aſs. pl. 39. 26 H. 8. 3. pl. 14.
[b] See the Books cited under this and the following Sections.
[c] Raſtal's Entries, 56. pl. 2.
[d] S. P. C. 168. Letter B. See L. Quinto, Ed. 4. 1:6 a. 40 Ed. 3. 42. pl 24.
[e] 20 Ed. 4. 6. pl. 5. 2 Inſt. 384.
[f] 26 H. 8. 3. pl. 14. 33 H. 6. 1. pl. 6. 40 Ed. 3. 42. 24. 14 H. 7. 2. pl. 8. 40 Aſs. pl. 18.
[g] 22 Aſs. pl. 39. 26 H. 8. 3. pl. 14. 33 H. 6. 1. pl. 6. 40 Ed. 3. 42 pl. 24 14 H 7. 2. pl. 8. 20 Ed. 6 pl. 5. 40 Aſs. pl. 18. Fitz. Damages 67.
[h] 40 Ed. 3. 42. pl. 24. 14 H. 7. 2. pl. 8.
[i] 21 Aſs pl. 77. 2 Inſt. 384.

the Books abovementioned, in which Damages seem of Course to be awarded against the Appellant, without any Inquiry whether his Appeal were Malicious or not; it may be answered, That the Books speak as generally in Relation to the Recovery of the Damages against the Abettors; and yet it seems [a] plain from the whole Purport of the Statute, That they are not within the Purview of it, unless their Abetment were founded on Malice. And some [b] seem to have gone so far as to hold, That the Heir who abets his Mother in bringing an Appeal for the Death of his Father, can be in no Case within the Statute, by Reason of such Abetment; because Nature and Duty oblige him, in such a Case, to abet his Mother. But this Reasoning, if strictly examined, seems to prove no more than this, That in such a Case the Heir shall *prima facie* be intended to have abetted the Appellant, rather out of Duty than Malice, and that therefore he shall not be taken to be within the Purview of the Statute, without very strong Evidence of his Malice. But surely it cannot be denied, That in some Cases it may be notorious, That an Heir abets such an Appeal, not out of Duty but Malice; as where he himself, without the least probable ground of Suspicion, is the first Promoter of the Prosecution; or where he causes it to be carried on by violent and unfair Methods, not for the Sake of Justice but Oppression, in which Cases it seems harsh to say, That he is not as well within the Meaning as Letter of the Statute.

[a] 2 Inst. 384. S. P. C. 168. Letter B. P. C. Com. 88 b. *seems contrary.* Vide Dy. 120 pl. 10.

[b] Fitz. Champerty 10. P. C. Com. 88. b. 2 Inst. 384.

Sect. 139 Secondly, In the Construction of the Words *Homicides and other Felonies*, in the Preamble of the Statute, it hath [c] been adjudged That the Purview of it extends to Rape, which was made a Felony by another [d] Branch of the same Statute; and it is [e] holden, both by *Coke* and *Staundforde*, That, it in like manner extends to Offences made Felonies by any subsequent Statute.

[c] Fitz. Coro. 275. 381. P. C. com. 124. b.

[d] Supra Sect. 59, 60.

[e] 2 Inst. 384. S. P. C. 198. Letter D.

Sect. 140. Thirdly, In the Construction of these Words, *When any being appealed of Felony surmised upon him, doth acquit himself in the King's Court in due Manner, either at the Suit of the Appellor, or of our Lord the King*; it seems to have been generally agreed, That no Acquittal is within the Intention of the Statute, [f] unless it be had on an Appeal, (either at the Suit of the Party, or of the King, after a Nonsuit of the Party,) and be of such a Nature as [g] finally to bar all other Prosecutions for the same Felony, whether at the Suit of the King, or of the same, or any other Party. And therefore it seems clear, That no Damages shall be recovered on the [h] Abatement of an Appeal, nor on the bare [i] Nonsuit of the Appellant, nor where the Appellant is barred, either by a [k] Demurrer, or by a [l] Plea, shewing that he is not intitled to the Appeal, nor on any Acquittal on an insufficient [m] Original; because in all these Cases the Appellee is liable to another Prosecution for the same Felony. And if a Person appealed of Murder, be found guilty [n] of Homicide by Misadventure, or *Se defendendo*, which will be a Bar of any other Prosecution for the same Killing, yet it hath been resolved that he shall not recover Damages, not [o] only because it appears that the Appeal was not groundless, but also because the Appellee is not totally acquitted. But it is [p] clear, That the Appellee is intitled to his Damages, where he is acquitted on an Appeal at the Suit of the King, after a Nonsuit of the Plaintiff, or where he vanquishes [q] the Appellant in a Trial by Battel. Also if two be appealed, the one as Principal, and the other as Accessary; and the Jury being

[f] S.P.C. 169. Letter B. 2 Inst. 385. Vide 14 H. 7. 2. pl. 8.

[g] S. P. C. 169.

[h] 4 Co. 47. b. S. P. C. 169. Letter A. 9 H. 4. 2. b. Vide 9 H. 5. 1. Pl. 3.

[i] 2 Inst. 385. Fitz. conspiracy 25. But 33 H. 1. pl. 6. Fitz. Coro. 102. 48 Ed. 3. 21. pl. 2. *seem doubtful in this Case.*

[k] 2 Inst. 385. Fitz. Coro. 12. S. P. C. 169. Letter A. [l] 27 Ass. pl. 25. 2 Inst. 385. S. P. C. 169. [m] 4 Co. 45. a. 47. a. Fitz. Coro. 444. 9 H. 5. 2. S. P. S. 169. [n] 22 Ass. pl. 77. 2 Inst. 385. S. P. C. 199. [o] Vide Supra Sect. 138. pl. 8. [p] 41 Ass. & 24. Fitz. Coro. 275. 381. Damages 77. [q] Fitz. Coro. 98. S. P. C. 169. Letter E.

ing

ing charged on the Acceſſary, as well as the Principal, do acquit the Principal; it ſeems to be [a] agreed, That the Acceſſary ſhall recover Damages, by the Intent of the Statute, without any expreſs Verdict concerning him, becauſe he is impliedly acquitted by the Acquittal of the Principal; for it is impoſſible that there ſhould be an Acceſſary where there is no Principal. And this Reaſon ſeems to hold as ſtrongly for the Damages, where the Acceſſary doth not appear on the Trial or Acquittal of the Principal, becauſe in ſuch Caſe the Acquittal of the Principal is as [b] much an Acquittal of the Acceſſary, as where he doth appear. But it is holden [c] by Sir *Edward Coke*, That ſuch an Acceſſary ſhall not recover Damages, becauſe no Jury can be retorned to aſſeſs them; and Sir *William Staundforde* [d] ſeems to be of Opinion, That ſuch an Acceſſary ſhall not recover Damages, unleſs he be expreſly acquitted by Verdict, after the Acquittal of the Principal. Yet whether [e] the Juſtices themſelves may not, in a Caſe of this Nature, if they think fit, aſſeſs the Damages, without any Jury, or elſe aſſeſs them by an Inqueſt of Office, may deſerve to be conſidered. Alſo it ſeems to be to little Purpoſe to require an actual Acquittal of a Perſon, where it appears by the Acquittal of another, that he could not be guilty. However it ſeems clear, That a Perſon appealed as Acceſſary to two Principals, ſhall not [f] recover Damages by the Acquittal of one of them; becauſe for what appears he might be acceſſary to the other. Neither [g] ſhall he recover Damages where he is diſcharged by the Death of the Principal, before his Attainder, becauſe it doth not appear but that he might have been guilty.

[a] P. S. P. 168. F. 169. 2 Inſt. 385. 33 H. 6. 1. pl 6.
[b] 33 H. 6. 1. pl. 6
[c] 2 Inſt. 385.
[d] S. P. C. 168. Letter F. Vide 41 Aſſ. pl. 24.
[e] Vide ſupra Sect. 52, 53.
[f] 2 Inſt. 385. Dyer 120. pl. 11. Fitz. coro. 463.
[g] S. P. C. 173. Letter A. 33 H. 6. 1. pl. 6.

Sect. 141. It ſeems at this Day, That if a Defendant, appearing upon erroneous Proceſs to a good Appeal, be acquitted, he ſhall recover Damages by the Intent of the ſaid Clauſe, becauſe ſuch an Acquittal is a good Bar of any other Proſecution for the ſame Felony, and the Life of the Appellee was put in Danger by the [h] Appeal. But there were formerly ſome Opinions, That the Appellee in ſuch a Caſe ſhould not recover Damages, becauſe his Life was not in Danger at the Time of the Trial, for that he might have taken Advantage of the Error in the Proceſs: But granting it to be a good Rule, That the Defendant ſhall not recover Damages where his Life is not in Danger at the Time of the Trial, which yet I find not confirmed by any Authority, beſides the Year-Book of 9 *H.* 5. 2. it may be anſwered, That in the Caſe in Queſtion the Defendant's Life is in danger at the Time of the Trial, becauſe the Error in the Proceſs is ſalved by his Appearance, as ſhall be ſhewn more at large in the Chapter concerning Proceſs.

[h] 9 H. 5. 2. 2 Inſt. 386. Quære S. P. C. 169. b. Fitz. coro. 444. Yelv. 204. Cro Jac. 284. 4 Co. 45. a.

Sect. 142. If a Perſon who has taken a Releaſe, or prayed the Benefit of the Clergy, waive ſuch Releaſe, or Benefit of Clergy, and put himſelf on his Trial and be acquitted; it is ſaid, [i] that he ſhall recover his Damages, notwithſtanding the Objection that the taking ſuch Releaſe, or making ſuch Prayer, ſeem to carry with them an implied Confeſſion of Guilt.

[i] S. P. C. 169. 173. Letter A. Vide Fitz. coro. 386. & 33 H 6. 1. pl. 6. ſupra Sect.

Sect. 143. Where-ever any Perſon is ſo far acquitted on an Appeal carried on at the Suit of the Party, as to be intitled to his Damages, [k] he ſhall have Judgment for them without any Proceſs to bring in the Party to anſwer to the Damages, becauſe he is ſtill in Court; but where he is ſo acquitted on an Appeal carried on at the Suit of the King after a Nonſuit of the Party, he ſhall not recover Damages, without a *Scire facias*, to bring in the Party, becauſe he was out of Court by the Nonſuit.

[k] S. P. C. 169. Letter C.

Fourthly, In the Construction of theſe Words, *The Juſtices before whom the Appeal ſhall be heard and determined ſhall puniſh the Appellor by a Year's Impriſonment, and the Appellor ſhall nevertheleſs reſtore to the Parties appealed their Damages, according to the Discretion of the Justices, having Respect to the Imprisonment or Arrestment, that the Party appealed hath sustained by Reason of such Appeals, and to the Infamy that they have incurred by the Imprisonment, or otherwise,* &c. the following Points have been holden.

Sect. 141. First, That Justices of *Nisi prius* [a] have no Power to give Judgment for such Imprisonment or Damages, upon an Acquittal before them, whether before or since the Statute of 14 *H.* 6; by which it is enacted, *That such Justices shall have Power in all Cases of Felony or Treason, to give their Judgments, as well where a Man is acquitted, as where he is attainted.* For [b] the Words abovementioned in the Statute of *Westminster* 2, are to be intended of such Justices only before whom the whole Plea of the Appeal is heard and determined, and therefore in Strictness can extend to the Justices of the King's Bench only, where the Appeal is commenced before them, (for that the whole Appeal is in such Case heard and determined before them, either in Person, or else by others delegated by, and representing them,) and not to the Justices of *Nisi prius*, who have nothing to do with the Appeal before the Trial, nor any Original Power to try it. And the Statute abovementioned of 14 *H.* 6. hath been construed to intend only to enable Justices of *Nisi prius* to give the Principal Judgment, and not to transfer to them from the Court of King's Bench, a Power in collateral Matters. Yet [c] Justices of *Nisi prius* have by Usage not now to be disputed, gained a Power to assess the Damages, and to inquire of the Sufficiency of the Plaintiff to answer them, and also of the Abettors. But I do not find that they have ever given Judgment for the Damages. Yet there is no Doubt [d] but, That if such Justices be also Justices of Assise, and as such have an Appeal commenced before them, they may, as Justices of Assise, upon the Acquittal of the Appellee, not only inquire of the Damages, &c. but also give Judgment for them, both by the Letter and Meaning of the Statute.

Sect 142. Secondly, That if a Jury give too small Damages to the Appellee, the Court may encrease [e] them; from which it seems to follow, That if a Jury give too large Damages the Court may abridge them. And surely no less can be implied by the Statutes ordering, That the Damages shall be given according to the Discretion of the Justices, Respect being had to the Imprisonment, &c. And this Construction also seems agreeable to the Rules of Law in other Cases, by which the Court is said [f] to have a general discretionary Power, except in some special Cases, as Local [g] Trespasses, &c. either to increase or abridge the Damages found by an Inquest of Office; and where a Jury which hath acquitted an Appellee inquires afterwards of the Damages, it seems in Respect of such Inquiry to be no more than an Inquest of Office, tho' it were returned to try the Cause.

Sect. 143. Thirdly, That if there be several Appellees, and all of them acquitted, the Damages ought to be severally [h] assessed as to every one of them; and this doubtless is agreeable both to the Letter and Meaning of the Statute, which provides that in the giving the Damages, Respect shall be had to the Imprisonment and Infamy, and other Damage sustained by Reason of the Appeal; and these being several, and receiving different Aggravations from the different Circumstances of each Person's particular Case, it cannot but be reasonable, That the Damages be assessed severally also.

[a] 10 Ed 4. 14. pl 12. 22 Ed. 4. 19 pl. 44. S. P. C. 169. Letter D. 2 Inst. 386.
[b] S P. C. 169 Letter D.
[c] 4 Co. 93 b. 2 Inst. 386. Dyer 120. pl. 10, 11, 12, 13. B. o. Appeal 113. Fitz. coro. 463. 8 H. 5. 6. pl. 26.
[d] 22 Ed 4. 19. pl. 44 B o. Appeal 113.
[e] Co El. 223. Vide 2 Inst. 387. 42 Ass. pl. 19. seems to be contrary.
[f] 3 H 6 29. b. 14 H. 4. 9 b. 8 H. 4. 23. pl 9. 3 H 4 4. pl. 16. 7 H. 6. 31. pl. 16. 19 H 6. 10. pl. 28. Bro. Abridment 36. Vide 27 H. 8. 2. pl. 8 & supra Sect 52.
[g] 27 H. 8. 2. pl. 8 19 H 6. 42. pl. 86. 19 H. 6. 10. pl. 28.

Vide 3 H. 6. 29. b. [h] S. P. C. 170. Letter A. Dyer 120. pl. 10. 11 H. 4. 16. b. 12 Co. 126. 2 Inst. 386. 41 Ass. pl. 24. Fitz. Damage 77. 8 H. 5, 6. pl. 26.

Sect. 144. Fourthly, That a Monk or Feme Covert, being appealed without the Abbot, or Husband, cannot have a Judgment for the Damages on their Acquittal, because they are disabled by the Law to recover any Damages without the Abbot or Husband; and the general Words of a Statute shall not be construed to enable Persons in a Point, wherein the Common Law hath disabled them. But the Authority of this Opinion, as to a Wife, is questioned by [a] *Hobart*, neither do any of those [b] who seem to give it greater Weight, bring any other Proof of it, than a Note in *Fitzherbert*'s Abridgment, of a Resolution to such Purpose, in the Time of *Edward* 3. as to the Case of a Monk, and an Assertion, that the Law is the same in the Case of a Wife: Against which it may be plausibly argued, That since the Imprisonment and Infamy sustained by a Feme Covert, in a malicious Appeal against her, are far from being less grievous in Respect of her Coverture, and are a good [c] Ground of a Writ of Conspiracy at the Common Law, brought by the Husband and Wife; and since the Wife may take any Thing to the Benefit of her Husband, and it appears to the Court that the Appellant by his own Act, without any Default either in the Husband or Wife, gives them a good Title to the Damages; and since no express Judgment can be given for the Husband, being not a Party to the Record, and it is most for his Advantage, as well as his Wife's, that a present Judgment be given: It may perhaps be thought no unreasonable Construction of the Statute, that in this particular Case Judgment should be given for the Wife to recover the Damages, which would as much enure, for the Benefit of her self and her Husband, as an express Judgment for them both, on a Writ of Conspiracy.

[a] Hobart 98.
[b] 2 Inst. 385. 11 Co. 77. b. 9 Co. 73 a. 1 Rol. Rep. 170. S. P. C. 170. Letter B. Fitz. coro. 276.
[c] 2 Inst. 386. 24 Ed. 3. 73. pl. 90. 1 Inst. 132 b.

However, it is certain, [d] That if the Husband and Wife are both of them appealed and acquitted, they shall have a joint Judgment for the Damage done to the Wife, for which the Wife alone shall sue Execution, if the Husband die without suing it, and the Husband alone shall have Judgment for the Damage done to himself.

[d] Fitz Judgment 108. 2 Inst. 385, 386. 11 H. 4. 16. b. 17. a. S. P. C. 170. Letter B.

Fifthly, In the Construction of the Words, *And if peradventure the Appellor be not able to recompence the Damages, it shall be inquired by whose Abetment, by Malice, the Appeal was commenced, if the Party appealed desire it. And if it be found by the same Inquest, that any Man is Abettor through Malice, he shall be distrained by a judicial Writ, at the Suit of the Party appealed to come before the Justices,* &c. The following Points have been holden.

Sect. 145. First, That [e] the Abettors are in no Case liable to render Damages, where the Appellant himself is not liable, tho' never so sufficient; and this is confirmed by Experience, and the manifest Purport of the Statute, which by directing that the Abettors be inquired of, where the Appellant appears insufficient to answer the Damages, plainly intimates that they are to be inquired of in such Cases only, wherein the Appellant must have answered them if he had been able; and agreeably hereto it seems to be settled, [f] That a Release of Damages to the Appellant will discharge the Abettors, if they can produce it.

[e] S. P. C. 170. Letter D. 171. Letter A. 2 Inst. 386.
[f] 2 Roll. 7. 7. b.

Sect. 146. Secondly, That [g] unless the Appellant be found by the Jury to be insufficient, the Abettors shall not be inquired of; and yet the Statute doth not expresly direct that the Jury shall inquire of the Sufficiency of the Appellant. But it being the general Method of the Law in other Cases, of like Nature, to make an Inquiry by a Jury, it is certainly a reasonable Construction of the general Words of the Statute, that such Inquiry may be made in the present Case. Yet, whether the Justices themselves may not, if they think fit, make such Inquiry without a Jury,

[g] 2 Inst. 386.

it being but an Inquiry of Office, may deserve to be considered for the Reasons in the 52 and 142 Sections of this Chapter. However, There can be no Doubt but that the Insufficiency of the Appellant must appear by one or the other of these Inquiries, before the Abettors can be inquired of.

Sect. 147. Thirdly, That [a] the Abettors may traverse the Jury's finding the Appellant to be insufficient, or that they abetted him, *&c.* For it is hard that a Man should be concluded by any Matter whatsoever, found to his Prejudice in an Action, to which he is no way Privy. Also it is holden by [b] *Staundforde*, That if a Jury on the Acquittal of one Defendant find that there were no Abettors, yet they may afterwards on the Acquittal of another Defendant find that there were Abettors, because there is no Reason that the first Inquest shall bind one who is not Privy to it, and has no Remedy against it. But the contrary hereto is holden in the Book of [c] Assizes, where the Court refused to inquire of the Abettors, on the Acquittal of a Defendant, because it had been found on the Acquittal of another, that there were no Abettors; but this Case, if thoroughly examined, seems repugnant to it self; for the Jury were permitted on the second Acquittal to tax the Damages, which yet are said to have been taxed before; but to what Purpose should this be done, unless it were first found that the Appellant was sufficient, or else that there were Abettors, which could not but control the first finding; as also the second Taxation of the Damages must do, unless it were wholly the same with the first.

Sect. 148. Fourthly, That [d] if the Appellant be found sufficient to render part of the Damages, and not the Whole, Judgment shall be given against the Abettors for the Whole, and not for Part against them, and for the other Part against the Apppellant; for that those Words of the Statute, *If peradventure the Appellor be not able to recompence the Damages*, must be understood of all the Damages.

Sect. 149. Fifthly, That [e] the Appellee after his Acquittal may sue for the Damages by Attorney.

Sect. 150. Sixthly, That [f] though the Statute expresly give only judicial Process for the Recovery of the Damages against the Abettors, yet the Appellee may, if he think fit, take out an Original Writ of Abetment, grounded on the Statute, and therein count to greater Damages than were found by the Jury; which in Respect of such Finding, being but in Nature of an Inquest of Office, shall not conclude the Appellee.

Sect. 151. Seventhly, That [g] if the Appellee chuse rather to proceed for the Recovery of his Damages by judicial Process, than by Original; it is safest for him to make use of a Distress, which is given by the express Words of the Statute; yet there is a Note [h] of an old Case, wherein a *Venire facias* was first awarded; but it is [i] questionable, whether this be justified by the Statute or not.

Sect. 152. Eighthly, That [k] it is time enough for the Appellee to shew the Time and Place of the Abetment, when the Abettors appear upon such Process; and by such Shewing he supplies the Omission of the Jury in not finding any Time or Place, on their Inquiry of the Abetment, *&c.*

Sect 153. Ninethly, That [l] the Nonsuit of an Appellee, either in an Original Writ, or Process against the Abettors, whether before or after Appearance, is no Bar of a second Writ or Process.

[a] S. P. C. 171. Letter A. Quære 8 Ed. 4. 3. pl. 5. 12 Co. 126. 2 Inst 386. Rastal's Entries 44. Bro. Appeal 96.

[b] S. P. C. 170. Letter F.

[c] 41 Ass. 24.

[d] 12 Co. 126. S. P. C. 170. Letter D. 8 Ed. 4. 3. pl. 5. 8 H. 5, 6. pl. 26. 26 H. 8. 3. pl 14. 2 Inst. 386. Fitz coro 29. 386. 463. Bro. Appeal 96 Contra 41 Ass. pl. 8. Fitz. Coro. 219 Bro. Appeal 74.

[e] Fitz. Coro. 13.

[f] Fitz. Action sur le Statute 28. 2 Inst. 386, 387.

[g] S. P. C. 171. Letter D. 2 Inst 139.

[h] S. P. C. 171. Letter B 2 Inst. 386, 387.

[i] Fitz Coro. 102.

[k] S. P C. 171. Letter B. 2 Inst. 386, 387.

[k] S. P. C. 171. Letter A. 2 Inst. 386. Fitz. Coro. 45. [l] S. P. C. 171. Letter C. 2 Inst. 139. Fitz. Coro. 386.

Sect.

[a] S. P. C. 170. Letter C. Fitz. Fines 2. 1 Ass. pl. 9. 22 Ass. pl. 39. 8 H. 4 17. pl. 2.
[b] See the Books cited the following part of this Section. Fitz. Coro. 137. 8 Co. 60. a. S. P. C. 170. Letter C. seems contrary.
[c] 40 Ass pl. 1. Fitz. Coro. 214.
[d] Fitz Fines 49. 41 Ass. pl. 8 Fitz. Coro. 219. Damages 77.

Sect. 154. As to the seventh general Point, *viz.* Where the Appellant is to be fined, there can be no Doubt but [a] that by the express Words of the above expounded Statute of *Westminster* 2, 18. Where-ever the Appellant, or his Abettors are by the Purport thereof to render Damages to an Appellee, they are also to be fined to the King, and imprisoned for a Year. Also it seems clear from the general Purport of the [b] Books, that an Appellant appearing to have brought an ill grounded Appeal, whether of Felony or [c] Maihem, shall be fined, in many Cases wherein he is not liable to render Damages by the Statute abovementioned; as where he is [d] Nonsuit, either against all or part [e] of the Appellees only, whether after, or, as some [f] have holden, before Appearance, or where the Writ abates through the [g] Default of the Appellant in willfully suing by a [h] wrong Name, or a [i] vitious Writ, *&c.* and even a *Feme Covert*, [k] suing an Appeal known by her to be groundless, as for the Death of a Husband whom she knows to be alive, shall be fined. But it is certain that where a Writ abates by the Act [l] of God, or for any other Cause, no way imputable to the Appellant, he shall neither be fined nor amerced. Also it is certain, That an Infant is in no Case to be fined for a false Appeal, but some [m] have holden that he may be amerced, which is contradicted by others, who say, [n] That an Infant can in no Case be amerced.

[e] 22 Ass. pl. 82. Fitz Coro. 182. [f] Fitz. Fines 107. [g] 8 Co. 60. a. [h] 9 H. 5. 1. pl. 3. Fitz. Fines 28. Bro. Fines 16. [i] Fitz. Coro. 121. [k] Bro. Appeal 25. 8 H. 4 17. pl. 2. [l] Fitz. Brief 612. [m] Bro. Fines for Contempt 37. 41 Ass. pl. 14. [n] Co. Lit. 127. Cro. Ca. 161. Vide 1 Danvers's Abridgment 462. L. pl. 1, 2. 463. pl. 8, 9, 10, 13.

CHAP. XXIV.

Of Approver.

[a] S. P. C. 142. 3 Inst. 129. H. P. C. 192.

Sect. 1. HAving gone through the several kinds of Appeals by innocent Persons, I am now in the second Place to consider the Nature of an Appeal by an Offender, confessing himself to be guilty, who is commonly called a Prover or [a] Approver in *English*, or *Probator* in *Latin*; because he must at his Peril prove his Appeal in every Point, and for so doing is pardoned of Course. And for the better understanding the Nature of such Appeal, I shall examine the following Particulars.

1. When a Man may be said to become an Approver.
2. Who may be admitted to be Approvers, and who not.
3. In what Cases.
4. Of what Offences.
5. Against what Offenders.
6. Before what Justices.
7. How they are to be ordered and demeaned, both before and after the Appeal.

8. What Process is to be awarded against the Appellees.
9. In what manner the Court is to proceed upon, and after the Trial.
10. How the Approver is to be rewarded for making good his Appeal.

Sect. 2. As to the first Point, *viz.* When a Man may be said to become an Approver, it seems [a] agreed, That a Man is then properly an Approver, when being indicted of Treason or Felony, before competent Judges, and in Prison for the same, and capable of being an Approver, he confesses the Indictment, and is sworn to reveal all the Treasons and Felonies he knows, and then before a Coroner enters his Appeal against all that were Partners with him in the Crime in the Indictment, being at the Time of the Appeal within the Realm.

As to the second Point, *viz.* Who may be admitted to be Approvers, and who not, I shall observe,

Sect. 3. First, That [b] a Peer of the Realm cannot be an Approver.

Sect. 4. Secondly, That [c] neither a Person attainted of Treason, or Felony, nor even one outlawed in a Personal Action, as some [d] say, can be an Approver, because by his Attainder or Outlawry, he is out of the Law and his Accusation shall not be of such Credit, as to put any Person upon his Trial.

Sect. 5. Thirdly, That [e] an Ideot, or Person born deaf and dumb, or any one that is *Non compos* at the Time, or an Infant under the Age of Discretion, cannot be an Approver, because no such Person ought to be admitted to take the Oath before the Coroner, without which there can be no Approvement.

Sect. 6. Fourthly, That it is holden both by [f] *Staunsforde*, [g] *Coke*, and [h] *Hale*, That no Woman, nor Infant, can be an Approver, but it is observable that the Opinions of *Staundforde* and *Coke*, seem chiefly to be grounded on this Foundation, that the Appellee may have such-like Exceptions against Approvers, as the Defendant may have in an Appeal brought by a lawful Person, and therefore may except that the Approver is within Age, or a Woman, *&c.* because such Persons cannot wage Battel; but it being settled at this Day, That these are no good Exceptions to an Appeal brought by a lawful Person, as hath been more fully shewn in the Precedent [i] Chapter, it seems to be justly questionable, whether they are now to be admitted as good Exceptions to an Appeal, by an Approver. To which may be added, That in the Opinion of [k] *Hale*, contrary to that of [l] *Staundforde*, and [m] *Coke*, a Man above the Age of seventy, or maimed, may be an Approver, though he cannot wage Battel; from whence it follows clearly, That in the Judgment of *Hale*, there is no Necessity that an Approver should be able to wage Battel.

Sect. 7. Fifthly, That it seems to be [n] agreed, That a Person in holy Orders cannot be an Approver, because it is a Rule that no Member of the Clergy can sue any Appeal whatsoever, in a Matter or Cause of Death.

As to the third Point, *viz.* In what Cases one may be admitted to be an Approver, I shall observe,

Sect. 8. First, That no [o] one shall be admitted to be an Appover, till he hath confessed the Crime charged against him in his Indictment.

Sect. 9. Secondly, That it is holden [p] in some Books, That he that hath once pleaded not Guilty, cannot be an Approver, but shall be hanged, because he is found false, and his Confession contradicts his former Plea; yet the contrary hereto is holden by [q] others, and [r] *Staundforde* admits that the

[a] H. P. C. 192. 3 Inst. 129, 130.
[b] 3 Inst. 129 H. P.C. 192.
[c] 3 Inst. 129. H. P. C. 192. S. P. C 146. Letter C.
Bro. Coro. 81. 211. Fitz. Coro. 112, 127, 167, 387, 443. 445. 11 Ass. pl. 27. 17 Ass. pl. 4.
[d] Bro. Appeal 57.
[e] Supra Ch. 23. Sect. 32. Fitz Coro. 175.
[f] 3 Inst. 129. S. P. C. 147. H. P. C 191. Vide Supra Ch. 23. Sect. 32.
[f] S P. C. 147. Letter D.
[g] 3 Inst. 129.
[h] H. P. C. 192.
[i] Sections 30 and 31.
[k] H. P. C. 192.
[l] S. P.C. 147. Letter D.
[m] 3 Inst. 129.
[n] S. P. C. 147. Letters A. B. D. H P C. 192. 3 Inst. 139.
[o] Fitz. Coro. 441. 431.
[p] 3 Inst. 129. H. P. C. 193. S. P. C. 144. Letter B. 145 a. Fitz. Coro. 440.

21 Ed. 3. 18 pl. 25. 19 H. 6. 47. pl. 103. [q] Finch 387. 12 Ed. 4. 10. pl. 26. Vide 2 H. 7. S. P. C. 145.

Court of Grace may admit ſuch Perſons to be Approvers; and this is as much as can be contended for in any other Caſe; for it ſeems [a] agreed, That the Court is not bound of Right, to admit any Perſon whatſoever to be an Approver.

Sect. 10. Thirdly, That it is [b] agreed, That any one indicted of Treaſon or Felony may be an Approver, but that unleſs the Crime with which a Perſon is charged, amount either to Felony or Treaſon, he cannot be an Approver.

Sect. 11. Fourthly, That it is alſo [c] agreed, That no Perſon accuſed of Treaſon or Felony, can be an Approver, unleſs he be actually indicted for it; becauſe his Confeſſion amounts not to a Conviction until he be indicted, and conſequently puts it not in the Power of the Court to give Judgment againſt him, when his Appeal ſhall be rejected or falſified, as every Approvement ought to do.

Sect. 12. Fifthly, That it ſeems alſo to be generally [d] agreed, That if a Perſon indicted be alſo appealed of the ſame Felony, he can no longer be an Approver, the Reaſon whereof ſeems to be, That though the King may in his Diſcretion, by admitting a Perſon to be an Approver, reſpite the Judgment and Execution of one proſecuted by Indictment, which is his own Suit, yet he cannot delay them in an Appeal, which is the Suit of the Party, and *à fortiori*, therefore it follows, That [e] if a Perſon be appealed only, and not indicted, he cannot be an Approver.

Sect. 13. Sixthly, That notwithſtanding the Appeal of an Approver, may in ſome Reſpects be looked upon as the Suit of the King, and equivalent to an Indictment, yet the Appellee [f] of an Approver cannot become an Approver himſelf, not only becauſe it would falſifie the Appeal of the firſt Approver, in ſuppoſing that he had omitted ſome of his Partners, but alſo becauſe it would cauſe an infinite Delay; for the Appellee of ſuch an Approver might as well become an Approver of others, and ſo on.

Sect. 14. As to the fourth Point, *viz.* Of what Offences a Perſon may be admitted to approve another, it ſeems [g] agreed, That no one can approve another of any other Offence, but the very Crime contained in the Indictment; and therefore that he cannot approve a Man of a Crime of a different [h] Nature, nor even of being acceſſory [i] before or [k] after to the ſame Crime, becauſe no Man can abet, or receive himſelf. But it ſeems alſo to be agreed, That inaſmuch as the Oath of an Approver is [l] general, to diſcover all the Treaſons and Felonies he knows, if he accuſe any Perſons of Crimes of a different Nature from his own, whether in the ſame, or a foreign [m] County, his Accuſation will be a reaſonable Ground to carry on a Proſecution againſt them for ſuch Crimes, though it [n] be not of it ſelf of Force ſufficient to put them upon their Trials.

Sect. 15. As to the fifth Point, *viz.* Againſt what Offenders a Perſon may be admitted to become an Approver, it ſeems [o] clear, That a Man may be an Approver againſt any Perſon whatſoever within the Realm, whether he live in the ſame or a foreign County, provided he be named of the County wherein he dwells. But it is ſaid, That if it appear either by the [p] Confeſſion of the Approver, or the Return [q] of the Sheriff, or the Teſtimony [r] of Perſons of Credit in the County, That [s] there are no ſuch Perſons, as ſome of thoſe named in the Appeal, *in rerum natura*, or within the [t] Realm, or even [u] within the County, whereof they are named in the Appeal, the Approver ſhall be hanged, unleſs the [x] Court in Mercy will ſpare him, becauſe his Appeal in reſpect of ſuch Perſons appears to be falſe, or to no purpoſe.

[a] 3 Inſt. 129. H. P. C. 194.
[b] 19 H. 6. 47. pl. 103. 3 Inſt. 129. 21 Ed. 3. 18. pl. 24. Finch 387. Fitz. Coro. 231. 448. Bro. Coro. 41.
[c] 3 Inſt. 129. H. P. C. 193. S. P. C. 143. b. Fitz. Coro. 231. Seems contrary.
[d] 3 Inſt. 129. Finch 387. H. P. C. 193. S. P. C. 147. Letter B. 181 Letter C.
[e] 2 Rich. 3. 22 pl. 53. 11 H. 7. 5. pl. 22. Bro. Coro. 228. Fitz. Coro. 442. 40 Aſs. pl. 39. Seems contrary.
[f] Fitz. Coro. 113. S. P. C. 147. Letter B. 11 H. 4. 93. pl. 54. Seems contrary.
[g] S. P. C. 143. Letter A. H. P. C. 194. 3 Inſt. 129, 130. 2 Inſt 629. Finch 387.
[h] Fitz. Coro. 127, 217. 40 Aſs. pl. 39. 11 H. 4. 93. pl. 54.
[i] 27 Aſs pl. 69. 10 Ed. 4. 14. pl. 8. Fitz. Coro. 35. 208. Bro. Coro. 154.
[k] Fitz. Coro. 126.
[l] 2 Inſt. 629. H. P. C. 194. 12 Ed. 4. 10. pl. 26. Fitz. Coro 37. 387.
[m] Fitz. Coro 437.
[n] Fitz Coro. 126, 127, 387.
[o] Fitz. Aſſiſe 446. Fitz. Coro. 460. S. P. C. 154.
[p] S. P. C. 145. Letter F. 1 Ed. 4. 16. pl. 4. Fitz. Coro. 153.
[q] H. P. C. 194. 21 H. 6. 34. pl. 1.
[r] H. P. C. 195. S. P. C. 145. Fitz. Coro. 133.
[s] Bro. Coro. 29. 21 H 6 34. pl. 1. H. P. C. 195.
[t] 1 Ed. 3 16. pl. 4. 1 Aſs pl. 2. S. P. C. 145.
[u] Fitz. Coro 46.
[x] S. P. C 145.

Sect. 16. As to the sixth Point, *viz.* Before what Justices a Person may be admitted to be an Approver, it seems to be a settled [a] Rule, That a Man may be an Approver before any Justices, who have Power to assign a Coroner to take the Appeal; and for this Reason it seems to be [b] agreed, That one may be an Approver before the Justices of the King's Brench, and Justices of Gaol-Delivery, and Justices in Eyre. And upon this Ground it is holden in Sir *Edward Coke*'s *third* [c] *Institute*, and also in Sir *Matthew Hale*'s [d] *Pleas of the Crown*, under the Chapter of Approver, That a Man may be an Approver before Justices of *Oyer and Terminer*. But the Foundation of this Opinion seems to be overthrown by what is said by both these [e] Authors in other Places, wherein it is holden that Justices of *Oyer and Terminer* cannot Assign a Coroner, because it is not within their Commission: And it seems to be a [f] general Rule, That those only can receive the Appeal of an Approver who can assign a Coroner to take it; and therefore it seems to be agreed, That neither a [g] Court-Baron, nor [h] Justices of Peace, nor any other special [i] Justices, can receive such Appeal, unless their Commission extend to it. And for the like Reason it seems to be the Opinion of [k] Sir *Edward Coke*, That the Lord High Steward of *England* cannot receive such an Appeal; but this is contradicted by [l] Sir *Matthew Hale*.

As to the sixth Point, *viz.* In what manner an Approver is to be ordered and demesned, both before and after the Appeal, the following Particulars seem most remarkable.

Sect. 17. First, That it seems to be [m] agreed, That where-ever a Person indicted of Treason or Felony confesses the Indictment, whether he appealed others or not, he puts it entirely in the Discretion of the Court, either to give Judgment, and award Execution against him, or to respite them till he shall have made good his Appeal.

Sect. 18. Secondly, That [n] whenever a Person is admitted to become an Approver, the Court shall assign a Coroner to receive his Appeal, and shall take an Oath from him to discover all the Treasons and Felonies that he knows.

Sect. 19. Thirdly, That [o] the Court which admits a Man to become an Approver, ought to limit him a certain Number of Days, to make his Appeal in, during which it is holden by [p] some, That he is to have a Penny a-day as his Wages from the King; but by [q] others, That he ought not to have it till he has made good his Appeal, by convicting the Appellees.

Sect. 20. Fourthly, That the Approver during all the Time assigned him for making his Appeal, ought [r] to be at his Liberty, and out of Prison; for [s] he may disavow an Appeal made by Duress of Imprisonment; but if he alledge that an Appeal was extorted from him by such Duress, and such Allegation be found to be false, either by the Examination of the Coroner, or by an Inquest of Office, the Approver shall be hanged.

Sect. 21. Fifthly, That [t] the Approver ought to make his Appeal before the Coroner, on every one of the Days limited for the making of it; for if he fail on any one of them, and the Coroner record such Failure, Judgment shall be given against him.

[a] 3 Inst. 130. S. P. C. 143. Letter C. H. P. C. 194.
[b] 3 Inst. 130. S. P. C. 143. Letter C. H. P. C. 194. Fitz Assise 446.
[c] 3 Inst. 130.
[d] H. P. C. 194.
[e] 4 Inst. 165. H. P. C. 162.
[f] H. P. C. 194. 3 Inst. 130. S. P. C. 143. Letter C.
[g] H. P. C. 194. S. P. C. 144.
[h] 9 H. 4. 1. pl. 1. 2 H. 4. 19. pl. 12. 10 Co. 76. b. Bro. Appeal 18. H. P. C. 194.
[i] S. P. C. 144.
[k] 3 Inst. 130.
[l] H. P. C. 194.
[m] 21 H. 6. 34. pl. 1. 19 H. 6. 35. pl. 74. Bro. Coro. 48, 49. Fitz. Coro. 66, 67, 447. H. P. C. 194. 3 Inst. 129.
[n] H. P. C. 194. 2 Inst. 629. S. P. C. 143. Letter A. Fitz. Coro. 37. 12 Ed. 4. 10. pl. 26.
[o] H. P. C. 195. S. P. C. 145. Letter C. 12 Ed. 4. 10. pl. 26. Fitz. Coro. 37. 439. 26 Ass. pl. 19.
[p] Fitz. Coro. 439. H. P. C. 194. S. P. C. 144. Letter B. Bro. Coro. 34. 11 H. 4. 93. pl. 54.
[q] 21 H. 6. 34. pl. 1.
[r] H. P. C. 195. Fitz. Coro. 439. S. P. C. 145. Letter D.
[s] Fitz Coro. 118, 169, 255. 12 Ass. pl. 29. S. P. C. 145. Letter D.
[t] H. P. C. 195. Bro. Coro. 99. 26 Ass. pl. 19. S. P. C. 145. Letter A.

[a] H. P. C. 195. S. P. C. 145. Letter E. 26 Aff. pl. 19.

And so shall it be [a] also, If after he have formed his Appeal, before the Coroner, he make the least Variation in his repeating it before the Court, and the Coroner record such Variation.

[b] H. P. C. 196. S. P. C 145. [c] Fitz. Coro. 462. 29 Ed. 3 42. [d] Supra ch. 9 Sect. 41, 43. [e] H P. C. 196. S P. C. 146. Fitz. coro. 460. [f] H. P. C. 196. S. P. C. 146

Sect. 22. As to the seventh Point, *viz.* What Process is to be awarded against the Appellees, it seems [b] agreed, That the Coroner may award Process to the Sheriff, against any Appellee in the same County, till it come to the Exigent; but it is certain, That [c] he cannot award it to any other Officer, except the Sheriff, nor to any Sheriff out of his own County.: And it seems [d] questionable, whether he be not restrained by the Statute of *Magna Charta*, Ch. 17. to award the Exigent to the Sheriff of his own County. But it seems [e] agreed, That the Justices of the King's Bench, or Justices in Eyre, might by the Common Law as well award Process of Outlawry, as any other Process, against Appellees in any County whatsoever.

And it is [f] certain, That Justices of Gaol-Delivery may award Process into any County, to apprehend and try them by Force of 28 *Ed.* 1. commonly called the Statute *de Appellatis*; but whether this Statute do impower such Justices to award Process of Outlawry into a Foreign County, may deserve to be considered.

As to the eighth Point, *viz.* In what manner the Court is to proceed upon, and after the Tryal, I shall observe,

[g] H. P. C. 196. S. P. C. 142. Letter D. 3 Inst. 130. 47 Ed 3. 5. pl. 10. [h] S. P. C 180. Letter E. H. P. C. 196. 47 Ed. 3. 5. pl. 10. 19 H. 6. 35. pl. 74. 3 Inst. 130. [i] H. P. C. 196. S. P. C. 74. Letter B. 106 Letter D. 149 Letter B. 180 Letter E. 11 H 4. 93. pl. 49. 21 H. 6. 34. b. 35. a. Bro. coro. 31. 49. 3 Inst. 130. Fitz. coro. 143. 7 Ed. 3. 12. pl. 29. [k] S. P. C. 180. Letter E. [l] Fitz. coro. 98. [m] 47 Ed. 3. 15 pl. 26. 47 Ed. 35. pl. 10. Fitz. coro. 103. H. P. C. 201. 3 Inst. 130. S. P. C. 149. Letter B. [n] H. P. C. 201. Bro. coro. 49. 21 H 6. [o] Fitz. coro. 128, 369. Fitz. Assise 421. H. P. C. 197. contra 21 Ed. 3. 17. pl. 21. Bro. coro. 38. Fitz. coro. 447. [p] Bro. Clergy 5. 26. 11 H. 4. 93. pl. 49.

Sect. 23. First, That it is in the Election [g] of the Appellee, either to put himself upon his Country, or to wage Battel with the Approver.

Sect. 24. Secondly, That let there be never so many Appellees, if they wage Battel, the Approver must fight them [h] all. But on the contrary, it seems to be generally [i] agreed, That if a Person appealed by several Approvers of one and the same Felony, vanquishes any one of them, he shall be acquitted against them all, and all of them shall be condemned, in the same manner as if every one of them had been actually vanquished. But if an Approver having appealed several of the same Crime, be vanquished by one of them, it seems to be [k] holden, That his Appeal is still in force against the rest; but the Note in [l] *Fitzherbert*'s *Abridgment*, which seems to be the Foundation of this Opinion, seems rather to be intended of an Appeal by an innocent Person, than of an Appeal by an Approver, in Relation to whom it seems to be a general Rule, That being once falsified as to any one of the Appellees, he ought to be condemned, as hath been more fully shewn in the 9th and 15th Sections of this Chapter.

Sect. 25. Thirdly, That if the King pardon the Approver or Appellee, hanging the Appeal, the Approvement [m] ceases, and the Appellee shall be discharged; for in the first Case, by the Pardon the Felony is extinct, and a Man can no longer be an Approver, than while he is under the Guilt of the Crime, whereof the Approvement is made, and liable to be condemned by the Court, whenever his Appeal shall be falsified, *&c.* And in the second [n] Case, it cannot be doubted but that the King's Pardon will discharge the Appellee, because an Approvement is rather the Suit of the King, than of the Party.

Sect. 26. Fourthly, That whether the Appeal of an Approver be falsified by the [o] Confession, or Vanquishment [p] of the Approver, or verified by the Conviction or Vanquishment of the Appellee, yet if the Offence be within the Benefit of the Clergy, neither the Approver in the first Case, nor the Appellee in the second, are excluded from it, any more than in the Case of an Indictment.

Sect. 27. As to the ninth Point, *viz.* How the Approver is to be rewarded for making good his Appeal; it is said, [a] That if an Approver convict all the Appellees, whether by Battel or Verdict, the King, *ex merito justitiæ*, ought to pardon him as to his Life, and also give him his Wages [b] from the Time of the Appeal to the Time of the Conviction. But [c] it seems, That anciently he ought not to be suffered to continue in the Kingdom. And it is recited by 5 *H.* 4. *ch.* 2. *That diverse notorious Felons, for Safeguard of their Lives, had become Provors, to the Intent, in the mean Time, by Brocage, and great Gifts to pursue and have their Pardons, and then after their Deliverance, had become more notorious Felons than they were before*; and thereupon it is enacted, *That if any Person pray or pursue, or cause to be prayed or pursued for any such Felon so attainted by his own Confession, to have any Charter of Pardon, the Name of him that pursues such Charter be put in the same Charter, making Mention that the same Charter is granted at his Instance. And if he to whom such Charter is granted become a Felon again, the Party who pursued the Charter shall forfeit* 100 l.

[a] H.P.C.197. S.P.C. 142. Letter D. 3 Inst. 129, 130. contra 19 H. 6. 35. pl. 74. Fitz. con. 6.
[b] Vide supra Sect. 19.
[c] S.P.C. 142. Letter D.

CHAP. XXV.

Of Indictment.

Sect. 1. AN Indictment is an Accusation, at the Suit of the King, by the Oaths of twelve Men of the same County wherein the Offence was committed, returned to inquire of all Offences in General in the County, determinable by the Court into which they are returned, and finding a Bill brought before them to be true; but when such Accusation is found by a Grand Jury, without any Bill brought before them, and [d] afterwards reduced to a formed Indictment, it is called a Presentment; and when it is found by Jurors returned to inquire of that particular Offence only which is indicted, it is properly called an Inquisition. And for the better understanding the Nature of such Proceedings, I shall consider the following Particulars.

[d] Lamb. B. 4. ch. 5.

1. Whether a Grand Jury may find Part of a Bill brought before them true, and Part false.
2. Whether an Indictment be merely the Suit of the King.
3. What Matters are indictable.
4. Where a Man may be tried at the Suit of the King for a capital Offence, without any Indictment.
5. Whether a Man may be arraigned on an Indictment while an Appeal is depending against him for the same Offence.
6. Who may and ought to be Indictors, and in what Manner they are to be returned.
7. Within what Place the Offences inquired of must arise.
8. What ought to be the Form of the Body of an Indictment.
9. What ought to be the Form of the Caption of it.
10. Upon what Proof it may be found.

11. In what Cases it may be quashed.
12. What may be pleaded to it, and in what Manner.

Sect. 2. As to the first Point, *viz.* Whether a Grand Jury may find Part of a Bill brought before them true, and Part false, it seems to be generally agreed, That they must either find *Billa Vera*, or *Ignoramus*, for the Whole; and that if they take upon them to find it specially, or conditionally, or to be true for Part only, and not for the rest, the Whole is void, and the Party [a] cannot be tried upon it, but ought to be indicted anew; and accordingly it hath been resolved, That if a Grand Jury indorse a Bill of Murder, [b] *Billa vera se defendendo*; or *Billa vera* for Manslaughter, [c] and not for Murder; or if they indorse a Bill upon the Statutes of News, *Billa vera*, [d] but whether *Ista verba prolata fuerunt maliciose, seditiose, vel econtra, ignoramus*; or if they endorse an Indictment of Forcible Entry, and Forcible Detainer, *Billa vera* [e] as to the Forcible Entry, and *Ignoramus* as to the Forcible Detainer; or if they indorse, [f] That if the Freehold were in *J. S.* or the Possession were in *J. S.* then they find *Billa vera*, the Whole is void.

[a] 2 Rol. Rep. 52. 3 Bulst. 206. 1 Rol Rep. 407, 408.
[b] 2 Rol. Rep. 52. Powle's Case.
[c] 3 Bulst. 206. 1 Rol. 408. 1 Sid. 230
[d] Leon. 287.
[e] Yelv. 99. 1 Sid. 414. Vide B. 1. c. 64 Sect. 40. Cro. Jac. 151. contra 1 Sid. 99.
[f] Yelv. 15.

Sect. 3. As to the second Point, *viz.* Whether an Indictment be merely the Suit of the King; it is every Day's Practice, That it is so far esteemed the King's Suit, that the Party who prosecutes it is a good Witness to prove it: Also it seems to be agreed, [g] That no Damages can be given to the Party grieved upon an Indictment, or any other criminal Prosecution, [h] notwithstanding the King, by his Commission erecting a New Court, expresly direct, That the Party shall recover his Damages by such a Prosecution. Also, where by Statute Damages are given to the Party grieved by the Offence intended to be redressed, it [i] seems that they cannot be recovered on an Indictment grounded on such Statute, unless such Method of recovering them be expresly given by the Statute; but that they ought to be sued for in an Action on the Statute in the Name of the Party grieved. But it seems [k] certain, That the Court of King's Bench, having the King's Privy Seal for that purpose, may give to the Prosecutor the third Part of the Fine assessed, on a criminal Prosecution, for any Offence whatsoever. Also, it is every Day's Practice of that Court, to induce Defendants to make Satisfaction to Prosecutors for the Costs of the Prosecution, and also for the Damages sustained by the Injury whereof the Defendants are convicted, by intimating an Inclination on that Account to mitigate the Fine due to the King.

[g] 1 Rol. Abr. 220. Letter B. 2 Rol. Abr. 83. Letter P. Cro. Car. 531, 558.
[h] Cro. Car. 558. Vide supra, Ch. 1. Sect. 3, 4, 6, 7, 8.
[i] 1 Rol. Ab. 220 Letter B. Jon. 380. Cro Car. 448.
[k] 1 Keb. 487. pl. 30.

Sect. 4. As to the third Point, *viz.* What Matters are indictable: There can be no Doubt, but that all capital Crimes whatsoever, and also all Kinds of inferior Crimes of a publick Nature, as Misprisions, and all other Contempts, all Disturbances of the Peace, all Oppressions, and all other Misdemeanours whatsoever of a publickly evil Example against the Common Law, may be indicted; but no Injuries of a [l] private Nature, unless they some Way concern the King. Also it seems to be a good general Ground, That where-ever a Statute prohibits a Matter of a publick Grievance to the [m] Liberties or Security of the Subject; or commands a Matter of publick [n] Convenience, as the repairing of the Common Streets of a Town, an Offender against such Statute is punishable, not only at the Suit of the Party aggrieved, but also by way of Indictment for his Contempt of the Statute, unless such Method of Proceeding do manifestly appear to be excluded by it. Yet if the Party offending have been fined to the King in the Action brought by the Party, as it is said [o] that he may in every Action for doing a Thing prohibited by Statute, it seems

[l] 27 Ass. pl. 20. Bro. Indictment 16, Presentment 26.
[m] 2 Inst. 55, 163. Cro Jac. 577.
[n] 1 Mod. 34. 1 Sid. 209.
[o] 8 Co. 60. b. 2 Inst. 131.

seems questionable, whether he may afterwards be indicted; because that would make him liable to a second Fine for the same Offence. Also, if a Statute extend only to private [a] Persons, or if it extend to all Persons in general, but chiefly concern Disputes of a private Nature, as those relating to [b] Distresses made by Lords on their Tenants, it is said that Offences against such Statute will hardly bear an Indictment. Also, where a Statute makes a new Offence, which was no way prohibited by the Common Law, and appoints a particular Manner of proceeding against the Offender, as by Commitment, or Action of Debt, or Information, *&c.* without mentioning an Indictment, it seems to be [c] settled at this Day, That it will not maintain an Indictment, because the mentioning the others Methods of proceeding only, seems impliedly to exclude that of Indictment. [d] Yet it hath been adjudged, That if such a Statute give a Recovery by Action of Debt, Bill, Plaint, or Information, or otherwise, it authorises a Proceeding by way of Indictment. [e] Also, where a Statute adds a farther Penalty to an Offence prohibited by the Common Law, there can be no Doubt but that the Offender may still be indicted, if the Prosecutor think fit, at the Common Law. And if the Indictment for such Offence conclude *contra formam statuti*, and cannot be made good as an Indictment upon the Statute, it seems [f] to be now settled, That it may be maintain'd as an Indictment at Common Law, as will be more fully shewn in the following Part of this Chapter.

As to the fourth Point, *viz.* Where a Man may be tried at the Suit of the King for a capital Offence without any Indictment, I shall endeavour to shew,

1. Where one may be so tried as having been taken with the Manner.
2. Where one may be so tried upon a Verdict.
3. Where upon an Appeal not prosecuted.
4. Whether one may be so tried upon a Sheriff's Return.

Sect. 5. As to the first Point, *viz.* Where one may be so tried as having been taken with the Manner: [g] It is said, That anciently if one guilty of Larceny had been freshly pursued and taken with the Manner, and the Goods so found upon him had been brought into the Court with him, he might be tried immediately without any Indictment; and this is said to have been the proper Method of proceeding in such Manors which had the Franchise of Insangthefe, but seems to be altogether obsolete at this Day.

Sect. 6. As to the second Point, *viz.* Where one may be so tried upon a Verdict: It is [h] said, That in an Action of Trespass in the King's Bench, *De muliere abductâ cum bonis viri*, if the Defendant be found guilty of having carried away the Woman and Goods with Force, and feloniously; or [i] in a Common Action of Trespass in the said Court, for Goods carried away, if it be found that the Defendant feloniously stole them, he shall be put to answer the Felony without any farther Accusation; for such a Charge by the Oath of twelve Men, on their Inquiry into the Merits of a Cause, in a Court which has Jurisdiction over the Crime, is equivalent to an Indictment; and the King being always in Judgment of Law present in Court, may take Advantage of any Matter therein properly disclosed for his Benefit. But such a Verdict in a Court which has [k] no Jurisdiction over criminal Matters, seems to be of little Force, because such Court has nothing to do with such Matters. And it seems, [a] that

a 1 Sid. 209. 1 Modern 34.
b 1 Modern 71, 288. 1 Lev. 299. Raym. 205. 1 Vent. 104. 2 Inst. 128, 131.
c Bond's Case, Michaelmas 3 Georgii. Shower 398, 399. 3 Keb. 34, 273. Cro. Jac. 643, 644. 3 Mod. 79. Palmer 388.
d Sid 434, 439. 6 Mod. 86. 2 Rol. Re 247, 248, 398.
d Dominus Rex versus Dixon Trin. 3 Georgii.
e 3 Modern 118. 1 Sid. 192. Seem contra.
f The Case of the County, of the City of Norwich, adjudged Pasch 3 Georgii.
g Vide supra ch. 15. sect. 41. 7 H 4. 43. pl. 9. 26 Ass. pl. 32. 1 Ed 3. 13. pl. 6. S. P. C. 25, 29, 148. Letter C. 179 Letter B. H. P. C. 198. Bro. Appeal 130.
1 Ass. pl. 5. Fitz. coro. 156, 357.
h H. P. C. 199. S. P. C. 94. Letter B. 95. Fitz cor. 122. Fitz utlgary 49. 13 Ass. pl. 5. Bro. coro 77.
i H. P.C. 199. S. P. C. 94. Letter B. Fitz. Indictment 31.
k S. P. C. 94 Letter B. Fitz. Indictment 31.

[a] that even in the King's Bench, if on any Indictment whatsoever, except only an Inquisition of Death found before a Coroner on View, a Person not mentioned in it be found guilty of the Crime whereof others are indicted, yet such finding shall not serve for an Indictment against him, because it was wholly extrajudicial. [b] But such finding of others guilty, whether in the King's Bench, or other Court of criminal Jurisdiction, upon an Inquisition of Death, found before a Coroner on View, is of greater Force, because the Jury acquitting the Party so indicted, [c] ought to inquire what other Person did the Fact; because it appears by a Record of the highest Credit, That a Person is killed. [d] Also, if a Person be declared against in a proper Court, for having been guilty of a Misdemeanor, *simul cum A. & B. & C.* and thereupon the Jury find *A. B.* and *C.* guilty; it seems that such Verdict will serve for an Indictment against them, because it was not wholly extrajudicial.

As to the third Point, *viz.* Where one may be so tried upon an Appeal not prosecuted, the following Particulars seem most remarkable.

Sect. 7. *First*, That an Appeal by an innocent Person, and an Appeal by an [e] Approver, are equally favoured in this Respect.

Sect. 8. *Secondly*, That regularly where a Person is indicted and appealed of the same [f] Crime, and the Appeal is not prosecuted, he shall not [g] be arraigned upon the Indictment, but upon the Appeal.

Sect. 9. *Thirdly*, [h] That if an Appellant be nonsuit in an Appeal by Writ, before he hath declared, the Appellee cannot be arraigned at the King's Suit on the Writ of Appeal; not only because it contains no Certainty of the Circumstances of the Fact, which it is the proper [i] Office of the Declaration to ascertain; but also, because, for what appears to the contrary by the Record, the Writ might [k] have been purchased by a Stranger. And therefore in such Case, it seems to be in the Discretion [l] of the Court, either to dismiss the Appellee, or to bail him, till it shall appear, Whether there will be any other Prosecution against him. But if an Appellant, by Writ, be nonsuit after Declaration, or any Appellant by Bill, or Approver, be nonsuit, it seems, [m] That regularly the Appellee shall be arraigned at the King's Suit, on the Bill or Declaration; because they must be as certain as an Indictment, and cannot be commenced but in Person.

Sect. 10. *Fourthly*, That it seems to be a settled Rule, That whereever an Appeal is once well commenced, and afterwards so far determined, without a full Acquittal, that neither the same, nor any [n] other Plaintiff, can ever bring another Appeal against the same Appellee, he may be arraigned upon the Bill or Declaration, at the Suit of the King; as where an Appellant, having a good Title to the Appeal, makes a Release [o] to the Appellee, hanging the Action, or suffers a [p] Nonsuit, or [q] *Retraxit*, or [r] demurs to a good Plea or Issue, tendered by the Appellee, which Demurrer is adjudged against him; or where such an Appellant or Approver [s] confess their Appeal to be false, [t] unless they make such Confession in the Field, upon a Trial awarded by Battel; for such Confession amounts to a Vanquishment of the Appellant or Approver, and consequently is a full Acquittal of the Appellee; after which his Life shall not be brought

[a] 13 Ed. 4. 3. pl. 7. Fitz. coro. 39.
[b] 13 Ed. 4. 3. pl. 7.
[c] Supra ch 9. sect. 33.
[d] Bro Indict. 13. 26 Ass. pl. 62.
[e] S. P. C. 147 Letter E. 148. H. P. C. 199, 200. Bro. Appeal. 53. Bro. coro. 3, 16, 49
[f] H. P C. 199 31 H. 6. 11. pl. 6. Fitz. coro. 18. S. P. C. 107. Letter A.
[g] H.P.C. 199 S. P. C. 147. Letter E. 33 H. 6. 1. pl 6. 4 Ed. 4. 10. pl. 14. Bro. Appeal. 92, 149. S. P. C. 107. Letter A. Fitz. coro. 114.
[h] S.P.C. 148. Letters A. B. C. H. P. C. 199, 200. Bro. Appeal 67, 130. Fitz. coro. 156, 198, 357, 384.
[i] See ch. 23. Sect. 86, 87, &c.
[k] See ch. 23. Sect. 26, 129.
[l] S.P.C. 148. Letter C. Bro. Appeal 67, 130. 27 Ass. pl. 7. 1 Ass pl 5. Fitz. coro. 156, 198, 357.
[m] S. P. C. 148. H. P. C. 199, 200 Bro. Appeal. 67.
[n] S. P. C. 148. Bro. Appeal 118. Fitz. coro. 369. Vide Bro. coro. 35. 9 H. 5. 2. pl. 7.
[o] S. P. C. 148. Letter B. H. P. C. 200. Bro. Appeal 27. Fitz coro. pl. 12.
[p] H. P. C. 199. S. P. C. 147. Letter E. Cro. Eliz. 460. Fitz. coro. 25, 381. Bro. nisi prius 28. Fitz. utlagary 47.
[q] S. P. C. 147. Letter E. 148. Letter B.
[r] Dyer 120. pl. 13.
[s] S. P. C. 148. Letter B. Fitz. coro. 103. 3 H. 6. 50. pl. 16. 13 Ass. pl. 10. H. P. C. 200. 47 Ed. 3. 5. pl. 10. Bro. coro. 3, 16, 49, 98. Bro. Appeal 53.
[t] 21 H. 6. 34. pl. pl. 1. S. P. C. 148. Letter B. H. P. C. 200.

again into Danger for the same Crime. And this seems to be the only Reason why after such a Vanquishment, or a Verdict in his Favour, an Appellee shall be discharged, as well against the Suit of the King, as that of the Party. But it seems, That in all other Cases whatsoever, an Appellee, in an Appeal well commenced; being wholly discharged of the Suit of the Party, may be arraigned upon the Appeal, at the Suit of the King, whether such Discharge were merely owing to the Act of the Party, as in the Cases above-mentioned, or to the Act of the Court; as [a] where an Approver is adjudged to be hanged before he hath perfected his Appeal; or partly to the Act of Law, and partly to the Act of the Party, as [b] where an Appeal by a Woman for the Death of her first Husband, is abated by her marrying a second; or where an Appellee is discharged of an Appeal, for not [c] having been made a Defendant in a former Appeal, brought by the same Appellant for the very same Fact; or whether such Discharge be merely owing to the Act of God; as [d] where an Appellant dies a natural Death, while his Appeal is depending. It seems indeed to be holden in the Year Book [e] of 4 *H. 6.* as a general Rule, That where-ever a Writ is abated, the Declaration depending upon it is determined also, and consequently, that the Appellee cannot be arraigned upon it; but to this it may be answered, that in the very same Place it is allowed, That after a Nonsuit in an Appeal, the Appellee may be arraigned at the Suit of the King; and it seems difficult to give a Reason, why a Writ is not as much determined upon a Nonsuit as upon an Abatement; to which may be added, that the Point adjudged, which was this, That where a Writ abates for a Misnosmer, the Defendant shall not be arraigned at the Suit of the King, seems plainly to go on this Ground, That where a Suit is ill commenced, the King shall not have a greater Advantage from it than the Party might have had; and therefore the Opinion above-mentioned, being also contradicted by the best [f] Authorities, seems to be of little Weight.

Sect. 11. *Fifthly*, That where-ever [g] an Appeal abates for Insufficiency of the Writ, or is barred for want of a good Title in the Appellant; or for any other Matter which shews it was ill commenced, the Defendant shall not be arraigned upon it at the Suit of the King, because it never had a good Foundation, and cannot give a greater Advantage to the King than to the Party himself who sued it; and therefore it seems to be agreed, That if an Appeal be abated for want of Form apparent in the Writ, as [h] for the Omission of the Word *Habeas*, or for false [i] *Latin*, or for any other [k] apparent Defect; or if it be abated for a Defect not apparent of it self, but disclosed by the Pleadings of the Parties, as for a [l] Misnosmer, or wrongful Addition, or any such like Insufficiency; or if it be abated on Account of the Disability of the Appellant, as by the Plea of Outlawry [m] for Felony or Trespass; or if it be put without Day upon a Plea of Excommunication of the Appellant; or [n] if it be barred by a Release made before the Commencement of the Suit, or by reason that the Time for bringing it was elapsed [o] before it was commenced, or because the Appellant appears to have never had any Right to bring it; as where in an Appeal by one as Wife, it is found that she was [p] never lawfully married to the Deceased; or in an Appeal by one as Heir [q] to

[a] S.P.C. 147. Letter E. 21 Ed. 3. 17. pl. 20.
[b] S P.C. 147. Letter E. H. P. C. 200.
[c] 47 Ed. 3. 16. pl. 27. Fitz. coro. 104.
[d] S.P.C. 147. Letter E. 47 Ed. 3. 5. pl. 10.
[e] 4 H 6 16. Bro. Appeal 44.
[f] S P C 147. Letter E. H P.C. 200,
[g] Bro. Appeal 5. Fitz coro 68. Bro. coro. 35. contra 41. Aff. pl. 14. Fitz. age 74.
[h] Fitz. coro. 121. S P. C. 149. Letter A. 13 Aff pl 13. Bro. Appeal 53. H. P. C. 200.
[k] Bro. coro. 78. S P. C. 148 Letter C.
[l] Bro. Appeal. 44 Fitz. coro. 12, 103. 4 H 6 15, 16. S. P. C. 148. Letter C. H. P. C. 200.
[m] S. P. C. 149. Letter A. H. P. C. 200, Fitz utl. 47 Bro. Appeal. 57, 118, 146. 17 Aff. pl. 26 Fitz. coro. 175.
[n] S. P. C. 148. Letter B. Fitz coro. 12. H. P. C. 200. Vide supra Sect. 10.
[o] S P.C. 149. Letter A. H. P. C. 200.
[p] S P. C. 149. Letter A. H. P. C. 200. Fitz. coro. 3.
[q] S. P. C. 149. Letter A. 27 Aff. pl. 25. Bro. Appeal. 68. H. P. C. 200. Fitz. coro. 201, 384. contra Bro. Appeal. 53. 13 Aff. pl. 10.

his Father, it is found that he hath an elder Brother alive by the same Father, *&c.* the Appellee shall not be arraigned upon the Appeal, at the Suit of the King, but shall be wholly discharged of it. But where an Appeal is put without Day on the Plea of [a] Excommunication, the Appellee shall be mainprised from Day to Day till the Plaintiff be absolved; and notwithstanding it seems to be holden generally in some [b] Books, That where an Appeal is abated for any of the Insufficiencies abovementioned, or barred, the Appellee shall be set at large, and be discharged, as well against the King as the Party; yet [c] surely this must be understood only of such Cases wherein it appears, That neither any Indictment is preferred, or intended to be preferred by the King, nor any other Appeal preferred, nor intended to be preferred by the same or some other Party; for otherwise surely it cannot but be intended, that it must be in the Discretion of the Court, upon Consideration of the Circumstance of the Case, either to commit or bail the Appellee for a reasonable Time, in order to answer such further Prosecution, or [d] to bind him to his Good Behaviour for a certain Time, *&c.*

Sect. 12. *Sixthly*, That whatsoever may be pleaded by an Appellee either in Bar or Abatement of an Appeal, while it is carried on at the Suit of the Party, may [e] as well be pleaded by him, when it is prosecuted at the Suit of the King; as [f] that the Appellant suing an Appeal of Death, as Wife to the Deceased, was never married to him, or [g] that she is outlawed, *&c.* which depends upon the Reason taken Notice of in the precedent Sections, *viz.* That an Appeal shall not give the King a greater Advantage than the Party himself who sued it.

Sect. 13. *Seventhly*, That [h] where ever an Appellee is arraigned upon the Suit of the King, he may plead the King's Pardon, in the same Manner as if he had been arraigned upon an Indictment: But if an Appellee, who by pleading such a Pardon discharges himself of an Appeal at the Suit of the King, be also indicted, it is adviseable [i] to take Care at the same Time when he is in such Manner discharged of the Appeal, to have a Cesser of Process entered on the Indictment, to prevent the Vexation of a causeless Prosecution upon it.

Sect. 14. As to the fourth Point, *viz.* Whether one may be tried at the Suit of the King for a capital Offence, without any Indictment upon a Sheriff's Return, it seems to be generally agreed, [k] That neither the Sheriff's Return of a Rescous, or Escape, or of any other Matter, nor any other Record whatsoever, except only an Appeal or Indictment, or something equivalent thereto, as the Verdict of twelve Men, finding a Man guilty in such Manner as is above set forth in the sixth Section of this Chapter, can at this Day put a Man upon his Trial for a capital Offence, as being contrary not only to the Common Law, but to [l] *Magna Charta*, and other [m] Statutes made in Affirmance of it.

Sect. 15. As to the fifth general Point of this Chapter, *viz.* Whether a Man may be arraigned on an Indictment, while an Appeal is depending against him for the same Offence, it seems [n] that it was the Common Practice before the Statute of 3 *H.* 7. 1. Whether any Appeal were depending or not, not to try any Man upon an Indictment of Murder, before the Year and Day were passed, lest thereby the Suit of the Party should be prevented. And if such Regard were had to an Appeal where none was depending, it cannot be thought but that much [o] greater was

[a] S.P.C. 149. Letter A. 13 Ed. 4. 8. pl. 3. 3 Ass. pl. 12. Fitz mainprise 6.
[b] 18 Ed. 3. 35. pl. 15. Bro Appeal. 146. 11 Ass pl. 27. 17 Ass pl 26. Fitz. utlagary 47. Fitz. coro. 12, 68, 167, 175, 201, 384. Bro. nonab. 23.
[c] H.P.C. 200. Vide S.P.C. 149. Letter A. Bro. Appeal. 67, 130. Fitz. coro. 156, 198, 357. Fitz. error. 52. 27 Ass. pl. 7. 1 Ass. pl. 5. 32 Ass. pl 8. 7 H. 7. 5 pl 7.
[d] Fitz. coro. 387. S.P.C. 149. Letter D.
[e] S P C 172. Letter B. Quære, Fitz coro. 452.
[f] Fitz. coro. 3.
[g] 21 Ed. 3. 17. pl. 20. Bro. coro 37.
[h] Fitz. monstrans de faits 128. H P.C. 201. S P.C. 104. Letters A B Fitz. coro. 25. 11 H 4. 41. pl 6. Vide supra ch. 24. Sect. 25
[i] S.P.C. 104. H P.C. 201. 4 Ed. 4. 10. pl. 14. Fitz. coro. 25.
[k] H P C. 201. 2 Inst. 50. S.P.C. 31. Letter C. 94. Letter B 95. 2 Ed. 3. 1. pl. 4. 1 H. 7. 6. pl. 2. Fitz. coro. 48, 149. Bro. coro. 130. Vide supra ch 19. Sect. 15.
[l] 9 H. 3. ch. 29.
[m] 25 Ed. 3. de proditionibus cap. 4. 28 Ed. 3. 3. 37 Ed. 3. 18.
[n] See the Preamble of 3 H. 7. 1. S. P. C. 107. Letter A. Fitz. coro. 44, 82. 7 H. 4. 36. a.
[o] 44 Ed. 3. 38. pl. 35. 31 H. 6. 11. pl 6. 21 Ass. pl. 4. 21 Ed 3 23. pl. 16. Fitz. coro. 18, 114. Fitz. respondet 36.

had

had to one actually depending, whether before or after the Year and Day were passed. [a] Yet it seems that the Court was never in any Case peremptorily bound to suspend the Proceedings on an Indictment in respect of an Appeal, but might always in Discretion, whenever it should seem proper, proceed on an Indictment, hanging an Appeal. And accordingly we find, that in many Instances [b] in the Old Books, when it was holden, That in an Appeal by an Infant, the Parol should [c] demur till his full Age, the Court have proceeded to try a Man upon an Indictment, while an Appeal by an Infant was depending against him, to prevent the Delay, which could not but be occasioned, if the Proceedings should be deferred till the Appellant should come to full Age. Also [d] where a Writ of Appeal of Robbery hath been sued out against a Person under an Indictment for the same Robbery, and ready to be tried, the Court have refused to put off the Trial of the Indictment in respect of such Writ of Appeal; because before the Appellant hath declared, it doth not judicially appear, that both the Indictment and Appeal are for the very same Fact. But if there were no such special Reason to induce the Court to proceed upon an Indictment while an Appeal is depending, it seems to have been the general [e] Practice to suspend the Proceedings on the Indictment till the Appeal were determined.

As to the sixth general Point of this Chapter, *viz.* Who may be, and ought to be Indictors, and in what Manner they are to be returned, I shall endeavour to shew,

1. How these Matters stand by the Common Law.
2. How by Statute.

Sect. 15. As to the first Particular, it seems clear, That by the Common Law every Indictment must be found by twelve [f] Men at the least, every [g] one of which ought to be of the same [h] County, and returned by the Sheriff, or other proper Officer, without the Nomination of any other Person whatsoever; and ought also to be a Freeman, and a lawful liege Subject; and consequently neither under an [i] Attainder of any Treason or Felony; nor a [k] Villein, nor Alien, nor outlawed, whether for a criminal Matter, or, as [l] some say, in a personal Action. And from hence it seems clear, that if it appear by the Caption of an Indictment, or otherwise, that it was found by [m] less than twelve, the Proceedings upon it will be erroneous. [n] Also, it seems that any one who is under a Prosecution for any Crime whatsoever, may, by the Common Law, before he is indicted, challenge any of the Persons returned on the Grand Jury; as being outlawed for Felony, *&c.* or Villeins, or returned at the Instance of a Prosecutor, or not returned by the proper Officer, *&c.*

Sect. 16. Also many Indictments in inferior [o] Courts have been [p] quashed for want of the Words, *Proborum & legalium hominum*, in the Caption of the Indictment, setting forth by what Persons it was found; [q] but this is said to be no Exception to an Indictment found in the Court of King's Bench, or Grand Sessions, or Counties Palatine, and hath been often [r] over-ruled, as to Indictments in other Courts, because all Men shall be intended to be honest and lawful, till the contrary appear.

[a] 4 Co. 45. b. 47. 7 H. 4 34. pl. 22, 35. pl. 4. 21 H. 6. 28, 29. Fitz. conspir 6. Fitz. coro. 82. Quære, Fitz. coro. 114. Bro. Appeal 41.
[b] Fitz. coro. 278, 279. 32 Ass. pl. 8. 41 Ass. pl. 14. Bro. Appeal 75. Quære, Fitz. coro. 114. 21 Ed. 3. 23. pl. 16. Bro. Appeal 105, 119.
[c] 13 Ass. pl. 10. Fitz. Age 41, 57 17 Ed. 4. 2. pl. 4. Bro. Appeal 105 Vide supra ch. 23. Sect. 30.
[d] 31 H. 6. 11. pl. 6. Fitz. coro 18.
[e] Dyer 296. pl. 20. *See the Books cited to the other Parts of this Section.*
[f] Cro. Eliz. 654. 3 Inst 30. 2 Inst. 387.
[g] See the Preamble of 11 H. 4 9. 3 Inst. 32, 33, 34. 12 Co. 99.
[h] 2 Rol. Re. 82.
[i] 3 Inst. 32.
[k] Popham 202. 1 Inst. 156. b.
[l] 3 Inst. 32. 21 H. 6. 30. pl. 17. Vide Fitz. Process 208. Quære, Cro. Car. 134, 147. 1 Jon. 198, 199.
[m] Cro. Eliz. 654. pl. 16.
[n] 11 H. 4. 41. pl. 8. Bro. coro. 189 Bro. indict. 2. 21 H. 6. 30. pl. 17. Quære, Cro. Car. 134, 135, 147.
[o] 1 Keb. 629. pl. 112. 2 Keb. 471. pl. 63.
[p] Cro. Eliz. 751. pl. 7. Cro. Jac. 635. Palm. 282, 389. 2 Rol. Rep. 400. 2 Rol. Ab. 82. pl. 7. 3 Mod. 122. Poph. 202.
[q] 1 Keb. 629. pl. 112. 2 Keb. 471. pl. 63. 1 Lev. 208.
[r] 2 Keb. 135, 284. 1 Keb. 50. pl. 5. Cro Jac. 41. 1 Sid. 106, 367. Quære, 2 Rol. Ab. 82. pl. 8.

11 H. 4. 41. pl. 8. Fitz. indict. 25 coron. 89. Bro. indict. 2. Vide infra Sect 26. [b] S. P. C. 88. 12 Co. 99. H. P. C. 202. 3 Inst. 32, 33, 34. Vide Cro. Car. 134, 135.

Sect. 17. It is resolved in the [a] Year-Book of 11 *H.* 4. by the Advice of all the Justices, That one outlawed on an Indictment of Felony, may plead in Avoidance of it, that one of the Indictors was outlawed for Felony, *&c.* But it seems to be the general [b] Opinion, That this Resolution is rather grounded on the Statute of 11 *H.* 4. *ch.* 9. which was made in the same Term, in which this Resolution was given, than on the Common Law; because it appears by the very same Year-Book, that when this Plea was first proposed it was disallowed; from whence, as I suppose, it is collected, that the subsequent Resolution was founded on the Authority of the said Statute, which may be intended to have been made after the Plea was disallowed, and before the subsequent Resolution, by which it was adjudged good. Yet, considering that the said Resolution was given in the Beginning of *Hilary* Term, and that the Parliament which made the said Statute was not holden before the Beginning of the same Term; and therefore it is not likely that the said Statute was so soon made; and also considering, that the said Resolution was given by Advice of all the Judges, who seem to have been consulted about the Validity of the Plea above-mentioned at the Common Law, and takes no manner of Notice of any Statute, but only of the Law in General, it may deserve a Question, Whether such Plea be not good at the Common Law?

Vide 2 Rol. Abr. 647, 648. Cro. Eliz. 413. Cro. Jac. 672.

Sect. 18. I do not find it any where holden, That none but Freeholders ought to be returned on a Grand Jury; but how far the Law is in this Respect altered by Statute, shall be shewn in the twentieth Section.

Sect. 19. As to the second Particular, *viz.* How the Matters above-mentioned stand by Statute, it is enacted by the Statute of *Westminster* 2, 28. *That old Men above the Age of seventy Years, Persons perpetually sick or infirm at the Time of the Summons, or not dwelling in the Country, shall not be put in Juries, or lesser Assises.* And the Equity thereof, and the Reason of the Thing, seem plainly so far to extend to Grand Juries, that if it shall appear that any of the Persons above-mentioned be returned on a Grand Jury, the Court, into which they are returned, will easily excuse their Non-appearance. But it seems clear, [c] that any such Persons being returned on a Grand Jury, may lawfully serve upon it, if they think fit; neither do I find that they can have an Action on the said Statute for being so returned; for the Writ [d] in the Register grounded on, and reciting the Statute, mentions the Prohibition of it to be, that Men above the Age of seventy Years shall not be put *in Assisis, juratis, vel recognitionibus aliquibus*, which Expressions seem proper for Petit Juries only; whereas the [e] Writ grounded on the Statute of *Articuli super chartas*, set forth more at large in the twenty-first Section, recites the Prohibition thereof to be, that none of the Persons in the Writ mentioned shall be put *in inquisitionibus nec juratis*, which Expression seems to be of a larger Extent, and to take in Grand as well as Petit Juries; by which it seems clearly to be implied, that in the Judgment of those who formed the said Writ, the Statute last mentioned is more general than the former.

[c] 2 Inst. 448. [d] Regist. 180. b. F. N. B. 166. D. Vide 2 Inst. 447, 448. [e] Regist. 178. F. N. B. 165. Vide 2 Inst. 561.

Sect. 20. It is farther enacted by the above-mentioned Statute of *Westminster* 2, 38. *That none shall be put in Assises or Juries, though they ought to be taken in the proper County, who have less Tenements than to the Value of twenty Shillings yearly.* And it is required by the Statute of 21 *Ed.* 1. commonly called the Statute *De his qui ponendi sunt in Assisis*, *That they should have Tenements to the Value of* 40s. *yearly; Provided, That before Justices in Eyre for Common Pleas in their Eyres, and also in Assises, and Juries, which shall be taken in Cities and Burghs, and other trading Towns, the same may be done as was accustomed:* And this Exception is likewise mentioned in the [a] Writ in the Register, which seems to be grounded on both these Statutes; by which it appears, That neither by the Common Law nor by these Statutes there was any Necessity in Proceedings before Justices in Eyre, *&c.* That Petit Jurors should be Freeholders; and if so, it seems probable that there is no greater Necessity that Grand Jurors making an Inquiry before them should be Freeholders; and if a Grand Juror before such Justices need not to be a Freeholder, why should there be a greater Necessity that a Grand Juror before other Justices should be a Freeholder? And it is farther remarkable, that the above mentioned Writ in the Register, which seems to be grounded on these Statutes, mentions only Persons put *in assisis, juratis, vel recognitionibus aliquibus:* To which may be added, That the [b] several subsequent Statutes, which require that none but Freeholders or Copyholders of Lands of such a Value shall be returned on Juries, expresly extend only to Juries returned for the Trial of Issues, except only the [c] Statutes concerning Indictments in the Sheriff's Torn, which require, that every Juror finding such Indictment shall have 20 *s.* yearly of Freehold, or 26 *s.* of Copyhold, and also except 3 *H.* 7. 1. which requires that every Juror of an Inquest by which Justices of Peace shall inquire of Concealments by other Inquests shall have Tenements of the yearly Value of 40 *s.* and also except 33 *H.* 6. 2. which requires that every Indictment in the County Palatine of *Lancaster*, of Persons supposed by the same Indictment to live in some other County, and also every Indictment in any other County, of Persons in the same Indictment, supposed to live in the said County of *Lancaster*, shall be taken by such Jurors only as have Lands to the yearly Value of one hundred Shillings: All which seems to make it doubtful, Whether there be any Necessity either by the Common Law or Statute, that a Grand Juror in in any other Case must be a Freeholder.

Sect. 21. It is enacted by 28 *Ed.* 1. commonly called the Statute of *Articuli super Chartas, cap.* 9. *That no Sheriff, nor Bailiff shall impanel in Inquests, nor in Juries over many Persons, nor others, nor otherwise than as is ordained by Statute: And that they shall put in those Inquests and Juries, such as be next Neighbours, most sufficient, and least suspicious.* And the like is enacted almost in the very same Words by 42 *Ed.* 3. 11. And it is farther enacted by the said Statute of *Articuli super Chartas, That he who doth contrary, and is attainted thereupon, shall pay unto the Plaintiff his Damages double, and shall be grievously amerced to the King.* And the said Statute of *Articuli super Chartas*, is said by Sir *Edward Coke*, to extend to all Suits or Proceedings, either criminal or civil, real, personal, or mix'd, publick or private, Assises or Enquests; and surely that Part of it which ordains, that the most sufficient and least suspicious shall be returned on all Juries, is so agreeable to common Right and natural Justice, that it cannot but be thought to be in Affirmance of the Common Law, and equally to extend to Grand and Petit Juries, and consequently if any Officer shall be wilfully guilty of an Offence against it in the Return of any Jury, he cannot but be punishable for his Contempt, at the Suit of the King. And it is enacted by 23 *E.* 3. 6. *That Justices of Assises shall have Commissions sufficient to inquire in their Sessions of Sheriffs,* &c. *for putting into Panels Jurors suspect and of evil Fame.* And it is farther enacted by 34 *Ed.* 3. 4. *That all Panels shall be made of the next People, which shall not be suspect nor procured. And that the Ministers which do against the same, shall be punished before the Justices who take the Inquest, according to the Quantity of their Trespass,*

[a] Register 181. a. F N B 165 D. Vide 2 Rol. Ab 647, 648. Cro. El. 413.

[b] 2 H 5. Stat 2 cap 3. 35 H 8 c 6. 27 El. c 6. 4 & 5 Gul. & Mar. c. 24. 7 & 8 Gul. 3. 32

[c] Vide supra, cap. 10. sect. 65, 66, 67, 68.

2 Inst. 561.

pass, as well against the King as against the Party for the Quantity of the Damage which he hath suffered in such Manner; and both these Statutes seem equally to extend to the undue Return of Grand and Petit Juries. But it is observable, that the Clause of the above recited Statute of *Articuli super Chartas*, which ordains that the Sheriff, *&c.* shall render double Damages, extends only to Juries returned in Suits between Party and Party; because it says, That he shall render them to the Plaintiff, which is a Denomination never given to the King or Prosecutor, where the Proceeding is by Way of Indictment; and accordingly we find that the Writs in the [a] Register grounded on this Statute expresly relate to Suits between Party and Party.

[a] Regist. 178. F.N.B. 165.

Sect. 22. But the principal Statutes relating to the Return of Grand Juries, are 11 *H.* 4. 9. and 3 *H.* 8. 12. the first whereof is as followeth, *Because, that now of late Enquests were taken at* Westminster, *of Persons named to the Justices, without due Return of the Sheriff, of which Persons some were outlawed before the said Justices of Record, and some fled to Sanctuary for Treason, and some for Felony, there to have Refuge, by whom, as well many Offenders were indicted, as other lawful liege People of our Lord the King, not guilty, by Conspiracy, Abetment, and false Imagination of other Persons, for their special Advantage and singular Lucre, against the Course of the Common Law used and accustomed before this Time: Our said Lord the King, for the greater Ease and Quietness of his People, will and granteth, that the same Indictment so made, with all the Dependance thereof, be revoked, adnulled, void, and holden for none for ever: And that from henceforth no Indictment be made by any such Persons, but by Enquests of the King's lawful liege People, in the Manner as was used in the Time of his noble Progenitors, returned by the Sheriffs, or Bailiffs of Franchises, without any Denomination to the Sheriffs, or Bailiffs of Franchises before made by any Person, of the Names, which by him should be impanelled, except it be by the Officers of the said Sheriffs or Bailiffs of Franchises sworn and known to make the same, and other Officers to whom it pertaineth to make the same according to the Law of* England: *And if any Indictment be made hereafter in any Point to the contrary, that the same Indictment be also void, revoked, and for ever holden for none.*

In the Construction of this Statute the following Points have been resolved,

Sect. 23. [b] First, That where a Person not returned by the Sheriff on a Grand Jury procures his Name to be read among those of others who were actually returned, whereupon he is sworn of the Grand Jury, *&c.* he may be indicted, either in the King's Bench [c] or before Justices of *Oyer* and *Terminer*, for his Contempt of the Statute; and being found guilty, may be fined and imprisoned; and yet the Statute doth not expresly provide that any such Person shall be any Way punished, but only that the Indictment shall be void, *&c.*

[b] 12 Co. 98, 99. 3 Inst. 33.

[c] Supra, cap. 5. Sect. 32.

Sect. 24. [d] Secondly, That Indictments of Offences not capital are as much within the Statute as Indictments of Treason or Felony; and also Indictments before Justices of Peace as much as Indictments before superior Justices; but it hath been [e] questioned whether a Coroner's Inquest be within the Purview of it.

[d] 12 Co. 98. 3 Inst. 33. Cro. Ca. 134.

[e] 1 Jon. 198, 199. Cro. Ca. 134, 147.

Sect. 25. Thirdly, That a Person arraigned upon any Indictment taken contrary to the Purview of the Statute, [f] may plead such Matter in Avoidance of the Indictment, and also plead over to the Felony.

[f] H.P.C. 202. 3 Inst. 34. Cro. Ca. 134, 147. 1 Jon. 198, 199.

Sect. 26. Fourthly, That a Person outlawed upon any such Indictment without a Trial, may also shew in Avoidance of the Outlawry, that the Indictment was taken contrary to the Purview of the Statute, as seems fully to appear from the [a] above-mentioned Year Book of 11 *H.* 4. 41. But if a Person who is tried upon such an Indictment, takes no such Exception before his Trial, it may be [b] doubtful whether he may be allowed to take such Exception afterwards, because he hath slipp'd the most proper Time for it; except it can be verified by the Records of the same Court wherein the Indictment is depending, as by an Outlawry in such Court of one of the Indictors, *&c.* in which Case it is [c] said, That any one, as *amicus Curiæ*, may inform the Court of it.

[a] Supra, Sect 17.
[b] 3 Inst. 34. Bro. Indict. 2.
[c] 3 Inst. 34.

Sect. 27. [d] Fifthly, That if any one of the Grand Jury who find an Indictment be within any one of the Exceptions in the Statute, he vitiates the Whole, tho' never so many unexceptionable Persons joined with him in finding it.

[d] 11 H. 4. 41. pl 8. H. P. C. 202. S. P. C. 88. 3 Inst. 33.

Sect. 28. Sixthly, That if a Prisoner indicted of Felony offer to take any such Exception, he shall upon his Prayer have [e] Counsel assigned him for his Assistance in it.

[e] Cro. Ca. 134, 147. 1 Jon. 198.

Sect. 29. [f] Seventhly, That the Court needs not admit of the Plea of the Outlawry of an Indictor, in Avoidance of any such Indictment, unless he who pleads it have the Record ready.

[f] 3 Inst. 34. Cro. Ca. 147.

Sect. 30. It seems somewhat questionable, [g] whether Outlawry in a personal Action be within the Purview of the Statute.

[g] 1 Jon. 198, 199. Cro. Ca. 134, 147.

Sect. 31. It is recited by the above-mentioned Statute of 3 *H.* 8. 12. *That many Oppressions had been, by the untrue Demeanour of Sheriffs and their Ministers, done to great Numbers of the King's Subjects, by Means of returning, at Sessions holden for the Bodies of Shires, the Names of such Persons, as for the singular Advantage of the said Sheriffs and their Ministers, would be wilfully forsworn and perjured, by the sinister Labour of the said Sheriffs and their Ministers: By Reason whereof many substantial Persons, (the King's true Subjects) had been wrongfully indicted of divers Felonies and other Misbehaviour, by their Covin and Falshood: And also somtimes by Labour of the said Sheriffs, divers great Felonies had been concealed, and not presented by the said Persons, by the said Sheriffs and their Ministers partially returned, to the Intent to compel the Offenders to make Fines, and give Rewards to the said Sheriffs and their Ministers.*

Vid. sup Sect. 15.

And thereupon it is enacted, *That all Panels to be returned, which be not at the Suit of any Party, that shall be made, and put in by every Sheriff and their Ministers afore any Justice of Gaol-Delivery, or Justices of Peace, whereof one to be of the* Quorum, *in their open Sessions, to enquire for the King, shall be reformed by putting to, and taking out of the Names of the Persons, which so be impanelled by every Sheriff and their Ministers, by the Discretion of the same Justices before whom such Panels shall be returned. And that the same Justice and Justices shall command every Sheriff, and their Ministers in his Absence, to put other Persons in the same Panel by their Discretions: And that the same Panels so reformed by the said Justices be good and lawful. And that if any Sheriff, or any their Minister, at any Time do not return the same Panels so reformed, that then every such Sheriff and Minister so offending, shall forfeit for every such Offence* 20 l. &c.

Sect 32. It hath been resolved that this Statute doth not take away the Force of the above-recited Statute of 11 *H.* 4. in any Point wherein it doth not expresly vary from it; from whence it follows, That if any of the Jurors who find an Indictment be outlawed, or returned by a Sheriff or Bailiff, at the Nomination of any other Person, the Indictment may be avoided in the same Manner as before, by Force of 11 *H.* 4. except

H. P. C. 202. 3 Inst. 33. Contra S. P. C. 88.

cept such Nomination be made by the Justices authorized by 3 *H.* 8. to reform that Panel.

Sect. 33. As to the seventh general Point of this Chapter, *viz.* Within what Place the Offences inquired of must arise, notwithstanding it were anciently [a] holden, That if one who had committed a Robbery in the County of *A.* were taken with the Manner in the County of *B.* he might be put to answer in the County of *B* (by which I suppose it is intended that he might be put to answer on an Indictment found in the County of *B.*) and then tried by a Jury from the County of *A.* Yet it seems to be generally [b] agreed at this Day, That by the Common Law, no Grand Jurors can indict any Offence whatsoever, which doth not arise within the Limits of the Precinct for which they are returned: And upon this Ground it hath been resolved to be a fatal Exception to an Indictment, that it doth not appear by it that the Offence arose within the [c] County, or [d] Riding, or [e] other special Division, or [f] Precinct, for which the Jury which found it was returned. And *à fortiori* therefore it must be a [g] good Exception, that it expresly appears by the Indictment that the Offence arose in a County, *&c.* different from that for which the Jury was returned. And it is [h] holden, That even the finding of a collateral Matter expresly alledged in the Indictment to have happened in a different County, is void. But [i] some have holden, That if the County be expressed in the Margent of an Indictment, the Vill or Vills in which the Offence is laid, shall be intended to be in the same County. But the greater [k] Number of Authorities require a greater Certainty, as by expressly alledging such Vill or Vills in the County named in the Margent, or *in comitatu prædicto*, which seems to be sufficient where but one County is named before; but to be [l] uncertain where a County is named in the Body of the Indictment different from that in the Margent. But it seems from the Authority of [m] *Band*'s Case, That if a Fact be alledged in *B. juxta D in Comitatu E.* being the same County for which the Jury is returned, the County is set forth with sufficient Certainty, because *B.* shall be intended to be in the same County with *D.* Also if one be indicted for a Rescous from an Arrest in the County of *B* it hath been [n] holden, that it is needless to express the County wherein the Rescous was done with greater Certainty, because it shall be intended to have been in the same County wherein the Arrest was; *à* [o] *fortiori* therefore, if a Fact be alledged at *B.* in the Parish of *C.* in the County of *D.* it cannot but be intended that *B.* as well as *C.* is in the County of *D.*

Sect. 34. But of whatsoever Nature an Offence indicted may be, whether local or transitory, as seditious Words, or Battery, *&c* it seems to be [p] agreed, That if upon Not guilty pleaded it shall appear that it was committed in a County different from that in which the Indictment was found, the Defendant shall be acquitted, as shall be shewn more at large in the Chapter concerning Evidence.

Sect. 35. And therefore at the Common Law, if a Man had died in one County of a Stroke received in another, it seems to have been the more [q] general Opinion, that regularly the Homicide was indictable in neither of them, because the Offence was not compleat in either, and no Grand Jury could inquire of what happened out of their own County. But this Inconvenience is remedied by 2 *&* 3 *Ed.* 6. 24. by which it is enacted, *That where any Person shall be feloniously stricken, or poisoned in one County, and die of the same Stroke or Poisoning in another County, that then an Indictment thereof found by Jurors of the County, where the Death shall happen, whether it shall be found before the Coroner, upon the Sight of such dead*

I Body;

[a] 26 Ass. pl. 32. Fitz Coro. 194. Vide supra, Sect. 5.
[b] 3 Inst. 49. H. P. C. 203.
[c] 1 Bulst. 203, 205. Cro. El. 137 pl. 8. Dy. 69. pl. 29. 2 Keb. 302. pl. 94.
[d] Cro Jac. 276.
[e] Cro Jac. 276.
[f] Keilw. 89, 33 pl 6.
[g] Stedman's Case, Cro. El. 137.
[h] Cro. Jac. 17.
[i] 1 Bulst. 203. 1 Sid. 312. Keilw. 33. pl 6. Cro. Jac. 167.
[k] 1 Sid 345, 346. Cro. El 606. pl 4. 677. pl. 6 738. pl. 10 751. pl. 7. Vide Cro Jac. 95, 276. 2 Keb. 302 pl. 94.
[l] Cro. El. 100. pl. 5. 184. pl. 1. 436. pl. 51.
[m] Cro. Jac 41
[n] Cro. Jac. 345 Vide Fitz. Coro. 45. Attachm. 1. Retorn de Viscount 32. Bro. Retorn de Brief 97.
3 H. 7. 11. pl. 3. 5 H. 7. 17. b. 18. a. 10 Ed. 4. 15. pl. 13. Dy. 69 pl. 29.
[o] Cro. El. 108, pl. 3.
[p] H. P. C. 203. Kelynge 15.
[q] Vide B. 1. Ch 31. S. 13. 6 H. 7 10. pl. 7. 10 H. 7. 28. pl. 20. Fitz. Indictment 23. *See the Preamble of* 2 & 3 Ed. 6. 24. Contra Fitz. Coro. 373. Indictm. 24. 7 H. 7. 8. pl. 1. 10 H. 7. 20. pl. 8. Fitz. Cor. 446.

Body; or before the Justices of Peace, or other Justices or Commissioners, which shall have Authority to inquire of such Offences, shall be as good and effectual in the Law, as if the Stroke or Poisoning had been committed and done in the same County where the Party shall die, or where such Indictment shall be so found.

Sect. 35. And it seems that by the Common Law, if a Fact done in one County prove a Nusance to another, it may be indicted in [a] either County.

[a] H.P.C. 203. Fitz Bar. 279. Assise 446. 19 Ass. pl. 6.

Sect. 36. Also by the Common Law if one guilty of Larceny in one County carry the Goods stoln into another, he [b] may be indicted in either, as hath been more fully shewn in the first [c] Book.

[b] Keilw. 160. b. 4 H. 7. 5. b. Fitz. Cor. 61.

[c] Ch. 33. S. 9.

Sect. 37. Also if a Man marry two Wives, the first in a foreign Country, and the second in *England*, it is [d] holden that he may be indicted and tried for it in *England* upon the Statute of 1 *Jac.* 1. 11. which makes it Felony; because the second Marriage alone was criminal, and the first had nothing unlawful in it, and was merely of a transitory Nature: But where the second Marriage is in a foreign Country, it hath been holden, That the Party is not triable on the Statute above-mentioned; but this seems contrary to the Purview of it, as hath been more fully shewn in *Book* 1. *Chap.* 43. *Sect.* 7.

[d] 1 Sid. 171. Kelynge 79, 80.

Sect. 38. Also if a Woman be taken with Force in one County, and carried into another, and there married, the Offender may be indicted and tried in the second County, upon the Statute of 3 *H.* 7. 2. against Forcible Marriage, because the Continuance of the Force in such County amounts to a Forcible Taking within the Statute. But if an Offence in stealing, taking away, withdrawing, or avoiding a Record, against the Purport of 8 *H.* 6. 12. be committed partly in one County and partly in another, so as not to amount to a compleat Offence within the Statute in either, it is said that the Party cannot be indicted for a Felony in either, but only for a Misprision.

Book 1. Ch. 42. Sect. 10.

Book 1. Ch. 45. Sect. 6.

Sect. 39. It is enacted by 26 H. 8. 6. *For the Punishment and speedy Trials, as well of the Counterfeiters of any Coin currant within this Realm, washing, clipping, or minishing of the same, as of all and singular Felonies, Murders, wilful burning of Houses, Manslaughters, Robberies, Burglaries, Rapes, and Accessaries of the same, and other Offences feloniously done, within any Lordship Marcher of* Wales, *that the Justices of the Gaol-Delivery, and of the Peace, and every of them for the Time being in the Shire or Shires of* England, *where the King's Writ runneth, next adjoining to the Lordship Marcher, or other Places in* Wales, *where such counterfeiting, washing, clipping, or minishing of any Coin currant within this Realm, or Murther shall be committed; or where any other Felonies or Accessaries shall be committed, shall have full Power at their Sessions and Gaol-Delivery, to enquire by Verdict of twelve Men of the same Shire or Shires next adjoining, within* England, *where the King's Writ runneth, there to cause all such Counterfeitors, Washers, Clippers of Money, Felons, Murderers, and Accessaries to the same, to be indicted, according to the Laws of this Land, in like Manner and Form, as if the same Petit Treasons, Murders, Felonies, and Accessaries to the same, had been done within any of the said Shires within the said Realm: And also to hear, determine, and judge the same, according to the Laws of the Realm.*

Sect. 40. And it seems generally to have been [e] holden, That the Power given by this Statute to the Justices of Gaol-Delivery and of Peace, in the adjoining *English* Counties, in relation to the Offences therein mentioned, is not repealed by 34 & 35 *H.* 8. 26. which impowers the Justices of the Grand Sessions in *Wales* to take Indictments of such Offences. But it hath been [f] resolved that an Acquittal on an Indictment

[e] 1 Mod. 64, 68. 2 Keb. 685. Cro. Car. 247. 331. See Book 1. Ch. 31. Sect. 14.

[f] 1 Lev. 118.

ment at the Grand Sessions is a good Bar of an Indictment for the same Crime in an *English* County.

Sect. 41. It is enacted by 28 *H.* 8. 15 which hath been more fully set forth and expounded in *Book* 1. *Ch.* 37. *That Treasons, Felonies and Robberies,* &c. *upon the Sea,* &c. *shall be inquired,* &c. *in such Places in the Realm as shall be limited in the King's Commission, in like Manner as if such Offences had been committed on the Land.*

Sect. 42. It hath been [a] resolved, That this Statute extends not to Offences done in Creeks or Ports within the Body of a County, because such Offences were always cognisable by the Common Law.

Sect. 43. Also it hath been [b] resolved, That the Force of this Statute, in relation to Treasons done upon the Sea, is not taken away by 35 *H.* 8. 2. more fully set forth in the forty-seventh Section.

Sect. 44. It was made a [c] Doubt upon this Statute, Whether one who was an Accessory at Land to a Felony at Sea, were triable by the Admiral within the Purview of it; but this is settled by [d] 11 & 12 *W.* 3. *c.* 7. which enacts, That Accessories to Piracy before or after, in such Manner as is set forth more at large in that Statute, shall be inquired of, tried, and adjudged according to the said Statute of 28 *H.* 8. 15.

Sect. 45. It is farther [e] enacted by the said Statute of 11 & 12 *W.* 3. *c.* 7. That all Piracies and Felonies upon the Sea, *&c.* may be tried at Sea, or upon the Land, in his Majesty's Plantations, in such Manner as hath been more fully set forth in the first Book.

Sect. 46. It seems to have been a great [f] Doubt before the making of the Statute of 35 *H.* 8. 2. in what Manner and in what Place High Treason done out of the Realm was to be tried; for some seem to have holden, That it was triable only upon an [g] Appeal before the Constable and Marshal; others, that it might be tried upon an Indictment, laying the Offence in [h] any County where the King pleased; and others, that it was triable by Way of Indictment in that County [i] only wherein the Offender had Lands: But surely it [k] cannot reasonably be doubted, but that it was triable some Way or other, for it cannot be imagined that an Offence of such dangerous Consequence, and expressly within the Purview of 25 *Ed.* 3. should be wholly dispunishable, as it must have been if it were no Way triable.

Sect. 47. *But for a plain Remedy, Order, and Declaration of this Matter,* it is enacted by 35 *H.* 8. 2. *That all Manner of Offences, being then already made or declared, or after to be made or declared, by any of the Laws and Statutes of this Realm, to be Treasons, Misprisions of Treasons, or Concealments of Treasons, and done, perpetrated, or committed by any Person or Persons, out of this Realm of* England, *shall be from thenceforth inquired of, heard and determined before the King's Justices of his Bench, for Pleas to be holden before himself, by good and lawful Men of the same Shire, where the said Bench shall sit and be kept; or else before such Commissioners, and in such Shire of the Realm, as shall be assigned by the King's Majesty's Commission, and by lawful Men of the same Shire, in like Manner and Form to all Intents and Purposes, as if such Treasons, Misprisions of Treasons, or Concealments of Treasons, had been done, perpetrated and committed within the same Shire, where they shall be so inquired of, heard and determined, as is aforesaid.*

In the Construction of this Statute the following Points have been resolved,

[a] Book 1. Ch. 37. Sect. 11. Quære Moor 121. pl 265.
[b] 3 inst 11, 112. 4 Inst. 124.
[c] Yel. 134, 135. 13 Co. 51, 52. Noy 131. Contra H. P. C. 77. 3 Inst. 112. Book 1. Ch. 37 Sect. 7.
[d] Book 1. Ch. 37. Sect 15.
[e] Book 1. Ch 37. Sect 12.
[f] 19 E. 4 6.b. *See the Preamble of* 35 H 8. 2.
[g] Vide supra, Ch 4 Sect. 9. *and* Ch 23. Sect. 29 Dyer 131. pl 75.
[h] 1 Inst. 261.
[i] H.P C. 204 3 Inst. 11.
[k] Contra Dyer 131. pl. 75. *and* 11 Co 63. a. 1 And. 262.

Sect. 48. First, That if the Court of King's Bench, or Commissioners appointed in pursuance of the Statute, after having taken an Indictment of a foreign Treason, remove into a different County from that in which the Indictment was found, the [a] Trial shall be by Jurors returned from the first County; and this is most agreeable to the general Course of the Common Law; which [b] requires, That Indictments shall be tried by Jurors of the same County in which they were found.

Sect. 49. Secondly, That the Commissioners and County for the Trial of such Treasons, are [c] sufficiently assigned by the King in Pursuance of this Statute, by his either writing his Name to the Commission that appoints them, or signing the Warrant to the Lord Keeper for the Commission.

Sect. 50. Thirdly, That a Treason done by an [d] *Irishman* in *Ireland*, is triable in *England* according to the Purview of this Statute; for *Ireland* being out of the Realm of *England*, a Treason committed [e] in it is certainly within the Letter of the Act; and nothing within the Letter of a Statute made for enlarging the Jurisdiction, and supplying the Defects of the Common Law, shall easily be construed out of the Meaning of it. And therefore it seems reasonable, That any Offence which by 25 *Ed.* 3. or any other subsequent Statute, either expressly extending to, or [f] received in *Ireland*, is equally Treason in *Ireland* and *England*, may be tried here by Vertue of this Statute. But if an Offence be made Treason by an *Irish* Statute, which is not Treason in *England*, I see not how it can be tried here; since being neither made nor declared to be Treason by any Law or Statute of this Realm, it is not within the Description of the Offences provided for by 35 *H* 8. To which may be added, That Offences beyond Sea, to be tried here by Vertue of that Statute, are to be inquired of and determined in like Manner as if they had been committed in such Shire wherein they shall be inquired of and determined; but if an Offence which is Treason in *Ireland* and not in *England*, had been committed in any *English* County, it is manifest that it could not be punished as Treason. Also it hath been [g] resolved, That no Treason committed in *Ireland* by an *Irish* Peer, is triable in *England*, because he is intitled to a Trial by his Peers, which cannot be had in *England*.

Sect. 51. Fourthly, That this Statute is not [h] repealed by 1 & 2 *Ph.* & *Mar.* 10. which enacts, *That all Trials hereafter to be had, award-d or made, for any Treason, shall be had and used, according to the Common Laws of the Realm, and not otherwise.* For it is the manifest Purport of this Statute to restore the ancient Course of the Common Law as to the Trial of Treasons in which great Innovations had been made by Statutes in the Reigns of King *Henry* VIII. and *Edward* VI. but it cannot be thought agreeable to the Intention of it to abrogate any Statute, which in a doubtful Case settled and confirmed the Jurisdiction of the Common Law, and gave a Method of Trial as agreeable as possible to its usual and ordinary Manner of Proceeding.

Sect. 52. It was a great Doubt at the Common Law, [i] Whether an Accessory in one County to a Felony in another, were indictable in either, but this is remedied by 2 & 3 *Ed.* 6. 24. by which it is enacted, That such an Accessory may be indicted and tried in the same County wherein he was Accessory. But intending more fully to treat of this Matter in the Chapter concerning the Arraignment of the Principal and Accessory, I shall refer the Reader thither for the farther Consideration of it.

[a] H.P.C. 204. 3 Inst. 34.
[b] S.P.C. 90. Letter B. Vid. Dy. 286. pl. 45.
[c] H. P. C. 16, 205. 3 Inst. 11.
[d] 3 Inst. 11. 1 And. 262, 263. H. P. C. 16, 205. 11 Co. 63. a. Vide 3 Keb. 560, 566. Warner's Case.
[e] See B 1. Ch. 17. Sect. 67.
[f] 1 And 263. 1 Sid. 357. pl. 11.
[g] Dyer 360. pl. 6. Vide 1 And. 262.
[h] 11 Co. 63. H. P. C. 205. 3 Inst. 24. 1 And 262. S. P. C. 90. Letter B. Dyer 131. pl. 75, 286. pl. 45, 298. pl. 29, 300. pl. 38.
[i] Keilw 67. Dyer 38.

As to the eighth general Point of this Chapter, *viz.* What ought to be the Form of the Body of an Indictment, I shall endeavour to shew:

1. What ought to be the Form of the Body of an Indictment at Common Law.
2. What of an Indictment upon a Statute.

As to the first of these Particulars I shall endeavour to shew,

1. How the Body of an Indictment at Common Law, ought to set forth the Substance and Manner of the Fact.
2. How the Persons mentioned or referred to in it.
3. How the Thing wherein the Offence was committed.
4. How the Circumstances of Time and Place.
5. Where it may be vitiated by false, or improper *Latin*, or the Use of *English* instead of *Latin*.
6. Where the Offence indicted may be laid jointly, and where severally, and where both jointly and severally, and where the Offences of several Persons may be laid in one Indictment.
7. Whether the Words *Vi & Armis* be in any Case necessary.
8. Whether it be necessary to lay the Offence *contra pacem*.
9. Whether it be necessary to lay it *contra coronam & dignitatem Regis*.
10. Whether it be necessary to lay it *in contemptum Regis*.
11. Whether it be necessary to lay it *illicitè*.
12. Whether a Defect in any of these Particulars be amendable.

As to the first Point, *viz.* How the Body of an Indictment at Common Law ought to set forth the Substance and Manner of the Fact, I shall endeavour to shew:

First, In what Manner it ought to set them forth in relation to the Offence of the Principal.

Secondly, In what Manner in relation to the Offence of the Accessory.

As to the first of these Particulars, *viz.* In what Manner the Body of an Indictment at Common Law, ought to set forth the Substance and Manner of the Fact, in relation to the Offence of the Principal, I shall observe,

Sect. 53. First, That no Periphrasis or Circumlocution whatsoever will supply those Words of Art which the Law hath appropriated for the Description of the Offence, as [a] *Murdravit* in an Indictment of Murder; [b] *Cepit*, in an Indictment of Larceny; [c] *Mayhemiavit*, in an Indictment of Maim; [d] *Felonicè*, in an Indictment of any Felony whatever; [e] *Burglariter* or *Burgulariter*, or else *Burgalariter*, in an Indictment of Burglary; [f] *Preditoriè*, in any Indictment of Treason; [g] *Contra ligeantiæ suæ debitum*, in an Indictment of High Treason against the King's Person.

Sect. 58. Secondly, That in an Indictment, as well as in an [h] Appeal of Rape, the Fact seems to be sufficiently ascertained by the Words *Felonicè rapuit*, without adding *carnaliter cognovit*, or first setting forth the special Manner of the Terror or Violence, and then concluding that the

[a] Supra Ch. 23. Sect. 77. Dyer 304. pl. 56. Bro Indict. 7. Cro. El 920
[b] Fitz. Coro. 119 Indictm. 2. 8. Bro. Coro. 76. 12 Ass pl 32 2 Ed. 3. 1. pl. 3. Supra Ch. 23. Sect. 77.

[c] Supra Ch. 23. Sect. 77. [d] 2 Ed. 3. 1 pl 3. 2 Ed 3. 18 pl. 1. Fitz. Indictment 3. Supra Ch. 23. Sect. 77. Bro. Indictment 36 Bro. Appeal 48 18 Ed. 4 10. pl 28 Cro. El. 193 pl. 7. 4 Co. 41. b. 5 Co. 121. b. See 9 Co. 69. a. [e] Dalison 22. 4 Co. 39 b. H P C 207. 5 Co. 121 b. Cro. El. 920. [f] H. P. C. 11. 3 Inst. 15. Fitz Coro. 55 S P. C. 3. Letter A 3 H 7 10. pl. 2. [g] 3 Lev. 396. Calvin's *Case*, 5, 6, 10. [h] Supra Ch. 23. Sect. 79. Letter I. Fitz. Indictment 18. 9 Ed. 4. 26.

Defendant *sic felonicè rapuit, &c.* Also it seems, That the like general Manner of setting forth the Offence, which is sufficient in an [a] Appeal of Larceny, will also be sufficient in an Indictment.

Sect. 59. Thirdly, That in other Cases it is [b] generally a good Rule in Indictments as well as Appeals, That the special Manner of the whole Fact ought to be set forth with such Certainty, that it may judicially appear to the Court, That the Indictors have not gone upon insufficient Premisses. And upon this Ground it seems to be agreed, That an Indictment finding that a Person hath feloniously broken Prison, without shewing the Cause of his Imprisonment, *&c.* by which it may appear that it was of such a Nature, that the breaking might amount to Felony, is [c] insufficient. Also [d] Indictments against Persons for refusing to be sworn Constables, after they had been *legitimo modo electi,* have been quashed for not shewing the Manner of the Election, that it might appear to have been such as obliged the Defendants to have undertaken the Office. Also it hath been [e] adjudged, That an Indictment of Burglary is insufficient without the Word *Noctanter.* Also it seems to be [f] agreed, That an Indictment charging a Man with a Nusance in respect of a Fact, which is lawful in it self, as the erecting of an Inn, *&c.* and only becomes unlawful from particular Circumstances, is insufficient, unless it set forth some Circumstances which make it unlawful: But it is said that this is needless where the Thing indicted is unlawful in its own Nature, as the keeping of a Bawdy-house, *&c.* Also it hath been [g] adjudged, That an Indictment for traiterously coining *Alkemy* like to the King's Money, without shewing what Money, is insufficient; of which this seems to be the plainest Reason, That it appears not whether it were made like to the King's gold or silver Coin, or only like to that in Brass or Copper, *&c.* and if it were made like to that of the latter Kind only, it [h] seems that the Offence could not amount to Treason. Also it [i] seems, That an Indictment of Perjury, not shewing in what Manner and in what Court the false Oath was taken, is insufficient, because for what appears it might have been extrajudicial, *&c.* Also it seems clear, That it is necessary both in Indictments and [k] Appeals of Maihem and Murder, to set forth particularly in what Manner the Hurt was given, and that an Omission thereof is not holpen by a general Conclusion, that the Defendant *sic felonicè Mayhemiavit* or *Murdravit, &c.* But having already shewn in the Chapter of Appeals, with what Certainty the Count in an Appeal of Death, must set forth the special Manner of the Fact, as by shewing in what [l] Part of the Body the Wound was given, and the [m] Length and Breadth of such Wound; and [n] that the Party died of it; and with what [o] Weapon it was given; and that the Word [p] *Percussit* cannot safely be omitted where the Truth of the Fact will bear it, I shall refer the Reader to the said Chapter of Appeals, for the Learning relating to these Points. It hath been [q] adjudged, That an Indictment of Extortion charging *J. S.* with the Taking of 50 *s.* as Bailiff of an Hundred, *colore officii,* without shewing for what he took it, is good at least after Verdict, for perhaps he might claim it generally as being due to him as Bailiff, in which Case the Taking could not be otherwise expressed. But this seems to be a special Case.

Sect. 60. Fourthly, That an Indictment charging a Man disjunctively is void, as where it finds that A. *Murdravit* B. *vel Murdrari causavit,* or that A. *Verberavit* B. *vel Verberari causavit;* or that A. [r] *Fabricavit talem cartam vel fabricari causavit,* for here are distinct Offences, and it appears not of which of them the Indictors have accused the Defendant.

[a] Supra Ch. 23. Sect. 79. Letter K.
[b] Cro. El. 147. pl. 11. 201. pl. 30. 9 Ed. 4. 26.
[c] Bro. Indictment 7. 9 Ed. 4. 26.
[d] Aleyn 78, 79. 1 Mod. 24. 5 Mod. 96, 129.
[e] Supra Ch. 10. Sect. 46.
[f] Cro. El. 583. pl. 12. 2 Roll. Rep. 345. Palm. 368, 374.
[g] Fitz Indictment 10. S. P. C. 95. Letter D H. P. C. 206. Vide 2 Roll. Rep. 12.
[h] Book 1. Ch. 17. Sect. 57.
[i] Cro. El. 137.
[k] Supra Ch. 23. Sect. 79. 2 Lev. 140, 141. Salk. 377. Kelynge 124.
[l] Supra Ch. 23. Sect. 80.
[m] Supra Ch. 23. Sect. 81.
[n] Supra Ch. 23. Sect. 83.
[o] Supra Ch. 23. Sect. 84.
[p] Supra Ch. 23. Sect. 82.
[q] 1 Sid. 91.
[r] 5 Mod. 137, 138. 1 Salk. 371. pl. 8.

Sect 61. Fifthly, That [a] regularly every Indictment muſt either charge a Man with ſome particular Offence, or elſe with ſeveral of ſuch Offences, particularly and certainly expreſſed, and not with being an Offender in general; for no one can well know what Defence to make to a Charge ſo uncertain, or to plead it either in Bar or Abatement of a ſubſequent Proſecution; neither can it appear that the Facts given in Evidence againſt a Defendant on ſuch a general Accuſation, are the ſame of which the Indictors have accuſed him; neither can it judicially appear to the Court, what Puniſhment is proper for an Offence ſo looſely expreſſed. And upon this Ground it hath been adjudged, That an Indictment is inſufficient which only charges a Man in general, with having [b] ſpoken divers falſe and ſcandalous Words againſt *J. S.* being Mayor of ſuch a Place; or with being a [c] common Defamer, Vexer, and Oppreſſer of many Men; or with being a common [d] Diſturber of the Peace, and having ſtirred up divers Quarrels as well among his Neighbours as others of the King's Subjects at ſuch a Place, to the great Loſs and Diſturbance of his Neighbours aforeſaid, and other the King's Subjects, *&c.* or with being a [e] common Oppreſſor and Diſturber of the Peace; or with having been and ſtill continuing to be a Man of evil [f] Behaviour; or with being a [g] common Deceiver of the King's People; or with being a [h] common Publiſher of the King's Secrets, and of his Own, and of divers other Perſons impanelled together with him to inquire for the Body of the County of divers Felonies, againſt his Oath, *&c.* or with being a [i] common Foreſtaller; or with being a [k] common Thief; or with being a [l] common Evil-doer; or with being a common [m] Champertor; or with being a common [n] Conſpirator, and ſuch like. It is holden indeed in a Note in *Fitzherbert*'s *Abridgment*, That an Indictment for Confederacy in general is good, but this is made a Query by the Reporter of the [o] Year-Book, from which the ſaid Note in *Fitzherbert* is taken, and is denied to be Law both by [p] *Brook* and [q] *Rolle*, nor do I any where find the leaſt Reaſon offered to diſtinguiſh this from the other Caſes above-mentioned. Alſo it is holden by Sir *Edward* [r] *Coke*, That the ancient Form of Indictments charging Men with having as Hereticks and Traitors, and Infeſters of the Highways, conſpired and confederated, *&c.* to deſtroy the Catholick Faith, and having daily publiſhed falſe and ſeditious Writings, *&c.* were utterly inſufficient, and yet ſuch Indictments ſeem to have been [ſ] frequent; as were alſo Indictments charging Men in general, as *Inſidiatores viarum, & depopulatores agrorum*, which [t] Words took the Benefit of the Clergy from the Perſons indicted, before the Statute of 4 *H.* 4. 2. by which it is enacted, That thoſe Words ſhall no more be put into Indictments, nor if they be, ſhall have ſuch Effect as to take from the Perſons indicted the Benefit of the Clergy; [u] and this Statute in this Reſpect ſeems to be in Affirmance of the Common Law, which ſeems generally to diſallow of ſuch uncertain Indictments, as appears from the Reaſons and Authorities above ſet forth. Yet it hath been adjudged, That a Man may be generally indicted as a common Barretor againſt the [x] Form of the Statute, and [y] againſt the Peace, without ſhewing any of the particular Facts in the Indictment, by which he appears to have been ſo; for Barretry is an Offence of a [z] complicated Nature, conſiſting in the Repetition of divers Acts in Diſturbance of the common Peace, all of which it would be too prolix to enumerate in the Indictment; and therefore [aa] Experience hath ſettled it to be ſufficient to charge a Man generally, as a common Barretor, (which is a [bb] Word of Art appropriated to

[a] Vide 1 Lev. 203. 1 Keb. 278. Shower 389, 390.
[b] 1 Roll. Re. 79. 2 Roll. Ab. 79 pl. 11.
[c] 2 Roll. Ab. 79 pl. 1, 2. 1 Mod. 71.
[d] 2 Roll. Ab. 79. pl. 10.
[e] 1 Mod. 71. 288. 1 Lev. 299. Raym. 205. 1 Vent. 104.
[f] 2 Roll. Ab. 79. pl. 12.
[g] 6 Mod. 311.
[h] Moor 302. pl. 451.
[i] Fitz Action ſur le Stat. 26. 29 Aſſ. pl. 45. Moore 302. pl. 451.
[k] 2 Roll. Ab. 79. pl. 5. Moore 302. pl. 451. 22 Aſſ. pl. 73.
[l] 22 Aſſ. pl. 73.
[m] 29 Aſſ. pl. 45.
[n] 29 Aſſ. pl. 45.
[o] 22 Aſſ. pl. 45.
[p] Bro. Indictment 12.
[q] 2 Roll. Ab. 79. pl. 8.
[r] 3 Inſt. 41.
[ſ] 3 Inſt. 41.
[t] 11 Co. 29. a. H. P. C. 206.
[u] Vide 3 Inſt. 41. Lambert, Book 4 Ch. 5. Fol. 4[illegible]4
[x] Book 1. Ch. 81, Sect. 10.
[y] Cro. Jac. 527. 2 Roll. Ab. 82. pl. 5.
[z] Book 1. Ch. 81. 8 Co. 36. b. 37.
[aa] 2 Roll. Ab. 79 pl. 3. Cro. Jac 527. 2 Keb. 409. pl. 33.
[bb] Book 1. Ch 81. Sect 10. 2 Lev. 208.

this

this Purpose,) and before the Trial to give the Defendant a [a] Note of the particular Matters which you intend to prove against him. Also it is [b] holden, That there is no need to name any particular Place where the Defendant was a Barretor, because he shall be supposed to have been guilty in divers Places, and the *Venire* is most proper from the Body of County. Also it is said that there is no need in the Conclusion of such an Indictment, to lay the Offence *ad nocumentum omnium ligeorum, &c.* but that [c] *Diversorum* is sufficient in such an Indictment as well as in an Indictment of a common Scold, *&c.* because it appears from the Nature of the Thing, that it could not but be a common Nusance. Also it seems to be [d] agreed, That an Indictment against one as a common Scold, is good without setting out the Particulars, for the same Reasons that such Indictment of Barretry is good.

[a] Book 1. Ch. 81. Sect. 13.
[b] Vide B. 1. Ch. 81. Sect. 11.
[c] 2 Keb. 409. pl. 33. See Book 1. Ch. 75. Sect. 5.
[d] 6 Mod. 311. Book 1. Ch. 75. Sect. 5.

Sect. 62. Sixthly, That the Charge must be laid positively, and not by Way of [e] Recital, as with a *Quod cum, &c.* and that the Want of a direct Allegation of any Thing material in the Description of the Substance, Nature, or Manner of the Crime, [f] cannot be supplied by any Intendment or Implication whatsoever: And upon this Ground it seems to be [g] generally holden, That an Indictment of Death having the Words *felonice murdravit, &c.* cannot amount to an Indictment of Murder, without the Words *Ex malitia precogitata*; and yet by the Word *Murdravit* it expresly charges the Party with Murder, and it is impossible that there could be a Murder, and no Malice prepense. Also it seems to be generally agreed, That no Indictment of Death can be good without an express Allegation, that the Deceased both received the Hurt which is laid as the Cause of his Death, and also that he died of the Hurt so received; and that the Want thereof cannot be made good by any Implication whatsoever, as hath been more fully shewn, *Ch.* 23. *Sect.* 82, 83. Also it hath been [h] adjudged, That an Indictment against *J. S.* for feloniously breaking such a Prison, and commanding *J. N.* who was therein imprisoned for Felony to escape, is not a good Indictment for a felonious Breaking, without expresly shewing that *J. S.* did escape; and yet the Breaking is expresly laid to be felonious, and it is impossible that it could be so, unless the Party did escape. But it will be needless to enumerate any more Instances of this Kind, which are so very frequent, that there is scarce any Case which mentions Exceptions taken to Indictments, without having some or other grounded on this Rule, That in an Indictment nothing material shall be taken by Intendment or Implication. Yet the Law will not admit of too great a Nicety of this kind, for it hath been adjudged, That if in the first Part of an Indictment of Death, the Assault be laid with Malice prepense, *&c.* there is no [i] need to repeat it in the following Clause, which shews the giving of the Wound, being joined with a Copulative to the precedent Sentence, and laid at the same Time and Place with the Assault. Also it hath been [k] adjudged, that where an Indictment sets forth, That *J. S.* was lawfully arrested by Vertue of a Plaint before such a Sheriff, *&c.* it shall be intended that there was a good Warrant. Also it hath been [l] adjudged, That where a Warrant is alledg'd, authorizing the Arrest of *J. S.* within the Liberties of *London*, and the Indictment lays the Execution of it in such a Parish and Ward in *London*, without expresly laying the Parish and Ward within the Liberties of *London*, yet the Indictment is good, for the Court will not admit of such a strained Exception, that a Parish in *London* may be out of the Liberties of *London*.

[e] Salk. 371. pl. 6.
[f] S. P. C. 96. Cro. Jac. 20. 4 Co. 42. 5 Co. 120. b.
[g] Dyer 99. pl. 63. & 65. H. P. C. 231. Vide 2 Lev. 140, 141. 4 Co. 41. b. Contra Dyer 68. pl. 28.
[h] Kellew. 87. Vide Supra Ch. 18. Sect. 11.
[i] 4 Co. 41. b.
[k] Cro. Jac. 473.
[l] 9 Co. 67. 5 Co. 120.

Sect.

a Cro. Jac 610. 2 Mod. 128. 2 Roll. Rep. 226. Moore 606. 2 Lev. 229. contra 2 Roll. Rep. 226. Quære Ray. 378. 1 Keb. 852.

b Book 1. Ch. 64. Sect. 38. Cro. Jac. 610. 2 Roll. Rep. 226. 2 Lev. 229. 2 Mod. 129.

Sect. 63. Also it hath been [a] adjudged, That where an Indictment finds that *J. S. existens* of such or such a Degree or Trade, *&c.* as brings him within the Purview of the Law whereon the Indictment is founded, committed such a Fact, it shall be intended that he was of such Degree, *&c.* at the Time of the Fact, without any express Allegation to that Purpose, because that is the most natural Construction of the Participle *existens*, going before the Verb to which it is the nominative Case; [b] yet where an Indictment of Forcible Entry, finds that *A.* disseised *B.* of such Land *existens liberum tenementum* of *B.* it seems agreed, That the Indictment is insufficient, because it stands indifferent, according to the common Rules of Construction, whether the Land were the Freehold of *B.* at the Time of the Disseisin, or at the Time of the finding of the Indictment, the Word *existens* not being the nominative Case to the Verb, but applied to the Thing which was the Subject of the Action. But I cannot find any certain general Rule, whereby it may be known in what Cases an Exception of this kind shall be taken to be so over nice, that the Court will not regard it. All therefore that I shall add on this Head is this, That as on the one Hand the Law will not suffer a Man to be condemned of any Crime whereof the Jury have not expresly found him guilty, by any Argument or Implication from what they have so found; so on the other Hand it will not suffer a Criminal to escape on so trifling an Exception, which it would be absurd and ridiculous to take Notice of; for *nimia subtilitas in jure reprobatur.* But the Judgment hereof cannot but be in a great Measure left to the Discretion of the Judges, who from the Circumstances of each particular Case, the Comparison of Precedents, and the plain Reason of the Thing, seem always to have endeavoured to have gone within these Rules as nearly as possible.

c 3 Mod. 104.

d See Book 1. Ch 64. Sect. 39.

e Supra Ch. 23. Sect. 88, and 89.

f 2 Roll. Ab. 81. pl. 5.

Sect. 64. Eighthly, That it is a certain Rule, That where one material Part of an Indictment is repugnant to another, the Whole is void, for the Law will not admit of such Nonsense and Absurdities in legal Proceedings, which, if suffered, would soon introduce Barbarism and Confusion; also it takes off much from the Credit of an Indictment, that those by whom it is found have contradicted themselves. And upon this Ground it hath been adjudged, That if an Indictment [c] charge the Defendant with having forged a certain Writing by which *A.* was bound to *B.* which is impossible if the Writing were forged; or if an Indictment of Forcible Entry set forth, That the Defendant disseised *J. S.* of Lands, wherein it appears by the Indictment it self, that he had no Freehold whereof he could be disseised; or that the Defendant entred peaceably on *J. S.* and then and there Forcibly disseised him; or that he disseised him of Land then being and ever since continuing to be his Freehold; [d] every such Indictment is void, for its manifest Inconsistency and Repugnancy. And upon the like Reason it hath been adjudged, That an Indictment of Death, laying the Stroke at *A.* and the Death at *B.* or the Stroke on the first of *May*, and the Death on the Tenth, and then concluding that the Defendant in such Manner murdered the Party at *A.* aforesaid, or on the first of *May* aforesaid, is insufficient for the Repugnancy, as hath been more fully shewn in the [e] Chapter of Appeals, because it supposes the Murder to have been committed at a Place in the first Case, and on the Day in the second; in which it appears by the Indictment it self, That the Party was not killed but only wounded. Also it hath been [f] adjudged, That an Indictment for selling Iron with false Weights and Measures, is void, not only because it is absurd to suppose that Iron could be sold by Measure, but also because it is repugnant and inconsistent that it should be so sold at the same Time when it was sold by Weight. Also if an Indictment at a Sessions holden the 13th of *January*, 30 *Car.* 2. find that the Defendant has been absent from Church six Months from the first of *January*, 30 *Car.* 2. it is [b] agreed, That it is void for the Impossibility, for there are but eleven Days between the 1st of *January*, and the holding of the Sessions. Also if an Indictment charge a Man with having feloniously done a Fact, which appears upon the Face of the Indictment to have been but a Trespass, as with feloniously cutting down and carrying away Trees, the Court will [c] not arraign him; yet where the Sense appears plain, the Court will often dispense with a small Impropriety in the Expression, as where one is indicted for having mowed *unam Acram fœni*, which is [d] said to be sufficient, and yet that which was mowed, could not at the Time of the Mowing be in Strictness called Hay, but Grass only.

As to the second Particular, *viz.* In what Manner the Body of an Indictment at Common Law must set forth the Substance and Manner of the Fact, in relation to the Offence of the Accessory, I shall observe,

Sect. 65. First, That a Repugnancy in setting forth such Offence is equally fatal as in setting forth that of the Principal; and therefore if an Indictment of Death which lays the Stroke on one Day, and the Death on a subsequent one, charge the Accessories with having abetted the Fact, at the Time of the Felony and Murder only, it is insufficient, as hath been more fully shewn in the [e] Chapter of Appeals, because it appears by the Indictment it self, that the Time of the Death, and consequently of the Murder, was subsequent to that of the Stroke, and therefore it is repugnant to alledge that the Defendant abetted the Stroke by being present at the Time of the Death.

Sect. 66. Secondly, That where several are present, and abet a Fact, and one only actually does it, an [f] Indictment may, in the same Manner as an [g] Appeal, either lay it generally, as done by them all, or specially, as done only by the one, and abetted by the rest. But it hath been resolved, That if an Indictment barely charge a Man with having been present when a Murder was committed, it is [h] void, because a Man may be innocently present, and shall not be presumed to have been a Party, where no Circumstance is found that makes him so.

Sect. 67. Also it hath been [i] adjudged, that an Indictment of *J. S.* as accessory to four, by these Words, that *J. S. sciens ipsos quatuor homines feloniam prædictam fecisse apud D. felonice receptavit*, is naught for not saying *eos receptavit*, for it doth not appear how many of them the Indictors have found him to have received, whether all four, or three, or two, or but one.

Sect. 68. It hath been [k] holden, That an Indictment charging a Constable with having voluntarily and feloniously suffered a Person arrested by him upon Suspicion of Felony to escape, without shewing what the Nature of the Felony was, and that it was actually committed, is void for the Uncertainty, not only because it appears not but that the Offence of which the Party was suspected, was never actually committed; in which Case the Escape could [l] not be criminal; but also because it appears not what the Felony was, and unless the Arrest were for a Felony, the Escape could not be felonious. But it is said, That an Indictment for knowingly receiving Persons outlawed for, or convicted of Felony, or for knowingly suffering such Persons to escape, [m] may be good, without shewing what the Felony was, or that it was actually committed, if the

[b] Raym. 434. Par. Case, 3 Keb. 655, pl. 8.
[c] 12 Aff pl. 32. Fitz. Coro. 171. Indictment 9 Bro. Coro. 76. Book 1. Ch. 33. Sect. 21.
[d] 2 Rol. A. 81. pl. 1. Parallel Cases. 2 Rol. Ab. 81 pl. 2, 3. Vide 18 Aff. pl. 15.
[e] Ch. 23. Sect. 88, 89. Supra Sect. 64.
[f] H. P. C. 265, 266. 9 Co 67. Plowd. Com. 97.
[g] Supra Ch. 23. Sect. 76.
[h] 14 H. 7. 31. pl. 7. Bro. Indictment 5.
[i] 30 H. 6. 2. pl. 10 Fitz. Indictment 13. S. P. C. 95. Letter B. H. P. C 206.
[k] Cro El. 752. pl. 10. Hetley 53. 8 Ed 4. 3 pl 6. H. P. C 206. S. P. C. 95. Letter A. Fitz. Indictment 16. Vide Fitz. Coro. 55, 76.
[l] Supra Ch. 12. Sect. 16, 17. Ch. 18. Sect. 7. Ch. 19. Sect. 2, 3.
[m] 8 Ed. 4. 3. pl. 6. Fitz. Indictment 16. Quære Keilw. 194. a.

the Record of the Outlawry or Conviction be set forth with convenient Certainty: And the most plausible Reason of this Opinion seems to be this, That it may be sufficiently made out by such Record, of what Kind the Felony was, and also that it was actually committed, *&c.* It is holden indeed by Sir *William* [a] *Staundforde*, That such a general Indictment for receiving a Person outlawed for Felony in the same County wherein he dwells is good, but not if it were in another, because a Man is bound at his Peril to take Conusance of an Attainder of Felony in his own County, but not in another. But I much question the Authority of this Distinction, since, as the Law seems now to be [b] holden, a Man is no more bound to take Conusance of such an Attainder in his own County, than in any other.

Sect. 69. It hath been [c] holden, That an Indictment finding that *J. S. scienter receptavit* such a one, being a Felon, is not good, for this Reason among others, because it doth not expresly find, that *J. S.* knew the Person so received by him to have been a Felon. But this is contradicted by other [d] Authorities, by which it is holden, that the Word *scienter* in such a Case shall be construed to go thro' the whole Sentence.

As to the second Point, *viz.* In what manner the Body of an Indictment at Common Law must describe the Persons mentioned in it, I shall endeavour to shew,

1. In what manner it must describe the Defendant.
2. How other Persons mention'd or referr'd to in the Indictment.

Sect. 70. As to the first Particular, it is said, That an Indictment that the King's Highway in such a Place is in Decay, thro' the Default of the Inhabitants of such a Town, is [e] good without naming any Person in certain: Also it is said, [f] That no Indictee can take any Advantage of a mistaken Surname in the Indictment, either by Plea in Abatement, or otherwise, notwithstanding such Surname have no manner of Affinity with his true one, and he was [g] never known by it; and in this Respect, an Indictment differs from an Appeal, whereof it is [h] certain that a Misnosmer of a Surname may be pleaded in Abatement, as well as any other Misnosmer whatsoever.

Sect. 71. But I do not find but that every other Misnosmer of the Defendant, except that of the Surname, and also every defective Addition, are as fatal in an Indictment as an Appeal; for it seems generally to be [i] holden that a Misnosmer of the Defendant's Name of Baptism may be pleaded in Abatement of an Indictment. Also it hath been [k] adjudged to be a good Plea in Abatement of an Indictment against one by the Name of Sir *J. S.* Knight, that he is a Baronet, and no Knight. Also it hath been [l] holden, that it is a good Plea in Abatement of an Indictment against Garter King at Arms, that he is not called Garter in the Indictment, because it is a Name of Dignity, being given him by the Words *creamus, coronamus,* and *nomen imponimus*; and from the Reason of this Case, it seems plainly to follow, that the Omission of any other Name of [m] Dignity may be pleaded in Abatement of an Indictment: [n] And if so, why should not the Omission of the Defendant's Name of Baptism be equally fatal?

Sect. 72. It seems to be agreed, that notwithstanding an Indictment be the Suit of the King, yet being within the express Letter of the Statute of 1 *H.* 5. 5. concerning Additions, set forth more at large in the Chapter

4 of

[a] S. P. C. 95. Letter G. Vide Fitz. Coro. 377. Dyer 355. pl. 36.
[b] H. P. C. 218.
[c] 7 H. 6. 42. b. Bro. Indictment 4. Fitz Indictment 11. 3 Keb. 760, pl. 45. S. P. C. 96. Letter G.
[d] 2 Lev. 208. 8 Ed. 4. 3 pl. 6. 1 Danv. Abridg. 19 pl. Letter H.
[e] 2 R. A. 79 L.
[f] 1 H. 5. 5. pl. 8. H. P. C. 243. S. P. C. 181. Letter D. Fitz. Misnosmer 9. Vide 3 H. 6. 25, 26. Theloal. lib. 11. cap. 5. Sect. 14.
[g] *Quære* Kelyng 11, 12.
[h] 1 H. 5. 5. pl. 8. Rastal's Entries, 50. pl. 10, 54 pl. 4. H. P. C. 243. S. P. C. 181. Letter D. Supra ch. 23. Sect. 102.
[i] Theloal. lib. 11. ch. 5. Sect. 12. 11 H. 4. 41. pl. 7. Fitz. coro 88. Misnosmer 18. H. P. C. 243. contra 3 H. 6. 26. a Bro. Misnosmer 6.
[k] Cro. Ca. 371. 1 Jon. 346.
[l] 2 Leon. 248, 249. *Quære* Cro. El. 542. pl. 8.
[m] Vide supra ch. 23. Sect. 102, 103. Shower 392, 393.
[n] Vide ch. 23. S. 103. Keilw. 25 b. 26 a. *Quære* Palm. 195.

of [a] Appeals, it [b] cannot be construed to be out of the Meaning of it. From whence it follows, that the Want of a sufficient Addition, within that Statute is as good an [c] Exception to an Indictment, if [d] Process of Outlawry lie on it, as it is to an Appeal. Also it hath been adjudged, that it is a [e] fatal Fault to apply such Addition to the Name which comes under the *Alias dictus* only, and not to the first Name: But it is said not to be material [f] whether any Addition be put to the Name which comes under the *Alias dictus* or not, because what is so express'd is not material. But it is so great a Fault to put no Addition to the first Name, that where several are indicted, such an Omission, in Respect of one of them, makes the Indictment [g] vicious as to all. And it may be probably argued, that there is the same Reason for the like Fault in an Appeal against divers, to abate it also as to all, but I do not find this Point [h] expresly agreed. But it seems clear, that generally the Law is the same in relation to Additions in Indictments and Appeals. Having therefore already treated in the Chapter of Appeals of the general Learning relating to this Subject, and shewn that an Addition in [i] *English* is as good as in *Latin*; and that where several Defendants have the same Addition, it is [k] safest to repeat it after each of their Names; and that the Son being of the same Name and Addition with the Father, ought to be distinguished with some [l] farther Description; and having also shewn what is a sufficient Addition of the [m] Estate, or Degree, or [n] Mystery, and also of the [o] Town, Hamlet, Place, and County, of the Defendant: And also how the Defect of an Addition may be [p] salved by the Appearance and Plea of the Defendant, I shall refer the Reader for all these Particulars to the Chapter of Appeals.

Sect. 73. As to the second Particular, *viz.* In what manner the Body of an Indictment at Common Law must describe the other Persons besides the Defendant mentioned or referred to in it: It is certainly safest to describe them with convenient Certainty, which will hardly be dispensed with, except in special Cases, and for special Reasons. For those general Indictments which [q] anciently seem to have been allowed for suffering divers Bakers to bake, *&c.* against the Assise, *&c.* nor for distraining divers Persons without Cause, *&c.* have by the later [r] Authorities been holden insufficient for their Uncertainty in not naming some Persons in particular who were so suffered to bake, or distrained, without which the Court cannot so well know what Fine will be proper; nor can the Defendant be so well enabled to make his Defence, nor to plead the Indictment to a subsequent Prosecution. And for the same Reasons among others, an [f] Indictment for taking divers Sums of divers Persons for such a Toll at such a Rate, without naming any Persons in particular, hath been adjudged naught. Yet where in common Presumption it may be very difficult, if not impossible, to know the Names of the Persons referred to in an Indictment, it [t] may be good without naming any of them; [u] as where one is indicted for having knowingly received and harboured divers Thieves, to the Jurors unknown; in which Case, such a general Charge is maintainable from the Necessity of the Thing, for otherwise a notorious Offender of this Kind, might be wholly dispunishable, for want of the Jurors knowing the Names of the Persons so received, and yet might be publickly known to carry on such a Practice, to the common Nusance of the Country, in which Respect it cannot but be reasonable in such a Case to punish him, tho' not as an Accessory to the Thieves, without shewing that he had received some of them in particular. And for the like Reason,

[a] Supra ch. 23 Sect. 104
[b] Bro. Addition 50 Long quinto Ed. 4. 33, 34. Finch 234.
[c] Bro. Additions, 23, 41. 2 Leon 183. Shower 392, 393. 9 Ed. 4 48. pl 2. Dyer 46. pl. 2, 3, 4
[d] Cro. El 38. pl 9 148. pl 16 Cro. Ja. 531.
[e] S. P. C. 68. 2 Leon 183. 30 H. 6. pl. 2. Cro. El. 583. pl. 12. Vide Dy. 88. pl. 107. 1 Ed. 4. 1. pl. 3.
[f] 30 H. 6. pl. 2. S P. C. 68 Fitz. Process 103. 1 Ed. 4. 1 pl. 3.
[g] 1 Bulf. 183.
[h] Vide supra ch. 23. Sect. 125. Fitz. Count 18.
[i] Supra, ch. 23. Sect 105.
[k] Supra, ch. 23. Sect. 165.
[l] Supra, ch. 23. Sect. 105.
[m] Supra, ch. 23 Sect. 106, 107, 108, 109, 110, 111.
[n] Supra, ch. 23. Sect. 112, 113, 114, 115, 116, 117.
[o] Supra, ch. 23 Sect. 117, 118, 119, 120, 121, 122.
[p] Supra, ch. 23. Sect. 123.
[q] 38 Ass. pl. 11, 12. Bro. Presentment 27.
[r] Bro. Indictment 21. 2 Rol. Ab. 80. pl. 1, 2.
[f] Shower 389, 390.
[t] Pl Com. 85. b. 129 a.
[u] 2 Lev. 298.

if a Stranger [a] unknown to the Country be found slain, or if the dead Body of a Person who was well known, be disfigured in such a Manner by its Wounds, that no one can discover whose it was, it is certain that an Indictment against the Offender, for having killed *quendam ignotum*, will be good. [b] And upon the same Ground, if a Stranger unknown to the Country be robbed, and will not come in to prosecute, nor discover his Name, it seems clear that an Indictment against the Offender for having robbed *quendam ignotum* is good. And if Goods be found upon one notoriously suspected of Felony, of which he can give no manner of Account, as where a Highwayman is apprehended with his Pockets full of Watches and Rings, it seems that he may either be indicted for stealing such Watches and Rings, being the Goods *quorundam ignotorum*, or, as some [c] say, for stealing them generally. Also in the Indictment of the Regicides for the Murder of King *Charles* I. it was [d] agreed that the Fact was well laid, as done *per quendam ignotum*, with a Vizor on his Face. And if one steal the Goods of an Abbey, *&c.* during a Vacancy, he may be indicted for stealing [e] *Bona Ecclesiæ*, and yet the Church can have no Property. But these seem to be special and extraordinary Cases, depending on particular Reasons, and grounded on manifest Necessity, without which, it seems that such Indictments cannot be maintained: For it seems to be taken as a Ground in [f] many Books, that regularly the Persons offended, as well as the Defendant, ought to be certainly described in every Indictment. And agreeably hereto it hath been [g] adjudged, That an Indictment for stealing *quandam peciam panni linei cujusdam J. S.* without adding *de bonis & catallis ejusdem J. S.* is insufficient, because it doth not expressly appear to whom the Goods stolen did belong. Also it was anciently [h] holden, That where one is indicted for the Death of a Person unknown, the Inquest ought to tell his Name to the Court; but surely this must be intended where they have some Means to know it. However, from the whole thus much seems plainly to follow, that where-ever the Person injured is known to the Jurors, his Name ought to be put into the Indictment. And therefore, as I take it, those [i] Books which seem generally to allow of Indictments of killing, or robbing Persons unknown, are to be understood with this Limitation, That such Indictments are then good when the Party is in Truth unknown to the Jurors. And agreeably hereto, others [k] who speak more fully of the Matter, seem plainly to go upon the Necessity of the several Cases. And the Want of such Necessity seems probably to have been the best Reason why Indictments not shewing to whom the Wrong was done, were disallowed in some of the [l] old Books. However, it is certain that an Appeal for the Death or Robbery of a Person unknown, is in no Case good, as hath been more fully shewn in the [m] Chapter of Appeals.

Sect. 74. It hath been [n] adjudged, That an Indictment of an Assault on *John* Parish-Priest of *D.* in the County of *C.* is good, without mentioning his Surname, for if a wrongful Surname of the Defendant himself will not vitiate an Indictment, as hath been more fully shewn. *Sect.* 71, surely *a fortiori*, the Omission of the Surname of any other Person will not vitiate it; especially where such Person is otherwise described with such Certainty, that it is impossible to mistake him for any other. But if an Indictment for a Wrong done to a Person well known describe him only by

[a] 1 Ed. 3. 20. pl 26. 1 Ass. pl. 7. Fitz. coro. 159. 23 Ass 94. Fitz. Indictment 10. S. P. C. 95. Letter G. Pl. Com. 85 b. 129. a. 9 H. 6. 45. b. Dyer 99. pl. 61. 285. pl. 38. Vide Fitz. coro 146, 183. Noy 85. Supra, ch. 23. Sect. 78.
[b] Fitz. Indictm. 12. 17. 9 Ed. 4. b. S. P. C. 95. Letter G. Dyer 99. pl. 61. Keilw. 25. Supra, ch. 23. Sect. 78. Bro. Indictment 11. Pl. Com. 85. b. 129 a. 18 Ass. 15. seems contrary.
[c] Fitz. Indictm. 9. 26. S. P. C. 95. Letter G. contra Fitz. Indictm. 27. Bro Indictment 20. 30 Ass. pl 37.
[d] Keling. 10.
[e] 7 Ed. 4. 14. pl. 1. Fitz. Indictment 15. S. P. C. 95. Letter
[f] Lamb. B. 4. ch. 5. Dalt. ch. 131. S. P. C. 95. Letter G.
[g] Cro. El. 489, 490.
[h] 1 Ed. 3. 20. pl. 26. 1 Ass. pl. 7. Fitz. coro. 159, 183. Vide Bro. Indictment 10.
[i] H. P. C. 207. Dy. 285. pl 38.
[k] S. P. C. 95. Letter G. Pl. Com. 85. b. 129. a. Keilw. 25. 9 H. 6. 45. b. Vide Dyer 99. pl. 61. Dalton ch. 131.
[l] Fitz. Indictment 27. 30 Ass. pl. 37. 18 Ass. pl. 15. 2 Leon. 39.
[m] Supra, ch. 23. Sect 78.
[n] Keilw. 25. Dyer 285 pl. 38.

his Name of Baptism, without some Addition to distinguish him from others of the same Name, it seems [o] questionable, Whether it be not insufficient for the Reasons given in the foregoing Section? It is [a] said, indeed, in a short Note of a Case in *Moore*'s Reports, That an Indictment against one *Cole, quod burglariter domum cujusdam Ricardi fregit*, was adjudged good, without the Surname; and it not being there mentioned, that there was any other Description of the Party but by his Name of Baptism, it may be argued that that alone is sufficient: But to this it may be answered, That the only Point taken Notice of as adjudged, is that the Surname is not necessary, and perhaps in the Record at large there might be some Addition: But granting that there was none, yet the Authority of this Case is the less to be regarded, because of the Books cited to support it [b] two seem to be directly against it; and the [c] third, which is most to the Purpose, only proves that an Indictment for stealing the Goods *cujusdam ignoti* is good, which seems by no means to come up to the Point in Question, as hath been more fully shewn in the precedent Section. Yet howsoever the Law may stand in relation to such an Uncertainty, it seems to be [d] agreed, That a Repugnancy or Absurdity in the Description of the Person injured will vitiate an Indictment, as where one is indicted for stealing *bona prædict. J. S.* where no *J. S.* was mentioned before, for tho' in Civil Actions, the Word *prædicit* hath been sometimes [e] rejected, as Surplus and void, where it could be referred to [f] no certain Antecedent, yet this may perhaps chiefly depend on the Statutes of *Jeofailes*, which in many Cases help Defects in Form in Civil Actions, but extend not to criminal Cases, wherein the greatest Exactness is required; and if an Award may be defeated by appointing a [g] Payment on a certain Day beforemention'd, where no such Day was mentioned before, it cannot well be imagined that the like Inconsistency will be less fatal in a criminal Proceeding.

Sect. 75. It hath been [h] adjudged not to be necessary in an Indictment of Death to alledge, that the Person killed was in the Peace of God, and of our Lord the King, *&c.* tho' such Words are commonly put into Indictments, for they are not of Substance, and perhaps the Truth might be that the Party was at the Time actually breaking the Peace.

Sect. 76. As to the third Point, *viz.* In what Manner the Body of an Indictment at Common Law must describe the Thing wherein the Offence was committed, it seems clear that no Indictment can be good which wants a convenient Certainty of this Kind: And therefore it is [i] said, That an Indictment for forging a Lease of certain Lands, without naming some one certain Parcel, is insufficient. Also it seems to be agreed, That an [k] Indictment for stealing *bona & catalla J. S.* without any farther Description of them is void for its Uncertainty, for the like Reasons for which Indictments charging a Man with being an Offender in general are void, as hath been more fully set forth in the sixty-first Section: And upon the like Ground it hath been [l] adjudged, that an Indictment for a Trespass in two Closes of Meadow or Pasture; or for diverting *quandam* [m] *Partem aquæ* running from such a Place to such a Place, without any farther Description; or for ingrossing [n] *magnam quantitatem straminis & fæni*, or [o] *diversos cumulos tritici*, without shewing how much of each; or for carrying away *duas* [p] *centenas casei*, without adding the Words *libras* or *uncias*, or some other Substantive to *centenas*; or for erecting several [q] Cottages *contra formam statuti*, without shewing how many, *&c.* are insufficient for their Uncertainty. As to the [r] Case of the King against *Wetwang*, wherein the Court disallowed an Exception to the Generality

 of

[o] Vide Dalton ch. 131. Lambert, Book 4. ch. 5.
[a] Moore, 466. pl. 662.
[b] 18 Ass. pl. 15. Fitz. Indictment 27.
[c] 9 Ed. 4. 1. b
[d] Lambert, Book 4. ch. 5. Folio 495. 9 Ed. 4. 1. b. Fitz. Indictment 17. Bro. Indictment 6. S. P. C. 95. b. Vide Cro. Ca. 465.
[e] 3 Levinz. 436. Cro El. 709. pl. 31.
[f] Vide Cro. Ja. 549, 550. pl. 11. 585, 586. pl. 7. 618. pl. 8. Yelv. 76. 111. Cro. Eliz. 658. pl. 2.
[g] Cro. Ja. 149. pl. 8. 1 Rol. A. 254. pl. 15. 263. pl. 6. Yelv 97, 98.
[h] 4 Co. 41. b.
[i] Hob. 272.
[k] Dalton, ch. 131. Lamb. B. 4. ch. 5. Fo. 496.
[l] 2 Rol. Ab. 81. pl. 4. 5 Mod. 138. Dalt. ch. 131. Parallel Cases B. 1. ch. 64. Sect. 37.
[m] 2 Rol. Ab. 80 pl. 14. 2 Buls. 119. Parallel Cases B. 1. ch. 76. Sect. 88.
[n] Cro. Ca. 380, 381. Vide 2 Bulst. 317. Shower 389 390.
[o] 1 Rol. R. 134. 135.
[p] Cro El. 754.
[q] 2 Rol. A. 80 pl. 13.
[r] 2 Keb. 178. 1 Lev. 203.

of an Indictment for taking *quosdam pisces*, without shewing how many, it may be answered, that this was contrary to the Opinion of Mr. Justice *Twisden*, and was only the sudden Opinion of two of the other Judges; neither does it appear that the Indictment was adjudged good, but only that the Court refused to quash it, and ordered the Defendant to plead to it. However, it seems clear from constant Experience, [a] That if an Indictment be uncertain as to some Particulars only, and certain as to the rest, it is void only as to those which are uncertainly expressed, and good for the Residue.

Sect. 77. If the Indictment be for a Larceny or Trespass on a living thing, as an Ox, Sheep, or Horse, *&c* it seems to be holden by [b] *Lambard*, and [c] *Dalton*, that it is most proper to express to whom the Property of it belonged, by calling it respectively the Ox, Sheep, or Horse of the Party injured, without using the Words *bona* or *catalla*: But that it is improper to use these Words, where the thing taken was not a living Creature. Also it is holden by [d] *Lambard*, that it is proper to shew the Worth of all living things, and also of such dead things as are sold by Weight or Measure, by expressing that they are of such a Price, and the Worth of other dead things, by expressing that they are of such a Value; yet no Instance is produced where any Indictment has been disallowed in either Case for a Variance from these Rules. And as to the first of them it is farther observable, that the [e] Precedents in *Crompton* of Indictments for Stealing of Horses, and Oxen, expresly alledge the Horse and Ox stol'n *de bonis & catallis cujusdam J. S.* &c. Also an Appeal of stealing Sheep in [f] *Rastal's Entries* expresly alledges them *de bonis & catallis* of the Appellant. And as to the second of the Rules abovementioned, it is observable, that the Directions in the [g] Register concerning this Matter, which seem to be the chief Foundation of the said Rule are thus express'd, that in a Writ of Trespass of immoveable Chattels, the Writ shall say, *Tants de chateux ad valentiam X. S.* But if it be brought of a moveable Chattel, it shall say, *precii X S.* and *non ad valentiam.* Yet it appears by the Register it self, that even in Writs of Trespass concerning which these Directions are given, the Worth of the things taken away is sometimes omitted for the [i] Whole, and sometimes for [k] Part. And it is said to have been [l] adjudged, That such Writs are good notwithstanding such Omissions. Also where things moveable and immoveable are mentioned together in the same Writ the Worth of all of them together is sometimes [m] expressed under the Words *ad valentiam*, &c. And sometimes the Worth of moveable Chattels, as that of [n] Corn in a Granary, *&c.* of [o] Wine in a Vessel, and of [p] Wool is expressed under the Words *ad valentiam*, From all which it seems to [q] appear, That the said Directions are not necessary to be observed, even in Writs of Trespass, concerning the Form whereof they are expresly given, and that it is not material whether the Words *ad valentiam* or *precii* are used, or whether any Value be set on the things taken away or not. And if so, why should it be a greater Fault not to observe the said Directions in Indictments, which are [r] not tied to the strict Forms of Writs? Therefore from the whole, it seems [s] questionable, whether it be needful to set forth the Value of the Goods in an Indictment of Trespass for any other Purpose than to aggravate the Fine, and whether it be necessary in an Indictment of Larceny for any other purpose than to

[a] Vide Poph c. 208.
[b] Lambard, B. 4. Ch. 5. fol. 196.
[c] Dalt. Ch. 131.
[d] Lambard, B 4. Ch. 5. fol. 497, 498. Vide Cro. Ja. 130.
[e] Crompton de pace, 247, 248.
[f] Rast. Entr. 55. pl. 6.
[g] Register, 93. b.
[i] Vide Register, 93. b. *in the Writ* de warrena fugata, &c. *and that* de parco fracto. *and* 94 a. *in the Writ* de equo & catallis arrestatis, 94. b. *in the Writ* de averiis imparcatis, &c. *and in that* de trangressione facta uxori, &c *and* 96 b. *in that* de equo percusso & 97 a. *in that* de ovibus fugatis, &c.
[k] Regist. 93 b. *in the Writ* de clauso fracto arboribus succisis 94. b. *in the Writ* de domo fracta, &c. *and in the Writ* de Jumento, &c. fugatis. *and in that* de equis imparcatis, *and* 95. b. *in that* de palis, &c. *and in that* de piscaria piscata, &c. *and in that* de domo fracta, &c. *and* 96. a. *in that* de ovibus tonsis, &c & 96. b. *in that* de warrena fugata, &c. & 97. a. *in that* de porcis fugatis, &c,
[l] Register, 97. b. Vide Cro. Ja. 130. 1 Sid. 39, 150.
[m] Register 94. a. *in the Writ* de piscaria piscata, &c. *and* 95. b. *in that* de piscata piscata, &c *and in that* de domo fracta, &c. & 96 de exclusis stagni.
[n] Register 95. b. *in the Writ* de bladis inundatis, &c. & 96. a. *in that* de clauso fracto, &c.
[o] Register 95. b. *in the Writ* de vino, &c.
[p] Register 96. *and in the Writ* de ovibus tonsis, &c.
[q] Vide f. n. b. 88 *Letter* m. Cro Ja. 130. 1 Sid. 39, 150, 121, 15.
[r] q. Dy. 4. 26. b.
[s] See Dalton, Ch. 131. Lambard, B. 4. Ch. 5. fol. 496, 497.

I

shew

ſhew that the Crime amounts to grand Larceny, and to aſcertain the Goods thereby the better to intitle the Proſecutor to a [a] Reſtitution.

As to the fourth Point, *viz.* in what manner the Body of an Indictment at Common Law muſt ſet forth the Circumſtances of Time and Place, I ſhall endeavour to ſhew,

1. How it ought to ſet forth the Circumſtance of Time.
2. How that of Place.

Sect. 78. And firſt as to the Circumſtance of Time. I find it no where holden, That it is neceſſary to mention the Hour in an Indictment. But on the contrary, it is ſaid, [b] That if there be any Neceſſity for it in an Appeal, which yet is [c] queſtionable, it is from the Statute of *Glouceſter*, and not from the common Law; and therefore I ſhall take it for granted, That it is not neceſſarily required in an Indictment; ſince it is certain, That there is no Statute that makes it ſo, and the Common Law ſeems to have required no greater Certainty in an Indictment than in an Appeal.

Sect. 79. But it is laid down as an undoubted Principle in all the Books [d] that treat of this Matter, That no Indictment whatſoever can be good, without preciſely ſhewing a certain Year and Day of the material Facts alledged in it. Alſo it hath been [e] adjudged, That the Sheriffs Return of a Reſcous, without ſhewing the Year and Day, are inſufficient; becauſe ſuch a Return is in Lieu of an Indictment. Alſo it is taken for granted in [f] *Dyer*, That an Indictment of Reſcous is not good, without expreſly ſhewing the Day and Year both of the Arreſt, and alſo of the Reſcous, and that the Time of the latter is not ſufficiently ſhewn, by [g] ſhewing that of the former. And where an Indictment of Reſcous ſet forth, That *J. S.* committed ſuch a Felony ſuch a Day, and Year, and Place, *per quod* A. B. *prædictum* J. S. *cepit & arreſtavit, & in ſalva cuſtodia ſua adtunc & ibidem eundem* J. S. *habuit & cuſtodivit*, it is made a [h] Query, Whether the Indictment be not inſufficient, becauſe no Time of the Arreſt is alledg'd in the ſame Sentence with it; and it is doubtful whether the Time of the Cuſtody which is alledged in the next Sentence, by Force of the Copulative be applied alſo to the Arreſt or not, and *Dyer* ſeems rather to incline to the contrary Opinion. However, it is certain, That if an Indictment lay the Offence on an [i] uncertain or impoſſible Day, as where it lays it on a [k] future Day, or lays one and the ſame Offence at [l] different Days, or lays it on a Day which makes the Indictment [m] repugnant to it ſelf, it is void. Alſo it hath been adjudged, That no [n] Defect of this kind can be help'd by the Verdict. Alſo it is ſaid, That an Indictment of Death laying an Aſſault at a certain Time and Place is [o] not ſufficient without repeating the Time and Place in the Clauſe of the Stroke, and the like Rule ſeems alſo to hold as to Indictments of other Felonies, in which reſpect ſuch Indictments differ from Indictments of Treſpaſs. Alſo it is [p] certain, That an Indictment of Death ought as well to ſet forth the Year and Day of the Death as of the Stroke, that it may appear that the Party died within the Year and Day. But theſe Matters having been more fully conſidered in the Chapter of Appeals, I ſhall refer the Reader thither for the better underſtanding of them.

Sect. 80. It ſeems to be [q] generally agreed, That the Words *adtunc & ibidem* in the ſubſequent Clauſes of an Indictment are of the ſame Effect as if the Year and Day mentioned in the former Part of it had been expreſly

[a] Supra, Ch. 23. Sect. 55, 56, 57.
[b] S. P. C. 80.
[c] Supra, Ch. 23. Sect 87. 1 Bulſt. 203.
[d] S. P. C. 95. Letter A. Lambard, B. 4. Ch 5. Dalt. Ch. 131. Fitz Indict. 28 Dyer, 164. pl. 60. H. P. C. 208. 8 H. 5, 8. pl. 4.
[e] Fitz. Coro. 45. Attachm. 1. Bro. Return de brief. 97. 3 H. 7, 11. pl. 3.
[f] Dyer, 164. pl. 60. Vide Fitz Return de Viſcount, 32, Dy 69 pl. 29. 10 Ed. 4, 15. pl. 13. Quære 5 H. 7, 17. b. 18. a.
[g] Yet the contrary is adjudged, 2 Bulſt. 208 Cro. Ja. 345.
[h] Dy. 164. pl. 60.
[i] Supra, Ch. 23. Sect. 88. Moor, 555. pl 753.
[k] Raſtals Entries, 263. pl 5.
[l] 2 H. 7. 7. pl. 22.
[m] Supra Sect. 64. & Ch. 23. Sect 88, 89.
[n] 1 Rol. Ab. 781. N. 1.
[o] Supra, Ch. 23. Sect. 88. Hetley, 35. 119, 120. 5 H. 7, 17. b. 18. a. 1 Bulſt. 203, 204.
[p] Supra, Ch. 23. Sect 90.
[q] Dy. 28. pl. 6. Vide Keilw. 100. ſupra Ch. 23. Sect 88. 4 Co. 41. b. Quære Dyer, 164. pl. 60.

[a] 7 H. 6. 39. pl. 4. Fitz. error. 17. Plow. Com. 122. b.
[b] Lamb. B. 4. Ch. 5. fol. 491.
[c] Lamb. B. 4. Ch. 5. fol. 491.
[d] Book 1. Ch. 10. Sect. 5. Lamb B. 4. Ch. 5. fol. 492.

presly repeated. Also it hath been [a] adjudged, That an Indictment laying the Offence on the *Thursday* after the Day of *Pentecost* in such a Year is good: And from the like Ground it seems to follow, That an Indictment laying it on the [b] *Utas* of *Easter*, *&c.* (which shall be taken for the very Eighth Day after the Feast.) or on the Tenth of *March* [c] last (if it may be ascertained by the Style of the Sessions before which the Indictment was taken) is as good as if it had shewn the Day and Year by expresly naming such a Day of such a Month, *&c*,

Sect. 81. And where an Indictment charges a Man with a bare Omission as the not scowring such a Ditch, *&c*, it is [d] said, That it needs not shew any Time.

Sect. 82. It is most [e] regular to set forth the Year by shewing the Year of the King, yet this may be dispensed with for special Reasons, if the very Year be otherwise sufficiently expressed, for that only is material; and therefore in the [f] Case of the Regicides no Year of any King was laid for the King's Murder, but the compassing of his Death was laid in the Twenty fourth Year of King *Charles* the first, and the Murder was laid on the Thirtieth Day *ejusdem mensis Januarii*, because if the Reign of either King had been expressed, it might have caused a Dispute Whether that of the other would not have been more proper.

[e] Supra, Ch. 23. Sect. 90. 1 Lev. 113. 1 Salk, 195.
[f] Keling. 11.

Sect. 83, It is [g] agreed, That a Mistake in not laying an Offence on the very same Day on which it is afterwards proved upon the Trial, is not material upon Evidence.

[g] Supra, Ch. 23. Sect. 87, 88. 91. 3 Inst. 230.

Sect. 84. If an Indictment charge a Man with having done such a Nusance such a Day and Year, *&c.* and on divers other days, it is void [h] only as to the Facts on those days which are nncertainly alledged, and effectual for the Nusance on the Day specified; but if it charge a Man generally with several Offences at several Times, without laying any one of them on a certain Day, [i] as with extorting divers Sums of divers Subjects for a Passage over such a Ferry, *&c.* between such a Day and such a Day, it hath been adjudg'd That it is wholly void. Yet it hath been solemnly resolved, That a Conviction of [k] Deer-stealing setting forth the Offence between the Eighth and Twelfth of *July*, *&c.* is sufficient.

[h] Rex, v. Dixon. Trin. 2 Geog. Vide Supra, Sect. 76.
[i] Shower, 389, 390.
[k] Dom. Reg. versus Simpson adjudged, Trin. 13. Annæ.

Sect. 85. As to the second Particular, *viz.* How an Indictment at Common Law must shew the Place where the Offence was done, it seems agreed by all the [l] Books, That no Indictment can be good without expresly shewing some Place wherein the Offence was committed; which must [m] appear to have been within the Jurisdiction of the Court in which the Indictment is taken, and must also be alledg'd in such a Manner as is perfectly free from all [n] Repugnance and Inconsistency, for if one and the same Offence be laid at two [o] different Places, or at the Town of *B.* [p] aforesaid, where no such Town was mentioned before; or if in an Indictment of Murder, the Stroke be laid at *A.* and the Death at *B.* and then it is [q] concluded that the Defendant *Sic felonicè murdravit* the Person deceased at *A.* the Indictment is void. And so is it also if it do [r] not lay a Place both of the Stroke and Death; or if the Place or Places so alledg'd, be not such from whence a [s] Visne may come, Yet it hath been adjudged, That a Fact laid in a Parish in *London*, with some other Addition, as in the Parish St. [t] *Michael* in *Woodstreet*, *London*, or in the Parish of St. [u] *Lorrence Jewry*, is good, without shewing the Ward in which

[l] 25 Ed. 3. 43 pl 36 Fitz. Indictment 1. Suggestion 7. 4 H. 7, 8. pl. 5. Kelw. 98. pl. 1. 1 Bulst. 124. *See the books cited Sect. 72. under the Letters* d, e, f, g, h.
[m] Vide Keil 33. pl. 6, 89 pl. 9 Cro. El 448.
[n] Vide Supr. Sect. 64 & 79. & Ch. 23. Sect. 88, 89, 91.
[o] 2 H. 7 7 pl. 22.
[p] Cro. Ca. 465. Vide Supra, Sect. 74.
[q] *See* Ch. 23. Sect. 88, 89, 91.
[r] Supra, Ch. 23. Sect. 92.. Hetley, 35. 118, 119. Dyer 68. pl. 28
[s] Supra, Ch. 23, Sect. 92, 93.
[t] 9 Co. 66. b. contra Cro. El. 732. Supra, Ch. 23. Sect. 92,
[u] 7 H. 6. 36. pl. 42.

the Parish lies. But these Matters having been more fully treated of in the [a] Chapter of Appeals, and also in the foregoing part of this [b] Chapter, relating to the Certainty of the Time of the Offence, I shall refer the Reader thither for the fuller Consideration of them.

Sect. 86. It seems, that there is no need in an Indictment on a Statute, setting forth the Descriptions which bring the Defendant within the Purview of it, to set forth any Place where those Things happened, which brought him within such Descriptions; and therefore where a Statute makes it High Treason for a Person born within the Realm, and in Popish Orders, to come into, or remain in the Kingdom, *&c.* there is no need in an [c] Indictment on such Statute to shew in what Place the Defendant was born or ordained. Also it seems to be [d] agreed, That a Mistake of the Place in which an Offence is laid will not be material upon the Evidence on not guilty pleaded, if the Fact be proved at some other Place in the same County. But if there be no such Place in a County as that wherein an Offence is laid in an Appeal or Indictment, all Process on such Indictment or Appeal is made void by the Statutes of 7 *H.* 5. and 9 *H.* 5. 1. and 18 *H.* 6. 12. By the last of which Statutes it is recited, *That in the Parliament holden in the ninth Year of* H. 5. *it was ordained, For that many People of Malice cause often the King's liege People to be appealed or indicted in diverse Counties of Treasons or of Felonies, supposing by the said Indictments or Appeals, that the said Treasons or Felonies were done in a certain Place in such a County,* &c. *where no such Place is in the same County, that the Process of the same shall be void; and that the Indictors, Procurators, and Conspirators shall be punished by Fine,* &c. *by the Discretion of the Justices, and also liable to Writs of Conspiracy, and by the present Statute the above recited Statute is made perpetual.*

87. It is observable, That the Statute made in the ninth Year of *H.* 5. herein referred to, seems to be wholly omitted by *Keble* and *Pulton*, who have no other Statute concerning this Matter made in the ninth Year of *Henry* V. excepting the first, which only confirms a Statute made in the seventh Year of the same King concerning Appeals and Indictments; and there is no other Statute whatsoever in the seventh Year of that King mentioned in *Keble* or *Pulton*, but only one which requires the Justices before the Award of any Exigent to inquire by Inquest of Office, Whether there be any such Place in the County as that wherein an Offence is laid in an Appeal or Indictment. But this Statute seems only to extend to the County of *Lancaster*, for it is directed to the Chancellor of that County, and recites, That Persons had been indicted and appealed in Places falsly alledg'd in the said County, and in the enacting Part speaks only of Justices who had Power to determine Felonies in the said County, and in the latter Part expresly commands the said Chancellor to cause it to be proclaimed in the same County, but mentions no other. From all which I see not how it can extend to any other County, and yet *Wingate* in his [e] Abridgment makes it equally extend to all Counties. However, [f] *Rastal* in his Collection of Statutes seems to have set down the very Statute which is referred to by the above recited Statute of 18 *H.* 6. 12. and this is certainly [g] still in Force.

As to the fifth Point, *viz.* Where the Body of an Indictment may be vitiated by false or improper *Latin*, or the Use of *English* instead of *Latin*, I shall endeavour to shew,

[a] Ch. 23. Sect. 88, 89, 91, 92 & 93.
[b] Supra, Sect. 78, 79, 80.
[c] Poph. 93, 94. B. 1. Ch. 17 Sect. 79, 80, 81, 82.
[d] Vide Supr. Sect. 83. & Ch. 23. Sect. 91. Kelynge, 15. Salk. 288. H. P. C. 264, 165.
[e] Wingate's Abridgm. of the Statutes under the Title of Conspiracy, Sect. 3.
[f] Rastal's Statutes, Consp. 3.
[g] Lamb. B. 4 Ch. 5. fol. 493. F. n. b. 115. G.

1. Where false *Latin* will vitiate an Indictment.
2. Where a Word which is not *Latin*.
3. Where such Faults are holpen by an *Anglicè*.

Sect. 88. As to the first of these Particulars, it seems to be holden generally in some [a] Books, that no false *Latin* will vitiate an Indictment, and it seems to be holden by my Lord [b] *Coke*, That an Indictment shall not be quash'd for any false Concord between the Substantive and Adjective, as *præfata Regi*, or *præfato Reginæ*, because tho' the Expressions be incongruous, yet they are *Latin* and significant; neither do I find this Opinion denied by any other Authority, and therefore I leave to be considered, Whether it may not still be maintained, especially [c] considering, That the Sense appears as fully, clearly, and expresly from such *Latin* as if it had been never so properly expressed. And it seems also, That the like Reason may be given for the Case in [d] *Yelverton*, wherein an Indictment of forcible Entry, finding that the defendant *unum mesuagium ingressum fecit*, without adding the Word *in* before *mesuagium*, was adjudged good; but it is said in the Book, That this is not false, tho' it be not fine *Latin*; by which it seems to be implied, That if it had been false *Latin*, it might have vitiated the Indictment. However, it seems to be settled at this day, That an Indictment against two or more, laying the Fact charged against them in the singular Number, is insufficient, as where it finds That *A.* and *B.* *insultum* [e] *fecit*; the Reason whereof perhaps may be this, That it appears somewhat doubtful upon the Face of the Indictment whether the Jurors intended to charge more than one, because the Fact is laid in the singular Number, which it seems absurd to apply to more than one, and therefore the Indictment is insufficient for its Uncertainty. As to [f] *Fulwood's* Case, wherein *Croke* reports the contrary to have been resolved, it is certain, That the Verb in the Record is in the plural Number. And as to the [g] Cases wherein Faults of this kind have been amended in original Writs, as *teneat conventionem* for *teneant*, and such like; it may be answered, That those Amendments were made by Vertue of the Statutes of [h] Amendments, which extend not to criminal Proceedings. And as to the Case in [i] *Bulstrode's* Reports, wherein it is said to have been resolved, That an Indictment of Felony against more than one in the singular Number was amended, and thereupon the Defendants were adjudged to be hanged, it may be answered, That it doth not appear in what Part of the Indictment the singular Number was put for the plural; neither is the said Resolution, in whatsoever Sense it be taken, reconcileable with the later Authorities, as shall be more fully shewn under the twelfth Point. But it is [k] said, That a Fault of this kind is made good by the Grand Jury's finding the Indictment *Billa vera* against one of the Defendants only; the Reason whereof perhaps may be this, That the Uncertainty of the Indictment is supplied by such an Indorsement. But this seems contrary to the Authorities relating to this Matter cited in the second Section. Also it hath been [l] adjudged, That where a Bill of Indictment lays the Fact in the plural Number against two, and it is found *Billa vera* as to one of them only, it is good; and yet the Verb in the plural Number in the Record must, after such a finding, be applied only to one Person; but to this it may be answered, That here is no Uncertainty either in the Bill or Indorsement. Also it hath been [m] adjudged, That the Word *Solvit* instead of *Solvat*, is not fatal in a Judgment; but that a new one shall be given.

[a] 5 Cro. 121. a. Cro. Ca. 465.
[b] 5 Co. 121. b. Vide Cro. El. 108. pl. 3.
[c] Vide Cro. El. 108 pl. 3.
[d] Yelv. 27, 28.
[e] Dominus Rex versus Dobson, Termino Hilarii, 3 Georgii, 2 Keb. 51. pl. 9. Vide Cro. Ca. 465, 573. Cro. El. 754. pl. 15.
[f] Cro. Ca. 489.
[g] 2 Vent. 173. Yelv. 224, 225. 2 Saund. 38. Cro. Ja. 306, 369.
[h] Salk. 51, 52. 6 Mod. 268.
[i] 2 Bulst. 35.
[k] 2 Keb. 51. pl. 9.
[l] Cor. Ca. 464. 465.
[m] 1 Sid. 219.

Sect. 89. As to the second Particular, *viz.* Where the Use of a Word which is not *Latin* will vitiate an Indictment, it seems generally [a] agreed, That an Indictment wholly in *English* is void, which seems to depend upon the Statute of 36 *Ed.* 3. 15. *By which 'tis enacted, That all Pleas which be pleaded in any of the King's Courts shall be entred and enrolled in Latin.* And from hence it seems clearly to follow, That if any material Part either of the Body or Caption of an Indictment be expressed in a Word which is not *Latin*, as by the Word [b] *erectaverunt* instead of *erexerunt*, or [c] *brachia sua dextra*, instead of *brachio*, or [d] *præsentant' existit* instead of *præsentat'* the Indictment is insufficient; (except in some special Cases herein after set forth,) for no one can say, That the bare giving a *Latin* Termination to a Word unknown in that Language, can make it become *Latin*; and if the Want of one material Word may be supplied, why not the Want of two, and so on? It hath indeed been [e] holden, That a Fault of this kind, as *imaginavit* for *imaginatus est*, *ave* for *avia* is amendable in an original Writ, which yet is denied by others, if it be in a [f] substantial Part. However, it seems certain, That such Amendment must depend upon the Statutes of Amendments, which extend [g] not to criminal Proceedings. Also it seems, That it is no less a Fault to make Use of a Word which is proper *Latin* in another Sense, whether entirely different, or of a much larger Extent, than that in which it is used, as of the Word [h] *collis* for *colli*, or [i] *mala ars* for *veneficium*. Also it seems agreed, That an Abbreviation not justified by legal Usage, as [k] *Dno* without a Dash, for *Domino*, [l] *R. Rs.* for *Regni Regis*; or the Expression of a Number in any Figures that are not [m] *Roman*, is equally fatal as it would have been wholly to have omitted what you endeavour in such Manner to express. Also it hath been [n] adjudged, That an Inquisition finding that *J. S. seipsum emersit*, &c. is insufficient, because *emergo* doth not signifie to put into, but rise out of the Water. [o] Also it is said, That an Indictment has been quashed for the Words *Pace Regia*, instead of *Pace Regis*; but it appears not what was the Nature of the Indictment, nor in what Part of it these Words were used, and therefore I would suppose it to have been in such Part of some Indictment wherein those Expressions are so material that they cannot be rejected as Surplus and immaterial; for it seems to be a settled Rule, That nothing which may be so rejected shall vitiate an Indictment; as where the Year of the Lord is written in common [p] Figures, but the Year of the King is well expressed, or where an Indictment is said to be taken before *J. S.* and *J. N.* [q] *duo Justiciariis*, &c. Also it seems, That the Use of a Word which is not proper *Latin*, as of the [r] Word *contrafacere*, for counterfeiting, may be made good by Precedents. And there can be no doubt but that [s] Terms of Art, which are necessary in all Institutions, as *Felonia*, *Murdrum*, *Burglaria*, and such like, are good, tho' they be not good classical *Latin*; for they are of such a complex and peculiar Signification as no proper *Latin* Word will come up to. Also it hath been [t] adjudged, That a literal Translation of a Statute into *Latin* is sufficient, if intelligible, let it be never so unelegant, as where it sets forth that the Defendant *super caput suum proprium*, did forge, Meaning, That he did it of his own Head.

[a] Cro. El. 85. pl. 4. *Quære* 3 Keb. 637.
[b] Cro El. 231. pl. 22.
[c] Cro. El. 137. pl. 10.
[d] 1 Sid. 175. Salk. 370. pl. 2.
[e] 8 Co. 159. b. 2 Bulst. 35. Moore 5. pl. 17. N. Bend. 33. pl. 53. 1 And. 24.
[f] 1 Lev. 1, 2. 5 Co. 45. Cro. El. 462.
[g] 1 Salk. 51, 52. 6 Mod. 268. Vide Supra, Sect. 88.
[h] 1 Bulst. 109.
[i] Noy. 85. 1 Jon. 144. Latch. 156.
[k] 1 Sid. 175.
[l] 1 Sid. 140.
[m] 1 Salk. 195. 1 Sid. 40. pl. 6. 3 Keb. 301. 2 Lev. 102. 1 Mod. 78.
[n] 2 Lev. 140. 3 Mod. 100. B. 1. Ch. 27. Sect. 15.
[o] 1 Sid. 140.
[p] 1 Salk 195. 1 Mod. 78.
[q] Cro. El. 108. pl. 3.
[r] 2 Jon. 49, 50.
[s] Dalt. Ch. 131. 10 Co. 133.
[t] 2 Lev. 221.

Sect. 90. As to the third Particular, *viz.* What Faults of this kind are holpen by an *Anglicè*. It seems to be holden generally in some Books, That the Use of a Word which is either not *Latin* at all, or not *Latin* in the Sense in which it is used, may in many Cases be holpen by an *Anglicè*, as [a] *crectaverunt, anglicè* did erect; [b] *Retes, anglicè* Nets; [c] *Pellices, anglicè* Skins; *Ollis* [d] *æriis, anglicè* brass Pots. But to this it may be answered, That as to the three first of these Instances what is said concerning this Matter is only spoken of by the By, and did not come into Judgment; and as to the last of them it may be said, That it doth not concern a criminal Proceeding, but a civil Action, and that after a Verdict: And if the Purport of it be that an *Anglicè* helps the Use of a Word that is not *Latin* in an Action of Trover, tho' Damage be expressly given for it, it is contradicted by many other express [e] Resolutions, in which it seems to have been taken as a settled Rule, That where Damages are expressly given for a Thing expressed by a Word that is not *Latin*, it is no way help'd by an *Anglicè*. Also it hath been [f] adjudged, That an Indictment for taking *octo discas, anglicè* Dishes, is insufficient; and this is agreeable to what is laid down as a settled Rule in many [g] Books, *viz*. That where there is a proper *Latin* Word for the thing intended to be expressed, no *Anglicè* will help an improper one, as it will do where there is [h] no proper *Latin* Word, because in such a Case there is such a Necessity either to use a feigned one or none at all. Also it hath been adjudged, That where there is a proper *Latin* Word, an *Anglice* cannot make good the Use of any other either in a more [k] special or [l] extensive Signification than the *Latin* Language will bear, as to make Words [m] *malas artes* signifie Witchcraft, or [n] *Riscus* a boxful of Linen, or [o] *fulcrum tecti*, a Field-bed with a Testern and Curtains, in which Cases the Judges will take [p] no manner of Notice of what comes under the *Anglicè* beyond the strict Signification of the *Latin*.

Sect. 91. As to the sixth Point, *viz*, Where the Offence indicted may be laid jointly, and where severally, and where both jointly and severally, and where the Offences of several Persons may be laid in one Indictment; it seems certain at this Day, That notwithstanding the Offence of several Persons cannot but in all Cases be several; because the Offence of one Man cannot be the Offence of another, but every Man must answer severally for his own Crime; yet if it wholly arise from any such joint Act, which in it self is criminal, without any Regard to any particular personal Default of the Defendant, as the joint [q] keeping of a Gaming-House, or the [r] unlawful hunting and carrying away of a Deer, or [s] Maintenance or [t] Extortion, *&c*. The Indictment or Information may either charge the Defendants jointly and severally, as thus: *Quod* [u] *custodiverunt, & uterq; eorum custodivit*; or, *quod* [x] *asportaverunt, & eorum uterque asportavit*; or may charge them jointly only, without charging them [y] severally, because it sufficiently appears from the Construction of Law, That if they joined in such Act, they could not but be each of them guilty; and from hence it follows, That on such Indictment or Information [z] some of the Defendants may be acquitted, and others convicted; for the Law looks on the Charge as several against each, tho' the Words of it purport only a joint Charge against all. But where the Offence indicted doth not wholly arise from the joint Act of all the Defendants, but from such Act joined with some personal and particular Defect or Omission of each Defendant, without which it would be no Offence, as the following a joint Trade without having served a seven Years Apprenticeship required by the Statute, in which Case it must be the particular Defect of each Trader which must make him guilty, and one of them may offend against the Statute, and the others not, the Indictment or Information [aa] must charge them severally

[a] Cro. El. 231. [b] Keilw. 100. 3 Bulst. 178. *seems contrary*. [c] 1 Sid. 318. [d] Cro. Ja. 129. [e] 1 Lev. 99, 129, 204. 1 Sid. 98. 318. Raym. 15. 3 Lev. 336. 10 Co. 130, 133. [f] 2 Keb. 779. pl. 4. [g] Noy. 85. Latch. 156. March. 16. 60. 1 Jon. 144. 10 Co. 133. Vide 1 Lev. 204. 1 Sid. 318. Yel. 68. [h] 10 Co. 133. Noy 85. Latch. 156. March. 16. 1 Sid. 81. 1 Jon. 144. [k] Noy. 85. 1 Sid. 60, 81. [l] Cro. Ja. 664, 665. [m] Noy. 85. Latch 156. 1 Jon. 144. [n] Cro. Ja. 664, 665. 2 Rol. Re. 254, 255. [o] 10 Co. 130, 132, 133. [p] Cro. Ja. 664, 665. 2 Rol. Rep. 254, 255. 10 Co. 130, 132, 133. [q] Dominus Rex versus Dixon & uxorem adjudged Trin. 2. Georgii. [r] Dominus Rex versus Howkins, adjudg'd Mich. 3 Georgii. [s] 1 Vent 302. [t] Salk. 382. [u] Dominus Rex versus Dixon & uxorem, adjudg'd Trin. 2. Georgii. [x] Dominus Rex versus Howkins, adjudg'd Mich. 3 Georgii. [y] Domina Regina versus Williams, adjudg'd Mich. 10. Annæ. Bear & White, 4to. Gulielmi. Cro. Car 380, 381. 2 Rol, Ab. 707. pl. 45, 48, 708. pl. 52. contra 2 Rol. Rep. 345. Palmer, 367, 368. [z] 2 Rol Ab. 707. pl. 45, 48, 708. pl 52. Bear & White, 4to Gulielmi. [aa] 2 Rol. Ab. 81. pl. 6. 5 Mod. 180.

verally and not jointly; for it is absurd to charge them joinly, because the Offence of each Defendant arises from a Defect peculiar to himself. And for the like Reason a joint Indictment against several for not [a] repairing the Street before their Houses hath been quashed. But I do not find it settled in what Cases several Offences of several Persons may be joined in one Indictment; for in some [b] Books Indictments against several for several Offences, as for Recusancy, [c] following a Trade without having served an Apprenticeship, not [d] repairing the Streets, *&c.* are mentioned without any Exception on this Account: And it is holden, That one Indictment against two Justices for not [e] inquiring of a Riot, and an Indictment against two Persons for speaking of the same [f] Words, may be maintained; and yet it is [g] agreed, That one Action lies not against several for the same Words; Also in [h] *Rolle*'s Reports an Indictment against several for having Inmates in their Houses is said to have been quash'd; because it was but one joint Indictment against them all, whereas there ought to have been several Indictments against them. Also in the sixth [i] Modern Reports, an Indictment against several for the Neglect of a Day of fasting appointed by Proclamation, is said to have been quashed for the like Reason. And this is certainly most agreeable to the Rule of bringing Actions upon penal Statutes, wherein several Offences shall not be joined, except it be in respect of some one Thing to which all of them have a Relation; as where several [k] join in a Suit in the [l] Admiralty for a Contract on Land, or in procuring or giving an untrue Verdict, or are privy to one another [m] in Maintenance of the same Cause.

Sect. 92. As to the seventh Point, *viz.* Whether the Words *Vi & armis* be in any Case necessary in the Body of an Indictment at Common Law; it is taken for granted in some [n] Books, That they were necessary at Common Law in all Indictments for Offences which amount to an actual Disturbance of the Peace, as Rescouses and Assaults, and such like; yet I do [o] not find it agreed, That they were ever necessary in such Indictments, wherein it would seem absurd to put them in, as in Indictments for [p] Conspiracies, [q] Cheats, Slanders, Escapes, and such like; or [r] Nusances committed in a Man's own Ground. However, there can be no doubt but that the Omission of them in Indictments of this kind, is made good by the Statute of 37 *H.* 8. 8. By which it is recited, *That in all Indictments of Felony and Trespass, and divers others, it was common to use the Words* Vi & Armis, *and in divers of them to declare the Manner of the Force and Arms, that is to say,* vi & armis videlicet baculis cultellis arcubus & sagittis, *or other such like Words; where of Truth the Parties indicted had no such Weapons at the Time of the Offence, yet for lack of such Words the said Indictments were taken as void, and had been avoided by Writ of Error or Plea,* &c. and thereupon it is Enacted, *That these Words* Vi & Armis, videlicet, cum baculis, cultellis, arcubus & sagittis, *or other such like, shall not of Necessity be put in any Indictment or Inquisition: Nor shall the Parties indicted have any Advantage by Writ of Error or Plea, or otherwise, to avoid any such Indictment or Inquisition for the Want of these or the like Words: But that the same Inquisitions and Indictments, and every of them, lacking the said Words, or any of them, shall be adjudged as effectual to all Intents, Constructions, and Purposes, as the same Inquisitions and Indictments having the same Words in them.*

Sect. 93. But notwithstanding this Statute seems to be so express as to all Indictments, yet it is [s] holden in many Books, That Indictments of Trespass, and such like, are still insufficient without the Words *vi & armis*, and many Indictments have accordingly been quash'd for want of them, where they are not implied in some others, as [t] *rescussit*, or *manu*

[a] 2 Rol. Ab. 81 pl. 7.
[b] 1 Leon 241.
[c] 2 Rol. Ab. 81 pl. 6. Salk. 382. 1 Vent. 302.
[d] 2 Rol. Ab, 81 pl 7.
[e] Stiles Rep. 245.
[f] Stiles Rep. 312.
[g] Cro. Ja. 647. 1 Rol. Ab. 781. O. pl. 1. Palm. 313. 1 Bulst. 15
[h] 2 Rol. Re. 164.
[i] 6. Mod 210.
[k] Brook Joinder in Actions 5, 47, 100, 108. f. n. b 171.
[l] Letters D, E. Fitz. decies tantum, 1, 4, 6, 8, 9.
[l] *Quære* Dy. 159. pl. 39.
[m] Brock Mainten. 26, 52.
[n] Cro. Ja. 473. 2 Lev. 221. *See the Books cited in the next Section.* *Quære* supra, Ch. 23 Sect. 85.
[o] *Yet see the Preamble of* 37 H. 8, 8.
[p] 1 Lev. 125 126. Dalt. Ch. 131.
[q] 1 Keb. 652. Dalt. Ch. 131.
[r] Poph. 206. Cro. Ca. 377.
[s] S. P. C. 94. 2 Lev. 221. 1 Sid 140. 1 Bulst. 205. 1 Lev. 126. 1 Keb. 101. 2 Keb. 154. Vide Poph. 206. Cro. Ca. 377, 378.
[t] Cro. Ja. 345 2 Bulst. 208. Book 1. Ch 64. Sect. 44. Dalt. Ch. 131.

 forti,

forti, &c. But it ſeems difficult to aſſign any Reaſon for theſe Opinions, unleſs it be, That becauſe the enacting Part of the Statute ſays, That the Words *vi & armis videlicet cum baculis cultellis*, &c. are not neceſſary, *&c.* the Meaning was only to take away the Neceſſity of thoſe ſuperfluous Words *baculis & cultellis*, &c. but not of the Words *vi & armis*, where they are proper and pertinent; but to this it may be anſwered, That the Preamble ſeems to complain of the Opinion, that the Words *vi & armis*, whether put by themſelves, or uſed with thoſe other Words, were in any Caſe thought neceſſary in Indictments; and it is moſt natural ſo to explain the enacting Part of a Statute as to make it extend to all the Miſchiefs complained of in the Preamble; beſides, the enacting Part of the Statute is expreſs, *That Indictments without thoſe Words* vi & armis videlicet, baculis, cultellis, arcubus & ſagittis, *or any of them, ſhall be as effectual as if they had them compriſed in them*; and ſurely the Words *vi & armis* cannot but be comprehended under thoſe Words, *or any of them*. It is ſaid [a] indeed in *Levinz*'s ſecond Reports, That the Words *vi & armis* are ſtill neceſſary, becauſe without them there can be no *Capiatur* entered, nor Fine to the King; but this is in Effect to contradict the Statute which ſays, That an Indictment without thoſe Words ſhall be as effectual to all Intents, Conſtructions, and Purpoſes, as an Indictment with them. Beſides, will any one ſay, That there can be no *Capiatur* nor Fine to the King upon Indictments of Cheats, Conſpiracies, and ſuch like? wherein yet it ſeems to be agreed, That thoſe Words are not neceſſary. And agreeably hereto, the Court of King's Bench has [b] often refuſed to quaſh Indictments of Treſpaſs for the Want of theſe Words. However, it is certainly ſafe and adviſeable to make uſe of them where they are proper and pertinent, if it be to no other Purpoſe than to aggravate the Offence.

Sect. 94. As to the eighth Point, *viz.* Whether it be neceſſary in the Body of an Indictment at Common Law to lay the Offence *contra pacem*, inaſmuch as all Offences whatſoever which are ſubject to a publick Proſecution ſeem in general to be ſo, as they are Breaches of the Law, and in that Reſpect tend to the Diſturbance of the quiet and peaceable Government of the King over his People; it ſeems to be a good general [c] Rule, That no Indictment or Information, for an Offence, capital or not capital, againſt the Common Law or Statute, can be good, except it expreſsly ſuppoſe ſuch Offence to have been done againſt the Peace of the King or Kings, in whoſe Reign or Reigns it was committed. And accordingly I find, That every Precedent of an Indictment in *Coke*'s Entries, whether for [d] Treaſon, or [e] Felony, or [f] inferior Offences, expreſly lays the Offence againſt the Peace of the King, except only in four Inſtances, whereof the one is, of an Indictment for a [g] Nuſance for not repairing the Highway, which if it may be maintained, ſeems to depend chiefly on this Reaſon, That the Offence is of ſuch a Nature, that a Man may be as well guilty of it in his own Ground as in that of another, and therefore it hath been [h] holden, That it needs not to be laid againſt the Peace, becauſe the laying it in ſuch a Manner may ſeem to imply ſomewhat of Force or Treſpaſs againſt the Perſon or Poſſeſſion of another; but it ſeems difficult to reconcile this Opinion with thoſe many Reſolutions taken Notice of in the following Part of this Section, by which Indictments, for want of theſe Words, *contra pacem*, have been adjudg'd inſufficient, where the Offences could on no other Account be ſaid to be againſt the Peace, than as they were Breaches of the Law, as all Nuſances certainly are. And one [i] other of the ſaid Inſtances in *Coke*'s Entries is, of an Indictment of *Homicide* by Miſadventure, and one other [k] of an Indictment of *Homicide* in Self-De-

[a] 2 Lev. 221.

[b] Cro. Ja. 472, 473. Vide Cro. Ja. 345. 2 Bulſt. 208. Dalt. Ch. 131. Lamb. Book 4. Ch. 5. fol. 502, 503.

[c] 3 Keb. 490. pl. 45. 1 Keb, 789. pl. 43. 2 Bulſt, 258. *See the Caſes cited in the following part of this Section. and* Cro. El 186. pl. 10. 6 Mod. 128.

[d] Coke's Entries 360. pl. 14, 15, 361. pl. 16.

[e] Cokes Ent. 351. pl, 1, 352. pl 2, 355. pl 7, 8. 356. pl. 9, 358. pl. 11, 12 359 pl. 13.

[f] Coke's Ent. 352, 353, 361 pl. 17. 362. pl. 18,

[g] Coke's Ent 358, pl. 10 *See* Raſtal's Entries, 263. pl. 7.

[h] 2 Roll. Ab. 82 pl. 9 83 pl 5. 6. Contra Cro. Ca. 584.

[i] Coke's Ent. 353 pl. 4.

[k] Coke's Ent. 354. pl. 5.

fence; but these Precedents, if they may be maintained, seem to depend chiefly on this Reason that such Offences are supposed to be owing rather to the Misfortune than Fault of the Party. And the † fourth of the said Instances is of an Indictment of Perjury on the Statute, which concludes in *contemptum Reginæ*, &c. *& contra formam statuti*, without adding *contra pacem*. But [a] *Rastal*'s Precedents, both of Indictments of Felony, and of inferior Offences do as often omit the Words *contra pacem*, as make use of them. However, certainly the much greater Number of Precedents expresly conclude *contra pacem*, and the Authority of these is much strengthened by those many Cases in the Reports, wherein Indictments and Informations appear to have been quash'd for want of the Words *contra pacem*; as Indictments and Informations for [b] Barretry, [c] Forgery, [d] retaining a Servant without a Testimonial from his last Master, [e] following a Trade without having served an Apprenticeship, [f] erecting a Cottage, [g] Assault and Battery, *&c.* But it seems clear from all the Precedents, That neither an Information [h] *qui tam*, on a penal Statute, nor an Information by the King for an [i] Intrusion, or other [k] Wrong of a Civil Nature done to his Lands, Goods, or Revenues, need the Words *contra pacem.*

Sect. 95. If the Offence indicted be expresly laid partly in the Reign of one King, and partly in the Reign of another, as where *J. S.* is indicted for having erected a Wear in the Time of Queen *Elizabeth*, and continued it in the Time of King *James*, and thereupon the Indictors conclude, That so the Wear was erected and continued *contra pacem Regis*, &c. without adding *contra pacem nuper Reginæ*, the Indictment is [l] insufficient, because it appears, That the Commencement of the Wrong, which is as much indicted as the Continuance, was in the Reign of Queen *Elizabeth*; and consequently, if a Crime, must have been against the Peace of her Reign. But if the Indictors had concluded only, That *J. S.* so continued the Wear *contra pacem Domini Regis*, &c. and had laid the Erection of it by way of Recital, or Inducement only, it is [m] said, That the Indictment had been good, because it should be taken as an Indictment for the Continuance only.

Sect. 96. As to the ninth Point, *viz.* Whether it be necessary in the Body of an Indictment at Common Law, to lay the Offence *contra coronam & dignitatem Regis*, it is observable, That all the Precedents of Indictments in *Coke*'s Entries, cited in the ninety fourth Section, which lay the Offence *contra pacem*, lay it also *contra coronam & dignitatem Regis*, &c. Yet not one of [n] *Rastal*'s Precedents doth so; neither do I find any one Case wherein an Indictment against which no other Exception could be taken, has been adjudged [o] insufficient for the Want of these Words. But on the contrary I find it expresly resolved in [p] *Holbrook*'s Case, That an Indictment of a Riot is good without them.

Sect. 97. As to the tenth Point, *viz.* Whether it be necessary in the Body of an Indictment, at Common Law, to lay the Offence *in contemptum Regis*, it is so laid in some Indictments of inferior Crimes in [q] *Coke* and *Rastal*, and in others [r] not. Also it is so laid, with the Addition of the Clause *contra leges suas*, in every Information of Intrusion upon the King's Lands in [s] *Coke* and [t] *Rastal*, and also in an Information in [u] *Coke* for a Trover and Conversion of the King's Goods. But in [x] two Informations for Mines claimed by the King, which are the only Precedents I find of

† Coke's Entries, 363. pl. 19.
[a] Rastal's Entries, 263.
[b] 2 Rol Ab. 82. pl. 5. Cro. Ja. 527. pl. 4.
[c] 2 Rol. A. 82. pl. 11.
[d] 1 Mod. 78.
[e] 3 Keb. 790. pl 45. 1 Keb. 501. pl 58, 848. pl. 48 6 Mod. 128,
[f] 1 Keb. 474. pl. 91.
[g] 2 Keb. 36. pl. 72. Vide 2 Keb. 779. pl 7. Yelv. 66.
[h] Rastal's Entries, 409 pl. 2. 1 Keb. 860. pl. 70. Coke's Entries *from* 364 *to* 372. 393. pl. 17.
[i] Rastal's Entries, 412. pl 4. Coke's Entries, *from* 372 *to* 390.
[k] Rastal's Entries, 410. pl. 3. Coke's Entries, 390. pl. 16.
[l] Yelv, 66. Vide 4 H. 6. 4 pl. 7. Fitz. brief. 25.
[m] Yelv. 66. 4 H. 6, 4. pl. 7. Fitz. brief. 25.
[n] See Rastal's Entries, 263.
[o] See 2 Bulst. 258. Aleyn, 49, 50.
[p] 2 Rol. Ab. 82. pl. 1.
[q] Coke's Ent. 353, 363. pl. 19. Rastal's Ent. 263. pl 9.
[r] Coke's Ent. 362. pl. 17, 18. Rastal's Ent. 263. pl. 6, 7, 11.
[s] Coke's Entries, 372. pl. 10, 376. pl. 11, 379. pl. 12. 381. pl. 13. 385. pl 14. 387. pl. 15. 1 Coke, 16. b. 26. b.
[t] Rastal's Entries, 412. pl. 4.
[u] Coke's Entries, 390. pl. 16.
[x] Rastal's Entries, 410. pl. 3. Pow. Com. 310.

this

this kind, the supposed Injury is laid only *ad damnum Regis*, without either of the said Clauses; neither do I find either of them in any Indictment of Treason or Felony, nor in any Information *qui tam* in *Coke* or *Rastal*; and though it seems to be admitted in the Year-Book of [a] 4 *H.* 6. that in an Action on a Statute it is necessary to conclude, *in contemptum Domini Regis*, yet in [b] *Lutwyche*'s *Entries* it is oftner omitted than us'd, and no Exception appears to have been taken for the Omission.

Sect. 98. As to the eleventh Point, Whether it be necessary in an Indictment at Common Law to lay the Offence *illicitè*, I cannot find this Word used in any one of *Coke*'s or *Rastal*'s Precedents of Indictments, neither do I find any clear and express [c] Authority, that it is in any Case necessary in an Indictment at Common Law; but on the contrary I find it expresly [d] adjudged, That it is not necessary in an Indictment of a Riot, because the Act it self contained in the Indictment so plainly appears to be unlawful. But where a Statute uses the Word unlawfully in the Description of an Offence, it is certain that an Indictment grounded on it must use the Word *illicitè*, or some other tantamount.

Sect. 99. As to the twelfth Point, *viz.* Whether a Defect in any of the Particulars above-mentioned be amendable, I take it to be [e] settled, That no criminal Prosecution is within the Benefit of any of the Statutes of Amendments; from whence it follows that no Amendment can be admitted in any such Prosecution, but such only as is allowed by the Common Law. And agreeably hereto I find it laid down as a [f] Principle in some Books, That the Body of an Indictment removed into the King's Bench from any inferior Court whatsoever, except only those of *London*, can in no Case be amended; but it is [g] said, That the Body of an Indictment from *London* may be amended, because by the City-Charter a Tenor of the Record only can be removed from thence. [h] And it seems, That by the Course of the King's Bench, a Rule may be made on any Coroner to amend even the Body of his Inquest by his Notes in a meer Matter of Form. But I do not find it any where holden, that this can be done after it is filed, by which it becomes a Record of the Court; and then the same Objections seem to lie against the Amendment of it, as of an Indictment. But it seems to be [i] agreed, That the Caption of an Indictment from any Place, may upon Motion be amended by the Clerk of the Assises or of the Peace, so as to [k] make it agree with the original Record at any Time during the same Term in which it came in, [l] but not in a subsequent Term. But I have known it holden, That the Caption of an Inquisition cannot be amended at any Time after it is filed, any more than the Body; the Reason whereof perhaps may be this, that the Caption being part of, and drawn at the same Time with the Inquisition, greater Exactness is required in it than in that of an Indictment, which is left as a Thing of Course to be drawn up by the Clerk of the Court, when occasion shall require. Also by the Opinion of two Judges against that of two, the Want of Continuances in the Record of an Attainder of Felony [m] cannot be amended by the Certificate of the Clerk of the Assises, especially if the King signify his Pleasure, that he doth not desire any Amendment. And it seems to be [n] settled at this Day, that no Discontinuance is amendable in any criminal Prosecution, [o] without Consent. But it hath been [p] adjudged, That a meer Misprision in the joining of an Issue in a criminal Prosecution, as where the Word *similiter*, *&c.* is omitted, may be

[a] 4 H. 6. 4. pl. 7. Fitz Brief 25.
[b] Lutw. 132, 133, 134 135, 139. 165, 167.
[c] *See* 1 Keb. 859. pl. 68. 2 Keb. 715. pl. 99.
[d] 2 Rol. A 82. pl. 4.
[e] 1 Jon. 421. 1 Salk. 51, 52. 6 Mod. 268, &c. Vide supra. Ch. 23. Sect. 127. 1 Sid. 66. pl 39.
[f] 1 Keb. 252. pl. 20. 2 Keb. 580. pl. 112. 1 Sid. 155. pl. 5. Vide 1 Keb. 45. pl. 120. 2 Keb. 141. pl. 13, 142. pl. 15. Contra 2 Bulst. 35.
[g] 1 Keb. 252. pl. 20. 1 Sid. 155. pl 5. 229, 230. 1 Keb. 571. pl. 26. Vide Hob. 135.
[h] *See* B. 1. Ch. 27. Sect. 16.
[i] 1 Saund. 249 1 Sid. 175. pl. 7. 1 Keb 656. pl. 36. 3 Mod. 167.
[k] Cro. Jac. 276, 277. Vide 1 Sid. 155
[l] 1 Sid. 155. pl 5. 1 Keb. 45. pl 120. 656. pl. 36 1 Sid. 175. pl. 7. 12 H. 7. 25. pl. 3. 10 Ed. 4. 15. pl. 15.
[m] 1 Rol. Ab 196. A. 1 Jon. 420.
[n] 1 Salk 51, 52. 6 Mod. 268. Bro. Amendment 10, 17, 66, 92. Fitz. Amendment 59. 29 E. 3. 32. Discontinuance de process 47.
[o] 21 H. 7. 40. pl. 65. Fitz. Amendment 78.
[p] Cro. Jac. 502, 529, 530. 2 Rol. Rep 59.

amended at any Time. Also it hath been [a] adjudged, That the Direction of a *Venire*, *Vicecomitibus* of such a Place, which is returned by *J. S. vicecomite*, may be amended on the Oath of *J. S.* that there is but one Sheriff of the Place, which is himself. Also it is every Day's Practice to amend [b] criminal Informations, and the Pleadings thereon by Rule of Court, while all is in Paper. And [c] *Quære* if the Record may not be so amended by the Paper-Book at any Time before Judgment? [a] 1 Keb. 900. pl. 71. 901. pl. 75. 1 Sid. 244. Vide 8 Co. 156. b. 3 Lev. 430. [b] 1 Salk. 47. pl. 1, 2, 3. [c] Salk. 47.

Sect. 100. It seems to have been anciently the common Practice where an Indictment appeared to be insufficient, either for its Uncertainty, or the Want of proper legal Words, not to put the Defendant to answer it; but if it were found in the same County in which the Court sate, to award Process against the Grand Jury, to come into Court and [d] amend it. And it seems to be the common Practice at [e] this Day, while the Grand Jury who found a Bill, is before the Court, to amend it by their Consent in a Matter of Form, as the Name or Addition of the Party, *&c.* pl. 2, 3. Salk. 50. pl. 10 Vide 1 Keb. 452. pl. 45. Cro Ca. 144. 1 Lev. 189. 3 Lev. 430. [d] 22 Ass. pl. 73. 2 Ed. 3 1. pl. 3. 8 H. 5. 8. pl 4.

Sect. 101. And now I am in the second Place to shew what ought to be the Form of the Body of an Indictment upon a Statute; for the better Understanding whereof, having premised, that the same Rules which have been already laid down concerning Indictments at Common Law, are generally applicable to Indictments on Statutes, I shall in this Place consider such Matters only as more peculiarly belong to the Form of the Body of an Indictment upon a Statute, under the following Particulars: S. P. C. 97. Letter A Fitz. Indictment 2, 3. 27. Vide 25 E. 3. 43. pl. 36. Bro. Indictment 12. [e] Kelynge 37.

1. Whether it be necessary that such Indictment recite the Statute whereon it is grounded.
2. What Mis-recitals of such Statutes are fatal.
3. How far it is necessary to bring the Offence indicted within the very Words of the Statute.
4. Whether an Indictment grounded on a Statute, which will not maintain it, may be made good as an Indictment at Common Law.
5. How far it is necessary to conclude *contra formam Statuti.*

Sect. 102. As to the first Particular, *viz.* Whether it be necessary that such Indictment recite the Statute whereon it is grounded, I take it to be [f] settled, that there is no Necessity in any Indictment or Information on a [g] publick Statute, to recite such Statute, whether the Offence be such only because prohibited, or be an Evil in its own Nature, and whether it be prohibited by more than one Statute, or by one only; for the Judges are bound *ex officio* to take Notice of all publick Statutes, [h] and where there are more than one by which an Indictment or Information may be maintained, they will go upon that which is most for the King's Advantage. [f] 5 H. 7. 17 b. Fitz. Action sur le Statute 7. 20. 2 Rol. A. 79. pl. 8. Plowd. Com. 1, 79, &c. 1 H. 6. 1. pl 2. 4 Co. 48. a.

As to the second Particular, *viz.* What Mis-recitals of such Statutes are fatal, I shall endeavour to shew: Cro. El. 236. pl. 1. Cro. Ca. 229. Dyer 155. pl. 19 346. pl. 9. Bro. Action sur le Stat. 4 Parliam. 15. *but* Cro. El. 187. pl. 12. 47 Ed. 3. 10. pl. 7.

1. Whether all Mis-recitals of the substantial Part of a Statute are fatal.
2. What Mis-recitals of the Place or Time at which the Parliament was holden.
3. Whether a Mis-recital of the Title of a Statute.
4. What other Mis-recitals are fatal.

Dyer 159. pl. 37. Bro Parliament 75. Bro. Champerty 1. Show. 337. F. N. B 55. C. *seem contrary.* Quære 6 Mod. 140, 141. [g] Moor. 468. pl. 669. Moor 699 pl. 972. 4 Co. 13. 76. Bro. Avowry 5. Bro. Parliament 15, 32. [h] Dyer 155 pl. 19. Dyer 346. pl. 9. 5 H. 7. 17. b. 6 Mod. 140. Vide Cro. El. 187. pl 12.

Sect. 103. As to the first of these Particulars, it seems to be settled, That notwithstanding there be no Necessity to recite a publick Statute; yet if the Prosecutor take upon him to do it, [a] and materially vary from a substantial Part of the Purview of the Statute, and conclude *contra formam Statuti prædicti*, he viciates the Indictment, because it judicially appears to the Court, that there is no such Foundation for the Prosecution, as that whereon it is expresly grounded; as where in an [b] Indictment with such a Conclusion on the Statutes which prohibit Entries with strong Hand, the Word *Vi* is put for *manu forti*; or where the Word [c] *nuncia* is put for *mendacia* in such an Indictment on the Statutes against the Tellers of Lies of great Men; [d] or where the Verb in a Statute which expresses the principal Act wherein the Offence consists, is expressed in such an Indictment on such a Statute, by a Word which is neither classical nor legal *Latin*; [e] or where a Statute in describing the Courts wherein it prohibits Persons to bring Actions in other Names without their Privity, calls them Courts wherein Pleas are holden in Actions personal, *&c.* and you in reciting it in such an Indictment call them Courts wherein Pleas are holden in any Actions.

Sect. 104. Yet it seems that the following Mis-recitals of the substantial Part of the Purview of a Statute in any Indictment are not fatal, as the Omission of a synonymous Word, having no other Meaning than what is fully expressed in the Words which are recited; or the joining of Words which are either wholly Synonymous, or much of the same Sense, as signifying such Things as generally include one another, (as [g] the Words *malitiosè & contemptuosè, &c.*) with a Copulative, where the Statute uses a Disjunctive, or the using the singular Number for the Plural, or the Plural for the Singular, where the Sense is the same; as where in [h] reciting a Statute speaking of Suits in any Courts, you Use the Words *in aliqua Curia*; or where in reciting the Statute against disturbing Persons in their open Preaching, you use the [i] Words *in apertis prædicationibus*.

Sect. 105. Also it [k] seems that no Advantage can be taken of a Variance from any Part of a private Statute, without shewing it to the Court in a proper Manner, because otherwise such a Statute shall be taken to be as it is recited.

Sect. 106. As to the second of the Particulars above-mentioned, *viz.* What Mis-recitals of the Place or Time at which the Parliament was holden, are fatal, [l] it seems to be generally agreed, That a Mis-recital of the Place or Day at which the Parliament was holden, vitiates an Indictment. [m] As if a Parliament be first holden on the twenty eighth of *April*, in the thirty-second Year of *Henry* VIII. and afterwards holden by Prorogation on the twelfth of *April* the next Year, and a Statute then made, be recited as made at a Parliament holden on the twenty-eighth of *April*, in the thirty-second Year of *Henry* VIII. Or if a Parliament be summoned to meet on the twenty-third of *January* in such a Year, and before the Meeting be prorogued to the twenty-fifth, and then holden, and a Statute made by such Parliament be [n] recited as made in a Parliament holden on the twenty-third; or if a Parliament first holden on one Year be continued by Prorogation to another, and then sit again, and a Statute made at such Sessions be [o] recited as made in a Parliament holden or begun at such second Year, (which is all one,) instead of saying that it was made at a Sessions of Parliament then holden, and the Indictment conclude *contra formam Statuti prædicti*, the Variances in Strictness are fatal; for the Court will not make any Case better than the Record has made it, and therefore where that expresly grounds it on the Act

[a] Pl. Com 79, 83. b. 84. Cro. El. 236, 245. pl. 4. Palm. 565. 4 Co. 48. *See the three next Sections.* 1 Ro. Rep. 50. Cro. Ca. 135, 136. 1 Jon. 194.

[b] Cro. El. 93. pl. 2. 2 Bulst. 258.

[c] 4 Co. 12. b. 13. Cro. Ca. 135

[d] 2 Jon. 49, 50. 3 Keble 661. pl. 11.

[e] Cro. El. 236.

[f] Cro Ja. 362. *See the 108th Section.*

[g] 2 Bulst. 47, 49, 50, 51, 52, 53.

[h] Cro. Ca. 522, 523.

[i] 2 Bulst. 47, &c.

[k] 4 Co. 13. Sid. 356.

[l] Bro. Parliament 87. Cro. El. 853. pl. 12.

[m] Plow. Com. 79, 83, 84. Cro. Ca. 136, 232. 3 Keb. 468. pl. 55. 2 Jon 50. Hob. 310. Cro. Ja. 139. Cro. El. 245. pl. 4. *But this is made a Query by* Coke *in* 2 Bulst. 53.

[n] Dyer 203. pl. 72, 73. Herly 129.

[o] Cro Ja. 111. pl. 9. 139. Lutw. 140. 4 Inst. 27. vide 1 Brown. 100 Yelv. 127 Dyer 95. pl. 36, 37, 38, 471. pl 6.

of a supposed Parliament, where there was no such Act, the Court will not find one out to make it good. Also it hath been [a] adjudged, That a Repugnancy in setting forth the Time when a Parliament was holden, is fatal, as if a Statute be recited as made on such a Day, in the first and second Years of such a King, for it is impossible that one and the same Day should be in two Years. Also it is holden in [b] *Croke*'s Reports, That an Indictment was discharged for not shewing in what County a Parliament was holden; but no Reason is given for this Opinion, [c] and it hath been adjudged, That the total Omission of the Day when the Parliament was holden, is no Fault in the Recital of a Statute. Also it seems to be [d] agreed, That a Mistake in supposing a Statute to have been made at a Parliament holden in such a Year, when in Truth it was then holden by Prorogation, may be help'd by the constant Course of Precedents upon such Statute. Also it seems to be [e] agreed, That not only a Mis-recital of the Day whereon the Parliament was holden, but even a Mis-recital of the Purview of a Statute may be salved by a general Conclusion *contra formam Statuti*, without adding *prædicti*, *&c.* [f] But I do not find it settled, Whether a Fault of this Kind can be help'd by the Defendant's Admittance, that there is such a Statute as is supposed; and it will be difficult to maintain that the Party's Admittance of what the Court judicially knows to be contrary to the Truth, can make good any Judgment.

Sect. 107. As to the third of the Particulars above-mentioned, *viz.* Whether the Mis-recital of the Title of a Statute be fatal, it is [g] said to have been holden by Sir *Matthew Hale*, That the Mis-recital of the entituling of an Act will not vitiate a Replication, because it is not Matter of Substance; and a Judgment is [h] said to have been lately given in the Court of Common Pleas agreeable to this Opinion; but the contrary is [i] said to have been since adjudged in the Court of King's Bench.

Sect. 108. As to the fourth of the Particulars above-mentioned, *viz.* What other Mis-recitals of a Statute are fatal, [k] it is said to have been often adjudged, That a Variance in reciting a Statute to commence after the making, where the Statute is express, that it shall commence after the End of the Sessions, is fatal. But I take it to be a settled Rule, That a Variance no Way altering the Sense of the Statute does [l] no hurt; as where in the Recital of an Oath prescribed by Statute, the Words *Sea of Rome* are put for *See of Rome*; and *I do declare in Conscience* instead of *I do declare in my Conscience*. Also it seems to be [m] agreed, That a Variance from an immaterial Part of a Statute does no hurt, [n] and therefore that where a Statute contains several Branches relating to several distinct Matters, an Omission of such Branches as no way relate to the Offence indicted does no hurt, because they are nothing to the present Purpose. Also it hath been adjudged, That every Mis-recital even of such Branch is not fatal; as if it vary only in such a Part of the Description of the Offence, as is put in only by Way of Flourish, and *ex abundanti*, and makes no necessary Ingredient in the Offence prohibited, nor needs any Proof; as if in a Prosecution on the Statute of 12 *R.* 2. the [o] Recital be that none shall devise, speak, or tell any false News, Lies, or other such false Things, *&c. unde discordia aut aliqua lis* (*Anglicè* Debates) *inter magnates vel inter magnates & communitatem dicti Regni oriri possint*; where the Words of the Statute are, *That none shall devise, speak, or tell any false News, Lies, or other such false Things*, &c. *whereof Discord or any Slander might rise within the said Realm*; for the first Words, *viz. That none shall devise*, &c. *any false News, Lies, or other such false Things*, &c. are only material.

[a] Moor 302. pl. 452.
[b] Cro. El. 106. pl. 21.
[c] Dyer 203. pl. 74.
[d] Yelv. 127. Brownl. 100. 2 Keb 34. pl. 68. Dyer 171. pl. 6.
[e] Cro. Car. 232, 233. Pal. 565. Raym. 191, 192. 3 Keb. 647, 648. Lutw. 140.
[f] Affirm'd Cro. Jac. 139. Denied Cro. El. 236.
[g] Hardress 324.
[h] 6 Mod. 62.
[i] 6 Mod. 62.
[k] 2 Rol. Abr. 465. Letter B.
[l] 1 Vent. 172.
[m] Cro. El. 186. pl. 10. 4 Co. 48. Palm. 565. Cro. Ca. 135, 136, 564. 1 Jon. 194.
[n] Plowd. Com. 65, 105. a. Dyer 203. pl. 7. Hob. 226. 3 Keb. 662.
[o] Cro. Car. 135, 136. Palm. 565. 1 Jon. 194.

material. Indeed as this Case is reported by *Croke*, there is a Mis-recital even in this Part, for instead of *other false Things*, the Recital is said to mention *other Things* generally, omitting the Word *false*; but I suppose that this is a Mistake of the Printer, and that there is no such Variance in the Record of the Case, because no Exception is reported to have been taken to it.

Sect. 109. But if a Mis-recital of such a Part of the Purview of a Statute be not fatal, it seems *à fortiori* to follow, That a Mis-recital of the Preamble is not material, where the substantial Part of the Purview is well recited. And upon this Reason chiefly, as I suppose, it hath been adjudged, That if in an Action on the [a] Statute of Hue and Cry for a Robbery, the Declaration recite the Preamble to speak of the Burning of Houses, where the Statute mentions Arsons generally, without any particular mention of the Arson of Houses; or in an Action for the Slander of an Earl, on 2 *R.* 2. 5. if the Declaration in reciting the Preamble, mention only what relates to Earls, *&c.* and omit the Clause concerning the other great Officers, [b] yet the Plaintiff may have Judgment, especially after Verdict. And these Resolutions seem to weaken the Authority of *Parker*'s Case reported by [c] *Hutton*, wherein it was said to have been holden by three Judges against the Opinion of *Hobart*, that the putting of the Word *indicari* for *indictari* in the Recital of the Preamble of the said Statute of Hue and Cry, in a Writ grounded thereupon, is fatal.

[a] Vide 3 Keb. 647. pl. 68. 661, 662. 2 Jon. 51.
[b] 2 Jon. 49, 50, 51. 3 Keb. 647. pl. 68. 3 Keb. 661, 662. Vide Cro. Jac. 139.
[c] Hutton 56, 57. 3 Keb. 648, 662. 2 Jon. 50, 51.

Sect. 110. If an Indictment on 8 *H.* 6. in reciting that Part of the Statute which declares in what Actions the Party grieved shall recover his Damages, after having mentioned Recoveries by Verdict, omit the [d] Words *or in any other Manner*; or use the [e] Words *Assisum nova disseisina* for *Assisam nova disseisina*; [f] or recite the Statute, as giving the Fine on a Recovery by Action *dicto Domino Regi*, where there is nothing to make good the Word *dicto*; [g] or recite the Statute relating to the bringing an Action to be, *if the Party after such Entry make any Feoffment*, &c. where the Words are, *if after such Entry any Feoffment be made*, or [h] recite it to be *if any Person be put out and disseised* in the Conjunctive, where the Words of the Statute are, *if any Person be put out or disseised* in the Disjunctive, the Variances have been adjudged fatal. Yet [i] it hath been holden, That the last of these is an immaterial Variance, because tho' the Words above-mentioned be disjunctive in the Statute, they have always been expounded in the Copulative. Also it may be questioned how far the rest of these Authorities may be Law at this Day, since of [k] late the Court has not been so strict in Recitals as formerly; and if an Indictment fully recite a Statute so far as it concerns Indictments, a Misprision in what concerns other Matters seems to be much help'd by the Authority of the Cases above-cited.

[d] Cro El. 186. pl. 10.
[e] Cro El. 93. pl. 2.
[f] 1 Bulst. 218.
[g] Cro. El. 307. pl. 10. *Parallel Case*, Cro. El. 697. pl. 10.
[h] Cro. El. 96. pl. 9. Vide Cro. El. 697. pl. 10.
[i] Cro. El. 307. pl. 10.
[k] 3 Keb. 662.

Sect. 111. It hath been [l] adjudged, That a total Omission of the Clause of a Statute which ordains what the Party shall forfeit, does no hurt. Yet if the Statute be wholly mis-recited in such Clause, as if the Words [m] *admitteret* or *forisfaceret* be used in such Clause for *amitteret* and *forisfaceret*, the Exception for the Variance seems to have greater Weight. Yet if the Word mis-recited be synonymous with the other which is rightly recited, and the [n] whole Purport of both as fully expressed in one Word, which is properly recited as if both had been used, as it certainly is in the Case above-cited, wherein the Word *forisfaceret* is rightly recited, and the Word *amitteret* mis-recited, it may perhaps be questioned whether such an Exception would be fatal at this Day, especially considering that it is in a

[l] 20 H. 6. 31, 32. *which seems mistaken in the Abridgments*, Fitz. Brief 86. Bro. Champerty 1. Vide Plowd. Com. 84. b. Dyer 160. pl 40.
[m] Cro. Jac. 133. pl. 5.
[n] Vide Cro. Jac. 362.

Part of the Statute which might as well have been omitted in the Recital; and there is no Variance but from a Word wholly nugatory and superfluous, and the Sense would be compleat by rejecting the Word mistaken, as surplus and insensible. But if in the Mis-recital of such a Clause, there be such a Variance as carries with it a plain material Repugnancy to the Intent of the Statute, [a] as where the Words, *whoever shall do the same, shall incur the Pain,* &c. are thus recited, *whoever shall do the contrary, shall incur the Pain,* &c. I do not well see how any Thing can be said to make it good; for it is a general Rule, That [b] Repugnancies in Indictments are fatal, and the Prosecutor himself declares, That not those who do the Thing indicted, but those who do it not are within the Penalty of the Statute.

Sect. 112. As to the third Particular, *viz.* How far it is necessary to bring the Offence indicted within the very Words of the Statute; I take it for a general Rule, That [c] unless the Statute be recited, neither the Words *contra* [d] *formam Statuti,* nor any *Periphrasis,* Intendment or [e] Conclusion will make good an Indictment, which does not bring the Fact prohibited or commanded, in the doing or not doing whereof the Offence consists, within all the material Words of the Statute. And upon this Ground it hath been resolved, That an Indictment of Rape finding that the Defendant such a Day and Place, *&c.* A. B. *felonicè cepit, & eam adtunc & ibidem carnaliter cognovit, &c. contra voluntatem suam, &c.* is not [f] sufficient without the Word *Rapuit*; because that is the Word used by the Statute which makes the Offence Felony. Also it hath been [g] adjudged, That Indictments for Perjury on 5 *El.* 9. omitting the Words *voluntariè & corruptè,* in setting forth the Swearing; and Indictments for striking in a Church on 5 & 6 *Ed.* 6. 4. [h] omitting the Words *to the Intent to strike,* &c. and Indictments for aiding the Procurers of the Pope's Bulls on 13 *El.* 4. [k] omitting the Words *To the Intent to set forth,* &c. *the usurped Power,* &c. and Indictments for Forestalling on 5 & 6 *Ed.* 6. 14. setting forth, That the Defendant bought certain Goods of *J. S.* which he was about to sell at such a Market; but [l] not expresly alledging, That *such Goods were then coming to such Market to be sold*; and [m] Indictments for ingrossing on the same Statute, setting forth, That the Defendant bought so much Corn, *&c.* without alledging, That *he ingrossed it,* &c. *by buying,* &c. and [n] Indictments for Treason in Compassing the King's Death, on 25 *E.* 3. having neither the Word *Compass* nor *Imagine,* *&c.* cannot be taken as Indictments on such Statutes. And the like hath been adjudged in many other [o] Cases.

Sect. 113. Neither doth it seem to be always sufficient to pursue the very Words of the Statute, unless by so doing you fully, directly and expresly alledge the Fact in the doing or not doing whereof the Offence consists, without any the least Uncertainty or Ambiguity; for it hath been [p] adjudged, That an Indictment for Perjury on 5 *El.* 9. setting forth, That the Defendant *tacto per se sacro evangelio falso deposuit, &c.* is not good without directly shewing that he was sworn. Also it hath been [q] adjudged, That an Information on 18 *H.* 6. 17. for not abating so much of the Price of Wine sold as the Vessels wanted of the Statute-Measure, is insufficient if it do not expresly shew how much they wanted. Also it is said, That an Indictment on the Statute of Usury setting forth, That the Defendant took more than five in the Hundred, is not good, without shewing in particular how much.

[a] 4 Co. 12. b. 13. a.
[b] Supra Sect. 64, 65.
[c] Cro. El. 535. 67. *See the Books cited to the later part of this Section,* Cro. El. 749. pl. 2. *seems contrary.*
[d] Dy. 363. pl. 25. 2 Ro. Re. 227, 263. 2 Leon. 211. 11 Co. 58. a.
[e] Cro. El. 147. pl. 11. Cro. El. 201. pl. 30. 2 Leon. 211.
[f] 9 Ed. 4. 26. Bro. Indictment 7. Vide supra ch. 23. Sec. 77.
[g] Cro. El. 147. pl. 11. Cro. El. 201. pl. 30. 2 Leon. 211. Vide Coke's Entries 367, 368.
[h] Cro. El. 231. pl. 23. 2 Leon. 188. Noy 171.
[k] Dy. 363. pl. 25.
[l] 1 Rol. Rep. 421. *See* Book 1. Ch. 80. Sect. 12, 13.
[m] 2 Leon. 39. *See* Book 1. Ch. 80. Sect. 15 & 20.
[n] Kelynge 8. B. 1. Ch. 17. Sect. 8.
[o] 11 Co. 58 a. Dyer 346. pl. 9. 2 Ro. Re. 227, 263. Sup. Sec. 106. 2 Rol. Ab. 81. pl. 15. 9 Ed. 4. 26, 27.
[p] Cro. El. 105. pl. 17. *See* 9 Ed. 4. 26.
[q] 2 Leon. 38, 39.

Sect. 114. As to the Description of the Person of the Defendant, in order to bring him within the Purview of a Statute, which extends only to such Kind of Persons as are specially mentioned in it; it is a good [a] general Rule, That every Indictment must bring the Defendant within all the Descriptions mentioned in the Body of the Act, except they are such as carry with them the bare Denial of a Matter, the Affirmation whereof is a proper and natural Plea for the Defendant; as where it is enacted, That all Persons having no reasonable Excuse to be absent, shall go to their Parish-Church, *&c.* in which Case it is said, that it is not necessary to shew, That the Defendant had no reasonable Excuse, for this will come most properly in question from the Plea of the Defendant. Also it seems that there is no need in describing the Defendant to set forth the Place where the Thing happened, which brought him within the Description, as hath been more fully shewn in the 86th Section. Also it hath been adjudged, That it is [b] sufficient in describing the Defendant to say, That he *existens* so and so, as the Statute mentions, did the Fact, without alledging that he was so at the Time of the Fact; for that shall be intended, as hath been more fully shewn in the sixty-third Section.

[a] Poph. 93, 94. *See* Book 1. Ch. 10. Sect. 2. 2 Leon. 5. Quære 2 Keb. 582. pl. 18.

[b] Moor 606. pl. 838. Cro. Jac. 610. 2 Leon. 5. 2 Lev. 229. 2 Ro. Re. 226. contra 2 Ro. Re. 263. Quære Raym. 378. 1 Keb. 852. pl. 55.

Sect. 115. It seems [c] agreed, That there is no need to alledge in an Indictment, that the Defendant is not within the Benefit of the Provisoes of a Statute whereon it is founded; and this hath been [d] adjudged, even as to those Statutes which in their Purview expresly take Notice of the Provisoes, as by saying, That none shall do the Thing prohibited, otherwise than in such special Cases, *&c.* as are expressed in the Act. But as I take it, a Conviction on a Penal Statute ought expresly to shew, that the Defendant is not within any of its Provisoes; for since no [e] Plea can be admitted to such a Conviction, and the Defendant can have no Remedy against it, but from an Exception to some Defect appearing in the Face of it, and all the Proceedings are in a summary Manner, it is but reasonable that such a Conviction should have the highest Certainty, and satisfy the Court, That the Defendant had no such Matter in his Favour as the Statute it self allows him to plead.

[c] Poph. 93, 94. 1 Jon. 157. 1 Lev. 26. Vide Savil 32. pl. 73.

[d] Poph. 93, 94.

[e] Quære 1 Salk. 181, 182.

Sect. 116. It seems to be laid down as a general Rule in [f] *Savil's* Report, which is also confirmed by the Year-Book of 11 *H.* 4. 14. That if the Statute whereon an Indictment is grounded be particularly recited; the general Conclusion, *contra formam Statuti*, after the Allegation of the Fact, will supply an Omission in it of a Circumstance mentioned in the Statute, which would be fatal without such a Recital and Conclusion; for since the Statute is particularly recited, and the Defendant charg'd with having done the Offence against the Form of it; and it is impossible that he could so have done, if any Circumstance expresly requir'd by the Statute had been wanting; it seems that the Offence may properly enough be said to be as fully set forth in the very Words of the Statute, as if such Words had been repeated in the Allegation of the Offence, according to the common Rule, that *Verba relata hoc maximè operantur per referentiam ut inesse videantur.* Neither do I find this contradicted by any of the Resolutions in the precedent Sections; for it does not appear that there was such a Recital and Conclusion in any of the Indictments therein referr'd to. Yet notwithstanding the Omission of a Circumstance mentioned in a Statute, may perhaps in such Manner be holpen; it seems that the Want of a certain Description of the Time or Place, or Things or Persons concerned, or of the Conclusion *contra pacem*, or of an express and direct Allegation of the Fact it self, cannot be so supply'd; for such Omissions [g] viciate an Indictment drawn in the very Words of the Act.

[f] Savil 33. pl. 78. Vide supra, ch. 23. Sec. 63. 2 Ro. Rep. 227. S.P.C. 81. C.

[g] 2 Rol. Rep. 226. *seems contrary.*

Sect. 117. As to the fourth Particular, *viz.* Whether an Indictment grounded on a Statute which will not maintain it, may be made good as an Indictment at Common Law; it seems formerly to have been [b] generally taken for granted, That no Indictment whatsoever which is grounded on a Statute, and concludes *contra formam Statuti*, and cannot be made good by any Statute, can be maintained as an Indictment of an Offence at Common Law; the chief Reason whereof seems to be this, That it appears that the Prosecution is intended to be grounded on a Foundation which will not support it. But the contrary seems to have been adjudged in [c] *Page*'s Case, wherein it was resolved, That if Persons be indicted specially on the Statute of Stabbing, and the Evidence be not sufficient to bring them within the Statute, they may be found guilty of general Manslaughter at Common Law, and that the Words *contra formam Statuti* shall be rejected as Senseless, where the Offence is prohibited by the Common Law only. And the same hath been since [d] adjudged as to other Statutes; and as I took it, was lately agreed in an Information against the City of [e] *Norwich*.

Sect. 118. As to the fifth Particular, *viz.* How far it is necessary for an Indictment on a Statute, to conclude *contra formam Statuti*, it seems that Judgment on a Statute shall in no Case be given on an Indictment, which doth not so conclude; for granting that such Judgment may in some Cases be given in an Action brought at Common Law, without Reference to any Statute, as it is [f] said, That Judgment on 8 *H.* 6 9. may be given on the old Common Law Writ of Assise of Novel Disseisin, yet it will not follow, That such a Judgment can in any Case be given on an Indictment drawn as for an Offence at Common Law without any Reference to Statute. For as to the said Case of an Assise of Novel Disseisin, it may be said that the Statute of 8 *H.* 6. expresly says, That the Party may recover by such Writ; and therefore since there is no special Writ of this Kind formed upon the Statute, and the Party has [g] no Authority to make out a Writ himself in a new Form, it is reasonable that he may recover by the old Writ. But it [h] seems that Judgment on this Statute cannot be given on an Action of Trespass in the Common Law Form. because there is a special Writ of Trespass in the [i] Register grounded on the Statute; and it seems to be [k] agreed, That where there is a special Writ grounded on a Statute, Judgment shall never be given on such a Statute in an Action brought at Common Law. And in like Manner, since every one who prosecutes an Indictment is at Liberty to draw it as he pleases, so that he observes the general Rules of Law concerning Indictments; it seems to be [l] taken as a common Ground, That a Judgment by Statute shall never be given on an Indictment at Common Law, as every Indictment which doth not conclude *contra formam Statuti*, shall be taken to be. And therefore [m] if an Indictment do not conclude *contra formam Statuti*, and the Offence indicted be only prohibited by Statute and not by Common Law, it is wholly insufficient, and no Judgment at all can be given upon it: But if the Offence were also an Offence at Common Law, I take it to be in a great Measure settled at this Day, That [n] Judgment may be given as for an Offence at Common Law, tho' the Indictment conclude *contra formam Statuti*, as hath been more fully shewn in the precedent Section.

[b] Cro. El 231. pl. 23. Cro. El 307. pl 10. Cro. El 697. pl. 10. 2 Leon. 188. Noy 71, 172. 5 Co 99. 2 Ro R. 263. Cro. Ca. 465. 2 Keb 36. pl 73. 2 Keb. 566. pl. 70 Vide 6 Mod. 17 *the same may be collected from* 2 Rol. Ab 82. pl. 2, 3. *and* 1 Jon. 379.

[c] H. P. C. 58. Alcyn. 43, 44. B 1. Ch. 30. Sect. 9

[d] 1 Sid. 420. 2 Keb. 138. pl 5. Vide 1 Salk. 212.

[e] *The King against the City of* Norwich, *adjudged* Hilar. 5. Georgii.

[f] 9 H. 6. 2. pl. 5. Bro. Action sur le Statute 6

[g] 2 Inst. 407.

[h] Vide 2 Inst. 200. Bro. Parliament 75.

[i] Register 289. a.

[k] 9 H. 6. 2. pl. 5 56. pl. 42. 19 H 6. 54. b. 47 Ed. 3. 10. pl. 7. 8 H. 4 13. b. 2 Ed. 4. 9. pl. 5. Bro. Action sur le Statute 6, 10. Parliam. 75. Fitz. Judgment 10. Cessavit 18. Attachment sur Prohibition 1, 3. Bendloe 57. pl. 92. Cro. El. 759, 760.

[l] *See the Authorities cited to the other Parts of this Section.*

[m] 2 Rol. Re. 38. 1 Saund. 249. 1 Sid. 409. 2 Keb. 506. pl. 79. 1 Salk. 370. pl. 3.

[n] *See the precedent Section* 2 Keb. 477. pl. 7. 1 Sid. 409. 1 Saund. 249, 250. 9 H. 6. 56. pl 42. Fitz. Attachment sur Prohibition 1, 3. But 2 Rol. Ab. 82. pl. 2, 3. 2 Keb. 566. pl. 70. 1 Jo. 379, 380. *seem contrary.*

Sect. 119. If there be more than one Statute concerning the same Offence, and the first of them were never discontinued, and the later [a] only continue the former without making any Addition to it; or only [b] qualify the Method of Proceeding upon it, without altering the Substance of its Purview; it seems agreed, That it is safe in an Indictment on any such Statute to conclude *contra formam Statuti*; and it hath been [c] holden, That a Conclusion *contra formam Statutorum*, will in such Cases vitiate the Prosecution; but where a Statute hath been wholly discontinued, and is afterwards reviv'd, there [d] seem to have been some Opinions, That a Prosecution on it ought to conclude *contra formam Statutorum*. Also where the same Offence is prohibited by several independent Statutes there are some [e] Authorities, that you must either conclude *contra formam Statutorum*, or *contra formam* of the particular Statutes naming them, and that if you barely conclude *contra formam Statuti*, the Indictment will be insufficient, for not shewing on which of the Statutes it was taken. But there are also strong [f] Authorities for the contrary Opinion, which is also most agreeable to [g] Precedents; to which may be added, That if it be a good Objection to such an Indictment, concluding *contra formam Statuti*, that it appears not on which of the Statutes the Prosecution is grounded, the same Objection may as well be made to an Indictment concluding *contra formam Statutorum*; for it no more appears from such a Conclusion on what Statute the Prosecution is grounded, than from the Conclusion *contra formam Statuti*; and yet it seems to be [h] generally admitted, That a Conclusion *contra formam Statutorum* is good where the Indictment is for an Offence prohibited by several Statutes. Also where such an Indictment concludes *contra formam Statuti*, without shewing what Statute is [i] intended, why may it not be said that such Statute shall be taken as is most for the King's Advantage, as well as where the Indictment concludes *contra formam Statutorum*, in which Case it seems to be admitted, that it shall be so taken. But where a later Statute ordains, That a former Statute shall be executed in a new Case not mentioned in the former, as 8 *H.* 6. 9. does, that 15 *Ric.* 2. 2. shall be executed in the Case of a Forcible Detainer, which is not mentioned in 15 *Ric.* 2. or where a new Statute adds a new Penalty to an Offence prohibited by a former Statute, as [k] 23 *Eliz.* doth that of 20*l.* for a Month's Absence from Church contrary to the Tenor of 1 *Eliz.* it seems, that it may with greater Reason be argued, That if the Indictment conclude *contra formam Statuti*, it will be [l] insufficient, because it may seem, that the Offence is not punishable by any one Statute only. Yet considering that the Precedents in these Cases generally conclude *contra formam Statuti*, and the Prosecution in Truth depends on the Addition made by the later Statute, which seems of it self alone sufficient to support it, it may be reasonably argued, and seems agreeable to the later [m] Opinions, That such a Conclusion may be allowed in these Cases also. However it seems safe in any of the Cases above-mentioned, to conclude *contra formam* [n] *Statut'*, which shall stand either for *Statuti* or *Statutorum*, or be rejected in such manner as will best maintain the Indictment.

Sect. 120. As to the ninth general Point of this Chapter, *viz.* What ought to be the Form of the Caption of an Indictment, I shall take it for granted, That every such Caption is erroneous, which doth not set forth with proper Certainty, both the Court in which, and the Jurors by whom, and also the Time and Place at which the Indictment was found; for the better understanding whereof I shall endeavour to shew what Certainty of this Kind is necessary,

[a] Cro. El. 750. pl. 6. Owen 135. 1 Lutw. 221.
[b] Yelv. 116. Cro. Jac. 187. pl. 9.
[c] Yelv. 116. See Cro. Jac. 187. pl. 9.
[d] Owen 135. 1 Lutw. 221.
[e] Cro. El. 760. pl. 6. 187. pl. 12. 2 Leon. 5. Cro. Jac. 142. pl. 19. Aleyn 49, 50. 2 Bulst. 258. Dalt. Ch. 131.
[f] Crompt. 104 pl. 49. 5 H. 7. 17. b. Cro. El. 186. pl. 10. 4 Co. 48. a.
[g] Vide 2 Rol. Ab. 79. pl. 3. 82. pl. 5, 6. Dalton Ch. 129. Aleyn 50. B. 1. Ch. 81. Sect. 10.
[h] Dyer 155. pl. 15. Cro. El. 750. pl. 6. Aleyn 49, 50. Lamb. B. 4. Ch. 5.
[i] Dy. 155. pl. 15. 347. pl. 9. 2 Rol. Re. 227. 5 H. 7. 17. b. Owen 135. Supra Sect. 92. Contra 2 Leon. 5. 2 Rol Re. 65.
[k] Vide Cro. Jac. 142. Cro. El. 750. pl. 6. 2 Leon. 5.
[l] Aleyn 49, 50.
[m] Vide 1 Mod. 191. 3 Lev. 61. 1 Lutw. 212.
[n] Aleyn 50. 6 Mod. 140.

1. In Respect of the Court, before which.
2. Of the Jurors, by whom.
3. Of the Time: And,
4. Of the Place, at which the Indictment was found.

Sect. 121. As to the first of these Particulars, it is certain, That every such Caption must shew, that the Indictment was taken before such a Court as had Jurisdiction over the Offence indicted; and therefore if it set forth, that any Indictment whatsoever was taken before *J. S.* [a] Steward, without shewing to whom he was Steward, or in what Court; or that an Inquisition of Death, upon View of the Body, was taken before *J. S.* [b] Mayor of *London*, or before *J. S.* Steward to [c] such a Person, and in such a Court, without adding, That he was a Coroner; or if it expresly call him Coroner, but do not also shew that he was such for the [d] District in which the Inquisition was taken, it is insufficient But it hath been [e] adjudged, that it is sufficient to set forth, that it was taken before *J. S.* a Coroner in the County, without saying, that he was a Coroner for the County, for that cannot but be intended.

Sect. 122. Where [f] the Caption of an Indictment alledges it taken at the General Sessions of the Peace of such a County, or Burgh, it doth not seem necessary to add, That such Sessions was holden for such County, or Burgh, because it could not but be so holden, if it were the General Sessions of such County, or Burgh; but if it had been only described as a General Sessions holden in such County, or Burgh, it is said [g] to be a fatal Exception, that it is not expresly alledged as holden for such County, or Burgh; but [h] *Quære*, if this be not helped by putting the County in the Margin.

Sect. 123. There are some [i] Authorities, that if the Caption of an Indictment before Justices of Peace take no Notice of their Commission to hear and determine Felonies, *&c.* which is generally done by the Clause, *necnon ad diversas Felonias, &c.* it is insufficient: But having already more fully considered this Matter, *Chap.* 8. *Sect.* 33. I shall refer the Reader to what is there said concerning it.

Sect. 124. There are also several Authorities, that the Caption of an Indictment before Justices of Peace is insufficient, unless either the Words [k] *Domini Regis*, or [l] *Publicæ*, be added after *Pacis*; and it hath been sometimes holden, That even the Words *Domini Regis*, are not sufficient without the Word [m] *nunc*, or some other, to shew whether it were the Peace of the present King, or of some of his Predecessors. And the chief Ground of these Opinions seems to be the Statute of 27 *H.* 8. 24. *Sect.* 4. by which it is enacted, *That in every Writ and Indictment that shall be made within any County-Palatine, or Liberty, whereby any Thing shall be supposed to be done against the King's Peace, it shall be supposed to be done against the King's Peace, his Heirs and Successors, and not against the Peace of any other Person whatsoever, any Statute, Grant, or Usage, to the Contrary notwithstanding.* From whence, I suppose, it may have been collected, that by Parity of Reason, Justices of Peace ought to be styled, in legal Proceedings, Justices of the King's Peace, that it may appear that the Peace of no other Person, but of the King, is intended. But since this is not expresly required by the said Statute; and it cannot but be intended, (especially at this [n] Day, when none but the King can appoint Justices of Peace) that all Justices of Peace must be Justices of the publick Peace, or of the King's Peace, which is the same Thing; and accordingly Exceptions for the want of these

[a] 22 Ed. 4. 19. b. Bro. Battail 7. Indictment 46.
[b] 22 Ed. 4. 13. a. H. P. C. 207. S.P.C. 96. F.
[c] 22 Ed. 4. 12. b.
[d] Cro. Eliz. 193. pl. 7. 2 Ro Rep. 82. 22 Ed. 4 19. b. Bro. Bat. 7. Indictment 46.
[e] Plcom 97. a. 76. b. 4 Co. 41. b.
[f] 1 Sid. 247. pl. 11.
[g] 1 Keb. 329. pl. 66, 668. pl. 59. 1 Lev. 304. 2 Keb. 133. pl. 99. 2 Keb. 128. pl. 83, 141. pl. 11. 1 Keb. 635. pl. 126. *seems contrary.*
[h] Cro. Eliz. 490.
[i] S. P. C. 96. Letter E. H P. C 207. 2 Keb. 160. pl 46. Bro. Indictment 32. *But this is left as a Query.* 22 Ed. 4. 12. b. 13. a. Bro. Error. 186. See Bro. Indictment. 50.
[k] 1 Lev. 175. 2 Keb. 647. pl. 84. 1 Sid. 247. pl. 11, 422. pl. 13.
[l] 1 Keb. 37. pl. 101. 1 Sid. 422. pl. 13.
[m] 1 Sid. 422. pl. 13. 2 Keb. 582. pl. 117.
[n] Vide Ch 5. Sect. 1.

these Words have been often [a] over-ruled; I take them to be obsolete at this Day, as it seemed to be lately settled between the [b] King and *Hawkins* on a Conviction of Deer-stealing.

Sect. 125. But it seems generally agreed, [c] That if the Caption of an Indictment, at a Sessions of the Peace, do not mention before whom it was holden, or if it set it forth [d] generally as holden before Justices, without shewing any Thing of the Nature of their Commission, or as holden before Justices [e] of the Peace, *&c.* without naming any of them, or shewing for what Place they were Justices, or if it [f] describe them as Justices *ad pacem in comitatu prædict. conservand'*, omitting the Word *assignat'*, it is insufficient. [g] Yet it hath been adjudged, That it is not necessary for the Caption of an Indictment taken at a General Sessions of the Peace, to style any of the Justices of the *Quorum*, because it sufficiently shews, that one or more of them were such by shewing, That the Sessions was a General one.

Sect. 126. It hath been adjudged, [h] That the Caption of an Indictment, setting it forth as taken *ad magnam curiam cum leta tentam*, is insufficient; the chief Reason whereof seems to be this, That such a Caption rather imports, that the Indictment was taken at the Court which had no Jurisdiction to take it, than at the proper one; for it seems to be express, that it was taken at the Court-Baron, and mentions nothing in Relation to the Court-Leet, but that it was holden together with the Court-Baron. And agreeably hereto it is said in the Year-Book of 10 *Edw.* 4. 15. That if the Caption had been *ad magnam Curiam & ad letam*, it had been some Sense, but that *cum leta* bears no Sense. From whence it may be argued, That if a Caption set forth an Indictment as taken at a Court-Baron and Court-Leet, it may be good, because the Court-Baron having no Manner of Jurisdiction in criminal Matters, and the Court-Leet having such Jurisdiction, it may well be [i] intended that the Indictment was taken at the Court-Leet, and not at the Court which had nothing to do with it. *A fortiori* therefore, if an Indictment be set forth as taken *ad vis. franci pleg. cum cur' baron' tent'*, it shall be intended to have been taken at the Court-Leet; as it is [k] said to have been holden by the late Chief Justice *Holt*, who yet seemed to be of Opinion, That if a Court-Baron had a Jurisdiction of such Matters as well as a Court-Leet, but in a different Manner, such a Caption would have been insufficient, for not shewing more expresly at which of the Courts the Indictment was taken.

Sect. 127. It hath been adjudged, [l] That the not setting forth in the Caption of an Indictment taken at a Leet, whether the Court were holden by Grant or Prescription, is holpen by the Multitude of Precedents.

Sect. 128. As to the second Particular, *viz.* What Certainty is necessary in the Caption of an Indictment in respect of the Jurors by whom it was found, it seems agreed, That no Caption of an Indictment whether found at a [m] Court-Leet, or other inferior Court, can be good, without expresly shewing, that the Jurors who found it were of the [n] County, City, or Burgh, or other Precinct, for which the Court was holden, and that they were at least [o] twelve in Number, and [p] also, that they found the Indictment upon their Oaths. Also, Indictments have been [q] quashed for an Omission of the Names of the Jurors in the Caption; but there is a [r] Precedent in *Saunders*'s Reports of a Caption, setting

[a] 2 Keb. 385 pl. 58. 1 Sid. 247. pl. 11. *It is made a Query*, 1 Keb. 656. pl. 36. 1 Sid. 175. pl. 7.
[b] *Adjudged* Term. Mich. 3 Georgii.
[c] 1 Mod. 24. 2 Keb. 580. pl. 112. Cro. Eliz. 738. pl. 10.
[d] 1 Bulst. 203.
[e] 2 Keb. 128. pl. 83. Cro. Eliz. 738. pl. 10. Vide Keilw. 192. b. 194. a. 2 Keb. 385. pl. 58. 22 Ed 4, 19. b. Bro Battail 7. Indictment 46.
[f] 1 Saund. 263.
[g] 1 Sid. 367. 3 Mod. 152. 2 Keb. 366. pl. 19.
[h] 10 Ed. 4. 15. pl. 15. Bro. Indictment 34. Fitz. Indictment 20. S. P. C. 95. Letter C. H P. C. 206. 2 Keb. 139. pl. 7.
[i] 1 Salk. 195. Supra Ch. 11. Sect. 6.
[k] 1 Salk. 195.
[l] 1 Salk. 200.
[m] 6 H. 4. pl. 4.
[n] Raym. 434. Cro. Eliz. 677. pl. 6. 2 Keb. 160. pl. 46. 3 Keb. 807. pl. 17. Vide Supra Sect. 33.
[o] Cro. Eliz. 654. pl. 16. Vide Supra Sect. 15. 6 H. 4. pl. 4. 41 Ed. 3. 31. pl. 36.
[p] 2 Keb. 676. pl. 54. 1 Sid. 140. 3 Mod. 201. 1 Keb. 629. pl. 112, 329. pl. 66. *See the Cases cited to Letters* a, b, c, d, e, f, g, *and* 1 Salk. 371. pl. 7.
[q] 2 Rol. Ab. 82. pl. 10. 2 Keb. 470. pl. 61. 6 H. 4. pl. 4. Qu. 2 R 3. 11. pl. 25. Vide Rast. Ent. 553, 606.
[r] 1 Saund. 249. Vide 13 H. 7. 20. a. 2 Keb. 366.

forth,

forth, That the Indictment was taken by twelve Men, *&c.* without naming them, and yet no Exception appears to have been taken on this Account. Also, many Indictments taken in inferior [a] Courts, have been quashed for want of the Words, *proborum & legalium hominum* in the Caption, but this Exception hath been often over-ruled, as hath been more fully shewn in the sixteenth Section of this Chapter. Also, many Indictments in such Courts have been quashed for want of the Words, [b] *jurat. & onerat.* in the Caption; and also for want of the Words [c] *adtunc & ibidem*, before the Words *jurat. & onerat'*; and also for [d] want of the Words *ad inquirendum pro dicto Domino Rege & pro corpore comitatus*; and also for want of the Words [e] *super sacramentum suum dicunt*, after the Words *jurat. & onerat'*; and also for expressing the [f] Oath to have been to inquire *pro corpore civitatis prædicta*, where the Offence arose in, and the Sessions was holden for a Burgh, *&c.* But it is [g] said, That in the Caption of an Indictment taken in the King's Bench, or at the [h] Grand Sessions, the Words *super sacramentum suum dicunt*, supply the Want of the Words *jurat. & onerat'*, *&c.* Also, it is said to have been [i] adjudged, That the Words *jurat. & onerat. ad inquirend. pro Domino Rege & corpore comitatus* are sufficient, without the Word *pro* before *corpore*; and that the Addition of the Words *ad largum* after *inquirend.* does no [k] hurt; and that there is no need of the Words *ad inquirendum pro corpore comitatus* in an [l] Inquisition taken for a particular Purpose; and that the Omission of the Word [m] *onerat.* is not fatal, if there be the Word *jurat'*, for that fully implies it.

Sect. 129. As to the third Particular, *viz.* What Certainty is necessary in the Caption of an Indictment, in respect of the Time when it was found? It seems [n] agreed, That such Caption must set forth a certain Day and Year when the Court was holden, before which the Indictment was found, and must record it as then found in the [o] Present Tense, and not in the Preterperfect; for it hath been [p] adjudged, That if it describe the Sessions at which the Indictment was taken, as holden *die Martis & die Mercurii*; or as holden on such a Day in such a Year of the King, without [q] ascertaining what King; or if it set forth the Style of the Day or Year in any [r] Figures but *Roman*, it is insufficient. But it seems to be [s] agreed, That it is sufficient to express the Year of the King, without adding that of the Lord: Also it seems, that [t] *extitit præsentatum* for *existit* is made good by the Multitude of Precedents.

Sect. 130. As to the fourth Particular, *viz.* What Certainty is necessary in the Caption of an Indictment in respect of the Place where it was found? It seems agreed, That if such Caption either set forth no [u] Place at all where the Indictment was found, or do not [x] shew with sufficient Certainty, that the Place set forth is within the Jurisdiction of the Court before which it was taken, as where it sets forth the Indictment as taken at a Sessions of the Peace holden for such a County, at *B.* [y] without shewing in what County *B.* is, otherwise than by putting the County into the Margin, it is insufficient: Also, if an Act of Parliament, whether it be in Print, or not, appoint, that the Quarter-Sessions of such a County shall be holden at such a Place only, and not elsewhere, except for Cause of the Plague, *&c.* it seems, [z] that the Caption of every Indictment taken at any such Sessions, is insufficient, unless it expresly shew, that it was holden at such Place. But it hath been [*] adjudged, That the Caption

[a] 1 Keb. 629. pl. 112. 2 Keb. 471. pl. 63. 2 Rol. Abr. 82. pl. 8. 2 Keb. 366. pl. 19.
[b] 1 Keb. 101. pl. 100, 524. pl. 14, 629, pl. 112, 852. pl. 55. 2 Keb. 367. pl. 20. Vide 3 Keb. 128 pl. 50. Contra 2 Keb. 59 pl. 28. 2 Jo. 180.
[c] 1 Mod. 26. 2 Keb. 583. pl. 121, 610, pl. 47.
[d] 2 Keb. 471. pl. 63. Show. 272. 6 Mod. 95, 180.
[e] 1 Sid. 140, 1 Keb. 498. pl. 51.
[f] 1 Saund. 249.
[g] 1 Keb. 629. pl. 112.
[h] 2 Keb. 471. pl. 63.
[i] 6 Mod. 180.
[k] 1 Sid. 140.
[l] Show. 272. 6 Mod. 95.
[m] Dom. Rex versus Gravenor, *adjudg'd* Hil. 3 Georg.
[n] Vide 1 Bulst. 203. Supra Ch. 10. Sect. 9.
[o] 1 Sid. 229, 230. 1 Keb. 37. pl. 101, 823. pl. 114. Vide 1 Mod. 81. 2 Saund. 393. 1 Vent. 170.
[p] 4 Co. 48. a.
[q] 2 Keb. 582. pl. 117, 118.
[r] Vide supra Sect. 89. 1 Mod. 78. 2 Keb. 128. pl. 83.
[r] Vide supra Sect. 82. & Ch. 23. Sect. 90.
[t] 1 Sid. 140, 368. 1 Keb. 37. pl. 101. 2 Keb. 367. pl. 20. 5 Co. 120. Fitz. Indictment 20. Bro. Indictment 34. 10 Ed. 4. 15. pl. 15.
[u] Dyer 69. pl. 29.
[x] Cro. Jac. 276, 277.
[y] Cro. Eliz. 137. pl. 9, 606. pl. 4, 738. pl. 10, 751. pl. 7.
[z] Dyer 135. pl. 14.
[*] 5 Co. 120. b. 121. Vide Poph. 208. Cro. Eliz. 490.

tion of an Inquisition as taken at *B.* before *J. S.* Coroner of the King's Liberty of *B.* aforesaid, is good, without expresly shewing that *B.* is within the Liberty of *B.* for it cannot but be intended.

Sect. 131. As to the tenth general Point of this Chapter, *viz.* Upon what Proof, and within what Time after the Offence, an Indictment may be found? It [a] seems, that before 1 *Ed.* 6. no certain Number of Witnesses was required upon the Indictment or Trial of any Crime whatever; for it seems to be generally [b] agreed, that the Statutes of 1 and 2 of *Philip* and *Mary*, 10 & 11, in restoring the Order of Trial by the Course of the Common Law, took away the Necessity of two Witnesses in all Cases within those Statutes; from whence it plainly seems to follow, that they were not required by the Common Law. It is holden [c] indeed by some, That by the ancient Common Law one Witness was not sufficient to convict any Person of High Treason, and this is said to be grounded on the Law of God, expressed both in the Old and New Testament. But granting that one Witness was not sufficient for a Conviction, it doth not follow but that he might be sufficient for an Indictment. Also, however the Law might have stood in Relation to these Matters before the Conquest, it seems to have been wholly altered long before the Statute of *Ed.* 6. And I rather incline to this Opinion, since I find it so little supported by the Generality of the Authorities cited by Sir *Edward Coke* for the Proof of the contrary, which wholly relate either to the Proof of an Essoin, or of a Summons [d] in a real Action, or [e] of the Default of Persons summon'd on a Jury, or [f] other Matters rather less to the Point. And as to the abovecited Passages of Scripture it may be answered, that those in the Old Testament concern only the judicial Part of the *Jewish* Law, which being framed for the particular Government of the *Jewish* Nation, doth not bind us any more than the ceremonial; and that those in the New Testament contain only prudential Rules for the Direction of the Government of the Church, in Matters introduced by the Gospel, and no way control the Civil Constitutions of Countries. To which may be added, That whatsoever may be said either from Reason or Scripture for the Necessity of two Witnesses in Treason, holds as strongly in other Capital Causes, and yet it is not pretended, that there is or ever was any such Necessity in relation to any other Crime but Treason.

[a] Vide 3 Keb. 68. pl. 7. Bro. coro. 220. 2 Jo. 233.
[b] Bro. coro. 220. S.P.C. 164. Dyer 132. pl. 75. 1 Jon. 233. Kel. 18, 49. Vide 3 Inst. 24, 25, 26. H.P.C. 208, 262.
[c] 3 Inst. 26. Raym. 408.
[d] Bract. 354. b.
[e] 35 H. 6. 46. b. 47. a.
[f] 48 Ed. 3. 30. pl. 17.
[g] 15 Ed. 44.

Sect. 132. But it is enacted by 1 *Ed.* 6. 12. *par.* 22. *That no Person or Persons, after the first Day of* February *then next to come, shall be indicted, arraigned, condemned, or convicted for any Offence of Treason, Petit Treason, or Misprision of Treason,* &c. *unless the same Offender or Offenders, be accused by two sufficient and lawful Witnesses, or shall willingly without Violence confess the same.*

Sect. 133. Also it is further enacted by 5 & 6 *Ed.* 6. 11. *par.* 8. *That no Person or Persons after the first Day of* June *then next coming, shall be indicted, arraigned, condemned, convicted or attainted, for any of the Treasons in the Act mentioned, or for any other Treasons that then were, or after should be, which should after be perpetrated, committed, or done, unless the same Offender or Offenders, be thereof accused by two lawful Accusers; which said Accusers at the Time of that Arraignment of the Party accused, if they be then living, shall be brought in Person before the Party so accused, and avow and maintain what they have to say against the said Party, to prove him guilty of the Treasons or Offences contained in the Bill of Indictment laid against the Party arraigned, unless the said Party arraigned shall willingly, without Violence, confess the same.*

Sect. 134. But it is enacted by 1 & 2 *Ph. & M.* 10. *That all Trials after that Statute to be had, awarded, or made for any Treason, shall be had and used only according to the due Order and Course of the Common Law.*

Sect. 135. Also it is enacted by 1 & 2 *Ph. & Ma.* 11. *That all and every Person and Persons who shall be accused or impeached of any of the Offences contained in that Statute, or of any other Offence or Offences concerning the impairing, counterfeiting or forging of any Coin Current within this Realm, shall and may be indicted, arraigned, tried, convicted or attainted by such like Evidence, and in such Manner and Form as has been used and accustomed within the Realm, at any Time before the first Year of the Reign of King* Edward 6.

Sect. 136. It is further enacted by 7 *W.* 3. 3. *That after the 25th Day of* March, *in the Year* 1696, *no Person or Persons whatsoever shall be indicted, tried, or attainted of High Treason, whereby any Corruption of Blood may, or shall be made to any such Offender or Offenders, or to any the Heir or Heirs of any such Offender or Offenders, or of Misprision of such Treason, but by and upon the Oaths and Testimony of two lawful Witnesses, either both of them to the same Overt Act, or one of them to one, and the other of them to another Overt Act of the same Treason, unless the Party indicted and arraigned, or tried, shall willingly, without Violence, in open Court, confess the same, or shall stand Mute, or refuse to plead; or in Cases of High Treason, shall peremptorily challenge above the Number of thirty-five of the Jury.*

Sect. 137. And it is further enacted by the said Statute, *That no Person or Persons whatsoever, (such only excepted as shall be guilty of designing, endeavouring, or attempting any Assassination on the Body of the King, by Poison, or otherwise,) shall be indicted, tried, or prosecuted for any such Treason as aforesaid, or for Misprision of such Treason, that shall be committed or done within the Kingdom of* England, *Dominion of* Wales, *or Town of* Berwick *upon* Tweed, *unless the same Indictment be found by a Grand Jury, within three Years next after the Treason or Offence done and committed.*

Sect. 138. But it is provided, *That nothing in this Act shall any Ways extend to any Impeachment, or other Proceedings in Parliament, nor to any Indictment of High Treason, nor to any Proceeding thereupon, for counterfeiting his Majesty's Coin, his Great Seal, or Privy Seal, his Sign Manual, or Privy Signet.*

Upon these Statutes the following Particulars seem most remarkable.

Sect. 139. *First*, That where the Statute of 1 *Ed.* 6. requires, That the Party be accused by two lawful Witnesses; and that of 5 & 6 *Ed.* 6. That he be accused by two lawful Accusers; they both mean the very [a] same Thing, because the Common Law admits of no other Accusers but Witnesses.

Sect. 140. *Secondly*, That according to the general [b] Opinion, it is not required either by the 1st, or 5th and 6th *Ed.* 6. That such Accusers or Witnesses be present with the Indictors in Person, but that they may send their Accusation to the Indictors in Writing under their Hands, which will be sufficient even after their Death. Also it is observable, That the Books which speak of this Matter do not expresly say, that such Accusation must be upon Oath, but surely this cannot but be intended; for how can any Accuser be said to be a lawful Witness, if he be not upon his Oath? But this is cleared by 7 *W.* 3. as to the Treasons within that Statute; for it expresly provides, That no Person shall be indicted thereof, but by and upon the Oaths and Testimony of two lawful Witnesses.

[a] Bro. coro. 220. 3 Inst. 25, 26. H. P. C. 208.

[b] S P.C. 164. Bro. coro. 220. H.P.C. 208. *But* 3 Inst. 25, 26. *seems contrary.*

Sect. 141. *Thirdly*, By the Judgment both of [a] *Coke* and [b] *Hale*, one who can only witness by Hearsay what he has heard a good Witness say, is not a lawful Accuser within any of these Statutes; for if this were to be allowed, nothing would be more easy than in any Case, where there is one Witness, to get a second, which would totally elude the Provision of the Statutes in requiring two lawful Witnesses, *&c.*

Sect. 142. *Fourthly*, That the Words, *unless the Party shall willingly, without Violence, confess the same*, in the 1st, and 5th, and 6th *Ed.* 6. are to be understood [c] where the Party accused upon his Examination, before his Arraignment, willingly confesses the same without Torture: But it is observable, that 7 *W.* 3. is thus expressed, *Unless the Party indicted and arraigned, or tried, shall willingly, without Violence, in open Court confess the same.*

Sect. 143. *Fifthly*, That one Witness to one, and another Witness to another Overt Act of the very same [d] Treason, have been construed to be sufficient, within the Statutes of the 1st, and 5th, and 6th *Ed.* 6. and the express Words of 7 *W.* 3. are agreeable hereto.

Sect. 144. *Sixthly*, That the Statute of 1 & 2 *Ph. & Ma.* 10. by enacting, That all Trials of Treason shall from thenceforth be according to the Course of the Common Law, doth not [e] take away the Necessity of two Witnesses upon an Indictment, required by the 1st, and 5th, and 6th *Ed.* 6. because the Indictment is no Part of the Trial, but is more properly the Accusation to be tried.

Sect. 145. *Seventhly*, [f] That the said Statute of 1 & 2 *Ph & Ma.* doth not extend to Misprision of Treason; but this is expresly provided for by 7 *W.* 3. as to such Treasons as are within that Statute, and therefore there must be two Witnesses to the Indictment, as well as Trial of every such Misprision.

Sect. 146. *Eighthly*, That [g] Petit Treason is within the 1st, and 5th, and 6th of *Ed.* 6. and 1 & 2 *Ph. & Ma.* 10. but not within the 7th of *W.* 3. from whence it follows, That two Witnesses are required to the Indictment, and not to the Trial of it, and that two Witnesses are not necessary even upon the Indictment, if [h] the Party, upon his Examination, confess it.

Sect. 147. *Ninthly*, That the Statute of 1 & 2 *Ph. & Ma* 11. which enacts, That all Persons accused of any Offences concerning the impairing, counterfeiting, or forging the Coin, shall be indicted and tried as at the Common Law, hath been construed [i] to extend to clipping, and all other Offences in impairing the Coin, which have been made Treasons since the said Statute of 1 & 2 *Ph. & Ma.* From whence it may be probably argued, That the Statute of 7 *W.* 3. by expresly providing, that nothing therein shall extend to High Treason for counterfeiting the Coin; intended in like Manner, that it should not extend to any other High Treason concerning the Coin.

Sect. 148. As to the eleventh general Point of this Chapter, *viz.* In what Cases an Indictment may be quashed. I take it to be [k] settled, That by the Common Law the Court may, in Discretion, quash any Indictment, for any such Insufficiency, either in the Caption, or Body of it, as will make any Judgment whatsoever, given upon any Part of it against the Defendant, erroneous; yet it seems, That Judges are in no Case bound, *ex debito justitiæ*, to quash an Indictment, but may oblige the Defendant either to plead or demur to it: And this they generally do where it is for a Crime of an enormous or publick Nature, as Perjury, Forgery, Sedition, Nusances to the Highways, and other Offences of the like

[a] 3 Inst. 25, 26.
[b] H P.C. 208. Contra Dyer 99. pl. 68. Vide S. P. C. 164. Bro. coro. 220.
[c] 2 And. 66, 67. 3 Inst. 25.
[d] Raym. 407, 408. Kel. 9.
[e] S P.C. 90, 164. 3 Inst. 24, 25, 26, 27. Bro. coro. 220.
[f] Bro. coro. 220. 3 Inst. 24.
[g] Bro. coro. 220. 3 Inst. 24.
[h] Vide supra Sect. 140.
[i] 2 Jo. 233. Vide Bro. coro 220. 3 Keb. 68. pl. 7.
[k] State Trials Volume 4. Page 135. 1 Sid. 54. pl. 19, 247. pl. 11. 2 Keb. 128. pl. 83. 1 Keb. 45. pl 120. Cro Car. 584. Palm. 389. Salk, 372. pl. 11. State Trials Volume 4. Page 134.

like Nature. [a] Neither will the Court quash an Indictment removed by *Certiorari*, if a Recognizance for the Trial of it hath been forfeited. [a] Salk. 380. pl. 26.

Sect. 149. Also it is enacted by 7 *W.* 3. 3. *That no Indictment for High Treason, or Misprision thereof, (except only Indictments for counterfeiting the King's Coin, Seal, Sign, or Signet,) nor any Process or Return thereupon, shall be quashed on the Motion of the Prisoner, or his Counsel, for miswriting, misspelling, false or improper* Latin, *unless Exception concerning the same be taken and made in the respective Court, where such Trial shall be, by the Prisoner, or his Counsel assigned, before any Evidence given in open Court upon such Indictment; nor shall any such miswriting, misspelling, false or improper* Latin, *after Conviction on such Indictment, be any Cause to stay or arrest Judgment thereupon: But nevertheless, any Judgment given upon such Indictment, shall and may be liable to be reversed upon a Writ of Error, in the same Manner, and no other than as if this Act had not been made.*

Sect. 150. It hath been settled * in the Construction of this Statute, that no such Exception can be taken, after Plea pleaded. * State Trials Volume 4. Page 135, 329.

Sect. 151. It is said [b] in *Siderfin*'s Reports, That the Court never [c] quasheth an Information exhibited by a Common Person, but that it will quash an Information exhibited by the Attorney General, or by the Master of the Crown-Office, upon Motion, if there be Cause: But this was denied in one [d] *Nixon*'s Case, wherein the Court seemed to be agreed, That they never have, or will quash any Information whatsoever. [b] 1 Sid. 152. Vide 1 Sid. 54. pl. 19: [c] Contra 1 Keb. 255. pl. 28. [d] King *versus* Nixon, Trin. 5 Georgii. Vide Salk. 372. pl. 11.

Sect. 152. As to the twelfth general Point of this Chapter, *viz.* What may be pleaded to an Indictment, and in what Manner? Having already shewn in this Chapter how a Defendant may plead [e] to an Indictment, that the Indictors were returned contrary to the Purview of 11 *H.* 4. 9. And having also [f] shewn, how he may plead a Misnosmer, or wrongful Addition; and intending in the following Part of the Book to shew, how he may plead a former Acquittal, Conviction, or Attainder, or a Pardon, or other special Plea, or the general Issue. I shall in this Place only take Notice, That the Defendant may plead any Plea in Abatement of an Indictment of Felony; and also plead over in Bar, and take [g] the general Issue also, in the same Manner as an Appellee may do, as hath been more fully shewn *Chap.* 23. *Sect.* 126, 135. [e] Supra Sect. 25. [f] Supra Sect. 70, 71, 72. Vide Ch. 23. Sect. 102. [g] Finch. 383. H P.C. 202, 249, 254.

CHAP. XXVI.

Of Information.

INformations are of two Kinds:

First, Such as are merely the Suit of the King.

Secondly, Such as are partly the Suit of the King, and partly the Suit of the Party.

And

And first, for the better understanding the first of these, I shall endeavour to shew,

First, In what Cases they lie.
Secondly, What ought to be the Form of them.
Thirdly, How the Law concerning them hath been altered by Statute.

Sect. 1. As to the first of these Particulars, *viz.* In what Cases such Informations lie: It hath been holden, That the King shall put no [a] one to answer for a Wrong done principally to another, without an Indictment or Presentment, but that he may do it for a Wrong done principally to himself. But I do not find this Distinction confirmed by Experience, for it is every Day's Practice, agreeable to numberless Precedents, to proceed by way of Information, either in the Name of the Attorney General, or of the Master of the Crown-Office, for Offences of the former Kind, as for [b] Batteries, [c] Cheats, seducing [d] a young Man or Woman from their Parents in order to marry them against their Consent, or for any other wicked Purpose; spiriting [e] away a Child to the Plantations, rescuing [f] Persons from legal Arrests, [g] Perjuries and Subornations thereof, [h] Forgeries, Conspiracies, (whether to accuse [i] an innocent Person, or to impoverish [k] a certain Set of lawful Traders, *&c.* or to [l] procure a Verdict to be unlawfully given, by causing Persons bribed for the Purpose, to be sworn on a *Tales*,) and other such like Crimes done principally to a private Person, as well as for Offences done principally to the King, as for [m] Libels, seditious Words, [n] Riots, false News, [o] Extortions, Nusances, (as in not [p] repairing Highways, or obstructing [q] them, or stopping [r] a Common River, *&c.*) Contempts, as in departing [s] from the Parliament without the King's Licence, disobeying [t] his Writs, uttering [u] Money without his Authority, escaping [x] from a legal Imprisonment on a Prosecution for a Contempt, neglecting to keep Watch and Ward, abusing [y] the King's Commission to the Oppression of the Subject, making a Return to a *Mandamus* of Matters [z] known to be false; and in general, any other Offences against the Publick Good, or against the first and obvious Principles of Justice, and Common Honesty.

Sect. 2. Also it seems, [aa] That of Common Right such an Information, or an Action in the Nature thereof, may be brought for Offences against Statutes, whether they be mentioned by such Statutes or not, unless other Methods of Proceeding be particularly appointed, by which all others are impliedly excluded.

Sect. 3. But I do not [bb] find it any where holden, That such an Information will lie for any capital Crime, or for Misprision of Treason.

Sect. 4. As to the second Particular, *viz.* What ought to be the Form of such Informations? Having already in the Chapter *of Inditements* incidentally shewn the principal Points relating to this Matter, I shall only take Notice in this Place, That seeing an Information differs from an Inditement in little more than this, that the one is found by the Oath of twelve Men, and the other is not so found; but is only the Allega-

[a] Thelo. B. 1. ch. 4. Sect. 9, 10, 11, 12, 13, 14. Finch. 336. Fitz. Action sur le Statute, &c.
[b] *See the Preamble of* 4 & 5 Will. & Ma. infra Sect. 5. Show. 116, 117, 118.
[c] Show. 110, 116, 117. 1 Sid. 431.
[d] Cro. Car. 557, 558. March 52, 53. 3 Keb. 101. 1 Lev. 257. 1 Sid. 387. 5 Mod. 221, 222. 2 Keb. 432. Raym. 473.
[e] Raym. 474.
[f] Raym. 231. Show. 109, 110, 113. Cro. Car. 579.
[g] Raym. 202. 5 Mod. 342.
[h] Show. 111.
[i] Raym. 417.
[k] 1 Sid. 174.
[l] *See the President of such an Information.* 1 Saund. 300, 301.
[m] Raym. 201. Show. 118, 119.
[n] 5 Mod. 459. Cro. Car. 252. Show. 106.
[o] Raym. 216.
[p] Raym. 384. Show. 110, 111, 112, 116. 1 Sid. 140.
[q] Show. 112, 116. [r] Show. 114, 118. [s] Ibid. [t] Cro. Car. 253. [u] Raym. 185. [x] Cro. Car. 209. [y] Show. 116. [z] Salk. 374. pl. 16. [aa] Show. 111, 115, 116, 117. 3 Mod. 117. 2 And. 128. Rast. Ent. 686. b. Vitail. 1. Vide 3 Leon. 237. & supra Ch. 24 2 And 127, 128. [bb] Vide Show. 109, 110.

tion of the Officer who exhibits it, whatsoever Certainty is requisite in an Indictment, the same at least is necessary also in an Information, and consequently, as all the material Parts of the Crime must be precisely found in the one, so must they be precisely alledged in the other, and not by Way of [a] Argument or Recital. Yet it hath been adjudged, That where an Information of Perjury was drawn in this Manner, *Memorandum quod* A. B. *&c. dat Curiæ hic intelligi & informari quod Termino Sancti Hill. &c. in Rotulis continetur sic, viz.* That such an Action was brought, and a Trial had thereon, *&c. Et quod,* the Defendant, at such Trial, took such an Oath which was false, *&c.* without adding, before such mention of the false Oath, *Et ulterius dat Cur. hic intelligi;* yet, by Reason of the late Precedents the Information is as [b] sufficient, at least after Verdict, as if those Words had been added; and it must be confessed, That this is the most reasonable Construction, for how can it be intended that it could be contained in the Record of the Trial, That such an Oath was taken at it, or that it was false?

[a] Salk. 375.

[b] Raym. 34, 35.

Sect. 5. As to the third Particular, *viz.* How the Law concerning such Informations hath been altered by Statute? it is recited by 4 & 5 *Wil. & Ma.* 18. *That divers malitious and contentious Persons had more of late, than in Times past, procured to be exhibited and prosecuted Informations in their Majesty's Court of King's Bench at* Westminster, *against Persons in all the Counties of* England, *for Trespasses, Batteries, and other Misdemeanors, and after the Parties so informed against had appeared to such Informations, and pleaded to Issue, the Informers had very seldom proceeded any further, whereby the Persons so informed against had been put to great Charges in their Defence; and altho' at the Trials of such Informations Verdicts had been given for them, or a* Nolle Prosequi *entred against them, they had no Remedy for obtaining Costs against such Informers.* And thereupon it is enacted, *That after the first Day of* Easter-Term, *in the Year* 1693, *the Clerk of the Crown, in the said Court of King's Bench, for the Time being, shall not without express Order, to be given by the said Court, in open Court, exhibit, receive, or file any Information for any of the Causes aforesaid, or issue out any Process thereupon, before he shall have taken, or shall have delivered to him a Recognizance from the Person or Persons procuring such Information, to be exhibited with the Place of his, her, or their Abode, Title, or Profession, to be entred to the Person or Persons against whom such Information or Informations, is, or are to be exhibited, in the Penalty of twenty Pounds, that he, she, or they will effectually prosecute such Informations or Information, and abide by, and observe such Orders, as the said Court shall direct; which Recognizance the said Clerk of the Crown, and also every Justice of the Peace of any County, City, Franchise, or Town corporate, (where the Cause of any such Information shall arise,) are, by the said Statute impowered to take: After the taking whereof by the said Clerk of the Crown, or the Receipt thereof, from any Justice of the Peace, the said Clerk of the Crown shall make an Entry thereof upon Record, and shall file a Memorandum thereof in some publick Place in his Office, that all Persons may resort thereunto without Fee; and in case any Person or Persons against whom any Information or Informations for the Causes aforesaid, or any of them, shall be exhibited, shall appear thereunto, and plead to Issue, and that the Prosecutor or Prosecutors of such Information or Informations, shall not at his and their own proper Costs and Charges, within one whole Year next after Issue joined therein, procure the same to be tried; or if upon such Trial a Verdict pass for the Defendant or Defendants, or in Case the same Informer or Informers procure a* Nolle Prosequi *to be entred; then, in any of the said Cases the said Court of King's Bench is authorised to award to the said Defendant or Defendants, his, her, or their Costs, unless the Judge, before whom such Information*

formation ſhall be tried, ſhall at the Trial of ſuch Information, in open Court, certify upon Record, That there was a reaſonable Cauſe for exhibiting ſuch Information; and in caſe the ſaid Informer or Informers ſhall not within three Months next after the ſaid Coſts taxed, and Demand made thereof, pay to the ſaid Defendant or Defendants the ſaid Coſts, then the ſaid Defendant and Defendants ſhall have the Benefit of the ſaid Recognizance, to compel them thereunto.

Sect. 6. But it is provided, *That nothing hereof ſhall extend, or be conſtrued to extend, to any other Informations than ſuch as ſhall be exhibited in the Name of their Majeſties Coroner, or Attorney, in the Court of King's Bench, for the Time being (commonly called the Maſter of the Crown Officer.)* From whence it follows, That Informations exhibited by the Attorney General remain as they were at the Common Law.

For the better Underſtanding this Statute, I ſhall endeavour to ſhew,

1. Whether it extend to all Kinds of Informations.
2. In what Caſes the Court will order an Information to be filed.
3. How the Party may be relieved againſt Proceſs iſſued againſt him, before any Recognizance given.
4. Where the Defendant ſhall have Coſts.

Sect. 7. As to the firſt of theſe Particulars: It ſeems clear, That this Statute extends to all Informations whatſoever exhibited by the Maſter of the Crown Office; and tho' it may be objected, That an Information in the [a] Nature of a *Quo Warranto*, being a proper Means to try a Right, is not within the meaning of the Statute, which mentioning *Treſpaſſes, Batteries, and other Miſdemeanors*, may be reaſonably conſtrued to intend ſuch other Miſdemeanors only as are of an inferior Nature, like to thoſe ſpecified, which are generally wrangling and frivolous ones; yet ſeeing this is a remedial Law, and therefore ought to be largely conſtrued, and ſuch Informations may be as vexatious as any other, and always ſuppoſe an Uſurpation of ſome Franchiſe, and every ſuch Uſurpation is certainly a Miſdemeanor, it hath been ſettled that this Statute doth extend to them.

[a] Salk. 376. pl. 19.

Sect. 8. As to the ſecond Particular, *viz.* In what Caſes the Court will order an Information to be filed. It ſeems to have been the general Practice not to make ſuch an Order, without firſt making a Rule upon the Perſon complained of to ſhew Cauſe to the contrary; which Rule is never granted, but upon Motion made in open Court, and grounded upon Affidavit of ſome Miſdemeanor, which if true, doth either for its Enormity, or dangerous Tendency, or other ſuch like Circumſtances, ſeem proper for the moſt publick Proſecution. And if the Perſon upon whom ſuch a Rule is made, having been perſonally ſerv'd with it, do not, at the Day given him for that Purpoſe, give the Court good Satisfaction, by Affidavit, that there is no reaſonable Cauſe for the Proſecution, the Court generally grants the Information; and ſometimes upon ſpecial Circumſtances, will grant it againſt thoſe who cannot be perſonally ſerv'd with ſuch Rule, as if they purpoſely abſent themſelves, *&c.*

Sect. 9. But if the Party on whom ſuch a Rule is made, ſhew to the Court a reaſonable Cauſe againſt ſuch Proſecution; as that he has been before indicted for the ſame Cauſe, and acquitted: or that the Intent of the [b] Proſecution is to try a Civil Right, as the Title to Land, *&c.* which is not yet determined; or that the Complaint is trifling, vexatious, or oppreſſive; or if he can ſhew to the Court (in Anſwer to a Motion for

[b] Cro. Jac. 212.

an Information, in the Nature of a *Quo Warranto*) that his Right to the Franchise, in question, had been already determined on a *Mandamus*; or that it hath been acquiesced in many Years, without any Dispute; or that it depends on the Right of those who voted for him, which hath not been yet tried; or that the Franchise no way concerns the Publick, (as all those which relate to the Government of a Corporation, or the Election of Members of Parliament, and Fairs, and Markets, *&c.* are said to do) but is wholly of a private [a] Nature, as a Cony-warren, *&c.* Or that the Election, by which he Claims, is agreeable to Charter; or that he has never acted under it; the Court will not grant the Information, unless there be some particular and extraordinary Circumstances in the Case, the Determination whereof being wholly left to the Discretion of the Court, cannot well come under any certain stated Rules.

[a] Vide Salk. 374. pl. 15.

Sect. 10. As to the third Particular, *viz.* How the Party may be relieved against Process issued against him, before any Recognizance given according to the Statute? It seems that he may move the Court [b] to set it aside, as having issued contrary to the Directions of the Statute.

[b] Salk. 376. pl. 19.

As to the fourth Particular, *viz.* Where the Defendant shall have Costs, I shall observe,

Sect. 11. *First*, That if the Information be tried at Bar, the Defendant can have no Costs within this Statute; for the Words are, [c] *That the Court is authorised to award Costs*, &c. *unless the Judge, before whom the Information shall be tried, shall at the Trial, in open Court, certify upon Record, that there was a reasonable Cause for exhibiting such Information.* Which is most naturally to be understood of a Trial at *Nisi Prius*; and it would be absurd to suppose, That the Statute intended that the Justices of the King's Bench, at a Trial before themselves, should make a Certificate to themselves: To which may be added, That where a Cause is of such Consequence as to be tried at the Bar, it may reasonably be intended to be out of the Purview of the Statute, which was chiefly designed against trifling and vexatious Prosecutions.

[c] Clerk's Case.

Sect. 12. *Secondly*, That if there be several Defendants, and any one of them found guilty, those who are acquitted cannot have [d] Costs within this Statute; and this is agreeable to the Construction made of the Statutes which give Costs to Defendants in civil Actions, by Force whereof no Defendant, in such like Case, could recover Costs before the Statute of 8 & 9 *Will.* 10.

[d] Salk. 194. pl. 5.

Sect. 13. *Thirdly*, That it hath been adjudged in the Construction of those Words, *The Court of King's Bench is authorized to award to the Defendant his Costs, where the Judge, who tries an Information, does not at such Trial certify, That there was a reasonable Cause for the Information* [e]. That the said Court is bound of Right, in every such Case, to award them, whether the Acquittal were upon the Merits, or only from a Slip in Point of Form, and howsoever notorious the Offence might be; for where a Court is authorized, by Statute, to do a Matter of Justice to the Party, upon certain Circumstances, it has no discretionary Power of considering, whether it ought to do it or not, when a Case appears to be within those Circumstances. To which may be added, That the Statute being general as to all Cases wherein the Judge, who tries the Information, doth not certify a reasonable Cause, seems to imply, That it shall be left to such Judge only for this Purpose to consider, whether the Prosecution were reasonable or not, and it is the Prosecutor's Folly not to apply to him.

[e] Dom. Regina *versus* Davis, adjudged Mich. 10 Anne. Vide 2 Chancery Cases 191.

Sect. 14. It is further enacted by 9 *Annæ*, 20. *That in case any Person or Persons shall usurp, intrude into, or unlawfully hold and execute the Office or Franchise of Mayor, Bailiff, Portreeve, or other Office within a City, Town corporate, Borough, or Place in* England *or* Wales, *it shall and may be lawful, to and for the proper Officer of the Court of Queen's Bench, the Court of Sessions of Counties Palatine, or the Court of Grand Sessions in* Wales, *with the Leave of the said Courts respectively, to exhibit one or more Information or Informations, in the Nature of a* Quo Warranto, *at the Relation of any Person or Persons, desiring to sue, or prosecute the same, and who shall be mentioned in such Information or Informations, to be the Relator or Relators against such Person or Persons, so usurping, intruding into, or unlawfully holding and executing any of the said Offices or Franchises, and to proceed therein in such Manner as is usual in Cases of Informations, in the Nature of a* Quo Warranto; *and if it shall appear to the said respective Courts, that the several Rights of divers Persons to the said Offices or Franchises may properly be determined on one Information, it shall and may be lawful for the said respective Courts to give Leave to exhibit one such Information against several Persons, in order to try their respective Rights to such Offices or Franchises, and such Person or Persons, against which such Information or Informations, in the Nature of a* Quo Warranto, *shall be sued or prosecuted, shall appear and plead as of the same Term or Sessions in which the said Information or Informations shall be filed, unless the Court, where such Information shall be filed, shall give further Time to such Person or Persons, against whom such Information shall be exhibited, to plead; and such Person or Persons who shall sue or prosecute such Information or Informations, in the Nature of a* Quo Warranto, *shall proceed thereupon, with the most convenient Speed that may be.*

Sect. 15. And it is further enacted and declared, *That in case any Person or Persons, against whom any Information or Informations, in the Nature of a* Quo Warranto, *shall, in any of the said Cases, be exhibited in any of the said Courts, shall be found or adjudged guilty of an Usurpation, or Intrusion into, or unlawfully holding and executing any of the said Offices or Franchises, it shall and may be lawful, to and for the said Courts respectively, as well to give Judgment of Ouster against such Person or Persons, of and from any of the said Offices or Franchises, as to fine such Person or Persons respectively, for his or their usurping,* &c. *And also to give Judgment that the Relator or Relators, in such Information named, shall recover his or their Costs of such Prosecution; and if Judgment shall be given for the Defendant or Defendants in such Information, he or they, for whom such Judgment shall be given, shall recover his or their Costs therein expended against such Relator or Relators, such Costs to be levied by* Capias ad Satisfaciendum, Fieri Facias, *or* Elegit.

Sect. 16. And it is further enacted, *That the Statute for the Amendment of the Law, and all the Statutes of* Jeofails *shall be extended to Informations, in Nature of a* Quo Warranto, *and Proceedings thereon, for any the Matters in the said Act mentioned.*

And now I am in the second Place to consider the Nature of such Information as is partly the Suit of the King, and partly the Suit of the Party, which is commonly called an Information *qui tam*, and this having a great Affinity with Actions on Statutes, I shall consider them together, and endeavour to shew,

1. In what Cases they lie.
2. What ought to be the Form of them.
3. In what Courts they may be brought.
4. In what County.
5. Within what Time.

6. Who are disabled to bring them.
7. Whether there may be a Nonsuit in them?
8. Whether the Informer or Defendant may appear by Attorney?
9. In what Cases there shall be Costs.
10. Whether the Defendant may wage his Law, or take Advantage of a Protection?
11. In what Manner the Defendant is to plead to such an Information or Action.
12. By whom the Replication shall be made.
13. In what Manner the Issue shall be joined, and where it shall be tried.
14. Where the Verdict may be found as to Part of the Information against the Informer, and as to other Part for him.
15. What Judgment on such an Information or Action is good.
16. Whether the Penalty of a penal Statute may be compounded or granted over?

Sect. 17. As to the first of these Particulars, *viz.* In what Cases an Information or Action *qui tam* will lie; I [a] take it for granted, that they lie on no Statute which prohibits a Thing as being an immediate Offence against the Publick Good in general, under a certain Penalty, unless the Whole, or Part of such Penalty be expresly given to him who will sue for it; because [b] otherwise it goes to the King, and nothing can be demanded by the Party. But where such Statute gives any Part of such Penalty to him who will sue for it by Action or Information, *&c.* I take it to be settled at this Day, That any one may bring such Action, or Information, and lay his Demand [c] *tam pro Domino Rege quam pro seipso.* [d] Also where a Statute prohibits, or commands a Thing, the Doing or Omission whereof is an immediate Damage to the Party, and also highly concerns the Peace, Safety, or good Government of the Publick, or the Honour of the King, or of his Supreme Courts of Justice; as the Statutes of the [e] Scandal of Great Men, of [f] Hue and Cry, and those that restrain certain Suits in the [g] Civil or Canon Law Courts, or even in inferior [h] Common Law Courts, it seems to have been the general Opinion, that the Party grieved may, and it is holden [i] by some that he ought to bring his Action on such Statute *tam pro Domino Rege quam pro seipso.* And it seems to be taken [k] as a Ground in some Books, That where-ever the King is to have a Fine on an Action on a Statute, the Action must be so laid; but not where the Defendant is only to be amerced. But I much question, Whether this be a good general settled Rule in Relation to this Matter? since in an Action on the Statutes of Hue and Cry, the Defendant shall [l] only be amerced; and yet such Action may certainly be laid *tam pro Domino Rege quam pro seipso.* Also in Actions, which by the Common Law a Man may bring *tam pro Domino Rege quam pro seipso,* as in those for Injuries to the Party, mix'd with a high Contempt to the King, (as where a [m] Judge refuses to allow the Benefit of the King's Pardon to a Prisoner, unless he will give him such a Bribe; or where one makes a [n] Rescous of one taken on a *Capias Utlagatum,* at the Suit of the Party, or the Sheriff suffers one taken on such a *Capias* to [o] escape) the Plaintiff is [p] said to have his Election to lay his Action this Way, but not to be compelled so to do. To which may be added, that the Plaintiff cannot so lay his Action for a Common Trespass at Common Law, and yet therein the Defendant is to be fined.

[a] 2 And. 127, 128.
[b] 2 And. 128. 2 Jon. 234. Vide 1 And. 139, 140.
[c] Vide Co. Ent 375, 376, 377.
1 Lutw. 133, 134, 138, &c. Dy. 95. pl. 36. 346. pl. 9. 1 And. 139, 140.
Long quinto Ed. 4. 117. b. 118. a.
[d] 4 Co. 13. a. 12 Co. 134.
[e] 4 Co. 13. a. 12 Co. 134. Hetl. 122. *Quære* 1 Sid. 233. 1 Lev. 148.
[f] Ra. Ent. 406, 407. Co. Ent. 348, &c.
[g] Ra. Ent. 226. dismes 23. b. pl. 1. 24 a. pl. 2. Cro. Jac. 134. Dy. 159. b. 1 Ro. Re. 203.
[h] Ra. Ent. 433. pl. 1, 2.
[i] 4 Co. 13. a.
[k] Cro. Jac. 134. Hetl. 121. Vide Moore 911, pl. 1285.
[l] Cro. Jac. 350.

[m] 1 Rol. A. 1. A. pl. 1. n. 1 Rol. A. 1 A. pl. 2. [o] 1 Rol. Re. 78. pl. 19. Cro. Jac. 360, 361, 532, 533. Cr. Eliz. 877. *Parallel Cases,* Noy. 22. 2 Rol. A. 93. pl. 14. 41 Ass. pl. 12. 27 Ass. pl. 49. [p] Cro. Jac. 619. pl 5.

Neither does the Opinion I would contend against, seem to be confirmed by the constant Course of Precedents; but on the contrary, many of those on the Statutes against [a] Forcible Entries, and on the Statutes against [b] Illegal Distresses, do not lay the Action *tam pro Domino Rege quam pro seipso*; and yet there are [c] Authorities in this last Case, as well as in the former, that the Defendant is liable to be fined. But the Case of an [d] Action on 2 & 3 *Ed.* 6. 13. wherein it seems clear that it is not necessary to lay the Action *tam pro Domino Rege quam pro seipso*, does not seem to come up to the Point; because it is generally holden, that the Defendant is only amerceable in such Action, being in Nature of an Action of Debt, and not finable, as it is said [e] that he may be in an Indictment or Information grounded on the [f] Contempt of the Statute.

Sect. 18. As to the second Particular, *viz.* What ought to be the Form of such Information or Action: Having in the precedent Chapter *Sect.* 94. endeavoured to shew that there is no need that such Information or Action conclude *contra pacem*; and in *Sect.* 97. Whether it be necessary for them to conclude *in contemptum Regis*; and in *Sect.* 102. That they need not recite the Statute whereon they are grounded; and in *Sections* 103, 104, &c. What Misrecitals of a Statute will be fatal; and in *Sect.* 112, 113, &c. How far it is necessary to bring the Case within the very Words of the Statute; and in *Sect.* 118, 119. How far it is necessary to conclude *contra formam Statuti*; and in *Sect.* 117. In what Cases one may have Judgment on a Statute, in an Action brought at Common Law; I shall in this Place observe only these following Particulars:

Sect. 19. *First*, If an Information contain several Offences against a Statute, and be well laid as to some of them, but defective as to the rest, the Informer may have Judgment for so much as is well laid. [g] As where the Words of the Statute are fully pursued in the Description of some of the Offences and not of others; [h] or where some of the Times that the Defendant hath offended against the Statute are expressed with convenient Certainty, and others not; as where it is alledged that the Defendant, for eleven Months, and more, from 10 *September*, in such a Year, unto 9 *September* in the Year following, used a Trade, without having been an Apprentice, &c. or was absent from Church, &c. in which Cases Judgment shall be given for the eleven Months. But if the whole Time be expressed inconsistently; as that the Defendant was an Offender eleven Months, from the first of *November* in such a Year, to the first of *August* following, the whole is void for the Repugnancy, as hath been more fully shewn, *Ch.* 25. *Sect.* 64.

Sect. 20. *Secondly*, It seems to be settled at this Day, That it is in the Election of him who brings an Action on a penal Statute, which gives one Moiety of the Forfeiture to the King, and another to the Informer, either to have a Writ against the Defendant, *Quod reddat* [i] *Domino Regi & A. B. qui tam, &c. quas eis debet*; or to have it in this Form, *Quod reddat A. B. qui tam, &c. quas ei debet.* Also it seems to be settled, That whether the Writ be in the one Form, or the other, it is well pursued by a Declaration in the Name of the Plaintiff only. [k] Also it seems to be doubtfull, whether there be any necessity that either the Writ, or Count, in any such Action, do express that it is brought by or for the King, as well as the Party, as hath been more fully shewn in the 17th *Section*; and there is a [l] Precedent of such an Action brought in the King's Name by *A. B. qui pro seipso in hac parte sequitur.* But it seems [m] agreed, that

[a] Co Ent 44. b. 146. a. Precedents both Ways.
[b] Ra. Ent. 226. b. pl. 1. 2 Inst. 132, 133.
[c] Co. Ent. 45. b. 35 H. 6. 6. 2 Inst. 131. 2 Rol. A. 222 pl. 12, 13. Quære Dy. 177. b. 1 Danv. 460. pl. 12. Cro. Ca. 559, 560.
[d] More 911. pl. 1285. 2 Rol. Abr. 223. pl. 17. Cro. El. 621. Hetl. 121, 122.
[e] Moore 911. pl. 1285. Vide Cro. Ja. 538, 631
[f] Vid. Sav. 62.
[g] Cro. Jac. 104.
[h] 1 Sid. 368. 2 Keb. 366, 367. 2 Rol. A. 696. pl. 7. Cro. Jac. 529, 530. Cro. El. 835.
[i] 1 Jon. 261, 262. Cro. Ca. 256. Pl. com. 77, 78. Dy. 95 pl. 36. 3 Lev. 374, 375. Quære Dalis. 66, 67 More 64. 65. Bro. Act. sur le Statute, 4. 27 H. 8. 23. pl. 20.
[k] Bro. Act. popular 5. Long quinto Ed. 4. 117. b. 118. a. See Rast. Ent. 686. Vit. 1. 427. pl. 4. 428. pl. 5.
[l] Rast. Ent 427. pl 3.
[m] Jo. 261, 262. Cro. Ca. 256. Co. Entr. 371. b.

every

every Information muſt be in this Form, That the Informer *tam pro Domino Rege quam pro ſeipſo ſequitur*, even where it is brought on a Statute which gives one third Part of the Penalty to a third Perſon. But I find ſome difference as to the Forms of ſuch Informations, as to ſome other Reſpects; for ſometimes they ſay, [a] That the Action accrues to the Informer *qui tam, &c.* to demand the Sum forfeited, for the King and himſelf; and [b] ſometimes that the Action accrues to the King, and to the Informer, *qui tam, &c.* and [c] ſometimes, that it accrues to the King, and to *J. S. &c.* (*viz.* where the Statute divides the Penalty into three Parts, *&c.*) and alſo to the Informer, *qui tam, &c.* and ſometimes they have no [d] Clauſe at all of this Kind. And * *Quære*, If it be not fatal to have any ſuch Clauſe where the Penalty is not recoverable by the Information, but requires a ſubſequent one, grounded on the Conviction? Alſo, ſometimes ſuch Informations pray Proceſs againſt the Defendant, to bring him in to [e] Anſwer to the Informer, *qui tam, &c.* only; ſometimes [f] to anſwer *tam Domino Regi quam A. B. qui tam, &c.* and [g] ſometimes to Anſwer *de & ſuper præmiſſis* generally, without expreſſing to whom.

Sect. 21. *Thirdly*, Regularly it is ſafeſt for every ſuch Information, or Action, to demand the very Sum due to the Informer, and neither more or leſs; for it hath been adjudged, [h] That if an Action on a Statute demand the whole Forfeiture for the Informer, where the Statute gives Part of it to the King, it is inſufficient: Alſo it hath been holden, [i] That if the Information make no Demand at all, or demand more or leſs for the Party than appears to be his Due, it is inſufficient as to him; yet [k] perhaps it may be good as to the Share of the Forfeiture given to the King. Alſo it hath been [l] adjudged, That it is ſufficient to demand the Share due to the Informer, without making any mention of that due to the King: Alſo, [m] where the *quantum* of the Forfeiture depends upon the finding of the Jury, as it does on the Statute of *Foreſtalling*, it hath been adjudged ſufficient to leave a Blank for the Sum. Alſo it hath been [n] adjudged, That a Popular Action may conclude *ad grave damnum*, without adding, *of the Plaintiff*; becauſe every Offence, for which ſuch Action is brought, is ſuppoſed to be a general Grievance to every Body.

Sect. 22. *Fourthly*, It is enacted by 18 *Eliz.* 5. *Par.* 1. *That none ſhall be admitted or received to purſue againſt any Perſon or Perſons, upon any penal Statute, but by Way of Information or Original Action, and not otherwiſe.* And it hath been adjudged, That no Popular Action, ſince this Statute, can be brought on a former Statute, either by [o] Bill in the King's Bench, or by [p] Plaint in an Inferior Court, but only by Original Writ, or Information; whether the Statute on which ſuch Action is grounded, [q] inflict a Penalty generally, without ſaying how it ſhall be recovered, or expreſsly give a Recovery by Bill or Plaint, *&c.* (as that of 4 *&* 5 *Ph. & M.* againſt [r] making Kerſeys, without having ſerved an Apprenticeſhip; and that of 5 *Eliz.* 4. againſt [s] following any other Trade without having ſerved an Apprenticeſhip.) Yet the contrary hath been ſince expreſsly adjudged [t] as to ſuch former Statutes as expreſsly give a Recovery by Bill or Plaint, becauſe the Statute of 18 *Eliz.* doth not mention original Writs, but original Actions; and a Suit by Bill or Plaint is an [u] original Action in the Court in which it is commenced, and therefore may reaſonably ſeem to be only within the Intent of the Statute, where it is removed into a ſuperior Court, and there proceeded upon. And if this be

[a] Co. Ent. 370. b. Ra. Ent. 430. pl. 13, 14. 431. b. pl. 15. 463. b. 5.
[b] Co. Entr 369 a. 366. a. b. 365 a. Raſt. 208. b.
[c] Co. Ent. 371. b.
Vide 2 Keb. 820. 2 Mod. 100.
[d] Co Ent. 370. a. 364. a. b.
* 1 Lutw. 162. Vide Sup. B. 1. Ch. 8. S. 10.
[e] Co. Ent. 364. b.
[f] Co. Entr. 370. a. 369. a. 366. a. b. 365. a.
[g] Co. Ent. 371, b. 372. a.
[h] Bro. Action ſur le Statute 4. 27 H. 8. 23. pl. 20. Vide Hob. 245.
[i] Hob. 245. Vide Cro. Ca. 330, 331.
[k] Cro. Ca. 330, 331.
[l] 1 Jon. 156, 157.
[m] 1 Jon. 156, 157.
[n] Bro. Action Popular, 2.
[o] Cro. Eliz. 76, 77. Mo. 247. pl. 390. 3 Inſt. 194.
[p] Cro. Eliz. 544. pl. 14.
[q] 23 H 6 10. Cro. El. 76, 77. Mo. 247. pl. 390. 3 Inſt. 194.
[r] 4 & 5 Ph. & M. 5. par. 32, 33, 34. 6 Co. 19. b. Mo. 412. pl. 565.
[s] 5 El. 4. par. 31, 39. Cro. El. 544 pl. 14. Noy. 60.
[t] 1 Rol. Ab. 537. pl 8. 9.
[u] Vide 2 Danv. Abr. 279, 280. 3 Leon. 237.

2 the

the Meaning of the Statute, I see not how any Suit whatever, by Bill or Plaint on any penal Statute, can be within the Purview of it, while such Bill or Plaint continue in the Court in which they were commenced, whether the Statute on which they are brought do expresly mention them, or leave the Method of suing to the general Construction of Law. To which may be added, That the Statute of 21 *Jac.* 1. 4. *Par.* 1. seems to suppose, that Actions on penal Statutes may indifferently be brought by Writ, Plaint, Bill, or Information; for the Words are, *That all Offences hereafter to be committed against any penal Statute, for which any Common Informer or Promoter may lawfully ground any Popular Action, Bill, Plaint, Suit, or Information, before Justices of Assise,* &c. *shall be commenced,* &c. *by way of Action, Plaint, Bill, Information, or Inditement in the proper County, before the Justices of Assise,* &c. However it seems clear, [a] That no Suit, by Bill or Plaint, by a Party grieved, suing upon a Clause, either expresly or impliedly relating to himself only, is within the said Statute of 18 *El.* For it is expresly provided, *Par.* 6. *That it shall not restrain any certain Person, Body Politick or Corporate, to whom, or to whose Use, any Forfeiture is limited by any Statute, and not generally to any Person that will sue; but that every such Person may sue as before.* [b] But where the Party particularly grieved by an Offence against a Statute, sues for a Forfeiture generally limited to any one who will sue for it, he seems to be as much within the Restraint of the said Statute, as if he were not the Party grieved.

[a] Cro. El. 434. pl. 45. 645. pl. 53. Vide Cro. El. 76, 77. 3 Leon. 237.

[b] Cro El. 76, 77. Vide 3 Leon. 237.

Sect. 23. *Fifthly,* [c] In an Action on a Statute, which requires some Officers at one certain Time after their Admission, and others at another, to qualify themselves by certain Acts, it is safest, expresly to shew the Time when the Defendant was admitted to his Office, and that he neglected to qualify himself in the Time limited; and also, That he actually exercised his Office after such Neglect.

[c] Lutw. 162.

Sect. 24. *Sixthly,* It is said, [d] That the Fact is sufficiently alledged after a *quod cum* in an Action on a Statute, but not in an Information.

[d] Show. 337.

Sect. 25. As to the Third Particular, *viz.* In what Courts such an Information or Action may be brought: Having already, *Ch.* 5. *Sect.* 32. endeavoured to prove, that where a Statute appoints that a Penalty shall be recovered in any of the King's Courts of Record, the Offence may be indicted before Justices of *Oyer* and *Terminer*, tho' not in a Court-Leet, or of [e] Pie-powders, or such others, instituted for special Purposes; and intending under the next Particular, incidentally to consider what Suits may be brought in the Courts of *Westminster-Hall*, on penal Statutes; I shall only take Notice in this Place, That where a Statute limits Suits by an Informer *qui tam* to other Courts, yet any [f] one may, by Construction of Law, exhibit an Information in the Exchequer for the whole Penalty for the Use of the King.

Contra Hutt. 99. 1 Jo. 193. Litt. 163. Vide Cro. Ca. 112. 1 Vent. 8.

[e] Cro. El. 530. pl. 59. 6 Co. 20. a.

[f] 2 And. 127, 128. Cro. Jac. 178, 179.

Sect. 26. As to the Fourth Particular, *viz.* In what County such Information or Action may be brought. It is enacted by 31 *El.* 5. *That in any Declaration, or Information,* ([g] *not being exhibited by such Officers of Record, as had in Respect of their Offices, before the Time of the said Statute, lawfully used to exhibit Informations, or sue upon penal Laws; and not* [h] *concerning Champerty, buying of Titles, or Extortion, or the King's Customs,* &c. *or Usury, or Forestalling,* &c.) *the Offence against any penal Statute shall not be laid to be done in any other County but where the Matter alledged to be the Offence, was in truth done: And that the Defendant may traverse, and alledge, That the Offence supposed to be committed, was not committed in the County where*

[g] Parag. 3.

[h] Parag. 4. B. 1. Ch. 80. S. 47.

where it is alledged; which being tried for the Defendant, or if the Plaintiff be thereupon nonsuit, the Plaintiff shall be barred in that Action or Information.

Sect. 27. It is further enacted, *Par.* 7. *That all Suits for using unlawful, or not using lawful Games, or for not having Bows or Arrows, or for using a Trade without having been brought up in it, shall be sued and prosecuted in the General Quarter-Sessions of the Peace, or Assises of the same County, where the Offence shall be committed, or otherwise enquired of, heard and determined in the Assises, or General Quarter-Sessions of the Peace of the same County where such Offence shall be committed, or in the Leet within which it shall happen, and not in any wise out of the same County, where such Offence shall happen, or be committed.*

In the Construction of this Statute, the following Particulars seem most remarkable.

Sect. 28. *First*, That it hath been adjudged, That the Defendant can have no Advantage of the above-recited Clause, which appoints, That all Offences against penal Statutes shall be laid in the proper Counties, but [a] only by way of Plea; and this Construction seems very agreeable to the Purport of the said Clause; the Words whereof are, *That the Defendant may traverse the County, &c. which being tried for him, or if the Plaintiff be thereupon nonsuit, the Plaintiff shall be barred, &c.* But *this Point is otherwise settled by 21 Jac. 1. 4. Par. 3.*

Sect. 29. *Secondly*, That the said Clause extends [b] not to any Suit by a Party grieved, or by the [c] Attorney General, but only by those brought by Common Informers.

Sect. 30. *Thirdly*, That the last recited Clause, concerning Suits for using a Trade without having been brought up in it, *&c.* which are appointed to be brought at the Assises, or Sessions, in the proper County, and not in any wise out of the County, restrains not an Information in the [d] King's Bench, or Exchequer, for such Offence happening in the same County where those Courts are sitting; for the negative Words of the Statute are not, That such Suits shall not be brought in any other Court, but, That they shall not be brought in any other County; and the Prerogative of these High Courts shall not be restrained without express Words. But where the Offence is in a different County, such Suits, in those, or any other Courts, out of the proper County, seem to be within the express [e] Words of the Statute: Yet it was long a very great [f] Question, Whether an Action of Debt or Information, in the Courts of *Westminster-Hall*, were not to be construed to be out of the Meaning of them? But this Point is now settled in the Construction of the Statute of 21 *Jac.* 1. 4. as shall be more fully shewn hereafter.

Sect. 31. It is enacted by the said Statute of 21 *Jac.* 1. 4. *That all Offences to be committed against any penal Statute, for which any Common Informer or Promoter may lawfully ground any Popular Action, Bill, Plaint, Suit or Information, before Justices of Assise, Justices of* Nisi Prius *or Gaol-Delivery, Justices of* Oyer *and* Terminer, *or Justices of Peace, in their General or Quarter-Sessions, (except Offences against the Statutes concerning* [g] *Recusancy,* &c. *or Maintenance,* &c. *or the King's Customs,* &c. *or transporting Gold, or Silver, or Munition, or Wool, or Leather,* &c.) *shall be commenced, sued, prosecuted, tried, recovered and determined, by Way of Action, Plaint, Bill, Information or Indictment, before the Justices of Assise, Justices of* Nisi Prius, *Justices of* Oyer *and* Terminer, *and Justices of Gaol-Delivery, or before the Justices of the Peace of every County, City, Borough or Town Corporate, and Liberty, having Power to enquire of, hear, and determine the same, in*

[a] 2 And. 180. the contrary adjudged. Cro. El. 735. 736.

[b] Cro. El. 645. pl. 53.

[c] 1 Vent. 8 Cro. Ja. 178

[d] Cro. Jac. 178, 179. Salk. 373. Hob. 184.

[e] Vide Hob. 184, 327. Cro. Jac. 85.

[f] 1 Keb. 584. pl. 46. 2 Keb. 99 pl. 23. 125. pl. 77. 3 Keb. 247. pl. 67. 448. pl. 8. 1 Sid. 303, 400.

[g] Vide Hob. 251. & B. 1. ch. 10. S. 5. Raym. 394.

England *or* Wales, *wherein such Offences shall be committed, in any of the Courts, Places of Judicature, or Liberties aforesaid, respectively, only at the Choice of the Parties who shall commence Suit, or prosecute for the same, and not elsewhere, save only in the said Counties, or Places usual for those Counties, or any of them: And that the like Process in every Popular Action, Bill, Plaint, Information or Suit, to be commenced, sued or prosecuted, by Force of, or according to the Purport of this Act, be had and awarded, to all Intents and Purposes, as in an Action of Trespass* Vi & Armis *at Common Law. And that all, and all manner of Informations, Actions, Bills, Plaints, and Suits whatsoever, to be commenced, sued, prosecuted, or awarded, either by the Attorney General, or by any Officer whatsoever, or by any Common Informer, or other Person whatsoever, in any of his Majesty's Courts at* Westminster, *for, or concerning any the Offences aforesaid, shall be void.*

Sect. 31. And it is further enacted, *That if on the General Issue the Offence be not proved in the same County in which it is laid, the Defendant shall be found not Guilty*, as shall be more fully shewn under the eleventh Particular.

Sect. 32. Also it is farther enacted, *That no Officer shall receive, file, or enter of Record, any Information, Bill, or Plaint, Count or Declaration, grounded on the said penal Statutes, or any of them, which by this Act are appointed to be heard and determined in their proper Counties, until the Informer or Relator hath first taken a Corporal Oath before some of the Judges of that Court, that the Offence or Offences laid in such Information,* &c. *was, or were not committed in any other County than where, by the said Information,* &c. *the same is, or are supposed to have been committed,* &c. *the same Oath to be there entred of Record.*

In the Construction of this Statute, I shall observe the following Particulars:

Sect. 33. *First*, That as the Law is now [a] settled, no Action of Debt, or Information, or other Suit whatever, can be brought in any Court of *Westminster-Hall*, on any penal Statute, made before the said Statute of 21 *Jac.* for any Offence not therein excepted, for which the Offender may be prosecuted in the Country, [b] unless such Offence shall be committed in the same County in which such Court shall sit; and surely this cannot but be thought most agreeable to the Meaning as well as the Letter of the said Statute; the whole Provision whereof would be to little purpose, if such Suits should be construed out of it. And as to the Objection, That if all Suits on penal Statutes should be wholly taken from the Superior Courts, all Offences against them would become dispunishable by the Offender's removing himself out of the County wherein he committed them; because the Courts in the Statute mentioned, have no Jurisdiction out of the Counties wherein they sit; it hath been [c] answered, That Process of Outlawry will lie against such Offenders, by Vertue of the above-recited Clause of the said Statute, which gives the like Process in all Suits prosecuted according to the Purport of it, as in Actions of Trespass at the Common Law.

Sect. 34. *Secondly*, That [d] where a subsequent Statute gives an Action of Debt, or any other Remedy, for the Recovery of a Penalty in any Court of Record generally, it so far impliedly repeals the Restraint of 21 *Jac.* and consequently leaves the Informer at his Liberty to sue in the Courts of *Westminster-Hall*.

[a] 1 Salk. 372, 373. 5 Mod. 425. 2 Lev. 204. 3 Inst. 192, 193. *See the contrary adjudged* 1 Vent. 8. 1 Lev. 249. 3 Lev. 71. 3 Keb. 804 pl. 7. 2 Keb 401, 447, 458. 1 Sid. 303, 400. *See the same Case doubted*, 1 Vent. 364. 2 Lev. 204. Latch. 192. Sup. Sect. 30. 1 Sid. 359, 360. 1 Lut. 165. 2 Keb. 340. pl. 10. Raym. 394.

[b] 1 Jon. 193. Sup Sect. 30.

[c] 1 Salk. 373. pl. 14.

[d] 1 Salk. 372. 373.

Sect.

Sect. 35. *Thirdly*, That the Statute of 21 *Jac.* gave [a] no Jurisdiction to the Courts therein mentioned, over any Offences, in relation to which they had none before; and [b] therefore that Suits for such Offences must be brought in the Courts of *Westminster-Hall*, in the same Manner as before.

Sect. 36. *Fourthly*, That [c] the said Statute hinders not the Removal of any Indictment into the King's Bench by *Certiorari*; after which it may be either tried there, or in the Country by *Nisi Prius*.

Sect. 37. *Fifthly*, That [d] it hath been adjudged, That an Officer by receiving an Information without such a previous Oath, That the Offence arose in the same County in which it is laid, doth not make the Proceedings upon it erroneous; for the Act is only directory to the Officer, but doth not intend that such Oath should be made Parcel of the Record; and therefore the Omission of it cannot be assigned for Error.; and yet the Act is express, That such Oath shall be entred of Record. But *Quære*, If the Court may not properly be [e] moved to set aside such Process, as having issued contrary to the Directions of the Statute?

Sect. 38. *Sixthly*, That no [f] Suit by a Party grieved is within the Restraint of the Statute.

Sect. 39. As to the fifth Particular, *viz.* Within what Time such Information or Action may be brought; it is to be observed, That all Popular Actions were limited to a certain Time by 7 *H.* 8. 3. But this [g] Statute being repealed by 31 *El.* 5. I shall take no farther Notice of it.

Sect. 40. But it is enacted by the said Statute of 31 *El.* 5. *Par.* 5. *That all Actions, Suits, Bills, Indictments, or Informations which shall be brought for any Forfeiture upon any Statute penal, made, or to be made, whereby the Forfeiture is, or shall be limited to the Queen, her Heirs or Successors only, shall be brought within two Years after the Offence committed; and not after two Years. And that all Actions, Suits, Bills, or Informations, which shall be brought for any Forfeiture, upon any penal Statute, made, or to be made, except the Statutes of Tillage, the Benefit and Suit whereof is, or shall be by the said Statute, limitted to the Queen, her Heirs or Successors, and to any other that shall prosecute in that Behalf, shall be brought by any Person that may lawfully sue for the same, within one Year next after the Offence committed; and in Default of such Pursuit, that then the same shall be brought for the Queen's Majesty, her Heirs or Successors, any Time within the two Years after that Year ended. And if any Action, Suit, Bill, Indictment, or Information, shall be brought after the Time so limited, the same shall be void. And it is provided, That where a shorter Time is limitted by any penal Statute, the Prosecution must be within that Time.*

Sect. 41. Also it is enacted by 18 *El.* 5. *Par.* 1. *That upon every Information which shall be exhibited on any penal Statute, a Special Note shall be made of the very Day, Month, and Year of the exhibiting thereof into any Office, or to any Officer, which lawfully may receive the same, without any Antedate thereof to be made; and that the same Information be accounted and taken to be of Record, from that Day forward, and not before: And that no Process be sued out upon such Information, until the Information be exhibited in Form aforesaid,* &c. *and that every Clerk making out Process contrary to this Act, shall forfeit* 40 s. &c.

Sect. 42. It is farther enacted by 21 *Jac.* 1. 5. *That no Officer shall receive, file, or enter of Record, any Information, Bill, Plaint, Count, or Declaration, grounded on any penal Statute (being* [h] *within the Provision of the said Statute of* 21 *Jac.) until the Informer or Relator hath first taken a corporal Oath, before some of the Judges of the Court, that he believes in his Conscience, the Of-*

4 *fence*

[a] 1 Vent. 8. Cro. Ca. 112. Hutt. 98, 99.
[b] Cro. Ca. 112. Litt. Rep. 163. Hutt. 98, 99. Vide 2 Keb. 106 pl. 42.
[c] 1 Jon. 193.
[d] Cro. Ca. 316. Vide 4 Inst. 272. 2 Inst. 193.
[e] Vide Salk. 376. pl. 19. Sup. Sect. 10.
[f] Cro. El. 645. Noy 71. Shower 164. 3 Leo. 237.
[g] Vide Bro. Action Popular, 6.
[h] For this Matter see the 37th Sect.

fence was committed within a Year before the Information or Suit, within the County where the said Information or Suit was commenced, &c.

In the Construction of these Statutes, I shall observe the following Particulars;

Hob. 270.

Sect. 43. *First*, That [a] if an Offence prohibited by any penal Statute, be also an Offence at Common Law, the Prosecution of it, as of an Offence at Common Law, is no way restrained by any of these Statutes.

[b] Shower's Rep. 353, 354.

Sect. 44. *Secondly*, That if a Suit on a penal Statute be brought after the Time limited, the Defendant needs not plead the Statute, but [b] may take Advantage of it on the General Issue.

[c] Cro. Co. 331. Cro. Jac. 366. Vide Dalis. 60. pl. 13.

Sect. 45. Thirdly, That if an Information *tam quam* be brought after the Year, on a penal Statute, which gives one Moiety to the Informer, and the other to the King, it is naught only [c] as to the Informer, but good for the King.

[d] Supra Sect. 38.

Sect. 47. *Fourthly*, That the Party grieved is [d] not within the Restraint of these Statutes, but may sue in the same Manner as before.

[e] Show. Rep. 353, 354.

Sect. 48. *Fifthly*, That it seems not [e] to be settled, Whether the suing of a *Latitat* within the Year be a sufficient Commencement of a Suit on a penal Statute, to avoid the Limitation of these Statutes?

[f] Show. 353, 354.

Sect. 49. *Sixthly*, That it [f] seems also to be questionable, Whether a Suit by a Common Informer, on a penal Statute, which first gives an Action to the Party grieved, and in his Default, after a certain Time, to any one who will sue, be within the Restraint of these Statutes?

Sect. 50. *Seventhly*, That it seems questionable, Whether the Clause in 31 *El. Par.* 4. by which it is enacted, *That nothing in the said Act contained shall entend to Champerty, King's Customs, or Forestalling,* &c. *but that every such Offence may be laid in any County; any Thing in the said Act to the contrary notwithstanding*, do except the said Offences, out of the above-recited Clause, relating to the Time within which Suits on penal Statutes must be brought? For the Words above-mentioned, *viz. But that every such Offence may be laid in any County*, seem to restrain the Generality of the precedent, which say *That nothing in the Act contained shall extend to such Offences.*

Sect. 51. As to the sixth Particular, *viz.* What Persons are disabled to bring such an Information or Action: It is enacted by 31 *El.* 5. *Par.* 1. *That no Person, other than the Party grieved, shall be received to inform, or sue upon any penal Statute, that before that Time hath been for any Misdemeanor, by any Order of any the Queen's Majesty's Courts, ordered not to follow or pursue any Suit upon any penal Statute.*

[g] Co. Litt. 139. b. Fitz. Nonsuit, 13. Bro. Nonsuit 68. Prerog. 116. [h] Co Litt. 139. b. Bro. Nonsuit 68. Prerog. 116.

Sect. 52. As to the seventh Particular, *viz.* Whether there may be a Nonsuit in such an Information or Action? It seems agreed, That notwithstanding the King [g] cannot be nonsuit in any Information or Action, wherein he himself is the sole Plaintiff; yet any [h] Informer *qui tam*, or [i] Plaintiff in a Popular Action, may be nonsuit, and thereby wholly [k] determine the Suit, as well in Respect of the King as of himself: Also it seems agreed, [l] That the Attorney General may enter a *Nolle Prosequi*, (which, as [m] some say, has the Effect of a Nonsuit) to any Information or Action brought by the King only.

[i] Bro. Nonf. 35. [k] 37 H. 6. 5. a. [l] Bro. Nonsuit 35. [l] Litt. 139. b. [m] Co. Lit. 139. b. Vide 1 Sid. 420. *Quære* Salk. 21. pl. 11.

Sect. 53. As to the eighth Particular, *viz.* Whether the Informer or Defendant may appear by Attorney? It seems agreed, That after [a] Plea pleaded to an Indictment, Information or Action, for any Crime whatsoever, under the Degree of [b] capital, the Defendant might always, by the Favour of the Court, be permitted to appear by Attorney: Also it seems, That generally the Court might always dispense with the personal Appearance of the Defendant, even before [c] Plea pleaded, [d] except in such Cases, wherein a personal Appearance is required by some Statute, as it is in [e] *Præmunire*, *&c.* in which Cases it seems generally agreed, That an Appearance by Attorney cannot be admitted, without some special Writ or Grant to that Purpose, whether the Defendant be a Peer [f] or Commoner. It is said indeed, in *Rolle's Rep.* That Sir [g] *Anthony Mildmay* was suffered to plead a Pardon to a *Præmunire* by Attorney, and no Mention is made of any such Writ or Grant: But I presume that there was a Clause to this Effect in his Pardon.

Sect. 54. It is enacted by 18 *El.* 5. Par. 1. *That every Informer, upon any penal Statute, shall exhibit his Suit in proper Person, and pursue the same only by himself, or by his Attorney in Court; and that he shall not use any Deputy or Deputies at all.*

Sect. 55. It is recited by 29 *El.* 5. Par. 21. *That divers of her Majesty's Subjects, dwelling in the remote Parts of the Realm, had been many Times maliciously troubled upon Informations and Suits, exhibited in the Courts of the King's Bench, Common Pleas, and Exchequer, upon penal Statutes, and had been drawn up upon Process out of the Countries where they dwell, and driven to attend and put in Bail, to their great Trouble, and Undoing; and for Reformation thereof, it is enacted, That if any Person or Persons, shall be sued or informed against, upon any penal Law, in any the said Courts, where such Person or Persons are bailable by Law, or where, by the Leave or Favour of the Court, such Person or Persons may appear by Attorney; in every such Case, the Person or Persons so to be impleaded or sued, shall, and may, at the Day and Time contained in the first Process served for his Appearance, appear by Attorney of the same Court where the Process is returnable, to answer and defend the same, and not be urged to personal Appearance, or to put in Bail for the answering such Suits.*

Sect. 56. And it is enacted by 31 *El.* 10. Par. 20. *That this shall extend only to the natural Subjects born, or to be born, within the Dominions of the Queen's Majesty, her Heirs or Successors, and to Persons made free Denizens, and to no others.*

[a] Bro. Attor. 53, 54. 63, 101. 9 Ed. 4. 2. pl. 8. 9 Ed. 4. 4. pl. 44. 22 Ass. pl. 73.
[b] Bro. Attor. 63.
[c] Dy. 346. 9. 1 Lev. 146. Vide 21 Ed. 4. 77. pl. 12. 7 H. 6. 21. a.
[d] Fitz Attor. 48, 53, 104. 3 Inst. 125. 39 Ed. 3. 7. 15 H. 7. 9. pl. 12. F. N. B. 66. Lett. H. & M. Vide Bro. Attorn. 69, 81, 82. 37 H. 6. 27. b. 3 H. 7. 6. pl. 4. Cro. Jac. 462, 616. 22 Ed. 4. 33, 34.
[e] See Cases cited to Lett. d.
[f] 15 H. 7. 9. pl. 12. 39 Ed. 3. 7.
[g] 1 Rol. Rep. 190. Vide 2 Bulst. 299.

As to the ninth Particular, *viz.* In what Cases there shall be Costs on such an Action or Information, I shall endeavour to shew,

1. Whether an Informer shall in any Case have his Costs.
2. In what Cases the Defendant shall have them.

Sect. 57. As to the first of these Particulars, I take it to be in a great Measure settled, [h] That an Informer upon a Popular Statute, shall in no Case whatsoever have his Costs, unless they be expresly given him by such Statute; for it is certain that he cannot recover them by the Common Law, for that doth not [i] give Costs in any Case: Neither can he recover them by the Statute of *Glocester*, 1. which gives the Demandant his Costs in all Cases wherein he shall recover his Damages; for this seems to suppose some Damage to have been done to the Demandant in particular, which cannot be said in any Popular Action; and therefore such Actions have always been construed to be out of the Benefit

[h] 2 Keb. 781. pl. 12. 1 Rol. A. 574. pl. 4. 1 Lutw. 200, 201. 1 Vent. 133. Salk. 206. pl. 4. Contra Moor 65. pl. 175. 3 Lev. 374.
[i] 2 Inst. 288.

[a] 2 Keb. 781. pl. 12. 1 Rol. Abr. 574. P. 1, 2, 3, 4. 1 Jon. 447. Cro. Ca. 559, 560. 1 Lutw. 200, 201. 2 Inst. 289.

nefit of this Statute. But it seems agreed, [a] That an Action on a Statute, by the Party grieved, for a certain Penalty given by such Statute, is within the Statute of *Gloucester*, because such Penalty is intended him by way of Recompence for his particular Damage by the Offence prohibited; and if he could recover that only, and no more, by way of Costs, it would be in most Cases in vain for him to sue for it, since the Costs of Suit would exceed it. But it is said, That no Costs shall be recovered in an Action on a Statute, which gives no certain Penalty to the Party grieved, but only his Damages in general, *&c.* if such a Statute be introductive of a new Law, and give a Remedy in a [b] Point not remediable at the Common Law. But there is not that Inconvenience in this Case as in the former; because no certain Sum being specified, the Jury may give the Plaintiff a full Satisfaction by way of Damages.

[b] 1 Rol. Ab. 574 pl. 1. 1 Lutw. 200, 201. 10 Co. 116. Cro. Ca. 560. Salk. 206. pl. 4.

Sect. 58. As to the second Particular, *viz.* In what Cases the Defendant shall have Costs: It is enacted by 18 *El.* 5. which is made perpetual by 27 *El.* 10. *That if any Informer or Plaintiff, on a penal Statute, shall willingly delay his Suit, or shall discontinue, or be nonsuit in the same, or shall have the Trial or Matter pass'd against him therein, by Verdict or Judgment of Law, that then, in every such Case, the same Informer or Plaintiff shall yield, satisfy, and pay unto the Party Defendant, his Costs, Charges, and Damages, to be assigned by the Court in which the same Suit shall be attempted,* &c.

In the Construction hereof, I shall take Notice of the following Particulars;

Sect. 59 *First*, That it seems to be agreed, That no Action on any Statute, by the Party [c] grieved, is within the Purview of this Statute, the whole Purport whereof seems clearly to relate only to Common Informers: Yet, if such Action, by the Party grieved, be *for any Offence or Wrong* [d] *personal, immediately supposed to be done to the plaintiff or Plaintiffs*; or whatsoever the Nature of the Action may be, *if the Plaintiff* [e] *might have Costs, in Case Judgment should be given for him*, he shall pay them on a Nonsuit or Verdict against him, *&c.* by Vertue of [f] 23 *H.* 8. 15. and 4 [g] *Jac.* 1. 3.

[c] 1 Salk. 30. 1 And. 116. Cro. El. 177 pl. 4. Noy 71. 2 Leon 116.
[d] Vide Cro. El. 177. pl. 4
[e] Hutt. 22.
[f] Vide 2 Danv. Abr. 224 pl. 1, 2, 3.
[g] Vide 2 Danv. 225. pl. 9

Sect. 60. *Secondly*, That it hath been holden, That where Judgment is given against an Informer, because the Court in which he [h] sues has no Jurisdiction of the Cause, or [i] because the Statute on which he grounds his Information is discontinued, yet he shall pay Costs within the Intent of the said Statute of 18 *Eliz.* which shall have a liberal Construction, and was intended to prevent all vexatious Informations; and surely such ill grounded Prosecutions cannot but be thought such.

[h] 2 Keb. 581. pl. 12. 1 Sid 311.
[i] 2 Keb. 106. 41. *Quære* Hutt. 35, 36.

Sect. 61. As to the tenth Particular, *viz.* Whether the Defendant, in such an Action or Information, may wage his Law, or take Advantage of a Protection? It is said [k] to have been ruled, That the Defendant ought not to be admitted to wage his Law in any such Action or Information, because they are founded on a Statute; nor do I find any Authority to the contrary. But perhaps it may be questioned, How far the Reason given for the Opinion above-mentioned may be conclusive, since such an Action or Information doth not seem so [l] properly to be grounded on a Statute, as on the Contempt of it. But as to the Question, Whether the Defendant can take Advantage of a Protection? There seems to be near the same Number of Authorities on each [m] Side. But there is no great

[k] 10 H. 7 18. pl. 18. Bro. Ley gage. 63, 106. Co. Lit. 295.
[l] Vide 21 H. 7. 15.

[m] *In the Affirmative*, Fitz. Protect. 98, 122. Keil. 135. b. *In the Negative*, Fitz Protection 61, 105: 21 Ed. 3. 13. pl 12, Co: Litt. 131. Vide 2 Rolle's Abr. 323. Letter G.

I need

need nicely to examine these Matters, since generally it is expresly provided by penal Statutes, That neither Wager of Law, nor Protection, shall be admitted in any Suit brought upon them.

Sect. 62. As to the eleventh Particular, *viz.* In what Manner the Defendant is to plead to such an Information, or Action, I shall take it for granted, That he must answer to the whole [a] Time laid in such Information or Action; and that if he have any [b] special Matter for his Excuse or Justification, he must set it forth with all convenient Certainty; and that if he plead the General Issue to the whole, he must depend upon it, and not [c] together with it plead also a special Plea either to the Whole or Part of the Charge; but for these Matters I shall refer the Reader to the Books which treat of Pleading in general; and in this Place shall only consider,

[a] Bridg. 115. [b] Vide Bridg. 114, 115. [c] 1 Ro. Re. 49, 50, 134.

1. Where a prior Suit depending may be pleaded to such an Information or Action.
2. Where a Pardon, or Release, or a Recovery in a former Suit.
3. What is a good General Issue; and where it may be pleaded.

Sect. 63. As to the first Point, *viz.* Where a prior Suit depending may be pleaded to such an Information or Action: It seems agreed, [d] That where-ever any Suit on a penal Statute may be said to be actually depending, it may be pleaded in Abatement of a subsequent Prosecution, being expresly averred to be for the same Offence. [e] Neither will it be any Exception to such a Plea, That the Offence in the subsequent Prosecution is laid on a Day different from that in the former. [f] Neither doth a Mistake in such a Plea of the very Day whereon the Suit pleaded as prior was commenced, seem to be material on the Issue of *Nul tiel Record*, if it appear in truth to have been commenced before the other, and for the same Matter. And if two Informations be exhibited on the very same Day, it seems [g] that they may mutually abate one another, because there is no Priority to attach the Right of the Suit in one Informer more than in the other. Also it seems, That an [h] Information or Bill [i] the same Day that they are filed, may be so far said to be depending, before any Process sued upon them, that they may be pleaded in Abatement of any other Suit on the same Statute. And from the same Reason it seems also, That a Writ of Debt may be so pleaded after it is returned; because then it seems to be agreed, That it may properly be said to be depending; and whether it may not also be so pleaded before it be returned, seems questionable; Because, according to some [k] Opinions, a Writ may be said to be depending as soon as purchased.

[d] Cro. El. 261. 1 Ro. Re. 49, 50, 134. [e] Cro. El. 261. Vide 1 Ro. Re. 49, 50. [f] Hob. 209. [g] Hob. 138. [h] Cro. El. 261. [i] 10 Ed. 4. 13. pl. 2. [k] Cro. El. 677. pl. 7. Cro. Jac. 11.

Sect. 64. As to the second Point, *viz.* Where a Pardon, or Release, or a Recovery in a former Suit, may be pleaded to such an Information, or Action? It seems agreed, That notwithstanding the King have such an Interest in every penal Statute, that he may [l] proceed in a Suit brought upon it by a Common Informer, after the Death, Release, or Nonsuit of such Informer, hanging the Prosecution; and may also totally prevent any such Suit, by first [m] suing for the whole Penalty himself; or may totally bar it by a Pardon or Release [n] precedent to its Commencement; yet if it be actually commenced before any Suit by the King, the Informer hath such an Interest in the Part of the Penalty assigned him by

5 Co. 48. a. b. 1 Rol. Re. 379 pl. 37. contr. Salk. 89. pl. 11. 2 Ed. 4. 11. pl. 3. 7 Co. 30. a. [l] 11 Co. 65. b. 66. a. 5 Co. 48. b. Noy 100. 3 Inst. 194. 2 Bulst. 261 262. Cro. El. 583. Moore 548. Cont. Cro. El. 138. pl. 13. 37 H. 6, 5 a. 20 H. 7. 5. b. 6 a. Bro. Attaint, 130. Vide 2 Ro. Re. 33. Hutt. 82. [m] Crompton Jurisdiction, 38. a. 3 Inst. 194. 11 Co. 65 b. 66. a. [n] Fitz. decies tantum, 5. Charter 21. Bro. Action Popular, 3, 4. 1 H. 7. 3. pl. 2. 37 H. 6. 4. 3 Inst. 194. 5 Ed. 4. 2, 3.

by the Statute, that the King can no [a] way discharge, or suspend the Suit, as to [b] such Part. Also it seems that the King can in [c] no Case bar the Suit of a Party grieved, nor proceed in it after the Death of the Plaintiff, *&c.* Also, it seems agreed, [d] That a Conviction or Acquittal *bona fide* in any Action or Information on a penal Statute, whether by the Party grieved, or a Common Informer, or a Release *bona fide*, from the Party grieved, or Common Informer, [e] after such a Conviction, hath always been a good Bar of any subsequent Prosecution for the same Offence. But for the better settling of these Matters, the Statute of 4 *H.* 7. 20. was made, by which it is recited, *That it had been usual for Offenders against penal Statutes, to cause Popular Actions to be commenced against them by Covin of the Plaintiffs, or else when such Actions had been commenced against them, to delay the same, either by Non-appearance, or by Traverse: and hanging the same, to cause the like Action Popular to be brought against them by Covin for the same Cause and Offence, and therein by Covin of the Plaintiff to be condemned, either by Confession, feigned Trial, or Release, which Condemnation or Release, so had by Collusion and Covin, did use to bar the Plaintiff in the Action sued in good Faith*; and thereupon it is enacted, *That if any Person sue with good Faith any Action Popular, and the Defendant plead any Manner of Recovery of Action Popular in Bar of the said Action; or else, that he before that Time barr'd the Plaintiff in any such Action Popular, that then such Plaintiff, with good Faith, may averr, That such Recovery or Bar were by Covin; and if such Collusion or Covin so averr'd, be lawfully found, such Plaintiff shall recover,* &c *and the Defendant condemned of Covin or Collusion, as aforesaid, shall have two Years Imprisonment,* &c *and that no Release of any Common Person to any such Party, whether before or after any Action Popular, or Indictment of the same, had, or commenced or made, hanging the said Action, shall be anywise available or effectual to let or surcease the said Action, Indictment, Process, or Execution. Provided always, That no Plaintiff or Plaintiffs be receiv'd to averr any Covin in any Action Popular, where the Point of the same Action, or else the Covin or Collusion, have been once tried, or lawfully found with the Plaintiff or Plaintiffs, or against them, by trial of twelve Men, and not otherwise.*

[a] Cro. El. 138 pl. 13. 1 Leon. 119. 1 H. 7. 3. pl. 2. 27 H. 6. 4. Hutt. 82. Bro. Action Popular 3, 4. 3 Inst. 194.
[b] Sav. 23.
[c] Noy 100. Moore 58.
[d] Fitz. decies tantum 4, 5. Bro. Act. popular, 4 7. 7 Cro. Jac. 482. 1 H. 7. 3. pl. 2. 11 Co. 65. b. 66. a. 9 Ed. 4. 4. pl. 15.
[e] 2 Ro Re. 33. Bro. Act. Popular, 7. 5 Ed. 4, 2, 3.

Sect. 65. It is [f] said, That if a Recovery in a former Suit be pleaded in Bar of any Popular Action, the Plaintiff may, by Reason of the express Words of the Statute, averr, That such Recovery was by Covin, without shewing wherein the Covin consisted; but otherwise such a general Pleading would be vicious.

[f] Pl. com. 49, b. 50.

As to the third Point, *viz.* What is a good General Issue, and where it may be pleaded? I shall observe the following Particulars;

Sect. 66. *First*, That if the Defendant plead *Nil debet* to an Action or Information *qui tam*, it is safest to say, That he owes [g] nothing to the Informer, nor to the King; because if he only plead, that he owes nothing to the Informer, it may be objected, [h] That the whole Declaration is not answered, which makes a Demand for the King as well as the Informer: Yet perhaps it may be a good Answer [i] to such Objection, That in the Plea, that he owes nothing to the Informer; it is necessarily implied that he owes nothing to the King, and therefore needs not be expressed.

[g] Vide Co. Ent. 165, b. 167. b.
[h] Hob. 327, 328. 1 Vent. 122.
[i] 3 Lev. 375. Vide Cro. Ca. 10, 11.

Sect. 67. *Secondly*, That if there be more than one Defendant, they ought [k] not to plead jointly that they are not guilty, but severally, That neither they, nor any of them, are guilty, *&c.*

[k] 21 H. 6. 20. pl. 37. Fitz. decies tantum 6. 2 Rol. Abr. 707. pl. 48.

Sect.

Sect. 68. *Thirdly*, That where-ever the Breach of the Statute, whereon such Suit is grounded, is alledged only from a Matter *in Pais*, and not from Matter of Record, the Defendant [a] may plead, that he owes nothing, or that he is not guilty, *&c.* but if it be alledged from a Matter of Record, such a Plea is not good; because a Record is not triable by the Country, but only by itself.

[a] 21 H. 7. 14. pl. 20. Bro. Issues joins, 23. Vide 21 Jac. 14 par. 4.

Sect. 69. *Fourthly*, That if the Defendant be within the Benefit of any *Proviso* of a penal Statute, he might, according to some, always give it in [b] Evidence on the General Issue, in a Suit on such Statute: But if he have Matter in his Discharge depending on a subsequent Statute, it hath been holden [c] (even since the Statute of 21 *Jac.* 1. 4.) That he must plead it specially, and cannot give it in Evidence. But this seems contrary to the express Purview of the said Statute; by which it is enacted, *That if any Suit shall be brought against any Person for any Offence against any penal Law, either by, or on the Behalf of the King, or by any other, or on the Behalf of the King, and any other, it shall be lawful for such Defendant, to plead the General Issue, that he is not guilty, or that he owes nothing, and to give such special Matter in Evidence to the Jury that shall try the same, which Matter being pleaded, had been sufficient in Law to have discharged the said Defendant against the said Suit, and the said Matter shall be then as available, to all Intents and Purposes, as if had been sufficiently pleaded in Bar.*

[b] 2 Rol. Abr. 683, pl. 10, 12. Cont. pl. 11.

[c] 2 Rol. Abr. 683, pl. 13.

Sect. 70. Also it is enacted by the same Statute, *Par.* 2. *That if the Defendant to any Suit, commenced by, or on the Behalf of the King, or any other, for any Offence against any penal Statute, plead, That he oweth nothing, or, that he is not guilty, and the Plaintiff or Informer, upon Evidence to the Jury, shall not prove the Offence laid in the said Suit, and that the same Offence was committed in the same County in which it is laid, the Defendant shall be found Not guilty.*

Sect. 71. It is provided by the last Paragraph of the said Statute, *That no Clause thereof shall extend to any Suit on any Law against Popish Recusants,* &c. *or against Champerty,* &c. *or concerning defrauding the King of his Customs,* &c. *or the transporting of Gold, or Silver, or Munition,* &c. *or Wool, or Leather, but that such Offence may be laid in any County, at the Pleasure of the Informer.* But *Quære*, If the last Words of this *Proviso*, *viz. but that such Offence may be laid in any County*, do not restrain the Exception intended by it to that Part of the Statute only which relates to the laying the Offence in the proper County? For if so, the Defendant in a Suit on the Laws mentioned in it, may give the special Matter in Evidence on the General Issue, as well as in a Suit on any other penal Statute.

Vide supra, Sect. 50.

Sect. 72. As to the twelfth Particular, *viz.* By whom the Replication is to be made in such an Information or Action: It seems agreed, [e] That regularly a Replication to a Special Plea to an Information in the Courts of *Westminster-Hall*, shall be made by the Attorney General only, who, in Respect of the King's Interest in the Suit, is presumed to be most proper to be consulted concerning it; and by the same Reason it [f] seems that such Replication in a Suit before Justices of Assize, shall be made by the Clerk of the Assizes only. Also it is said, [g] That the Replication to a General Issue in an Information *qui tam* in the Courts of King's Bench or Exchequer, may be made in the Name of the Attorney General only, by the Usage of those Courts. But in most of the [h] Precedents I can find of Actions *qui tam*, the Replication is made by the Plaintiff only. Also I find a Demurrer by the Informer only to a Plea in Bar to an [i] Information *qui tam*, without any mention of the Attorney General. And if the Attorney General, *&c.* shall absolutely refuse to make a Replication to any

[e] 6 Co. 20. a. Vide Cro. Jac. 538. Cro. El. 138. pl. 13. 2 R. Re. 33. Bro. Attaint, 127. Co. Ent. 365, a. 366, a. 367, a. 368, a. 395. a. Ra. Ent. 410. a.

[f] Vide Cro. Jac. 502.

[g] 1 And. 49.

[h] Co. Ent. 159, b. 163, a. b. 165, b. 166, a. 167. b.

[i] Co. Entr. 371. a.

[a] Vide supra, Sect. 64. 5 Co. 48. b.

any Plea to an Information, surely the Informer may be [a] admitted to make it himself; for otherwise it would be in the Power of the Attorney General, *&c.* by refusing to make a Replication, wholly to defeat the Suit.

Sect. 73. As to the thirteenth Particular, *viz.* In what Manner the Issue is to be joined in such an Information or Action, and where it shall be tried: It hath been laid down [b] as a settled Rule, That where the King is to have no Part of the Thing demanded in an Action on a penal Statute, but only a Fine or Amercement, there is no necessity either in the joining of the Issue or *Venire facias*, to use the Words *qui tam pro Domino Rege, &c.* but that it is sufficient simply to Name the Party, as in Actions at Common Law; for the King seems to have little more Interest in such Suits than in Actions at Law. Yet where-ever the Plaintiff may declare *tam pro Domino Rege quam pro seipso*, it seems, [c] That it can be no Fault to use those Words as well in the joining of the Issue, *&c.* as in the beginning of the Suit. And if the King be to have Part of the Penalty demanded, it hath been [d] adjudged to be a fatal Fault, and not amendable after Verdict, not to mention that the Plaintiff sues *tam pro Domino Rege quam pro seipso*, in the joining of the Issue. But *Quære*; for there are many [e] Precedents where the Issues in such Actions have not mentioned the Plaintiff, as suing for the King; but have simply named him by his Proper Name, as in other Actions. And where he is expresly named in the Declaration, as suing for the King as well as for himself, Why it should be intended that he sues otherwise in the Progress of the Action?

[b] Cro. Ca. 336, 337. Vide Coke's Ent. 160, b. 161, b. 164, a. 348, b. 350. b.

[c] Ra. Ent. 406, b. 407. a. Co. Ent. 349. b.

[d] 1 Vent. 122. 2 Keb. 788. Vide supra, Sect. 17, 20.

[e] Co Entr. 159, b. 163, a. b. 165, b. 166. a. 167. b. Vide supra, Sect. 17, 20.

Sect. 74. As to the Place where such Issues shall be tried, it is enacted by 18 *El.* 5. *That no Jury shall be compelled to appear in any of the Queen's Courts at* Westminster, *for the Trial of any Issue in any Suit* (by a Common [f] Informer) *upon any penal Law, for any Offence committed above thirty Miles from the City of* Westminster; *except in Case where the Attorney General for the Time being, for some reasonable Cause in that Behalf to be shewed, shall require the same to be tried at the Bar, in any of the Courts of the Queen's Majesty, her Heirs or Successors, at* Westminster *aforesaid: Which Request shall be noted on the Backside of the Writ of* Distringas *thereupon awarded, to the End the Sheriff, or his Bailiff, may, and shall signify the same to the Jury that are in such Case impanelled.*

[f] *See the three last Sections of the Statute, and the 22d, 47th and 49th Sections of this Chapter.*

Sect. 75. As to the fourteenth Particular, *viz.* Where a Verdict may be found as to Part against the Informer, and as to Part for him: It seems, [g] That regularly, if an Offence against a Statute be of such a Nature that it may be committed by a single Person, without the Concurrence of any other, and several Persons be jointly charged in one Information, for one Act done by them all against such Statute, one of them only may be found guilty, and the rest acquitted; because, tho' the Words of the Information seem to import a joint Charge against all the Defendants, yet in Judgment of Law each of them is charged severally for his own Offence, which cannot but be several, whether the Act, in the doing whereof it consisted, were done by one or more; and accordingly the Issue must be, that [h] neither they, nor any of them, are guilty. And for the like Reasons, if one be informed against for having offended against a Statute for more Times, or in a higher Degree than can be proved; as for not coming to Church during the Space of ten Months, where he can be proved to have been absent but eight Months, *&c.* or for [i] ingrossing 1000 Quarters of Wheat, where the Evidence amounts but to 700, he may be found guilty so far as the Evidence goes, and Not guilty for the

[g] 2 Rol. Abr. 707, pl. 45, 48. 708 pl. 50. Lane 19, 59, 60.

[h] Supra Sect. 67.

[i] 2 Rol. Abr. 707. pl. 48. Lane 59, 60.

the Residue; for such Offences are not in the Nature of entire Contracts, which regularly must be fully proved in the same Manner as they are alledged, but are in the Nature of Trespasses, which it is sufficient to prove for any Part. But if the Offence against a Statute consist in making a Contract contrary to the Purview of it; as in the Case of Usury, it is [a] said, That if it be alledged as having been made by two, it must be so proved likewise, because it is a Rule of Law, That if Contracts be not proved as they are laid, they shall not be taken to be the same.

Sect. 76. As to the fifteenth Particular, *viz.* What Judgment on such an Information or Action is good? It hath been adjudged, That where a Statute (as that of Recusancy, for instance) ordains that the Offender shall forfeit such a Sum, and that the Sum so forfeited shall be divided into three Parts; whereof one Third shall go to the King, and one to the Informer, and the other to the Poor, *&c.* and that if the Offender do not pay, *&c.* within such a Time, that he shall be committed, *&c.* the Judgment on an Information *qui tam* on such Statute may be general, that the [b] King and Informer shall recover the whole [c] Sum, without making any mention how it shall be distributed, or that the Party shall be committed [d] for Non-Payment, *&c.* But on such an Information if the Judgment for the Recovery of the Forfeiture be given wholly for the Informer, without any mention of the King, it hath been holden, [e] That it is totally erroneous. Yet it hath been adjudged, That if on an Information *qui tam*, wherein, as it is laid, the Informer hath no Right to any Part, but the King ought to have the Whole, Judgment be given that the Defendant shall forfeit the Sum mentioned by the Statute, and that the King shall have one Moiety, and the Informer the other, such Judgment is erroneous [f] only as to the latter Part, wherein it awards to whom the Penalty shall go; but shall stand for the Clause concerning the Forfeiture, which sufficiently entitles the King to the Whole. And it hath been adjudged, [g] That if there be no Clause at all concerning the Forfeiture in a Conviction on a penal Statute, but only a Judgment *Quod Convictus est*, it is sufficient, for the Forfeiture is implied.

Sect. 77. As to the sixteenth Particular, *viz.* Whether the Penalty of a penal Statute, may be compounded or granted over? It is enacted by 18 *El.* 5. *That no Informer, or Plaintiff, shall, or may compound or agree with any Person or Persons, that shall offend, or shall be surmised to offend against any penal Statute, for an Offence committed or pretended to be committed; but after Answer made in Court unto the Information or Suit in that Behalf exhibited, or prosecuted: Nor after Answer, but by the Order or Consent of the Court in which the same Information or Suit shall be depending; on Pain that whosoever shall offend, in making of Composition, or other Misdemeanor, contrary to the true Intent and Meaning of this Statute, or shall by Colour or Pretence of Process, or without Process, upon Colour or Pretence of any Matter of Offence against any penal Law, make any Composition, or take any Money, Reward, or Promise of Reward, for himself, or to the Use of any other, without Order or Consent of some of her Majesty's Courts at* Westminster, *and shall be thereof convict, shall stand on the Pillory,* &c. *and for ever be disabled to pursue, or be Plaintiff or Informer in any Suit or Information upon any Statute Popular or Penal; and shall also forfeit ten Pounds,* &c.

Sect. 78. It seems [h] clear, both from the Preamble and the whole Tenor of the Statute, that it extends only to Suits by Common Informers, and not to those by a Party grieved.

Sect.

[a] Line 19, 59, 60.

[b] 1 And. 139, 140. Vide Style Rep. 329, 330.

[c] 2 Rol. Abr. 102. Lett. K. Vide 2 Keb. 820 pl. 30.

[d] 1 And. 139, 140.

[e] Styl's Rep. 329, 330.

[f] 2 And. 128, 129, 130.

[g] Dominus Rex versus Howkins Mich. 3. Geo.

[h] *See the three last Sections of the Statute, and the 22d, 47th, and 49th Sections of this Chapter.*

[a] Hutt. 35. *Sect.* 78. But it hath been [a] holden, That it extends as well to subsequent penal Statutes, as to those which were in being when it was made. [b] And also that it extends to the compounding of Suits commenced in Courts which have no Jurisdiction, as much as if they had a Jurisdiction.

[b] 1 Keb. 106. pl. 42. 1 Sid. 311.

Sect. 79. It is enacted and declared by 21 *Jac.* 1. 3. (which, as to these Matters, appears both by the Preamble, and Body of the Statute, and many former [c] Resolutions, to be made in Affirmance of the Common Law) *That all Commissions, Grants, Licences, Charters, and Letters Patents, made or to be made to any Person or Persons, Bodies politick or Corporate whatsoever, of Power, Liberty, or Faculty, to dispense with any others, or to give Licence or Toleration, to do, use, or exercise any Thing against the Tenour or Purport of any Law or Statute, or to give or make any Warrant for any such Dispensation, Licence, or Toleration to be had or made, or to agree, or compound with any others for any Penalty or Forfeitures limited by any Statute, or of any Grant or Promise of the Benefit, Profit, or Commodity of any Forfeiture, Penalty, or Sum of Money, that is or shall be due by any Statute, before Judgment thereupon had, and all Proclamations,* &c. *any way tending to the furthering of the same, are altogether contrary to the Laws of this Realm, and shall be utterly void,* &c. And it is farther enacted, *That all such Commissions,* &c. *shall be examined, heard, tried and determined by, and according to the Common Laws of this Realm, and not otherwise.*

[c] 7 Co. 36, 37. Moore 763. Hob. 183. 3 Inst. 186, 187. 2 Rol. Abr. 187. pl. 12. *seems contrary.*

Sect. 80. But is provided, *That this Act shall not extend to any Warrant or Privy Seal, made or directed by the King to the Justices of either Bench, or the Exchequer, or of Assise, or of* Oyer and Terminer *and Gaol-Delivery, or Peace, or other Justices for the Time being, having Power to hear and determine Offences done against any penal Statute, to compound for the Forfeitures of any penal Statutes, depending in Suit and Question before them, or any of them respectively, after Plea pleaded by the Defendant.*

[d] 3 Inst. 178. *Sect.* 80. It is said by Sir [d] *Edward Coke*, That such Justices, by such Warrant, *&c.* can make such Composition for the Use of the King only; However it seems, That by 18 *El.* they may give Leave to an Informer to [e] compound with a Defendant after Plea pleaded.

[e] Vide supra, Sec. 64, 65, 66.

Sect. 82. Also it is provided, *That the said Act shall not extend to any Grants, Letters Patents, or Commission heretofore granted, of, for, or concerning the licensing of the keeping of any Tavern or Taverns, or selling, uttering or retailing of Wines to be drunk, or spent in the Mansion-House or Houses, or other Place, in the Tenure or Occupation of the Party or Parties, so selling or uttering the same; or for or concerning the making of any Compositions for such Licences, so as the Benefit of such Compositions be reserved and applied, to and for the Use of his Majesty, his Heirs or Successors, and not to the private Use of any other Person or Persons.*

CHAP. XXVII.

Of Proceſs.

AND now I am come to ſuch Proceſs as is to be awarded upon an Appeal, Indictment, or Information; for the better underſtanding the Nature whereof, (having premiſed that it ſeems plain, from the Nature of the Thing, that there can be [a] no need of it where the Defendant is preſent in Court, but only where he is abſent,) I ſhall conſider it,

[a] Lamb. B. 4. Ch. 8. Dalt. Ch. 132. Cromp. 150. a.

1. In General; without any particular Regard to Proceſs of Outlawry.
2. In Particular; with Regard to ſuch Proceſs only.

And *Firſt*, I ſhall examine the Nature of ſuch Proceſs in general, without any particular Regard to Proceſs of Outlawry, under the following Particulars;

1. Where it is well awarded into a County different from that wherein the Court ſits from which it is awarded.
2. What kind of Proceſs ſhall iſſue on an Indictment, Appeal, and Information.
3. In what Manner it is to be executed.
4. What is required by Statute, in Relation to Proceſs on Informations.
5. What is the proper Proceſs on a Default.
6. What after a Removal by *Certiorari*.
7. Where it ſhall be ſaid to be diſcontinued, or miſcontinued, or put without Day.
8. How far an Error in Proceſs is fatal.

Sect. 1. As to the firſt Particular, *viz.* Where ſuch Proceſs is well awarded into a County different from that wherein the Court ſits from which it is awarded: It ſeems [b] to be a good general Rule, That no Proceſs without Writ can be well awarded on any Indictment, or Appeal, *&c.* from any Court, out of the County wherein it ſits: But it ſeems agreed, [c] That ſuch Proceſs by Writ may, by the Common Law, be well awarded into any County of *England*, either by the Court of King's Bench, or by Juſtices of *Eyre*, upon an Indictment, *&c.* before them. Alſo it is clear, That Juſtices of *Oyer* and *Terminer* have the ſame Power, in Relation to Perſons indicted or appealed before them of Felony, by Force of 5 *Ed.* 3. 11. whereby it is recited, *That in Times paſt ſome Perſons appealed or indicted of divers Felonies in one County, or outlawed in the ſame County, had been dwelling, or received in another County, whereby ſuch felonious Perſons indicted and outlawed, had been encouraged in their Miſchief, becauſe they might not*

[b] 19 Aſs. pl. 6. Fitz. Barr. 279. Bro. Juriſ. 105. Vide Fitz. Aſſiſe, 446.

[c] S.P.C. 146. a. H. P. C. 196. Vide ſupra, Ch. 24. Sect. 22.

not be attached in another County; and thereupon it is enacted, *That Justices assigned to hear and determine such Felonies, shall direct their Writs to all the Counties of* England, *where need shall be to take such Persons indicted.*

Sect. 2. It is observable, That the Mischief complained of in the Preamble of this Statute relates as well to Persons appealed, as to those who are indicted; and therefore it seems reasonable to construe them also to be within the Meaning of the Purview, tho' they be not within the Letter of it, which extends only to Persons indicted.

Sect. 3. It seems questionable, [a] Whether Justices of Peace, being assigned [b] by their Commission to hear and determine Felonies, are as well within the Meaning as Letter of this Statute? For, as on the one Side it may be argued, That this being a remedial Law, ought to receive as favourable and large an Interpretation as the Words will admit; so on the other Side it may be said, That the Preamble of the Statute making mention as well of Persons appealed, as of those who are indicted, cannot be thought to have any manner of Regard to Justices of the Peace, before whom no Appeal lies; and nothing can be more reasonable than to construe one Part of a Statute by another.

[a] Vide Crom. Justice, 149. b. Lamb. B. 4. Ch. 8.
[b] Vide supra, Ch 8 Sect. 32.

Sect. 4. But by 22 *H.* 8. 5. Par. 5. *Justices of Peace of the Shire,* &c. *wherein any decayed Bridge shall be,* &c. *shall make Process into every Shire within this Realm, against any Persons who ought to amend such Bridge, being presented before them to be decayed,* &c. Also they have the like Power by other Statutes in many other Cases, for which, not being so proper for this Treatise, I shall refer the Reader to the [c] Authors which more particularly treat of the *Office of a Justice of Peace.*

[c] Crompton's Justice, 151, 152. Lamb. B. 4. Ch. 8.

As to the second Particular, *viz.* What Kind of Process shall issue on an Appeal, Indictment, and Information; I shall endeavour to shew,

First, Where such Process ought to have the Clause of *Non omittas.*

Secondly, In whose Name, and under what *Teste*, it is to be made.

Thirdly, What is the proper Process on Indictments for Crimes of an Inferior Nature.

Fourthly, What is the proper Process on Informations.

Fifthly, What is the proper Process on Appeals, and on Indictments of Treason, Felony and Mayhem.

Sixthly, How many Days there ought to be between the *Teste* and Return of such Process.

Sect. 5. As to the first Point, *viz.* Where such Process ought to have the Clause of *Non omittas*: It is laid [d] down in some Books as a general Rule, That in every Suit, to which the King is a Party, the Process ought to have the Clause, *Non omittas propter aliquam libertatem, &c.*

Sect. 6. But I do not find this Rule observed as to all Kinds of Suits by the King, in the best Precedents; for tho' the said Clause is mentioned in every Award of Process on [e] Indictments (except only [f] one) and even on [g] Informations *qui tam*, in *Coke's Entries*; yet it is omitted in all the Awards of Process I can find on Informations of [h] Intrusion on the King's Lands, or of [i] Trover and Conversion of his Goods; and yet these are at least as much, if not more properly, the Suits of the King, than the former.

[d] Crompton's Just. 149. b. Lamb B. 4. Ch 8. Dalt. Ch. 132. 41 Ass. 17. Bro. Franc. 18. Process, 102. Fitz. Prerog. 21. Vide infra, Sect. 17.

[e] Coke's Ent *from* 352, *to* 363. [f] Co. Ent. 358. b. [g] Co. Ent. 365, a. 366, a. 367, a. 368. a. [h] Co. Entr. 372, a. 376, a. 379, a. 381, a. 387. b. 1 Co. 16, 17. [i] Coke's Entr. 390. b.

Sect. 7. As to the ſecond Point, *viz.* In whoſe Name, and under what *Teſte* ſuch Proceſs is to be made. It is expreſly [a] enacted by 27 *H.* 8. 24. *Par.* 3. *That all manner of Proceſs upon Indictments of Treaſon, Felony, or Treſpaſs to be made in every County-Palatine, and other Liberty, ſhall be made only in the Name of the King; and that every Perſon having ſuch County-Palatine, or any other ſuch Liberty, to make Proceſs,* &c. *ſhall make the* Teſte *in the Name of the Perſon that hath ſuch County-Palatine,* &c.

Sect. 8. And as to Proceſs on Indictments in any other Courts, there can be no [b] Doubt but that it ought alſo to be in the Name of the King: And if it iſſue from the Court of King's Bench, it ſeems [c] clear, That it ought to be under the *Teſte* of the Chief Juſtice, or of the Senior Judge of the Court, if there be no Chief Juſtice; and if it iſſue from any other Court, there ſeems to be the ſame Reaſon that it ought to be under the *Teſte* of the firſt in the Commiſſion; and that ſuch a *Teſte* will be ſufficient. It is holden indeed by [d] *Lambard,* That every Proceſs on an Indictment before Juſtices of Peace, ought to be under the *Teſte* of ſome two Juſtices: But there are Precedents to the contrary in [e] *Crompton;* and even in [f] *Lambard.* Neither do the [g] Authorities cited by *Lambard* ſeem to come up fully to his Point; for they ſeem to amount to no more than this, That one Juſtice of the Peace cannot award Proceſs on an Indictment, but that two of them at the leaſt muſt do it, and that ſitting the Court in the Seſſions: And indeed it ſeems plainly to appear, from the [*] Commiſſion itſelf, That one Juſtice has no Authority either to take an Indictment, or to proceed upon it: But I do not ſee the Conſequence, That becauſe an Indictment cannot be taken, nor proceeded upon, by leſs than two, therefore the Proceſs cannot be teſted by leſs than two.

Sect. 9. As to the third Point, *viz.* What is the proper Proceſs on Indictment or Crimes of an inferior Nature. It ſeems clear, both from the [h] Books which ſpeak of this Matter, and the conſtant Courſe of [i] Precedents, That a *Venire Facias* (which is but in Nature of a Summons to cauſe the Party to appear) is a proper Proceſs to be firſt awarded on an Indictment for any Crime (whether againſt the Common Law, or Statute) under the Degree of Treaſon, Felony, or [k] Maihem, except in ſuch Caſes wherein other [l] Proceſs is directed by ſome Statute. Alſo ſuch a *Venire* ſeems to be the firſt proper Proceſs on an [m] Information in the Crown-Office, for a Debt claimed by the King, as having been forfeited by a *felo de ſe.*

Sect. 10. If it appear by the [n] Return to ſuch *Venire,* that the Party has Lands in the County whereby he may be diſtrained, the [o] Diſtreſs infinite ſhall be awarded from Time to Time, till he do appear, and by Force hereof he ſhall [p] forfeit on every Default ſo much as the Sheriff ſhall return upon him in Iſſues. But if a *Nihil* be returned on ſuch a *Venire,* a [q] *Capias, alias* and *pluries,* ſhall iſſue, *&c.*

Sect. 11. It is ſaid in *Fitzherbert's* [r] *Abridgment, That in* Oyer *and* Terminer, *if the Party at the firſt Day make Default, a Man may have a* Venire Facias, *or a* Pone per vadios, &c. *at his Election;* the Meaning whereof perhaps may be this, That if the Defendant, being ſummoned on the *Venire,* do not appear, the Proſecutor may either take out a ſecond *Venire,* or a [s] *Pone per vadios, &c.* But I cannot [t] find any expreſs Authority, or Precedent, to juſtify the making either a *Pone per vadios, &c.* or a *Ca-*

[a] Vide 4 Inſt. 205.

[b] Vide Lamb. B. 4. Ch. 8. Dalt Juſt. Ch. 132.

[c] Finch of Law, 436. Cro. Ca. 393.

[d] Lamb. B. 4. Ch. 8. *See* Dalt. Juſt. Ch. 132.

[e] Crompton, 232, 233.

[f] *See the printed Precedents in the End of his Eirenarcha.*

[g] Bro. Peace, 6, 7. Vide 14 H. 7. 8. b. Crompt. 151. b.

[*] Vide ſupra, Ch. 8. Sect. 24, 25. Dalt. Ch. 132.

[h] Crompt. 150, b. 151. Dalt. ch. 132. Lamb. B. 4. Ch. 8. Fitz. Aſſiſe, 17. 32 H. 6. 10. b.

[i] Co. Entr. 358, pl. 10. 362, pl. 17, 18. 363. a.

[k] Finch of Law, 356.

[l] Vide ſupra, Ch. 23. Sect. 151. Ra. Ent. 263. pl. 11.

[m] 1 Saund. 271.

[n] Crompt. 150, 151. Lambert, B. 4. Ch. 8. Dalt. Juſt. Ch. 132. Dalt. Sheriff, Ch. 34, 78.

[o] Regiſter Judicial, 1. Finch, 352, 353. Dalton's Sheriff, Ch. 34, 78. Dalt. Juſtice, Ch. 132.

[p] Vide 2 Danv. Ab. 296, f. 5. 2 Inſt. 453, 454.

[q] Lamb. B. 4. ch. 8. Crompt. 150, 151. Fitz. Treſpaſs, 232. Dalt. Juſt. Ch. 132. 11 H. 6. 4. a. Finch of Law. 352.

[r] Fitz. Proceſs, 188.

[s] Vide Finch of Law. 352.

[t] Vide ſupra, Sect. 9, 10. Fitz. Pro. 213. Treſ. 232. 29 Ed. 4. 18. a. b.

pias,

pias, the first Process on any Indictment under the Degree of Maihem, or Felony, *&c.* except only where such Process is expressly given by some Statute.

Sect. 12. As to the fourth Point, *viz.* What is the proper Process on Informations: It seems, That a *Capias* against a [a] Commoner, and a [b] *Distringas* against a Peer, are the first proper Processes on an Information for an Intrusion on the King's Lands, or for a [c] Trover and Conversion of his Goods: And either an * Attachment or [d] *Subpœna*, at the Election of the Informer, were by the Common Law proper Processes on all Informations *qui tam* on Popular Statutes. And so was a [e] Summons in all Originals in Debt on such Statutes, in the same Manner as in an Action of Debt at [f] Common Law; and an [g] Attachment, or *Pone per vadios, &c.* in other Actions on such Statutes, in the same Manner as in Actions upon the Case, and in Actions of Trespass at [h] Common Law.

Sect. 13. And it is enacted by 21 *Jac.* 1. 4. By which all Popular Suits on penal Statutes are restrained to their proper Counties, as is shewn at Large in the precedent [i] Chapter of Informations, *That the like Process in every Popular Action, Bill, Plaint, Information, or Suit, to be commenced, sued or prosecuted, by Force of, or according to the Purport of the said Act, be had and awarded, to all Intents and Purposes, as in an Action of Trespass* Vi & Armis *at the Common Law.* And [k] consequently the Process in all such Suits must now be by Attachment or *Pone per vadios, &c.* and after by Distress infinite, where by the Return, the Party appears to be sufficient, [l] otherwise by *Capias.*

Sect. 14. It is as I take it, the usual Practice of the Crown-Office, on a Criminal Information, first, to award a *Subpœna*; and after the Return thereof, if no Appearance be entred in four Days, and an Affidavit be made of the Service of the *Subpœna*, to make out a *Capias* of Course, where the Defendants are informed against in their private Capacity, and a [m] *Distringas*, where they are sued as a Corporation aggregate.

Sect. 15. As to the fifth Point, *viz.* What is the proper Process on Appeals, and on Indictments of Treason, Felony and Maihem: It seems certain, That a *Capias* is the first Process in all Indictments of [n] Treason or Felony, and in [o] all Appeals, whether of Maihem or Felony; from whence it seems reasonable to conclude, That it ought also to be the first Process in an Indictment of Maihem, as well as of Felony or Treason.

Sect. 16. As to the sixth Point, *viz.* How many Days there must be between the *Teste* and Return of all such Process: It seems agreed, That there ought to be at least fifteen Days between the *Teste* and Return of every Process awarded from the King's Bench into any [p] Foreign County: But that this is not required in Process awarded into the same County where in the Court sits.

Sect. 17. As to the third Particular, *viz.* In what Manner such Process is to be executed: It is laid down as a [q] general Rule, That wherever the King is a Party to the Suit, (as he certainly is to all Informations and Indictments) the Process ought to be executed by the Sheriff himself, and not by the Bailiff of any Franchise, [r] whether it have the Clause *Non omittas, &c.* or not, and whether the Defendant be within a Franchise, or in the County at large; for the King's Prerogative shall be preferred to any Franchise: But it is said, [s] That this is to be intended only where in the Grant of the Franchise, no mention is made of Causes to which the King is a Party.

[a] Coke's Ent. 372, a. 376, a. 379, a. 381, a.
1 Co. 16. b.
[b] Co. Entr. 387. b.
[c] Co. Ent. 390. b.
* Coke's Ent. 365, a. 366, a. 367, a. 368.
[d] Co. Ent. 370, b. 371, b. 395, a.
1 And. 48.
[e] Co. Entr. 158, a. 164, b. 166. a.
Ra. Entr. 599. pl. 2, 3.
[f] Finch of Law, 352.
[g] Co. Entr. 43, b. 44. pl. 3. 46, a. 348, a. 349, a. 350, a. 351. a.
Ra. Ent. 406. a. b.
[h] Finch of Law, 355.
[i] Vide Ch. 26. Sect. 31 to Sect. 38.
[k] See Finch of Law, 345, 352, 355.
[l] 1 Rol. Abr. 463, pl. 11. 780. pl. 6. 793, pl. 4. *the same Case.*
Palm. 449.
1 Keb. 159, pl. 109.
2 Rol. Abr. 277. D.
[m] Vide Salk 174. pl. 15.
[n] 3 Mod 265.
[o] Co. Ent. 50. pl. 1.
Fitz. Exigent 28.
Finch of Law. 246. 351.
Ra. Entr 45. pl. 1. *there is a Precedent seemingly contrary.*
[p] Co. Litt. 134, b.
Salk. 174 pl. 15.
1 Lev. 61
9 Co. 118 b.

[q] Dalt. Ch. 132. Bro. Franchise, 18. [r] 41 Ass. 17. Bro. Process, 102. Fitz. Prerog. 21. [s] Bro. Prerog. 109. Franch. 31.

Sect.

Sect. 18. As to the fourth Particular, *viz.* What is required by Statute in Relation to Process on Informations: It is enacted by 4 & 5 *Will.* & *M.* 18. That no Process shall issue on any Information to be exhibited by the Master of the Crown-Office, till the Prosecutor have given such a [a] Recognizance as by the said Act is directed. Also it is enacted by 18 *El.* 5. That [b] no Process shall issue on any Information on a penal Statute, till a special Note be made of the Time when such Information was exhibited, *&c.* But these Matters having been already handled in the Chapter of *Informations*, in the Places cited in the Margin, I shall refer the Reader thither, for the fuller Consideration of them.

Sect. 19. As to the fifth Particular, *viz.* What is the proper Process upon a Default: It seems, That if a Defendant appear to an [c] Indictment or [d] Appeal of Felony, and afterwards, before issue joined, make an Escape, whether from his [e] Bail, or from an actual [f] Prison, the Common *Capias*, *alias* and *pluries*, *&c.* shall be awarded against him, unless there had been an Exigent before, in which Case a new [g] Exigent shall be immediately awarded. And if a Defendant, against whom no Exigent had been before awarded, make such Default after Issue joined, and an Inquest awarded to try it, it seems [k] that a *Capias*, *&c.* shall be awarded again him *ad audiendum juratam*, *&c.* and, as I take it, the same Day on which the *Capias* is returnable, shall be given to the Inquest, (for it seems [i] agreed, That the Inquest shall never be taken by Default in the Case of Felony, as it may for an inferior Crime.) But in such Case, if the Exigent had before been awarded, it [k] seems, That a new Exigent in the Common Form shall be awarded; and that thereby both the Issue and Inquest are without Day. And it is said in some [l] Books, That such Exigent shall be *Ad audiendum judicium*: But this seems questionable; since it seems to be [m] agreed, That the Defendant may save himself from Judgment by a Render at any Time before the Return of the Exigent.

Sect. 20. It is said [n] by Sir *Mathew Hale*, That the Defendant in such Case appearing on the Exigent, shall plead *de novo*, because the Issue and Inquest are *sine die* by the Award of the Exigent; but this seems to be made a Query by [o] *Staundforde*, and the [p] Authorities whereon it seems to be chiefly founded, are very obscure; and as it seems may well be understood in this [q] Sense, That the Court may cause the same Inquest to come to try the same Issue, which (according to [r] *Brook*) tho' it be put without Day by the Exigent, is not waived by it, unless the Defendant fail to render himself before the Return of it.

Sect. 21. Before I proceed to the sixth Particular, *viz.* What is the proper Process to be awarded after a Removal by *Certiorari*, it may not be improper to premise some Things concerning the Nature of a *Certiorari*; as,

1. To what Courts it lies.
2. Where the Court of King's Bench uses a Discretionary Power in granting, denying, and filing it.
3. What Restraints are put upon it by Statute.
4. How the *Fiat* for it is to be signed.
5. To whom it ought to be directed.

[a] Vido supra, Ch. 26. Sect. 5, 6, 10.
[b] Vide supra, Ch. 26. Sect. 39, 40, 41, 43, 44, 46, 47.
[c] H. P. C. 211.
[d] 16 Ass. pl. 13. 26 Ass. pl. 51.
[e] 16 Ass pl. 13. Fitz Exigent 10. But this is made a Query, Crompt. 150. b.
[f] 26 Ass. pl. 51.
[g] 19 H. 8. 1. pl. 1. Bro. Process, 1. seems to be contrary.
[h] S. p. C. 70. Lett. E. F. Bro. waiver de Choses, 39. Fitz. Exigent 10. Process, 113, 127.
[i] S. P. C. 70. Letter E. Fitz Exigent 10. Coro. 173. Bro. waiver de choses, 39. 16 Ass pl. 13. Bro. Appeal, 54.
[k] 26 Ass pl. 51. S. P C. 70 Letters E. F. H. P. C 211. Bro. waiver de choses, 39. Fitz. Exigent 10. Coro. 196.
[l] 26 Ass. 51. Crompt. 150. b. Fitz. Croro. 196.
[m] Fitz. Exigent, 10. Bro. waiver de choses, 39. Coro 192. H P C. 211.
[n] H. P. C. 211.
[o] S. P. C. 70. Letters E. F.
[p] Fitz. Exigent 10. 16 Ass pl. 13.
[q] Vide Fitz. Coro. 173.
[r] Bro. waiver de choses, 39. Process, 148. Exigent 67

6. Where

6. Where a Record may be removed into the Court of King's Bench without it.

7. What is be done by a Defendant before the Allowance of it.

8. How far it is a *Supersedeas* to the Court below.

9. In what Manner it is to be returned.

10. Where a Record is removed by it.

11. What is to be done by the Court above, where the Record is not removed.

As to the first Point, *viz.* To what Courts a *Certiorari* lies: I shall endeavour to shew,

1. Whether it lie to all inferior Courts in general.
2. Whether to those of the *Cinque-Ports*.
3. Whether to those of *Wales*.
4. Whether to those of *London*.

Sect. 22. As to the first Point, *viz.* Whether regularly it lie to all inferior Courts in general: It seems agreed at this Day, That regularly the Court of King's Bench having a general [a] Superintendency over all other Courts of Criminal Jurisdiction, whether they be of an antient or [b] newly created Jurisdiction, may award a *Certiorari* as well as the Court of Chancery, to remove the Proceedings before any such Courts, unless the Statute or [c] Charter which erects them, expresly give them an absolute Judicature, exempt from such Superintendency; as the [d] Statutes concerning the Commissioners of the *Cambridgshire Fens, &c.* are said by some to have done.

Sect. 23. And accordingly it seems to be agreed, That such a *Certiorari* lies to [e] Justices in *Eyre*, and also to those of [f] Gaol-Delivery, or of a [g] County-Palatine, and to the [h] College of Physicians, having a special Power by Statute to fine and imprison for certain Offences, and to Justices of Peace, *&c.* even in such [i] Cases which they are impowered by Statute finally to hear and determine, and also to [k] Commissioners of Sewers, notwithstanding the Clause in 13 *El.* 9. *Par.* 5, *That the said Commissioners shall not be compelled to make any Certificate or Return of their Commissions, or of their Ordinances, Laws, or Doings, &c.* For it hath been adjudged, [l] That this is intended to exempt them from returning their Orders into Chancery, as by the Statute of *H.* 8. they were obliged to do, and shall not be construed to take away the Superintendency of the Court of King's Bench, without express Words.

Sect. 24. As to the second Point, *viz.* Whether a *Certiorari* lie to the Courts of the *Cinque-Ports*? It hath been adjudged, That such a *Certiorari* lies to such Courts to remove an [m] Indictment of Sodomy there found, or an [n] Order made by the Justices of Peace at a Sessions there holden. It is said indeed, by [o] *Rolle*, That the Reason why such an Indictment may be removed is, because the Offence is made Felony by a late Statute, and therefore the Courts of the *Cinque-Ports* cannot hold Plea of it without a new Charter; by which it seems to be implied, That in his Opinion Indictments in such Courts of Crimes whereof they have Jurisdiction, are not removable. But the other Books above-cited, seem to speak generally of all Indictments, and to lay it down as a Rule, That the Privilege

[a] S. P. C. 70. 1 Salk. 144, pl. 3. 146, pl. 7. 148. 2 Lev. 86. 1 Lev. 312. Contr. 41 Ass. pl. 22. Br. Coro. 193. Certiorari, 8.
[b] 1 Salk. 145. pl. 3.
[c] Cro. Ca. 265. 3 Mod. 93, 94.
[d] 1 Sid. 296. Contra 1 Keb. 43. pl. 87. 2 Keb. 722. pl. 124.
[e] 1 Sid. 226. 2 Keb. 81, 82. 4 Inst. 294, 295.
[f] 1 Salk. 144. pl. 2.
[g] 3 Mod. 229, 230. 2 Lev. 223. 1 Salk. 146, pl. 7. 148.
[h] 1 Rol. Abr. 395 pl. 4, 5. Alcyn. 49. 5 & 6 Guil. & Mar. 11. Par. 5.
[h] 1 Salk. 144. pl. 3.
[i] 3 Mod. 93, 94.
[k] 1 Salk. 145. pl. 6. 1 Keb. 429. pl. 85. March. 196, 197, 199. Raym. 186.
[l] 1 Mod. 44, 45. 1 Lev. 288. 1 Ventr. 66, 67, 68.
[m] Cro. Ca. 252, 251, 264, 291. 1 Rol. Ab. 395. pl. 6. Style 14.
[n] 2 Lev. 86. Sid. 356. 2 Keb. 154.
[o] 1 Rol. Ab. 395. pl. 6.

vilege of the Courts of the *Cinque-Ports*, used Time out of Mind, that the King's Writ doth not run there, is to be intended only of Civil [a] Causes between Party and Party.

Sect. 25. As to the third Point, *viz.* Whether a *Certiorari* lie to the Courts of *Wales*? It seems to be settled, That such a *Certiorari* lies to remove any Indictment taken in *Wales* for a Crime not capital, either at the [b] Grand Sessions, or at a [c] Sessions of the Peace: But it is [d] said, That it hath never been granted to remove an Appeal from *Wales*; [e] neither doth it seem to be clearly settled, That it lies to remove an Indictment of Felony from thence; for such Indictments are never [f] quashed, as Indictments for inferior Crimes are. Neither do I find it agreed [g] in what Manner the King's Bench shall proceed on any Indictment removed from *Wales*. But it is said, That an Indictment of Felony so removed, may be tried in the next [h] *English* County, by force of [i] 26 *H.* 8. But it seems [k] agreed, That this Statute extends not to Appeals.

Sect. 26. As to the fourth Point, *viz.* Whether a *Certiorari* lie to the Courts of *London*? It seems to be admitted in the late [l] Reports, That a *Certiorari* may be granted to remove any Indictment from *London* or *Middlesex*; but it is [m] said, That he who prays it ought to give three Days Notice to the other Side: Also it is said, [n] That by a *Certiorari* to *London*, the Tenour of the Indictment only shall be removed by the City-Charters. And it seems, [o] That anciently that City insisted on a Privilege, That all Indictments and Proceedings for any Cause, except Felony, should be tried and determined there, and not elsewhere.

Sect. 27. As to the second Particular, *viz.* Where the Court of King's Bench uses a Discretionary Power, in granting, denying and filing a *Certiorari*. It hath been [p] adjudged, That where-ever a *Certiorari* is by Law grantable for an Indictment, the Court is bound of Right to award it at the Instance of the King, because every Indictment is the Suit of the King, and he has a Prerogative of suing in what Court he pleases. But it seems to be agreed, That it is left to the Discretion of the Court either to grant or deny it at the Prayer of the Defendant: And agreeably hereto, it is laid [*] down as a general Rule, That the Court will never grant it for the Removal of an Indictment before Justices of Gaol-Delivery, without some special Cause; [q] as where there is just Reason to apprehend that the Court below may be unreasonably prejudiced against the Defendant; [r] or where there is so much Difficulty in the Case, that the Judge below desires that it may be determined in the King's Bench, [s] or where the King himself gives a special Direction that the Cause shall be removed; or where the [t] Prosecution appears to be for a Matter not properly criminal.

Sect. 28. It seems, [u] That the Court will not ordinarily, at the Prayer of the Defendant, grant a *Certiorari* for the Removal of an Indictment of Perjury, or Forgery, or other heinous Misdemeanor; for such Crimes deserve all possible Discountenance, and the *Certiorari* might delay, if not wholly discourage their Prosecution.

Sect. 29. Also it is said, [x] That the Court of King's Bench will never grant a *Certiorari* for a Conviction of Recusancy upon a Default at Sessions; be-

[a] Vide Cro. El. 910, 911. Palm. 54, 55. 56, 96. Cro. Jac. 531. 1 Sid. 432. pl. 21. Hardr. 475, 476.
[b] 1 Rol. Abr. 394. pl. 1, 2. 2 Ro. Re. 28, 29. Cro. Jac. 484. Poph. 144. 2 Keb 471. pl. 63. Cro. Jac. 248.
[c] 1 Salk. 146. pl. 7.
[d] Cro. Jac. 248. 2 Keb. 797, 798.
[e] 1 Mod. 64, 68. 2 Keb. 685, pl. 8. 724. Cro. Ca. 331, 332. 1 Rol. Abr. 394 pl. 3. 1 Ventr. 93, 146.
[f] Vide Ch. 25. Sect. 148.
[g] Vide 1 Rol. Abr. 394. Br 1, 2, 3. 2 Keb. 685, pl 8, 724.
[h] 2 Keb. 798, 799. 1 Vent. 146. Quære 1 Rol. Abr. 394, 395.
[i] Supra, Ch. 25. Sect. 39, 40.
[k] Cro. Ca. 248. 2 Keb. 797, 798. 1 Vent. 146. See B. 1. Ch. 31. Sect 41.
[l] Raym. 74. 1 Keb. 352. pl. 20. 3 Mod 230, &c. Hardr. 409, 410. 6 Mod. 246. Vide 5 & 6 W. & M. 11.
[m] Raym. 74
[n] 1 Keb 252. pl. 20. 1 Sid. 155, 230. Vide Supra, Ch. 25. Sect 99.
[o] Cro. Ca. 128, 265.
[p] Term. Pasch. 5 Georg. Vide 1 Vent. 63. 1 Mod. 41.
[*] 1 Salk. 144. pl. 2. 1 Keb. 4.
[q] 1 Salk. 150. pl. 18.
[r] 1 Salk. 149. pl. 15.
[s] 1 Vent. 63. 1 Mod. 41.
[t] 1 Salk. 151. pl. 20.
[u] 1 Sid. 54 pl. 19.
[x] 1 Salk. 145. pl. 5.

cause

cause by the * Statute such Convictions are to be removed into the Exchequer, and from thence Process is to be awarded upon them. But the Court of King's Bench cannot proceed upon them, and therefore will not suffer them to come thither, lest the Statute should be evaded.

* 3 Jac. 1. 4. Par. 9. Vide B 1. Ch. 10. Sect. 23.

Sect. 30. It seems from the *Year-Book* of 16 *E.* 4. That it is a good Objection against the granting a *Certiorari,* that issue is joined in the Court below, and a *Venire* awarded for the Trial of it; for it appears by that [a] Book, where a *Certiorari* had been granted in such a Case, that the Court being afterwards apprised of the Matter, remanded the Cause.

a 16 Ed 4, 5 pl. 3. Bro. Co 10. 162.

Sect. 31. It seems [b] agreed, That a *Certiorari* shall never be granted to remove an Indictment or Appeal after a Conviction, unless for some special Cause; as where the Judge below is doubtful what Judgment is proper to be given; for unless there be some such Reason, the Judge who tried the Cause, shall not be prevented from giving Judgment in it; for it cannot be intended but that he is best acquainted with the Circumstances of it, and consequently best able to judge what Fine, or other Punishment is proper for it.

b 1 Salk. 149 pl. 15. 6 Mod. 17.

Sect. 32. But it hath been adjudged, [c] That a *Certiorari* for the Removal of a Presentment before Justices in *Eyre,* of a Matter which is inquirable and punishable by the Forest Law only, shall not be granted before, but only after Conviction; for if it should be granted before, the Offence would be dispunished; but it may be granted after Conviction, in order to give the Party, the Right of whose Freehold is concerned in it, an Opportunity so far to [d] traverse it.

c 1 Sid. 296. 2 Keb. 81, 82.

d Vide Fitz Ass 442. 4 Inst. 294, 295. 21 Ed. 3. 48 pl. 70. Bro. Forest 3.

Sect. 33. The Court has [e] refused to grant a *Certiorari* to remove a Recognizance of Appearance before Justices of *Oyer* and *Terminer, &c.* because the Court below is most proper to judge, upon the whole Circumstances of the Case, which are equitably to be considered, whether it ought to be estreated or not.

e 1 Sid. 296 2 Keb. 81, 82.

Sect. 34. There is a Rule in the Court of King's Bench, That no Order of Commissioners of Sewers ought to be filed without Notice given to the Parties concerned. Also it is every [f] Day's Practice of that Court, before it will suffer the Return of a *Certiorari* for the Removal of the Orders of such Commissioners to be filed, to hear Affidavits concerning the Facts whereon they are grounded; and if the Matter shall still appear doubtful, to direct the Trial of feigned Issues, and either to file the Return, or supersede the *Certiorari,* and grant a *Procedendo,* as shall appear to be most reasonable for the Trial of such Issues, and to give [g] Costs against the Prosecutor of the *Certiorari,* if it appear to have been groundless.

Dominus Rex versus Combs. Hill. 1 Georgii

f Vide 1 Salk. 145. pl. 5. 2 Keb. 137. pl. 1. *seems contrary*

g Vide 2 Keb. 500. pl. 63.

Sect. 35. As to the third Particular, *viz.* What Restraints have been put by Statute upon the granting a *Certiorari.* It is enacted by 1 & 2 *Ph. & M.* 13. pl. 7. *That no Writs of* Habeas Corpus, *or* Certiorari, *shall be granted to remove any Prisoner out of any Goal, or to remove any Recognizance, except the same Writs be* [h] *signed with the proper Hands of the Chief Justice, or in his Absence, of one of the Justices of the Court out of which the same Writ shall be awarded or made, upon Pain that he that writeth any such Writs, not being signed, as is aforesaid, to forfeit for every such Writ five Pounds.*

h Vide Salk. 150. pl. 19

Sect. 36. Also it is enacted by 5 & 6 *Will. & Ma.* 11. *That in Term-Time, no Writ of* Certiorari *whatsoever, at the Prosecution of any Party indicted, be granted out of the King's Bench, to remove any Indictment or Presentment from any General or Quarter-Sessions, before Trial, but upon Motion of Counsel, and by Rule of Court made in open Court.* But it is provided, *That in Vacation such Writ may be granted by any Justices of the said Court, whose Names shall be endorsed thereon, and also the Name of the Person at whose Instance it is granted.*

Sect. 37. It is enacted by 22 *Ca.* 2. 12. Par. 4. *That all Defects of Repairs of Causeys, Pavements, Highways, or Bridges, shall be presented in the County only where such Causeys,* &c. *lie, and not elsewhere; and that no Indictment or Presentment shall be removed by* Certiorari, *or otherwise, out of the said County, till such Indictment or Presentment shall be traversed, and Judgment thereupon given.* And it is farther enacted by 3 & 4 *W. & M.* 11. *That all Matters concerning Highways,* &c. *shall be determined in the County where they lie, and not elsewhere; and that no Presentment, Indictment, or Order made by Vertue of that Act shall be removed by* Certiorari, &c. But it is enacted by 5 & 6 *W. & M.* 11. *That if the Right or Title to repair such Causeys,* &c. *may come in Question, upon Suggestion and Affidavit of the Truth thereof, a* Certiorari *may be granted to remove such Indictment or Presentment into the King's Bench,* &c. upon the like Recognizance as is required by the said Statute as to other [a] *Certiorari's*, for the Removal of Indictments from Sessions, for which I shall refer the Reader to the forty-sixth and following Sections. Also it hath been adjudged, That if the Sessions manifestly exceed their Authority, in making Orders concerning Highways, such [b] Orders may be removed by *Certiorari* into the King's Bench, and quashed.

[a] *See the Statute of* 13 & 14 *Car.* 2. 6. *Par.* 16

[b] *See* B. 1. Ch. 67. Sect. 10.

Sect. 38. It is enacted by 7 & 8 *Will. & M.* 6. Made for the Recovery of small Tithes before Justices of Peace, *That no Proceedings or Judgment by Vertue thereof shall be removed or superseded by any Writ of* Certiorari *out of any Court whatsoever, unless the Title of the Tithes,* &c. *shall come in Question.* And in the Construction hereof, it hath been adjudged, [c] That if the Party insist on any Matter of Law before the Justice of Peace, which is any way doubtful, as on a Custom in a Parish to be discharged of a certain kind of Tithe, *&c.* the Order may be removed within the Intent of the Statute.

[c] *Dominus Rex ver.* Furnace. *Termino Hil. sexto Georgii.*

Sect. 39. And it is enacted by 12 *Car.* 2. 23. Concerning the Excise, *Par.* 35. *That no Writ of* Certiorari *shall supersede Execution or other Proceedings, upon any Order by Justices of Peace in pursuance of that Statute, but that Execution, and other Proceedings, shall and may be had thereupon, any such Writ, or Allowance thereof notwithstanding.* And the like is generally enacted by other Statutes concerning the Revenue; for which I shall refer the Reader to the several Statutes.

Vide 1 Keb. 818. pl. 10.

Sect. 40. As to the fourth Point, *viz.* How the *Fiat* for a *Certiorari* is to be signed: It is said, [d] That if a *Certiorari* be taken out in Vacation, and tested of the precedent Term, the *Fiat* for it must be signed by some Judge of the Court, some Time before the Essoin-Day of the subsequent Term, otherwise it is irregular, and the Court upon Motion will order a *Procedendo.* But it is said, That there is no need for any Judge to sign the Writ of *Certiorari* it self, but only in such Cases wherein it is required by Statute.

[d] 1 Salk. 150. pl. 19.

Sect. 41. As to the fifth Point, *viz.* To whom the Writ of *Certiorari* is to be directed. It seems, That notwithstanding [e] regularly it ought to be directed to the Judge of the inferior Court, yet in some Cases it may be directed to the proper [f] Officer known to have the Custody of the Record to be removed, and in some other Cases to [g] others, as shall be most agreeable to the usual Course of approved Precedents, which [h] seems to be the best Guide whereby to judge of this Matter. And accordingly

[e] 3 Keb. 13. pl. 17.

[f] 4 H. 6. 15. b. 16 a. S. P. C. 64. Letter B. Hob. 135. Dalt. ch. 134. Style 371. Rast. Entr. 110. pl 4. 2 Lev. 223.

[g] *See the Cases cited in the other Parts of this Section.*

[h] Dyer 163. pl. 56.

cordingly it seems, That for an Indictment or Confession of an Approver before a Coroner, it shall be directed to the Coroner alone [a], and for an Appeal, both [b] to the Sheriff and Coroner; and for an Indictment in the *Cinque-Ports*, to the [c] Mayor and Jurats; and for an Indictment at an Assise in a County-Palatine, to the Chancellor of such [d] County, who shall send for it to the Justices of Assise.

Sect. 42. If the Person who ought to certify a Record, as a Justice of [e] Peace, *&c.* who hath taken a Recognizance, *&c.* or a [f] Judge of *Nisi Prius*, who hath taken a Verdict, or a [g] Coroner, who hath taken an Inquest, *&c.* happen to die, having such a Record in his Custody, it seems, That a *Certiorari* may be directed to his Executor or Administrator to certify it. [h] Also it hath been adjudged, That it may be directed to a Justice of Assise to certify a Record of Assise taken before his Companion in his Absence.

Sect. 43. All the Precedents, I am able to find, of *Certiorari's* for the Removal either of [i] Indictments, or [*] Recognizances from Sessions, are directed either to the Justices of Peace for the County generally, or to some of them in particular by Name, and not to the *Custos Rotulorum*; and according to [k] *Lambard*, they are never directed to him: Yet it is taken for granted in the [l] *Year-Book* of *H.* 7. That after a Recognizance for the Peace is brought in to the *Custos Rotulorum*, it shall be certified by him. But surely, if the *Certiorari* be directed generally to the Justices of the County, or any one of them, it may be as well returned by any of them, as by the *Custos Rotulorum*. And I question whether it can be well [m] returned by him, unless he do it as Justice of Peace, naming himself such? But if there are sufficient Precedents to warrant the directing the *Certiorari* to him as *Custos Rotulorum*, there can be no Doubt but that a Return by him as such will be good.

Sect. 44. As to the sixth Point, *viz.* Where a Record may be removed into the Court of King's Bench without any Writ of *Certiorari*: It seems agreed, † That if a Justice of Peace, or other Judge of Record, having taken a Recognizance, or Inquisition, or recorded a Riot, or done any other executory Matter, within his Jurisdiction, have still continued in the same Commission, *&c.* without any Interruption, the Court of King's Bench shall receive such Record from his Hands, without any Writ of *Certiorari*. Also it seems to be [n] agreed, That upon the Death of both the Justices of Assise, the Clerk of Assise may, without any *Certiorari*, bring in the Records of the Verdicts of *Nisi Prius*: But that the [o] Executors or Administrators of a Judge, can in no Case bring in a Record without a Writ to authorise them to do it. Also it seems to be [p] agreed, That no Record which is executed, as by Acquittal, *&c.* can be brought into a higher Court without a Writ. And it seems to be the stronger [q] Opinion, That neither a Justice who is out of Commission at the Time, nor one who has been out of Commission, but is afterwards restored, can certify any Record without a Writ of *Certiorari*.

Sect. 45. As to the seventh Point, *viz.* What is to be done by a Defendant before the Allowance of a *Certiorari*: It is enacted by 21 *Jac.* 8. *Par.* 7, 8. *That all Writs of* Certiorari *for the Removal of any Indictment of Riot, Forcible Entry, or of Assault and Battery, at any Quarter-Sessions of the Peace, or otherwise, shall be delivered at some Quarter-Sessions of the Peace in*

[a] Register Judic. 74. b. 78. a. Rast Ent. 55. a. 263. b.
[b] Register Judic. 76. Supra, Ch. 9. Sect. 42.
[c] Cro. Ca. 252, 253, 264.
[d] 2 Lev. 223. 3 Keb. 279.
[e] 2 Keb. 750. pl. 4.
8 H. 4. 3, a. 5. b.
Cro. Jac. 669. 21 H. 7. 21. pl. 4.
[f] Dyer 163. pl. 54, 55, 56. Rast. Entr. 439. pl. 14. 2 Inst 424. 2 Rol. Abr. 629. Lett. S.
[g] Bro. Certiorari, 9. Indictment, 23. 43 Ass pl. 40.
[h] Bro. Rec. 81. 11 H. 7. 5. pl. 21.
[i] Register Judic. 76. b. 77. a. Rast. Ent. 263. b.
[*] Register Origin. 90. F. N. B. 81. c.
[k] Lamb. B. 4. Ch. 7.
[l] 2 H. 7. 1. pl. 2.
[m] Vide Hob. 135.
† Dalt. Ch. 134. Lamb. B. 4. Ch. 7. 8 Ed. 4. 18. pl. 28. Bro. Record, 17. 64. 8 H. 4. 4. a. 5. b. Crompt. 132, 133. b.
[n] Dyer 163. pl. 54, 55, 56. 2 Inst. 424. See March 118, 119.
[o] Dyer, 163 pl. 54, 55, 56. Rastal's Entr. 439 pl. 14. 8 H. 4. 4. a. [p] 8 Ed. 4. 18. pl 28. Lamb. B. 4. Ch. 7. S. 317. Cromp. 133. b. [q] Dalt. Ch. 134. 8 H. 4. 4. a. 5 b. Bro. Garrantie d'Attorney, 9. Bro. Record, 17, 64. Bro. Certiorari, 9. Dyer, 163. pl. 54. Rast. Ent. 438. a. b.

open

open Court; and that the Party indicted shall, before the Allowance thereof, become bound to the Prosecutor in 10 l. *with such sufficient Sureties as the Justices of Peace, at their Quarter-Sessions, shall think fit, with Condition to pay unto such Prosecutor within one Month after Conviction, such reasonable Costs and Damages as the said Justices of Peace of such Counties where such Indictments shall be found in the said Sessions of the Peace, shall assess or allow; and in Default thereof, it shall be lawful for the said Justices to proceed to Trial of such Indictments, any such Writs of* Certiorari *notwithstanding.*

Sect. 46. And the like Recognizance in the Sum of 40 *l.* is required by 13 & 14 *Car.* 2. 6. *Par.* 16. concerning the Highways, on the Removal of every Indictment, *&c.* on that Statute.

Sect. 47. It is observable, That these Statutes do not [a] extend to all Indictments at Sessions in general, but only to those particular Ones therein mentioned: But this Defect was in a great Measure [b] supplied by the Rules of the Court of King's Bench, which, upon the Removal of an Indictment from *London* or *Middlesex*, required a Recognizance from the Defendant to carry down the Record to Trial the same Term, on which the *Certiorari* was returnable, or the Sittings after; and on the Removal of an Indictment from other Counties [c] required such Recognizance for a Trial at the next Assises.

[a] 1 Keb. 225. pl. 38. 727. pl. 69.

[b] Vide 1 Keb. 33. pl. 88. 6 Mod. 246. 2 Salk. 526. pl. 3.

[c] Show. Rep. 336.

Sect. 48. And agreeably hereto, it is enacted by 5 & 6 *W.* & *M.* 11. and 8 & 9 *Guil.* 3. 33. *That all the Parties indicted at a General or Quarter-Sessions of the Peace, prosecuting a* Certiorari, *before the Allowance thereof, shall find two sufficient Manucaptors, who shall enter into a Recognizance in the Sum of* 20 l. *before one or more Justices of the Peace of the County or Place, (or* [d] *else before one of the Judges of the King's Bench, in which Case such Judge shall make mention of it under his Hand, on the Back of the Writ) and the Recognisance shall be with Condition, at the Return of such Writ, to appear and plead to the Indictment or Presentment in the Court of King's Bench, and at his own Costs to procure the Issue that shall be joined upon the said Indictment or Presentment, or any Plea relating thereto, to be tried at the next Assises for the County wherein the Indictment was found, after such* Certiorari *shall be returnable, if not in* London, Westminster, *or* Middlesex; *and if there, then to cause it to be tried the next Term after wherein such* Certiorari *shall be granted, or at the Sitting after the said Term, if the Court of King's Bench shall not appoint any other Time for the Trial thereof: And if any other Time shall be appointed by the Court, then at such other Time, and to give due Notice of such Trial to the Prosecutor, or his Clerk, in Court; and* [e] *also, That the Party or Parties, prosecuting such* Certiorari, *shall appear from Day to Day in the said Court of King's Bench, and not depart until he or they shall be discharged by the said Court: And such Recognizances,* Certiorari's, *and Indictments, shall be filed in the King's Bench, and the Name of the Prosecutor (if he be the Party grieved or injured) or some Publick Officer, endorsed on the Back of the Indictment; and if the Person prosecuting such* Certiorari, *being the Defendant, shall not, before Allowance thereof, procure such Manucaptors to be found as aforesaid, the Justices of Peace shall, and may proceed to Trial of the Indictment notwithstanding such* Certiorari.

[d] Viz. by Force of 8 & 9 Guil. 3. 33.

[e] Viz. by 8 & 9 Guil. 3. 33.

Sect. 49. And it is farther enacted by the said Statute of 5 & 6 *W.* & *M.* 11. *That if the Defendant prosecuting such* Certiorari, *be convicted, the King's Bench shall give reasonable Costs to the Prosecutor, if he be the Party grieved or injured, or be a Civil Officer who shall prosecute on Account of any Fact that concerned him as Officer to prosecute or present; which Costs shall be taxed according to the Course of the said Court; and the Prosecutor for the Recovery of such Costs, shall within ten Days after Demand made of the Defendant, and Refusal of Payment on Oath, have an Attachment granted against the Defendant by the said Court for such his Contempt; and the said Recognizance shall not be discharged till the Costs so taxed shall be paid.*

[a See the fifth Parag.]

Sect. 50. And the like in effect is [a] enacted by the said Statute of 5 & 6 *W.* & *M.* 11. concerning the Removal of Indictments by *Certiorari* within the Counties-Palatine of *Chester*, *Lancaster* and *Durham*.

In the Construction of these Statutes, the following Points seem most remarkable.

[b 1 Keb. 225, pl. 38. 231, pl. 51. 598, pl. 68. 903. pl. 1. 1 Sid. 70.]

Sect. 51. *First*, That notwithstanding by the express Words, Justices of Peace may proceed to Trial of the Indictments, notwithstanding the *Certiorari*, if a proper Recognizance be not given; yet they will be in Contempt to the Court that awarded the *Certiorari*, if they make no [b] Return to it; for all Writs must be obeyed unless good Cause be shewn to the contrary; and the proper way of shewing it is to return it.

[c 6 Mod. 246]

Sect. 52. *Secondly*, That it appears from the manifest Purport of these Statutes, That they extend only to *Certiorari's* procured by Persons indicted; from whence it follows, That those which are procured by the Prosecutor of an Indictment remain as they were at [c] Common Law.

[d 2 Salk. 564. pl. 3.]

Sect. 53. *Thirdly*, That [d] these Statutes, being in the Affirmative, as to the taking of Recognizances, do not take away the Power which the Justices of the King's Bench have by the Common Law of taking Recognizances upon their granting *Certiorari's*, from whence it follows, That if any such Justice, granting a *Certiorari*, shall take a Recognizance variant from that prescribed by the Act, either as to the Sum or Condition, *&c.* Such Recognizance will have the same Force as it would have had, if these Statutes had not been made; but it is said, That the *Certiorari*, if procured by the Defendant, will not in such Case be a *Supersedeas* to the Proceedings below, as it would have been at the Common Law; for the Statutes seem to be express, That the Sessions may proceed notwithstanding any *Certiorari* procured by a Defendant whereon such Recognizance is not given, as is expresly prescribed.

[e March, 27.]

Sect. 54. *Fourthly*, That if the Persons offering to be Sureties, appear to be worth 20 *l.* the Justices [e] cannot refuse them.

[f March, 27.]

[g 1 Keb. 231. pl. 51.]

Sect. 55. *Fifthly*, That if divers be indicted [f] in the same Indictment, and some of them find Sureties, and others not, the Indictment ought to be removed as to those who find Sureties (because they shall not be prejudiced by the Default of the others.) And, as [g] some say, It shall be removed as to the others also.

[Vide 6 Ed. 6. 5. a. March, 111.]

[h 1 Salk. 55. pl. 5.]

Sect. 56. *Sixthly*, [h] That the Master of the Crown-Office, in taxing the Costs, ought only to consider those which are subsequent to the *Certiorari*.

[i 1 Salk. 55. pl. 5.]

Sect. 57. *Seventhly*, That the Prosecutor, by accepting the Costs so taxed, is not restrained from aggravating the Fine to be set on the Defendant, because he has a Right to such Costs by the express Words of the Statute; and therefore the Defendant can claim no Indulgence from having paid them: But in other Cases, after a Prosecutor has accepted Costs from a Defendant, he cannot by the Rules of the Court, aggravate his Fine; because in such Cases, having no Right to demand Costs, if he take them at all, he must take them by way of Satisfaction of the Wrong, after which it is unreasonable in him to harrass the Defendant. And this I take to be a Common Practice; tho' in [i] *Salkeld's Reports* there seem to be a Note to the contrary.

Sect. 58. *Eighthly,* [a] That notwithstanding the Condition of the Recognizance seem to be express, That the Defendant shall procure a Trial at the next Assises, *&c.* yet it shall not be forfeited, unless the Prosecutor of the Indictment give Rules according to the Course of the Court.

[a] 1 Salk. 370 pl. 4.

Sect. 59. *Ninthly,* That after such [b] Recognizance is forfeited by the Defendant's not procuring a Trial according to the Purport of the Condition, the Court will not hear any Motion to quash the Indictment, or *Certiorari.*

[b] 1 Salk. 380. pl. 26. *Dominus Rex versus* Somers Mich. 6 Geo.

Sect. 60. It is enacted by 3 *&* 4 *W. &* *M.* 10. against Deer-stealers, *That no* Certiorari *shall be allowed to remove any Proceedings on that Act, unless the Party convict shall become bound, with good Sureties, in* 50l. *to pay full Costs and Damages within one Month after the Conviction shall be confirmed, or a* Procedendo *granted.*

Sect. 61. And the like in effect is enacted by 4 *&* 5 *W. &* *M.* 23. and 5 *Anna Sess.* 2. *Ch.* 14. in Relation to Convictions, on those Acts, of Offences concerning the Game.

Sect. 62. As to the eighth Point, *viz.* How far a *Certiorari* is a *Supersedeas* to the Court below: It is [c] agreed by all the Books, That after it is allowed by such Court, it makes all its subsequent Proceedings on the Record that is removed by it, erroneous. Also it seems to be generally [d] agreed, That a *Certiorari,* for the Removal of an Indictment of Forcible Entry found at a Sessions of the Peace, being delivered to any one Justice of Peace of the same Place, before the Statute of 21 *Jac.* 1. set forth more at Large *Sect.*45. which requires, That every such *Certiorari* shall be delivered at some Quarter-Sessions in open Court, did (by such Delivery without more) so far supersede the Power of the Sessions, that all its subsequent Proceedings thereon, and even an Execution of a prior Award on the same Indictment, would have been erroneous. And it seems to be generally [e] agreed, That any one such Justice, to whom such *Certiorari* should be delivered, might and ought thereupon immediately to have awarded a *Supersedeas* to the Sheriff in order to have stopped the Execution of any prior Award of such Court upon such Indictment.

[c] Cro. Ca. 261, 262. 1 Salk. 148, 149.

[d] Cro. El. 915, 916. 2 Keb. 306, pl. 5. Moor. 677. pl. 921. 1 Salk. 158. pl. 22.

[e] Cro. El 915, 916. Moore, 677. pl. 921. *This seems to be a Quære,* F. N. F. 237. Lett. E. Dalt. Ch. 134.

Sect. 63. It seems to be the better [f] Opinion, That a *Supersedeas* on such a *Certiorari,* being delivered to the Sheriff before he hath begun to put a Process in Execution, will make his subsequent Execution of it wholly void; because it is a ministerial Act, and not a judicial one. But if such *Supersedeas* be not delivered to the Sheriff till after he have in Part executed such Award, it [g] seems, That he may afterwards be authorised to go through with it by a Writ of *Venditioni exponas,* in the same Manner as he may in the like Case after a Writ of Error; but I [h] question, Whether he can lawfully proceed after such *Supersedeas* actually delivered to him, without the Writ of *Venditioni exponas?*

[f] Cro. El. 915, 916. Moore, 677. pl 921.

[g] Dy. 98. pl. 57. Yelv. 6. Cro. Eliz. 597 pl. 2. 1 Rol. Abr. 894. pl. 4. 2 Rol. Abr. 491. D. 5, 6. 3 Keb. 169. pl. 4. 174. pl. 9. 309. pl. 51.

[h] *See the Books next above-cited,* and Moor, 542. pl. 718. 1 Salk. 147, pl. 12.

Sect. 64. It seems to be the stronger Opinion, That a *Certiorari,* being once delivered, makes all subsequent Proceedings on the Record that ought to be removed by it, [i] erroneous, by Force of those Words, *Coram nobis terminari volumus, & non alibi,* whether such Proceedings are before or after its Return; and notwithstanding the Party who prosecuted it never make any other Suit to have the Record certified, but only by causing the *Certiorari* to be delivered. And in this Respect a *Certiorari* hath a stronger Force than a Writ of Error; for that becomes [k] of no Effect

[i] Yel. 4. Ch. 7. fol. 32. Dy. 245. pl. 63. 6 H. 7. 15. b. 16. a. Bro. Recordare, 8. Dalt. Ch. 134. Lamb. B. 4. Ch. 7. fol. 516 Cont. Crompt. 132. b. 133. a. [k] Dyer 245. pl. 63, 1 Keb. 14. pl. 35. 54. pl. 12. 107. pl 123. 118. pl. 25. 1 Sid. 268. pl. 20. 2 Rol. Abr. 491. pl. 7.

Moore 73. pl. 199. 1 Keb. 93 pl. 79. [b] Dy. 222, 223. Mo. 73. pl. 199 1 Inst. 128 b. [*] Cro. Jac. 282. pl. 2. Vide supra, Ch. 5. S. 7, 8, 9, 10. Cro. El. 152. pl. 29. 915, 916. Cro. Jac. 43. pl. 10. Yelv. 32, 57, 121. Cro. Ca. 79. 2 Jon. 209. [c] 1 Salk. 144. pl. 1. 150. pl. 17. [d] 1 Keb. 944. pl. 3. [e] Vide supra, Sect. 45 to 62. || 2 R. A. 492. Lett. F. pl. 12. Dalt. Ch. 75 [f] Cro. Jac. 282. Yelv. 207. 1 Bulst. 155, 156. [g] 16 Ed. 4. 5. pl. 3. Vide Bro. Discontinuance de Process, 52. [h] Raym. 186. 1 Vent. 66. 1 Salk. 144, 145. [i] *Agreed by the Court of King's Bench, in the Case of the King against* Whitlow, Hil. 6. Geo. [k] Lamb. B. 2. Ch. 2 107, 108 [l] Dalt. Ch. 73. and 134. [m] Cro. El. 821. pl. 17. [n] 1 Lev. 311. ||| 2 Salk 479. [o] 1 Rol. Ab. 752. pl. 27. 754. pl. 14. 2 Keb 385. pl. 56. † *Cited* 2 Keb. 385. pl. 56. [p] 1 Sid. 64. 1 Lev. 50.

if the Party who prosecuted it, neglect to get the Record certified in a reasonable Time. Also it seems to be holden in some [a] Books, That the very issuing of a *Certiorari* is of itself a *Supersedeas* to the inferior Court, whether the *Certiorari* be ever delivered or not: In the same Manner as an Appearance in the Court above, and a *Supersedeas* purchased there, will avoid [b] an Outlawry pronounced after, though such *Supersedeas* were not delivered to the Sheriff before the *quinto exactus*; but the Contrary hereto, in relation to a *Certiorari*, seems more agreable to the general Tenor of the * Books, and the Reason of the Thing. And it hath been [c] adjudged, That if a *Certiorari* for the Removal of an Indictment before Justices of Peace be not delivered, before the Jury be sworn for the Trial of it, the Justices may proceed. Also it hath been [d] holden, That a *Certiorari* is of no Effect, unless it be delivered before its Return is expired. And it is certain that by force of the Statute it cannot at this Time be any [e] *Supersedeas* to the Proceedings on an Indictment at Sessions, without a proper Recognizance, *&c.*

Sect. 65. It hath been || holden, That a *Certiorari* for the Removal of a Recognizance for the Good Behaviour, or for an Appearance at Sessions, will supersede its Obligation. But this would be highly inconvenient; and the contrary Opinion seems to be supported by the better [f] Authority.

Sect. 66. It [g] seems, That if an Indictment be removed by *Certiorari* after issue joined, and afterwards remanded, the Inferior Court shall proceed to Trial, in the same Manner as it would have done if no *Certiorari* had been granted.

Sect. 67. I shall take it for [h] granted, That inferior Courts proceeding after a *Certiorari* delivered, where by Law they ought not, are punishable for a Contempt; as hath been more fully shewn, *Chap.* 22. *Sect.* 28.

Sect. 68. Also it seems, That by the Common Law if a *Certiorari* be once filed, the Proceeding below can [i] never be revived by any *Procedendo*.

Sect. 69. As to the ninth Point, *viz.* In what Manner a *Certiorari* is to be returned: I shall refer the Reader to the Form in which it is to be done, to [k] *Lambard* and [l] *Dalton*, and shall farther take Notice only of these following Particulars;

Sect. 70. *First*, That every such Return ought to be under the Seal [m] of the inferior Court, or of the Justice, or Justices to whom it is directed; and if such Court have no proper Seal, it seems, [n] That the Return may be well made under any other.

Sect. 71. *Secondly*, That every such Return must be made by the very same Person to whom the *Certiorari* is directed; for if it be directed to the Justices of Peace of such a Place, and the ||| Clerk of the Peace only return it; or to the Constable, or to the Recorder of *B.* and the [o] Deputy Constable, or Deputy Recorder, return it, (without shewing in the Return that the Principal had Power to make a Deputy); or to the Steward of St. *Paul's*, and the Steward of the Church of St. †*Peter* and St. *Paul* return it, nothing is removed. Yet it is [p] certain, That if it be directed to the Justice of *Chester*, it may be returned by *A. B.* Chief Justice; for the same Officer is known to be meant, in the Writ and Return, and his Description in both is in Substance the same. Also it is [q] said, That if a Writ of Error be

2 Salk. 452. 1 Keb. 165. pl. 120. 187. pl. 168. [q] Yelv. 212. Cro. Jac. 254. 255. 1 Sid. 349. 1 Keb. 941. pl. 62. 2 Keb. 385 pl. 56 1 Rol. Abr. 753, 754.

directed to several Justices, and returned by Part of them only; yet if it [a] truly recite the Record, it so far removes it, that a new Writ of Error lies, *de recordo quod coram nobis residet, &c.* And [b] *Quære* how the Court shall proceed upon the like Mis-return of a *Certiorari?*

Sect. 72. *Thirdly*, That [c] regularly a Recognizance taken by a Justice of Peace, whether it still actually continue in the Hands of such Justice, or [d] have been sent by him to the Clerk of the Peace, ought to be certified on a *Certiorari* for the Removal of it by such Justice only, until it be made a Record of the Sessions, [e] after which it shall be certified in the same Manner as the other Records thereof shall be.

Sect. 73. *Fourthly*, That it is [f] adviseable, That a Return to a *Certiorari* directed to Justices of Peace, for the Removal of an Indictment taken before them, have the Clause *Necnon ad diversas Felonias, &c.* as well in the [g] Description of the Justices who make the Certificate, as of those before whom the Indictment is said to be taken in the Caption; which Matter hath been already considered, *Chap.* 8. *Sect.* 33. and *Chap.* 25. *Sect.* 123, 124, 125.

Sect. 74. *Fifthly*, [h] That the Person to whom a *Certiorari* is directed, may make what Return to it he pleases; and the Court will not stop the filing of it on Affidavits of its Falsity, except only where the Publick Good requires it, (as in the Case of the [i] Commissioners of Sewers) or for some other special Reason: But regularly the [k] only Remedy against such a False Return, is an Action on the Case at the Suit of the Party injured by it, and an Information, *&c.* at the Suit of the King.

Sect. 75. *Sixthly*, [l] That whatsoever Matters are put into the Return of a *Certiorari*, by way of Explanation or otherwise, besides those which are expressly ordered to be certified, are put in without any Warrant or Authority, and consequently shall be no more regarded by the Court above, than if they had been wholly omitted.

Sect. 76. *Seventhly*, That [m] generally the Return to a *Certiorari* ought to certify the Record itself, or the Tenour of it, or the [n] Tenour of the Tenour, [o] according as the Writ requires: And agreeably hereto it hath been [p] adjudged, That if on a *Certiorari* to return an Order of Justices of Peace, the Tenour of such Order be certified, the Return is naught; yet a Return of the Tenour of an Indictment from *London* on a *Certiorari* to remove the Indictment itself, is good by the City-Charter, as hath been already shewn, *Sect.* 26. Also, it [q] seems to have been generally holden, That where-ever the Purport of a *Certiorari* is not to proceed upon the Record to be removed, but only to try an Issue of *Nul tiel Record*, it is sufficient to certify the Tenour of the Record, whether the *Certiorari* require a Certificate of the Record itself, or of the Tenour of it only. However, I take it to be clear, That if the Court which awards such a *Certiorari*, have no Jurisdiction to proceed on the Record thereby ordered to be removed; as where the Court of [r] Common Pleas award a *Certiorari* for the Removal of an Indictment on the Issue of *Nul tiel Record*, concerning such Indictment, the Court below ought only to certify the Tenour of it, lest there should be a Failure of Justice.

Sect. 77. As to the tenth Point, *viz.* Where a Record is removed by a *Certiorari*: Having premised that nothing can be removed by it where it is improperly [s] directed, or [t] returned, for which I shall refer the Reader to the foregoing Parts of this Chapter; I shall in this Place observe only the following Particulars;

[a] Vide Yelv. 6, 7.
[b] 28 H. 6. 12. pl. 24.
[c] 1 Rol. Abr. 753 Lett. Q. 754.
[d] Vide F. N. B. 71. Letter d.
[e] 21 H. 7. 21. pl. 4. Cro Jac. 669. 2 H. 7. 1. pl. 2. Supra Sect. 43.
[f] Domina Reginæ versus Randal, Pasc. 13 Annæ.
[g] Vide supra Sect. 43.
[h] Register Origin, 90, 151, b. 283, b. 284, &c. F. N. B. 81. Letter c. 2 H. 7. pl. 2, Bro. Peace, 11. Dalt. Ch. 70. Crompton, 131, b. 132. a. Lamb. B. 4. Ch. 7. fol. 516, 517. Dalt. Ch. 134. 22 Ed. 4. 12, b. 13. a. 12 H. 7. 25. pl. 3. 2 R. 3. 9. pl. 20. Bro. Indictment, 32, 50. Cause a Remover Plea, 27. Vide 1 Keb. 263. pl. 48.
[i] 6 Mod. 90. Domina Reginæ versus Norton, Pasc. 11 Annæ.
[k] Supra Sect. 34.
[l] 6 Mod. 90. 2 Salk. 492, 493.
[m] Register Origin, 151, a. 169 a. b. F. N. B. 245. Letter B.
[n] F. N. B. 245. Lett. B. 3 Keb. 13. pl. 17.
[o] F. N. B. 245. Lett. B. Cromp. 131. b. Dalt. Ch. 134. Lamb. B. 4. Ch 7. f. 515.
[p] 1 Salk. 147 pl. 10. 2 Salk. 492, 493.
[q] 3 Hob. 135. Keb. 13. pl. 17. Dyer 187. pl 4. 1 Keb 107. pl. 127.
[r] 1 Rol. Ab. 394, pl. 2. 395 pl. 1, 2.
[s] Vide Supra Sect. 41 42, 43.
[t] Vide Supra Sect. 69, &c.

Sect.

Sect. 78. *First*,[e] That it seems to be settled at this Day, That as a Writ of [a] Error may remove a Judgment given; and a [b] *Recordare* may remove a Plaint entred, after its *Teste* and before its Return: So likewise a [c] *Certiorari* may remove a Record that shall come within its Description before the Time of its Return, tho' there were no such Record *in esse* at the Time of its *Teste*, [d] nor at the Time when it was first delivered to the Court below.

Sect. 79. *Secondly*, That as a *Recordare* will remove a Plaint that was [e] discontinued below, because the Court above will proceed only on the Plaint, and all the other Proceedings thereon below are to no Purpose; there seems to be the like Reason that a *Certiorari* also may remove an Indictment which was discontinued below.

Sect. 80. *Thirdly*, That as a Writ of Error can remove no Record which materially varies from the Description set forth in such Writ, so neither can a *Certiorari*, as in the following Instances;

Sect. 81. *First*, Where the Writ describes an Indictment or other Record, taken before *A. B.* and eight others, and that certified appears to have been taken before [f] *A. B.* and seven others only, or [g] before him and the other eight mentioned, and others also besides them; or where the Writ describes a Record, [h] *coram A. & B. & sociis suis*, and the Record certified appears to have been taken *coram C. D. & sociis suis*; or [i] where the Writ calls the Justices, before whom the Record is taken, *Justiciarios nostros*, and in the Record certified they appear to have taken it as Justices of a former King.

Sect. 82. *Secondly*, Where the Writ describes an Indictment for stealing [k] two Horses, and that certified is for stealing one Horse only.

Sect. 83. *Thirdly*, [l] Where the Writ describes an Order concerning Foreign Salt, and that certified is concerning Salt in general.

Sect. 84. *Fourthly*, [m] Where the Writ describes on Order concerning the Town of *Needham-Market*, or concerning the Manor of [n] *Ansly*, and an Order concerning the Town of *Needham*, or the Manor of *Anesly*, is returned, without shewing in the Return that they are both the same Town.

Sect. 85. *Fifthly*, Where the Writ mentions only [o] Orders against *A. B. & C.* or Indictments wherein *A. B. & C.* are indicted, and those certified are against *A.* only, or against *A. & B.* only. Yet [p] it is taken for granted in many Books, neither do I find it any where denied, That a *Certiorari* for the Removal of all Indictments against *A.* may remove one wherein the said *A.* is indicted, together with twenty others, so far as it concerns him; because in Judgment of Law it is a several Indictment as to every one of the Persons indicted. But I do not find it [q] agreed, Whether in such a Case the Indictment shall be removed so far as it concerns the other twenty?

Sect. 86. *Sixthly*, Where there is a [r] material Variance between the Writ, and the Record certified, in the Names or Additions of the Parties; as where the Writ gives the Defendant the Surname of [s] *Giggure*, and the Record certified that of *Giggeer*; or where the Writ commands the Removal of all Convictions against [t] *Henry*, Coachman, *quocunque no-*

[a] 1 R. 3. 4. pl. 8. Bro. Recordare, 9. 1 Mod. 112. 3 Keb. 308. pl. 51. Cont. Noy, 54. 1 Rol. Abr. 749. M. 1.
[b] 1 R. 3. 4. pl. 8. Bro. Recordare, 9.
[c] 1 R. 3. 4. pl. 8. Dy. 222. pl. 23. 1 Vent. 63. Bro. Recor. 9 1 Mod. 41. 1 Salk. 149. pl. 3. Lamb. B 4. Ch. 7. fol. 517. Crompt. 132. b. Dalt. Ch. 134. 1 Mod. 112. Yelv. 32. Cont. 1 Sid. 317. 2 Keb. 141. pl. 13. 142. pl. 15. Noy 54. 1 Rol. Abr. 749. M 1.
[d] 1 Rol. Abr. 395. B 1.
[e] 3 H. 6. 30. pl. 17. F. N. B. 71. Lett. A. Fitz. Recordare, 2.
[f] Cro. Jac. 254, 255. Yelv. 42. Plow. Com. 392.
[g] Vide Bro. Error, 13. 28 H. 6. 11. pl 24. 1 Keb. 129. pl. 51. 282. pl. 86. 102. pl. 106.
[h] 1 Sid 148. *Parallel Case*, 1 Rol. Abr. 753 pl. 14 1 Rol. Abr. 753. pl. 3.
[i] 1 Roll Abr. 754. pl. 7, 13. Dyer 105. pl. 6. Yelv. 212.
[k] 2 Ass. pl. 3. S. P. C. 70. Lett. C. Bro. Varriance, 62. Lamb. B. 4. Ch. 7. fol. 518. Bro. Coro. 69. Crompt. 132. b. 1 Bulst. 155.
[l] 1 Salk. 145. pl. 4.
[m] 2 Salk. 452. See Cro. El. 882. pl. 14.
[n] 12 Ass. pl. 2. Bro. Variance, 66.
[o] 1 Salk. 146. pl. 9. 151. pl. 21. Domina Regina, *v.* Hotspurt, Hill. 12 Annæ. Cont. 1 Rol. A 395. B. 2.
[p] 6 Ed. 4 5. pl. 13. Record Bro. 57. Lamb. B 4. Ch. 7 f. 517. Crompt. 132. a. Dalt. Ch. 134. March, 112.
[q] *Affirmed* 6 Ed. 4. 5. pl. 13. Record Bro. 57. Lamb. B. 4. Ch. 7. f. 517. Crompt. 132. a. Dalt. Ch. 134. *Denied*, March, 112. 1 Keb. 231. pl. 51.
[r] Vide 1 Rol. Abr. 754. pl. 5, 6.
[s] Salk 264. pl. 8.
[t] *Adjudged Mich. tertio Georgii.*

mine; censeatur, and those certified are against *Henry Manton*, Coachman; or where the Writ calls the Defendant *John* [a] *of Stiles*, and the Record *John Stiles*; or where the one calls him [b] Knight and Baronet, and the other Baronet only; or the one [c] *Garret Ma ines*, and the other *Gerrard Malines*; or the one *J. S.* [d] *nuper de B.* and the other *J. S. nuper de C.* or the one *J. S.* of *B.* [*] *Sadler*, and the other *J. S.* of *B. Salter*. Yet if the Variance be only in the Spelling, and the Words have the very same Sound either way, as [e] *Bird* and *Burd*, [f] *Shelbury* and *Shellery*, it seems that it will not be material; because it appears not by any Record of the Court, but that the Name in the *Certiorari* may be the true Name, and the Record certified describing one by a Name of the same Sound, shall be intended to mean the same Person. Also, if a *Certiorari* name the Party without any Addition, and the Record certified, name him with an Addition; yet it seems that it may be probably argued, that the Record may be well removed by such Writ, in the same Manner as it may be by a Writ of [g] Error, which has the like Variance. But if a Writ of Error describe a Person with an Addition, which is omitted in the Record certified, it hath been [h] lately adjudged contrary to the Opinion in Sir *Edward Coke*'s [i] Third Report to the contrary (which seems to be rather contradicted than supported by the [k] Authorities cited to maintain it) that it cannot remove the Record; and the Reason seems to be the same in Respect of a *Certiorari*.

Sect. 87. As to the eleventh Point, *viz.* What is to be done by the Court above, where the Record mentioned in a *Certiorari* is not removed by it: It is [m] said, That such Court cannot in such Case proceed upon the Record; because in Judgment of Law it still remains in the Court below, but will either [n] quash the Writ, and [o] award a new one, or suffer the Court below to proceed in the Cause, and take such [p] Order in Relation to the Defendant's Appearance either in the one Court, or the other, to answer the farther Prosecution of the Cause against him, as shall in Discretion appear to be most proper.

Sect. 88. And now I shall consider the sixth Particular, *viz.* What Process is to be awarded after the Removal of a Record by *Certiorari* into a superior Court: As to which I take it to be agreed, That, after such Removal, if the Defendant do not appear in the Court of King's Bench, the same [q] Kind of Process lies against him as if the Cause had been originally commenced there. Also I take it to be [r] agreed, That seeing by such Removal the Cause below is wholly put without Day, there is no Way to nonsuit the Plaintiff, before he hath appeared in the Court of King's Bench, but by taking out a *Scire facias* to warn him to prosecute his Appeal in that Court; whereupon if the Sheriff return a *Scire feci*, he shall be nonsuit. And if the Sheriff return a *Nihil*, a *Scire facias sicut alias* shall be awarded; whereon, if the Sheriff return a second *Nihil*, I do not find it [s] agreed what ought farther to be done.

Sect. 89. As to the seventh Particular, *viz.* Where the Process on an Appeal, Indictment, or Information shall be said to be discontinued, or miscontinued, or put without Day; having premised, that it seems

[a] 26 Ass. pl. 31.
[b] Cro. Ja. 633.
[c] Vide Cro. Ja. 477.
2 Rol. Abr. 329. pl. 17.
Such a Variance between a Protection and the Writ adjudged fatal.
[d] *Adjudged in a Writ of Error between* Ainsworth *and* Wilson, Hil. 5 Geo.
Par Case, 1 Sid. 193 pl. 123.
[*] Dy. 173. pl. 16.
1 Rol. Ab. 753. pl. 4.
[e] Cro. El. 172. pl. 14.
Cont. 25 Ed. 3. 43. pl. 3.
[f] Vide Cro. El. 172. pl. 14.
1 Rol. Abr. 797. Lett. H.
2 Rol. Ab. 329, pl. 14.
[g] 1 Sid. 193. pl. 23.
9 H. 6. 1. pl. 3.
Dyer 25. pl. 161.
[h] Shute *and* Car, *adjudged Hill. Tertio Georgii.*
9 H. 6. 1. pl. 13.
Bro. Variance. 6.
Vide Dy. 25. pl. 161.
Cont. 1 Sid. 104.
2 Rol. Abr. 328, 329.
[i] 3 Co. 2. a.
1 Rol. Abr. 752. a.
[k] 9 H. 6. 1.
7 Ass. pl. 5.
26 Ass. pl 31.
[m] 12 H. 7. 25. pl. 3. 2 R. 3. 9. pl. 20. 3 Ass. pl. 3. Vide 1 Sid. 193. pl 23. 2 Keb. 142. pl. 15. [n] 1 Keb. 102. pl. 106. 1 Salk. 147. pl. 10. [o] Vide 3 Ass. pl. 3. [p] Vide 12 H. 7. 25. pl. 3. 3 Ass pl. 3. 2 R. 3. 9. pl. 20. Bro. Indictment 50. Bro. Coro. 69. 2 Keb. 142. pl. 15. Lamb. B. 4. Ch. 7. f. 518. Supra, Ch. 25. Sect. 11. [q] S. P. C. 70. Lett. D. E. H. P. C. 211. [r] S. P. C. 70. Lett. D. H. P. C. 211. 48 Ed. 3. 22. pl. 2. 48 Ass. pl. 3. 1 Salk. 61, 62. 6 Mod. 246. Bro. Appeal, 15, 140. Fitz. Coro. 105. [s] Vide S. P. C. 70. Lett. D. E. 72. Lett. A. 48 Ed. 3. 22. pl. 2. 48 Ass. pl. 3. Bro. Appeal, 15, 140. Fitz. Coro. 105.

to be agreed, That every Suit, whether Civil or Criminal, and also every Process in such Suit against Jurors, ought to be properly continued from Day to Day, from its Commencement to its Conclusion, without any the least Gap or Chasm; and that the suffering any such Gap or Chasm, is properly [a] called a Discontinuance; and the continuing of the Suit by [b] improper Process, (as by a *Capias* instead of a *Distringas*) or by giving the Parties an [c] illegal Day, is properly called a Miscontinuance: I shall for the more distinct understanding of the Learning of this Kind, endeavour more particularly to shew;

First, In what particular Instances Process is generally said to be discontinued.

Secondly, Where to be miscontinued.

Thirdly, Where to be put without Day.

And first, Process is generally said to be discontinued in the following Instances,

Sect. 90. *First*, Where the second is not tested on the very same [d] Day on which the first is returnable; as where a *Venire facias* is returnable on the 23 of *January*, and the *Distringas* is tested on the 24th, or any other subsequent Day.

Sect. 91. *Secondly*, Where there is a Term intervening between the *Teste* and Return of a [e] *Capias*; for the Law will not suffer any such *Capias*, lest thereby the Defendant should be imprisoned an unreasonable Time; but an Original may be continued by any [f] other Process, except a *Capias*, tho' it have a Term or more intervening between its *Teste* and Return. [g] Neither is it any Objection to an Exigent, That it is not made returnable on the next Term after its *Teste*, because it must allow Time enough for five Counties to be holden between its *Teste* and Return.

Sect. 92. *Thirdly*, [h] Where, after Issue or Demurrer, the Court give the Parties a Day to a distant Term, without making any Continuance to that immediately following.

Sect. 93. *Fourthly*, Where the Term to which the Suit is continued is adjourned, and the Suit is [i] not adjourned accordingly.

Sect. 94. *Fifthly*, Where any of the Parties are described in any Continuance of the Suit, whether on the [k] Roll, or by [l] Process, by a Name or Addition variant from those in the Original, *&c.* tho' [m] only in one Letter.

Sect. 95. *Sixthly*, Where after Issue joined the Process is [n] not continued from Time to Time against the Jurors, returnable on the same Days to which the Suit is continued on the Roll against the Parties.

Sect. 96. *Seventhly*, Where [o] a joint *Venire* is first awarded for the Trial of all the Defendants together, and afterwards several *Venires* for the Trial of each of them.

Sect. 97. *Eighthly*, Where [p] a *Venire* omits Part of the Issue, or Issues to be tried.

[a] Fitz. Judgment 12. Finch of Law 431. Co. Litt. 325, a. Bro. Amend. 17. Fitz. Process, 124. 127. 1 H. 7. 2. b. 22 E. 3. 2. pl. 12. 22 E. 4 3. pl. 12. 12 H 4. 3. pl. 5.

[b] 21 H 7. 16. pl. 27. 8 H. 6 29. pl. 24 12 H. 4. 3. pl 5. 10 H. 7. 21. pl. 15. Keilw. 36 Finch of Law 431, 432. Co. Litt. 325. Bro. Discontinuance de Process, 11. 23, 50, 57, 61. 12 H. 4. 18. pl. 15. Cont. 40 E. 3. 16. pl. 5. Fitz. Amend. 12.

[c] Bro. Discontinuance de Process, 23. 21 H. 7. 16. pl. 27.

[d] 1 Bulst. 141, 142, 143. Yelv. 204, 205. Cro. Ja. 283, 284. 6 Mod. 281, 282, 283. 1 Salk 51.

[e] 8 Ed. 4. 13. pl. 10. Dy. 175, pl. 23. Cro. El. 467. *the first.* Fitz. Continuance, 3.

[f] 8 Ed. 4. 13. pl. 10. Dalis. 108. Dyer 175. pl. 23. *Quære* Bro. Discontinuance de Process, 23. 21 H. 7. 16 pl. 27. [g] Dalis. 108. 1 Rol. Abr. 484. pl. 1, 3. [h] Cro. Ja. 236. Yelv. 169. 21 H. 7. 16. pl. 27. 1 Rol. Abr. 584. pl. 8, 9, 10. Cont. 1 Bulst. 144. 3 Bulst. 233. [i] Vide 1 Danv. Abr. 243. 4 E 4. 40. Fitz. Discontinuance, 27. [k] Fitz. Discontinuance, 1. Bro. Amendm. 22. 4 H. 6. 6. pl. 17. 40 E. 3. 18. pl. 10. [l] Fitz. Amendm. 13, 17, 21, 27, 69, 77. Discontinuance, 7, 12, 17, 40, 42. Error, 15. Bro. Discontinuance de Process, 46. Amendm. 50. 38 E 3 22. b. 39 E. 3. 21. a. 40 E. 3. 31. pl. 9. 34. pl. 18. 8 H. 5. 2. pl. 9. 7 H. 6. 27. pl. 20. 9 H. 6. 39. a. [m] *Quære* 4 H. 6. 6. b. Bro. Amendm. 45. Fitz. Amendm. 21. [n] 21 Ed. 4. 20. pl. 27. Bro. Discontinuance de Process, 53. Continuance, 82. [o] *Quære*, 22 H. 6. 3. b. 4. a. Fitz Discontinuance, 11. Vide 7 H. 6. 27. pl. 19. [p] Fitz. Discontinuance 14, 35. 12 H 5. 3. pl. 16. Vide Bro. Discontinuance de Process, 63. *Quære* Cro. El. 622. pl. 14.

Sect. 98. *Ninthly,* † Where a *Venire* omits any of the Parties.

Sect. 99. *Tenthly,* Where a Juror is named in the *Habeas Corpora,* by a Name [a] different from that in the Panel returned on the *Venire*; or where a Juror returned on ſuch a Panel is wholly omitted in the *Habeas Corpora*; but in theſe Caſes, if the Juror ſo miſnamed, or * omitted, be not ſworn at the Trial of the Cauſe, it is [b] queſtionable, Whether there be any Diſcontinuance at all?

Sect, 100. *Eleventhly,* Where a *Venire* or *Diſtringas* are iſſued without any [c] Award on the Roll to warrant them.

Sect. 101. It [d] ſeems, That before the making of the Statutes of 11 *H.* 6. 6. and 1 *E.* 6. 7. all Pleas and Proceſſes before Juſtices of Aſſiſe, Gaol-Delivery, *Oyer* and *Terminer,* or *Peace,* or other the King's Commiſſioners, were diſcontinued by the making a new Commiſſion, or Aſſociation, or by altering the Names of the Juſtices or Commiſſioners; but this Miſchief is fully remedied by thoſe Statutes.

Sect. 102. If an [f] Indictment be removed by *Certiorari,* after Iſſue joined, and Proceſs awarded for the Trial; *Quære,* If it ſhall be diſcontinued, if not remanded before the Return of ſuch Proceſs?

Sect. 103. As to the ſecond Point, *viz.* Where Proceſs is generally ſaid to be miſcontinued: It ſeems, That where-ever an Error in Proceſs doth not amount to a Diſcontinuance, it is generally called a Miſcontinuance; and this ſeems agreeable to the proper Notion of the Word; for as a Cauſe may then properly be ſaid to be diſcontinued, when there is either nothing at all done to continue it, or nothing but what is as to this Purpoſe merely void in Law; ſo it ſeems to be properly ſaid to be miſcontinued, where it is continued amiſs, or by an [g] erroneous and not void Continuance. And agreeably hereto, the Books which ſpeak of Errors in Proceſs, ſeem generally to include them all, without [h] Exception, under the general Heads of Miſcontinuance and Diſcontinuance. And this, as I apprehend, was alſo the Opinion of the greater Part of the Court of King's Bench, in the late Caſe of [i] *Widdrington* and *Charleton.*

Sect. 104. As to the third Particular, *viz.* Where Proceſs ſhall be ſaid to be put without Day: It ſeems [k] agreed, That by the Common Law all Proceedings upon any Indictment, Information, or Popular Action, whereon no Judgment had been given, were wholly determined by the Demiſe of the King, and that nothing remained but the Indictment or Information, Original Writ, or Bill, which were put without Day till re-continued by Re-attachment to bring in the Defendants to plead *de novo.* But this is fully [l] provided for by 4 & 5 *W.* 3. 18. and 1 *Anne* 8. By which it is enacted, That ſuch Proceſs, &c. ſhall continue in the ſame Force after the King's Demiſe, as it would have had if he had lived.

Sect. 105. As for Appeals, [m] I do not find it any where ſaid, That the Pleas, and other Proceedings therein, being put without Day by the Demiſe of the King might not be revived by a ſpecial Re-attachment, in the ſame Manner as in any other Action: However it is certain at this Day, That by Force of 1 *Ed.* 6. 7. and 1 *Anne* 8. neither the Writ nor Bill, nor any Plea, nor Proceeding therein, ſhall be any way diſcontinued or put without Day by ſuch Demiſe.

† Fitz. Diſcontinuance, 10, 35. 1 Rol. Re. 22. pl. 30. 3 Bulſt. 311. Winch, 73. Br. Amendm. 50. 39 E. 3. 21. a. [a] Fitz Repleader, 4. Amendm. 26. 4 H 6. 7, 8. pl. 20. 19 H. 6. 39. a. 9 Ed. 4. 13. pl. 7. 27 H. 6. 5. pl. 33. Bro. Diſcontinuance, 47. Vide 1 Danv. Ab. 330, 331. 5 Co. 42. a. b. * Fitz. Amendm. 57. 37 H. 6. 12. a. b. Br. Amendm. 51. [b] 1 Sid. 66. 1 Keb. 182, 191, 198, 215. 6 Mod. 285. Fitz. Diſcontinuance, 4. *ſeems to make it no Diſcontinuance.* But 19 H. 6. 39. a. 34 H. 6. 20. pl. 39. 27 H. 6. 5. pl. 33. Fitz. Enqueſt, 18. 5 Co. 36. b. 37 a. Fitz Diſc. 37, 38. Br. Amendm. 10, 37, 92. *are to the contrary.* Vide Cro. E. 586 pl. 17. [c] Fitz. Error, 16. 7 H. 6. 28. [d] Vide ſupra, Ch. 5. Sect. 5, 6, 7, 8, 9, 10, 11, 12. Ra Ent. 77. pl. 2, 3. [f] Vide Bro. Diſcontinuance de Proceſs, 52. 15 Ed. 4, 5. pl. 3. Supra. Sect. 66. [g] Vide Finch of Law, 431. Sup. Sect. 89. 11 47, 50, 57. 21 H. 7. 16. pl. 27. 39 E. 3. 20. b. [h] 21 H. 7. 16. pl. 27. Bro. Diſcontinuance de Proceſs, 30, 31. Cro. Amendment, 17. Cro. Jac. 283, 284. 1 Bulſt. 142, 143. [i] Trin. 11 Annæ. [k] 7 Co. Jac. 14. Moore 748. [l] Vide Supra, Ch. 1. Sect. 12, 13. [m] Vide 7 Co. 30.

Sect. 106. It seems to be holden by [a] some, That all Causes, whether Civil or Criminal, are discontinued ; and by [b] others, who seem to speak more accurately, That they are put without Day, by the Justices before whom they were depending, not coming on the Day to which they are continued, whether such Absence were occasioed by [c] Death, or any other Cause. But it seems to be agreed by all, That a Cause so discontinued, or put without Day, cannot be revived without a Re-summons, or Re-attachment ; which if they are [d] Special, may revive the whole Proceedings ; but if general, the original Record only. Nor do I find that any Statute hath remedied this Mischief, except in the Case of Assises, and *Juris utrum*, which are provided for by 1 *E.* 6, 7.

Sect. 107. As to the eighth Particular, *viz.* How far Errors in Process are fatal : It seems to be generally taken [e] as an undoubted Principle, That a Discontinuance, by suffering a total Chasm in the Proceedings, whether on the Roll or in the Process, by not giving a fresh Continuance *instanter* upon the Determination of the precedent, shall never be aided by an Appearance and pleading over: And the Book [f] of 9 *H.* 5. 2. *pl.* 7. seems to have an Opinion, That the Misreturn of a Sheriff, as where he returns a *Cepi* on the Award of an Exigent, is not saved by the Defendant's pleading over ; but this is [g] questioned by *Staunsforde*, and seems contrary to the general Tenour of the other [h] Books, and contradicted both by [i] *Brook* and [k] *Fitzherbert*, in their Abridgment of this very Case. And in all probability the Book is misprinted ; for as it stands at present, it is hardly Sense, or reconcileable with [l] itself. But if a Defendant appearing on erroneous Process, expresly except to it before he have pleaded over, there have been many [m] Authorities, that he ought to be discharged, and that [n] new Process shall issue where the Defect first happened. But there is a greater [o] Number of Authorities to the contrary ; by which it appears, That if the Original be good, and the Defendant present in Court, he shall be compelled to answer it, let the Process whereon he came in, or the Execution of it, be never so erroneous, or defective, so that it never were discontinued ; for the End of Process is to compel an Appearance ; and that End being served, and a legal Charge appearing against the Defendant no way discontinued, the Law will not so far Regard a Slip in the Process, as to let the Defendant out of Court in order only to have him brought in again in better Form. And therfore where a Defendant hath excepted to the Process whereon he hath appeared, that he was [p] never served with it, or that [q] no such Process lies in the Case, or that it bore [r] *Teste* before the Original, or that

[a] Dy. 226, pl. 38. Keil. 2. pl. 3. Cro. E. 12. pl. 1. Bro. Discontinuance de Process, 29. 25 Ass. pl. 5. Vide 1 Co. 38.

[b] Co. Litt. 135. b. Finch of Law 432. 433. Ra. Ent. 77. pl. 1. Fitz. Discontinuance, 19 Re-attachment, 1, 17, 23, 24. 9 H. 6. 40 a. 24 E. 3. 23. pl. 17. 28 Ass pl. 42. 30 Ass pl. 39. Bro. Discontinuance de Process, 2.

[c] Vide Bro. Re-attachment, 18. 4 H. 7. 7. pl. 6. F. N. B. 111. d. 187, b 188. a.

[d] 7 Co. 29. b. Fitz. Re-attachment, 1.

[e] 1 Bulst. 143. Yelv 204. Cro. Ja. 283, 284. 8 H. 6. 29. pl. 24. 21 H. 6. 16. pl. 27. 12 H. 4. 17. pl. 15. 34 H. 6. 20. pl. 39. 18 H. 6. 15. a. b. Co. Litt. 325. a. Bro. Discontinuance de Process, 4, 11, 47. Amendment, 17. Fitz. Process 127. Discontinuance, 40. Amendment, 27. 38 E. 3. 22. b. 19 H. 6. 39. a *See* Bro. Error, 3. Repleader 2 and Disc. 1. *Where the contrary Opinion is said to have been holden ; but this seems not to be warranted by the Case at Large in the Year-Book.* [f] Vide Supra, Ch. 23. S. 141. [g] S. P. C. 169. b. [h] 5 Co. 45. a. Fitz. Coro. 444 Co. Litt 325. a. Salk. 59. pl 2. 1 Sid. 260. pl. 7. 1 Rol. Ab 779 Letter L. 780. Yelv. 158. Cro. El. 582. pl 6 Cro. Jac 311. pl. 10. *See the Books cited to the other Parts of this Section. In* 1 Rol. Ab. 380. pl. 6. *Notice is taken of three Resolutions that a* Capias *where it lies not, is not aided by an Appearance and pleading-over. and of a subsequent one contradicting them.* [i] Bro Restitution. 8. [k] Fitz. Coro 68. *But in another Part of his Book he abridges this Case, without taking any Exception to it.* Fitz Damage, 50. [l] *Also it is cited in* Yelv. 204. Cro. Jac. 284. 1 Bulst. 142. *for the Proof of the contrary Opinion.* [m] 40 E. 31 pl. 10. 47 Ed. 3. 14. pl. 16. 18 H. 6. 15. a. b. 3 H. 6 9, a. Fitz. Repleader, 1. Amendm. 14. Process. 154 Error, 82. Bro Discontinuance de Process, 50, 57 Default and Appearance, 11 1 Rol. Abr. 779. L. 3. 3 Mod. 265. *But the Year-Book of* 8 H. 6. 29 b. *from which the above-cited Authority in* Brook Discontinuance, 50. *is taken, seems rather to contradict than warrant it.* [n] 8 H. 6. 29 pl. 24. 12 H 6. 18 pl. 15. 18 H. 6. 15. b. 47 E. 3, 14. pl. 16. Bro. Discontinuance de Process, 11, 50, 57. Fitz. Process, 127. Discontinuance, 17. [o] 21 H 7. 16. pl. 27. Fitz. Error, 47. 46 E. 3. 30. pl. 28. Bro. Error, 28. Responder, 12. Faux Judgment, 4. 10 H. 7. 21. pl. 15. Yelv. 158. 1 Sid. 100. pl. 10. 260. pl. 7. *and see the other Books under-cited.* [p] Fitz. Discontinuance, 36. 9 H. 5. 3. pl. 8. 1 Rol. Ab. 779. L. 1, 2. 46 E. 3. 30. pl. 28. Bro. Faux Judgment, 4. [q] 10 H. 7. 21. pl. 15. 12 H. 4. 18. pl. 15. Bro. Error 109. Process 173. Jour. 36, 54. 21 H. 7. 16. pl. 27. 8 H. 6. 29. pl. 24. Fitz. Process, 127. [r] 1 Sid. 406. pl. 16.

it was not awarded into the * proper County, or that it was † not returnable at a proper Day, or that it was || directed to one who was no Officer, or that it had not so many Days as it ought ¶ between its *Teste* and Return, or for any [u] other such like Defect; yet he hath been compelled to answer the Original. And agreeably hereto it was lately [a] resolved, upon great Deliberation by the Court of King's Bench, against the Opinion of Mr. Justice *Powell*, That the Defendant in an Appeal of Death, coming in upon an Exigent, which was erroneous for want of the Words *de morte viri, &c.* had salved the Error by his Appearance, notwithstanding he had done all he could to take Advantage of it, by craving *Oyer* of the Process, and then demurring. And [b] *Note*, That in all the *Year-Books* above-cited to this Point, except ** one, it is said generally, That such Errors are salved by an Appearance, without any mention of any Amendment: But in that one it is said, That they shall be amended. Also it seems, That where-ever Process is awarded [c] *instanter* from Time to Time, without any the least Break or Chasm, and the Parties have [d] always a Day upon the Roll, all other Kinds of Errors whatsoever that come under the Name of Discontinuances, are [e] salved by an Appearance; for there are [f] Cases by which it appears, That Defendants appearing, and taking Exceptions to such Errors, have been compelled to answer to the Original, which they wou'd not have been if such Original had been taken to have been discontinued by such Errors, as they certainly are by an Error, in suffering a total Chasm in the Continuance. And if the Original be not discontinued by such Errors, Why should they not be as much salved by an Appearance, as any of the other Errors above-mentioned? For would it not be altogether as trifling in this, as in any other Case, to dismiss a Person only in order to send for him again? And in Criminal Cases this cou'd not but be of the utmost ill Consequence, by giving the Defendant, who is actually in the Power of the Court, an Opportunity of escaping.

Sect. 108. But it seems agreed by all the [g] Books, That any other Discontinuance in the Process against Jurors, shall have the same Effect as a Discontinuance in suffering a Chasm in the Process; but it seems, That no such [h] Discontinuance, whether in the Process or in the Roll, shall in any Case discontinue or abate the Original Suit; but if it appear before Trial, shall cause [i] new Process to be awarded where the first Fault happened; and if after Trial, a new [k] *Venire* to have the whole [l] Issue tried over again; because the first *Venire* was executed, and the whole Trial unwarranted. But [m] if Judgment be given on a Verdict by Jurors appearing on a Process any way erroneous, it will be totally erroneous; because the Trial was wholly unwarranted, and consequently the Issue mistried.

Sect. 109. Also, as I apprehend, any other Error in the Process against the Jurors, who actually try a Cause, will make a [n] Mistrial, as much as those which are called Discontinuances: as where such Process of this Kind is awarded which is not [o] proper in the Case, or where it is directed to a [p] wrong Officer, or has a [q] wrong Visne, or [r] misrecites the

* 38 E. 3. 20 b. 29 E. 3. 31. Fitz. Discontinuance, 39.
† 21 H. 7. 16. pl. 27. Cont. 40 E 3. 31. pl. 10. Fitz. Amendment, 14. Cro. El. 582. pl 6.
¶ Bro. Jour. 36, 54. Discontinuance, 23. Error, 169. Amendment, 60. Fitz. Jour. 37, 38. 12 E. 4. 21. pl. 1. 9 E. 4. 18. pl. 20. 2 H 7. 11. pl. 11.
[u] Fitz. Discontinuance, 51. 3 H. 4. 10. pl. 10.
[a] *Witherington versus Charlton.* Trin. 11 Anne. Vide 1 Salk. 59, 60.
[b] Vide 40 E. 3. 31. pl. 10. Fitz Amendment. 14. 59.
** 2 H. 7. 11. pl. 11.
[c] Vide 1. Bulst. 141, 142, 143. Yelv. 204, 205. 6 Mod. 281, 282, 283, 285, 286. 1 Salk. 51. Cro. Jac. 284.
[d] 1 Rol. Abr. 779 L. 3. 12 H. 4. 18. pl. 15. 21 H. 7. 16. pl. 27. 38 E. 3. 20. b. 12 H. 4. 3. pl. 5. Bro. Discontinuance de Process, 11. Fitz. Discontinuance, 39.
[e] Cro. Jac. 311. pl. 10.
[f] 38 E. 3. 22. b. Fitz. Discont. 40. 19 H. 6. 39. a. Amendment, 27. Bro. Repleader, 2. Discontinuance de Process, 1. Error, 3. 3 H. 6. 9. a.
[g] Fitz. Amendment, 26. Bro. Amendment, 10, 92. Discontinuance de Process, 4. 19 H. 6. 39. a. 27 H. 6. 5. pl. 33. 3 H. 6. 20. pl. 39.
[h] 30 Ass. pl. 36. Cont. Bro. Discontinuance, 47. *But his Note is not warranted by the Books at Large, which are* 27 H. 6. 5. pl. 33. and 34 H. 6. 20 pl. 39.
[i] 19 H. 6. 39. a 34 H. 6. 20. pl. 39. Fitz Amendment, 26, 57. Enquest. 18. 29 E. 3. 31. Bro. Amendm. 10. Discontinuance, 50. 30 Ass. pl. 36.
[k] 6 Mod. 286, 287. Fitz. Discontinuance, 24, 38. 22 H 6. 3. b. 4. a.
[l] 2 H. 5. 3. pl. 16. Fitz. Disc. 35. Vide 9 H. 4. 7. b. Bro. Enquest, 98.
[m] Faux Judgment, 12. Error, 16. 22 E. 3. 2. pl. 12. 7 H. 6. 28. 19 E. 3. 31. a.
[n] Vide 1 Danv. Abr. 334, 335, 352, 357, 455, 456.
[o] 7. H. 6. 28. Fitz. Error, 16.
[p] 1 Brow. 134. Cro. El. 574. pl. 15. 586. pl. 16. Moor 356. pl. 482. Yelv. 15. 5 Co. 36. b.
[q] Cro. El. 468. the first. Vide supra, Ch. 24. Sect. 92. 2 D. Abr. 455, 456. 21 Jac. Ch. 13. 16. and 17 Car. 2. 8.
[r] Cro. Jac. 89. pl. 15.

former Process, or is [a] misreturned, or [b] not returned at all, &c. For if Errors of this Kind have such Effect even in Civil Actions, where they are not within some of the Statutes of *Amendments* or *Jeofails*, as it seems to be admitted that they have, it plainly follows, That they must always have it in Criminal Proceedings, since [c] no such Proceedings are within the Benefit of any of those Statutes. But if an Error of this Kind, owing wholly to the Misprision of the Clerk, be discovered before Trial, and the Amendment of it will set the whole Matter right, perhaps it may be [d] amended by the Common Law. And it hath been [e] holden clearly, That even a Discontinuance of Process may be amended by Consent of the Parties.

Sect. 110. Howsoever an Error may be so far salved by the Party's Appearance, that he shall be as much compellable to answer the Original, as if there had been no such Error: Yet if he were subject to any Disadvantage in Respect of having such Process awarded against him; as to the Loss of his Goods upon an Exigent, or to the Forfeiture of the Privilege of Appearance by Attorney upon a *Pluries*, he [f] shall wholly avoid such Disadvantage when such Award, which should have caused it, appears to be any way erroneous, whether in Respect of a Discontinuance, or Miscontinuance, or otherwise.

Sect. 111. Also, for the like Reason, it seems to be [g] agreed, That if a Man be outlawed, or condemned by Default, for not appearing to Process, which is any way erroneous, he may take Advantage of the Error in Avoidance of such Outlawry, or other Condemnation; for no one shall be condemned barely for not appearing, where that which shou'd have compelled him to have appeared is defective. But it [h] seems, That a Defect in Process in an Outlawry, may be salved by the Defendant's purchasing a Pardon, and shewing it to the Court; for that supposes that there was such an Outlawry against him, as needed a Pardon, which, if it were erroneous, it would not do.

Sect. 112. How far a Discontinuance of one Appeal will be a bar to another, hath been already considered, *Chap.* 23. *Sect.* 130.

And now I am in the second Place particularly to consider the Nature of Process on a Criminal Accusation, with a particular Regard to Process of Outlawry only; and for the better understanding thereof, shall consider the following Points;

1. Whether Process of Outlawry lie in all Criminal Cases?
2. In what Manner it is to be awarded in general.
3. What is particularly required in the Award of it against the Principal and Accessory.

Sect. 113. As to the first Point, *viz.* Whether Process of Outlawry lie in all Criminal Cases: I take it to be certain, That it lies in all Appeals, [i] whether of Felony or Maihem, and in all Indictments of Treason or Felony, and on all [k] Returns of a Rescous; and also in all Indictments of [l] Trespass *Vi & Armis.* Also it seems probable, That it lies on an Indictment of [m] Conspiracy, or [n] Deceit, or any other Crime of a higher Nature than a Trespass with Force and Arms, but [o] not on any Indictment for a Crime of an inferior Nature.

[a] Cro. Jac. 467. pl. 14. 1 Danv. Ab. 357, 354, 355. [b] Vide 21 Ja. 13. 1 Danv. Ab. 340. pl. 2, 3. 341. pl. 4, 5. 8 Co. 163. a. [c] 6 Mod 283, 284, 285. 1 Salk. 51. [d] Long quint. E. 4. 140. Bro. Amend. 10, 17, 66, 92. Discontinuance de Process, 4. 47. Vide Fitz. Amendment, 59, 75. 29 E. 3. 32. [e] 21 H 7. 40. pl. 65. Fitz Amendment. 78. [f] 10 H. 7. 21. pl. 15. 12 H. 4. 18. pl. 15. 19 H. 6 29. a. 3 H 4. 10. pl. 10. S. P. C. 184. Letter D. Vide Bro. Att. 82, 84. Exigent, 20. H. P. C. 271. Fitz. Amendment, 27. Discontinuance, 40, 51. Error, 82. But 8 H. 5. 2. pl. 9. 43 E. 3. 17. b. 18 a. 34 pl. 47. Fitz Amendment, 77. Bro Appeal, 7. *seem contrary.* [g] 3 H 7. 8, b. 9. a. Fitz Replead. 1. Error, 47. Discontinuance de Process, 17. 1 Sid. 100. pl. 3. 260. pl. 7. Bro. Restitution, 8. Amendment, 60. 9 E. 4. 18. pl. 20.

[h] 3 H. 7. 10. pl. 10. Fitz. Charter, 25. Discontinuance 51. [i] Finch of Law, 346. Theloal digest of Writs, B. 1. ch. 15. pl. 1. 35 H. 6. 6. pl. 9. [k] 13 H. 7. 21. pl. 5. 2 Inst. 665. Cont. Fitz. Process, 56, 213. 29 E. 3. 18 a b. [l] 22 E. 4. 11. pl. 31. Finch of Law, 355. Bro. Exigent, 51. 35 H. 6. 6. pl. 9. [m] 8 H. 6. 9. pl. 21. Fitz. Pro. 89. Bro. Exigent, 25, 28, 46. S. P. C. 172. 22 H. 6. 7. pl. 11. [n] 35 H. 6, 6. pl. 9. [o] Vide 22 E. 4. 11. pl. 31 35 H. 6. 6. pl. 9. Cont. 8 H. 6. 9. pl. 21. Theloal B. 1. Ch. 15.

Sect. 114. It ſeems [a] agreed, That it lies not on any Action on a Statute, unleſs it be given by ſuch Statute, either expreſly, as in the Caſe of a [b] *Præmunire*, and many other Caſes; or impliedly, as where a Recovery is given by an Action wherein ſuch Proceſs lay before. And agreeably hereto it hath been adjudged, That it lies not in an Action on the Statutes of [c] Liveries, or of [d] Maintenance, nor in a [e] *decies tantum*, and that it lay not in a Writ of [f] Entry on 5 *Ric.* 2, 7. till it was given by 23 *H.* 8. 14. But that it lies on a Writ of Treſpaſs for a [g] Forcible Entry on 8 *H.* 6. 9. becauſe the Statute expreſly gives a Recovery by ſuch Writ, and ſuch Proceſs lies in it by the Common Law. It ſeems to be holden in the [h] *Year-Book* 8 *H.* 6. That it lies on all Indictments on Statutes; but the contrary is adjudged in [i] 22 *E.* 4. as to the Statutes againſt *Foreſtalling*; and it is there laid down as a general Rule, That it lies not on an Indictment any more than in an Action on a Statute, unleſs it be expreſly or impliedly given by ſuch Statute.

As to the ſecond Point, *viz.* In what Manner Proceſs of Outlawry is to be awarded in general: I ſhall obſerve the following Particulars;

Sect. 115. *Firſt*, That it ſeems to be agreed [k] That in every Indictment or Appeal, for any Crime under the Degree of Capital, there muſt be three *Capias's* to the Sheriff of the ſame County wherein the Proſecution is commenced, before the Exigent ſhall be awarded, unleſs it be after [l] Judgment; in which Caſe one *Capias* is ſufficient. And [m] *Quære*, If three *Capias's* be not ſtill neceſſary in an Appeal of Rape, as they were at the Common Law, notwithſtanding it be made [n] Felony by Statute?

Sect. 116. *Secondly*, That it ſeems to be [o] agreed, That one *Capias*, before the Award of the Exigent, hath always been ſufficient in an Indictment or Appeal of Death, or High Treaſon; but that it ſeems [p] doubtful, whether two *Capias's* were not required by the Common Law, in all Indictments and Appeals of any other Felony. However it is certain, That they are required in all Indictments of any other Felony, by 25 *E.* 3. 14. by which it is accorded, *That if after any Man be indicted of Felony, before the Juſtices in their Seſſions, to hear and determine, it ſhall be commanded to the Sheriff, to attach his Body by Writ or by Precept, which is called a* Capias; *and if the Sheriff return that the Body is not found, another ſhall be incontinently made, returnable at three Weeks after, wherein it ſhall be compriſed, that the Sheriff ſhall cauſe to be ſeiſed his Chattels, and ſafely to keep them till the Day of the Writ or Precept returned. And if the Sheriff return, That the Body is not found, and the Indictee cometh not, the Exigent ſhall be awarded, and the Chattels ſhall be forfeit, as the Law of the Crown ordaineth. But if he come and yield himſelf, or be taken by the Sheriff, or by other Miniſter, before the Return of the ſecond* Capias, *then the Goods and Chattels ſhall be ſaved.* It ſeems to have been the general [q] Opinion, That this Statute extends to Appeals as well as Indictments, tho' it mention only the later; but that it extends not to any Indictment or Appeal of Death, tho' it ſpeak of Felony in general.

Sect. 117. *Thirdly*, [r] That after the Sheriff hath returned a *Cepi*, if he have not the Body at the Day, the Court will not award an Exigent on the Suggeſtion of an Eſcape, unleſs the Sheriff will return one.

[a] 22 E. 4. 11. b. 8 H. 6. 9 pl. 21. Fitz. Proceſs 81. Bro. Proceſs. 57. Exigent, 25. [b] Fitz. Proceſs, 106. 9 E. 4. 2. pl. 8. *See the Statute againſt Provijors*, 27 E. 3. [c] 8 H. 6. 9 pl. 21. [d] 22 E. 4. Cont. Fitz. Proceſs, 89. 22 H. 6. 7. pl. 11. *Quære* Bro. Exigent, 28. [e] 8 H. 6. 9 pl. 21. 35 H. 6. 6. pl. 9. Bro. Proceſs, 145. [f] 35 H. 6. 6. pl. 9 Fitz. Proceſs, 101. Bro. Proceſs, 16. [g] Bro. Exigent 35. 37. H. 6. 23. pl. 11. [h] 8 H. 6. 9. pl. 21. Fitz. Proceſs, 81. [i] 22 E. 4. 11. b. Bro. Exigent, 51. Vide 35 H. 6. 6. pl. 9. 37 H. 6 23. pl. 11. [k] Finch of Law, 351, 355. Raſt. Entr. 188, pl. 18. 302, pl. 1, 2, 3. 26 E. 3. 72. pl. 13. Fitz. Exigent 30. Utlagary 17. Error 82. Vide 3 H. 6. 9. a. 3 H. 4. 11. pl. 10. [l] 40 E. 3. 25. pl. 28. Exigent 7. 27. Finch 476. [m] 1 Vide 16 Aſſ. pl. 13. Fitz. Exigent 10. Coro. 173. Bro. Proceſs, 148. Exigent, 67. [n] Vide ſupra, Ch. 23. Sect. 59, to 70. [o] S. P. C. 67. a. H. P. C. 209. Fitz. Coro. 234. 1 H. 5. 5. pl. 8. Finch 351. [p] Fitz. Coro. 184. 234. 22 Aſſ. pl. 97. Cont. 8 H. 5, 6. pl. 25. Fitz. Exigent, 3. [q] S. P. C. 67. H. P. C. 209. Vide Fitz. Exigent, 3, 28, 30. Proceſs 226. 8 H. 5. 6. pl. 25. 1 H. 5. 6. pl. 8. [r] S. P. C. 70. Lat. G. Fitz. Exigent, 25. 30. Aſſ. pl. 23.

Sect.

Sect. 118. *Fourthly*, That if there be several Appellees, some of which appear, and others make Default, and those who appear plead a Plea in Abatement of the Writ, or any such Plea in Bar as goes to the Whole, the Suit [a] shall be continued against those who made Default by *Capias* only, and no Exigent shall issue till such Plea or Pleas shall be determined.

Sect. 119 *Fifthly*, That an Exigent shall [b] never be awarded to the Sheriff of any other County than that wherein the Offence is laid; and that by the [c] Common Law there was no [d] necessity of a *Capias* to the Sheriff of any other County. But the Law relating to this Matter, having been altered by several Statutes, I shall set forth those Statutes in particular, and endeavour to shew how they are to be understood.

Sect. 120. And first it is enacted by 6 *H.* 6. 1. *That before any Exigent be awarded against Persons indicted in the King's Bench, of Treason or Felony, Writs of* Capias *shall be directed as well to the Sheriff or Sheriffs of the County wherein they be indicted, as to the Sheriff or Sheriffs of the County whereof they be named in the Indictments, the same* Capias *having the Space of six Weeks at the least, or longer Time, by the Discretion of the said Justices, if the Case require it, before the Return of the same; which Writs so returned, the Justices shall proceed in the Manner as they had done before the Statute: And if any Exigent be awarded or any Outlawry pronounced against such Persons before the Return of the said Writs, the same Exigent, so awarded, with the Outlawry thereof pronounced, shall be void, and holden for none.*

Sect. 121. And it is farther enacted, by 8 *H.* 6. 10. *That upon every Indictment or Appeal, by the which any Subject dwelling in other Counties than where such Indictment or Appeal shall be taken, of Treason, Felony, and Trespass, before the Justices of Peace, or before any other, having Power to take such Indictments or Appeals, or other Commissioners or Justices, in any County, Franchise or Liberty, of* England, *before any Exigent awarded, presently after the first Writ of* Capias *returned, another Writ of* Capias *shall be awarded, directed to the Sheriff of the County whereof he, who is so indicted, is or was supposed to be conversant by the same Indictment, returnable before the same Justices, before whom he is indicted, or appealed, at a certain Day, containing the Space of three Months, from the Date of the said last Writ, where the Counties be holden from Month to Month; and where the Counties be holden from six Weeks to six Weeks, the Space of four Months, until the Day of the Return of the said Writ; by which Writ of second* Capias, *the Sheriff shall be commanded to take him which is so indicted or appealed, by his Body, if he can be found within his Bailiwick: And if he cannot be found within his Bailiwick, to make Proclamation in two Counties before the Return of the same Writ, that he which is so indicted or appealed, shall appear before the said Justices,* &c. *at the Day contained in the said Writ, to answer,* &c. *After which Writ so served and returned, if he which is so indicted or appealed, come not at the Day of such Writ returned, the Exigent shall be awarded. And that every Exigent and Outlawry otherwise awarded, or pronounced, shall be holden for none, and void.*

Sect. 122. But it is expresly provided, *That the above-recited Statute, concerning Process to be made before the King in his Bench, stand in force. And that this present Statute shall not extend to Indictments or Appeals taken within the County of* Chester. *And that if any Persons shall be indicted or appealed of Felony or Treason, and at the Time of the same Felony or Treason supposed, was conversant within the County, whereof the Indictment or Appeal makes mention, the like Process be made against them as was used before.*

[a] H.P.C. 210. S.P.C. 70. Lett. B.

[b] Fitz. Exigent, 26. Default 10, 97. 22 E. 3. 11, pl. 4. 30 H. 6. 2. pl. 7. 11 H. 4. 72. pl. 6.

[c] Fitz. Process, 4. 34. See the Preamble of 6 H. 6. 1. and 8 H. 6. 10.

[d] Vide Fitz. Process, 1, 3, 34, 155, 164. 22 E 3. 11. pl. 4. 47 Ed. 3. 4. pl. 7. Dyer 295 pl. 18. 30 H. 6. 2. pl. 7. 11 H. 4. 72. pl. 6.

4

Sect.

Sect. 123. And it is farther enacted by 10 *H.* 6. 6. *That such second* Capias, *as is required by* 8 H. 6. 10. *shall be awarded upon Indictments or Appeals, removed into the King's Bench, or elsewhere, by* Certiorari *or otherwise.*

Sect. 124. It is observable that it seems to be holden generally in many [a] Books, That every Outlawry whatever, on an Indictment or Appeal against a Person living in a County different from that wherein th Court sits, is erroneous, if no such *Capias*, with a Command to the Sheriff to make Proclamation, as is given by 8 *H.* 6. were awarded to the Sheriff of the County wherein the Party is supposed to be conversant before the Award of the Exigent: And there are [b] Precedents wherein Outlawries in Appeals, originally commenced in the King's Bench, have been reversed for want of such a *Capias.* Yet it seems, That on the other Side it may be probably argued, That Indictments of Treason or Felony, originally commenced in the King's Bench, are expresly provided for by the [c] Statute of 6 *H.* 6. which requires, That a *Capias*, having the Space of six Weeks or more, shall be awarded to the Sheriff of the County whereof the Indictee shall be named; and this Statute is taken Notice of by that of 8 *H.* 6. which expresly enacts, That it shall stand in its full Force, and therefore cannot well be imagined to intend either to supersede or repeal it. Especially, considering that it begins with Justices of Peace, and makes no express mention of the King's Bench; And it is a [d] general Rule, in the Construction of Statutes, That where Things of an inferior Degree are first mentioned, those of a higher Dignity shall not be included under subsequent general Words. Also it appears from the Preamble of 10 *H* 6. 6. That neither Indictments nor Appeals, removed into the King's Bench by *Certiorari*, were within the Benefit of 8 *H.* 6. 10. before the making of that Statute, which expresly provides for Indictments and Appeals so removed; and there seems at least as good Reason, that Indictments and Appeals, originally commenced in the King's Bench, shall not be taken to be within the Benefit of it. To which may be added, That it seems to have been admitted in the *Year-Book* of [e] 31 *H.* 6. that an Appeal, originally commenced in the King's Bench, is within the Equity of 6 *H.* 6. 1. and that an Outlawry thereon is erroneous, if there were no *Capias* containing the Space of six Weeks, directed to the Sheriff of the County whereof the Appellee is named, as that Statute requires; by which it seems to be implied, That such an Appeal is not within the 8 but 6 *H.* 6. and that the same is still in force.

[a] 1 E. 4. 1. pl. 3. 19 H. 6. 2. pl. 2. S. P. C. 67, 68, 69. H P. C. 209. Fitz. Process, 103. 39 H. 6. 1. pl. 2.
[b] Ra. Entr. 304, pl 2. 3. Vide 19 H. 6. 2. pl. 2. Fitz. Error, 26. Ra. Ent. 58. pl. 1, 2.
[c] Vide supra, Sect. 120.
[d] 2 Co. 46. b.
[e] 31 H. 6. 11: pl. 8.

Sect. 125. It seems to have been [f] agreed, That by Force of these Statutes, a *Capias* shall be awarded into a County-Palatine, where the Defendant is named of any Place in such County, in any Indictment or Appeal; and it seems, That such *Capias* shall be directed to, and returned by the [g] Chancellor of such County; and it hath been [h] said, That if he will not return it, the Exigent may be awarded as well as if he had returned it; because the Court cannot compel him to return it, and the Prosecution might be unreasonably delayed, if the Proceedings were to be stayed till he should return it. But [i] *Staundeforde* makes a *Quære*, Whether the Court of King's Bench may not enforce a Return of the Writ?

[f] S P. C 68. Letter D. H. P. C. 209, 210. 19 H. 6. 2. 31 H 6. 11: pl 11. Fitz Cor. 19. Bro. Cinque-Ports, 22. Sed vide 1 H. 6. 10.
[i] Ra. Entr. 52. pl. 1, 2. 19 H 6. 2. 31 H. 6. 11. Cont. S. P. C. 68. Letter, D. Fitz. Process, 197

Sect. 126. If a Defendant be expresly named of the same County wherein he is indicted or appealed, and be also named under an *alias dictus* of another, it hath been [k] adjudged, That there is no need of any *Capias*, with

[g] Bro. Cinque-Port, 22 [h] 31 H 6. 11. pl 8. [i] S. P. C. 69. a. Vide Cro. Ca. 252, 253. [k] 4 E. 4. 1. pl. 3. Fitz. Process, 103. Dyer 214. pl. 44. Bro. Proclamation, 5. S. P. C. 68. b.

with a Command for Proclamation, according to 8 *H.* 6. because that which comes under the *alias dictus* is [a] no way traversable nor material. Also if a Defendant be named of *B.* and late of C. there is [b] no need of any *Capias* to the Sheriff of the County wherein C. lies, because it appears that the Defendant is at present conversant at *B.* But if a Defendant be named of no certain Place at present, but only late of B, and late of C, and late of *D. &c.* being all of them in Counties different from that wherein the Prosecution is commenced, a *Capias* shall go the Sheriff of [c] every one of those Counties.

[a] Supra Ch. 25 Sect. 72. [b] S. P. C. 68. Lett. B. Fitz. Process, 192. Crompton, 152. [c] H. P. C. 210.

Sect. 127. Notwithstanding the Words are express, That any Outlawry pronounced contrary to the Directions of the Statutes, shall be void: Yet it seems to be agreed, [d] That it is not to be taken to be utterly void, but only voidable by Writ of Error.

[d] 39 H. 6. 1. pl. 2. Bro Utlagary 34. Error, 16. 19 H. 6. 2. pl. 2. Fitz Error, 26. Cro. El. 179. pl. 10. 3 Co. 59. b. Plow. Com. 137. b.

Sect. 128. As to the third Point, *viz.* What is particularly required in the Award of Process of Outlawry against the Principal and Accessary, it is recited by the Statute of *Westminster*, 1. 14. *That it had been used in some Counties to outlaw Persons being appealed of Commandment, Force, Aid or Receipt, within the same Time that he which is appealed for the Deed is outlawed: And thereupon it is provided, That none be outlawed upon Appeal of Commandment, Force, Aid or Receipt, unless he that is appealed of the Deed be attainted: So that one like Law be used therein thro' the Realm; nevertheless, he that will so appeal, shall not, by Reason of this, intermit or leave off to commence his Appeal at the next County against them, no more than against their Principals, which be appealed of the Deed, but their Exigent shall remain, until such as be appealed of the Deed be attainted by Outlawry or otherwise.*

In the Construction of this Statute, the following Particulars seem most remarkable;

Sect. 129. *First*, That it seems to be [e] agreed, That it extends as well to Indictments as to Appeals, not only because the Word [f] Appeal in the Statute may, in a large Sense, be taken for any Accusation in general; but because Indictments are certainly as much within the Reason of the Statute, as Appeals; and the Common Law, for the [g] Settling whereof this Statute was made, did [h] not make any Distinction in this Respect between Appeals and Indictments.

[e] H. P. C. 210. 2 Inst. 183. S. P. C. 46, 69 Lett. A. [f] 9 Co. 119 a. [g] S. P. C. 44. Lett. G. 46. Lett. A. 69. Lett. B. [h] Bract. f. 127. b. 128. a. See Britt. f. 5. 2 Inst. 183.

Sect. 130. *Secondly*, That it seems also to be [i] agreed, That whereever some of the Defendants are expresly charged as Principals, and others as Accessories, before the Award of the Exigent, the Outlawry thereon of those charged as Accessories, cannot but be reversible; because it appears upon the Record, That the Exigent issued contrary to the Directions of the Statute. But if several be outlawed on a Writ of Appeal, which [k] chargeth them all alike, without any Distinction, I see [l] not how any Advantage can be taken of the Appellant's not having pursued the Statute, since it appears not but that he might have charged them all as Principals.

[i] 43 E. 3. 17. b. 18. a. 34. pl. 47. 44 Ass. pl. 16. Ra. Entr. 48. b. [k] Vide H. P. C. 210. 2 Inst. 183. S. P. C. 46. Lett. B. 70. Lett. A. 148. Lett. A. [l] Vide 43 E. 3. 17. b. 18. a. 34. pl. 47. 44 Ass. pl. 16. Bro. Appeal, 7. 79. Bro. Exigent, 44. Fitz. Forfeiture, 14.

Sect. 131. *Thirdly*, That it is holden both by [m] *Staundforde*, [n] *Coke*, and [o] *Hale*, That if an Appellant take out the Exigent at the same Time against all the Defendants he must when they appear, count against them all as Principals, and shall be concluded to count against some as

[m] S. P. C. 46. Lett. B. 70. Lett. A. [n] 2 Inst. 183. [o] H. P. C. 210. *The Principal Authorities in the Old Books for the Maintenance of this Opinion seem to be* 7 H. 4. 27. Fitz. Coro. 80. 20 E. 3. 7. b.

Principals, and others as Acceſſories, becauſe he has taken out ſuch Proceſs againſt them which is erroneous, where all are not Principals. But granting that an Exigent taken out at the ſame Time againſt all the Defendants, appear to have been erroneous, when by the Declaration it appears that ſome of the Defendants are accuſed only as Acceſſories, and therefore ought not to have had an Exigent awarded againſt them, till the Principal had been attainted. Yet ſeeing this is only an Error in the Proceſs to bring in the Defendant, and all ſuch Errors are ſalved by an Appearance, as the Law ſeems to be now ſettled, and hath been more fully ſhewn *Sections* 107, *&c.* It ſeems[a] queſtionable at this Day, Whether an Appellant may not be at liberty to declare as he pleaſes againſt Defendants appearing on ſuch an Exigent? However it is certainly ſafeſt, [b] and moſt adviſeable for an Appellant when he comes to the Exigent to ſhew which of the Defendants he intends to charge as Principals, and which of them as Acceſſories, and to take out the Exigent againſt the former only, and a *Capias* againſt the others.

Sect. 132. *Fourthly*, That it ſeems the better [c] Opinion, That where there are more than one Principal, the Exigent ought not to iſſue till all of them are attainted.

[a] See 40 Aſſ. pl. 25. *where it appears that Perſons appealled as Acceſſories, and brought in by an Exigent, were ſtill proceeded againſt as Acceſſories. See alſo* 43 E. 3. 17. b. 18. a. 35. pl. 47. 44 Aſſ pl. 16. Bro. Appeal, 7. Exigent, 44. Fitz. Forfeiture, 14.

[b] Bro. Appeal 107. 20 E. 3. 7. b.

[c] 2 Inſt. 183. Plowd. Com. 29 a. dubitatur 7 H. 4. 36. pl. 5. Bro. Appeal, 22. Contr. Fitz Exigent, 4.

CHAP. XXVIII.

Of Arraignment in general.

HAving ſhewn in what Manner a Perſon under a Criminal Accuſation is to be brought into Court; I ſhall in the next Place endeavour to ſhew in what Manner he is to be arraigned or put upon his Trial; and this I ſhall conſider,

Firſt, As it relates to all Criminals in general.
Secondly, As it relates to Principal and Acceſſories in particular.

And firſt, As to the Arraignment of all Criminals in general: Having already ſhewn in the Twenty-fifth [d] Chapter, That regularly the Court will not arraign a Man upon an Indictment while an Appeal for the ſame Crime is depending againſt him; I ſhall here conſider only the following Particulars;

[d] Sect. 15.

Firſt, In what Manner a Criminal is to be arraigned.
Secondly, Whether the Omiſſion of it will be Error.
Thirdly, Where a Perſon ſhall be arraigned upon ſeveral Appeals or Indictments.

As to the first Particular, *viz.* In what Manner a Criminal is to be arraigned, I shall observe,

Sect. 1. *First*, That every Person, at the Time of his Arraignment, ought to be used with all the [a] Humanity and Gentleness which is consistent with the Nature of the Thing, and under no other Terror or Uneasiness than what proceeds from a Sense of his Guilt, and the Misfortune of his present Circumstances; and therefore ought not to be brought to the Bar in a contumelious Manner; as with his [b] Hands tied together, or any other Mark of Ignominy and Reproach; nor even with Fetters on [c] his Feet, unless there be some Danger of a Rescous or Escape. It seems indeed to have been holden by [d] some, That this is a particular Privilege of Persons in Holy Orders. But it seems the [e] better Opinion, That the Law makes no Distinction in this Respect, between them and Laymen.

Sect. 2. *Secondly*, That there is no necessity that a Prisoner at the Time of his Arraignment hold up his Hand at the Bar, or be commanded so to do; for this is [f] only a Ceremony for making known the Person of the Offender to the Court; and if he answer that he is the same Person, it is all one.

Sect. 3. *Thirdly*, That on every Indictment the Arraignment must be in *English*, by Vertue of 37 *E.* 3. 15. by which it is enacted, *That all Pleas which shall be pleaded in any Courts whatsoever, before any of the King's Justices whatsoever, or in his other Places, or before any of his other Ministers whatsoever, or in the Courts and Places of any other Lords whatsoever within the Realm, shall be pleaded, shewed, defended, answered, debated, and judged in the* English *Tongue, and entred and inrolled in* Latin. But it seems to have been always taken, That Appeals are not within this Statute, but that they are to be arraigned, and the Plea of the Defendant to be read, in [g] *French*, in the same Manner as antiently; and thus I have often known it done in my own [h] Experience; but upon what Reason this Difference between Appeals and all other Prosecutions is grounded, I have never heard.

Sect. 4. *Fourthly*, [i] That an Appeal in the King's Bench ought to be arraigned on the Plea side, unless it come in by *Certiorari*, in which Case it is said, That it ought to be arraigned on the Crown-side.

Sect. 5. *Fifthly*, That where a Writ of Appeal is abated, the Prisoner shall not [k] be arraigned on the Count, at the Suit of the Party, because the Count depends upon the Writ, and that being determined, all [l] falls to the Ground. Yet it seems certain, That if the Writ were good, the Appellee may in many Cases be arraigned at the Suit of the King upon the Count, as hath been more fully shewn, *Ch.* 23. *Sect.* 7, 8, 9, 10, 11, 12, 13.

Sect. 6. As to the second Particular, *viz.* Whether the Omission of an Arraignment will be Error: It is said in the Third [m] *Modern Report* That an Attainder of High Treason was reversed for this and other Errors. Neither do I find any Precedent of an Attainder in *Coke's Entries*, on an

[a] 3 Inst. 34, 35. 2 Inst. 315, 316.

[b] Bracton, 137. pl. 3. Briton. 14, 17. Fleta Lib. 1. cap 31.

[c] Bracton, 137 pl. 3. 3 Inst. 34, 35. H P C. 212. Kely. 10.

[d] Fitz Coro. 432. S. P. C. 133 Lett. H.

[e] 3 Inst. 34, 35. H. P C. 212. 2 Inst. 315. Briton, 14, 17. Bracton, 137 pl 3. S. P. C 133. Letters F. G Kely. 10.

[f] *Agreed by all the Judges in the Lord* Stafford's *Case*. Raym. 408.

[g] 1 Sid. 324. pl. 4. 2 Jon. 210. Cro. El. 69. pl. 22. 1 Salk. 61.

[h] *As in the Case of* Smith *and* Bowen, *Mich.* 7 *Anne And that of* Widderington *and* Charlton. *Trin.* 11 *Anne. And that of* Reeve *and* Trundal, *Pasche* 3 *Geo.*

[i] 2 Jon. 210. 1 Sid. 324 pl. 4. 1 Salk. 62.

[k] Style's Rep. 7.

[l] Bro. App. 44. 4 H. 6. 16. Vide supra, Ch. 23. Sect. 10.

[m] 3 Mod. 265. Vide Raym. 408.

Indictment of [n] Treason or [*] Felony, in which it is not expressed either in these Words, *Ad barram hic dictus in propria persona sua committitur mareschallo, &c. & statim de præmissis* (in Case of Felony, or *de altis proditionibus*, in Case of High Treason) *ei superius impositis allocutus qualiter se velit inde acquietare dicit, &c.* or in Words [a] tantamount. And therefore it is certainly safest to express it in every Record of such Attainder, where the Party appears and is condemned, whether upon Confession or Verdict, or standing Mute, *&c.* Yet I find it wholly omitted in every Attainder upon an [b] Appeal in *Coke's Entries*, and much oftner [c] omitted than expressed [d] in such Attainders in *Rastal.*

Sect. 7. As to the third Particular, *viz.* Where a Person shall be arraigned upon severall Appeals or Indictments: It seems, That by the Common Law, if a Man be appealed of divers Robberies at the Suit of divers Persons, he may be severally [e] arraigned on each Appeal, and then severally tried on each, that each Appellant may be equally intitled to the Restitution of his Goods, upon the Conviction of the Apellee. And in like Manner at this Day a Person charged with several [f] Indictments of Robbery at the Prosecution of several Persons, may be severally arraigned and tried on each Indictment; because the Prosecutor since the Statute of 21 *H.* 8. 11. is intitled to a Restitution of his Goods upon a Conviction on such an Indictment, in the same Manner as the Plaintiff is upon a Conviction in an Appeal. And it is holden both by [g] *Staundforde* and [h] *Hale*, That even a Person attainted of Robbery at the Suit of one Person, may be arraigned and tried at the Suit of another, if such Suit were commenced before the Attainder: But *Quære*: For of the Authorities cited for the Maintenance of this Opinion two [i] seem to be directly against it; and the [k] other, which seems most to the Point, does not come up to it.

Sect. 8. It is made a *Quære* by [l] *Staundforde*, Whether a Prisoner before his Attainder shall answer to divers Appeals of Death or Rape, in the same Manner as in the Case of Robbery?

[n] Coke's Ent. 360, pl. 14, 361. pl. 15, 16.

[*] Coke's Entr. 352. pl. 2, 3. 354. b. 355, pl. 7, 8, 356, pl. 9. 358, pl. 11, 360. pl. 13.

[a] See Rast. Ent. 42. pl. 1.

[b] See Coke's Entr. *from f.* 53 *to* 60.

[c] See Ra. Ent. 47, a. b. 48, a. b. 49, a. b. 50, a. b. 52, a. 54, a. 55. b.

[d] See Rast. Ent. 42. pl. 2. 53. pl. 6.

[e] 4 E. 4. 11. pl. 18. H. P. C. 212. S. P. C. 66. Letters A. B. 107. Letter B. 160. b. Fitz. Coro. 26, 27.

[f] S. P. C. 66. Letter E. H. P. C. 212.

[g] S. P. C. 66. a. b. [h] H. P. C. 212, 248. [i] Fitz. Coro. 379. 7 H. 4. 31. pl. 16. *Abridged* Fitz. Coro. 81. [k] 4 E. 4. 11. pl. 18. *Abridged* Fitz. Coro. 26, 27. *See* 44 E. 4. 44. pl. 57. *Abridged* Fitz. Coro. 95. *See also Chap.* 23. *Sect.* 53 *and the Chapter concerning the Plea of Auterfoits convict and attaint.* [l] S. P. C. 66. Letter C.

CHAP. XXIX.

Of the Arraignment of the Principal and Accessary.

AND now I am in the second Place to consider the Nature of Arraignment, so far as it particularly relates to Principals and Accessaries; for the better understanding whereof, it may not be improper to consider,

1. In what Cases, in Judgment of Law, a Man shall be said to be a Principal, and in what Cases he shall be said to be an Accessary.
2. Where he shall be adjudged an Accessary before.
3. Where an Accessary after.

Sect. 1. And *First*, For the better understanding in what Cases a Man shall be said to be a Principal, and in what an Accessary; having premised, That where a Felony is committed by divers Persons, the [a] same Man may be a Principal and Accessary in it, and so charged in the [b] same Indictment or Appeal; as where *A.* commands *B.* to kill *C.* and afterwards actually joins with him in the Fact. And having also farther premised, That it is agreed by all the Books, That a Man may be an Accessary after the Fact, by [c] receiving one who was an Accessary before, as well as by receiving a Principal; and that there seems to be the same [d] Reason, that a Man may be an Accessary before the Fact, by procuring another to be in such Manner an Accessary to the Principal, I shall endeavour to shew,

1. In what Offences there can be no Accessaries, but all must be Principals, if any way guilty.
2. Where those who only abet a Fact shall be esteemed as much Principals in it as those who actually do it.
3. Where those who are actually absent when a Fact is committed may be esteemed Principals in it.
4. Where one shall be adjudged a Principal in an Offence against a Statute.
5. Whether the Offence of an Accessary can ever rise higher than that of the Principal.

[a] H. P. C. 219. 3 Inst. 139. Keilw. 107. Fitz. Coro. 80.
[b] 7 H. 4. 27. pl. 4. Fitz. Coro. 80. Vide Fitz. Coro. 176, 285.
[c] Lamb. B. 2. Ch. 7. f. 291. 26 Ass. pl 52. Bro. Coro. 104. Fitz. Coro. 196. Crompt. Just. 42. pl. 24. S P. C. 43. Letter D.
[d] *See the Books above-cited, and* H. P. C. 219.

Sect. 2. As to the first Particular, *viz.* In what Offences there can be no Accessaries, but all must be Principals, if any way Guilty: It seems to have been always an uncontroverted Maxim, That there can be no Accessaries in [e] High Treason, or [f] Trespass. Also it seems to have been always agreed, That whatsoever will make a Man an Accessary before in

[e] 3 Inst. 20, 21, 138. Dalis. 16. pl. 81. H. P. C. 215. 12 Co. 81, 82. 2 Inst. 183. Bro. Treason, 19. 3 H. 7. 10. pl. 2. Fitz. Coro. 55. 19 H. 6. 47. pl. 103. S. P. C. 3. Lett. A. 40. Lett. C. Bro. Coro. 135. Dalt. Ch. 108. Crompt. 42. pl. 19. Co. Litt. 57.
[f] 12 Co. 81, 82. 2 Inst. 183. Bro. Rape, 3. Co. Litt. 57.

Fe-

Felony, will make him a Principal in [a] High Treason and Trespass; as [b] Battery, [c] Riot, Rout, [d] Forcible Entry, and even in [e] Forgery and [f] Petit Larceny. And therefore, where-ever a Man commands another to commit a Trespass, who afterwards commits it in pursuance of such Command, he [g] seems by necessary Consequence to be as Guilty of it, as if he had done it himself; from whence it follows, That being in Judgment of Law a Principal Offender, he may be tried and found [h] Guilty, before any Trial of the Person who actually did the Fact.

Sect. 3. It was formerly a [i] Question, Whether the same Receipt of an Offender, which will make the Receiver an Accessary after the Fact in the Case of Felony, will make him a Principal in High Treason, as it seems to be [k] settled at this Day that it will? For if it shou'd be adjudged a Misprision only, as [l] some have contended, a Man wou'd be subject to a less Punishment for receiving a Traitor than for receiving a Felon; for he who receives a Felon is certainly liable to Judgment of Death, as being an Accessary to the Felony, but he who receives a Traitor wou'd be liable only to Fine and Imprisonment, as being guilty of a Misprision only.

Sect. 4. It seems [m] agreed, That whosoever agrees to a Trespass on Lands or Goods done to his Use, thereby becomes a Principal in it. But that no one can become a Principal in a Trespass on the Person of a Man by any such Agreement. Also it seems [n] agreed, That no one shall be adjudged a Principal in any Common Trespass, or inferior Crime of the like Nature, for barely receiving, comforting and concealing the Offender, tho' he know him to have been Guilty, and that there is a Warrant out against him, which by Reason of such Concealment, cannot be executed. And if he cannot be punished as a Principal, it is certain that he cannot be punished as an Accessary; because in such Offences, all who are punished as Partakers of the Guilt of him who did the Fact, must be punished as Principals in it, or not at all. Yet if a Man knowing that there is a Warrant against such Offender, advise and persuade him to absent himself, [o] perhaps he may be indictable for a Contempt of the Law in hindring the due Course of Justice.

Sect. 5. It is certain, That in [p] Petit Treason, and also such Felony as shall have [q] Judgment of Death, there may be Accessaries both before and after the Fact, who must be proceeded against as such, and not as Principals, as shall be more fully shewn in the following Part of this Chapter. Also it seems, [r] That there may be Accessaries before the Fact in Mayhem, but that the Appellant hath his [s] Election to proceed against them either as Principals, or as Accessaries. [t] But I find it no where holden, that there can be Accessaries in Mayhem after the Fact.

Sect. 6. I do not find it agreed, [u] Whether there can be any Accessaries in *Præmunire*?

Sect. 7. As to the second Particular, *viz.* Where those who only abet a Fact, shall be esteemed as much Principals in it as those who actually do it: It seems to have been [x] anciently the more prevailing Opinion, That

[a] 19 H. 6 47. pl. 103. Bro. Treason, 9. Fitz. Coro. 8. 3 Inst. 138. [b] 38 Ass. pl. 9. Keilw. 55. pl. 4. [c] Co. Litt. 57. [d] B. 1. Ch. 64. S. 22. Co. Litt. 57. Fitz. Gard. 99. [e] Moore 666. pl. 913. Vide 1 Sid. 312. pl. 25. [f] Cro. E. 750. pl. 4. 2 Inst. 183. 12 Co. 81. Cont. H. P. C. 223. [g] Moore 787. H. P. C. 217. Pl. Com 475. Vide Infra, Sect. 7. Fitz. Coro. 314, 433. S. P. C. 41. Lett. D. *Quære* Moor, 53. pl. 155. [h] Bro. Tres. 256. 1 Lev. 124. 29 Ass. pl. 59. Fitz. Ass. 291. Cont. 27 Ass. pl. 4. *Quære* Vaugh. 115, 116. [i] Dyer 296. pl. 21. 12 Co. 81, 82. 3 Inst. 138. Dalt. Ch. 89. 108. Crompt. 42. pl. 19. Vide 3 H. 7. 10. pl. 2. S. P. C. 3. Lett. A. [k] H. P. C. 215. 3 Inst. 138. Dalt. Ch. 108. Crompt. 42. pl. 19. Vide supra, Sect. 2. and B. 1. Ch. 20. Sect. 3. 4. S. P. C. 3. Lett. A. Bro. Treason, 19. Bro. Coro. 135. [l] Dyer 296. pl. 21. [m] Cro. El. 824. 38 Ass. pl. 9. Bro. Disseisor, 98. Bro. ejectione Custodiæ, 8. Bro. Trespass, 256. 38 E. 3. 18. a. b. Co. Litt. 180. b. Fitz. Gard. 89. [n] Popham 134. 2 Rol. Abr. 75. Letter A. pl. 3. [o] 2 Rol. Ab. 75. Lett. A. pl. 4. [p] Dalis. 16. pl. 11. 3 Inst. 20, 21. Crompton, 42. pl. 19. S. P. C. 40. Lett. C. B. 1. Ch. 32. Sect. 5, 6. [q] 12 Co. 81, 82. Cro. El. 750. pl. 4. 2 Inst. 183. [r] *See the Citations to the next Letter.* [s] 22 Ass pl. 82. Fitz. Coro. 11, 182, 215, 221. Cont. Cont. Bro. Appeal, 154. [s] Vide supra Ch. 23. Sect. 19. 22 Ass pl. 82. Fitz. Coro. 11, 182, 215, 221. Cont. Bro. Appeal, 154. [t] Vide Supra, Sect. 4. [u] Vide S. P. C. 44. Lett. F. Dalt. ch. 108. Bro. Præmunire, 4, 6. Pl. Com. 97. b. [x] Pl. Com. 99 b. Fitz. Coro. 90, 216. 40 Ass. pl. 8 & 25. Bro. Coro. 11. 40 E. 3. 42. pl. 22. S. P. C. 48. Lett. G. H. 41. Lett. A. B. 44 E. 3. 38. pl. 35. See Bract. B 3. Ch. 12. Sect. 10, 11, 13. Ch. 19. S. 11. Ch. 21. Sect. 8, 10, 11. Lamb. B. 2. ch. 7. fol. 283. Stat. of West. 1. ch. 14. Contr. Fitz. Coro. 433.

those

those only were to be adjudged Principals in Felony who actually did the Fact; as in Murder, those only who gave the mortal Blow; in Rape, those only who actually ravished the Party, *&c.* and that those in the Company who were only present and abetted and encouraged the Doing it, were to be esteemed Accessaries; or at most Principals in the [a]second Degree only. But I take it to be settled at this Day, That all those who [b]assemble themselves together with a felonious Intent, the Execution whereof causes either the Felony intended, or any other to be committed, or with an Intent to commit a [c]Trespass, the Execution whereof causes a Felony to be committed, and continue together abetting one another till they have actually put their Design in Execution; and also all those who are [d]present when a Felony is committed, and abet the Doing of it, as by holding the [e]Party while another strikes him; or by [*]delivering a Weapon to him that strikes, or by moving [f]him to strike, are Principals in the highest [g]Degree, in Respect of such Abetment, as much as the Person who does the Fact, which in Judgment of Law is as [h]much the Act of them all, as if they had all actually done it; [i]and if there were Malice in the Abettor, and none in the Person who struck the Party, it will be Murder as to the Abettor, and Manslaughter only as to the other.

Sect. 8. It doth not seem necessary to the making an Abettor a Principal, that the Person on whom the Felony is committed shou'd be under any [k]Terror from the Abetment, and by Reason thereof discouraged from making that Defence which otherwise he might have made; but it seems to be sufficient for this Purpose, that the Person who does the Fact is encouraged and emboldened in it from the Hopes of present and immediate Assistance from the Abettor, whether he be within View of the Fact, or [l]not. And upon this Ground it hath been adjudged, [m]That where Persons combine together, to stand by one another in a Breach of the Peace, with a general Resolution to resist all Opposers, and in the Execution of their Design a Murder is committed, all of the Company are equally Principals, tho' at the Time of the Fact some of them were at such a Distance as to be out of View. Also upon the same Reason it hath been adjudged, [n]That where a Company of Rogues assault a Man in the Highway, who escapes from them, and then one of them rides from the rest, in the same Highway, and robs another out of the View of his Companions, and then returns to them, they are all of them equally Principals. And the like hath been [o]adjudged in Relation to all those who accompany one another with an Intent to commit a Burglary, in the Execution whereof some stand to watch only in the adjacent Places, and the rest actually break, and enter the House.

Sect. 9. But [p]where divers Persons accompany one another in the doing of a lawful Act, and one of them happens to kill a Man, he that gives the Wound is only guilty of the Homicide, and the rest of the Company shall neither be esteemed Principals nor Accessories. [q]Also if

[a] Pl. Com. 97. [b] 11 H. 4. 13 pl. 30. Fitz. Coro. 86, 228. Bro. Appeal, 32. Moore 53. pl. 155. 9 Co. 67 b. Kely. 47. Pl. Com. 97, 98. 4 Co. 42. *See the Cases cited to the other Parts of this and the next Section. And* B. 1. ch. 31. Sect. 31. ch. 32 Sect. 5. and ch. 41. Sect. 6. [c] B. 1. ch. 31. Sect. 46. H. P. C. 216, 217. Fitz. Coro. 60, 314, 350. 433. Bro. Coro. 172. Keil. 161. Kely. 47. Salk. 334, 335. S. P. C. 40. Lett. D. E. [d] See B. 1. ch. 32. Sect. 6. Moor. 53. pl. 155. 2 Inst. 182. 3 Inst. 138. 59. Bro Appeal, 19, 132. Bro. Coro. 19, 167, 188. S. P. C 40. Lett. D 44. Lett. B C. 41 Lett. B.

10 E 4. 14. pl. 8. H. P. C. 215, 216. Fitz. Coro. 99, 309, 433. Dalt. ch 108. Lamb. B. 2. ch. 7. fol. 283. 7 H. 4 27 pl. 4. *Presence holden not to be necessary foe this Purpose.* Fitz. Coro. 60. 4 H 7. 18. pl. 10. [e] H. P. C. 216. Fitz Coro. 135. S. P. C. 40. Lett. F. 13 H. 7. 10. pl. 7. [*] H. P. C. 216. 2 Inst. 41, 82. [f] Fitz. Coro. 60. S. P. C 40. Lett. D. H. P. C. 216. 4 H. 7. 18. pl. 10. Bro. Coro. 141. Bro. Appeal 85. [g] H. P. C. 215, 216. Pl. Com. 98. Supra ch. 23. Sect. 76. ch. 25. Sect. 66. [h] Pl. Com. 98 100. Fitz. Coro. 60. Bro. Coro. 141. Bro. Appeal 85. 4 H. 7 18. pl. 10. 9 Co. 67. b. [i] B. 1. ch. 31. Sect. 49 *to* Sect. 54. [k] *But this seems required in* Pl. Com 98. [l] Fitz. Coro. 60. H. P. C. 216, 217. 4 H. 7. 18. pl. 10. Salk. 334. 335. B 1. ch. 35. Sect. 7. ch. 38. Sect. 8. [m] See B. 1. ch. 31. Sect. 46. H. P. C. 216, 217. Bro. Coro. 172. Salk. 334 335. Keilw. 161. a. Fitz. Coro. 60, 314, 350, 433 S. P. C. 40. Lett. D E. Vide Kely. 47. [n] B. 1. ch. 35. Sect. 7. Vide Moore 53. pl. 155. S. P. C. 40. Lett. D. E. [o] B. 1. ch. 38. Sect. 8, 9. 11 H. 4. 13. 30. Vide Moore, 53. pl. 155. [p] Keilw. 161. a. [q] Kely. 47.

the Act intended tho' unlawful, were a bare Treſpaſs, and one of the Company be guilty of Larceny, it is a Felony in ſuch Offender only, becauſe it is a Crime of a Nature entirely different from that intended, and not cauſed by the Execution of it.

Sect. 10. Alſo thoſe who by accident are barely preſent when a Felony is committed, and are merely paſſive, and neither any Way encourage it, nor endeavour to hinder it, nor to apprehend the Offenders, ſhall [a] neither be adjudged Principals nor Acceſſaries; [b] yet if they be of full Age, they are highly puniſhable by Fine and Impriſonment for their Negligence, both in not endeavouring to [c] prevent the Felony, and in not endeavouring to [d] apprehend the Offender. And [e] if they any way ſhewed an Aſſent to the Felony, it ſeems, That they may be puniſhed as Principals in it; becauſe the ſhewing ſuch an Aſſent cou'd not but give Encouragement to it.

Sect. 11. As to the third Particular, *viz.* Where thoſe who are actually abſent when a Felony is committed may be eſteemed Principals in it: I take it to be a ſettled Rule, That where-ever a Man procures a Felony to be committed, and is abſent at the Time when it is committed, and no other Perſon but himſelf can be adjudged a Principal in it, he ſhall be eſteemed as much a Principal as if he had been preſent; for no one can be [f] puniſhed as a Felon, but either as a Principal or as an Acceſſary; and therefore where the Procurer of a Felony cannot be puniſhed as an Acceſſary, becauſe there is no other to whom he can be an Acceſſary, he muſt be puniſhed as a Principal, or not at all. And upon this Ground, it ſeems to be clear, That if a Man [g] perſuade another to drink a Poiſonous Liquor, under the Notion of a Medicine, who afterwards drinks it in his Abſence; [h] or if *A.* intending to poiſon *B.* put Poiſon into a Thing, and deliver it to *C.* who knows nothing of the Matter, to be by him delivered to *B.* and *C.* innocently deliver it accordingly in the Abſence of *A.* or if one [i] incite a Madman to kill another, who afterwards kills him in the Abſence of the Perſon that incited him; In all theſe, and the like Caſes, the Procurer of the Felony is as much a Principal as if he had been preſent when it was done. And ſo [k] likewiſe all thoſe ſeem to be who were preſent when the Poiſon was infuſed, and privy to, and conſenting to the Deſign. But [l] thoſe who only abetted their Crime by their Command, Counſel or Advice, but were abſent when the Poiſon was infuſed, are Acceſſaries, and not Principals. Alſo if *A.* intending to poiſon *B.* deliver a poiſonous Thing to *C.* to be by him delivered to *B.* and *C.* knowing it to be poiſoned deliver it to *B.* in the abſence of *A.* In this Caſe *C.* [m] only is a Principal in the Felony, and *A.* an Acceſſary.

Sect. 12. By force of 3 *H.* 7. 2. All thoſe who are Acceſſaries before to the forcible taking away of a Woman, made Felony by that Statute, whether they were preſent or abſent at the Time of the Taking, or Acceſſaries after, by wittingly receiving the Woman ſo taken away, ſhall be puniſhed as [n] Principals; but this depends on the expreſs Words of the Statute, and not on any Conſtruction from the Reaſon of the Common Law.

[a] S. P. C. 40. Lett. D, E. H. P. C. 216. Fitz. Coro. 92, 197, 395. Bro. Indict. 5. 14 H. 7. 31. pl. 7. Cont. Fitz. Coro. 314. 197. Lamb. B. 2. ch. 7. f. 289. Vide ſupra, Ch. 23. Sect. 66.
[b] S. P. C. 40. Lett. E. Fitz. Coro. 395.
[c] Noy, 50. Dalt. Ch. 108.
[d] Supra, Ch. 12. Sect. 1, 2, 3, 4.
[e] Vide infra, Sect. 15.
S. P. C. 40. Lett. D E. H. P. C. 217. Fitz. Coro. 150. Dalt. ch 108. Lambl B. 2. ch. 7. f. 282. *My Pleas of the Crown*, B. 1. Ch. 20. Sect 3. *But* Fitz. Coro. 92. *and* Crompt. 41. pl. 7. 8. *ſeems contrary.*
[f] 4 C. 44. b. Pult. 122. a.
[g] 4 Co 44. b. 2 Inſt. 183. Crompt. 44. pl. 43 H. P. C. 216. Pult. 122. a. Dalt. ch 108.
9 Co. 81. 3 Inſt. 138.
[h] H P. C. 218. 9 Co. 81. Kely. 52, 53.
[i] See B 1. ch. 1. S. 7.
[k] H. P. C. 216.
[l] 4 Co. 44. b. Crompt. 44. pl. 43.
[m] Kely. 52, 53.
[n] See B. 1. Ch. 42. Sect 8, 9. and H. P. C. 217.

Sect. 13. As to the fourth Particular, *viz.* Where a Man shall be adjudged a Principal in an Offence against a Statute: It seems to have been always [o] generally agreed, That notwithstanding all penal Statutes are to be construed strictly; yet where-ever a Statute ordains, That those who are guilty of the Thing prohibited by it, shall be adjudged Traitors or Felons, it by a necessary Implication makes all the Procurers and Abettors of it Principals or Accessories before, upon the same Circumstances which will make them such in a Treason or Felony at Common Law; because such Persons may properly be said to have done the Thing in such a Manner caused by them, and consequently to come within the very Words of the Statute. And therefore it seems to have been generally unquestionable, That those who procure the [a] Clipping of the King's Coin, or other Offence, made High Treason by Statute, in such a Manner as will make them principal Traitors in a Treason at Common Law, shall be adjudged principal Traitors by the Statute. And that those who abet a [b] Petit Treason, or a Felony by Statute; as a [c] Rape, or [d] Buggery, *&c.* shall be adjudged Principals if present when it was committed, and Accessaries if absent, in the same Manner as in Felonies at Common Law, unless the Statute expresly provide otherwise; as that of 3 *H.* 7. 2. does, as hath been shewn in the foregoing Section.

Sect. 14. But there [e] seem to have been formerly some Opinions, That the Receivers of a Felon by Statute, shall not be adjudged Accessaries to the Felony after the Fact, in the same Manner as the Receivers of a Felon at Common Law; because such Persons can in no Propriety of Speech be said to have done the Thing prohibited, as the Procurers of it may be said to have done: But this [f] seems to have been more strongly holden in Respect of those Statutes which expresly provide that Accessories before to the Offence prohibited, shall be punished as Felons, *&c.* but say nothing of Accessaries after; from which Words it may be argued, That they must be either intended to exclude Accessaries after the Fact, or have no manner of Effect. Yet I take it to be settled at this Day, That in these, and all other Cases, where a Statute makes any Offence [g] Treason or [h] Felony, it involves the Receiver of the Offender in the same Guilt with himself, in the same Manner as in Treason or Felony at Common Law, unless there be an express Provision to the contrary. For since it is agreed, That such new Treason or Felony shall have the same Construction with a Treason or Felony at Common Law to all other [i] Intents and Purposes, Why should it not also have the same in Relation to those who are to be esteemed Principals and Accessories in it? And as to the Objection, That the Receivers of the Offender cannot thereby be so properly said to have done the Offence, as the Accessaries before, it may be answered, That they may properly enough be said to be Partakers in the Guilt of the Offender; and what Crime such a Partaking shall be adjudged to amount to, is most reasonably determined by the Rules of Law in other Cases of like Nature. And as to the Objection, That a Statute by expressing Accessaries before, must be intended to exclude Accessaries after, or to have no manner of Effect, it may be answered, That nothing is more common than for Statutes to express those Things which the Law would have implied, in which Cases it seems a very reasonable Construction, That *Expressio eorum quæ tacite insunt nihil operatur.*

[o] S. P. C. 44. Lett. A. B. C. 19 H. 6. 47. pl. 103. 3 Inst. 45, 59, 72. B. 1 ch. 40. Sect. 4. Crompt. 42. pl. 13. Dalt. ch. 108. Lamb. B. 2. ch. 7. f. 286, 287. Dalis. 11. pl. 12. 22. pl. 3. H. P. C. 215. *Quære* Dy. 88. pl. 105.
[a] Dalis. 11. pl. 12. H. P. C. 223, *in the Additions printed in the second Edition.*
[b] Vide supra, Sect. 2. B. 1. ch. 17. S. 55. 19 H. 7. 47. pl. 103. S. P. C. 3. Lett. A. H. P. C. 18.
[c] See B. 1 ch. 32. Sect. 5, 6. H. P. C. 187, 215. See B. 1. ch. 41. Sect. 6. S. P. C. 44. Lett. B. 11 H. 4. 13. Dalis. 22. pl. 3. Fitz. Coro. 86, 228. Bro. Rape, 2, 3.
[d] 3 Inst. 59. H. P. C. 215. See B. 1. ch. 38. Sect. 18.
[e] Vide S. P. C. 44. Lett. C. and supra, Sect. 3.
[f] Vide S. P. C. 44. Lett. C. Lamb. B. 2. ch. 7. fol. 284, 285.
[g] Vide supra, Sect. 3. Bro. Treason, 19. S. P. C. 3. Lett. A. 3 H. 7. 10. pl. 2.
[h] H. P. C. 215. Dalis. 22. pl. 3. Lamb. B. 2. ch. 7. f. 284, 285. 3 Inst. 45, 61, 72, 73.
[i] See B. 1. ch. 40. S. 4. Sup. a, ch. 18. Sect. 12. S. P. C. 168. Lett. D. H. P. C. 230, 231.

Sect. 15. As to the fifth Particular, *viz.* Whether the Offence of the Acceſſary can ever riſe higher than that of the Principal: I take it to be an uncontroverted [a] Rule, That it never ſhall; it ſeeming incongruous and abſurd that he who is puniſhed only as a Partaker of the Guilt of another, ſhou'd be adjudged guilty of a higher Crime than the other. And therefore it ſeems clear, [b] That if a Wife or Servant cauſe a Stranger to murder the Husband or Maſter, and are abſent when the Murder is committed, they cannot be ſaid to be Acceſſaries to Petit Treaſon, but to Murder only, becauſe the Offence of the Principal is but Murder. But if ſuch Wife or Servant had been [c] preſent when the Murder was committed, they would have been guilty of Petit Treaſon, and the Stranger of Murder; becauſe in Reſpect of ſuch [d] Preſence they would have been Principals in killing, as hath been more fully ſhewn *B.* 1, in the Chapter of *Petit Treaſon, Sect. 6.*

16. As to the ſecond Point, *viz.* In what Caſes a Man ſhall be adjudged an Acceſſary before: It ſeems to be [e] agreed, That thoſe who by Hire, Command, Counſel or Conſpiracy; and it ſeems to be generally [f] holden, That thoſe who by ſhewing an expreſs Liking, Approbation or Aſſent to another's felonious Deſign of committing a Felony, abet and encourage him to commit it, but are ſo far [g] abſent when he actually commits it, that he could not be encouraged by the Hopes of any immediate Help or Aſſiſtance from them, are all of them Acceſſaries before the Fact, both to the Felony intended, and to all other Felonies which ſhall happen in and by the Execution of it, if they do not [h] expreſly retract and countermand their Encouragement, before it is actually committed.

Sect. 17. But it doth not ſeem neceſſary in any Indictment or Appeal againſt a Man as Acceſſary before the Fact, to ſet forth the Special Manner by which he abetted it, but only to charge him [i] generally, *Quod Felonice, &c. abettavit, incitavit & procuravit, &c.* Alſo the like general Way of ſetting forth the Aid given to a Felon, ſeems to be ſufficient both as to thoſe who are * Principals, by being preſent when the Felony is committed, and alſo as to thoſe who are † Acceſſaries after.

Sect. 18. It cannot be doubted, But that if a Man adviſe a Woman to kill her Child as ſoon as it ſhall be born, and ſhe kill it in purſuance of ſuch Advice, he is an [k] Acceſſary to the Murder, tho' at the Time of the Advice, the [l] Child not being born, no Murder cou'd be committed of it; for the Influence of the felonious Advice continuing till the Child was born, makes the Adviſer as much a Felon as if he had given his Advice after the Birth. Alſo it ſeem [m] agreed, That if I command another to beat a Man, and he beat him in ſuch a Manner that he dies thereof, I am an Acceſſary before to the Felony; [n] becauſe it happened in the Execution of a Command, which naturally tended to endanger the Life of the other. And [o] *a fortiori* therefore it follows, That if a Man commands another to rob a Man, and he in robbing him kill him; or to burn the Houſe of *J. S.* and he by burning it, burn alſo the Houſe of *J. N.* the Commander is as much an Acceſſary to the ſubſequent Felony, as to that which was directly commanded. Alſo it is ſaid, [p] That if I command

[a] 3 Inſt. 20, 139. H. P. C 215. Bro. Coro. 119. Vide Kielw. 34. pl. 9. and inf. S. 21. 22.
[b] 3 Inſt. 20. Dalſ. 16. pl. 11. Dyer, 254, pl. 103, 332, pl. 25. 128. pl. 57. H. P. C. 24, 25, 215. Crompt. 19. pl. 8. Bro. Coro. 119. *But 40 Aſſ 25. whereof this Note in* Brook *is an Abridgment, ſeems contrary See alſo* Fitz. Coro. 216. *which is an Abridgment of the ſame Caſe.*
[c] 3 Inſt. 20. H. P. C. 24, 25. Dy. 128, pl. 57. 254, pl. 103 332. pl. 25. Crompt. 19. pl. 8. Moore 91. pl. 227. Dalſ. 16. pl. 11
[d] Vide ſupra Sect 7.
[e] 3 Inſt. 182. Dalt. Ch. 108. Lamb. B. 2. ch. 7. S. P. C. 40. Lett. D. Crompt. 41. pl. 1, 7, 8. H. P. C. 217.
[f] 2 Inſt. 182. Dalt. ch. 108. Lamb B. 2. ch. 7. f. 286. H. P. C. 217. Pl. Com. 475. b. Cont Cromp. 41. pl. 7, 8.

[g] Vide ſupra, Sect. 7, 8. S. P. C. 40. Lett. D E. &c. Bro. Appeal 19. Bro. Coro. 188. Crompt 42 pl. 16. H. P. C. 217, 218. Lamb. B. 2 ch. 7. f. 289. Dalt. ch. 108. Pl. Com. 475. a. 476 b. [h] 3 Inſt. 51. [i] Coke's Ent. 56, pl. 5. 57. pl. 6. Ra. Ent 51. pl. 6. Fitz. Coro. 433. *ſeems ſomewhat contrary.* * 4 Co. 41. Cok. Ent, 57. pl. 6. † Cok. Ent 56. pl. 5. Ra. Ent. 48. pl. 4. 52. pl. 15. [k] Dyer 186 3 Inſt. 51. Dalt. ch 108. Lamb B. 2. ch. 7. f. 286 Crompt. 41. pl. 2. [l] See B. 1. ch. 31. Sect 16, 17. [m] H. P. C. 217. Pl. Com. 475 b. Lamb. B. 2. ch. 7. fol. 386. Pl. Com. 475. [n] S. P. C. 41. Lett. D. Fitz. Coro. 314. Vide Pl. Com. 475. b. Dalt. ch. 108. Cromp. 43. pl. 35. [o] Pl. Com 475. b. [p] Pl. Com 475 a. b. Dalt. ch. 108. Lamb. B. 2. ch. 7. f 286. Crompt. 42. pl. 34, 35.

a

a Man to rob another, and he kill him in the Attempt, but do not rob him, I am guilty of the Murder, because it was the direct and immediate Effect of an Act done in Execution of my Command to commit a Felony. But if I persuade *A.* to poison *B.* and *A.* accordingly give Poison to *B.* who eats Part of it, and gives the rest to *C.* who is killed by it, I am guilty of a great Misdemeanor only in Respect of *C.* but not [a] an Accessary to his Murder, because it was not the direct and immediate Effect of the Act done in pursuance of my Command, but happened accidentally thro' the Act of *B.* to which I being no way Privy, cannot be made Accessory by Reason of it. Yet in this Case *A.* is certainly guilty of the Murder of *C.* as hath been more fully shewn, *Book* 1. *Chap.* 31. *Sect.* 42, 43.

[a] Pl. Com. 474, 475. Dalton ch. 108. Lambart, B. 2. ch. 7. f. 288. Crompt. 42. pl. 10.

Sect. 19. It seems to be holden generally in some * Books, That whereever a Felony ensues, and follows upon any unlawful Act commanded by another, and executed in the same Manner as it was commanded, the Commander is an Accessary to the Felony. But this [b] seems to be too large a Rule and liable to great Difficulties, unless limited by some Distinctions; but finding little in the Books concerning this Matter, I shall leave it to be farther considered by others.

* Plow. Com. 475 a. Moore 487. Dalt. ch. 108. 3 Inst. 51.

[b] S P. C. 41. Letter D. Fitz. Coro. 314. Dalt. ch. 108. Moore 53 pl. 155.

Sect. 20. It seems to be [c] agreed, That if the Felony committed be the same in Substance with that which was intended, and variant only in some Circumstance, as in Respect of the Time or Place, at which, or the Mean whereby it was effected, the Abettor of the Intent is altogether as much an Accessary as if there had been no Variance at all between it and the Execution of it; as where a Man advises another to kill such a one in the Night, and he kills him in the Day, or to kill him in the Fields, and he kills him in the Town, or to poison him, and he stabs or shoots him.

[c] Pl. Com. 475 b. H. P. C. 217. Lamb. B. 2. ch. 7. f. 287. 3 Inst. 51. Crompt. 42. pl. 14. Dalt. ch. 108.

Sect. 21. But if a Man command another to commit a Felony on a particular Person or Thing, and he do it on [d] another; as to kill *A.* and he kill *B.* or to burn the House of *A.* and he burn the House of *B.* or to steal an Ox, and he steal an Horse; or to steal such an Horse, and he steal another; or to commit a Felony of one kind, and he commit another [e] of a quite different Nature; as to rob *J. S.* of his Plate as he is going to Market, and he break open his House in the Night, and there steal the Plate; it is said, That the Commander is not an Accessary, because the Act done varies in Substance from that which was commanded.

[d] H. P. C. 217. Pl. Com. 475. Dalt. ch. 108. Lamb. B. 2. ch. 7. f. 287. Crompt. 42. pl. 11.

[e] Pl. Com. 475. 3 Inst. 51. Dalt. ch. 108. Lambard, B. 2. ch. 7. fol. 287, 288. Crompt. 42. pl. 11.

Sect. 22. But it is observable, That [f] *Plowden*, in his Report of *Saunders*'s Case, which seems to be the chief Foundation of what is said by others concerning these Points, in putting the Case of a Command to burn the House of *A.* which shall not make the Commander an Accessary to the burning the House of *B.* unless it were caused by burning that of *A.* states it in this [g] Manner, *If I command a Man to burn the House of such an one, which he well knows, and he burn the House of another, there I shall not be Accessary, because it is another distinct Thing, to which I did not give Assent*, &c. By which it seems to be implied, That it is a necessary Ingredient in such a Case to make *B.* no Accessary, that he knew the House which he was commanded to burn; for if he did not know it, but mistook another for it, and intending only to burn the House which he was commanded to burn, happen by such Mistake to burn the other, it may probably be argued, That the Commander ought to be esteemed an Accessory to such burning, because it was the direct and immediate

[f] Pl Com. 475 b.

[g] *But this Case is not stated in this Manner, either by* Lambard, Dalton *or* Crompton, *See* Lamb. B. 2. ch. 7. fol. 287. Dalt. ch. 108. Crompt. 42. pl. 36.

Effect of an Act wholly influenced by his Command, and intended to have pursued it.

Sect. 23. It seems to be generally agreed, [a] That he who barely conceals a Felony, which he knows to be intended, is guilty only of a Misprision [b] of Felony, and shall not be adjudged an Accessary.

Sect. 24. It seems to be certain, That no one can be any [c] way punished as an Accessary to Homicide *per infortunium*, or *se defendendo*, because they are not Felonies; from whence it follows, That if he who is indicted or appealed, as a Principal in Murder, be found guilty of such Homicide only, those who are only charged as his Accessaries before or after, shall be discharged. [d] And so also shall those who are charged only as Accessaries before, where the Principal is found guily of Manslaughter; because that necessarily supposes the Fact to have happened on a sudden; for if it had been done upon Premeditation, it wou'd have been Murder. And *Quare*, If they who are charged as Accessaries [e] after, should not also be discharged at Commom Law where the Principal was found guilty of Manslaughter, and admitted to the Benefit of his Clergy, because in such Case it could not appear by any Judgment that there was a Principal; but the Law in this Respect seems to be altered by 1 *Anna* 9. set forth more at large in the following Part of this Chapter, which makes a Conviction equivalent as to this Purpose to an Attainder.

[a] Lamb. B. 2. ch. 8. f. 289. Moore 8. pl. 29. S. P. C. 37. Letter C. H. P. C. 129, 2 9. 3 Inst. 139, 140. 2 Inst. 183. *But this is made a Quare by* Dalton, *ch.* 108.
[b] See B. 1. ch. 59.
[c] Fitz. Coro. 116, 172. Bro. Coro. 33, 80. 15 Ass. pl. 7. 11 H. 4. 93. pl. 53. Crompt. 43. pl. 38. Bro. Forfeiture, 13.
[d] 4 Co. 43, 44. H. P. C. 217. Moore 461, pl. 645. Cro. El. 540. pl. 4. Crompt. 43. pl. 40. Dalt. ch. 108. See B. 1. ch. 30.
[e] Vide Crom. Just. 44. pl. 41. 3 Inst 55. Moore 461, pl. 645. Cro. El. 540. pl. 4.

Sect. 25. Before the Statute of 11 & 12 *W.* 3. Accessaries to Piracy were not within the Purview of 28 *H.* 8. by which Piracy is triable according to the Course of the Common Law; but for this I shall refer the Reader to B. 1. *Ch.* 37.

As to the third Point, *viz.* In what Cases a Man shall be adjudged an Accessary after: I shall endeavour to shew,

1. What Kind of Receipt of a Felon will make the Receiver such an Accessary.
2. Whether it be necessary that such Receiver know of the Felony.
3. Where the Receivers of a Felon shall be excused in Respect of the Relation they bear to him.
4. How far the Felony must be complete at the Time of the Receipt, to make the Receiver an Accessary.

Sect. 26. As to the first Particular, *viz.* What kind of Receipt of a Felon will make the Receiver an Accessary after the Fact: It seems agreed, [f] That generally any Assistance whatsoever given to one known to be a Felon, in order to hinder his being apprehended or tried, or suffering the Punishment to which he is condemned, is a sufficient Receipt for this Purpose; as where one assists him with a [g] Horse to ride away with, or with Money or Victuals to support him in his Escape; or where one harbours and [h] conceals in his House a Felon under Pursuit by Reason whereof the Pursuers cannot find him; and much more, where one harbours in his House and openly [i] protects such a Felon, by Reason whereof the Pursuers dare not take him.

[f] 2 Inst. 183. S. P. C. 41. Letter E. Dalt. ch. 108. Lamb. B. 2. ch. 7. f. 289, &c. H. P. C. 218. Dalt. ch. 108. Crompt. 43. pl. 39.
[g] H. P. C. 218. Dalt. ch. 108. Crompt. 43. pl. 39.

[h] Dalt. ch. 108. Fitz. Coro. 427. Lamb. B. 2. ch. 7. f. 291. S. P. C. 43. Letter C. Crompt. 42. pl. 20.
[i] 26 Ass. pl. 47. *Adjudged* Bro. Coro. 130. Fitz. Coro. 195.

Sect. 27. Alſo I take it to be ſettled at this Day, That whoever reſcues a Felon from an Arreſt from the Felony, or voluntarily [b] ſuffer him to eſcape, is an Acceſſary to the Felony: [c] Alſo ſome have ſaid. That all thoſe are in like Manner guilty who oppoſe the apprehending of a Felon; but for theſe Matters I ſhall refer the Reader to the former Part of this Book, wherein they are more fully handled.

Sect. 28. It ſeems to be holden both by [d] *Brook* and [e] *Staundforde*, That the bare receiving into one's Houſe a Perſon known to be a Felon, is ſufficient without any farther Circumſtances to make a Man an Acceſſary to the Felony: And this ſeems to be favoured by the *Year-Books* of [f] 25 *E.* 3. and [g] 7 *H.* 6. Alſo it ſeems to be holden both by [h] *Staundforde* and [i] *Dalton*, That not only ſuch a Receipt of ſuch a Felon into one's Houſe, but any other Favour or Aid voluntarily afforded him, as by relieving him with Money, Meat or Drink, is ſufficient for this Purpoſe. But it is obſervable, That the Caſe in the Book of [l] *Aſſiſes*, whereon *Dalton* ſeems chiefly to ground his Opinion, and which is more accurate than any other *Year-Book* I meet with on this Subject, is of one who was indicted *for having received a Felon, and for that no one by Reaſon of him dared to take him:* Whereupon it is ſaid by *Shard, If one receive a Felon in Favour and Aid of the Felony, I hold ſuch a one an Acceſſary to the Felony.* Alſo it is farther obſervable, That the *Year-Book* of 9 [m] *H.* 4. on which the above-mentioned Opinion of *Brook* ſeems to be grounded, ſeems to prove only that every Receiver of a Felon, knowing him to be ſuch, is indictable, but not that he is indictable for Felony; and the chief Purport of the Caſe is to ſhew, That one who having a Felon in his Houſe, voluntarily ſuffers him to go at Large, is not guilty of a felonious Eſcape, unleſs he had arreſted him. To which may be added, That [n] *Lambard* doth not ſay generally, That all thoſe who receive a Felon, knowing him to be ſuch, are Acceſſaries after; but all thoſe who feloniouſly, and with an evil Mind, receive a Felon, *&c.* And Sir *Edward Coke*, in his [o] *Second Inſtitute*, deſcribes ſuch Acceſſaries, as thoſe who knowing a Felony receive the Felon, and not only conceal his Offence, but favour and aid him, that he be not known. And in his [p] *Third Inſtitute* he ſaith, If one receive a Thief, and aid and maintain him in his Felony, he is an Acceſſary; by which Expreſſions it ſeems to be implied, That there ought to be ſome other Circumſtance beſides that of the bare ſuffering of a Perſon known to be a Felon to be in one's Houſe, to make a Man an Acceſſary.

Sect. 29. However it ſeems to be [q] agreed, That no one ſhall be adjudged an Acceſſary to a Felony for receiving into his Houſe a Perſon under Bail for ſuch Crime, or for relieving with Money or Victuals a Perſon ſo bailed, or in Priſon; and the Reaſon given by [r] *Dalton* is, becauſe the Felony cannot be concealed, nor the Trial hindred by it. And if this be a ſufficient Reaſon, Why may not any other Receipt or Relief of a Felon, whereby the Felony is not concealed, nor the Trial, *&c.* hindred, come under the like Rule? As it ſeems [ſ] agreed That the ſending a Letter to procure the Deliverance of a Felon, or the inſtructing him to [t] read, in order to entitle him to the Benefit of the Clergy, ſhall do; and even the [u] adviſing his Friends to perſuade Witneſſes not to come againſt him at

[a] Supra ch. 21. Sect. 7, 8. Fitz. Coro. 158, 433. H. P. C. 116. Cont. Fitz. Coro. 48. S. P. C. 43. Lett. D. Dalt. ch. 108. 1 H. 7. 6. pl. 2. Bro. Coro. 130.

[b] Supra. ch. 19 Sect. 10, 22, 26.

[c] Supra, Sect. 10. and Ch. 17. Sect. 1.

[d] Bro. Eſcape 43.

[e] S. P. C. 41. Lett. E.

[f] 25 E. 3. 39. pl. 2. *Abridged* Fitz. Coro. 126.

[g] 7 H. 6. 42. pl. 18. *Abridged* Bro. Indictm. 4. Fitz. Indict. 11.

[h] S. P. C. 41. Lett. E.

[i] Dalt. ch. 108. *See alſo* Crom. 42 pl. 25.

[l] 26 Aſſ. pl. 47. *Abridged* Bro. Coro. 103. Fitz. Coro. 195.

[m] 9 H. 4. 1. pl. 3. *Abridged* Fitz. Coro. 76. Bro. Coro. 26 Bro. Eſcape. 43.

[n] Lamb. B. 2. ch. 7. f. 289.

[o] Page 183.

[p] Page 134.

[q] H. P. C. 218. Dalton ch. 108. Crompt. 42. pl. pl. 25.

[r] Dalt. ch. 108. Crompt. 42. pl. 25. *and* Lamb. B. 2. fol. 209. *are to the ſame purpoſe.*

[ſ] 26 Aſſ. pl. 47. Bro. Coro. 103. Fitz. Coro. 195. S. P. C. 41. Lett. E. H. P. C. 219. Lamb. B. 2. ch. 7. fol. 289, 219. [t] 3 Inſt. 139. H. P. C. 219. [u] 3 Inſt. 139. H. P. C. 219.

his Trial; and also the [a] labouring of Witnesses in pursuance of such Advice. And yet the two last of these Practices are certainly very highly criminal; and tho' they do not tend totally to prevent the Trial, yet are the most likely Means to make it fruitless and ineffectual. Also it seems to be agreed, That the suffering a Felon to escape [b] without arresting him,[c] or the bare Concealment of a Felony, tho' they are Crimes of a very high Nature, do not make a Man an Accessary.

Sect. 30. Also I take it to have been generally agreed, before the Statute of 3 & 4. *W. & M.* 9. That neither the receiving of [d] other Mens Goods, known to have been stolen, nor the taking of one's * own Goods again, from one that had stolen them, on an Agreement not to prosecute him, nor the taking of any other [e] Reward on such an Agreement, did make a Man an Accessary to the Felony, unless he also had received the Thief. But now it is enacted by that Statute, *That if any Person or Persons shall buy or receive any Goods or Chattel that shall be feloniously taken or stolen from any other Person, knowing the same to be stolen, he or they shall be taken and deemed an Accessary, or Accessaries, to such Felony, after the Fact, and shall incur the same Punishment as an Accessary or Accessaries to the Felony, after the Felony committed.* And it is farther enacted by 1 *Anne* 9. That such Persons may be prosecuted for a Misdemeanor, before the Principal shall be convicted, as shall be shewn more at large in the following Part of this Chapter.

Sect. 31. It doth not seem to be settled, [f] Whether the Receipt of a Felon, who is pardoned by the King, but still liable to an Appeal, may not make the Receiver an Accessary.

Sect. 32. As to the second Particular, *viz.* Whether it be necessary that a Man know of the Felony, in order to make him an Accessary by receiving the Felon: There can be no Doubt but that it is necessary that such Receiver have [g] Notice of the Felony either express or implied; and therefore it is the settled Form of all [h] Indictments and Appeals [i] against Accessaries after the Fact, expresly to charge them with having known that the Person received by them, had committed the Principal Felony.

Sect. 33. But it is not clearly settled, Whether in some Cases an implied Notice of the Felony be not sufficient for this Purpose? As where a Man receives a Person attainted of Felony, in the same County wherein he is attainted, in which Case it hath been [k] holden, That he is an Accessary to the Felony, whether he had actually Notice of the Attainder or not; because it appears by Matter of Record in the same County, whereof every Man is said to be conusant. But to this it may be answered, That Felony implies in it something of Wilfulness and Baseness; something [l] *felleo animo perpetratum*; and that it wou'd be extremely hard, by such a forced way of Reasoning, to presume a Man guilty of it, who probably may be entirely innocent: And to this Opinion the greater Number of [m] Authorities seem to incline.

[a] 3 Inst. 139.
[b] H. P. C. 219. Supra, Sect. 10. and 27. Moore 8. pl. 29.
[c] Supra, Sect. 10. and 27. B. 1. ch. 59.
[d] Aleyn. 57. Style, 91. Cro El. 888. pl. 1. Yelv. 4, 5. Lamb. B. 2. ch. 7. f. 290, 291. 1 Rol. Abr. 68. pl. 29. H. P. C. 218. 25 E. 3. 39. pl. 2 *Abridged* Fitz. Coro 126. 27 Ass. 69. *Abridged* Fitz. Coro. 208. Bro. Coro. 114 Cont. Cromp. 42, pl. 3. 43. pl. 37, 39. *It is made a Quare*, Crom. 42. pl. 17. *and* S. P. C. 43. Lett. C.
* H. P. C. 130. Dalt. ch. 108. Moore 8. pl. 29. Crompt. 41. pl. 5. 42 pl. 23. Lamb B. 2. Ch. 7. fol. 290. 1 Rol. Ab. 67. pl. 27. Cro. El. 486. pl. 3. Vide Noy. 90.
[e] H. P. C. 130. 3 Inst. 134, 138. B. 1. ch. 59.

Sect. 5, 6, 7. Cont. Crompt. 41. pl. 4, 5. Lamb. B. 2. ch. 7. f. 290. 2 And. pl. 35. *It is made a Quare*, More, 8 pl. 29 *and* Dalt. ch 108 [f] Vide Pl. Com. 476. Dalt. ch. 108. [g] S. P. C. 41. Lett. B. H. P. C. 218. [h] 7 H. 6. 42 pl. 18 *Abridged* Bro. Indictm. 4. 3 H 7. 10. pl. 2. Bro. Coro. 150. Fitz. Cor. 55, 285, 429. 22 Ass. pl 55. H P. C. 218. [i] Ra. Ent. 43, b. 54 pl. 3, 4. 51. pl. 15. Coke's Ent. 56, pl. 5. 57. pl. 6. [k] S P. C. 41. Lett. E. 96. Lett. G. Crompt. 43. pl. 29, 31, 32. H. P. C. 218. Dyer, 355. pl. 36. Fitz. Coro 377. Dalt. ch. 108. *Quare* 7 H. 6. 42. b. 43. a. [l] Co. Litt. 391. a. [m] S. P. C. 41. Letter E. Dalt. ch. 108. Lamb. B. 2. ch 7. f. 293. H. P. C. 218.

Sect. 34. As to the third Particular, *viz.* Where the Receivers of a Felon shall be excused in Respect of the Relation they bear to him: It seems agreed,[a] That the Law hath such a Regard to that Duty, Love, and Tenderness, which a Wife owes to her Husband, as not to make her an Accessary to Felony by any Receipt whatsoever given to her Husband; yet if she be any way guilty of [b] procuring her Husband to commit it, it seems to make her an Accessary before the Fact in the same Manner as if she had been Sole. Also it seems agreed, That no other Relation besides that of a Wife to her Husband, will exempt the Receiver of a Felon from being an [c] Accessary to the Felony; from whence it follows, That if a Master receive a Servant, or a Servant a Master, or a Brother a Brother, or even a Husband a Wife: they are Accessaries in the same Manner as if they had been mere Strangers to one another.

Sect. 35. As to the fourth Particular, *viz.* How far the Felony must be complete at the Time of the Receipt, to make the Receiver an Accessary: It seems to be clearly agreed, [d] That a Man shall never be construed an Accessary to a Felony, in Respect of the Receipt of an Offender, who at the Time of the Receipt was not a Felon, but afterwards becomes such by Matter subsequent; as where one receives another who has wounded a Person dangerously, that happens to die after such Receipt; for tho' the Offender be for special Reasons adjudged to some Purposes guilty of Homicide *ab initio*, yet he shall not be so esteemed in Respect of any others but himself; for Fictions of Law shall never be carried farther than the Reasons which introduce them necessarily require.

Having thus shewn who are to be esteemed Principals, and who Accessaries; I am now to shew in what Manner they are to be arraigned, and shall endeavour to shew,

1. How far it is necessary that the Principal be actually attainted or convicted before the Accessary shall be proceeded against.
2. Whether the Accessary shall in any Case be arraigned or tried before any Principal hath appeared.
3. Whether a Person charged as Accessary to more than one, may be tried before all the Principals have appeared.
4. Whether the Principal and Accessary may be both tried by the same Inquest, and in what Manner they have are to be tried.
5. In what Manner the Accessary shall be tried, where his Offence arises in a different County from that of the Principal.

Sect. 36. As to the first Point, *viz.* How far it is necessary that the Principal be actually attainted [f] or convicted before the Accessary shall be proceeded against: It seems clear, That whatsoever the Nature of the Felony be, if the Principal be in such Manner [g] acquitted of it, [h] whether at the Suit of the King, or of the Party, that he may plead such Acquittal in [i] Bar of any subsequent Prosecution for the same Felony, the Accessary shall not be arraigned, but shall be discharged, according to the Rule, *Ubi factum* [k] *nullum, ibi fortia nulla.*

[a] Lamb. B. 2. ch. 9. Bract. B. 3. ch. 32. S. 9. Dalt. ch. 108. H. P. C. 219. Crompt. 42. Sect. 22. S. P. C. 26. *See* B. 1. ch. 1. Sect. 9, 10.
[b] Bract. Lib. 3. ca. 32. Sect. 9, 10. Dalt. ch. 108. *See* B. 1. ch. 1. Sect. 11, 12. Fitz. Coro. 383.
[c] Dalt. ch. 108. Crompt. 42. Sect. 22. H. P. C. 219. S. P. C. 26. Lett. C.
[d] 21 H. 7. 34. pl. 34. *See* Bro. Coro. 62. H. P. C. 219 Crompt. 42. pl. 15. Dalt ch. 108. Lamb. B. 2. ch. 7.
[e] Supra ch. 18. Sect. 13. ch. 19 S. 25.
[f] Vide 9 Ass pl. 5. Bract. 128. pl. 13, 14. *and the Notes to the fourth of these Points.*
[g] Fitz. Ass. 291. Conspiracy, 4. H. P. C. 221. S. P. C. 47. Lett. F. 48. Lett. A. Supra, ch. 23. Sect. 140. Fitz. Coro. 222. 33 H. 6. 1. pl. 6. 29 Ass pl. 59. Ra. Ent. 57. pl. 6. Raym. 477. Fitz. Office de Court, 23.
[h] Fitz. Coro. 277.
[i] Vide supra. ch. 23. Sect. 140.
[k] 4 Co. 43. b. S. P. C. 47. Lett. F.

Sect. 37. How far the Accessary shall be discharged upon the Principal's being found guilty of Manslaughter, *&c.* hath been already shewn *Section*, 24.

Sect. 38. It is certain that the Exigent shall not be awarded against the Accessary before the Principal is attainted, as hath been more fully shewn, *Ch.* 27. *Sect* 128, *&c.*

Sect. 39 It seems also to be clear, That where the Law requires the Attainder or Conviction of the Principal before the Accessary shall be convicted, it requires that such Attainder and Conviction of the Principal be on the [a] same Suit, and for the same Crime, of which the Accessary is to be convicted; for it is agreed, That an Attainder of the Principal at the Suit of the [b] King no way helps the Proceedings against the Accessary at the Suit of the Party, and *sic e converso:* Also it seems to be agreed, That the Attainder of the Principal of one Felony is no way [c] material as to the Proceedings against the Accessary for another.

Sect. 40. But where the Principal is actually attainted, tho' erroneously, of the same Felony with which the Accessary is charged, it seems [d] agreed, That such Attainder, while it stands unreversed, is as sufficient for this Purpose as it would have been if there had been no Error in it. Yet it seems [e] certain, That if the Principal be attainted, and then the Accessary, the Reversal of the Attainder of the Principal, *ipso facto* reverses the Attainder of the Accessary; and that the Heir may have an Assise of *Mortdancester* against the Lord of the Fee, having entred into the Lands of such an Accessary, as having escheated to him by Reason of the Attainder.

Sect. 41. It seems to have been in a great Measure settled [f] before the Statute of 1 *Annæ* 9. notwithstanding the great Variety of Opinions in the *Old Books* concerning this Matter, That where-ever the Attainder of the Principal was prevented by his [g] Death, or [h] standing Mute, or challenging [i] peremptorily above the Number allowed him by Law, or being admitted [k] to the Benefit of the Clergy, or [l] pardoned, whether before or after his Conviction, the Accessary should not be arraigned.

Sect. 42. But it seems to have been generally always agreed, [m] That after the Principal is actually attainted, whether after a Conviction by Verdict, or by [n] Outlawry, *&c.* his Death or Pardon, *&c.* subsequent, will no way avail the Accessary.

[a] Bro App. 19.
[b] 2 Inst. 184. Plowd. 98, b. 99. a. H P. C. 221. S P. C. 47. Lett. A. Bro. Coro. 19. 7 H. 4 27. Vide Dyer, 133. pl. 4.
[c] 40 Ass. pl. 25 H. P. C. 222. 22 Ass. pl. 40.
[d] Fitz. Coro. 58. 2 R. 3. 21, b. 22. a. H. P. C. 222, 223. 2 Inst. 184. Crompt. 43. pl. 29. Bro. Coro. 164 or 5. 174 or 5. S. P. C. 47. Lett. D 7 H. 4. 16. pl. 5. 9 Co. 68. b. 119.
[e] H. P. C. 164. 270. Bro. Coro. 18 E 4. 9. pl. 16.

Cromton's Justice, 41. pl. 9. 1 Rol. Ab. 777. pl. 10. 9 Co. 119 b. Fitz Mordancester, 46. [f] *See the Preamble of* 1 Annæ, 9. [g] Bro. Appeal, 19. Coro. 86 7 H. 4. 27. pl 4. Fitz Coro. 378. Conspiracy, 4. Responder, 35. F. N. B. 115. Lett. F. H. P. C. 221. 44 E. 3. 7. pl. 6. 33 H. 6. 1, 2 pl. 6. 21 H. 7. 31. pl. 15. 22 Ass. pl. 40. [h] H. P. C. 221. 2 Inst. 184 Cont. Fitz Coro. 58 *this is made a Quære* S. P. C. 47. Lett. C. [i] *See the Statute of* 1 Annæ 9. *But this is made a Quære* S. P. C. 47. Letter C. Fitz Coro. 51. 3 H. 7. 12 pl. 5, 8. [k] Cro El. 541. 4 Co. 43, b, 44 a. H. P. C. 221. 3 Inst. 114, 139. 3 H. 7. 1. pl. 3. Cro. Ca. 566, 567 Crompton's Justice, 43, pl. 26, 44. pl. 42. Raym. 477. Fitz. Coro. 145, 176, 193, 252, 376, 450. Bro. Coro. 18, 70, 71, 83, 84, 101, 131 or 132, 137 or 138. 18 Ass. pl. 13. 26 Ass. pl. 27. 5 Assise, pl. 5. 7 H. 4. 16. pl. 5. Bro. Clergy, 15. Cont. Fitz. Coro. 58, 53, 270, 466. Crompton's Justice, 42. pl. 26. 10 H. 4, 5 pl. 17. Bro. Coro. 157 or 158. *Quære* 3 H. 7. 12 pl. 10. S. P. C. 47. H. 48. A. [l] H. P. C. 221. F. N B. 115. Lett. F. Cro. El. 541. Fitz Coro. 53. Fitz Conspiracy, 4. 33 H. 6. 1. pl. 6. Bro. Coro. 18. 4 Co 43, b 44 a. 3 Inst. 139. Cromp. Justice, 44. pl. 42. 3 H. 7. 12. pl. 10. 7 H. 4. 16. pl. 5. Raym. 477. *This is made a Quære*, Crompton's Justice, 42. pl. 26. and S. P. C. 47. G. Cont. Fitz. Coro. 151, 260. Bro. Coro. 70. 3 Assise, pl. 14. Vide Dyer, 88. pl. 105. [m] Cro. Eliz. 541. 4 Co. 43, b. 44. a. H. P. C. 221. Raym. 477. Cont. Fitz Cor. 450. [n] 4 Co. 43. b. Dy. 120. pl. 10. Fitz. Coro. 58, 93. 40 Assise pl. 8. 43 E. 3. 17. pl. 21. 3 H. 7. 1. pl. 3. 9 H. 4. 8, b. 9. a. Bro. Coro. 164 or 5. 174 or 5. Bro. Mainprise, 58. Cont. *as to Abjuration*, 7. H. 4. 16. pl. 5. Bro. Coro. 18.

Sect. 43. And it is enacted by the said Statute of 1 *Anne* 9. Par. 1. *That if any principal Offender shall be convicted of any Felony, or shall stand Mute, or shall peremptorily challenge above the Number of twenty Persons, returned to serve on the Jury, it shall and may be lawful to proceed against any Accessary, either before or after the Fact, in the same Manner as if such principal Felon had been attainted thereof, notwithstanding any such principal Felon shall be admitted to the Benefit of his Clergy, pardoned, or otherwise delivered before his Attainder*; *and such Accessary shall suffer the same Punishment, if he or she shall be convicted, or shall stand Mute, or peremptorily challenge above the Number of twenty Persons returned to serve on the Jury, as he or she should have suffered if the Principal had been attainted.*

Sect. 44. And it is recited by the same Statute, *Par.* 2. *That the Buyers and Receivers of stolen Goods had oftentimes conveyed away and concealed the Principal Felons, so that they could not be convicted of such principal Felony, and thereby such Buyers and Receivers had escaped all Manner of Punishment, which had greatly encouraged the Buying and Receiving of such stolen Goods*; and thereupon it is enacted, *That it shall and may be lawful to prosecute and punish every such Person or Persons buying or receiving any stolen Goods, knowing the same to be stolen, as for a Misdemeanor, to be punished by Fine and Imprisonment, altho' the principal Felon be not convicted before of the said Felony, which shall exempt the Offender from being punished as Accessary, if the Principal shall be afterwards convicted.*

Sect. 45. As to the second Point, *viz.* Whether the Accessary shall in any Case be arraigned or tried before any Principal hath appeared: Notwithstanding the numerous [a] Authorities in the Old Books, that an Accessary shall not be compelled to answer before the Principal have appeared and answered, I take the contrary Opinion to be in a great Measure [b] settled at this Day. And yet it seems to have been always agreed, [c] That his Plea cannot be tried before such Appearance or Attainder, [d] unless he desire it himself; in which Case it is agreed, That he may be tried without the Principal, according to the Rule that *Quilibet potest renunciare juri pro se introducto.*

Sect. 46. As to the third Point, *viz.* Whether a Person charged as Accessary to more than one Principal, may be tried before all of them have appeared: It seems to be holden by Sir [e] *Matthew Hale*, agreeably to what seems to be the stronger [f] Opinion in *Plowden*, That if a Man be indicted as Accessary to more than one, and one of the Principals appear and be convict, the Court may, if they please, try the Accessary, as being Accessary to such Principal, and also condemn him if the Issue be found against him; and if it be found for him, may afterwards arraign and try him as Accessary to the other when they shall appear, But the contrary Opinion is certainly supported by great [g] Authorities; neither do I find any Instance in the Books wherein the Court hath actually proceeded to the Trial of an Accessary in such a Case before all the Principals have either appeared, or been attainted: And [h] unless there be some very particular Circumstances in the Case, it cannot be doubted but that it will be a weighty Motive to induce the Court in Discretion to respite the Trial of an Accessary, to shew that some of those to whom he is charged as an Accessary, are neither attainted, nor have appeared; for

[a] Bro. Coro. 11, 20, 118. 9 H. 7. 19 pl. 14 Bract. 128, pl. 11. 139, pl. 11. 142, pl. 8. 148. pl. 4 Fitz. Responder, 35, 36. Coro. 33, 82, 90, 135, 135, 216, 350. Trespass 199. 44 E. 3. 38, pl. 35. 9 E. 4. 48. pl. 1. 40 E. 3. 42. pl. 22. 44 E. 3. 7 pl. 6. 25 E. 3. 44. pl. 14. 40 Ass. pl. 8. 25. Bro. Appeal, 9. 189. 2 R. 3. 21. pl. 50. Bro. Mainprise, 58. S. P. C. 46. D. *'Tis said that the Law was so anciently but that it is now changed.* The Dalton ch. 108. *seems to be for the old Opinion.* [b] H. P. C. 222. 9 H. 4. 3. a. Fitz. Coro. 77. Bro. Appeal 28. S. P. C. 46. Lett. D. [c] H. P. C. 222. Bro. Appeal, 28. 9 H. 4. 3. a. Fitz. Coro. 77. S. P. C. 46. Letter D. 1 And. 109. [d] Fitz. Coro. 12, 124, 463. H. P. C. 222. S. P. C. 46. Letter D. [e] H. P. C. 222. [f] Plowd. Com. 98, b. 99. [g] S. P. C. 46. G. *See the Books cited to Section* 47. 7 H. 4. 36. pl. 5. *Quære* Bro. Appeal 22. 7 H. 4. 36, pl. 5. Keil. 107. [h] Plow. Com. 99 b. 7 H. 4. 36. pl. 5.

it must be owned, That it is a strong Objection against the trying him immediately, as Accessary to those who do appear, that thereby the Country may be subject to the Trouble of attending two Trials where one might do as well; and the Person tried may be subject to the Hardship and Hazard of two Trials for his Life, which is contrary to the general Course of the Law, (as shall be more fully shewn under the Chapter concerning the Plea of *Auterfoits acquit*,) whereas if the Trial should be deferred till all the Principals be attainted or appear, he would be tried but once. [a] But if there be several Principals, and a Person be charged as Accessary to one of them only, it seems clear, That it is no Objection against his being tried as Accessary to such a Principal, that the others have not yet appeared, nor are attainted, *&c.*

Sect. 47. As to the fourth Point, *viz.* Whether the Principal and Accessary may be both tried by the same Inquest, and in what Manner they are to be so tried: It seems [b] to be settled at this Day, That if the Principal and Accessary appear together, and the Principal plead the general Issue, the Accessary shall be put to plead also; and that if he likewise plead the general Issue, both may be tried by [c] one Inquest; but that the Principal must be [d] first convicted; and that the Jury shall be charged, that if they find the Principal not guilty, they shall find the Accessary not guilty. But it seems agreed, That if the Principal plead a Plea in Bar, or to the Writ, the Accessary shall not [e] be driven to answer till such Plea be determined.

Sect. 48. As to the fifth Point, *viz.* In what Manner the Accessary shall be tried, where his Offence arises in a different County from that of the Principal: It seems to have been [f] agreed antiently, That by the Common Law, if a Town extended into more than one County, and a Felony were committed in that Part of it which lay in one County, and there were Accessaries in that Part of it which lay in another County, an Appeal might be brought against the Accessaries as well as the Principals, in that County in which the principal Felony was committed; and where the Counties were at a Distance, it seems that it may be probably argued, [g] That an Appeal might be brought in like Manner against all in the County wherein the principal Felony was committed; because in an Appeal the Trial may be by a Jury returned from each County. But where one of the Counties can not join with any other in taking an Inquest; as that of *London*, *&c.* it [h] hath been adjudged, That an Appeal against the Accessary could not be brought in either. Also, because there can be no [i] Joinder of Counties for the finding of an Indictment, it seems to have been very [k] doubtful at the Common Law, where the Offence of the Accessary arose in a different County from that of the Principal, whether it could be indicted at all; because the County in which it arose could

[a] S. P. C. 46. Lett. G.

[b] H. P. C. 222. Dy. 120 p. 10. 2 Inst. 184. 28 E. 3. 94. pl. 3. Fitz. Coro. 10. 17. S. P. C. 46. Lett. F. Rast. Ent. 50. pl. 18. 52, a. pl. 15. 54. pl. 5. Fitz Exigent, 4. Mainprise, 3. Cont. Bract. 128, pl. 13, 139, pl. 11, 142, pl. 8, 148 pl. 4. 44 E. 3 7 pl. 6. Fitz. Coro. 82. 90, 135, 216, 350. Trespass 199. 40 E. 3. 42. pl. 22. 25 E. 3. 44. pl. 14. 40 Ass. pl 8. 25. 44 E. 3. 8. pl. 35. Bro. Appeal, 9. Coro. 11, 118. Mainprise, 58. 2 R. 3. 21. pl. 50. *In all which Books it seems to be holden, That the Accessary is not compellable to answer till all the Principals be convict.*

[c] *See the Books cited to Letter* b. Cont Fitz. Coro. 10, 77, 82. 9 H. 4. 3. a. 7 H 4. 36. pl. 5. Dyer 120. pl. 10, 11. S. P. C. 46 Lett. D. E. F. G. [d] H. P. C. 222. Fitz. Coro. 10. Rast. Entr. 50, b. 51. a, 52, pl. 15. 54. b. 9 Co. 117. [e] Bro. Peremptory, 43. 2 Inst. 184. S. P. C. 46. Lett. F. [f] 44 Ass. pl. 16 43 E. 3. 17. pl. 21. and f. 34. b. Fitz Coro. 93. Bro. Coro. 125. 45 Ass. pl. 9. Bro. Appeal, 80. *But* S. P. C 63. Lett. H. *this Case seems to be cited with some Doubt.* [g] 3 H. 7. 12. pl. 4. *See* B. 1. ch. 31. Sect. 18. *and* Dyer 38, 39, 40. 7 Co. 2. b. *But* Fitz. Coro. 93. *and* Bro. Coro. 125 *or* 6 *and* Bro. Appeal, 7. *and* 45 Ass. pl. 9. S. P. C. 63. Lett. H. *seems to be contrary. And in* S. P. C. 65. Lett. D. *there is an Opinion, That in this Case there shall be several Appeals in the several Counties. But now one Appeal is sufficient, in the Case of Murder, by Force of* 2 *&* 3 E. 6. 24. *set forth more at large in the next Section. See* H. P. C. 188. *Quære* 44 Ass pl. 16. 43 E. 3. 17. pl. 21. and f. 34. b. [h] Dyer 38, 39. 40. 7 Co. 2. b. [i] Finch of Law, 411. B. 1. ch. 31. Sect. 13. [k] Kielw. 67. *the Accessary in such Case is said to be indictable in the County in which the principal Felony was committed. But in the Year-Book of* 9 E 4. 48 pl. 1. *Abridged* Fitz. Coro. 33 and Brook Indictm. 52 *the Accessary was indicted in the County in which he was Accessary, and the Court wrote to the Justices of the County wherein the principal Felony was committed, to certify whether the Principal were indicted before them And in* S. P. C 90. Let. C. *this Case is holden to be Law. See also* 3 Inst. 49, 135. *but in* S. P. C. 63. Lett. H. *It is said, That there was no Remedy at Common Law against the Accessary where his Offence was in a different County from that of the Principal.*

not

not take Conusance of the principal Felony arising in another County, without which they could not find that of the Accessary.

Sect. 49. But these Matters are fully cleared by the Statute of 2 & 3 *E* 6. 24. by which it is enacted, *Par.* 3. *That an Appeal of Murder may be sued in the same County where the Party feloniously striken or poisoned shall die, as well against the Principals as Accessaries, in whatsoever County or Place the Accessaries shall be guilty; and the Justices before whom any such Appeal shall be commenced, sued and taken, within the Year and Day after such Murder and Manslaughter committed and done, shall proceed against such Accessaries in the same County where such Appeal shall be so taken, in like Manner and Form, as if the same Offence of Accessaries had been committed in the same County where such Appeal shall be so taken, as well concerning the Trial by the Jurors, or twelve Men of such County where such Appeal shall be taken upon the Plea of not guilty, as otherwise.*

Sect. 50. And it is farther enacted, *Par.* 4. *That where any Murder or Felony shall be hereafter committed and done in one County, and another Person, or more, shall be Accessary or Accessaries in any Manner of wise, to any such Murder or Felony in any other County, that then an Indictment found or taken against such Accessary or Accessaries upon the Circumstances of such Matter before the Justices of the Peace, or other Justices or Commissioners, to inquire of Felonies in the County where such Offences of Accessary or Accessaries in any manner of wise, shall be committed or done, shall be as good and effectual in the Law, as if the said principal Offence had been committed or done in the same County where the same Indictment against such Accessary shall be found: And that the Justices of Gaol-Delivery, of* Oyer *and* Terminer, *or two of them, of or in such County where the Offence of any such Accessary shall be hereafter committed and done, upon Suit to them made, shall write to the* Custos Rotulorum, *or Keepers of the Records, where such Principal shall be attainted or convict, to certify them whether such Principal be attainted, convicted, or otherwise discharged of such principal Felony; who upon such writing to them, or any of them, directed, shall make sufficient Certificate in Writing, under their Seal or Seals, to the said Justices, whether such Principal be attainted, convicted or otherwise discharged, or not: And after they that so shall have the Custody of such Records, do certify that such Principal is attainted, convicted or otherwise discharged of such Offence by the Law; that then the Justices of Gaol-Delivery or of* Oyer *and* Terminer, *or other thereto authorised, shall proceed upon every such Accessary, in the County where such Accessary or Accessaries became Accessary, in such Manner and Form, as if both the said principal Offence and Accessary had been committed and done in the same County where the Offence of Accessary was, or shall be committed or done: And that every such Accessary shall answer upon his Arraignment, and receive such Trial, Judgment, Order and Execution, and suffer such Forfeitures, Pains and Penalties, as is used in other Cases of Felony; any Law or Custom to the contrary before used in any wise notwithstanding.*

In the Construction of this Statute, the following Points seem most Remarkable, *viz.*

a 8 Co. 118. a. Vide supra, ch. 25. Sect. 62.

Sect. 51. *First*, An Indictment against an Accessary, in pursuance of this Statute, in the County wherein he was Accessary, ought expresly to recite that the Principal did the Felony in the other County, and not barely that he was indicted for it; for that is only an Argument, and no direct Affirmation that he did it.

Sect. 52. *Secondly,* The Court of [a] King's Bench in Relation to a Person, there indicted, as an Accessary in the County wherein the said Court happens to sit, to a Felony in another County: And the Lord [b] High Steward, in Relation to a Peer to be tried before the Lords on an Indictment against him as Accessary in one County to a Felony in another, are within the Purview of the said Statute; not only because it is a remedial Law, and made to supply a very mischievous Defect of the Common Law, which oftentimes necessarily occasioned a Failer of Justice, and therefore ought to have a beneficial Construction: But also because the Court of King's Bench being the [c] supreme Court of *Oyer* and *Terminer,* and Gaol-Delivery, may naturally be included in the very Words of a Statute which gives such Justices any new Power; or if it be not thought to be strictly within the Words, it is at least within the Meaning of them, which otherwise would give a higher Privilege to an inferior Court than to a superior: And the like in Effect may be said in the Case of the Lord [d] Steward, who by the Words of his Commission, as well as the Nature of the Thing, seems to be a Justice of *Oyer* and *Terminer,* and within the very Words of the Statute, or at least within the Meaning. To which may be added that those Words in the latter Part of the Statute, *That then the Justices of Gaol-Delivery, or of* Oyer *and* Terminer, *or other there authorised, shall proceed against such Accessaries,* &c. seem plainly to imply, That such other so authorised may also send for a Certificate of the Record relating to the Principal; for nothing can be more Natural than to expound one Part of a Statute by another. As to the Objection, That the Words of the Statute are, that the said Justices, *or two of them,* shall write to the *Custos Rotulorum,* &c. And therefore that the Lord Steward cannot do it, because he is but one, it may be [e] answered, That those Words are to be thus construed, That where there are two or more such Justices, they must write, &c. but not where there is but one.

Sect. 53. *Thirdly,* Not only the Justices of the King's Bench, the Pleas before whom are properly styled [f] *Placita coram Rege,* and not *coram Justiciariis,* but any other Justices, writing for a Certificate in pursuance of the Statute, ought to do it by Writ in the King's Name, and not by a Precept in their own Names, and under their own Seals; and the Reason given by *Dyer* is because it is a Writing from Justices to Justices.

Sect. 54. *Fourthly,* Where some of those supposed to have been Accessaries to a Felony in a different County, are proceeded against in the King's Bench, in pursuance of the Statute, if there be a likelihood that others will be in the same Manner proceeded against in another Court, it seems most adviseable [g] to send for the Record relating to the Principal by a special Writ formed upon the Matter according to the Words of the Statute, and not by *Certiorari,* because that would wholly [h] remove the Record from the Court below into the Court of King's Bench, which might cause a Doubt, whether either the Court below, or that of King's Bench could certify it upon a subsequent Writ; for as to the Court below, it might be objected, That being no longer a Record of that Court, it cannot be certified by it; and as to the King's Bench, it might be objected, That the Principal was neither attainted nor convicted there: Whereas the Words of the Statute are, *That the Justices shall write to the Keepers of the Records where such Principal shall be attainted or convicted.* But these Doubts are avoided by [i] directing a special Writ to the Court below,

[a] 3 Inst. 49. 135. 9 Co. 118. H. P. C. 223. See the Notes to Section 48. under Lett. x.

[b] 3 Inst. 49. 135. H. P. C. 223.

[c] Vide supra, Ch. 3. Sect. 11.

[d] 3 Inst. 136.

[e] 3 Inst. 136.

[f] Dyer 253, pl. 103, 254. a. 12 Co. 32. H. P. C. 223. *But Sir Edw. Coke in* 3 Inst. 49. 135. *seems to make it necessary for the Justices of the King's Bench only to write in the King's Name.*

[g] 3 Inst. 49. 136.

[h] Vide supra, Ch. 27. Sect. 62 to 69. and Sect. 77 to 87.

[i] 3 Inst. 49. 136. Vide H. P. C. 223.

below, on which a ſpecial Certificate ſhall be made in purſuance of the Statute, and the Record ſhall ſtill remain below, and conſequently may be certified from thence on a ſubſequent Writ.

CHAP. XXX.

Of ſtanding Mute.

HAving ſhewn in what Manner a Priſoner is to be arraigned, I am in the next Place to examine in what Manner he is to be dealt with afterwards; and to that End ſhall endeavour to ſhew what is to be done with him,

1. Upon his ſtanding Mute.
2. Upon his Confeſſion.
3. Upon his Pleading.

And firſt, as to the Priſoner's ſtanding Mute, I ſhall conſider,

1. Where he ſhall be ſaid to ſtand Mute.
2. How it ſhall be tried whether he do ſo of Malice, or by the Act of God.
3. What ſhall be done where one is found to ſtand Mute by the Act of God.
4. Where he who ſtands Mute ſhall be awarded to the ſame Execution as if he had not ſtood Mute, and where he ſhall be adjudged to his Penance.
5. What is the Nature of ſuch Penance.
6. What he ſhall forfeit, and to whom.
7. Whether the Proſecutor of an Indictment or Appeal of Larceny be intitled to a Reſtitution of the Goods ſtolen, upon the Defendan's ſtanding Mute.
8. Where one that ſtands Mute ſhall have the Benefit of the Clergy.

Sect. 1. As to the firſt Point, *viz.* In what Caſes a Man ſhall be ſaid to ſtand Mute: I take it to be agreed, That he who anſwers impertinently, or ineffectually, or refuſes to put himſelf upon his Trial in ſuch Manner as the Law directs, may as properly be ſaid to ſtand Mute as he who makes no Anſwer at all; as where a Man [a] refuſes to plead a Plea in Chief, or the General Iſſue, but inſiſts on ſome frivolous Defence, or even to plead a good [b] dilatory Plea, and refuſes to plead over to the Felony, in which Caſe, after ſuch Plea is found againſt him, he ſhall not [c] be admitted to plead in Chief, but ſhall be adjudged to his Penance in the ſame Manner as if he had made no Plea at all. And ſo ſhall he be

[a] Dy. 241, 49. H. P. C. 226. S. P. C. 150. Letter, E.
[b] Keilw. 70. a. Vide Bro. Coro. 22.
[c] Keilw. 70. a.

4 who

who pleads a good Plea in Chief, or the General Iſſue, but [a] refuſeth to put himſelf upon the Inqueſt (that is, to be tried by God and his Country if a Commoner, or by God and his [b] Peers, if a Lord) or to wage Battle where ſuch Trial is [c] allowed.

Sect. 2. It ſeems to be holden in the [d] ſecond *Inſtitute*, and alſo in the latter Part of Sir *Mathew Hale*'s *Pleas of the* [e] *Crown*, That if a Priſoner on his Trial peremptorily challenge above the Number allowed him by Law, he ſhall not be dealt with as one that ſtands Mute, but ſhall be hanged: But this very Point is made a *Quære* in another [f] Part of *Hale*'s *Pleas of the Crown*; and alſo in [g] *Kelynge*, and the contrary is holden in the third [h] *Inſtitute*: Neither does it ſeem eaſy to aſſign a Reaſon why he who challenges more Jurors than he ought, ſhall, in Reſpect of an implied Refuſal of a legal Trial, be thought worthy of a greater Puniſhment than he who obſtinately, directly, and expreſly refuſes it. To which may be added, That there ſeems to be but one * full Authority in the Old Books for the Maintenance of this Opinion, whereas there is a great [i] Number of the other Side.

Sect. 3. But it is clear, [k] That he who demurs in Law to an Indictment or Appeal, ſhall not be eſteemed to ſtand Mute, nor be dealt with as ſuch, as having refuſed a Trial by his Country, for he puts himſelf upon a Trial by the Court, which is the proper Trial of a Matter in Law.

Sect. 4. Alſo it ſeems clear, That after a Man hath † confeſſed himſelf guilty, or pleaded, and put himſelf upon his [l] Country, he ſhall not afterwards be demeaſned as one that ſtands Mute, in Reſpect of his ſubſequent Silence: But the Jury ſhall be charged, and the Trial ſhall proceed, and the like Judgment ſhall be given as in Common Caſes.

Sect. 5. As to the ſecond Point, *viz.* In what Caſes, and in what Manner it ſhall be tried, whether one who ſtands Mute do ſo of Malice, or of the Act of God: It ſeems agreed, [m] That where a Priſoner wholly ſtands Mute without making any Anſwer at all, the Court ſhall take an Inqueſt of Office by the Oath of any [n] twelve Perſons that [o] happen to be preſent, whether he do ſo of Malice, or by the Act of God. But [p] after an Iſſue hath been joined, if the Priſoner ſtand Mute when the Jury are in Court, if there be any need for ſuch Inquiry, it ſhall be made by them, and not by an Inqueſt of Office.

Sect. 6. Where [q] a Man anſwers, but not effectually, it ſeems needleſs to make any Inquiry whether his Refuſal be owing to his Malice or not, becauſe it is apparent.

Sect. 7. As to the third Point, *viz.* What ſhall be done where one is found to ſtand Mute by the Act of God: It is agreed, [r] That in ſuch a Caſe, the Judges of the Court, (who are always to be of Counſel with the Priſoner, to ſee that he have Law and Juſtice) ſhall not only cauſe the Felony to be enquired of, but alſo whether the Priſoner be the ſame Perſon, and all other Matters which he might have pleaded in his Defence. And ſuch Inquiry ſhall be made, as I ſuppoſe, not by an Inqueſt of Office,

[a] Bro. Pain. 2, 14, 15. S P. C. 150. Lett. E. Bro. App. 93. 2 Inſt. 178. H. P C. 226. Fitz. Coro. 27. 30, 359. 4 E. 4. 11. pl. 18. 7 E. 4. 29 pl. 13. 14 E. 4. 7. pl. 10. 3 Inſt. 227. Vide Bro. Coro. 149 8 E. 4. 3. pl 6.
[b] Kely. 57.
[c] *For this ſee Chapter of the Trial by Battel, and* S. P. C. 81. Lett. E.
[d] 2 Inſt. 178.
[e] H. P. C. 259.
[f] H. P. C. 226.
[g] Kely. 36.
[h] 3 Inſt. 227.
* 3 H. 7. 12. pl. 5. *Abridged* Fitz. Coro. 56. *And* Bro. Cor. 135 *or* 6. *And* Bro. Pain 5. *And Note, there is no other Authority cited for this Opinion by* Coke, Hale, *or* Kelynge. 2 Inſt. 178. H. P. C. 259. Kely. 36.
[i] Fitz Coro. 359. 3 H. 7. 12. pl. 8. *Abridged* Fitz. Fitz Coro. 51. *and* Bro. Clergy, 27. *And Note that this Caſe is the more remarkable, becauſe of the very ſame Year with the former, and ſubſequent to it.*

Vide Kely. 36. 3 H. 7. 2. pl. 5. *the like is ſaid to be adjudged by all the Juſtices but* Keble; *and this Caſe is abridged* Bro. Appeal 82. Pain, 4. [k] *See the next Chapter, Sect.* 5. † S. P. C. 150. Lett. C. *Same Point admitted* 8 H. 4. 3. pl. 5. *which is abridged,* Bro. Pain, 2. *but in theſe Books it is incidently holden, That where a Man does not confeſs, but pleads not Guilty, and after ſtands Mute, he ſhall be put to his Penance.* [l] Kely. 36, 37. H. P. C. 225, 226. 15 E. 4. 33 pl. 19. *Abridged* Bro. Penance, 19. and Bro. Coro. 51. Cont. 8 H. 4. 3. pl. 5. *for which ſee the Note next above.* [m] H. P. C. 225. S. P. C. 150. Lett. C. 2 Inſt. 177, 178. 8 H. 4. 1. pl. 2. Fitz. Coro. 71, 225. 43 Aſſ. pl. 30. Bro. Appeal, 24. [n] Ra. Ent. 385. pl. 3. [o] 8 H. 4. 1. pl. 2. Fitz. Coro. 71. Bro. Appeal, 24. [p] S. P. C. 150. Lett. D. *from the Authority of* 8 H. 4. 3. *for which ſee the Notes to the precedent Section.* [q] Vide H. P. C. 225, 226. S. P. C. 150. Lett. D. 2 Inſt. 177, 178. [r] S. P. B. 150. Lett. D. 2 Inſt. 177, 178. H. P. C. 225.

but

but by a Jury returned by the Sheriff in the same Manner as if the Defendant had actually pleaded; for since it is no way his Fault that he did not so plead, there is no Reason why his Trial should be in a more loose and summary Manner, or any way less regular, or solemn, than if he had. To which may be added, That Sir *Mathew Hale* saith, [a] *That the Felony shall be enquired of*, &c. *in the same Manner as if the Prisoner had pleaded Not guilty*; from which Words it seems plain, That in his Opinion the Inquiry ought to be by an Inquest returned by the Sheriff as in other Trials at the Mise of the Parties, because if the Defendant had pleaded, it must certainly have been so. And therefore it seems reasonable, That where Sir *William Staundforde* [b] having spoken of such Inquiry, adds immediately, That it is but an Inquest of Office, ought to be understood, not of the Inquiry of the Felony, whereof he had last spoken, but of the Inquiry whether the Prisoner stood Mute of Malice, or by the Act of God, whereof he had spoken in the Sentence next before. And I the rather incline to think that this is his Meaning, because the [c] Books cited by him, to this Point, relate to this Inquiry only.

[a] H. P. C. 225.

[b] S. P. C. 150. Lett. D.

[c] Fitz. Coro. 225. 43 Ass. pl. 30. 8 H. 4. 1. pl. 2.

As to the fourth Point, *viz.* In what Cases he that stands Mute shall be awarded to the same Execution as if he had not stood Mute, and where he shall be adjudged to his Penance, I shall consider,

1. What shall be done to him who stands Mute after an Attainder.
2. What to a Person arraigned for High Treason.
3. What to one arraigned for Petit Larceny.
4. What to one arraigned for a Felony by Statute.
5. What to one arraigned upon an Appeal.
6. What to one indicted of a capital Felony, or Petit Treason.

Sect. 8. As to the first Particular, *viz.* What is to be done to him who stands Mute after an Attainder: It seems to be settled [d] at this Day, That where-ever one who is attainted, either by Judgment on a Verdict, or Confession, or by Outlawry, or Abjuration, stands Mute to the Demand why Execution should not go against him, he shall not be awarded to his Penance, but to the same kind of Execution, if any, that wou'd have been awarded if he had not stood Mute. Yet there seems to be this Difference, That where one who hath always continued in Prison, after an Attainder by Verdict or Confession, stands Mute to the Demand why Execution should not go, it shall be awarded [e] against him, without any Inquiry whether he stand Mute by Malice, or otherwise, or whether he be the same Person who is so attainted or not; because it sufficiently appears that he is the same Person, and that is sufficient to justify an Award of Execution against him, where nothing appears to the contrary. But if a Person so attainted, be re-taken after an Escape; or if one be taken after an Outlawry or Abjuration, and stand Mute to the Demand, Why Execution should not go against him? it shall be inquired whether he stand Mute of Malice, or of the Act of God; and if it be found of Malice, it seems that Execution shall be awarded without any farther inquiry: [g] But if it be found to be of the Act of God, it seems That it ought to be also inquired, whether he be the same Person or not, in the same Manner as where one stands Mute by the Act of God, when first brought upon his Trial.

[d] H. P. C. 226. Kely. 36. S. P. C. 150. Lett. C. D. *So adjudged*, 8 H. 4. 3. pl. 5. *Abridged* Bro. Pain, 2. Coro. 22 *as to the Case of Abjuration or any other Attainder after a Confession; but the contrary is insinuated as to other Attainders But* in 26 Ass. pl. 19 *Abridged* Fitz. Coro. 191. Bro. Pain 12. Coro. 99 *one who had abjured standing Mute, was put to his Penance, and not hang'd.*

[e] S. P. C. 150. Lett. C. D. 10 E. 4. 19. pl. 26. Fitz. Coro. 36. Bro. Coro. 155.

[g] S. P. C. 150. Lett. C. D 10 E. 4. 19. pl. 26. Fitz. Coro. 36. Bro. Coro. 155.

Sect. 9. As to the second Point, *viz.* What is to be done to one who stands Mute to an Arraignment for High Treason: It is clearly settled [a] at this Day, That standing Mute upon an Arraignment for High Treason is equivalent to a Conviction by Verdict, or Confession, and consequently subjects the Criminal to the same Kind of Judgment and Execution as such a Conviction would do. But I take it for granted, That such standing Mute must in [b] like manner appear to be obstinate; and that if it be found to be the Act of God, the whole Matter shall in like Manner [c] be inquired of, as hath been more fully shewn in the former Part of this Chapter. But where such Prisoner appears to stand obstinately Mute, I do not find it any where holden, That there is any Necessity that he probably appear to be Guilty, or that any Evidence be examined to prove him so, before he shall be condemned or executed. But this is adviseable, where one stands obstinately Mute on an Arraignment for Felony by Statute, as shall be more fully shewn in the fourteenth and fifteenth *Sections.*

Sect. 10. As to the third Particular, *viz.* What is to be done to one who stands Mute to an Arraignment for Petit Larceny: I take it to be agreed, [d] That if a Man appear to stand obstinately Mute on an Arraignment for Petit Larceny, he shall have the like Judgment, *&c.* as if he had confessed the Indictment.

Sect. 11. As to the fourth Particular, *viz.* What is to be done to those who stand Mute to an Arraignment for Felony by Statute: It is expressly enacted by 33 *H.* 8. 12. *Par.* 12. *That if a Person indicted, and arraigned of Treason, Misprision of Treason, Murder, Manslaughter, or Bloodshed,* &c. *against that Act, within the Verge of the Court, shall obstinately refuse to answer directly, or shall stand Mute, he shall have like Judgment,* &c. *as if he were found Guilty,* &c, But [e] where a Statute, as that of *Piracy, &c.* ordains a Trial by the Common Course of the Law, it hath been adjudged, That the Criminal shall have Judgment of his Penance, *&c.* as in other Felonies.

Sect. 12. As to the fifth Particular, *viz.* What is to be done to one who stands Mute to an Arraignment on an Appeal: It is holden by Sir *Matthew Hale,* [f] That an Appellee of Felony standing Mute shall not have Judgment of Penance, but to be hanged; but this is made a *Quære* in [g] *Staundforde,* and [h] *Brook*; and the contrary Opinion seems to be favoured by Sir [i] *Edward Coke,* and is expresly holden by [k] *Kelynge,* and supported by several [l] Resolutions in the Old Books. Whereas the *Year-Book* of 21 [m] *E.* 3. seems to be the only Resolution in favour of the other Side; to which it may be answered, Not only that three of the abovecited Resolutions to the contrary, are much later, but also that the Appellee in this Case appears to have been taken with the Manner, [n] which probably might be a Circumstance of considerable weight in the Judgment.

Sect. 13. As to the sixth Particular, *viz.* What is to be done to one who stands Mute to an Indictment of a Capital Felony, or a Petit Treason: It is enacted by the [o] abovementioned Statute of *Westminster,* 1. 12. *That notorious Felons which openly be of evil Fame, and will not put themselves*

[a] H. P. C. 226. Savil. 56. pl. 121. Kely. 57. Dyer 205. pl 4. 2 Inst. 177, 178. Bro. Pain, 19 Co. Litt. 391 3 Inst. 14. S. P. C. 150. Lett. C. Cont. Fitz. Coro. 283. [b] Vide supra, Sect. 5, 6. 18 E. 3. pl 26. S. P. C. 150. Lett. D [c] Vide supra, Sect. 7. S. P. C. 150. Lett. D. [d] 2 Inst. 177.

[e] Dyer 241. Pl. 49. 3 Inst. 114. B. 1. Ch. 37. pl. 9. S. P. C. 150. Lett. C. H. P. C. 226. [f] H. P. C. 226. [g] S. P. C. 150. Lett. B. [h] Bro. Pain. 8, 19. [i] 2 Inst. 178, 179. [k] Kely. 37. [l] 8 H. 4. 1. pl. 2. *Abridged* Bro. Pain, 1. Forfeiture, 11. Appeal, 24. Fitz. Coro. 71. 4 E 4. 11 pl. 18. *Abridged* Fitz. Coro. 71. Bro. Appeal 93. Pain, 14. 43 Ass. pl. 30. *Abridged* Bro. Pain, 13. Appeal, 78. Coro. 123 *or* 124 Fitz. Coro. 225. 14 E. 4. 7. pl. 10. *This Point is made a Quære; but in the very next folio* pl. 17. *abridged* Bro. Coro. 160 *or* 161. *it is adjudged by all the Justices, That the Appellee in such Case should have his Penance.* [m] 21 E. 3. 18. pl. 26. *Abridged* Bro. Pain, 8. Appeal, 40. Coro. 43. *But neither* Fitz Coro. 56. *nor* 3 H. 7. 2. pl. 5. *nor* 3 H. 7. 12. pl. 5. *cited by* Staundforde, *seem to come up to this Point, but rather to be Authorities of the other Side.* *See* Bro. Coro. 82. [n] Vide supra Ch. 25. 41. [o] Vide 2 Inst. 177, 178.

in Enquests of Felonies, that Men shall charge them with before the Justices at the King's Suit, shall have strong and hard Imprisonment, as they which refuse to stand to the Common Law of the Land. But this is not to be understood of such Prisoners as be taken on light Suspicion.

[a] 2 Inst. 177.

Sect. 14. Sir [a] *Edward Coke*, in the Construction of this Statute, saith, That no Person shall be put to this Punishment, unless the Matter be evident, or probable, which it is the Duty of the Judge to look into; and Sir *William* [b] *Staundforde*, saith, That there ought to be evident or probable Matter to convince the Party of the Crime whereof he is arraigned, or otherwise that he be a notorious Felon, or openly of bad Fame; and therefore he advises the Judge, for the satisfaction of this Statute, and discharge of his Duty, to examine the Evidence which proves the Prisoner Guilty of the Fact, before he proceed to the Judgment of *Pain fort & dure.* Yet I cannot find any Book which takes Notice of any Examination of this Kind, or of any Entry that the Defendant appeared to be a notorious Felon, before such Judgment given against him, upon his standing Mute, whether upon an [c] Indictment or [d] Appeal: But all the Books cited in the Margin seem to intimate, That the standing Mute is of itself a sufficient Ground for such Judgment. Yet all that can be inferred from thence seems to be this, That it is not necessary to make any thing of this Kind Part of the Record, it being a Matter left to the Discretion and Conscience of the Judge, and to be presumed where it is not expressed. But as to all Capital Appeals whatsoever, and all Indictments and Appeals of Petit Treason, perhaps it may be said, That [e] not being within this Statute, but remaining as they were at the Common Law, the Obstinacy of a Criminal in standing Mute to them, may be of it self, without more, a sufficient Inducement to a Judge to award him to his Penance. But considering that such Appeals and Indictments are within the same Reason with those mentioned in the Statute; and it is uncertain how the Common Law stood in Relation to these Matters, as appears by the best Authors, [f] differing among themselves concerning them; and seeing the Method prescribed by the Statute is very just and equitable, it seems prudent at least in a Judge to observe the same Rules in all Cases of this Kind.

[b] S. P. C. 150. Letter A. Vide H. P. C. 226.

[c] Ra. Ent. 385. pl. 2, 3. Keilw. 70. a. 7 E. 4. 29. pl. 13. 3 H. 7. 12. pl. 5, 8.

[d] 8 H. 4. 1. pl. 2. 4 E. 4. 11. pl. 18 14 E. 4. 7. pl 10. 43 Aff pl. 30. 21 E. 3. 18. pl 26. 3 H. 7. 2 pl. 5.

[e] S. P. C 150. Lett. B. C. 2 Inst. 177, 178, 179 *And the Books cited Sect. 12 under Lett.*

[f] S P. C. 149 Lett. F. 2 Inst. 178, 179.

Sect. 15. I do not find it said in any Book, what shall be done to a Prisoner who obstinately standing Mute to an Arraignment, shall appear to be charged upon very light Suspicion; but I take it for granted, That he may be severely fined and imprisoned for his Contempt.

Sect. 16. As to the fifth Point, *viz.* What is the Nature of the Penance to which a Prisoner is to be adjudged upon his obstinately standing Mute: It is observable, That the above-cited Statute of *Westm.* 1. says only in general, That Felons standing Mute shall be put *in Prison fort & dure*, without saying any thing of the Manner of it, which it seems to leave as a known Thing to the usual Practice in such Cases; which we shall best find from the Books of Entries, and other Law Books, all of which generally agree, That the Prisoner shall be remanded [g] to the Place from whence he came, and put [h] in some low dark Room, [i] and

[g] H P. C. 227. S. P. C 150. Lett. E. Kielw. 70. a. 4 E. 4 11. pl. 18. 14 E. 4. 8. pl. 17. *Abridged* Bro. Coro. 160. 2 Inst. 178. Ra. Ent. 385. pl. pl. 17. 8 H. 4. 1. pl. 2. [h] *This Clause is omitted in* Keilw. 70. a. 4 E. 4. 11. pl. 18. *but is mentioned in all the other Books above cited, but with this Difference, That* 14 E. 4. 11. pl 17. *says only that he shall be put in a Chamber, without adding that it shall be low or dark.* [i] *In this all the Books above cited seem to agree. And* 14 E. 4. 8. pl. 17. *and* S. P. C. 150. Lett. E. *and* 2 Inst. 178 *add, That he shall lie without any Litter or other thing under him, and that one Arm shall be drawn to one quarter of the Room with a Cord, and the other to another, and that his Feet shall be used in the same Manner. But these Clauses are wholly omitted in all the other Books above cited, except* H P. C. *which takes Notice of the Latter of them only And* Ra. Ent. 385. pl. 2. *adds, That a Hole shall be made for the Head, and* Keil. 70. a. *says, That the Head shall not touch the Earth; but none of the other mention either of these Clauses.*

there laid on his Back, without any manner of Covering, except for the Privy Parts, and * that as many Weights shall be laid upon him as he can bear, and more, and that he shall have no manner of Sustenance but of the worst [a] Bread and [b] Water, and that he shall [c] not eat the same Day in which he drinks, nor drink the same Day on which he eats; and that he shall so continue till he [d] die. But it is said [e], That anciently the Judgment was not, That he should so continue till he should die, but till he should answer, and that he might save himself from the Penance by putting himself on his Trial, which he cannot do at this Day after the Judgment of Penance is once given.

Sect. 17. It seems clear, [f] That Women upon standing Mute, are liable to such Penance as well as Men.

Sect. 18. It is said [g] to be the constant Practice at *Newgate* Sessions, where a Prisoner refuses to plead, to endeavour to compell him to do it by tying his Thumbs together with Whipcord, and not to proceed to the Judgment of Penance, before all Methods of persuading him to plead, are found ineffectual.

Sect. 19. As to the fifth Point, *viz.* What he who obstinately stands Mute shall forfeit, and to whom: There is no doubt but that in Case of [h] High Treason he shall forfeit both Lands and Goods, in the same Manner as if he had been attainted any other way. Also I take it for granted That in the Case of Felony and Petit Treason, where a Person by standing Mute shall not avoid being attainted for such Crimes, he shall forfeit his Lands and Goods in the same manner as on other Attainders. But where-ever a Person standing Mute is adjudged to his Penance, and thereby prevents that Attainder which otherwise he might have incurred, it seems agreed, [i] That he forfeits his Chattels only, and not his Lands.

Sect. 20. It is agreed in the *Year-Book* of 8 [k] *H.* 4. That the Goods so forfeited ought not to be delivered to any Person claiming them under a Grant from the Crown, till he have shewed a good Title to them in the King's Court, by some Grant sufficient to pass them.

Sect. 21. And it seems [l] That such Goods will not pass by Grant of all Felons Goods, having no Words specially extending to the Goods of those who stand Mute, &c. because a Person adjudged to his Penance for standing Mute, does not seem to suffer as a Felon, being neither attainted nor convicted of any Felony, but as a Person refusing to stand to the Law of the Land. And it seems rather the stronger Opinion, [m] That they pass not by the Grant of *all Goods of Felons and Fugitives of all Persons within such a District; so that if such Persons for any Trespass or other Fault ought to lose Life or Member; or shall fly and refuse to stand to Judgment, or do any other Trespass for which they ought to lose their Chattels.*

Sect. 22. As to the sixth Point, *viz.* Whether the Prosecutor of an Indictment or Appeal of Larceny be intitled to a Restitution of the Goods stolen, upon the Defendant's standing Mute: It seems agreed, [n] That by the Common Law, where a Person stands Mute to an Appeal of Larceny, it is proper to charge the same Inquest which is to enquire whether the standing Mute be of Malice or not, to inquire also whether the Goods mentioned in the Appeal are the Goods of the Appellant, and whether the Defendant were taken upon a fresh Suit [o] made by such Appellant,

* *In this all the Books above-cited agree.*
[a] *But* 14 E. 4. 8. pl. 17. S. P. C. 150. Lett. E. *and* 2 Inst. 178. *are, That he shall only have three morsels of Barley Bread a Day,* Keilw. 70. a. *that he shall have only Rye Bread; and* Ra. Ent. 385. pl. 2 *and* 2 H. 4 1. pl. 2. *generally that he shall have of the worst Bread.*
[b] 14 E. 4. 8. pl. 17. S. P. C. 150. Lett. E. 2 Inst. 178. *and* 8 H. 4. 1. pl. 2. *and* Kielw. 70. a. *are, That he shall have the Water next the Prison, so that it be not current; but* Ra. Ent. 385. pl. 5. *is general, That he shall have the worst Water.*
[c] *This is omitted in* Keilw. 70. a. *and in* 8 H 4 1. pl. 2.
[d] *This is omitted in none of the Books above cited, except* 14 E. 4. 11. *and* H. P. C. 227 *but neither of these Books give the whole Judgment at Large.*
[e] S. P. C. 150. Lett. F. 151. Lett. E. Briton 11.
[f] 2 Inst. 177.
[g] Kely. 27, 28.
[h] *See the Books cited to Sect* 9.
[i] 14 E. 4. 7. p. 10 H. P. C. 226, 227. Co. Litt 391. Fitz Esc. 10. Co. 10. 51. Ass. 421. S. P. C. 151. a. Bro. Forfeiture, 11, 64. Appeal, 24. 8 H. 4. 1. b. 2. a. b. 3 H. 7. 12. pl. 8.
[k] 8 H. 4. 2. a. Bro. Appeal, 24.
[l] Dy. 268 pl. 18. 8 H. 4. 2. a. b. Bro. Forfeiture, 11.
[m] Dy. 268. pl. 18. 8 H. 4. 2. a b, Bro. Forfeit. 11.
[n] Vide supra Ch. 23. Sect. 53. Lett. F. 8 H. 4. 1. pl. 2. *Abridged* Bro. Appeal, 24. S. P. C. 166.
[o] Vide ch. 23. Sect. 50, 51, 52.

which

which Points being found [p] for him, he ſhall have an Award of Reſtitution to ſuch Goods, and to ſuch only, [q] in whoſe Hands ſoever [r] they are found. And it is ſaid in general in ſome Books, [a] That in an Appeal of Larceny there ſhall be a Reſtitution of the Goods, upon the Appellee's ſtanding Mute, without ſaying any thing of any Inquiry concerning the Property, or freſh Suit: But I take it for granted, That where it is ſo omitted, it is taken as a Thing known, and done of Courſe, and therefore needleſs to be expreſly mentioned.

Sect. 23. But it ſeems queſtionable, Whether the Proſecutor of an Indictment of Larceny, be in like manner intitled to a Reſtitution, upon the Defendant's ſtanding Mute? Becauſe it ſeems agreed, [b] That by the Common Law there could be no ſuch Reſtitution upon any other Proſecution but an Appeal; and it is certain, That the Proſecutor of an Indictment is not intitled to a Reſtitution by the expreſs Words of 21 * *H.* 8. 11. which require, *That the Felon be found guilty, or otherwiſe attainted,* &c. And I do not know that he is intitled to it by any other Statute, or any equitable Conſtruction of this.

Sect. 24. As to the ſeventh Point, *viz.* Where one who ſtands Mute ſhall have the Benefit of his Clergy: It ſeems clear, [c] That unleſs it happen to be otherwiſe ſpecially provided by ſome Statute, where-ever he ſhall be allowed it upon a Conviction, by Verdict or Confeſſion, he ſhall have it upon his ſtanding Mute. Alſo I take it to be agreed, [d] That a Statute taking away the Benefit of the Clergy from thoſe who ſhall be convicted of a Crime, doth not thereby take it away from thoſe who ſtand Mute on an Indictment or Appeal for ſuch Crime. But it is enacted by 3 & 4 *W.* & *M.* 9. ſet forth more at Large in the Chapter of *Clergy, That if any Perſon ſhall be indicted of any Offence, for which by Vertue of any former Statute, he is excluded from the Benefit of his Clergy, if he had been thereof convicted by Verdict or Confeſſion, if he ſtand Mute he ſhall not be admitted to it.* But Appeals, and Offences excluded from the Benefit of the Clergy by ſubſequent Statutes, ſeem not to be within the Purview of this Statute, for the fuller Conſideration whereof I ſhall refer the Reader to the Chapter of *Clergy.*

[p] Supra Ch. 23. Sect. 53.
[q] Supra Ch. 23. Sect. 57.
[r] Supra Ch. 23. Sect. 54.
[a] 21 E. 3. 18. pl. 26. *Abridged* Bro. Appeal, 40. 43 Aſſ. pl. 30. *Abridged* Bro. Appeal, 78. Coro. 123 *or* 124. Fitz Coro. 225. Vide 40 Aſſ. pl. 39. *Abridged* Fitz. Coro. 217.
[b] Supra Ch. 23 Sect. 55, 56.
* *Set forth more more at large*, Ch. 23. Sect. 55.
[c] Fitz. Coro. 233, 283. Aſſ. 421. 8 H. 4 3. pl. 5. H. P. C. 231. Moore 550. pl. 738. 3 H. 7 12. pl. 8 *Abridged* Bro. Clergy, 27. Fitz. Coro. 51. 3 H 7. 12. pl. 10. *Abridged* Fitz. Coro. 53. Fitz Cor. 58. *ſe ms contrary. but I cannot find any thing in* 3 H. 7. 1. *Which is the* Year-Book *cited to this Note to warrant this Opinion.*
[d] *See* H. P. C. 232 *to* 238.

CHAP.

CHAP. XXXI.

Of Confeſſion and Demurrer.

AND now I am to conſider what is to be done to a Priſoner upon his Confeſſion, which may be either,

1. Expreſs, or,
2. Implied.

Sect. 1. An expreſs Confeſſion is where a Perſon directly confeſſes [a] the Crime with which he is charged, which is the higheſt Conviction that can be, and may be received [b] after the Plea of Not Guilty recorded, notwithſtanding the Repugnancy; for the Entry is, That the Defendant *poſtea*, or *relicta verificatione, cognovit indictamentum.*

Sect. 2. Such a Confeſſion carries with it ſo ſtrong a Preſumption of Guilt, that an Entry [c] on Record *quod cognovit indictamentum, &c.* in an Indictment of Treſpaſs, eſtops the Defendant to plead not Guilty to an Action brought afterwards againſt him for the ſame Matter. But it ſeems queſtionable, Whether ſuch Entry of a Confeſſion of an Indictment of a Capital Crime, will in like Manner eſtop a Defendant to plead Not Guilty to an Appeal, becauſe in Caſe of Life, the Court will be very tender in going upon Preſumptions. And where a Perſon upon his Arraignment actually confeſſes [d] himſelf guilty, or unadviſedly diſcloſes the Special [e] Manner of the Fact, ſuppoſing that it doth not amount to Felony, where it doth, yet the Judges, upon probable Circumſtances, that ſuch Confeſſion may proceed from Fear, Menace, or Dureſs, or from Weakneſs or Ignorance, may refuſe to record ſuch Confeſſion, and ſuffer the Party to plead Not guilty.

Sect. 3. An implied Confeſſion is where a Defendant in a Caſe not Capital, doth not directly own himſelf Guilty, but in a Manner admits it by yielding to the King's Mercy, and deſiring to ſubmit to a ſmall Fine; in which Caſe, if the Court think fit to accept of ſuch Submiſſion, and make an Entry that the Defendant *poſuit ſe in gratiam Regis*, without putting him to a direct Confeſſion, or Plea, (which in ſuch Caſes ſeems to be left to Diſcretion) the Defendant ſhall [f] not be eſtopped to plead Not guilty to an Action for the ſame Fact, as he ſhall [g] be where the Entry is *quod cognovit indictamentum.*

Sect. 4. I take it for granted, That no Confeſſion whatever ſhall, before final [h] Judgment, deprive the Defendant of the Privilege of of taking Exceptions in Arreſt of Judgment to Faults apparent in the Record; [i] for the Judges muſt *ex officio* take Notice of all ſuch Faults, and any one, as *amicus Curiæ*, may inform them of them.

[a] Vide S. P. C. 142. Lett. C. Lamb. B. 4. Ch. 9. Finch of Law 38.
[b] Kely. 11. *Quære if the Law be the ſame in Civil Actions. Affirmed* Cro. E. 144. pl. 3. *Denied* 2 Jon. 156.
[c] 9 H. 6. 60. a. Fitz. Eſtopp. 24. 102. 11 H. 6. 65. pl. 21. Lamb. B. 4. ch. 9. Trial per Pais 25.
[d] S P. C. 141. Lett. C.
[e] 22 Aſſ. pl. 71. *Abridged* Fitz. Coro. 180. 27 Aſſ pl 40.
[f] 9 H. 6. 60. a *Abridged* Fitz. Eſtoppel, 24. 11 H. 4. 65. pl. 21. Lamb. B. 4. Ch. 9.
[g] Supra §. 2.
[h] 1 Salk. 77, 78.
[i] Finch of Law, 226 2 Danv. Abr. 252. 2 Lev. 223.

Sect. 5. It seems to be taken for granted, both by [a] *Brook* and [b] *Staundforde*, [c] *Coke* and [d] *Hale*, speaking as I suppose, of a general Demurrer, That it amounts so far to a Confession of the Indictment as laid, that if the Indictment be good, Judgment and Execution shall go against the Prisoner. But it is observable, That no adjudged Case is cited for the Maintenance of this Opinion, nor any Authority from the Old Books except the *Year-Book* of 14 *Ed.* 4 *pl.* 9. in which it is reported to have been said by *Choke*, That if a Defendant demur to a Plea, he shall be hanged, *quod fuit concessum*. But to this it may be said, That it was only spoken incidentally, and not a Point adjudged; and besides that it is so short and obscure that it is scarce intelligible, which appears by *Brook*'s abridging it in different Senses; for in one Place [e] he seems to understand it of a Demurrer by a Defendant to a Plea in Bar, which seems impossible; and in another [f] Place he seems to understand it in a different Sense. And therefore perhaps the Meaning of it may be only this, That after a Defendant hath pleaded such a Bar, as confesses the Fact, and concludes him to plead the General Issue afterwards, as some Pleas are said [g] to do; if he afterwards demur to a Replication to such Plea, he shall be condemned if the Demurrer be adjudged against him, and the Indictment or Appeal be good.

Sect. 6. But howsoever the Law may stand in Relation to a [h] General Demurrer concluding in Bar of an Appeal, or Indictment, as in Common Demurrers in Civil Actions, or a Demurrer to a Plea in Bar, [i] which admits the Fact, or to a * Replication to such a Plea: It hath been adjudged, That if an Appellee demur in Law to an Appeal by Reason of the [k] Insufficiency of the Declaration, or generally demur to the Declaration, with a [l] Conclusion *& petit judicium de narratione illa & quod narratio illa cassetur*; or having prayed [m] Oyer of the Writ and Process, demand Judgment of the Appeal, *quia dicit quod breve de appello prædict. & process. inde minus sufficient' in lege existunt ad ipsum W. C. ad dictum breve de Appello respondere compellend' & hoc parat. est verificare prout Cur', &c. unde petit judicium de brevi de Appello prædict. & petit inde allocationem, & quod breve illud de Appello cassetur*; such Demurrer shall not conclude him from pleading over to the Felony, either at the same Time [n] with the Demurrer, or [o] after it shall be adjudged against him.

Sect. 7. But it seems, That in Criminal Cases not Capital, if the Defendant demur to an Indictment, *&c.* whether in Abatement or otherwise, the Court will not give Judgment against him to answer over, but final [p] Judgment; for it seems, That in such Cases there can be no Demurrer properly in Abatement, except [q] it be to a Plea in Abatement, or to a [r] Replication to such a Plea.

Sect. 8. A Demurrer to an Appeal hath been [s] received after Issue joined: But it hath been adjudged, [t] That a Demurrer to an Indictment ought not be received after Verdict.

[a] Bro. Peremptory, 86. [b] S. P. C. 150. Lett. C. [c] 2 Inst. 178. [d] H. P. C. 243.

[e] Bro. Demurrer, 17. [f] Bro. Peremptory, 86.

[g] Vide supra, Ch. 23. Sect. 135.

[h] *See the precedent Section.* [i] Vide Bro. Peremptory, 86. Fitz. Coro. 12. * Vide Bro. Perempt. 86 [k] Dyer 38. pl. 51. 39 pl. 65. Cro. Eliz. 196 pl. 13. [l] *As it was done in the Case of* Smith *and* Bowen. Mich. 7 Ann. Vid. Salk 59. pl. 2. [m] *As it was done in the Case of* Widdrington *and* Charlton, Hill 10 Ann. [n] Smith *and* Bowen, Mic. 7 Annæ. *In which Case the Demurrer was continued on the Record with a* Cesset. triatio exitus, &c. *and after the Demurrer was determined against the Defendant, a* Venire *was awarded.* [o] Dyer, 38. pl. 51. Salk 59, 60. Cro. E. 196 pl. 13. [p] Vide Salk. 220. [q] Salk. 218. [r] Ra. Entr. 160. pl 1, 2, 3. 611. [s] Cro. E. 196. pl. 13. [t] 1 Sid. 208. *wherein the Precedent in* Co. Ent. 363. b. *to the contrary it is denied to be Law.*

CHAP.

CHAP. XXXII.

Of Sanctuary.

BEFORE I consider in the third Place, how a Prisoner is to be demesned upon his Pleading; I shall examine the Nature of the several Kinds of Pleas in Criminal Cases, which are either,

1. Dilatory, or,
2. In Chief.

Dilatory Pleas are either,

1. Declinatory, or,
2. In Abatement.

Declinatory Pleas are either,

1. Of the Privilege of Sanctuary, or,
2. Of the Benefit of the Clergy.

Sect. 1. As to the Plea of the Privilege of Sanctuary, the Learning relating to it being made is a great Measure useless by the Statute of 21 *Jac.* 1. 28. *Par* 7. by which it is enacted, *That no Sanctuary or Privilege of Sanctuary shall after that Time be admitted or allowed in any Case.* I shall but briefly consider it under the following Heads,

1. What was the Nature of the Privilege of Sanctuary.
2. What Authority was necessary for the creating it.
3. To what Matters it extended.
4. At what Time and in what Manner it was to be pleaded.

Sect. 2. As to the first Point, *viz.* What was the Nature of the Privilege of Sanctuary: It seems to be agreed, [a] That so far as a Place was allowed to have it, it gave all those who fled to it for Safeguard, and continued within its [b] Precincts, a [c] Freedom from being apprehended, or compelled to answer in any Court of Justice, and a Right to be remanded, if taken out against their Will.

[a] Finch of Law, 374. S. P. C. 108. Lett. B.

[b] *What those Precincts were* Keilw. 189. a. b. 191. 9 H. 7. 20. pl. 15. S. P. C. 113. a. Bro. Sanctuary, 10.

[c] Keilw. 188, 189, 190, 191. 8 H. 6. 4. b. *Abridged* Fitz. Coro. 5. 1 H. 7. 23. b. *Abridged* Fitz. Coro. 49. 9 E. 4. 28. b. *Abridged* Fitz. Coro. 32. Keilw. 107, 188.

Sect. 3. As to the second Point, *viz.* What Authority was necessary for the creating it: It seems, that it belonged of Common [a] Right to every Church and Churchyard, for the Space of Forty Days, but could not be claimed for a longer Time, either by Force of any Bull from the [b] Pope, nor even by [c] Prescription, ([d] especially in the Case of High Treason) but only by a Grant [e] from the King, made, or at least confirmed [f] or allowed [g] in *Eyre*, since the Time of Memory. But it is said, That it did not gain *the Name of a Sanctuary till it had the Pope's Bull, tho' it had the † full Privilege of one, as to all Exemption from Temporal Courts, by the King's Grant only.

Sect. 4. As to the third Point, *viz.* To what Matters it extended. It seems agreed, That it never was any farther a Protection against any Action merely Civil, [h] than to save the Defendant from Execution of his Body. Also it seems to be generally agreed, That if it were granted by general Words, it extended not to [i] High Treason. But it seems agreed, [k] That in such Case it extended to all Felonies except [l] Sacrilege, and to all inferior Crimes, except such as were committed by a Sanctuary Man [m] within the Sanctuary, or even [n] out of it, *sub spe redeundi.*

Sect. 5. As to the fourth Point, *viz.* At what Time, and in what Manner it was to be pleaded: It seems agreed, That the Defendant lost the Benefit of it, unless he pleaded it before any [o] other Plea, and properly made out his Case; but for this Matter I shall wholly refer the Reader to the Old [p] Books.

Sect. 6. For the learning of Abjuration, [q] depending much upon that of Sanctuaries, and seeming to be of very little Use at this Day, I shall refer to *Staundforde's Pleas of the Crown, Book* 2. *Chap.* 40. and to what hath been said already concerning that Matter, in the Chapter concerning *Coroners*, *Sect.* 44.

[a] 32 H. 8. ch. 12. Finch of Law 368. 3 H. 7. 12 pl. 6. *Abridged* Fitz. Coro. 54. 21 E. 3. 17. pl. 21. *Abridged* Bro. Sanctuary, 2. Supra Ch. 9. Sect. 44. Keilw. 189. a. Bro. Sanctu. 11, 14, 16. Rast. Entr. 583. pl. 1, 2. [b] Keilw. 189, 190, 191. S. P. C. 110. b. 111. Lett. A. Bro. Sanctu. 6. 15. 5 Co. de jure Regis ecclesi. 26. [c] 1 Inst. 114. Keilw. 188, &c. *But Quære if such Prescription were confirmed by King, or allowed in* Eyre *since Time of Memory.* Keilwey, 188, 189, 190, 191. [d] S. P. C. 112. a. 1 H. 7. 23, 25, 26. *Abridged* Fitz. Coro. 49. Prescription, 20. Vide Ra. Entr. 584. pl. 3, 4, 5. [e] S. P. C. 108. Lett. B. 110, 111. 1 H. 7. 25. b 26. Bro. Sanctuary, 7. Keilw. 189, 190, 191. [f] Keilw. 189, 190. 1 H. 7. 23. 2 Rol. Abr. 268. 269. [g] Keilw. 189, 190. 2 Rol. Abr. 268, 269. 1 H. 7. 23. Bro. Sanctuary, 7. 15. *this is made a Quære.* S. P. C. 112. * Finch of Law, 375. † Finch of Law, 374, 375. [h] Bro. Sanctuary, 3, 11. 7 H. 6. 8. pl. 34. *Abridged* Fitz. Jurisdiction, 2. Dyer. 295. pl. 11, 12. [i] 21 E. 3. 17. pl. 21. *Denied*, 29 Ass. pl. 24. *Abridged*, Fitz. Grant, 77. Bro. Sanctuary, 6. 1 H. 7. 23, 25, 26. *Abridged* Fitz. Coro. 49. Prescription, 20. Cont. Keilw. 190, 191. *Quære* Finch, 374. [k] *See the Books cited to the other Parts of this Section. Quære if in such Case it extended to Petit Treason.* Bro. Sanctuary, 2. [l] 3 Inst. 115. Fitz. 420. [m] *Agreed by all the Canonists*, Keilw. 191 b. [n] *Denied by many of the Canonists*, Keilw. 191. b. [o] S. P. C. 113. Lett. B. Fitz. Coro. 438. Bro. Sanctuary, 5. 21 E. 3. 17. pl. 21. *Abridged* Bro. Sanctuary, 2. Fitz. Coro. 447. 9 E. 4. 28. b. *Abridged* Fitz. Coro. 32. [p] Keilw, 90, 107, 188, 189. S. P. C. 113. a. 1 H. 7. 23, 24, 25, 26. 9 H. 7. 20. pl. 15. Ra. Ent. 584, pl. 3, 4, 5. 683. pl. 3. [q] 3 Inst. 115. Fitz. Aiel, 5.

CHAP.

CHAP. XXXIII.

Of Clergy.

FOR the better underſtanding the Nature of the Benefit of the Clergy, (or rather of the [a] Statute at this Day) I ſhall endeavour to ſhew,

[a] *See the latter Part of this Chapter.*

1. By what Kind of Perſons it is demandable.
2. For what Crimes.
3. At what Times.
4. Whether it ſhall be allowed where it is not demanded.
5. Who is to judge whether the Perſon who demands it have a Right to it or not.
6. How far the Ordinary was puniſhable at Law for demanding or refuſing a Clerk againſt Law.
7. In what Manner at the Common Law a Clerk was to be delivered to the Ordinary, and what is be done to him afterwards.
8 What is to be done to him at this Day, and how far it ſhall be to his Benefit.

Sect. 1. As to the firſt Point, *viz.* By what Kind of Perſons the Benefit of the Clergy, (or rather of the Statute at this Day) is demandable: It may not be improper to look a little back into the Original of it, whereby we ſhall find, That anciently the Clergy [b] ſtrongly inſiſted, that by the Law of God their Perſons were ſo ſacred, that they could not, without a Violation of that Law, be convened before, and much leſs puniſhed with the Loſs of Life or Member by any ſecular Judge, for any Crime whatever. But there ſeems to be ſo little [c] Colour for any Pretence of this Kind from Scripture, that I almoſt wonder how it was poſſible that any Perſons could be ſo far prejudiced, as ſeriouſly to be perſuaded that it is deducible from thence.

Sect. 2. But it ſeems agreed; [d] That all Perſons in Holy Orders, have this Privilege by the Canon Law; but this Law being no farther in [e] Force here than as it hath been received, and is conſiſtent with the Common or Statute Law; it will be proper to ſhew how far it hath

[b] Keilw. 181, 182, 183, 184, 185.

[c] Keilw. 181, &c.

[d] *See* Lyndw. *Book* 2. *in the Chapter* De foro Competente Kely. 99, 100, 101. Keilw. 180, &c. S. P. C. 123, 124. Finch of Law, 462, 463.

[e] Keilw. 181, *&c.* Kely. 99, &c. 5 Co. de jure Regis eccleſ. 13, &c.

been received, and is consistent with those Laws; which I shall at present consider under this Head, so far as it relates to the Persons intitled to this Privilege; and shall farther consider it as to other Matters, in the following Part of this Chapter.

Sect. 3. It seems agreed, That before the Statute of *Articuli cleri, Ch.* 15. made in the ninth Year of *Edw.* 2. it was [a] generally denied to those who had abjured, or who had any other way confessed themselves Guilty: But by a favourable Interpretation of that Statute, which expresly extends only to those who fly to the Church for Safeguard, it hath been allowed [b] to all those who have confessed themselves guilty, upon their Arraignment or otherwise, in the same Manner as if they had not confessed.

Sect. 4. Also it seems, That notwithstanding the Clergy [c] contended That the Word *Clericus* (which is the Word generally used by the [d] Canon Law as well as ours, [e] to express those who are intitled to this Privilege) did include those of the Inferior Orders,* as well as Bishops, Priests and Deacons: Yet it seems, [f] That the Temporal Judges sometimes denied it to those in Inferior Orders, as well as to mere [g] Laymen, before the Statute of 25 *E.* 3. *Ch.* 4. which reciting, *That the Prelates had grievously complained, That secular Clerks, as well Chaplains, as other Monks, and other People of Religion, had been drawn and hang'd by Award of the secular Justices, in prejudice of the Franchise of Holy Church,* &c. *doth enact, That all Manner of Clerks, as well Secular as Religious,* &c. *shall freely enjoy the Privilege of Holy Church,* &c.

Sect. 5. It seems that by a favourable Interpretation of this Statute, which universally prevailed soon [h] after it was made, not only those actually admitted into some inferior Order of the Clergy, [i] but also those who were never qualified to be admitted into Orders, (which was tried [k] by putting them to read a Verse) have been taken to have a [l] Right to this Privilege, as much as Persons in Holy Orders, whether they were Persons lawfully born, or †Bastards, [m] Aliens or Denizens, in the Communion of the Church or [n] Excommunicate, within the Common Benefit of the Law, or ||Outlaws, *&c.* so that they were not [o] Hereticks convict, nor [p] Jews, Mahometans, nor Pagans; nor under [q] a perpetual Disability of going into Orders, admitting of no Dispensation, as [r] blind and maimed Persons formerly were, and Women [s] still are; nor liable to the Objection of Bigamy, *viz.* (of having [u] married two different Women successively, or a Widow) which by a Constitution of the Council of *Lyons,* [x] received in this Kingdom, was a Bar to the Demand of the Privilege of the Clergy; and by Force of 18 *E.* 3. 2. was triable by the Certificate [y] of the Bishop.

Sect. 6. But it is expresly enacted by 1 *E.* 6. 12. *Par.* 16. *That any Person who by the Law of this Realm ought to have the Benefit of his Clergy, shall be admitted to it, altho' he have been divers Times married to any single Woman*

[a] Fitz Coro. 155. 11 Co. 29 b. S. P C. 124. Lett. G. Vide Keilw. 186. b. Seldon's Janus Anglor'. Ch. 10.

[b] Bro. Clergy, 3, 7, 8. 9 E. 4. 28. pl. 40. 8 H 4, 3 pl. 5. 1 Ass pl. 4. 27 H 6, 7. b. Fitz Coro. 191.

[c] Kely. 99, 100.

[d] Lyndw. B. 2. *in the Chapter* De foro competente.

[e] *See the Statute of* Marlb. Ch. 28. *and* Westm. 1. Ch. 2. *and* Articuli cleri, Ch. 15. *and the Old Books cited,* 2 Inst. 633, 634 &c. * Keilw. 181, Kely. 99. 100.

[f] Kely 99, 100.

[g] Fitz Coro. 233. *But they sometimes allowed it to mere Laymen, being able to read.* Fitz. Coro. 117.

[h] *Yet it was holden the next Year after the Statute* quod literatura non facit clericum nisi habeat sacram tonsuram. 26 Ass. pl. 19. *Abridged* Fitz. Coro. 191. S P. C. 124. Lett. B. [i] Kely. 100, 101, 102. Bro. Clergy, 7, 20. [k] Kely. 100, 101. Finch, 462, 463. S P. C. 133. Letters A. B. C. D. 34 H. 6. 49. pl. 16. Fitz. Coro. 44. *See the Cases cited to the fourth general Point of this Chapter.* [l] 9 E. 4. 28. pl. 40. *Abridged* Bro. Clergy, 7. † Bro. Clergy, 22. [m] Bro. Clergy, 20. [n] Bro. Clergy, 20. H. P. C. 229. 11 Co. 29. b. || *See* 3 & 4 W. & M. 9. 11 Co. 29. b. [o] S. P. C. 133. Lett. B. Bro. Clergy, 20. 11 Co. 29. b. [p] Bro. Clergy, 20. 11 Co. 29. b. H. P. C. 229. [q] 11 Co. 29. b. [r] 11 Co. 29 b. H. P. C. 229. Cont. Bro. Clergy, 21. [s] Finch, 463. 11 Co. 29. b. *See the Preambles of* 21 Ja. 1. Ch. 6. and of 3 & 4 W. & M. 9 Par. 7. *Yet 'tis admitted* Fitz. Coro. 461. *That a Woman might claim the Benefit of the Clergy.* [u] S. P. C. 134, 135. Ra. Ent. 106. a. b. [x] *See the Statute of Bigamy,* 4 E. 1. Ch. 5. 5 Co. De Jure Regis ecclesiastico, 13. S. P. C. 125. Lett. F. [y] Ra. Ent. 160. a. b. S. P. C. 134, Lett. C. 135. b. 11 H. 4. 11. pl. 24. *Abridged* Fitz. Coro. 85. 40 E. 3. 42. pl. 23. *Abridged* Fitz. Attorney, 39.

or single Women, or to any Widow or Widows, or to two Wives or more. But it bore some [z] Question whether this Statute were not impliedly repealed by 1 & 2 *Ph. & Ma.* 8. while it stood in Force, *Which repealed all Clauses, &c. against the See of* Rome.

Sect. 7. As to Women it was enacted by 21 *Jac.* 1. 6. *That on a Conviction of Grand Larceny under the Value of* 10 s. *being no Burglary, nor Robbery in or near the Highway, nor a felonious private taking from the Person,* &c. *but only such an Offence for which a Man might have his Clergy, they shall be burnt in the Hand, and imprisoned,* &c.

Sect. 8. But it is enacted by 3 & 4 *W. & M.* 9. Par. 7. *That where a Man being convicted of any Felony may demand the Benefit of his Clergy; if a Woman be convicted for the same, or the like Offence, upon her Prayer to have the Benefit of this Statute, Judgment of Death shall not be given against her upon such Conviction, or Execution awarded upon any Outlawry for such Offence, but she shall suffer the same Punishment as a Man should suffer, that has the Benefit of his Clergy allowed him in the like Case; that is to say, shall be burnt in the Hand by the Gaoler in open Court, and farther be kept in Prison for such a Time as the Justices in their Discretion shall think fit, so as the same do not exceed one Year's Imprisonment.*

Sect. 9. It seems, [a] That one who had been guilty of Sacrilege, or of breaking the Prison of the Ordinary, had no Right to the Benefit of the Clergy, but at the [b] Discretion of the Ordinary.

Sect. 10. It seems clear, [c] That before the Statute of 4 *H.* 7. 13. He who had been admitted to the Benefit of the Clergy, might have it a second Time as well as the first, unless he had broken the Prison of the Ordinary, to which he was committed when the Clergy was first allowed him; in which Case it seems, [d] That he could not save himself from a second Prosecution, tho' for the very same Felony for which he was before convicted, unless he could shew a Purgation.

Sect. 11. But it is enacted by 4 *H.* 7, 13. *That every Person, not being within Orders, who hath once been admitted to the Benefit of his Clergy, eftsoons arraigned of any such Offence, be not admitted to have the Benefit or Privilege of the Clergy,* &c. *And it is provided, That if any Person at the second Time of asking his Clergy, because he is within Orders, hath not there ready his Letters of his Orders, or a Certificate of his Ordinary, witnessing the same: That then the Justices afore whom he is so arraigned, shall give him a Day by their Discretion to bring in his said Letters or Certificate; and if he fail, and bring not at such a Day his said Letters or Certificate, then the Person to lose the Benefit of his Clergy as he shall do that is without Orders.*

[z] Vide S.P.C. 134.b Dalis. 21. pl. 1. Dyer 201 pl. 67. Bro. Clergy, 20 H. P.C. 229.

[a] S. P. C. 31. Lett. F. 32. Lett. A. 123. Lett. D. 124. Lett. A. 132. Lett. B. Fitz. Coro. 112, 117, 120, 250, 257. 4 Inst. 314. 12 Ass. 39. *Abridged* Bro. Clergy, 10. 17 Ass. pl. 4. 17. E. 3. 13. pl. 47. *Abridged* Fitz. Coro. 112. 9 E. 4. 28. pl. 40. *Abridged* Bro. Clergy, 7. 27 Ass. 42. *Abridged* Fitz. Coro. 205. Bro. Clergy, 13. 11 Co. 29. b.

[b] *Yet it seems to be holden* 26 Ass. pl. 19. and 27. *Abridged* Bro. Clergy, 11, 12. Fitz. Coro. 191, 193, *That one who had been guilty of Sacrilege might demand it as well as any other. And it seems to be holden* Fitz. Coro. 232, 250, 419. *That one who had broken the Prison of the Ordinary had no manner of Right to it.* Vide 12 Ass. 39. *Abridged* Bro. Clergy, 10. *This Point is made a Quære* 9 E. 4. 28. pl. 40. *Abridged* Bro. Clergy, 7.

[c] H. P. C. 230. S. P. C. 31. Lett. F. 32. Letter A. 107. Letter B. 124. Letter C. 135. Letters B D. *See the Preamble of* 4 H. 7. 13. *But* 17 Ass. pl. 4. 17 E. 3. 13. pl. 47. *Abridged* Fitz. Coro. 112. *It seems to have been doubted where the Clerk was attainted before he first had the Benefit of the Clergy.*

[d] Fitz. Coro. 232. *and to the Books cited to Letter C. and to the former Section.*

Sect.

Sect. 12. But it is enacted by 28 *H.* 8. *Par.* 7. *That Persons within Holy Orders, shall be under the same Pains and Dangers for the Offences referred to by that Statute, and be used and ordered to all Intents and Purposes, as other Persons, not being within Holy Orders. And it is farther enacted by* 32 H. 8. 3. Par. 8. *That Persons within Holy Orders who shall be admitted to their Clergy, shall be burnt in the Hand in like Manner as lay Clerks, and shall suffer and incur all such Pains Dangers, and Forfeitures, and be ordered and used for their Offences of Felony, to all Intents, Purposes and Constructions, as Lay Persons admitted to their Clergy, be, or ought to be,* &c.

Sect. 13. But it is enacted by 1 *E.* 6. 12. *par.* 10. That in all Cases of Felony, other than those in that Act mentioned, every Person who shall be found Guilty, or confess, or stand Mute, or not answer directly, shall have the Benefit of his Clergy, in like Manner and Form as before the first Year of King *Henry* VIII. And therefore it seems plain, That where Lay Persons are not excluded from the Benefit of the Clergy the first Time; Persons in Holy Orders may have it as often as they want it, in the same Manner as they might upon the Foot of the said Statute of 4 *H.* 7. 13. [a] except they shall be outlawed, or challenge above the Number of twenty, in which Case they are not within the Purview of 1 *E.* 6. which extends only to those who shall be found Guilty, or confess, or stand Mute, *&c.* But [b] where the Crime itself charged against a Person in Holy Orders, is by any Statute generally excluded from the Clergy, such Person shall no more have the Benefit of it than if he were a mere Layman.

[a] H. P. C. 238, 239. S. P. C. 135. Letter B.

[b] S. P. C. 135. Let. D. 136, H. P. C. 235, 236.

Sect. 14. It is recited by 34 *&* 35 *H.* 8. 14. *That divers Persons had been indicted and attainted, and some of them Clerks convict, and some of them Clerks attainted,* &c. *before Justices of Peace, Gaol-Delivery,* &c. *within divers Cities, Counties and Franchises,* &c. *the Records of which Attainders and Convictions often, by Negligence of the Clerks,* &c. *having the Rule and Keeping thereof, had been imbezilled, and not ready to be objected against such Persons, being newly arraigned before other Justices,* &c. *And for that it had not been known certainly whether to resort for the same Records, because they were not certified into any Place certain, such Offenders had often had the Benefit of the Clergy where they ought not,* &c. And thereupon it is enacted, *That the Clerk of the Crown, Clerks of the Peace, and Clerks of Assise, where any such Attainder, or Conviction shall be so had, shall certify a Transcript, briefly containing the Effect of every such Indictment,* &c. *and Clerk attainted,* &c. *that is to say, the Name, Surname, and Addition of every such Person,* &c. *and the Certainty of the Offence,* &c. *and the Day and Place of his Attainder or Conviction,* &c. *and the Day and Place of his Offence,* &c. *before the King in his Bench at* Westminster, *there to remain of Record for ever, within forty Days after such Attainder,* &c. *if the Term be then, and if not, then within twenty Days after the next Term,* &c. *on Pain of* 40 s. &c. *And that the Clerk of the Crown in the King's Bench, shall receive the same without Fee, under the like Pain.*

Sect. 15. *Provided, That if there be more Persons contained in any such Indictment, other than such Person so attainted or convicted, that then such Clerk shall certify such Transcript only* [c] *concerning the Persons or Persons so attainted or convicted, which shall be as effectual against such Person and Persons against whom it shall be so objected, alledged or pleaded, as if the very Record were present.*

[c] Note, *That this is omitted in* Keble's *Statutes.*

1

Sect.

Sect. 16. And it is farther enacted, *That the said Clerk of the Crown in the King's Bench, shall at all such Times as the Justices of the Gaol-Delivery, or Justices of the Peace, in every County within this Realm of* England, *do write unto him for the Names of such Persons, which be so attainted, or convict, and certified in the said Bench, shall incontinently certify the said Names and Surnames of the said Persons, with the Causes why and wherefore they were convicted or attainted, unto the Justices of Gaol-Delivery, or Justices of the Peace,* &c. *on Pain of* 40 s.

Sect. 17. But it is provided, *That this Act shall not extend to the Clerks of the Crown,* &c. *in* Wales, *or* Chester, *or Counties-Palatine of* Lancaster *and* Durham, *to make any Transcript of any such Attainder or Conviction, before the King's Justices of his Counties in* Wales, &c.

Sect. 18. It seems, [a] That the Justices may, by Force of this Act, write in their own Names to the Clerk of the Crown in the King's Bench, for a Certificate of the Transcript of an Attainder or Conviction, and need not do it by Writ in the King's Name under their *Teste, &c.* which is required [b] by the Construction of 2 *&* 3 *E.* 6. 24. where the Justices of one County write to those of another for the Certificate of the Attainder, or Acquittal of the Principal, in order to proceed against the Accessary. And the Reason of the Difference is, because in this last Case Justices write to Justices, but in the former to an Officer only.

Sect. 19. It is farther provided by 3 *&* 4 *W. & M.* 9. *Par.* 8. as followeth, *Forasmuch as such Men and Women who have once had their Clergy,* &c. *may happen to be indicted for an Offence committed afterwards in some other County, Be it therefore enacted, That the Clerk of the Crown, Clerk of the Peace, Clerk of the Assises where such Man or Woman shall be convicted, shall, at the Request of the Prosecutor, or any other in their Majesties Behalf, certify a Transcript briefly, and in few Words, containing the Effect and Tenor of every Inditement and Conviction of such Man or Woman, of his or her having the Benefit of the Clergy,* &c. *and Addition of every such Person or Persons, and the Certainty of the Felony and Conviction, to the Judges and Justices in such other County where such Man or Woman shall be indicted, which Certificate being produced in Court, shall be sufficient Proof that such Man or Woman have before had the Benefit of Clergy,* &c.

As to the second Point, *viz.* For what Crimes the Benefit of the Clergy, or rather of the Statute may be demanded, I shall premise,

Sect. 20. *First,* That it seems to be generally agreed, That by the Common Law it is demandable as well upon an [c] Appeal as Indictment, for any Crime whatsoever, which subjects the Offender to the [d] Loss of Life or Member, except [e] High Treason, (whether against the King's Person or [f] not,) and Sacrilege; for the first of which the Common Law seems to give the Offender no manner of Right to the Benefit of his Clergy, and for the latter to have it left to the Discretion of the Ordinary, as hath been more fully shewn, *Sect.* 9.

[a] Dy. 253, pl. 103.

[b] Vide Sup. Ch. 29. Sect. 53.

[c] 11 Co. 29. b.

[d] S. P. C. 124. Lett. B. Bro. Clergy, 19. Finch of Law 462, 463.

[e] S. P. C. 124. Lett. E. Fitz. Coro. 283. 19 H. 6. 47. pl. 103. *Abridged* Fitz. Coro. 8. Bro. Clergy, 6. Vide 2 Inst. 634.

[f] *So it appears from the Books cited to Letter* E. *Yet* H. P. C. 330. *and* 11 Co. 29. b. *and* Bro. Clergy, 25, 31. *it seems to be holden, That by the Common Law Clergy was excluded from such High Treason only as was against the Person of the King. But* Quaere *upon what Ground this is holden. And see* 25 E. 3. De Clero, ch. 5.

Sect. 21. *Secondly*, That it seems to be doubtful, [a] whether it were demandable at the Common Law for Petit Treason; but this was settled by 25 *E.* 3. *de clero, Ch.* 4. which expresly allows it for *any Treasons, or Felonies, touching other Persons than the King himself, or his Royal Majesty.*

Sect. 22. *Thirdly*, That after this a Construction [b] prevailed, That Clergy might be denied to Felons charged as *insidiatores viarum, & depopulatores agrorum*, but this is remedied by 4 *H.* 4. 2.

From these Premisses it seems to be generally agreed, [c] That the following Conclusions necessarily follow;

Sect. 23. *First*, So far as a Person, who in Respect of his Orders or Learning, or otherwise, is qualified to be admitted to the Benefit of the Clergy, is denied it in Respect of his [d] Crime, not amounting to High Treason or Sacrilege; such Denial must be grounded on some Act of [e] Parliament, made since 25 *E.* 3.

Sect. 24. *Secondly*, Where-ever an Offence is made Felony by Statute, it [f] shall have the Benefit of the Clergy, unless it be expresly excluded from it.

Sect. 25. *Thirdly*, Where-ever a Person is denied the Benefit of the Clergy, in Respect of a Statute, excluding it from the Crime charged against him, the [g] Indictment or Appeal, and the [h] Evidence thereon, must expresly bring his Case within the Words of such Statute: And therefore, if a [i] Murder be not expresly laid, and proved to have been done of Malice prepense; and the Offence of an Accessary [k] before, to have been done maliciously; and that of a [l] Cut-purse *clam & secrete a persona, &c.* the Offender shall have his Clergy. And agreeably hereto it hath been adjudged, [m] That an Indictment of Robbery *in quadam via Regia pedestri ducent' de* London *ad* Islington, shall not oust the Offender of the Benefit of his Clergy; because the Words of the Statutes [n] to this Purpose are *In, or about, or near the Highway.* Yet it hath been adjudged [o] That an Indictment against a Man as Accessary to Murder before the Fact, by the Words *malitiose excitavit, movit, & procuravit, &c.* is sufficient to out the Offender of the Benefit of the Clergy, by Force of 4 & 5 *Ph. & M.* the Words whereof are *That all Persons who shall maliciously command, hire, or counsel any Person*, &c. which are not expresly pursued in such Indictment. But the counselling another being necessarily included in the moving, procuring, and exciting him, which therefore are tantamount in Sense, and different only in the Manner of Expression, such an Indictment is as [p] much within the Statute as if it followed the very Words. Also it hath been [q] adjudged, That in order to oust a Man of the Benefit of the Clergy by Force of a Statute, which takes it away from a Capital Offence at Common Law, there is no need that the Indictment or Appeal conclude *contra formam Statuti*, because the Statute doth no way alter the Nature of the Offence, but only leaves it to its proper Judgment, and takes away a personal Privilege of Exemption from such Judgment.

Sect. 26. *Fourthly*, A Statute excluding the Principals from the Benefit of the Clergy, doth [r] not thereby exclude the Accessaries before or after; Neither [s] doth a Statute, excluding the Accessaries, thereby exclude

[a] Vide S.P.C. 124. Lett. E. H.P.C. 230. Finch of Law 463. 11 Co. 29. b.
[b] Supra Ch. 25. Sect. 61. S.P.C. 124. Lett. D
[c] H.P.C. 230, 231.
[d] S.P.C. 124, 125, &c. H.P.C. 232, 233, &c.
[e] H.P.C. 230.
[f] H.P.C. 230.
[g] H.P.C. 231. 11 Co. 37. S.P.C. 114. Lett. A. 130. Lett. B.
[h] S.P.C. 130. Lett B. Dy. 261. pl. 26. 224. pl. 30.
[i] H.P.C. 231. S.P.C. 130. Lett. B Dyer, 261. pl. 26. Vid 23 H. 8. Ch. 1. 1 E. 6. 12. par. 10.
[k] H.P.C. 231. 1 And. 195. 11 Co. 37. Dyer 183. pl. 59. Vide 4 & 5 Ph. & M. 4.
[l] H P.C. 231. 8 El. Ch. 4.
[m] Moore 5. pl. 16.
[n] 23 H. 8. Ch. 1. Par. 3. 1 E 6. Ch. 12. Par. 10. 4 & 5 Ph. & M. 4.
[o] 1 And. 195.
[p] See B. 1. Ch. 32. Sect. 3.
[q] See B. 1. Ch. 30. Sect. 9. 1 Vent. 13.
[r] See B. 1. Ch. 3. Sect. 4. 183. pl. 59.
Ch. 30. Sect. 7. H. P. C. 7, 58, 231. 11 Co. *from* 29 to 36. 1 And. 195. Dyer 99. pl. 59.
See 4 & 5 Ph. & Ma. 4. [s] 11 Co. *from* 29 *to* 36. Sav. 46. pl 98.

the

the Principals. And it seems agreed, [a] That where a Statute excludes those from the Clergy who shall be found guilty of Petit Treason, Murder, Burglary, Robbery, or any other Kind of Crimes, it shall be construed to intend only to exclude the Principals, and not Accessaries before or after, notwithstanding they are certainly in a high Degree Partakers in the Guilt of the principal Offender, as hath been more fully shewn *Chap.* 29. *Sect.* 13, 14. Yet inasmuch as such Statutes taking away a Privilege of so high a Consequence to the Subject, ought to receive the strictest Interpretation; and the Words of them may, without any manner of Strain, or Repugnance to the general Rules of Law, be taken in such a Sense as will include the Principals only, I do not know that they have ever been carried farther.

Sect. 27. *Fifthly*, Where Clergy is allowable, it shall be as much allowed to one who stands [b] Mute, or challenges peremptorily [c] above the Number of twenty, or is [d] outlawed, *&c.* as to one who is convicted by Verdict, or Confession, *&c.*

Sect. 28. *Sixthly*, A Statute taking the Benefit of the Clergy from those who shall be found guilty, doth not [e] thereby take it from those who stand Mute, or challenge peremptorily above the Number of twenty, or are outlawed, *&c.* But it seems [f] clear, That a Statute taking it away from those who shall be found Guilty, extends as well to those who shall confess themselves guilty upon Record, as to those who shall be found guilty by Verdict; for as the latter are found guilty by a Jury, so are the former by the Court, and their Conviction being from their own Mouths, is of the highest Nature possible.

Sect. 29. And now I shall endeavour to shew for what Crimes Persons are excluded from the Benefit of the Clergy by Statutes made since 25 *E.* 3. which being somewhat perplexed and intricate, I shall, for the better clearing of this Matter, first take a general View of those Statutes so far as they are in Force at this Day, and then shall more distinctly consider them, as they particularly concern the several Kinds of Capital Crimes.

Sect. 30. The first of those Statutes I shall take Notice of, is 23 *H.* 8. *Ch.* 1. by which it is enacted, *Par.* 3. *That no Person who shall be found guilty, after the Laws of this Land, for any manner of Petit Treason, or for any wilful Murder of Malice prepensed, or for robbing any Churches, Chapels, or other Holy Places, or for robbing of any Person or Persons, in their Dwelling Houses, or Dwelling Place, the Owner or Dweller in the same House, his Wife, his Children, or Servants, then being within, and put in Fear and Dread by the same, or for robbing of any Person or Persons in or near about* [*] *the Highways, or for wilfull burning of any Dwelling-Houses or Barns, wherein any Grain of Corn shall happen to be; nor any Person or Persons being found guilty of any Abetment, Procurement, Helping, Maintaining, or Counselling of, or to any such Petit Treasons, Murders or Felonies, shall be admitted to his Clergy; such as be within Holy Orders only excepted.*

Sect. 31. *Note*, That this Statute extends [g] as well to Appeals as to Indictments, and to those who shall confess [h], as much as to those who shall plead and be found Guilty; for the Words are general, *That no Person who shall be found guilty, after the Laws of this Realm*, &c. *shall be admitted to his Clergy*, &c. But it extends not [i] to Persons outlawed, and was easily evaded [k] by Persons brought to their Trials, by standing Mute, or challenging peremptorily above the Number of twenty, whereby they prevented their being found guilty.

[a] H. P. C. 7. 58. 1 And. 195. Dy. 99. pl. 59, 183. pl. 59.

[b] H. P. C. 231. 25 H. 8. 3. Pa. 2. Supra, ch. 30. Sect. 24. Moore 550. pl. 738. Cont. Fitz. Coro. 283.

[c] 3 H 7. 12. pl. 8. *Abridged* Bro: Clergy 27. Fitz. Coro. 51. H. P. C. 231. 25 H. 8. 3. Par. 2. 3 & 4 W. & M. 9.

[d] 11 Co. 29. b. *See* 3 & 4 W. & M. 9.

[e] *See* 25 H. 8. 3. Par. 2. 3 & 4 W. & M. 9. 11 Co. Poulters *Case*.

[f] 11 Co. 29. a.

[*] So Rastal's *Statutes; but* Pulton *omits the Word* about, *and* Keble *the Word* near.

[g] 11 Co. 30. b.

[h] Supra Sect. 28.

[i] 11 Co. 30. b

[k] *See the Preamble of* 25 H 8. 3. *And* 11 Co. 30. b.

Sect. 32. But these two last Defects are provided for by 25 *H.* 8. *Ch.* 3. by which it is enacted, Par. 2. *That every Person who shall from thenceforth be indicted of Petit Treason, willful burning of Houses, Murder, Robbery or Burglary, or other Felony, according to the Tenour and Meaning of* 23 H. 8. *and thereupon arraigned, and do stand Mute of Malice or froward Mind, or challenge peremptorily above the Number of twenty, or else will not, or do not answer directly to the same Indictment and Felony, whereupon he is so arraigned, shall from thenceforth lose the Benefit and Privilege of his Clergy, in like Manner and Form as if he had directly pleaded to the same Petit Treason, Murder, Robbery, Burglary, or other Felony, whereupon he is so arraigned, and thereupon had been found guilty, after the Laws of the Land.*

Sect. 33. But this Statute extends not [a] to those who are outlawed, any more than 23 *H.* 8. neither doth it extend to Appeals, nor to Accessaries before, both of which are included in 23 *H.* 8.

Sect. 34. After came the Statute of 1 *E.* 6. 12. Par. 10. *That no Person who shall be in due Form of the Laws attainted or convicted of Murder, of Malice prepensed, or of Poisoning, of Malice prepensed, or of breaking of any House by Day or by Night, any Person being then in the same House where the same Breaking shall be committed, and thereby put in Dread; or of robbing any Person in the Highway, or near the Highway; or for felonious stealing of Horses, Geldings, or Mares; or of felonious taking of any Goods out of any Parish-Church, or other Church or Chapel; or being indicted or appealed of any of the same Offences, and thereupon found guilty by Verdict of twelve Men, or shall confess the same upon his Arraignment; or will not answer directly according to the Laws of this Realm, or shall stand wilfully, or of Malice, Mute, shall not be admitted to the Benefit of his Clergy, And that in all other Cases of Felony, all Persons that shall be arraigned, or found guilty upon their Arraignment, or shall confess, or stand Mute, in Form aforesaid, or will not answer directly in Form aforesaid, shall have their Clergy in the same Manner as before the first Year of King* Henry, VIII.

Sect. 35. *Note*, That this Statute extends as well to [b] Appeals as to Indictments, in which Respect it is more fully penned than 25 *H.* 8, And that it extends to Persons in Holy [c] Orders, as much as to Lay-men, and to all Persons attainted in general, and consequently to those who are outlawed, in which Respects it is more fully penned than either, [d] 23 or [e] 25 *H.* 8. Yet it hath several considerable Defects; as,

Sect. 36. *First*, In that it doth not exclude those from the Benefit of the Clergy, who challenge above the Number of twenty; so that it is easily made ineffectual [f] by taking such Challenges, as to Crimes excluded from the Benefit of the Clergy, by this Statute, and no other. But as to Crimes within 25 *H.* 1. it [g] seems plain, That a Person that takes such Challenges might be excluded from his Clergy by force of that Statute even before it was reviv'd by 5 & 6 *E.* 6. set forth more at Large *Sect.* 42, &c. because 1 *E.* 6. restores the Benefit of the Clergy, as it was before the Reign of *Henry* 8. to such only as shall be found guilty, or confess, or stand Mute, or not answer directly, and consequently [h] those who challenge above the Number of twenty, seem clearly to be excluded in the same Manner as if 1 *E.* 6. had never been made.

[a] 11 Co. 31, 32.
[b] 11 Co. 32. b.
[c] 11 Co. 31, 32.
[d] Supra Sect. 30.
[e] Supra Sect. 32.
[f] 11 Co. 32. a. Sup Sect. 27, 28. *But* S. P. C. 126 Lett. A. *it is made a Quære whether those who challenge more than twenty, are not included under the Word Convict.*
[g] *But in* 11 Co. 32. a. *it seems to be otherwise holden.*
[h] Vide H. P. C. 239.

Sect. 37. *Secondly,* In that it omits Acceſſaries in the Clauſe which takes away Clergy, but includes them in that which reſtores it, which is general as to all Caſes of Felony, not mentioned in the Act, whereof any Perſon ſhall be found guilty, and conſequently as to Acceſſaries wholly takes off the Force of 23 *H.* 8. which extends [i] only to thoſe who ſhall be found guilty, and is the only Statute in this Reign which excludes Acceſſaries from the Clergy. And accordingly we find, [a] That after this Statute Acceſſaries were admitted to their Clergy, in the ſame Manner as before the Reign of *Henry* 8. till the making of 4 *&* 5 *Ph. &* *Mar.* ſet forth more at large *Sect.* 45.

Sect. 38. *Thirdly,* In that it alſo omits Arſon in the Clauſe which takes away Clergy, but includes it in the general Words of that which reſtores it, and conſequently reintitled thoſe [b] Convict of it to the Clergy, in all Caſes but that of challenging more than twenty, till the making of 5 *&* 6 *E.* 6. as ſhall be more fully ſhewn hereafter.

Sect. 39. *Fourthly,* In that the Clauſe which ouſts Horſe-ſtealers of their Clergy is worded in ſuch a Manner as makes it doubtful whether it extend to thoſe who ſteal but one, which occaſioned the making of 2 * *&* 3 *E.* 6. 33. which declares, *That a Perſon feloniouſly ſtealing one Horſe, Gelding, or Mare, ſhall be put from his Clergy in the ſame Manner as if he had been indicted, or appealed for ſtealing of two,* &c.

Sect. 40. *Fifthly,* In that the Clauſe which ouſts Houſe-breakers of their Clergy, is not worded in ſuch a Manner as fully brings their Offence under the Notion of Felony; for it is thus expreſſed, *Any Perſon who ſhall be attainted,* &c. *of breaking any Houſe by Day or Night, any Perſon being therein and put in Fear or Dread,* &c. But ſuch a Breaking, even in the Night, is no Felony unleſs it be done with an Intent to commit a Felony, which makes it Burglary; neither can it be Felony if done in the Day with any Intent whatſoever; for tho' a Felony follow, which may make the Houſe-breaking, done with an Intent to commit it, properly enough to be called felonious: Yet it ſeems, That it cannot make it become [c] a Felony, becauſe it is not reducible to any Species of Felony. And therefore the Statute muſt be ſupplied by a reaſonable Intendment, and [d] conſtrued to mean ſuch Houſe-breaking only as amounts to, or is attended with Felony.

Sect. 41. It is [e] holden by Sir *Edward Coke,* That Piracy was reſtored to the Benefit of the Clergy by this Statute; but as to Piracy on the High Sea, the contrary hath been ſolemnly * adjudged, and confirmed by conſtant Experience, and is certainly agreeable to the [f] legal Notion of Piracy in other Caſes; which being a Capital Offence by the Civil Law only, (even after the Statute of 28 *H.* 8. 15. which altered not the Nature of the Offence, but only the Manner of the Trial) ſhall not be included in a Statute ſpeaking generally of Felonies, which ſhall be conſtrued only of thoſe Felonies which are ſuch by our Law; as thoſe Piracies are [g] which are committed in a Creek or Port within the Body of a County, but no other.

Sect. 42. The next general Statute relating to theſe Matters, is 5 *&* 6 *E.* 6. 10. which firſt recites the above-mentioned [h] Clauſe of 23 *H.* 8. concerning Clergy, and takes Notice that it was defective in omitting thoſe who rob, *&c.* in one County, and remove the Thing taken into another, and there are tried, *&c.* and that this Omiſſion was ſupplied by 25 *H.* 8. and that the ſaid Statute of 25 *H.* 8. was in this Reſpect made ineffectual by 1 *E.* 6. 12. which reſtored Clergy as it ſtood before the Reign of *H.* 8. to all the Felonies not therein mentioned; and that by Reaſon

[i] Vide ſupra, Sect. 30, 33.
[a] 11 Co. 31. b. Dyer 133. pl. 4.
[b] 11 Co. 31, 32, &c. Vide ſupra, Sect. 36.
* Vide infra Sect. 61.
[c] *Yet Quære, for this Matter is Doubtfully expreſſed,* S. P. C. 126. Lett. A *and* 11 Co. 31. b. 31 a.
[d] S. P. C. 125. Lett. D. 126. Lett. A. 11 Co. 31. b. 32. a.
[e] 11 Co. 31. b.
* Moore 756. pl. 1044. Vide 3 Inſt. 111.
[f] B. 1. ch. 37. Sect. 6, 7.
[g] B. 1. ch. 37. Sect. 11.
[h] Vide ſupra, Sect.

son of the said Statute of 1 *E.* 6. divers Persons had committed Robberies, *&c.* in one County, and after had been taken *&c.* and tried in another, and there had their Clergy, which they would not have had if the said Statute of 25 *H.* 8. had stood in Force; and then goes on in these Words, *For Redress whereof from henceforth to be had, be it enacted, &c. That the said Act made in the said 25th Year, touching the putting of such Offenders from their Clergy; and every Article, Clause and Sentence, contained in the same, touching Clergy, shall from henceforth, touching such Offences, from henceforth to be committed and done, stand, remain and be in full Strength and Vertue, in such Manner and Form, as it did before the making of the said Act in the first Year of the Reign of our Sovereign Lord the King that now is: Any Clause, Article, or Sentence compris'd therein to the contrary notwithstanding.*

Sect. 43. It was for some Time a great Question, Whether this Statute revived 25 *H.* 8. for the Whole, or only for such Part of it which relates to Felons removing the Thing feloniously taken into a different County from that wherein they took it, and there tried, *&c.*? And Sir [a] *William Staunforde* inclines to the latter Opinion; because the Words are, *That the said Act made in the said 25th Year, touching the putting such Offenders from their Clergy, shall be revived,* &c. where the Word *such* shall have Relation only to the Offenders mentioned before; which are those who steal in one County, and remove the Thing stolen into another; and this Objection is strengthened [b] by the Title of the Act, which is only this, *That such as rob in one Shire and fly into another, shall not have their Clergy.* To which it may be added, That all Statutes which take away Clergy, are to be construed strictly *in favorem vitæ.* Yet it hath been adjudged [c], and is, as I take it, fully [d] settled, That this Statute revived 25 *H.* 8. as to every other Part of it, as well as that concerning Felons carrying the Thing stolen from one County into another; for granting that the Makers of the Statute of 5 & 6 *E.* 6. had the Case of such Felons principally in their View; which appears pretty plainly, not only from the Title of the Statute, but also from the Preamble and Purview, for the Preamble expressly takes Notice of no other Mischief from the Repeal of 25 *H.* 8. but only this, That thereby many of such Felons had their Clergy; and then follows the enacting Clause, which begins in these Words, *For Redress whereof,* and then goes on, *be it enacted,* &c, *That* 25 *H.* 8. *touching such Offenders, and such Offences, remain in full Force.* Yet considering that the Statute of 5 & 6 *E.* 6. begins with a Recital of the whole Clause of 23 *H.* 8. wherein there are several other Offences contained, and that the Words, *Such Offenders, and such Offences* in the enacting Clause of 5 & 6 *E.* 6. may properly enough refer to them, as well as to the Offence of the Felons mentioned next immediately before: And farther considering that the Words, *Such Offenders and such Offences,* may properly enough be taken to include *all such in Mischief, and such in Inconvenience,* according to the received [e] Construction of the Word *such,* in some other Statutes, and *a fortiori,* those in greater Mischief and greater Inconvenience, as almost all the other Offences specified in 25 *H.* 8. are, as for instance, Petit Treason, Murder, Arson, *&c.* and it is a received [f] Construction of penal Statutes, to extend them to all Cases that come within the Meaning of the Words. And it would be absurd to imagine that the Makers of the Statute intended to put those who carried Goods stolen into a different County, in a worse Case in such County than in that wherein they stole them, as they must be if 25 *H.* 8. were only revived against them where they carried the Thing stolen into a different County;

[a] S. P. C. 128. Lett. A.

[b] Vide 11 Co. 33. a.

[c] 11 Co. 33, 34, 35.

[d] H. P. C. 232 to 237. See Rastal's Statutes, Title Clergy, Par. 16.

[e] 11 Co. 33. b.

[f] 11 Co. 33, 34. Vide supra, Sect. 25. and B. 1. ch. 32. Sect. 3.

County; for by such a Construction they would have been excluded from the Clergy, in the County wherein they committed the Robbery by 1 *E.* 6. 12. only, which not extending to those who challenge above the Number of twenty, might easily be evaded; whereas in a different County they would be excluded from it in such Case, by 25 *H.* 8. To which may be added, [a] That the first Sentence of the Purview of 5 & 6 *E.* 6. *viz. That the said Act of* 25 *H.* 8. *touching the putting such Offenders from their Clergy*, had been sufficient if no more had been intended but the excluding those who rob in one County and fly into another; and therefore it is most natural to intend that it was the Meaning of the Makers of the Statute, by adding those farther Words, *That every Article, Clause, and Sentence in the same, touching Clergy, shall touching such Offences, remain*, &c. to revive the whole Statute so far as it related to Clergy. [a] 11 Co. 34.

Sect. 44. And since the whole Statute of 25 *H.* 8. is revived, it follows by a necessary Consequence, That so much of 23 *H.* 8. also as is expresly affirmed by it, is revived also. And therefore since 25 *H.* 8. having recited the Clause of 23 *H.* 8. concerning Clergy, and the Mischief that it extended only to those who are found Guilty, expresly enacts, *That whoever shall be indicted of Petit Treason, willful burning of Houses, Murder, Robbery, or Burglary, or other Felony, according to the Tenour and Meaning of the said Statute, and stand Mute, or challenge peremptorily above twenty*, &c. *shall lose the Benefit of the Clergy, in like Manner as if he had pleaded, and been found guilty*; whereby it affirms and inforces the 23 *H.* 8. as to those found guilty of such Crimes; it follows by a necessary Consequence, That Persons not in Holy Orders found guilty of Petit Treason, or [b] Arson, which were omitted by 1 *E.* 6. are excluded from the Clergy by 23 *H.* 8. thus affirmed and enforced by 25 *H.* 8, and consequently revived by 5 & 6 *E.* 6.

[b] 11 Co. 34, b 35. a. H. P. C. 232, 233. Cont. Savil 46. pl. 98 S. P. C. 125.

Sect 45. But it is observable, That the said Statute of 25 *H.* 8. wholly omits [c] Accessaries, as well as 1 *E.* 6. But to remedy this Defect, it is enacted by 4 & 5. *Ph.* & *M.* 4. *That every Person that shall maliciously command, hire, or counsel any Person or Persons, to commit or do any Petit Treason, willful Murder, or to do any Robbery in any Dwelling-House or Houses, or to commit or do any Robbery in or near the Highway in the Realm of* England, *or in any other the Queen's Dominions, or to commit or do any Robbery in any Place within the Marches of* England *against* Scotland, *or willfully to burn any Dwelling-House, or any Part thereof, or any Barn then having Corn or Grain in the same, that then every such Offender, being outlawed thereof, or being thereof arraigned and found guilty by the Order of the Law, or being otherwise lawfully attainted or convicted of the same Offence; or being arraigned thereof, do stand Mute of Malice or froward Mind, or do challenge peremptorily above the Number of twenty Persons, or will not answer directly to such Offence, shall not have the Benefit of his Clergy.*

[c] Vide supra, Sect. 33.

Sect. 46. It is observable, 1. That this Statute is general as to all Robberies in any Dwelling-House: Yet it seems to have been always taken as a [d] reasonable Construction, That it shall be restrained to such Robberies of this Kind as were excluded from the Benefit of the Clergy, by some former Statute; for it cannot be well imagined that the Makers of this, or any other Statute, intended in any Case to take away Clergy from the Accessary, where the Principal is left to the full Benefit of it.

[d] 11 Co. 35, 36, 37. Vide H. P. C. 235, 236, 237. Cont. Savil, 46. pl. 98.

Sect. 47. 2dly, That an Indictment, or Appeal, in order to oust an Accessary of his Clergy by force of this Statute, must expresly pursue it, in Substance [a] at least, as hath been already shewn, *Sect.* 25.

[a] Vide Dy. 186. pl. 2, 3. *That the Words* Wilful Murder, *in an Indictment on the Statute are sufficiently pursued by laying the Murder* done ex malitia præcogitata.

Sect. 48. It is farther enacted by 3 & 4 *W. & M.* 9. Par. 3. *That if any Person or Persons whatsoever be indicted of any Offence, for which by Vertue of any former Statute, he or they are excluded from having the Benefit of his or their Clergy, if he or they had been thereof convicted by Verdict or Confession, if he or they stand Mute, or will not answer directly to the Felony, or shall challenge peremptorily above the Number of twenty Persons returned to be on the Jury, or shall be outlawed thereupon, shall not be admitted to the Benefit of his or their Clergy.*

Sect. 49. But *Note*, That this Statute extends not to Appeals, nor to Offences made Felonies by subsequent Statutes.

And now I am in the second Place more distinctly to consider the several Statutes which take away the Benefit of the Clergy, so far as they particularly relate to the several Kinds of Crimes; for the better Illustration whereof having referred the Reader, as to the Felonies made such by Statute, to the several Chapters in the first Book wherein such Felonies are handled, I shall here consider the Statutes which take away Clergy from Capital Offences at the Common Law, under the following Heads, as they relate,

1. To Petit Treason.
2. To Homicide.
3. To Larceny.
4. To Sacrilege.
5. To Robbery.
6. To Burglary.
7. To Arson.

Sect. 50. And first as to Petit Treason: It is certain, that by force of 23 & 25 *H.* 8. revived [b] by 5 & 6 *E.* 6. the Principal not being a [c] Clerk in Holy Orders, is excluded from the Benefit of the Clergy, upon a [d] Conviction, [e] standing Mute, or Challenge of more than twenty, upon an [f] Indictment.

Sect. 51. And Sir [g] *Matthew Hale* seems to be of Opinion, That the Principal is likewise ousted of his Clergy, by 23 *H.* 8. in Appeal of Petit Treason, if he be convict by Verdict or Confession, but not in other Cases: But *Quære*, How this can be? For since so much [h] only of 23 *H.* 8. seems to be revived, as is affirmed and enforced by 25 *H.* 8. and that no way extends to Appeals but only to Indictments, it seems difficult to make out that any Part of 23 *H.* 8. so far as it relates to Appeals, is revived by 25 *H.* 8.

Sect. 52. But I would rather incline to think that the Principal in an Appeal of Petit Treason may be excluded from his Clergy by 1 [i] *E.* 6. 12. in all Cases except that of challenging above the Number of twenty, under the Words *Murder of Malice prepensed* in that Statute; because all Petit Treason, in the very Notion of it, necessarily [k] includes such Murder and more.

[b] Vide supra, Sect. 43, 44. H. P. C. 232.
[c] Vide supra, Sect. 13.
[d] Vide supra, Sect. 30, 31.
[e] Vide supra, 32, 33.
[f] Vide supra, Sect. 33.
[g] H. P. C. 232.
[h] Vide supra, Sect. 43, 44.
[i] Vide supra, Sect. 34, 35, 36.
[k] B. 1. ch. 2. Sect. 6.

Sect.

Sect. 53. However the Makers of 4 [a] & 5 *Ph. & M.* 4. seem plainly to have been of Opinion, That the Principals in Petit Treason are excluded from the Clergy in all Cases as well upon an Appeal as Indictment; because they have in all Cases expresly excluded the Accessaries maliciously before, as well upon an Appeal as Indictment; and [b] it cannot be well imagined that they intended to make the Law more severe against them than against the Principals.

[a] Vide supra, Sect. 45.
[b] Vide 11 Co. 35. a. And supra Sect. 46.

Sect. 54. *Secondly,* As to Homicide: It is certain that willful Murder of Malice prepensed is excluded from the Benefit of the Clergy upon Indictments in all Cases by [c] 23 & [d] 25 *H.* 8. and by 1 [e] *E.* 6. 12.

Sect. 55. Also it seems [f] to be the Opinion of Sir [g] *Matthew Hale,* That it likewise is excluded from the Clergy in all Cases as well upon Appeals as Indictments, but this seems questionable; for Appeals are certainly not [h] within 25 *H.* 8. and [h] therefore since so much only of 23 *H.* 8. is revived by 5 & 5 *E.* 6. as is affirmed and enforced by 25 *H.* 8. I do not see how it can be revived as to any Appeal. From whence it seems to follow, That the only Statute which expresly excludes them is 1 *E.* 6. 12. which [i] omits the Case of challenging more than twenty. Neither is this Defect supplied by 3 & 4 *W. & M.* 9. for this extends [k] only to Indictments.

[c] Vide supra, S. 25, 30, 31.
[d] Vide supra, Sect. 32, 33.
[e] Vide supra, Sect. 34, &c.
[f] H.P.C. 232.
[h] Vide supr. Sect. 42, 43, 51.
[i] Vide supra, Sect 34, 36.
[k] Supra Sect. 48, 49.

Sect. 56. But Accessaries maliciously before to such Murder are expresly excluded from the Clergy in all Cases, as well upon Appeals as Indictments by 4 & 5 *P. & M.* 4 and how far the Principal may † hereby in like Manner be implicitly excluded also in all Cases, I shall leave to be considered.

† Vide 11 Co. 35. a. and supra, Sect. 46, 53.

Sect. 57. By 1 *Jac.* 1. 8. He that shall be convicted by Verdict of twelve Men, or Confession, or otherwise according to the Laws of this Realm, of Homicide, by Stabbing, (but not those who abet them, *&c.* for which I shall refer to *Book* 1. *Chap.* 30. *Sect.* 4, 5, *&c.*) shall be excluded from the Benefit of his Clergy, *&c.*

Sect. 58. And this Statute seems plainly to extend as well to Appeals as Indictments, but not to the Case of standing Mute, or challenging above twenty, *&c.* But those who are indicted of such Manslaughter are excluded from the Clergy in all such Cases, as well as on a Conviction, by 3 & 4 *W & M.* 9.

Supra Sect. 48, 49.

Thirdly, Larceny is excluded from the Benefit of the Clergy in the following Cases,

1. In that of a felonious secret Taking from the Person.
2. In that of Horse-stealing.
3. In that of stealing from a Shop or Dwelling-House, *&c.*
4. In that of stealing Woollen Manufactures from the Tenters.
5. In that of stealing the King's Naval Stores.

59. And first, As to a felonious secret Taking from the Person: It is enacted by 8 *Eliz.* 4. *That no Person who shall be indicted or appealed for felonious taking of any Money, Goods, or Chattles, from the Person of any other, privily without his Knowledge, in any Place whatsoever, and thereupon found guilty by Verdict of twelve Men, or shall confess the same upon his or their Arraignment, or will not answer directly to the same, according to the Laws of the Realm, or shall stand wilfully or of Malice, or obstinately Mute, or challenge peremptorily above the Number of twenty, or shall be upon such Indictment or Appeal outlawed, shall be admitted to his Clergy,* &c.

Uuuu Sect.

Vide Sect. 26, 45, 46. *Sect.* 60. But *Note*, That this Statute extends not to any Accessaries before or after.

Sect. 61. *Secondly*, As to Horse-stealers: It seems that they are [a] ousted of their Clergy in all Cases, as well upon Appeals as Indictments, by 1 *E.* 6. 12. and 2 & 3 *E.* 6. 33. by the latter of which Statutes it is enacted, *That all Persons feloniously taking or stealing any Horse, Gelding, or Mare, shall not be admitted to the Privilege of the Clergy, but shall be put from the same, in like Manner and Form as though they had been indicted or appealed for felonious stealing of two Horses, two Geldings, or two Mares, of any other, and thereupon found guilty by Verdict of twelve Men, or confessed the same upon their Arraignment, or stand wilfully or of Malice Mute.*

[a] Vide supra, Sect. 34, 39

Sect. 62. It seems a reasonable [b] Construction of this Statute to extend it as well to those who are outlawed, or challenge more than twenty, as to those who are found guilty by Verdict, *&c.* because it is general, That all such Persons *shall be put from their Clergy*, &c. *in such Manner as if they had been found guilty*, &c. and if they had been found guilty, it is certain that they wou'd have been ousted of their Clergy by the express Words of 1 *E.* 6. 12. *Par.* 10.

[b] S. P. C 125. Letters B. C. H. P. C. 238.

Supra, 34, &c.

Sect. 63. But I do not find that any [c] Statute excludes any Accessaries to this Offence from their Clergy.

[c] H. P. C. 238.

Vide supra, Sect. 26, 45, 46. *Sect.* 64. *Thirdly*, As to Larceny from a Dwelling-House, Shop, *&c.* It is enacted by 10 & 11 *W.* 3. 23. *That all Persons who by Night or Day, shall in any Shop, Ware-house, Coach-house or Stable, privately and feloniously steal any Goods, Wares, or Merchandizes, of the Value of* 5 s. *or more, though such Shop*, &c. *be not broke open, and tho' the Owner, or any other Person be not in such Shop*, &c. *or that shall assist, hire or command any Person to commit such Offence, being thereof convict, or attainted by Verdict or Confession, or being indicted thereof shall stand Mute, or challenge above twenty of the Jury, shall be excluded from the Benefit of the Clergy.*

Sect. 65. But this Statute seems Defective in neither mentioning Persons [d] outlawed, nor [e] Accessaries; neither is it help'd by 3 & 4 *W.* & *M.* 9. because [f] it is subsequent to it.

[d] Vide Sect. 26, 27, 28.

[e] Vide supra, Sect. 26, 45, 46.

[f] Vide supra, Sect. 48, 49.

Sect. 66. It is enacted by 12 *Anne* 7. *That every Person who shall feloniously steal any Money, Goods, or Chattels, Wares, or Merchandises, of the Value of* 40 s. *or more, being in any Dwelling-house, or Out-house thereunto belonging, although such House or Out-house be not actually broken by such Offender, and altho' the Owner of such Goods, or any other Person or Persons, be or be not in such House or Out-house, or shall assist, or aid any Person or Persons, to commit any such Offence, being thereof convicted or attainted by Verdict or Confession, or being indicted thereof shall stand Mute or will not directly answer to the Indictment, or shall peremptorily challenge above the Number of twenty returned to be of the Jury, shall be absolutely debarred of and from the Benefit of Clergy*, &c.

Sect. 67. But it is provided, *That nothing in this Act shall extend to Apprentices under the Age of fifteen Years, who shall rob their Masters as aforesaid.*

Vide Sect. 26, 27, 28, 64, 65. *Sect.* 68. This Statute seems also Defective like the former, as to Persons outlawed, and Accessaries.

Sect. 69. *Fourthly*, As to those who shall feloniously steal Woollen Manufactures from the Tenters: It is enacted by 22 *Car.* 2. 5. *That no Person who shall be indicted for feloniously cutting and taking, stealing or carrying away of any Cloth or Woollen Manufactures from the Rack or Tenter in the Night Time, and thereupon found guilty by Verdict of twelve Men, or shall confess the same on Arraignment, or will not answer directly to the same, according to the Laws* of *of the Realm, or shall stand wilfully or of Malice Mute, or challenge peremptorily above the Number of twenty, or shall be upon such Indictment outlawed, shall be admitted to the Benefit of the Clergy,* &c.

Sect. 70. *Fifthly*, As to those who steal Naval Stores: It is observable, That those who *shall steal or imbezil any of his Majesty's Sail, Cordage, or any other his Majesty's Naval Stores*, are in the like Manner excluded from the Clergy by 22 *Car.* 2. 5. as those who steal Woolen Manufactures from the Tenters, *&c.*

See the precedent Section.

Sect. 71. But *Note*, That this Statute extends neither to Appeals, nor to [a] Accessaries.

Sect. 72. As to Sacrilege: It is observable, That all Persons not in Holy Orders, who shall be indicted, whether in the same County wherein the Fact was committed, or in a [b] different County, of *robbing any Church, Chapel, or other Holy Place*, are excluded from their Clergy by [c] 23 *H.* 8. 1. and 25 [d] *H.* 8. 3. revived [e] by 5 *&* 6 *E.* 6. 10. upon a Conviction, standing Mute, or peremptory Challenge of more than twenty; and by 3 *&* [f] 4 *W. & M.* 9. upon an Outlawry.

Sect. 73. But the Word *Robbing* [g] being always taken to carry with it some Force, as shall be more fully shewn *Sections* 88, 92, 96. It seems that no Sacrilege is within any of these Statutes, which is not accompany'd with the actual breaking of a Church, *&c.*

Sect. 74. But by 1 *E.* 6. 12. [h] *Par.* 10. all Persons in general are ousted of their Clergy for the *felonious taking of any Goods out of any Parish Church, or other Church or Chapel*, in all Cases, except that of challenging more than twenty; and by 3 *&* [i] 4 *W. & M.* 9. upon such a Challenge, as well as upon a Conviction, *&c.* upon an Indictment, [k] whether in the same County wherein the Sacrilege was committed, or in a different one.

[a] Vide Sect. 26, & 45, 46.
[b] Infra, 80, 81, 82.
[c] Vide supra, Sect. 30, 31.
[d] Vide supra, Sect. 34, 33.
[e] Vide supra, Sect. 42, 43, 44.
[f] Vide supra, Sect. 48, 49.
[g] Kely. 58, 69, 70. Dyer 224, pl. 30.
[h] Vide supra, Sect. 34, 35, 36, 37.
[i] Vide supra, Sect. 48, 49.
[k] Infra, 80, 81, 82.

Sect. 75. But it seems, That Accessaries to such a Robbery, or felonious taking are excluded from their Clergy by no Statute; for tho' they are expresly mentioned by 23 *H.* 8. 1. yet since they are omitted by 25 *H.* 8. 3. and so much only [l] of 23 *H.* 8. 1. is revived as is affirmed and enforced by 25 *H.* 8. 3. they seem to remain in the same Case as if they had been wholly omitted by 23 *H.* 8. 1. which is the only Statute I know of which extends to them, except the Offence amount to Burglary, in which Case Accessaries before are ousted of their Clergy by 3 *&* 4 *W. & M.* 9.

[l] Vide supra, Sect. 43, 44, 52, 55.

Sect. 76. But *Quære* if there be need of any Statute to exclude them, since the Common Law seems to have given no Person whatsoever, any Right to Demand the Privilege of the Clergy for Sacrilege, but only at the Discretion of the Ordinary, as hath been more fully shewn *Section* the ninth.

Fifthly, As to Robbery, I shall particularly consider the Statutes excluding it from the Clergy, as they relate,

1. To Robbery in or near the Highway.
2. To Robbery in a Dwelling-House, Booth or Tent.
3. To Robbery in general.

Sect. 77. And first, as to Robbery in or near the Highway: It is observable, That all Persons, not in Holy Orders, who shall be indicted [m] of *Robbing any Person or Persons in or about the Highways*, are ex-

[m] Vide supra, Sect. 33.

[a] Vide supra, Sect. 30, 31. [b] Vide supra, Sect. 32, 33. [c] Vide supra, S. 42, 43, 44. [d] Vide supra, Sect. 48, 49. † Vide supra, Sect. 34, 35, 36, 37.

excluded from the Clergy by 23 [a] *H.* 8. 1. and 25 [b] *H.* 8. 3. revived [c] by 5 & 6 *E.* 6. 10 upon a Conviction, standing Mute, or peremptory Challenge of more than twenty; and by 3 & 4 [d] *W. & M.* 9. upon an Outlawry.

Sect. 78. And *Note*, That all Persons in general, *who shall be guilty of robbing any Person or Persons in the Highway, or near to the Highway*, are excluded from the Clergy both upon an Appeal and Indictment by † 1 *E.* 6. 12. *Par.* 10. in all Cases except that of challenging more than twenty; and by 3 & 4 *W. & M.* 9. upon such a Challenge upon an Indictment.

Sect. 79. *Note*, That no Robbery is within these Statutes, but such as is laid in the Indictment to have been committed in or near the [e] Highway, [f] and to have [g] put the Person robbed in Fear.

[e] Vide supra, Sect. 25. [f] Supra Sect. 73. and Dy. 224 pl. 30. and B. 1. Ch. 35. Sect. 13. [g] Vide supra Sect. 43, 44. [h] Vide B. 1. Ch. 33. S. 9.

Sect. 80. It is recited by 25 *H.* 8. 3. revived [g] by 5 & 6 E. 6. 10. *That divers Felons and Robbers that had committed many heinous Robberies and Burglaries in one Shire, and conveyed the Spoil and Robbery into another Shire, and had been there* [h] *taken, indicted and arraigned upon Felony, and felonious taking of the same Goods, and not upon the same Robbery nor Burglary; for that it was not committed nor done in the same Shire where they had been so indicted and arraigned, and by Reason thereof the same Felons, Robbers, and Burglars had enjoyed the Privilege of their Clergy.* And thereupon it is enacted, *That if any Person or Persons be indicted of Felony for stealing of any Goods or Chattels, in any County within this Realm of* England, *and thereupon arraigned and be found guilty or stand Mute of Malice, or challenge peremptorily above the Number of twenty Persons, or will not directly answer to the Law, shall lose and be put from the Benefit of the Clergy, in like Manner and Form as they should have been if they had been indicted and arraigned, and found guilty in the same County where the same Robbery or Burglary was done or committed; if it shall appear to the Justices before whom any such Felons or Robbers be arraigned, by Evidence given before them, or by Examination, that the same Felonies, whereupon they were so arraigned, had been such Robberies or Burglaries, in the same Shire wherein such Robberies or Burglaries were committeed or done, by Reason whereof they should have lost the Benefit of their Clergy by Force of* 23 H. 8. *in Case they had been found guilty thereof in the same Shire where such Robberies or Burglaries were so committed and done.*

[i] 11 Co. 31. a.

Sect. 81. But *Note*, That this Statnte extends [i] not to those who are outlawed; nor to those who are indicted out of the Realm of *England*; nor to those who are indicted of such stealing as is excluded from the Clergy by subsequent Statutes; nor to Appellees; but the three first of these Defects are supplied by 3 & 4 *W. & M.* 9. by which it is enacted, *That if any Person or Persons be indicted of Felony for stealing of any Goods or Chattels in any County within this Realm of* England, *Dominion of* Wales, *or Town of* Berwick *upon* Tweed, *and thereof be convicted or attainted, or upon his or their Arraignment shall stand Mute, or will not directly answer to the Indictment, or shall challenge peremptorily above the Number of twenty Persons returned to be of the Jury, he or they shall be totally excluded from having the Benefit of his or their Clergy, if it appear upon Evidence or Examination before the Justices, that the said Goods or Chattels were taken by Robbery or Burglary, or in any other Manner, in any other County, whereof if such Person or Persons had been convicted by a Jury of the said other County, he or they are excluded by Vertue of this or any other Act from having the Benefit of his or their Clergy.*

Sect.

Sect. 82. *Note,* That [a] the Words *If it shall appear upon Evidence before the Justices,* &c. are to be intended where the Party pleads Not guilty, and is found guilty by the Jury, and the Words *If it shall appear upon Examination,* &c. are to be intended where he stands Mute, or challenges peremptorily above the Number of twenty, or is outlawed, or confesses [b], *&c.* And it hath been [c] adjudged, That there is no need to make any Entry on the Record, that it appears by such Evidence, or Examination, that the Felony was originally commenced in a different County, and was of such a Nature that the Offender cou'd not have his Clergy. But it is said, [d] That it is usual to write in the Margent of the Indictment, that it is for Robbery, *&c.* in another County.

Sect. 83. It is said to [e] have been holden by all the Justices, That if the Felony whereof a Man is found guilty in the County wherein he is indicted, be such as doth not need the Benefit of the Clergy, as amounting only to Petit Larceny, *&c.* the Offender shall have only the proper Judgment for such Offence, and no other, in Respect of the Robbery, *&c.* proved upon the Evidence, *&c.* in the first County, for being convicted of no Offence which will warrant a Judgment of Death, and consequently having no need to demand his Clergy, he cannot be hurt by being excluded from it.

Sect. 84. It is enacted by 3 *&* 4 [f] *Ph. & M* 4. *That those who shall maliciously command, hire or counsel any Person or Persons to commit or do any Robbery in or near any Highway in this Realm of* England, *or in any other the Queen's Dominion, shall be ousted of their Clergy, on a Conviction, standing Mute, peremptory Challenge of more than twenty, or Outlawry.*

Secondly, As to Robbery in a Dwelling-house, Booth or Tent, I shall consider the Statutes concerning it as they relate,

1. To such Robbery putting some Person in Fear.
2. To such Robbery putting no Person in Fear.

Sect. 85. *First,* As to such Robbery putting some Person in Fear: It is observable, That all Persons not in Holy Orders, *who shall rob any Person or Persons in their Dwelling-houses, or Dwelling-place, the Owner or Dweller in the same House, his Wife, his Children or Servants then being within, and put in fear and dread by the same,* and indicted, [g] are excluded from their Clergy by 23 *H.* 8. 1. and 25. *H.* 8. 3. revived by 5 *&* 6. *E.* 6. 10. upon a Conviction, standing Mute, or peremptory Challenge of more than twenty, and by 3 *&* 4. *W. & M.* 9. upon an Outlawry.

Sect. 86. And *note,* * That by 25 *H.* 8. 3. and 3 *&* 4 *W. & M.* 9. they are excluded from their Clergy on an Indictment in a Foreign County. And their Accessaries before are excluded in all Cases by 3 *&* 4 || *Ph. & Ma.* 4.

Sect. 87. And by 1 † *Ed.* 6. 12. *Par.* 10. all Persons in general who shall *break any House by Day or by Night,* (*viz.* [h] who shall break a House burglarily, if in the Night, or shall break a House and commit a Felony therein, if in the Day) [i] *any Person being then in the same House where the same breaking shall be, and thereby put in Fear or Dread,* are excluded from their Clergy, as well upon an Appeal as an Indictment, in all Cases, [k] except that of challenging more than twenty; and by 3 [l] *&* 4 *W. & M.* 9. upon such a Challenge, as well as upon a Conviction, *&c.* upon an Indictment, whether in the same County wherein the breaking and Felony

[a] 11 Co. 31.

[b] Vide supra, Sect. 28, 31. 11 Co. 31. Cont. 1 And. 114.

[c] 1 And. 114.

[d] H. P. C. *in the old Edition printed in the Year,* 1678.

[e] Moo. 550. pl. 739. H. P. C. 242.

[f] Vide supra, Sect. 45, 46. *How such Offence must be laid in the Indictment.*

Vide supra, Sect. 25.

[g] Vide supra, Sect. 30, 31, 32, 33, 42, 43, 44, 48, 49, 72, 77.

* Vide supra, Sect. 80, 81, 82, 83.

|| Vide supra, Sect 45, 46.

† Vide supra, Sect. 34, &c.

[h] Vide supra, Sect. 40. 11 Co. 36. a. b.

[i] Vide infra, Sect. 93.

[k] Vide supra, Sect. 36.

[l] Vide supra, Sect 48, 49.

[a] Vide supra, Sect. 80, 81, 82. 83.
* H. P. C. 236. Supra Sect. 45. 46.
[b] Vide supra, Sect. 73. And infra, Sect. 88, 92, 96.
† Supra Sect. 48, 49.
[c] Kely. 58, 59. 70. Supra, Sect. 73, 87 infra, S. 92, 96. H. P. C. 237, 238.

was committed, or in a [a] different County; and the Accessaries before to such a breaking if accompanied with stealing in a Dwelling-house, are ousted of their Clergy in all * Cases by 4 & 5 *Ph.* & *M.* 4. because the felonious taking being accompanied with a Breaking, seems properly [b] enough to come under the Notion of Robbery in a Dwelling-house, all Accessaries to which before the Fact are expresly excluded from their Clergy by that Statute, as Accessaries before to Robbery in general are by 3 & †4 *W.* & *M.* 9.

Sect. 88. But [c] no Breaking is within the Statute of 1 *E.* 6. which doth not amount to an actual breaking of an House, or of some Part of it; as of a Cupboard or Door, *&c.* fixed to the Freehold; and therefore the breaking of a Trunk or Box, *&c.* seem plainly not be within the Statute. But by 3 & 4 *W.* & *M.* 9. *Every Person or Persons that shall feloniously take away any Goods or Chattel, being in any Dwelling house, the Owner, or any other Person being therein, and put in Fear, or shall comfort, aid, abet, assist, counsel, hire, or command any Person to commit such Offence, being thereof convicted or attainted, or indicted, and standing Mute, or peremptorily challenging above twenty, shall be ousted of the Benefit of their Clergy.*

Secondly, As to such Robbery, putting no Person in Fear: I shall consider the Statutes concerning it as they relate,

1. To such Robbery in a House, which some Person is in at the Time.
2. To such Robbery in a House, which no Person is in at the Time.

Sect. 89. As to the first of these, it is enacted by 5 & 6 *E.* 6. 9. *That if it happen any Person or Persons to be found guilty according to the Laws of this Realm, for robbing of any Person or Persons in any Part or Parcel of their Dwelling-houses, or Dwelling-places, the Owner or Dweller in the same House, or his Wife, his Children or Servants being then within the same House or Place where it shall happen the same Robbery and Felony to be committed and done, or in any other Place within the Precinct of the same House or Dwelling-place, that such Offenders shall in no wise be admitted to their Clergy, whether the Owner or Dweller in the same House, his Wife or Children then and there being, shall be waking or sleeping.*

Sect. 90. *And that no Person or Persons which shall happen to be found guilty after the Laws of this Realm, of and for robbing any Person or Persons, in any Booth or Tent, in any Fair or Market, the Owner, his Wife, his Children, or Servants or Servant then being within the Booth or Tent, shall not be admitted to the Benefit of his or their Clergy, but utterly be excluded thereof,* &c. *without having any Respect or Consideration whether the Owner or Dweller in such Booths and Tents, his Wife, Children or Servants being in the same Booths or Tents at the Time of such Robberies and Felonies committed, shall be sleeping or waking.*

[d] H. P. C. 236, 237.

Sect. 91. This Statute [d] seems plainly to extend to all who shall be convicted by Verdict or Confession, whether upon an Appeal or Indictment; but not to those who shall be outlawed, or stand Mute, or challenge peremptorily above twenty Jurors; but these Defects are supplied as to Indictments by 3 [e] & 4 *W.* & *M.* 9.

[e] Vide supr. Sect. 48, 49.

Sect.

I

Sect. 92. It seems to be generally agreed, That no Robbery is within this Statute which is not accompanied with an actual [a] breaking of an House, or of some Part of it.

Sect. 93. Also it seems to be agreed, [b] That a Sojourner's being in a House at the Time of the Robbery doth not bring it within this Statute; for the Words are *The Owner or Dweller in the same House, or his Wife, his Children, or Servants, being then within the same House,* &c. Yet it is said in [c] *Hale's Pleas of the Crown* to have been ruled by Advice of the Justices, That where one entered into the Lodging of Sir *H. Hungate*, being Parcel of *Whitehall*, and broke open a Chamber and took away his Goods, his Case was within this Statute, and that the Indictment ought to be for breaking the King's House, called *Whitehall*, and for stealing the Goods of Sir *H. H.* divers Persons being in the House: But *Note*, That this Case is wholly omitted in the first Edition of *Hale's Pleas of the Crown*, and I cannot but think that it is misprinted in the Second; because such a Robbery seems by no Means within the Purview of this Statute, which extends only to such Robberies as are done to a Man in such a Place as may be called *his Dwelling-house or Dwelling place, his Wife, Children, or Servants being at the same Time within the same.* But in the State of this Case it seems to be admitted, That *Whitehall*, wherein the Felony was committed, could not properly be called, nor ought to be laid in the Indictment as the Dwelling-house or Dwelling-place of the said Sir *H. H.* who was the Person robbed, but of the King: Also it seems to be admitted, That it is sufficient to set forth generally in the Indictment that divers Persons were in the House, without shewing that they were under any Relation to the Person robbed, as his Children or Servants, *&c.* which [d] seems to be necessarily required by 5 *&* 6 *E.* 6. 9. And therefore I take it, that the Statute here intended is not 5 *&* 6 *E.* 6. 9. but rather 1 *E.* 6. [e] 12. *Par.* 10. or 39 [f] *El.* 15. Yet *Quære*; for neither of these Statutes seem to extend to this Case as it is here put. However 3 *&* 4 *W. & M.* 9. seems fully to extend to it. By which it is enacted, *That all those who shall rob any Dwelling-house in the Day-Time, any Person being therein, or shall comfort, aid, abet, assist, counsel, hire, or command any Person to commit such Offence, being thereof convicted or attainted, or indicted, and standing Mute, or challenging peremptorily above twenty, shall be ousted of their Clergy.* But I do not [g] find that any Statute excludes those from their Clergy who are Accessaries to a Robbery in a Booth or Tent, except it be from the Person of a Man, in which Case the Accessaries before the Fact seem to be excluded from their Clergy by 3 *&* 4 *W. & M.* 9. as shall be more fully shewn hereafter.

[a] *For this* vide supra, Sect. 73, 87, 88, 96.

[b] H. P. C. 237, 238. *Yet in* Pop 84. *there is a Case seemingly contrary.* [b] Hetley 64. S. P. C. 129. H. P. C. 236, 237. ·iqu· 11 Co. 35. b.

[c] Folio 237, 238.

[d] Vide Hetl. 64. H. P. C. 235, 236. 11 Co. 36. b. S. P. C. 129. b. Popham 84.

[e] Vide supra, Sect. 87.

[f] Vide infra, S. 95, 96, 97.

[g] *See the Statute of* 3 *&* 4 Ph. & M. supra, Sect. 45. 46.

Sect. 94. It seems plain, That those who are guilty of a Felony within these Statutes, are excluded from their Clergy by 3 *&* 4 *W. & M.* 9. on an Indictment in a Foreign County, in the same Manner as if they had been convicted in the first County, as hath been more fully shewn, *Sect.* 80, 81, 82, 83.

Sect. 95. *Secondly*, As to such Robbery in a House which no Person is in at the Time: It is recited by 39 *El.* 15. *That then of late divers lewd and felonious Persons, understanding that the robbing of Houses in the Day-time, no Person being therein at the Time, is not so penal as where some Person is therein, had been emboldened to take their Opportunity to commit many heinous Robberies, in breaking and entring divers Houses,* &c. and thereupon it is enacted, *That if any Person shall be found guilty, and convicted by Verdict, Confession, or otherwise, according to the Laws of this Realm, for the felonious taking away in the Day-time, of any Money, Goods or Chattel, being of the Value of* 5 s. *or upwards, in any Dwelling-house or Houses, or any Part thereof, or any Out-house or Out-houses, belonging and used to and with any Dwelling-house or Houses, altho' no Person shall be in the said House or Out-houses at the Time of such Felony committed, then such Person shall not be admitted to the Benefit of his Clergy.*

Sect. 96. Notwithstanding the Words of the Purview of this Statute seem plainly to include all felonious Takings to the Value of 5 *s.* out of a House, *&c.* whether with or without Force; yet since the Mischief complained of in the Preamble, and intended to be redressed is the frequent committing of many *heinous Robberies in breaking and entring,* &c. and since all other [a] Statutes excluding the Benefit of the Clergy from Robberies in Houses, have been construed to extend to such Larcenies only as are accompanied with a breaking of a House, or of some Part of it; it seems agreed, [b] That this Statute also shall extend only to such a felonious taking as is accompanied with the like breaking.

Sect. 97. It seems agreed, [c] That a Chamber in one of the Inns of Court, wherein a Person usually lodges, is properly a Dwelling-house within this Statute, and may be so called in an Indictment, because every Owner of such a Chamber hath a separate Interest in it. But that a Lodging in *Whitehall* or *Somerset-house* is not [d] a Dwelling-house within this Statute; from whence it seems to follow, That a Robbery in such a Lodging is not excluded from the Clergy by this Statute, if any Person were at the Time in any other Part of the Palace, because the whole is but one Dwelling-house.

Sect. 98. It seems agreed, [e] That no Accessary is ousted of his Clergy by this Statute. Also it hath been adjudged, [f] That he who stands by and abets another while he breaks and enters the House, and afterwards divides the Money with him, but doth not actually enter the House himself, is not within the Statute, the Reason whereof seems to be this, That the Words, *If any Person shall be convicted,* &c. *of a felonious taking,* &c. *in a Dwelling-house,* &c. shall in so penal a Law be intended only of an actual taking, and not of a constructive one. But this seems an extremely nice Case, and if it were a new Point, and not confirmed by Experience, the Authority of it might perhaps be justly questioned; for if the Person who only stood by and entred not the House, had actually entred it, and the other only had taken the Money, and had not given him any Part of it till both had gone out of the House; in this Case, as well as in the other, it might be said, That he who actually received not any Part of the Money till he was gone out of the House, was guilty only of a constructive taking in the House, and consequently not within this Statute. But I cannot easily perswade my self but that in such a Case both must be adjudged equally within the Statute; and why not as well in the other, it seeming an uncontroverted * Rule, That where divers are present and abet one another in committing any Felony, the Act of one shall be looked on as the Act of all. And upon this Ground, as I take it, it hath been always agreed, That those who are present, and abetting, when a Murder is committed, are all of them equally excluded from their Clergy, whether they actually gave the stroke or took the Money or not; and yet the Statutes to this Purpose mention only those who shall be found guilty of Murder or Robbing, *&c.* Nor do I find any Resolution to the contrary on any other Statute concerning Clergy, except only the [g] Statute of *Stabbing,* whereon it hath been adjudged, [h] That the Person only who gives the Stab is within the

[a] Supra Sect. 73, 87, 88, 92, 96.
[b] Kely. 30, 58, 69, 70. H. P. C. 237, 238. 11 Co. 36. b. Cro. Ca. 473, 474.
[c] Cro. Ca. 473, 474. 1 Jon. 394. H P. C. 83, 237. Kely. 27, 52. *See* B. 1. ch. 38. Sect. 13.
[d] Kely. 27, 52. Vide supra, Sect. 93.
[e] H. P. C. 237. Supra Sect. 45, 46.
[f] Cro. Ca. 473, 474. *Note, that the same Case is in* 1 Jon. 394. *but this Point is not taken Notice of.*
* Vide supra, Ch. 29. Sect. 7, 8, 13.
[g] 1 Jac. 1. 8.
[h] Aleyn 44. H P. C. 58. B 1. ch. 30. Sect. 71.

the Purview of it: But this seems plainly to depend on the particular Circumstances of this Offence, which is excluded from the Clergy in Respect of the Cruelty and Bloody Mind of him who gives the Stab, which certainly is peculiar to himself.

Sect. 99. However it is certain at this Day, *That whoever shall comfort, aid, abet, assist, counsel, hire or command any Person or Persons to break any Dwelling-house, Shop, or Ware-house thereunto belonging, or therewith used, in the Day-time, and feloniously take away any Money, Goods, or Chattel of the Value of* 5 s. *or upwards therein being, altho' no Person shall be within such Dwelling-house, Shop or Ware-house, being convicted or attainted, or being indicted and standing Mute, or challenging peremptorily above twenty, shall be excluded from their Clergy, by the express Words of* 3 & 4 W. & M. 9.

Sect. 100. But *Note*, That this Clause mentioning only a felonious taking in a Dwelling-house, Shop, or Ware-house thereunto belonging, and not mentioning Out-houses in general, as 39 *El.* doth, seems to have done it with a View to leave Out-houses to the same Construction which prevailed before; and therefore I take it that an Assistant to such a Felony in an Out-house, not being such a Shop or Ware-house, without entring into it, is clearly intitled to the Benefit of his Clergy since this Statute, however it might be disputed before. Vide supra, Sect. 98.

Sect. 101. *Note* also, That the Accessaries before to such a Felony in any Out-house, not being such a Shop or Warehouse, are still intitled to the Benefit of their Clergy, because the only [a] Law which excludes them is the [b] above-cited Clause of 3 *&* 4 *W. & M.* 9. which extends only to such Felonies in a Dwelling-house, Shop or Ware-house thereunto belonging.

[a] H. P. C. 227.
[b] Supra Sect. 99.

Sect. 102. But all Principals in any Felony within the said Statute of 39 *El.* are excluded from their Clergy by the same Statute upon any Conviction, whether upon an Indictment or Appeal; and by the said Statute of 3 [*] *&* 4 *W. & M.* upon an Outlawry, standing Mute, or peremptory Challenge of more than twenty, upon an Indictment, whether in the same County in which the Felony was first committed, or in a different [c] County.

[*] Supra Sect. 48, 49.
[c] Supra Sect. 81, 82, 83.

Sect. 103. *Thirdly*, As to Robbery in general, it is enacted by 3 *&* 4 *W. & M.* 9. *That all and every Person or Persons that shall rob any other Person, or shall comfort, aid, abet, assist, counsel, hire or command any Person or Persons to commit such Offence, being thereof convicted or attainted, or being indicted and standing Mute, or challenging peremptorily above twenty, shall not have the Benefit of his Clergy.*

Sect. 104. *Sixthly*, As to Burglary: [d] If any Person be in the House at the Time of the breaking, and thereby put in fear, the Principal is excluded from his Clergy by 1 *E.* 6. 12, *Par.* 10. in all Cases, except that of challenging more than twenty, and by 25 *H.* 8. revived [e] by 5 *&* 6. *E.* 6. or at least by 3 *&* 4 *W. & M.* 9. upon such a Challenge, upon an Indictment.

[d] Vide 11 Co. 35. b. 36. Supra Sect. 34, 36, 40.
[e] Vide supra, Sect. 42, 43, 44.

Sect. 105. Also the Principal in every Burglary, whether [f] any Person were in the House at the Time or not, is excluded from his Clergy by 18 *El.* 7. upon a [g] Conviction by Verdict, Outlawry, or Confession; and by 3 *&* 4 *W. & M.* upon standing Mute, or challenging peremptorily more than twenty upon an Indictment.

[f] Poph. 42, 52. 1 And. 302. Moor 660. 4 Co. 40. a. B. 1. ch. 38. Sect 11.
[g] 11 Co 35 b. H. P. C 233.

Sect. 106. Also by [a] the same Statute of 3 & 4 *W. & M.* 9. *Every Person who shall counsel, hire or command any Person to commit any Burglary, being thereof convicted, or attainted, or being indicted, and standing Mute, or challenging peremptorily above twenty, shall not have his Clergy.*

Sect. 107. *Seventhly,* As to Arson: It hath been clearly [b] settled, since *Poulter's* Case, that the Principal [c] not being in Holy Orders, is excluded from the Clergy upon an Indictment in all Cases, except Outlawry, by 23 *H.* 8. and 25 *H.* 8. as [d] revived by 5 & 6 *E.* 6. 10. And it is certain that he is excluded upon an Outlawry on an Indictment by 3 & 4 *W. & M.* 9.

Sect. 108. Also Accessaries to the Fact before, maliciously, are excluded in all Cases by 3 [*] & 4 *Ph. & M.* 4.

Sect. 109. *Note,* That by 1 *E.* 6. 12. *Par.* 14. [e] Every Lord of Parliament is allowed his Clergy in all Cases, wherein others are excluded by that Act, except wilful Murder, and consequently cannot be denied his Clergy for any other Felony wherein it was grantable at Common Law, unless it be ousted by some Statute made since the first Year of *Edward* 6. or [†] revived by 5 & 6 *E.* 6. 10.

Sect. 110. As to the third general Point of this Chapter, *viz.* At what Time the Benefit of the Clergy is demandable: It seems, [f] That it might be demanded by the ancient Common Law as soon as the Prisoner was brought to the Bar, before any Indictment or other Proceeding against him; for it is plain, That anciently the Clergy claimed, and were in a great measure indulged a Privilege of being wholly [g] free from secular Jurisdiction for Crimes punishable with loss of Life or Member. But after the Stat. of *Westm.* 1. *Ch.* 2. which strictly enjoined the Ordinaries not to suffer Clerks who have been indicted by solemn Inquests to be delivered without due Purgation, the Judges soon made a settled Rule [h] not to deliver any Clerk to the Ordinary, before he had been first indicted and arraigned, and his Offence had been inquired of and found by an Inquest of Office, which was done both to the end that if the Prisoner were found guilty, he [i] might absolutely forfeit his Goods, (which anciently were saved by a Purgation) and also that the Court might be apprised, whether it were proper from the Circumstances of the Case, disclosed upon such an Inquiry, to deliver the Clerk to the Ordinary generally, in which Case he was allowed to make his Purgation [k], or specially, [l] *absque purgatione facienda.* But this Practice being found inconvenient to Prisoners, because they lost their Goods if found guilty by such Inquiry, and yet could take no Challenge to any of the Jury, it being but an Inquest of Office, it hath been the general Practice [m] ever since the Reign of *H.* 6. to oblige those who demand the Benefit of the Clergy to plead and put themselves upon their Trial, under [n] Pain of being dealt with as those that stand Mute, whereby they forfeit their Goods [o] without any Inquiry concerning their Crime; but yet [p] cannot be denied their Clergy, where they should be intitled to it in case they were convicted, unless they be specially excluded by some Statute. But after a Clerk hath put himself upon his Trial, and the Inquest are charged with him, it is said that he [q] may, if he desire it, be admitted to his Clergy, before the Jury come back; but shall not forfeit his Goods unless they find him guilty.

[a] Vide 11 Co. 36. a. H. P. C 233, 234.
[b] H. P. C. 233. 11 Co. 29, &c.
[c] Vide supra, Sect. 10, 11, 12, 13, 30, 32.
[d] Vide supra, Sect. 43. 44.
[*] Supra Sect. 25, 45.
[e] S. P. C. 130.
[†] Supra Sect. 42, 43, 44.
[f] *See the Statute of* Marl. Ch. 28. Westm. 1. Ch. 2. Articuli Cler. Ch. 15. 2 Inst. 150, 163, 164, 633. S. P. C. 123. Lett. C. 130. b. 131. a. 185. Bract. lib. 3. Ch. 9. Supra, Ch. 15. Sect. 83. Hob. 288, 289. *Yet in* Kely. 100 *the contrary seems to be holden.*
[g] Vide Bract. lib. 3. Cap 9. Articuli Cleri ch. 15. S. P. C. 138. Lett. E. 139. Lett. A. 140. Supra Sect. 1, 2. Fitz. Coro. 128.
[h] S. P. C. 131, 185. 2 Inst. 164, 633, 634. H. P. C. 239. Finch of Law 463. Fitz. Coro. 376, 232, 382, 386. 417. *But this seems to be doubtful* Fitz. Coro 233. [i] S. P. C. 131, 185. 5 Co. 110. Regist. 68. Pl. Com 262 b. Cont. 40 Ass 42. pl. 23. *Abridged* Fitz. Coro. 91. Bro. Forfeiture 5. Hob. 289. *'tis holden, That the Goods are not forfeit without a Conviction.* [k] H. P. C. 240. Hob. 288, 289. S. P. C. 139. Lett. D. 5 Co. 109. [l] Vide Fitz. Coro 119, 417. H. P. C. 240. Rast. Ent. 121. pl. 1. Hob. 288, 289. Kely. 100. [m] H. P. C. 239. 2 Inst. 164. Fitz. Coro. 53, 58. S. P. C. 131. Salk. 61. Finch of Law. 463. Hob. 288. [n] Fitz Coro. 58. *So said in a Note of a Case in* 3 H. 7. 1. *but I do not find it made out by the Books at large. But this is clearly holden,* 3 H. 7 12. p 10. *Abridged* Fitz. Coro 53. [o] Supra Ch. 30. Sect. 19. [p] 8 H. 4. 3. pl. 5. *Abridged* Fitz. Coro. 72. Supra, Ch. 30. Sect. 24. [q] S. P. C. 131. a. b. Finch of Law. 463.

Sect. 111. Also I take it to be generally agreed in the latter [a] Books, That a Person may demand his Clergy after a *Non legit* recorded; and also after Judgment given against him, whether of [b] Death, or of [c] *pain fort & dure*, or of [d] Outlawry, *&c.* as well as before Judgment, and even [e] under the Gallows, if there be a Judge there who has Power to allow it; as a Justice of the King's Bench, if the Party were condemned there; or a Justice of Gaol-Delivery if he were condemned before him, and the Commission of Gaol-Delivery be not [f] yet adjourned, and according to some [g] Opinions, even tho the Commission were adjourned.

Sect. 112. As to the fourth general Point of this Chapter, *viz.* Whether the Benefit of the Clergy shall be allowed where it is not demanded: I take it to be generally agreed, That notwithstanding it was anciently the [h] usual Method for the Ordinary to demand the Criminal as his Clerk, before the Court allowed him the Benefit of his Clergy; Yet there was no [i] Necessity that any such Demand should be made by the Ordinary; But the Court might without it admit a Person to the Benefit of his Clergy, upon sufficient Evidence of his being a Clerk, as upon his producing Letters of Orders, or reading as a Clerk, *&c.* except he appears to have been guilty of Sacrilege, or of breaking the Prison of the Ordinary, in which Cases it is said to have been in a great Measure left to the [k] Discretion of the Ordinary, whether he should have his Clergy or not. And as there is no necessity that the Ordinary should demand the Benefit of the Clergy for a Clerk; so [l] neither doth there seem to be any that the Prisoner himself should demand it, where it sufficiently appeared to the Court that he has a Right to it in Respect of his being in Orders, *&c.* in which Case, if the Prisoner does not demand it, it seems to be left to the Discretion of the Judge, whether he will allow it him or not.

Sect. 113. As to the fifth general Point of this Chapter, *viz.* Who is to judge whether a Person who demands the Benefit of the Clergy, have a Right to it or not: I take it, That in all Cases the temporal Judge is to determine both, whether the Crime be within the Benefit of the Clergy, and also whether the Person who demands it be qualified to demand it or not; for notwithstanding it had its [m] original Commencement from the Canon Law, yet it being no [n] otherwise to be allowed here than as it hath been received by, and is agreeable to the Common or Statute Law, whereof the temporal Courts are the Judges, it seems very reasonable that all Questions [o] of this kind be determined by those Courts. And therefore even in those Cases, wherein by the old Books the Ordinary seems to have been allowed a discretionary Power of demanding or refusing a Clerk, as where he hath been guilty of [p] Sacrilege, and also in Cases wherein it is said generally, That a Prisoner hath no Right to his Clergy, as where he is convict of [q] Heresy, *&c.* it seems to be taken as a Ground by *Staundforde*, That the temporal Judge, where the Ordinary refuses a Prisoner, has a Power to determine whether still he may be allowed his Clergy or not. And this seems to be ground-

[a] H. P. C. 239, 240. S. P. C. 132. Lett. B. Finch of Law 463, 464. Fitz. Coro. 99, 109. Dy. 205. pl. 6. *This seems doubtful* 12 Ass. pl 15. *Abridged* Fitz. Coro. 117. Cont. Fitz. Coro. 233.
[b] 40 Ass. 42. pl 23. *Abridged* Fitz. Coro. 91. Dy. 183. pl. 89. 34 H. 6. 49. pl. 16. *Abridged* Fitz. Coro. 20. Bro Cler. 1.
[c] H P. C. 239. Supra Ch. 30. Sect. 24.
[d] 9 E. 4. 28. 8 H 4 3 pl. 5. *Abridged* Fitz. Coro. 72.
[e] 34 H. 6. 49. pl. 16. *Abridged* Fitz. Fitz. Coro. 20. Bro. Cler. 1. H. P. C. 239, 240. Dy. 205. pl. 5, 6. S. P. C. 132. Lett. B. Crompt. Jurisd. 126. a.
[f] S P. C. 132. Lett. B. H. P. C. 240. Cro. Jurisd. 126, a.
[g] *As it seems from* Dy. 205. pl. 5, 6.
[h] Bra B. 3. c. 9. West. 1. ch 2. 2 In. 163, 164. S P. C. 130. b. 9 E. 4. 28. 12 Ass pl. 15. 34 H. 6. 49 pl. 16. Kely. 99.
[i] S. P. C 131. b. 132, 133. Hob. 289, 290. Fitz Coro. 117. Bro. Clergy, 1. 9. *See the following Section. But this Matter seems to be left doubtful,* 12 Ass pl. 15. *Abridged* Bro. Clergy, 9. 34 H 6. 49 pl. 16. Kely. 99 Fitz Coro 44, 120, 191. 9 E. 4 28. F. N. B. 66. Lett. B
[k] Vide supra, Sect 9. Fitz Coro 112, 120. S. P. C. 133. b. 27 Ass pl. 42. *Abridged* Fitz. Coro. 205.
[l] S. P. C. 131. b. Fitz Coro. 191, 254 26 Ass. pl 19. H P. C. 239. Bro. Clergy, 1, 9. Bro. Clergy, 1, 9. Coro. 73. Hob. 288, 289.
[m] Vide supra, Sect. 2 Hob. 288
[n] Vide Supra Sect. 2, 110. Hob. 288.
[o] Vide 1 E. 3 13. pl. 8. 1 Ass pl. 4. *Abridged* Fitz. Coro 155. Bro. Cler. 8. *Where the Court refused to deliver to the Ordinary a Clerk who had abjured, till he should get the King's Pardon of his Return into the Land without Licence. See* Kely. 28.
[p] S. P. C. 133 Lett. B. Supra Sect. 9
[q] S. P C 133. Lett B *But* 21 E. 4. 21. pl. 1. *Abridged* Bro. Clergy, 18. 9 E 4. 28 pl. 41. *Abridged* Bro. Clergy, 7 *seem to be contrary where the Ordinary assigns no particular Cause of Refusal.*

ed

ed on good Reafon; for otherwife in fuch Cafes the Ordinary by fuch Pretences might have an abfolute Power of controlling the Temporal Courts in a Matter properly determinable by fuch Courts. And therefore whatever Point it may turn upon, whether a Prifoner ought to have his Clergy or not, as the Validity of his Letters of Orders, or his being a Heretick convict, *&c.* howfoever the Temporal Courts may pay the higheft Regard to the Certificate of the Ordinary; yet I take it to be generally [a] holden, That they only are finally to determine whether upon the whole the Prifoner be well intitled to his Clergy, or not, becaufe the Ordinary is not in this Refpect efteemed as a Judge, but [b] only as a Minifter to the Court. However it was certainly the [c] fettled Practice (while the Method of trying the Prifoner's Capacity of receiving Orders was by putting him to read a Verfe,) for the Judges of the Common Law to over-rule the Ordinary as to the Point, Whether the Prifoner read as a Clerk or not; and to record a *Legit* or *Non legit*, according to their own Judgment.

Sect. 114. But the neceffity of fuch an Ability to read in the Cafe of a Peer, was taken away by 1 *E.* 6. * 12. *Par.* 15. by which it is enacted, *That in every Cafe where any of the King's Subjects fhall upon his Prayer have the Privilege of his Clergy,* &c. *every Lord having Place and Voice in Parliament, fhall by Vertue of that Act, of Common Grace, upon his Requeft or Prayer, alledging that he is a Lord or Peer of this Realm, and claiming the Benefit of this Act tho' he cannot read, without any burning in the Hand, lofs of Inheritance, or corruption of Blood, be judged, deemed, taken and ufed for the firft Time only, to all Intents, Conftructions and Purpofes as a Clerk convict, and fhall be in Cafe of a Clerk convict, which may make Purgation, without any further or other Benefit or Privilege of Clergy, to any fuch Lord or Peer from thenceforth, at any Time after, for any Caufe to be allowed,* &c.

Sect. 115. The neceffity of fuch reading is alfo taken away, as to every common Perfon, by 5 *Anne* 6. by which it is enacted, *That if any Perfon convict of fuch Felony, for which he ought to have the Benefit of Clergy, pray the Benefit of that Act, he fhall not be required to read, but fhall be punifhed as a Clerk convict.*

Sect. 116. As to the fixth general Point of this Chapter, *viz.* How far the Ordinary was punifhable at Law for demanding or refufing a Clerk againft Law: It feems agreed, [d] That anciently this was fuch a Contempt for which his Temporalities might be feifed: But fince the Statute of 25 *E.* 3. 6. which provides, *That Prelates fhall be admitted to pay a reafonable Fine for Contempts to Writs of* Quare non admifit, *and fuch like*, it feems to have been generally [e] agreed, That the Ordinary is liable only to be fined; but to no fuch Seizure for a Contempt of this kind, as in obftinately [f] perfifting to return that a Prifoner reads as a Clerk, or the contrary, *&c.* againft the declared Senfe of the Court.

[a] Hob. 290. *See the Notes to the other Parts of this and the foregoing Section, yet* 9 E. 4 28. *Abridged* Bro. Clergy, 7. *This Matter feems to be left doubtful.* Vide Fitz. Coro. 44. F. N. B. 66. Letter B. [b] 7 E. 4. 29. pl. 12. *Abridged* Fitz. Fines, 24. Bro. Clergy, 17. Ordinary, 16. 34 H. 6. 49. pl. 16. *Abridged* Fitz. Fines, 19. Bro. Clergy, 1. 7 H. 4 41. pl 6. *Abridged* Bro. Clergy, 2. Ordinary, 20. 15 H. 7. 9 pl. 8. *Abridged* Fitz. Imprifonm. 28. Bro. Ordinary, 11. Kely 89 51. Finch of Law 463, 464. S. P. C. 131. Lett. C. 132. Lett A. B. C. D. 133. Lett. A B C. D. 141 Lett. B. H. P. C. 240. 21 E 4 21. pl. 1. *Abridged* Bro. Clergy, 18 [c] Kely. 28, 51. 9 E. 4. 28. pl. 41. *Abridged* Fitz. Coro 32. Bro Ordin. 12. *See the Cafes cited to the precedent Letter.* [*] Vide fupra, Sect 109. S. P. C. 129, b. 130. [d] Fitz Coro. 32, 191 233. 9 E. 4. 28. pl 41. Vide 21 E. 3 3. pl. 7. Bro Contempt 19. S. P. P. 132. Letter D. Hob 290. 2 Inft 164 *See the Notes under the next Letter.* [e] 9 E 4 28. a. *Abridged* Fitz. Coro. 32. Bro. Clergy, 7. 7 E 4 29 pl. 12. *Abridged* Fitz. Fines 24. Bro. Clergy 17. Ordinary, 16. 34 H. 6 49 pl. 16. *Abridged* Fitz Fines 19 Bro. Clergy, 1. 15 H 7. 9. pl. 8. *Abridged* Fitz Imprifonm. 28 Bro. Ordinary, 11. Kely 28, 51. Finch of Law, 463. 2 Inft. 164. *Yet fee the contrary holden the very next Year,* 26 Aff. pl. 19. *Abridged* Fitz. Coro. 191 *And alfo* 7 H. 4 41. pl. 6. *Abridged* Bro. Clergy, 2. Ordinary, 20. And S. P. C. 132. Lett D. [f] *See the Books cited to the other Parts of this Section.*

Sect. 117. As to the seventh general Point of this Chapter, *viz.* In what Manner a Clerk was to be delivered to the Ordinary, and afterwards demesned by the Common Law: It seems [a] plain, That anciently where-ever a Clerk was delivered to the Ordinary by a temporal Judge, his Person ought to be kept in the Ordinary's Prison, till [b] he had been tried before him by a Jury of twelve Clerks; for the Clergy never pretended to an absolute Exemption from all kind of Punishment for their Crimes, but only to a Privilege of being tried only by Ecclesiastical Judges; and this was anciently so far indulged them, that after they had been once delivered to the Ordinary, they could not afterwards be remanded to any temporal Court, before the Statute of 8 *Eliz.* 4. set forth more at large *Section* 122, *&c.* either for the same Crime wherewith they had been charged in such Court, nor for any other [c] committed before the Time when the Benefit of the Clergy was allowed them, whether such other Crimes were within the Benefit of the Clergy or not. And if they could acquit themselves on their Trial before the Ordinary of the Crimes for which they had been arraigned in the Temporal Courts, which Acquittal was called a Purgation, [d] they anciently claimed a Right not only to be delivered out of Prison, but also to be restored [e] to their Goods, *&c.* But to render such Purgation the more difficult, and also to delay the Delivery of Great Offenders as much as possible, the Judges anciently often refused [f] to deliver them to the Ordinary till they had been arraigned for all the Crimes whereof they stood indicted. But after the Statute of [g] 25 *E.* 3. the Judges could not refuse the Delivery of Clerks Convict in Respect of any Crime whereof they had not been actually arraigned; and therefore they used to arraign them at once for all the Crimes whereof they stood indicted.

Sect. 118. And if such Clerks could not purge themselves upon such a Trial, I do not [h] find that they were anciently liable to any greater Punishment than Degradation, and the [i] Loss of their Goods, and the Profits of their Lands, unless they had been guilty of Apostacy, *&c.* But afterwards, [k] by a Provincial Constitution, if they were notoriously scandalous, they were to be kept in perpetual Prison, on slender Diet, *&c.*

Sect. 119. If the Ordinary had refused to admit a Clerk delivered to him to make his Purgation, he might be compelled [l] by a special Writ for that Purpose.

Sect. 120. But this Privilege was often very much abused; and therefore after the Statute of *Westminster*, 1. Ch 2. which requires that no Clerk shall be delivered without due Purgation, the Courts of Common Law would never deliver over a Clerk to the Ordinary, without a [m] previous Inquiry into or Trial of his Crime, whereupon if the Clerk were found Guilty, he absolutely forfeited his Goods, and the Judges would [n] often in their Discretion make a Special Delivery, *absque purga-*

[a] Bract. lib. 3, c 9. S.P.C. 137. C. [b] *See the Statute of West.* 1. ch. 2. 2 Inst. 163, 164. S P. C. 137. Lett. C. 138. Lett. A B. *If the Ordinary suffered a Clerk to go at large without making such Purgation, he might be fined by the temporal Courts.* 15 H. 7. 9 pl. 8. 9 E. 4. 28. a. [c] *And this Privilege was expresly confirmed* 25 E 3. ch. 5. *and appears from the recital of* 8 E. 4. Vide Dyer 214. pl. 48. 215. pl. 49: H. P. C. 213, 249, And 114. S P. C 108. Lett. A. Finch of Law 464. Poph. 107. [d] Finch of Law, 464, 465. [e] H. P. C. 241. 5 Co. 110. b. S. P. C. 185. *In the Register,* 68. b. *there are three Writs to this Purpose.* S P C 52. Lett. C. 185, 192. Lett. B. 193. Reg. 68. b. Vide 1 Rich. 3. ch. 3. [f] Fitz. Coro. 394, 461. Bro. Clergy, 24, 30. S. P. C. 66 Lett. D. 108. Lett. A. H. P. C. 213. Bro. Coro. 11. [g] S. P. C. 108. Lett. A. 142. Lett. B. Dy. 214, 215. [h] Bract. Lib 3. c. 9. Sect 2. S. P. C. 138. Lett. B. [i] H. P. C. 241. 5 Co. 110. b. Bracton *and* Staundforde *in the Places cited to the precedent Letter seem to hold generally, That Degradation was the only Punishment; but I suppose that they mean the only Punishment to the Person.* [k] S. P. C. 140, 141. *See* Cro. Ja. 431. [l] Bract. Lib. 3. cap. 9. Sect. 3. S. P. C. 137. Lett. C. 138. Lett. A. 15 H. 7. 9. pl. 8. Cro. Jac. 431. Bro. Coro. 223. [m] Vide supra, Sect. [n] H. P. C. 240. 2 Inst. 165. Hob. 289.

tione facienda; as where it appeared that a Prisoner was a common [a] Thief, *&c.* or where in an Appeal of Robbery a Restitution of the Goods stolen had been awarded [b] to the Appellant, which Judgment they would not suffer to be contradicted by a Purgation. And both in such a Case, and also *a fortiori* where a Clerk is admitted to his Clergy after an Attainder, whether by an express Judgment or by Outlawry, *&c.* or even after a Confession [c], though he were not specially delivered *absque purgatione facienda*, the Ordinary seems by the stronger * Opinions to have been liable to an Escape, if he had admitted him to his Purgations because it could not but contradict a Judgment, or the Party's own Confession, which is the highest Conviction. Neither was any Purgation thought lawful without a previous Notice to the [d] King of the Time when it was intended to be made.

Sect. 121. As to the eighth general Point of this Chapter, *viz.* What shall be done to one who is allowed the Privilege of the Clergy at this Day, and how far it shall be for his Benefit: It is enacted by 4 *H.* 7. 13. *That if any Person, not in Orders, shall be convict of Murder, he shall be mark'd with an* M. *and if of any other Felony, with a* T. *on the Brawn of the Left Thumb, in open Court, before he shall be delivered to the Ordinary.* And it is said by [e] *Hale*, That by 3 *H.* 7. 1. A Clerk convicted of Manslaughter shall be committed, or bailed at Discretion till the Year be passed. But the contrary hath been [f] adjudged; for the said Statute mentions only those who are acquitted of Murder at the King's Suit, within the Year and Day, in which Case it directs that they shall be committed or bailed, till the Year and Day be passed, that they may be forthcoming, in order to answer to an Appeal, if brought within that Time. But it admits the Clergy once had to be a good Bar to an Appeal, even after an Attainder, and therefore cannot be thought to have intended to make Provision in any Case for the Parties being forthcoming to answer an Appeal after Clergy hath been allowed him, which makes it ineffectual. But it is certain that any Person who hath his Clergy may be committed for any Time within a Year by 18 *Eliz.* 7. *Par.* 3. set forth more at large, *Sect.* 125.

Sect. 122. It is recited by 8 *Eliz.* 4. *Par.* 3. *That divers Persons had oft-times committed sundry detestable Felonies, for the which Clergy is not allowable, and afterwards had fled to Places remote where they were not known, and committed some other Felony within the Benefit of the Clergy, and being arraigned for the same had had their Clergy allowed them, and thereupon been committed to the Custody of the Ordinary, the former Offence being then not known, and so by that Means could not after be impeached for the same, to the great encouraging of Offenders, using such Practices of Fore-knowledge and set Purpose, for their Discharge of the same.*

Sect. 123. *For reformation whereof it is enacted, That every Person or Persons, who shall hereafter upon his or their Arraignment for any Felony, be admitted to the Benefit of his Clergy, and delivered to the Ordinary for the same, and shall make his due Purgation for the same Offence or Offences, whereupon he was so admitted to his Clergy, and shall before the same Admission to his Clergy, have committed any other such Offence, whereupon Clergy is not allowable, and not being thereof indicted and acquitted, convicted, or attainted or pardoned, shall and may be indicted or appealed for the same, and thereupon put to answer, and ordered and used in all Things according to the Laws and Statutes of this Realm, in such like Manner and Form, as tho' no such Admission of Clergy had been; any Law, Custom, or Usage to the contrary notwithstanding.*

[a] S. P. C. 139. Lett. D. Hob. 289. Fitz. Coro. 247.
[b] Finch of Law, 464. S. P. C. 139. Lett. B. Fitz Coro. 109, 247.
[c] *But this is left a Quære,* S. P. C 138. Lett. E. 139 Lett. A. *but it seems agreed, That a Clerk might be admitted to his Purgation after a Conviction by Verdict.* Fitz. Coro. 393. 5 Aff. pl. 5. *Abridged* Fitz. 145. Cont. Fitz. Coro. 417.
* S. P. C. 48, 138. Lett. C. 27 H 6. 7. b. *Abridged* Fitz. Coro. 16. 13 E. 4. 3. pl. 6. *Abridged* Bro. Coro. 158. Fitz. Coro. 38. 3 H. 7. 12. pl. 5. *Abridged* Fitz. Coro. 56. 136. 9 E. 4. 28. a. *Abridged* Bro. Coro. 55. Bro. Coro. 4. Finch 464, 465. Cont. Hob. 289. Fitz Coro. 109, 128, 450, 247. 18 Aff pl 13 *Abridged* Fitz. Coro. 176. Utlagary, 2. Theloal, B. 1. ch. 15. Sect 26.
[d] Finch, 454. S. P. C 138. Lett. B. Fitz. Coro. 152.
[e] H. P. C 240.
[f] Kely. 25.

Sect. 124. *And for the avoiding of sundry Perjuries and other Abuses, in and about the Purgation of Clerks Convict, delivered to the Ordinaries, it is enacted by* 18 Eliz. 7. *That every Person, who shall be admitted to his Clergy, shall not thereupon be delivered to the Ordinary, but after such Clergy allowed, and burning in the Hand, according to the* [a] *Statute in that behalf provided, shall forthwith be enlarged and delivered out of Prison by the Justices before whom such Clergy shall be granted, that Cause notwithstanding.* [a] 4 H. 7. 13. for which see Sect. 121.

Sect. 125. But it is provided, Par. 3. *That the Justices before whom any such Allowance of Clergy shall be had, shall and may for the further Correction of such Persons to whom Clergy shall be allowed, detain and keep them in Prison for such convenient* [b] *Time, as the same Justices in their Discretions shall think convenient, so as the same do not exceed one Year's Imprisonment.* [b] 2 Bulst. 137.

Sect. 126. And it is farther provided, Par. 5. *That all Persons admitted to their Clergy, shall notwithstanding such Admission, be put to answer to all other Felonies whereof they shall be indicted or appealed, and not being thereof before acquitted, convicted, attainted or pardoned, and shall in such Manner and Form be arraigned, tried, adjudged, and suffer such Execution for the same, as they should have done, if, as Clerks Convict, they had been delivered to the Ordinary, and there had made their Purgations; any thing in this Act contained to the contrary notwithstanding.*

Upon these Statutes the following Points seem most remarkable.

Sect. 127. *First*, Inasmuch as it plainly appears, not only from the Preamble, but also from the express Words of the above-recited Clause of 8 *Eliz.* 4. That it had nothing else in View but only to prevent the Inconvenience that Offenders should be discharged of Crimes not within the Benefit of the Clergy, by being admitted to their Clergy for Crimes within the Benefit of it, as they were [c] before this Statute; and inasmuch as the above-recited *Proviso* of 18 *Eliz.* 7. tho' it be more largely worded than 8 *Eliz.* 4. hath a plain Relation to it, and therefore may reasonably receive the same Construction; it seems to have been agreed [d] ever since these Statutes, That a Conviction for a Felony within the Benefit of the Clergy, and an Allowance of Clergy thereon, is as much a Discharge of all precedent Felonies within the Benefit of the Clergy (tho' not of any others) as it was before these Statutes. [c] Vide supra, Sect. 117. [d] H.P.C. 213, 249. 1 And. 114. Poph. 107.

Sect. 128 *Secondly*, Inasmuch as the Statute of 18 *Eliz.* 7. is express, *That every Person admitted to his Clergy, shall not be delivered to the Ordinary, but after such Clergy allowed, and burning in the Hand, shall forthwith be enlarged and delivered out of Prison*, &c. *with a* Proviso *nevertheless, that for further Correction he may be kept in Prison*, &c. *and also with a farther* Proviso, *that he shall answer to all former Felonies, in the same Manner as if he had made his Purgation.* It seems to be the more prevailing Opinion, [e] That a Clerk Convict being admitted to his Clergy, may either be taken to have a kind of a Statute-pardon, or else to be in the same Case as if he had made his Purgation at the Common Law. And both of these Constructions seem reasonable. For as to the first it may be said, That the Statute by ordaining that the Party shall be forthwith enlarged and delivered out of Prison, under certain *Provisoes*, seems plainly to imply that he shall be liable to no other Punishment, and consequently in Effect pardons him. And as to the second it may be said, That the Statute seems only to intend to take away the Practise of making Purgation, which had been so much abused, but not the Benefit accruing to the Subject by it [e] Vide Kely. 37, 102.

it, but rather to make it more univerſal, by giving the ſame Advantage to all by a direct and expreſs Law, attended with no Inconvenience, which before ſome only gained by an uſurped Practice, very frequently abuſed, and highly derogatory from the Honour of the Common Law. But [a] Sir *Edward Coke* is of Opinion, That it ſhall enure by way of Purgation in Reſpect of ſuch Perſons only who might be admitted to make their Purgation before the Statute, and in Reſpect of others by way of Pardon. And [b] *Hobart* argues, That becauſe many Offenders before the Statute might have their Clergy, who yet could not be diſcharged by making their Purgation; and the Statute intends that all in general who are admitted to their Clergy ſhall be diſcharged, *&c.* And alſo becauſe all Purgations diſcredited a Trial at Law, therefore it is not reaſonable to intend that the Statute meant that ſuch a Diſcharge ſhould enure by way of a Purgation, but only by way of a Statute-pardon. But to this it ſeems a reaſonable Anſwer, That it doth by no Means follow, that becauſe the Statute intended that ſuch Diſcharge ſhould extend to Perſons who could not have the Benefit of a Purgation, therefore it did not intend that it ſhould have the Effect of a Purgation; neither doth it ſeem to follow, That becauſe a Purgation diſcredited the Acts of a Jury, therefore ſuch a Diſcharge, if it have to ſome purpoſes the ſame Effect as a Purgation, muſt diſcredit them likewiſe.

[a] 5 Co. 110. a. b.

[b] Hob. 292, 293.

Sect. 129. *Thirdly*, Taking the Statute to enure either by way of a Statute-pardon, or Purgation, it ſeems that it reſtores [c] the Party to his Credit, and conſequently enables [d] him to be a good Witneſs; which it hath been queſtioned whether a Pardon by the King can do, as ſhall be ſet forth more at large in the Chapter of *Pardon*. Alſo it ſeems agreed, That it gives him a Capacity to purchaſe [e] Goods, and to retain the [f] Profits of his Land, but gives him no Right to be reſtored to thoſe which he had at the Time of the Conviction, which being veſted in the King by the Forfeiture upon the Conviction, [g] ſhall not be deveſted either by a [h] Pardon or [i] Purgation. For it is certain that a Pardon never avoids [k] any precedent legal Act, as ſhall be more fully ſhewn in the Chapter of *Pardon*. Neither would the Common Law endure that Purgation, which was introduced by a Connivance, or rather tolerated than allowed, ſhould ſo far control its Proceedings.

Sect. 130. *Fourthly*, Whether the Statute enure as a Pardon or Purgation, it [l] ſeems to take from the Spiritual Court the Power of depriving the Party for the Crime for which he has had his Clergy. For if it enure as a Pardon, ſurely it cannot be doubted but that it frees the Party from all ſubſequent Puniſhment, and conſequently from a Deprivation. And if it enure as a Purgation, which is admitted [m] to have been a good Bar to a Deprivation before the Statute, why ſhould it not have the ſame Effect as a Purgation had formerly, in this as well as in other Reſpects. Yet [n] *Watſon*, in his *Clergyman's Law*, holds an Opinion on the Authority of [o] *Croke's Second Report*, that a Clergyman may be deprived for Manſlaughter after he has had his Clergy, not obſerving, as I ſuppoſe, that what is

[c] H P. C. 241.
[d] Kely. 37. Raym. 369, 370, 380. Vide 1 Sid. 222. State Trials, Vol. 2. 523. Vol. 4. 379 to 386. 5 Mod. 15.
[e] H. P. C. 241. 5 Co. 110. Hob. 293.
[f] 5 Co. 110. Fitz. Coro. 393. Forfeit. 34.
[g] 12 Co. 121. 5 Co. 110. b. H. P. C. 241. Co. Lit. 391. a. 3 H. 7. 12. pl. 10. Fitz. Coro. 53, 365, 356, 393. Fitz. Forfeit. 23, 34. Bro. Forf. 11. 8 H. 4. 2. b. Plow. Com. 262. b. S. P. C. 185. 20 E 4. 5. pl. 3. Bro. Coro. 166. *But it is holden* 40 E. 3. 42. pl 23. *Abridged* Fitz. Coro. 91. *and* Bro. Forfeit. 5. *That nothing is forfeited unleſs there be an Attainder, Alſo 'tis ſaid, that the Profits of Lands are not forfeited,* 20 E. 4. 5. pl. 3. Bro. Coro. 166.
[h] 1 Saund. 362. 1 Lev. 8. 120.
[i] Vide ſupra Sect. 110. Fitz. Coro. 356. Finch. 464. Cont. Fitz. Coro. 365. Bro. Forfeit. 113. F. N. B. 66. Lett. A. Bro. Clergy, 28.
[k] 1 Saund 362. 1 Lev. 8. 120.
[l] Hob. 292, 293. 2 Roll. Ab. 305. pl. 3.
[m] Cro. Jac. 431.
[n] Ch. 6. fol. 35, 36. *in the Folio Edition.*
[o] Cro. Jac. 430, 431.

said in this Book was only on the sudden on a Motion for a Prohibition in the King's Bench; and that in the same Case a Prohibition was afterwards actually brought and declared on in the [a] Common Place, and Judgment thereupon solemnly given for the Plaintiff upon open Argument by all the Judges.

Sect. 131. *Fifthly*, It seems agreed, That where a Person exempt from burning in the Hand, (either in Respect of his [b] Peerage or [c] Orders, or a [d] Special Pardon,) is admitted to the Benefit of his Clergy, he shall have the same Advantage of the Statute without being burnt in the Hand, as others shall have upon such burning; for the Words of the Statute, that the Party *after such Clergy allowed, and burning in the Hand, shall be enlarged*, &c. shall have this Construction, That he shall be enlarged, *&c.* upon burning where burning ought to be.

Sect. 132. It is holden, That after a Man is admitted to his Clergy, it is [e] actionable to call him Felon, *&c.* because his Offence being pardoned by the Statute, all the Infamy and other Consequences of it are discharged.

Sect. 133. How far a Person convicted of a Crime within the Clergy, and praying or being ready to pray it, but not actually admitted to it, shall be within these Statutes shall be considered, *Ch.* 37.

Sect. 134. It is enacted by 5 *Anne* 6. *That where any Person shall be convict of Larceny, the Judges shall at their Discretion award him to the Work-house, or House of Correction, there to be kept without Bail, not less than six Months, nor more than two Years from the Conviction; an Entry whereof is to be made of Record,* &c. *And if such Offender escape, he shall be committed to some such House. there to remain not less than twelve Months, nor more than four Years,* &c.

Sect. 135. It is enacted by 4 *Geo.* 11. and 6. *Geo.* 23. *That where any Person or Persons shall be convicted of Grand or Petit Larceny, or any felonious stealing or taking of Money, Goods, or Chattels, either from the Person, or the House of any other, or in any other Manner, and who by the Law shall be intitled to the Benefit of Clergy, and liable only to the Penalties of burning in the Hand or whipping, (except Persons convicted for receiving or buying stolen Goods, knowing them to be stolen) it shall and may be lawful for the Court before whom they were convicted, or any Court held at the same, or any* * *other Place with the like Authority, if they think fit, instead of ordering any such Offenders to be burnt in the Hand, or whipt, to order and direct that such Offenders shall be sent, as soon as conveniently may be, to some of his Majesty's Colonies, and Plantations in* America, *for the Space of seven Years: And that Court before whom they were convicted, or any subsequent Court, with like Authority as the former, shall have Power to convey, transfer, and make over such Offenders, by Order of Court, to the Use of any Person or Persons who shall contract for the Performance of such Transportation, to him, or them, and his and their Assigns, for such Term of seven Years. And where any Persons shall be convicted of any Crimes for which they are excluded their Clergy, and the King shall extend his Mercy to them, upon Condition of Transportation to any Part of A*merica, *and such Intention of Mercy be signified by a Principal Secretary of State, it shall be lawful for any Court, having proper Authority to allow such Offenders the Benefit of a Pardon, to order and direct the like Transportation, to any Person (who will contract for the Performance thereof) of any such Offenders, as also of any Person convict of receiving or buying stolen Goods, knowing them to be stolen, for the Term of fourteen Years, in Case such Condition of Transportation be general, or else for such other Term as shall be made Part of such Condition; and such Person so contracting, and his Assigns, shall have an Interest in the Service of the said Offenders for such Term of Years.*

[a] Hobart 288. 2 Roll. Abr. 305. pl. 3. *also a Prohibition was granted in the like Case*, 27 & 28 Eliz. Rotulo 2574. *cited.* Hob. 294.
[b] 1 Lev. 180.
[c] Hob. 294.
[d] 5 Co. 110. b.
[e] Hob. 294. Vide Hob. 67. 81. 1 Danv. 163. pl. 6. *and the Chapter of Pardon.*
* *Vid.* by 6 Geo. ch. 23.

And if any such Offender return into Great Britain *or* Ireland *before the End of his Term, he shall be liable to be punished as any Person attainted of Felony, without the Benefit of* Clergy, &c. *Provided, That the King may pardon and dispense with any such Transportation, and allow of the Return of such Offender, paying his Owner at the Time, such Sum as shall be adjudged reasonable by any two Justices of the Peace where such Owner dwells; and where any such Offenders shall be transported, and shall have served their Terms, such Services shall have the Effect of a Pardon, as for the Crimes for which they were transported,* &c.

Sect. 136. And it is farther enacted, That *every such Person to whom any such Court shall order any such Offenders to be transferred or conveyed, shall before such Offenders shall be delivered to them, contract with such Person as shall be appointed by such Court, and shall give sufficient Security to the Satisfaction of such Court, for the transporting such Offenders to some Plantation in* America, *to be ordered by such Court, and the procuring an authentick Certificate from the Governour or Chief Custom-House Officer of the Place, of the Landing of such Offenders,* &c. *and their not returning by the wilful Default of such Contractor.*

Sect. 137. And it is farther enacted by 6 *Geo.* 23. *That the Court may nominate two or more Justices of the Peace for the Place where such Offenders shall be convicted, who shall have Power to contract with any Person or Persons for the Performance of the Transportation of such Offenders; and to order such and the like Security as the said former Act directs to be taken by Order of Court, and to cause such Felons to be delivered to such Contractors; which said Contracts aud Security shall be certified by the said Justices to the next Court held with the like Authority, to be filed,* &c.

Sect. 138. And it is farther enacted, *That all Charges in or about such Contracts,* &c. *shall be born by each County,* &c. *for which the Court was held, and that the respective Treasurers shall pay the same. And that all Securities for Transportation shall be by Bond in the Name of the Clerks of the Peace,* &c. *and the Money recovered shall be to the Use of the respective Counties,* &c.

Sect. 139. And it is farther enacted, *That the Persons so contracting,* &c. *may carry such Offenders towards the Sea Port,* &c. *and that if any Person shall rescue such Offenders, or aid them in making their Escape,* &c. *they shall be deemed guilty of Felony, without Clergy. And that if any Felon ordered for Transportation shall be afterwards at large within any Part of* Great Britain, *without some lawful Cause, before the Expiration of his Term, and be lawfully convict thereof, he shall suffer Death without Clergy. And may be tried before Justices of Assise,* Oyer *and* Terminer, *or Gaol-Delivery, for the County where he shall be apprehended,* &c. *or from whence he was ordered to be transported,* &c. *and that the Clerk of Assise, and Clerk of the Peace, where such Orders of Transportation shall be made, shall on Request of the Prosecutor,* &c. *certify briefly a Transcript containing the Tenor of every Indictment, Conviction and Order of Transportation to the Justices of Assise,* &c. *which shall be a sufficient Proof of such Conviction and Order of Transportation.*

2

CHAP.

CHAP. XXXIV

Of Pleas in Abatement.

AND now I come to *Pleas in Abatement*, which having already considered so far as they particularly relate to Appeals, Indictments, and Informations, in the several Chapters concerning them, and shewn in *Chap.* 23. from *Section* 101. to *Section* 126. what Pleas are good in Abatement of an Appeal; and in *Sections* 126, and 135, That an Appellee may plead as many of them as he pleases, unless they be repugnant to one another, and afterwards take the General Issue; and in *Chap.* 25. *Sect.* 12. That the same Matters may be pleaded to an Appeal on an Arraignment thereon at the Suit of the King, as on an Arraignment at the Suit of the Party, and in the same Chapter, *Sections*, 70, 71, 72, 73. what Misnosmers, *&c.* may be pleaded in Abatement of an Indictment; and in *Chap.* 26. *Sections*, 63, 64, 65. what Pleas are good in Abatement of an Information; and having considered Demurrers in Abatement, *Chap.* 31. *Sect.* 5, 6, 7. I shall in this Place take Notice only of the following Particulars;

Sect. 1. *First*, That it hath been holden [a] that it is no good Plea in Abatement of an Indictment, as it is of an Appeal [b], or Information, [c] that there is another Indictment against the Defendant for the same Offence. But in such [*] a Case the Court in Discretion will quash the first Indictment if any Fault can be found in it.

Sect. 2. *Secondly*, That where an Indictment of a Capital Crime is abated for a Misnosmer of the Defendant's [d] Christian Name, the Court will not dismiss him, but cause him to be indicted *de novo* [e] by his true Name, and arraign him again on such new Indictment. For I take it to be settled [f] at this Day, That regularly a Defendant shall not be dismissed for an Insufficiency in an Indictment or Appeal for a capital Crime.

Sect. 3. *Thirdly*, That a Defendant appearing *Gratis*, and by Attorney to an Information, may [g] plead a Misnosmer in Abatement, as well as if he had appeared in proper Person; for if he be not the Person intended, the Attorney General may reject the Plea, and sign Judgment on a *nihil dicit*; but if he accept the Plea, he thereby admits him that pleads it to be the Person concerned to make a Defence, and therefore shall not afterwards say that it doth not appear but that the Plea might be put in by a Stranger.

[a] 1 Jon. 199. Cro. Ca. 147.
[b] Ch. 23. Sect. 124.
[c] Ch. 26. Sect. 63.
[*] Cro. Car. 147. 1 Jo. 199.
[d] Vide Ch. 25. Sect. 70, 71.
[e] H. P. C. 243. Cro. Ca. 371, 372.
[f] Vide Ch. 23. Sect. 4. 131. Ch. 25. Sect. 9, 10, 11. Cont. 11 H. 4. 41. pl. 7. Fitz. Misnos. 18. Coro. 88. Bro. Misnos. 23. *See the Books cited* Ch. 23. Sect. 131. Lett. a.
[g] *Adjudged* Trin. 4 Geo. *between the* King *and* Westby.

CHAP.

CHAP. XXXV.

Of the Plea of Autrefoits acquit.

PLeas in Chief are either,

1. In Bar, or
2. The General Issue.

As to Pleas in Bar, having shewn already, *Chap.* 23. *Sect.* 128. what Pleas of this Kind to an Appeal are good, which shew that the Plaintiff had never any Right to bring it; and in *Sections* 129, 130, 131. where a *Retraxit*, Nonsuit, Discontinuance, or Abatement, of one Appeal may be pleaded in Bar of another; and in *Section* 132. where the bringing of an Appeal against one Person will be a Bar to a subsequent one against another Person not named in the First; and in *Section* 133. where a Release will bar an Appeal; and in *Section* 134. where an Appellant may be barred as to one Appellee, and continue his Suit against the rest; and in *Section* 135. what Pleas of this Kind are consistent with the General Issue, and in *Ch.* 26. *Sect.* 64, 65, what is a good Plea in Bar to an Information, I shall in this Place only consider,

1. The Plea of *Autrefoits acquit.*
2. The Plea of *Autrefoits attaint* or *convict.*
3. The Plea of a Pardon.

Sect. 1. And first of the Plea of *Autrefoits acquit*, which is grounded on this *Maxim*, [a] That a Man shall not be brought into Danger of his Life for one and the same Offence, more than once. From whence it is generally taken, by all the Books, [b] as an undoubted Consequence, that where a Man is once found Not guilty on an Indictment or Appeal free [c] from Error, and [d] well commenced before any [e] Court which hath Jurisdiction of the Cause, he may by the Common Law in all [f] Cases whatsoever plead such Acquittal in Bar of any subsequent Indictment or Appeal for the same Crime. But for the more distinct understanding hereof I shall particularly consider,

1. How far he who pleads this Plea must be ready to produce the Record of his former Acquittal.
2. Where a Variance between the Record of the former Acquittal and the Indictment or Appeal to which it is pleaded, may be helped.
3. How far other Discharges of a former Prosecution have the same Effect as an Acquittal by Verdict.

[a] S.P. C. 105. Lett. A. 4 Co. 40. a. 45. a 47. a. 9 H. 7. 19. pl. 14. Fitz. Pard. 3. Bro. Appeal, 9, 12, 89. Coro. 11. Cromp. Just. 111. pl. 1.

[b] *See the Authorities cited to all the other Parts of this Chapter, and* 5 E. 3. 25. pl. 36.

[c] Vide infra Sect. 8.

[d] Vide infra Sect. 9.

[e] Vide infra, Sect. 10.

[f] 25 E. 3. 44. pl, 16. *Abridged* Fitz. Coro. 136. 41 Ass. 9. *Abridged* Fitz. Coro. 220. Bro. Coro. 120 or 121. 2 Leon. 161. Vide infra, Sect. 14, 15. 47 E. 3. 16. pl. 27. *Abridged* Fitz. Coro. 104 Bro. Appeal, 14.

4. How far it is necessary that the Indictment or Appeal in the Record of Acquittal be free from Error, and well commenced.

5. Whether an Acquittal in any Court which has a Jurisdiction be sufficient for this Purpose.

6. How far an Acquittal of a Person as Principal will bar a subsequent Prosecution against him as Accessary, *& e converso*, how far a an Acquittal of a Man as Accessary will bar a Prosecution against him as Principal.

7. How far the Law is altered in these Respects as to an Indictment of Death, by 3 *H.* 7. 1.

Sect. 2. As to the first Particular, *viz.* How far he who pleads this Plea must be ready to produce the Record of his former Acquittal, I take it to be [a] agreed, That such Plea being a Plea in [b] Bar, and the Record not in the Custody of, nor the Property of him that pleads it, there is no need to plead with a *profert sub pede sigili*; but the Defendant shall have a [c] Day given him to bring it in. And there is in *Brook* a Note of a [d] Case in the Time of *Edw.* 3. wherein a Plea of *Autrefoits acquit* was disallowed, because the Defendant shewed forth the Record when he pleaded it; and the Book gives this Reason, That *the Record ought to come before the Court by Writ.*

Sect. 3. As to the second Particular, *viz.* Where a [e] Variance between the Record of the former Acquittal, and the Indictment or Appeal to which it is pleaded may be helped: I take it to be clear, That if the Nature of the Crime be in [f] Substance the same, a Variance may generally be helped by proper [g] Averments. And therefore if a Man be named in the first Record *Yeoman*, and in the second *Gentleman*, yet it seems [h] clear, that he may make good the Variance, with an Averment that he only was meant under each Addition. Also if a Man be acquitted of an Indictment of Murder or Robbery *cujusdam* [i] *ignoti*, and afterwards arraigned on an Indictment for the same Fact, describing the Person killed or robbed by his proper Name; yet it hath been holden, [k] That he may plead the Acquittal in Bar, averring that both the Indictments are for the very same Felony. Also if the Person killed be described by his proper Name and Surname in the first Indictment, and by the same Christian, but by a different Surname in the second, yet it hath been [l] adjudged, That he may plead an Acquittal on the first in Bar of the second Indictment, averring that the Person so differently named was one and the same Person. But it seems [m] adviseable in such Case to add a farther Averment, That the Person killed was known as well by the Name in the first, as by that in the second Indictment; for if he were never known by the Name in the first Indictment, I much question whether the Defendant cou'd be found guilty upon it; and if he cou'd not, it seems plain that his Life having never been in danger by it, the Acquittal upon it [n] cannot be any Bar to a subsequent Indictment. But if there be no other Variance between the first and second Indictment but only as to the [o] Times when the Crime is alledged to have been committed, or as to the [p] Places being both in the same County, there is no doubt but

[a] S. P. C 105. Lett. A. H. P. C. 245. Fitz. Coro. Fitz. monstrans de faits 33. Vide Rast. Entr. 385. pl. 4 *seems contrary.*
[b] Co. Litt. 128. *See the Chapter of Pardon.*
[c] Co. Lit. 128. b. Fitz. Coro. 232.
[d] Bro. Coro. 218. *But* 26 Ass. pl. 15. *Abridged* Fitz. Coro. 189. 11 H. 4. 41. pl. 6. *Abridged* Fitz. Mostrans de faits 128. Bro Coro. 29. 9 H. 7. 19. pl. 14. *Abridged* Bro. Appeal, 189. *seems contrary.*
[e] Vide 2 Keb. 705. pl. 71.
[f] 14 H. 7. 2. pl 8. S. P. C. 168. Lett. B.
[g] S. P. C. 105. H. P. C. 246.
[h] Vide Keil. 58 a.
[i] Vide supra, Ch. 25. S. 73.
[k] Keilw. 25. b. Dy. 285. pl. 38. Vide Fitz. Coro. 159.
[l] 26 Ass. pl. 15. *Abridged* Bro. Coro. 198. Fitz. Coro. 189. Crompt. Just. 112. pl. 12. S. P. C. 105. Letter C. 1 Roll. Rep. 368. pl. 22.
[m] Vide H. P. C. 246. S. P. C, 105. Lett. C. Crompt. Just. 112. pl. 12.
[n] Vide supra, Sect. 1. & infra Sect. 8. 9, 10.
[o] Dy. 285. pl. 38. H. P. C. 246. Vide 22 Ass. pl. 55. *Abridged* Fitz. Coro. 179. S. P. C. 105. Lett. C. 11 H. 4. 41. pl. 6. *Abridged* Bro. Coro. 29. Variance 31. Fitz. Monstrans de faits 128. 25 E. 3. 44 pl. 16. *Abridged* Fitz. Coro. 136. 3 Ass. pl. 15. *Abridged* Fitz. Coro. 166. Crompt Just, 112. pl. 13.
[p] H. P. C. 246. S. P. C. 105. Lett. C. 106. Lett. A

that regularly it may be help'd by an Averment, that the Felony in both is one and the ſame, becauſe neither the Time nor Place laid in an Indictment, *&c.* are material upon Evidence, ſo that the Defendant be proved guilty at any other [a] Time before the Indictment, or at any other Place [b] within the County. And it is holden by [c] *Staundforde*, That an Acquittal of Murder in one County may be pleaded in Bar of a ſubſequent Indictment in another County for the ſame Murder. But this ſeems queſtionable, becauſe all Indictments are local; and therefore if the firſt were laid in an improper County, the Defendant could not be found guilty upon it, and conſequently was in no danger of his Life, and therefore [d] cannot plead an Acquittal upon it in Bar of a ſubſequent Indictment in the proper County: But if the firſt Indictment were in the proper County, the ſecond cannot but be in an improper one, and conſequently the Defendant not being liable to be found guilty upon it, cannot be ſaid to be reduced by it to the Inconvenience of being twice brought into danger of his Life for one and the ſame Offence, the avoiding of which Inconvenience [e] ſeems the Chief Inducement for which the Law allows the Plea of *Autrefoits acquit.*

Sect. 4. But if a Man ſteal Goods in one County, and then carry them into another, in which Caſe it is certain [f] that he may be indicted and found guilty in either, it ſeems very reaſonable, that an Acquittal in the one County for ſuch ſtealing may [g] be pleaded in Bar of a ſubſequent Proſecution for the ſame ſtealing in another County, becauſe the Defendant may be altogether as well convicted in the one County, as in the other; and therefore if he could not bar the ſecond Proſecution by the Acquittal on the firſt, his Life would be twice in danger from that which is in Truth but one and the ſame Offence, and only conſidered as a new one by a meer Fiction or Conſtruction of Law, which ſhall hardly [h] take Place againſt a Maxim made in favour of Life. And as to the [i] Objection, That the Jurors of the one County can take no Manner of Conuſance of what is done in the other, and conſequently cannot try whether the Felony whereof the Party is indicted in the ſecond County be the very ſame with that of which he was acquitted in the firſt, it may be anſwered, That it appears from the old Books, that anciently the Judges often ſatisfied themſelves of the Truth of an Averment that the Offences in both Indictments were the ſame, by [k] Witneſſes, or by an [l] Inqueſt of Office, without putting it to a Trial by Jury, upon an iſſue joined, on the Denial thereof by the Proſecutor, which ſeems [m] to have been of later Years the uſual Method. But granting that it is to be tried by ſuch Jury, I do not ſee how it follows, That becauſe they cannot convict a Defendant upon Evidence of a Fact done out of their own County, therefore they cannot collaterally inquire whether an Offence laid in their own County be in Subſtance the ſame with that done in another, ſince it cannot be denied but that in abundance of Caſes a Jury of one County may receive Evidence of Facts done in another. To which may be added, That in the *Year-Book* of 4 *H.* 7. 5. *pl.* 1. which is the [n] Chief Authority for the contrary Opinion, it is admitted that an Acquittal on an Appeal of Larceny in the one County, may be pleaded in Bar of a ſubſequent Appeal in the other; becauſe ſuch an Appeal intitles the Plaintiff to a Reſtitution of the Goods, whereof being once

[a] H P.C. 264. Salk. 288.

[b] *See the Chapter of Evidence; and* H. P. C. 264.

[c] S. P. C 105. Lett. C. *See* Crompt. Juſt. 112. pl. 9.

[d] Vide Sect. 1, 8, 9, 10.

[e] Supra, ſect. 1, 8, 9, 10.

[f] Supra Ch. 23. Sect. 47. Ch. 25. Sect. 36. *and* B. 1. Ch. 33. Sect. 9.

[g] 41 Aſſ. pl. 9. Fitz. Coro. 220. *But this is left doubtful* S. P. C. 105. Lett. C. 106 Lett. A. H. P. C. 246. Crompt Juſt. 112. pl. 9. Bro. Coro. 139 or 140. 4 H. 7 5. pl. 1. Fitz. Coro. 62.

[h] Vide ſupra, Ch. 18. Sect. 13. *and* Ch. 19. Sect. 25. *and* Ch 29. Sect. 35.

[i] 4 H. 7. 5 pl. 1. Fitz. Coro. 62.

[k] 26 Aſſ pl. 15. *Abridged* Fitz Coro. 189. Bro Coro. 98. 41 Aſſ. pl. 9 *Abridged* Fitz. Coro. 220.

[l] 3 Aſſ. pl. 15. *Abridged* Fitz. Coro. 166. *See the ſixth Section.*

[m] 9 H. 7. 19. pl. 14. *Abridged* Bro. Appeal, 89.

[n] Vide Bro. Coro. 139 or 140. Fitz. Coro. 62. S. P. C. 106. H. P. C. 246.

bar-

barred he is barred for ever. But granting this to be a good Reason, which yet it seems difficult to make out, the very same may be said at this Day as to an Indictment, which since * 21 *H.* 8. 11. intitles the Prosecutor to a Restitution also. Besides, taking the Law as it stood formerly, why may not a Jury of one County try whether a Felony therein indicted, be the same whereon the Party was before acquitted in another County, in the Case of a second Indictment, as well as of a second Appeal?

Sect. 5. It seems [a] that it is no Plea to an Appeal of Larceny, That the Defendant hath been found Not guilty in an Action of Trespass brought against him by the same Plaintiff for the same Goods; for Larceny and Trespass are entirely different: Also it seems a general [b] Rule, That a Bar in an Action of an inferior Nature, will not bar another of a superior. Yet it seems, [c] That an Acquittal in an Indictment of Murder, will be a good Bar of an Indictment of Petit Treason, because both Offences are in Substance the same. But it is clear that an Acquittal of one Felony is [d] no manner of Bar to a Prosecution for another in Substance different, whether committed before or at the same Time with that of which he is acquitted; and therefore if a Man commit a Burglary, and steal the Goods of *A.* and *B.* and be indicted for the Burglary, and stealing the Goods of *A.* and acquitted; it hath been adjudged, [e] that he cannot plead such Acquittal to an Indictment for stealing the Goods of *B.* But it seems agreed, That he may plead it to a second Indictment for the Burglary.

Sect. 6. As to the third Particular, *viz.* How far other Discharges of a legal Prosecution have the same Effect as an Acquittal by Verdict: Having shewn already in the [f] Chapter of *Appeals*, how far the Discharge of one Appeal will bar another, I shall only add in this Place, That notwithstanding the [g] Allowance of a Pardon, or any other Bar of one Indictment, seems to be pleadable in Bar of another; and by the like Reason, whatever hath been allowed a good Bar of one Appeal may be pleaded in Bar of another: Yet it seems that no other Discharge of an Indictment will bar an Appeal, and no other Discharge of an Appeal will bar an Indictment, but only an [h] Acquittal by Battel, or an Acquittal by Verdict on the general Issue, finding the Defendant's [i] Innocence; as where it finds him Not guilty on such an Issue, on an Indictmet or Appeal of any Felony whatsoever; or where it finds † him guilty of Homicide *se defendendo*, or *per infortunium*, on an Indictment of Murder. But it hath been adjudged, [k] That where a Demurrer by an Appellant to a Tender of Battel, or to a Plea, hath been adjudged against him, yet the Appellee may be afterwards arraigned at the Suit of the King.

Sect. 7. It it said by Sir *Matthew Hale* in the [l] Chapter of *Autrefoits acquit*, That an Acquittal by Battle in an Appeal is no Bar of an Indictment. But I find no other Authority to this Point but a Note in *Fitzherbert* [m] of a Case to this Purpose in the Time of King *Edward* the Second. To which it may be answered, That this Matter is only spoken of incidently, and not adjudged. And that *Staundforde* in the same Place [n] where he cites it, makes a *Quære* whether it be Law or not, And it is expresly holden by *Bracton*, [o] That an Appellee who vanquishes the Appellant in Battel, shall go quit not only from all other Appeals, *but also from the Suit of the King; because by this he clears his Innocence against all, in the same manner as if he had put himself upon his Country and his Country had acquitted him.* Also it is admitted by Sir *Matthew Hale* in the

P Chapter

* Vide sup. Ch. 23. Sect. 55, 56.

[a] 2 Ric. 3. 14. a. Bro. Appeal. 121. Vide infra. Ch. 36. Sect. 7.

[b] Co. Litt. 146. a. 2 Ric. 3. 14, 15.

[c] 3 Inst. 213. H. P. C. 246.

[d] S. P. C. 105. Lett. A. H. P. C. 244. Bro. Coro. 11.

[e] Kely. 30, 52.

[f] Ch. 23. Sect. 129, 130, 131.

[g] 11 H. 4. 41. pl. 6. *Abridged* Fitz. monstrans de faits, 128. Bro. Coro. 29. Appeal, 33. Variance, 31. Vide S. P. C. 106. Lett. B.

[h] *See the next Section.*

[i] S. P. C. 169. a.

† 3 Inst. 213. Crompt Just. 111. pl. 6. 4 Co. 46. b.

[k] Dy. 120. pl. pl. 13. Crompt. Just. 112. pl. 18.

[l] H. P. C. 245.

[m] Fitz. Coro. 375.

[n] S. P. C. 106. Lett. D.

[o] Lib. 3. cap. 19. Sect. 8.

[a] Chapter of *Indictments*, That if an Approver be vanquished in Battel joined on his Appeal, he shall be hanged, and the Appellee discharged, without being arraigned at the Suit of the King. Also it hath been [b] adjudged, That upon such a Vanquishment the Appellee is intitled to his Damages against the Appellant, as being *legitimo modo acquietatus*, which seems [c] necessarily to imply that he is finally acquitted as well against the King as against the Party.

Sect. 8. As to the fourth Particular, *viz.* How far it is necessary that the Indictment or Appeal in the Record of Acquittal be free from Error, and well commenced: I take it to be settled [d] at this [e] Day, That where-ever the Indictment, or Appeal, whereon a Man is acquitted, is so far erroneous (either for want of Substance in setting out the Crime, or of Authority in the [f] Judge before whom it was taken,) that no good Judgment could have been given upon it against the Defendant, the Acquittal can be no Bar of a subsequent Indictment or Appeal, because in Judgment of Law the Defendant was never in danger of his Life from the first; for the Law will presume *prima facie* that the Judges would not have given a Judgment, which would have been liable to have been reversed. But if there be no Error in the Indictment or Appeal, but [g] only in the Process, it seems agreed, That the Acquittal will be a good Bar of a subsequent Prosecution, notwithstanding such Error; the best Reason whereof seems to be this, That such Error is [h] salved by the Appearance.

Sect. 9. It seems agreed, [i] That an Acquittal on an Appeal brought by one who had no Right to bring it, as by any other Woman [k] except the Wife of the Deceased, or by any other Man [l] except the next Heir, is no more a Bar to an Appeal by another Appellant, or to an Indictment, then an Acquittal on an insufficient Appeal or Indictment would have been.

Sect. 10. As to the fifth Particular, *viz.* Whether an Acquittal in any Court which has a Jurisdiction be sufficient for this Purpose: Notwithstanding the [m] Opinion in the Book of *Assizes*, That no Acquittal in any other Court can be any Bar to a Prosecution in the Court of King's Bench, because that is the highest Court, I take it to be settled [n] at this Day, That an Acquittal in any Court whatsoever, which has a Jurisdiction of the Cause, is as good a Bar of any subsequent Prosecution for the same Crime, as an Acquittal in the highest Court. And therefore it hath been adjudged, [o] That an Acquittal of Murder at a Grand Sessions in *Wales*, may be pleaded to an Indictment for the same Murder in *England*. For the [p] Rule is, That a Man's Life shall not be brought into Danger for the same Offence more than once.

[a] H. P. C. 200. Vide supra, ch. 25. Sect. 10. Lett. e. 21 H. 6. 34. pl. 1. S. P. C. 148. Lett. B.

[b] Fitz. Coro. 98. S. P. C 168. Letter E. Supra ch. 23. Sect. 140.

[c] S. P. C. 169. Supra ch. 23. Sect. 140.

[d] 4 Co. 45. a. 47. a. H. P. C. 244, 245. 3 Inst. 214. Fitz. Coro. 444. Supra ch. 23. Sect. 140. Crompt. Just. 112. pl 14, 15, 16, 19. 20 H. 11. b. 12. a. 9 H 5. 2. pl. 7. *Abridged* Bro. Appeal, 39. Coro. 35. Fitz. Coro. 68.

[e] *But* Staundforde *seems to be of Opinion, That an Acquittal on an erroneous Appeal, is a good bar to an Indictment till it be reversed by Error.* S. P. C. 106. Lett. B. *cited in* Crompt. Just. 112. pl. 15. *But this seems repugnant to all other Books, and to what is said by* Staundforde *himself, in the very same page. Indeed in the second Addition of* Hale's *Pleas of the Crown, there is a Note to the same Effect with what is said in* Staundforde; *but this is manifestly misprinted, and the Word* Acquit *put for* Attaint.

[f] Crompt. Just. 111. pl. 4, 5. Supra ch. 9. Sect. 15, 16. 4 Co. 46. [g] Fitz. Coro. 444. 9 H. 5. 2. pl 7. *Abridged* Bro. Appeal, 39. Coro. 35. Fitz. Coro. 68. S. P. C. 106. Lett. B. 169 Lett. A. Crompt. Just. 112. pl. 15. [h] Supra ch. 27. Sect. 107. [i] 20 H. 7. 11. b. 12. a. 21 H. 6. 28 b. 29. a. *Abridged* Bro. Appeal, 41. Crompt. Just. 112. pl. 14. S. P. C. 106. Lett. B. H. P. C. 245. [k] Supra ch. 23. Sect. 36, 37, 38. [l] Supra, ch. 23. Sect. 39, 40, 41, 42. [m] 9 Ass. pl. 15. [n] 4 Co. 45. b. Rast. Ent. 385. pl. 4. 11 H. 41, pl. 6. *Abridged* Fitz. monstrans de faits, 128. 25 E. 3. 44. pl. 16. *Abridged* Fitz. Coro. 136. 41 Ass. pl. 9. *Abridged* Bro. Coro. 120 *or* 121. Crompt. Just. 112. pl. 8. Fitz. Coro. 220. [o] 1 Lev. 118. 1 Sid. 179. Supra, ch. 25. Sect. 39, 40. Supra Sect. 1, 8, 9.

Sect. 11. As to the sixth Particular, *viz.* How far an Acquittal of a Person as Principal will bar a subsequent Prosecution against him as Accessary; *& è converso*, how far an Acquittal of a Man as Accessary will bar a Prosecution against him as Principal: It seems to be [a] settled at this [b] Day, That an Acquittal of a Man as Principal is no Bar of a subsequent Prosecution against him as Accessary after the Fact, because such Acquittal clears him only of the Charge of having committed the Fact, which being a Crime entirely different from that of receiving him that hath committed it, there seems no more Reason that the Acquittal of it should bar a Prosecution for the Receipt, than if they were Offences that bore no Manner of Relation to one another. But it is [c] holden in many Books of good Authority, (contrary to what is admitted [d] to have been the ancient Law,) that the Acquittal of a Man as Principal is a good Bar of a subsequent Prosecution against him as Accessary before; for it is said, That such an Accessary is in some measure [e] guilty of the Fact; and therefore that an Acquittal which clears a Man from being guilty of the Fact, doth by Consequence clear him from being such an Accessary. And this seems reasonable upon the Supposition that a Man may be found guilty of an Indictment against him as Principal, upon Evidence which only proves him to have been an Accessary before. But if a Man cannot be found guilty of such an Indictment upon such Evidence, as it is strongly [f] holden that he cannot, it may with great Reason be said, That the Acquittal of him as Principal no way acquits him as Accessary before; for if so, he might save himself by a mere Slip in the Indictment, and bar all other Prosecutions by an Acquittal on a Trial, which in truth never brought him into [g] Danger of his Life. And it is upon this Supposition, as I suppose, That it is holden in some [h] Books, contrary to those above-cited, That one who has been acquitted as Principal may be tried again as Accessary before, as well as after.

Sect. 12. But it seems [i] agreed, That an Acquittal of a Man as Accessary before, or after, is no Bar to a subsequent Prosecution against him as Principal.

Sect. 13. Also it hath been holden, That an Acquittal of a Man as Accessary to one Principal, will not save him from being arraigned afterwards as Accessary to another in the same Fact; but for this I shall refer to *Chap.* 29. *Sect.* 46.

Sect. 14. As to the seventh Particular, *viz.* How far the Law is altered in these Respects as to an Indictment by 3 *H.* 7. 1. It seems agreed, [k] That by the Common Law an Acquittal on an Indictment might be pleaded in Bar of an Appeal of Death, in the same Manner as an Acquittal of any other Felony might be pleaded in Bar of a subsequent Prosecution, and therefore in favour of Appeals a general Practice was introduced, [l] not to try any Person on an Indictment of Death, till after

[a] Kely 25, 26. H. P. C. 244. S. P. C 105. Lett. A. Crompt. Just. 42. pl. 18. 112. pl. 7. 27 Ass. pl 10. *Abridged* Fitz. Coro. 200. Bro. Coro. 105. Lamb. B. 2. ch. 7.

[b] Cont. Fitz. Coro. 282.

[c] S. P. C. 44. Lett. C. 105. Lett. A. B. Kely. 25, 26. Lamb. B. 2. ch. 7. H. P. C. 224. 244. Crompt. Just. 42. pl. 18. 112 pl. 7. *But the Principal Authority in the old Books is* 2 E. 3. 20. pl. 14. *Abridged* Fitz. Coro. 150. *which seems inconsistent with itself; for the Words are for an example, That a Man may in such Case be twice put to answer, We award that you go quit. And* Fitz. Coro. 282. *is contradicted by all other Books; for it says, That a Man acquitted as Principal, cannot be so much as arraigned as an Accessary after. And* 27 Ass pl. 10. *Abridged* Bro. Coro. 105. *and* Fitz Coro. 200. *extend only to the Case of an Accessary after. And* 8 H. 5. 6. pl. 26. *Abridged* Fitz. Coro. 463. *expressly goes upon the Supposition, That a Man may be found guilty as Principal, upon Evidence which only proves him Accessary.*

[d] S P C 105. Lett. B. Fitz. Coro. 424.

[e] Vide supra ch. 29. Sect. 13, 14.

[f] H. P. C. 266. Keilw. 107. Dalis. 14.

[g] Vide supra Sections 1, 8, 9, 10.

[h] Kielw. 107. Dalis. 14. Lamb. B. 2. ch. 7.

[i] Crompton's Justice, 43. pl. 30. Bro. Coro. 186.

[k] Vide supra, ch. 25. Sect. 15. 21 H. 6. 28, 29. *Abridged* Bro. Appeal, 41. 44 E. 3. 25. pl. 36. *Abridged* Bro. App. 12. H. P. C. 244, 245. 47 E. 3. 16 pl. 27. *Abridged* Fitz. Coro. 104. Bro. Appeal 33, 55, 102. 2 Leon. 161. *But this is made a Quære* 17 Ass. pl. 1.

[l] Vide supra, ch. 25. Sect. 15. Crompt. Justice, 111. pl. 2, 3. Kely. 95, 96, 97, 98. 2 Leon. 161. H P. C. 244, 245. S. P. C. 107. Lett. A. Bro. Appeal, 9. 42 Ass. pl. 8. *Abridged* Bro. Appeal. 119. 45 E. 3. 25. pl. 36. *Abridged* Bro. Appeal 12. 11 H. 4. 94. pl. 56. *Abridged* Bro. Appeal 36. 41 Ass. pl. 14. *Abridged* Bro. Appeal. 75.

the Year and Day had been paſſed, by which Time it often happened that all was forgotten; and *for Reformation thereof it is enacted, That if any Man be ſlain or murdered, and therefore the Slayers, Murderers, Abettors, Maintainers and Comforters of the ſame, be indicted, that the ſame Slayers and Murderers, and all other Acceſſaries of the ſame, be arraigned and determined of the ſame Felony and Murder at any Time at the King's Suit, within the Year after the ſame Felony or Murder done, and not tarry the Year and Day for any Appeal to be taken for the ſame Felony or Murder. And if it happen any Perſon named as Principal or Acceſſary to be acquitted of any ſuch Murder at the King's Suit, within the Year and Day, that then the ſame Juſtices before whom he is acquitted, ſhall not ſuffer him to go at large, but* [a] *either to remit him again to the Priſon, or elſe to let him to Bail after their Diſcretion till that Year and Day be paſſed. And if it fortune the ſame Felons or Murderers, and Acceſſaries ſo arraigned, or any of them to be acquit, or the Principal of the ſaid Felony, or any of them to be attainted, the Wife or next Heir to him ſo ſlain, as ſhall require, may have their Appeal of the ſame Death and Murder, within the Year and Day after the ſame Felony and Murder done againſt the ſaid Perſons ſo arraigned and acquit, and all other their Acceſſaries, or againſt the Acceſſaries of the ſaid Principal, or any of them, ſo attainted, or againſt the ſaid Principals ſo attainted, if they be on live, and the Benefit of the Clergy thereof before not had; and that the Appellant ſhall have ſuch and like Advantage, as if the ſaid Acquittal or Attainder had not been, the ſaid Acquittal or Attainder notwithſtanding.*

Sect. 15. It ſeems [c] agreed, That this Statute ſhall not be conſtrued to extend to any other Appeal but of Death, nor to any other Acquittal but upon an Indictment; from whence it follows, That an Acquittal on an Indictment, or Appeal, for any other [d] Felony except Death, may ſtill be pleaded in Bar of an Appeal for the ſame Crime, and that an Acquittal on an Appeal of Death [e] may ſtill be pleaded in Bar of an Indictment, in the ſame Manner as by the Common Law.

Sect. 16. How far a Perſon found guilty of Manſlaughter, or of Homicide *ſe defendendo*, on an Indictment of Murder, is liable to be tried again upon an Appeal by force of this Statute, ſhall be conſidered in the next Chapter.

[a] Vide ſupra, ch. 33. S. 121. F. N. B. 251. Lett. G. Crompt Juſt. 111. pl. 2. 3.

[b] *This ſeems miſprinted in* Keble's *Statutes*, Vide S. P. C. 107. *and* Raſt. *Statutes title* Murder, 2

[c] H. P. C. 244, 245. S. P. C. 107. Lett. A.

[d] H. P. C. 244, 245. S. P. C. 107, Lett. A

[e] H. P. C. 244, 245. S. P. C. 107. Lett. A Crompton's Juſtice, 111, pl. 2, 3.

CHAP.

CHAP. XXXVI.

Of the Plea of Autrefoits attaint *or* convict.

Sect. 1. IT ſeems to be generally agreed, [a] That where-ever a Man is attainted of Felony, either by Judgment upon a Verdict, or by [b] Outlawry, or Abjuration, whether upon an Indictment or Appeal, he may plead ſuch Attainder to any ſubſequent Indictment or Appeal, for the ſame or any other Felony. And two Reaſons are given for ſuch Plea to a ſecond Proſecution for the ſame Felony; Firſt, [c] Becauſe the Life of the Defendant was in danger by the firſt; and it is againſt a Maxim of Law to bring a Man into ſuch Danger more than once for one and the ſome Offence: 2dly, [d] Becauſe generally the proceeding in ſuch ſecond Proſecution cannot be to any Purpoſe, becauſe the Party is dead in Law by the firſt Attainder, and hath forfeited all that he can forfeit, and therefore it is ſaid, That it is equally abſurd to attaint him a [e] ſecond Time, as to attempt to kill one who is already dead. And this is the only [f] Reaſon I find any where given for the Plea of *Autrefoits attaint* of one Felony to a Proſecution for another. But where both of theſe Reaſons fail in the firſt Caſe, and the latter of them in the ſecond; and alſo in ſome other Caſes, for ſpecial Reaſons, the Plea of *Autrefoits attaint* ſeems to be of little Effect, as in the following Inſtances.

Sect. 2. *Firſt*, Where the firſt Attainder is reverſed for Error, after which it can neither be pleaded to a Proſecution for the ſame or any other Felony; becauſe by ſuch Reverſal the Attainder is of no [g] more Force than if it had never been: And if an Acquittal on an erroneous Indictment or Appeal will not bar a ſubſequent Proſecution, ſurely *a fortiori* an Attainder reverſed will not do it. But it is agreed to be a good Bar while it ſtands unreverſed, becauſe it is not void but voidable only.

Sect. 3. *Secondly*, Where the Attainder was at the Suit of the King and [h] pardoned, and after the Party is proſecuted upon an Appeal; for it is an allowed Maxim, That the King cannot bar the Suit of the Subject, and if he cannot bar an Appeal by pardoning the Offender before it appear whether he be guilty or innocent, there cannot but be much leſs Reaſon that he ſhould bar it after the Guilt appears by a Judgment upon Record.

[a] H. P. C. 247. S. P. C. 107. Lett. B. 12 Co. 100. 6 Co. 13. b. 3 Inſt. 213, 214. Supra, ch. 23. Sect. 38.
[b] *Yet this is made a Quære* 28 E. 3. 90. pl. -3. *but no Notice is taken of the Quære in the Abridgment of the Caſe in* Fitz. Coro, 136. Vide 18 H. 8. 2. pl. 12. 12 Co. 100.
[c] 9 H. 7. 19. pl. 14. *Abridged* Bro. Appeal. 89. Coro. 11.
[d] S. P. C. 107. Lett. B. H. P. C. 247. 12 Co. 100. Cro. El. 516. Cromp. 113. pl. 1.
[e] Bro. App. 9. 44 E. 3. 44. pl. 57. *Abridged* Fitz. Coro. 95. 6 H. 4. 6. pl. 29. *Abridged* Fitz. Coro. 227. Bro. Appeal, 10. Popham, 107. 7 H. 4. 31. pl. 16. Fitz. Eſcheat, 14. Bro. Coro. 11. Fitz. Coro. 81. 95. Cont. 4 E. 4. 11. pl. 18. Fitz Coro. 27. *See the Chapter of* Judgment.
[f] *See the Books cited to the precedent Letter.*
[g] S. P. C. 106. Letter B. 12 Co. 100. H. P. C. 247. 4 Co. 45. a.
[h] Bro. Coro. 11. 28 E. 3. 90. pl. 3. *Abridged* Fitz. Coro. 139. S. P. C. 107. Lett. B. 3 Inſt. 213. Crompton's Juſtice, 113. pl. 3. 6 H. 4. 6. pl. 29. *Abridged* Fitz. Coro. 227. Bro. Appeal. 10. Cont. 12 Co. 100.

Sect.

I

Sect. 4. *Thirdly*, Where a Person attainted of Felony, is afterwards indicted of High Treason, whether before or after his * Attainder; for the Judgment of Death in High Treason is not only different from that in Felony, but the Forfeiture is also more general, (extending to Land in Tail as well as to Land in Fee-simple, since [a] the Statutes of 26 *H.* 8. 13. and 33 *H.* 8. 20.) But if the Felony were first committed, it seems [b] agreed, That the Title of Escheat to the Felons Lands in Fee-simple, vested in the Lords of whom they are holden from the Time of the Felony, shall not be devested by the subsequent Attainder for the Treason, as it would be if the Treason had been first committed.

Sect. 5. *Fourthly*, Where an Appellee of Larceny hath a second Appeal brought against him hanging the first, and afterwards is attainted in the first, in which Case, according to some [c] Opinions the Court may, in order to entitle the second Appellant to a Restitution, enquire by an Inquest of Office, and according to other [d] by an Inquest taken at the Mise of the Parties, whether such Appellee be guilty of the Larceny or not. And the Law seems to be the same in Relation to an Indictment of [e] Larceny since the Statute of 21 *H.* 8. 11. which entitles the Prosecutor to a Restitution of his Goods, upon the Offender's being found guilty, *&c.* in the same Manner as upon an Appeal. Also it hath been [f] adjudged, That a Person attainted is as liable to answer a Personal Action, as if he had not been attainted. For otherwise his Attainder would give him a Privilege and Protection, which the Law is far from intending in allowing the Plea of *Autrefoits attaint* to a second Prosecution for a new Crime, which is chiefly grounded on this Reason, That the Law will not suffer an absurd and vain Thing in attainting one who is attainted already.

Sect. 6. *Fifthly*, Where a Person attainted of one Felony, is afterwards prosecuted as a Principal in another, and others are also prosecuted together with him as his Accessaries, in which Case it is said, [g] That for the Benefit of Publick Justice he is compellable to plead, *&c.* to the second Prosecution in the same Manner as if he had not been attainted, because otherwise the Accessaries to such second Felonies could not [h] be brought to their Trials for want of a Conviction of their Principal.

Sect. 7. It seems [i] clear, That a Judgment against a Man on an Indictment or Action of Trespass, is no Bar to an Indictment or Appeal of Larceny, for the same taking, because Trespass and Larceny are Offences of a different Nature, and the Judgment for the one entirely differs from that for the other. Also I take it to be in a great measure [k] agreed, That the Judgment of *Pain fort & dure* in one Felony is no Bar to a Prosecution for another; because such Judgment neither corrupts the Blood, nor forfeits the Lands, as an Attainder doth. But it seems questionable, whether it may not bar a second Prosecution for the same Felony, because the Life of the Party was brought into danger by the first.

Sect. 8. It is [l] said, That *Autrefoits attaint* or *convict* was no Plea for one who had broken the Prison of the Ordinary; but for this I shall refer to the Books cited, *Ch.* 33. *Sect.* 9, 10.

* 1 H. 6. 5. 22. *Abridged* Bro. Treason, 11. Fitz Coro. 2. 3 Inst. 213. Popham, 107. H. P. C 213, 241. *And the Observation to the contrary in* 2 Inst. 590. *and* S. P. C. 107. Lett. B. Crompt. Just. 113. pl. 2. *on the above-cited Year Book of* H. 6. 5. *to the plain purport of it, seems repugnant.*

[a] Co. Lit. 372, 392. *See the Chapter of Forfeiture.*

[b] 3 Inst. 213. S. P. C. 137. Lett. B.

[c] Vide supra ch. 23. Sect. 53. *and* ch. 28. Sect. 7. Fitz. Coro. 379. 7 H. 4. 31. pl. 16. *Abridged* Fitz. Coro. 81. Bro Appeal, 21. Vide 44 E. 3. 44 pl. 57. *Abridged* Bro. Appeal, 11. Fitz. Coro. 95.

[d] 4 E. 4. 11. pl 18. S. P. C. 66. Lett. E. H. P C. 213. 248. Bro. Appeal, 93. Fitz. Coro. 26 Vide 6 Ed 4. 4. *Abridged* Bro. Coro 147.

[e] Vide supra, ch. 23. Sect. 55, 56. H. P. C. 212, 248.

[f] 3 Inst. 213, 215. Cro. El. 516. Cont. Cro. El. 213.

[g] Poph. 107.

[h] Vide supra, Ch. 29. *from* Sect. 36 *to* Sect. 45.

[i] Vide supra, ch. 35. Sect. 5. 7 H. 4. 35. pl. 4. Fitz. Coro. 82.

[k] 3 Inst. 213 Crompt. Just. 113. pl. 4 Dy. 308. pl. 73.

[l] S. P. C. 31, 32.

Sect. 9. It is certain that an Attainder on an Indictment of Death is no Bar to an Appeal, by Reaſon of 3 *H.* 7. 1. ſet forth more at large in the precedent Chapter, which gives an Appeal againſt Perſons attainted of Death, the Benefit of Clergy thereof being not had, as it is certain that it cannot at this Day. But it ſeems [m] agreed, That in all other Caſes the Plea of *Autrefoits attaint* is ſtill of the ſame Force as it was by the Common Law.

Sect. 10. The Plea of *Autrefoits convict*, ſeems chiefly to depend on this Reaſon [a] That the Party ought [b] not to be brought twice into Danger of his Life for the ſame Crime. Upon which Ground it ſeems [c] agreed, That a Conviction on an Appeal or Indictment of Burglary, or other Felony, may be pleaded to an Indictment or Appeal for the ſame Felony; And that a Conviction of Manſlaughter in an Appeal of Death may be pleaded in Bar of a ſubſequent Indictment or Appeal of the ſame Death; and that the Reaſon why ſuch a Conviction on an Indictment of Death cannot be pleaded to an Appeal as well as to an Indictment (unleſs the Perſon ſo convicted be admitted to his Clergy, or at leaſt have prayed it,) [d] depends entirely on 3 *H.* 7. 1. which expreſsly giving an Appeal againſt a Perſon attainted on an Indictment of Death, who hath not had his Clergy, cannot but be thought to give it as well againſt a Perſon convicted, ſince every Attainder includes a Conviction and more, and it is wholly owing to the Default of the Court which ſhall not prejudice any one, that a Perſon convicted is not attainted [e]. But I do not find any Authority that a Conviction of one Felony may be pleaded in Bar of another; but on the contrary it is plain, That it was anciently the uſual [f] Practice, where a Clerk was indicted of ſeveral Felonies, and tried and convicted of one of them, and demanded by the Ordinary, not to deliver him upon ſuch Demand, but to detain him in Priſon till he had been arraigned of all the Felonies whereof he ſtood indicted. Alſo it ſeems [g] agreed, That even after the Statute of 25 *E.* 3. 5. *de clero*, a Clerk convict of one Felony, might immediately, while he ſtood at the Bar, be arraigned of any other.

Sect. 11. But it ſeems to be admitted [h] as a general Rule, That after a Clerk convict was once delivered to the Ordinary, he could not afterwards be impeached either for the ſame, or any other Felony committed before ſuch Delivery to the Ordinary, whether it were within the Benefit of the Clergy or not: And tho' this be ſo far remedied [i] by 8 *Eliz.* 4. and 18 *Eliz.* 7. That a Perſon admitted to his Clergy, for any Felony, ſhall not in Reſpect thereof bar a ſubſequent Proſecution for another Felony not within the Benefit of the Clergy; yet, as I take it, the Law generally ſtill continues as it was, as to the Felony whereof the Party who is admitted to his Clergy is convicted, and alſo as to other Felonies within the Benefit of the Clergy committed before ſuch Admittance, whereof it ſeems agreed, That regularly one admitted to his Clergy ſhall not be afterwards arraigned.

Sect. 12. It ſeems to have been long ſettled, That not only he who hath been admitted [k] to his Clergy on a Conviction of Manſlaughter, upon an Indictment of Murder, but alſo that he who being called to Judgment on ſuch a Conviction, hath [l] prayed his Clergy, but hath not

[m] H. p. C. 247.

[a] Vide ſupra, Sect. 1.

[b] Vide 4 Co. 39 b. 40. a. 47. a. 2 Leon. 83.

[c] 4 Co. 39. b. 40. a. 2 Leon. 83. Crompt Juſt. 113. pl. 5. Kely. 94, 98. 4 Co. 46. 1 Salk. 62, 63. Cro Ca. 147.

[d] Vide 1 And. 68. 4 C. 46. 3 Mod. 156, 157. Infra, Sect. 17.

[e] Vide S. P. C. 108. Lett. A. H P. C. 247, 248. Crompt. Juſt. 113.

[f] Fitz. Coro. 394, 461. S. P. C. 108. Lett. A. Supra, ch. 33. Sect. 117.

See the Preamble of 25 E. 3. 5.

[g] S. P. C. 108. Lett. A. Dy. 215. pl. 49.

[h] Dy. 214, 215. H. P. C. 248, 249. Supra, ch. 33. Sect. 117 *to* 121. 18 H. 8. 2. pl. 12. 3 Inſt. 131. Kely. 93, 103. Crompt. Juſt. 113 pl. 8, 9, 10. Fitz. Coro. 232.

[i] Vide ſupra, ch. 33. *from* Sect. 221. *to* Sect. 130.

[k] 4 Co 40. Wetherel's *Caſe.* 45. b. 46. Crompt. Juſt. 102, pl. 10. Vide Cro. Ja. 282. 1 And. 68. 2 Roll. Rep. Yelv. 204, 205. 1 Bulſt. 241. *See the Caſes cited to the next Letter.*

[l] 2 Leon. 160, 161. 4 Co. 45. b. 46. a. Kely 93, *&c.* 3 Inſt. 161. Coke's Entr. 554 b. *This is left doubtful,* 478.

been actually admitted to it, may bar any subsequent Appeal for the same Death, as he might by the Common Law. And as to the Objection from the seeming Absurdity, that if the Law be so he that hath his Clergy on a Conviction of Manslaughter will be in a better Case than if he had been wholly acquitted, it may be answered, That this doth not depend on any Reasoning from the Nature of the Thing, but from the Statute of 3 *H.* 7. 1. which expresly takes away the Plea of *Autrefoits acquit* in this Case, but by suffering even Persons attainted on an Indictment of Death, who have been admitted to their Clergy to plead such Admission in Bar of an Appeal, plainly seems to have intended to leave the Benefit of the Clergy, as it stood before.

Sect. 13. Also it hath been adjudged, [a] That it is not material whether the Appeal, in Bar whereof such Conviction and Clergy are pleaded, were depending at the Time of such Conviction or not; since the Judges [b] may, if they think fit in their Discretion, proceed on an Indictment of Death, notwithstanding an Appeal thereof be depending; and therefore as on the one Side the Party is liable to be hanged if found guilty of Murder on a Verdict against him on such Indictment, pending an Appeal, it cannot but be equitable, that on the other Side he should have the full Benefit of the Verdict if found in his Favour.

Sect. 14. But there have been many [c] Opinions, That unless the Court call a Man to Judgment on a Conviction of Manslaughter on an Indictment of Murder, he cannot demand the Privilege of his Clergy, and consequently cannot plead such Conviction and Clergy thereon had, or prayed, in Bar of an Appeal. And accordingly it was solemnly resolved * by all the Judges, except one, in the latter End of the Reign of King *James* the second, That the Court might delay the calling a Convict to Judgment, to hinder him from praying his Clergy, (especially if an Appeal be depending.) in order to make him liable to an Appeal. But the contrary seems [d] to be fully settled in the Case of *Armstrong* and *Lisle*, wherein it was adjudged upon great Deliberation, That a Conviction of Manslaughter on an Indictment of Murder, and the [e] Prayer of Clergy thereupon, may be pleaded in Bar of an Appeal of the same Death, whether such Prayer were made upon the Party's being called to Judgment or not. For it seems to be [f] admitted, even by those of the contrary Opinion, That the Delay of the Court in not admitting a Man to his Clergy who prays it when called to Judgment, shall no way prejudice him, but that he may bar an Appeal by pleading the Conviction and Prayer of Clergy as much as if he had been actually admitted to it. And why should it be more reasonable that the Delay of the Court in not calling a Man to Judgment, should put it in the Power of the Court to make so high a Privilege in favour of Life, wholly precarious and discretionary? To which may be added, That a Demand of Clergy by a Convict before he is called to Judgment, seems in Strictness to be as legal as a Demand after a Call to Judgment; since whenever a Person appears to have a Right to his Clergy, as he seems plainly to do, when his Crime is found to be such as is within the Benefit of it, it seems a necessary Consequence that he has a Right to pray it. And it seems [g] agreed, That by the ancient Common Law, Clergy might be demanded upon the Prisoner's first Arraignment. And tho' afterwards for special Reasons, the Judges made it a Rule not to admit any one to it till after he had pleaded; yet I find it no where holden in the old Books,

[a] Salk. 63. Kely. 91, 92, 94. 104, 107, 108. *But the contrary seems to be holden in* 3 Inst. 131.

[b] Supra, ch. 25. Sect. 15. *and the Notes to ch.* 35. Sect. 14. Kely. 94, 95, 96, 97, 98.

[c] 1 Sid. 316. Kely. 106. Vide Dyer, 214. pl. 48. 215. pl. 49. 296 pl. 60.

* 3 Mod 156, 157, 158. Kely 106.

[d] Kely. 93. 103, 104, 105, 107. Salk. 62, 63.

[e] *But Note that in this Case the Party was actually admitted to his Clergy in the King's Bench.*

[f] Vide supra, Sect 12.

1 And. 68. 4 Co. 45, 46. Kely. 105. Salk 63.

[g] Supra, ch 33. Sect. 110, 111.

Books, That a Man could not legally demand it till called to Judgment. Neither doth the [a] Opinion to the contrary, in the Report of the Case of *Armstrong* and *Lisle*, grounded upon the Authority of [b] *Searl's* Case, seem to be all made out by that Case.

[a] 1 Salk. 63. Kely. 105.
[b] Hob. 289.

Sect. 15. But it seems clearly settled, That whenever the Record on which a Man is convicted of Manslaughter, and admitted to his Clergy, on an Indictment or Appeal of Murder, is erroneous, either in Respect of Insufficiency [c] in the Indictment or Appeal, or for a [d] Mis-trial, *&c.* so that his Life was not in Danger at the Trial, *&c.* he cannot plead such Conviction and Clergy thereon had, in Bar of a second Indictment or Appeal.

[c] 4 Co. 39. b. 40. a. 47. a. Crompt. Just. 111. pl. 4, 5.
[d] 6 Co. 14. b.

Sect. 16. It hath been adjudged, [e] That the Conclusion of a Plea of *Autrefoits convict* of Manslaughter, and Clergy thereon, *&c.* may be either *petit judicium si prædict' A. B. iterum de eadem morte, de qua semel convictus est, respondere compelli debeat*, or thus, [f] *petit judicium si prædict' A. B. appellum suum prædict. versus eum de morte prædict. habere seu manutenere debeat.*

[e] 3 Inst. 131.
[f] Coke's Entr. 55. b. 3 Inst. 131.

Sect. 17. It is said [g] to have been adjudged in *Holcroft's* Case, That a Verdict finding a Man guilty of Homicide *se defendendo* on an Indictment of Murder may be pleaded to an Appeal of the same Death; but this was certainly not the very Point [h] in Question in that Case; neither do I find it expresly taken Notice of in any Report of it. However, since it seems clear, That such a Conviction wou'd be a good Bar of an Appeal at the Common [i] Law; and since it is not within the Letter of 3 *H.* 7. 1. which mentions only Persons acquitted or attainted, it shall not easily be construed to be within the Meaning of it, [k] being in this Respect a penal Statute, and derogatory from a Maxim of the Common Law in favour of Life. And tho' it be in a great measure [l] agreed, That the Statute in giving an Appeal against a Person attainted of Murder doth by necessary Consequence give it as well against one convict of Murder, because every Person attainted is convict and more; and if an Appeal shou'd not lie against a Person convicted until he were attainted, it wou'd be wholly in the Power of the Court by delaying to give Judgment on a Person convicted to bar an Appeal. Yet since these Reasons hold not in the Case of one convict of *Homicide se defendendo* only, it may well be argued, That a Conviction thereof may still be a good Bar of an Appeal.

[g] Crompt. Just. 111. pl. 6.
[h] Coke's Ent. 55. 4 Co. 45. b. 46. 3 Leon. 160, 161. 3 Inst. 131. 1 And. 68.
[i] Vide supr. Sect. 10.
[k] Vide 3 Inst. 131. Kely. 104.
[l] 1 And. 68. 4 Co. 46. Supra, Sect. 10.

CHAP.

CHAP. XXXVII.

Of Pardon.

BEFORE I proceed to consider in what Manner a Pardon is to be taken advantage of, it may not be improper to premise some Things concerning the Nature of Pardon in general, as,

1. By whom it is grantable.
2. Where it is grantable of Right.
3. What is the Nature of a Pardon of Grace.

Sect. 1. As to the first Point, *viz.* By whom a Pardon is grantable: It seems that anciently the Right of pardoning Offences within certain Districts was claimed by the Lords Marchers and others, who had *Jura regalia*, by ancient Grants [a] from the Crown, or by Prescription; but it is enacted by 27 *H.* 8. 24. *Par.* 1. *That no Person or Persons, of what Estate or Degree soever they be, shall have Power to pardon or remit any Treasons or Felonies whatsoever, nor any Accessaries to the same, nor any Outlawries for such Offences, whether committed in* England *or* Wales, *or the Marches of the same; but that the King shall have the whole and sole Power and Authority thereof united and knit to the Imperial Crown of this Realm, as of good Right and Equity it appertaineth.*

[a] *See the Statute of* 27 H. 8. ch. 24. Co. Citt. 114. b. Crompt. Just. 116. pl. 19. S. P. C. 104. Lett. C. 3 Inst. 233.

As to the second Point, *viz.* Where a Pardon is grantable of Right, I shall endeavour to shew where it is to be so granted,

1. To Persons found guilty of excusable Homicide.
2. To an Approver who hath convicted an Appellee.
3. To Robbers, Clippers, Burglars, *&c.* who shall discover two or more guilty of Robbery, *&c.*

Sect. 2. And first, As to Persons found guilty of excusable Homicide, it is enacted by the Statute of *Glocester*, 9. *That in case it be found by the Country, that a Person tried for the Death of a Man, did it in his Defence, or by Misfortune, then by the Report* [b] *of the Justices to the King, the King shall take him to his Grace, if it please him.* By which at first Sight it seems to be implied, That it is left to the Discretion of the King, whether he will grant a Pardon in such Case or not. And agreeably hereto it is said in four several Notes [c] in *Fitzherbert*'s *Abridgment* of Cases in the Time of *Edward* 3. That a Person found guilty of Homicide *se defendendo* is to be remitted to Prison in order to attend the King's Grace: And yet in two other Notes of [d] Cases in the very same Year, it is said,

[b] *For the Form of a* Certiorari *in such Case, and a Pardon thereon.* See Reg. 109.

[c] Fitz. Coro. 284, 286, 287, 354. *Also* Fitz. Coro. 305. *and* 44 Ed. 3. 44. pl. 55. *Abridged* Fitz. Coro. 94. *and* 2 H. 4. 18. pl. 5. *Abridged* Bro. Forfeiture 9. *are to the same Purpose.*

[d] Fitz. Cor. 297, 361.

That in such a Case if the Prisoner cause the Record to come into the Chancery, the Chancellor will make him a Charter of Pardon, without speaking to the King; and this seems to be [a] settled at this Day, and agreeable to the ancient [b] Common Law, which shall not without express Words be restrained by a Statute which seems to be made in Affirmance of it. And therefore those Words in the Statute, *If it shall please the King*, shall be taken as spoken only out of Reverence to him, and not as intended to make the Right of the Subject to such a Pardon precarious. And the Cases above-cited, which seem to be contrary, may be reconciled with the others, by intending them to mean only the Grant of the King's Pardon to a Person represented to him as guilty of Homicide *se defendendo* only, without any Certificate of the Verdict upon Record; for none of those Cases make any mention of such Certificate, as the others do; and if there be no such Certificate, it seems plain that the Grant of a Pardon is a meer matter of Favour. However it seems to have been always [c] agreed, That the Forfeiture of Goods by such Homicide may be saved by a Pardon, (which in this particular Case seems to purge the Offence *ab initio*). And it hath been [d] adjudged, That such a Pardon is as necessary for one who is indicted only of Homicide *se defendendo* and confesses it, as for one who is found guilty of Homicide *se Defendendo* on an Indictment of Murder. And if he were found guilty of having fled [e], *&c.* I question whether the Pardon will save the Forfeiture of the Goods by Reason of the Flight; for that is grounded not on the Homicide, but on the Contempt of the Law in not standing to it's Judgment.

Sect. 3. Secondly, In what Manner an Approver who convicts the Appellee is intitled to a Pardon, hath been already shewn, *Ch.* 24. *Sect.* 27.

Sect. 4. Thirdly, As to Robbers, Clippers and Coiners, and Burglars, *&c.* who shall discover two or more guilty of Robbery, *&c.* it is enacted by 4 *&* 5 *W. & M.* 8. *That if any Person or Persons, being out of Prison, shall after the 25th Day of March,* 1691. *commit any Robbery, and afterwards discover two or more, who then had, or afterwards shall commit any Robbery, so as two or more of the Persons discovered shall be convicted of such Robbery, any such Discoverer shall himself have, and is hereby entitled to the gracious Pardon of their Majesties, their Heirs and Successors, for all Robberies which he or they shall have committed at any Time or Times before such Discovery made, which Pardon shall be likewise a good Bar to any Appeal brought for any such Robbery.*

Sect. 5. Also it is enacted by 6 *&* 7 *W.* 3. 17. *That if any Person or Persons, being out of Prison, shall after the first Day of May,* 1695. *be guilty of clipping, coining, counterfeiting, washing, filing, or otherwise diminishing the Coin of this Realm, and afterwards discover two or more who then had, or afterwards shall commit any of the said Crimes, so as two or more of the Persons discovered shall be convicted of the same, any such Discoverer shall himself have, and is hereby intitled to the gracious Pardon of his Majesty, his Heirs and Successors, for all such his Crimes, which he or they have committed at any Time or Times before such Discovery made.*

Sect. 6. Also it is enacted by 10 *&* 11 *W.* 3. 23. (which excludes [f] all Persons from their Clergy who shall by Night or Day, in any Shop, Warehouse, Coach-house or Stable, privately and feloniously steal any Goods, Wares or Merchandizes, being of the Value of 5 *s.* or more, altho' such Shop, *&c.* be not actually broken open, and altho' no Person be therein, or shall

[a] S. P. C. 15. Lett. C. 16. Lett. D. 2 Inst. 316, 317. H. P. C. 250. Book 1. ch. 29 Sect. 24. Bro. Chart. de Pardon, 65. Keilw. 108. pl. 27.

[b] Vide Kely. 122, 123. Bract. Lib. 3. cap. 17. Book 1. ch. 29, *from* Sect. 19 *to the end of the Chapter.*

[c] *See the Books cited to the other Parts of this Section, and* 4 H. 7. 2. pl. 3. *Abridged* Fitz. Coro. 61. Bro. Coro. 138 *or* 139. Forfeit. 51. 2 H. 4. 18. pl. 6. *Abridged* Fitz. Coro. 69. Bro. Forfeit. 9.

[d] Keilw. 53. pl 8. 4 H. 7. 2. pl. 3. *Abridged* Fitz. Coro. 61.

[e] Vide Fitz. Coro. 286, 287, *and* infr. *in the Chapter of Falsifying Attainders.*

[f] Vide supra, ch. 33. Sect. 64, 65.

assist, hire or command any Person to commit such Offence,) *That if any Person or Persons after the twentieth Day of* May 1699. *shall commit any Burglary, House-breaking, or Felony in stealing of any Horse or Horses, or any Money, Wares or Goods, from whom the Benefit of the Clergy is by the said Act taken away, and being out of Prison, shall discover two or more, who then had or after shall commit any such Burglary, Horse-stealing or Felony, as aforesaid, and shall be convicted thereof, or cause to be discovered and apprehended two or more, who shall be convicted, as aforesaid, every such Discoverer shall have, and is hereby intitled to his Majesty's most gracious Pardon for the Burglaries, House-breakings, Horse-stealings or Felonies as aforesaid, which he or she or they shall have committed at any Time or Times before such Discovery made; which Pardon shall be likewise a good Bar to any Appeal for any such Burglary,* &c.

Sect. 7. And it is farther enacted by 5 *Annæ* 31. *That every Person who shall be guilty of Burglary, or of the* * *felonious breaking and entring any House in the Day-time, and after shall discover two who shall have committed such Burglary or Felony, so as they be convict,* &c. *shall have* 40 l. &c. *and be entitled to a Pardon of all Burglaries and Felonies, except Murder and Treason; which Pardon shall be a Bar to any Appeal,* &c.

* Vide Ch. 33. *from* Sect. 85. to Sect. 106.

As to the third Point, *viz.* What is the Nature of a Pardon of Grace, I shall consider the following Particulars;

1. Where such a Pardon is good in Law.
2. What is the Effect of it.
3. Whether it may be waived.

As to the first Point, *viz.* Where such a Pardon is good in Law, I shall consider,

1. What is required to make a good Pardon of Felony in general.
2. What is particularly required in a Pardon of Treason, Murder, or Rape.
3. How far the Pardon of one Man may discharge another.
4. How far it is necessary that the Pardon of several Persons for Felony, be several.
5. Whether the King's Grant of a Protection, or of a Place of Trust to a Traitor or Felon, carry with it an implied Pardon of his Crime.
6. What is required to make a good Pardon of Offences not capital.
7. Whether any Offence can be pardoned before it is committed.
8. Whether there be any Offence which cannot be pardoned after it is committed.
9. How far a Pardon may be of Force against the private Interest of the Subject.
10. Whether it may be conditional.
11. Where a Pardon is void in Respect of a wrong Recital.

Sect. 8. As to the first Particular, *viz.* What is required to make a good Pardon of Felony in general: It seems to be laid down as a general Rule in many Books, That where-ever it may be reasonably intended that the King, when he granted such Pardon, was not fully [a] apprized both of the Heinousness of the Crime, and also how far the Party stands convicted thereof upon Record, the Pardon is void, as being gained by Imposition upon the King. And this is very agreeable to the Reason of the Law, which seems to have intrusted the King with this high Prerogative, upon a special Confidence that he will spare those only whose Case, could it have been foreseen, the Law it self may be presumed willing to have excepted out of its general Rules, which the Wit of Man cannot possibly make so perfect as to suit every particular Case. And upon this ground it hath been holden, [b] That if one be indicted by these Words, That he had slain a Man for having sued him in the King's Court, and the King make him a Charter of all Manner of Felonies; this Charter shall not be allowed, because it shall be intended that the King was not acquainted with the Heinousness of the Crime, but deceived in his Grant. Also where one outlawed in an Appeal of Felony prayed his Clergy, which was counterpleaded on the Account of Bigamy, *&c.* and afterwards purchased a Pardon, and sued a *Scire facias* against the Appellant, *&c.* it is [c] said, That the Pardon was not allowed, because it made no mention of the Bigamy. Also it seems agreed by all [d] the Books That if a Man be attainted of any Felony, whether by Abjuration, or Outlawry, or otherwise, and afterwards get a Pardon which doth not expressly mention the Attainder, the Pardon will not avail him; [e] because it shall be intended that the King had not Conusance of the Attainder, but was deceived in his Grant, which shall not grieve him when he has true Notice of the Matter. And upon the like Ground it hath been holden [f] That the Pardon of one who is convicted by Verdict of a Felony is not good, unless it recite the Indictment and Conviction. Also it hath been [g] questioned, whether the Pardon of one who is barely indicted of Felony be good, if it do not mention the Indictment. But this hath been [h] adjudged to be helped by the Words *sive indictatus sive non.*

Sect. 9. It hath been holden, That anciently [i] a Pardon of all Felonies, included all Treasons, as well as Felonies whatsoever, and might be pleaded to an Indictment for them: And it seems to be taken for granted, in many [k] Books, that a Pardon of all Felonies in general, without describing any one particular Felony, may even at this Day, if the Party be neither [l] attainted nor indicted, be pleaded in Bar of any Felony whatsoever, coming within the general Limitations of the Pardon, except Murder or Rape, and that the only [m] Reason why it cannot be also pleaded to Murder or Rape, is because the Statute of 13 *R.* 2. set forth more at large under the next Point, requires an express Mention of them. But I find this Point no [n] where solemnly debated; neither doth it seem easy to reconcile it with the general Rules concerning Pardons, agreed to be good in other Cases; for if a Felony cannot be

[a] 8 H. 6. 20. a. *Abridged* Bro. Charter of Pardon, 19. 8 H. 6. 21. *Abridged* Bro. Patents, 15. 6 Co. 13. 3 Inst. 238.

[b] 8 H. 6. 20. a. *But Note, that* Brook *in abridging this Case in the Title of Charter of Pardon,* 19. *omits the Words, because he sued him in the King's Court.*

[c] Fitz. Charter, 16. S. P. C. 102. Lett. C. Crompt Just. 115. pl. 4. *from the Authority of the Year-Book of* 11 H. 4. 11. pl. 24. *and* 48. pl. 23. *where on the Debate of this Case it seems admitted that the Pardon was not good because it made no mention of the Bigamy, and yet it is said that upon the Non appearance of any one to maintain the Appeal, the Pardon was afterwards allowed* Ergo Quære.

[d] 8 H. 6. 21. *Abridged* Bro. Patents, 15. 9 Ed. 4. 28. pl. 41. *Abridged* Fitz. Charter, 23. Bro. Charter, 23. 6 Ed. 4. 4.

1 Ed. 3. 23. pl. 8. 1 Ass. pl. 4. *Abridged* Fitz. Coro. 155. *Same Point admitted* 36 H. 6. 25. a. b. 26. a. *Abridged* Bro. Charter. 25. 6 Co. 13 b. Fitz. Coro 124. Crompt. Just. 115. pl. 1, 2. 3 Inst. 238. H. P. C. 251. S. P. C. 102. Lett. C. 123. Lett. A. Dalt. ch. 94. Kely. 28. [e] *These are the very Words of* 8 H. 6. 21. *Abridged* Bro. Patent, 15. [f] 1 Sid. 366. pl. 2. 430. pl. 18. 2 Keb. 363. pl. 11. 3 Keb. 694. pl. 24. [g] 2 Jon. 56. 3 Keb. 30. pl. 55. [h] 2 Jon. 56. 3 Keb. 30. pl. 55. 694. pl. 24. Crompt. Just. 115. pl. 11. [i] 10 Ed. 4. 10. pl. 14. Co. Litt. 391. a. 3 Inst. 236. Vide 22 Ass. pl. 49. S. P. C. 2. Lett. E. 102. Lett. F. Fitz. Charter, 13. Dy. 124. pl. 39. March 214, *&c.* [k] Keilw. 91. b. Bro. Coro. 147. Co. Lit. 391. a. S. P. C. 2. Lett. E. 102. Lett. F. 3 Inst 236. 22 E. 4. 7. pl. 22. *See the Books cited to the other Parts of this Section.* [l] 8 H. 6. 21. *Abridged* Bro. Patents, 15. Fitz. Coro. 24. 2 Keb. 574. pl. 92. 10 Ed. 4. 10. pl. 14. 36. H. 6. 25. a. b. 26. a. H. P. C. 251. 2 Jon. 56. 6 Ed. 4. 4. Bro. Chart. Pardon, 10. [m] Keilw. 91. b. 9 Ed. 4. 26. b. Crompton's Justice, 115. pl. 12. [n] Vide 2 Keb. 363. pl. 11. 415. pl. 45. 574. pl. 92.

well

a See the precedent Section.

well a pardoned where it may be reasonably intended that the King, when he granted the Pardon was not fully apprised of the State of the the Case, much less doth it seem reasonable that it should be pardoned where it may be well intended that he was not apprised of it at all. And if a Felony whereof a Person be attainted cannot be well pardoned, even tho' it appear that the King was informed of all the Circumstances of the Fact, unless it also appear that he was informed of the Attainder, much less doth it seem reasonable that a Felony should be well pardoned where it doth not appear that he knew any Thing of it: For by this Means, where the King in Truth intends only to pardon one Felony, which may be very proper for his Mercy, he may by Consequence pardon the greatest Number of the most heinous Crimes, the least of which, had he been apprised of it, he would not have pardoned. And for these Reasons, as I suppose, general Pardons are commonly made by Act of Parliament; and have been of late Years b very rarely granted by the Crown, without a particular Description of the Offence intended to be pardoned, As to the c Precedents of such general Pardons in *Rastal's Entries*, it may be answered, That their Authority seems to be of less weight when compared with those many Precedents of Pardons in the Register, every d one of which particularly describe the Offence which is pardoned, and even those which relate to e Homicide by Lunaticks, or Infants, or in Self-Defence, *&c.* except only one which pardons Escapes, but expressly excepts all voluntary ones. And therefore where the Books speak of Pardons of all Felonies in general as good, perhaps it may be reasonable for the most Part to intend that they either speak of a Pardon by Parliament, or that they suppose f that the particular Crime is mentioned in the Pardon, tho' they do not express it.

b Vide 2 Keb. 575. pl. 92.
c Rast. Ent. 455. pl. 1, 2, 3. 459. pl. 21.
d Register of Original Writs from fol. 308 to 313.
e Register of Original Writs 309.
f See Dyer 124. pl. 39 Vide 22 Ass. 47 Abridged Fitz. Chart. 14.

Sect. 10. It is enacted by 27 *E.* 3. 2. *That in every Charter of Pardon of Felony, which shall be granted at any Man's Suggestion, the said Suggestion and the Name of him that makes it shall be comprised; and if after the same Suggestion be found untrue, the Charter shall be disallowed. And the Justices before whom such Charters shall be alledged, shall enquire of the same g Suggestion, and if they find it untrue, shall disallow the Charters so alledged.* And it is enacted by 5 *H.* 4 2. That if an Approver become a Felon again after a Pardon, he who procured the Pardon shall forfeit 100 *l.*

g Vide Raym. 13 1 Sid. 41.

Sect. 11. It is certain that a general Pardon of Felonies extends not to Piracy, as hath been more fully shewn, *Book* I. *Ch.* 37. *Sect.* 6.

Sect. 12. It seems a settled Rule, That no Pardon of Felony shall be carried farther than the express Purport of it; and therefore where a Man was attainted on an Appeal of Robbery, and the King reciting the Attainder pardoned the Execution, it is said, h That because the Pardon did not expressly mention the Felony, it was disallowed. But it does not appear how it was pleaded, nor to what purpose it was attempted to be made use of, nor how far, or in what Respect it was disallowed; and therefore tho' i some Books seem to hold generally on the Authority of this Case, that such a Pardon is no way good, yet I do not well see how any more can be proved from it than this, That it shall neither amount to a Pardon of the Felony itself, nor of any other Consequence of the Attainder besides the Execution. But it seems difficult to give a Reason why it should not well pardon the Execution, since the King doth not appear to have been any way deceived; and k it hath been clearly adjudged, that the King may if he think fit pardon the Execution, and no more,

h 8 H. 4. 21. Pl. 7. Abridged Fitz. Chart. 26. Bro. App. 27. Charter de Pardon 13 Coro. 24. 6 Co. 13. b. S. P. C. 102. Lett. C.
i Compt. Just. 115 pl. 3. H. P. C. 251.
k 6 H. 4. 6. pl. 29 Abridged Fitz. Coro. 227. See the Chapter of Execution and Reprieve. State Trials, Vol. 1. f. 261.

Sect. 13. It seems [a] agreed, That where a general Act of Pardon excepts some particular Kinds of Felony, such Exception extends as well to those whereof any Persons are attainted as to others; for if those whose Guilt appears not on Record are excepted, much greater Reason is there that those whose Guilt appears in so high a Manner should be excepted; and therefore being within the Letter of the Exception, they cannot but be intended to be within the Meaning of it also. Neither doth it follow, that because the Pardon of a Felony whereof a Person is attainted is not [b] good without mentioning the Attainder, therefore such a general Exception of all Felonies shall not extend to those whereon there hath been an Attainder; for the Case of such a Pardon depends on this special Reason, That the King ought to be fully apprised of the Proceedings against the Party before he pardons him, as hath been more fully shewn, *Sect.* 8.

Sect. 14. As to the second Particular, *viz.* What is particularly required in a Pardon of Treason, Murder or Rape: I do not [c] find that the Common Law required any Thing particular in the Form of Pardons of such Crimes, which was not equally requisite in the Pardon of any Felony whatever. But it being enacted by the Statute of 2 *Ed.* 3. 2. which is confirmed by several [d] subsequent Statutes, *That Charters of Pardon of Manslaughters shall not be granted, but only where the King may do it by his Oath, that is to say, where a Man slayeth another in his own Defence, or by Misfortune.* And there being no Precedent in the Register [e] of a Pardon of any other Homicide, but such as is done either in Self-defence, or by Misadventure, or by Infants or Madmen; [f] some have gone so far as to hold that the King's Pardon of any other Homicide is not good, unless it be confirmed by Parliament, or at least have a *non obstante* of these Statutes. But this seems contrary not only to the general Tenour of the Books, which clearly [g] admit the King's Power to pardon any Homicide in general, but also to the express Purport of 13 *Rich.* 1. which by shewing in what Form the King shall make a Pardon of Murder, plainly allows that he has a Power to make it. Besides, the same Reasons hold as strongly against the King's Power to pardon Manslaughter as Murder, which yet I never knew disputed. However it seems reasonable that thus much at least be allowed to follow from the Arguments above-mentioned, that too great Caution cannot well be [h] taken in the Grant of Pardons of any Homicide, that there be some such favourable Circumstances in Extenuation of it, as may bring it some way within the Equity of the Cases in the Register, and those old Statutes.

Sect. 15. It is recited by the Statute of 13 *Rich.* 2. 1. *That the Commons had grievously complained of the outragious Mischiefs which had happened to the Realm, for that Treasons, Murders, and Rapes had been commonly done, and the more because Charters of Pardon had been easily granted in such Cases, and that hereupon the Commons had requested the King that such Charters might not be granted, to which the King had answered, That he would save his Liberty and Regality, as his Progenitors had done*; and thereupon it is enacted, *That no Charter of Pardon shall from thenceforth be allowed before any Justice for Murder, or for the*

[a] 6 Co. 13. b. H. P. C. 251. 3 Inst. 235.

[b] Vide supra, Sect. 8, 9.

[c] Vide supra Sect. 9. Moor, 752. pl. 1033. 3 Mod. 37, 38. Fitz. Chart. 13. Coro. 25. Keilw. 91.

[d] 4 Ed. 3. Ch. 13. 10 Ed. 3, 2. 14 E. 3. 14.

[e] Regist. 309.

[f] S. P. C. 101. Lett. A. 3 Inst. 236. Style, 375, 377. March 217. Bract. 133. a. Show. Rep. 283, 284. 1 Keb. 67. 1 Lev. 8.

[g] 11 H. 4. 11. pl 24. *Abridged* Fitz. Chart. 16. 4 Ed. 4. 10 pl. 14. *Abridged* Fitz. Coro. 25. 9 H. 7. 5. pl. 1. *Abridged* Fitz. Scire fac. 56. 9 H. 4. 1. pl. 2. *Abridged* Fitz. Scire fac. 63. 13 H. 4. 6. pl. 14. *Abridged* Fitz. Coro. 266. Dy. 34 pl. 20. *in all which Books it is clearly admitted, That an Outlawry in an Appeal of Death may be pardoned by the King so far as the publick Justice is concerned in it. See also,* Show. Rep. 283, 284. 2 Jon. 56. Kely. 24, 25. 1 Sid. 366. pl. 2. Moore 752. pl. 1033. Raym. 13. 2 Keb. 363. pl. 11. 415. pl. 45. 574. pl. 92. 3 Keb. 30. pl. 55. 694. pl. 24. 3 Mod. 37.

[h] *See* Bracton, 133. a.

Death of a Man slain by Await, Assault, or Malice prepensed, Treason, or Rape of a Woman, unless the same Murder, Death of a Man slain by Await, Assault or Malice prepensed, Treason, or Rape of a Woman, be specified in the same Charter. And if the Charter of the Death of a Man be alledged before any Justices, in which Charter it is not specified, That he of whose Death any such is arraigned, was murdered, or slain by Await, Assault, or Malice prepensed, the same Justices shall enquire by a good Inquest, of the Visne where the Dead was slain, if he were murdered or slain by Await, Assault or Malice prepensed; and if they find that he was murdered, or slain by Await, Assault or Malice prepensed, the Charter shall be disallowed, and further it shall be done as the Law alloweth.

Sect. 16. Also the said Statute required that the Name of him who sued for such a Charter should be endorsed upon the Bill under a great Penalty, *&c.* But as to this, and all other Matters, except only what is contained in the precedent Section, it is repealed by 16 *Rich.* 2. 6.

Sect. 17. It so fully appears from the express Words of 13 *Rich.* 2. That the King's Pardon of Murder, Rape, or Treason cannot be good, without a Clause of *non obstante*, unless the Crime be specified in the Pardon, that I do not [a] know that it hath ever been disputed. But it hath been formerly often [b] adjudged, That a Murder might be well pardoned under the general Description of a felonious Killing, if the Charter had the Clause of *non obstante* of this Statute. Which Construction seems in a great measure to evacuate so excellent a Law, by barely changing the Form of the Charter. But it seems difficult to give a good Reason why this Statute should so easily be evaded, which was made for the Prevention of such great Mischief, and no way tends to abolish the King's Prerogative, but only to put such a Restraint upon the Abuse of it, which every one must own to be reasonable. But if such Opinions were founded on the King's Power of dispensing with Statutes, they seem to have been of [c] little Force since the Statute of 1 *Will. & Mar. Sess.* 2. *ch.* 2. *by which it is declared and enacted, That from and after that Session, no Dispensation by* non obstante *of or to any Statute, or any Part thereof, shall be allowed*, &c.

Sect. 18. But it seems plain, That Pardons of Manslaughter, or any other Felony, except Murder or Rape, remain as they were at Common Law, for which I shall refer to *Sections* 8,9,10,11,12,13. from whence it follows, that the Pardon of the [d] felonious Killing of *J. S.* may be well pleaded to an Indictment of Manslaughter for killing him. But where such a Pardon hath been pleaded to an Indictment of Manslaughter by the Coroner's Inquest, the Court in Prudence hath refused [e] to allow it till the Fact hath been found Manslaughter only, by a Jury directed by a higher Court.

Sect. 19. It hath been [f] adjudged, That where a general Act of Pardon expresly pardons all Petit Treasons, but excepts Murders, it cannot be avoided by indicting one for Murder only, without the Word *Proditorie, &c.* who has been guilty of Petit Treason; for the less Offence being included, and consequently drowned in the greater, cannot but be pardoned by a Pardon of it; and therefore the Exception of Murder in such a Pardon must be construed of such Murder only as is specially so called, and doth not amount to Petit Treason.

[a] Vide Bro. Charter. of Pardon, 10. Crompt. Just. 115. pl. 12. Keilw. 91. b. Cro. Ja. 495. March 213, 214. &c. *Yet in* Rast. Ent. 455. *there are Precedents of Pardons of all Murders in general, without any* non obstante, *and in* Dy. 124. pl. 39. *there is mention of a Pardon of all Treasons,* &c. *but I suppose that the particular Treason was also expresly pardoned; for it appears that the Attainder for it was expresly mentioned.*

[b] 2 Keb. 363. pl. 11. 574. pl. 92. Show. Rep. 283, 284. 1 Sid. 366. pl. 2. 3 Mod. 37, 38. Kely. 24, 25. Moor, 752. pl. 1033. 12 Co. 18. 2 Jon. 56. Rast. Ent. 455. pl. 3. *the same Point is admitted and complained of* S. P. C. 132. Lett. A. H. P. C. 250. Vide 3 Inst. 236. 2 H. 7. 6. b. March. 214. Sty. Rep. *Rickabee's Case*

[c] Show. Rep. 283, 284.

[d] 2 Keb. 363. pl. 11. 574. pl. 92. Kely. 24, 25. 2 Jon. 56.

[e] 2 Keb. 415. pl. 45.

[f] Dy. 50. pl. 4, 5. 235. pl. 19. 6 Co. 13. b. Crompt. 115. pl. 5, 6, 8.

Sect.

Sect. 20. Alſo it hath been [a] adjudged, That a general Act of Pardon of all Felonies, *&c.* except Murder, ſhall extend to a *felo de ſe*; for notwithſtanding his Offence may in Strictneſs be called Murder, and conſequently may ſeem naturally enough to come within the Exception, yet ſince the general Words of an Act of Parliament are to be expounded according to the Common Uſe of them, and the Offence of *felo de ſe* and Murder are generally underſtood as diſtinct Offences, and as ſuch are diſtinctly treated by all Authors, who when they uſe the Word Murder, as ſignifying a certain Species of Offences, always mean by it the Murder of another; and farther, ſince there is greater Reaſon to except the Murder of another out of a Pardon, than that of a Man's ſelf, becauſe both the Law of God and Nature ſeem generally to require Blood for Blood, which can be applied only to the Murder of another, the Word Murder ſhall in ſuch an Exception be taken only to ſignify the Murder of another.

Sect. 21. Alſo it hath been [b] adjudged, That if a general Act of Pardon extend to all Felonies, Offences, Injuries, Miſdemeanors, and other Things done before ſuch a Day, it pardons a Homicide from a Wound given before the Day, whereof the Party died not till after the Day, becauſe the Stroke which is the Cauſe of the Death being pardoned, all the Effects of it are conſequently pardoned.

Sect. 22. As to the third Particular, *viz.* How far the Pardon of one Man may diſcharge another: it ſeems to be generally [c] agreed, That notwithſtanding all Felonies are [d] ſeveral, and conſequently a Pardon of one Man cannot be a direct Diſcharge of another, yet in ſome Caſes the Felony of one Man may be ſo far dependent upon that of another, that the Pardon of the one will by a neceſſary Conſequence enure to the Benefit of the other. As where the Principal pleaded his [e] Pardon, and was allowed it at the Common Law, [f] before his Attainder, or where he pleads and is allowed it at this Day before his [g] Conviction, in which Caſe it ſeems that the Acceſſary may by a neceſſary Conſequence take Benefit of it, becauſe he cannot be arraigned till after the Principal is convicted.

Sect. 23. It is [h] agreed, That if a Man be bound to the King as Surety for another, for the Payment of a certain Fine or other Debt due to the Crown, the Pardon of the Principal is a Diſcharge of the Surety alſo. But it ſeems to have been [i] holden as a general Rule, That where a Man is bound as Surety for another for the Performance of a future Act, the Diſcharge of the Principal before the Time of the Performance will not diſcharge the Surety, becauſe nothing was due to the King at the Time of ſuch Diſcharge: But this ſeems extremely nice; neither do the Caſes [k] brought for the Proof of it ſeem any way to come up to it. For as to the firſt of them, *viz.* that of the King's Releaſe of a Recogniſance for the Peace to the Principal, before it is forfeited, which ſhall not diſcharge the Sureties, it may be anſwered, that it will [l] not ſo much as diſcharge the Principal. And as to the other Caſe [m] cited for this Purpoſe, *viz.* that of the King's pardoning *J. N.* the building of ſuch a Houſe, for his building whereof *J. S.* is bound to the King, which ſhall be no Diſcharge to *J. S.* it may be anſwered, that as this Caſe is put, *J. N.* doth not ſeem to be bound

[a] 1 Lev. 8. 120. 1 Syd. 150. 1 Keb. 66. 548.

[b] Pl. Com. 401. Crompt. Juſt. 116 pl. 20. *This is left a Quære*, Dyer 99. pl. 65.

[c] Vide ſupr. Ch. 29. Sect. 41. Lett. l. 34 H. 6. 9. pl. 19. 42 Aſſ. pl 16. Bro. Charter of Pardon, 33. Coro. 122 or 123. Fitz. Charter 15.

[d] Cro. Eliz. 30, 31. 22 Ed. 4, 7. pl. 22. *See the next Section*, Dyer, 34. pl. 21, 22.

[e] F. N. B. 115. Lett. e. 7 H. 4. 16. pl. 5. Supra Ch. 29, Sect. 41. Lett. l.

[f] Supra, Ch. 29. Sect. 41, 42.

[g] Supra Ch. 29. Sect. 43.

[h] 1 H. 7. 10. pl. 12. Fitz. Pardon, 4. Bro. Charter of Pardon, 36.

[i] *See the Books next above-cited.*

[k] *See the Books next above cited.*

[l] See Book 1. Ch. 60. Sect. 17.

[m] 1 H. 7. 10. pl. 12. &c.

at

3

at all, but only *J. S.* who therefore doth not seem to come under the Notion of a Surety, but of a Principal.

Sect. 24. As to the fourth Particular, *viz.* How far it is necessary that the Pardon of several Persons for Felony be several: It seems [a] agreed, That the Pardon of *A. B.* & *C.* of all Felonies by them done, without adding, or any of them, is void; because it supposes them jointly guilty, and extends to no other but joint Felonies, whereas all Felony is several [b] in each Offender, and cannot be joint. And the *Year-Book* of [c] 22 *E.* 4. goes so far as to hold, That the Addition of the Words, *or any of them*, will not help a Pardon beginning with such joint Words, But this is [d] said to be misreported, and contrary to the Roll, and seems to be agreed [e] not to be Law at this Day.

Sect. 25. As to the fifth Particular, *viz.* Whether the King's Grant of a Protection, or of a Place of Trust to a Traitor or Felon, carry with it an implied Pardon of his Crime: It is generally [f] agreed, That a Protection granted to a Felon shall be so far from enuring as a Pardon, that it shall not so much as privilege him from answering immediately to an Indictment, in the same Manner as if he had no Protection at all. But there is a short [g] Note of a Case in *Fitzherbert*'s *Abridgment*, where one being indicted and found guilty of Felony, produced a Charter whereby it appeared that the King had hired him to go into *Gascoign*, to the Army, whereupon the Court allowed the Charter. And Sir *Edward Coke* [h] supposes that the Offence was specially recited in the Charter, and that such Recital varies this Case from that of a Protection, which must be a formed Writ, and therefore can have no such Recital. But however such a Charter may enure as a [i] Suspension of the Proceedings against a Felon for a Time, I do not see how it can be collected from this Case, that it shall enure as a Pardon of the Felony by Implication, which seems contrary to the Rule [k] of Law in other Cases which will not suffer a Pardon of Felony to be carried beyond the express Purport of it. However it was solemnly adjudged [l] in Sir *Walter Raleigh*'s Case, That the King's Grant of a military Command to a Person attainted of High Treason, wherein he called him his true and loyal Subject, and gave him judicial Power over the Lives of others, did not pardon the High Treason, because every Pardon of High Treason requires an express mention of it, if not by the Common Law, yet at least by the Statute of 13 [m] *R.* 2. Besides if the Offence had been but Felony, yet after an Attainder it could not have been pardoned without an express Mention both of the [n] Felony, and also of the [o] Attainder.

Sect. 26. As to the sixth Particular, *viz.* What is required to make a good Pardon of Offences not capital: It hath been adjudged, That a Pardon of all Misprisions, Trespasses, Offences and Contempts, will pardon a Contempt in making a [p] False Return, &c. and a [q] Striking in *Westminster-Hall*, and * Barretry, and even a [r] *Præmunire*: And it hath been laid down as a [s] general Rule, That it will pardon any Crime which is not capital. But it is said [t] to have been holden, That such a Par-

[a] 22 Ed 4. 7. pl. 22. Bro Charter of Pardon, 51. Dyer 34. pl. 21, 22. S. P. C 102. Lett. D.
[b] *See the precedent Section.*
[c] 22 E. 4. 7. pl. 22.
[d] Bro. Charter of Pardon 51. Dy. 34 pl. 21, 22 S. P. C. 102. Lett. D.
[e] Dyer, 34. pl. 21, 22. H. P. C. 252.
[f] S P. C 104. Lett. D. Co. Litt. 130. b. 7 Ed. 4. 29. pl. 13. *Abridged* Fitz. Coro. 30. 3 Inst. 239. 240. 2 Roll. Abr. 323. Lett. G. Fitz. Coro. 61. *But* Fitz. Coro. 122. *seems contrary.*
[g] Fitz. Coro. 239 *cited* 3 Inst. 239. 240. S. P. C. 104 Lett. D 2 Roll. Rep. 50.
[h] 3 Inst. 240.
[i] Vide S. P. C. 104 Lett D 3 Inst. 239, 240. 2 Roll Rep. 50.
[k] Vide supra, Sect. 12, &c.
[l] Cro. Ja. 494. 2 Roll. Rep. 50. State Trials, Vol. 1. fol. 187, 188, 877.

[m] Supra Sect. 15. [n] Vide supra Sect 8, 9. [o] Vide supra Sect 8, 9. [p] 36 H. 6. 24. pl. 21. 37 H. 6. 21, 22, *Abridged* Fitz. Charter, 22. Bro. Charter of Pardon, 25. [q] 1 Lev. 106. 1 Sid. 211. 1 Keb. 852. pl. 56 * 1 Mod. 102. [r] Cro. Jac. 336. 2 Bulst. 299. [s] 1 Mod. 102. Vide Kielw. 159 198 pl 2. Fitz. Coro. 122. [t] Watson's Clergyman's Law, Ch. 5. 1 Sid. 170, 222. *the same Case is in* Keble 780 *but this Point is not taken Notice of. And the contrary seems to be admitted,* Cro. Eliz. 685. pl. 21. Moor, 916. pl. 1299. *And is agreed,* 2 Mod 52

don will not extend to Simony, because it is *malum in se*; but this seems to be no good Reason; for Barretry, and the injurious Striking of another, and generally all Offences at Common Law, are also *mala in se*; and yet it seems clear, that unless they be Capital, they may be pardoned by such a Pardon.

Sect. 27. It hath been questioned * whether a general Pardon of all Trespasses extends to Champerty or Confederacy.

Sect. 28. As to the seventh Particular, *viz.* Whether any Offence can be pardoned before it is committed: It seems agreed [b], That the King can by no previous Licence, Pardon, or Dispensation whatsoever, make an Offence dispunishable which is * *malum in se, i. e.* unlawful in itself, as being either against the Law of Nature, or so far against the Publick Good, as to be indictable at Common Law. For a Grant of this Kind tending to encourage the Doing of Evil, which it is the Chief End of Government to prevent, is plainly against Reason, and the Common Good, and therefore void. Yet it seems to have been adjudged [c], That the King's Grant to the Bishop of *Salisbury*, and his Successors, having the Custody of a Prison, that they shall be quit from all Escapes, *&c.* having been allowed in *Eyre*, shall be a good Discharge from any Fine for a negligent Escape out of such Prison. And yet it is admitted that such a Grant is no Discharge of a voluntary Escape; but it is said, that it shall discharge a negligent one, because it is punishable only by a pecuniary Penalty; and it is a general Rule, That the King may discharge a [d] Possibility of an Interest before it happens; as where the Tenants of his Manor are to be amerced for a Default in Respect of their Tenures, which the King may pardon beforehand. But if it be a good Rule that the King cannot pardon an Offence which is *malum in se* before it happens, and the negligent keeping of a Prison be such an Offence, which I think cannot be denied; and farther if it be also a good Rule, That where the King's Grant is plainly against the Common Good, as a Grant of this Kind seems to be, as tending to make a Gaoler less diligent in his Duty, by taking off the legal Punishment of his Negligence, I do not well see how this Case can be maintained. For it seems by no Means to follow that because the King can discharge his Right to an Amercement before it happens, for a Default of his Tenants in a Matter relating barely to the Revenue of the Crown, which it is admitted that in the like Case any other Lord may do as well; therefore he can discharge a pecuniary Penalty for an Offence of a publick Nature before it happens. Neither doth it seem that a negligent Escape is only punishable by a pecuniary Penalty; for in some [e] Books it is said to be fineable, by which it is implied, that the Offender may be imprisoned. Besides it seems [f] agreed, That many negligent Escapes will forfeit the Office of keeping a Gaol, and therefore it is plain that a pecuniary Penalty cannot be said to be their only Punishment. However this is the only Case I [g] meet with which looks like an Exception out of the General Rule, That the King cannot pardon an Offence that is *malum in se* before it happens.

Sect. 29. But where [h] a Thing, which is lawful in its own Nature, is made unlawful by the Prohibition of an Act of Parliament only, as the carrying [i] Bell-metal or [k] Beer, *&c.* out of the Realm, importing [l] certain Merchandises in Foreign Ships, *&c.* selling [m] Wines beyond a

* 7 H. 4. 9. pl. 11.

[b] Finch of Law, 234, 235. 19 H. 6. 62. b. 37 H. 6. 4. b. 5. a. 11 H. 7. 11. 12. pl. 35. Bro. Charter de Pardon, 76. Davis's Rep. 75. 5 Co. 35. b. 12 Co. 29, 30.

* *But Chief Justice* Vaughan *in* Sorrel's *Case*, fol. 332, *&c. seems to find fault with the Distinction between* malum in se *and* Prohibitum, *as not fully answering all the Cases concerning Dispensations.*

[c] 3 H. 7. 15. pl. 30. *Abridged* Fitz. Grant, 37. Bro. Patents 51. *Cited* S. P. C. 102. Lett. E.

[d] Dy. 52. pl. 2. 19 H. 6. 62, 63, 64. *Abridged* Bro. Patents, 16.

[e] Vide supra, 19. Sect. 31.

[f] Supra, Ch. 19. Sect. 29, 30.

[g] *But Chief Justice* Vaughan *in* Sorrel's *Case*, 335, 336. *seems to argue to the contrary.*

[h] Dav. Rep. 75, 76. Finch, 234, 235.

[i] Dyer 52. pl. 1, 2. [k] Dyer 92. pl. 18. [l] Dyer 54. pl. 17. 18. [m] Dyer 270. pl. 22.

certain Price, [a] exporting Wool to any other Place than *Calais*, selling [b] Wines without a Licence, multiplying [c] Gold or Silver, [d] Coining Money of a base Alloy, and [e] other Matters of the like Nature, it seems to have been formerly taken [f] for granted, that generally the King might dispence with it as to a [g] particular Time, or Place, or Person, or even a * Corporation aggregate, *&c.* so far as the Publick was concerned in it. Yet where such Dispensation cou'd not but be attended with a great Inconvenience, as the introducing a Monopoly, or frustrating the End for which the Law was made, as the licensing [h] a particular Person to import Foreign Cards or Wines prohibited by Parliament, and [i] *a fortiori* if it tended to suspend the whole Statute in general, it was commonly agreed to be void. Also where-ever an Act of Parliament gives a particular Interest, or Right of Action, to the Party [k] grieved by the Breach of it, as the Statutes of [l] *Mortmain*, which give an Entry to the next immediate Lord for an Alienation to a Corporation, the [m] Statutes against Maintenance, Forcible Entries, carrying Distresses out of the Hundred, [n] suffering one in Execution to escape, *&c.* which give an Action to the Party grieved by the Offence prohibited; it seems to have been always agreed, That no Charter by the King can be of any Force to bar the Right of the Party grounded upon such Statute, because it is a settled Rule, that the King cannot prejudice the Interest of the Party. Also where a Statute is express, that the King's Charter against the Purport of it, whether with or without a Clause of *non obstante*, shall be void; it is said by Sir [o] *Edward Coke*, that no Clause of *Non obstante* can dispense with it, unless it tend to restrain some Prerogative, solely and inseparably incident to the Person of the King, as the Right of pardoning, or of commanding the Service of the Subject, for the publick Weal, which being, [p] as he seems to argue, founded on the Law of Nature, are so far inseparable from the King, that by a Clause of *Non obstante* he may dispense with any Statute whatsoever, which tends to deprive him of them. And on this Ground the Resolution of the Judges in the [q] *Year Book* of *H.* 7. is said to be maintainable, whereby it was adjudged, without any Difficulty, That where the Statute of 23 *H.* 6. *ch.* 8. expresly enacts, That Patents to Sheriffs to continue longer than a Year shall be void, and the Party disabled to bear the Office of Sheriff notwithstanding any Clause of *Non obstante*, yet the King by the Clause of *Non obstante*, might make a good Patent of such Office for Life. Which is in Effect to say that let there be never so good Reasons for the making a new Law for the Restraint of the Prerogative in any Particular relating to the Service of the Subject, yet it is not in the Power of the Legislature to make such a Law; and yet no one will deny that where-ever the Law of Nature leaves a Matter indifferent, there the Law of Man ought to prevail. Neither is there any Pretence to say that the King has a Right by the Law of Nature to appoint Sheriffs, since it is plain that before the [r] Statute of 9 *Ed.* 2. the Freeholders chose them, unless they had a Fee in their Office. And what Reason can there be that the Statute-Law which gives the Crown the Power of making Sheriffs, may not also qualify that Power as shall be thought convenient? But it is observable, that the Resolution abovementioned, does not go upon any particular Reason which may di-

[a] 2 Rich. 2. 11. 12. pl. 26. 11 H. 7. 11, 12. pl. 35. 37 H. 6. 4. 2 H. 7. 6. b. Bro Charter, de Pardon, 24, 76. Parliament, 98. 13 H. 7. 8. b. Fitz. Charter, 21. Grant, 33.
[b] Vaughan, 330. 1 Lev. 217. 1 Sid. 6, 7.
[c] Vaughan,
[d] 11 H. 7. 11. pl 26. Vaugh 344.
[e] 2 Rich. 3. 12. a. 2 H. 7. 6. b 12 H. 3. a. by Martyn. Dyer 224. pl. 31. 225. pl. 35. 303. pl. 49.
[f] See the Books above cited to the other Parts of this Section, and State Trials, Vol. 3. f. 799 to 810. f. 845.
[g] 11 Co. 88. a. 7 Co. 36. b. 1 Lev 218. Co. Litt 99. a. Vide 3 Lev. 389.
* Vaugh. 352, 1 Lev. 217.
[h] Vauhg 344. 11 Co. 88. See the Books above-cited.
[i] State Trials, Vol. 3. fol. 793, 796, 808. 809
[k] Supra, ch. 26. Sect. 64. 37 H. 6. 4. a. b. 2 Rich. 3. 12. a. Vaugh. 342. 343. Infra, S 34.
[l] 11 Co. 98, 99. Vide Keilw. 134. pl. 15.
[n] Dyer 162. pl. 50. 297. pl. 24.
Fitz Grant, 33. Bro. Patents, 102. Vide Finch of Law, 234, 235. 13 H. 7. 8. b. Plow. Com. 502. b.
[r] Inst. 558, 559

But now by 7 & 8 W. 3. 37. such Licence may be granted by the King alone. [m] Vaugh. 342, 343. [o] 12 Co. 18. 19. [p] 7 Co. *Calvin's Case*, 14. a. [q] 2 H. 7. 6 b. *Abridged*

stinguish

ſtinguiſh the Caſe of a Sheriff, from any other Caſe, but only on the King's Power by *Non obſtante* to diſpenſe with the Statutes concerning the tranſporting Wool, the pardoning of Murder, and the expreſſing the Quantities of the Land granted by the King's Patents, and ſuch like, which becauſe they may be diſpenſed with by Clauſes of *Non obſtante*, it is taken for granted, that the Statute of 23 *H.* 6. might as well be diſpenſed with by them; as if it were a plain Conſequence that becauſe Statutes which ſay nothing concerning the Clauſe of *Non obſtante*, may be diſpenſed with by it; therefore a Statute which expreſsly provides againſt it, may alſo as well be diſpenſed with by it.

Sect. 30. It is [a] ſaid, That the King may diſpenſe with the Statutes of *Mortmain*, without any Clauſe of *Non obſtante*; and this ſeems very reaſonable, becauſe thereby he only gives up that Right of Entry which thoſe Statutes give him for the Forfeiture, which every meſne Lord might alſo do as well ſo far as he had a Right by thoſe Statutes. Alſo it ſeems to be holden [b] by ſome Books, That the Clauſe of *Non obſtante* was only requiſite in Reſpect of ſuch Statutes which expreſsly ſaid it ſhould be void. But the far greater Number of [c] Authorities ſeem to be to the contrary.

Sect. 31. But the diſpenſing Power was carried ſo very high in a late Reign, and found to be of ſuch dangerous Conſequence, as to make the Execution of the moſt neceſſary Laws in Effect precarious, and merely dependent on the Pleaſure of the Prince. And it ſeeming highly incongruous that the King ſhould have a kind of abſolute unlimited Power, in diſpenſing with Laws wherein the Church and State have the higheſt Intereſt, when at the ſame Time he has no Power at all to diſpenſe with any Law which veſts the leaſt Right or Intereſt in a Private Subject, it was found by Experience neceſſary to *declare and enact by* 1 Will. & Mar. Seſſ. 2. Ch. 2. *That no Diſpenſation by* Non obſtante *of or to any Statute, or any Part thereof, be allowed, but that the ſame ſhall be held void and of none Effect, except a Diſpenſation be allowed in ſuch Statute. But it is provided that no Charter, Grant, or Pardon, granted before* 23 October, 1699, *ſhall be any ways impeached or invalidated by that Act, but that the ſame ſhall be and remain of the ſame Force and Effect in Law, and no other, as if the ſaid Act had never been made.*

Sect. 32. It hath been always [d] agreed, That the King never could diſpence with a Statute before it was made.

Sect. 33. As to the eighth Particular, Whether there be any Offence which cannot be pardoned after it is committed: I take it to be a ſetled Rule [e], That the King may pardon any Offence whatever, whether againſt the Common or Statute Law, ſo far as the Publick is concerned in it, after it is over, and conſequently [f] may prevent any popular Action on a penal Statute by a Pardon of the Offence before any Suit commenced by an Informer. But while a Publick Nuſance continues unreformed, it ſeems * agreed, That the King cannot wholly pardon it, becauſe ſuch Pardon would take way the only Means of compelling a Redreſs of it. But it hath been [h] holden by ſome, That a Pardon of ſuch Offence will ſave the Party from any Fine for the Time precedent to the Pardon.

[a] Co. Litt. 99. Plowd. Com. 502. b. Dyer 269. pl. 19. *where the Grant is made ex certa Scientia.*

[b] Cont. *by* Dy. *in* Plow. Co. 502. Vide Raſt. Ent. 302. a. Fitz. Grant, 36. Entry congeable, 28. Plow. Com. 334. b. Finch 234, 235. Plow. Com. 502.

[c] 2 H. 7. 6. b. *Abridged* Bro. Patents, 109. Fitz. Charter 33. 2 Rich. 3. 12. a. 43 Aſſ. pl. 19. Vide Dyer 52. pl. 1. 54. pl. 17. 29. pl. 17, 18. 270. pl. 22. 303. pl. 49. 352. pl. 25. Fitz. Aſſiſe, 445. Keilw. 134. pl. 15. 12 Co. 29, 30. State Trials, Vol. 1. fol. 578.

[d] Finch. 235. 1 Sid. 6. Dy. 52. pl. 2.

[e] *See the Books cited to the other Parts of this and the next Section.*

[f] Vide ſupr. ch. 26. Sect. 64.

See the following Section.

* 3 Inſt. 237. Vaugh. 333. 37 H. 6. 4. b, Plow. Com. 487. Vide

[h] 12 Co. 30.

Sect. 34. As to the ninth Particular, *viz.* How far a Pardon may be of Force against the Private Interest of the Subject: I take it to be a [a] settled Rule, That the King cannot by any Dispensation, Release, Pardon or Grant whatsoever, bar any Right, whether of Entry, or Action, or any legal Interest, Benefit or Advantage whatsoever before vested in the Subject; and upon this Ground it seems clear, That the King can no way bar any Action on a Statute by the Party [b] grieved; nor even a popular [c] Action by a Common Informer, if commenced before his Pardon or Release; and that he cannot discharge a Recognizance [d] for the Peace, before it is forfeited.

Sect. 35. And upon the same Ground, it seems to be clearly agreed, That as the Release of a Person robbed, or of the Wife or Heir of a Person killed, will not [e] bar an Indictment, or a Demand of Execution at the Suit of the King, so neither will a Pardon [f] by the King be any Bar to an Appeal, except only where it is carried on at the Suit of the King, after a Nonsuit of the Party, in which Case it may be barred by a [g] Pardon in the same Manner as an Indictment. But if one who appears to be attainted of Felony, whether by Outlawry, or otherwise, on an Appeal carried on at the Suit of the Party, get a Pardon from the King, he [h] must sue a [i] *Scire facias* against the Appellant before the Pardon shall be allowed, unless the Appellant appear [k] *gratis,* and confess that he will sue no farther, *&c.*

Sect. 36. If the Appellant appear on the *Scire facias*, it is [l] certain that he may pray Execution notwithstanding the Pardon: But if the Sheriff have returned a [m] *Scire facias*, or two [n] *Nihils*, and the Appellant appear not [o] upon Demand, the Appellee shall be discharged. Yet if the Appeal be of Death, and the Sheriff return the Appellant dead, there are some [p] Authorities that a *Scire facias* ought to go against the next Heir to the deceased, but the greater Number of [q] Authorities seem to be to the contrary.

Sect. 37. There is said [r] to be no need of any *Scire facias* on such a pardon against the Lords mediate or immediate, because the Pardon no way tends to reverse the Attainder, and consequently can do no Hurt to their Title of Escheat, *&c.* grounded on the Attainder, but rather affirms it.

[a] Sup. S. 29. 8 H. 6. 19. *Abridged* Fitz. Grant, 4. 37 H. 6. 4. b. *Abridged* Bro. Charter de Pardon, 24. 2 Rich. 3. 12. a. Pl. Com. 487. a. b. Fitz Assise, 445. Cro. Ca. 199. 2 Roll. Abr. 178. Lett. S. 304. Lett. S. Cro. Ja. 159. [b] Supra ch. 26. sect. 64. 2 Rich. 3. 12. a. Vide Keilw. 134 pl. 15. Fitz. Chart. 21. [c] Supr. ch. 26. Sect. 64. 37 H. 6. 4. a. b. *Abridged* Fitz. Grant, 21. Bro. Charter de Pardon, 24. 2 Rich. 3. 12. a. 5 Ed. 4. 3. pl. 25. [d] 37 H. 6. 4 b. Fitz. Charter, 21. Pardon, 4, 5. Bro. Charter de Pard. 24. Recognis. 22. 11 H. 7. 12. pl. 35. 12 Co. 29, 30. Book 1. ch. 60. Sect. 17. [e] 8 H. 4. 22. pl. 17. *Abridged* Fitz. Charter, 26. Bro. Charter de Pardon, 13. Appeal 27, 33, 41, 128. 11 H. 4. 16. pl. 36. [f] *See the Authorities cited to the other Parts of this Section, and* Bro. Appeal 150. 3 Inst. 237. [g] Supra Ch. 25. Sect. 13. Bro Appeal, 33. [h] Dy. 34. pl. 20. S. P. C. 104. Lett. B. H. P. C. 251. 11 H. 4. 11. pl. 24. 11 H. 4. 48 pl. 23. 9 H. 7. 5. pl. 1. 2 Rich. 3. 8. pl. 17. 9 H. 4. 1. pl. 2. 13 H. 4. 6. pl. 14. 38 H. 6. 13. pl. 26. *and the Authorities cited to the other Parts of this Section.* [i] *That the Appellee may have such a* Scire facias *of Course on such a Pardon, without producing a Release or other Deed from the Appellant.* 9 H. 7, 5. pl. 1. *Abridged* Fitz Scire facias, 56. Bro. Scire facias, 166. 2 Rich. 3. 8. pl. 17. S. P. C. 104. Lett. B. Cont. 11. H. 4. 16. pl. 36. *Abridged* Bro. Sci' fa' 73. *That there was no need of any* Scire facias *where an Appeal was abated by the King's Death, and the Year and Day were passed.* 2 H. 7. 10. pl. 5. Bro. Charter of Pardon, 69. [k] 11 H. 4. 16 pl. 36. Fitz. Coro. 87. *Same Case* Bro. Confession, 12. *and* Jour in Court. 21. *But 'tis made a Wonder that a* Scire facias *was not awarded.* [l] S. P. C. 104. Lett. B. H. P. C. 251. 11 H. 4. 1. pl. 2. [m] S. P. C. 104. Lett. B. H. P. C. 251. [n] Finch 477. Vide Dy. 168 pl. 17. 172. pl. 10. 11. [o] 2 Rich. 3. 8. pl. 17. 9 H. 4. 1. pl. 2. *Abridged* Fitz. Scire facias 63. Bro. Charter de Pardon, 14. [p] 11 H. 4. 11. pl. 24. 11 H. 4. 48. pl. 23. 19 H. 4. 6. pl. 14. *Abridged* Fitz. Coro. 266. Vide Fitz. Coro. 85. Supra ch. 23. Sect. 38, & 41. [q] 9 H. 7. 5. pl. 1. *Abridged* Fitz. Scire fac' 56. Bro. Scire facias 166. Appeal 88, 144. 38 H. 6. 13. pl. 26. Bro. Appeal, 141. Charter de Pardon, 28. Supra Ch. 23. Sect. 38, 41. [r] Dyer 34. pl. 20.

Sect. 38. If several Persons be outlawed in an Appeal, and one of them be pardoned, and get his Pardon allowed on the Non-appearance of the Appellant on a *Scire facias, &c.* and afterwards another of them get his Pardon, it seems that he shall take no [a] Advantage of the Appellant's Default on the first *Scire facias*, but must sue out his *Scire facias, &c.* in the same Manner as if there had been no such Default.

Sect. 39. It is holden by great * Authorities, That if a Person be convicted of Manslaughter upon an Appeal of Death, the King may pardon the burning in the Hand; for which this Reason is given by Sir *Edward Coke*, that it is no Part of the Judgment at the Suit of the Party, but a collateral and exemplary [b] Punishment inflicted by the Statute of 4 *H.* 7. 13. But this is made a *Quære* by [c] others, and the principal Case wherein it is said to have been resolved, is very differently [e] reported, and was never [f] adjudged; And the Ground laid down that the King may pardon it because it is no Part of the Judgment at the Suit of the Party, by which it seems admitted, that if it were part of the Judgment, the Law wou'd be otherwise, seems rather to make against it than for it; for there are [g] Precedents of express Judgments, *quod cautarisetur in manu sua læva.* Also it is [h] admitted, That where a Defendant is to have a certain Imprisonment, *&c.* at the Suit of the Party upon a Statute, the King cannot dispense with it, except in some special [i] Cases, wherein it may be reasonably intended that such Imprisonment was given by the Statute, by way of Satisfaction to the Publick Justice only, in which Case it seems agreed, [l] That the King may dispense with it, as it is said that he may, with finding of Sureties by one convict on the Statute against Trespasses in Parks. But it seems duobtful, whether the Statute of 4 *H.* 7. 13. which appoints the burning of the Hand can well admit of such a Construction; for the Words are, *Whereas upon Trust of the Privilege of the Church, diverse have been more bold to commit Murder,* &c. *because they have been admitted to their Clergy as oft as they have offended; for avoiding of such presumptuous Boldness, it is enacted, That every Person not being in Orders, who hath been once admitted to his Clergy, be not again admitted thereto, and that every such Person convict,* &c. *shall be marked,* &c. from whence it seems plain, That the Statute expresly intends such Marking as a Discouragement of the Offence; and it seems difficult to give a Reason why it should be construed to mean it only as a collateral and not as a direct Punishment. Neither doth it seem a plain Reason, that because the Statute intended it as an exemplary Punishment, the King may dispense with it; for surely the Execution of an Appellee attainted of Murder, and the perpetual imprisonment of a Clerk delivered to the Ordinary upon a Conviction on an Appeal, who cou'd not make his Purgation, were alsso exemplary Punishments; and yet it is generally [m] agreed, That the King never cou'd dispense with them. And therefore upon the whole this seems to be a Point that deserves to be farther considered.

Sect. 40. But granting that the King may pardon the burning the Hand in an Appeal, it seems a very reasonable [n] Consequence that the Party shall immediately be delivered by Force of the Statute of 18 *Eliz.* which says, That after burning he shall be delivered, which ought to have this Construction, that he shall be delivered after burning, where he is to be burned.

[a] 1 H. 4. 1. pl. 2. Fitz. Scire facias 63. *But* Bro. Charter de Pardon, 14. *in the Abridgment of the same Case holds the contrary.*

* H. P. C. 251. 3 Inst. 237. Hob. 294. Cited State Trials, Vol. 4. fol. 382.

[b] *But my Lord* Hobart *f.* 294. *says, That it is no Part of the Judgment, nor so much as in the Nature of the Punishment, but only a Mark to notify that the Party may have his Clergy but once.*

[c] Raym. 369, 370. Dyer 202. pl. 68. 261. pl. 26. Cro. Eliz. 464. *the first*, pl. 13.

[e] Biggins Case, 5 Co. 50. Cro. Eliz. 632. pl. 27. 682. pl. 14. Moor 571. pl. 782.

[f] Raym. 371.

[g] Rast. Ent. 1. b. pl. 2. 56. a. pl. 1. *Yet it is omitted* 55. b. pl. 6.

[h] 5 Co. 50. b. Dy. 261. pl. 26. 323. pl. 28.

[i] 3 Inst. 171. 237. 2 Inst. 200, 439.

[l] Dy. 238. pl. 34, 35. 3 Inst. 171. 2 Inst. 200.

[m] Vide supra Sect. 35. 5 Co. 50. b. Dy. 261. pl. 26. *Yet 'tis made a Quære,* Dy. 200, pl. 68. *whether the King cou'd not pardon such Imprisonment.* Cro. Ca 596, 597. Hob. 294.

[n] 5 Co. 50. b. Vide Ch. 33. Sect. 131.

Sect. 41. It seems to have been always agreed, [a] That the King's Pardon will discharge any Suit in the Spiritual Court *ex officio*; Also it seems to be [b] settled at this Day, That it will discharge any Suit in such Court *ad instantiam partis pro reformatione morum*, or *salute animæ*, as for Defamation, or laying violent Hands on a Clerk and such like; for such Suits, like those in the Star-Chamber, are in Truth the Suits of the King, tho' prosecuted by the Party. Also it seems to be [c] agreed, That if the Time to which such Pardon hath Relation be prior to the Award of Costs to the Party, it shall discharge them: And it seems to be the general [d] Tenour of the Books, That tho' it be subsequent to the Award of the Costs, yet if it be prior to the Taxation of them, it shall discharge them; because nothing appears in certain to be due for Costs before they are taxed. [e] Also if a Person be imprisoned on a Writ of *Excommunicato capiendo* for his Contumacy in not paying Costs, and afterwards the King pardon all Contempts, it seems that he shall be discharged of such Imprisonment without any *Scire facias* against the Party, because it is grounded on the Contempt which is wholly pardoned; and the Party must begin anew to compel a Payment of the Costs.

Sect. 42. But it seems agreed, [f] That a Pardon shall not discharge a Suit in the Spiritual Court, any more than in a Temporal, for a Matter of Interest or Property in the Plaintiff, as for Tithes, Legacies, Matrimonial Contracts, and such like. Also it is [g] agreed, That after Costs are taxed in a Suit in such Court at the Prosecution of the Party, whether for a Matter of Private Interest, or *pro reformatione morum*, or *pro salute animæ*, as for Defamation, *&c.* they shall not be discharged by a subsequent Pardon.

Sect. 43. If the Offence be pardoned after Costs are taxed, and then the Defendant appeal to a Superior Court, which gives new Costs, whether upon the Affirmance or Reversal of the first Sentence, they shall * not be avoided by Reason of the Pardon, because they are not given in Respect of the Offence, but of the Award of the former Costs, which being taxed before the Pardon, are not avoided by it, and therefore the Appeal was proper for determining whether they were well given or not. But if the Offence for which the Suit was in the Spiritual Court be pardoned, hanging an Appeal, and such Pardon relate to a Time precedent to the Award of the Costs, and after such Pardon the Appellant desert his Appeal, and the Spiritual Court award Costs against him in Respect of such Desertion, it seems, [h] That he may have a Prohibition, because the Pardon having discharged the Costs of the first Suit as well as the Offence, made the Appeal to be to no Purpose. It is [i] said, That Costs taxed to the Party grieved for a Contempt in a Court of Equity are not discharged by a general Pardon of all Contempts, because it is the Common Course of a Court of Equity to award such Costs at the Pleasure of the Judge. But it hath been questioned whether Costs taxed by the Prothonotary upon an Attachment to the Party grieved be not discharged by a general Pardon of all Contempts.

Sect. 44. It was insisted † by the House of Commons in the Earl of *Danby*'s Case, and is enacted by 12 & 13 *W.* 3. *Ch.* 2. *That no Pardon under the Great Seal be pleaded to an Impeachment by the Commons in Parliament.*

Sect. 45. As to the Tenth particular, *viz.* Whether a Pardon may be conditional: It seems agreed, [k] That the King may extend his Mercy on what Terms he pleases, and consequently may annex to his Pardon any Condition that he thinks fit, whether precedent or subsequent, on the Performance whereof the Validity of the Pardon will depend.

[a] 5 Co. 51. Cro. Eliz. 684. pl. 18. Cro. Ca. 113, 114.
[b] 5 Co. 51. Winch. 125. Cro. Ja. 335. Hob. 81. Cont. Cro. El. 684. pl. 18.
[c] Cro. Jac. 335. Cro. Ca. 9. Vide Cro. Ca. 667, 668.
[d] 2 Roll. Abr. 304. pl. 1. 299 pl. 8. 5 Co. 51. Latch 190. Noy 85, 91. Cro. Ca. 46, 47. Vide Cro. Ca. 9. *wherein 'tis holden that an Award of Costs, tho' they have not been taxed, shall not be avoided by a Pardon, but the other Books seem contrary.*
[e] 1 Jon. 227. 2 Rol. 178. Lett. S. *Contra adjudged* Cro. Jac. 159. *And 'tis made a Quære* Cro. Ja. 212. *whether an Excommunication can be discharged by the King's Pardon*, 8 Co. 68, 69.
[f] 5 Co. 51.
[g] Latch 190. 5 Co. 51. Cro. Ca. 46, 47. *and the Authorities cited to the precedent Section.*
* Cro. Co. 46, 47. Winch 125.
[h] 2 Roll. Ab. 304. pl. 2. Noy 85. Latch 155.
[i] 2 Vent. 194.
† State Trials, Vol. 2. fol. 199, 723.
[k] Moor 466. pl. 662. Co. Lit. 274. b.

Sect. 46. As to the eleventh Particular, *viz.* Where a Pardon is void in Respect of a wrong Recital: It being a general Rule, [a] That where ever the King appears to have been deceived his Grant is void, I take it to be agreed, That if it appear from the Recital of a Pardon, that the King was misinformed either as to the [b] Nature of the Case, or the Proceedings thereupon, the Pardon is void; as where the [c] King pardons a Man for a Felony whereof he stands indicted, or indicted or attainted, and in Truth he never was indicted, *&c.*

Sect. 47. How a Pardon of Felony shall be avoided by Statute in Respect of a wrong Suggestion, hath been already shewn, *Sect.* 10.

Sect. 48. As to the second general Point, *viz.* What is the Effect of a Pardon: I take it to be settled at this Day, That the Pardon of a Treason or Felony even after a Conviction or Attainder, does so far clear the Party from the Infamy and all other * Consequences of his Crime, that he may not only have an Action [d] for a Scandal in calling him Traitor or Felon after the Time of the Pardon, but may also be a good Witness notwithstanding the [e] Attainder or Conviction; because the Pardon makes [f] him as it were a new Man, and gives him a new Capacity and Credit.

Sect. 49. And it hath been [g] admitted that the King's Pardon of the burning of the Hand on a Conviction of Manslaughter hath the same Effect as to this Purpose, as the burning would have had, which is [h] agreed to restore the Party to his Credit.

Sect. 50. But it hath been adjudged, [i] That a Pardon is of no Manner of Force, as to this Purpose, till it have passed the Great Seal.

Sect. 51. Also it is said, [k] That the Pardon of a Felony will not make an Arrest for it, by one who did not know of the Pardon, unlawful, because such Arrests being for the Publick Good are to be favoured; and therefore shall not be actionable by Reason of such a Pardon, as scandalous Words shall be, because they deserve no Favour.

Sect. 52. I do not [l] find it clearly settled, Whether the Pardon of a Conviction of Perjury make the Party a good Witness.

Sect. 53. If a Man be convicted, or deprived, or otherwise punished for an Offence during a Session of Parliament, and at the same Session an Act passeth which pardons the Offence: It seems agreed, [m] That the Conviction or Deprivation, *&c.* are *ipso facto* avoided, because the Act taking Effect from the first Day of the Session, it now appears that the Offence was pardoned at the Time of the Conviction, *&c.* Also it hath been adjudged, That where an Act of Parliament expressly pardons such and such Crimes from a certain Day before the Session, it thereby avoids all [n] Convictions and [o] Deprivations, and [p] Awards of Costs and Amerciaments, [q] *&c.* for such Crimes, whether such Convictions, *&c.* were before or after the Session, because it appears to be the Intent of the Parliament that such Crimes shall no way be punished, which cannot take Effect if such Convictions, *&c.* continue in Force.

[a] Yelv. 43, 47, 48. Cro Jac. 18, 34. 2 Roll. Abr. 188. Lett. N. O. Dy 351. pl. 26. Cro Ja. 548. [b] Raym. 13. 1 Sid. 41. [c] 3 Inst. 238. H. P. C. 251.

* Vide 1 Keb. 940. pl. 59. Fitz Coro. 154, 281. 1 Ass. 3. Cro. Ca. 55. 1 Sid 222. 5 Co. 49. [d] Hob. 67, 81, 82. Moor 863 pl. 1187. 872. pl. 1213. 1 Roll. Abr. 87. pl. 6. Owen, 150. 1 Brownl. 10. Raym. 23. Cont. Cro Ja. 622. pl. 14. [e] State Trials Vol. 2. f. 269. Vol. 3. f. 552, 553 585, 596, 610. Vol. 4. 119. 5 Mod. 15, 16. Raym. 369, 370 *But the contrary is holden* Bulst. 154. *and* State Trials, Vol. 2. 520 *to* 524. Raym. 379, 380. [f] State Trials, Vol. 4. 119. [g] State Trials, Vol. 4. 379 *to* 386. [h] Supra Ch. 33. Sect. 129. [i] *By the Lords in the Earl of* Warwick's *Trial*, State Trials, Vol. 4. 379 *to* 386. [k] Hob. 67, 82. [l] Vide State Trials, Vol. 2. 520 *to* 524. 1 Keb. 780. pl. 24. 5 Mod. 15, 16. Raym. 369, 370, 379, 380. Kely. 37, 38. 1 Sid. 52, 221, 222. 3 Lev. 426. [m] Cro. Eliz 41. pl. 4. Watson's Clergyman's Law, Ch. 6. *pag.* 31. *in the Folio Edition.* Vide Latch. 22. [n] 6 Co. 14. a. Cro. Ca. 67, 68, 114, 115. Vide Latch, 22, 141. 8 H. 5. 2. pl. 6. 35 H. 6. 1, 2. Fitz. Fines, 21. Pardon, 6. [o] Burton's Case. 6 Co. 13. b. 14. a. *But this Case hath often been denied to be Law*, 1 Keb. 780. pl. 24. 1 Sid. 164, 222. [p] Latch, 190. Noy 91. Cro. Ca. 47. [q] 36 H. 6 24, 25. 37 H. 6. 21 Fitz. Charter 22. 5 Co. 49. Co. Litt. 126 b. Cro. Ja. 64. Moor, 394, pl. 511. Cro. Eliz. 768, 778. *Whether an Excommunication be pardon'd by a general Pardon of all Contempts, &c.* Supra Sect. 41.

Sect.

Sect. 54. But it seems to be a settled [a] Rule, That no Pardon by the King, without express Words of Restitution, shall divest, either from the King or [b] Subject, an Interest either in Lands or Goods, vested in them, by an Attainder or Conviction precedent. Yet it seems [c] agreed, That a Pardon prior to a Conviction, shall prevent any Forfeiture either of Lands or Goods.

Sect. 55. It hath been adjudged, [d] That a Clause of Release of all Judgments and Executions in a general Pardon, extends as well to Debts due to the King by Assignment or Forfeiture, as to those originally due to him, and that it doth not restore them to the Person who assigned or forfeited them, but extinguishes them in the Hands of the Debtor.

Sect. 56. It seems agreed, That notwithstanding the King's Pardon to a Simonist coming into a Church contrary to the Purport of 31 *El.* 6. or to an Officer coming into his Office by a corrupt Bargain, contrary to the Purport of 5 & 6 *Ed.* 6. 16. may save [e] such Clerk or Officer, from any Criminal Prosecution in Respect of the corrupt Bargain; yet shall it not [f] enable the Clerk to hold the Church, nor the [g] Officer to retain the Office, because they are absolutely disabled by Statute.

Sect. 57. Also it seems [h] agreed, That the King's Pardon cannot salve the Corruption of Blood by Attainder of Treason or Felony.

Sect. 58. As to the third general Point, *viz.* Whether a Pardon may be waived: I take it to be [i] agreed, That a general Pardon by Parliament cannot be waived, because no one by his Admittance can give to a Court a Power to proceed against him, when it appears that there is no Law to punish him.

Sect. 59. But it is [k] certain, that a Man may waive the Benefit of a Pardon under the Great Seal, as where one who has such a Pardon doth not plead it, but takes the General Issue, after which he shall not resort to the Pardon.

And now I am to shew in what Manner a Pardon is to be taken Advantage of, which I shall consider,

1. In Relation to a general Pardon by Parliament.
2. In Relation to a particular Pardon under the Great Seal.

Sect. 60. And first, as to the pleading of a general Pardon by Parliament: It seems [l] agreed, That if any Persons are excepted out of it, the Court is not bound, and some [m] have holden that it hath no Power in Discretion to give any Person the Benefit of it, unless it be pleaded. Also it seems generally agreed, That if the Body of such a Pardon either excepts divers particular Persons by Name, or excepts all those who come under a general Description, as all those who adhered to *J. S.* &c. no one can demand the Benefit of it, without expresly shewing in the [n] first Case that he is not one of the Persons excepted; and in the latter [o] Case, that he is not included in such Description. And if he

[a] 1 Lev. 8. 120. 2 Mod. 53. 1 Keb. 695, 757, 921, 817, 922. 3 Mod. 101. 241, 242. 1 Saund. 362, 363. 1 Sid. 167, 168, 264. Theloal lib. 1. ca 15. Sect. 8.
[b] Dy. 34. pl. 20. Finch of Law 467. Theloal. lib. 1. ca. 15. Sect. 3.
[c] 5 Co. 110. b. Owen. 87. State Trials Vol. 4. 119. 2 Mod. 53.
[d] 1 Lev. 120, 12[illegible] 1 [illegible] 695, 757, 817, 921, 922. 1 Saund. 362, 363. 1 Sid. 167, 168, 264
[e] Supra Sect. 26, 33. Owen, 87, 88.
[f] Hetl. 104. Co. Lit. 120, a. 3 Inst. 154. Watson's Clergyman's Law, *ch.* 5. *pag.* 28. *in the Folio Edition.*
[g] 3 Inst. 154. 3 Bulst. 90, 91. *See* B. 1. ch. 67. Sect. 5. 1 Keb. 781. pl. 24
[h] Co. Litt. 8 a. 391. b. 3 Inst. 233, 240, 241.
[i] *See* B. 1. ch. 64. Sect. 63. S. P. C. 173. Lett. A. 169. 103. Lett A. Bro. Notice, 1. 26 H. 8. 7. pl. 34. 11 H. 4. 41. pl. 8. Bro. Coro. 30. 200. Indictment, 2. Fitz Coro. 89. Crompt. Just. 115. pl. 13,
[k] S. P. C. 173. Lett. A. 169. N Bro. Coro. 200. Kely. 24, 25.
[l] H. P. C. 252. 8 E. 4. 7. pl. 1. Cro. Ca. 32. Crompt. Just. 115. pl. 13. 14. Cro. El. 768. pl. 9. 778. pl. 11. 6 Co. 79. b. Moor, 770. pl. 664. Raym. 23. 2 Inst. 234. 2 Roll. Rep. 307. Cro Eliz. 4. pl. 2. Moor, 619. pl. 845.
[m] 1 Leon. 300. Cro. Eliz 125. pl. 4. Cont. Lane 71. Moor 394. Vide 5 Co. 49. Cro. Ca. 32. Yel. 126.
[n] 8 E. 4. 7 pl. 1. S. P. C. 103. Lett. A. Fitz. Pardon 3. Bro. Pleadings, 124. Cont. 2 Leon. 26.
[o] 8 E. 4. 7 pl. 1. S. P. C. 103. Lett. A. Fitz. Pardon 3. Plowd. Com. 103. a. 484. b. Bro. Chart. 66. 4 H. 7. 8. pl. 9. Dy. 27. pl. 180. State Trials, Vol. 2. fol. 5.

hap-

happen to be of the same Name with one of the Persons excepted by Name, it is said that it will not [a] be sufficient for him to aver that he was none of the Persons excepted, without adding that he is a different Person from such other of the same Name. Which, how it can be tried, unless it appear by some Additions to the Name in the Statute, may deserve to be considered. But if the Body of a Statute be general as to all Persons whatsoever, and afterwards some are excepted in the Provisoes, [b] perhaps it may be sufficient to plead such a Pardon, without any Averment That he who pleads it is none of the Persons so excepted; it being a [c] general Rule, That where a Man is within the general Words of the Body of a Record or Deed, which is qualified by subsequent Provisoes, it is sufficient for him to bring his Case within such general Words, and that the Exceptions in such Provisoes ought to be shewn of the other Side.

Sect. 61. But it seems agreed, [d] That the Court is so far bound to take Notice *ex Officio* of a general Pardon by Parliament, which extends to all Persons in general without Exception, That it cannot proceed against any Person whatsoever as to any of the Offences pardoned, tho' he be so far from pleading it, or praying the Benefit of it, that he does all he can to [e] waive it.

Sect. 62. Also where a general Act of Pardon excepts certain Kinds of Crimes, there is [f] no need to aver that the Crime whereof a Person is indicted is not one of such excepted Crimes; but the Court ought judicially to take Notice whether it be excepted or not.

Sect. 63. Also where such a Statute excepts only one Particular Person, it hath been [g] said, That there is no need of an Averment that a Person indicted is not such Person; but that the Court is to take Notice whether he be or not.

Secondly, As to the taking Advantage of a particular Pardon under the [h] Great Seal, I shall observe only the following Particulars.

Sect. 64. First, That it will be [i] Error to allow a Man the Benefit of such a Pardon, unless it be pleaded.

Sect. 65. Secondly, That he who pleads such a Pardon, ought to [k] produce it *sub pede sigilli*, tho' it be a Plea in Bar, because it is presumed to be in his Custody, and the [l] Property of it belongs to him. Yet if a Man plead such Pardon without producing it, it seems [m] that the Court may in Discretion indulge him a farther Day to put in a better Plea; and that at such Day he may perfect his Plea by producing the Charter. Also it seems [o] agreed, That there is no need in a Plea of *Autrefoits acquit, &c.* to produce the Record immediately, because it is pleaded in Bar, and he that pleads it hath neither the Custody nor Property of it.

[a] 8 E. 4. 7. pl. 1. S. P. C. 103. Lett. A. Fitz. Pardon, 3.
[b] Vide 1 Lev. 26. 4 H. 7. 8. pl. 9. Raym. 23.
[c] 1 Lev. 26, 88. Raym. 65. Cro. Ca. 515.
[d] H. P. C. 252. Plow. Com. 83. b. 26 H. 8. 7. pl. 34. Bro. Notice 1. Dy. 28. pl. 188. 5 Co. 49. 3 Inst. 234. 11 H. 4. 41. pl. 8. Bro. Coro. 30. Indictment, 2. 2 Roll. Rep. 307.
[e] Vide supra Sect. 58.
[f] Noy, 100. Black versus Allen. Cro. Ca. 449. Moor, 620, pl. 845. Vide 2 Leon. 26. Crompt. Just. 116. pl. 17. 8 Co. 68. 3 Inst. 234. 1 Cro. Eliz. 125. pl. 4. Vide 2 Leon. 26.
[h] That no such Pardon is good unless under the Great Seal, and consequently that Articles of Surrender cannot be pleaded as amounting to a Pardon, State Trials, Vol. 1. fol. 578, &c. [i] Cro. Eliz. 153. pl. 33. [k] H.P.C. 252. S. P. C. 103. Lett. B. 11 H. 4. 41. pl. 6. [l] See the Books above-cited, and Cro. Ja. 70, 317. Cro. Ca. 441, 442. 1 Jon. 377. 1 Sid. 311. Cro. El. 217, pl. 2. 547, pl. 21. 716. pl. 42. [m] 11 H. 4. 41. pl. 6. S. P. C. 103. Lett. B. [o] Vide Supra, Ch. 35. Sect. 2.

Sect. 66. Thirdly, That if there be a Variance [a] between the Record on which a Man is convicted or attainted, and his Charter of Pardon; yet if there be no Repugnancy to intend that the same Person or Thing are meant in both, it may be supplied by proper Averments: And therefore if one be indicted by the Name af *J. S.* [b] Yeoman, and pardoned by the Name of *J. S.* Gentleman, or indicted by the Name of *B.* the Tasker, and pardoned by the Name of *B.* the Son of *W.* he may make good the Variance by averring, that he is the same Person intended in such Indictment and Pardon: Or if in an Indictment [c] of the Death of *J. S.* the Stroke be supposed to have been given on the first of *August*, and in the Pardon on the third, the Party may aver that the Death of one and the same *J. S.* are intended in both. And if such a variant Pardon be pleaded without any such Averment, it seems that the Court may in Discretion give the Party a farther Day either to [d] perfect his Plea, or to [e] purchase a better Pardon. And there are some [f] Instances in the old Books, where upon such Variance the Court took an Inquiry of Office, whether the same Person were meant in both Records.

Sect. 67. Fourthly, That no such Pardon can be pleaded together with, or after the General Issue, unless it be of a Date subsequent to the Time of the pleading such Issue, because otherwise it is waived by it; as hath been more fully shewn, *Sect.* 58.

Sect. 68. Fifthly, [g] That the Party shall not be obliged to lay the Stress of his Case on any particular Words or Clause in such Pardon, but may take Advantage of the whole.

Sect. 69. Sixthly, That after an [h] Amerciament in the King's Bench hath been estreated into the Exchequer, and the Party being taken upon Process from thence hath insisted upon a Pardon, and been denied any Benefit from it, yet he may be brought by a *Habeas Corpus cum causa* to the King's Bench, because the Record remains there, and the Transcript is only sent into the Exchequer, and may plead the same Pardon in the King's Bench; and if it be adjudged sufficient, may have a *Supersedeas* to the Barons, *&c.*

Sect. 70. Seventhly, That while the Statute of 10 *Ed.* 3. 2. stood in Force, (which required all Persons pardoned for Felony to find Sureties for their Good Behaviour before the Sheriff and Coroners within three Months, *&c.*) no Pardon of [i] Felony could be allowed, without a Writ out of Chancery, commonly called a Writ of Allowance, testifying that the Party had found [k] Sureties, *&c.* according to that Statute, unless it were dispensed with by a Special Clause of *Non obstante, &c.* But the Necessity hereof is taken away by 5 *&* 6 *W. & M.* 13. which hath repealed the said Statute of 10 *Ed.* 3. *but hath provided, That the Justices before whom any Pardon for Felony shall be pleaded, may at their Discretion, remand, or commit the Person that pleads it to Prison, till he or they shall enter into a Recognizance with two sufficient Sureties for the Good Behaviour for any Time, not exceeding seven Years. Provided that if such Person be an Infant or Feme-covert, he or she may find two sufficient Sureties, who shall enter into a Recognizance for his or her, being of the Good Behaviour, as is aforesaid.*

[a] H. P. C. 253. Supra Ch. 35. Sect. 3, 4, 5. 3 Inst. 240. S. P. C. 104 Lett. a. Crompt. Just. 116. pl. 18. [b] Keilw. 58. a. Dy. 34. pl. 20. 1 Roll. Rep. 368. Fitz. Coro. 294. *but* 18 E. 3. 33. pl. 11. *Abridged* Fitz. Brief, 364. *seems contrary* [c] 11 H. 4. 41. pl. 6. *Abridged* Fitz. monstrans de faits, 128. Bro. Variance 31. Coro. 29. Charter de Pardon, 15. *But note, That none of these Books make mention of any Averment, but seem to imply that the Pardon was allowed without it, notwithstanding the Variance.* [d] 11 H. 4. 41. pl. 6. Fitz. monst. de faits, 128. [e] 3 Inst. 240. 1 Sid 41. 26 Ass. pl. 46 Raym. 13. Fitz. Office de Court, 34. Bro. Charter de Pard. 32. Office de Court, 25. [f] Fitz. Coro. 294. 3 Ass. pl. 15. *Abridged* Fitz. Coro. 166. Bro. Cor. 190, *or* 191. Variance, 63. *But* Bro. *in abridging this Case under the Title of Charter of Pardon,* 29. *makes this Remark,* quod mirum mihi. [g] 37 H. 6. 4 a. Fitz. Chart. 21. [h] 36 H 6. 24, 25. Fitz. Chart. 22. Bro. Charter 25. [i] S. P. C. 103. Lett. C. Crompt. Just. 115. pl. 15. 3 H. 7 pl. 5. Plow. Com. 502. b. 1 Keb. 9. pl. 11. 1 Sid. 41. Raym. 13. 3 Inst. 234, 235. *But there never was any Necessity for such Writ upon a Pardon of Treason,* Cro. Eliz. 814. pl. 2. Noy. 31. [k] *That a Breach of the Recognizance avoided the Pardon.* 3 H. 7. 7. pl. 5. S. P. C. 103. Lett. C. Crompt. Justice, 115. pl. 16.

Sect.

Sect. 71. Eighthly, That the Judges may insist on the usual Fee of Gloves [a] to themselves and Officers, before they allow a Pardon.

[a] Fitz Coro. 294. 4 E. 4. 10. b. 2 Jon. 56. 1 Sid. 452. pl. 18. Kely. 25 Pulton de pace, 88. a.

CHAP. XXXVIII.

Of the General Issue.

Sect. 1. HAving shewn already, *Ch.*23.*Sect.*126 and 135. that the General Issue is pleadable in capital Cases, together with any other Plea in Bar or Abatement, which is not repugnant to it; and that it may also be pleaded even after such Plea found against a Defendant; and having also shewn, *Ch.* 37. *Sect.* 59. That the Plea of the General Issue amounts to a Waiver of a Pardon; and *Ch.* 26. *Sect.* 66. *&c.* what is a good General Issue to an Information on a penal Statute; and in the same Chapter, *Sect.* 73, 74. In what Manner the Issue is to be joined on such an Information, and where it is to be tried, I shall in this Place take Notice only of the following Particulars;

Sect. 2. First, That in a criminal Information or Indictment in the [b] King's Bench, for a Misdemeanor, and also in an Indictment before [c] Justices of the Peace, the Issue is well joined for the King by the Words *A. B. qui pro Rege sequitur similiter, &c.* without any Addition, shewing that *A. B.* is the proper Officer for this Purpose; for it shall be intended that he was sufficiently known to be such by the Court. But in all [d] Precedents I meet with of Informations of Intrusion, the Issue for the King is joined by the Attorney General, naming himself such.

Sect. 3. Secondly, That in Indictments of [e] capital Crimes, after the Defendant hath pleaded *quod ipse in nullo est inde culpabilis, & inde de bono & malo ponit se super patriam,* (which is the general Form of pleading the General Issue in capital Cases, both in [f] Indictments and [g] Appeals,) the Usage seems to have been immediately to award Process against the Jury, without any express joining of Issue on the Part of the King. But in the Precedents of Appeals of Felony, whether by an [h] Appellant or [i] Approver, generally the Issue is expresly joined by the Appellant and Approver as well as the Appellee.

Sect. 4. Thirdly, That it seems [k] the better Opinion, that if an Issue be joined in Process on a Recognizance for the Peace, whether the Defendant killed *J. S.* and such Issue be found for the King, yet shall it not estop the Defendant to plead Not guilty to an Indictment or Appeal for the Death of the same *J. S.*

[b] 1 Sid. 230, 231. Coke's Entr. 363. a.
[c] Cro. Ca. 315.
[d] 1 Co. 17. a. 27. a. Coke's Entr. 372. a. 379, a. 381, a. 385, a. 387, b. 390. b. Rast. Ent. 412. a.
[e] Coke's Ent. 352, a. 353, b. 354, b. 355, b. 356, b. 358, a. 360, a. 361. a. Rast. Ent. 385. pl. 5. 9.
[f] *See the Precedents above-cited*
[g] Coke's Ent. 57. b. Rast. Ent. 47, a. b 48, a. 49. a. b. 50. a. b. 51. a. 52, a. 53, a. 54, a. 55. b.
[h] *See the Precedents cited to immediately the precedent Letter. But in* Rast. Ent. 43. b. *after the General Issue with an* &c. *the Process is awarded against the Jury.*
[i] Rast. Ent. 42. b.
[k] 7 H. 4. 35. b. Bro. Appeal 19.

CHAP. XXXIX.

Where a Prisoner shall be allowed Counsel, and a Copy of the Indictment, &c.

A Person having pleaded Not guilty is to be tried either,

1. By his Country, or
2. By his Peers, or
3. By Battle.

But before I consider what is proper to each of these in their Order, I shall endeavour to shew,

1. In what Cases a Prisoner may have Counsel to assist him in his Defence.
2. Where he may have a Copy of the Indictment.

Sect. 1. As to the first of these Particulars, I take it to be a settled [a] Rule at Common Law, That no Counsel shall be allowed a Prisoner, whether he be a [b] Peer or Commoner, upon the General Issue, on an Indictment of Treason or Felony, unless some Point of Law arise, proper to be debated.

Sect. 2. This indeed many have complained of as very unreasonable; yet if it be considered, that generally every one of Common Understanding may as properly speak to a Matter of Fact, as if he were the best Lawyer; and that it requires no manner of Skill to make a plain and honest Defence, which in Cases of this Kind is always the best; the Simplicity and Innocence, artless and ingenuous Behaviour of one whose Conscience acquits him, having something in it more moving and convincing than the highest Eloquence of Persons speaking in a Cause not their own. And if it be farther considered that it is the [c] Duty of the Court to be indifferent between the King and Prisoner, and to see that the Indictment be good in Law, and the Proceedings regular, and the Evidence legal, and such as fully proves the Point in Issue, there seems no great Reason to fear but that, generally speaking, the Innocent, for whose Safety alone the Law is concerned, have rather an Advantage than Prejudice in having the Court their only Counsel. Whereas on the other Side, the very Speech, Gesture and Countenance, and Manner of Defence of those who are Guilty, when they speak for themselves, may often help to disclose the Truth, which probably would not so well be discovered from the artificial Defence of others speaking for them.

[a] 3 Inst. 29. 137. 7 H. 4. 35. b. Finch, 386. 2 Bulst. 147. Bro. Coro. 54. Fitz. Coro. 31. Cro. Ca. 147. S. P. C. 151. B. 9 E. 4. 2 pl. 4. 1 Lev. 86. Dr. & Stud. B 2. ch. 48. State Trials, Vol. 1. f. 70. V. 2. f. 1002. *See the Books cited to the other Parts of this Chapter.*

[b] State Trials, Vol. 1. f. 70. 265. 614. Vol. 4. f. 355. 3 Inst. 29. Rushworth's Collections, Part 2. Vol. 1. f. 94.

[c] 2 Bulst. 147. 3 Inst. 29.

Sect. 3. But the Law allows a Defendant the same Benefit of Counsel in an [a] Appeal, whether Capital or not Capital, as in any other Action. Perhaps for this Reason among [b] others, because Appeals are presumed to be generally carried on with greater Heat and Spleen than Indictments, and yet are not so much to be favoured as being for the most Part rather grounded on a Desire of private Revenge than of publick Justice; and therefore the Defendant shall have at least the same Advantage in them as in Common Actions.

Sect. 4. Also upon Indictments, the Court will never refuse to assign a Prisoner Counsel to argue a doubful Point of Law, happening to arise at or after his Trial; as where it shall appear questionable whether the Facts proved, if true, fully [c] amount to the Crime charged against him; or whether the Persons offered to be Evidence against him be [d] legal Witnesses in Respect of such or such Exceptions against them; or whether certain Persons returned [e] of his Jury can be lawful Jurors, in Respect of certain Objections against them; or whether the † Indictment or ¶ Process, *&c.* be strictly legal: In all which Cases the Prisoner must [f] propose the Point, and [g] if the Court think it will bear a Debate, they will assign him Counsel to argue it.

Sect. 5. Also where-ever a Prisoner hath a [h] Pardon or other [k] Special Matter to plead to an Indictment, or an [l] Error to Assign in order to reverse an Outlawry, the Court will of Course assign him Counsel. And it is [m] said, That for such collateral Matters any one may be of Counsel for a Prisoner without any Assignment.

Sect. 6. But if a Question arise on the Trial of a Peer concerning the Course of Parliamentary Proceedings, the Lords will not [n] suffer it to be argued by Counsel, but will debate it among themselves.

Sect. 7. There is a Case in the *Year-Book* of [o] *H.* 7. Where a Serjeant at Law, as *amicus Curiæ*, offered his Opinion to the Court, concerning the Trial of an Indictment of Death, That it was not proper to proceed in it till the Year and Day were passed, nor doth he appear to have been any way reprehended for it. [p] But it is not safe for any one to be either Counsel or Solicitor to one in Prison for a capital Crime, in order to prepare him for his Trial, without an Assignment from the Court. But by Leave of the Court Prisoners have sometimes been indulged the Assistance of Counsel, not only to [q] advise them in Prison, but [*] also to stand by them at the Bar: But it is said, [r] That in Strictness they ought not to be prompted by them as to Matters of Fact, [s] nor to have the Assistance of any Papers drawn up by Counsel to prepare them for their Trial.

Sect. 8. After a Prisoner hath had Counsel assigned him, the Court will not [t] discharge them without his Consent, tho' they desire it, but will sometimes add others to them.

Sect. 9. It is [u] said, That the Court cannot assign an Appellee any of the King's Counsel; but that if they will they may be either for or against him.

[a] S. P. C. 151. B. Dr. & Stud. B. 2. ch. 48. Dy. 296. pl. 20. Keilw. 176. b. Finch of Law 386. 1 Bulst. 85. 9 E. 4. 2. pl. 4. Bro. Coro. 54. Fitz. Coro. 31.
[b] Dr. & Student, B. 2. ch. 48.
[c] 3 Inst. 137.
[d] State Trials, Vol. 1. f. 569. Rushworth's Stafford 671.
[d] State Trials Vol. 2. 520.
[e] State Trials, Vol. 3. f. 135.
† 3 Inst. 29. 1 Lev. 68. Cro. Ca. 147.
¶ 3 Inst. 29. 137. 6 Co. 14.
[f] 3 Inst. 137. State Trials, Vol. 2. f. 762.
[g] State Trials, Vol. 2. 694, 701, 709, 763, 764. Vol. 3. 867.
[h] 3 Inst. 29, 137. Vide 26 Ass. pl. 46. Fitz. Office de Court, 34.
[k] 1 H. 7. 23. a. Bro. Coro. 128, 129. Finch of Law 386.
[l] 2 Jo. 180. Cro. Ca. 365. Yet in the Year-Book of 1 H. 7. 13. the Court refused it, because the Party was of very bad Fame.
[m] 2 Jo. 180.
[n] State Trials, Vol. 2. 694, 699.
[o] 7 H. 4. 36 a. S. P. C. 151. B. 3 Inst. 29, 137.
[p] State Trials, Vol. 2. fol. 272, 273, 712, 743, 763, 768.
[q] State Trials, Vol. 3. f. 133.
[*] State Trials, Vol. 2. fol. 614.
[r] State Trials, Vol. 2. fol. 614.
[s] State Trials, Vol. 1. f. 732. Vol. 2. f. 743, 762, 763, 770.
[t] State Trials, Vol. 2. f 711, 712.
[u] 1 Bulst. 85.

Sect. 10. It having been found by Experience that Prisoners have been often under great Disadvantages from the want of Counsel, in Prosecutions of High Treason against the King's Person, which are generally managed for the Crown with greater Skill and Zeal than ordinary Prosecutions, it is enacted by 7 *Wil.* 3. 3. *That all and every Person and Persons whatsoever, that shall be accused and indicted for High Treason, whereby any Corruption of Blood may or shall be made to any such Offender or Offenders, or to any the Heir or Heirs of any such Offender or Offenders, or for Misprision of such Treason, shall be received and admitted to make his and their full Defence by Counsel learned in the Law: And in Case any Person or Persons so accused or indicted shall desire Counsel, the Court, before whom such Person or Persons shall be tried, or some Judge of that Court is authorised and required, immediately upon his or their Request, to assign to such Person and Persons, such and so many Counsel, not exceeding two, as the Person or Persons shall desire, to whom such Counsel shall have free Access at all seasonable Hours; any Law or Usage to the contrary notwithstanding.*

Sect. 11. But it is provided, *S.* 3. *That any Person being indicted of such Treason may be outlawed,* &c. *and where by the Law, after such Outlawry, he may come in and be tried, he shall upon such Trial have the Benefit of the said Act.*

Sect. 12. And it is farther provided, *S.* 12, 13. *That nothing in the said Act shall extend, or be construed to extend to any Impeachment or other Proceedings in Parliament whatsoever. And also that it shall not any ways extend to any Indictment of High Treason, nor to any Proceedings thereupon, for counterfeiting his Majesty's Coin, his Great or Privy Seal, his Sign Manual, or Privy Signet.*

Sect. 13. As to the second Particular, *viz.* Where a Prisoner may have a Copy of the Indictment against him: It is said, [a] That by the Common Law it is always denied in Cases of Treason or Felony. Yet if a Prisoner take a legal Exception to an Indictment, it is said [b] that the Court will grant him a Copy of so much as concerns his Exception. Also if he have such Matter to plead which cannot well be put into Form without Knowledge of the Charge against him as laid in the Indictment, as *Autrefoits acquit, &c.* it is [c] said that the Court will give him the Heads of the Indictment, to enable him to have his Plea so drawn as to suit the Charge against him.

[a] 1 Lev. 68. Moor, 666. State Trials, Vol. 1. f. 644. Vol. 2. fol. 711, 763. Vol. 3 fol. 861, 862, 863, 864. Show. 131. 1 Sid 85.
[b] Lev. 68. 1 Sid. 85.
[c] State Trials Vol. 2. fol. 711.

Sect. 14. But it is enacted by 7 *W.* 3. *That every Person and Persons indicted for High Treason, except for counterfeiting the Coin, or the Great or Privy Seal, or Sign Manual or Privy Signet, shall have a true Copy of the whole Indictment, but not the Names of the Witnesses, five Days at the least before Trial, to advise with Counsel thereupon, to plead and make their Defence, his or their Attorney, or Agent, requiring the same, and paying the Officer his reasonable Fees for writing thereof, not exceeding five Shillings for the Copy of every such Indictment.*

Sect. 15. What Exceptions may be taken to such Indictment, and when, hath been shewn, *Chapter* 25. *Sect.* 148, 149, 150, 151.

CHAP.

CHAP. XL.

From what County the Jury is to be returned, &c.

FOR the better understanding what more particularly relates to a Trial by the Countrey in capital Cases, having shewn *Ch.* 5. *Sect.* 18. That by Vertue of a special Commission, Justices of *Oyer* and *Terminer* may sit in one County, for the Trial of a Fact in another by the proper Jurors. And having also shewn, *Ch.* 23. *Sect.* 92. what is a proper Place from whence a Visne may come, I shall in this Place only consider,

1. From what County the Jury is to be returned.
2. By Vertue of what Process.
3. Before what Court.
4. How they may be challenged.

As to the first of these Particulars, *viz.* From what County the Jury is to be returned: I shall endeavour to shew,

1. From what County they are to be returned for the Trial of the General Issue.
2. From what County for the Trial of a Foreign Plea.

Sect. 1. As to the first Point, *viz.* From what County a Jury is to be returned for the Trial of the General Issue: I take it to be [a] agreed, That [b] regularly by the Common Law they must be returned in all Cases, for the Trial of the General Issue from the same County wherein the Fact was committed. And it is said, That in an Appeal of Death, where the Wound was given in one County and the Party died in another, the Jury [c] ought to be returned from each County before the Statute of 2 & 3 *Ed.* 6. 24. since which the whole may be tried either upon an [b] Indictment or Appeal, in the County wherein the Death happens.

Sect. 2. But it is enacted by 33 *H.* 8. 23. *That if any Person being examined by the King's Council, or three of them, upon any Manner of Treasons, Misprisions of Treasons, or Murders, do confess any such Offences, or that the said Council, or three of them, upon such Examination, shall think any Person so examined, to be vehemently suspected of any Treason, Misprisions of Treasons or Murder, That then in every such Case by the King's Commandment, his Majesty's Commission of* Oyer *and* Terminer *under the Great Seal, shall be made by the Chancellor of* England *to such Persons and into such Vills and Places as shall be named and appointed by the King, for the speedy Trial, Conviction, or Delivery of such Offenders; which Commissioners shall have Power to enquire, hear and determine all such Treasons, Misprisions of Treasons and Murders, within the Places limited by their Commission, by such good and lawful Persons as shall be returned before them by the Sheriff, or his Minister, or any other having Power to return Writs and Process for that Purpose, in whatsoever other Shire or Place within the King's Dominions, or without*

[a] S.P.C. 154. Dy. 132. pl. 75. 286. pl. 5. Fitz. Coro. 194. 3 Inst. 27. 26 Ass pl, 32. Vide supra, Ch. 5. Sect. 18.

[b] Vide infra, Sect. 5.

[c] Book 1 Ch. 31. Sect. 13. Supra, Ch. 23. Sect. 35. Fitz. Coro. 59, 60.

[d] Vide supra, Ch. 25. Sect. 35.

without, such Offences were done or committed, and that in such Cases, no Challenge for the Shire or Hundred shall be allowed.

Sect. 3. It hath been [a] adjudged, That this Statute so far as it relates to Treason done within the Realm, is repealed by 1 & 2 *Ph. & Ma.* 10. which enacts, That all Trials for Treason shall be according to the Common Law. But as to [b] Murder and [c] Misprision of Treason, it still seems to continue in Force. And as to High [d] Treason done without the Realm, it doth not seem material whether it it be in Force or not, because that is fully provided for by 35 *H.*8.2. as hath been more fully shewn *Ch.*25. *Sect.* 47, 48, 49, 50, 51.

Sect. 4. It hath been [e] adjudged, That the Word *Murder* in this Statute shall have the same strict Construction as in the [f] Statutes which take away the Benefit of the Clergy from Murder, and consequently shall not extend to one examined before the Council as Accessary only, and not as Principal; for Murder is one Offence, and the being Accessary to it is another.

Sect. 5. Having shewn already that he who steals [g] Goods in one County and carries them into another, or does a Fact in one County which proves a [*] Nusance to another, may be indicted or appealed in either, from whence it follows, that he may be also tried in either: Having also [h] shewn, that he who marries two Wives, the first in a Foreign Country, and the second in *England*, may be indicted and tried in *England*; and that he who takes a Woman by Force out of one County, and carries her into another and there marries her, [i] may be indicted and tried in the second County: And that Felonies in [k] *Wales* may by Force of 26 *H.* 8. 6. be indicted and tried in the next adjoining *English* County: And that Treasons upon the Sea, [l] or in a Foreign [m] Country, and Felonies [n] and Piracies upon the Sea, may be indicted and tried in any County in *England*; and that an [o] Accessary in one County to Murder in another, may be appealed and tried in the County wherein the Stroke was given; and that an Accessary to Murder, or any other Felony in one County, may be indicted [†] and tried in the County wherein he was Accessary; I shall refer to the Places cited in the Margin for the farther Consideration of these Matters.

Sect. 6. As to the second Point, *viz.* From what County the Jury is to be returned for the Trial of a Foreign Plea, That is, the Plea of issuable Matter alledged in a different County from that wherein the Party is indicted or appealed, as where a Man indicted in the County of *A.* [p] pleads that he was taken out of a Sanctuary in the County of *B.* Or where one appealed by a Woman for the Death of her Husband in one County, [q] pleads That since the Death of her Husband she hath married *J. S.* in another County; it is [r] agreed, That by the Common Law such Pleas can only be tried by Juries returned from the Counties wherein they are alledged: And therefore if Issue be joined on such Matters before a Court which hath no Jurisdiction out of the County wherein it sits, there seems to be [s] no Remedy by the Common Law, but to remove the Proceedings by *Certiorari* into the King's Bench, which having a Jurisdiction throughout the whole Kingdom, will award proper Process for the Trial.

[a] 1 And. 104, 105.
[b] 1 And. 194, 195.
[c] Vide supra, Ch. 25. Sect. 145. Bro. Coro. 220. 3 Inst. 24.
[d] Vide Dyer, 286, pl. 45.
[e] 1 And. 194. 195.
[f] Supra Ch. 33. Sect. 26. B. 1. Ch. 31. Sect. 11.
[g] B. 1. Ch. 33. Sect. 9. Supra, Ch. 23. Sect. 47. Ch. 25. Sect. 36.
[*] Supra, Ch. 25. Sect. 35.
[h] B. 1. Ch. 43. Sect. 7. Supra Ch. 25. Sect. 37.
[i] B. 1. ch. 42. Sect. 10. Supra, Ch. 25. Sect. 38.
[k] B. 1. Ch. 31. Sect. 14. Supra, Ch. 25. Sect. 39, 40.
[l] Supra, Ch. 25. Sect. 41, 42, 43.
[m] Supra Ch. 25. Sect. 46 to 52.
[n] B. 1. Ch. 37. Sect. 12, 12, 13, 14, 15. Supra, Ch. 25. Sect. 41 to 46.
[o] Supra, Ch. 29. Sect. 49.
[†] Supra, Ch. 25. Sect. 52. and Ch. 29. Sect. 50, 51, &c.
[p] Keilw. 175. pl. 10.
[q] Dyer 296. pl. 20.
[r] 3 Inst. 27. S. P. C. 154. Keilw. 175. pl. 10. Dy. 296. pl. 20. H. P. C. 255. Vide 23 H. 8. 14. Sect. 5.
[s] Keilw. 175. pl. 10. Dy. 296. pl. 20. Vide Dyer 286. pl. 5.

Sect. 7. But *for the more speedy Trials of Murders and Felonies, it is enacted by* 23 H. 8. 14. Par. 5. *That all Manner of Foreign Pleas triable by the Countrey, upon any Indictment for any Petit Treason, Murder or Felony, shall be forthwith tried before the same Justices afore whom the Party shall be arraigned, and by the Jurors of the same County that shall try the Petit Treason, Murder or Felony, whereof he shall be so arraigned, without any further Respite or Delay, in whatsoever County or Counties, Place or Places of this Realm, the Matter of the same Pleas be supposed or alledged.*

Sect. 8. But this Statute extending neither to Indictments of High Treason, nor to Appeals, it [a] is said, That a Foreign Issue therein must still be tried by the Jury of the County wherein it is alledged.

[a] 3 Inst. 27. S. P. C. 154. H. P. C. 255. Vide Dyer, 296. pl. 20.

CHAP. XLI.

Of Process against Jurors.

FOR the better understanding the Nature of Process against Jurors in Criminal Cases, I shall endeavour to shew,

1. Where a Panel may be returned without any Precept by a bare Award.
2. In what Manner the Process is to be returnable.
3. Where a *Venire* may be joint or several.
4. What Process may be awarded by *Proviso*.
5. In what Cases, and in what Manner a *Tales* is grantable.
6. Where it is necessary to return a Panel into Court, before an Inquest can be taken upon it, and where the Prisoner may have a Copy of it.

Sect. 1. As to the first Point, *viz.* Where a Panel may be returned without any Precept by a bare Award, it is [b] agreed, That Justices of [c] Gaol-Delivery, may have a Panel so returned by the Sheriff, without any Precept or Writ; and the [d] Reason given for it is, That before their coming they always make a general [e] Precept to the Sheriff in Parchment under their Seals, *to bring before them at the Day of their Session's twenty-four out of every Hundred,* &c. *to do those Things which shall be injoined them on the Part of the King,* &c. And therefore it is said that they need not make any other Precept for the Return of a Jury, for the Trial of any Issue joined before them, But that their bare [f] Award that the Jury shall come is sufficient, because there are enow for that Purpose supposed to be present in Court, whom the Sheriff may return immediately whenever the Court shall require their Service. Also it is said, [g] That a Jury may be so returned before Justices of Peace at their Sessions, because the [h] Precept for

[b] Fitz. Inquest, 55. 3 Inst. 168. 2 Inst. 568. H. P. C. 158. 256. Crompt. Jur. 128. S. P. C. 155. Lett. E.

[c] *Yet 'tis said that the Law is (otherwise if they have a Special Commission.* Fitz. Inq. 55. 3 Inst. 168. Crompt. Jurisd. 128.

[d] Fitz. Inq. 55. Crompt. Jur. 128. 3 Inst. 168. 2 Inst. 568.

[e] Vide Rast. Ent. 384. b. 385. a. pl. 1. Cro. C. 448.

[f] *For the Form of such an Award see* Rast. Ent. 385. pl. 5. 6. State Trials, Vol. 4. fol. 182.

[g] 2 Inst. 568. *Adjudged* 1 Sid. 364. pl. 11.

[h] *See* Lambard's Just. B. 4. Ch. 2. *and* Crompt. Justice, 232.

for the Summons of the Sessions hath a Clause to the same Effect for the Summons of twenty four out of every Hundred, *&c.* Yet I much question whether this Matter do not rather depend on [a] Practice, and the constant Course of Precedents, then any Argument from the Reason of the Thing. For the [b] Precept to the Sheriff from Justices of *Oyer* and *Terminer*, in order for the holding of their Sessions, hath in Effect the very same Clause for the bringing of twenty-four before them, out of each hundred, at the Day of their Sessions, *&c.* And yet it seems [c] agreed, That they cannot have a Jury returned for the Trial of an Issue joined before them, by Force of a bare Award, but ought to make a particular Precept to the Sheriff for that Purpose under their Seals.

Sect. 2. It seems [d] agreed, That by the Course of the King's Bench no Jury can be returned into it from a Foreign County, without proper Process, under the [e] Seal of the Chief Justice, *&c.* But [f] *Quære* if it may not be returned for the Trial of an Indictment, *&c.* in the same County wherein it sits, by a bare *praceptum est*, *&c.*

Sect. 3. As to the second Point, *viz.* In what Manner the Process against Jurors is to be returnable, it seems agreed, That it may be returnable immediately into the Court of King's Bench for the Trial of an Indictment in the same County wherein it sits, whether for a Crime committed in such County, or for a [g] Treason, *&c.* beyond the Sea. But that for the Trial of Indictments removed thither by *Certiorari* from other Counties, there [h] ought to be fifteen Days between the *Teste* and Return of every Process.

Sect. 4. Also it is [i] agreed, That Justices in *Eyre*, or of Gaol-Delivery, may order a Jury to be returned immediately for the Trial of a Prisoner arraigned before them. Also it is clearly [k] holden by Sir *Edward Coke*, and hath been often [l] adjudged, That Justices of *Oyer* and *Terminer*, for the Trial of any Issue joined before them, might award a *Venire* returnable the same Day on which the Party is arraigned. Also it is holden by Sir [m] *Edward Coke*, and hath been [n] adjudged, That Justices of the Peace may do the like; but there are very [o] strong Authorities to the contrary, unless the Crime amount to [p] Felony, or the Party [q] consent to be tried immediately.

Sect. 5. *Quære* how far the Law is altered as to these Points by 4 & 5 *Will. & M.* 24. and 7 & 8 *W.* 3. 32. which by requiring that Jurors shall be summoned six Days before they are to appear, seem to make it necessary whenever a [r] *Venire* or particular Precept is required for the Return of a Jury, [s] that there be six Days between its *Teste* and Return.

Sect. 6. It hath been [t] adjudged, That a *Venire* before Justices of *Oyer* and *Terminer* returnable at a Day certain is erroneous, unless the Sessions appear to have been [u] adjourned to the same Day; because otherwise it shall not be intended that their Commission continued till such Day, and if it did not, their Authority to try the Issue was determined. But it is admitted [x] that such *Venire* may be made returnable at the next Assises, and then tried by Vertue of [y] 1 *E.* 6. 7.

[a] Vide 3 Inst. 164. 1 Sid. 364. pl. 11.
[b] Rast. Ent. 443. b. pl. 1, 2.
[c] H. P. C. 162, 256. 3 Inst. 164. 2 Inst. 568.
[d] S. P. C. 154. Lett. B. Vide 27 H. 6. 10. pl. 4. Supra, Ch. 27. Sect. 16.
[e] Supra, Ch. 27. Sect. 8.
[f] Vide Dyer 118. pl. 78.
[g] Vide Ch. 25. Sect. 47. 1072.
[h] 2 Roll. A. 626. pl. 4, 5. Supra Ch. 3. Sect. 12. and Ch. 27. Sect. 16.
[i] 2 Inst. 568. State Trials, Vol. 4. fol. 214.
[i] Keilw. 159 b. H. P. C. 256. Crompt. Just. 152. a. Cro. Ca. 315. 1 Sid. 335 pl. 20. Fitz. Inq. 55. Vide Kely. 7.
[k] 2 Inst. 568. 3 Inst. 164.
[l] Cro. Ca. 340, 583. 2 Roll. A. b. 96. pl. 1. H. P. C. 161. *Admitted* 2 Keb. 212, pl. 49 292, pl. 75. 718, pl. 109. 1 Keb. 433. pl 13. 1 Sid. 334. pl 20. 1 Roll. Abr. 96. pl. 1. Cro. Ca. 340, 583. Cont. Keilw. 159. b. Trial per pais, 26. 2 Roll. Ab. 625. pl. 2. H. P. C. 266. [m] 2 Inst. 568. 3 Inst. 164. [n] Cro Ja. 404. pl. 2. *and in this Book it is said that Common Experience is so.* [o] Fitz Coro. 44. Keilw. 159. b. 1 Jon. 379. pl. 10. S. P. C. 156. a. 1 Keb. 433. pl 3. Trial per Pais, 25, 26. 2 Keb. 212. pl. 49. Crompt. Justice, 152. a. 1 Sid 99, pl. 2. 335. pl. 20. Cro. Ca. 438, 448. 2 Roll Abr. 625. L. 1. 3. H. P. C. 256 [p] 1 Sid. 335, pl. 20. *In* Crompt Justice, 150. b. *'Tis said that the Sessions for the Peace may award Process for the Trial of an Indictment of Felony, the next Day after it is traversed. Quære if the Party's being in Gaol make no Difference?* Cro. Ca 340 2 Roll. Abr. 96 pl. 1. 1 Sid. 335. pl. 20. [q] 1 Keb. 433. pl. 3. 1 Sid. 99, pl. 2. 334 pl. 20, [r] Vide supra, Sect. 1. [s] State Trials, Vol. 4. fol 99, 100. [t] 1 Sid. 348. pl. 15. 2 Keb. 284 pl. 53. 292, pl. 75. 718, pl. 109. 854. pl. 6. *And in these Books such Error is said not to be helped by the next Assises happening to fall on the same Day.* [u] Vide supra, Ch. 5. Sect 6. 13. [x] 1 Sid. 348. pl. 15. 2 Keb. 284 pl. 53 718. pl. 109 854 pl. 6. Cro Ca. 340 [y] Vide Ch. 5 Sect. 11.

Sect. 7. It hath been [a] adjudged, That the Award of a *Venire* returnable at a certain Day before Justices of *Oyer*, *&c.* needs not expresly mention before what Justices it shall be returnable; for it cannot but be intended that it ought to be before the same Court which awards it.

Sect. 8. As to the third Point, *viz.* Where a *Venire* may be joint or several: It seems agreed, That where several Persons are arraigned upon the same [b] Indictment or [c] Appeal, and severally plead not guilty, it is in the [d] Election of the Prosecutor, *&c.* either to take out [e] joint *Venires* against them all, or [f] several against each of them. But in an Appeal, if one plead Not guilty, and the other plead a Release made at *A.* it seems [g] that there must be several *Venires*.

Sect. 9. It seems generally [h] agreed, That where the same Jury is returned on such a Joint Process against several Defendants, if a Juror be challenged by any one Defendant, and the Challenge allowed, and the Juror thereupon [i] drawn, he is by necessary Consequence drawn as to all the other Defendants also, because there being but one Panel, the same Person cannot at the same Time be taken from it, and yet continue in it. But where one Jury is jointly returned for the Trial of several Defendants before Justices of Gaol-Delivery, it is [k] certain that they may afterwards sever the Panel, if they find it expedient, for the Prevention of this Inconvenience. But I do not find [l] that this can be done in any other Case. And it seems agreed, That after an Appellant hath taken out a joint *Venire* against all the Appellees, he cannot [n] afterwards take out several ones, tho' the first be never returned; and the Reason seems to be because it wou'd amount to a [o] Discontinuance.

Sect. 10. As to the fourth Point, *viz.* Where Process may be taken out by the Defendant in Criminal Cases by *Proviso*. (*i. e.* with a [p] Clause that if two Writs come to the Sheriff he shall execute one of them only.) I take it to be agreed, [q] That it may be so awarded in any Appeal, whether Capital or not Capital, in the same Manner as in other Actions, after the Appellant hath made Default in [r] relation to the very same Kind of Process. And therefore if the Appellant, after Issue joined, either neglects to take out any [s] *Venire* the same Term, *&c.* or takes one out but doth not [*] get it returned, it seems that the Defendant may take one out by *Proviso*, *&c.* And in like Manner if the Appellant make the like Default in suing out an *Habeas Corpora*, or other subsequent Process, the Defendant may sue out the like Process by *Proviso*. But where the Defendant hath sued out any Process by *Proviso*, there are [t] Authorities that

[a] 29 Ed. 3. 30. b. 31. a. *In* Dy. 315. pl. 99. *the same Case is taken Notice of, and it is there said, That the* Venire *itself needs not shew before what Justice it is returnable; but this seems not to be warranted by the Book at large.* Vide 2 Keb. 855. pl. 6. [b] H. P. C. 256. [c] State Trials, Vol. 4. fol. 100. H. P. C. 256. S. P. C. 155. a. 1 Jo. 425. *But* Cro. Eliz. 541. pl. 4. *it is said to be the Course to try the Defendants in Appeal by several* Venires. S. P. C. 155. a. *it is said, That where there are three Defendants the Plaintiff may join 2 of them in one* Venire, *and take out another against the third.* [d] *See the Books above-cited. and* 1 Jon. 425. *and* Fitz. Quare impedit, 199. 21 H. 6. 22. pl. 46. [e] *See the Books above-cited. Also the same is adjudged,* 1 Jon. 425. *where one Appellee was charged with doing the Fact* proditorie, *the others* Felonice. *See* Fitz. Quare impedit, 199. Visne, 11, 14. Keilw. 106. b. [f] Dy. 120. pl. 10. 131. pl. 72. Cro. Eliz. 541. pl. 4. [g] 50 E. 3. 1. pl. 1. Bro. Visne 27. Vide 11 H. 7. 5 pl. 9. Bro. Disc. de Process, 62. Fitz. Execut. 114. Nisi prius, 7, 8. [h] S.P.C. 155. a. H. P. C. 256. 9 Ed. 4. 27. pl. 40. Moor, 13. pl. 48. Co. Litt. 156. b. Dyer 246 pl. 70. Plowd. Com. 100. Bro. Challenge, 84. *Parallel Case* Co. Litt. 130. b. 4 H. 4. 4. a. Dyer 246. pl. 70. 50 Ed. 3. 1. pl. 1. Fitz. Protection, 21, 126. 3 H. 4. 5. pl. 24. Crompt. Just. 113. b. pl. 1. *But this is made a Quære* Dyer 152. pl. 8. *and denied in the same Case in* Dalis. 25 pl. 11. [i] *But if no Judgment be given that the Juror who is challenged by one shall be drawn, but only that he shall stand aside for a Time, it is said that he may try those who do not actually challenge him,* Dyer 120. pl. 8. Cont. Bendloes, 58. pl. 95. [k] Kely. 7. H. P. C. 256. Plow. Com. 100. 9 Ed. 4. 27. pl. 40. Crompt. Just. 113. b. pl. 2. [l] Plow. Com. 100. [n] 8 Co. 66. a. S. P. C. 155. Lett. A. 27 H. 6. 4 pl. 28. Fitz. Process, 94, S. P. C. 155. Lett. A. Bro. Venire facias 32. 9 Ed. 4. 27. pl. 40. Fitz. Challenge 56. Vide Fitz. Inquest, 59. Executors, 114. [o] Supra Ch. 27. Sect. 96. [p] 8 H. 6. 6 pl. 14. Fitz. Process, 79. Vide 2 Roll. Ab. 656. B. 1. 2. Rast. Ent. 625. pl. 7. [q] H. P. C. 257. S.P.C. 155. Lett. B. Fitz. Process 211. 15 H. 7. 9. pl. 10. Keilw. 176. pl. 10. [r] *See the Books cited in the other Parts of this Section.* 33 H. 6. 14. a. [s] Dyer 215 pl. 51, 52. Cro. Ca. 484. Vide. Dyer, 284. pl. 34. 3.9 pl. 13. 2 Roll Ab. 666. B. 1. 2. 2 Jon. 38. Keilw. 176. pl. 11. [*] 8 H. 6. 6. pl. 14. Fitz. Process, 79. Bro. Nisi prius, 13. [t] 15 H. 7. 9. pl. 10. 14 H. 7. 7. pl. 16. Fitz. Process, 211. Dyer, 316. pl. [illegible] H. P. C. 257. Cro. Ca. 484. 2 Roll. Ab. 666. pl. 1, 2, 3. 4. Bro. Octo Tales, 8. S. P. C. 71. Lett. A. 155. Lett. G. Dyer, 284. pl. 34. 193. pl. 28. Cont. Fitz. Process, 68. Dyer 215. pl. 51, 52. 217. pl. 51.

the

the Plaintiff is to sue out the proper subsequent Process upon it in the same Manner as if he had sued out the first; and that it is irregular for a Defendant to take out any such subsequent Process till the Plaintiff has made a [a] Default in Respect of the same Kind of Process, except only in such Actions wherein the Defendant is an Actor as well as the Plaintiff, as in [b] Replevin, or [c] Error, or [d] *Quare impedit* against the Patron only, or [e] Prohibition, *&c.* in which Actions the Defendant may either take out Process by *Proviso*, without any Default in the Plaintiff, or [f] may, if he think fit, take it out in the same Manner as the Plaintiff, without any Clause of *Proviso*. But it seems agreed, That neither in Actions wherein the King is sole [g] Party, nor in [h] Indictments, there can be any Process taken out by *Proviso*, because no Laches is imputable to the King. Also it hath been [i] questioned, whether there can be any such Process in Informations *qui tam*, because the King is in some Sort a Party.

As to the fifth Point, *viz.* In what Cases, and in what Manner a *Tales* is grantable, I shall observe the following Particulars.

Sect. 11. 1. That if a full Jury appear not in an Appeal whether by Reason of the [k] Death of some of the Persons returned, or for any other Cause, or if so many be [l] challenged and drawn that there do not remain enow to make a Jury; or if after the Jury is charged, one [m] or more of them die, the Appellant [n] may pray a *Tales*, in the same Manner as a Plaintiff in other Actions. And so also may the Appellee, if the Appellant neglect to pray one the same [o] Term, *&c.* But it seems that a Defendant cannot regularly pray it till there has been a Default in the Plaintiff.

Sect. 12. 2. That in Capital Cases, a *Tales* may be granted for a larger Number than the first Process, as for [p] sixty, or forty, or any other even [q] Number that the Court thinks proper, in order to prevent the Delay, which may be occasioned by the Defendant's peremptory Challenges. And in this Respect the Law in Respect of a *Tales* in Capital Cases is different from what it is in any other Case; it being an allowed Rule, that in all [r] other Cases the *Tales* must be for a less Number than the first Process.

Sect. 13. 3. That every subsequent *Tales*, in Capital as well as in all [s] other Cases, must be for a [t] less Number than the former, except the former were quashed, in which [u] Case the next may be for the same Number.

[a] Dyer 215. pl. 51, 52. Bro Nisi prius, 40. 6 Mod. 246. [b] Dy. 193 pl. 28. 21 H. 6. 22. pl. 2. 16 H. 7. 14. pl. 10. Fitz. Nisi prius, 9. Bro. Nisi prius, 40. [c] 2 Lev. 5, 6. 2 Saund. 336. [d] 6 Mod. 245. Fitz Nisi prius, 6. [e] Par. Case, 2 Roll. Abr. 666. Lett. R. Fitz. Nisi prius, 3. [f] 2 Lev. 5, 6. 16 H. 7. 14. pl. 10. Bro. Nisi prius 40. 21 H. 6, 22. pl. 2. Bro. octo Tales, 17. 2 Saund 336. [g] 2 Leon. 110. [h] 6 Mod. 246, 247. 1 Keb. 195. pl. 184. Cont. 1 Sid. 316. [i] 2 Leon. 110. [k] S. P. C. 155. Lett F. 10 Co. 104 b. H. P. C. 257. 20 Ed. 3. 11. pl. 13. [l] State Trials, Vol. 1. f 502. *and the Books next above cited.* [m] S. P. C. 155 Lett. F. 12 H. 4. 10. a. S. 10 Co. 104. b. *Quære* 2 Rol. Abr. 671. pl. 2. [n] H. P. C. 257. S. P. C. 155. Lett. C. 14 H. 7. 7. pl. 16. [o] Cro. Ca. 484. 14 H. 7 7. pl, 16. 10 Co 104 b. *See the Books cited to the precedent Section, under the Letter* [l] *Yet 'tis said in* Dyer 359. pl. 2. *That if a full Jury do not appear, and the Plaintiff pray a* Distringas *without praying any* Tales, *the Court ought to grant it at the Prayer of the Defendant.* Vide 2 Roll. Abr. 671. N. [p] 14 H 7, 7. pl. 16. H P. C. 257. S. P. C. 155. Lett. C. Finch 415. Bro. octo Tales, 6, 8, 19. Keilw. 176. pl. 10. Dyer 213. pl. 43. 1 Bulst. 121. 15 Ed. 4. 33. pl 19. 16 Ed. 4 5. pl. 3. 10 Co. 104, b. 105. a. [q] 10 Co. 105. a. Finch of Law, 414 *But a* Tales de circumstantibus *may be of any uncertain Number*, 10 Co. 105. a. [r] 14 H 7. 7. pl. 16. Finch of Law, 414. 10 Co. 104, b. 105. a. 2 Roll. Abr. 672. Lett. Q. 37 H. 6. 12. pl. 1. Bro. octo Tales, 11. 16. Fitz. Inquest, 20, 40. 18 Ed. 4. 6 pl. 31. [s] Finch of Law, 414. 2 Roll. Abr. 672. Letters Q S. Bro. octo Tales, 15, 16. Bro. attaint, 7. 10 Co. 105. 47 Ass pl. 10. 14 H. 7. 2. pl. 6 [t] S. P. C. 155. Lett. C. H. P. C. 257. Keilw. 176. pl. 10. 10 Co. 105. a. Fitz. Inquest, 40. *it is said, That there may be* 12 Tales, *but this is contrary to all the other Books.* [u] S. P. C. 155. Lett. C. H. P. C. 257. Fitz. Challenge, 36. 20 H. 6. 38. pl. 2.

Sect. 14. 4. That the quashing the Array of the principal Panel doth [a] not quash that of the *Tales*, but the Inquest shall be taken of those returned on the *Tales* if there be enow, and if not, others shall be added to them by a new *Tales*. Yet it seems [b] agreed, That if all the Persons returned on a *Habeas Corpora*, be challenged and drawn, there shall not be a *Tales* awarded, but a new *Venire facias*; for the Word *Tales* plainly refers to some others, to whom the Persons returned are to be like. Also it seems agreed, [c] That if the first *Habeas Corpora* be quashed, the *Habeas Corpora* with a *Tales* cannot but be quashed with it, and the Party must go on in the same Manner, as if the *Venire* had been only returned, and nothing done upon it; for where a Process is quashed, all that follows it and depends upon it, seems of Course to fall with it.

Sect. 15. 5. That it seems the stronger Opinion, That a *Tales* is not grantable upon the Return of a *Venire*, but only [d] upon the Return of a *Habeas Corpora* or *Distringas*, because it appears not before such Return, but that a full Jury may appear.

Sect. 16. 6. That the [e] *Distringas*, or [f] *Habeas Corpora*, with a Command to add so many more to those summoned on the *Venire*, is the first Process against the *Tales*; but it is [g] said not to be grantable with a *Nisi prius*, without having been first returned into the Court.

Sect. 17. 7. That [h] if a Juror be with-drawn after a Trial is commenced whereon a *Tales de Circumstantibus* was awarded, and afterwards a new *Habeas Corpora* be taken out with a *Tales*, it shall appoint such *Tales* to be added to the Jurors returned on the first *Venire*, and also to those returned on the *Tales de circumstantibus*; because the Court above will take judicial Notice of what is done at *Nisi prius* being entred on Record.

Sect. 18. 8. That the [i] Statutes which authorise Justices of *Nisi prius* to award a *Tales de circumstantibus*, extend [k] as well to all Capital Cases, whether of Treason or Felony, as to others. But it seems that such a *Tales* cannot be prayed for the King upon an Indictment, or Criminal Information, without a [l] Warrant from the Attorney General, or an express [m] Assignment from the Court before which the Inquest is taken. But for the fuller Understanding of these Matters, not being so proper for this Treatise, I shall refer to the Statutes in the Margin.

Sect. 19. 9. That it hath been [n] questioned whether any *Tales* be grantable by Justices of *Oyer* and *Terminer*; and it hath been [o] holden, That it is not grantable by Justices of Gaol-Delivery: And therefore if a Trial before such Justices be put off for Want of a sufficient Number of Jurors, it seems the usual Practise for the Court not to order a *Tales*, but a [p] larger Panel, whereon the former Jurors shall be returned in the same Order as before, and called to be sworn as they stand without any more Regard to those who were sworn before than to the others. Which is the Method likewise to be observed in the like Case, as to the swearing of a Jury returned with a *Tales*.

[a] Fitz. Inquest, 30. S. P. C. 155. Lett. G. Dyer 245. pl. 64. 10. Co. 104. b. 105. a.
[b] S. P. C. 155. Lett. E. Finch, 414.
[c] 34 H. 6. 20. pl 39. Fitz. Inquest, 20.
[d] Cro. Eliz. 502, 503. 27 H. 6. 10. pl. 4 Bro Nisi prius, 1. and Octo Tales 1. 34 H 6. 21. pl. 39. 2 Roll. Abr. 671. O. pl. 2. Cont. Bro. octo Tales, 10. 15 H. 7. 9. pl. 10.
[e] 1 Roll. Ab. 798. pl 9.
[f] 27 H. 6. 10. pl. 4. Bro. Nisi prius, 1. and octo Tales 1.
[g] 27 H. 6. 10. pl. 4. Bro. Nisi prius, 1. and Octo Tales 1. 1 H 5. 11. pl. 22.
S. P. C. 157. a.
[h] Cro. Ja. 677.
[i] 35 H. 8. 6. Par. 6, 7, 8. made perpetual by 2 & 3 Ed. 6. 32. 4 & 5 Ph. & Ma. 7 14 El 9.
[k] Raym. 357. 1 Lev. 223. 1 Keb. 490. pl. 30.
[l] 1 Lev. 223.

[m] *See the Statute of* 14 Eliz. 9. [n] State Trials, Vol. 4. fol. 179 *to* 182. [o] State Trials, Vol. 4. fol 179 *to* 182. *Yet there is an Instance in* Keilw. 176. pl. 10. *of the* Tales *awarded in an Appeal before such Justices and the like was done* Plow. Com. 100. *upon an Indictment of Murder.* [p] State Trials, Vol. 4. fol. 179 *to* 182. [q] Yelv. 23.

Sect. 20, As to the sixth Point, *viz.* Where it is necessary to return a Panel into Court, before an Inquest can be taken upon it, and where the Prisoner may demand a Copy of it. It is recited by 42 *Ed.* 3 11. *That divers Mischiefs had happened, because that the Panels of Inquests which had been taken before Justices by Writ of* Scire facias, *and other Writs, had not been returned before the Sessions of the Justices at the* Nisi prius, *and otherwise, so that the Parties could not have knowledge of the Names of the Persons which should pass in the Inquest, whereby divers of the People had been disherited and oppressed, and thereupon it is ordained that no Inquest* [c] *but Assises and Deliverances of Gaols, be taken by Writ of* Nisi prius, *nor in any other Manner, at the Suit of the Great or Small, before the Names of all them that shall pass in the Inquest, be returned in the Court.*

Sect. 21. It seems [f] agreed, That this Statute extends as well to Writs of *Nisi prius* in Criminal Cases as in Civil, and to [g] Jurors returned upon a *Tales* as well as to those returned upon a Principal Panel.

Sect. 22. But it seems [h] that in Trials before Justices of Gaol-Delivery the Prisoner has no Right to a Copy of the Panel before the Time of his Trial, except only in Cases within the Purview of 7 & 8 *W.* 3. 3. which enacts, *That every Person indicted and tried for High Treason, or Misprision thereof (except it be for counterfeiting the Coin,* &c.) *shall have a Copy of the Panel of the Jurors, who are to try him, duly returned by the Sheriff, and delivered unto him two Days at least before he shall be tried.*

Sect. 23. It hath been [i] adjudged to be sufficient within the Intent of this Act to deliver to a Prisoner a Copy of a Panel array'd by the Sheriff before it is returned into Court, if the very same Panel be afterwards returned.

c *Note that* 6 H. 6. ch. 2. *provides also for Assises*, 3 Inst 175.

f S.P.C. 156, 157.

g H. P. C. 258. *Quære, If the Statute extend to Justices of* Oyer *and* Terminer, *for it is said to be the Practice for Trials before them for Treason to be on the* Venire *and not to award any* Habeas Corpora. St. Trials, Vol. 4. fol. 102.

h State Trials, Vol. 2. fol 762. Vol. 3. fol. 4. 856, 867 Vol. 4. fol. 6.

i State Trials, Vol. 4. fol. 101 *to* 104.

CHAP.

CHAP. XLII.

Before what Court the Jury is to be returned.

Sect. 1. AND now I am to consider before what Court the Process against Jurors in Criminal Cases is returnable: As to which there can be no [a] Doubt but that by the Common Law it is returnable only into the Court wherein the Prosecution was depending.

Sect. 2. But the Statute of [b] *Westm.* 2. *Ch.* 30. having ordained that all Pleas in either Bench, which require only an easy Examination, shall be determined in the Country before the Justices of Assise, by Vertue of the Writ prescribed by that Statute, commonly called the Writ of *Nisi prius*, it seems to have been universally agreed, [c] That an issue joined in the King's Bench upon an [d] Indictment or [e] Appeal, whether for Treason or [f] Felony, or a Crime of an inferior [g] Nature, committed in a different County from that wherein the Court sits, may be tried in the proper County by Writ of *Nisi prius* by Vertue of the said Statute.

Sect. 3. Yet inasmuch as the King is not expressly named in this Statute, and it is a general Rule, That he shall not be bound by a Statute which doth not expressly name him; it seems to have been generally holden, That where-ever the King is a Party it is irregular to grant a Trial by *Nisi prius* without his [h] special Warrant, or the [i] Assent of his Attorney. But I do not find it denied, [k] but that regularly the Court may grant it in an [l] Appeal in the same Manner as in any other Action.

Sect. 4. Having shewn already, *Ch.* 7. *Sect.* 17, 18. and *Ch.* 23. *Sect.* 141, the 2d. that Justices of *Nisi prius* have Power by 14 *H.* 6. 1. to give Judgment in Felony and Treason, and how far they have Power to give Damages in an Appeal, and having also shewn *Ch.* 25. from *Sect.* 7 *to* 14. in what Cases they may arraign an Appellee at the Suit of the King, after a Nonsuit of the Party, I shall refer to what is there said concerning these Matters.

[a] Vide 4 Inst. 159.

[b] 2 Inst. 421, 423, 424. Cro. Ca. 349.

[c] 2 Inst. 424. 4 Inst. 160. *See the Books cited to the other Parts of this Section.*

[d] Bro. Coro. 231.

[e] 4 Co. 43. pl. 9. 4 Inst. 160. Dy. 46. pl 8. 261. pl. 26. 21 H. 7. 34. pl 35. Rast. Ent. 47. a. 55. a. Vide supra, Ch. 7. Sect. 18. Ch. 23. Sect. 141, 201.

[f] Bro. Coro. 231. 4 Inst. 160. Raym. 367.

[g] Cro. Ca. 348, 349. 6 Mod. 246, 247.

[h] Fitz. Nisi prius, 16. 2 Leon. 110. 2 Inst. 424. F. N. B. 241. Lett. A. Bro. Nisi prius, 16.

[i] 2 Inst. 424. F. N. B. 241. Lett. A. Crompt. Jurisf. 211. b. 6 Mod. 246, 247. S. P. C. 156. Letter A. H. P. C. 258. *In* Cro. Ca. 348, 349. *In an Indictment of Barretry, which seemed to require great Examination, the Court refused to grant a Trial by* Nisi prius *at the Motion of the Attorney General, till the King by his Letters, had signified his Pleasure that it should be so tried.* Vide 6 Mod. 123.

[k] *But not where the Jury is to be from two Counties,* Dy. 46. pl. 6.

[l] *See the Books cited to the precedent Section under Letter. e.*

CHAP.

CHAP. XLIII.

Of Challenges.

AND now I am to shew in what Manner the Jurors returned for the Trial of a Criminal may be challenged, which I shall consider,

1. So far as it relates to all Persons in general.
2. With Regard to Aliens only.

Sect. 1. As to the Learning of this Kind, so far as it relates to all Persons in general, having premised that no Challenge [a] can be taken, either to the Array or to the Polls, till a full Jury have appeared; and that no Juror can be [b] challenged either by the King or Prisoner, without [c] Consent, after he hath been sworn, whether on the same Day, or (according to the greater Number of [d] Authorities,) on a former, on the same Trial, unless it be for some Cause which happened [e] since he was sworn, I shall endeavour to shew,

1. How Jurors may be challenged on the Part of the King.
2. How on the Part of the Prisoner.

Sect. 2. And first, as to such Challenges on the Part of the King: It seems [f] agreed, That by the Common Law the King might challenge peremptorily as many as he thought fit, of any Jury returned to try any Cause in which he was a Party. But this is remedied by 33 *Ed.* 1. commonly called an Ordinance for Inquests, which is enacted as followeth, *Of Inquests to be taken before any of the Justices, and wherein our Lord the King, is Party, howsoever it be: It is agreed and ordained by the King and all his Counsel, that from henceforth, notwithstanding it be alledged by them that sue for the King, that the Jurors of those Inquests, or some of them be not indifferent for the King, yet such Inquests shall not remain untaken for that Cause, but if they that sue for the King will challenge any of those Jurors, they shall assign of their Challenge a Cause certain, and the Truth of the same Challenge shall be inquired of according to the Custom of the Court.*

[a] Hob. 235. [b] Yelv. 23. Cro. Ca. 291. Co. Litt 158. a. 22 Ed. 3. 8. pl. 20. 2 Roll Abr. 658. pl. 5, 6, 7, 8, 9. 659. pl. 4, 5. 661. Lett. Q. 12 H. 4. 10. a. Fitz. Challenge, 64. 14 H. 7. 6. pl. 13. Bro. Challenge 73. 9 H. 5. 7. pl. 21. *Abridged* Fitz. Challenge 72. Bro. Challenge, 50. 14 H. 7. 19. pl. 8. *Abridged* Bro. Challenge 75. State Trials, Vol. 3. fol. 379. *Neither can a Challenge be taken to the Array after any of the Jurors are sworn.* Hob. 235. [c] Cro. Ca. 291. State Trials, Vol. 3. fol. 379. [d] 22 Ed. 3. 8. pl. 20. 2 Roll. Ab. 658. pl. 5, 6, 7, 8. 659. pl. 4, 5. 661. Lett. Q. 12 H. 4. 10. a. 14 H. 7. 6. pl. 14. Bro. Challenge 50, 73, 130. Fitz. Challenge, 143. 28 Ass. pl. 44. Yelv. 23. *Yet adjudged, That a Juror after he is sworn may be peremptorily challenged another Day, tho' not on the same wherein he is sworn* 32 H. 6. 26. pl. 14. *Abridged* Bro. Challenge, 193. 14 H. 7. 19. pl. 8. *Abridged* Bro. Challenge, 75. S. P. C. 158. 2 Rich 3. 19. pl. 34. *Abridged* Bro. Challenge, 194. [e] 22 Ed. 3. 8. pl. 20. Yelv. 23. 2 Roll. Abr. 658. pl. 5, 6, 7, 8, 9. Bro. Challenge, 130. 28 Ass. pl. 44. Co. Litt. 158 a. 14 H. 7. 6 pl. 14. Bro. Challenge 50, 73, 75. Fitz. Challenge, 64, 72, 143. [f] Co. Litt. 156 b. H. P. C. 259. S. P. C. 162. Lett. A. 2 Roll. Ab. 645. X. pl. 2, 3.

Sect. 3. It seems to be clearly settled [a] at this Day, That this Statute being general, extends as well to all criminal as civil Causes: However if the King challenge a Juror before the Panel is perused, it is [b] agreed that he needs not shew any Cause of his Challenge till the whole Panel be gone thro', and it appear that there will not be a full Jury without the Person so challenged. And if the Defendant, in order to oblige the King to shew Cause, presently challenge *touts paravaile* [c], yet it hath been adjudged that the Defendant shall be first put to shew all his Causes of Challenge, before the King need to shew any.

Sect. 4. As to the second Point, *viz.* How Jurors may be challenged on the Part of the Prisoner: Having premised that a [d] Peer can take no Challenge to any of his Peers; and that where several are tried on a joint [e] *Venire*, a Juror challenged and drawn as to one, cannot but be drawn as to all, I shall farther endeavour to shew,

1. How Jurors may be challenged peremptorily.
2. How they may be challenged for Cause.

As to the first Particular, *viz.* How Jurors may be challenged peremptorily, having premised that the Prisoner must take all such Challenges himself, [f] even in such Cases wherein he may have Counsel, I shall endeavour to shew,

1. In what Cases a peremptory Challenge is allowable.
2. How many Jurors may be so challenged.

Sect. 5. As to the first Particular, I take it to be agreed, That a peremptory Challenge was allowable by the Common Law, in all [g] capital Cases both upon Indictments and [h] Appeals, and also in [i] Misprision of High Treason; but it was enacted by 33 *H.* 8. 23. *Par.* 3. *That it should not be allowed in any Cases of High Treason, nor Misprision of High Treason.* Nor do I know that any Statute hath revived it as to the latter of these; for it is said that the Statute of 1 *Ph. & M.* 10. which by restoring the old Course of the Common Law as to Trials of Treason, has revived [k] such Challenge as to Treason, doth not [l] extend to Misprision of High Treason.

Sect. 6. It hath been anciently [m] adjudged, and is holden both by [n] *Staundforde* and [o] *Coke*, That a Man shall have the same peremptory Challenges on an Issue joined upon collateral Matter alledged in Avoidance of an Outlawry for a capital Crime, as he may on the general Issue: But the contrary is holden by [p] *Hale*, and is said to have been [q] adjudged in the Case of *Okey* and *Barkstead*.

Sect. 7. As to the second Particular, *viz.* How many Jurors may be challenged peremptorily: It seems to have been the settled [r] Rule of the Common Law, where-ever such Challenge was allowed, to suffer the

[a] Moor. 595. pl. 869. S. P. C. 162. Lett. A. H P. C. 259. Co. Litt. 159. b. *and the Books cited to other Parts of of this Section. Yet premptory Challenges were taken for the Queen in* Throckmorton's *Trial*, 1 Mar. State Trials Vol. 1. fol. 48.
[b] 1 Ventr. 309, 310. S. P. C. 162. Lett. A. State Trials, Vol. 2. 744. Vol 3. fol. 52. 869. H. P. C. 259.
[c] State Trials Vol. 3. fol. 52. Raym. 473, 474. *See* State Trials, Vol. 3. f. 4. Vol. 4. f. 177, 407.
[d] Rushw. Collections, 2 V. 1. f. 94. Moor 621, 622. Co. Litt. 156. b. State Trials, Vol. 1. fol. 164, 265. Trial per pais Ch. 9.
[e] Supra, Ch. 41. Sect. 9.
[f] State Trials, Vol. 4. f. 105. Vol. 1. fol. 601. V. 2. fol. 743, 744.
[g] Co. Litt. 156. b. Moor 12, pl. 46.
[h] Moor, 12. pl. 46. Bendl. 42. pl. 77. 9 H. 5. 7. pl. 21. *Abridged* Fitz. Challenge 72. Bro. Challenge, 50. 14 H. 7. 7. pl. 16. Bro. Challenge, 74, 75, 211. 3 H. 7. 2 pl. 5.
[i] 3 Inst. 27. *But in no other Case that is not Capital.* State Trials, Vol. 2. fol. 254.
[k] 3 Inst. 227. S. P. C. 157 Lett B 158. 1 And. 107, 108. Co. Litt. 156. b. State Trials, Vol. 2. fol. 764, &c. *But this is made a Quære* Savil, 57.
[l] Supra, Ch. 25. Sect. 145. *Yet* 3 Inst. 27. a. *it is said that for Misprision of Treason one may peremptorily challenge* 35.
[m] Fitz. Challenge, 153, 165.
[n] S. P. C. 163. Lett. A. *Yet the same Point is made a Quære,* S. P. C. 158.
[o] Co. Litt. 157. b.
[p] H P C. 259.
[q] 1 Lev. 61. *But the other Books which report the same Case take no Notice of this Point.* 1 Sid 72. Kely. 13.
[r] Co. Litt. 156. b. Crompt. Just. 114. pl. 4. 9 H. 5. 7. pl. 21. 14 H. 7. 7. pl. 16. Bro. Challenge, 70, 74, 75, 217. 19 Ed. 4. 33. b. 3 H. 7. 2. pl. 5. *Abridged* Bro. Challenge 211. 17 Ass. pl. 6. 17 Ed. 3. 23. pl. 8 *Abridged* Bro. Challenge 105. Trial per pais, Ch 9. S. P. C. 157, b. 158. *See the Books cited,* Ch. 30. Sect 2. Lamb. B. 4. Ch. 14. *says That it was doubtful at Common Law how many might be challenged.*

Prisoner to challenge as many as he thought fit under the Number of three full Juries, *i. e.* not amounting to more than thirty-five. But if a Criminal challenge more than that Number, [a] it seems the more prevailing Opinion that he is to be dealt with as one that stands Mute.

Sect. 8. It is enacted by 22 *H.* 8. 14. *Par.* 7. made perpetual by 32 *H.* 8. 3. *That no Person arraigned for any Petit Treason, Murder or Felony, be admitted to any peremptory Challenge above the Number of twenty.* But it seems [b] agreed, That 1 & 2 *Ph. & Ma.* 10. which restores the Course of the Common Law as to Trials of Treason, has revived the old Challenge of 35 in Trials of Petit Treason.

Sect. 9. It seems to have been holden by Sir [c] *Edward Coke*, That he who challenges more than twenty upon an Arraignment of Felony, since the above-mentioned Statute of 22 *H.* 8. shall [d] neither forfeit his Goods, nor have Judgment of Death, nor of *pain fort & dure*, but shall only be over-ruled as to his Challenges so far as they exceed twenty, and put upon his Trial. But this seems to have been doubted by Sir *Matthew* [e] *Hale*, and the contrary is holden by [f] *Crompton*, and seems more agreeable to the most natural Construction of 22 *H.* 8. which seems to have intended no Alteration as to the Nature or Effect of peremptory Challenges, but only as to their Number. To which may be added, That nothing is more Common than for [g] subsequent Statutes which take from Felons the the Benefit of the Clergy, [h] expresly to exclude those who challenge more than twenty, which would be needless if their Challenge were only to be over-ruled, and did not subject them to Judgment of [i] Death, &c.

Sect. 10. As to the second Particular, *viz.* How Jurors may be challenged for Cause, having premised that it is a [k] general Rule, That where-ever [l] the King is a Party, as he is in every [m] Indictment, and in some Sort also in [n] Appeals of Felony, he who takes a Challenge for Cause must shew it presently, and shall not have Time till the Panel is perused, as the King shall where he takes a Challenge, as hath been more fully shewn, *Sect.* 3. and having also farther premised that after a Prisoner hath challenged a Juror for Cause, and his Cause hath been disallowed, or found against him, he may [o] challenge the same Juror peremptorily, before he is [p] sworn, I shall endeavour to shew,

1. What shall be a good Challenge of a Juror, in Respect of his Honour or Insufficiency.
2. What in Respect of his Unindifferency.

And first as to the Challenge of a Juror for his Honour or Insufficiency; having premised that it is agreed to be a good Challenge of this Kind that a Juror is an [q] Alien, [r] Minor, or [s] Villain, I shall more fully endeavour to shew,

[a] Supra, Ch. 30. Sect. 2.
[b] Bro. Challenge, 217. H. P. C. 260. 3 Inst. 227. Vide supra, Sect. 5. *and* Ch. 25. Sect. 134, 146.
S. P. C. 158. a. Co. Litt. 156. b.
[c] 3 Inst. 227.
[d] Vide Ch. 30. Sect. 19. Staund. Prer. 46. a.
[e] H. P. C. 260.
[f] Crompton's Just. 114 pl. 4.
[g] Supra, Ch. 33. Sect. 32, 45, 48, 59, 64, 66, 69, &c.
[h] Vide supra, Ch. 33. Sect. 27, 36.
11 Co. 31, a. 32, a. 35. b. S. P. C. 126. Lett. A.
[i] Vide Ch. 33. Sect. 20.
[k] Co. Litt. 158. a. Fitz. Challenge 128. State Trials, Vol. 3. f. 235. S. P. C. 162. Letter C. 2 Roll. Abr. 659. pl. 6, 7, 8. 38 Ass. pl. 22. 1 Sid. 244. Cont. 19 Ass. pl. 6. *Abridged* Bro. Challenge, 107.
[l] *Except in Inquests*, Fitz. Challenge, 105, 107. 2 Roll. Abr. 659. pl. 9. 660 N. 2.
[m] *That Cause must be shewn presently on Indictments.* Co. Litt. 158. a. 1 Sid. 244. 1 H. 5. pl. 1. *Abridged* Fitz. Challenge, 70
[n] *That Cause must be shewn presently in Appeals.* Co. Litt. 158. a. *This is left a Quære* S. P. C. 162 Lett. D.
[o] Co. Litt 158. a. 37 H 6. 8 pl. 17, *Abridged* Fitz. Challenge, 48. Bro. Challenge, 86. Cont. 10 H. 4, 9. pl. 7. *Abridged* Fitz. Challenge, 180.
[p] Vide supra, Sect. 1.
[q] Co. Litt. 156. b. Theloal B. 1. ch. 6. Sect. 14. 14 H. 4. 19. pl, 23. Bro Challenge, 48. Fitz. Challenge, 91. 2 Roll. Abr. 656. pl. 2. Calvin's Case, 18. b.
[r] Co. Litt. 157. b. 172. b. Litt. Sect. 259.
[s] 2 Roll. Abr. 657. pl. 1. Co. Litt. 156. b. 9 Ed. 4. 16. pl. 16. 26 Ass. pl. 28. F. Challenge 135. Bro. Challenge, 64, 118. *But the contrary is holden in the Year-Book of* 10 H. 7. 20. *Abridged* Bro. Challenge, 220. *and a Quære by the Reporter and* Brook.

1. Where Peerage is a good Cauſe of Challenge.
2. Where the Want of Freehold.
3. Where Infamy.
4. Whether old Age, Sickneſs, or Non-Reſidence in the County be in any Caſe a good Cauſe of Challenge.

Sect. 11. As to the firſt Particular, *viz.* Where Peerage is a good Cauſe of Challenge, it is [a] agreed, That if a Peer be returned on a Jury and bring a Writ of Privilege, he ſhall be diſcharged. Alſo it ſeems to have been [b] holden, That even without ſuch a Writ he may either challenge himſelf, or be challenged by the Party. *Quære.*

Sect. 12. As to the ſecond Particular, *viz.* Where the Want of Freehold is a good Cauſe of Challenge: It ſeems to be admitted by the Statute of 21 E. 1. *de his qui ponendi ſunt in Aſſiſis*, and alſo by the Regiſter, That at the Common Law there was no [c] neceſſity that Jurors ſhou'd have any Freehold as to Inqueſts before Juſtices in *Eyre*, or in Cities or Burghs, as hath been more fully ſhewn, *Chap.* 25. *Sect.* 20. Alſo it ſeems [d] agreed, That the Common Law doth not require that a Juror ſhould in any Caſe have a Freehold of any certain Value; and upon this Ground it hath been adjudged, That a Freehold worth but [e] 20*s.* or [f] 5 *s.* or even a [g] Penny, is ſtill a ſufficient Qualification for a Juror in ſuch Caſes as are not within the Statutes which require a Freehold of a greater Value. Alſo it hath been [h] adjudged, That the Common Law did not require that a Juror ſhould in any Caſe have any Freehold. But this is not only contrary to what ſeems implied by all the Authorities above-cited, which in ſaying that the Common Law did not require a Freehold of any certain Value, plainly ſeem to ſuppoſe that it required ſome Freehold, but hath been alſo contradicted by many expreſs [i] Authorities; agreeably to which it ſeems to be [k] ſettled at this Day, That the Want of Freehold is a good Challenge of a Juror in all Caſes not otherwiſe provided for by [l] Statute, and conſequently in a Trial for High Treaſon in *London* as well as in any other County.

Sect. 13. But it ſeems agreed, That where-ever the Letter of the Common or Statute Law require that a Juror ſhould have a Freehold, the Meaning is fully ſatisfied, by his having the [m] Uſe of a Freehold; and that it is not material whether he have it in his own or his [n] Wife's Right, or whether it be [o] Abſolute or upon Condition, or an Eſtate of Inheritance, or only [p] for Term of one's own or another's Life, ſo that it be in the ſame [q] County, wherein the Suit is brought, and actually continue in the Juror [r] till the Time when he is ſworn.

[a] 48 Aſſ pl. 6. 48 Ed. 3. 30. pl. 18. Bro. Challenge, 18, 37, 209. Dy. 314. pl. 98. 35 H. 6. 46. pl. 8. Moor, 767. Regiſt. 179. F. N. B. 165. E. 166.

[b] 22 E. 3. 18. pl. 75. Fitz. Challenge, 119. 2 Roll. Abr. 646. Y. 1, 2. *but his Notes are not warranted by the Books at large.* Co. Litt. 157. b. 9 Co. 49. 27 H. 8. 22. pl. 18. Cont. 35 H. 6. 46. pl. 8. Bro. Challenge, 8. Finch of Law 506. 6 Co. 53. a. Fitz. Challenge, 44. 1 Jon. 153. F. N. B. 166.

[c] Vide Raym. 485, 486. 1 Vent. 366. Infra, Sect. 21.

[d] Keilw. 46. pl. 2 54, pl. 19. 92. pl. 5. Cro. El. 413. *See the Citations to the next three Letters, and* Litt. Sect 464 *and* 2 Rol. Abr. 647, 648.

[e] 10 H. 6. 7. pl. 24. *Abridged* Fitz. Challenge, 29. Bro. Challenge, 189. 19 H. 6, 9. pl. 21. *Abridged* Fitz. Challenge, 32. Bro. Challenge, 60. 2 H. 7, 13. pl. 17. Bro. Challenge, 152. 10 H 6. 18. pl. 59. Bro. Challenge, 192.

[f] 3 H. 4, 4 pl. 14. *Abridged* Fitz. Challenge, 78. Bro. Chall. 32.

[g] Keilw. 46 pl. 2.

[h] 28 Aſſ. pl 15. *Abridged* Bro. Challenge, 106. 10 H. 7. 13. pl. 7. State Trials, Vol. 3. f. 135 *to* 140. Vide 16 H. 7. 14. pl. 10. 7 H. 6. 44. pl. 23. *Abridged* Fitz. Challenge, 24. Bro. Challenge, 57. *It ſeems to be holden that by Common Law it is a Challenge only to the Favour.*

[i] Cro. Eliz. 413. pl. 4. Trial per pais, ch. 9. 3 H. 4. 4. pl. 14. *Abridged* Fitz. Challenge, 78. Bro. Challenge, 32. 4 H. 4. 1. pl. 2. Vide Keilw. 54. pl. 14. Co. Litt 156. b. 157. a. 2 Roll. Abr. 647. pl. 9, 10. 7 H. 4. 1. pl. 4. *Abridged* Bro. Challenge 34. Fitz. Challenge, 58. 21 H. 7. 29. pl. 10. *Abridged* Bro. Challenge, 90. 10 H. 7, 11. pl. 30. *It ſeems taken for granted that Iſſues in all Caſes are to be returned upon Juroos, by which it ſeems to be implied that they ought to have Land,* &c.

[k] State Trials, Vol. 3. 869. Vol. 4. fol. 874.

[l] Vide infra, Sect. 19, *&c.*

[m] Keilw. 46, pl. 2. 92. pl. 5. Dyer 9. pl. 26. Fitz. Challenge 27. 13 H. 7, 7 b. 5 Ed. 4, 7. pl. 15. Bro. Challenge, 165. Co. Litt. 272. Plow. Com. 58. a. 15 H. 7. 13. b. S. P. C. 160. Lett. b. Bro. Jurors, 14

[n] Fitz. Challenge 27. 9 H. 7. 1. pl. 2. Bro. Challenge, 157. 12 H. 7. 4 pl. 2. Bro Challenge 160. Co. Litt. 156. b.

[o] Co. Litt. 156. b. Keilw. 167, 168. 2 Roll. Abr. 648. pl. 20. Cont. 7 H 4. 1. pl. 4. Fitz. Challenge, 158. *But* Bro. *in abridging this Caſe in Title* Challenge, 34 *ſays* quod mirum.

[p] 9 H. 7. 1. pl. 2. 12 H. 7. 4. pl. 2. Bro. Challenge, 160. Co. Litt. 156. b. Bro. Challenge, 157. *See* F. N. B. 14. Lett. e. 166. Lett. f.

[q] 9 H. 7. 1. pl. 2. Bro. Challenge, 157. Co. Litt. 157. a. Raſt. Ent. 118. b. 19 H. 6. 9. pl, 21.

[r] 12 H. 7. 4. pl. 2. Bro. Challenge, 160. Co. Litt. 157. a. 7 H. 4, 1. pl. 4. *Abridged*, Fitz. Challenge, 158.

Sect.

Sect. 14 It is enacted by the [a] Statutes of *Westminster*, 2. 38. and 21 *Ed.* 1. *de his qui ponendi sunt in Assisis*, that none shall be put in Assises or Juries, except in Cities, Burghs, or trading Towns, who have not Tenements to the yearly Value of 40 *s. &c.* But it seems to have been [*] generally agreed that a Juror can neither be challenged by the Parties for being returned contrary to these Acts, nor alledge such Matter himself for his Discharge, but must take his Remedy by Action against the Sheriff, or by Writ of Privilege for his Discharge.

Sect. 15. It is farther enacted by 2 *H.* 5. 3. *That no Person shall be admitted to pass in any Inquest upon Trial of the Death of a Man, nor in any Inquest betwixt Party or Party in Plea real, nor in Plea personal, whereof the Debt or the Damage declared amount to forty Marks, if the same Person have not Lands or Tenements of the yearly Value of forty Shillings, above all Charges of the same; so that it be challenged by the Party, that any such Person so impanelled in the same Cases, hath not Lands or Tenements of the yearly Value of forty Shillings above the Charges as afore is said.*

Sect. 16. It hath been [c] adjudged, That this Statute extends as well to a Collateral Issue, as to the General one, but not to an Indictment or Information for a Crime not [d] Capital, for the Words are, *Upon Trial of the Death of a Man, nor in any Inquest between Party and Party in Plea real or Personal*, &c.

Sect. 17. It seems [e] agreed, That a *Cestuy que use* of any Freehold in the same County, of the yearly Value of 40 *s.* is a good Juror within this Statute. And some have [f] holden, That the Law is the same as to a Feoffee of such Land in Trust for another, or a [g] Remainder Man of a State of Freehold expectant on a Lease for Years. But this seems not to be maintainable, because the Statute in requiring that a Juror shall have Lands of the yearly Value of 40 *s.* above all Charges, plainly seems to intend that he ought to have Lands of the clear [h] Income whereof at the Time he can expend so much. But a Man cannot expend any Thing out of Lands whereof he is infeoffed to the Use of another, or wherein he has only a dry Remainder.

Sect. 18. It hath been [i] adjudged, That this Statute is repealed as to Treasons by 1 [k] *&* 2 *Ph. & Ma.* 10. which enacts that all Trials for Treason shall be according to the Common Law.

Sect. 19. It is recited by 23 *H.* 8. 13. *That Trials in Murders and Felonies in Cities, Boroughs, and Towns corporate within this Realm having Authority to proceed in the Deliverance of such Offenders, had been oftentimes deferred and delayed, by Reason of Challenge of such Offenders, for lack of Sufficiency of Freehold, to the great hindrance of Justice.* And thereupon it is enacted, *That every Person and Persons being the King's natural Subject born, which either by the Name of a Citizen, or of a Freeman, or any other Name, doth enjoy and use the Liberties and Privileges of any City, Borough or Town corporate where he dwelleth or maketh his Abode, being worth in movable Goods and Substance to the clear Value of forty Pounds, be admitted in Trial of Murders and Felonies in every Sessions and Gaol-Delivery, to be kept and holden in and for the Liberty of such Cities, Boroughs, and Towns Corporate, albeit they have no Freehold; any Act, Statute, Use, Custom or Ordinance to the contrary hereof notwithstanding.*

Sect. 20. *Provided that this Act no way extend to any Knight or Esquire, dwelling, abiding, or resorting in or to any such City*, &c.

[a] Vide supra, Ch. 25. Sect. 29, 20 21.

[*] 2 Inst. 448. 28 Ass. pl. 15. *Abridged* Bro. Challenge, 106. 3 H. 4. 4 pl. 14. *Abridged* Bro. Challenge 32. Fitz. Challenge, 78. F. N. B. 166, State Trials, Vol. 2 fol. 744. *But* 38 Ass. pl. 19. *is contrary.*

[c] Keilw. 92. pl. 5. 16 H. 7. 14. pl. 10. 2 Rol. Abr. 647, 648.

[d] Cro Eliz. 413. pl. 4. Raym. 485, 486.

[e] Vide supra, Sect. 13.

[f] Keilw. 92. pl. 5. *and* Bro. Challenge, 202. Jurors, 14. *in an Abridgment of the Year-Book of* 15 H. 7. 13. pl. 1. *but I do not find this Point in the Book at large.*

[g] Keilw. 168. pl. 2.

[h] Vide Keil. 92. a. 18 Ed. 4, 13. pl. 8. 19 H. 6. 9. pl. 21. Fitz. Challenge, 32. 36 H. 6, 23. pl. 16. 2 Roll. Abr. 647, pl, 11, 648, pl. 28, 649 pl. 29.

[i] State Trials, Vol. 3. f. 135 *to* 140.

[k] Vide ch 25. Sect. 134, 144, 145, 146.

Sect. 21. Also special Provision is made by 11 *H.* 7. 21. and 4 *H.* 8. 3. for Jurors in *London* in real and personal Actions above the Value of forty Marks, for which I shall refer to the Statutes at Large.

Sect. 22. It is enacted by 4 *&* 5 *Will. & M.* 24. *That all Jurors* (*other than Strangers upon Trials* per medietatem linguæ) *who are to be returned for Trials of Issues joined, in any of the Courts of King's Bench, Common Pleas or Exchequer, or before Justices of Assise or* Nisi prius, Oyer *and* Terminer, *Gaol-Delivery, or General Quarter-Sessions of the Peace in any County of this Realm of* England, *shall every of them have in their own Name, or in Trust for them within the same County, ten Pounds by the Year at least above Reprises, of Freehold or Copyhold Lands or Tenements, or of Lands or Tenements of ancient* [a] *Demesne, or in Rents, or in all or any of the said Lands, Tenements, or Rents, in Fee-simple, Fee-tail, or for the Life of themselves, or some other Person; and that in every County in* Wales *every such Juror shall have in the same County six Pounds by the Year at least, in Manner aforesaid above Reprises.*

Sect. 23. But it is provided *that it shall be lawful to return any Person on a* Tales *in* England, *who shall have five Pounds by the Year, or in* Wales, *who shall have three Pounds by the Year, in Manner aforesaid.*

Sect. 24. Also there is a Saving to all [b] Cities, Boroughs, and Towns Corporate, of their ancient Usage of returning Jurors of such Estate, and in such Manner as before had been used and accustomed. But there is no express Saving of any Trial contrary to the Purview of this Statute and made good by some other; and therefore it may be argued that the Trial of Felonies in Towns by Jurors worth 40 *l.* in Goods by Vertue of the above-cited Statute of 23 *H.* 8. is no longer lawful, it not being a Trial by Usage, but by Statute. Yet seeing 4 *&* 5 *Gul. & Mar.* seems plainly to have a View to Trials in Counties only, and the Statute of 16 *&* 17 *Ca.* 2, 3. which is penned almost in the very same Words, was taken [c] no way to alter the former Method of Trials in Towns, lest it should cause a Failer of Justice; and it being generally impracticable to get a sufficient Number of such Freeholders as the Statute requires in Towns, it seems a reasonable Construction of 4 *&* 5 *W. & M.* That the Trial by 23 *H.* 8. still continues lawful as before. But it hath been [d] agreed, That for Trials in *London* for High Treason, every Juror ought to have such Freehold or Copyhold as is required by 4 *&* 5 *Wil. & Ma.*

Sect. 25. As to the third Particular, *viz.* Where Infamy is a good Cause of Challenge, it seems that it is a good Challenge of a Juror that he is [e] outlawed, or that he hath been [f] adjudged to any corporal Punishment whereby he becomes infamous, or that he hath been convicted of Treason, or [g] Felony, or [h] Perjury, or [i] Conspiracy, or of [k] Forgery on 5 *Eliz.* 14. or attainted in an [l] Attaint for giving a false Verdict. And it hath been [m] holden that such Exceptions are not salved by a Par-

[a] *But by the Common Law a Freehold in Ancient Demesne was not sufficient.* 9 H. 7, 1. pl. 2. Bro. Challenge, 157. Co. Litt. 156. b.

[b] Vide supra, Sect. 12. *and there is the like Exception in* 27 Eliz. 6. Par. 7. *and in* 16 *&* 17 Ca. 2, 3. Par. 4.

[c] 1 Vent. 366.

[d] State Trials, Vol. 4. f. 186. *and in* Francia's *Trial.*

[e] Co. Litt. 158. a. 21 H. 6, 30. pl. 17. 11 H. 4, 41. pl. 8. Bro. Indictment 2. 2 Rol. Abr. 657. pl. 3. Bro. Challenge, 64. Fitz. Process, 208. Cro. Ca 134. Trials per pais, ch. 9. [f] Co Litt. 6, b. 156. a. Trials per pais ch. 9. [g] Co. Litt 6 b. 158. a. 2 Bulst. 154 State Trials Vol. 2. fol. 521 *to* 524. Trials per pais, ch. 9. Cont. 1 Lev. 263. [h] Bract. Lib. 4 cap. 19. Sect. 2 Fleta lib. 4. cap. 8. Sect. 2. Trials per pais, ch. 9. [i] *See* B. 1. ch. 72. Sect. 9 Co. Litt. 6. b. 158. a. *it seems to be holden, That the Conviction for Conspiracy ought to be at the King's Suit.* *But* 33 H. 6 55. pl. 45. Bro. Challenge, 15. Fitz. Challenge, 41. *make no such Distinction.* [k] C. Litt. 6. b *and the Reason seems to be because the Statute is express that the Offender shall be set on the Pillory,* &c. *but it was adjudged,* 33 H 6. 55. pl. 45. *Abridged* Fitz. Challenge, 41. Bro. Challenge 15. 2 Roll. Abr. 649. pl. 5. *That a Conviction on* 1 H. 5. 3. *was not a good Challenge to a Juror, because it was not a Conviction on an Action at the Common Law.* Vide 44 Ed. 3. 39. pl. 39. Fitz. decies tantum, 11, 12. [l] *See the Authorities under the precedent Letter.* [m] State Trials, Vol. 2. f. 521 *to* 524. 2 Bulst. 154 Vide sup. ch. 37. S. 48 *to* 53.

don. And it was anciently [a] holden that Excommunication was alſo a good Challenge. Yet it [b] ſeems that none of the above-cited Challenges are principal ones, but only to the Favour, unleſs the Record of the Outlawry, Judgment or Conviction be produced, if it be a Record of another Court, or the Term, *&c.* be ſhewn, if it be a Record of the ſame Court.

Sect. 26. As to the fourth Particular, *viz*, Whether old Age, or Sickneſs, or Non-reſidence in the County be in any Caſe a good Cauſe of Challenge of a Juror, I take it to be agreed, That notwithſtanding the [c] Statute of *Weſtm.* 2. 38. be expreſs that neither old Men above the Age of Seventy Years, nor Perſons perpetually Sick, nor thoſe who are infirm at the Time of their Summons, nor thoſe who do not reſide in the County, ſhall be put in Juries, or in the leſſer Aſſiſes; and therefore ſuch Perſons may ſue out a Writ of [d] Privilege for their Diſcharge, grounded on this Statute; yet if they be [e] actually returned and appear, they can neither be challenged by the Party, nor excuſe themſelves from not ſerving if there be not enow without them.

Sect. 27. As to the ſecond Point, *viz.* What ſhall be a good Challenge of a Juror in Reſpect of his Unindifferency: It is expreſsly enacted by 25 *Ed.* 3. *ch.* 3. which ſeems to have been made in [f] Affirmance of the Common Law, *That no Indictor ſhall be put in Inqueſts upon Deliverance of the Indictees of Felonies or* [g] *Treſpaſs, if he be challenged for that ſame Cauſe by him which is ſo indicted.* And this Exception againſt a Juror that he hath found an Indictment againſt the Party for the ſame Cauſe, hath been adjudged good, not only upon the Trial of [h] ſuch Indictment, but alſo upon the Trial of another Indictment or Action, [i] wherein the ſame Matter is either in Queſtion, or happens to be material, tho' not directly in Iſſue.

Sect. 28. It hath been allowed a good Cauſe of Challenge on the Part of the Priſoner, That the Juror [k] hath a Claim to the Forfeiture, which ſhall be cauſed by the Party's Attainder or Conviction; or that he hath declared his [l] Opinion before-hand that the Party is guilty, or will be hanged, or the like. Yet it hath been [m] adjudged that if it ſhall appear that the Juror made ſuch Declaration from his Knowledge of the Cauſe, and not out of any Ill-will to the Party, it is no Cauſe of Challenge.

Sect. 29. But it hath been [n] adjudged to be no good Cauſe of Challenge, that the Juror hath found others guilty on the ſame Indictment; for the Indictment is in Judgment of Law ſeveral againſt each Defendant, for every one muſt be convicted by particular Evidence againſt himſelf.

Sect. 30. It hath been [o] ruled to be a good Challenge of a Juror, on the Part of the King, that he hath given his Dogs the Names of the King's Witneſſes.

[a] Co. Litt. 158.
[b] Co. Litt. 157. b. 33 H. 6. 55. pl. 45. 43 Aſſ. pl. 46. 8 H. 5. 11. a. 21 Ed. 4. 74. b. pl. 5. 2 Roll. Abr. 650, pl. 11. 649 pl. 13. 658. Lett. K. 33 H. 6. 1. pl. 1. Bro. Challenge, 15, 147.
[c] 2 Inſt. 446, 447, 448.
[d] F. N. B. 165, b. 166 D. Regiſter 179, 180.
[e] State Trials, Vol. 2. f. 744. 2 Inſt. 448.
[f] 12 Aſſ. pl. 36. 19 Aſſ. pl. 6. Bro. Challenge, 101, 107. S. P. C. 158. Lett. B.
[g] *Yet in* 7 Ed. 4. 4. pl. 11. *Abridged* Bro. Challenge, 166. Fitz. Challenge, 53 *its is holden to be no principal Challenge in Treſpaſs.*
[h] State Trials, Vol. 2. fol. 379. Vol. 4. fol. 186. *In the Year-Book of* 40 Aſſ. pl. 10. *Abridged* Bro. Challenge, 142. *an Indictor being returned on the Petit Jury and giving a Verdict, was fined becauſe he did not challenge himſelf. Yet* 27 Aſſ. pl. 13. *Abridged* Bro. Challenge, 120. *and* Fitz. Challenge, 137. *'tis not allowed to be a principal Challenge even upon the Trial of the ſame Indictment.*
[i] 8 H. 4. 2. pl. 4. *Abridged* Bro. Challenge, 42. Fitz Challenge, 79. Co. Litt. 157. b. 1 Sid. 244. 2 Roll. Ab. 649. pl. 9.
[k] State Trials Vol. 1. fol. 502.
[l] 21 H. 7. 29. pl. 10. Bro. Challenge, 90. State Trials, Vol. 4. fol. 184, 185. *and ruled that the Priſoner ſhall not examine a Juror concerning ſuch Matter on a* voier dire, *becauſe it ſounds in Reproach.* Vide 49 Ed. 3. 1. pl. 2. *Abridged* Bro. Challenge, 25. Fitz. Challenge, 100,
[m] 7 H. 7, 25. pl. 8. *Abridged* Bro. Challenge 55. Fitz. Challenge, 22. 20 H. 6. 40. 2 Roll. Abr. 657. Lett. I. Vide 49 Ed. 3, 1. pl. 2. *Abridged,* Bro. Challenge. 25. Fitz Challenge, 100.
[n] Kely. 9. State Trials, Vol. 4. fol. 141, 175.
[o] State Trials, Vol. 2. 738.

Sect, 31. It seems to be [a] settled, That where the King is a Party he may take either a principal Challenge, or to the Favour.

Sect. 32. It is [b] said, That the Subject cannot take a Challenge for the Favour against the King, because every one is bound by his Allegiance to favour the King. But if [c] no more be meant by these Books, than that such a Challenge is not good without shewing some actual Partiality in such Sheriff or Juror, or some particular Cause in Respect whereof the King may influence them, it seems not clearly settled how the King in this Respect hath a greater [d] Privilege than the Subject, which yet it seems agreed [e] that he hath.

Sect. 33. It hath been [f] said to be no principal Challenge where the King is a Party, that a Juror is of the King's Livery, or his immediate Tenant; but it is said that a Challenge for such Cause ought to conclude to the [g] Favour. But these Matters seeming to be unsettled, I shall leave them to be farther considered by others.

For other Matters relating to Challenges, being not so proper for this Treatise, I shall refer to the [h] Books which more particularly treat of them.

Sect. 34. And now I am in the second Place to consider the Learning of Challenges, so far as it particularly relates to Aliens; as to whom it is enacted by 28 *Ed*. 3. 13. *Par*. 2. *That in all Manner of Inquests and Proofs, which be to be taken or made amongst Aliens and Denizens, be they Merchants or* [i] *other, as well before the Mayor of the Staple as before any other Justices or Ministers, altho' the King be Party, the one half of the Inquest or Proof shall be Denizens, and the other half of Aliens, if so many Aliens and Foreigners be in the Town or Place where such Inquest or Proof is to be taken, that be not Parties, nor with the Parties in Contracts, Pleas, or other Quarrels, whereof such Inquests or Proofs ought to be taken: And if there be not so many Aliens, then shall be put in such Inquests or Proofs, as many Aliens as shall be found in the same Towns or Places which be not thereto Parties, nor with the Parties, as afore is said, and the Remnant of Denizens, which be good Men, and not suspicious to the one Party nor to the other.*

Sect. 35. It is declared by 9 *H*. 6. 29. that the above-recited Statute of 2 *H*. 5. which requires that Jurors in certain Cases shall have Tenements to the yearly Value of 40*s*. *shall be no wise prejudicial to this Statute of* 28 *Ed*. 3. *nor extend itself but only to the Inquests to be taken between Denizen and Denizen*, Also it seems agreed [k] that the subsequent Statutes which require that Jurors shall have Tenements to a greater Value no way repeal the said Statute of 28 *E*. 3. Yet it seems [l] that the *English* Half of the Jury ought to have Tenements to the same Value as in other Cases. And it hath been [m] adjudged, that the Words *quorum quilibet habeat quatuor libratas terræ, &c.* shall be applied to the *English* only.

Sect. 36. It seems [*] agreed, That there is no need that any of those who find an Indictment against an Alien should be Aliens.

[a] Co. Litt. 156. a. 4 H. 7, 8. pl. 7. Fitz. Challenge, 63. 44 Ed. 3. 38. pl. 32. Bro. Challenge, 22. 2 Roll. Abr. 645. pl. 5.
[b] Fitz. Challenge, 63, 65. Co. Litt. 156. a. 2 Roll. Abr. 646. pl. 8. 4 H. 7, 8. pl. 3. Trials per pais, ch. 9. State Trials, Vol. 3. fol. 235, 236. Vol. 4. fol. 70, 661. Cro. Eliz. 663. pl. 12.
[c] Vide 2 Rol. Ab. 646. pl. 8. 640. pl. 6. 1 Vent. 309.
[d] *For in the Year Book of* 20 H. 6. 40. a. *Abridged* 2 Roll. Abr. 641. pl. 5, 6. *It is holden in the Case of the Subject to be no Cause of Challenge, that the Sheriff hath Malice against the Party without shewing some particular Instance of Partiality.*
[e] *See the Books cited to the other Parts of this and the next Section.*
[f] Fitz. Challenge, 17. S. P. C. 162. Lett. C. 2 Roll. Abr. 646. pl. 10. *It is said generally in some Books that it is a good Challenge of a Juror that he is the King's menial Servant, or a Valet of the Crown.* Co. Litt. 156. a. Fitz. Cor. 63. Trials per pais ch. 9. 2 Roll. Abr. 646. pl. 11. *But* State Trials, Vol. 3. f. 235, 236. V. 4. f. 70. *and in other Books the contrary is ruled.* Bro. Challenge 154. 4 H. 7. 3. pl. 5. Cro. Eliz. 663. pl. 12.
[g] Vide supra Sect. 33.
[h] Co. Litt. 157, 158. Trials per pais, ch. 9. 2 Roll. Abr. 635, *to* 666.
[i] Fitz. Inquest, 22. 3 Ed. 4. 11. pl. 3.
[k] Cro. El. 272. Vide H. P. C. 260, 261.
[l] Cro. Eliz. 272.
[m] Cro. Eliz. 272. 841, pl. 18.
[n] H. P. C. 260. S. P. C. 159.

Sect.

Sect. 37. Also it hath been adjudged, [o] That the said Statute of 28 *E.* 3. is repealed as to Trials for Treason, by [p] 1 & 2 *Ph. & Ma.* 10. which enacts that all Trials for Treason shall be according to the Course of the Common Law. Yet it seems that the [q] King may, if he thinks fit, make a special Grant to an Alien to be tried for Treason by a Jury whereof the one half shall be Aliens.

Sect. 38. [a] Also it hath been adjudged that the said Statnte of 28 *Ed.* 3. doth not extend to an Appeal, or other Action by an Alien against an Alien, for the Words are *all Inquests*, &c. *between Aliens and Denizens.*

Sect. 39. It is [b] holden, That by Denizens in this Statute are meant not only those who are born within the King's Ligeance, but also those who are made Denizens by the King's Letters Patents.

Sect. 40. It seems to be [c] settled, That no Alien, whether he be Plaintiff or Defendant, can take any Advantage of the Statute, unless he [d] pray it in Time; and that if he have neglected to pray it before the Return of a Common *Venire*, he can neither except to such *Venire*, nor pray a *Tales* or other Process *de medietate lingua.*

Sect. 41. It was [e] holden, even before the Union of the two Kingdoms under King *James* the first, that no *Scot* was an Alien within the Meaning of this Statute, not only because the *Scotch* Language is the same with the *English*, but also [f] because the *Scots* were never reckoned Aliens, but rather Subjects.

Sect. 42. *Note*, That [g] some of the Precedents for the Award of a *Venire* of a Jury of half Denizens and half Aliens, in pursuance of 28 *E.*3. mention, that the Aliens shall be of the same Country whereof the Party alledges himself; and others direct [h] generally that one half of the Jury shall be Aliens, without specifying any Country in particular. And this Form seems most agreeable to the Statute which speaks of Aliens in general, and seems to be confirmed both by late * Practice, and the greater Number of † Authorities.

Sect. 43. If on a *Venire* of half Denizens and half Aliens, the Sheriff return 12 as Aliens, and among them some who in Truth are not such, it ¶ seems that the Party shall not be concluded by such Return, but may notwithstanding challenge the Array for Want of a sufficient Number of Aliens.

Sect. 44. It seems [l] agreed, That the Return of a *Venire* of half Denizens, and half Aliens, ought to specify which of the Jurors are Denizens and which Aliens, and that a full number of each must appear to be sworn.

Sect. 45. If one or more be wanting to make up the full Number of six Denizens or Aliens, the Justices of *Nisi prius*, by a reasonable [m] Construction of the Statutes which give a *Tales de circumstantibus* may award such a *Tales* for so many Denizens or Aliens as shall be wanting.

Sect. 46. It is expresly enacted by 2 & 3 *P. & M.* and 4 & 5 *Eliz.* 20. set forth more at large *B.* 1. *Ch.* 54. that those adjudged Felons, as *Egyptians* by Vertue of those Statutes, shall be tried by the Inhabitants of the County or Place where they shall be taken, and not *per medietatem lingua.*

[o] Dalis. 22. Dy. 144, 145. pl. 61. Inst. 27. H. P. C. 260. [p] Vide supra Ch. 25. Sect. 134, 144. 146. [q] S. P. C. 158. Fitz. Trial, 71. 22 Ed. 3. 14. pl. 38. [a] 21 H 6. 4. pl. 10 Fitz. Trial, 32. Bro. Trial, 42. S P. C. 260. Lett. C. H. P. C. 261. *But by 27 Ed. 3. 8. it is enacted, that in Pleas between Aliens concerning the Staple there shall be a Jury of none but Aliens.* S. P. C. 159 Lett. C. [b] Bro. Den. 4. [c] Dy. 28, pl. 180, 145. pl. 60, 61. 304. pl. 51. 357. pl. 45. 3 Ed. 4, 11, pl. 3. 22 Ed. 3. 14. pl. 38. 2 Roll. Abr. 643. P. 1. Fitz. Inq. 22. Trial. 71. H P. C. 261. Bro. Panel, 3. Cont. 21 H. 7, 32, pl. 23. Bro. Deniz. 4. S. P. C. 259. *'Tis holden* Cro. Eliz 869 pl. 3 *by two Judges aginst one, that tho' the Defendant appear by the Declaration to be alien, yet the Common* Venire *is well awarded, unless a* Venire de medietate *be prayed.*

[d] *For the Form of such a Prayer* Rast. Ent. 7, a. pl. 2, 158, b. 159, a. 264. b. pl. 1, 2. 265 a. Dy. 144. pl. 60. S. P. C. 259. Plow. Com 2. b. [e] Dyer 304. pl. 51. H. P.C. 261. [f] *But Quære of this Reason, for it seems contrary to what is admitted in the whole Argument of* Calvin's *Case,* 7 Co. *See* State Trials, Vol. 1. fol. 572, 573. Vol. 4. fol. 652. *&c.* [g] Dyer 144. pl. 60. Rast. Ent. 7. b. pl. 2. 159, a. 264 b. pl. 1, 2. [h] Rast. Ent. 265. a. 10 Co. 104. a. * State Trials, Vol. 3. fol. 2. † H. P. C. 261 S. P. C. 158 Lett. C. Bro. Denizen, 4. Bro. Panel, 3. Cont. Fitz. Trial, 30. *By five Judges against one.* ¶ 2 Roll. Abr. 643. pl. 2. Vide S. P. C. 158. Lett. C. [l] Cro. El. 818, pl. 10. 841. pl. 18. *But this being only a mis-return is help'd by Verdict in Cases within the Statutes of* Jeofails. [m] 10 Co. 104. a. Cro. Eliz. 305, pl. 3. 818. pl 10. 841. pl. 18.

CHAP. XLIV.

Of a Trial by Peers.

AS to a Trial by Peers, having ſhewn already, *Ch.* 39. *Sect.* 1. That a Peer has no more Privilege than a Commoner as to having the Benefit of Counſel. And *Ch.* 43. *Sect.* 4. That a Peer cannot challenge any of his Peers, I ſhall now endeavour to ſhew,

1. The particular Form and Solemnity to be obſerved in ſuch a Trial.
2. Who are to be Triers.
3. Who are to be ſo tried.
4. As to what Crimes.
5. Upon what Suits and Pleas.
6. Whether a Peer can waive a Trial by his Peers.
7. In what Manner the Peers may require the Opinion of the Lord Steward or of the Judges.
8. Whether the Court may be adjourned.

And firſt of the particular Form and Solemnity to be obſerved in ſuch a Trial.

Sect. 1. When an Indictment is found againſt a Peer for a Crime for which he ought to be tried by his Peers, the King by his Commiſſion under the Great Seal reciting the Indictment, conſtitutes ſome [a] Peer High [b] Steward of the Kingdom *pro hac vice*, and by the ſame Commiſſion gives him Power to receive and proceed on ſuch Indictment, and requires the Peers to be attendant on him, and the Lieutenant of the Tower to bring the Priſoner before him.

Sect. 2. Alſo * a *Certiorari*, (which may either have the ſame Date with the Steward's Commiſſion, or a ſubſequent one) goes out of Chancery to certify the Indictment before the Steward *indilate*; and the Steward by his Precept under his Seal, directed to thoſe before whom the Indictment was found, appoints a certain Day and Place at which it ſhall be certified. And another Writ goes out of Chancery to the Lieutenant of the Tower, *&c.* to bring the Priſoner before the Steward at ſuch Day and Place as he ſhall appoint, and thereupon the Steward by his Precept under his Seal directed to the Lieutenant, *&c.* appoints the Day and Place.

Sect. 3. Alſo the Steward makes [c] another Precept under his Seal to the Serjeant at Arms, appointed to ſerve him during the Time of his Commiſſion, to ſummon the [d] Peers before him at ſuch a Place, Day, and Hour, *&c.*

[a] Supra, ch. 2.
[b] 1 H. 4. 2. 3 Inſt. 28. 13 H. 8. 11. pl. 1. S. P. C. 152. *the Neceſſity of making a High Steward for the Trial of an Impeachment for High Treaſon was denied by the Houſe of Commons in the Earl of* Danby's *Caſe.* State Trials, Vol. 2. fol. 198, 199.
* 3 Inſt. 28.
[c] *This is to be intended when the Parliament is not ſitting, but is either diſſolved or prorogued.* State Trials, Vol. 3. fol. 659 to 663. 3 Inſt. 28.

S. P. C. 152. a. 13 H. 8. 11. pl. 1.

[d] *'Tis ſaid* 13 H. 8. 11 pl. 1. S. P. C. 157. a. *That the Steward ſhall make ſuch Precept to cauſe* 20 *or* 18 *Peers to come before him, but* Sir Edward Coke, 3 Inſt. 28. *ſays that the Precept doth not mention any certain Number; and now by* 7 W. 3 *all the Peers are to be ſummoned.*

Ppppp Sect.

Sect. 4. At the Time appointed the Steward, attended with [a] six or [b] seven Serjeants at Arms carrying Maces before him, and by the King at Arms, and the Usher of the Black Rod, enters the Place of Trial uncovered, and ascends a Chair of State which always is [c] provided for that Purpose, and then the [d] Clerk of the Crown, or a [e] Master in Chancery delivers to him his Commission, and he delivers it again to the Clerk [f] of the Crown, and then a Serjeant at Arms makes three [g] Oyes, and a Proclamation for Silence in the Name of the Steward, and then the Lord Steward and all the other Lords [h] standing up uncovered, the Commission is read, and then the [i] Usher on his Knees delivers to the Steward a White Rod, who redelivers it to him or to a Serjeant at Arms, who holds it by him during the Trial: Then an [m] Oyes is made, and a Command given in the Name of the Steward to all Justices and Commissioners to certify all Indictments, *&c.* which being delivered into Court, the Clerk of the Crown reads the Return. Another Oyes is made that the Lieutenant of the Tower, *&c.* return his Writ and Precept, and bring the Prisoner to the Bar, and then the Prisoner is brought to the Bar, the [n] Gentleman-Gaoler of the Tower carrying the Axe before him, which being [o] done the Clerk reads the Return.

Sect. 5. All things being thus prepared, the High Steward [*] acquaints the Prisoner with the Nature of the Crime, and such like Matters proper for such an Occasion, and then the Clerk of the Crown arraigns him, [q] but is not to insist on his holding up his Hand.

Sect. 6. After the Prisoner hath pleaded and put himself upon God and his Peers, the King's Counsel go thro' with their Evidence; and after the Prisoner hath made his Defence, and the King's Counsel have been fully heard, the Prisoner is withdrawn from the Bar, and the Lords go together to consider of their Evidence; and when a Majority of them are agreed, they return to the Place of Trial, and the Lord Steward demands of them one by one, beginning with the Puisne, whether the Person arraigned be Guilty or Not Guilty, and they [r] all answer one by one, not upon their Oaths but on their [s] Honours and Ligeances. And the Lord Steward gives Judgment according to the Determination of the [t] Majority being more than twelve, but gives no Vote himself on a Trial by [u] Commission, but only on a Trial by the House of Peers, while the Parliament is sitting.

Sect. 7. As to the second Point, *viz.* Who are to be Triers: It is agreed, [x] That none but Lords, who have a Vote in Parliament can pass on such a Trial; and before 7 *W.* 3. 3. when the Trial was by Commission, it seems to have been the Practice for the Lord Steward to cause as many Temporal Lords to be summoned as he thought fit; and for the Lords so summoned alone to pass on the Trial. But this is remedied by that Statute set forth more at large in the next Section.

[a] 3 Inst. 28.
[b] Rushw. Collections, Part, 2. Vol. 1. fol. 96. Vide 2 Jon. 54.
[c] 3 Inst. 28. S. P. C. 152. 1 H. 4. 1. 13 H. 8. 11. pl. 1.
[d] 3 Inst. 28.
[e] Rushw. Collections, Part 2. Vol. 1. fol. 96.
[f] 3 Inst 28. Rushworth's Collections, Part 2. Vol. 1. fol 96.
[g] 1 H. 4. 1. 3 Inst. 28.
[n] State Trials, Vol. 3. f. 955. Vol. 4. fol. 350.
[i] 3 Inst. 28. Rushworth's Collections, Part 2. Vol. 1. fol. 96.
[m] 3 Inst. 28.
[n] State Trials, Vol. 3. f. 955. Vol. 4. fol. 355.
[*] *By* 3 Inst. 28. *All this is to precede the Call of the Peers and their seating themselves; but* 1 H. 4. 1. *and* 13 H. 8. 11. b. *and* S. P. C. 152 a. *and* State Trials, Vol. 1. f. 266. Vol. 3. f. 955, 956. *and* Vol. 4. f. 353 *to* 355. *and* 2 Jon. 55. *are contrary.*
[o] 3 Inst. 29. S. P. C. 152. a. 2 Jon. 55. *and the other Books cited to the precedent Section.*
[q] Raym. 408. State Trials, Vol. 3. fol. 658, 957. Vol. 2. 702, 703.
[r] 3 Inst. 30. 2 Inst. 49. Fitz. Coro. 34. 1 H. 4. 1. a. S. P. C. 152. 13 H. 8. 12. 2 Jon. 55. 56. 10 Ed. 4. 61. pl. 17.
[s] *See the Books above-cited, and* 1 Co. 30. b. 2 Inst. 49.
[t] 1 H. 4. 1. 13 H. 8. 12. S. P. C. 153. E. 3 Inst. 30. Moor 622.
[u] State Trials, Vol. 2. fol. 702. Vol. 3. fol. 657, 679.
[x] 2 Inst. 48. Co. Litt. 156.

Sect. 8. It is agreed, That at a Trial before the House of Peers, every Temporal Lord who has a Right to vote in that House, has a Right to pass on such Trial, But is is said in the *Year-Book* of 10 *Ed.* 4. 6. [a] *pl.* 17. That upon the Trial of a Peer in Parliament, the Bishops shall make a Procurator, because they cannot consent to the Death of a Man; but this is [b] said to be wholly grounded on a Canon not in Force at this Day, neither do I find any Precedent wherein they have been excluded against their Consent, or have withdrawn themselves without a Protestation of their Right, or making a Proxy; and the Judgment against the *Spencers*, was expresly reversed for this Reason among others, because the Bishops were not present; and in the Precedents chiefly insisted on of the other Side, it is not expresly said that they were not present, and it doth not clearly appear, but that they might be included under the Word Peers. However it hath been always [c] admitted that they have a Right to vote in a Bill of Attainder: Also in the Earl of *Danby*'s Case, they were adjudged[d] by the House of Lords to have a Right to vote in Questions previous to the Trial of a Peer, tho' this was strongly opposed by the House of Commons. And their Right to vote at the Trial itself, if they think fit, seems fully implied in 7 *W.* 3. 3. which enacts, *That upon the Trial of any Peer or Peeress for Treason or Misprision, all the Peers who have a Right to sit and vote in Parliament shall be summoned twenty Days at least before every such Trial, to appear at every such Trial, and that every Peer so summoned and appearing, shall vote at the Trial, every such Peer first taking the Oaths of Allegiance and Supremacy, and subscribing and repeating the* [*] *Declaration against Popery.*

Sect. 9. As to the third Point, *viz.* What Persons are to be thus tried: It is [f] agreed, That no Lord of any [g] other Country, or even of [h] *Scotland,* before the Union under Queen *Anne*, or of [h] *Ireland*, nor the Son and Heir [i] apparent of any Peer, nor any other Man whatsoever, who is not at the Time a Lord of Parliament, hath any Right to such a Trial in this Kingdom. But that every Lord of Parliament hath a Right to such a Trial [k] by Vertue of that Clause in *Magna Charta, ch.* 29. *Nec super eum ibimus, nec super eum mittemus, nisi per legale judicium parium suorum vel per legem terræ.*

Sect. 10. It is recited by 20 *H.* 6. 9. *to have been a Doubt in the Law of* England *how Ladies of great Estate in Respect of their Husbands, Peers of the Land, married or sole, that is to say, Dutchesses, Countesses or Baronesses, shall be put to answer, and judged upon Indictments of Treasons and Felonies, because they are not mentioned in the said Statute of* Magna Charta, ch. 29. *and thereupon to put out such Doubts, it is* [l] *declared, That such Ladies so indicted of any Treason or Felony, whether they be married or sole, shall thereof be brought to answer, and judged before such Judges and Peers of the Realm, as Peers of the Realm should be, if they were indicted or impeached of such Treasons or Felonies.*

Sect. 11. It seems [m] agreed, That a Queen, the King's Consort, and also a Queen Dowager, whether she continue sole after the King's Death, or take a second Husband, be he a Peer or Commoner; and also all Peeresses by Birth, whether they be sole or [n] married to Peers or Commoners; and also all Marchionesses and Viscountesses, are intitled to a Trial by the Peers, tho' none of them be expresly mentioned in this Act, or in *Magna Charta.* But it is [o] agreed, that a Peeress by Marriage loses her Dignity by marrying a Commoner.

[a] *Abridged* Fitz. Coro. 34. *Cited* S. P. C. 153. Lett. B. Brook *in a Note of the same Case*, Coro. 153. *says that they shall make Proxies.* *Sir* Edward Coke, 3 Inst. 31. *says that they must withdraw and make their Proxies.*

[b] *See Bishop* Stillingfleet, *of the Bishops Jurisdiction in Criminal Cases*, Ch. 2, 3. *and* Hunt's *Argument*, Ch. 9, 10, 11.

[c] *See* Hunt's *Argument for the Right of Bishops*, &c. Ch. 12. *and* Stillingfleet *of the Bishops Jurisdiction in Capital Cases*, Ch. 1. Sect. 3. *and* Ch. 2.

[d] State Trials, Vol. 2. f. 179 *to* 202.

[*] B. 1. Ch. 14. Sect. 1.

[f] 2 Inst. 48. 3 Inst. 30. Co. Lit. 156. b.

[g] Vide Fitz. Brief, 473. 20 Ed. 4. 6. pl. 6. Bro. nosme de Dignity, 49.

[h] 9 Co. 117. Vide 39 Ed. 3. 35. b. Bro. nosme de Dignity, 29. † Vide supra Ch. 25. Sect. 50.

[i] Bro. Treason, 2.

[k] *Such Trial is said to be very ancient.* 2 Inst. 50. [l] 2 Inst 45. 50. [m] 2 Inst. 50. Crompt. Jurisd. 33. b. [n] *See the Citations to the next Letter.* [o] 2 Inst. 50. Co. Litt. 16. b. 6 Co. 53. b. Dy. 79 pl. 51.

Sect. 12. It is said by [a] *Staundforde* and [b] *Coke*, That those who are Lords of Parliament, not in Respect of their Nobility, but of their Baronies which they hold of the Crown, as Bishops now do, and some Abbots and Priors [c] did formerly, are not within the Intent of *Magna Charta*, to be tried by the Peers. And [d] *Selden* seems clear, That this is the only Privilege which Bishops have not in Common with other Peers. And those who seem [e] most for the contrary Opinion admit that the Law hath been generally so taken. Neither do they produce any Precedent where a Bishop or Abbot has been tried by the Peers upon a Commission; but on the contrary admit that there are [f] two Precedents of their being tried by the Countrey. And it is said by [g] others, That there are divers Precedents of this Kind; yet *Selden*, with his utmost Diligence, seems able to produce but two, which clearly and fully come up to his Point, *viz.* those of Archbishop *Cranmer* and Bishop *Fisher*. However it seems to be [h] agreed, that while the Parliament is sitting a Bishop shall be tried by the Peers.

Sect. 13. As to the fourth Point, *viz.* As to what Crimes a Peer is to be tried by his Peers: I take it to be [i] agreed, That he has a Right to be so tried upon an Indictment of Treason or Felony, [k] whether such Treason or Felony be made such by the Common Law, or by Statute; and also upon an Indictment for a Misprision of Treason or Felony; but it [l] seems that regularly he is to be tried by the Country for all other Crimes, out of Parliament, as [m] *Præmunire*, [n] Riot, [o] seducing a young Lady from her Parents in order to debauch her, *&c.*

Sect. 14. As to the fifth Point, *viz.* Upon what Suits and Pleas a Peer is to be tried by his Peers, it hath been [p] adjudged, That he shall not be so tried upon an Appeal of Felony, but only upon an Indictment; and the Reason given for it is, that those Words in *Magna Charta, ch.* 29. *nec super eum ibimus, &c.* are to be intended only of the Suit of the King, and not of the Suit of the Subject.

Sect. 15. Also it hath been [q] adjudged, and appears from constant [r] Experience, That neither the said Clause of *Magna Charta*, nor any other Law privileges a Peer from being indicted by a Grand Jury of Commoners, either in the King's Bench, or before Commissioners of *Oyer*, or the Coroner, *&c.*

Sect. 16. Also it seems [s] to be clear, That if a Peer absent himself, and cannot be found, he may be outlawed *per judicium coronatorum, &c.*

Sect. 17. Also it is said that the Court of King's Bench may allow a [t] Pardon pleaded by a Peer to an Indictment in that Court: But that it cannot receive either his Plea of Not guilty, or Confession, but only the Lord Steward on an Arraignment before the Lords.

Sect. 18. It seems clear, That if a Peer be * attainted of Treason or Felony, he may be brought before the King's Bench and demanded, What he has to say why Execution should not be awarded against him? And if he plead any Matter to such Demand, his Plea shall be discussed and Execution awarded by the said Court, upon its being adjudged against him.

S. P. C. 152. A
[b] 3 Inst. 30. *But in* Fitz. Coro. 161 *it seems admitted that a Bishop shall be tried by the Peers in Cases proper for such Trial. and* Brook *tit.* Trial, 142. *cites a Note from* Fitz. Challenge, 115. *wherein he says it was holden, That Bishops shall be tried by the Peers, but this is mistaken, for there is no such Opinion there holden.*
[c] Co Litt 97. Fuller's Ch. History. B. 6. fol. 292.
[d] Selden of Baronage, p. 152. Titles of Honour, 1*st Edit. pa.* 347.
[e] Hunt's *Argument for the Bishops Right in Capital Cases*, Ch. 18. Gibson's Codex, 154. Stillingfleet *of the Bishops Jurisdiction in Capital Cases*, Ch. 4
[f] Bro. Trial, 142. *See* Hunt's *Argument* Ch. 18. *and* Stillingfleet *of the Bishops Jurisdiction in Capital Cases.*
[g] S. P. C. 153. Lett. A. Seld. Barona. 142 *to* 155. Vide 3 Inst. 30.
[h] *See* Hunt's *Argument*, Ch. 18. Trials per pais Ch. 2. para. 8.

State Trials, Vol. 1. f. 374. Stillingfleet *of the Bishops Jurisdiction in Capital Cases.* [i] 3 Inst. 30. 2 Inst. 49.
S. P. C. 153. Lett. D. 1 Bulst. 198. [k] S. P. C. 158. Lett. D. E. F. 1 Bulst. 198. [l] *See the Books above-*
cited. State Trials, Vol. 2. f. 3. Fitz. Coro 161. [m] 1 Bulst. 198, 199. 3 Inst. 30. 12 Co 93.
[n] State Trials Vol. 3. fol. 79. [o] State Trials, Vol. 3. fol. 52. 12 Co. 93. [p] 10 Ed. 4 6. pl. 17. Fitz.
Coro. 34. Bro. Coro. 153. S. P. C. 152. Lett. A. 2 Inst. 49. 3 Inst. 30. Rast. Ent. 50. pl. 7. [q] 3 Inst.
26, 28. 2 Inst. 49. [r] 1 H. 4. 1. State Trials, Vol. 3. fol. 52, 79, 657, 951. Vol. 4. f. 351, &c. [s] 3 Inst. 31.
2 Inst. 49. [t] 2 Inst. 49. * 1 H. 7. 22, 23. pl. 15. Bro. Coro 119. Treason, 18. Fitz. Coro. 49.

Sect. 19. As to the sixth Point, *viz.* Whether a Peer can waive a Trial by his Peers, it hath been [a] adjudged, That if a Peer on an Arraignment before the Lords refuse to put himself upon his Peers, he shall be dealt with as one that stands Mute; for it is as much the Law of the Land that a Peer be tried by his Peers, as a Commoner by Commoners. Yet if one who has a Title to Peerage, be indicted and arraigned as a Commoner, and plead Not guilty, and put himself upon his Country, it hath been [b] adjudged that he cannot afterwards suggest that he is a Peer, and pray a Trial by his Peers.

Sect. 20. As to the seventh Point, *viz.* In what Manner the Peers may require the Opinion of the Lord Steward, or of the Judges: It was [c] resolved by all the Judges in the Lord *Dacre*'s Case, who was tried by Commission, that no Question ought to be asked of the Lord Steward or of the Judges in the Absence of the Prisoner. And it was [d] adjudged by the Lord Steward, in the Earl of *Warwick*'s Case, who was tried by the House of Peers in Parliament, that that no Question ought to be asked of the Judges in the Absence of the Prisoner. But in the Lord *Audley*'s Case, who was tried by Commission, the Lords Triers, [e] after they were withdrawn, consulted with the Lord Chief Justice four several Times, and also sent to consult with the Lord Steward. Yet, notwithstanding this Precedent, the Judges [f] resolved in the Lord *Morley*'s Case, who was likewise tried by Commission, that if after the Lords were withdrawn they should send for any of the Judges to desire their Opinions on a Point in Law, and the Lord Steward should permit them to go, they wou'd tell the Lords, if they should ask them any Question, that they were not to give any private Opinion, without Conference with the rest of the Judges, and that openly in Court. But they resolved that if the Lord Steward shou'd ask them any Question in open Court, tho' in the Absence of the Prisoner, they wou'd answer it, because they are called to assist the Court, and the Demand of any Question in such Case is to be referred to the Discretion of the Lord Steward.

Sect. 21. When a Peer is tried before the House of Peers in Parliament, the Lord Steward [g] withdraws with the rest of the Lords, and consults with them.

Sect. 22. As to the eighth Point, *viz.* Whether the Court may be adjourned: It is agreed, [h] That where a Peer is tried by the House of Lords in full Parliament, the House may be adjourned as often as there is Occasion, and the Evidence taken by Parcels: Also it hath been [i] adjudged, That where the Trial is by Commission, the Lord Steward, after a Verdict is given, may take Time to advise upon it, and that his Office continues till he has given Judgment. Also it is [k] said to have been agreed by the Judges in the Lord *Dacre*'s Case, that on such a Trial the Court might be adjourned, and that if the Lords Triers did not agree, it was holden by some they ought to be kept together all Night, and by others that they might go to their several Houses. But it is said, [l] That there is no Precedent of the Lords Triers ever having separated upon a Trial by Commission, after the Evidence has been given for the King; and it is said to have been [m] resolved by all the Judges in the Case of the Duke of *Norfolk*, That the Peers in such Case must continue together till they agree to give a Verdict, and the like was [n] adjudged by the Lord Steward in the Lord *Delamere*'s Case.

[a] Rushw. Collections, Part 2. Vol. 1. fol. 94. 3 Inst. 30. Kely. 57. *Yet there is said to be a Record in* 4 Edw. 3. *That* T. *Lord* Berkley, *put himself on his Country, and was tried by a Jury of Kts.*

[b] Dalis. 16.

[c] 3 Inst. 29, 30. 2 Inst. 49. Kely. 57. State Trials, Vol. 3. fol. 679.

[d] State Trials, Vol. 4. fol. 381.

[e] Rushw. Collections, Part 2. Vol. 1. fol. 101. State Trials Vol. 1. fol. 171.

[f] Kely. 54.

[g] State Trials, Vol. 3. fol. 679.

[h] State Trials, Vol. 2. f. 654. Vol. 3. f. 677 to 680.

[i] Rushw. Collections, Part 2. Vol. 1. fol. 95. State Trials, Vol. 1. f. 265. *But* Moore, 622. *seems contrary.*

[k] Kely. 57. *But* Moore, 622, *in a Report of the very same Case it is said that the contrary was holden.*

[l] State Trials Vol 3 fol 678. *But see* Moore 622.

[m] 3 Inst. 30. *in the Margent.*

[n] State Trials, Vol. 3. fol. 677 to 680.

C H A P. XLV.

Of Trial by Battle.

Sect. 1. A Trial by Battle, at the [a] Defendant's Choice, is allowable in Appeals [b] of Treason before the Constable and Marshal, and in Appeals [c] of Felony, whether by Appellants or [d] Approvers.

Sect. 2. For the Manner of waging Battle in an Appeal of Treason, being according to the Civil Law, I shall refer to *Rushworth's Collections, Part* 2. *Vol.* 1. *fol.* 112 *to* 128.

Sect. 3. When an Appellee of Felony wages Battle, he pleads [e] that he is Not guilty,, and that he is ready to defend the same by his Body, and then [f] flings down his Glove, and if the Appellant will join Battle, he replies that he is ready to make good his Appeal by his Body upon the Body of the Appellee, and takes up the Glove: And then the Appellee lays his [g] right Hand on the Book, and with his left Hand takes the Appellant by the Right, and [h] swears to this Effect, *Hear this thou who callest thy self* John *by the Name of Baptism, that I, who call my self* Thomas *by the Name of Baptism, did not feloniously murder thy Father* W. *by Name, (on the Day of in the Year of* at B. *as you surmise, nor am any way guilty of the said Felony; so help me God,* (and then he shall kiss the Book and say) *and this I will defend against thee by my Body as this Court shall award.* And then the Appellant lays his right Hand on the Book, and with the left Hand takes the Appellee by the Right, and swears to this Effect, *Hear this thou who callest thy self* Thomas *by the Name of Baptism, that thou feloniously (on the Day of in the Year of* at B.) *didst murder my Father,* W. *by Name, so help me God,* (and then he shall kiss the Book and say) *and this I will prove against thee by my Body, as this Court shall award.* And then the Court shall [i] appoint a Day and Place for the Battle, and in the mean while the Appellee shall be kept in the [k] Custody of the Marshal, and the Appellant shall find [l] Sureties to be ready to fight at the Time and Place, unless he be an Approver, in which Case [m] he shall also be kept by the Marshal. And the [n] Night before the Day of Battle, both Parties shall be arraied by the Marshal, and shall be brought into the Field before the [o] Justices of the Court where the Appeal is depending, at the rising of the Sun, [p] bare-headed, and bare-legged from the Knee downwards, and bare in the Arms to the Elbow, and armed only with Bastons an Ell long, and four cornered Targets, and before they engage they shall both take this [q] Oath, *Hear this ye Justices, that I, A. B. have neither eat nor drunk, nor done any Thing else, nor any other for me, by which the Law of God may be depressed, and the Law of the Devil exalted.* And then after [r] Proclamation for Silence under Pain of Imprisonment for a Year and a Day,

[a] Finch of Law, 421. S.P.C. 176. Letter F. Fleta, lib. 1. ch. 34. S. 27. Trials per pais, ch. 2. Sect. 19.
[b] Vide supra, Ch. 23. S. 29. Crompt. Jur. 82, b. 88. a. Bro. Battle 15.
[c] Rast. Ent. 50. pl. 10. Cro. Eliz. 69. pl. 22. Dyer 120. pl. 10. S. P. C. 176. ch. 13, 14. *and the Books cited to the other Parts of this Chapter.*
[d] Rast. Ent. 42. pl. 3. S. P. C. 178. b. 9 Co. 31. b.
[e] Cro. Eliz. 69 pl. 22. Rast. Ent. 42. pl. 3. 50. pl. 10. Dyer, 120. pl. 10. 9 H. 4. 3. pl. 16
[f] S.P.C. 178. Lett K. Fitz. Coro. 385. Vide 1 H. 6, 6. b.
[g] Bro. Battle, 1, 6. 9 H. 4, 3. pl. 16. 17 Ass pl. 1. 17 Ed. 3, 2. pl. 6. Britton, 41. S. P. C. 178. A.
[h] Fleta B. 1. ch. 34. S. 28, 29. 9 H. 4, 3. pl. 16. 17 Ass pl. 1. Bro. Battle 1, 6. 17 Ed. 3, 2. pl. 6. Britton, 41. Bract. B. 3. Ch. 21. S. 2.
[i] Rast. Ent. 42. b. pl. 2. S. P. C. 178. B.
[k] Fleta, B. 1. ch. 33. S. 28. Rast. Ent. 42. b. pl. 2. 9 H. 4, 3. pl. 16. S. P. C. 178. Bro. Battle, 1. Fitz. Coro. 78, 111.
[l] Fleta, B. 1. Ch. 34. S. 28. 9 H. 4. 3. pl. 16. 17 Ass. pl. 1. S. P. C. 178. Let B. Fitz Cor. 78, 111. Bro. Battle, 1, 6. 17 Ed. 3, 2. pl. 6. Bract B. 3. Ch. 21. S. 3. *says that both Parties shall be kept in Custody.*
[m] Rast Ent. 42 b. pl 2.
[n] 9 H. 4, 3. pl. 16. Bro. Battle. 1.
[o] Fleta B. 1. Ch. 34. Sect. 30, 31. Dyer 301. Bro. Battle. 15 S. P. C. 177, 178. Bract B. 3. C. 21. Sect. 4, 5. Britt. 40. Cont. 37 H. 6. 20.
[p] Britt. 41. *By some the Appellant's Head shall be covered.* 9 H. 4. 3. pl. 16. Bro. Battle, 1. Vide 1 H. 6, 6 7. Dy. 301.
[q] Fleta, B. 1. Ch. 34. S. 30. Bract B. 3. Ch. 21 Sect. 4. Britt. f. 40.
[r] Fleta, B. 1. Ch 34. S. 31.

&c.

&c. they ſhall begin the Combat, wherein if the Appellee be ſo far vanquiſhed that he cannot or will not fight any longer, he may be adjudged to be* hanged immediately; but if he can maintain the Fight till the Stars appear, he ſhall have [b] Judgment to go quit of the Appeal. And if the Appellant become Recreant, that is a Crying Coward, or Craven, the Appellee ſhall not only recover his Damages, but may alſo, as it † ſeems, plead his Acquittal in Bar of a ſubſequent Indictment or Appeal, and the Appellant [c] ſhall for his Perjury loſe his *liberam legem.* Yet if there be other Appellees in the ſame Appeal, it hath been adjudged, [d] that it ſhall ſtill ſtand in Force againſt them. But for theſe Matters I ſhall refer to *Ch.* 24. *Sect.* 24.

Sect. 4. In Appeals each Party muſt fight in proper [e] Perſon, and not by Champions. And therefore if the Appellant be under an apparent Diſability of fighting, as being a [f] Woman, or in [g] Holy Orders, or under [h] Age, or of the Age of [i] ſixty, [k] or maimed, or [l] blind, he may counterplead the Wager of Battle, and compel the Appellee to put himſelf upon his Country. [m] Alſo if an Appellant become blind by the Act of God after he has waged Battle, the Court will diſcharge him of the Battle; and in ſuch Caſe it is [n] ſaid that the Appellee ſhall go free.

Sect. 5. Alſo if a [o] Peer of the Realm, and much more if the King, bring an Appeal, the Defendant ſhall not be admitted to wage Battle, by Reaſon of the Dignity of their Perſons.

Sect. 6. Alſo the Citizens of *London* have a ſpecial [p] Privilege by Charter, that in Appeals brought by any of them, there ſhall be no Wager of Battle.

Sect. 7. Alſo any Plaintiff may counterplead a Wager of Battle, by alledging ſuch Matters againſt the Defendant as induce a violent Preſumption of Guilt; as in an Appeal of Robbery, by ſhewing [q] that the Defendant was taken with the Manner, *&c.* And in an Appeal of Death, that he was [r] found lying upon the Deceaſed with a bloody Knife in his Hand; and in any Appeal by ſhewing that the Defendant being under an Arreſt for the Crime charged againſt him, [ſ] brake the Priſon, or [t] eſcaped, unleſs ſuch Breaking or Eſcape be [u] pardoned. For the Law will [x] not oblige a Plaintiff to make good his Accuſation in ſo extraordinary a Manner, when in all appearance he may prove it in the ordinary way. It is alſo a good Counterplea of Battle that the Defendant hath been [k] indicted for the ſame Fact, unleſs the Indictment were inſufficient.

Sect. 8. It is enacted by 6 *Ric.* 2. That the Defendant ſhall not be received to wage Battle in an Appeal of Rape.

* S P.C. 178. b. *See where this is done accordingly.* 19. H. 6. 35. pl. 75. Fitz Coro. 6. Bro. Coro. 46. Bract. B. 1. Ch. 21. S. 6. [b] Trials per pais, ch. 2. Sect. 19. 3 Inſt. 221. Fleta, B. 1. Ch. 34. Sect. 32. Bract. B. 3. Ch. 21. S. 5. † Supra, ch. 23. Sect. 140. *and* ch. 35. Sect. 6. Fitz. Coro. 98. Fleta, B. 1. Ch. 34. S. 32. [c] 3 Inſt. 221. Co. Lit. 6. b. [d] Fitz. Coro. 98. [e] Finch of Law, 421, 422. 9 Co. 31. b. 3 Inſt. 221. Plow. Com. 335. b. Trials per pais, ch. 2. Sect. 19. [f] Keilw. 120. pl. 66. Fleta, B. 1. ch. 34. S. 25. S. P. C. 180. Lett. A. [g] Britton, 40. [h] Keilw. 120. pl. 66. Finch of Law 423. Fitz droit, 3.

S P. C. 60. Lett. D. 180. Lett. A. 22 Ed. 4. 20. a. Fleta, B. 1. Ch. 34. Sect. 25. [i] S. P. C 60. Let. D. 180. Lett. A Fitz. Coro. 385. 22 Ed. 4. 20. a. Trials per pais, ch. 2. Sect. 19. Fleta B. 1. ch. 34. Sect. 25. [k] Finch of Law, 423. Fitz. Coro. 230, 268. S. P. C. 180. Lett. A. 22 Ed. 4. 20, a. Trial per pais, ch. 2. Sect. 19. Fleta, B. 1. ch. 34. Sect. 25. [l] Fitz. droit, 57. 3 Inſt. 158, 159. [m] Fitz droit 57. 3 Inſt. 158, 159. [n] 3 Inſt. 158, 159. [o] Finch of Law, 423. S. P. C. 152. Lett. A. Plow. Com. 335. b. Fleta, B. 1. Ch. 34. Sect. 25. [p] S. P. C. 180. Lett. C. Fitz. Coro. 125, 187. [q] Finch of Law, 422, 423. S. P. C. 179. Fitz. Coro. 100, 125, 144, 157, 230, 268, 375. 4 Aſſ. pl. 1. 22 Ed. 4. 19. b. Bro. Battle, 5, 7. Appeal, 114. 20 H. 7, 8. pl. 18. Vide ſupra, Ch. 15. Sect. 41. [r] Finch of Law, 179. S. P. C. 179 Fitz Coro. 411. [ſ] Finch of Law, 422. S. P. C. 180. 1 Aſſ. pl. 3. 6. Hob. 82. Fitz. Coro. 154. 157, 164, 251, 281. [t] Finch of Law, 422. Hob. 82. S. P. C. 80. Bro. Battle, 3. 1 Aſſ. pl. 6. Fitz Coro. 164, 251. [u] S. P. C. 180. Hob. 82. Fitz. Coro. 154, 281. Bro. Battle, 3. 1 Aſſ. pl. 3. [x] Trials per pais, Ch. 2. S. 19. [y] Finch of Law, 422. 22 Ed. 4. 19. b. Bro. Battle, 7, 11. Appeal, 114. 20 Ed. 4, 6. pl. 5. Raſt Ent. 50. pl. 10.

CHAP. XLVI.

Of Evidence.

Sect. 1. AS to the Nature of Evidence, so far as it more particularly concerns Criminal Cases, having premised that it is a settled Rule, That in Cases of Life no [a] Evidence is to be given against a Prisoner but in his Presence; and that it hath been [b] adjudged, That no Bill of Exceptions is grantable on an Indictment of Treason or Felony, the Statute of *Westminster* 2. 3. *Cum aliquis implacitatus, &c. proponat exceptionem, &c.* having never been thought to extend to any such Case, it being plain that it could not but cause an infinite Delay of Justice if it should; I shall more fully consider the following Points,

1. How many Witnesses are required in Criminal Cases.
2. What is to be allowed as Evidence.
3. Who may be Witnesses.
4. In what Manner the Witnesses for the Defendant are to give their Evidence.
5. Whether a Defendant have Right to Process to bring in his Witnesses.
6. What Evidence maintains an Indictment, *&c.*
7. What may be given in Evidence on the Part of the Defendant.

Sect. 2. As to the first Point, *viz.* How many Witnesses are required in Criminal Cases: Having already endeavoured to shew that the Common Law did [c] not require any certain Number of Witnesses for the Trial of any Crime whatsoever, I shall only add in this Place, That it seems to have been the more * prevailing Opinion, that 1 [d] *E.* 6. 12. and 5 *&* 6 *E.* 6. 11. which required two Witnesses in Treason, were not repealed by 1 *&* 2 *Ph. & M.* 10. which ordered that all Trials of Treason should be according to the Course of the Common Law; and therefore that it was still necessary in all Trials of High Treason, not concerning the Coin, to have either two Witnesses to the [d] same Overt-Act, or one Witness to one, and another [e] Witness to another Overt-Act of the same kind of Treason, or at least one Witness to an Overt-Act, and [f] another to a material Circumstance to prove it. In Relation to which Matters the Law seeming to be settled by 7 [f] *W.* 3. which is express, *That no Person shall be indicted, tried or attainted for High Treason, but upon the Oaths of two lawful Witnesses, either both of them to the same Overt-Act, or one of them to one, and the other of them to another Overt-Act of the same Treason*; it will be needless

[a] State Trials, Vol. 4. fol. 277, 310.

[b] *Sir* Henry Vane's *Case*, State Trials, Vol. 1. fol. 938. *wherein it is said that such Bill never was nor ought to be allowed in any Capital Case, and as this Case is reported in* 1 Sid. 85. 1 Keb. 384. *it seems to have been holden that it is not grantable on any Indictment, and as it is reported in* 1 Lev. 68. *and* Kely. 15. *That it is not grantable in any Criminal Case whatsoever.* Vide 2 Inst. 427.

[c] Ch. 25. Sect. 131.

* H. P. C. 262. *and the Authorities cited to the other Parts of this Section.* Cont. State Trials, Vol. 1. fol. 180, 181, 636. V. 2. fol. 408. *and* supra Ch. 25. Sect. 131.

¶ *For these Statutes, and their Exposition See* ch. 25. Sect. 132 *to* 148.

[d] Raym. 407, 408. State Trials, Vol. 2. fol. 533. Vol. 3 fol. 688, 689.

[e] State Trials, Vol. 1. fol. 697, 723, 724. Vol. 2. fol. 317, 695, 785, 829, 830. Vol 3. fol. 149, 156, 228. Vol. 4. f. 86, 87, 88, 117. Raym. 407, 408. Kely. 9.

[f] State Trials, Vol. 2. fol. 408. Vol. 3. fol. 228, 229, 688, 689, 894 *to* 901. 928, 929, 930. Vide State Trials, Vol. 1. fol. 636. *But* State Trials, Vol. 1. fol. 180, 181. *'tis holden that Circumstantial Evidence alone is sufficient.*

[f] Vide Ch. 25. Sect. 136 *to* 148.

less

less at this Day to examine how far these Opinions were reconcileable with 1 *Ph. & Ma.*

As to the second Point, *viz.* What is to be allowed as Evidence in Criminal Cases, I shall consider,

1. Where the Confession of the Defendant or the Depositions of others out of Court may be allowed as Evidence.
2. How far Hearsay is Evidence.
3. Whether Similitude of Hands be any Evidence in Criminal Cases.

Sect. 3. As to the first Particular, *viz.* Where the Confession of the Defendant, or the Depositions of others, out of Court, may be allowed as Evidence: It seems that the Confession of the Defendant himself, whether taken upon an [a] Examination before Justices of Peace, in pursuance of 1 & 2 *Ph. & M.* 13. or of 2 & 3 *Ph. & Ma.* 10. upon [b] a Bailment or [c] Commitment for Felony, or taken by the Common Law upon an Examination before a Secretary of State, or other Magistrate, for [d] Treason, or [e] other Crimes, not within those Statutes, or in [f] Discourse with private Persons, hath always been allowed to be given in Evidence against the Party confessing, but [g] not against others.

Sect. 4. Also it was [h] holden, That two Witnesses of a Confession of High Treason, upon an Examination before a Justice of Peace, were sufficient to convict the Person so confessing, within the Meaning of 1 *E.* 6. 12. and 5 & 6 *E.* 6. 11. which required two Witnesses in High Treason, *unless the Offender should willingly without Violence confess the same*; But this is remedied by 7 *W.* 3. 3. which requires two Witnesses, *unless the Party shall willingly, without Violence, in open Court confess, &c.*

Sect. 5. It [i] seems an established Rule, that where-ever a Man's Confession is made use of against him, it must all be taken together, and not by Parcels.

Sect. 6. It seems [k] settled, That the Examination of an Informer taken upon [l] Oath, and * subscribed by him either before a [m] Coroner upon an Inquisition of Death in pursuance of 1 & 2 *Ph. & M.* 13. or before [n] Justices of Peace in pursuance of 1 & 2 *Ph. & M.* 13. and 2 & 3 *P. & M.* 10. upon a [o] Bailment or [p] Commitment for any Felony, may be given in Evidence at the Trial of such Inquisition, or of an Indictment for the same Felony, if it be made out by Oath to the Satisfaction of the Court, that such Informer is [q] dead, or unable to [r] travel, or kept [s] away by the Means or Procurement of the Prisoner, and that the Examination offered in Evidence is the very same [t] that was sworn before the Coroner or Justice, without any Alteration whatsoever.

[a] H. P. C. 102, 262, 263, 264. State Trials, Vol. 1. fol. 265. Vol. 3. fol. 8, 9.

[b] Supra Ch. 15. Sect. 58, 59, 60, 61.

[c] Supra, ch. 15. Sect. 11, 12.

[d] State Trials, Vol 1. f. 87, 181, 963. Francia's Trial. Kely. 18.

[e] 5 Mod. 164, 165. State Trials, Vol. 2. fol. 426. Vol. 3. fol. 131, 132.

[f] Dyer 215. pl. 50. H. P. C. 102, 193.

[g] Kely. 18, 19. State Trials, Vol. 3. fol. 8, 9. Vol. 4. f. 33. *See the contrary practised* State Trials, Vol. 1. *in Sir* Jervis Ellis's *Trial, and in* Throgmorton's *Trial*, fol. 49 *to* 56. *Duke of* Norfolk's *Trial*, fol. 73 *to* 85 *and* 97, 98. *Other Trials from* fol. 118 *to* 122. *Earl of* Essex's *Trial*, 167, 168. *Sir* Walter Raleigh's *Trial*, fol 177, 178, 181.

[h] Kely. 18. Supra, ch. 25. Sect. 142.

[i] 5 Mod. 165. Cont. State Trials, Vol. 1. fol. 53. Throgmorton's *Trial.*

[k] Kely. 55. H. P. C. 262, 263. 1 Lev. 180. Salk. 281. pl. 8. 2 Keb. 19. Vide Cro. El. 901. Dalt. ch. 111, 112, 113.

[l] State Trials, Vol. 1. fol. 265. H. P. C. 262, 263. * H. P. C. 262, 263.

[m] Supra, ch. 9. Sect 31. 2 Jon. 53.

[n] *See the Books above-cited; but* 2 Jon. 53. *'tis adjudged that Depositions before a Coroner may be read, but said that those taken before a Justice of Peace can in no Case be read.*

[o] Supra, ch. 15. Sect. 59, 60, 61.

[p] Supra, ch. 16. Sect. 11.

[q] Kely. 55. 1 Lev. 180. 2 Keb. 19 pl. 39. H. P. C. 263.

[r] Kely. 55.

[s] Kely. 55. *in* Harrison's *Case*, State Trials, Vol. 3. f. 941. *such an Examination was read in Evidence, upon Proof that the Witness had been enticed away, tho' it did not directly appear to have been done by the Procurement of the Prisoner.*

[t] Kely. 55. 2 Keb. 19. pl. 39. H. P. C.

Sect. 7. But it hath been [a] adjudged, That it is not sufficient to authorize the Reading such an Examination, to make Oath that the Prosecutors have used all their Endeavours to find the Witness, but cannot find him.

Sect. 8. Also it hath been [b] adjudged that Depositions taken before a Coroner upon an Inquisition of Death *super visum corporis*, cannot be given in Evidence upon an Appeal for the same Death, because it is a different Prosecution from that wherein they were taken.

Sect. 9. There are many [c] Instances in the Reigns of Queen *Elizabeth* and King *James* I. wherein the Depositions of absent Witnesses were allowed as Evidence in Treason and Felony, even where it did not appear but that the Witnesses might have been produced *viva voce*. And it was adjudged in [d] the Earl of *Strafford*'s Trial, that where Witnesses could not be produced *viva voce*, by Reason of Sickness, *&c.* their Depositions might be read for or against the Prisoner on a Trial of High Treason, but not where they might have been produced in Person. And it was admitted [e] in the Lord *Stafford*'s Trial, that the Depositions taken by a Witness before a Justice of the Peace might at the Prisoner's Desire be read at the Trial, in order to take off the Credit of the Witness by shewing a Variance between such Depositions and the Evidence given in Court *viva voce*. And for the same Reason it seems [f] agreed, That where a Witness at one Trial varies from his own Evidence at another in relation to the same Matter, such Variance may also be given in Evidence to invalidate his Testimony at the second Trial.

Sect. 10. But it is § said to have been adjudged in the seventh Year of *Will.* 3. by the Court of King's Bench upon Advice with the Justices of the Common Pleas, upon an Indictment for a Libel, that Depositions taken before a Justice of Peace relating to the Fact could not be given in Evidence, tho' the Deponent were dead; and that the Reason why such Depositions may be given in Evidence in Felony depends upon the Statutes of *Ph. & Ma.* And that this cannot be extended farther than the particular Case of Felony. But in the Report of this Case in 5 [g] *Mod.* it is said that the Reason why such Depositions could not be read was, because the Defendant was not present, when they were taken, and therefore had not the Benefit of a Cross Examination.

Sect. 11. However it was [h] agreed in Sir *John Fenwick*'s Case, That the Information of a Witness taken upon Oath before a Justice of Peace, being joined with the Evidence of one other Witness only *viva voce* could not in the ordinary Course of Justice, amount to sufficient Evidence within the 7th of *W.* 3. which requires two Witnesses in High Treason; and therefore it was thought necessary to proceed in that Case by Bill of Attainder in Parliament, whose Power can be restrained by no Rules but those of natural Justice.

Sect. 12. And in the same Case it was [i] agreed, That the Evidence given by a Witness at one Trial, could not in the ordinary Course of Justice be made use of, against a Defendant on the Death of such Witness, at another Trial.

[a] Kely. 55.
[b] 2 Rol. Rep. 460, 461. Vide 1 Sid. 325. 2 Keb. 384. pl. 54.
[c] State Trials, Vol. 1. *Duke of* Norfolk's *Trial*, f. 84 Abington's *Trial*, f. 118, 119. Udal's *Trial*, fol. 148, 149. *Earl of* Essex's *Trial*, fol. 166. *Sir* Walter Raleigh's *Trial*, fol. 181, 182. *and the like was admitted in the Lord* Aud[illegible] *Case on an Indictment for a Rape on his own Lady.* State Trials, Vol. 1. fol. 268, 269.
[d] Rushw. Stafford, fol. 231, 526 *to* 531.
[e] State Trials, Vol. 2. fol. 622 *to* 627, 644, 647, 651. *See* Vol. 1. f. 911.
[f] State Trials, Vol. 2. f. 343, 344, 528, 529. *See* Sect. 12.
§ Salk. 286. Vide supra, Sect. 3.
[g] 5 Mod 165. Vide Rushw. Strafford, 524 *to* 531. *and* State Trials, Vol. 2. fol. 420. *and* Vol. 4 fol. 261. *and* 2 Rol. Rep. 460, 461.
[h] State Trials, Vol. 4. f. 237, *&c.*
[i] State Trials Vol. 4. fol. 265 *to* 272. Vide supra Sect. 9. 1 Sid, 325. 2 Keb. 384. pl. 54.

Sect.

Sect. 13. Also it seems clear that Depositions taken in the Spiritual Court in a Cause of Divorce for a Forcible Marriage cannot * be given in Evidence upon an Indictment for such Marriage on the [k] Statute of 3 *H.* 7. 2.

Sect. 14. As to the second Particular, *viz.* How far Hearsay is Evidence: It seems [a] agreed, That what a [b] Stranger has been heard to say is in Strictness no Manner of Evidence either for or against a Prisoner, not only because it is not upon Oath, but also because the other Side hath no Opportunity of a cross Examination; and therefore it seems a settled Rule, That it shall never be made use of but only by way of Inducement [c] or Illustration of what is properly Evidence; yet it seems [d] that what the Prisoner hath been heard to say at another Time may be given in Evidence for him, as well as against [e] him, and also what a † Witness hath been heard to say at another Time, may be given in Evidence in order either to invalidate or confirm the Testimony which he gives in Court.

Sect. 15. As to the third Particular, *viz.* whether Similitude of Hands be any Evidence in Criminal Cases: It is observable that this with other Circumstances in [f] *Algernoon Sydney*'s Case was ruled to be good Evidence of his having written a Paper charged against him as an Overt-act of High Treason: Yet in the Trial of the seven [g] Bishops, the Court was divided in Opinion, whether Similitude of Hands were Evidence of the Defendants having signed the Paper charged against them as a Libel; and the Parliament having declared an Opinion in the Reversal of *Algernoon Sydney*'s Attainder, that Comparison of Hands is no Evidence of a Man's Hand-Writing in Criminal Cases: It seems to have been generally holden [h] since that Time, that is not Evidence in any Criminal Case, whether capital or not capital.

As to the third Point, *viz.* who may be Witnesses in criminal Cases, I shall endeavour to shew,

1. Whether a Husband or Wife may be Witnesses for or against one another.
2. Whether a Judge or Juror may be a Witness.
3. Where an Accomplice in the Crime charged against a Prisoner may be a Witness against him or for him.
4. Where a Person shall be disabled to be a Witness in Respect of his having been attainted or convicted of a Crime.
5. Where it is a good Exception against a Witness that his Interest is concerned.
6. What other Exceptions are good against a Witness.

Sect. 16. As to the first of these Particulars, *viz.* Whether a Husband or Wife may be Witnesses for or against one another: It seems [i] agreed, That the Husband and Wife being as one and the same Person in Affection and Interest, can no more give Evidence for one another in any Case whatsoever than for themselves; and that regularly the one shall not be admitted to give Evidence against the other, nor the Examination of the one be made Use of against the other, by Reason of the implacable Dissension which might be caused by it, and the great Danger of Perjury from taking the Oaths of Persons under so great a Biass, and the extreme Hard-

* H.P.C. 263.
[k] Vide B. 1. ch. 42.
[a] State Trials, Vol. 2. f. 332, 414, 415, 761, 802, 803. Vol. 3. fol. 145, 210, 252. Vol. 4. f. 33.
[b] Vide supra, Sect. 3.
[c] State Trials, Vol. 2. f. 325, 328, 332, 333, 414, 415. Vol. 3. fol. 144, 145, 209, 210. Vol. 4. fol. 33.
[d] State Trials, Vol. 3. f. [illegible], 255.
[e] Vide supra, Sect. 3.
† State Trials, Vol. 2. fol. 529 802, 803. Vol. 3. fol. 218 to 222. 428, 429. Vol. 4. fol. 51, 52, 53. Vide Supra, Sect. 9. & 12.
[f] State Trials, Vol. 3. f. 213, 216, 217, 226, 230.
[g] State Trials, Vol. 3. fol. 762 to 767.
[h] Vide State Trials, Vol. 3. fol. 892, 893 Vol. 4. fol 271, 272. and Francia's Trial.
[i] Co. Litt. 6. b. 2 Rol. Abr. 686. pl. 4. H. P. C. 263. 1 Brownl. 47. Hutton, 116. Raym. 1. 2 Keb. 403. pl. 12. State Trials, Vol. 4. fol. 698.

Hardship of the Case: And therefore it hath been [a] adjudged, That the Husband cannot be a Witness against the Wife, nor the Wife against the Husband, to prove the first Marriage on an Indictment on the Statute of 1 [b] *Jac.* I. 11. for a second Marriage. Yet [c] some Exceptions have been allowed to this general Rule in Cases of evident Necessity, as in the Lord [d] *Audley*'s Case, who held his Wife's Hands and Legs while his Servant, by his Command, ravished her; or where a Man is indicted for a [e] Forcible Marriage against the [f] Purport of 3 *H.* 7. or where either a Husband or Wife have Cause to demand [g] Sureties of the Peace against the other, *&c.*

Sect. 17. As to the second Particular, *viz.* Whether a Judge or Juror may be a Witness: It seems [h] agreed, That it is no Exception against a Person's giving Evidence either for or against a Prisoner, that he is one of the Judges or Jurors who are to try him. And in the Case of [i] *Hacker*, two of the Persons in the Commission for the Trial came off from the Bench, and were sworn and gave Evidence, and did not go up to the Bench again during his Trial.

Sect. 18. As to the third Particular, *viz.* Where an Accomplice in the Crime charged against a Prisoner may be a Witness against him or for him: It has been long settled [k], That it is no Exception against a Witness that he hath confessed himself guilty of the same Crime, if he have not been [l] indicted for it; for if no Accomplices were to be admitted as Witnesses, it would be generally impossible to find Evidence to convict the greatest Offenders. Also it hath been often [m] ruled, That Accomplices who are indicted, are good Witnesses for the King until they be convicted. Also it hath been [n] adjudged, That such of the Defendants in an Information against whom no Evidence is given, may be Witnesses for the others. It hath been also [o] adjudged that where *A. B.* and *C.* are sued in three several Actions on the Statute for a supposed Perjury in their Evidence concerning the same Thing, they may be good Witnesses in such Actions for one another.

Sect. 19. As to the fourth Particular, *viz.* Where a Person shall be disabled to be a Witness in Respect of his having been attainted or convicted of a Crime: It seems agreed, That a Conviction, and therefore a *fortiori* an Attainder, or Judgment of [p] Treason, [q] Felony, [r] Piracy, [s] *Præmunire* or † Perjury, or of Forgery [u] on 5 *Eliz* and also a [x] Judgment in Attaint for giving a false Verdict, or in Conspiracy at the Suit of [y] the King, and also [z] Judgment for any * Crime whatsoever to stand in the Pillory, or to be whipt or branded, being in a Court which had a ¶ Jurisdiction, are good Causes of Exception against a Witness, while they continue in force.

[a] Raym. 1. *and the same Point was admitted in* Fielding's *Trial.* State Trials, Vol. 4. f. 754
[b] Vide B. 1. Ch. 43.
[c] *In* Raym. 1. *There is an Opinion that a Husband and Wife may be Witnesses against one another in Treason, but the contrary is adjudged,* 1 Brownl. 47. See 2 Keb 403.
[d] State Trials, Vol. 1. f. 265, 269. Hutt. 116. Rushw. Collections, part 2. Vol. 1. fol. 94, 99. *But this Case is denied to be Law,* Raym 1.
[e] Cro. Ca. 488. State Trials, Vol. 4. fol. 588. 3 Keb. 193. pl. 43.
[f] *See* B. 1. ch. 42.
[g] *See* B. 1. ch. 60. Sect. 4. Hutt. 116.
[h] State Trials, Vol. 2. fol. 257, 632, 674. Kely. 12. 1 Syd. 133. pl. 6.
[i] Kely. 12.
[k] State Trials, Vol. 1 f. 96, 696, 697, 723. Vol. 2. fol. 334, 501. Vol. 3. fol. 161, 217, *&c.* 595, 668, 669. Vol. 4. fol. 12, 33. *See* Hale's *Opinion to the contrary* arguendo. State Trials, Vol. 1. fol. 724 *and* Bracton 118. b.
[l] State Trials, Vol. 1. fol. 96. Vol. 2. fol. 501.
[m] State Trials, Vol. 1. fol. 966. Vol. 4. f. 12. Kely. 17, 18. 3 Keb. 136. pl. 70. Vide Vol. 1. fol. 697.
[n] 1 Sid. 237. pl. 4. Vide Trials per pais, 148. Style 401. 12 Ass. 12. Savil 34.
[o] 2 Rol. Abr. 685. pl. 3.
[p] 5 Mod. 16. Kely. 33.
[q] Raym. 369. Co. Litt. 6. b. 2 Bulst. 154.
[r] 2 Roll. Abr. 686. H. 2. 3.
[s] Co Litt. 6. b.
† Raym. 32. infra, §. Sect. 22, 23. Supra Ch. 37. Sect. 52. Co. Lit. 6. b. H. P. C. 263.
[u] Co. Litt. 6. b. Vide supra, Ch. 43. Sect. 25. 33 H. 6. 55. pl. 45. *But* H. P. C. 263. *'tis said in general that one attaint of Forgery cannot be a Witness.*
[x] Co. Litt. 6 b. 2 Roll. 684. pl. 4.
[y] 33 H. 6. 55. pl. 45. 24 E. 3. 34. pl. 34. Vide supra, Ch. 43. Sect. 25. B 1. ch. 72. Sect. 9. Co. Litt. 6. b *But* H. P. C. 263. *'tis said in general that one attaint of Conspiracy cannot be a Witness.*
[z] *That it is not material whether such Judgment were actually executed.* 2 Salk. 689. 3 Inst. 219. 3 Lev. 426. *But* Co. Litt. 6. b. Kely. 37, 38. H. P. C. 263. 5 Mod. 75, 76. *seem to make the Execution of the Judgment material*
* 2 Salk 689. 3 Lev. 426. *This Point is made a Quære* 5 Mod. 15, 16, 75, 76. *And it is said that by the Civil and Canon Law no such Judgment disables a Witness, unless the Nature of the Crime be infamous.* 3 Lev. 426, 427.
¶ 1 Sid. 51. pl. 16, Raym. 32.

Sect.

Sect. 20. But it is || agreed, That no ſuch Conviction or Judgment can be made uſe of to this Purpoſe, unleſs the Record be actually produced in Court. Alſo it is a general Rule that a ** Witneſs ſhall not be asked any Queſtion the anſwering to which might oblige him to accuſe himſelf of a Crime; and that his Credit is to †† be impeached only by general Accounts of his Character and Reputation, and not by Proofs of particular Crimes, whereof he never was convicted.

Sect. 21. It ſeems clear [a] at this Day, That Outlawry in a perſonal Action is not a good Exception againſt a Witneſs, as it is againſt a Juror. And that a Perſon convicted of Felony, who is admitted to his Clergy and [b] burnt in the Hand, is thereby re-enabled to be a Witneſs.

Sect. 22. It ſeems [c] agreed, That the King's Pardon of Treaſon or Felony after a Conviction or Attainder, reſtores the Party to his Credit: Alſo it was holden by the late Chief Juſtice [d] *Holt*, That the King's Pardon will remove a Man's Diſability to be a Witneſs in all Caſes whatſoever, wherein it is only the Conſequence of the Conviction or Judgment againſt him, and not an expreſs Part of the Judgment, as it is in Conſpiracy [e] at the Suit of the King, and in Perjury on the Statute. But this Matter [f] ſeems not to be fully ſettled.

Sect. 23. It hath been [g] ruled, That a Conviction of Perjury doth not diſable a Man from making an Affidavit in Relation to the Irregularity of a Judgment.

Sect. 24. As to the fifth Particular, *viz.* Where it is a good Exception againſt a Witneſs that his Intereſt is concerned: It ſeems an uncontеſted [h] Rule, in all Caſes whatſoever, That it is a good Exception againſt a Witneſs, that he is either to be a Gainer or Loſer by the Event of the Cauſe; whether ſuch Advantage be direct and immediate, or conſequential only. And this ſeems to be the Reaſon why he who is Bail for the Defendant, [i] cannot be an Evidence for him without Conſent. Alſo upon the ſame Ground it is [k] agreed, That he who borrows Money upon an uſurious Contract, cannot be a Witneſs upon an Information for the Uſury (unleſs he [l] hath paid the Money) whether ſuch Information be brought by himſelf or any other; for if in ſuch Caſe a Man might be a Witneſs, he would in Effect ſwear for himſelf, by proving a Matter which may avoid his own Contract. And upon the like Reaſon it hath been [m] ruled, That he who by a Slight has been impoſed upon to ſet his Hand to a Note for more Money than he intended, is no good Witneſs on an Information for the Cheat; becauſe a Conviction may be a Means to avoid the Note, by being made uſe of by the Party when ſued upon it as a Motive to influence the Jury, which cannot well be prevented, tho' in Law it be no [n] Evidence. And for the like Reaſon I take it to be generally * agreed, That he whoſe Property may be prejudiced by a Forgery, is no Evidence to prove it on an Indictment or Information. And if it be a Forgery within 5 *Eliz.* a farther Reaſon may be offered why ſuch a Perſon cannot be an Evidence becauſe he may have an Action on the Statute; and upon this Reaſon alone it hath been [o] adjudged, That he againſt whom a Verdict is given, cannot be a Witneſs to prove Perjury in the Evidence. And yet it appears from daily Experience, That [p] a Perſon beaten, and generally any other Perſon to whoſe [q] Damage a criminal Information concludes, is a good

|| State Trials, Vol. 1. f. 268. Vol. 2. f. 307, 436, 445. Vol. 3. f. 425. Vol. 4. f. 130.

** State Trials, Vol. 2. f. 268, 472. Vol. 3. f. 387, 1010. Vol. 4. f. 44. Cont. Ruſhw. Strafford, 605. & *ibid.* 558. *one was not admitted to ſpeak to clear himſelf.*

†† State Trials, Vol. 3. f. 256, 257, 680. Vol. 4. f. 129. 130. Vide Vol. 2. fol. 151, 267, 297.

[a] Co. Lit. 6 b. *But* 33 H. 6. 32. pl. 2. *taken Notice of*, 2 Rol. Abr. 675. pl. 4. *ſeems contrary.*

[b] Supra, Ch. 33. Sect. 129. Ch. 37. S. 49.

[c] Supra, Ch. 37. Sect. 48, 49, 50.

[d] 2 Salk. 514, 689. *But ſee* 2 Brow. 47.

[e] B. 1. Ch. 72. Sect. 9.

[f] Vide ſupra, Ch. 37. Sect. 52.

[g] 2 Salk. 461. pl. 3.

[h] Co. Lit. 6. 1 Sid. 237. pl. 5. 1 Keb. 836. pl. 17.

[i] State Trials, Vol. 3. fol. 253.

[k] Co Lit. 6. b. 2 Rol. Abr. 685. pl. 2.

[l] Raym. 191. Vide 2 Keb. 384. pl. 54.

[m] 1 Salk. 283. *Tet between the King and* Paris, 1 Sid. 431. 2 Keb. 572. pl. 84. 1 Vent. 49. *the contrary was ruled in a ſtronger Caſe, by* 3 *Judges againſt the Opinion of* Twyſden.

[n] 1 Salk 283. pl. 12. 1 Sid. 325.

* Salk. 283. pl. 12.

[o] 2 Rol. Ab. 685. pl. 4. *and the ſame Point is taken for granted.* 1 Sid. 237. pl. 5. 1 Keb. 836. pl. 17. Vide 1 Salk 283. pl. 12.

[p] 2 Rol. Ab. 685. pl. 5. 2 Keb. 572. pl. 84.

[q] 1 Sid. 237. pl. 5. 2 Keb. 384. pl. 54. 572. pl. 84. 1 Keb. 836. pl. 17. 1 Salk. 286. pl. 20. 1 Sid. 211. pl. 8.

good Evidence to prove ſuch Battery or other Miſdemeanor, notwithſtanding the Objection that he may have an Action. And therefore, upon the Whole, the Rules of Evidence concerning this Matter ſeem not to be clearly ſettled.

Sect. 25. It ſeems [a] agreed, That it is no good Exception againſt a Witneſs, That he has a Maintenance from the King; for every one may maintain his own Witneſſes. Alſo it hath been [b] adjudged to be no good Exception againſt a Witneſs, That he has received a Reward for having made a Diſcovery of the Crime to be proved againſt the Priſoner. Alſo it hath been [c] ruled to be no good Exception, That a Witneſs hath the Promiſe of a Pardon or other Reward on Condition of giving his Evidence, unleſs ſuch Reward be promiſed by way of Contract for giving ſuch and ſuch particular Evidence, or full Evidence, or any way in the leaſt to biaſs him to go beyond the Truth; which not being eaſily avoided in Promiſes or Threats of this Kind, it is certain that too great Caution cannot well be uſed in making them.

Sect. 26. As to the ſixth Particular, *viz.* What other Exceptions are good againſt a Witneſs: It ſeems [d] agreed to be a good Exception, That a Witneſs is an Infidel; that is, as I [e] take it, That he believes neither the Old nor New Teſtament to be the Word of God, on one of which our Laws require the Oath ſhould be adminiſtred.

Sect. 27. Alſo it is [f] certain, That want of Diſcretion is a good Exception againſt a Witneſs; on which Account alone it [g] ſeems that an Infant may be excepted againſt; for in ſome Caſes an Infant of nine Years of Age has been allowed to give Evidence.

Sect. 28. But it ſeems agreed, That it is no good [h] Exception againſt a Witneſs that he is an Alien, or Villain, or Bondman, &c.

Sect. 29. As to the fourth Point, *viz.* In what Manner the Witneſſes for the Defendant are to give their Evidence: It hath always been [i] agreed, That the Evidence for the King muſt in all Caſes be upon Oath, and alſo that the Evidence for the Defendant in an [k] Appeal, whether capital or not capital, or in an Indictment or Information for a [l] Miſdemeanour, muſt alſo be upon Oath. And it is ſaid by Sir *Edward* [m] *Coke*, *That we never read in any Statute, ancient Author, Book-caſe or Record, that in criminal Caſes the Party accuſed ſhould not have Witneſſes ſworn for him, and therefore that there is not ſo much as* ſcintilla juris *againſt it.* And it is ſaid by Sir [n] *Matthew Hale*, That there is no known Law againſt it. However there having been a conſtant immemorial [o] Practice not to ſuffer Witneſſes to be ſworn againſt the King upon Indictments of capital Crimes, [*] except in ſome Caſes ſpecially provided for by Statute; and the Judges being always tender of departing from the ſettled Practice of their Predeceſſors, and generally chooſing rather to preſume it originally founded on ſome Statute or other good Foundation, than to ſuffer the Reaſonableneſs of it to be nicely inquired into, which might be an Inlet to endleſs Uncertainties, it was thought neceſſary to enact by 1 *Anna* 9. *Par.* 3. *That after the twelfth of* February 1702. *every Perſon who ſhall be produced or appear as a Witneſs on the Behalf of the Priſoner, before he or ſhe be admitted to depoſe, or give any Manner of Evidence, ſhall firſt take an Oath to depoſe the Truth, the whole Truth, and nothing but the Truth, in ſuch Manner as the Witneſſes for the Queen are by Law obliged to do; and if convicted of any wilful Perjury in ſuch Evidence, ſhall ſuffer all the Puniſhments, Penalties, Forfeitures, and Diſabilities, which by any of the Laws and Statutes of this Realm, are or may be inflicted upon Perſons convicted of wilful Perjury*

[a] State Trials, Vol. 2. f. 334, 335, 691, 693.
[b] State Trials Vol. 1. f. 723, 724. Vol. 2. f. 334, 335. Vol. 4. fol. 121. Kely. 18.
[c] Kely. 18. State Trials, Vol. 2 f. 334, 335. 693. V. 3 f. 221, 222. *But Sir Mathew Hale of a different Opinion.* Kely. 18. Vide State Trials, Vol. 4. fol. 121.
[d] Co. Lit 6. State Trials, Vol. 4. f. 131.
[e] Vide Trigls per pais, 165. 2 Keb. 314. pl. 23.
[f] Co. Lit. 6.
[g] H P.C. 263. 1 Brownl 47.
[h] State Trials, Vol. 1. f. 253.
[i] H. P. C. 264. 2 Bulſt. 147.
[k] State Trials, Vol. 2. f. 737. 1 Sid. 325.
[l] 1 Sid. 211.
[m] 3 Inſt. 79.
[n] H. P. C. 264.
[o] Cro. Ca. 292. 2 Bulſt. 147. State Trials, Vol. 1. f. 55. 148. Vol. 2. fol. 296, 737. H. P. C. 264.
[*] Vide 31 El. Ch. 4. 4 Jac. ch. 1.

I Sect.

Sect. 30. As to the fifth Point, *viz.* Whether a Defendant in criminal Cases have Right to Process to bring in his Witnesses: I take it that in Prosecutions for [a] Misdemeanours the Defendant may take out *Subpœna's* of Course, but that in Capital Cases he hath no [b] Right by the Common Law to any Process against his Witnesses without a [c] special Order of the Court. But it is enacted by 7 *W.* 3. 3. *Par.* 7. *That all Persons Persons accused and indicted for any High Treason, whereby any Corruption of Blood may ensue, shall have the like Process of the Court where they shall be tried, to compel their Witnesses to appear for them at any such Trial or Trials, as is usually granted to compel Witnesses to appear against them.* And it seems that since the Statute of 1 *Anne* 9. set forth more at large in the precedent Section, which ordains, That the Witnesses for the Prisoner shall be sworn, Process may be taken out against them of course in any Case whatsoever.

Sect. 31. As to the sixth Point, *viz.* What Evidence maintains an Indictment, *&c.* Having already shewn, *Ch.* 25, *Sect.* 117. and *Book* 1. *Ch.* 30. *Sect.* 9 That according to the later Opinions, where one is indicted upon a Statute, and the Evidence doth not bring the Case within the Statute, but yet proves the Offence in the Indictment as it is an Offence at the Common Law, the Defendant may be found guilty at the Common Law, and the Words *contra formam Statuti* rejected as Surplus; having also shewn, *Ch.* 35. *Sect.* 11. That it is strongly holden that a Man cannot be found Guilty of an Indictment against him as Principal, upon Evidence which only proves him to have been Accessory before, but shall be discharged of the Indictment; I shall in this Place take Notice only of the following Particulars.

Sect. 32. *First*, That it is a settled Rule [d] in all Cases, whether capital or not capital, That the Day laid in the Indictment or [e] Appeal is not material upon Evidence, but that the Defendant may be convicted upon Proof of a Fact at any other Time, whether before or after the Day laid; so [f] that it were before the Time when the Indictment or Appeal were preferred. And agreeably hereto Sir [g] *Henry Vane* was found guilty of an Indictment of High Treason laid on the 30th of *May* 11 *Car* 2. upon Evidence of a Fact done the 30th of *January*, 1 *Car.* 2.

Sect. 33. *Secondly*, That where the Time proved varies from that laid in the Indictment or Appeal the Jury [g] may either find the Defendant guilty generally, in which Case the Forfeiture shall relate to the Time laid, till the Verdict be falsify'd by the Party interested, (as it may be in this [h] Respect, tho' not as to the Point of the Offence,) or they may [i] Specially find him Guilty on the Day on which the Fact is proved, whether before or after the Day laid in the Indictment or Appeal, in which Case the Forfeiture shall relate to the Day so specially found. But where a Verdict expressly finds a Defendant guilty before the Time laid in the Indictment or Appeal, whether it may be falsified, as to the Time, by the Party interested, as it may be where it finds him guilty generally of the Offence in the Indictment or Appeal, upon Evidence of a Fact after the Time laid, may deserve to be consider'd.

Sect. 34. *Thirdly*, That where a certain [k] Place is made Part of the Description of the Fact which is charged against the Defendant, the least Variance as to such Place between the Evidence and Indictment is fatal; as where a Trespass in taking away Goods, or any other Offence is alledged in such a Parish in the House of *J. S.* or in such a Parish in a Play-House in *Lincoln's-Inn-Fields*, and upon Evidence it appear to have been done at the House of a different Person, or that there is no Play-House in *Lincoln's-Inn-Fields*. But it is a settled [l] Rule, That a Place laid

[a] State Trials, Vol. 1. f. 969. Vol. 3 f. 238, 252, 420.

[b] Vide State Trials, Vol. 1. f. 969. Vol 3. f. 1002, 1003.

[c] *But in Turner's Case*, State Trials, Vol. 1 f 995. *'Tis said that the Court can't grant the Prisoner any Precept to bring in his Witnesses.* &c.

[d] H. P. C. 264. 3 Inst. 230. 1 Salk. 288. Kely. 16. 2 Inst. 318, 319. State Trials, Vol. 4. fol. 9.

[e] H. P. C. 187.

[f] 1 Salk. 288. State Trials, Vol. 4. f. 9.

[g] Kely. 16.

[g] H. P. C. 264. 2 Inst. 318. 3 Inst. 230,

[h] H. P. C. 264, 270. 3 Inst. 230. *and* infra, *in Chapter* 51.

[i] Kely. 16. H. P. C. 264. 2 Inst. 318. 3 Inst. 230.

[k] Salk. 385, 661.

[l] H. C. C. 264, 265. Salk. 288. State Trials, Vol. 4. f. 9. Kely. 15, 33.

laid only for a Venue in an Indictment or Appeal is no way material upon Evidence; but that a Proof of the same Crime at any other Place in the [a] same County, maintains the Indictment or Appeal as well as if it had been proved in the very same Place. Also it hath been [b] adjudged, That after a Crime hath been proved in the County in which it is laid, Evidence may be given of other Instances of the same Crime in another County, in order to satisfy the Jury. Also it was [c] adjudged in Sir *Henry Vane*'s Case, That where one is indicted for High Treason in compassing the Kings Death in the County of *M.* and the levying of War in the same County is laid as an Overt-Act of such Treason, and [c] proved in the same County by one Witness, the levying of War in another County may also be proved by another Witness. But it seems to have been [d] agreed at the same Time, That where the levying of War is the Treason for which the Party is indicted, it must be fully proved in the County in which it is laid. Also it seems, That at this Day the levying of War can in no Case be given in Evidence as an Overt-Act in any County in which it is not laid, unless it tend to prove some Overt-Act that is expressly laid; for it is enacted by 7 *Wil.* 3. 3. *Par.* 8. *That no* [e] *Evidence shall be admitted or given of any Overt-Act that is not expressly laid in the Indictment against any Person or Persons whatsoever.* In the Construction whereof it hath been [f] adjndged, That where one is indicted for High Treason in adhering to the King's Enemies, and certain Acts of Hostility done by him in a certain Ship called the *Clencarty*, are laid as the Overt-Acts of such Adherence, no Evidence can be given of any other distinct Act of Adherence, having no Relation to, nor any way tending to prove, what was done in the *Clencarty*, tho' it conduce to prove the same Species of Treason; and therefore that on such an Indictment no Evidence can be given of the Prisoner's having run away to the Enemy in a Custom-House boat, *&c.* But it hath been [g] adjudged, That where one is indicted for High Treason in compassing the King's Death, and a Consult and Agreement to assassinate the King is laid as one of the Overt-Acts of such Treason, the Defendant's giving about among the Conspirators a List of the Persons Names who were intended to be employed in the Assassination, may be given in Evidence against him upon such Indictment, because it naturally tends to prove his Agreement to the intended Assassination, which Agreement is one of the Overt-Acts laid in the Indictment. Also it hath been been [h] adjudged, That where the writing of several treasonable Letters is laid as an Overt-Act of High Treason in Compassing the King's Death, and the Purport of such Letters is only set forth in the Indictment without a particular Recital or Description of any of them, the particular Letters making good such Charge may be read at the Trial.

Sect. 35. *Fourthly*, That where several Overt-Acts are laid in an Indictment of High Treason, the Proof of any [i] one of them maintains the Indictment as much as if every one of them were proved.

Sect. 36. *Fifthly*, That where one is indicted for writing a [k] Libel *secundum tenorem sequentem*, or for forging a Deed so and so described, any the least Variance between the Libel recited or Deed described, and those given in Evidence, is fatal; but that where the Substance only of a Libel is set forth in *Latin*, it is sufficient if the Libel be proved to have the same Sense as is set forth. Yet it seems [l] agreed, That it is no Evidence in any criminal Case, that the Defendant said so and so, or Words to the like Effect; because the Court must know the very Words to judge of their Force and Effect.

[a] *See the Books above-cited, and* Supra, ch. 25. Sect. 34 *to* 52. *and* Cro. Eliz 911.
[b] Kely. 33.
[c] Kely. 14, 15. State Trials, Vol. 1. f. 932. Vol. 2. f. 317, 776, 785. Vide Vol. 1. f. 843. Vol. 4. f. 78.
[c] *For it is necessary that some Overt-act be proved in the same County; for otherwise the compassing cou'd no way be said to be proved in the County wherein it is laid. See the Books above-cited.*
[d] Kely. 15.
[e] Vide State Trials, Vol. 1. f. 843.
[f] State Trials Vol. 4. f. 331, 332, 333.
[g] State-Trials, Vol. 4. f. 124, 125, 132, 133, 134.
[h] Francia's Trial. Vide Vol. 1. fol. 617, 950. Vol. 2. f. 98, 99, 112, &c. 322, 323. Vol. 3. f. 857, 1009. *Yet in some Indictments the very Words charged to have been treasonable have been set forth.* State Trials, Vol. 2. fol. 746. Vol. 3. fol. 204, 219.
[i] State Trials, Vol. 1. f. 843, 851. V. 2. fol. 430. Vol. 4. f. 159.
[k] Salk 660, 661. H[illegible] 272.
[l] [illegible]. 294.

Sect. 37. *Sixthly*, That a Variance between an Indictment or Appeal of Death, and the Evidence as to the instrumental Cause mentioned in such Indictment or Appeal, is no [a] way material, so that the Party be proved to have died by the same kind of Death as is alledged in the Indictment or Appeal. And therefore it is [b] agreed, That if one be indicted or appealed for killing another with a Sword, and upon Evidence it appear that he killed him with a Staff, Hatchet, Bill or Hook, or any other Weapon with which a Wound may be given, he ought to be found guilty; for the Substance of the Matter is, whether he gave the Party a Wound of which he died, and it is not material with what Weapon he gave it, tho' for Form's sake it be [c] necessary to set forth a particular Weapon. And on the same Ground it hath been also [e] adjudged, That an indictment, or Appeal for poisoning a Man with one kind of Poison, may be maintained by Evidence of a different kind of Poison; for the Substance of the Matter is whether the Defendant did poison the Deceased or not. [f] Yet it seems clear, That Evidence of poisoning, burning, or famishing, or any other kind of killing wherein no Weapon is used, will not maintain an Indictment or Appeal of Death by killing with a Weapon; and that Evidence of killing with a Weapon will not maintain an Indictment or Appeal of Poisoning, *&c.* because they are different Kinds of Deaths; and in like Manner that an Indictment of Treason could [g] never be maintained by Evidence of Treason of a different Species.

Sect. 38. *Seventhly*, That it seems a [h] general Rule, That wherever a Variance between an Indictment or Appeal, and the Evidence brought to support them, is material or immaterial in Respect of the Principal; in the same Cases also it will be material or immaterial in Respect of the Accessary.

Sect. 39. *Eighthly*, That it is [i] settled at this [k] Day, That if an Indictment or Appeal against *A. B.* and C. for the Death of *D.* charge *A.* as having given the mortal Blow, and *B.* and C. as having been present, procuring and abetting, and the Evidence prove that *B.* and *C.* gave the Blow, and that *A.* was only present procuring and abetting; yet it maintains the Indictment, because in such a Case in the [k] Judgment of Law, the Act of any of them is the Act of all.

Sect. 40. *Ninthly*, That it hath been [l] resolved, That if one be indicted as Accessary to two, and upon Evidence appear to have been Accessary to one of them only, yet he shall be found guilty. But it is [m] holden by Sir *Edward Coke*, That if an Appeal be brought against two as Principals, and against another as Accessary to them, and one of those charged as Principals be found not guilty, the Accessary is discharged, for which he gives this Reason, That because the Plaintiff made him Accessary to two, he cannot be found Accessary to one. But no Authority is cited for the Maintenance of this Opinion; neither doth it seem easy to reconcile it with the Resolution above-mentioned, unless the Rules of Evidence on an Appeal differ from those on an Indictment, which I do not [n] find that they do as to other Variances.

[a] 9 Co. 67. 2 Inst, 319. 3 Inst. 135. H. P. C 265.
[b] *See the Books above-cited, and* supra Ch. 23. Sect. 84.
[c] Vide supra, Ch. 23. S. 84.
[d] 3 Inst. 135. H. P. C. 265. 3 Inst. 319.
[e] H. P. C. 265. 2 Inst. 319.
[f] State Trials Vol 4 f. 9.
[h] H. P. C. 265. 3 Inst. 165.
[i] *But there were anciently some Opinions to the contrary.* Supra Ch. 29. Sect. 9 Lett. x. S. P. C 41. Lett. A. B.
[k] Plow Com. 98, 100, a. 1 Salk. 334, 335. 3 Mod. 121. 9 Co. 67. b. 4 H. 7. 18. pl. 10. *Abridged* Fitz. Coro. 60. Bro. Appeal, 85. Coro. 140 *or* 141, S. P. C 41. Lett. A. B. Supra, Ch. 23. Sect. 76. Ch. 25. Sect. 66.
[k] *See the Books above-cited, and* B. 1. Ch. 32. Sect. 6.

Ch. 31. Sect 31. *and* 50. Ch. 34. Sect. 7. Ch. 38. Sect. 8, 9. Ch. 41. Sect. 6. H. P. C. 222, 265. Vide Keilw. 107. *and* supra, Ch. 29. Sect. 46, 47.

[l] 9 Co. 119. a.
[m] 2 Inst. 183.
[n] Vide supra, Sect. 32, 34, 37, 38. 39.

[o] 9 Ch 67.b. Cro Jac 280. H P.C. 266.
[p] See B. 1. Ch. 31. Sect. 18, 19, and S. 40 to 43.
[q] 9 Co. 67.
[a] 9 Co. 62, 63, 67.

Sect. 41. *Tenthly*, That it hath been [o] agreed, That if a Person be generally indicted for the Murder of another *ex malitia præcogitata*, and no express Malice appear upon the Evidence but only [p] Malice implied by Law, yet he shall be found guilty. Also it hath been [q] adjudged, That where an Indictment sets forth all the special Matter in Respect whereof the Law implies Malice, a Variance between the Indictment and Evidence, as to the Circumstances doth no Hurt, so that the Substance of the Matter be found. As [a] where an Indictment for the Murder of a Serjeant of Mace in *London* upon an Arrest, supposes that the Sheriff made a Precept to such Serjeant for the Arrest, and upon the Evidence it appears that there was not any such Precept, but that the Serjeant made the Arrest *ex Officio* at the Plaintiff's Request upon the Entry of the Plaint, according to the Custom of the City; for the Substance of the Matter is whether the Defendant killed an Officer in the lawful Execution of legal Process.

[b] Co. Litt. 6. b. S P. C. 179. Lett. A. Vide supra, Ch. 45. Sect. 10. and State Trials, Vol. 1. fol. 181, 636. Vol. 2. fol. 408. Vol. 3. f. 228, 229, 688, 689, 894 to 901, 928, 929, 930.
[c] Co. Litt. 6. b.

Sect. 42. *Eleventhly*, That violent [b] Presumption from plain Circumstances is in some Cases taken for full Proof; as where a Man is stabbed in a House, and another runs out with a bloody Knife in his Hand, and no one else is in the House at the Time; also it is [c] said, That a probable Presumption is of some Weight, but that a light one is not to be regarded at all.

[d] Kely. 32.
[e] Kely. 32, 33.
[f] Kely. 32.
[g] Kely. 33.

Sect. 43. *Twelfthly*, That it is enacted by 21 *Jac.* 27. *That if any Woman be delivered of any Issue of her Body, Male or Female, which being born alive should by the Laws of this Realm be a Bastard, and that she endeavour privately, either by drowning, or secret burying thereof, or any other way, either by herself or the procuring of others, so to conceal the Death thereof, as that it may not come to light, whether it were born alive or not, but be concealed; in every such Case, the said Mother so offending shall suffer Death as in Case of Murder, except such Mother can make Proof by one Witness at the least, that the Child whose Death was by her so intended to be concealed was born dead.* In the Construction whereof it hath been [b] adjudged, That in order to convict a Woman by Force of this Statute, there is no need that the Indictment be drawn specially, or conclude *contra formam Statuti*; but that it is the better way to set forth only that the Defendant *infantem masculum vivum parturiit, qui quidem infans masculus adtunc & ibidem vivus existens natus per legem hujus regni Angliæ Spurius fuit, Anglice* a Bastard, and then to go on in the ordinary Way to shew that she murdered him, *&c. contra pacem, &c.* for the Statute doth not make a new Offence, but only make such Concealment an undeniable Evidence of Murder. Also it hath been [c] agreed, That where a Woman appears to have endeavoured to conceal the Death of such Child within the Statute, there is no need of any Proof that the Child was born alive, or that there were any Signs of Hurt upon the Body, but it shall be undeniably taken that the Child was born alive and murdered by the Mother. But it hath been [d] adjudged, That where a Woman lay in a Chamber by herself, and went to Bed without Pain, and waked in the Night, and knocked for Help but could get none, and was delivered of a Child and put it in a Trunk, and did not discover it till the following Night, yet she was not within the Statute, because she knocked for Help. Also it hath been [e] agreed, That if a Woman confess herself with-child before-hand, and afterwards be surprised and delivered, no Body being with her, she is not within the Statute, because there was no Intent of Concealment. And therefore in such Cases it must appear by Signs of Hurt upon the Body, or some other way, that the Child was born alive.

Sect. 44. As to the ſeventh Point, *viz.* What may be given in Evidence on the part of the Defendant: It ſeems [f] agreed, That *ſon aſſault Demeſne* may be given in Evidence on the General Iſſue in an Indictment, but not in an Action of Battery. Alſo it ſeems to have been always [g] agreed, that the Defendant in an Information on a Penal Statute may give in Evidence any Exception in his Favour in the Body of the Act. And it hath alſo been [h] holden that he may give in Evidence any ſuch Exception in a *Proviſo* of the Act, (becauſe any ſuch Exception ſhews that he did not act againſt the Form of the Statute;) but that he cannot [d] give in Evidence any Clauſe of Exemption in a later Statute, but ought to plead it.

[a] B. 1. Ch. 62. Sect. 3.
[b] Savil, 32. pl. 75.
1 Jon. 157.
2 Rol. Abr. 683. pl. 11.
[c] 2 Roll. Ab. 683. pl. 10, 12.
But this is left a Quære Savil, 32. pl 75.

Bro General Iſſue, 3. Vide Supra Ch. 25. Sect. 115. [d] 2 Roll. Abr. 683. pl. 13.

CHAP. XLVII.

Of Verdict.

FOR the general Learning of Verdicts I ſhall refer to other Books, and in this Place take Notice only of the following Particulars;

Sect. 1. 1*ſt.* That it ſeems to have been [e] anciently an uncontroverted Rule, and hath been allowed, even by thoſe [f] of the contrary Opinion, to have been the general Tradition of the Law, That a Jury ſworn and charged in a capital [g] Caſe, cannot be diſcharged (without the [h] Priſoner's Conſent) till they have given a Verdict. And notwithſtanding ſome [i] Authorities to the contrary in the Reign of King *Charles* II. this hath been holden for clear Law both in the Reign of King [l] *James* II. and [m] ſince the Revolution.

Sect. 2. 2*ndly*, That it ſeems to have been * always agreed, That in all † capital Caſes the Jury muſt give their Verdict openly in Court, and cannot give a privy Verdict.

Sect. 3. 3*dly*, That it is ſettled, [n] That the Jury may give a ſpecial Verdict in any criminal Caſe, whether capital or not capital, as well as in a Civil.

Sect. 4. 4*thly*, That it hath been [o] adjudged, That where the Jury find a Man not guilty of an Indictment or Appeal of Murder, they are not bound to make any Inquiry, whether he be guilty of Manſlaughter, *&c.* But that if they will they may, according to the Nature of the Evidence, find him guilty of [p] Manſlaughter or [q] Homicide *ſe defendendo*, or *per infortunium*; for the killing is the Subſtance, and the Malice but a Circum-

[e] Co. Litt. 227. b.
3 Inſt. 110.
1 And. 103, 104.
H. P. C. 267.
[f] Raym. 84.
[g] *And the ſame is holden by* Coke *as to Larceny, and any Caſe of Member.*
3 Inſt 110.
Co. Lit. 227. b. *but as to Caſes of an Inferior Nature, the contrary hath been adjudged,* Raym. 84.
[h] 1 And. 103, 104.
[i] Kely. 47, 52.
State Trials, Vol. 1. fol. 978. Vol. 2. fol. 155, 277, 389.

Raym. 84. [l] State Trials Vol. 3. f 678. Vide ſupra Ch. 44. Sect. 22. [m] State Trials, Vol 4. fol. 110, 178, 179. * Co Lit. 227. b. 3 Inſt. 110. Raym. 193. † *The ſame is holden by Sir* Edward Coke, *as to Larceny, and any Caſe of Member,* 3 Inſt. 110. Co. Lit. 227. b. *And it is ſaid in* Raym. 193. *That no privy Verdict can be given in any Caſe where the Jury are to look upon the Priſoner when they give it.* [n] S. P. C 165. Lett. C. 1I P. C. 267. 9 Co. 12. b. 63. 1 Bulſt. 87. Vide infra, Sect. 6. *But it is ſaid,* Kely. 29, 30. *That it is diſhonourable for the Court to ſuffer a ſpecial Verdict in a plain Caſe.* [o] Cro. Eliz. 276, pl. 5. 296, pl. 2. 464. pl. 13. [p] Dyer, 261. pl. 26. 4 Co. 43. b. 9 Co. 81. Daliſ. 14. H. P. C. 267. Latch, 126. Pl. Com. 101. Cro. Eliz. 276. pl. 5. 296, pl. 2. 464, pl. 13. Moor 407. pl. 546. Bro. Coro. 121 *or* 122. *But* 2 Roll. Re. 461, *this was queſtioned as to an Appeal of Death.* [q] Bro. Coro. 1. H. P. C. 267. Daliſ. 14. S. P. C. 165. Lett. A. *See the Books cited to the following Section.*

ſtance

stance, a [r] Variance as to which hurts not the Verdict. Yet the Books seem to make this Difference, That where the Jury find the Defendant guilty of Manslaughter on an Indictment of Murder, they may give their Verdict [s] generally, without setting out any of the Circumstances of the Fact: But that they shall not [a] be received to find him guilty generally of Homicide *se defendendo*, or *per infortunium*, but must set out the whole Circumstances of the Fact, and in the [b] Conclusion shew of what Crime they find the Defendant guilty, wherein if they be mistaken, it is [c] said, That the Court may notwithstanding give such Judgment as shall appear to be proper from the Circumstances of the Fact specially set forth.

Sect. 5. *5thly*, That it hath been [d] adjudged, That if the Jury on an Indictment or Appeal of Murder find the Defendant guilty of Manslaughter, without saying any thing expresly as to the Murder, it is insufficient and void, as being only a Verdict for Part. And *Quære* if the Law be not the same where the Jury upon such an Indictment find that the Defendant killed the Deceased *se defendendo* or *per infortunium*, and do not expresly find that he did not murder him, according to the Generality of the ancient [e] Authorities.

Sect. 6. *6thly*, That it is agreed, That on an Indictment for stealing Goods of a certain Value above 12 *d.* the [f] Jury may find the Defendant guilty, but that the Goods are but of the Value of 10 *d.* &c. But it seems that if a Man be indicted for Felony, generally, and upon the Evidence it [g] plainly appear that the Fact amounts to no more than a bare Trespass, he cannot be found guilty of the Trespass, but ought to be indicted anew. Yet if the special Circumstances of the Case be set forth in an Indictment for an Offence laid as Felony, and the Defendant be found guilty generally, and afterwards the Court be of Opinion that the Fact doth not amount to Felony, but only to an enormous Trespass, it seems [h] agreed, That Judgment may be given as for a Trespass only. Also if the Jury find a special Verdict on a general Indictment for Felony; and the Crime be adjudged upon such Verdict to be but a Trespass, [i] Judgment may be given upon it as for a Trespass only. Also if on an Indictment of Trespass the Fact appear to have been felonious, it hath been [k] adjudged, That the Defendant may be found guilty of the Indictment as it is laid, because the King may proceed against the Offender as he thinks fit, either as a Trespasser or Felon. But the contrary is [l] said to have been holden by the late Chief Justice *Holt*; and it hath been [m] adjudged, That if it appear in an Action of Trespass that the Taking was felonious, no Verdict ought to be taken unless the Defendant have been before tried for the Felony, because the suffering such Actions might be a Means to prevent Prosecutions for Felonies.

[r] 1 Bulst. 87. *'Tis holden by two Judges against one, That where the Appeal mentioned three Wounds and the Verdict found but one, yet the Variance was immaterial.* Vide Ch. 46. Sect. 37.

[s] *See the Books cited under Letter* p.

[a] H. P. C. 267. S. P. C. 15. Lett B. 165. Lett. A. 3 Inst. 56. 26 H. 8. 5. a. Aleyn 12.

[b] Fitz. Coro. 264, 286, 287, 305. Vide Benl. 47. 1 And. 41.

[c] 43 Ass. pl 31. Fitz. Coro. 226. Crompt. Just. 114 pl. 1. S. P. C. 165. Lett. A. Vide Bendl. 47 1 And. 41.

[d] 1 And 103. 104. *and note, That in all the Books cited under the precedent Section to Lett.* p. *where the Defendant is found guilty of Manslaughter on an Indictment of Murder, he is expresly acquitted of the Murder. but other Books which speak of this Matter, say in general, That the Defendant may be found guilty of Manslaughter on an Indictment of Murder, without saying any thing as to the Necessity of giving an express Verdict upon the Murder.* 9 Co. 67 b. Crompt. Just. 114. pl. 5. H P. C. 267. *See* 4 Co. 40. a. 46. b.

[e] Fitz Coro. 284, 285, 287. Sed Vide 44 E. 3. 44. pl. 55. Fitz. Coro. 94. Benl. 47. 1 And. 41.

[f] Fitz. Coro. 115, 177, 451. 18 Ass. pl 14. H. P. C. 267. S. P. C. 165. Lett. B. Crompt. Just. 114. pl. 2. B 1. Ch. 35. Sect 4

[g] Kely 29, 30. Cro. Ca. 332. *'Tis made a Quære* 2 H. 7. pl. 22. *and* 10 pl. 6. *whether where an Indictment of Larceny is insufficient as to the Felony, the Party may be found guilty of the same taking as for a Trespass.*

[h] Kely 29, 30. Cro. Ca. 376, 377. 1 Jon. 351.

[i] Cro. Ja. 497, 498.

[k] 18 Ed. 4. 10. pl. 28. 2 Lev. 208. Vide supra, Ch. 35. Sect 5. *and* Ch. 36. Sect 6. *That an Acquittal or Judgment against a Man in an Action or Indictment of Trespass is no Bar on an Indictment or Appeal of Larceny.* Kely. 30.

[l] 6 Mod. 77.

[m] 2 Roll. Abr. 556, pl. 19. 557. pl. 20, 21, 22, 23. 24. Noy 18. Vide 1 Jon. 147. Noy 82. Latch, 145. 1 Mod. 283. Cont. Bract. *cited* S. P. C. 28 a. 83. b.

Sect. 7. *7thly*, That it hath been holden, That a Verdict acquitting a Defendant of the Death of a Man found against him by the Coroner's Inquest, ought not to be received unless it shew what other Person did the Fact; but for this I shall refer to *Ch.* 9. *Sect.* 33.

Sect. 8. *8thly*, That on an Indictment for a Riot against three or more, if a Verdict acquit all but two and find them guilty; or on an Indictment for a Conspiracy, if the Verdict acquit all but one, and find him guilty, it is repugnant and [n] void as to the two found guilty in the first Case, and as to the one found guilty in the second, unless the Indictment charge them with having made such Riot, or Conspiracy, *simul cum aliis, juratoribus ignotis*; for otherwise it appears that the Defendants are found guilty of an Offence whereof it is impossible that they should be guilty; for there can be no Riot where there are no more Persons than two, nor can there be a Conspiracy where there is no Partner. Yet it seems [a] agreed, That if twenty Persons are indicted for a Riot or Conspiracy, and any three found guilty of the Riot, or any two of the Conspiracy, the Verdict is good; And that [b] where several are indicted for Treason or Felony, or other Crime, which may be as well done by one only, as by more, a Verdict [c] may find one of the Defendants only guilty, and acquit all the rest. And in like Manner it seems [d] agreed, That a Verdict on an Information on a penal Statute against several Persons jointly charged with the Offence against the Statute, may acquit some and find others guilty; because tho' the Words of the Information be joint, yet in Judgment of Law, each Defendant is severally charged for his own Offence. And in like Manner it [e] seems, That the Defendant in such Information may be found guilty for a less Time, or Degree than is laid, unless the Offence consist in the doing some entire Thing which must be precisely proved in the same Manner as it is laid.

Sect. 9. *9thly*, That the Court in judging upon a special Verdict is confined to the Facts expresly found, and cannot supply the Want thereof, as to any material Part by any Argument or Implication from what is expresly found; and therefore where an Indictment set forth that the Defendant discharged a Gun against *J. S.* and thereby give him a mortal Wound, *&c.* and the Special Verdict found that he discharged a Gun and thereby killed *J. S.* but did not expresly say that he discharged it against *J. S.* it was [f] adjudged, That the Court could not take it from the other Circumstances of the Fact, which were expresly found, tho' they were as full to the Purpose as possibly they could well be, that the Defendant discharged the Gun against *J. S.*

Sect. 10. *10thly*, That it hath been [g] adjudged, That where an Indictment found at the Assises is removed into the King's Bench by *Certiorari*, and there the Defendant pleads Not guilty, *& de hoc ponit se super patriam, &* T. F. *Miles coronator & attornatus Dom' Regis, &c. similiter*, and thereupon the Defendant is found Guilty of the Offence *in Indictamento prædict' interius ei imposit' prout prædict.* T. F. *interius versus eum queritur*, the Verdict is good; for those Words *prout prædict.* T. F. *interius versus eum queritur* shall be rejected as Surplus, [h] repugnant and void, and the Verdict is compleat without them.

[n] Poph. 202. 1 Salk. 385. State Trials, Vol. 2. f. 60, 61. Vol. 4. f. 160, 161. *In the Year-Book of* 11 H. 4. 2. pl. 3. *Abridged* Fitz. Verdict, 18. *It is agreed, That such a Verdict is repugnant, and therefore the Court would not receive it, but sent the Jury back again, where upon they found both the Defendants guilty.*

[a] State Trials Vol. 4. fol. 160, 161.

[b] State Trials, Vol. 4. f. 160, 161.

[c] *Yet it hath been holden, That on an Indictment of Burglary and other Felony against* A *and* B. *the Jury cannot upon the very same Evidence against both, find* A. *guilty of the Burglary, and* B. *of the Felony only*, 1 Sid. 171. pl. 4.

[d] Vide supra, Ch. 26. Sect. 75.

[e] Vide supra, Ch. 26. Sect. 75. *and* State Trials, Vol. 4. fol. 160, 161.

[f] Kely. 111.

[g] 2 Saund. 308.

[h] *See* B. 1. Ch. 30. Sect. 9. *What is a good Verdict on an Indictment of Forgery*, B. 1. Ch. 70. Sect. 27.

Sect. 11. 11*thly*, That it hath been [a] adjudged, That if the Jury acquit a Prisoner of an Indictment of Felony against manifest Evidence, the Court may, before the Verdict is recorded, but [b] not after, order them to go out again and reconsider the Matter; but this is by many thought hard, and seems not of late Years to have been so frequently practised as formerly. Also there are [c] Instances where Defendants acquitted against plain Evidence, of Felonies and other enormous Crimes, have been bound to their Good Behaviour. However it is settled, That the Court cannot set aside a Verdict which [d] acquits a Defendant of a Prosecution properly criminal, as it seems that they may a Verdict that [e] convicts him for having been given contrary to Evidence, and the Directions of the Judge, or any Verdict whatever for a [d] Mistrial.

[a] 1 And. 104. Crompt Just. 114. pl. 6. Aleyn, 12. Vide State. Trials, Vol. 2. f. 60, 61. [b] Crompt. Just. 114. pl. 6. Fitz. Coro. 108. [c] Cro. Ca. 292. *against the Opinion of* Cro. *and* Berkely, *and* Cro. Ja. 507. Vide State Trials, Vol. 2. fol. 60, 61. *where the Court upon the Acquittal of the Defendants of the Indictment against them for a Riot, committed them for their contempt to the Court during the Trial.* [d] *Agreed in the Case of the* King *and* Bennet, Hill. 4 Georgii, *wherein it was holden by six of the Judges against six. That a new Trial was not grantable upon an Acquittal on an Information in the Nature of a* Quo Warranto, *because it sounds in the Criminalty.* 1 Keb. 124. pl. 33. 2 Keb. 403, pl. 14. 404. pl. 18. *Whether it be grantable for a corrupt Practice in obtaining a Verdict,* 1 Lev. 9, 10, 124. 1 Sid. 153, 154. 1 Keb. 546, pl. 47. 568, pl. 16. 590. pl. 54. 3 Keb. 179. pl. 2. 409. pl. 31. Shower 336. *That it is not grantable where the Acquittal was occasioned by a slip in an Indictment of Perjury in varying from the Original Record,* 2 Keb. 409 pl. 31. [e] *Adjudged* 2 Jon. 163. 3 Keb. 525. 1 Lev. 9. *But it is doubted* 1 Keb. 124. pl. 33. 127. pl. 43. 5 Mod. 350. 1 Sid. 49. pl. 12. *and the contrary is ruled* 2 Keb. 396, pl. 81. 403. pl. 14. [f] *See* 6 Co. 14. b. 1 Keb. 546. Supra, Ch. 23. Sect. 92. *and* Ch. 36. Sect. 15.

CHAP. XLVIII.

Of Judgment.

Sect. 1. HAving shewn already what Judgment is good on an Information, or Action *qui tam*, and *Ch.* 33. *Sect.* 135, *&c.* where it may be saved by an Award of Transportation, and *Ch.* 25. *Sect.* 149. That Judgment in High Treason, not being for counterfeiting the Coin, or Seal, *&c.* shall not be arrested for Miswriting or Misspelling, or false or improper *Latin*: Having also premised, That by the Course of the Court of King's Bench, upon every Conviction in that Court, of a Crime [f] capital or not [g] capital, whether by * Verdict or Confession, the Party is to have four Days to move in [h] Arrest of Judgment, if there be so many Days remaining of the Term; and if not, [i] then the longest Time that can be had in the Term: Having also premised, That on a Conviction of Homicide *se defendendo*, or *per infortunium*, no [k] Judgment at all is to be given, but the Party let to Mainprize in Order to purchase his Pardon, I shall farther endeavour to shew the Nature,

[f] Algernoon Sidney's *Case*, State Trials, Vol. 3. fol. 207, 231. Rosewell's *Case*, State Trials, Vol. 3. Knightley's *Case*, State Trials, Vol. 4. fol. 215. [g] State Trials Vol. 3. fol. 77. * State Trials, Vol. 4. fol. 210. [h] *But in* Saund. 301, 302. *Chief Justice* Hale *refused to hear any Motion in Arrest of Judgment of a scandalous Conspiracy; but in my own Experience I never knew such a Motion refused to be heard.* [i] State Trials, Vol. 4. fol. 217. *Yet in the Lord* Grey's *Case*, State Trials, Vol. 3 fol. 77. *the Court would not give Judgment on a Conviction for a Misdemeanour, because there were not four Days left of the Term.* [k] H. P. C. 269. B. 1. Ch. 29. Sect. 24. Supra, Chh. 37. Sect. 2.

1. Of Judgments by express Sentence to the Punishment proper for the Crime.

2. Of Judgments without any such Sentence.

Of Judgments by such express Sentence in criminal Cases there are two Kinds.

1. Such as are fixt and stated, and always the same for the same Species of Crimes.

2. Such as are discretionary and variable according to the different Circumstances of each Case.

Sect. 2. And first of fixt and stated Judgments; as to which it seems [a] agreed, That the Law makes no Distinction between a Peer and a Commoner, or between a common and ordinary Case, and one attended with extraordinary Circumstances; for which Reason it was [b] adjudged in *Felton*'s Case, who was convicted by Confession of the Murder of the Duke of *Buckingham*, that the Court could not order his Hand to be [c] cut off, nor make it part of the Sentence that his Body should be hanged in Chains, but that the Body after Execution being at the King's Disposal might be hanged in Chains, or otherwise ordered as the King should think fit.

Of such fixt and stated Judgments, the most remarkable are those for Treason and Felony, *Præmunire* and Misprisions.

Sect. 3. The settled [d] Judgment at [e] this Day against a Man for High Treason, not relating to the Coin, seems to be, That he shall be [f] carried back to the Place from whence he came, and from thence be [g] drawn to the Place of Execution, and be there hanged by the [h] Neck, and cut [i] down alive, and that his [k] Entrails be taken out and [l] burnt before his Face, and his Head cut off, and his Body divided into four Quarters, and his Head and Quarters disposed of at the King's Pleasure. And I find little or no Variation in Substance from this Judgment, but only in some Circumstances, for which I shall refer to the Notes in the Margin and the *State Trials*.

[a] State Trials Vol. 2. fol. 704. 3 Inst. 31.
[b] Hetl. 126. Litt. Rep. 237. Rushworth's Collections, Part 1. fol. 640, 641.
[c] *Agreed* 3 Inst. 140. 12 Co. 71. *That the Court cannot order the Hand to be cut off in any Case wherein it is not the stated Judgment.* See B. 1. Ch. 21. Sect. 1 *to* 7.
[d] 3 Inst. 210. 211. H P. C. 268. S. P. C. 182. Lett. E. Plow. Com. 387. b. Co. Entr. 361. b.
[e] *In the Time of* Will. Ru-

fus *Judgment was given against two convicted of High Treason that one should have his Eyes put out, and the other* in crucem tollatur. Madox *History of the Exchequer*, fol. 6. [f] S. P. C. 182. Lett. E. *But this Clause is wholly omitted in* H. P. C. 268. *and* 3 Inst. 210. *and in* Plowd Com. 387. b *it is thus expressed*, quod duceretur per præfat' constabular' usque dictam turrim *London*, &deinde, &c. *And in* Co Entr. 361. b. *it is thus*, Quod præd. *T. B.* ducatur per præfat. Maresc' usque prisonam Mar' Maresc' Domini Regis, &c. [g] S.P. C. 182. Lett. E. *It is expressed, That he shall be drawn upon an Hurdle. And* Plow. Com. 387. b. *it is, That he shall be drawn thro' the middle of the City of* London, *to the Gallows at* Tyborn. *Also in* Co Entr. 361. b. *and* 3 Inst. 110. *a particular Place of Execution is mentioned.* [h] S. P. C. 182. b. *and* 3 Inst. 110. *But* Plowd. Com 387. b. Co. Entr. 361. b *and* H. P. C. 268. *it is only said*, Quod suspendatur, *without adding* per collum. [i] 3 Inst. 110. S. P. C. 182, Lett. E. Plow. Com. 387. b. Co. Entr. 361. b. *But this is omitted* H. P. C. 268. [k] *This Clause is thus expressed*, 3 Inst. 210, 211. Plowd. 387. b. Co. Entr. 361. b. Quod interiora sua extra ventrem suum capiantur, *without mentioning the cutting off of the Privy Members; and so is* H. P. C. 268. *and the later Precedents. But* S P.C. 182. Lett. E. *is express that they shall be cut off.* [l] S. P.C. 108. Lett. E. *But in* Plowd. Com. 387. b. Co. Entr. 361. b. 3 Inst. 211. *it is thus expressed* ipsoque vivente, comburantur.

Sect.

Sect. 4. It hath been always agreed to be the proper Judgment against a Man for High Treason at Common Law, in counterfeiting the King's [a] Coin or [b] Seal, That he shall be drawn to the Place of Execution, and there hanged by the Neck till he be dead. But there have been [c] great Opinions, That the Judgment against a Man for Clipping, and other Offences against the Coin, made Treason by Statute, shall be to be drawn, hanged and quartered, as for other High Treasons; because it is a general [d] Rule, That where a Statute makes an Offence Treason or Felony, it gives it the like Incidents that belong to a Treason or Felony by the Common Law; yet inasmuch as High Treason at Common Law in counterfeiting the Coin had Judgment only of Drawing and Hanging; and it is a reasonable Construction, That the Makers of the Statutes, which made other Offences concerning the Coin High Treason, intended to give such Offences the like [e] Incidents with High Treasons against the Coin at the Common Law, and not to make inferior Offences of this Kind subject to a heavier Punishment than the greater; it seems to be [f] settled at this Day, That the Judgment for such Offences shall be the same as for counterfeiting the Coin, *&c.* at the Common Law, *i. e.* of Drawing and Hanging, without Quartering.

Sect. 5. It hath been [g] long [h] agreed, That the Judgment against a Man for Petit Treason is the same with that for counterfeiting the Coin, *viz.* That he shall be [i] drawn to the Place of Execution and there hanged by the Neck till he be dead.

Sect. 6. The Judgment against a [k] Woman, in all Cases of Treason, whether High or Petit Treason, is, That she shall be drawn to the Place of Execution, and there burnt.

Sect. 7. The Judgment against a Man or [l] Woman for Felony of Death, hath always been the same [m] since the Reign of *H.* 1. *viz.* That he or she be [n] hanged by the [o] Neck till [p] dead, which in the [q] Roll is shortly entered thus, *Sus. per coll.*

Sect. 8. For the Judgment of *Pain fort & dure* upon an Offender's standing Mute, I shall refer to *Ch.* 30. *Sect.* 16.

Sect. 9. Judgment in *Præmunire* at the Suit of the [r] King, against a Defendant, being in [*] Prison, is, That he shall be out of the King's Protection, and that his Lands and Tenements, Goods and Chattels shall be forfeited to the King, and that his Body shall remain in Prison at the King's Pleasure; but if the Defendant be condemned upon his [s] Default in not appearing, whether at the Suit of the King or [t] Party, the same Judgment shall be given as to the being out of

[a] S. P. C. 182. Lett. E. 3 Inst. 17. H. P. C. 268. Cro. Ca. 383. 19 H. 6. 47. b. pl. 103. *Abridged* Fitz. Coro. 8. Bro. Tresf. 9. [b] Fleta, B. 1. Ch. 22. Sect. 1. [c] S. P. C. 182. Lett. E. 3 Inst. 17. H. P. C. 19. [d] *See* B. 1. Ch. 40. Sect. 4. [e] *See* 2 Jon. 233. Supra Ch. 25. Sect. 147. [f] Dy. 230. pl. 55. 2 Lev. 98. 2 Jon. 233. 3 Keb. 278. pl. 27. Raym. 234. [g] *But* Bract. 104. b. *it is said, That they are burnt*, qui saluti dominorum suorum insidiaverint. [h] 3 Inst. 211. H. P. C. 268. S. P. C. 182. Lett. F. 19 H. 6 47. pl. 102. *Abridged* Fitz Coro 7. Bro. Treason 8. 33 Ass. pl 7. *Abridged* Bro. Treason, 15. Fitz. Coro. 210. [i] *See* 21 E. 3. 17. pl. 21. *Abridged* Fitz. Coro. 447. Bro. Coro. 38. *where an Approver becoming Nonsuit, had Judgment to be hanged only, and not drawn, tho' he stood indicted of Petit Treason. But the Case is obscure both in the Reports and Abridgments.* [k] *Preface to the 6th Report.* H. P. C. 268. 3 Inst. 211. S. P. C. 182. Lett. F. Fitz. Coro. 383. 23 Ass. pl. 2. *Abridged* Bro. Treason, 26. 12 Ass. 30. *Abridged* Bro. Coro. 73 *or* 74. Treason, 12. Fitz. Coro. 170. 1 Rich. 3. 4 pl. 5. *Abridged* Fitz. Coro. 46. [l] 1 Ric. 3, 4. pl. 5. *Abridged* Fitz. Coro. 46. [m] 3 Inst. 53. [m] S. P. C. 182. Lett. G. H. P. C. 268. 3 Inst. 211. Fitz. Coro. 227. *See the Citations to the next Letter.* [o] *The Words* per collum *are omitted* Co. Entr. 60. b. 352. b. pl. 2. 353, b. pl. 3. 355, b. pl. 7. 360. pl. 13. *and* Rast. Ent. 42, b. pl. 2. 53, b. pl. 6. 55. b. pl. 6. [p] 3 Inst. 53, 211. H. P. C. 268. 6 E. 4, 4. *But this is omitted,* 6 H. 4. 6. b. S. P. C. 182. Lett. G. *and in* Rast. Ent. 42, b, pl. 2. 53, b. pl. 6. 55. b. pl. 6. *the Precedents in* Coke's Entr. *cited to Letter* o. *comes only under an* &c. [q] S. P. C. 182. Lett. G. [r] Co. Litt. 129. b. *'tis agreed,* 30 E. 3. 11. *Abridged,* Fitz. Judgment, 145. *And* in 8 H. 4. 6. b. 7. a. *Abridged* Fitz. Forfeiture, 13. Bro. Forfeiture, 12. Præmunire, 6, *and* 20. *That such Judgment shall not be given at the Suit of the Party, on* 27 Ed. 3. *but in the two last Citations 'tis holden, That the same Judgment shall be given at the Suit of the Party on* 16 Rich. 2. [*] 3 Inst. 218. Supra B. 1. Ch. 19. S. 14, 45. Co. Litt. 129. b. 130. a. [s] Vide B. 1. Ch 19. Sect. 14. Rast. Entr. 466, b. 467. b. 3 Inst. 125, 218. Dalt ch. 90. [t] 8 H. 4, 6. b. 7. a. *Abridged* Fitz. Forfeiture, 13. Bro. Forfeiture, 12. Præmunire, 6, 20. 30 E. 3, 11. b. *Abridged* Fitz. Judgment, 145. 44 E. 3 7. pl 6. *Abridged* Fitz. Respender, 35. 39 E. 3, 37. *Abridged* Fitz. Retorn de viccunt, 61. Attorney, 36. 8 H. 6. 3. pl. 8. *Abridged* Bro. Premunire, 8. 20.

the

the King's Protection, and the Forfeiture; but instead of the Clause, that the Body shall remain in Prison, there shall be an Award of a *Capiatur.*

Sect. 10. The Judgment against a Man for Misprision of High Treason [a] is, That he shall be imprisoned during his Life, and forfeit all his Goods, and the Profits of his Lands during his Life.

Sect. 11. The Judgment against a Man for drawing a Sword on a Judge, or striking any Person in the [b] Presence of the King's Higher Courts, is, That he shall be imprisoned during Life, and forfeit his Goods, and the Profits of [c] his Lands during Life, and that his [d] Right Hand shall be cut off at a certain Place.

Sect. 12. For the Judgments for [e] striking in the King's Palace, for [f] rescuing a Prisoner from the Superior Courts, [g] for Perjury, or [h] Forgery on the Statute, and for the villainous [i] Judgment in Conspiracy at the Suit of the King, I shall refer to the Citations in the Margin.

Sect. 13. The Entry of the Judgment for a Defendant upon an Acquittal by Verdict, or upon the Plea of a Pardon is, *ideo consid' est quod præd'* A B. *de* [k] *præmissis eat inde die,* or *eat sine die,* omitting [l] *de præmissis*; or *de proditionibus prædictis eat inde* [m] *quietus*; or [n] thus, *Quod sit inde quietus, &c. & quod ipse eat inde sine die*; and upon the Plea of a Release to an Appeal, and in other Cases of like Nature, it is, *ideo consid' est quod* [o] *præd'* A. *quoad sectam præd'* B. *in præmissis eat inde sine die.* And [p] *Staundforde* says, That upon the Acquittal of one arraigned of Treason or Felony, the Judgment is no other, but that the Court discharges the Defendant paying his Fees.

Sect. 14. Secondly, As to Judgments by express Sentence, which are discretionary and variable according to different Circumstances, I shall observe in general, That for Crimes of an infamous Nature, such as Petit [q] Larceny, [r] Perjury, or [f] Forgery at Common Law, gross [t] Cheats, Conspiracy not requiring a villainous Judgment, keeping a Bawdy-house, bribing [u] Witnesses to stifle their Evidence, and other Offences of the like Nature, against the first Principles of natural Justice, and common Honesty, it seems to be in great Measure left to the Prudence of the Court to inflict such corporal Punishment, and also such Fine and Lien to the Good Behaviour for a * certain Time †, *&c.* as shall seem most proper and adequate to the Offence, from the Consideration of the Baseness, Enormity, and dangerous Tendency of it, the Malice, Deliberation and Wilfulness, or the Inconsideration, Suddenness and Surprize with which it was committed, the Age, Quality and Degree of the Offender, and all other Circumstances which may any way aggravate or extenuate the Guilt.

[a] H. P. C. 128, 169. 3 Inst. 36, 218. Bro. Treason, 19, 25. [b] *See* B. 1. Ch. 21. Sect. 3. *to* Sect. 6. [c] *So is* H. P. C. 131. *And in* 41 Aff. pl. 25. *Abridged* Bro. Fines, 11. Forfeiture, 41. Restitut. 32. Scire facias, 160. 2 Roll. Abr. 76. pl. 3. *Judgment was given, That the Lands shou'd be seised into the King's Hands, and the King answered of the Profits; after which the King granted over the Lands as forfeited, and then pardoned the Offence; and the Heir was restored upon a* Scire facias. *By which it appears that the Inheritance of the Lands was not forfeited.* (Vide supra, ch. 37. Sect. 54) *But in* 1 Keb. 751. *the Judgment is, That the Lands shall be forfeited during Life; and* Dalison 23. *a Quære is made by what Law the Lands shall be forfeited any farther than during Life: Yet* 3 Inst. 140, 218. *and* 39 Aff. pl. 1. *Abridged* Bro. Contemp s, 9. Fitz. Assise, 333. Dyer, 188. pl. 10 Fitz Judgment, 174. Coro. 280. S. P. C 38. Lett. B. Owen, 120. Cro. Eliz. 405. Dalison, 23. *say, in general, That the Land shall be forfeited without adding for Life; and* 22 Ed. 3. 12. pl. 26. *Abridged* Fitz Forfeiture, 21. *That the Offender shall be disinherited.* [d] *In this Part of the Judgment the Books above cited generally agree.* [e] B. 1. Ch. 21. Sect. 1, 2. [f] B 1. Ch. 21. Sect. 5. [g] B 1. Ch. 69. Sect. 11, 13. [h] B. 1. Ch. 70. Sect 12. [i] B. 1. Ch. 72. Sect 9 [k] Co. Entr. 356. b. Rast. Ent. 47. b. pl. 3. 48. a pl. 4. [l] Co. Entr. 358. a pl. 9, 10. 359. b. Rast. Entr. 51. b. pl. 12. 56. a. pl. 5. 57. pl 7. [m] Co. Entr. 360. b. Rast. Entr 51 pl. 11. [n] Rast Ent. 49. b pl. 6. 57. pl 7. [o] Rast Entr. 43. pl 8. 50. pl. 10. [p] S P. C 182. Lett. I. [q] 3 Inst. 218. B. 1. Ch 33. Sect 36 State Trials, Vol. 3. fol. 487. 488. Hob. 62. [r] Raym. 81. 1 Sid. 142, 278. 3 Leon. 170 [t] Cro. Ja 498. 2 Roll. Ab. 78 H 1 1 Keb. 849. Noy 99 103. [u] State Trials, Vol. 2 fol. 272. Raym. 376 * 1 Sid. 214 pl. 14. † *See* Cro Ca 55. *a Decree of the Star Chamber against a Judge for Bribery, that he should be incapable of any Office of Judicature.*

Sect. 15. And at this Day by Force of 5 *Annæ* 6. and 4 *Georg.* 11. and 6 *Georg.* 23. set forth more at large, *Ch.* 23. *Sect.* 134 *to* 139. the Judges upon a Conviction for Larceny, may in their Discretion award the Offender to the House of Correction, and for that and other Felonies within the Benefit of the Clergy, instead of giving the usual Sentence, *&c.* may direct that the Offender be transported.

[a] Daliſon, 20.
[b] 2 Inſt. 47, 201. Co. Lit. 135.
[c] Salk. 56, 400.

Sect. 16. But it [a] seems that the Court cannot be authorised by any Letters Patents, but only by Act of Parliament, to inflict a Punishment unknown to our Laws, as of [b] Banishment, *&c.*

Sect. 17. [c] *Note,* That the Court may assess a Fine, but cannot award any corporal Punishment against a Defendant, unless he be actually present in the Court.

[d] 11 Co. 43, 44. 1 Roll. Rep. 74, *&c.* Supra Ch. 9. Sect. 16. 1 Lev. 126.

Sect. 18. *Note also,* That where there are several Defendants, a joint Award of one Fine against them all is [d] erroneous, for it ought to be several against each Defendant; for otherwise one who hath paid his proportionable Part might be continued in Prison till all the others have also paid theirs, which would be in Effect to punish him for the Offence of another.

[e] Dy. 232. pl. 6.
[f] Co. Litt. 127. a.

Sect. 19. It hath been [e] adjudged, That where a Man is to make Fine and Ransom, the Ransom must be treble the Fine at least; but Sir [f] *Edward Coke* strongly argues, That Fine and Ransom are in legal Understanding the same Thing under different Names, called a *Fine,* because it makes an End of the Business, and a *Ransom,* because it redeems from Imprisonment; for if they were different Things, it would follow that where the Books say, That a Man shall make a Fine and Ransom, they must be taken to intend that he ought to pay two different Sums, of which there is no Precedent.

[g] Co. Litt. 260. a. *Adjudged* Raym. 376, 377. *and there said that* Cro. Ca. 251. *is to be thus understood.*

Sect. 20. A Fine is under the Power of the Court, during the Term in which it is set, and [g] may be mitigated as shall be thought proper; but after the Term it admits of no Alteration.

2*dly.* Of Judgments without an express Sentence to the Punishment proper to the Crime, there are two Kinds,

1. Outlawry.
2. Abjuration.

[h] Finch of Law, 356. Dy. 223. pl. 24. Bro Coro. 166.
3 Inſt. 212.
[i] *If the Judgment appear not by the Return of the Exigent to have been given by the Coroner it is erroneous, except in* London, *where the Mayor by Custom is Coroner, and the Judgment is given by the Recorder.* Co. Litt. 288. Bro. Utlagary, 31. Dy. 217. pl. 6. 8 Co. 126. a. 21 H. 7. 33. Cro. Eliz. 648 pl 3.

Sect. 21. Judgment of Outlawry is [h] given by the [i] Coroner at the fifth County-Court upon the Party's not appearing to the Exigent, (which is a [k] Writ commanding the Sheriff to cause the Defendant to be demanded from County-Court to County-Court until he be outlawed, *&c.*) and such Judgment is [l] entred thus, *Ideo, &c. per judicium coronatoris Domini Regis comitatus prædict' utlagatus est.*

Sect. 22. It seems [m] agreed, That when a Judgment of Outlawry for Treason or Felony appears of Record by the Sheriff's Return of the Exigent; and it hath been [n] holden, That if it appears not by such Return, but only by the Coroners Return of a [o] *Certiorari* to them directed to certify whether the Party were outlawed or not, the Party is as much [p] at-

[k] Reg. Jud. 2. a. [l] 3 Inſt. 212. [m] Co. Litt. 128, b. 288. b. 28 Aſſ. pl. 49' *Abridged,* Bro. Nonability, 25. 3 Inſt. 212. Theloal, B. 1. Ch. 15. S. 20. [n] Co. Litt. 288. a. *But the contrary seems to be holden,* Dy. 223, pl. 23, 25. *and it is made a Quære,* 38 E. 3. 14. a. b. [o] Vide Raſt. Ent. 332, a. b. [p] Finch of Law, 467. 3 Inſt. 52, 212. State Trials, Vol. 3. fol. 324. Bro. Coro. 166.

tainted,

tainted, and shall forfeit and lose as much as if Sentence had been given against him upon a Verdict or Confession.

Sect. 23. If such [a] Outlawry appear to the Court to be erroneous, whereof any one as *amicus Curiæ* may inform them, the Party shall have Counsel assigned him to take Advantage of the Error; but if he will neither bring a Writ of Error, nor plead, in convenient Time, and the Outlawry be voidable only and not void, the proper Execution shall be [b] awarded against him, but no Sentence pronounced, because the Outlawry is a Judgment, and no Man shall have [c] two Judgments for one Offence.

Sect. 24. For the Nature of Abjuration, (which was also an [d] Attainder of itself) being wholly obsolete at this Day, I shall refer to the Citations [e] in the Margin.

Sect. 25. It seems to be generally [f] agreed, That a Man can no other way be attainted of Treason or Felony at this Day, but only by Judgment by express Sentence, or by Outlawry or Abjuration; and therefore where an Appellee was slain in the Field upon a Wager of Battle, [g] Judgment was given, *Quod suspendatur per collum* in order to intitle the Lord to his Escheat. But I know of no other Case wherein it is clear at this Day, that a Man may be attainted after his Death: It is said indeed in a Note in *Fitzherbert*'s [h] *Abridgment* of a Case in the Time of *Edward* III. that, in *Eyre* it hath been seen that a Man hath been attainted by Presentment after his Death; also it was holden by * *Markham* in the Time of *Henry* IV. That if he who levies War against the King be slain in Battle, his Lands may be seised by the King. And it is said in the [k] *Fourth Report*, That if one aiding the King's Enemies be slain in open Rebellion, and the Chief Justice of the King's Bench, who is the Sovereign Coroner of *England*, make a Record of it upon the View of the Body, and return it into the King's Bench, he shall forfeit his Lands. And this seems agreeable to 34 *E.* 3. 12. whereby the King expresly reserves his Prerogative as to Forfeiture of Wars, but grants that he will in no other Case seize Lands for Treason whereof the Party is not attainted in his Life. Yet the contrary Opinion seems to be holden in the *First* and *Third* [m] *Institutes*, and also by [n] *Hale*; and to this [o] *Staundforde* seems also to incline.

[a] 3 Inst. 212, 213. [b] State Trials, Vol. 3. f. 323, 324. 334, 335. [c] Finch of Law, 389, 467. S. P. C. 34. Letter C. 217 Lett. C. Fitz. Coro. 313, 335. 11 H. 7, 4. pl. 10. *Abridged* Bro. Coro. 226 *or* 227. 27 Ass. pl 54. *Abridged* Bro. Coro. 110. 9 Ed. 4, 28. b. pl. 41. *Abridged* Bro. Coro. 55. 12 Co. 100. Fitz. Escheat, 14. Supra Ch. 23. Sect. 53. Ch. 36. Sect. 1. *Yet Sentence was given upon one Outlawed of Felony*, 3 H. 7, 7. pl. 5. *Abridged* Bro. Coro. 134 *or* 135. [d] Finch of Law, 389, 467. S. P. C. 34. Lett. C. 117. Lett. C. 122. Lett. C. Fitz. Coro. 313. 335. 3 Inst. 216, 217. [e] Supra, Ch, 9. Sect. 44. *and* Ch. 32. Sect. 6. 3 Inst. 216, 217. [f] Bro. Coro. 166, *and the other Books under-cited.* [g] Fitz. Judgment, 225. Co Litt. 390. a. 3 Inst. 212. 2 Inst. 283. Plowd. Com. 261, b. 262. a. Bro. Escheat, 24. [h] Fitz. Petition, 2. Co. Lit. 390, a. Vide Fitz. Coro. 290, 312. *and the next Chapter, Sect. 16. where a Felon killed in the pursuit forfeited his Chattels, and the Year, Day and Waste, and the mesne Profits of his Lands from the Time of the Felony.* * 7 H. 4, 46. b. *but denied by* Gascoign; *and 'tis said by* Brown, *in* Plowd. Com. 263. a. *that the antient Law was so. See also* Plowd. Com. 262. a. *and* Dalt. Ch. 89. [k] 4 Co. 57. b. [m] 3 Inst. 27. Co. Litt. 13. [n] H. P. C. 12. [o] S. P. C. 188. 180

CHAP.

CHAP. XLIX.

Of Forfeiture of Lands and Goods, Loss of Dower, and Corruption of Blood.

AND now I am to shew the Consequences of an Attainder or Conviction of Treason and Felony, which I shall consider under the following Particulars.

1. What shall be forfeited by the Offender.
2. Where his Wife loses her Dower.
3. How far his Blood is corrupted.

As to the first Point, I shall endeavour to shew,

1. What is forfeited by the Common Law,
2. What by Statute.
3. To what Time the Forfeiture shall relate,
4. What shall be done with the Goods of an Offender before they are actually forfeited.

As to the first Particular, *viz.* what is forfeited by the Offender, by the Common Law, I shall endeavour to shew,

1. Where his Lands are forfeited by the Common Law.
2. Where his Goods.

[a] 3 Inst. 19. 3 Co. 2, 3.
[b] 3 Inst. 19. 3 Co. 2, 3.
[c] *See the Statute of* 25 Ed. 3, 2.
[d] Co. Litt. 2. 4 Co. 58, a. 1 Leon. 21. *and* infra S. 23.
[e] 3 Co. 10. Co. Litt. 2. S.P.C. 191, D. Bro. Coro. 208, 210 1 Leon. 21. Infra S. 23.
[f] S.P.C. 191. D. Fitz. Trav. 48. Assise, 166.

Sect. 1. And first as to the Forfeiture of Lands, it seems agreed, That by the Common Law all Lands of Inheritance whereof the Offender was [a] seised in his own Right, and also all Rights of [b] Entry to Lands in the Hands of a Wrong-doer, are forfeited to the [c] King by an Attainder of High-Treason, and to the Lord of whom they are immediately holden, by an Attainder of Petit Treason or Felony: And that the Lands whereof a Person attainted of High Treason dies [d] seized of an Estate in Fee are actually vested in the King without any Office, because they cannot descend, the Blood being corrupted, and the Freehold shall not be in Abeyance.

Sect. 2. But it seems [e] agreed, That by the Common Law such Lands were not vested in the actual Possession of the King during the Life of the Offender without an Office.

Sect. 3. Also it [f] seems clear, That the Lord cannot enter into the Lands holden of him upon an Escheat for Petit Treason or Felony, without a special Grant, till it appear by due Process that the King hath had his Prerogative of the Year, Day and Waste.

Sect.

Sect. 4. It is [a] said, That the Inheritance of Things not lying in Tenure, as of Rents-Charge, Rents-Seck, Commons, *&c.* shall be forfeited to the King by an Attainder of High Treason, and that the Profits of them shall be also forfeited to the King by an Attainder of Felony during the Life of an Offender, and that the Inheritance shall be extinguished by his Death; for it cannot escheat, because there is no Tenure, nor descend because the Blood is corrupted.

Sect. 5. But it is [b] said, That no Right of Action whatsoever to Lands of an Estate of Inheritance are forfeited, either by the Common Law, or by the Statute; and it seems agreed, That no [c] Right of Entry into such Lands whereof there is a Tenant by Feoffment, or other Title, nor [d] Use, (except only Lands convey'd [e] fraudulently with an Intent to avoid a Forfeiture,) nor [f] Condition, were liable to be forfeited before the Statute of 33 *H.* 8. and that [g] Land in Tail could not be forfeited after the Statute of *Westminster* 2. but only for the Life of the Tenant in Tail, till the Statute of 26 *H.* 8. 13.

Sect. 6. It [h] seems, That the Profits of such Lands whereof a Person attainted of Felony is seised of an Estate of Inheritance in the Right of his Wife, or of an Estate for Life only in his own Right, are forfeited to the King, and that nothing thereof is forfeited to the Lord.

Sect. 7. It seems [i] agreed, That by Force of a special Custom a Copyhold of Inheritance may be forfeited by an Attainder or Conviction of Treason or Felony: Also it hath been [k] holden, That by Custom it may be forfeited for Treason or Felony, even without a Conviction; also it [l] seems the stronger Opinion, That it shall be forfeited by an Attainder of Treason or Felony of common Right, without any special Custom, but [m] not by a Conviction only.

Sect. 8. It seems [n] agreed, That by the Common Law upon an Attainder of Felony, the King had a Right utterly to waste the Lands holden of any but himself, whereof the Person attainted was seised of an Estate of Inheritance, either in his own or in his [o] Wife's Right. [p] And it is said by some, That the King had both this Right, and also a Right to hold such Lands for a Year and a Day; but it is holden by others, That the Right to hold over the Lands for a Year and a Day was given to the King in Lieu of the Waste; and this seems [q] implied in *Magna Charta, Ch.* 22. which saying, That the King shall not hold over the Lands of those convicted of Felony but for one Year and a Day, and making no mention of the Waste, seems plainly to intimate that at the Time of the making of that Statute the King was thought to have no other Right but only to the Year and Day. Yet the Statute of *Prerogativa Regis* made in the 17th of *Ed.* 2. having declared the King's Right to the Year and Day, and also to the Waste; it seems to have been the more general [r] Opinion since that Time that he hath a Right to both. Indeed if this Statute had been against the express Purview of *Magna Charta*, it would have been clearly repealed by those many subsequent Statutes which repeal all Statutes contrary to *Magna Charta*; but

[a] 3 In. 19, 21.
[b] 3 Co. 2, 3. 7 Co. 13. Vide infra, S. 23, 24, 25.
[c] Fitz Entry congeable 28. 3 Co. 2, 3. 3 Inst. 19.
[d] 3 Inst. 19.
[e] 2 Roll. Abr. 34. pl. 1, 2.
[f] 3 Inst. 19.
[g] 3 Inst. 19. S. P. C. 187. Plow. Com. 554. 555. Dy. 289. pl. 55. Co. Litt. 130, 372, 391.
[h] 3 Inst. 19. Fitz. Assize, 166. Forfeiture, 23. 4 Ass. pl. 4.
[i] 2 Jon. 151. 1 Lev. 263. 1 Leon. 1.
[k] 1 Bulst. 13. 2 Brownl. 217, 218, 219, 220. *See* Godbolt, 267. 2 Vent. 38, 39.
[l] 2 Jon. 189. 2 Ventr. 38, 39. 5 Co. 117. b. 2 Keb. 451. pl. 23. Coke's Copyholder, Sect. 58.
[m] 1 Lev. 263. 2 Keb. 451. pl. 23.
[n] 4 Co. 124. b. S. P. C. 190, 191. Staundf. Prerog. 48, 49, 50.
[o] Fitz. Coro. 327. Vide Fitz. Coro. 332.

[p] Vide 2 Inst. 36, 37. S. P. C. 190, 191. Staundf. Prerog. 48, 49, 50. [q] *See the Books abovecited, yet it seems admitted* 8 Ed. 3. Fitz. Traverse, 489. Prescription 50. *That the King was intitled to the Waste as to the Year and Day since this Statute.* [r] Bro. Coro. 206, 208, 209, 210. Fitz. Coro. 290, 308, 310, 312, 327, 358. Register, 165. Fitz Traverse, 19. S. P. C. 190, 191. Staundf. Prerog. 48, 49, 50. 49 Ed. 3, 11. pl. 3. 4 Co. 124. b. *But* 49 Ass. pl. 21. *the contrary seems to be holden.* 2 Inst. 36, 37. Fitz. Utlagary, 2. *See also* Fitz. Coro. 285, 390, 332, 344. *and it seems agreed, That the King's Prerogative of the Waste is not grantable over, except only as to such Interests which by Vertue of it are actually vested in him.* Fitz. Coro. 310. S. P. C. 191. Lett. E. Staundf. Prerog. 50.

being not contrary to the expreſs Words of it, but only to what is argumentively drawn from it, it may be well argued that it is ſtill in Force.

As to the ſecond Point, *viz.* Where the Goods of the Offender ſhall be forfeited for Treaſon or Felony, I ſhall endeavour to ſhew,

Firſt, What Goods are liable to ſuch Forfeiture.
Secondly, In what Caſes.

Sect. 9. As to the firſt of theſe Particulars, it ſeems [a] agreed, That all Things whatſoever which are comprehended under the Notion of a perſonal Eſtate, whether they be in Action or Poſſeſſion, which the Party hath, or is intitled to in his own Right, and not as Executor or Adminiſtrator to another, are liable to ſuch Forfeiture.

Sect. 10. Alſo it [b] ſeems to be ſettled, That a Bond taken in another's Name, or a Leaſe made to another in Truſt for a Perſon who is afterwards convicted of Treaſon or Felony, are as much liable to be forfeited, as a Bond made to him in his own Name, or a Leaſe in Poſſeſſion.

Sect. 11. Alſo it [c] ſeems to be in a great Meaſure ſettled, That the Truſt of a Term granted by a Man for the Uſe of himſelf, his Wife and Children, *&c.* is liable in like Manner to be forfeited, if fraudulently made with an Intent to avoid a ſubſequent Forfeiture; but that it ſhall be forfeited ſo far only as it is reſerved to the Benefit of the Party himſelf, if made *bona fide*, whether before or after Marriage, for good Conſideration without Fraud, which is to be left to a Jury on the whole Circumſtances of the Caſe, and ſhall never be preſumed by the Court where it is not expreſly found.

Sect. 12. It hath been [d] adjudged, That a Power of Revocation of the Truſt of a Settlement reſerved to the Grantor is not liable to be forfeited, if it depend on ſomething Perſonal to be done by the Grantor himſelf, as the making the Deed of Revocation under his own Hand and Seal.

2. Perſonal Things liable to Forfeiture ſhall be forfeited in the following Caſes.

Sect. 13. *1ſt*, Upon a [e] Conviction of Treaſon or Felony.

Sect. 14. *2ndly*, Upon a *fugam fecit* found before a Coroner, upon an Inquiſition of Death taken upon View of a dead Body; as to which it is [f] agreed, That where-ever a Perſon found Guilty by ſuch Inqueſt either as a Principal or as an Acceſſary [g] before the Fact, is found alſo to have fled for the ſame, he forfeits his Goods abſolutely, and the Iſſues of his Lands till he be acquitted or pardoned. Alſo it is [h] agreed, That where one indicted of any capital Felony, either as Principal or Acceſſary before or after, before Juſtices of *Oyer, &c.* is acquitted at his Trial, but found to have fled, he ſhall incur the like Forfeiture of his Goods but not of the Iſſues of his Lands, becauſe by the Acquittal the Land is diſcharged, and conſequently the Iſſues. And it hath been [i] hol-

[a] Staundf. Prerog. 45, 46. S. P. C. 187. D. Cro. Ca. 566. 12 Co. 121. *It is holden,* Staundf. Prerog. 45. b. *and* S. P. C. 188. Ch. 28. *That a Felon ſhall forfeit the Goods of others ſtolen by him, but the Authorities cited to this Point,* viz. 44 Ed. 3. 44. Fitz. Coro. 317, 318, 319, 323, 334, 379, 380. *do not ſeem fully to come up to it, except where ſuch Goods are waived, or of ſuch a Nature as not to be diſtinguiſhable from others of the like Kind, as Corn out of a Bag,* &c. Vide 2 Leon. 5, 6. 1 And. 19. Moor, 100. Dy. 309, 310. *That a Term limited to Executors, and not veſted in the Party himſelf, is not forfeitable.*

[b] Cro. Ja. 312, 313. Hob. 214. *and the Books cited to the following Section.*

[c] 2 Keb. 564, 608, 644, 763, 772. 1 Lev. 279. Lane, 54, 113. 1 Mod. 16, 38. Hardr. 466. 1 Ander. 294. Raym. 120. 2 Roll. Abr. 34. pl. 1, 2. 1 Roll. Abr. 343 F. 5, 6, 7. March, 45, 88. 1 Sid. 26., 403. 1 Keb. 909.

[d] 2 Keb. 564, 644, 763, 772. 1 Lev. 279. 1 Mod. 16, 38. Vide infra, Sect. 26.

[e] 5 Co. 109. Supra ch. 33. Sect. 129. *and the Books cited to the three foregoing Sections.*

[f] S. P. C. 183, 184, 191, c. 192 a. H. P. C 271. Staundf Prer 46. Keilw 68. b. Dyer 239. pl. 36. 5 Co. 110.

[g] Secus *if he be found Acceſſory after, for the Indictment is ſo far void.* S. P. C. 184. A B. Supra ch. 9. Sect. 26.

[h] S. P. C. 184. A. B. 191. G. H. P. C. 271. Keilw. 68. b. 5 Co. 110. Fitz. Forfeit. 35.

[i] H. P. C. 271. S. P. C. 184. B. Fitz. Coro. 206.

den, That the Law is the same as to the finding of a *fugam fecit* upon an Acquittal of an Indictment of Petit Larceny. But it is [a] certain, That the Party may in all Cases, except that of the Coroner's Inquest, traverse the finding of a *fugam fecit*. Also it seems [b] agreed, That whenever the Indictment against a Man is insufficient, the finding a *fugam fecit* will not hurt him; and that in all Cases the Particulars of the Goods found to be forfeited may be traversed.

Sect. 15. 3*dly*, Upon a Default till the Award of an Exigent, as to which it is [c] agreed, That if one make such a Default either upon an Appeal or Indictment of a capital Felony, he forfeits his Goods unless he was pardoned before the Exigent was awarded; and it hath been [d] holden, That the Law is the same as to such a Default upon an Indictment of Petit Larceny: However it is clear, That where-ever Goods are so forfeited, they are not saved by an Acquittal at the Trial. But it seems [e] agreed, That they are saved by a Reversal of the Award of the Exigent, for an Error either in Fact or in Law; as for the Imprisonment of the Defendant at the Time when the Exigent was awarded, or for a Defect in the Indictment, Appeal or Process.

Sect. 16. 4*thly*, Upon a [f] Presentment by the Oaths of twelve Men, That a Person arrested for Treason or Felony, fled from, or resisted those who had him in Custody, and was killed by them in the Pursuit or Scuffle.

Sect. 17. 5*thly*, By being [g] waived or left by a Felon in his Flight, from those who either actually do pursue him, or are apprehended by him so to do, whereby he forfeits the Goods so waived, whether they be his own [h] proper Goods, or the Goods of others stoll'n by him, which shall not be restored to the right Owners but upon a proper Prosecution, as hath been more fully shewn, *Chap.* 23. from *Sect.* 49 *to* 58.

Sect. 18. As to the second Particular, *viz.* What is forfeited by Statute: It is enacted by 26 *H.* 8. 13. *That every Offender and Offenders being hereafter lawfully convicted of any Manner of High Treasons by Presentment, Confession, Verdict or Process of Outlawry, according to the due Course and Custom of the Common Laws of this Realm, shall lose and forfeit to the King, his Heirs, and Successors, all such Lands, Tenements and Hereditaments, which any such Offender or Offenders shall have of any Estate of Inheritance in Use or Possession, by any Right, Title, or Means, within the Realm of* England, *or elsewhere within any the King's Dominions, at the Time of any such Treason committed, or any Time after. Saving to every Person and Persons, their Heirs and Successors, other than the Offenders in any Treasons, their Heirs and Successors, and such Person and Persons as claim to any their Uses, all such Rights Titles, Interests, Possessions, Leases, Rents, Offices and other Profits, which they shall have at the Day of committing such Treasons, or at any Time before, in as large and ample Manner as if this Act had never been had nor made.* And the same is enacted in near the same Words by 5 & 6 *Ed.* 6. 11.

Sect. 19. And it is farther enacted by 33 *Hen.* 8. *That if any Person or Persons shall be attainted of High Treason by the Course of the Common Laws, or Statutes of this Realm, in every such Case every such Attainder by the Common Law shall be of as good Strength, Value, Force and Effect, as if it had been done by Authority of Parliament; And that the King, his Heirs and Successors, shall have as much Benefit and Advantage by such Attainder, as well of Uses, Rights, Entries, Conditions, as Possessions, Reversions, Remainders, and all other Things*

[a] H. P. C. 271. 36 H. 6. 28.
[b] Vide supra, Ch. 9. Sect. 51, 52. Fitz. Coro. 22.
[c] H. P. C. 271. S. P. C. 184. 47 Ed. 3. 26. pl. 72. *Abridged* Fitz. Traverse, 18. Bro. Coro. 17.
[d] Fitz. Coro. 181. Forfeiture, 28.
[e] S. P. C. 183, 184. D. Staundf. Prerog. 47. Bro. Coro. 8. Finch 352. 1 Roll. Abr. 793.
[f] 41 Ass. pl. 13. 22 Ass. pl. 81. Cro. Eliz. 4, 72. 5 Co. 110. b. 111.
[g] H. P. C. 271.
[h] 5 Co. 110. b. 111. 43 Ed. 3. 17, 18. H. P. C. 271. 1 Roll. Abr. 743. D. S. P. C. 184. D. Co. Litt. 259. Staundf. Prerog. 47. Cro. Ja. 464.
[i] 5 Co 109 b. Fitz Coro. 289, 290, 291, 312. S. P. C. 184. Lett. C. 189, 191. Lett. B. 192 A. 3 Inst. 56, 227.
Plowd. Com. 260. b. *But* Staundf. *makes a Quare whether the Law in this Point be not altered by* 34 E. 3. 12. *taken Notice of above* Ch. 48. Sect. 25. Staundf. Prerog. 46. a. [g] S. P. C. 186. Ch. 25. 5 Co. 109. Cro. Eliz. 611. pl. 18. 693. pl. 3. [h] S. P. C. 186. Ch. 25. *and* 29 E. 3. 29 b. *Abridged* Fitz. Avowry 253. *seems express to this Purpose; but* 3 Inst. 227 *and* 5 Co. 109 b. *it is said, That the Felons proper Goods are not forfeited as Waifs, but as the Goods of a Fugitive.*

as if it had been done and declared by Authority of Parliament, and ſhall be deemed and adjudged in actual and real Poſſeſſion of the Lands, Tenements, Hereditaments, Uſes, Goods, Chattles, and all other Things of the Offenders ſo attainted, which his Highneſs ought lawfully to have, and which they being ſo attainted ought or might lawfully loſe or forfeit if the Attainder had been done by Authority of Parliament, without any Office, or Inquiſition to be found of the ſame, any Law, Statute, or Uſe of the Realm to the contrary thereof in any wiſe notwithſtanding.

Sect. 20. Saving to all and every Perſon and Perſons, and Bodies Politick, and their Heirs, Aſſigns and Succeſſors, and every of them (other than ſuch Perſon and Perſons which hereafter ſhall be attainted of High Treaſon, and their Heirs and Aſſigns and every of them, and all and every other Perſon and Perſons, claiming by them or any of them, or to their Uſes, or to the Uſes of any of them after the ſaid Treaſons committed,) all ſuch Right, Title, Uſe, Poſſeſſion, Entry, Reverſions, Remainders, Intereſts, Conditions, Fees, Offices, Rents, Annuities, Commons, Leaſes, and all other Commodities. Profits and Hereditaments, whatſoever they or any of them ſhould, might or ought to have had if this Act had never been had nor made.

In the Conſtruction of theſe Statutes the following Points ſeem moſt conſiderable.

Sect. 21. 1*ſt.* It is [a] ſettled, That they are not repealed by 1 *Ma. Seſſ.* 1. *ch.* 1. which enacts, *That no Pains of Death, Penalty, or Forfeiture in any wiſe enſue or be to any Offender or Offenders, for the doing or committing any Treaſon, Petit Treaſon or Miſpriſion of Treaſon other than ſuch as be in the Statute* 25 Ed. 3. *ordained and provided*; for the Words, *other than ſuch as be within the Statute of* 25 *Ed.* 3. *&c.* ſhall not be taken to refer to the Pains, Penalties and Forfeitures which are mentioned in the Beginning of the Sentence, but to Treaſons, Petit Treaſons, and Miſpriſion of Treaſon, which are laſt mentioned.

Sect. 22. 2*ndly*, It is [b] agreed, That Eſtates in Tail are forfeited by Force of thoſe Words in 26 *H.* 8. *of any Eſtate of Inheritance*, which muſt be void if they do not include Eſtates in Tail, for Eſtates in Fee-ſimple were forfeited before. Alſo it hath been [c] adjudged, That where Lands are given to a Man and his Wife, and the Heirs of their two Bodies, the Intail is forfeited by his Attainder, and the Heir as much diſabled as if the Gift had been made to the Heirs of his Body in general.

Sect. 23. 3*dly*, It was [d] ſettled in the Marqueſs of *Wincheſter*'s Caſe, That the Right to a Writ of Error to reverſe an erroneous Common Recovery is not forfeited by theſe Statutes; alſo it is [e] agreed, That a meer Right of Action to Lands in the Hands of a Stranger, as of a Diſcontinuee, or of the Heir of a Diſſeiſor, is not forfeited: [f] But, That a Right of Entry into Lands to which a Perſon attainted of High Treaſon is intitled, is as much forfeited as Lands in Poſſeſſion, but yet that the King ſhall [g] not be adjudged in Poſſeſſion of ſuch Lands without an Office, and *Scire facias*, or Seizure on ſuch Office; for the Words, *That the King ſhall be deemed in Poſſeſſion without Office* ſhall have this Conſtruction, That he ſhall be in Poſſeſſion without Office in the ſame Manner as he ſhould have been upon an Office found at Common Law: But at the Common Law if a Diſſeiſee had been attainted of High Treaſon, and the Seiſin found by Office, the King ſhould not have been in Poſſeſſion, without a *Scire facias*, or a Seiſure at leaſt.

[a] S. P. C. 187. 3 Inſt. 19. Dyer 28.

[b] S. P. C. 187. Co. Litt. 372, 391. *and the Books cited to the following Sections.*

[c] Dy. 322. pl. 27.

[d] 3 Co. 2, 3. 1 Leon. 270, 271. Moor, 125. Hob. 340, 341. Cro. Eliz 389. *cited and agreed*, Cro. Ca. 428. 7 Co. 13. Moor, 323. Litt Re. 100.

[e] 3 Co. 2, 3. Hob. 340, 341. 7 Co. 13. 4 Co 58. a.

[f] 3 Co 2, 3, 10.

[g] 3 Co. 11. a. 4 Co. 58 a. 1 Leon. 21. 9 Co. 95. a. Supra, Sect. 1, 2.

Sect. 24. *4thly*, After two contradictory Judgments upon the same Point, it was at last [a] settled, by a Majority of the Judges in *Stone* and *Newman*'s Case, That where a Tenant in Tail of the Gift of the Crown makes a Feoffment in Fee, the Reversion being still in the Crown, and afterwards is attainted of High Treason, the Right of the Intail is forfeited to the Crown; because the Reversion continuing always in the Crown, the Intail could not be discontinued, but the Heir might have entered after the Death of the Feoffor without bringing any Action; and tho' the Intail by such a Feoffment be put in Abeyance as to any Benefit which the Feoffor himself may claim from it; yet since it is not turned to a Right of Action, and wou'd have continued still in him for the Benefit of the Heir, if he had not been attainted, (as appears from the Form of a Writ of *Formedon*, which supposes that the Right descended to the Heir from the Feoffor, and consequently that it was in him at his Death,) it shall likewise continue in him for the Benefit of the King.

Sect. 25. *5thly*, It was solemnly adjudged in the Exchequer-Chamber in [b] *Sheffield*'s Case, and a Judgment to the contrary in the Exchequer reversed, That where one attainted of High Treason is seised of a defeasible Estate in Tail, and hath at the same Time a Right to an ancient Intail which is discontinued, he forfeits both the Intail in Possession, and the Right to the old Intail; for the first is within the express Words of 26 *H.* 8. and the latter within those of 33. And it by no Means follows, that because naked Rights of Action to Lands in the Hands of the Heir of a Disseisor, or of a Discontinuee, are not within the Meaning of the Statute, as it is [c] settled that they are not; therefore also a Right to Lands in the Hands of the Person attainted himself is not within the Meaning of it; for the Forfeiture of such naked Rights, might not only be of dangerous Consequence in unsettling Possessions, but might also be highly prejudicial to Strangers whom the Statute by an express Saving plainly intends to favour; but the Forfeiture of the Offender's Right to his own Lands can be of no Prejudice to any but himself and his Heirs, to whom the Statute is so far from intending any Favour, that it expresly excludes them from all the Benefit of the saving Clause.

Sect. 26. *6thly*, It seems [d] agreed, That a Power of revoking the Uses of a Settlement may be forfeited by Force of 33 *H.* 8. if the Execution of it require nothing but what may be as well performed by any other Person, as by the Party himself, by whom it was reserved, as the Tender of a Ring, *&c.* Also it was adjudged in [e] *Englefield*'s Case, That the Mention of such Considerations and Inducements for the reserving of such a Power of Revocation in the Preamble of it, as are inseparable from the Person, do not alter the Case if nothing of this Kind be inserted in the Proviso it self, by which it is reserved. But it is agreed, That if the Proviso by which such a Power is reserved require something inseparably annexed to the Person, it keeps it out of the Statute; and therefore in the [f] Duke of *Norfolk*'s Case, where there was this Proviso, That if the Duke should be minded to alter and revoke the Uses, and signify his Mind in Writing under his Hand and Seal, that then, *&c.* it was clearly adjudged, That the Power of Revocation was not forfeitable, because it depended on the Duke's signifying his Mind in Writing under his proper Hand and Seal, which none but himself could do. Also it was adjudged in [g] *Main*'s Case, That the Law is the same where such Proviso doth not expresly require the Party's signifying a Change of Mind, but only that the Deed of Revocation be under his proper Hand

[a] Cro. Ca. 427. Vide Plowd. Com. 552.

[b] Hob. 334, &c. Palmer, 358, &c. 2 Rol. Rep. 305, &c.

[c] Supra Sect. 23.

[d] 7 Co. 12, 13. Poph. 18. 1 And. 293. Moor 303. 4 Leon. 135. Palmer, 433, &c. 1 Ro. Rep. 142.

[e] 7 Co. 12. and the other Books above-cited. Cited and agreed 2 Keb. 566, 763, 773. 1 Lev. 279. Lane, 44. 1 Rol. Rep. 142.

[f] 7 Co. 13. Cited and agreed 1 Lev. 279. 2 Keb. 566, 763, 773. 3 Inst. 19.

[g] Supra, Sect. 12.

Hand and Seal. [a] But if such Proviso require only the Tender of a Ring by the Feoffor, *ipso adtunc declarante* that the Tender is to the Intent to avoid the Feoffment, it seems unsettled, whether it come within the same Construction.

Sect. 27. *7thly*, It [b] seems, That an Annuity granted to a Man *pro consilio impendendo*, is not forfeitable by these Statutes; Also it seems [c] doubtful whether an Office granted to a Man for Life, and requiring Skill and Confidence, be forfeitable; but if it be [d] granted in Fee, it seems clear that it may be forfeited even by the Common Law; because the Grantor in giving such an Estate, which shall descend to all the Heirs of the Grantee however unqualified, seems plainly not to have been induced to make his Grant from any Consideration of the peculiar Merit of the Persons who are to execute the Office.

Sect. 28. It hath been [e] adjudged, but not without great Difficulty, That an Act of Parliament that certain Persons shall forfeit all their Lands, Possessions, Rights, Interests and Hereditaments, and other Things of what Nature soever, extends to Estates in Tail, by Force of the Words *all Interests of what Nature soever*. Yet it is [f] agreed, That the Statutes of *Præmunire*, which give a general Forfeiture of all the Lands and Tenements of the Offender extend not to Land in Tail.

Sect. 29. It is [g] holden, That a Saving against the Corruption of Blood in a Statute concerning Felony, doth by a necessary Consequence save the Land to the Heir; because the Escheat to the Lord for Felony is only *pro defectu tenentis*, occasioned by the Corruption of Blood. Also it is holden, That a Saving of the Land to the Heir prevents the Corruption of Blood, and also the Loss of Dower. But it hath been [h] adjudged, That a Saving against the Corruption of Blood in a Statute concerning Treason doth not save the Land to the Heir, because in Treason the Land goes to the King by way of immediate Forfeiture, and not by Escheat.

Sect. 30. As to the third Particular, *viz.* To what Time the Forfeiture shall relate: It seems [i] agreed, That the Forfeiture upon an Attainder either of Treason or Felony, shall have Relation to the Time of the Offence, for the avoiding of all subsequent Alienations of the Lands, but to the Time of the [k] Conviction, or *fugam fecit* found, *&c.* only as to Chattels; unless the Party were [l] killed in flying from or resisting those who had arrested him; in which Case it is said, That the Forfeiture shall relate to the Time of the Offence.

Sect. 31. But it seems [m] unsettled, Whether in *Præmunire* it shall relate to the Time of the Offence, or only to that of the Judgment.

Sect. 32. It seems the better [n] Opinion, That no Attainder whatsoever shall have any Relation as to the mean Profits of the Lands of the Person attainted, but only from the Time of the Attainder.

Sect. 33. As to the fourth Particular, *viz.* What shall be done with the Goods of an Offender both before and after they are actually forfeited: It seems to have been always [o] agreed, That one indicted or appealed of Treason or Felony may *bona fide* sell any of his Chattels real or

Palmer, 429.

[b] Plow. Com. 381, 382.

[c] Plow. Com. 379, *&c.*

[d] Plow. Com. 379.

[e] 2 Lev. 169. 3 Keb. 459, 651, 712. 2 Mod. 130, 131. 2 Jon. 57.

[f] Co. Litt. 130, *and the Books above-cited.*

[g] H. P. C. 8. 3 Inst. 47, 90. Salk. 85.

[h] Salk. 85.

[i] Fitz. Forf. 3. 30. 30 H. 6. 5. a. S. P. C. 192. ch. 31. Fitz. Counterplea de voucher, 30. Co. Litt. 2 b. 8 Co. 170. 38 Ed. 3. 32. a. Plow. Com. 488. b.

[k] Fitz. Forfeiture 30. Staundf. Prerog. 48. S. P. C 192. ch. 31. Bro. Relation, 31. Exposition, 26. Forfeit. 119. Fitz. Coro. 296.

[l] Vide supra Sect. 16. S. P. C. 192. a. Fitz. Coro. 290.

[m] Cro. Car. 172, 173. 1 Jon. 217.

[n] 8 Co. 170. Plowd. Com. 488. b. 38 Ed. 3. 32. a. *But this is made a Quære* S. P. C. 191. Lett. D. *and the contrary seems holden*, Fitz. Coro. 290, 344. *See also* Fitz. Forfeiture, 16. Coro. 374. Finch 326, 327.

[o] Bract. B. 3. Ch. 8. Sect. 5. *and* Ch. 18. Sect. 1, 2. Fleta, B. 1. Ch. 26. Sect. 1, 2. 8 Co. 171. b. 7 H. 4. *in the last Case.* S. P. C. 193. a. State Trials, Vol. 1. fol. 994, 995. Vol. 4. fol. 65, 66, 454.

per-

personal for the Sustenance of himself and Family until they be actually forfeited.

Sect. 34. Also it seems [a] agreed, That the Goods of such Person can in no Case be lawfully removed out of his House until they be forfeited.

Sect. 35. Yet according to the general Tenour of the old [b] Books, the Goods of one [c] arrested for Treason or Felony, may by the Purview of an ancient Statute, which * seems to continue still in Force, be immediately inventoried and appraised, after which, and on Surety found that they shall be forth-coming, they shall be kept by the Bailiffs of the Party arrested, and for want of such Surety by his Neighbours, till he be convicted, or found to have fled, *&c.* whereby they are actually forfeited.

Sect. 36. Also it was enacted by the Statute *de Officio Coronatoris,* (set forth more at large, *Ch.* 9. *Sect.* 19, 20.) That where one is found guilty of Murder by a Coroner's Inquest upon View of a dead Body, the Coroner shall inquire what Goods he hath, and cause them to be valued and delivered to the Township, *&c.* But so much of this Statute as enables the Coroner to seise the Goods, [cc] seems to be repealed by 1 *Rich.* 3. (set forth more at large *Sect.* 38) unless the Party indicted be found also to have fled.

Sect. 37. Also it was enacted by 25 *Ed.* 3. 14 (set forth more at large *Ch.* 27. *Sect.* 116.) That in the second *Capias* given by that Statute on the Return of a *Non inventus,* it shall be comprised, That the Sheriff shall cause the Party's Chattels to be seised, and safely kept till the Day of the Writ or Precept returned, *&c.* and this is still in [d] Force notwithstanding the Statute of 1 *R.* 3. 3. for this prohibits only the seising of the Goods of those who are arrested; and so far as it relates to this Purpose, is enacted as followeth.

Sect. 38. *And that no Sheriff, Under-Sheriff nor Escheator, Bailiff of Franchise, nor any other Person, take or seise the Goods of any Person arrested or imprisoned for Suspicion of Felony, before that the same Person so arrested and imprisoned be convicted or attainted of such Felony according to the Law, or else the same Goods otherwise lawfully forfeited, upon Pain to forfeit the double Value of the Goods so taken, to him that is so hurt in that Behalf, by* [e] *Action of Debt,* &c.

Sect. 39. This Statute is said to be in [f] Affirmance of the Common Law, and hath been [g] adjudged to extend as well to the Seizure of Money as of any other Chattel.

Sect. 40. It seems plain from this Statute, That Goods may be seised as [h] soon as they are forfeited; and it seems the whole Township is answerable [i] for them to the King, and may seise them [k] where-ever they can be found.

[a] *See the Citations to the foregoing and following Section.*
[b] Fleta, B. 1. ch. 26. S. 2. Bract. B. 3. ch. 18. S. 2. Britton, f. 4. S. P. C. 52. Lett. C. 192. Lett. B. Staundf. Prerog 47, b. 48. a. *It is said* 26 Aff. pl. 32. *Abridged* Bro. Coro. 102. *That Justices* of Oyer, &c. *shall put the Chattels of Felons in Estreat presently,* &c. *and deliver them to the Towns,* &c. *to answer to the King in Eyre. But this seems intended of the Chattels of one convict of Felony.* *And in* 44 Aff. pl. 13. *and* 43 E. 3. 24. pl. 1. *Abridged* Bro. Coro 9. Forfeiture, 7. Reseiser, 3. Office *and* Officer, 3. Fitz. Tresp. 7. Bar, 196. *the* 2*d, it is said, That no Minister of the King ought to take the Chattels of an Appellee of Felony away with him, but to seise them, and cause the Party to find Surety that they shall not be eloigned,* &c. *and if the Party cannot find Surety, he ought to deliver them to the Neighbours,* &c. *And in the last Case of* 7 H. 4. *Abridged* Fitz Coro. 83. *and* Bro. Forfeit. 10. *It is said, That where one is indicted of Felony until he be attainted, his Goods shall not be removed out of his House, but shall be kept by his Neighbours until,* &c. *and in the mean Time the Felon ought to live upon his Goods,* Vide 41. Aff. pl. 13. *Abridged* Fitz. Process, 183. Bro. Forfeiture, 40. 13 H. 3. 13. pl. 6 *in which Books it is said, That Goods shall not be seised till they be forfeited* [c] *The old Writ recited* Bract. B. 3. Ch. 18 Sect. 2. *and* Fleta, B. 1. ch. 26. Sect. 2. *is express to this Purpose, Yet in* 3 Inst. 228 *it is said, That the Goods of any Delinquent cannot be inventoried, and the Town charged therewith before the Owner is indicted of Record; and a Note in* H. P. C. 269 *seems to be to the same Effect.* * State Trials, Vol. 1. fol. 994, 995. Vol. 4 fol. 65, 66. S P. C 139. [cc] S. P. C. 52. Lett. C. [d] S P. C 193 Staundf. Prerog. 48. [e] *For Precedents of such Actions, See* 1 Lutw. 132. Cro. Eliz. 749 [f] Vide supra, S. 33, 35, 34. S. P. C. 193. [g] Raym. 414. [h] Co. Litt. 391. [i] Fitz. Coro. 300, 347, 366. 13 H. 4. 13 pl. 6. *Abridged* Fitz. Forfeit. 32. 22 Aff. pl. 81. *Abridged* Fitz Coro. 181. Bro. Charge, 45. Forfeiture, 32. S P. C. 193. B. 94. A. B Staundf. Prerog. 47. b 47 E. 3 26 a. b. [k] 22 Aff. pl 81. *Abridged* Fitz. Coro. 181. Bro. Charge, 45. Forfeiture 32. Staundf. Prerog. 47. b.

Sect.

Sect. 41. And at the Common Law it was no [l] Plea for such Township, That the Goods were delivered to the Custody of *J. S.* who imbezilled them, *&c.* But it is enacted by 31 E. 3. 3. *That if any Man or Town be charged in the Exchequer by Estreats of the Justices of the Chattels of Fugitives and Felons, and will alledge in discharge of him another which is chargeable, he shall be heard, and Right done to the other.*

Sect. 42. As to the second Point, *viz.* Where the Wife loses her Dower: It is agreed, That before the Statute of 1 *Ed. 6. ch.* 12. the Wife not only lost her Dower at Common [a] Law, but also her Dower [b] *ad ostium ecclesiæ*, or *ex assensu patris*, or by Special [c] Custom (except that of [d] Gavelkind) by an Attainder of any Treason or [e] capital Felony, whether [f] committed before or after the Marriage, and whether the Land were in the Hands of a [g] Feoffee, or forfeited to the King, or escheated to the Lord of the Fee: And tho' the [h] Attainder were pardoned, *&c.*

Sect. 43. But it [i] seems that the Wife never forfeited Lands given jointly to her Husband and her, whether by way of Frank-marriage or otherwise, but only [k] for the Year and Day and Waste.

Sect. 44. Also it hath been [l] adjudged, That if a Husband having levied a Fine with Proclamations, is afterwards erroneously attainted of High Treason, and the five Years pass after his Death, and then the Outlawry is reversed, the Wife may pursue her Title of Dower within five Years after such Reversal; because being barred of her Dower by the Attainder while it stood in Force, which Attainder she could no way reverse, she had no Remedy to pursue her Title of Dower within the five Years, and therefore shall not be barred by her Non-claim.

Sect. 45. It is enacted by 1 *Ed. 6. 12. Par.* 17. *That albeit any Person shall be attainted of any Treason or Felony whatsoever, yet that notwithstanding every Woman that shall fortune to be Wife of the Person so attainted, shall be endowable and enabled to demand, have, and enjoy her Dower in like Manner and Form as tho' her Husband had not been attainted,* &c.

Sect. 46. But this is repealed as to Treason by 5 *&* 6 *Ed.* 6. 11. *Par.* 9. by which it is enacted, *That the Wife whose Husband shall be attainted of any Treason whatsoever, shall in no wise be received to ask, challenge, demand, or have Dowry of any the Lands, Tenements, or Hereditaments of the Person so attainted during the said Attainder in Force.* And this hath been construed [m] to extend as well to an Attainder of Petit Treason, as of High Treason.

As to the third Point, *viz.* How far the Blood is corrupted by an Attainder of Treason or Felony, the following Particulars seem most remarkable.

Sect. 47. 1*st*, It is [n] agreed, That by [o] such an Attainder, the Blood is so far stained or corrupted that the Party loses all the Nobility or Gentility he might have had before, and becomes ignoble.

Sect. 48. 2*dly*, It is also [p] agreed, That he can neither inherit as Heir to any Ancestor, nor have an Heir.

Sect. 49. 3*dly*, It is also farther [q] agreed, That where-ever it is necessary for any one who would make a Title to another, to derive the De-

[l] Fitz. Coro. 300, 347. S. P. C. 194. Lett. B.

[a] S. P. C. 194. D. Co. Litt. 31, a, 37, a. 41, a. 392. b. Litt. §. 747. 3 Inst. 47, 211.

[b] Co. Litt. 37. a. 41. a. S. P. C. 195. A. Bract. 311. pl. 13.

[c] Co. Litt. 41. a. Bract. 311. pl. 13. Winch, 27.

[d] Bract. 311. pl. 13.

[e] Co. Litt. 41. a.

[f] Co. Litt. 31. a.

[g] 3 Inst. 216. Savil, 54, 55. Co. Litt. 41. a. Benl. 55, 56, 57. Dy. 140. pl. 42. Moor, 639. pl. 879. Cont. by Vavasor. Litt. Sect. 55.

[h] 1 Leon. 3.

[i] Co. Litt. 37. 3 Inst. 216. Bract. 129. pl. 14. 130. pl. 23.

[k] Bract. 129. pl. 14. Supra Sect. 8. Cont. Bract. 130, pl. 23.

[l] 3 Inst. 216. Moor, 639. pl 879.

[m] S. P. C. 195. Dyer, 140. pl. 42. Co. Litt. 37. a. 392. b.

[n] 3 Inst. 211. S. P. C. 195. B.

[o] But an Attainder of Piracy, (B. 1. Ch. 37. Sect. 6, 8. Co. Litt. 391.) or Petit Larceny corrupts not the Blood. B. 1. Ch. 33. Sect. 36. 3 Inst. 211, Co. Litt. 41. a. Noy, 170.

[p] Co. Litt. 8. a. 391. b. 392. S. P. C. 195. B. Bro. Nonability, 21. Coro. 60.

[q] Cro. Ca. 543. Litt. Rep. 28. 1 Vent. 413, 417. Noy, 159, 166, *&c.* 1 Lev. 60. 1 Sid. 200, 201.

2 scent

scent thro' him, the Attainder is a Bar to such Title, [a] unless the Land were intailed. And therefore if there be Grandfather, Father and Son, and the Father be attainted, it is clear, That the Son [b] cannot claim as Heir to the Grandfather of the Lands in Fee-simple, because he must of Necessity derive the Descent thro' the Father, which by Reason of the Attainder he cannot do. And for the same Reason, if there be two Brothers, and one of them having issue a Son be attainted, and either the Son or Uncle purchase Land and die without Issue, the other [c] cannot be his Heir, because the Blood of the Father thro' whom the Descent must be convey'd, is corrupted. But it seems a [d] general Rule, That the Attainder of a Person who needs not be mentioned in the Conveyance of the Descent, does no hurt, let the Ancestor be never so remote; and *a fortiori* therefore it seems clearly to follow, That where one may claim as immediate Heir to another, without deriving the Descent thro' any other, he shall not be barred by the Attainder of any other. And therefore it seems [e] agreed, That if the Son of one attainted purchase Land, and have a Son and die, such Son shall inherit him, because he derives his Descent immediately from him. And for the like Reason it hath been [f] settled, That if a Man hath two Sons, and then be attainted, and one of the Sons purchase Lands and die without Issue, the other shall be his Heir, because he may make his Title without mentioning the Father.

But Sir *Edward Coke* [g] says, That the Reason of this Case is, *because the Attainder of the Father corrupts only the lineal Blood, and not the collateral Blood between the Brethren which was vested in them before the Attainder*; but he saith, *That some have holden that if a Man after he be attainted have Issue two Sons, the one cannot be Heir to the other, because they could not be Heir to their Father, for that they never had any inheritable Blood in them.* But the Ground of this Opinion seems to be overthrown by the Resolution in the Case of *Collingwood* and *Pace*, wherein it was adjudged [h] in the Exchequer-Chamber by seven Judges against three, That the Sons of an Alien might be Heirs to one another if born in *England* or naturalized; and yet it is certain that they could not be Heirs to their Father. Also it seems to [i] be the better Opinion, That where a Person attainted hath Issue by a Woman seized of Lands of Inheritance, such Issue may inherit the Mother, tho' he never had any inheritable Blood from the Father.

Sect. 50. 4thly. It seems clear, That notwithstanding a Person attainted be to many Purposes looked upon as dead in Law, yet he hath a Capacity to [k] purchase Land, which the King shall have upon Office found. Also if the Father of a Person attainted die seised of an Estate of Inheritance during his Life, no [l] younger Brother can be Heir, but the Land shall rather escheat; for the elder Brother, tho' attainted, is still a Brother, and no other can be Heir to the Father while he is alive: But it seems [m] agreed at this Day, That if he die before the Father, the younger Brother shall be Heir.

[a] 3 Co. 10. b. Litt. S 746, 747. 8 Co. 166. a. [b] 1 Vent. 416, 418. Dalis. 14 pl. 3. Co. Litt. 392. [c] Cro. Ca. 543. Dy. 274. pl. 40. 1 Vent. 413, 416, 425. [d] Cro. Ca. 543. 1 Vent. 413, 417, &c. Litt. Re. 28. Noy, 159, 166, &c. 1 Lev. 60. 1 Sid. 200, 201. Vide Bract. B. 3. Ch. 14. Sect. 17. [e] 1 Vent. 416. [f] Co. Litt. 8. a. 4 Leon. 5. Cro. Ja. 539. 1 Roll. Abr. 625, pl. 5. Cro. Ca. 543. 1 Vent. 425. Palm. 19. 1 Lev. 59. 2 Rol. Re. 193. 2 Sid. 25, 27. *This is left doubtful* Moor 569 pl. 775. Noy, 158, &c. Cont. Litt. Rep. 28. [g] Co. Litt. 8. a. 1 Rol. Abr. 625. pl. 5. [h] 1 Sid. 193. Hard. 224. 1 Vent. 413. 1 Lev. 59. [i] 1 Sid. 201. 1 Vent. 422, 426. Noy 159, 167, 168, 169. 2 Sid. 248. *This also appears from* 13 H. 7. 17. *cited* S. P C. 196. *Abridged* Bro. Tenant by Curtesy, 15 *and wherein it is holden, That if the Husband of an Inheritrix have Issue, and be attainted of Felony and pardoned, he shall not be Tenant by Curtesy by Reason of the Issue born before the Pardon, but by Reason of Issue born after he shall; from whence it necessarily follows, that such Issue must be inheritable to the Wife. Also it is admitted,* Co Litt 84 b *That the Issue of an Inheritrix by an Alien or a Person attainted may be in Ward, which could not be unless he could inherit the Mother.* Vide Cro. Ja. 539. Litt. Rep. 28. 1 Lev. 59, 60. *But the contrary was anciently holden.* 3 Co 41. Bract. B 3 Ch. 13. Sect. 19, 20. [k] Co. Litt. 2. b. [l] Fleta B. 1. Ch 28. Sect. 9. Co Litt. 8. a. 13. a. Bro. Mordancester, 36. S. P. C. 195. B. Bract. B. 5. Ch 6. Sect 7. Fitz. Petition, 20. Mordancester, 28. Discent, 7. 1 Vent 413, 417. 1 Lev. 60. Descent, 17. 29 Ass. pl. 11. Noy 166, 170. 1 Sid. 195. 26 Ass. pl. 2. [m] *See the Books next above cited, and* Bro. Discent, 64. Cont. Bract. B. 3. Ch. 14. Sect. 17.

Sect. 51. *5thly,* It is clear, That the Corruption of Blood from an Attainder is so high that it cannot be absolutely salved but by Act of Parliament; for it seems [a] agreed, That the King's Pardon cannot restore the Blood so as to make the Person attainted capable either of inheriting others, or of being inherited himself by any one born before the Pardon. [b] Yet if such Person have a Son born after the Pardon, and purchase Lands and die, such Son may be his Heir, unless he have an elder Brother alive born before the Pardon; for a Pardon doth as it were make a Man a new Creature, and give him a new Capacity, in Respect whereof his Issue born after the Pardon may be his Heirs, as to Lands purchased after the Pardon, in the same Manner as if he had never been attainted.

[a] Co. Litt. 8. a. 391. b. 392. a. S. P. C. 195. B. 3 Inst. 233. Dalis. 14 p[illegible]. Cont. 9 H. 5. 9. a.

[b] *See the Books next above-cited.*

CHAP. L.

Of avoiding Judgments in Criminal Cases.

FOR the better understanding the Learning concerning the avoiding of Judgments in criminal Cases, I shall endeavour to shew,

1. How such Judgments may be avoided.
2. The Effect of such Avoidance.

And first, such Judgments may be avoided either,

1. Without Writ of Error.
2. By Writ of Error.

They may be avoided without Writ of Error two Ways.

1. For Faults apparent in the Record.
2. For other Matters *dehors* the Record.

Sect. 1. And first I shall endeavour to shew where such Judgments may be avoided by Plea without any Writ of Error for Faults apparent in the Record; as to which it is observable, That notwithstanding it be the allowed Practice of the Court of Common Pleas to suffer a Defendant coming in by [c] *Capias Utlagatum* the same [d] Term in which an Exigent is returnable, to avoid the Outlawry without Writ of Error, by shewing that he purchased a [e] *Supersedeas* out of the [f] same Court, and

[c] Co. Litt. 259. b. 1 And. 36. pl. 92. Vide infra, Sect. 9. Secus *if he comes in* gratis. Dyer 192. pl. 25. Cont. 39 H. 6. 27. b. *Abridged* Fitz. Responder, 52. Bro. Utlagary, 35. Vide 14 H. 4. 27. a. b. Fitz. idempnitate nominis, 3. Bro. Uulagary, 28. 30 H. 6, 3. a. [d] 8 H. 6, 37. pl. 8. *Abridged* Fitz. Error, 19. 19 H. 6, 2. a. *Abridged* Fitz Error, 26. *But some have holden, That an Outlawry cannot be avoided for this or any other Cause in another Term.* Co. Litt. 259. b. 37 H 6, 17. a. b. *Abridged,* Fitz. Utlagary, 28. Bro. Error, 97. 37 H. 6, 17. a. b. *Abridged* Fitz. Utlagary, 28. Bro. Error, 97. 8 H. 6. 37. a. b. Con. *adjudged* 1 And. 36. pl 93. [e] 19 H. 6. 44. a. b. *Abridged,* Fitz Utlagary, 20 Bro. Utlagary, 21. 33 H. 6. 1. b. *Abridged* Fitz. Utlagary, 27. Bro. 2. 30 H. 6, 3. a. *Abridged* Fitz Protection, 11. Bro. Utlagary, 74. 12 H. 4. 18. a. *Abridged* Bro. Utlagary, 14. 7 H. 4, 1. a. *Abridged* Bro. Utlagary, 5. 8 H. 6, 7. a. b. Fitz. Error, 42. 11 H. 4. 34. 33 H. 6. 1. b. 45. a. *Abridged* Fitz. Utlagary, 27. 1 And. 36. pl. 93. *But* 1 Roll. Abr. 743. pl. 2. *the contrary is said to have been holden* 39 Eliz. [f] 30 H. 6, 3. a. *Abridged* Fitz Protection, 11. Secus *if the* Supersedeas *were from the Chancery,* 7 H. 4, 5. b. *Abitdged* Fitz. Supersedeas, 10. Bro. Utlagary, 65. Supersedeas, 8. Vide 18 H. 6, 18. a. b. *Abridged* Fitz. Error 24. 7 Ed. 4. 9. b. *Abridged* Fitz. Exigent, 1. Bro. Supers. 31. F. N. B. 236. A.

[a] delivered it to the Sheriff before the *quinto exactus, &c.* or by ſhewing any [b] other Matter apparent on Record which makes the Outlawry erroneous, as the Want of an [c] Original, or the [d] Omiſſion of Proceſs, or Want [f] of Form in a Writ of Proclamation, *&c.* or a [g] Return by a Perſon appearing not to be Sheriff, or a [h] Variance between the Original and Exigent or other Proceſs, or the Want of ſuch Addition as is [i] required by 1 *H.* 5. Yet it is ſaid in many [k] Books, to be the conſtant Courſe of the Court of King's Bench, never to reverſe an Outlawry on the Crown-ſide either in the ſame or a different Term, for [l] theſe or other Errors of the like Nature (as the [m] Want of a *Capias* to the Sheriff of the County whereof the Party is named, or a [n] Fault in the Indictment) without a Writ of Error; yet ſince Sir *Edward* [o] *Coke* ſeems to be of another Opinion, and ſince alſo it is clearly holden, That one may plead even a Matter of Fact in the King's Bench in Avoidance of an Outlawry of Felony which cannot be pleaded in Avoidance of any other Outlawry, as ſhall be more fully ſhewn, *Sect.* 6. I ſhall leave this Point to be farther conſidered. However it is [p] agreed, That a Conviction of Felony whereon the Party hath had his Clergy may be diſcharged by Exception to the Indictment, becauſe no Writ of Error lies of ſuch a Conviction, not being a Judgment.

Sect. 2. As to the ſecond Particular, *viz.* Where a Judgment may be avoided without Writ of Error for Matters *dehors* the Record, it is [q] holden, That he who purchaſes Land of a Perſon who afterwards is [r] outlawed of Felony, or condemned upon his own [s] Confeſſion, may falſify the Record not only as to the Time wherein the Felony is ſuppoſed to have been committed, but alſo as to the Point of the Offence. But it is [t] agreed, That where a Man is found guilty by Verdict, a Purchaſer cannot falſify as to the Point of the Offence, but that he may falſify for the Time where the Party is found Guilty generally of the Offence in the Appeal or Indictment; becauſe the Time is not material upon Evidence.

Sect. 3. Alſo it ſeems [u] agreed, That any Judgment whatſoever given by Perſons who had no good Commiſſion to proceed againſt the Perſon condemned, may be falſify'd by ſhewing the Special Matter without Writ of Error, becauſe it is void; as where a Commiſſion authoriſes to proceed on an Indictment taken before *A. B. C.* and twelve others, and by Colour thereof the Commiſſioners proceed on an Indictment taken before eight Perſons only.

Sect. 4. Alſo it ſeems [x] agreed, That if the Treaſon or Felony of which a Man is attainted, be afterwards pardoned by Parliament, the Attainder may be falſify'd by himſelf or his Heir without Plea.

[a] 14 H. 4 9 a. b. *Abridged,* Bro. Utlagary, 15. Long quinto Ed. 4. 5. *Abridged* Bro. Error, 155. Dyer 222, pl. 23. 223. pl. 26. *and it is ſaid not to be material whether it were delivered to the Sheriff or not;* Co. Lit. 128. b. Bro Utlag. 8. 4 E. 4, 42. a. Cont. Fitz. Error, 77. Vide Fitz. Error, 42. [b] Co. Litt. 259. b. 33 H. 6, 1. b. 45. a. *Abridged* Fitz. Utlagary, 27. [c] 11 H. 7, 4. b. *Abridged,* Bro. Utl. 78. 16 E, 4, 9. b. *Abridged* Bro. Error, 172. Fitz. Utl. 41. Vide 19 Ed. 4. 8. b. *But it is agreed, That an Outlawry without any Original is not void, but voidable only.* Fitz. Color, 45. Utlagary, 18. V. 7 H. 7, 5. b. *Abridged* Fitz. Error, 52. Keilw. 19 b. Bro. Utlagary, 45. Long quinto Ed. 4. 116. b. [d] 33 H. 6, 1.

b. 45 a. *Abridged* Fitz. Utl. 27. 8 H. 6. 37. pl. 8. *Abridged* Fitz. Error. 19. Bro. Utlagary, 19. 19 H, 6. 2. a. *Abridged* Fitz Error, 26. Long quinto Ed. 4, 116. b. Bro. Utlagary, 45. [f] Dy. 206. pl. 10. 11 H. 4, 34. a. [g] Dy. 41. pl. 7. [h] Fitz. Utlagary. 41. 38 H. 6. 31. a. *Abridged* Fitz Utlagary, 31. 21 Ed. 3. 56. b. *Abridged* Fitz. Diſcontiuance, 3. 16 Ed. 4, 9. b. Bro. Error, 172. Fitz. Diſcontinuance, 17. 20 H. 6, 18. *Abridged* Fitz Diſcontinuance, 22. 2 Rich. 3. 13. b. Bro. Miſnoſmer, 80. Variance, 90. [i] 8 H. 6. 37. a. *Abridged* Fitz Error, 19. 1 And. 36. pl. 92. 1 Roll. Abr. 743. pl. 6, 7. 2 Inſt. 670. Cont. Bro. Utlagary, 34. 39 H. 6 1. b. [k] 1 Roll. Abr. 743. Lett C. 37 H. 6, 17. b. *Abridged* Fitz Utlagary, 28. 4 E. 4, 42, a. b. 43. *Abridged* Bro. Error, 158. Utlagary, 67. 19 H. 6. 2. a. *Abridged* Fitz Error, 26. Vide Palmer 43. Contra, 11 H. 7, 4. b. *Abridged* Bro. Utlagary, 78. [l] *Not for the Want of an Addition,* 19 H. 6. 2. a. *Abridged* Fitz. Error, 26. 11 H. 6, 15. b. 54. [m] Supra, Ch. 27. Sect. 127. 9 H. 6, 15. b. Bro. Utlagary, 20, 34. 39 H. 6, 1. b. [n] 1 Bulſt. 109 1 Sid. 144. [o] Co Litt. 259. b. Vide 11 H. 7. 4. b. Bro. Utlagary, 78. 33 H. 6, 1. b. *Abridged* Fitz Utlagary 27. 8 H. 6, 37. a. b. *Abridged* Bro. Utlagary, 19. [p] Cro. Eliz. 489. 490. [r] H. P. C. 270. 3 Inſt. 230. *Yet the contrary ſeems holden* 49 Ed. 3, 11. 49 Aſſ. pla. 2. Bro. Coro. 205 *or* 6. 207 *or* 8. Fitz Traverſe, 19. [s] H. P. C. 270. 3 Inſt. 231. Bro. Traverſe de Office, 35. 7 Ed 4 1, 2. Fitz. Eſtopel 91. [t] *See the Books above-cited.* [u] H. P. C 270. 3 Inſt. 231. Plow. Com 392, &c [x] 3 Inſt. 232. H. P. C. 271. 8 Co. 79 b Vide Supra Ch. 37. S. 53. Cro. El. 72. Cro. Eliz. 4. *'tis ſaid that a Writ of Error lies on ſuch a Pardon. But this is contrary to* 3 Inſt. 231. *and* 6 Co. 14. a. *for the avoiding of an Outlawry by the King's Pardon.* Vide ſup. ch 49 S. 15. Fitz. Chart. 27. Bro. Err. 56. 18 Ed. 3, 38. Bro App 7. 92. 9 H. 5. 14, b. 15 a.

Sect.

y 29 Ed. 3. 25. a. z Rol. A. 489 Letter Y. z Co.L 269.b. V. 1 c H 4. 7. a. *Abridged* Fitz. Respon. 101. * Fitz. Utl. 2, 11, 18, 27. 33 H. 6. 1. b. 7 H. 6 25. a. Br Utl. 18, 40. 38 Ass pl. 17. 27 Ass pl. 47. Vide Fitz. Coro. 123. 8 H. 4, 13 b. 3 Inst. 32. Cont. 21 Ed. 4. 73. b Bro. Utl. 57. 1 H. 7. 13. Bro. Utlaga. 68 Coro. 128. *That he who pleads this Plea must shew in whose Custody he was, and in what County, and must also aver his Plea; and* by 5 Ed. 3. 13. *an Averment is given against the Testimony of a Sheriff or others, having no Record testifying such Imprisonment.* † Fitz. Utl. 11. 2 E. 4. 1. a. b. *Abridged* Fitz. Respond, 54. 9 H. 4. 3. a. Fitz. Scire Facias, 64

Sect. 5. But it hath been [y] adjudged, That the King's Letters Patents reversing an Attainder are void, unless they be afterwards made good by Act of Parliament.

Sect. 6. It seems generally agreed, That by the Common Law, in [z] *favorem vitæ*, an Outlawry of Treason or Felony might be avoided by Plea that the Defendant was in * Prison, or in the King's Service beyond the † Sea, *&c.* at the Time of the Outlawry ** pronounced against him. But I take it to be generally [a] agreed, That no Outlawry for any other Crime, (against a Party [b] rightly described) can be avoided by the Plea of any Matter [c] of Fact whatsoever.

Sect. 7. And it is enacted by 26 *H.* 8. 13. and 5 *&* 6 *Ed.* 6. 11. *That all Process of Outlawry to be had or made within this Realm, against any Offenders in Treason, being resiant or inhabited out of the Limits of this Realm, or in any of the Parts beyond the Seas at the Time of the Outlawry pronounced against them, shall be as good and effectual in Law to all Intents and Purposes, as if such Offenders had been resident and dwelling within this Realm at the Time of such Process awarded, and Outlawry pronounced.* [d] *Provided, That the Party so to be outlawed, shall, within one Year next after the said Outlawry pronounced,* [e] *yield himself to the Chief Justice of* England *for the Time being, and offer to traverse the Indictment or Appeal whereupon the said Outlawry shall be pronounced as is aforesaid, that then he shall be received to the same Traverse, and being thereupon found Not guilty by the Verdict of twelve Men, he shall be clearly acquitted and discharged of the said Outlawry, &c.*

Sect. 8. And it hath been [f] resolved, That these Statutes extend as well to Treasons by subsequent Statutes as to those within 25 *Ed.* 3.

Sect. 9. It seems generally agreed, That any Outlawry whatsoever may be avoided by a Defendant's coming in upon the [g] *Capias Utlagatum*, and pleading a [h] Misnosmer either of the Name, or Addition in the Writ, *&c.* as by shewing that whereas he is called by such a Name of [i] Baptism, or [k] Surname, he hath been always known by a different one, and not by that in the Writ, *&c.* or whereas he is named of such Estate, Degree, or Mystery, that he hath some other [l] Addition, and not that in the Writ, *&c.* Also it is said in many [m] Books, that he may plead, That there is no such Town as that whereof he is named. And it seems clearly agreed, That he may plead that at the Time of the Writ purchased, and ever since, he hath made his Abode at some [n] other Town, and not at that in the Writ, *&c.*

11 H. 7 5. a. Bro Utl. 79. 4 Ed 4 10. b. Cont. Fitz. Coro. 123. Vide 10 H. 4 7. a. *Abridged* Fitz. Ref. 101. 8 Co. 107 9 Co. 207. Co. 31. b. Co. Litt. 74. a. ** Fitz. Utlagary, 2, 48. Forfeiture, 19. Respond. 54. 101. 7 H. 6. 25. a. *Abridged* Bro. Utlagary, 18. 16 Ed. 4, 6. a. [a] Co. Litt. 259. b. [b] Vide infra, Sect. 9. [c] *Not by the Plea of Imprisonment.* Fitz Utl. 27, 47. 33 H. 6. 1. b 45 a. *nor by the Plea of being beyond Sea.* Fitz Utl. 27. 33 H. 6. 1. 45. a. [d] 5 & 6 E 6. 4. [e] Vide State Trials, V. 3. f. 335. 3 Mod. 47. 4 Mod. 366. *Sir* Tho. Armstrong's *Case.* [f] 3 Inst 32, 216. *But see* Dyer, 287. pl 48. *See also* 2 Jon. 180. *Error assigned for the Reversal of an Outlawry of High Treason, That the Defendant was beyond Sea at the Time.* [g] 33 H. 6. 1. b. 38, 45. a. Fitz. Utlagary, 22, 23, 26, 27, 29, 32, 35, 37, 44. Nonsuit, 6. Estoppel, 47, 54, 67. Dyer 192. pl. 25. Bro. Utlagary, 1, 22, 23, 24, 25, 26. Misnosmer, 52. 1 Ed. 4. 2. b. 21 H. 6, 50. b. 5 H. 7, 16. a. 7 Ed. 4. 1. 27 H. 8 11, 12 22 H. 6. 23. a. 19 H 6, 80. a. b. 5 H. 5. 7. b. 28 H. 6. 2. b. Vide Fitz. Variance, 74. 19 H. 6, 58. a. 22 Ed. 4, 37. 38. [h] 33 H. 6. 1. b. 45. a. *But in the Abridgment of this Case,* Bro. Utlagary, 2. *the contrary seems to be holden* Fitz Utlagary, 27. [i] Fitz. Utlagary, 44. Bro. Utlagary, 1. 27 H. 8. 11, 12. [k] 14 Ed. 4. 6 b. Bro. Utlagary, 53. 19 Ed. 4, 24, 25. Bro. Scire Facias, 132. Misnosmer, 1. 27 H. 8. 11, 12. 12 H 6. 7 b. *So if one be called in the Writ the Son of* J. S. *he may plead that he is the Son of* W. S. 10 Ed. 4, 12. b. Bro. idempnitate nominis, 9 [l] Fitz. Nonsuit, 6. Estoppel, 47. 67. 1 Ed. 4. 2. b. 21 H. 6 50 b. 28 H. 6. 2. b. Fitz. Utlagary, 32, 35, 37. Bro. Utlagary. 15, 24, 78. Misnosf. 52. 5 H 7. 16. a. 7 Ed. 4. 1. 5 H. 5, 7. b. *Abridged* Bro. Utl. 15. Fitz. Utl 37. *But 'tis there said That some were of Opinion, That the Party shou'd be put to his Writ of Error, because he is the same Person.* See 38 H 6. 1. Bro. Utl. 32, 51. 10 Ed 4. 16. a. Bro. Scire Facias, 132. 9 Ed. 4. 24, 25. [m] Fitz. Utl. 23, 26. 22 Ed. 4. 37. b. 22 H 6 23. a. 33 H. 6. 51. a. Bro. Utl. 26 *the 2d.* Vide Rast. Entr. 300, pl. 24. 301. pl. 25, 26. *But the contrary is holden.* 33 H. 6. 1. b. *because such Plea wou'd avoid the Outlawry against all Persons.* Bro. Utl. 29. *there is an Opinion to the contrary, but it seems not warranted by the Year Book.* [n] Fitz. Utl. 22, 23, 25, 29, 30, 33. Estoppel, 54. Error, 23. 38 H. 6. 1. a. b. 28 H. 6. 2. a. b. 33 H. 6. 38. 22 H. 6, 7. a. 16. a. 23. a. b. 19 H. 6, 80. a. b. Dyer, 192. pl. 25. 2 E. 4. 1. b. Bro. Utl. 22, 25, 32. 33. 58. 21 Ed. 4 79. Keil. 101. *such Matter is pleaded without any Traverse of the Place in the Indictment.* Vide 22 E. 4. 37, 38. 20. H 6. 19 b. *It is adjudged* 28 H. 6. *Abridged* Fitz. Utl. 25. *That it is no Plea for one named of the Parish of* C. *that there are* 3 *Vills in the same Parish,* viz. D. E. F. *and that he was commorant at* D. *and therefore ought to have been named of it.*

and

and it is [p] said, That by such Plea the Outlawry shall only be avoided as to the Person who pleads it (who shall [q] not be intended to be the Person meant) and shall stand in Force against the Person of the Name and Addition in the Record. But it is said, That a Person of the same Name and Addition as are mentioned in a Record of Outlawry, [r] cannot avoid it by averring that there are two Persons of such Name and Addition, and that the Person intended is the Elder, and he himself is the Younger, but shall be put to his Writ of *idempnitate nominis*, which is said by some to be the [s] only Remedy in such Case after an Outlawry returned. And it seems, That notwithstanding in Civil Causes [t] before an Outlawry is returned one of the same Name may come into Court, and shew [u] that he is not the Person intended; whereupon if the Plaintiff confess it, the Diversity of the Names shall be entred on the Roll, and a new Exigent shall issue with a fuller Description of the Person intended; Yet this * cannot be done upon an Indictment, without a Writ of *idempnitate nominis*, because it would make the Process variant from the Indictment, which cannot be altered without the Consent of the Jurors.

And now I am to shew how Judgments in Criminal Cases may be avoided by Writs of Error; as to which having shewn already, *Ch.* 29. *Sect.* 40. That the Reversal of the Attainder of the Principal *ipso facto* reverses that of the Accessory, I shall in this Place only observe the following Particulars.

Sect. 10. 1*st*, That it seems to be in a great Measure [a] settled, That a Writ of Error to reverse an Attainder of Treason or Felony may be brought as well by the Executor as by the Heir of the Party, but [b] no other Person whatsoever.

Sect. 11. 2*dly*, That a Person attainted of Treason or Felony, before he can have a Writ of Error to reverse his Attainder, must [c] assign his Errors, and thereupon have Leave from the Court to prosecute his Writ of Error.

Sect. 12. 3*dly*, That no Writ of Error for the Reversal of an Attainder of Treason or Felony is to be [d] allowed without an express Warrant from the King, or the Consent of the Attorney General.

Sect. 13. 4*thly*, That an Attainder of Felony of a Person who had any Lands, shall never be reversed by Writ of Error [e] without a *Scire facias* against all the Ter-tenants, and Lords mediate and immediate; but it is [f] settled, That such *Scire Facias* is not necessary in the Case of High Treason. Also it is [g] said, That it is not necessary in the Case of Felony when it suggested on the Roll that the Party had no Lands, and the Attorney General confesses it.

Sect. 14. 5*thly*, That it hath been [h] settled, That the Statute of 33 *H.* 8. 20. which enacts, *That if any Person shall be attainted of High Treason by the Course of the Common Laws or Statutes of this Realm, that in every such Case, every such Attainder by the Common Law shall be of as good Strength, Value, Force and Effect, as if it had been done by Authority of Parliament*, is to be intended of lawful Attainders by due Course of the Common Law, and not of erroneous and void Attainders, which therefore may be avoided in the same Manner as before.

[p] 39 H. 6. 1. b. Bro. Utl. 34. 73. 10 H. 6. 4. b. 30 H. 6. 2 pl. 9. Fitz. Err. 23. [r] 21 H. 7. 13. pl. 16. *But it is said*, 21 H. 6, 21. b. *Abridged* Fitz. Fitz. Scire facias. 55. Bro. Utl. 23. *That a* Cap. ad Satisfaciendum *the Judgment is affirmed or disaffirmed by the Affiance or Avoidance of the Outlawry*. Vide 22 H. 6. 16. a. Bro. Utl. 25. 19 H. 6. 58. a. b. Fitz. Utl. 21. [q] *And for this Cause this is a good Plea in Avoidance of the Plea of Outlawry in Disability*. Fitz. Nonability, 14. 21 H. 7, 13. pl. 16. 7 E. 4. 1. Br. Nona. 50. [r] 21 H 7. 13. pl. 16. 14 H. 4. 27. a. b. Fitz. idempnitate nominis, 2, 3. Vide Bro. Utl. 29, 55, 56. 21 Ed. 4, 15. a. 54 a. 13 H. 6, 7. b. Fitz. Utl. 1, 24, 43. Variance, 74. [s] Fitz Utl. 6, 16. Resp. 21. Nonab. 17. [t] 21 E 4. 15, a. 13 H. 7 12. a. Bro idempn. nominis, 3, 5, 7, 8. Fitz. idemp. nomi. 3, 6, 7. Cont. F.N.B. 268. Lett. B.

[a] F. N. B. 268. Letter A. Bro. idempnitate nominis, 3, 4, 11. 14 H. 4, 27. Fitz idempnitate nominis, 5. 21 Ed. 3, 36. b. Cont. Fitz. idempn. nominis 4. Bro idempn. nominis 6. Long quinto Ed. 4, 51. * Fitz. idemp. nominis 3. F.N.B. 268. Lett. B. Bro. idempn. nominis 2, 11. 9 H. 4. 3. [a] Cro. El. 225, 273, 558. 5 Co. 111. a. Owen, 147, 148. 1 Leon, 325, 326. Salk. 295. Shower. 13. [b] Vide Salk. 60, 61. [c] 1 H. 7. 13. b. Bro. Error, 135. [d] 1 Sid. 69. 1 Bulst. 71. 3 Mod. 42. 1 Ro Re. 175. [e] Dyer 34 pl. 20. 1 Keb. 141. pl. 11. 1 Syd. 316. 22 E. 4. 37. b. 3 Keb. 29. 4 E. 4, 10 pl. 14. Fitz Error, 52. 7 H. 7. 5. b. 4 Ed. 4, 10. pl. 14. [f] *The Queen and* Strafford. Mich. 12. Annæ *upon Examination of all the Precedents*. [g] 2 Salk 495. Vide 3 Keb. 29. [h] 3 Inst. 214, 215.

Sect. 15. *6thly*, That it is also clear, That the Statute of [a] 28 *Eliz.* 2. which enacts, *That no Record of Attainder that then was of High Treason, where the Party is or hath been executed, shall be reversed, avoided or impeached by any Plea or Writ of Error*, extends not [b] to Attainders since that Time.

Sect. 16. *7thly*, [c] That it hath been holden, That a Writ of Error lies in the King's Bench of an Attainder before the Lord High Steward.

[a] *Which is called the 29th in the printed Statutes by a Mistake.* 3 Lev, 333.
[b] 3 Inst. 213.
[c] 1 Sid. 208.

And now I am in the second Place to shew the Effect of the Avoidance of a Judgment, as to which I shall take Notice only of the following Particulars.

Sect. 17. *1st*, That it is [d] agreed, That after an Outlawry of Treason or Felony is reversed, the Party shall be put to [e] plead to the Indictment, for that still remains good.

Sect. 18. *2ndly*, That it is said [f] by Sir *Edward Coke*, If the Judgment be erroneous, both that and the Execution thereupon, and all former Proceedings shall be [f] reversed by Writ of Error; but if the Execution be erroneous that only shall be reversed.

Sect. 19. *3dly*, That it hath been [g] adjudged, That if the King grant over the Lands of a Person outlawed for Treason or Felony, and afterwards the Outlawry be reversed, the Party may enter on the Patentee, and needs neither to sue a Petition to the King, nor a *Scire facias* against the Patentee.

[d] Bro. Coro. 27, 143 *or* 144. 164 *or* 165. 7 H. 7. 5 pl 7. 18 Ed. 4. 9. pl. 16. 3 Mod. 42. Cro. Ja. 464 Fitz. Error, 52. Cro. Ca. 365.
[e] *That the Law is the same in Civil Causes.* Fitz. Error, 41. 37 H. 6. 17. Bro. Utlagary 28. 20 H 6. 3. a. *Abridged* Fitz. Protection, 11. Bro. Utlagary, 74. Cont. 21 H. 6. 50. pl. 3. *Abridged* Fitz. Nonsuit, 6. Bro. Utlagary, 24. Vide Bro. Utlagary, 35.
[f] 3 Inst. 2. 10.
[g] 1 And. 188.

CHAP. LI.

Of Execution and Reprieve.

AND now nothing remains but to shew in what Manner a Person condemned is to be executed or reprieved; as to which, having shewn already, *Ch.* 30. *Sect.* 8. That a Person attainted, standing Mute to a Demand why Execution shall not go against him, shall not be awarded to his Penance, but to the ordinary Execution proper for the Crime, I shall farther observe only the following Particulars,

Sect. 1. *First*, That the Court of King's Bench hath not only Power to award Execution against Persons attainted there, but also against Persons attainted in [h] Parliament, or any other [i] Court, the Record of their Attainder or a Transcript thereof being first [k] removed into the Court of King's Bench, and themselves brought thither by *Habeas Corpus*.

[h] 1 Sid. 72. 1 Lev. 61. 1 Keb. 244. Supra, Ch. 44. S. 18.
[i] Popb. 131. Cro. Ca. 176. Cro. Ja. 495.
[k] Cro. Ca. 176. Cro. Ja. 495. 1 Sid. 72. 1 Lev. 61. 1 Keb. 244.
[l] Cro. Ca. 176. Cro. Ja. 495. 1 Sid. 72, 73.

Sect. 2. 2*ndly*, That Execution ought [a] not to be awarded into a different County from that wherein the Party was tried and convicted, except only where a Record of Attainder is removed into the Court of King's Bench, which [b] may award the Execution in the same County wherein it sits.

Sect. 3. 3*dly*, That where a Person attainted hath been at Large after his Attainder, and afterwards is brought into Court and demanded why Execution should not be awarded against him, [c] if he deny that he is the same Person it shall be [d] immediately tried by a Jury returned for that Purpose.

Sect. 4. 4*thly*, That the Court [f] may command Execution to be done without any Writ.

Sect. 5. 5*thly*, That it is [g] holden by *Coke* and *Hale*, That no Execution can be warranted unless it be pursuant to the Judgment, and therefore that it cannot be altered by the King, as from hanging to beheading. Yet since there is a great Number of Precedents, where [o] Men condemned to be hanged for Felony, and Women condemned to be burnt [p] for Treason, have been beheaded by Force of a special Warrant from the King to that Purpose; and since [q] *Bracton* and [r] *Staundforde* and the [s] *Year-Book* of 35 *H.* 6. speaking of this Matter, are not so express as *Coke* and *Hale*, but say only in general, That the Sheriff cannot lawfully behead a Man who is only condemned to be hanged, by which they may perhaps intend no more than that he cannot lawfully do it of his own Authority; I shall leave this Matter to be farther considered. However it is agreed, That where beheading is Part of the Judgment, as in Case of High Treason, the King may [t] pardon all the rest, and consequently in such Case the Judgment will be well executed by beheading only.

Sect. 6. 6*thly*, That it seems [u] agreed at this Day, That an Execution cannot be lawfully executed by any but the proper Officer.

Sect. 7. 7*thly*, That it is [x] clear, That if a Man condemned to be hanged, come to Life after he be hanged, he ought to be hanged again; for the Judgment was not executed till he was dead.

Sect. 8. 8*thly*, That it seems agreed, That every Court which has Power to award an Execution, has also of Common Right a discretionary Power of granting a Reprieve; as [*] where a Person pleads a Pardon defective in Point of Form, but sufficiently shewing the King's Intention of Mercy; or where it is [**] doubtful whether the Offence be not included in a general Statute-Pardon; or [y] whether as it is laid in the Indictment, it amounts to so high a Crime as that with which the Prisoner was charged. And it seems [z] agreed at this Day, that Judges continue to have this Power after their Commission is determined.

[a] Cro. Ca. 176. 3 Mod. 124, 125.
[b] Cro. Ca. 176. Cro. Ja. 495.
[c] Vide Poph. 131. Cro. Ca. 176. Cro. Ja. 495. Crompt. Just. 183. b.
[d] 1 Sid 72. 1 Lev. 61. *Whether the Party may have peremptory Challenges on such a Trial* Supra Ch 43. Sect 6.
[f] Finch of Law, 478. 3 Mod. 42. *But sometimes Execution is commanded by Writ, as in* Sir Walter Raleigh's *Case.* Cro. Ja 496. *and in* Lord Stafford's *Case*, State Trials, Vol. 2. fol. 704, 705. *being both in the Custody of the Lieutenant of the Tower, and beheaded only.*
[g] 3 Inst. 52, 211, 212, 217, 12 Co. 130. H. P. C 272. *and accordingly Lord* Dacres, *Lord* Stourton, *and* Sanchar, *a* Scotch *Lord, were hanged for Murder.*

212. 9 Co. 121. b. [o] *Lord* Hungerford *in* 32 H. 8. 3 Inst. 211. *Duke of* Somerset *in* 5 Ed. 6. 3 Inst. 211, 211. *Lord* Audley *in* 6 Car. 1. State Trials, Vol. 1. fol. 271. [p] *Queen* Catherine Howard, *Lady* Jane Grey, *Countess of* Salisbury, *Lady* Alice Lisle. [q] Bracton 104. b. Vide 3 Inst. 217. [r] S. P. C. 13. a. [s] 35 H. 6. 38. [t] H. P. C. 273 3 Inst. 31, 52, 212. 12 Co. 130. Supra, ch. 37. Sect. 12. 3 Inst. 31. *it is said, That such a Pardon must be under the Great Seal; but it seems admitted that it may be by Writ.* State Trials, Vol. 2. f. 704, 705. [u] *See* B 1. Ch. 28 Sect. 8, 9. [x] 6 Ed. 4. 4. Fitz Coro. 335. Finch of Law, 389, 467. Vide Supra, Ch. 48. Sect. 7. [*] 26 Ass. pl. 46. *Abridged* Fitz. Office de Court, 34. [**] Dyer 235. pl. 19. [y] Dyer 296. pl. 21. [z] Dyer 205. pl. 5. Supra Ch. 6. Sect. 7.

Sect.

Sect. 9. 9thly, That it is clear, That if a Woman quick with Child be condemned either for [a] Treason or [b] Felony, she may alledge her being with Child in order to get the Execution respited, and thereupon the Sheriff [c] or Marshal shall be commanded to take her into a private Room, and to impanel a Jury of [g] Matrons to try and examine whether she be quick with Child or not; and if they find her quick with Child, the Execution shall be respited [h] till her Delivery. But it is agreed, That a Woman [i] cannot demand such Respite of Execution by Reason of her being quick with Child more than once; and that she can neither save herself by this Means from [k] pleading upon her Arraignment, nor from having [l] Judgment pronounced against her upon her Conviction. Also it is said both by [m] *Staundforde* and *Coke*, That a Woman can have no Advantage from being found with Child, unless she be also found quick with Child.

[a] H. P. C. 272. 3 Inst. 17.

[b] Quære if *before Justices of Peace*, Kejl. 51. a.

[c] S. P. C. 198. Lett. C. 22 Ass. pl. 71. *Abridged* Fitz. Coro. 180. Bro. Coro. 88.

[g] 3 Inst. 17. Finch of Law 478. S. P. C. 198. Letter C.

[h] State Trials Vol. 4. fol. 612. S. P. C. 198. Letter C. 3 Inst. 17. State Trials, Vol. 4. f. 612. Fitz. Coro. 253, 410. 23 Ass. pl. 2. *Abridged* Bro. Coro. 97. Fitz. Coro. 188. 25 Ed. 3. 42. b. *Abridged* Fitz. Coro. 130. 12 Ass. pl. 11. *Abridged* Fitz. Coro. 168. Bro. Coro. 72. Bro. Pain, 11.

[i] Finch of Law, 478. S. P. C. 198. Letter C. Fitz. Coro. 168, 253. 3 Inst. 17. H. P. C. 272, 23 Ass. pl. 2. *Abridged* Bro. Coro. 97. Fitz. Coro. 188. 25 Ed. 3. 42. b. *Abridged* Fitz. Coro. 130. 12 Ass. 11. Bro. Coro. 72 Pain, 11.

[k] Finch of Law, 478. 3 Inst. 17. 22 Ass. pl. 71. *Abridged* Fitz. Coro. 180. Bro. Coro. 88.

[l] State Trials, Vol. 4. fol. 611. S. P. C. 198. Lett. C. 3 Inst. 17.

[m] 3 Inst. 17. S. P. C. 198. Lett. C. *and in* 22 Ass. pl. 71. *Abridged* Fitz. Coro. 180. Bro. Coro. 88. *it is expresly said, That the Inquiry was whether the Woman were enseint with a Live Child or not. See also* H. P. C. 272. *and* Finch of Law, 478. *Yet* Fitz. Coro. 130, 168, 188, 240, 410 22 Ass. pl. 2. 25 Ed. 3. 42. b. 12 Ass. pl. 11. Bro. Coro. 72. Bro. pain, 11. *'tis said only, That the Woman was found enseint or pregnant.*

F I N I S.

2

An Alphabetical

INDEX

OF THE

Principal Matters

Contained in this

BOOK.

I N D E X.

Abettors.

Abjuration.

Accessary and Principal.

A.

B.

C.

Se-

In

INDEX.

Amer-

INDEX.

I N D E X.

Ap-

INDEX.

What

INDEX.

If

INDEX.

Eeeeee By

INDEX.

Association.

Attachment.

Attainder.

Attorney. See *Premunire.*

Averment.

Autrefoits acquit.

A.

B.

C.

D.

Award.

I N D E X.

INDEX.

Bailiffs

I N D E X.

Burgess.

I N D E X.

Nor

Challenge.

A.

B.

C.

D.

E.

Whe-

I N D E X.

INDEX.

Whe-

INDEX.

Con-

INDEX.

D. Whe-

INDEX.

INDEX.

D. Whe-

I N D E X.

INDEX.

Damages.

INDEX.

Whether

INDEX.

Escape.

INDEX.

Eyre.

INDEX.

A Va-

INDEX.

INDEX.

Whether

INDEX.

Whether

INDEX.

INDEX.

Mmmmmm *Garter*

I N D E X.

4 Whether

Whe-

B.

C.

D.

E.

F.

INDEX.

G.

H.

I.

K.

L.

Whether

INDEX.

INDEX.

D.

Jurisdiction.

Jurors.

A.

B.

C.

Justices.

INDEX.

See

INDEX.

Whether

INDEX.

INDEX.

Qqqqqq

Where

I N D E X.

Pain

INDEX.

Whether

INDEX.

INDEX.

Whether

INDEX.

INDEX.

INDEX.

Whether

INDEX.

Ttttt *Severe.*

INDEX.

Whether

Sug-

Whether

INDEX.

INDEX.

Whether

INDEX.

I N D E X.

INDEX.

Whether

I

FINIS.